Reference and Research Guide to
Mystery and Detective Fiction

**Recent titles in the
Reference Sources in the Humanity Series**

The Performing Arts: A Guide to the Reference Literature
Linda Keir Simons

American Popular Culture: A Guide to the Reference Literature
Frank W. Hoffman

Philosophy: A Guide to the Reference Literature, Second Edition
Hans E. Bynagle

Journalism: A Guide to the Reference Literature, Second Edition
Joe A. Cates

Children's Literature: A Guide to Information Sources
Margaret W. Denman-West

Reference Works in British and American Literature, Second Edition
James A. Bracken

Reference Guide to Mystery and Detective Fiction
Richard Bleiler

Linguistics: A Guide to the Reference Literature, Second Edition
Anna L. DeMiller

Reference Guide to Science Fiction, Fantasy, and Horror, Second Edition
Michael Burgess and Lisa R. Bartle

Reference and Research Guide to Mystery and Detective Fiction

Second Edition

Richard J. Bleiler

University of Connecticut

Reference Sources in the Humanities

A Member of the Greenwood Publishing Group

Westport, Connecticut • London

Library of Congress Cataloging-in-Publication Data

Bleiler, Richard.
     Reference and Research guide to mystery and detective fiction / Richard J.
     Bleiler.—2nd ed.
          p. cm.—(Reference sources in the humanities)
     Includes bibliographical references and index.
     ISBN 1–56308–924–6 (alk. paper)
     1. Detective and mystery stories—Bibliography. 2. Detective and mystery
     stories—Reference books—Bibliography. I. Title. II. Reference sources in the
     humanities series.
     Z5917.D5B59 2004
     [PN3448.D4]
     016.80883'872—dc22   2003058905

British Library Cataloguing in Publication Data is available.

Library of Congress Catalog Card Number: 2003058905
ISBN: 1–56308–924–6

First published in 2004

Libraries Unlimited, 88 Post Road West, Westport, CT 06881
A Member of Greenwood Publishing Group, Inc.
www.lu.com

Printed in the United States of America

The paper used in this book complies with the
Permanent Paper Standard issued by the National
Information Standards Organization (Z39.48–1984).

10   9   8   7   6   5   4   3   2   1

Contents

Introduction

Except through tautologies and generalities, it is not possible to provide an entirely satisfactory definition of either *detective fiction* or *mystery story* in the space of this introduction. The first term typically describes the activities of a detective, usually a person whose abilities at solving puzzles and interpreting evidence (clues) lead to a formal resolution of a problem, often a crime, frequently murder. The second generally involves a story in which a formally stated mystery and its equally formal resolution are central to the development and execution of a plot.

Numerous qualifications can, should, and must be made to the preceding statements. More than one detective may be present and may provide a different but equally viable solution to the crime; or no crime may have been committed and the story is nothing more than an exercise in logic and extrapolation; or the detective may solve nothing and bungle everything; or the detective may not be human and, indeed, may not even be of this planet. Furthermore, the existence of "mystery" is not limited to those works in which a detective or detectives appear, and mysteries are found in literary genres as seemingly disparate as weird fiction, science fiction, horror fiction, gothic fiction, espionage fiction, religious fiction, suspense fiction, and western fiction.

Despite the problems described here, there exists a substantial body of work that is commonly understood to be detective and mystery fiction, and numerous writers have written and continue to write detective and mystery fiction. This volume addresses itself to this body of work and to the accomplishments of these writers. It is in large part an annotated guide to the reference works that document and describe the primary and secondary literatures of mystery and detective fiction. Reference work should here be understood to include the encyclopedias, dictionaries, companions, vade mecums, bibliographies, bio-bibliographies, checklists, indexes, directories, handbooks, guides, and annotated editions intended and produced for an adult audience that were published in or prior to 2002. (A few publications from 2003 have however been included.)

No attempt has been made to describe the catalogues of book dealers, ephemeral in-house lists produced by libraries for their patrons, and works listing materials intended for juvenile readers, and reference works in languages other than English only occasionally have been annotated. Also omitted are the many biographies, monographs, and miscellaneous essay collections studying and criticizing the mystery and detective story and those who write it. I must add that I have not hesitated to make exceptions to those rules, especially when noteworthy and readily obtainable publications might otherwise be neglected.

This second edition differs significantly from the first edition. First, more than a third of the monographic citations are new. A surprising and gratifying number of reference works devoted to mystery and detective fiction were published between 1998 and 2002. These include genre encyclopedias, biographical dictionaries, genre studies, national bibliographies, media studies, and general reader's guides.

Next, in the case of author bio-bibliographies, the first edition's deliberate bias toward separate publications has been eliminated. Some notable authors have been the recipients of separately published reference books. When this is the case, these books are listed in the authors section, which annotates separately published reference works and a (very) few notable Web sites. Relatively few authors, however, have been the recipient of separately published bibliographies, whereas literally thousands of them have been accorded bio-bibliographic profiles in a variety of specialized reference books. The majority of these bio-biographical data are not accessible on the Internet, nor are they indexed through such databases as the H. W. Wilson's Biography Index and Gale's Biography and Genealogy Master Index. These data are frequently the only significant record of the author's accomplishments, and to leave them unremarked and inaccessible does a disservice not only to the researcher wanting a starting place but also to the casual reader who desires merely a list. This second edition thus indexes all the English-language bio-bibliographic and biocritical reference books that in the first edition were merely annotated, as well as those that are new to this volume: *American Hard-Boiled Crime Writers; And then There Were Nine . . . More Women of Mystery; The Art of Murder; Australian Crime Fiction; The Big Book of Noir; British Mystery Writers, 1860–1919; British Mystery Writers, 1920–1939; British Mystery and Thriller Writers since 1940, First Series;* both editions of *By a Woman's Hand; Canadian Crime Fiction; Colloquium on Crime; Corpus Delecti of Mystery Fiction; The Craft of Crime: Conversations with Crime Writers; Critical Survey of Mystery and Detective Fiction; Designs of Darkness; Detecting Men;* the three editions of *Detecting Women; Encyclopedia Mysteriosa; The Encyclopedia of Murder and Mystery; The Encyclopedia of Mystery and Detection; The Fatal Art of Entertainment; Great Women Mystery Writers; Hardboiled Mystery Writers; Latin American Mystery Writers: An A to Z Guide; The Mammoth Encyclopedia of Modern Crime Fiction; Murder Ink; Murder off the Rack: Critical Studies of Ten Paperback Masters; Murderess Ink; Mystery and Suspense Writers; 100 Masters of Mystery and Detective Fiction; The Oxford Companion to Crime and Mystery Writing; St. James Guide to Crime and Mystery Writers,* 4th edition; both volumes of *Speaking of Murder; Talking Murder; Ten Women of Mystery; They Wrote the Book; 13 Mistresses of Murder; Twelve Englishmen of Mystery;* the three editions of *Twentieth-Century Crime and Mystery Writers; Whodunit? A Who's Who in Crime & Mystery Writing; Women Authors of Detective Series;* and *Women of Mystery.* The contents of these works are listed in the appendix to this volume. As of this writing, *Latin American Mystery Writers: An A to Z Guide* has not been published, and the indexing of contents was based on the data provided by its editor, Dr. Darrell B. Lockhart.

In the first edition I recognized that the boundaries of literary genres were fluid; I established borders and made no effort to provide data on authors outside those borders whose works were classical thrillers, adventure stories, espionage stories, gangster tales, historical novels, westerns, and true crime stories. This is no longer the case, for the indexed works frequently differed radically in their methodology and approach, and although I would contend that the works of John Buchan, Tom Clancy, Len Deighton, Ian Fleming, Geoffrey Household, and Robert Ludlum are classifiable only sporadically (if at all) as mystery and detective fiction, one can find in the appendix references to bio-bibliographic data on them. (One also may find a reference to William Shakespeare, accorded an entry herein because of his appearance in *The Oxford Companion to Crime and Mystery Writing.*)

Although it would have been tempting to obtain and annotate every separate work on every author listed in the appendix, common sense and recognition of space considerations make that quite impossible. (Indeed, a full annotated list of the reference works devoted to William Shakespeare would comprise a lengthy volume in its own right.) Thus, although the author section in this second edition includes citations to many more monographs than appeared in the first edition, it cannot claim to be exhaustive. Researchers interested in whether a specific author has received genre attention must examine the appendix and work through the cited volumes in order to learn whether relevant additional materials exist.

In this second edition, I also have greatly expanded coverage of genre magazines and the sources that index them. Again, the intentional bias toward separate publications was relaxed, for although hundreds of magazines have been indexed, relatively few have been the subject of separately published indexes. Genre indexes are frequently the only detailed record of a magazine's contents and existence, and the contents of these indexes frequently are inaccessible through any electronic resource, although cover images can occasionally be found on the World Wide Web (and are obtainable on a variety of CD-ROMs). Much genre history awaits study in these magazines, the publications of many fine writers await rediscovery, and to leave this material inaccessible does everybody a disservice. One example of this need will suffice. In 2001, I posted the contents of the newly discovered second issue (vol. 1, no. 2) of *Verdict Crime Detection Magazine* to a discussion group, from whence it was added to a Web site devoted to indexing fiction magazines. A recent www.google.com search for "Verdict Crime Detection Magazine" yielded results in the very low double figures, almost all related to my earlier posting; a researcher interested in the magazine would learn nothing of its history or relative status. *Verdict Crime Detection Magazine* is, however, discussed at respectable length in Michael L. Cook's *Mystery, Detective, and Espionage Magazines* (Westport, Conn.: Greenwood, 1983) and partially indexed in Cook's *Monthly Murders: A Checklist and Chronological Listing of Fiction in the Digest-Size Mystery Magazines in the United States and England* (Westport, Conn.: Greenwood, 1982). This edition thus indexes the contents of the English-language genre magazine indexes and studies that in the first edition were merely annotated. These include *Monthly Murders; Mystery, Espionage, and Detective Fiction; Mystery, Espionage, and Detective Magazines; Mystery Fanfare;* the four series of *The Pulp Magazine Index;* and Street & Smith's *Hero Pulp Checklist.*

On the other hand, although I have expanded the coverage of material discussing radio programs, motion pictures, and television shows, no monographic sources are available that replicate the depth and variety of responses that can be retrieved from a search through www.google.com or through such sources as the Internet movie database (www.imdb.com). One example of this exhaustiveness: during the 1970s, I recall watching an English television show, *My Partner, the Ghost.* A recent www.google.com search for "My Partner, the Ghost" yielded 145 results, the first of which referenced the original English title: *Randall and Hopkirk (Deceased).* A search on "Randall and Hopkirk (Deceased)" yielded 4,100 results. The World Wide Web excels at providing media coverage; less so at providing bio-bibliographic and bibliographic data.

As before, this guide includes a number of the sources that index and describe the pulp magazines, and particular attention is paid to the works describing the hero pulps, a variety of pulp magazine that described the actions of a single heroic character and his assistants. The activities of these heroes often were set against backgrounds that amalgamated elements found in the adventure story, the science fiction story, and the espionage story, but it must be stressed that, despite their frequently sensationalistic trappings and often fantastic overtones, many of the stories in the pulp magazines were structured as traditional mysteries and concluded with the hero—Doc Savage, The Phantom Detective, Operator #5, The Spider, or The Shadow—unmasking the true villain and providing a rational explanation to the hitherto baffling mysteries and murders.

It is fervently hoped that the monographic citations will provide sufficient bibliographic data necessary to locate a publication. The citations begin by listing the author, authors, or editor(s); these are followed by the title, the place of publication, publisher, and year of publication of the first edition; pagination is provided, as are the series title and a statement as to whether an index or indexes are present. Works published only in paperback are so noted, and citations conclude with the work's Library of Congress number and its ISBN, when such exist and are present. If the work was first published abroad, the primary publication data are noted, and the American edition is referenced, if one exists. If the work has been revised and updated, the earlier editions are listed and the most recent edition available is described, with a note indicating that the later edition is described. Anonymous works are listed by their titles.

Following the preceding data are a description of each work's intent, organization, and content and (when appropriate) an evaluative opinion. These latter have proved somewhat controversial. James Harner, for example, stated positively that they were "uncompromisingly frank," and Geoff Bradley (reasonably enough) took me to task for my assessment of Maxim Jakubowski's *100 Great Detectives*. My firm belief is that an evaluative opinion serves a definite purpose, for although a reference book may be many things to many people and may contain data that are unique, it is ultimately—paramountly and inescapably—something that researchers must rely upon to answer their questions or to further their researches. Compilers of reference works must strive to make their data as close to 100 percent accurate as possible and to present these data in such a way as to make them as readily accessible as possible. I do not hesitate to comment if these data cannot be obtained immediately and with ease, or if I do not believe that they cannot be relied upon. I do not, of course, believe that there is only one way to present material, but I feel it is important to comment if a volume does not contain an index when one would assist the user, if it indexes something without providing relevant pagination, or if it neglects or omits data while claiming to be comprehensive. In addition, I have commented when a volume is physically defective, poorly bound, badly printed, awkwardly laid out, or in some way idiosyncratic or frustrating in its presentation of data. These are relevant in the assessment of a reference work.

In addition to describing and annotating paper publications, I have cited a number of the World Wide Web sites that are devoted to detective and mystery fiction and those who write it. The first edition made the mistake of attempting to describe the Web sites, and changes in content, shifts in Internet service providers (ISPs), collapses of ISPs, and other alterations in Uniform Resource Locators (URLs) rendered entirely too many citations out-of-date even before the volume was published. Thus, when URLs are listed in this volume, their annotations are deliberately brief. Although they are suffixed as commercial sites (.com), the personal Web sites of authors are referenced, but I have not attempted to reference or describe the majority of the general commercial Web sites currently accessible, for the primary intent of these tends to be the marketing of merchandise rather than the independent recognition of the author or genre.

ACKNOWLEDGMENTS

The majority of the items described in this bibliography came from my own collections, but for obtaining those materials that I do not own, I am indebted to Joe Natale, the Interlibrary Loan Librarian at the University of Connecticut's Homer Babbidge Library, and to his nonpareil assistants Lana Babbij, Judy DeLottie, Erika McNeil, and Lynn Sweet. These wonderful people consistently work miracles, routinely obtaining the unobtainable.

For taking the time to look for Polish publications, I would like to thank Joanna Koc.

For taking the time from his writing to answer my questions and to look for Indian genre publications, I would like to thank Ashok Banker.

For providing me with an advance copy of *Crime Fiction IV: A Comprehensive Bibliography, 1749–2000* and answering questions patiently, kindly, and promptly, I would like to thank Bill Contento and Allen J. Hubin, gentlemen and scholars both.

For providing me with data and a description of *Latin American Mystery Writers: An A to Z Guide,* a work that is certain to be groundbreaking, I would like to thank Dr. Darrell B. Lockhart.

For taking the time to share his Finnish publications, I would like to thank Juri Nummelin.

For generously sharing their expertise, collections, and publications, I wish to express gratitude to noted bibliographers and scholars Walter Albert, J. Randolph Cox, Kate Derie, David Skene-Melvin, Norbert Spehner, and Norman Stevens.

Special gratitude is due to my friend Sue Grzyb, whose extensive knowledge of the used and rare book trade provided me with examination copies of items I would not otherwise have been able to obtain. Enormous gratitude is due to Barbara Ittner of Libraries Unlimited, whose editorial acuity is matched only by her good humor and kindness.

My very special thanks to my father E. F. Bleiler, who shared generously of his time and collections, and to my dear Cheryl, who patiently reminded me when it was late and when I needed to eat, and who makes Connecticut a nicer place to live.

All omissions and errors are of course my own responsibility. Corrections and additions should be sent to the author at the Collections Services, U-1005, Homer Babbidge Library, University of Connecticut, Storrs, CT 06269-1005.

1

Encyclopedias and Dictionaries

Scope note: This chapter includes publications that call themselves encyclopedias and the general dictionaries of mystery and detective fiction. Dictionaries and encyclopedias of specific subjects—authors, characters, motion pictures and television shows, and so forth—are listed under their respective subject headings later in this book.

---

1.   Ashley, Mike. **The Mammoth Encyclopedia of Modern Crime Fiction.** New York: Carroll & Graf, 2002. xii, 780 p. Paperback. ISBN 0-7867-1006-3.

Despite its title, this is not a formal encyclopedia but several distinct encyclopedic dictionaries, offering information about the writers, media, and awards of contemporary mystery fiction and with cross-references linking the sections.

Following a very useful introduction to the different genres of modern crime fiction, the first dictionary discusses more than 500 contemporary writers. Entries are arranged alphabetically by writer's last name and give nationality and a biocritical description. In small type at the conclusion of each entry are the writer's full name and a selective bibliography that lists novels, short stories, and nonfiction, as well as series information, plus information on where to start reading, writers of "similar stuff," awards won, personal Web sites, and a cheerfully personal "final fact" about the author.

The media dictionary discusses more than 400 major television shows and motion pictures. Entries for television shows tell country of origin, years of broadcast, number of episodes, creator, producer(s), director(s), and stars; entries for motion pictures tell country of origin, year of release, director(s), producer(s), screenplay writer (as well as the work it was based on), and stars. The discussions are lively and informative.

The awards dictionary is treated as an appendix although it is nearly 60 pages long. Each award is described, and all winners (in all categories) are listed for the Agatha Award, the Arthur Ellis Award, the Barry Award, the Chester Himes Award, the Crime Writers' Association Awards, the Derringer Award, the Dilys Award, the Edgar Award, the Grand Prix de Littérature Policière, the Hammett Prize, the Herodotus Award, the Lambda Literary Award, the Lefty Award, the Macavity Award, the Maltese Falcon Award, the [Philip] Marlowe Award, the Ned Kelly Award, the Nero Wolfe Award, the Swedish Academy of Detection, the Shamus Award, the Sherlock Award, and the Trophy 813 Award. There are also appendixes listing current genre magazines and key Web sites and key characters and series.

This is a monumental accomplishment, a fact that was not lost on the Mystery Writers of America, which in 2003 awarded it the Edgar for Best Nonfiction Work. It belongs in all reference libraries.

2.   DeAndrea, William L. **Encyclopedia Mysteriosa: A Comprehensive Guide to the Art of Detection in Print, Film, Radio, and Television.** New York and London: Prentice Hall, 1994. x, 405 p. Cloth. LC 94-2075. ISBN 0-671-85025-3.

Although nearly 20 years had elapsed since Chris Steinbrunner and Otto Penzler compiled their *Encyclopedia of Mystery and Detection,* no comprehensive attempt had been made to update their efforts. DeAndrea—an award-winning author of mysteries—began writing this book because he saw a need for it: "A lot has happened since 1975. Writers so popular now as to seem forces of nature had not begun their careers then; there has been a decade and a half of (sometimes excellent) movies and TV shows, as well. It was time to get up-to-date." The result is a volume similar in appearance to the old *Encyclopedia,* an alphabetical list of approximately 1,400 entries containing numerous cross-references, a number of illustrations, and 11 separate signed essays on special aspects of the detective and mystery story. The volume concludes with three appendixes ("Bookstores," "Organizations and Awards," and "Magazines and Journals"), and a glossary of terms specific to the mystery story.

Like the earlier *Encyclopedia,* DeAndrea's *Encyclopedia Mysteriosa* is a genuine encyclopedia, and its entries attempt an encyclopedic thoroughness. A number of thriller writers are profiled, as well as a number of mainstream writers who contributed significantly to the genre and writers more noted for their work in other genres. The *Encyclopedia Mysteriosa* differs significantly from its inspiration in that the majority of its entries is for fictional characters or for the film, radio, and television presentations of crime and mystery. The first three pages of the volume contain 13 entries, 9 of which concern characters or media presentations, and this percentage remains consistent throughout the book.

Oddly enough, the most significant flaws in the *Encyclopedia Mysteriosa* are those that faced Penzler and Steinbrunner. First, because DeAndrea's concentration is on the more contemporary material, he fails to mention many of the older writers; a historian is likely to wonder, however, whether it was wise to neglect writers such as Archibald Clavering Gunter and Thomas Hanshew (to say nothing of John Collier and Thomas Cook) in favor of such television shows as the *A-Team.* Next, although there are occasional entries for European writers, the *Encyclopedia Mysteriosa* focuses almost entirely on the literature produced in Great Britain and America; additional entries (or a companion volume) surveying the mystery and detective literature produced around the rest of the world are needed.

These caveats aside, the *Encyclopedia Mysteriosa* belongs on all reference shelves.

3.   Denton, William. **Twists, Slugs and Roscoes: A Glossary of Hardboiled Slang.** http://www.miskatonic.org/slang.html

This Web site provides definitions of slang words and terms commonly found in hard-boiled detective fiction. A lighthearted introduction explains that "this is the language spoken by Philip Marlowe, Sam Spade, Mike Hammer and the Continental Op. When Cagney, Bogart, Robinson and Raft got in a turf war, this is how they talked." The list begins with "Ameche" (a telephone), concludes with "Zotzed" (killed), and includes definitions for such classics as "gunsel" and "gooseberry lay," as well as for several hundred additional terms. Except in the case of e-mail submissions, attributions are provided for each term. The list of sources from which the terms were derived concludes the dictionary. A well-done and very helpful dictionary.

4. Herbert, Rosemary, et al., eds. **The Oxford Companion to Crime and Mystery Writing.** New York and London: Oxford University Press, 1999. xxiii, 535 p. Cloth. LC 99-21182. ISBN 0-19-507239-1.

Unquestionably the best of the encyclopedic surveys of the genre, *The Oxford Companion to Crime and Mystery Writing* contains 666 entries discussing such subjects as the major authors, the significant characters, the notable character types, the recurrent themes and scenes, the frequently used plot devices, various important terms, and crucial historical elements. The essays range in length from 150 to 1,500 words and are signed; they tend to be written by experts and are clear and insightful. Cross-references are plentiful, and the volume concludes with a thorough index.

Excellent though it is, *The Oxford Companion* is limited primarily to the Anglo-American manifestations of mystery and detective fiction. The introduction is forthcoming about this, stating that the book is "designed for readers of the English language around the world, [and] its focus is upon works of crime and mystery writing published in English. A limited number of international writers whose first language is not English—such as the Belgian Georges Simenon and the Swedish writing team of Maj Sjöwall and Per Wahlöö—are accorded entries of their own, since their work, which has been readily available in English translation, has contributed to the development of the genre as a whole." One wishes, however, that the focus had been expanded and that instead of lengthy essays on such topics as the one titled "Europe, Crime and Mystery Writing in Continental," the volume had actually provided entries on the significant authors, characters, character types, recurrent themes and scenes, and so forth.

This criticism aside, *The Oxford Companion to Crime and Mystery Writing* has something for everyone and belongs in all libraries.

5. Herbert, Rosemary. **Whodunit? A Who's Who in Crime & Mystery Writing.** Preface by Dennis Lehane. New York: Oxford University Press, 2003. xix, 235 p. Index. LC 2002-029791. ISBN 0-19-515763-3 (hc); 0-19-515761-3 (pb).

Whodunit? is a badly titled volume, for it is not simply a book about crime and mystery writers and their characters, though some hundreds of these are described and discussed in occasionally lengthy essays that are complete with cross-references. *Whodunit?* is, instead, an encyclopedic work; it reuses some of the entries published in Herbert's earlier *Oxford Companion to Crime and Mystery Writing* (q.v.), although it is far from a simple reprint—it contains many new entries. All entries are signed, though the concluding index does not provide access by contributor.

For all that it is an excellent work, *Whodunit?* often leaves one wanting more. Although any volume will be hampered by space considerations, one wishes for more author entries. There likewise are no entries for such important and relevant subjects as cozy, locked-room, noir, and pulp magazines, significant omissions, particularly since the entries profile writers of all of these subjects. A revised and expanded second edition would be appreciated.

6.   Murphy, Bruce F. **The Encyclopedia of Murder and Mystery.** New York: St. Martin's Minotaur, 1999. xiv, 543 p. Cloth. LC 99-25316. ISBN 0-312-21554-1.

Murphy's introduction states that *The Encyclopedia of Murder and Mystery* surveys the "authors, characters, terminology, famous criminal cases, slang, subgenres and plot devices, murder techniques and poisons" that are part of the matter and context of crime and murder literature. To provide this survey, Murphy has written approximately 2,000 articles, ranging in length from 50 to 500 words. The entries begin with "Aarons, Edward S[idney]." and conclude with a cross-reference to "Zubro, Mark Richard." Additional cross-references are plentiful, and articles frequently conclude with selective bibliographies. There is, alas, no index.

Murphy—who edited the fourth edition of *Benet's Reader's Encyclopedia*— is a very capable writer, and the entries in the *Encyclopedia* frequently sparkle. It is thus unfortunate that the *Encyclopedia* has several lethal shortcomings. First, the field of mystery and detective literature is simply too large for one person to provide a viable encyclopedic survey of it. Although Murphy's *Encyclopedia* is in many ways superior to DeAndrea's *Encyclopedia Mysteriosa,* it has many of the earlier work's problems, chief among them is that apart from a few of the major established international writers (Dürrenmatt, Gaboriau, Simenon, Sjöwall and Wahlöö), the focus is primarily on the Anglo-American writers, history, and terms.

Next, Murphy's *Encyclopedia* is absolutely riddled with errors, on the order of almost one per page. Some of these errors are reasonably minor—critic E. F. Bleiler is not English but American; and some of these errors are typographical— Fredric Brown did not spell his first name "Frederic"; and some of these are errors of omission— Dashiell Hammett's unlisted first name was Samuel; and some of these are errors of fact—the first pulp magazine did not appear in 1889; and some of these are errors of ignorance—"Seeley Regester"'s *The Dead Letter* (1867) has not been forgotten but has been reprinted with a critical introduction; and some of these are absolutely unforgivable—Doyle's "A Study in Scarlet" categorically was not "serialized in 1887."

The Encyclopedia of Murder and Mystery was published at approximately the same time as *The Oxford Companion to Crime and Mystery Writing* (q.v.), and although the *Oxford Companion* is not perfect, it is much more reliable than Murphy's *Encyclopedia*.

7.   Steinbrunner, Chris, and Otto Penzler, eds. **Encyclopedia of Mystery and Detection.** New York, St. Louis, San Francisco: McGraw-Hill, 1976. 436 p. Cloth. LC 75-31645. ISBN 0-07-061121-1.

The *Encyclopedia of Mystery and Detection* was the first sustained attempt at providing the readers of what the editors call "the country's favorite literary genre" with a comprehensive reference work. It was partially inspired by the success of the *Detectionary* (q.v.), which was written by (among others) the editors of the *Encyclopedia,* but at 300,000 words, the *Encyclopedia* is more than five times the length of the *Detectionary*. It is a genuine encyclopedia, an alphabetical listing of nearly 600 articles, the majority of which concentrates on the authors of detective and mystery fiction, herein defined broadly enough to include writers of thrillers (John Buchan, Ian Fleming, and Geoffrey Household), writers traditionally considered mainstream (Theodore Dreiser, Fyodor Dostoyesky, and Victor Hugo), and writers significant in other literary genres (John Collier, Arthur Machen, and Ann Radcliffe). In addition, important characters are accorded entries of their own: Arthur Upfield's Inspector Napoleon Bonaparte and

Ian Fleming's James Bond share a page, and other odd juxtapositions can be located easily. A significant number of the author entries include an author photograph and conclude with chronologically arranged checklists of the author's fiction and descriptions of the significant motion picture, radio, and television adaptations. Characters entries describe their earliest appearance as well as their media appearances, and they often include checklists of publications in which the character appears and photographs of actors portraying the character. Finally, there are copious cross-references and a number of signed entries for such thematic subjects as those titled "Collecting Detective Fiction," the "Had-I-but-Known School," "Locked-Room Mysteries," and "Pulp Magazines."

The two greatest flaws in the *Encyclopedia* are those of inclusiveness and consistency. The editors recognize the former problem in their introduction by stating, reasonably enough, that "this is a big book, by any reasonable standard, but a line had to be drawn somewhere. If the reader insists, 'But X is just as important as Y,' he may be right. There are scores of borderline entries in this book, and hundreds of borderline omissions." This is quite correct. The problem of consistency is less noticeable but equally relevant: the entry on Pierre Chambrun concludes with a list of the publications in which he appears, but the entry for the vastly more significant Charlie Chan does not. Additionally, it is to be regretted that the checklists provide merely title and publication date; more bibliographical data would have been welcome. Nevertheless, despite its age, the strengths of the volume far outweigh its weaknesses. The *Encyclopedia* defined a field of literature; it remains a landmark volume.

8.   Turner-Lord, Jann. **Bob's Your Uncle: A Dictionary of Slang for British Mystery Fans.** Santa Barbara, Calif.: Fithian Press, 1992. 62 p. Paperback. LC 92-3858. ISBN 1-56474-022-6.

The cover of this slim paperback describes Jann Turner-Lord as "a confirmed anglophile and mystery-addict," and Turner-Lord's preface states that she was inspired to create this dictionary by reading Jonathan Gash, whose character Lovejoy "uses more slang than I've ever seen." Sources of inspiration aside, *Bob's Your Uncle* defines approximately 800 terms that Turner-Lord has located through her reading. None of her definitions provides attributions or sources, making the volume useless for determining whether a usage is historical or modern and for whether a word or phrase originated with a specific author. Furthermore, many of the terms defined by Turner-Lord are neither English slang nor limited to British mystery novels. A number of standard English abbreviations are defined, as are such readily understandable terms as "flummox," "petrol tin," "queue," "row," and "smarmy." *Bob's Your Uncle* was obviously a labor of love, but this does not excuse its deficiencies.

9.   Walter, Klaus-Peter, ed. **Lexikon der Kriminalliteratur: Autoren, Werke, Themen/Aspekte.** 5 vols. Meitingen, Germany: Corian-Verlag, 1993–. Looseleaf. ISBN 3-89048-600-2.

One need not read German to appreciate Walter's effort: his *Lexikon der Kriminalliteratur* is as of this writing the most comprehensive work on its subject, a massive multivolume series containing thousands of signed essays written by experts. Furthermore, the *Lexikon* was published as a looseleaf series, permitting the easy updating and correction of the contents. The result is accessible, easy to use, and thoroughly international in its approach. (Researchers familiar with the *KLG*—the *Kritisches*

Lexikon der deutschsprachigen Gegenwartsliteratur—will recognize the style and format of the *Lexikon der Kriminalliteratur.*)

Although there is additional material that is mentioned later, each portion of the *Lexikon* contains in essence three separate sections. The first discusses individual authors (i.e., Arthur Conan Doyle, Ian Fleming, Patricia Highsmith, Don Pendleton, Georges Simenon, Martin Cruz Smith, Edgar Wallace, and Cornell Woolrich). Each essay begins with a picture of its subject and concludes with lengthy bibliographies that cite the title and date (in boldface type) of the first edition of the work followed by lists of its appearances in German.

The *Lexikon*'s second section discusses individual works and their relative genre importance. These sections are pleasantly idiosyncratic; they include works by such genre authors as Dorothy Cannell, Max Allan Collins, Friederich Dürrenmatt, Ian Fleming, John Gardner, John Grisham, Thomas Harris, Stuart Kaminsky, Elmore Leonard, and Sara Paretsky. Researchers will, however, note the appearance of essays on works by such less familiar names as Michail Djomin, Gerhard Johann, Josef Skvorecky, Jurij Mamlejew, and Anatolij Rybakow, to name but a few. Each discussion concludes with a useful bibliography of secondary sources.

The *Lexikon*'s third section discusses themes and genre history; that is, the Classic Detective, women detectives and mystery writers, the *Black Mask Magazine,* and crime detection in utopian and fantastic literature. These discussions are not always prose: they at times include lengthy bibliographies, but they also can be historical surveys and critical assessments.

In addition to the preceding, the *Lexikon* contains lengthy lists of pseudonyms and their users, discussions of genre films, and lists of prize-winning authors and works. (These latter are international.)

The *Lexikon* belongs in all research libraries.

2

Reader's Guides and Genre and Theme Listings

Scope note: This chapter has in it works that are selective and general lists (i.e., lists of the 100 best books), the works that survey more than one genre, and the works that are useful or important general histories.

Surveys of individual genres are listed separately, and bibliographies intended to record an entire genre or subgenre, or that document a nationality's literary output, are listed in the genre and bibliography chapters, even when they are extensively annotated.

GENERAL

10.   Barnes, Melvyn. **Best Detective Fiction: A Guide from Godwin to the Present.** London: Clive Bingley, 1975; Hamden, Conn.: Linnet Books, 1975. 121 p. Index. Cloth. LC 75-22344. ISBN 0-208-01376-8.

Best Detective Fiction differs from the other guides in this section by being a bibliographic essay describing the books that Barnes considers "key contributions to the genre." In his preface, Barnes states that his criteria for determining this were "excellence of plot, writing and/or characterisation, or a degree of innovation which has established or enhanced a trend." He generally excluded thrillers and spy stories from his discussion, although he made exceptions for significant titles.

The essay, a chronological (rather than thematic) history, starts with discussion of two of the more significant pre-Poe detective stories, William Godwin's *Things as They Are; or, the Adventures of Caleb Williams* (1794) and the first English edition of Eugène François Vidocq's *Memoirs of Vidocq, Principal Agent of the French Police until 1827* (1828–1829). Successive chapters discuss Arthur Conan Doyle and his contemporaries and imitators; the writers of the 1920s; the hard-boiled writers; the writers of detective stories during the 1930s, 1940s, 1950s; and so forth. The essay concludes with mention of such writers as "Anthony Gilbert," Andrew Garve, Laurence Meynell, and Dick Francis. In all, about 125 authors and 225 books are mentioned, and for each of the latter Barnes cites the first English-language edition, as well as the first British edition if there is a difference. A checklist of books mentioned that is effectively an author index concludes the volume; there is no title index.

Although Barnes's preface specifically states that his volume "is not intended as a complete history of detective fiction," students having no background in the subject may find Barnes a useful introduction, for his judgments are solid and conventional, likely to surprise neither critics nor scholars. On the debit side, *Best Detective Fiction* contains virtually nothing that cannot be found elsewhere, and his omissions are significant. The only work of Raymond Chandler mentioned is *The High Window,* and such vital writers as R. Austin Freeman, John Dickson Carr, Dashiell Hammett, and Erle Stanley Gardner have only two works (apiece) cited. Worst of all, *Best Detective Fiction* is lifeless, dated in a way that Jacques Barzun and Wendell Hertig Taylor's *A Catalogue of Crime* and Bill Pronzini and Marcia Muller's *1001 Midnights* (q.q.v.) are not. Its successor (which follows) is superior.

11.   Barnes, Melvyn. **Murder in Print: A Guide to Two Centuries of Detective Fiction.** London: Barn Owl Books, 1986. xii, 244 p. Index. Cloth. ISBN 0-9509057-4-7.

Murder in Print was originally conceived as the second edition to Barnes's *Best Detective Fiction* (noted earlier), but while revising the book, Barnes realized that "the field [of detective fiction] has changed over the years to a degree that cannot be ignored. If the full picture is to be shown, there must be greater coverage of the modern crime novel in all its manifestations. Similarly, various subgenres, while mentioned in the earlier book, now warrant considerable sections of their own." *Murder in Print* thus presents "the result of further extensive research and an examination of the best authors to have emerged in the past twenty years. All material which appeared in the original volume has similarly been comprehensively revised, reorganized and expanded."

Like *Best Detective Fiction, Murder in Print* is a bibliographic essay, citing the first British and first American edition of the books it discusses. Nevertheless, *Murder in Print* contains a greater awareness of thematic developments than the first book, and its later chapters are thematic discussions rather than chronological lists. *Murder in Print* begins with the discussion of William Godwin's *Things as They Are* (1794) and the first English edition of Eugène François Vidocq's *Memoirs of Vidocq* (1828–1829). Later chapters discuss significant mystery and detective stories written prior to the advent of Sherlock Holmes, and significant chapters discuss Arthur Conan Doyle and his contemporaries. Thematic discussions include women detective and mystery writers and the writers of hard-boiled detective stories, police procedurals, and historical mysteries. As before, thrillers and spy stories generally are excluded from discussion, although Barnes makes occasional exceptions for significant titles. In all, approximately 260 authors and nearly 500 books are discussed. A checklist of books featured, a select but useful bibliography, and a combined author/title index conclude the volume.

Murder in Print is vastly superior to *Best Detective Fiction.* Authors neglected in the earlier volume are discussed at length in *Murder in Print,* and Barnes's critical assessments are sharper and shrewder. *Murder in Print* is substantially shorter than either Jacques Barzun and Wendell Hertig Taylor's *A Catalogue of Crime* and Bill Pronzini and Marcia Muller's *1001 Midnights* (q.q.v), but it has the virtue of offering its criticism in a historical context.

12. Barnett, Sandy, and Newfront Productions. **The History of the Mystery: An Interactive Journey.** http://www.mysterynet.com/timeline

As its title indicates, this Web site provides an interactive history of the mystery, from the days of Cicero until the present. The material is very well presented and offers numerous illustrations. Unfortunately, it also contains entirely too many errors, none of which have been corrected since this entry was first written. These include the misspelling of the name of Poe's pioneering detective, a claim that "The Purloined Letter" was a novel, an assertion that Mickey Spillane wrote only six novels featuring Mike Hammer, a claim that Erle Stanley Gardner began his writing career with stories for *Black Mask,* and a statement that *The Mysterious Affair at Styles* featured both Poirot and Marple. One continues to hope for corrections.

13. Barzun, Jacques, and Wendell Hertig Taylor. **A Book of Prefaces to Fifty Classics of Crime Fiction 1900–1950.** New York: Garland, 1976. viii, 112 p. Cloth. LC 76-26751. ISBN 0-8240-2425-7. 250 copies printed.

This annotated bibliography began its existence as the prefaces to 50 classic mystery stories, originally published between 1900 and 1950, that Garland reprinted around the time of this book's publication. The contents are arranged alphabetically by the author's name. Each annotation discusses the work, providing a brief but critical appreciation of its significance. As one would anticipate, the book lists familiar works by such authors as Raymond Chandler, G. K. Chesterton, Agatha Christie, R. Austin Freeman, Erle Stanley Gardner, Dorothy L. Sayers, Rext Stout, and Arthur Upfield (to name but a few), but it nevertheless contains surprises: Barzun and Taylor praise such lesser-known works as Gerald Bullett's *The Jury,* C. W. Grafton's *Beyond a Reasonable Doubt,* Thomas Kindon's *Murder in the Moor,* Dermot Morrah's *The Mummy Case,* and Henry Kitchell Webster's *Who Is the Next?* A brief biographical statement concludes each entry.

14a. Barzun, Jacques, and Wendell Hertig Taylor. **A Catalogue of Crime [Being a Reader's Guide to the Literature of Mystery, Detection, & Related Genres].** New York: Harper & Row, 1971. xxxi, 831 p. Indexes. Cloth. LC 75-123914. ISBN 06-010263-2.

14b. Barzun, Jacques, and Wendell Hertig Taylor. **A Catalogue of Crime [Being a Reader's Guide to the Literature of Mystery, Detection, and Related Genres].** New York: Harper & Row, 1989. xxxvi, 952 p. Indexes. Cloth. LC 88-45884. ISBN 0-06-015796-8.

The two editions of *A Catalogue of Crime* are among the most significant annotated bibliographies of the detective and mystery story. They are also among the most idiosyncratic of bibliographies, combining seemingly arbitrary inclusions, poorly presented citations, and a most unhelpful and often frustrating layout with intelligent, witty, and waspish opinions. The first edition differs significantly from the second not only in the number of citations but also because the first edition's final chapter is devoted to ghost stories, studies and reports of the supernatural, psychical research, and extrasensory perception (ESP).

This annotation concentrates on the *Catalogue*'s second edition, which contains the following five sections: novels of detection, crime, mystery, and espionage; short stories, collections, anthologies, magazines, pastiches, and plays; studies and histories of the genre, lives of writers, and the literature of *Edwin Drood;* true crime: trials, narratives of cases, criminology and police science, espionage, and cryptography; the literature of Sherlock Holmes: studies and annotations of the tales, nonfiction parodies, and critical pastiches. All entries are numbered, and in all 5,045 works are annotated, an impressive 3,549 of these being the novels of detection, crime, mystery, and espionage. Each section is arranged alphabetically by the author's or editor's last name; when multiple books by an author are annotated, the titles are listed alphabetically. The annotations are of necessity terse, most being no more than 75 to 100 words and the briefest being a mere 2 (Miles Burton's *Murder at the Moorings* is "Very poor!"). A combined author/title index concludes the volume.

A *Catalogue of Crime* is an authoritative (one could justifiably say authoritarian) annotated bibliography. Although the quality of prose is high, the accuracy of the annotations is sometimes surprisingly low, as in (for example) the case of the utterly erroneous dismissal of Joel Townsley Rogers's *The Red Right Hand* as "an overwritten, often illiterate attempt to portray a split personality involved in multiple killings and mutilations." In addition, crucial bibliographical data are consistently abbreviated, necessitating constant reference to nine pages of abbreviations at the book's beginning until such abbreviations as CCC, CCD, CUP, C&B, C&E, C&H, C&S, and C&W (to list but a few) are internalized. Furthermore, the names of individual authors are set in small capital letters but are not otherwise distinguished from the text, and the volume contains no running heads. In the case of prolific writers, this makes the location of information very difficult. Finally, Barzun and Taylor never state their methods for determining the contents of *A Catalogue of Crime.* Is this list based solely on the books they have read? based on their personal libraries? derived from the recommendations of friends and acquaintances?

Despite their idiosyncrasies, errors, and quirks, neither edition of *A Catalogue of Crime* may be dismissed. No other guide considered here offers anything approaching the breadth and depth of the *Catalogue,* and the critical judgments tend to be models of perception and concision, expressing in but a few words what others need a page to say. The revised and expanded edition of *A Catalogue of Crime* is a cornerstone of any reference collection and belongs in all libraries.

Genial though the annotations are, the research value of this book is unfortunately slight.

15.   Bourgeau, Art. **The Mystery Lover's Companion.** New York: Crown, 1986. 311 p. Cloth. LC 86-4511. ISBN 0-517-55602-2.

In his introduction Bourgeau, proprietor of Philadelphia's Whodunit? Bookstore, states that he is frequently asked to recommend mysteries, and to assist his customers, he compiled this annotated list of approximately 2,500 mysteries. The volume begins with an introduction in which Bourgeau briefly presents his criteria for determining quality ("a good mystery contains four vital elements: the main character, the plot, the action, and the atmosphere"). The body of the book contains four sections: "The American Mystery"; "The English Mystery"; "The Thriller"; and "The Police Procedural." Each section begins with a brief essay defining the term, after which the annotations are arranged alphabetically by author's last name. Authors represented by more than one volume have their books listed chronologically. Apart from the publication year, bibliographic data are not given, and the annotations are terse, the longest being no more than 100 words. Finally, Bourgeau rates each book using daggers: one is the lowest ("only read this one when you're drunk") and five is the highest ("a true classic").

Bourgeau often writes engagingly, but this volume is unfortunately less than satisfactory as a reference work. It contains no indexes, effectively rendering it useless to a reader who remembers only a title, and it is far from comprehensive: Fredric Brown (here spelled Frederic Brown) is represented by only four books; such significant work as *The Screaming Mimi* (1949) is unmentioned. Because such authors as Trevanian wrote in and are present in more than one genre, cross-references are necessary, yet none has been provided. Most sadly, the contents are dated in a way that Jacques Barzun and Wendell Hertig Taylor's *A Catalogue of Crime* and Bill Pronzini and Marcia Muller's *1001 Midnights* (q.q.v.) are not.

16. Breen, Jon L. **Twenty-Five Best Private Eye Novels of All Time.** http://www. thrillingdetective.com/trivia/triv16.html

This site reprints the list given by Breen in *The Fine Art of Murder* (q.v.).

17. Carr, John Dickson. **John Dickson Carr's Favourites.** http://hem.passagen.se/ orange/jdclist.htm

This Swedish site contains three lists originally compiled by critic and writer Carr: the top 10 mystery and detective short stories (undated), the 10 best detective novels (from 1946), and the 10 best detective novels (from "a later date"). The lists present their contents in no particular order and contain the Swedish titles of the books.

18. Cataio, Joseph. **Mystery Checklist.** Chicago: Reference Books, 1978. 57 p. Paperback. OCLC 5465563.

The *Mystery Checklist* lists the mystery books by 13 popular mystery writers: Raymond Chandler, Agatha Christie, Erle Stanley Gardner, Dashiell Hammett, John D. MacDonald, Ross Macdonald, Ngaio Marsh, Ellery Queen, Dorothy Sayers, Georges Simenon, Maj Sjöwall and Per Wahlöö, Mickey Spillane, and Rex Stout. The arrangement is alphabetical by author. Beneath each author's name are lists of that author's mystery novels, grouped by series character; there are two lists, one arranged alphabetically, the other chronologically. Nonseries books are listed after the lists. Short story collections are referenced in as many sections as necessary; anthologies and omnibus collections of separately published novels are excluded. In all cases, publishers, places of publication, pagination, and other bibliographic data have been omitted; titles are accompanied by only the date of first publication. In the case of Georges Simenon, only the English-language translations of the Inspector Maigret series are included; in the case of Ngaio Marsh, the American and the English titles are listed when they were published in the same year; and in the case of Ellery Queen, only those titles by Frederic Dannay and Manfred B. Lee are listed.

Though well put together and attractively laid out, the similar work by Pamela Granovetter (q.v.) offers more.

19. Charles, John, Joanna Morrison, and Candace Clark. **The Mystery Readers' Advisory: The Librarian's Clues to Murder and Mayhem.** ALA Readers' Advisory Series. Chicago and London: American Library Association, 2002. x, 227 p. Index. Paperback. LC 2001-1055083. ISBN 0-8389-0811-X.

The Mystery Readers' Advisory is intended for a more specialized audience than the majority of the works in this section. Its introduction states forthrightly that "the purpose of this book is to provide library staff with an introduction to the mystery genre as well as offer tips and techniques for providing mystery readers' advisory services in your library. This book was not intended to be a comprehensive bibliography of the mystery genre." Nevertheless, within the parameters it establishes, *The Mystery Readers' Advisory* is a capable introduction. Its first half discusses detective and mystery stories in pleasantly general terms that are likely to benefit public librarians who have never seen or read a mystery book (or who have just received their Master of Library Science [MLS] degrees). Three appendixes list books by subgenre (i.e., "amateur sleuths," "private investigator mysteries," "police procedural mysteries," and "historical mysteries") and theme ("classic mysteries," "mysteries for a book discussion group," "ecclesiastical mysteries," and "culturally diverse detectives") and provide a list of the print and electronic resources likely to be useful. The volume concludes with a selective bibliography and an index of authors and titles and broad genres.

20. Cooper, John, and B. A. Pike. **Detective Fiction: The Collector's Guide.** Lydeard, England: Barn Owl Books, 1988. x, 212 p. Cloth. GB 88-32237. ISBN 0-9509057-5-5. 2nd ed.: Aldershot, England: Scholar Press, 1994. x, 341 p. ISBN 0-85967-991-8.

Unlike Eric Quayle's similarly titled *The Collector's Book of Detective Fiction* (q.v.), this volume is not so much a literary history as it is a handbook for collectors: Cooper and Pike arrange their guide by author and describe the works of 144 significant authors and writing partnerships. All entries follow a similar format. Each gives the author's name, followed by a brief biographical statement that includes relevant pseudonyms; these are followed by a sometimes lengthy bibliographic description of the author's detective and mystery fiction. Binding colors are noted, dust wrappers are described, and unique points of the first edition are mentioned. Entries conclude with chronological lists of the first editions of the writer's detective and mystery novels (occasionally arranged by detective) and of uncollected mystery stories. Each entry is accompanied by a black-and-white photograph of one of the author's books; a section of color plates occupies the middle of the volume. The volume concludes with 13 appendixes that offer a subject guide to the output of the profiled writers; list the anthologies of the Crime Writers' Association (CWA) of Great Britain and the Mystery Writers of America (MWA); list the CWA and MWA award winners for the best novel(s) of each year from 1955 (CWA) and 1953 (MWA) until 1993; provide the names and addresses of specialist dealers in the United Kingdom and the United States; provide a glossary of terms used by book collectors and dealers; offer a selective guide to publishers' practices for designating first editions; list the names and addresses of specialist journals; provide the addresses of societies, journals, and newsletters devoted to individual writers; and give brief information on dust wrapper artists.

Cooper and Pike state in their introduction that "we are amateurs in bibliography, with no training or specialized knowledge of this field." This lack of background is the book's greatest weakness, for the descriptions almost invariably concentrate on the external appearance of the book and not on the textual and typographical elements that distinguish a first edition. Similarly, although their discussions are generally thorough, Cooper and Pike occasionally miss relevant titles. Nevertheless, Cooper and Pike obviously enjoy collecting and reading mystery and detective fiction, and their enthusiasm permeates this pleasurable volume.

21. **The Crown Crime Companion: The Top 100 Mystery Novels of All Time, Selected by the Mystery Writers of America.** Annotated by Otto Penzler. Compiled by Mickey Friedman. Introduction by Peter Ginna and Jane Cavolina. New York: Crown Trade Paperbacks, 1995. 190 p. Paperback. LC 94-43825. ISBN 0-517-88115-2.

Inspired by Susan Moody and the British Crime Writers' Association's *Hatchards Crime Companion* (q.v.), the Mystery Writers of America surveyed their members and compiled a list of their 100 best mystery novels of all time. The results of the survey, annotated by noted bibliographer Otto Penzler, are presented in the first section of *The Crown Crime Companion*. Accompanying these annotations are various lists that emerged during the compilation: the favorite female/male writer, the favorite female/male sleuth, favorite cities for murder, favorite murder weapon, favorite hiding place for a body, favorite animal in a mystery novel, and favorite mystery movie.

The second section assigns the mysteries to one of 10 categories, and an expert discusses the contents of each category: classics (H. R. F. Keating), suspense (Mary Higgins Clark), hard-boiled/private eye (Sue Grafton), police procedural (Joseph Wambaugh), espionage/thriller (John Gardner), criminal (Richard Condon), cozy/traditional (Margaret Maron), historical (Peter Lovesey), humorous (Gregory McDonald), and legal/courtroom (Scott Turow).

The third and concluding section provides lists of the Edgar nominees: the Grand Master, the Best Novel, the Best First Novel by an American Author, the Best Original Paperback, the Best Fact Crime, and the Best Critical/Biographical Work. Data in this last section are current as of 1994; winners are listed in boldface.

Surprisingly, the technical problems with this volume are identical to those of the *Hatchards Crime Companion*. Nowhere do the compilers provide simple alphabetical lists of the authors, titles, or detectives, and the volume is unindexed. Furthermore, the compilers failed to define what they meant by a mystery or a novel, and as a result their lists include works that are neither mysteries nor novels (e.g., short story collections). Equally seriously, the lists have been compiled by active writers, rather than people who have made a serious and concentrated study of the genre, and the preponderance of the titles listed are those published in the last half of the twentieth century, a number of which were best-sellers. One cannot fault the Mystery Writers of America for reading best-sellers (or wanting to write them), but when they include such works as Tom Clancy's *The Hunt for Red October,* Ira Levin's *Rosemary's Baby,* Jack Finney's *Time and Again,* and Bram Stoker's *Dracula* (!), while completely neglecting such writers as Margery Allingham, Lawrence Block, James Lee Burke, Fredric Brown, Dick Francis, R. Austin Freeman, Helen MacInnes, Ngaio Marsh, Robert B. Parker, Ellery Queen, Georges Simenon, and Cornell Woolrich, one is left wondering about the critical acumen of this supposedly august body.

The list of the top 100 mystery novels of all time is available on the Web: http://www.id-online.de/ufo/co3-crow.htm.

22. **Detective Mysteries: A Reader's Checklist and Reference Guide.** CheckerBee Checklist. Middletown, Conn.: CheckerBee, 1999. 95 p. Paperback. ISBN 1-5859-8001-3.

Not seen.

23.　　Eames, Hugh. **Sleuths, Inc. Studies of Problem Solvers: Doyle, Simenon, Hammett, Ambler, Chandler.** Philadelphia and New York: J. B. Lippincott, 1978. 228 p. LC 78-15990. ISBN 0-397-01294-2.

Sleuths, Inc. is an eccentric volume, with five of its six chapters studying the lives and works of the authors listed in the title; the sixth chapter provides an account of the life of Pat Garrett, who achieved fame by killing Billy the Kid. Eames's writing is punchy and direct—it is almost journalistic—but the essays tend to be disorganized, and there are a number of typographical errors. Furthermore, the chapter on Garrett is so remarkably out of place that one wonders why Eames included it. This is not to say *Sleuths, Inc.* does not deserve to be read. Although biographical data in most of the essays are dated and occasionally erroneous—all of his subjects have since died and additional biographical data have emerged—Eames has genuine insights into the works he describes. In order that the reader may be better aware of Brigid O'Shaughnessy's viciousness, for example, Eames recounts the events of *The Maltese Falcon* in chronological order. Similarly, so the reader may understand the Los Angeles of Philip Marlowe, Eames provides a lengthy history of the city. Although there is a selected bibliography for each chapter and a general bibliography, the volume is unindexed.

24.　　Gorman, Ed, Lee Server, and Martin H. Greenberg, eds. **The Big Book of Noir.** New York: Carroll & Graf, 1998. ix, 386 p. Index. Paperback. ISBN 0-7867-0574-4.

It is hard to define *noir* as it is used when referencing literature and motion pictures, but those works that are classed as noir tend to be bleak in outlook, stark in imagery, unsentimental in approach, proletarian in character, and unredemptive in resolution. The editors of *The Big Book of Noir* likewise recognize the problems in attempting such a definition and state that their volume "is a first and informal attempt to chart . . . the various strands of the noir vision in popular entertainment, from its vague beginnings in American pulps and European movie studios to the modern proliferation in mainstream cinema and fiction." *The Big Book of Noir* thus contains four sections, three of which contain chapters written by the editors and by such noted writers as Max Allan Collins, Barry Malzberg, Stephen King, James Sallis, Bill Pronzini, Bill Crider, and Jon L. Breen.

The first section, on film, discusses motion pictures and their creators, reprinting interviews with writers and directors. It concludes with a lengthy list of essential noir films. The second section, on fiction, discusses noted noir writers, among them Cornell Woolrich, Fredric Brown, Jim Thompson, Gil Brewer, Harry Whittington, Mickey Spillane, Chester Himes, and Donald Westlake, and the sources that published their output. It concludes with a lengthy list of noir authors. The third section, on comic books, is an essay by Ron Goulart. Although Goulart is an excellent writer and very knowledgeable, this section is too brief. Other writers should have been found. The fourth section, on radio and television, contains but four chapters, one discussing radio noir and three discussing noir television shows and those who wrote them.

There is much to praise about *The Big Book of Noir*. Though it is not exhaustive, it nevertheless attempts to provide something for almost everyone. At the same time, it is a work that must be used carefully, for many of its chapters were first published elsewhere and have not been revised for inclusion therein. The first chapter is Gene D. Phillips's "Fritz Lang Remembers," whose opening sentence is "high above Beverly Hills, beyond Benedict Cañon Drive, Fritz Lang lives in a splendid, secluded home overlooking Los Angeles." In point of fact, Lang had been dead for 22 years prior to the publication of

The Big Book of Noir, and it is only through checking the acknowledgments that one learns that Phillips's work was first published in 1975.

25.   Gorman, Ed, et al., eds. **The Fine Art of Murder: The Mystery Reader's Indispensable Companion.** New York: Carroll & Graf, 1993. x, 390 p. Index. Paperback. LC 93-21930. ISBN 0-88184-972-3.

This most enjoyable companion arranges its contents thematically, with 22 chapters offering what the back cover refers to as "the perfect accessory to any crime imaginable: a hefty, handsome, one-volume look at mystery fiction of all kinds, from the traditional mystery as written by Charlotte MacLeod and Lilian Jackson Braun, to the serial killer novels of Thomas Harris and Jim Thompson." The contents: American mysteries, traditional mysteries, the Black detective, religious mysteries, private eye mysteries, gay mysteries, British mysteries, dark suspense, women's suspense, police procedurals, hard-boiled mysteries, thrillers and other mysteries, young adult mysteries, short stories, true crime mysteries, the writing life, fandom, television mysteries, comic books, nostalgia, organizations, and mystery bookstores. Illustrations are plentiful, and the volume concludes with a well-done author/title index.

At their lengthiest, the chapters contain significant essays, interviews, discussions, and appreciations. The sections on American mysteries and traditional mysteries, for example, contain 17 and 22 different subsections, respectively. On the other hand, the section devoted to the Black detective contains only an essay titled "Chester Himes and the Black Experience" and a bibliography; and the chapters devoted to dark suspense, women's suspense, thrillers and other mysteries, young adult mysteries, and true crime mysteries contain but three sections apiece. The quality of the essays varies, but the contributors include Robert Bloch, Lawrence Block, Jon Breen, Simon Brett, Dorothy Cannell, Dorothy Salisbury Davis, Carolyn G. Hart, Joan Hess, Edward D. Hoch, H. R. F. Keating, Stephen King, John D. MacDonald, Charlotte MacLeod, Margaret Maron, Warren Murphy, Joan Lowery Nixon, Nancy Pickard, Bill Pronzini, and Margaret Yorke. All entries are lively and readable.

On the debit side, there are some notable omissions. Homage is repeatedly paid to the hard-boiled masters and *Black Mask* is mentioned a few times, but almost nothing is said about the pulps per se. Furthermore, the focus is almost exclusively on Anglo-American mystery writers, with little said about mysteries and mystery writers from other cultures and traditions.

These complaints aside, the considerable strengths of *The Fine Art of Murder* far outweigh its weaknesses. It is a volume that will have something for most people.

26a.   Granovetter, Pamela. **The Copperfield Checklist of Mystery Authors: The Complete Crime Works of 100 Distinguished Writers of Mystery and Detective Fiction.** Copperfield Collection, vol. 1. New York: Copperfield Press, 1987. 128 p. Paperback. ISBN 0-9617037-1-7.

26.5.   Grape, Jan, Dean James, and Ellen Nehr, eds. **Deadly Women: The Woman Mystery Reader's Indispensable Companion.** New York: Carroll & Graf, 1998. xv, 336 p. Paperback. Index. LC 97-21435. ISBN 0-7867-0468-3.

Deadly Women is, like *Murder Ink* (q.v.), a work that strives to provide something for everybody. It contains numerous brief and well-illustrated chapters, the majority by such professional writers and noted critics as Robert Randisi,

Bill Pronzini, Bill Crider, Ed Gorman, Marcia Muller, Margaret Maron, Carolyn G. Hart, Joan Hess, Toni L. P. Kelner, Edward D. Hoch, and Marlys Millhiser, and the book's focus is on the female role in mystery and detective fiction, not merely the women writers or the female characters. As such it provides histories of the overall genre, with discussion of some notable developments, including lesbian detectives and the emergence of the female hard-boiled protagonist. Individual writers are discussed, as are notable female characters, not all of whom were created by male writers: there are appreciations of Kinsey Millhone, Nancy Drew, Judy Bolton, and—surprise!—Carter Brown's Mavis Seidlitz. It provides interviews with such writers as Mary Higgins Clark, Dorothy Cannell, Elizabeth Peters, Sharan Newman, Val McDermid, Marian Babson, Minette Walters, Elizabeth George, Janet Evanovich, Nancy Pickard, Mary Wings, J. A. Jance, Sara Paretsky, Marcia Muller, Laurie King, and Charlotte MacLeod. All essays are lively, although there are occasional errors (or disputable facts), as in the statement that Craig Rice "was the first mystery writer to be so honored" by appearing on the cover of *Time* magazine in 1946: she may have been the first *female* mystery writer so honored, but Edgar Wallace was featured on the cover of *Time* on 15 August 1929. *Deadly Women* belongs in most libraries.

26b. McCallum, Karen Thomas, and Pamela Granovetter. **The Copperfield Checklist of Mystery Authors: The Complete Crime Works of 100 Distinguished Writers of Mystery and Detective Fiction.** Copperfield Collection, vol. 2. New York: Copperfield Press, 1990. 160 p. Paperback. ISBN 0-9617037-1-7.

Intended as a checklist for the collector and reader rather than as a bibliography for the scholar, this slim volume lists the novels written by 100 of the most notable detective and mystery writers. Arrangement is alphabetical by the author's name; the book titles are listed chronologically beneath the name. Publication data include only the date of the first edition; the publisher is not given. Next to each title are three boxes that readers can check to indicate whether they have read the book, own the book, or are uncertain. Omnibuses and collections of shorter works are included, as are (often) the contents of omnibuses. References to known alternate titles, lists of pseudonyms, and books in which the writer was a contributing author are given; award-winning titles are noted with a star. Uncollected short stories, the titles of individual short stories in collections, contributions to anthologies, edited works, and nonfiction titles are not given. Concluding the volume are blank pages for addenda and a directory of specialty dealers. The second edition updates all data through 1991.

Lovers and collectors of mystery and detective fiction will appreciate this checklist. It is portable, clearly arranged, and designed for use. Additional editions are anticipated.

27. Gray, Philip Howard. **Mean Streets and Dark Deeds: The He-Man's Guide to Mysteries (Critical Evaluations of a Thousand Best Private Eye, Detective, Murder, Spy and Thriller Novels of Recent Times).** Bozeman, Mont.: Badger Press, 1998. x, 338 p. Indexes. LC 98-070575. ISBN 0-9663734-0-5. 450 copies printed.

Mean Streets and Dark Deeds is a rarity: a book whose silly title is completely and utterly belied by the contents, which are shrewd, savvy, expertly researched, and enormously enjoyable. The volume begins with a lively introduction in which retired academic Gray explains how and why he decided to compile his bibliography and explains his terms, definitions, arrangements, and classifications. Following this are annotations for 1,001 novels, arranged alphabetically by the book's title, given in bold capital letters. Each citation includes the author's name, the publisher of the first edition, the audience for which the volume is intended, the detective's name and profession, the novel's genre (Gray identifies 18 subgenres), and a numerical ranking of the book's plot, language, action, mystery, and excitement: each of these can count for up to 3 points, meaning a score can be no higher than 15. An annotation of 100 to 300 words provides a discussion of the book, after which are the citation number, lists of the major awards the book has won, and a note indicating whether the book was cited by Keating in *Crime and Mystery,* Jacques Barzun and Wendell Hertig Taylor in *A Catalogue of Crime,* Symons in *Bloody Murder,* Haycraft in *The Art of the Mystery Story,* or Bill Pronzini and Marcia Muller in *1001 Midnights* (q.q.v.). These are followed by an author index to the references, a chronological index that ranks the titles by date and scores, a discussion of Gray's list and the lists cited previously as compared to the winners of the Edgar Awards, a subgenre index, a list of the 100 best mysteries by the 100 best authors, and a ranking of the novels by Gray's scores.

Mean Streets and Dark Deeds is not perfect: Gray misspells Fredric Brown's first name, and occasional errors have crept into the descriptions. At the same time, the book is addictive in the way of *1001 Midnights.* Gray is a demanding reader and pulls no punches in his annotations—his comment on Gore Vidal's *Death in the Fifth Position,* for example, states that "there is no doubt in my own mind that Vidal held the honor of authoring the Best-Written-Most-Boring-Murder-Mystery award until Margaret Truman came along to relieve him." He is exceptionally acute when firearms are misdescribed. Furthermore, for all that Gray is cheerfully politically incorrect, he is also discerning enough to create four awards for "annoying circumstances": the "Glazed Thundermug" for "unnecessary displays of scurrilous language, consisting primarily and uncreatively of two banal words"; the "Leaky Condom Award" given "to any overly boring description of sexual activity which is too pathetic to be humorous and not adequately described to be titillative"; the "Mad Dog Award," in which "we have villains so implausible that even Batman would rather go have a milkshake than to fight them"; and the "Polish Pistol Award," for "wrong statements about firearms, often with conclusions about physical laws, particularly Newtonian, which any good grade school pupil should be able to refute."

Academic libraries seriously collecting detective and mystery fiction should acquire and treasure *Mean Streets and Dark Deeds.*

28. Gribbin, Lenore S. **The Case of the Missing Detective Stories: A List of Books Desired in the Detective Fiction Collection of the University of North Carolina Library.** Chapel Hill: University of North Carolina Library, 1966. [iv], 135 p. Paperback.

Despite its title, this is not merely a desiderata list of the books desired by the library at the University of North Carolina. It is, instead, a checklist of the first English and American editions of the fiction of 60 of the most significant writers of mystery and detective fiction. The list is arranged alphabetically by subject's name, given in capitals and often accompanied by dates of birth and death. The titles are listed alphabetically beneath the subject's name, each title accompanied by the place of publication, publisher, year of publication, and pagination; there are separate entries for the English and American editions. The University of North Carolina's library holdings (as of 1966) are indicated with an unobtrusive asterisk. On the debit side, retitlings have not always been caught, and edited works have not been included.

Had it been widely distributed, this list could have been a significant reference work. It is now a historical document.

29. Grost, Michael E. **A Guide to Classic Mystery and Detection.** http://members. aol.com/MG4273/classics.htm

Grost describes his Web site as "an educational site containing reading lists and essays on great mysteries, mainly of the pre 1960 era." It is this and far more besides, for he has provided a guide that links hundreds of writers and their books by genre. The discussion begins with nineteenth-century mystery fiction and links to the writers and genres. There are sections and links devoted to turn-of-the-century mystery fiction and its writers and genres; golden age writers and genres; noted pulp fiction writers and genres; contemporary mystery fiction writers and genres; and general discussions of the canons of mystery fiction and observations on mystery writers. Subsections are used in the discussion of the golden age writers, which has separate discussions of the groups in what Grost terms "the Intuitionist School," "the Van Dine School," "the Realist School," and "the Bailey School." Grost's bibliographic data are based on his readings rather than authoritative lists, and he provides no illustrations, but his site nevertheless provides an excellent guide to significant publications.

30a. Haycraft, Howard, ed. **The Art of the Mystery Story: A Collection of Critical Essays.** New York: Simon and Schuster, 1946. ix, 545 p. Cloth. LC 47-30017.

30b. Haycraft, Howard, ed. **The Art of the Mystery Story: A Collection of Critical Essays.** New York: Biblo and Tannen, 1976. ix, 565 p. Index. Cloth. LC 75-28263. ISBN 0-8196-0289-2.

Neither this collection of essays nor Haycraft's earlier *Murder for Pleasure: The Life and Times of the Detective Story* (q.v.) is, strictly speaking, a reference book akin to the other reference books in this section. Nevertheless, *The Art of the Mystery Story* is a landmark work, for it established not only that serious criticism could be written about what had hitherto largely been dismissed as a substandard literary genre, but also that critical standards could be applied to works in this genre, and that many of these works could withstand this critical scrutiny.

The Art of the Mystery Story contains 8 sections and, in all, 53 chapters, several of which were written specially for Haycraft. The first section, "Mystery Matures: The Higher Criticism," consists of eight generally appreciative essays by historically important critics and writers, including G. K. Chesterton, R. Austin Freeman, Dorothy L. Sayers, Marjorie Nicolson, H. Douglas Thomson, Vincent Starrett, and Haycraft.

The second section, "The Rules of the Game," reprints S. S. Van Dine's "Twenty Rules for Writing Detective Stories," Ronald A. Knox's "Detective Story Decalogue," and the semihumorous oath of the Detection Club. Lighthearted though these rules are, they nevertheless successfully criticize the way too many detective and mystery stories are written.

The third section, "Care and Feeding of the Whodunit," contains work by Erle Stanley Gardner, Dorothy Sayers, Raymond Chandler, Craig Rice, Anthony Boucher, James Sandoe, John Dickson Carr, and Ken Crossen, among others. These authors discuss what Haycraft terms "the craft of mystery fiction," and not only is their prose eminently readable, their conclusions are magisterial.

The fourth section, "The Lighter Side of Crime," contains poems by Ogden Nash and Richard Armour and reprints, among others, "Watson Was a Woman," Rex Stout's classic piece of silliness; Stephen Leacock's "Murder at $2.50 a Crime"; and Ben Hecht's "The Whistling Corpse." Other works in this section are by S. S. Veendam and Christopher Ward, Robert J. Casey, E. V. Lucas, and Pierre Véry.

The fifth section, "Critics' Corner," consists of discussions by professional critics and reviewers and is, with the possible exception of the third section, the strongest portion of the book. Not only do the critics include the favorably inclined reviewers (among them Will Cuppy, Anthony Boucher, Ellery Queen, and Nicholas Blake), but among them is Edmund Wilson, whose mordant "Who Cares Who Killed Roger Ackroyd?" remains one of the finest attacks on the genre.

The sixth section, "Detective Fiction vs. Real Life," contains only four articles, but one of them—Dashiell Hammett's delightful "From the Memoirs of a Private Detective"—does much to show that truth is often infinitely stranger, sillier, and more ominous than detective and mystery fiction, for truth need not follow the rational lines of a literary plot. The "Inquest on Detective Stories" by the pseudonymous R. Philmore examines the validity of complicated killings in five recent novels and examines the psychological motives for the fictional crimes.

The seventh section, "Putting Crime on the Shelf," offers an article on collecting detective fiction by John Carter, a historical survey of the detective short story by Ellery Queen, and a lengthy list by James Sandoe of works "designed to sketch the form's history, but even more to gather its excellencies and its varieties in puzzling, literacy, and vigor." Haycraft prefaces Sandoe's presentation with a lengthy essay, offering support for and disagreement with Sandoe's choices.

The eighth and concluding section, "Watchman, What of the Night?" contains predictions for the future of the detective and mystery story written by novelist Harrison R. Steeves, critic Philip Van Doren Stern, and Haycraft.

Despite its age, this belongs in all libraries. Later printings are indexed, and the second edition has an introduction by noted scholar Robin W. Winks.

31a. Haycraft, Howard. **Murder for Pleasure: The Life and Times of the Detective Story.** New York: D. Appleton-Century, 1941. xviii, 409 p. Index. Cloth. LC 41-16907.

31b. Haycraft, Howard. **Murder for Pleasure: The Life and Times of the Detective Story.** Newly enlarged and revised ed., with **Notes on Additions to a Cornerstone Library** and **The Haycraft-Queen Definitive Library of Detective-Crime-Mystery Fiction.** New York: Biblo and Tannen,1968. xviii, [14], 409 p. Index. Cloth. LC 68-25809. ISBN 8196-0216-7.

Neither general histories nor collections of miscellaneous essays have been included in this section, but exceptions have been made for this book and for Haycraft's later *The Art of the Mystery Story* (profiled earlier). *Murder for Pleasure* is not the first book-length study of the genre, but it is the work that defined the genre, showing that it was a genuine form of literature and that its history and development were worthy of criticism and study. The 1974 edition contains the additional information promised by its title, and it moves to the end of the volume the illustrations that formerly accompanied the text.

For the first half of the book, Haycraft's approach is essentially historical. His coverage begins with the 1841 appearance of Poe's "The Murders in the Rue Morgue" and concludes with appreciative discussions of Poe's significant numerous English and American contemporaries. Many of the writers he discusses are now forgotten, but few of his judgments have been seriously challenged or overruled.

The second part of *Murder for Pleasure* is thematic in approach. Haycraft formulates the (hitherto largely unwritten) rules for writing a detective story, explaining structures and sources, the need for unity, the creation of the detective, whether there is a need for a sidekick, the viewpoint from which the story should be written, and so forth. In addition, he provides a lengthy list of the criticism written about the detective story, with separate sections for material in books and material in magazines, and he provides a briefer but still important list of the significant books. Finally, he discusses the probable future of the detective story, offers a still-challenging quiz, and provides a who's who in detection (i.e., an alphabetical list of the detectives, sidekicks, antagonists, paired with their creators).

Many histories have since been written, but this one belongs in all libraries.

32.   Huang, Jim, ed. **100 Favorite Mysteries of the Century.** Selected by the Independent Mystery Booksellers Association. Carmel, Ind.: Drood Review, Crum Creek Press, 2000. 159 p. Paperback. ISBN 0-9625804-6-5.

This slim and enjoyable volume began when the members of the online Independent Mystery Booksellers Association (IMBA) were asked to nominate their 100 favorite books. Over 700 titles were nominated, then winnowed by additional voting. This book contains three parts, the first of which lists the 100 favorite mysteries chronologically, then alphabetically by author. The alphabetical list provides signed appreciation of the book. Bibliographic data are confined to providing the author, title, and date of the first monographic edition in boldface type.

The second part provides booksellers' comments and additions to the first list: dealers and fans were permitted to list up to 5 titles that didn't make the top 100 but that they felt should have. Authors and titles are in boldface type, but dates are not provided.

The third part provides information about the IMBA member businesses. The contributors are listed alphabetically by bookshop: the name of the bookshop is given in boldface type, followed by its contact information (address, e-mail, and Web site), the store type, and the author described. A full list of the IMBA member businesses follows, arranged geographically, alphabetically by state, and then alphabetically by city within the state. A few Canadian stores are listed, and the book concludes with a list of currently available paperback editions (with publisher, ISBN, and price) of the books listed.

The list—but not the annotations—is available online at http://www. mysterybooksellers.com/favorites.html.

33.   Huang, Jim, ed. **They Died in Vain: Overlooked, Underappreciated and Forgotten Mystery Novels.** A Drood Review Book. Carmel, Ind.: Crum Creek Press, 2002. 192 p. Paperback. ISBN 0-9625804-7-3.

They Died in Vain contains 103 essays on mystery novels that a variety of mystery booksellers and reviewers considered to be somehow "overlooked, underappreciated or forgotten." The resulting volume contains three sections, the first and lengthiest of which is a list arranged alphabetically by subject's last name. The data for each work give the title, author, and original publication year in boldface type; the essays are signed. The entries range in date from 1878 (Anna Katharine Green's *The Leavenworth Case*) to 2000, although the majority is from the latter quarter of the twentieth century. (The entry for Charlotte Perkins Gilman's *Unpunished* is dated 1929 although the book did not see publication until 1997.)

The volume's second section provides information on the contributors; this includes contact information for a number of bookstores. The third section, described as a "shopping list," is really a checklist providing purchasing information on the titles that are currently in print.

34. Keating, H. R. F. **The Bedside Companion to Crime.** London: O'Mara, 1989. 192 p. Index. Cloth. GB-35501. ISBN 0-9483-9753-5. First American edition: New York: Mysterious Press, 1989. 192 p. Index. Cloth. LC 89-43167. ISBN 0-89296-416-2.

Noted crime writer and critic Keating maintains that it is for enjoyment that people read crime fiction versus fiction with crimes in it. In this sense of enjoyment—and to defend a genre that he sees as being attacked by people who want to make crime fiction into something it is not—he has assembled *The Bedside Companion to Crime*. It contains 11 chapters, their numbering beginning with 10 and counting down to zero. Numerous sidebars and rare photographs are present throughout.

The first chapter, "10 Little—Well, Ten Little Whats?" discusses Agatha Christie titles that have been changed upon republication in America: *And Then There Were None* began its life as *Ten Little Niggers* and has also been titled *Ten Little Indians; The Sittaford Mystery* became *The Murder at Hazlemoor,* and so forth. The chapter "9 Sly Glances" discusses, among other topics, dull books ("dull, nicely dull, books are what we the reading public want for a great deal of the time"), round-robin novels, his own errors, 20 great crooks, and some prolific authors (Leonard Gribble, Erle Stanley Gardner, Edgar Wallace, Leslie Charteris, Rex Stout, and John Creasey). The chapter "8 Kinds of Criminosity" surveys the genres that dominate mystery and detective fiction; "7 Songsters Singing" presents verse, in order of diminishing quality, by W. H. Auden, Ogden Nash, Reginald Hill, Julian Symons, John Heath Stubbs, Gawain Ewart, and Roger Woddis (whose "A Hell of a Writer" states that "The world has cause to celebrate / That day in 1888 / When Raymond Chandler was born"). The chapter "6 Beginnings" discusses the early careers of six writers; "5 Favourites" provides appreciations of five classic novels: *The Moonstone, The Hound of the Baskervilles, The Maltese Falcon, The Talented Mr. Ripley,* and *A Taste for Death.* The chapter "4 Good Old Boys" profiles R. Austin Freeman, Melville Davisson Post, Edgar Wallace, and Jacques Futrelle, whereas "3 Good Old Girls" profiles Mary Roberts Rinehart, Gladys Mitchell, and Margery Allingham. The chapter "2 into One" discusses the collaborative efforts behind Ellery Queen and Emma Lathen; and "1 Fearful Yellow" surveys the works of John D. MacDonald. The last chapter, "And then There Were None," brings the companion full circle, analyzing the form and structure of the typical Agatha Christie novel. An excellent index concludes.

Whether this volume can be considered a reference book is debatable, but it shares the same spirit as Dilys Winn's *Murder Ink* and *Murderess Ink* (q.q.v.), and Keating's intelligence, literacy, and wit make it thoroughly enjoyable.

35.   Keating, H. R. F. **Crime & Mystery: The 100 Best Books.** Foreword by Patricia Highsmith. London: Xanadu, 1987. 218 p. Index. ISBN 0-94776125-X.
New York: Carroll & Graf, 1987. 218 p. Index. LC 87-17377. ISBN
0-88184-345-8.

As its title indicates, this is an annotated list of the 100 works that Keating considers the best crime and mystery books. The list is arranged chronologically, the first title being Edgar Allan Poe's *Tales of Mystery and Imagination* (1845) and the last being
P. D. James's *A Taste for Death* (1986). Each work is presented in a pithy essay that describes its salient characteristics and reveals why Keating chose it; each essay concludes
with bibliographic data on the first English and American editions. The volume concludes with the publisher providing an annotation to a 101st book from Keating's own
oeuvre and a well-done index.

Keating provides an enjoyable introduction in which he reveals how he made his
decisions and that he (wisely) chose not to include "books with crime in them that are not
pure thrillers, nor espionage novels, nor horror stories, nor stories of pure suspense. And
certainly not novels proper that happen to have a crime in them. Sorry, Dostoievski." At
the same time, Keating chose to exclude books by such deserving names as R. Austin
Freeman, for Freeman can be hard to obtain and Keating states, "I see little point a book
praising authors if no one is going to be able to get hold of the books I have praised them
for." This is a less defensible attitude, for a good research library should hold these
books, and even in 1987, interlibrary loans could be arranged. Furthermore, by ignoring
these authors, Keating further marginalizes them and makes it even less likely that they
will be brought back into print. (And there is now a complete R. Austin Freeman available from the Battered Silicon Dispatch Box.) These objections aside, *Crime & Mystery*
is a delight: Keating's prose is witty and succinct, his taste impeccable, and his
judgments magisterial.

A chronological version of his list is available online at http://hem.passagen.
se/orange/bestlist.htm.

36.   Keating, H. R. F., ed. **Whodunit? A Guide to Crime, Suspense and Spy Fiction.** London: Windward, 1982. 320 p. Index. Cloth. ISBN 0-711202-29-4. New
York: Van Nostrand Reinhold, 1982. 320 p. Index. Cloth. LC 82-8616. ISBN
0-442-25438-5.

With assistance from 22 leading novelists and critics, Keating has assembled
one of the most enjoyable reader's guides, a volume that offers historical essays, critical
discussions of genres, biocritical data on noted writers and their books, and information
on some of the noted characters in mystery, detective, and suspense fiction. The volume
is illustrated throughout with pictures of authors, actors, manuscript pages, and
renderings of noted characters.

Keating's introduction discusses the differences among crime fiction, crime
fact, and mainstream fiction. The first section, "Crime Fiction and Its Categories," consists of essays from writers surveying the history and genres of detective and mystery
fiction. Reginald Hill provides a prehistory of the detective story. Keating writes "The
Godfather and the Father"; Robert Barnard, "The English Detective Story"; Julian
Symons, "The American Detective Story"; Hillary Waugh, "The American Police Procedural"; Michael Gilbert, "The British Police Procedural"; Eleanor Sullivan, "The
Short Story"; Jessica Mann, "The Suspense Novel"; Jerry Palmer, "The Thriller";
Michele Slung, "The Gothic"; and John Gardner, "The Espionage Novel." All contribu-

tors are excellent writers as well as experts in their fields; their essays are brief and insightful, though not completely free from error: Symons, for example, states, "*Red Harvest* is the only Continental Op novel," neglecting *The Dain Curse*.

The second section, "How I Write My Books," is autobiographical, with statements from Stanley Ellin, P. D. James, Desmond Bagley, Dorothy Eden, Patricia Highsmith, Gregory McDonald, Lionel Davidson, Len Deighton, Eric Ambler, and H. R. F. Keating. Brief though these essays are, they nevertheless reveal unexpected similarities: Ambler and McDonald make virtually identical statements regarding the importance of the Idea.

The third section, "Writers and Their Books: A Consumers' Guide," is the lengthiest. Written by Keating, Dorothy B. Hughes, Melvyn Barnes, and Reginald Hill, it provides biographical data on some 500 (predominantly) Anglo-American writers of some 1,500 books. Listed beneath each author are the titles of representative books, "recommended as an introduction to the author in question." The characterization, plot, readability, and tension of each book are separately rated, with up to 10 stars awarded for each. This awkward rating system is unintentionally made more difficult by the small size of the stars. Furthermore, though one can argue about the choice of subjects and representative books—Jacques Futrelle is represented only by a 1973 collection, Robert Van Gulik by only *Necklace and Calabash*—the rankings are most objectionable. One senses that the coauthors did not talk much among themselves or else they would not have permitted Arthur Reeve's *The Poisoned Pen* to rank higher in tension than Ruth Rendell's *Put on by Cunning,* nor would they have undervalued woefully R. Austin Freeman's tension, overrated Carter Brown's tension, and similarly overrated the characterizations of Mary Higgins Clark. Neither is this section error-free: *Rogue Male* was not Geoffrey Household's second book; the first name of Fredric Brown is misspelled; and so forth.

Keating is sole author of the fourth section, "The People of Crime Fiction," an illustrated guide to 90 of the best-known detectives and criminal figures, from "Abner, Uncle" to "Wolfe, Nero." Each character is briefly and wittily described; each entry concludes with the name of the character's creator. The brief concluding section is by Philip Graham, professor of child psychiatry at the Institute of Child Health, London, and consultant psychiatrist at the Hospital for Sick Children, Great Ormond Street; he attempts to address the subject of "Why People Read Crime Fiction." His theories, which involve releases of childhood fantasies and compulsive personalities, are very debatable.

Despite the occasional errors and the weak last section, this is one of the better reader's guides. The concluding index is excellent.

37.   Kelleghan, Fiona, ed. **100 Masters of Mystery and Detective Fiction.** Pasadena, Calif., and Hackensack, N.J.: Salem Press, 2001. 2 vols. 757 p. Index. LC 2001-032834. ISBN 0-89356-973-9 (vol. 1); 0-89356-977-1 (vol. 2); 0-89356-958-5 (set).

The 100 essays in the two volumes of *100 Masters of Mystery and Detective Fiction* were derived from Salem Press's *Critical Survey of Mystery and Detective Fiction* (q.v.), but the essays on living authors have been expanded and updated, as have the bibliographies accompanying them. The format of these volumes is the same as that of the *Critical Survey,* which is to say that the essays are arranged alphabetically by the subject's last name. All essays are signed, range in length from 2,500 to 6,000 words, and begin with ready-reference information that provides the subject's name, birth and death places and dates, notable pseudonyms, types of plot most commonly used, and the names of principal series. (In the case of Nick Carter and Ellery Queen, entries begin by listing the authors who have written using these names.) These are followed by a statement listing the subject's contribution to the genre, a brief biography, an analysis of the author's works and themes, and an occasionally lengthy primary and secondary bibliography. The second volume concludes with a glossary defining several hundred genre terms, a time line, and indexes by series characters and plot types.

This set is in most ways superior to its source, and Kelleghan is to be commended for her efforts, which bring an editorial focus and significant intellectual rigor to a set that badly needed these. On the debit side, there remain some small errors: T. S. Stribling and Carolyn Wells remain absent, as are such contemporary writers as Thomas Cook and Minette Walters; the glossary is better than it was but not yet what it could be; and Kelleghan's introduction, although intelligent and thought provoking, strikes this reader as being overly restrictive in its thesis and the accompanying exegesis. These cavils aside, these two volumes belong in all libraries that own the *Critical Survey of Mystery and Detective Fiction.*

38. la Cour, Tage, and Harald Mogensen. **The Murder Book: An Illustrated History of the Detective Story.** Foreword by Julian Symons. New York: Herder and Herder, 1971. 192 p. Index. Cloth. LC 71-150304.

Originally published as *Mordbogen* (Copenhagen: Lademann Forlagsaktieselskab, 1969), this is far more than the coffee-table book it initially resembles. It is instead a very well-illustrated history of the detective story, from Edgar Allan Poe to Georges Simenon. What makes it intriguing is that it is written from a Danish perspective. Many of its illustrations are by Scandinavian artists, and a number of its references are to English and European writers who have been either ignored or neglected by American historians. The text is full of informed, intriguing, and occasionally debatable commentary: Israel Zangwill, for example, is claimed as "the first writer to put a living personality into his book—no less a person, in fact, than Mr. Gladstone, the Prime Minister." Surely an earlier example can be found in Dickens?

The book concludes with a thoroughly international bibliography and a well-done index. Only slightly dated, this work remains relevant and enjoyable.

39. Landrum, Larry. **American Mystery and Detective Novels: A Reference Guide.** American Popular Culture. Westport, Conn.: Greenwood, 1999. xxii, 273 p. Indexes. LC 98-22916. ISBN 0-313-21387-9. ISSN 0193-6859.

Despite its title, this volume is not so much a reference guide as it is an extended series of bibliographic essays discussing predominantly American mystery and detective novels. There are five chapters—historical outline, related formulas, criticism and theory, authors, and reference—each of which contains numerous subsections. The historical outline section, for example, discusses among other subjects the European influence, story papers and dime novels, "classic" detective novels, pulp magazines, hard-boiled fiction, and contemporary diversity, and related formulas discusses seven of the major genre formulas: gothics, gangster novels, suspense novels, thrillers, courtroom dramas and lawyer novels, police procedurals, and postmodern detective novels. The authors sections is a largely chronological presentation, with a survey of early writers followed by a decade-by-decade discussion of the notable writers from the 1920s to the

1990s. A lengthy bibliography and separate indexes for the names and subjects and titles discussed or mentioned are included.

American Mystery and Detective Novels is a highly uneven work. When Landrum is discussing contemporary authors and their works, he often is excellent, presenting the subject neatly and concisely, using a minimum of words to convey strengths and weaknesses; his discussions of criticism and theory are likewise very enjoyable. On the other hand, his discussions of the historical material are deeply and repeatedly flawed; errors abound. In his discussion of dime novels, for example, he states, "The most famous dime novel figure was Nick Carter. Over 100 Nick Carter novels have been reprinted recently in paperback. [Not so; these paperbacks merely use a character with the same name.] The *Nick Carter Weekly* began in 1891, and as late as 1933 there were still 400 paper volumes in print. [The *Nick Carter Weekly* began publication on 2 January 1897.]" Similarly, Landrum's discussion of the pulp magazines starts, "Pulp magazines such as *Argosy* and *Blue Book* appeared around 1896," when in fact the first issue of *Blue Book* appeared under another title nearly 10 years later.

One hopes for a corrected and revised second edition.

40.   Mackler, Tasha. **Murder . . . by Category: A Subject Guide to Mystery Fiction.** Metuchen, N.J.: Scarecrow, 1991. xiii, 470 p. Cloth. LC 91-37638. ISBN 0-8108-2463-9.

Like Menendez and Olderr (q.q.v.), Mackler has compiled a subject index to mystery fiction; unlike them, she has annotated her bibliography, confining her focus "to mystery stories that are readily available as recently-released hardcovers and paperbacks, or as titles kept on a publisher's backlist." Mackler thus classifies and annotates approximately 2,400 titles, using subject headings ranging alphabetically from "Academics" to "Writers and Their Conventions." Mackler's 80 subjects include "Anthropology and Archaeology," "Corruption," "Espionage, the Industrial Kind," "Libraries," "Manuscripts," "Old Crimes and Murders," "Psychics, with a Touch of Magic," "Suicide or Murder," and "Witches, Curses, and a Little Voodoo," and geographic locations (Africa, Americans in England, Canada, Hollywood, etc.) are also referenced. Each citation provides publication data for the book's first hardcover and paperback editions; entries for paperback originals are distinguished by "PBO." Entries for books featuring series characters are numbered (1st, 2nd, 3rd, etc.). Books that can be classified into more than one subject are cross-referenced with the primary entry listing the secondary subject; the secondary subject references the primary entry. Concluding the volume are a list of British women mystery writers, a lengthier list of female detectives who are series characters, lists of the Edgar, Anthony, and Shamus Awards winners up to 1989, a brief bibliography, and an author index.

On the debit side, this volume is not error free: Susan Moody's *Penny Black* and *Penny Dreadful* are both listed as the second volume in the Penny Wanawake series, and additional errors are readily discernible. Furthermore, Mackler's citations occasionally are frustrating in their use of cross-references, and she is often inconsistent in her revelation of pseudonyms. Reference is made to Erle Stanley Gardner writing as A. A. Fair, but a user knowing of only A. A. Fair will find no linking cross-reference because references to Fair occur only under Gardner. Similarly, nowhere is it stated that Barbara Michaels and Elizabeth Peters are the same person, and although titles are cited by writers such as Ellis Peters and Dell Shannon, nowhere are their real names listed. Most annoying, there is no title index.

These problems do not prevent the contents of this volume from being accessible, and that Mackler chose to annotate only recently published and generally available titles is simultaneously one of this book's major strengths and weaknesses. She provided contemporary readers with a readily accessible list of books, but the majority of Mackler's entries are now out of print, and this bibliography is primarily of historic importance.

41.   Magill, Frank N., ed. **Critical Survey of Mystery and Detective Fiction.** Pasadena, Calif.: Salem Press, 1988. 4 vols. xii, 1748, xliv p. Index. Cloth. LC 88-28566. ISBN 0-89356-486-9 (set).

Critical Survey of Mystery and Detective Fiction provides biocritical surveys of the lives and prose of more than 270 authors chosen because they were pioneers in the development of the detective and mystery story, because they did their most notable work in the genre, or because they contributed to the genre even while having significant reputations in fields of other literary endeavor. This last criterion is a dubious one, allowing for the inclusion of such figures as Arnold Bennett, Jorge Luis Borges, Fyodor Dostoyevsky, William Faulkner, W. W. Jacobs, Stephen King, and Frank R. Stockton. Also included are critical surveys of writers of gothic fiction, espionage fiction, the police procedural, the psychological thriller, the hard-boiled, and the romantic suspense story.

The four volumes are arranged alphabetically by the subject's last name. Each article begins with ready-reference information that provides the subject's name, birth and death places and dates, notable pseudonyms, types of plot most commonly used, and the names of the author's principal series. This is followed by a section describing the principal series character(s). The next section provides a critical statement, of no more than 200 words, detailing the subject's contribution to the genre; it is followed by a brief biography of the author that is also rarely more than 200 words. A section titled "Analysis" provides descriptions of the author's major contributions to the genre, the focus being (more often than not) on plot summary rather than criticism. Entries conclude with separate sections listing the subject's principal mystery and detective books, other major works, and a brief bibliography of secondary sources. All entries are signed; few are more than 2,500 words in length, though writers of exceptional importance warrant longer entries; and the entry format described earlier is not followed in the case of such writers as Ellery Queen and Nick Carter, whose names have "served as house names for a shifting and sometimes large number of authors." The fourth volume concludes with a glossary of mystery/detective terms, indexes for the plot genres and series characters, as well as a general author/title index.

The *Critical Survey* will satisfy most high school students and undergraduates, but its four volumes are far from flawless. One may object to an editorial approach that accords entries to such noninfluences as Dean Koontz but neglects such historical figures as T. S. Stribling and Carolyn Wells. The articles tend to overpraise their subjects, providing appreciations rather than analyses, and errors in the plot summaries are sometimes significant. On occasion, the analyses focus exclusively on one series and neglect other more worthy publications. The bibliographic data list only titles and dates of publication, and these are presented as a group; even if the author has written under a pseudonym or in collaboration, these publications are not separately identified. For example, the entry for Leslie Charteris states, "Charteris often contented himself with polishing and giving final approval to a story written largely by someone else," but one cannot locate these stories in this set. Finally, the glossary is woefully inadequate, failing to define even such basic terms as "cozy" and erring in its definition of such terms as "gunsel" and "hard-boiled."

One hundred of the essays in the *Critical Survey* have been updated in *100 Masters of Mystery and Detective Fiction,* edited by Fiona Kelleghan (q.v.).

42. McLeish, Kenneth, and Valerie McLeish. **Bloomsbury Good Reading Guide to Murder, Crime Fiction, and Thrillers.** London: Bloomsbury, 1990. ix, 200 p. Indexes. Paperback. ISBN 0-7475-0732-5.

The first section of this guide describes the work of some 250 crime, thriller, and espionage writers, the majority of whom are from Great Britain or America. Arranged alphabetically by writer, each entry has the writer's birth year and nationality and provides a mildly critical but generally appreciative statement about the writer's oeuvre. Often an exemplary work is described in slightly more depth, though bibliographic data are generally confined to the book's title and its year of publication. Cross-references abound, and sidebars beside each author list other books by that author and related books by authors. Some 66 "special menus" scattered throughout the book list authors and titles by genres ranging alphabetically from "The Art of Crime" to "War Stories" and including such diverse subjects as "Big Money," "Christmas," "Filthy Rich," "Houses," "Junk Bonds," "Pensioners," "Special Skills Required," and "Unusual Locations." Following the first section, a two-page glossary defines eight related terms, a who's who lists the name of the character and the name of his or her creator, and the volume concludes with a capably done author/title index.

The contents of this guide were chosen because they reflected the enthusiasms of the McLeishes, and one cannot fault them for that. One can, however, argue that they should have cast their nets wider. A guide to good reading that mentions Michael Avallone and Tom Clancy but neglects Fredric Brown, R. Austin Freeman, Sue Grafton, Faye Kelleman, and Phoebe Atwood Taylor (to name but a few) cannot be considered definitive.

43a. Menendez, Albert J. **The Subject Is Murder: A Selective Subject Guide to Mystery Fiction. Volume 1.** Garland Reference Library of the Humanities, vol. 627. New York: Garland, 1986. x, 332 p. Index. Cloth. LC 85-45134. ISBN 0-8240-8655-4.

43b. Menendez, Albert J. **The Subject Is Murder: A Selective Subject Guide to Mystery Fiction, Volume 2.** Garland Reference Library of the Humanities, vol. 1060. New York: Garland, 1990. x, 216 p. Index. Cloth. LC 85-45134. ISBN 0-8240-2580-6.

Recognizing that people collect, read, and sell mystery and detective fiction by the book's perceived subject, Menendez offers subject access to nearly 6,000 mystery and detective novels: more than 3,800 books are classified in the first volume, and nearly 2,100 are classed in the second. In the first volume, 25 subject classifications are used; the second volume uses 29, with subclassifications in such areas as "sports and hobbies," in which 25 subcategories have been identified. Both volumes are arranged alphabetically by the subject heading, with the citations listed alphabetically by author's name. Both volumes number their citations, which provide title, place of publication, publisher, and year of publication; both conclude with an index to the authors. The first volume, however, includes a list of stores specializing in detective and mystery fiction, whereas the second volume drops the list, provides a statistical ranking of books "by category," a cross-reference index to the first volume, and a title index. Neither volume identifies pseudonyms or offers cross-references.

There is a need for subject access to mystery fiction, but at best these volumes can be considered but a beginning, for Menendez's subject headings are inadequate. Worse yet, each book is indexed only once. A reader thus hoping to find mysteries featuring cats (or dogs or pets) will find some of Lilian Jackson Braun's Cat volumes listed under "journalism" and others classed under the subjects of "art," "antiques," and "Christmas," but there is no subject access for locating Braun's most notable and recurring narrative device. Similarly, although Menendez's subject headings include "Circuses and Carnivals," "Cooking," "Hotels and Inns," "Musical Murders," "Politics and Murder," and "Weddings and Honeymoons," those novels that use female detectives cannot be located, for there is no listing for "Women Detectives" (or any variant term). Finally, Menendez's classifications occasionally are erroneous: R. Austin Freeman's *The Uttermost Farthing* is classed as an archaeological mystery, though the story involves a doctor hunting for the murderer of his wife, a hunt that has the doctor capturing burglars and anarchists, shrinking their heads according to the best Mundurucus recipes, and mounting their skeletons in his personal museum. Archaeology plays no role in this gleefully black-humored novel.

A revised, expanded, and corrected edition of these volumes is needed.

44. Moody, Susan, ed. **The Hatchards Crime Companion: 100 Top Crime Novels Selected by the Crime Writers' Association.** London: Hatchards, 1990. xvii, 153 p. Paperback. GB 90-42224. ISBN 0-904030-02-4.

During the late 1980s, members of the Crime Writers' Association of England voted on what they considered to be the 100 top crime novels of all time. The annotated list of their rankings occupies approximately the first third of this volume. The list begins with Josephine Tey's *Daughter of Time* and concludes with Edgar Wallace's *Four Just Men;* it includes such familiar names as Chandler, Hammett, Sayers, and James, but there are also some surprises: the Crime Writers' Association took a very broad view of their charge, and browsers of this section will find such titles as Richard Condon's *The Manchurian Candidate* and John Fowles's *The Collector*. The bibliographic data are limited, however; apart from the author, title, and publication year, the only information provided is the availability of a paperback or hardcover edition. Printed as sidebars throughout the annotated list are supplementary lists of the CWA's favorite male and female writers and favorite male and female detectives.

The second section consists of 10 essays that provide guides to the different genres of detective and mystery fiction, and the third section contains four essays on the nature of a good crime book. All essays are readable; all provide excellent introductions to their subjects; none will surprise anybody who has read substantially.

The fourth and concluding section to the volume provides information about the CWA. A history is provided, as is an extensive list of the volumes that have won the awards issued by the association: the Crossed Red Herrings Award, the Gold Dagger, the Silver Dagger, and the Diamond Dagger.

Despite its breeziness, this volume is inferior in organization and content to such "best of" lists as Maxim Jakubowski's *100 Great Detectives* (q.v.). Nowhere does Moody provide simple alphabetical lists of the authors, titles, or detectives; the annotations are brief and not particularly insightful, and the volume is unindexed. Were it not for its information on the CWA and its distinguished awards, this book would be without value.

45. Most, Glenn W., and William W. Stowe, eds. **The Poetics of Murder: Detective Fiction and Literary Theory.** San Diego: Harcourt Brace Jovanovich, 1983. xvii, 394 p. Index. LC 82-23429. ISBN 0-15-172280-3 (hc); 0-15-672312-3 (pb).

The last two words of the subtitle provide an indication of the focus of this collection of 20 essays, this volume unabashedly providing works of literary theory that discuss the detective story. No one theoretical school is espoused, and readers can find essays from thinkers proffering sociological, psychoanalytical, philosophical, Freudian, and semiotic perspectives. A significant number of the critics have international origins, and almost all of the essays have seen prior publication and have been translated for this volume; the only two original essays are Most's discussion of John le Carré and Stowe's essay on modes of detection in Doyle and Chandler. Among the more noted critics represented in the volume are Umberto Eco, Frank Kermode, Stephen Knight, F. R. Jameson, Jacques Lacan, and Roland Barthes, although it perhaps should be mentioned that the work of the latter two is virtually inaccessible, so dense, word-clogged, needlessly obscure, and self-referential as to seem parodic is it. Barthes's "Delay and the Hermeneutic Sentence," for example, contains the following sentence, which is (alas) all too typical: "Whence, in the hermeneutic code, in comparison to these extreme terms (question and answer), the abundance of dilatory morphemes: the *snare* (a kind of deliberate evasion of the truth), the *equivocation* (a mixture of truth and snare which frequently, while focusing on the enigma, helps to thicken it), the *partial answer* (which only exacerbates the expectation of the truth), the *suspended answer* (an aphasic stoppage of the disclosure), and *jamming* (acknowledgment of insolubility)." Similarly, Lacan's "Seminar on 'The Purloined Letter'" manages to say very little about its subject and says it in an extraordinarily involuted fashion, starting, "Our inquiry has led us to the point of recognizing that the repetition automatism (*Wiederholungszwang*) finds its basis in what we have called the *insistence* of the signifying chain."

The book concludes with a brief bibliography and an inadequate index.

46. Murch, A. E. **The Development of the Detective Novel.** London: Peter Owen, 1958. 272 p. Index. New York: Philosophical Library, 1958. 272 p. Index. Westport, Conn.: Greenwood, 1968. 272 p. Index. LC 69-10138. ISBN 1-08371-0581-1.

Murch concludes her introduction by stating, "The purpose of this book is to examine the evolution of this 'fixed form' [the detective novel] and its accepted variations, from the opening of the nineteenth century; to trace the sources of its recognizable elements and discover the stages by which it arrived at its present popularity." She thus provides a largely historical discussion of the detective story, beginning her literary survey by mentioning Elizabethan and seventeenth-century writers, the picaresque novels, the Newgate Calendar, and such writers as Daniel Defoe and the Chevalier de Mailly, whose 1719 *Le Voyage et Les aventures des Trois Princes de Serendip, traduit du Persan* contains the anecdote later used by Voltaire in *Zadig* (1750). Successive chapters discuss the establishment of certain features used in the detective story, the rise of the *roman-feuilleton* and themes in the work of Balzac, Sue, and Dumas. Her discussion of Poe's accomplishments and international influence is lively and readable, but when she reaches the end of the nineteenth century, her work starts to flag: errors of all kinds occur with increasing frequency. She seems unaware of the existence of the pulp magazines, which did much to create, define, and develop the different genres of mystery and detective story, and because she neglects to discuss the social implications of the modern literature, the volume ends on a weaker and more inconclusive note than it should. It nevertheless remains well worth reading.

47.   Niebuhr, Gary Warren. **Make Mine a Mystery: A Reader's Guide to Mystery and Detective Fiction.** Westport, Conn.: Libraries Unlimited, 2003. xv, 603 p. Indexes. ISBN 1-56308-784-7.

Intended largely for librarians, *Make Mine a Mystery* contains three sections, the first two of which consist of three chapters. The relatively brief first section is an introduction to the genre that provides useful definitions and explanations. An overview of the book is offered, as is useful advice for the librarian who wishes to engage in readers' advisory activities. Niebuhr's definitions are reasonable and intelligent, and his justifications are valid, but errors creep in when he provides a history of the mystery: he dates Poe's "The Murders in the Rue Morgue" to 1845 without explaining that the story first appeared in 1841 and that the 1845 date is its first book publication; he states that R. Austin Freeman's Dr. Thorndyke is an eccentric detective; he states that Ellery Queen and Rex Stout were important during the 1920s, whereas the first Queen mystery did not appear until 1929 and Stout's *Fer de Lance* was not published until 1934.

The second and very lengthy section is devoted to the genre literature. The different chapters document the various types of amateur detectives, public detectives, and private detectives. Each entry begins with a description of the author's work and series character and, in boldface type, a one- or two-word description of the detective type: that is, hard-boiled, traditional, historical, and so forth. For each entry, the book's title is given in boldface type followed by the publisher and publication year; the annotation describes the plot without revealing the solution, and each citation concludes with the geographical setting in italic type. Although one can always recommend additions, Niebuhr's choices are well presented and quite defensible, and the biggest problem with this second section is one of book design: there are no running heads, making it quite difficult to determine where one is in an alphabetical sequence.

The third section is a lengthy appendix that contains a very useful bibliography, information about conventions, lists of bookstores, journals, and online resources. The volume concludes with well-presented indexes for author, title, subjects, and geographical setting.

Despite the preceding criticisms, *Make Mine a Mystery* contains a wealth of data and is one of the best reader's guides considered in this chapter.

48.   Olderr, Steven. **Mystery Index: Subjects, Settings, and Sleuths of 10,000 Titles.** Chicago: American Library Association, 1987. xiv, 492 p. Cloth. LC 87-1294. ISBN 0-8389-0461-0.

Public librarian Olderr has indexed the authors, titles, detectives, and the subjects and settings of approximately 10,000 British and American detective and mystery books. Why these and not others were selected for indexing is stated in neither Olderr's preface nor his acknowledgments, although many if not all of the books apparently came from the collections of the Riverside (Illinois) Public Library, Olderr's place of employment. The index is clearly reproduced from typed copy and is easy to use, but in its presentation of data and in its principles of compilation, this is an eccentric book, one for which every statement must be qualified.

A "Main Entry Section" lists the books by their author and gives also the title, publisher, and date of publication. If the U.K. edition has a different title or publisher or both, these are provided. Each citation concludes with the name of the detective or the primary characters; a number after the character's name indicates the order of the character's appearance in a series. Although this material is not error free, the worst problem with this section is that Olderr opted to index by only the American titles, regardless of author's nationality or publication precedence, and did not include cross-references. In the case of prolific writers, this decision means that uncertain users must check the title index, for Olderr's lists are difficult to browse.

The title index lists all titles and retitlings, but it does not state which title the book has been indexed under, and occasionally it indexes titles that are nowhere present in the main entry section. A user curious about Agatha Christie's novel that began life as *Ten Little Niggers* will find an entry for that title, preceded by an entry for *Ten Little Indians,* but neither references the title under which the book has been indexed *(And Then There Were None)*, and the entry for *And Then There Were None* does not mention *Ten Little Indians.*

The subject and setting index and the character index conclude the volume. The former is perhaps the best part of the book: the subject headings are well chosen and offer access to the novels by terms as varied and intriguing as "Burglars as Detectives," "Camels," "Postal Inspectors as Detectives," "Transsexuals," and "Witch Doctors as Detectives." The settings range alphabetically from the Adirondack Mountains to Zanzibar. There are numerous helpful cross-references. The character index lists the detectives by their last names, giving the author. When the author used more than one detective or main character, individual titles also are given. Useful though this section could be, Olderr has been inconsistent in his indexing of detectives and main characters. Series detectives may be listed, but series narrators—those who observe and report on the activities of the detective—are not, with the exception of John Watson, M.D. The researcher hoping to find the R. Austin Freeman stories narrated by Jervis, or Hercule Poirot stories narrated by somebody other than Hastings, will be thoroughly frustrated, for although these characters have the force, if not the status, of main characters, they (and thousands of other narrators) are nowhere mentioned.

If all Olderr offered were indexes by author, title, and detective, this flawed volume would have been thoroughly superseded by Hubin's monumental achievements (q.v.). Olderr's indexing of subjects and settings, however, is far superior to that offered by Hubin, and until such time as a superior subject and setting index are compiled to detective and mystery fiction, this book remains a necessary acquisition.

49.   Ousby, Ian. **Guilty Parties: A Mystery Lover's Companion.** New York: Thames & Hudson, 1997. 224 p. Index. Paperback. LC 97-60242. ISBN 0-500-27978-0.

The title page of this lavishly illustrated guide states that it contains 195 illustrations, 31 in color. Indeed, the illustrations dominate the volume, which is in many ways reminiscent of la Cour and Mogensen's *Murder Book, Murder Ink,* and *Murderess Ink* edited by Dilys Winn, and Waltraud Woeller and Bruce Cassiday's *The Literature of Crime and Detection* (q.q.v.).

Ousby's history is gracefully written, but it is not without its share of factual errors. His discussion of the pulp magazines, for example, opens by stating that pulp magazines began "in the 1880s," that they sold largely by subscription, that their pages were grey, that Dr. Fu-Manchu was a creation of the dime novel, that the pulp series character

The Shadow was Lamont Cranston, and that Dashiell Hammett first appeared in *Black Mask* in 1923: errors all. Similar errors exist throughout. Equally seriously, Ousby's history is unbalanced, mentioning such historically important writers as Edgar Wallace only in passing.

The reference material given by Ousby includes lists of material about Sherlock Holmes; Locked Room mysteries; Ronald Knox's 1929 "Ten Commandments"; mysteries set at Oxford, Cambridge, and Harvard; books about Agatha Christie; the first and last appearances of golden age detectives; a brief "hard-boiled" dictionary; books and movies about Simenon and Maigret; films connected with crime and mystery fiction; and notable women writers. A map of the United States indicates settings of private eye novels; sad to say, Ousby can find only one Philadelphia private eye. The volume concludes with lists of award-winning detective and mystery fiction produced in the United States, United Kingdom, and France. A brief and inadequate bibliography of secondary sources is included, as well as a historical chronology and a well-done index.

Though *Guilty Parties* is amiable, it is not the book it could and should have been. Ousby's *Bloodhounds of Heaven* (1976) shows that he is capable of superior work.

50.   Pronzini, Bill. **Gun in Cheek: A Study of "Alternative" Crime Fiction.** Introduction by Ed McBain. New York: Coward, McGann & Geoghegan, 1982. 264 p. Index. Cloth. LC 82-5172. ISBN 0-698-11180-X.

The majority of the reader's guides in this section lists and describes the best writers and writings, but as Ed McBain's introduction makes immediately clear, this is not one of them: Pronzini's desire is to survey the truly terrible mysteries written by the unashamedly bad writers, for these works have been inexplicably neglected by both academics and aficionados. Pronzini's survey ranges wide, providing summaries of plots that should never have been hatched, samples of dialogue that should not have been written (and could not have been spoken), descriptions of behavior patterns that are improbable (and inimitable), and attitudes and approaches toward subjects that are perhaps best described as "politically incorrect." One chapter, "The Saga of the Risen Phoenix," assays the entire output of the low-budget Phoenix House, because "in less than twenty years, Phoenix published almost as many wonderfully bad novels as *all* the other publishers combined."

As in any guide, opinions are paramount and disagreements with these are inevitable. Pronzini is quite correct in stating, "What makes [William] Le Queux a classicist are his often-farfetched plots, his ability to pad them out interminably with description and repetitive conversation, and his unsurpassed ear for stilted dialogue." Pronzini is equally correct in damning Sydney Horler and Mickey Spillane (among others) for meretricious attitudes, impossible plotting, and generally poor writing. On the other hand, it is unfair to Michael Avallone, Robert Leslie Bellem, Carter Brown, and Richard Prather to include them here. All have styles uniquely their own and are in many ways self-parodic; indeed, critics such as S. J. Perelman recognized that Bellem's prose was unique, a cheerfully ribald parodying of all the pretensions and conventions of a genre. Avallone's mangling of metaphors and improbable plots and Prather's perpetual descriptions of tumescence (and equally improbable plots) are good-humored, lightweight, and intentionally silly.

Neither, alas, is *Gun in Cheek* free from error. In opening his discussion of the amateur detective ("AD"), Pronzini states, "Beginning with Jacques Futrelle's Professor F. X. Van Duesen [*sic*], 'The Thinking Machine,' in this country, and, somewhat later,

Chesterton's Father Brown in England, the AD has seen more bloodletting, faced more peril, and unraveled more mysteries than all professional detectives in public and private, combined." Futrelle most certainly did not invent the amateur detective, and the character of the Thinking Machine did not engage in physical activity but epitomizes the armchair detective. Neither (as Pronzini states elsewhere) was writer Tom Roan from Alabama; Pronzini undoubtedly meant Arizona.

Though these errors are jarring, they do not inhibit the pleasures given by this book. Pronzini's first chapter states,"The purpose of this book is threefold: first to rectify the neglect of these writers and their books, to give them the critical attention they deserve; second, to provide a different historical perspective on crime fiction—its detectives, its genres, its publishers—and on the social attitudes it reflects (which are often more pronounced in the bad mystery than in the good one); and third, to add a few chuckles—perhaps even a guffaw or two—to the heretofore sobersided field of mystery criticism." In all of these, he succeeds admirably.

51.   Pronzini, Bill. **Son of Gun in Cheek.** New York: Mysterious Press, 1987. x, 229 p. Index. Cloth. LC 87-7872. ISBN 0-89286-287-3.

A compilation in the same vein as *Gun in Cheek* (profiled earlier), this gleeful celebration of bad writing examines the output of Harry Stephen Keeler and works by Sydney Horler, Anthony Rud, Murray Leinster, Peter C. Herring, Michael Avallone, and Arnold Grisman, to name but a few. The overwrought blurbs used to promote these books are examined ("loaded to the gunwale with superpowered quake-stuff to make your withers quiver" concludes one gem), and unintentional examples of bad writing by good writers are presented. Finally, as before, Pronzini examines unintentionally hilarious sex scenes and the output of numerous (deservedly) unsuccessful presses.

The pulp writer Florence Mae Pettee in particular is excoriated. (States Pronzini, "She seemed to believe that substituting big words for little words, and/or colorfully offbeat words for common words, was the key to Good Writing.") Pettee's mystery, the 1929 *The Palgrave Mummy* is described at (hilarious) length, and a locked room mystery "Death Laughs at Walls" is reprinted in its entirety from the January 1930 *Detective Classics.* (States Pronzini: "I think I can guarantee that after you've read it, you'll never again feel quite the same about either the mystery short story or the English language.")

As before, a small number of errors creep in that in no way inhibit the pleasures given by the book, and as before, one might ask if it is wise to use the same standards to compare Michael Avallone and Robert Leslie Bellem with Sydney Horler and "Michael Morgan." Apart from this, *Son of Gun in Cheek* should be read and enjoyed by all.

52.   Pronzini, Bill, and Marcia Muller. **1001 Midnights: The Aficionado's Guide to Mystery and Detective Fiction.** New York: Arbor House, 1986. 879 p. Cloth. LC 85-30817. ISBN 0-87795-622-7.

The introduction to *1001 Midnights* begins by stating that the book was written by "aficionados, collectors, and students of this form of popular literature" to "provide other aficionados, collectors, as well as casual and new readers, with a reference guide to one thousand and one individual titles; to additional works by their authors; and to books of a similar type (whodunit, thriller, police procedural, etc.) by other writers." It closes by stating that *1001 Midnights* is a celebration of a genre, and it is this latter attitude—celebration—that offers the key to *1001 Midnights.* Unlike Barzun and Taylor, whose *Catalogue of Crime* shows no mercy to those books deemed inadequate, the 28 writers of the 1,001 entries know how to appreciate the terrible. They realize that without bad books—books that are "inspired nonsense" (those of Sydney Horler), that feature "creative butchery of the English language through phonetic spellings and some of the weirdest idioms ever committed to paper" (those of James O'Hanlon), and that are told through "one of the dullest, most annoying protagonists the genre has yet produced" (those of H. F. Heard)—there would be no way to identify the great books. The writers thus revel in the botched prose of such writers as Michael Avallone and "Michael Morgan," even as they celebrate the finer efforts by the genre's better writers.

The 1,001 annotations in *1001 Midnights* are arranged alphabetically by the subject's name; when the writer is represented by more than one book (as is often the case), the arrangement is alphabetical by title; novels and collections are represented. Bibliographic data are kept to a minimum, each citation listing only the first American edition (or the first British edition if no American edition exists). In addition, a simple code (e.g., *A* for action and adventure; *C* for comedy; *E* for espionage; *PP* for police procedural) classifies the contents. Notable titles and cornerstone titles are identified with one and two asterisks, respectively. The annotations provide a brief plot synopsis and a critical commentary that places the work in the context of the author's other works; all annotations are signed. Anglo-American authors predominate, but Georges Simenon is represented, as are Robert van Gulik, Janwillem van de Wetering, and Maj Sjöwall and Per Wahlöö. Citations for translations list only the first American publication and do not provide the name of the translator.

Although *1001 Midnights* has a few errors of fact—the entry for "Trevanian," for example, states that it is a pseudonym used by three writers—its most serious flaws lie elsewhere. First, Pronzini and Muller fail to state their basis for inclusions, and a user may well wonder why Robert Bloch's enormously important *Psycho* is mentioned only in passing, whereas *Psycho II* is excoriated at length. And if the deathly prose of "Michael Morgan" is accorded space, why were the Prince Zaleski stories, the lunatic lapidary creations of M. P. Shiel, neglected? Furthermore, the book lacks a title index, an oversight in a volume that is "a reference guide to one thousand and one individual *titles*." Nevertheless, any library that purchases *A Catalogue of Crime* would do well to locate and purchase the long out of print *1001 Midnights* as a companion; it conveys the joy of reading detective and mystery fiction.

53.   Quayle, Eric. **The Collector's Book of Detective Fiction.** Photographs by Gabriel Monro. London: Studio Vista, 1972. 143 p. Index. Cloth. LC 73-154663. ISBN 0-289-70263-1.

Sometimes listed as a reference work, this affectionate and heavily illustrated guide is reminiscent of Waltraud Woeller and Bruce Cassiday's *The Literature of Crime and Detection* (q.v.) in that it offers a roughly chronological history of the detective story. Where Quayle differs from his peers is that he remains constantly conscious of the financial worth of his books: "It would be difficult to find a sounder financial investment than copies of some of the works I shall describe in the following pages," states Quayle's introduction. The numerous illustrations are taken largely from volumes in his own collection.

The Collector's Book of Detective Fiction is engagingly written and enjoyable reading; its illustrations often are fascinating, though sometimes they do not occur in conjunction with their text. Also on the debit side, Quayle provides no bibliographies apart from citations in his text, and some of his statements are inaccurate (i.e., Quayle states that "most of the 'S. S. Van Dine' tales are melodramatic in the extreme and crammed with the high-speed violence and blood-letting commonly found in American crime novels of this and later periods"). The last section of the book, "Collecting First Editions," warns of "the squirrel instinct," which occurs when "a consuming desire sometimes grips an otherwise quite rational bibliophile: he starts to hoard every edition of every procurable title in the various field of literature in which he maintains an avid interest."

54a.   Queen, Ellery. **Queen's Quorum: A History of the Detective-Crime Short Story as Revealed by the 106 Most Important Books Published in This Field since 1845.** Boston: Little, Brown, 1951. ix, 132 p. Index. Cloth. LC 51-1258.

54b.   Queen, Ellery. **Queen's Quorum: A History of the Detective-Crime Short Story as Revealed in the 106 Most Important Books Published in This Field since 1845**. 2nd ed. Supplements through 1967. New York: Biblo and Tannen, 1969. ix, 146 p. Index. Cloth. LC 68-56450.

Probably the most influential annotated bibliography in this section, *Queen's Quorum* began as a list published at the conclusion of *Twentieth Century Detective Stories,* edited by Ellery Queen (Cleveland: World Publishing, 1948). From June 1949 through July 1950, it was reprinted as a series of columns in *Ellery Queen's Mystery Magazine,* after which it appeared in book form. The column was revived and continued in the November and December 1968 issues of *Ellery Queen's Mystery Magazine,* following which the second edition was published. The trivia-minded should note that the subtitle in both editions is in error: in the first edition it should be increased by one, for the book contains entries numbered 73 and 73a; in the second edition, entries 73 and 73a remain, and the number of entries is 125. This annotation concentrates on the second edition.

Like many of the bibliographies and readers' guides that succeeded it, the *Queen's Quorum* is simultaneously an appreciative history, a bibliographic essay, and an annotated bibliography of the most significant works published in the fields of detective, mystery, suspense, and criminal literature. Though it concentrates predominantly on the Anglo-American writers, European writers are not slighted. The volume begins with a chapter titled "The Incunabular Period," which mentions criminous elements in the works of writers from Cicero through Voltaire, and scattered throughout the bibliography are entries for Gaboriau's *Le Petit Vieux des Batignolles,* Maurice Leblanc's *Arsène Lupin, Gentleman-Cambrioleur,* and Balduin Groller's *Detektiv Dagoberts Taten und Abenteur.*

The annotations begin in the second chapter, "The Founding Father," which cites the 1845 edition of Poe's *Tales.* Thereafter, the entries proceed largely chronologically, with chapters titled "The First Fifty Years," "The Doyle Decade," "The First Golden Era," "The Second Golden Era," "The First Moderns," "The Second Moderns," "The Renaissance," "Renaissance and Moderns," and "Renaissance and Moderns Continuing," annotating the most significant literature produced during these times. The last annotation is Harry Kemelman's *The Nine Mile Walk* (1967), a collection of eight Nicky Welt stories.

Each citation provides publication data for the book's first edition and assigns each a code (H, Q, R, S) that indicates the book's historical significance, the book's quality (in terms of literary style and originality of plot), and the rarity or scarcity (or both) of the first edition. The annotations vary enormously in content—some are lengthy discussions of the detective, others are equally lengthy discussions of printing history, and still others cite other publications by the author; all are lively and well written. The first edition concludes with a separate checklist of the *Queen's Quorum* titles and an index merging the authors, titles, and characters; the second edition maintains the index and checklist but offers separate indexes for the titles and characters listed in the supplement.

Although now somewhat dated, and rather cumbersome in its arrangement, this remains a landmark publication. Some of its conclusions may be debated, but few have been overturned.

The 125 titles are available from a number of Web sites, but the following Swedish site also lists the four best short story collections and the four best novels according to Queen: http://hem.passagen.se/orange/equlist.htm.

55. Rennison, Nick, and Richard Shepard, eds. **Waterstone's Guide to Crime Fiction.** Brentford, England: Waterstone's, 1997. 171 p. Index. Paperback. ISBN 0-9527405-6-7.

In their brief introduction, the editors state, "The aim of the *Waterstone's Guide to Crime Fiction* is, primarily, to offer a generous selection of authors and titles currently available to those readers who enjoy reading novels that fall into the genre, broadly defined, of crime fiction."

The resulting volume lists nearly 200 historical and contemporary detective and mystery writers. Dead writers have their birth and death dates provided; no dates are given for living writers. A brief biocritical discussion of each author's influence, style, and recurrent themes is given, followed by an alphabetical list of their volumes available for sale in the United Kingdom; publishers, prices, and ISBNs are listed for approximately 1,400 books. Also present in the *Guide,* and making it more than merely an elaborate book dealer's catalogue, are interviews with Elmore Leonard and Lawrence Block, articles by Nicholas Blincoe on British hard-boiled fiction and Val McDermid "on the rise of the dyke detective," and an article by Rennison about P. C. Doherty's historical mysteries. Finally, numerous illustrations and cover reproductions are included, and appendixes list winners of the Crime Writers' Association's Gold Dagger Award, significant crime anthologies available at Waterstone's, the authors arranged by 22 subgenres (i.e., pioneers, golden age of English crime fiction, modern British, psychological drama, American classics, contemporary American noir, etc.), and a list of the services and locations of the nearest Waterstone's.

Apart from the interviews and articles, the *Guide* has little that is likely to assist American researchers, but it is nevertheless enjoyable.

56. Roth, Marty. **Foul and Fair Play: Reading Genre in Classic Detective Fiction.** Athens: University of Georgia Press, 1994. xv, 284 p. Index. LC 93-30367. ISBN 0-8203-1622-9.

Roth's volume is neither history nor reader's guide but a study that utilizes elements from both based on an analysis of 138 primary works. Roth's preface defines his intent by quoting Julian Symons's dictum about the differences among detective stories, spy stories, and thrillers: "It would be absurd to consider John Buchan and Eric Ambler together with R. Austin Freeman and Agatha Christie," wrote Symons. Roth cheerfully states, "This book is Symon's absurdity," adding that while he acknowledges "three general categories of detective fiction—the analytic, the hard-boiled, and the spy thriller—I not only consider Buchan, Ambler, Freeman, and Christie together, but also find they illuminate one another." *Foul and Fair Play* thus attempts to isolate the elements that comprise and define these three genres, asking such questions as why the detective must be an amateur and how one is to consider the concept of authorial "fair play," locked rooms, and the placement and nature of clues. The volume concludes with a bibliography of the 138 primary works and a useful index.

Roth's readings are wide-ranging; he discusses authors as varied as Eric Ambler, Raymond Chandler, G. K. Chesterton, Arthur Conan Doyle, Dashiell Hammett, Nathaniel Hawthorne, and Geoffrey Household. At the same time, his readings occasionally verge on the utterly risible, as when he states that "a compelling reading of *The Maltese Falcon* reflects the scatological dimensions of mystery fiction. In this reading, the black bird can be identified through its rhyme, as a black turd—what the French criminologist, Reiss of Lyons, called the 'criminal's *carte de visite odorante.*' " Contemporary reviewers do not seem to have responded to this reading, but unrefuted does not mean irrefutable.

Roth's *Foul and Fair Play* is worth reading. His judgments, however, do not need to be accepted.

57a.   Shibuk, Charles. **A Preliminary Check List of the Detective Novel and Its Variants.** (N.p., 1966?). 5 leaves. Mimeographed. OCLC 26462850.

57b.   Shibuk, Charles. **A Preliminary Check List of the Detective Novel and Its Variants. Supplement One.** (N.p., 1967?). 6 leaves. Mimeographed.

57c.   Shibuk, Charles. **A Preliminary Check List of the Detective Novel and Its Variants. Supplement Two.** (N.p., 1968?). 2 leaves. Mimeographed.

It is doubtful whether these lists were formally published, but because they appear every so often in bibliographies (Albert #241), they are here annotated.

Shibuk's lists are reproduced on legal-sized paper and contain approximately 120 annotations. Each checklist is arranged in rough alphabetical order by the author's name (given in capital letters), after which a paragraph comments briefly upon the major work(s) of the author, listing titles in capital letters, often with an abbreviated form of a publication date following them. For instance, the annotation for Vera Caspary states in its entirety "the 'corpse' comes back to life in LAURA ([19]43), a literate and witty mystery narrated by a variety of its characters." Very important works are indicated with an asterisk (*). There is nothing wrong with Shibuk's choices, but this work is no more than a curiosity.

58.   Stevenson, W. B. **Detective Fiction: A Reader's Guide.** Readers Guides. London: Published for the National Book League by Cambridge University Press, 1949. 20 p. Paperback.

Like Julian Symons's list of eight years later (q.v.), this bibliography is hardly more than a pamphlet. Stevenson's bibliography, however, is prefaced with a 10-page introduction that provides a brief but still useful survey of the detective story. Stevenson's annotations are arranged alphabetically, with each citation providing the author's name in regular type, the book's title in capital letters, the publisher of the first edition in italics, and the year of publication in regular type. The annotations tend to be terse, one or two sentences in length. Significant and standard British and American authors are represented equally, though Stevenson's list is varied and includes such largely unfamiliar names as H. C. Branson, Mary Fitt, and David Frome, as well as such surprises as Frances and Richard Lockridge and Phoebe Atwood Taylor. A bibliography of books about detective fiction concludes the pamphlet. Unindexed and now virtually unobtainable, at one time this could be purchased for one shilling.

59.   Stewart, R. F. **. . . And Always a Detective: Chapters on the History of Detective Fiction.** Newton Abbot and London: David & Charles, 1980. 351 p. Index. ISBN 0-7153-7922-4.

The title of this witty and enjoyable history is taken from the concluding line of "How to Make a Novel," a humorous poem first published in *Blackwood's Magazine* in May 1864, and the opening chapter follows cheerfully in this vein, for Stewart's goal is not so much to set rules and establish boundaries as it is to ask questions about the rules and wonder about the limitations that boundaries cause. He thus asks, "Does 'detective' in detective fiction refer to the person of the detective or to the activity of detection or to both in some proportion to be haggled over? The question may seem trivial, but that it has exercised writers' minds and coloured their views can be seen from the varying degrees of emphasis in their definitions." Following his discussion of the usefulness of the definitions that have been proposed by other critics, the first part of this volume describes the fiction that Stewart considers most significant in exemplifying the development of the form. The volume's second section is devoted to discussing the development of the detective. Rather surprisingly, Stewart focuses very heavily on Emile Gaboriau's *L'Affaire Lerouge, Le Crime d'Orcival, Le Dossier No. 113,* and *Monsieur Lecoq* as models and paradigms; Gaboriau becomes the measuring stick against which a great many writers are judged and found wanting. (He is also the last word of the text.)

There are two appendixes. The first is lengthy, offering "some notes, corrections, and comments" on *Victorian Detective Fiction: A Catalogue of the Collection Made by Dorothy Glover and Graham Greene* (q.v.); the second and briefer offers the answers to a quiz on pp. 75–76 in which Stewart challenges the reader to distinguish between older and newer quotations. The volume concludes with a useful bibliography and an excellent index.

60a.   Stilwell, Steven A. **What Mystery Do I Read Next? A Reader's Guide to Recent Mystery Fiction.** Detroit: Gale, 1997. xix, 545 p. Indexes. Cloth. LC 96-47713. ISBN 0-7876-1592-7.

60b.   Stilwell, Steven A. **What Mystery Do I Read Next? A Reader's Guide to Recent Mystery Fiction.** 2nd ed. Detroit: Gale, 1999. xvii, 806 p. Indexes. Cloth. ISBN 0-7876-4477-3. ISSN 1525-7266.

The second edition is described. It is not an original catalogue but the cumulation of the detective and mystery data that appeared as part of the first 10 editions of Gale's annual *What Do I Read Next?* This second edition of *What Mystery Do I Read Next?* attempts to serve as a reader's advisor, "describing in detail over 2,500 recommended mystery titles published between 1989 and 1999." The volume begins with lists of the winners (since 1990) of the Edgar Allan Poe Awards, the Shamus Awards, the Agatha Awards, the Anthony Awards, and the Macavity Awards. The data in these lists have not been integrated with the entries in the body of the volume.

The 2,527 entries in *What Mystery Do I Read Next?* are arranged alphabetically by author. Each entry is separately numbered, and the data presented include the book's title, place of publication, publisher, publication date, the series name (if any), the story type within the genre, the names and descriptions of up to three characters in the work, the time period of the story, the locale, a brief (three or four sentences) plot summary, and a listing of up to five books that utilize similar themes. Pseudonyms and coauthors are identified. A series of indexes provides access to the stories by series name, time period, geographic setting, story type, character name, character description, author, and title. It should be mentioned that the index to story type uses some 16 genres, ranging from "action/adventure" to "traditional" to classify its fiction, that the index to character description includes occupation (actress, librarian, publisher, etc.) as well as a plot function (i.e., counselor, cowboy, criminal), and that the index to geographic location offers reference not only to countries and continents but also to specific cities and even to imaginary places.

As with any work of this size, there is much to debate. The public library orientation makes the volume perhaps unduly positive about all works described and unnecessarily chatty in its presentation of data. Similarly, the limitations of the series mean that only works published since 1989 are described, though many of the books listed in the "other books you might like" section were published prior to 1989. Occasionally, works that have nothing to do with the genre (such as those of Tom Clancy) are referenced and described. There are odd omissions: Thomas Cook's acclaimed *Breakheart Hill* is not referenced, and but one book of Iain Pears's enjoyable Flavia di Stefano/Jonathan Argyll series is mentioned although the series appeared during the 1990s. Finally, a problem noted in the first edition reoccurs in somewhat reduced fashion in this edition: there does not appear to have been adequate proofreading, and readers curious to find works set in the deep south will be partially disappointed, for the section devoted to Alabama in the geographic index is incomplete.

Public libraries will find *What Mystery Do I Read Next?* a necessary acquisition. Academic libraries supporting studies in popular culture may find the indexing aids researchers. It also should be mentioned that the contents of this volume, along with quarterly updates and the contents to the other volumes in Gale's *What Do I Read Next?* are available (for a fee) through Galenet.com.

61. Stout, Rex. **Rex Stout's Favourites.** http://hem.passagen.se/orange/stoutlist.htm

Between 1938 and 1947, in 1951, and in 1956, Rex Stout chose the 10 best mystery books of all time. This Swedish site provides three tables listing these books, as well as the titles under which they were published in Sweden.

62. Symons, Julian. **The Hundred Best Crime Stories.** London: Sunday Times, Kensley House, [1959]. 20 p. Paperback. GB 59-8761.

Although hardly more than a pamphlet, this annotated bibliography provides a solid and occasionally surprising list of the 99 books that Symons—"with the help of distinguished critics and crime novelists, who have contributed lists, made notes on books they admired, and generally helped to enlighten my own ignorance"—considered to be the finest or most representative of their genre. The hundredth volume was chosen by readers of the *Sunday Times.*

Symons's list contains four sections: "The Begetters," "The Age of the Great Detective," "Novels of Action," and "The Modern Crime Novel." The citations in each section are arranged chronologically, with each entry providing the book's title in capitals, the year of publication, and the publishers and costs of the first English hardcover and paperback editions; the translators of such works as Dostoyevsky's *Crime and Punishment* are not noted. Symons's annotations are terse but helpful, and the curious reader will find mentioned virtually every significant British and American mystery, detective, or crime story writer from the first century of the genre's existence, plus works by such authors as Arthur Machen and William Faulkner.

What is particularly intriguing about *The Hundred Best Crime Stories* is that there is almost no overlap of contents between it and W. B. Stevenson's similar work of only 10 years earlier (q.v.). Had tastes changed so significantly in such a short time, or was Symons making a conscious attempt to be different from his predecessor? In any event, this volume is unindexed and now virtually unobtainable, although at one time additional copies could be had by sending 2s. 10d. to the London *Times*. Its contents have been reprinted in *The Armchair Detective Book of Lists,* edited by Kate Stine (q.v.).

Note: The pamphlet is undated, and the publication preceding date is taken from that given in *Julian Symons: A Bibliography* (q.v.).

63.   Symons, Julian.

63a.   First U.S. ed.: **Mortal Consequences, a History: From the Detective Story to the Crime Novel.** New York: Harper & Row, 1972. xii, 269 p. Index. LC 72-138767. ISBN 0-06-014187-4.

63b.   First U.K. ed.: **Bloody Murder: From the Detective Story to the Crime Novel: A History.** London: Faber and Faber, 1972. 254 p. Index. LC 181478. ISBN 0-571-09465-1.

63c.   Second U.S. ed.: **Bloody Murder: From the Detective Story to the Crime Novel: A History.** New York: Viking, 1985. 261 p. Index. LC 84-51885. ISBN 0-670-800961.

63d.   Second U.K. ed.: **Bloody Murder: From the Detective Story to the Crime Novel: A History.** Harmondsworth, England: Viking, 1985. 261 p. Index. LC 84-51885. ISBN 0-670-80096-1.

63e.   Third U.S. ed.: **Bloody Murder: From the Detective Story to the Crime Novel: A History.** New York: Mysterious Press, 1993. xiv, 349 p. Index. LC 92-54127. ISBN 0-89296-496-0.

63f.   Third U.K. ed.: **Bloody Murder: From the Detective Story to the Crime Novel: A History.** London: Papermac, 1992. 295 p. Index. ISBN 0-333-57049-9. (*Note:* This is also the fourth U.K. paperback edition.)

Symons opens the third edition of this excellent survey by stating, "This is the work of an addict, not an academic, and is a record of enthusiasm and occasional disappointment, not a catalogue or an encyclopedia. It is meant for reading, consultation, argument, reasoned contradiction." Having said this, however, Symons shows none of the signs of the addict and, instead, offers a stylish, reasonably balanced, and frequently acerbic assessment of the detective and mystery story, from its earliest days (Godwin,

Vidocq, and Poe) to the early 1990s. His history carefully distinguishes between puzzle stories, crime stories, and gothic novels, and although he provides a reasonable assessment of Vidocq's importance, he states unequivocally that "the first detective stories were written by Edgar Allan Poe," adding later, "Poe was the founding father whose genius suggested the themes to be followed by other writers." Successive chapters provide a largely chronological description of the development of the detective story, but this structure is abandoned about half way through, when Symons discusses Simenon and Maigret, then—in a chapter titled " 'Mr. Queen, Will You Be Good Enough to Explain Your Famous Character's Sex Life, If Any?' "—moves to discuss the writers who "humanized" their detectives and the ways by which they did so. Symons then discusses what he believes is the decline in the short story's quality and quantity, analyzes the relationships between the crime novel and police procedural, critiques some best-selling authors and their works ("Big producers and big sellers"), provides a short history of the spy story, assesses the successes of his earlier predictions, and concludes with a "postscript for the nineties." The volume is well indexed.

There is much to commend in Symons's work, idiosyncratic though it can be. At the same time, it is not a work without some flaws. Occasional errors in dates (Erle Stanley Gardner's death date), occasional errors of fact (the first woman to write a detective novel was not Anna Katharine Green), and occasional errors of judgment (as when Symons almost completely neglects *The Maltese Falcon* in favor of *The Glass Key*) occur. Equally seriously, he omits discussion of such writers as Harry Stephen Keeler, although the work of C. Daly King is examined. These criticisms aside, this remains a magisterial assessment of the genre; it belongs in all libraries.

64.   Winn, Dilys, et al. **Murder Ink: The Mystery Reader's Companion.** New York: Workman Publishing, 1977. xx, 520 p. Index. LC 77-5282. ISBN 0-89480-003-5 (hc); 0-89480-004-3 (pb).

A best-seller when it appeared, this heavily illustrated volume and its companion, *Murderess Ink* (profiled later), are still useful. In part, this is because *Murder Ink* contains something for almost everybody. It has autobiographical reminiscences by people as diverse as Penelope Wallace (daughter of Edgar Wallace) and Ian Carmichael (television's definitive Lord Peter Wimsey), and chapters on living with a mystery writer (by Abby Adams, whose husband is Donald Westlake) and on little old lady detectives; Peter O'Donnell reminisces about creating Modesty Blaise, H. R. F. Keating writes about initials ("I.N.I.T.I.A.L.S."), and Isaac Asimov contributes eight original limericks ("Verses for Hearses"). In all, there are more than 150 original contributions, ranging from the lighthearted to the serious. This is certainly the only book to contain not only an article on forensic odontology written by one of the country's leading forensic dentists and illustrated with (mercifully faded) photographs of bitten homicide victims, but also illustrations of a disguised Freddy the Pig, useful rules for drafting poison pen letters, a comparison of Oxford and Cambridge mysteries, a reprinting of the 1951 Haycraft-Queen definitive library of detective-crime-mystery fiction, and a delightful table enabling the curious to tell Spade from Marlowe from Archer.

This is not to say that the volume is problem free. Occasional factual errors occur, and the arrangement is frustrating—the heavily illustrated table of contents is spread over 10 pages, and the 14 sections are neither intuitively obvious nor readily accessible. On the other hand, Winn and her co-perpetrators clearly realized that mystery literature should not only be fun, it should be fun to read about, and this book was clearly assembled with that concept foremost in mind. The last pages contain statements about the book's typeface (Baskerville, of course) and that the color of the endpaper "exactly matches the color of arterial blood," and a tipped-in booklet reveals the solutions to 10 classic mysteries. The indexing is quite good.

65.   Winn, Dilys, et al. **Murderess Ink: The Better Half of the Mystery.** New York: Workman Publishing, 1979. xiv, 304 p. LC 79-64783. ISBN 0-89480-108-2 (hc); 0-89480-107-4 (pb).

Following the success of *Murder Ink* (see preceding), what could be more natural than to do a book devoted to the female of the species, one that (in the words of its dust wrapper) "proves, beyond a reasonable doubt, that women in the mystery are found dead as often as men, commit just as many murders as men, make just as many wisecracks as men, drink just as much booze as men, and that, in the final analysis, the female is not only deadlier than the male, but wackier." The resulting collection thus contains over 100 pieces by more than 50 writers on subjects as varied as the gothic, the first women mystery and detective writers, female private eyes, and the wives of private eyes and detectives. As in the first volume, illustrations are plentiful and subject variety abounds: Stephen King writes on how to scare a woman to death, and Tabith King writes about living with Stephen King; a pictorial shows Agatha Christie being measured for her waxwork at Madame Tussaud's; Jane Langton contributes illustrations of the clothing worn by Dorothy Sayers's characters; Jo April provides helpful hints for removing annoying (and incriminating) spots and marks; and Roger Lang provides illustrations for building a secret compartment.

Although some of this material is significant, this volume is by no means as useful as its predecessor. There are occasional factual errors, and the book has the same frustrating organizational problems, with eight thematically arranged sections that are neither intuitive nor obvious and a heavily illustrated table of contents that is six pages in length. Equally seriously, the book's tone comes across as calculatedly lightweight rather than irreverent. As before, the book is set in Baskerville, although this time the color of the endpaper "exactly matches the color of venous blood," and as before, the indexing is quite good.

66.   Woeller, Waltraud, and Bruce Cassiday. **The Literature of Crime and Detection: An Illustrated History from Antiquity to the Present.** New York: Ungar, 1988. 215 p. Index. Cloth. LC 86-16040. ISBN 0-8044-2983-9.

First published in 1984 as *Illustrierte Geschichte der Kriminalliteratur* (not seen), this enjoyable illustrated history offers a survey of detection and the detective story from classical antiquity to the writers of the early 1980s. Although more a history than a reader's guide, it is mentioned here because, like Tage la Cour and Harald Mogensen's *The Murder Book: An Illustrated History of the Detective Story* (q.v.), it offers a different perspective, being written from a German standpoint. The nineteenth-century writers and texts discussed include those by the standard American and British writers, but Karl May's *Der verlorene Sohn oder der Fürst des Elends,* Annette von Droste-Hülshoff's *Die Judenbuch,* and Jodocus D. H. Temme's *Wer war der Mörder?* are also mentioned. The coverage concludes with lists of significant American writers of the 1980s, data on whom appear to have been added during the translation. Though containing some unfortunate typos (Dr. Thorndyke has become "Mr. Thorndyke") and too many exclamation points, and occasionally providing lists rather than discussions, this nevertheless remains a useful volume. A selective bibliography cites English and German sources, and the author index is annotated, providing biographical data in addition to paginations.

Scope note: This section is for mysteries "about" a certain subject. Monographs surveying or discussing more than one subject are described in the section devoted to readers' guides.

SPECIFIC GENRES AND THEMES

Academic Mysteries. *See* College Mysteries

African American Mysteries

67.   Bailey, Frankie Y. **Out of the Woodpile: Black Characters in Crime and Detective Fiction.** Contributions to the Study of Popular Culture, no. 27. Westport, Conn.: Greenwood, 1991. xiii, 188 p. Index. LC 90-45804. ISBN 0-313-26671-9.

Although not a reference book, Bailey's study of African Americans in mystery fiction nevertheless offers a symposium of writers' views on creating Black characters, the results of a Mystery Writers of America (MWA) survey on Black characters, and a lengthy section titled "Directory: Black Characters in Crime and Detective Fiction, Film, and Television." Also, a substantial bibliography lists materials for further study.
     One should also mention such works as these:

> Stephen F. Soitos. **The Blues Detectives: A Study of African American Detective Fiction** (Amherst: University of Massachusetts Press, 1996).

> Daniels, Valarie L. **African American Mystery Page.** http://www.aamystery.com

> Henry, Angela. **MystNoir.** http://mystnoir0.tripod.com/MystNoirDir/

68.   Reader's Advice. **African-American Mysteries.** http://www.readersadvice.com/readadv/000291.html

A bare-bones list of authors and titles, but lengthy and accessible.

69.   Springfield Library. **The Black Detective: African-American Mystery Fiction.** http://www.springfieldlibrary.org/reading/blackdetectives.html

Arranged alphabetically by author's last name. Each work or series is briefly annotated.

American Novel of Detection

70.   Lachman, Marvin. **A Reader's Guide to the American Novel of Detection.** Reader's Guides to Mystery Novels. New York: G. K. Hall, 1993. xii, 435 p. Indexes. Cloth. LC 92-25726. ISBN 0-8161-1803-5.

This volume is the second in a series that started with Susan Oleksiw's *A Reader's Guide to the Classic British Mystery* (q.v.), and like its predecessor, this is an oddly inconsistent collection. Lachman's preface states that his focus is on the amateur detectives, those who "do not earn a living by solving crimes," although there are some exceptions, Rex Stout's Nero Wolfe and Arthur Reeve's Craig Kennedy being the most notable. Lachman also states that his focus is on the detectives of North America, allowing him to discuss books by Canadian writers; that he generally includes all relevant novels by any author he discusses, and that he generally includes all the books in which a particular series detective appears. In all, he references "the work of 166 authors, many of whom also have one or more pseudonyms, and 1,314 books." However, the methodology Lachman used to determine these authors and titles remains questionable. Why, for example, is there no mention of Professor Augustus S. F. X. Van Dusen, the famous "Thinking Machine" created by Jacques Futrelle? Where are the writings of Margaret Maron?

Questions of content aside, the majority of the guide consists of the annotated bibliography of the North American novel of detection. Although the guide's initial arrangement is alphabetical by author, the titles are arranged neither alphabetically nor chronologically by publication date but in what Lachman deems to be their internal chronology. In the case of prolific writers, this system makes locating information on a particular title rather problematic; the dates of books featuring John Dickson Carr's Dr. Gideon Fell, for example, appear in the following order: 1941, 1938, 1940, 1938, 1939, 1944, 1941, 1946, 1947, 1949. Each citation provides the title in boldface, place of publication, publisher, and date of publication; the major series detective is listed, as are the first English edition and subsequent retitlings. The annotations are well presented, stating the problem but not the solution.

In addition to the bibliography, the volume contains a list of pseudonyms and their users, an alphabetical list of creators and their most famous series character, an alphabetical list of the series characters, a listing of the occupations of the series characters, a listing by the story's chronological setting, a geographic locations index, and a settings index. An index for "miscellaneous information" provides thematic information about the novels, a "holiday index" lists the books involving specific holidays, and the book concludes with Lachman's list of 100 notable novels of detection. There is no title index.

As with the other volumes in this series, a revised and expanded edition would be helpful.

Animal Mysteries: Cats, Dogs, Horses, and Other Animals

Cats

71.   **Cats in Mystery Fiction.** http://www.geocities.com/Heartland/Meadows/3786.html

A lively and well-illustrated site.

72. Reader's Advice. **Cat Mysteries.** http://www.readersadvice.com/readadv/
     000023.html

     A bare-bones listing of authors and titles, but very accessible.

Dogs

73. **Mystery Fiction Featuring Dogs.** http://www.geocities.com/Heartland/Meadows/
     3786/dog.html

     A lively and well-illustrated site.

74. Reader's Advice. **Dog Mysteries.** http://www.readersadvice.com/readadv/
     000024.html#Dogs

Horses and Horseracing

75. Reader's Advice. **Horses and Horseracing Mysteries.** http://www.readersadvice.
     com/readadv/000024#Horses

Other Animals

76. Reader's Advice. **Animal Mysteries (Non-Cat).** http://www.readersadvice.
     com/readadv/000024.html

Archaeological Mysteries

77. Reader's Advice. **Archaeological Mysteries.** http://www.readersadvice.
     com/readadv/000333.html

     The usual bare-bones listing of authors and titles, but very accessible.

Art Mysteries

78. Reader's Advice. **Art Mysteries.** http://www.readersadvice.com/readadv/
     000332.html

     The usual bare-bones listing of authors and titles, but as always, very accessible.

Asian American Mysteries

79. Marple, Laural. **Asian American Mysteries List.**

     Available as part of the archives maintained by the DorothyL listserv. To obtain:
send an e-mail message to listserv@listserv.kent.edu; type "get asian.american" in the
subject line.

Baseball Mysteries. *See* Sports Mysteries

Bibliomysteries

80. Available as part of the archives maintained by the DorothyL listserv. To obtain: send an e-mail message to listserv@listserv.kent.edu; type "get biblio.mystery" in the subject line.

81. Ballinger, John. **Biblio-Mysteries.** Catalogue 8. Williamsburg, Va.: Bookpress, 1984. 88 p. Paperback.

As a rule the dealers' catalogues have not been included in this work, but with *Biblio-Mysteries* an exception must be made, for despite an apparently sizable reader interest in bibliomysteries—mysteries that in some way make use of the worlds and arcana of librarianship, the used or rare book trade, or the publishing industry—this catalogue is apparently the only separately published bibliography of bibliomysteries.

Ballinger's catalogue cites 554 works, the majority of which is books. The arrangement is alphabetical by author; last names are given in boldface and are capitalized. Titles are in regular type. Publication data are italicized and include the place of publication, publisher, and year of publication. Furthermore, each title is briefly annotated, Ballinger's note indicating why the title is a bibliomystery. A few citations are to multiple editions and states of the work. The citation to Lawrence Block's *The Burglar Who Studied Spinoza,* for example, makes reference to the original typed manuscript and setting copy; the galley proofs corrected by the author, including master set, first and second passes, author's set, and final set; the page proofs from which the book was photographed for printing and the blue-ink proof copy; and a presentation copy of the first edition.

Some years later Ballinger wrote *Collecting Bibliomysteries* (Williamsburg, Va.: Bookpress, 1990), a history of his collection. This urbane and witty pamphlet culminates with Ballinger's account of selling his collection and writing *The Williamsburg Forgeries,* a bibliomystery published by St. Martin's Press.

82. McCurley, Marsha. **Bibliomysteries.** http://www.bibliomysteries.com

A delightful site, offering information on collecting bibliomysteries and extensive bibliographic detail of the literature. These can be accessed by authors, but there are also lists of short stories, juvenile books, media adaptations, references, detectives and series, and authors in bibliographies. There are numerous links to related sites.

83. Reader's Advice. **Books and Publishing Industry Mysteries.** http://www. readersadvice.com/readadv/000248.html

A bare-bones site listing authors and titles, but very accessible.

Blind-Accessible Mysteries

84a. **Mysteries.** Washington, D.C.: Library of Congress, 1982. 205 p. Indexes. Paperback. LC 82-600158. ISBN 0-8444-0394-6. SuDoc LC 19.11:M99. Also available on disc, cassette, or in Braille.

84b.   **More Mysteries.** Washington, D.C.: National Library Service for the Blind and Physically Handicapped, Library of Congress, 1992. vi, 164 p. Indexes. Paperback. LC 92-30160. ISBN 0-8444-0763-1. SuDoc LC 19.11:M9912. Also available on disc and in Braille.

Mysteries and *More Mysteries* are annotated bibliographies of the detective and mystery stories available through the network library collections provided by the National Library Service for the Blind and Physically Handicapped at the Library of Congress. *Mysteries* cites those works that are available through disc, cassette, and in Braille up to 1982. *More Mysteries* lists the works available through cassettes and in Braille that were produced following the 1982 publication of *Mysteries*. The paper form of each volume is in large print.

Both bibliographies begin with a section listing the mysteries of prolific authors. In *Mysteries,* a prolific author has seven or more titles available through the National Library Service; in *More Mysteries,* a prolific author has six or more titles. These titles are separated by their medium and listed alphabetically. Each entry provides the work's title and order number in boldface, describes (in regular type) the size of the work (i.e., two cassettes, 3 discs, 3 volumes), and provides a descriptive annotation with occasional evaluative comments (e.g., "strong language and explicit descriptions of sex"). The name of the detective is always given.

The second section of *Mysteries* is titled "More Mysteries"; the second section of *More Mysteries* lists the works of other authors; and both list the works of less-prolific authors in the format described earlier. *Mysteries,* however, has sections listing mystery anthologies, an index titled "British-Sounding Narrators," and separate title indexes for the discs, cassettes, and Braille works. *More Mysteries* has a section listing single-author collections of short stories, lists its anthologies under the heading "Multiple Authors," and includes separate title indexes to the cassettes and Braille publications. Both volumes conclude with an order form.

An updated volume is certainly needed, but with the ready accessibility of books on tape, it is improbable that one will be produced.

Boating and Sailing Mysteries

85.   Reader's Advice. **Boating and Sailing Mysteries.** http://www.readersadvice.com/readadv/000292.html

A bare-bones listing of authors and titles, but very accessible.

Christmas Mysteries

86.   **Mysterynet.com Christmas Mysteries.** http://www.mysterynet.com/christmas/xmas_main.shtml

This congenial site provides an article about Christmas mysteries by Vicki Cameron; links to short mystery stories by Bill Pronzini, Marcia Muller, and Edward D. Hoch; links to classic Christmas mysteries by (among others) Arthur Conan Doyle and O. Henry; and a list of Christmas mystery books that may be ordered.

87.   Menendez, Albert. **Mistletoe Malice: The Life and Times of the Christmas Murder Mystery.** Silver Spring, Md.: Holly Tree Press, 1982. 35 p. Paperback.

"There is a whole body of literature featuring assorted varieties of crime and mayhem at the Happiest Time of the Year," writes Menendez in his brief introduction to this cheerful study of the mystery novels that in some way use Christmas. Menendez identifies the eight varieties of Christmas Murder Mysteries (CMM), describing them in the following categories: Country House Party Thriller, the Police Procedural (with its subcategory, the Lonely Cop), the Big-City Private Eye, the Village, the Department Store Glitter, the Spy Caper, the Lunatic on the Loose, and the Christmas as Background. The novels that exemplify these categories are annotated, and Menendez carefully refrains from providing the solutions. The pamphlet concludes with a checklist of 89 CMMs that lists the first American or British editions of each book.

A delightful achievement.

88.   MyShelf.com. **Mystery Christmas Titles at MyShelf.com.** http://www.myshelf.com/holiday/pages/xmasmystery.htm

Containing more references to primary literature than the Mysterynet's Christmas Mysteries site (profiled earlier), MyShelf.com's site offers a lengthy list of Christmas-related mysteries, including anthologies.

89.   Reader's Advice. **Holiday Mysteries.** http://www.readersadvice.com/readadv/000276.html

A bare-bones list of authors and titles, but lengthy and very accessible.

90.   Wolfe, S. J. **A Bibliography of Christmas Mysteries.**

Available as part of the archives maintained by the DorothyL listserv. To obtain: send an e-mail message to listserv@listserv.kent.edu; type "get xmas.mystery" in the subject line.

Classic British Mysteries

91.   Oleksiw, Susan. **A Reader's Guide to the Classic British Mystery.** Boston: G. K. Hall, 1988. xiii, 585 p. Indexes. Cloth. LC 88-1735. ISBN 0-8161-8787-8. Also: New York: Mysterious Press, 1989. xiii, 585 p. Indexes. LC 88-43489. ISBN 0-89296-969-5 (cl); 0-89296-968-7 (pb).

A novice to the study of detective and mystery fiction is likely to be frustrated rather than enlightened by Oleksiw's effort, for although she describes and annotates more than 1,440 titles by 121 authors, nowhere does she define the criteria that make one book a classic British mystery and render its neighbor unfit for inclusion. Why, for example, does Oleksiw list Reginald Hill's thriller *Fell of Dark,* yet not cite its apparent model, John Buchan's *The Thirty-Nine Steps*?

Questions of definition aside, Oleksiw's bibliography references books published after 1900; the sole exception is Fergus Hume's *The Mystery of a Hansom Cab.* These citations are arranged alphabetically by their author's last name. When the author wrote more than one volume, the entries are listed chronologically; when the author used more than one character, the entries are listed chronologically by series character. Pseudonyms and cross-references are provided. Each citation gives the title, publisher, and publication date for the book's first British and American editions and provides the name of the investigating detective. The annotations range in length from approximately 30 to more than 100 words, give away no plot twists, and reveal no endings.

The annotated bibliography dominates the volume, but there are indexes for characters and their creators, creators and their characters, occupations of series characters, time periods during which the stories occur, locations of stories occurring outside England, settings, and novels in which specialized technical information plays a significant role. A concluding list lists "one hundred classics of the genre," and there is an essay on the metropolitan police and local forces and a list of the ranks within the British class system. Oddly enough, there is no title index.

A revised and expanded edition of this study is needed.

92.   Reader's Advice. **British Mysteries.** http://www.readersadvice.com/readadv/000020.html

A bare-bones listing of authors and titles, less lengthy than Oleksiw's work but more accessible.

Clerical Mysteries

93.   Breen, Jon L., and Martin H. Greenberg, eds. **Synod of Sleuths: Essays on Judeo-Christian Detective Fiction.** Metuchen, N.J.: Scarecrow, 1990. viii, 161 p. Index. Cloth. LC 90-21025. ISBN 0-8108-2382-9.

Concentrating on surveying Judeo-Christian detective and mystery stories, this collection of five bibliographic essays is less concerned about theological problems than Spencer's work on the same subject (q.v.). Breen contributes two of the essays, "Protestant Mysteries" and "Mormon Mysteries"; Edward D. Hoch writes an essay titled "Priestly Sleuths"; Marvin Lachman contributes one titled "Religious Cults and the Mystery"; and in an essay titled "Is This Any Job for a Nice Jewish Boy?" James Yaffe discusses Jews in detective fiction. The book's final chapter is a "symposium" consisting of transcripts to questions answered by Ellis Peters, William X. Kienzle, Harry Kemelman, and Sister Carol Anne O'Marie. The book concludes with a bibliography of the works discussed in the body of the book and a well-done index.

Although some of the essays are dated, this remains a highly readable work, and the contributors—professional writers, all—do not hesitate to judge the works they are describing. The concluding bibliography is especially useful, since it provides the author and title and the place, publisher, and year of publication; separate sections list the works of fiction and drama discussed in the essays, anthologies, and secondary sources.

94.   Harper, Carol. **Nuns in Mysteries.**

Available as part of the archives maintained by the DorothyL listserv. To obtain: send an e-mail message to listserv@listserv.kent.edu; type "get nun.mysterys" in the subject line. Focus is on nuns, whereas that of Kristick's list (which follows) is on ecclesiastics.

95.   Kristick, Laurel. **Saintly Sleuths.**

Available as part of the archives maintained by the DorothyL listserv. To obtain: send an e-mail message to listserv@listserv.kent.edu; type "get saintly.sleuths" in the subject line.

96.   Spencer, William David. **Mysterium and Mystery: The Clerical Crime Novel.** Studies in Religion, no. 6. Ann Arbor, Mich.: UMI Research Press, 1989. xi, 344 p. Indexes. Cloth. LC 88-39773. ISBN 0-8357-1936-7. Also: Carbondale: Southern Illinois University Press, 1992. xi, 344 p. Indexes. LC 91-28207. ISBN 0-8093-1809-1.

It is debatable whether *Mysterium and Mystery* should be included here, for it is not a reference work in the way that the other works considered herein are. Nevertheless, this is one of only two substantial studies of its subject, the genre crime novel in which a clerical figure plays the role of the detective, and for this reason it warrants inclusion. Furthermore, it contains substantial bibliographies.

Mysterium and Mystery began its life as Spencer's Th.D., granted in 1986 from Boston University, and it is still as much a work of theology as it is a study of the clerical crime novel. It opens with a defense of the genre: Spencer states in his first chapter, "If some Christians question whether a mystery story can be a Christian story, they do not know their own faith thoroughly enough. And every detective of the full implication of any mystery ends in the mysterium that comes from this great source, which is the well-spring of morality as well."

Following Spencer's defense, the volume is divided into three major sections, the first of which, "Rabbis and Robbers," begins with a discussion of the elements of crime and detection found in *Bel and the Dragon* and the story of *Susannah* and concludes with a discussion of Harry Kemelman's Rabbi Small series. "Priests and Psychopaths" discusses the clerical crime novels of Umberto Eco, Ellis Peters, E. M. A. Allison, G. K. Chesteron, Anthony Boucher, Henry Catalan, Margaret Ann Hubbard, Leonard Holton, Ralph McInerny, Dorothy Gilman, Sister Carol Anne O'Marie, William X. Kienzle, and Andrew Greeley. Concluding the body of the book is the chapter titled "Ministers and Murderers," which analyzes the novels of Vicar Whitechurch, C. A. Alington, Margaret Scherf, Stephen Chance, Barbara Ninde Byfield, Isabelle Holland, Matthew Head, Charles Merrill Smith, and James L. Johnson. An appendix provides a graph of the clerical crime novel in English, and a lengthy bibliography and an index to fictional characters follow. A combined author/title/subject index concludes the volume.

This is a substantial contribution to the field, a scholarly examination of a hitherto disparate body of work, with the results presented in clear and cogent prose.

97.   Reader's Advice. **Clerical Mysteries.** http://www.readersadvice.com/readadv/000128.html

A bare-bones list of authors and titles, but very accessible.

College Mysteries

98.   Kramer, John E., Jr., and John E. Kramer III. **College Mystery Novels: An Annotated Bibliography, Including a Guide to Professorial Series-Character Sleuths.** Garland Reference Library of the Humanities, vol. 360. New York: Garland, 1983. xvii, 356 p. Indexes. Cloth. LC 82-48291. ISBN 0-8240-9237-6.

Many academics are fond of detective and mystery novels, and (perhaps coincidentally) many detective and mystery novels involve academics and have an academic setting. The college mystery novel is a direct descendant of the English "cozy," with the campus replacing the small English village and the large rural country house. A campus setting allows the author to create a small and insular world with its own government and political systems and to populate it with academic eccentrics, geniuses, and (frequently naive and nubile) young people. A crime then disrupts this world, exposing its political infighting and petty concerns to the investigators. Often there is a sense of satire, the author delighting in the depiction of academics feuding over the interpretation of a line of Milton or the "true" authorship of Shakespeare's dramas.

After defining the college mystery novel as "a full-length work of mystery or suspense fiction which is set at an institution of higher education and/or has as a principal character a student, a faculty member, or an administrator at a college or university," the father and son team of the Kramers identify 632 titles published between 1882 and 1982 that fulfill their definition. These are then divided into two groups: the "professorial series-character sleuths" and the "free-standing college mystery novels." Fifty-one series characters are identified and have their adventures described; each series character's entry concludes with the books in which he or she appears. The section devoted to free-standing college mystery novels annotates 308 volumes that do not have a series character. An appendix lists "outstanding" college mystery novels, and well-done indexes for authors, titles, and series characters conclude the volume.

Although the Kramers' annotations are critically perceptive, *College Mystery Novels* is irksome and inconsistent as a bibliography. For example, R. Austin Freeman's 1914 *The Uttermost Farthing* is listed in the "series-character" section despite being Freeman's only novel featuring Humphrey Challoner (a one-book series?). Furthermore, Challoner's connection with academe is at best tenuous: long prior to the start of the story, he was involved with anthropology and has maintained a small museum of oddities. In both sections the citations are listed chronologically, effectively frustrating those users who do not know the date of the series character's first book appearance or first publication date of a book. (Neither are these dates consistent: Arthur B. Reeve's Craig Kennedy is listed as 1912, whereas the first book cited is dated 1911 [and, for what it is worth, Craig Kennedy had appeared in magazine form in 1910].) Finally, historians and scholars can complain about omissions (Edwin Balmer's and William MacHarg's "Luther Trant" is not among the detectives surveyed), typographical errors (Charlotte Armstrong's *A Dram of Poison* "won the Edgar Allen Poe Award," and Fredric Brown's first name is given as "Frederic"), and the lack of an index for campus locations.

Despite these problems, *College Mystery Novels* is not insignificant. It is the first book-length attempt at describing a recurrent genre in crime and mystery fiction, and because much of the book is very capably done, the flaws mentioned previously are all the more noticeable. The second edition, described later, is not merely a continuation of this volume but an entirely new work.

99.   Kramer, John E. **Academe in Mystery and Detective Fiction: An Annotated Bibliography.** Lanham, Md.: Scarecrow, 2000. xiv, 426 p. Indexes. Cloth. LC 00-32230. ISBN 0-8108-3841-9.

Kramer's *Academe in Mystery and Detective Fiction* is the second edition of *College Mystery Novels* (described previously), although the majority of *Academe*'s 486 annotations are new and have not been carried forward from the earlier volume. In this volume, Kramer opens with a reasonable definition of "college mystery" novel, and the body of the book consists of the annotations of the Anglo-American detective novels that are either set "at an institution of higher education, or [that] feature characters from these institutions who act within their academic roles in off-campus locales." Bibliographic data are given entirely in capital letters, and biographical data are incorporated into the entries. The annotations are followed by an annotated bibliography of secondary sources, and the volume concludes with indexes for title, author, character, and the colleges and universities that serve as setting. (Oxford and Cambridge lead, followed distantly by Harvard/Radcliffe.)

Like the first edition, *Academe* can be a frustrating work. Kramer has arranged his entries chronologically, but under this arrangement, individual novels can be located only through the index, and in the case of such prolific authors as Colin Dexter, Carolyn Heilbrun, and Michael Innes, a researcher must look in multiple locations. There is also no linkage between the first edition and the second edition, though a number of authors are referenced in both volumes. Furthermore, any dedicated reader of mysteries will notice lacunae and wonder why Kramer has not included certain works. Most seriously, Kramer's research and methodologies must be questioned: he concludes the first annotation (William Johnston and Paul West's *The Innocent Murders* [New York: Duffield, 1910]) by stating, "The identity of Paul West is unknown." It took the present writer fewer than 15 *seconds* to confirm the identity of Paul West and find his birth and death dates (1871–1918). These criticisms aside, public libraries and academic libraries supporting studies in this particular aspect of popular culture may find that *Academe* receives use.

100. Kuhlenschmidt, Sally. **A Bit of Whimsey: Mysteries and Academia.**
http://www.msc.wku.edu/Dept/Support/AcadAffairs/CTL/mystery.htm

A well-done site maintained by Western Kentucky University's Center for Teaching and Learning. Oddly enough, this site does not appear to be aware of the works done by Kramer and the Kramers.

101. Reader's Advice. **Academic Mysteries.** http://www.readersadvice.com/readadv/000306.htm

A bare-bones list of authors and titles, but lengthy and accessible.

Courtroom Fiction and Legal Thrillers

102a. Breen, Jon L. **Novel Verdicts: A Guide to Courtroom Fiction.** Metuchen, N.J.: Scarecrow, 1984. xiv, 266 p. Index. LC 84-14110. ISBN 0-8108-1741-1.

102b. Breen, Jon L. **Novel Verdicts: A Guide to Courtroom Fiction.** 2nd ed. Lanham, Md.: Scarecrow, 1999. xiv, 276 p. Index. LC 99-35315. ISBN 0-8108-3674-2.

The first edition of Jon Breen's *Novel Verdicts* describes 421 English and American books that Breen considers "courtroom fiction," which is to say, fiction in which a percentage of the narrative occurs in a courtroom. The second edition is nearly twice the size of the first and annotates some 790 works, including a number of legal thrillers by such authors as John Grisham and Scott Turow; most works have been published prior to 1998. Breen introduces his subject by providing clearly articulated criteria for judging whether a work should be included, and the body of the volume consists of the annotations. As in the first edition, the arrangement is alphabetical by author; when the author has written more than one work—as in the case of such familiar names as Erle Stanley

Gardner, John Grisham, and Scott Turow—the arrangement is chronological. Citations provide bibliographic data for the first American and English editions, and a symbol indicates the percentage of the work that involves a trial or courtroom activity; the annotations are concise yet informative. Pseudonyms are identified and cross-references are provided as necessary. The volume concludes with a general index that lists authors, titles, and real people and cases; separate indexes to cause of action and jurisdiction are provided.

Delightful though the second edition is, it is not without some shortcomings. The book is poorly laid out; because citations are not boldfaced or otherwise typographically distinguished, locating an individual reference can be difficult. There are lacunae: Breen cites, for example, Charles Dickens's *The Posthumous Papers of the Pickwick Club* (reasonably omitting the subtitle) and mentions in passing *Bleak House*—but why is there no mention of *The Old Curiosity Shop,* which has a magnificent trial scene? Why is there no mention of contemporary writers Stephen Hunter and Richard Speight?

These flaws are minor and acceptable. The volume proves that a knowledgeable writer can bring to life even the most abstruse of subjects, and *Novel Verdicts* belongs in all libraries in which there is an interest in mystery and detective fiction.

103.   Campbell, Heather. **Legal Thrillers.**

Available as part of the archives maintained by the DorothyL listserv. To obtain: send an e-mail message to listserv@listserv.kent.edu; type "get legal.thriller" in the subject line.

104.   Gemmette, Elizabeth Villiers, ed. **Law in Literature: An Annotated Bibliography of Law-Related Works.** Troy, N.Y.: Whitston, 1998. 331 p. Index. LC 97-61546. ISBN 0-87875-498-9.

Intended as a teaching tool for the instructors of lawyers-in-parvo rather than the mystery aficionado, this volume annotates some 250 novels, novellas, and plays that illustrate some aspect of the law. The annotations are arranged alphabetically by the subject's name, followed by the title and the date of the work's first publication; these data are in boldface type. In the case of international works (i.e., Bertolt Brecht's *The Caucasian Chalk Circle*), the original title is also given, as are dates of first English and German performances and the date of the publication of the revised text. A description of the work follows; each annotation concludes with a list of the legal and law-related topics that the instructor may wish to get the students to discuss and the signature of its author. It is important to note that the works annotated tend to be from the mainstream rather than the genre: there are no entries for works by Scott Turow and Erle Stanley Gardner and but two for John Grisham, and the authors and works presented include writers as varied as Maya Angelou (*I Know Why the Caged Bird Sings*), Aristophanes (*Lysistrata*), Jane Austen (*Persuasion* and *Pride and Prejudice*), and Paul Auster (*Moon Palace*). The browser can find entries for William Shakespeare, Bernard Shaw, Thomas Hardy, Nathaniel Hawthorne, Jane Smiley, C. P. Snow, Frederick Douglass, and Harriet E. Wilson. An occasional work of science fiction (Frank Herbert, *The Dosadi Experiment;* Aldous Huxley, *Brave New World;* and Robert Silverberg, *Downward to the Earth*) enliven and add depth to the annotations. The volume concludes with an index of the legal and law-related topics, and biographical data on the contributors are provided.

Though *Law in Literature* is intended for a specialized audience and makes no attempt at comprehensiveness, lovers of genre fiction may find the volume's contents lead to works that might otherwise be neglected.

105.   Reader's Advice. **Courtroom Mysteries.** http://www.readersadvice.com/readadv/000289.html

106.   Reader's Advice. **Legal Thrillers.** http://www.readersadvice.com/readadv/000011.html

Bare-bones list of authors and titles, but lengthy and very accessible.

Cozy Mysteries

107.   Reader's Advice. **Cozy Mysteries.** http://www.readersadvice.com/readadv/000200.html

A bare-bones list of authors and titles, but lengthy and accessible. The DorothyL archives no longer offer Helen Androski's well-done list.

Fantasy Mysteries. *See* Science Fiction and Fantasy Mysteries

Food Mysteries

108.   Reader's Advice. **Food Mysteries**. http://www.readersadvice.com/readadv/000013.html

A bare-bones list of authors and titles, but useful and accessible.

Garden and Gardening Mysteries

109.   Reader's Advice. **Gardening Mysteries.** http://www.readersadvice.com/readadv/000290.html

A bare-bones list of authors and titles, but very accessible.

110.   St. Charles Public Library. **Digging for Clues: Mysteries in the Garden.** http://www.st-charles.lib.il.us/arl/booklists/clues.htm

This list of 44 mysteries (or series) featuring gardens and gardening is arranged alphabetically by author and provides only the title of the book. Although now somewhat dated, the list is nevertheless cleanly presented.

Gay and Lesbian Mysteries

111.   Reader's Advice. **Gay Male Mysteries.** http://www.readersadvice.com/readadv/000112.html

112.   Reader's Advice. **Lesbian Mysteries.** http://www.readersadvice.com/readadv/000117.html

Bare-bones lists of authors and titles, but very accessible.

113.　Slide, Anthony. **Gay and Lesbian Characters and Themes in Mystery Novels: A Critical Guide to Over 500 Works in English.** Jefferson, N.C.: McFarland, 1993. vii, 199 p. Indexes. Cloth. LC 92-56695. ISBN 0-89950-798-0.

Slide's introduction to this occasionally intriguing annotated bibliography begins by noting that "prior to the 1980s gay and lesbian characters and themes were introduced in only a small number of mystery novels, and that the portrayal of gay characters was generally unsympathetic." The remainder of his introduction speculates about the relationship between Nero Wolfe and Archie Goodwin, provides a historical survey of the use of homosexuals as characters in mysteries, and discusses the historical usage of the word *gay* to describe homosexuals.

The bibliography is arranged alphabetically by author's last name, given in bold capitals; biographical data are occasionally provided. The annotations list the title of the work(s) in boldface italics and provide reasonably thorough descriptions of the gay characters or themes: characters are named, themes are elaborated, plots are described, locations are specified. Endings and solutions are rarely revealed. When the author has written more than one work, the citations are arranged chronologically. Bibliographical data on the works are limited to parenthetical asides listing the publisher and publication year, and thematic entries for such subjects as AIDS are included. Numerous cross-references provide access to authors using similar themes and to subjects that Slide thinks are relevant to the gay and lesbian communities; some of these include Gay Activists Alliance, gay/lesbian bars, gay pride parades, gays/lesbians as heroes/heroines, gays/lesbians as murder victims, gays/lesbians as villains, gays/lesbians in the military, hairdressers—male; and the Hollywood entertainment industry. The book concludes with a list of the specialist publishers of gay and lesbian fiction, a brief bibliography, and indexes to gay and lesbian characters and titles. In all, approximately 500 works are cited.

Surprisingly, a number of readily apparent omissions occur whose presence might have added greater depth to the book: gay characters may be found in the work of Mickey Spillane, and Slide should have included them, not merely dismissed Mike Hammer as a latent homosexual; similarly, the sympathetically presented lesbian in Trevanian's *The Main* deserves mention but receives none. Furthermore, if the relationship between Wolfe and Goodwin can be interpreted as homosexual, surely the more intriguing relationship between E. W. Hornung's Raffles and Bunny warrants examination. Finally, there are occasional errors: H. F. Heard's *Dopplegangers: An Episode of the Fourth, the Psychological, Revolution* is science fiction and does not feature Mr. Mycroft as a detective.

Worse, too often Slide twists evidence. His discussion of Philip Marlowe, for example, claims that Marlowe might be gay because "Philip Marlowe practises sexual abstinence, has longstanding friendships only with men, and often displays an almost ingrained repugnance for the women whom he encounters." This is no evidence of anything except a literary tradition common to detective stories, particularly those first published in pulp magazines. Similarly, in discussing *The Big Sleep,* Slide states that Marlowe's revulsion at finding the naked Carmen Sternwood in his bed "is the action only of a misogynist," a misreading of ludicrous proportions: would Slide have Marlowe behave like Dan Turner? Marlowe declines to bed the disturbed Carmen Sternwood because he is not enslaved by his libido, because she is the daughter of his well-paying client (professional ethics and common sense govern his actions), and because he feels no sexual attraction to her (she is the most loathsome character in a novel filled with loathsome characters).

There remains a need for a reliable bibliography of gay and lesbian characters and themes in mystery novels.

Golf Mysteries. *See* Sports Mysteries

Gothic Mysteries

114. Radcliffe, Elsa J. **Gothic Novels of the Twentieth Century: An Annotated Bibliography.** Metuchen, N.J.: Scarecrow, 1979. xvi, 272 p. Index. Cloth. LC 78-24357. ISBN 0-8108-1190-1.

The gothic novel in its earliest state combined elements of crime with stronger elements of horror and fantasy, but the genre is more properly considered a branch of fantastic fiction than it is a genre of mystery fiction, and reference books surveying the "pure" gothic are thus not considered here. Elsa Radcliffe's work concentrates not on the historical gothic but on the crime novels of the twentieth century that traditionally feature young women in peril. Using criteria put forth by Montague Summers's *The Gothic Quest* (New York: Russell & Russell, 1938), Radcliffe's introduction divides the contemporary gothic into five categories: the historical gothic, the sentimental gothic, the horror gothic, the exotic gothic, and the whimsical gothic. In all of these works, states Radcliffe, there are elements involving the supernatural; a quest or a wrong to be righted; a setting that includes an old dwelling (a castle); a fantasy of wealth suddenly acquired or an inheritance; mystery, suspense, and intrigue; a fantasy of romantic love in some form; romanticism of the past and a historical setting; and confrontations between the forces of Good and Evil.

Radcliffe's bibliography is arranged alphabetically by author's last name (given in capital letters); biographical data are occasionally provided. Titles of works are underlined, and the place of publication, publisher, and year of publication are given; paperback series numbers also are listed. Many citations are annotated. When more than one title exists by the same author, the arrangement is alphabetical. Pseudonymous works tend to be listed under the author's original name, and cross-references abound. References are consecutively numbered, and the bibliography cites 1,973 books. The concluding index offers title access to the works.

Gothic Novels of the Twentieth Century is the only substantial work on its subject, and it is a shame that it is a work that is riddled with the most egregious of errors. Errors abound in the biographical data, bibliographic citations, and annotations. Too often, Radcliffe has included works on the strengths of their titles (i.e., Frank Belknap Long's *The Goblin Tower* and *The Horror from the Hills*) when minimal research would have indicated that the former is poetry and the latter is a short Lovecraftian horror novel. Too often, too, Radcliffe has knowingly included works that are not gothic; and although she forthrightly states that these are not gothic, what is their purpose in a bibliography devoted to the contemporary gothic?

A comprehensive bibliography of the contemporary gothic remains to be done.

Hard-Boiled Mysteries

115.   Goulart, Ron. **An Informal Reading List.** http://www.miskatonic.org/rara-avis/
biblio/goulart_checklist.html

This list of the works of 15 authors of hard-boiled novels originally appeared as
an appendix to Ron Goulart's fiction anthology *The Hardboiled Dicks* (Los Angeles:
Sherbourne Press, 1965). No additional bibliographical data are given, but the list is
clearly presented. Nevertheless, prefer the lengthier list provided by O'Brien (q.v.).

116.   Marling, William. **Hard-Boiled Detective Fiction.** http://www.cwru.edu/
artsci/engl/marling/hardboiled.index.html

The most comprehensive and enjoyable of the hard-boiled Web sites listed in
this section, this site provides an extensive history of the genre, with discussions of such
subjects as the *Black Mask* school and some of its more notable writers. The development of the narrative is examined, as are characteristics of the genre, and major works
are discussed. Also, a lengthy bibliography of secondary sources is included, as well as a
glossary and a section listing "ideas for papers."

117.   O'Brien, Geoffrey. **The Hardboiled Era: A Checklist, 1929–1958.** http://www.
miskatonic.org/rara-avis/biblio/checklist.html

Reprinted from the appendix to Geoffrey O'Brien's *Hardboiled America* (New
York: Van Nostrand Reinhold, 1981), this chronologically arranged list of hard-boiled
novels published between 1919 and 1958 is designed to show that the hard-boiled detective novel is not a series of isolated works but belongs to a long-standing tradition. As
many as 15 authors and the titles of their works are listed in each year. No additional bibliographical data are given, but the list is lengthy, clearly laid out, and well chosen.

118.   Reader's Advice. **Hardboiled Detectives.** http://www.readersadvice.com/
readadv/000022.html

A bare-bones list of authors and titles, but very accessible.

119.   Sandoe, James. **The Hard-Boiled Dick: A Personal Check-List.** Chicago: Arthur Lovell, 1952. 9 p. Paperback.

This pamphlet is historically significant as the first separately published reference work on its subject. It is a selective, annotated bibliography, with Sandoe using as
his criteria for selection the concepts of literary quality: "The reader who, having
Hammett and Spillane to choose between, prefers the former, may find some use in the
titles and notes which follow. The list is selective, not comprehensive, and some celebrated names are absent by design, but I hope that none is absent by choice."

Sandoe's entries are arranged alphabetically by author's name, and they provide
the book's title (underlined) and the year of first book publication (in parentheses). A
brief annotation follows, and the entry concludes with the name of the detective. Only in
the entries for Chandler and Hammett does this format differ, with Sandoe providing
more detailed annotations and, in the case of the latter, a lengthy excerpt from Anthony
Boucher's review in the *New York Times* of 10 August 1952. The majority of the entries
is for novels, although S. J. Perelman's "Somewhere a Roscoe" and "Farewell, My
Lovely Appetizer" are praised, and Joseph Shaw's *The Hard-Boiled Omnibus* is dis-

cussed. Sandoe concludes his annotations by stating (perhaps disingenuously), "The writers and tales noted here are themselves of very unequal merit and it's quite possible that the quality which appeared to me to rescue an otherwise routine imitation from boredom will not affect another reader in the same way."

This important bibliography is now superseded with regards to its content and bibliographic data but not with regards to its critical judgments. Because the original publication of this bibliography is now virtually impossible to obtain, it should be noted that this list has been reprinted in its entirety in *The Armchair Detective Book of Lists* (q.v.). A slightly revised version of Sandoe's list—it is prefaced with a significantly longer introduction—can be found in the chapter titled "The Private Eye," published in *The Mystery Story,* a collection of essays edited by John Ball (Del Mar: University Extension, University of California, San Diego, in cooperation with Publisher's Inc., 1976).

120a. Skinner, Robert E. **The New Hard-Boiled Dicks: A Personal Checklist.** Brownstone Chapbook Series, vol. 2. San Bernardino, Calif.: Borgo Press, 1987. 60 p. ISBN 0-941028-04-6.

120b. Skinner, Robert E. **The New Hard-Boiled Dicks: Heroes for a New Urban Mythology.** Brownstone Mystery Guides, vol. 2. San Bernardino, Calif.: Brownstone Books, 1995. 192 p. Indexes. LC 93-16090. ISBN 0-941028-13-5 (cl); 0-941028-13-3 (pb).

The first edition of this survey of the writers of hard-boiled fiction was intended as a direct continuation of the work of Sandoe (q.v.) and consisted of essays on the 10 authors and 1 artist that Skinner believes represent the best of the newer generation of hard-boiled writers. The authors thus profiled are Andrew Bergman, James Crumley, Loren D. Estleman, Stephen Greenleaf, Donald Hamilton, Chester Himes, Stuart Kaminsky, Elmore Leonard, Robert B. Parker, "Richard Stark" (Donald Westlake), and Ernest Tidyman. The artist is Jim Steranko.

The second edition revised and expanded the previous essays, dropped the essay on Ernest Tidyman, and expanded the contents with the inclusion of studies of James Lee Burke, Robert Campbell, James Colbert, Michael Collins, Sue Grafton, Joseph Hansen, Andrew Vachss, and Chris Wiltz. The introductory chapter has changed from the terse "The Hard-Boiled Dick Past and Present" to the lengthier "The Hard-Boiled Hero: Evolution of an Urban Myth." The first edition contains no indexes and brief bibliographies; the second contains indexes to the authors, titles, and characters and lengthier (although not comprehensive) bibliographies of the works of the authors being studied. The essays in both editions tend to the appreciative rather than critical.

Although not as magisterial in judgment as Sandoe's work, and arguably not a reference work, the second edition of *New Hard-Boiled Dicks* is nevertheless one of the first volumes to acknowledge the accomplishments of some of the finest contemporary writers of the hard-boiled genre.

Historical Mysteries

121. Choi, Soon Y. **Soon's Historical Fiction Site.** http://uts.cc.utexas.edu/~soon/histfiction

Soon's Historical Fiction Site is nicely arranged and very pleasantly thorough, offering links to information about specific authors, historical fiction in general, and historical fiction by era. A master list of historical fiction writers contains biographies, bibliographies, and links to Web pages, and there are many additional links to other lists surveying the historical mystery.

The list of mysteries is available as part of the archives maintained by the DorothyL listserv. To obtain: send an e-mail message to listserv@listserv.kent.edu; type "get history.listing" in the subject line.

122. Cramme, Stefan. **Historische Romane über das alte Rom.** http://home.t-online. de/home/Stefan.Cramme/hr-title.html

Cramme's bibliography of novels set in old Rome references approximately 3,350 titles, though only a percentage of these is mystery and detective fiction. The list is alphabetically arranged by author, although selected persons, locations, and subjects are also listed. Cramme states that the bibliography is "in preliminary form," making this a site to watch.

123. Doyle, Noreen. **Ancient Egypt in Mysteries and Thrillers.** http://members. aol.com/wenamun/Egyptmyst.html

A very well designed Web site listing the mysteries with significant elements "drawn from ancient, and most especially pharaonic, Egypt."

124. Heli, Rick. **The Detective and the Toga.** http://spotlightongames.com/roman/ romys.html

125. Heli, Rick. **Mysteries Personal Reading List.** http://spotlightongames.com/ mysteries/personal.html

The Detective and the Toga begins with links to newly published mysteries set in ancient Rome, offers information on new editions of works, and provides information on forthcoming titles. The list is arranged by time period, starting with lists of mysteries set during the founding of Rome and concluding with mysteries set during the Byzantine era. The citations are to titles, each title being linked to information providing the author, publisher, year and place of publication, and ISBN; translations also are listed. These lists are international, mixing titles written in English with those in other languages, and Heli's site permits searchers to list the contents by writings in Dutch, English, French, German, Italian, Russian, and Spanish. There are links to profiles of the authors, to a publishing chronology of Roman mysteries, to Roman mysteries in anthologies (with a separate section for German anthologies), to Roman mysteries in magazines, to biblical retellings, and to novels on audiotape.

The Mysteries Personal Reading List offers access to mysteries by time and locale. Both sites are gratifyingly thorough and accessible.

126. Historical Mystery Appreciation Society. **Murder: Past Tense.** http:// mywebpages.comcast.net/monskshould/hmas-index.html

Home page of the Historical Murder Appreciation Society, run by Sue Feder.

127. Hurt, Nance S. **Medieval Mysteries.** http://members.tripod.com/~BrerFox/ medieval.html

Hurt's most useful Web site is arranged alphabetically by author; titles and publication dates are provided, as are the time period during which the story occurs and the location.

128a.   Lovett, Gayle. **Historical Mysteries, the Ancient and Classical World: Egypt, Greece, Rome and the Near East.** Woden, A.CT.: Gaslight Books, 1998. 27 p.

128b.   Lovett, Gayle. **Historical Mysteries, Britain: From Roman Occupation to Henry VIII: An Annotated Checklist.** Woden, A.CT.: Gaslight Books, 1998. 42 p.

128c.   Lovett, Gayle. **Historical Mysteries, Britain: From Elizabeth I to the Regency Period.** Woden, A.CT.: Gaslight Books, 1998. 36 p.

128d.   Lovett, Gayle. **Historical Mysteries, Britain: Victorian and Edwardian.** Woden, A.CT.: Gaslight Books, 1998. 53 p.

128e.   Lovett, Gayle. **Historical Mysteries, Europe, African Continent, China, Japan, Australia.** Woden, A.CT.: Gaslight Books, 1998. 39 p.

128f.   Lovett, Gayle. **Historical Mysteries, United States of America and Canada.** Woden, A.CT.: Gaslight Books, 1998. 46 p.

128g.   Lovett, Gayle. **The Miscellanea: Updates to Nos. 1–6 to August 2001, Anthologies, General References, Index to Series Characters, Etc.** Woden, A.CT.: Gaslight Books, 2002. 100 p.

These seven checklists have not been available, but they are freely available online at http:///www.gaslightbooks.com.au/checklists/histmyst.htm.

129.   Lowe, Nick. **Ancient Greece in Fiction.** http://www.sun.rhbnc.ac.uk/Classics/NJL/novels.html

A monumentally thorough list, with different sections offering bibliographic data on the fiction, ranging chronologically from the Bronze Age to the time of Cleopatra. No attempt is made at distinguishing mysteries and detective fiction from straight historical novels.

130.   Mench, Fred. **Fictional Rome.** http://www.stockton.edu/~roman/fiction

Mench's site offers, among other things, a searchable database; access to authors, essays, and reviews; a useful glossary of Latin words used in novels; information about historical figures likely to appear in the novels; and a well-done time line. It contains fewer titles than the work of Cramme (q.v.), but they are better accessible.

131.   Orgelfinger, Gail. **Medieval and Renaissance Mysteries.**

Available as part of the archives maintained by the DorothyL listserv. To obtain: send an e-mail message to listserv@listserv.kent.edu; type "get medieval.mystery" in the subject line.

132.   Reader's Advice. **Historical Mysteries.** http://www.readersadvice.com/readadv/ 000025.html

Much more elaborate than the usual bare-bones list of authors and titles, with divisions permitting one to locate mysteries set in ancient Egypt, ancient Greece and the Hellenistic world, ancient Rome, the various centuries of the Middle Ages, the Renaissance, the Elizabethan age, the seventeenth century, the eighteenth century, the Victorian era, the nineteenth century in general, the twentieth century, and various eras.

133.   Reader's Advice. **Past and Present Mysteries.** http://www.readersadvice.com/ readadv/000247.html

A special subgenre of the historical mystery in which the historical setting and characters in some way interact with those of the present. A surprisingly lengthy list.

Hollywood Mysteries

134.   Slide, Anthony. **The Hollywood Novel: A Critical Guide to over 1200 Works with Film-Related Themes or Characters, 1912 through 1994.** Jefferson, N.C.: McFarland, 1995. vii, 320 p. Index. Paperback. LC 95-15512. ISBN 0-7864-0044-7.

Following an introduction that defines the meaning of "Hollywood novel," *The Hollywood Novel* contains a chronology of the Hollywood novel from 1912 through 1994, in which the date is listed in bold numbers, beneath which are given the authors and titles of Hollywood novels. (It is amusing to note that the first listed is Victor Appleton's *Tom Swift and His Wizard Camera.*) The majority of the volume, however, is arranged by author: names are given in bold capital letters, followed by birth date and death date, after which are given a brief biographical statement and a discussion of the works in which figure Hollywood or some aspect of movies and moviegoing. Titles of these books are given in bold italics, followed by the book's first publisher and the date of publication; motion picture adaptations are mentioned, and reactions of contemporary reviewers are occasionally quoted. Following this section are sections listing works about "the television novel" and "the radio novel," after which are given a brief general bibliography and a title index. A subject index offers access by such subjects as "academy awards presentations," "actors/actresses," and (relevant for this volume) "mystery novels."

There are many inaccuracies, errors, and omissions in *The Hollywood Novel.* The description of Joe Lansdale's *The Drive-In* neglects the hyphen in the title, errs in its description, and fails to mention the 1990 sequel, which takes the protagonists into the world of the makers of the movie. (Indeed, it is arguable whether Lansdale's works should have been included, for they have nothing to do with Hollywood and only peripherally concern movies and moviemaking.) Similarly, Raoul Whitfield is misidentified as the pseudonym for Temple Field, and his *Death in a Bowl* (dated 1931 by Slide, though serialized in 1930) is described as "dime novel stuff," a confusion of dime novels with pulp magazines.

These caveats aside, Slide should be commended for providing data on more than 1,200 works, most of which are only peripherally known when they are known at all. Readers interested in the Hollywood mystery novel will find much to choose from.

Humorous Mysteries

135.   Wittman, Pat. **Humorous Mysteries.**

Available as part of the archives maintained by the DorothyL listserv. To obtain: send an e-mail message to listserv@listserv.kent.edu; type "get humor.mystery" in the subject line.

136.   Reader's Advice. **Humorous Mysteries.** http://www.readersadvice.com/readadv/ 000059.html

137.   Reader's Advice. **Mysteries with a Light Touch.** http://www.readersadvice.com/ readadv/000054.html

Bare-bones lists of authors and titles, but lengthy and accessible.

Jack the Ripper

Works of true crime generally have not been included in this bibliography, but speculation about the identity of the person (or people) who committed the bloody murders in Whitechapel between 31 August and 9 November 1888 remains endlessly fascinating.

138a.   Begg, Paul, Martin Fido, and Keith Skinner. **The Jack the Ripper A to Z.** Foreword by Donald Rumbelow. London: Headline, 1991. x, 335 p. Index. Paperback. ISBN 0-7472-0424-1.

138b.   Begg, Paul, Martin Fido, and Keith Skinner. **The Jack the Ripper A–Z.** New ed. Foreword by Donald Rumbelow. London: Headline, 1992. 544 p. Index. Paperback. ISBN 0-7472-3676-3.

138c.   Begg, Paul, Martin Fido, and Keith Skinner. **The Jack the Ripper A–Z.** Rev. ed. Foreword by Donald Rumbelow. London: Headline, 1994. xvi, 538 p. Index. Paperback. ISBN 0-7472-4445-6.

138d.   Begg, Paul, Martin Fido, and Keith Skinner. **The Jack the Ripper A–Z.** New rev. ed. Foreword by Donald Rumbelow. London: Headline, 1996. xviii, 519 p. Index. Paperback. ISBN 0-7472-5522-9.

The new revised edition is described here.

The literature on Jack the Ripper is voluminous, and *The Jack the Ripper A–Z* is occasionally cited as one of the finest works on its subject. Kelly (q.v.) describes it as "the definitive reference work dealing with the case (as well as the only one devoted entirely to the crimes) . . . the *A to Z* is also good value as an account of the murders and theories, albeit rather staccato in its presentation." The *A–Z* is also one of the volumes that Coville and Lucanio (q.v.) perused prior to writing their work.

The Jack the Ripper A–Z is effectively an encyclopedic dictionary listing the names of all people and organizations who were in some way involved with the murders attributed to Jack the Ripper, as well as significant theories and presentations that have since been advanced. These include the police, private detectives, various suspects, motion pictures, lists of books, the contents of the Home Office Files, and such subjects as

"Inquests: Jurisdictional Disputes Over," "Metropolitan Police," and "Swanson Marginalia, The." The entries are informative, containing cross-references when appropriate, and the volume concludes with a full index. There are a number of fascinating black-and-white photographs, although no maps and no time line.

This remains an excellent work, though Evans and Skinner's *The Ultimate Jack the Ripper Companion* (q.v.) is in many ways its equal.

139.   Coville, Gary, and Patrick Lucanio. **Jack the Ripper: His Life and Crimes in Popular Entertainment.** Jefferson, N.C.: McFarland, 1999. ix, 193 p. Index. LC 99-24751. ISBN 0-7864-0616-X.

According to the preface, the primary objective of this volume is "to offer a descriptive study of the literature about Jack the Ripper, since little has been done to articulate the Ripper's appearances in various kinds of popular works, both nonfiction and fiction." The secondary objective is to "analyze the meaning and value of representative fictional works."

Coville and Lucanio have examined the work of Begg, Fido, and Skinner and Kelly (q.q.v.), and they discuss a gratifyingly large number of the portrayals of the Ripper, from the earliest fictional appearances to various media appearances. An entire section is spent on the material pitting Sherlock Holmes against Jack the Ripper, after which there are lengthy alphabetical lists of the major films, radio programs, television programs, and "miscellaneous media" that in some way make use of Jack the Ripper or the images associated with him. The volume concludes with a capable index.

Intriguing though the discussions are, the volume is often less satisfying than it could be. This is in part because Coville and Lucanio for some reason fail to provide a comprehensive bibliographic listing of the works they discuss. This is also in part because Coville and Lucanio's stated secondary objective occasionally dominates and skews the presentation of data; a work that states, "We can say that Jack the Ripper's symbolic identity is revealed here for the first time: he is us" simply cannot be taken too seriously.

140.   Evans, Stewart P., and Keith Skinner. **The Ultimate Jack the Ripper Companion: An Illustrated Encyclopedia.** London: Robinson, 2000. xii, 692 p. Paperback. ISBN 1-8411-9225-2. New York: Carroll & Graf, 2001. x, 758 p. Paperback. LC 00-711560. ISBN 0-7867-0926-X.

Unlike the other volumes in this section, *The Ultimate Jack the Ripper Companion* does not discuss the fiction associated with the murders. It instead reprints the complete contents of the Scotland Yard files, extensive press reports, witness statements and extracts from police notebooks, and such useful documents as the reports of the inquests held on the victims. The data are given largely in chronological order, starting with the material associated with the 3 April 1888 murder of Emma Smith and concluding with the 23 February 1894 naming of suspects by Chief Constable M. L. Macnaghten. Later sections, however, discuss missing suspects files and additional suspects, and the volume offers two appendixes, a chronicle of events and notes on senior police and Home Office officials; it concludes with an excellent bibliography of sources and a well-done index.

The Ultimate Jack the Ripper Companion does not have as many illustrations as *The Jack the Ripper A–Z* (q.v.), nor does it discuss such hoaxes as the Maybrick diaries and the supposedly spurious Best letters. But its presentation permits readers to see the growing hysteria that associated itself with the murders, and the volume concentrates on original data. Although there are no maps, the index identifies the roads, passages, and buildings that figured in the murders. It remains an excellent work.

141a.   Kelly, Alexander Garfield. **Jack the Ripper: A Bibliography and Review of the Literature.** Introduction by Colin Wilson. London: Association of Assistant Librarians, 1973. 55 p. Index. LC 73-167860. ISBN 0-902238-03-0.

141b.   Kelly, Alexander. **Jack the Ripper: A Bibliography and Review of the Literature.** 2nd ed. Introduction by Colin Wilson. London: Association of Assistant Librarians, 1984. 83 p. Index. LC 86-141915. ISBN 0-902248-11-1.

141c.   Kelly, Alexander, and David Sharp. **Jack the Ripper: A Bibliography and Review of the Literature.** 3rd ed. Introduction by Colin Wilson. London: Association of Assistant Librarians, 1995. 186 p. Index. ISBN 0-900092-90-4.

The third edition is described. Kelly's volume contains two sections: the relatively brief first part consists of Wilson's introduction, which ably describes the crime and summarizes the major theories, although this is followed by another section in which Kelly describes additional speculations. The second part of the volume consists of the bibliography and review of the literature: separate sections list contemporary publications, works discussing facts and theories, the biographies and autobiographies of people involved in the crimes, and creative works (fiction, drama, music, and media adaptations) using the crime as the basis. The annotations are not numbered, but a headnote states that 186 creative works have been listed. Citations are arranged alphabetically by author's last name; titles are given in italics; place of publication, publisher, and year of publication are given; and "a few highly recommended items" are listed in boldface type. The volume concludes with an author/title index.

Jack the Ripper is easy to use, and its contents are readily accessible. More: Kelly's annotations are authoritative, opinionated, and delightful reading.

Law Mysteries. *See* Courtroom Fiction and Legal Thrillers

Lesbian Mysteries. *See* Gay and Lesbian Mysteries

Library Mysteries. *See also* Bibliomysteries

142.   Gwinn, Nancy E. **Library Mysteries: A Halloween Sampler.** Washington, D.C.: Center for the Book, Library of Congress, 1992 (Halloween). Unpaged [8 p.]. Paperback.

Compiled by Gwinn to celebrate "Mystery at the Library of Congress," the Library of Congress's First Annual Halloween Mystery Celebration, this slim pamphlet lists a handful of the detective and mystery books and short stories that are set in libraries. Gwinn's citations are arranged alphabetically; book titles are given in italics, followed by place of publication, publisher, and year of publication. Citations to periodical publications give the title in quotation marks, followed by the periodical title in italics, the volume, month and year of publication, and the pagination. All citations are annotated.

Though incomplete and brief, Gwinn's is the only separate paper publication on its subject. Special and affectionate mention should be made of Edward F. Ellis's *The British Museum in Fiction: A Check-List* (Portland, Maine: Anthoensen Press, 1981), which attempts to list all the books in which the British Museum has been mentioned. Ellis cites the first British and first American editions of each book, indicating retitlings when necessary. The references to the British Museum are indicated not by page but by chapter and are followed by the text in which the mention is made; the book concludes with a title index. Ellis does not limit his contents to detective and mystery stories, nor does he provide a subject index, but users can nevertheless readily find references to the British Museum in works by August Derleth, Arthur Conan Doyle, R. Austin Freeman, and Inez Haynes Irwin, among many others.

143.   Hall, Alison. **Library Mysteries Bibliography.**

Available as part of the archives maintained by the DorothyL listserv. To obtain: send an e-mail message to listserv@listserv.kent.edu; type "get library.mystery" in the subject line. Although it needs updating, it has not been superseded by the much lengthier bibliography on the same subject maintained by Candy Schwartz (q.v.).

144.   Schwartz, Candy. **Mysteries Involving Libraries, Librarians, Etc.**

Available as part of the archives maintained by the DorothyL listserv. To obtain: send an e-mail message to listserv@listserv.kent.edu; type "get biblio.mystery" in the subject line. More data than that compiled by Hall, but Hall still contains some references that are not listed by Schwartz.

Lizzie Borden Mysteries

145.   Flynn, Robert A. **The Borden Murders: An Annotated Bibliography.** Preface by David Kent. Portland, Maine: King Philip, 1992. xiv, 113 p. Index. LC 91-075384. ISBN 0-9614811-3-7. 1,000 copies printed.

Works of true crime generally have not been included in this bibliography, but the 1892 murders in Fall River, Massachusetts, have created a veritable cottage industry of speculation about identity of the culprit. This enjoyable bibliography documents these materials, with separate sections surveying the nonfiction books; nonfiction articles and essays; reference works; miscellaneous; novels; short stories; plays, videos, and television shows; opera and ballet adaptations; poetry and rhymes; and music based on the murders. An index to names concludes the volume.

The sections describing the creative works are arranged alphabetically by author's last name, given in boldface capital letters. For novels, titles are given in italic capital letters, followed by the place of publication, publisher, and year of publication, after which Flynn provides a brief annotation describing the book's connection to the murders. For short stories, the author's last name is in boldface capital letters, the title of the work is in italic capital letters followed by the title of the book in which the story was published, the editor(s), place of publication, publisher, year of publication, and pagination. Original periodical publication data are often provided. For media adaptations, the works are listed under the name of the writer, given in boldface capital letters, followed by the title in italic capital letters, after which publication data for the play or basic data about the adaptation are given.

Scholars and experts will doubtless know of additional works, but Flynn provides a useful beginning and can be browsed with pleasure.

Locked Room Mysteries

146a. Adey, Robert. **Locked Room Murders and Other Impossible Crimes.** London: Ferret, 1979. 190 p. Indexes. Cloth.

146b. Adey, Robert. **Locked Room Murders and Other Impossible Crimes: A Comprehensive Bibliography.** 2nd ed. revised and expanded. Minneapolis, Minn.: Crossover Press, 1991. xliii, 411 p. Indexes. Cloth. LC 94-212600. ISBN 0-9628870-0-5.

Like a great many bibliographies, this one began as a labor of love. Adey wanted to document the stories he loved, and in 1972 he "hit upon the idea of listing all impossible crime novels and short stories known to me." The result was a bibliography of some 1,280 novels and short stories, all featuring crimes that could not have been committed but somehow were, all taxing the reader's ingenuity to solve the mystery before the investigator.

Following a lengthy and informative introduction, the first part of Adey's bibliography is arranged alphabetically by author; when the author contributed more than one work to the locked room genre, the arrangement becomes alphabetical by title. Each entry is numbered, provides the work's title (listing alternative titles when they are known) and the place of publication, publisher, and year of publication. Publication data on the first British and American editions are provided; if a book was simultaneously published in England and America, the English edition is cited first. Concluding each entry are the detective's name and a brief (and frequently intriguing) statement of the nature of the locked room problem. The second part of the volume contains the solutions. Each solution is numbered and keyed to its counterpart in the first part of the bibliography. A brief list titled "Foreign Language Books" concludes the volume.

Had Adey been content not to provide a second edition, the first edition would be inestimably useful and fascinating to browse. The second edition, however, is a tour de force, a list of 2,019 locked room stories. Although it is nearly three times as thick as the first edition, and thoroughly supersedes the earlier volume, its arrangement is largely similar to the first edition: all sections have been expanded, and titles new to the second edition are indicated with a check mark. A section listing the contents of locked room anthologies has been added.

Neither edition of this book contains a title index, and a chronological index might have been helpful. These oversights aside, the second edition will assist researchers as well as those who enjoy reading by genre.

147. Shortling, Grobius. **Golden Age of Detective Stories: "Locked-Room" Mysteries and Other Impossible Crimes.** http://www.mysterylist.com/lockedrm.htm

Shortling's essay provides informed commentary on the types of locked room mystery; exemplary authors and their titles are given.

148. Wopenka, Johan. **Locked-Room Mystery Recommendations.** http://hem.passagen.se/orange/roomlist.htm

Swedish critic and expert Wopenka provides a list of the genre cornerstones arranged chronologically; the Swedish title of the work is also provided.

Magic and Magician Mysteries

149.   Canick, Michael. **Magic in Fiction: A Short-Title Checklist.** New York: Volcanick Press, 1998. 40 p. Paperback.

Although it does not limit itself to mystery and detective fiction, *Magic in Fiction* is apparently the only separately published work on its subject: the use and appearance of magic and magicians in novels, short stories, plays, and poetry. The bibliography opens with a brief statement of the criteria Canick used for determining whether a work was "magic fiction." Following this, the bibliography contains two sections, the first of which lists materials by subject: literary fiction; mystery, detective, thriller fiction; science, speculative, horror, and fantasy fiction; children's fiction; miscellaneous magic fiction; circus, carnival, and sideshow fiction; gambling, cheating, fraud, and con fiction; hypnotism fiction; ventriloquism fiction; and occult fiction. In all, approximately 1,500 works are listed. Citations are arranged alphabetically by the author's last name, with the titles listed alphabetically beneath. These are followed by the year of publication (or the earliest date of which Canick has a record) and the publisher's name (often abbreviated).

The bibliography's second section is an author/title list of books that, in Canick's words, fall into "three types: 1) those whose existence I cannot verify; 2) those which may not be fiction; or 3) those which may not have any magic content." The citations do not indicate which is which, and one wonders why Canick referenced them, particularly since publications in the second and third categories are not relevant to this bibliography.

Canick offers much more than users can obtain through such volumes as Olderr's *Mystery Index* and the different editions of *What Mystery Do I Read Next?* (q.q.v.).

Married Protagonist Mysteries

150.   Griffith, Thomas H. **A List of Married (Fictional) Sleuths.**

Available as part of the archives maintained by the DorothyL listserv. To obtain: send an e-mail message to listserv@listserv.kent.edu; type "get married.sleuths" in the subject line.

Medical Thrillers

151.   **Medical Thrillers.** http://www.medical-thriller.com/

A list of more than 270 books, but accessible by author, title, and medical topic (e.g., pandemics, epidemics, infections, transplantations, forensic medicine). Very enjoyable.

Medieval Mysteries. *See* Historical Mysteries

Men Detective Mysteries

152.   Heising, Willeta L. **Detecting Men: Pocket Guide.** Dearborn, Mich.: Purple Moon Press, 1997. 144 p. Paperback. ISBN 0-9644593-4-5.

Detecting Men: Pocket Guide was created to accompany *Detecting Men* (q.v.), but it contains none of the biographical data or indexes of the full-sized volume and is an author/title list. Only living men who wrote series characters are listed, though several authors who died in 1996 are included, for new titles by them may yet appear. The *Pocket Guide* is arranged alphabetically by author's last name, given in boldface; pseudonyms are indicated by the letter *P,* but the real name is revealed in *Detecting Men.* The series character's name is listed beneath the author's name, and the series titles are listed in order, with the year of publication given in parentheses; only series titles are listed, although retitlings are given. Starred titles indicate award winners; solid stars are used for winners, open stars for nominees. A notepad is provided. Although not free from error, collectors and those needing lists will find the *Pocket Guide* to be extraordinarily helpful.

Mountie Mysteries

153.   Drew, Bernard A. **Lawmen in Scarlet: An Annotated Guide to Royal Canadian Mounted Police in Print and Performance.** Metuchen, N.J.: Scarecrow, 1990. xx, 276 p. Index. Cloth. LC 90-8388. ISBN 0-8108-2330-6.

No separately published bibliography of Mountie detective and mystery fiction appears to exist, but the character of the Royal Canadian Mounted Policeman, frequently resplendent in his red coat, is documented in this annotated guide of more than 200 motion pictures and approximately 500 books. Although many of these books are simply adventures, romances, and "Northerns," a significant percentage of these books features the Mountie as a detective, solving crimes and righting wrongs.

The bibliography is divided into two sections, the first referencing print sources and the second referencing dramatic adaptations. The entries in the former include books, magazine fiction, pulp magazines, comic books, comic strips, and Big Little Books. The initial arrangement is alphabetical by author's last name; titles are then listed alphabetically beneath the name. Citations include a biographical sketch, the book's title, publication data for the first North American and the first British editions, and frequently a lively annotation; titles that Drew was unable to examine are merely listed. All citations are keyed to a bibliography listing the references from which Drew derived his listings.

The dramatic adaptations cite the motion pictures, television programs, radio shows, musicals, plays, and operas in which Mounties appear. Citations are arranged alphabetically by title, and the presented data vary according to the material being described; for example, motion picture citations include studio, year the film was released, major cast and credits, and a content annotation.

In his *Canadian Crime Fiction* (q.v.), David Skene-Melvin characterizes this book as "regrettably flawed, for it could have been a valuable tool." Skene-Melvin's work includes an excellent index to Mountie novels, but Drew remains the only separately published work on its subject.

Music Mysteries

154.   Boettcher, Bonna J. **Music/Musicians/Musical Mysteries.**

A bare-bones list available as part of the archives maintained by the DorothyL listserv. To obtain: send an e-mail message to listserv@listserv.kent.edu; type "get music.mystery" in the subject line.

155.   Reader's Advice. **Musical Mysteries.** http://www.readersadvice.com/readadv/000234.html

A bare-bones list of authors and titles, but very accessible.

Native American Mysteries

156.   Macdonald, Gina, Andrew Macdonald, and MaryAnn Sheridan. **Shaman or Sherlock? The Native American Detective.** Contributions to the Study of Popular Culture, no. 74. Westport, Conn.: Greenwood, 2002. x, 284 p. Indexes. LC 2001-1023335. ISBN 0-313-30841-1.

The majority of the Macdonalds' volume is a study of the way in which Native Americans are depicted in mystery and detective fiction. The bibliography, which concludes the volume, however, is 10 pages long and contains separate lists of primary sources, juvenile detective fiction, and Native American detective fiction and mythologies. The citations are arranged alphabetically by author and provide the title (in italics), the place of publication, publisher, and year of publication. The resulting list is far more comprehensive than the following list.

157.   Reader's Advice. **Native American Mysteries.** http://www.readersadvice.com/readadv/000302.html

A bare-bones list, but accessible, very useful, and with numerous genre links.

Numerical Mysteries

158.   Reader's Advice. **Numbers in the Title.** http://www.readersadvice.com/readadv/000301.html

A bare-bones list of authors and titles that contain numbers. The list is accessible, but it is more of an exercise in trivia than anything else.

Nurse Mysteries

159.   Mikucki, Eleanor. **Nurse Sleuths.** http://www.geocities.com/Athens/3777/sleuths.html

More than a mere list of nurses who served as sleuths, this clearly produced Web site provides significant information on each of the nurses, their authors, and gives for each nurse an annotated list of the works in which she appeared. Arrangement is alphabetical by the name of the nurse; in all, arrangement of the bibliographies is chronological but additional publication data are not provided. Cover reproductions are given, as are links to related sites. The author compiled the Web site devoted to nurse-sleuth Cherry Ames (q.v.), and this Web site is equally enjoyable.

Paranormal Mysteries. *See also* Science Fiction and Fantasy Mysteries

160. Reader's Advice. **Paranormal Mysteries.** http://www.readersadvice.com/readadv/000212.html

A bare-bones list of authors and titles, and accessible. The present writer recognizes the existence of the genre but tends to regard stories involving paranormal powers as supernatural fantasies, hence the preceding cross-reference.

Past and Present Mysteries. *See* Historical Mysteries

Police Detective Mysteries

161. Kristick, Laurel. **Police Detectives.**

Available as part of the archives maintained by the DorothyL listserv. To obtain: send an e-mail message to listserv@listserv.kent.edu; type "get police.detective" in the subject line.

Police Procedurals

162. Reader's Advice. **Police Procedurals.** http://www.readersadvice.com/readadv/000019.html

A lengthy list of authors and titles. Useful and accessible.

163. Vicarel, Jo Ann. **A Reader's Guide to the Police Procedural.** Reader's Guides to Mystery Novels. New York: G. K. Hall, 1995. xiv, 402 p. Cloth. LC 94-33650. ISBN 0-8161-1801-9.

In her preface, Vicarel offers a definition of the police procedural, stating in part that "the main difference between a police procedural and a traditional mystery is that the procedural is a novel about police life and work first, and a mystery second. Sometimes the crime is secondary to the personal lives of the police." Using this definition as her basis, Vicarel provides an annotated bibliography of 1,115 police procedural novels written by 271 authors. Her entries are arranged alphabetically by the author's last name; when the author is present with more than one book, the entries are listed chronologically. Pseudonyms and cross-references are provided. Each citation gives the title, publisher, and publication date for the book's first edition and provides the name and rank of the investigating officer or officers; the annotations range in length from fewer than 20 to more than 100 words but give away no plot twists and reveal no endings.

Although the annotated bibliography dominates the volume, there are additional chapters listing pseudonyms and their users, series characters and their creators, and periods during which the story occurs. In addition, there are indexes for story location, novels featuring serial killers, "lighter" books, and authors "who have been identified as ex-police officers, currently serve on a police force, or have a close working relationship with a department." An essay discussing the differences between the police agencies of the United States and the United Kingdom and Vicarel's list of her favorite 100 police procedurals conclude the volume.

A Reader's Guide to the Police Procedural has its flaws. Thomas Harris's Red Dragon is listed, but not his Silence of the Lambs, yet the former's Will Graham is listed in the series character list (a one-book series?). More seriously, Vicarel's preface states, "Read Sci Fi or The Far Away Man to understand this literary technique [of lightness]," yet she fails to include a title index, forcing the curious to read every entry in the section devoted to "lightness" or to go elsewhere for the relevant information.

These complaints aside, A Reader's Guide to the Police Procedural is a thoroughly impressive achievement. Vicarel's efforts permit the identification and location of a large and disparate body of work, and for this she deserves commendation.

Private Eye Mysteries

164. Baker, Robert A., and Michael T. Nietzel. **Private Eyes: One Hundred and One Knights: A Survey of American Detective Fiction 1922–1984.** Introduction by Bill Pronzini. Bowling Green, Ohio: Bowling Green State University Popular Press, 1985. vi, 385 p. LC 85-70857. ISBN 0-87972-329-7 (hc); 0-87972-330-3 (pb).

This is one of two significant volumes on the private eye published in 1985, the other being David Geherin's The American Private Eye: The Image in Fiction (q.v.). Although the contents of the two books overlap to some degree, Baker and Nietzel's is lengthier, and, perhaps more significantly, a significant percentage of their content is derived from a 1983 questionnaire that surveyed the membership of the Private Eye Writers of America (PWA). "The ratings of the PWA membership guided our selection of authors for this book," states the introduction to Private Eyes. The authors add a little later that "of the 80 questionnaires that were distributed, 27 were completed and returned." The results of this survey are presented in the first chapter, but validity of data derived from such a minuscule group is never seriously questioned.

The metaphor of the private eye as knight errant dominates the book's arrangement and the chapter names, but statistics and nomenclature aside, Private Eyes is essentially a historical survey of significant private eye detectives. Starting with the writings of Hammett and Chandler, Baker and Nietzel discuss the private eyes created by Ross Macdonald, John D. MacDonald, Mickey Spillane, Fredric Brown, Erle Stanley Gardner, Rex Stout, William Campbell Gault, Bill Pronzini, Marcia Muller, George Chesbro, and scores of others. In all, 101 private detectives are described; an appendix cites 101 additional private eyes. The book concludes with useful indexes of authors and characters.

As a guide, Private Eyes has more than its share of typos, an occasional unattributed quote, some factual errors, and too much appreciation and not enough criticism. For Baker and Nietzel to praise Michael Avallone's "Ed Noon" as "the most James Bond-like of all our PIs," without mentioning Avallone's unique prose style, does disservice to series and to reader. Worse yet, in an apparent effort to be informal, Baker and Nietzel undermine their academic credibility through such sentences as "he exercises his one-eyed wonder worm at every opportunity and the opportunities abound" (p. 161).

Since 1983 many hitherto inaccessible pulp private eye stories have been reprinted, and many writers have created new and memorable private eyes. An updated and more comprehensive survey, and a correspondingly rewritten version of Private Eyes, might be in order.

165. Geherin, David. **The American Private Eye: The Image in Fiction.** New York: Frederick Ungar, 1985. xii, 228 p. Index. LC 84-15251. ISBN 0-8044-2243-5 (hc); 0-8044-6184-8 (pb).

One of two books on the private eye to appear in 1985—the other being *Private Eyes: One Hundred and One Knights* by Robert A. Baker and Michael T. Nietzel (q.v.)—this book surveys only 27 private eyes, but a number of these are not discussed by Baker and Nietzel. Unlike Baker and Nietzel, Geherin chose his writers not by survey but through personal knowledge "on the basis of their influence on the genre, their enormous popularity, or as in the case of several of the lesser-known writers, a desire to pay long overdue recognition to their creative contributions to the growth and vitality of the genre."

Geherin begins his study by discussing two of the earliest private eyes, Carroll John Daly's Race Williams and Dashiell Hammett's the Continental Op. Following sections discuss six notable pulp private eyes, four private eyes who had a life beyond the pulps, five private eyes who became active following World War II, four private eyes who were "compassionate" in one way or another, and six contemporary private eyes. An appendix, "An Enduring Hero," offers a theoretical understanding of the enduring popularity of the private eye, and the book concludes with a well-done index.

Geherin's decision to include private eyes who were active in the pulps allows him to discuss such figures as Robert Leslie Bellem's Dan Turner and John K. Butler's Steve Midnight, neither of whom is discussed by Baker and Nietzel, and Geherin provides a welcome appreciation of the four Paul Pine novels written by Howard Browne, another private eye writer neglected by Baker and Nietzel. Furthermore, Geherin is a lively and perceptive critic, and his assessments are consistently cogently expressed. An updated survey would be welcome.

166. Niebuhr, Gary Warren. **A Reader's Guide to the Private Eye Novel.** Reader's Guides to Mystery Novels. New York: G. K. Hall, 1993. xv, 323 p. Indexes. Cloth. LC 93-22212. ISBN 0-8161-1802-7.

This is the third in a series that began with Susan Oleksiw's *A Reader's Guide to the Classic British Mystery* and continued with Marvin Lachman's *A Reader's Guide to the American Novel of Detection* (q.q.v.), and like its predecessors, this is an oddly inconsistent work. Following the preface, in which he provides a reasonable series of criteria for defining a private eye novel, Niebuhr provides an annotated bibliography of approximately 1,100 works by 90 authors published up to and during 1992. The overall arrangement is alphabetical by author. For each work, Niebuhr provides the title in boldface and the names of the series characters in italics. Beneath the title are the place of publication, publisher, and publication year of the first American and first English editions. The annotations are in the 75- to 100-word range; collections of short stories are cited and listed, but their contents are not annotated. The citations are arranged by series character, after which they are ordered by what Niebuhr deems to be their internal chronology.

The annotated bibliography dominates the volume, but additional chapters list pseudonyms and their users and series characters and their creators, and indexes for the periods during which the stories occur, locations, settings, and miscellaneous information are provided. The volume concludes with a list of 100 classics and highly recommended titles. As with the other volumes in this series, there is no title index.

Although one can argue that Niebuhr should have chosen additional authors and works for annotation, the greatest weakness of *A Reader's Guide to the Private Eye Novel* is that it does not stand alone particularly well. It is best used in conjunction with the other books published in this series, in particular Lachman's *A Reader's Guide to the American Novel of Detection* and Vicarel's *A Reader's Guide to the Police Procedural* (q.q.v.). It is nevertheless a useful volume.

A revised and expanded edition would be helpful.

167. Siegel, Jeff. **The American Detective: An Illustrated History.** Dallas, Tex.: Taylor Publishing, 1993. vii, 168 p. Index. Cloth. LC 93-7189. ISBN 0-87833-829-2.

Although heavily illustrated, this history and discussion of significant American detectives manages to be more than a coffee-table book. Siegel's six chapters—"150 Years of Gumshoes," "The Shamuses," "The Snoops," "The Sheriffs," "The Shysters," and "The Spooks"—are lively, engagingly written, and contain frequently thought-provoking linkages, as between Nick Carter and Meville Davisson Post's Uncle Abner. Siegel's text frequently contains sidebars offering definitions and explanations, and there are some amusing but reasonable lists—"The Gumshoe Hall of Fame," "The Ten Silliest Cop Shows in Television History." Siegel discusses detectives in film as well as literature, linking, for example, the original *Dragnet* to the police procedurals of Hillary Waugh, Lawrence Treat, and Ed McBain. Nor, despite his introductory claims, does Siegel succeed in limiting his discussion to American detectives. Numerous references are made to the English detectives, and Rumpole in particular is praised: "He is such a marvelous character . . . that he deserves to be an American." (One suspects that John Mortimer could imagine a higher honor for his Q.C.!)

Following the text is a bibliographic essay, "Tracking the Sources," that describes and recommends the notable reference books about the genre, and Siegel provides a list of the winners of the Mystery Writers of America Edgar Allan Poe Awards from 1946 through 1993 (without explanations of the significance of the Raven, the Ellery Queen Award, and the Robert L. Fish Award). The book concludes with a capable index.

Like many popular histories, the book is weakest in documenting the material written between the creations of Poe and the advent of the pulp magazines. Virtually none of Siegel's quotations and references are documented, and the book contains no bibliography.

Science Fiction and Fantasy Mysteries

168. Frants, Marina. **F and SF Mystery.**

Available as part of the archives maintained by the DorothyL listserv. To obtain: send an e-mail message to listserv@listserv.kent.edu; type "get fandsf.mystery" in the subject line.

169. Grost, Michael. **Supernatural Detectives.** http://members.aol.com/MG4273/weirdmen.htm

Part of Grost's impressive site devoted to "reading lists and essays on great mysteries, mainly of the pre 1960 era," this bibliography provides data on the more significant writers of supernatural detective stories.

170.   Herald, Diana Tixier. **Detection in Science Fiction & Fantasy.** http://www. genrefluent.com/SFdetect.htm

Derived from *Genreflecting,* a work whose contents are by no means limited to mystery and detective fiction, this bibliography lists six anthologies, but the majority of the citations is to the more than 150 books by approximately 70 authors that offer a blend of science fiction and fantasy. The list is alphabetical; titles are italicized; and many entries are accompanied by ISBNs to permit easy ordering. Lengthier than the list compiled by Frants (q.v.) and briefer but more bibliographically reliable than the work of Lovisi (q.v.).

171.   Lovisi, Gary. **Science Fiction Detective Tales: A Brief Overview of Futuristic Detective Fiction in Paperback.** Brooklyn, N.Y.: Gryphon Books, 1986. 107 p. Paperback. ISBN 0-936071-01-X.

This is not a bibliography but an extended bibliographical essay, with Lovisi, a prolific writer of hard-boileds and paperback enthusiast, surveying the works that straddle the borders of science fiction and detective story. For each work discussed, Lovisi provides the publisher, publication date, series number, price, and pagination of each of the editions that were available to him.

What could have been a very worthwhile project is unfortunately a thoroughly botched job. The volume is reproduced from typed copy, the writing is thoroughly amateurish, and the number of typographical errors is unbelievable. On the first page alone are references to Harold Q. Masur's "Scott Jordon," "Earle Stanley Gardner," "Hercule Periot," and "Miss Marble." There is no separate list of the works discussed, and the volume lacks an index.

Readers interested in the intersection of the detective story and science fiction might wish to examine Hazel Beasley Pierce's *A Literary Symbiosis: Science Fiction/Fantasy Mystery* (Westport, Conn.: Greenwood, 1983). Though lacking a cumulative bibliography, it is capably written and well indexed.

172.   Reader's Advice. **Fantasy Mysteries.** http://www.readersadvice.com/readadv/0003344.html

173.   Reader's Advice. **SF Mysteries.** http://www.readersadvice.com/readadv/000355.html

Bare-bones lists of authors and titles, but very accessible.

Sports Mysteries

174.   Reader's Advice. **Sports Mysteries.** http://www.readersadvice.com/readadv/000239.html

A lengthy list, with links to various sports offering access to authors and titles.

Baseball

175.   Gants, Susan E. **Baseball Mysteries List.**

Available as part of the archives maintained by the DorothyL listserv. To obtain: send an e-mail message to listserv@listserv.kent.edu; type "get baseball.mystery" in the subject line.

176. Morris, Tim. **Guide to Baseball Fiction.** http://www.uta.edu/english/tim/baseball

Morris's *Guide to Baseball Fiction* references a number of baseball mysteries, although it does not provide them with a separate section and lists them along with the other creative works having baseball as their source or theme. Separate lists for adult novels, short stories, children's books, films, and criticism dealing with baseball fiction are provided.

Golf

177. Leininger, John. **Golf Mysteries.**

Available as part of the archives maintained by the DorothyL listserv. To obtain: send an e-mail message to listserv@listserv.kent.edu; type "get golf.mystery" in the subject line.

178. Taylor, Thomas. **The Golf Murders Collection: A Readers' and Collectors' Illustrated Guide to Golf Mystery Fiction.** Westland, Mich.: Golf Mystery Press, 1997. 206 p. Cloth. LC 96-95338. ISBN 1-8902230-0-X. 400 copies printed; not all signed.

Taylor states in his introduction, "It started with a love of mystery fiction . . . to that add a love of golf." He thus scoured the field looking for books that combined the two, and the result is *The Golf Murders Collection,* an annotated bibliography listing approximately 200 mysteries with golf in them. The bibliography contains five sections, the first of which is an alphabetical listing of full-length golf mysteries: the arrangement is by author (given in boldface type), followed by the title (in boldface capital letters), the publication data (publisher, place and date of publication), whether the book was paperbound, and sometimes the pagination. The annotations are full and chatty, describing the nature of the mystery and the amount of golf the mystery involves.

The second chapter consists of color reproductions of 144 dust wrappers from the books described in the first section. The arrangement is alphabetical by author's last name. This chapter is separately numbered and paginated (pp. 97–112) in the table of contents but occurs in the middle of the first chapter, which encompasses pages 27 to 172.

The third chapter is an alphabetical annotated list of 21 books that did not make the cut; that is, were not sufficiently golf-related to include in the first chapter. The fourth chapter is an annotated list of 24 short stories that involve golf; it is arranged by the author's last name and provides the original publication data of the short story: periodical title, month, and year of publication. The fifth chapter consists of charts permitting one to locate stories by their type, the amount of golf played, the author's sex, the protagonist's sex, and the story's setting. The volume concludes with an index.

Apart from rather too many typographical errors—Taylor has a recurrent problem in using apostrophes and commas—this is a capable labor of love. One wishes there was mention of Elmore Leonard's *City Primeval,* which has murders occurring on a golf course and thus should have at least been given as a title that did not make the cut, but this is hardly a flaw. On the other hand, the volume's subject matter is so specialized that it is hardly a necessary publication.

179.   Waterboro Public Library. **Golfing Mysteries.** http://www.waterboro.lib.me.us/
golfmyst.htm

A lengthy list, arranged alphabetically by author's last name. An introduction
explains that not all of the titles are available at the Waterboro Public Library, but they
can be obtained through interlibrary loan.

Spy Fiction

180.   McCormick, Donald, and Katy Fletcher. **Spy Fiction: A Connoisseur's Guide.**
New York: Facts on File, 1990. 346 p. Index. LC 89-29524. ISBN 0-8160-
2098-1.

This volume generally does not concern itself with espionage fiction, a distinct
literary genre that has its own authors and canon. Nevertheless, the effort of McCormick
and Fletcher deserves mention because (unlike Smith, which follows) they are selective,
attempting to create a canon that describes the efforts and accomplishments of the finest
writers of spy fiction. Their volume has two sections and begins with an introduction that
discusses the history of espionage fiction, defining it while defending it against those
who would dismiss it as a lesser branch of fiction. After this is an alphabetical list of
approximately 200 authors. For each, the name is given in boldface capital letters, followed by (in regular type) biographical data that include the author's nationality, birth
date and place, and death date and place; pseudonyms are also listed. Beneath these are
listed in chronological order the first English and American editions of their works;
place of publication, publisher, and publication date(s) are given. A brief biography is
then provided, after which an occasionally lengthy critical analysis explains the writer's
merits. When relevant, brief lists of media adaptations are given, though these include
only the title, the name of the issuing studio, and the year in which it was issued.

The second section of *Spy Fiction* consists of eight short essays: a brief history
of American spy fiction: before and after 1945; fiction from fact: the treatment of real
events in the spy novel; the role of the mole and the treatment of treachery; writers of spy
fiction worldwide; future directions of the spy novel; cross-fertilizations: the relationship between writers and the world of intelligence; adaptations to the screen; state of the
"Art": the modern spy novel. Following these is a glossary of several hundred entries,
defining terms ranging from "Ag & Fish" to "Zoo." The volume concludes with a
lengthy bibliography and a useful index.

Spy Fiction remains consistently useful.

181a.   Smith, Myron J. **Cloak-and-Dagger Bibliography: An Annotated Guide to
Spy Fiction, 1937–1975.** Metuchen, N.J.: Scarecrow, 1976. xi, 225 p. Index.
LC 75-44319. ISBN 0-8108-0897-8.

181b.   Smith, Myron J. **Cloak and Dagger Fiction: An Annotated Guide to Spy
Thrillers.** 2nd ed. Santa Barbara, Calif.: ABC-Clio, 1982. xxxvi, 431 p. Index.
LC 82-6655. ISBN 0-87436-328-4.

181c.   Smith, Myron J., and Terry White. **Cloak and Dagger Fiction: An Annotated
Guide to Spy Thrillers.** 3rd ed. Bibliographies and Indexes in World Literature,
no. 45. Foreword by Julian Rathbone. Preface by Joe Poyer. Westport, Conn.:
Greenwood, 1995. xl, 849 p. LC 94-22017. ISBN 0-313-27700-1. ISSN 0742-
6801.

As stated earlier, this volume generally does not concern itself with espionage fiction. Smith's volume deserves mention because it is the best of its kind. The third edition provides annotations to more than 5,800 novels and collections published from the first quarter of the twentieth century until the 1990s. These are presented in two sections: the first and by far the briefest annotates spy thrillers written prior to 1940, the latter annotates the spy thrillers written after 1940. Arrangement in both is alphabetical by the author's last name; titles are given in italic type; and the place of publication, publisher, and publication year are listed. Alternate titles are indicated, as are pseudonyms, and biographical data on the author frequently are provided. A series of descriptive symbols indicates whether the book exists exclusively in paperback (*P*), portrays no graphic sexuality (*), is suitable for a young adult readership (*y*), is humorous (*H*), and uses a historical plot, characters, or setting (*HI*). The citations occasionally discuss series novels en masse, but individual entries can be more than 300 words. There are five appendixes: "Craft Notes" provides excerpts from the writings of spies; and there are guides to pseudonyms, series characters, intelligence and terrorist organizations, and espionage jargon ("spookspeak"). The volume concludes with indexes for authors and titles.

Cloak and Dagger Fiction is an occasionally difficult volume to use, for Smith and White did not use catchwords, making the location of individual works occasionally difficult. It is nevertheless a monumental accomplishment.

182.   Stone, Nancy-Stephanie. **A Reader's Guide to the Spy and Thriller Novel.** Reader's Guides to Mystery Novels. New York: G. K. Hall, 1997. xv, 533 p. Indexes. LC 96-40454. ISBN 0-8161-1800-0.

Like all the other volumes in this series, this is an oddly inconsistent collection. Stone's preface provides a reasonable history of the spy novel, although her assessment that despite their difference in subject matter, " 'spy story' and 'spy thriller' are generally used interchangeably," strikes this reader as a missed opportunity to establish critical foundations. This complaint aside, Stone provides a list of 1,380 books published prior to 1996. Her volume begins with three alphabetical lists: the first provides pseudonyms and the real names of the users; the second, the creators and their series characters; and the third, the series characters and their creators. The majority of the volume is devoted to the annotated list of spy and thriller novels, arranged alphabetically by author's last name. A typical entry provides the author in boldface type, with an asterisk indicating an incomplete listing of the author's works. The title of the book is also given in boldface type, and beneath it are first American and first English publication data: place of publication, publisher, and year of publication. The annotations are arranged chronologically, with series character volumes listed first, followed by nonseries books, also listed chronologically.

Successive sections provide indexes to the "period of story," locations, and by miscellaneous motifs (i.e., AIDS, art, brainwashing, gambling, magic, mercenaries, and weapons). There are indexes for intelligence and security agencies used, a list of 100 representative titles, and a list of selected film and television adaptations. There is no index to titles, and there are no catchwords, making it occasionally difficult to locate a specific annotation.

Stone's *Reader's Guide* is capably done, but it is not without flaws. Surely it might have been better to list all works by an author together, rather than cross-referencing? And although the annotations reference a gratifyingly diverse number of publications, including a wide variety of paperback originals, there are some odd omissions:

surely Trevanian's *Shibumi* belongs in this volume as a thriller? And although Geoffrey Household's *Rogue Male* remains one of the greatest of all thrillers, he wrote many additional thrillers, none of which are listed. Finally, there are some errors in the annotations, including an almost unforgivable one in the aforementioned *Rogue Male*.

As with the rest of the volumes in this series, one hopes for an expanded second edition.

Stamp Mysteries

183. Hedman, Iwan. **Detektiver på Frimärken.** DAST Dossier Nr. 5. Introduction by Sigurd Tullberg. Strangnas, Sweden: DAST Forlag AB, 1978. 48 p. Cloth. 500 copies printed.

Swedish publications are generally beyond the scope of this section, but Hedman's bibliography deserves mention as a unique achievement. The Nicaraguan government in 1973 issued 12 postage stamps of varying denominations to commemorate the fiftieth anniversary of Interpol; each stamp featured a different literary detective. Hedman lists these stamps alphabetically by their subject. Each entry reproduces the stamp (in enlargement), a picture of the author, and a dust wrapper from a Swedish edition of the book. Annotations (in Swedish) provide information on the detective, a brief bibliography of secondary literature about the author and/or the detective, and a two-column bibliography citing the first Swedish and English editions of the books featuring this detective.

As has been observed by others, Hedman does not provide information on the origin of the stamps, which were created on the basis of a poll conducted by the readers of *Ellery Queen's Mystery Magazine,* and he does not provide information on the backs of the stamps, which contained statements about the importance of the detective. These complaints aside, this is an oddly delightful little publication, but its research value is slight.

Supernatural Detectives. *See* Science Fiction and Fantasy Mysteries

Suspense Novels

184. Jarvis, Mary J. **A Reader's Guide to the Suspense Novel.** Reader's Guides to Mystery Novels. New York: G. K. Hall, 1997. ix, 316 p. Indexes. Cloth. LC 96-40455. ISBN 0-8161-1804-3.

This volume is the fourth in the series that began with Susan Oleksiw's *A Reader's Guide to the Classic British Mystery* (q.v.), and, like its predecessors, it is an oddly balanced and somewhat inconsistent work. Jarvis offers annotated entries to some 750 suspense novels by 150 authors as diverse as James Hadley Chase, Mary Higgins Clark, Frederick C. Davis, Bruno Fischer, Patricia Highsmith, Henry James (!), Dean Koontz, Holly Roth, and Edgar Wallace. Rather surprisingly, names that one would anticipate finding in a work such as this—John Buchan, Ian Fleming, Ken Follett, Geoffrey Household, Alistair MacLean, Sapper, Shane Stevens, and Trevanian, to name but a few of the better-known writers of suspense—are not present.

The problematic contents aside, *A Reader's Guide to the Suspense Novel* contains 11 indexes: series characters and creators; creators and series characters; occupations of series characters; pseudonyms; suspense novels; period of story; location of story; setting; miscellaneous information and special subjects; the suspense event; and notable suspense novels.

The first four chapters are relatively brief, and chapter 5 dominates the volume. It is arranged alphabetically by author's name, given in boldface type; if the name is a pseudonym, the original name is listed below in parentheses. An asterisk by the author's name indicates whether Jarvis has annotated only a portion of the author's output. The citations are arranged chronologically; each gives the title in boldface, and the place of publication, publisher, and date of publication of the first English and American editions of the book. The major series detective is listed, as are retitlings. The annotations are brief and very well written.

The contents of the remaining chapters are largely routine, but chapter 10 deserves mention for attempting to codify and itemize the initial causes of the suspense in the novels. There is no title index.

An expanded edition of this guide would be welcome.

Theater Mysteries

185.   Reader's Advice. **Theater Mysteries.** http://www.readersadvice.com/readadv/000308.html

A surprisingly lengthy list of authors and titles. Very useful.

True Crime. *See also* Jack the Ripper and Lizzie Borden Mysteries

186.   Borowitz, Albert. **Blood & Ink: An International Guide to Fact-Based Crime Literature.** Note by Jacques Barzun. Foreword by Jonathan Goodman. Kent, Ohio: Kent State University Press, 2002. xviii, 524 p. Index. LC 2001-000570. ISBN 0-87338-693-0.

Discussions of true crime are in general beyond the scope of this work, but Borowitz's guide—whose introduction states that it "documents the interrelations between crime history and literature"—in fact cites and describes many creative works (novels, plays, operas, and verse) from around the world that are based on actual criminal cases. Following an introduction and a statement of methodology, the bibliography is arranged alphabetically by author's last name. Entries are numbered, the numbering starting anew with each letter; the number and the author's last name are given in bold type. These are followed by the title of the work in italics, the place of publication, publisher, and date of the first edition, although later editions and translations also are cited when useful. The annotations that follow are gratifyingly full and explanatory. The concluding index provides access by author, title, and subject, permitting researchers to locate works based on such subjects as assassinations, Athenian criminal cases, Lizzie Borden, Jack the Ripper, and "spouses and lovers' murders." One can easily enough locate works missed by Borowitz—his discussion of Agatha Christie mentions only *By the Pricking of My Thumbs,* although there is common agreement that the first part of Christie's *Murder on the Orient Express* is based on the Lindbergh kidnapping, and Edgar Wallace is cited only in passing, whereas he fictionalized the life of Charlie Peace and ghostwrote the life of Evelyn Thaw—but *Blood and Ink* is generally an exemplary work, and it will provide an excellent starting place for those interested in reading fictionalized accounts of crimes.

Women Character Mysteries

187. Androski, Helene. **Women Mystery Writers: Strong, Independent Female Lead Characters.**

Available as part of the archives maintained by the DorothyL listserv. To obtain: send an e-mail message to listserv@listserv.kent.edu; type "get women.series" in the subject line. It contains three sections. The first, "Mean Streets," cites works that feature "gritty realism or hard-boiled atmospherics"; the second, "Tea at the Vicarage," cites works that "feature a minimum of violence or other distressing subject matter"; and the third section, "Making a Statement," cites the works that "comment about social or environmental issues." Citations in all sections are arranged alphabetically by author; often her nationality and birth date are given. The series character is named, and her profession is provided; the settings are given, as are the time; and the title and publication date of the first book in the series are indicated. Very well done.

188a. Heising, Willetta L. **Detecting Women 2: Pocket Guide: A Checklist for Mystery Series Written by Women.** Dearborn, Mich.: Purple Moon Press, 1996. 128 p. Paperback. ISBN 0-9644593-2-9.

188b. Heising, Willetta L. **Detecting Women Pocket Guide: Checklist for Mystery Series Written by Women.** 3rd ed. Dearborn, Mich.: Purple Moon Press, 1999. 220 p. Paperback. ISBN 0-9644593-7-x.

The *Pocket Guide*s were created to accompany *Detecting Women 2* and *Detecting Women 3* (q.v.). They contain none of the biographical data or indexes of the full-sized volume and are author/title lists.

The third edition is arranged alphabetically by author's last name, given in boldface; pseudonyms are indicated by the letter *P,* but the author's real name is given only in *Detecting Women 2*. The series character's name is listed beneath the author's name, and the series titles are listed in chronological order, with the year of publication given in parentheses. Retitlings are given, and starred titles indicate award winners: solid stars are used for winners and open stars for nominees. The second edition provided a notepad, but the third edition contains no notepad, for it is significantly larger. It lists more than 200 authors more than the second edition; this translates to more than 800 series detectives and over 3,700 mystery titles in series order. Collectors and those needing lists will find the *Pocket Guide* to be extraordinarily helpful.

189. James, Dean. **The Feminine Perspective: Crime Fiction by and about Women.**

Available as part of the archives maintained by the DorothyL listserv. To obtain: send an e-mail message to listserv@listserv.kent.edu; type "get women.listing" in the subject line. A lengthy and useful list.

190. Reader's Advice. **Spunky Women Sleuths.** http://www.readersadvice.com/readadv/000204.html

191. Reader's Advice. **Sweet Old Lady Sleuths.** http://www.readersadvice.com/readadv/000202.html

Bare-bones, but lengthy and accessible.

Young Adult Mysteries

192. Aubrey, Irene E. **Mystery and Adventure in Canadian Books for Children and Young People/Romans Policiers et Histoires D'Aventures Canadiens pour la Jeunesse.** Ottawa: National Library of Canada, 1983. 18 p. Index. Paperback. C83-090083-7E. ISBN 0-662-52484-5.

Prepared to accompany a display of juvenile mystery and adventure books shown in the National Library of Canada, this brief bilingual catalogue contains no prefatory material but is divided into two sections, the first listing the English-language publications and the second listing the French-language publications. Both sections are arranged alphabetically by author's last name. Titles of books are in capital letters and underlined; illustrators are provided, as are place of publication, publisher, year of publication, and pagination. Translations are listed, and the names of translators are given. Beneath each citation are two columns of annotations—one in English, the other in French—describing the story and noting its awards (if any); the English annotation occurs first for the English publications, and the French annotation is given first for the French publications. An index to titles concludes the volume. Only about 40 titles are annotated.

193. Kokomo Howard County Public Library. **Young Adult Mysteries.** http://www.kokomo.lib.in.us/ya_mysteries.html

Although a number of fine writers of mysteries for young adults exist, relatively few Web sites are devoted to young adult mysteries. This site is a selective list of the works available for circulation. It is arranged alphabetically by author's name, followed by a brief annotation; for example, the annotation for Caroline Cooney's *The Face on the Milk Carton* states, "Janie's life is turned upside down when she recognizes herself in a picture of a missing child on a milk carton. Sequels are *Whatever Happened to Janie? The Voice on the Radio,* and *What Janie Found.*"

194. Sisters in Crime. **Young Adult Mysteries.** http://www.sistersincrime.org/yajuv

A lengthy list, alphabetical by author, listing titles that may be read by juveniles and young adults. Several hundred titles are listed, along with their ISBNs and initial prices, making this a very useful starting place.

3

General Bibliographies and Library Catalogues

Scope note: This section contains only the books that reference the primary texts of detective and mystery fiction. National bibliographies, subject bibliographies, indexes to short stories, indexes to magazines, and publisher bibliographies are found under their respective subject headings.

GENERAL

195.   Flanagan, Maurice. **British Gangster and Exploitation Paperbacks of the Postwar Years.** Introduction by Stephen Holland. Westbury, England: Zeon Books, 1997. 104 p. Paperback. ISBN 1-874113-08-4.

British Gangster and Exploitation Paperbacks of the Postwar Years began as a catalogue of paperbacks, but as Flanagan states, "It outgrew its roots almost from the outset." The resulting volume is idiosyncratic, but it provides capsulated histories of the publishers and their wares, accounts of such artists as Reginald C. W. Heade and H. W. Perl, and descriptions of the more notable writers. There are hundreds of black-and-white illustrations but, alas, no index. More comprehensive information can be found in Steve Holland's *The Mushroom Jungle* (q.v.).

196.   Gribbin, Lenore S. **Who's Whodunit.** University of North Carolina Library Studies, no. 5. Chapel Hill: University of North Carolina, 1969. x, 174 p. Paperback. LC 68-65305.

It was Gribbin's intention to list in this book the "names used by all American and British authors of book-length detective stories from 1845 [the year Poe's *Tales* was published] through 1961." Naturally, she fails in this attempt, but this does not diminish the ambition of her effort.

Following an introduction in which Gribbin defines the scope of her work, the majority of the volume provides a list of the names of the authors of book-length detective stories. When the name is genuine, the pseudonyms used by that author are listed beneath it. When the name is a pseudonym, it is cross-referenced to the person who used it; joint pseudonyms are referenced to both authors. In all cases, Gribbin cites the source that indicated the author wrote detective stories; these are listed in a bibliography. Because several of these sources erred in their attributions (Henry Kuttner did not use the pseudonym Jack Vance), Gribbin perpetuates the errors. The most significant problems with the volume, however, are not factual but bibliographic, for Gribbin cites no titles, making it impossible to determine which works by prolific authors (such as Georgette Heyer and Aldous Huxley) were detective stories. *Who's Whodunit* has been thoroughly superseded by such volumes as Hubin's (q.v.) and is now best seen as a period piece.

197.   Hagen, Ordean. **Who Done It? A Guide to Detective, Mystery and Suspense Fiction.** New York: R. R. Bowker, 1969. xx, 834 p. Index. Cloth. LC 69-19209. ISBN 0-8352-0234-8.

It is dangerous to attempt to be all things to everyone, and in the field of bibliography, it is equally dangerous to claim to be comprehensive. In this substantial volume Hagen does both, and the results are dire.

Who Done It? is divided into two sections, the first of which is titled "A Comprehensive Bibliography of Mystery Fiction, 1841–1967." This section is alphabetically arranged by author's last name, beneath which is an alphabetical listing of titles. The publisher of the first edition is given, as is the year of publication; reprint editions are sometimes cited. Beside each author's name is a classification: (D) for detective, (M) for mystery, and (S) for suspense. Despite having been partially compiled by Allen J. Hubin, the listings are far from comprehensive.

The second half of the volume is titled "A Bibliographic Guide to Mystery Fiction" and contains eight sections: a subject guide to mysteries; the mystery novel on the screen; mystery plays; the scene of the crime; heroes, villains, and heroines; anthologies and collections; award-winning mysteries; and writing on the mystery novel. An appendix offers "a murder miscellany" of material including a listing of organizations and societies, pseudonyms, title changes, quotations, collaborations, a dictionary, pulp magazines, and the mystery novel abroad. A title index to the comprehensive bibliography concludes the volume.

None of these sections can be considered complete or thorough. The subject guide, for example, contains only 28 subject classifications, and although works of Helen Traubel and Dick Francis are cited in the introduction, there are no sections devoted to their fields of interest (respectively, opera and/or music and horseracing), although Francis is mentioned by name in the subject classification for sports.

In a review titled "The Book, the Bibliographer and the Absence of Mind" (*American Scholar* [Winter 1969–1970]: 138–48) Jacques Barzun pilloried *Who Done It?* and denounced Hagen for being insufficiently familiar with his material and with the concepts of bibliography. Barzun concluded his castigation by stating, "This would-be bibliography is a product of uncontrolled promiscuity among twenty-five thousand cards. Both the text and the compiler's acknowledgments to his family and friends suggest that the work was put together from notes absent-mindedly taken, then transcribed by amanuenses who were willing but uncomprehending slaves (see Cobblestone)."

Barzun's review cannot be considered unduly harsh, for Hagen simply attempted to do too much. Substantial bibliographic errors occur in all sections. The book's first section fails to address the problems inherent in identifying the writers of detective, mystery, and suspense stories. Barzun states, "Amid the promised (D) (M) (S), he [the putative user] will find technical criminology (Cherrill), sea stories (Hammond Innes), ghost stories, famous trials, adventure stories (*Beau Geste*), stories of ethical struggle (Balchin, Cozzens), as well as the bare listing of the complete works of O. Henry, Ambrose Bierce, Henry James and Jorges [*sic*] Luis Borges. Is this bibliography? But editorial insouciance does not stop there. Since, as is well known, everything in French literature is mysterious, we are given titles at random from the translated works of Michel Butor, Marcel Aymé and Alain Robbe-Grillet; and for good measure, the somber sex-and-religious tale by Georges Bernanos called in English *Crime.*" Barzun elsewhere addresses the misidentifications of retitled works, inconsistencies in citations, and the problems inherent in classifying authors (rather than their works) as (D), (M), and (S).

Hagen died shortly before the publication of *Who Done It?* Had he lived, it is possible that later editions would have resolved the problems raised in the first edition. As it is, *Who Done It?* has been completely superseded by such works as Hubin's and Albert's (q.q.v.), and it remains at best a sadly flawed and badly dated volume, an unreliable series of lists that offer nothing that cannot be readily obtained elsewhere.

198. Holland, Steve. **The Mushroom Jungle: A History of Postwar Paperback Publishing.** Foreword by Brian Stableford. Westbury, England: Zeon Books, 1993. 196 p. Index. Paperback. ISBN 1-874113-01-7.

The Mushroom Jungle is the first systematic study of the British postwar (i.e., World War II) paperback. Like the American paperbacks of this period, the British paperbacks had delightfully lurid covers and generally have been deplored by establishment critics. Holland discusses the history and origins of the postwar British paperback—they originated out of the paper shortages of the Second World War—and provides accounts of those he describes as the "mushroom" publishers and their most notorious product, the works published as by "Hank Janson." The result is a clearly written survey supplemented by hundreds of black-and-white illustrations and two-color inserts. It is not a reference book in that it does not provide bibliographical lists, but it is essential reading for anybody who would like to know of the English popular reading from the 1940s through the 1950s and, occasionally, later.

Note: Holland has compiled and assisted in the compilation of dozens of the bibliographies of these mushroom publishers. These are listed in the section devoted to publishers.

199. Huang, Jim, ed. **The Drood Review's Mystery Yearbook.** Boston: Crum Creek Press, 1989. Paperback. OCLC 21012436.

Published in 1989, 1990, 1991, and 1997, *The Drood Review's Mystery Yearbook* was intended to list all of the mystery and detective books published during the previous year; short story collections and secondary studies also were included among the citations. The 1989 volume thus has as its focus the works published in 1988. In addition, the *Mystery Yearbook* lists the awards presented during the previous year, the bookstores specializing in mysteries (alphabetically and by state), and the periodicals publishing mystery and detective fiction. Many of these data were derived from second-hand sources, but the *Mystery Yearbook* collocates these and makes them accessible.

200a. Hubin, Allen J. **The Bibliography of Crime Fiction 1749–1975: Listing All Mystery, Detective, Suspense, Police, and Gothic Fiction in Book Form Published in the English Language.** Del Mar: University Extension, University of California, San Diego, in Cooperation with Publisher's Inc., 1979. xiv, 697 p. Indexes. Cloth. LC 78-23929. ISBN 0-89163-048-1.

200b. Hubin, Allen J. **Crime Fiction: 1749–1980: A Comprehensive Bibliography.** 2nd ed. New York: Garland, 1984. xv, 712 p. Indexes. Cloth. LC 82-48772. ISBN 0-8240-9219-8.

200c. Hubin, Allen J. **Crime Fiction III: A Comprehensive Bibliography 1749–1990.** 3rd ed., completely revised and updated. 2 vols. New York: Garland, 1994. xxix, 1,568 p. Indexes. Cloth. LC 93-41230. ISBN 0-8240-6891-2.

Although an advance reading copy of the fourth edition is noted later, this description concentrates on the third (1994) edition, a remarkable bibliography for which superlatives must be used. Hubin's introduction is exemplary; he defines his subject (crime fiction) and explains his coverage and its limitations and exclusions. It should be mentioned that Hubin has striven for comprehensiveness: the bibliography includes "mystery, detective, suspense, thriller, gothic (romantic suspense), police, and spy fiction" and covers "all such fiction in the English language published in book form (both soft and hard covers) through the end of 1990. Magazine and dime novel fiction, juvenile and children's material, omnibus collections, and anthologies are not included."

The third edition contains eight sections: an author index; a title index; a settings index; a series index; a series character chronology; a film index; a screenwriters index; and a directors index. In all editions, the author index is the longest and most comprehensive section, and in the third, it comprises some 887 triple-columned pages. Each entry lists the author's name in capital letters and provides (in regular type) reference to the sources from which further biographical data can be obtained. Also listed are the author's pseudonyms and birth and death dates; collaborators are cross-referenced. Series characters are identified and assigned a code based on their initials. Beneath the author's name, citations are alphabetical; the publisher and publication year of the first edition in English are given. Retitlings are indicated, and similar publication data are given for them; cross-references link title changes to the original title. The series character code indicates whether the series characters appeared in the book, and a note indicates whether the work is a novel, play, or short story collection. In addition, the contents of short story collections are identified, as are the settings of novels. Finally, if the work was adapted for the motion pictures, the citation provides the year and title of the film, its screenwriters, and director.

The other indexes are derived from the author index and are relatively brief. The title index lists only the book's author. The settings index begins with "Academia," concludes with "Zurich," and lists the books alphabetically by author and alphabetically by title beneath author. In all, approximately 150 settings are identified and scope-matched to the book; books set in Stockholm are not also indexed under Sweden, although cross-references are provided. The series index lists the series character's name and the name of the author or authors who used the character. The series character chronology lists the year in which the series character first appeared, the type of work done by the character, the country in which the character appeared, whether the character appeared primarily in hardcover or paperback books, the number of books in which the character appeared, and the author(s) who wrote about the character (the exception being Arthur Conan Doyle's Sherlock Holmes). The film index provides the title of the film, the studio in which it was made, the year in which the film was released, the names of the directors and screenwriters, the source author and work, and the series character. The screenwriters index lists the name of the screenwriter in capital letters and in regular letters beneath it the name of the motion picture, the author of the original work, and the title of the work if it differs from the motion picture. The director's index lists the director's name in capital letters and in regular letters beneath it the name of the motion picture, the author of the original work, and the title of the work if it differs from the name of the motion picture.

Crime Fiction is incontestably the most significant bibliography in its field, and it is a monumental achievement. Nevertheless, its very thoroughness raises several important and intriguing questions, most significant of which is, At what point does a work become "crime fiction"? The only work of Robert Graves to be cited is *They Hanged My Saintly Billy,* but this book argues that William Palmer was innocent of the murders attributed to him. Similarly, F. Scott Fitzgerald's *The Apprentice Fiction of F. Scott Fitzgerald, Bits of Paradise,* and *The Mystery of the Raymond Mortgage* are cited, but surely *The Great Gatsby*—whose titular hero is a minor thug who consorts with gamblers and bootleggers and is murdered by his mistress's husband—deserves inclusion under the guidelines Hubin established for himself.

Note: In late 2003, an electronic advance reading copy of the fourth edition was examined. It covers the crime fiction published from 1749 to 2000: 106,091 first editions are cited, as are 33,605 reprints; the contents of more than 6,600 collections are indexed, and more than 4,500 movies are listed. Included is a cumulative name index, and books may be located by author and title; specific stories are accessible by author and title, and movies can be located by book author and movie title. Entries can display their data chronologically as well as alphabetically. Also included are indexes for publishers and studios and lists for chronology, series, and setting; statistics about the contents of the database are provided. It is perhaps worth noting that the entry for F. Scott Fitzgerald now includes reference to *The Great Gatsby* and that the entry for Robert Graves references other works in addition to *They Hanged My Saintly Billy.* It is certainly worth noting that while Hubin includes enormous numbers of works published from 1990 to 2000, he also has found a number of overlooked earlier titles, including such hitherto forgotten works as Eugene N. Davis, *The Axe with Three Nicks* (Boston: Christopher, 1929). The CD-ROM of the fourth edition will be available from the Locus Press; the paper edition will be available from the Battered Silicon Dispatch Box.

201. Mercantile Library. **Bibliography of Mysteries from the 1920's and 1930's.** New York: Mercantile Library, 1984? 27 leaves. Index. OCLC 13490887.

Containing no prefatory material and perhaps never formally published, this bibliography lists mysteries published during the 1920s and 1930s. It is arranged alphabetically by author's name; titles are underlined, and, when more than one title is listed, they are listed alphabetically. The place of publication, publisher, and year of publication are given. It is worth noting that the publication data provided are for the first American edition; although a number of writers included here were British, data for the first British editions are not indicated. A concluding list provides the author's name, date of birth and death, pseudonyms used, and lists the page on which the entries can be found. Despite its rarity, this list contains only familiar names, neglects to mention several major writers, and offers nothing that cannot be readily abstracted from other bibliographies.

SPECIFIC LIBRARIES' HOLDINGS

202.   Hügel, Hans-Otto, Regina Urban, and Hermann Hoffmann. **Mord in der Bibliothek: eine Ausstellung des Studiengangs Kulturpädogogik der Universität Hildesheim.** Marbacher Magazine, no. 73. Vorwort von Fred Breinersdorfer. Marbach am Neckar: Deutsche Schillergesellschaft, 1996. xvi, 104 p. LC 96-152451. ISBN 3-9291463-0-4.

German publications are beyond the scope of this work, but one need not read German in order to appreciate *Mord in der Bibliothek,* the catalogue of a display devoted to the history of the detective story. English and American displays might pay lip service to Voltaire (*Zadig*) and Godwin's *Caleb Williams,* but the display would effectively begin with Poe's "The Murders in the Rue Morgue." *Mord in der Bibliothek,* however, possesses a European outlook, and the catalogue begins by discussing Friedrich Schiller's *Verbrecher aus Infamie* (1786), after which it describes Christian August Vulpius's *Rinaldi Rinaldini* (1799), E. T. A. Hoffmann's "Das Fräulein von Scuderi" (1820), Richmond's *Scenes in the Life of a Bow Street Runner* (1827), Wilhelm Hauff's *Abner, der Jude, der nichts gesehen hat* (1827), and Bulwer-Lytton's *Eugen Aram* (1832). Poe is cited as the sixth element in the display, and although some of the following names are likely to be well known—Dickens, Collins, and Doyle, for example—discussions of works by such authors as Jodokus Donatus Hubertus Temme, Adolf Streckfuß, and Auguste Groner, writers likely to be unfamiliar to most Americans, are included. At the same time, the display concludes with a discussion of Sue Grafton's *A Is for Alibi,* whose opening sentences are quoted: "Mein Name ist Kinsey Millhone. Ich bin Privatdetektiv mit einer Lizenz vom Staat Kalifornien."

203.   Osborne, Eric. **Victorian Detective Fiction: A Catalogue of the Collection Made by Dorothy Glover & Graham Greene.** Bibliographically arranged by Eric Osborne. Introduction by John Carter. Preface by Graham Greene. London, Sydney, Toronto: Bodley Head, 1966. xviii, 149 p. Indexes. 500 copies printed and signed by Dorothy Glover, Graham Greene, and John Carter.

If one has money, energy, dedication, and (especially) time enough, a fine collection of anything usually can be assembled. The Dorothy Glover/Graham Greene collection of Victorian detective fiction is case in point. After rereading *The Moonstone,* Glover and Greene set themselves the goal of collecting all of the mystery and detective fiction published between 1841 (the advent of Edgar Allan Poe's "The Murders in the Rue Morgue") and 1900–1901 (a convenient stopping point). In more than 20 years, Glover and Greene compiled a collection of 471 books and occasional periodical issues; dime novels are not among these, and although translations into English were acquired, Glover and Greene did not seek works initially published in languages other than English.

The catalogue begins with a delightful introduction by John Carter on the history of collecting of premodern detective fiction, followed by a brief bibliography of sources used for bibliographic attribution and verification. The entries themselves are numbered and arranged alphabetically by the author's last name, given in boldface; the title is given in bold italics. The publisher's name and the publication date are followed by an edition statement that provides the pagination, a description of the binding's color and salient points, and the illustrator; the name of the detective is given, as is (when relevant) the information on whether the book is a translation and part of a series. First edition data are given if the volume owned by Glover and Greene is not a first edition, and the entries note whether the volume is not held in the British Museum and (when relevant) reference it to the sources listed in the initial bibliography. An appendix written by Eric Sinclair Bell discusses the publishing history of Fergus Hume's *The Mystery of a Hansom Cab,* whose first edition is one of the rarest books in detective and mystery fiction. Indexes to detectives, illustrators, and titles conclude the volume.

Although some of its inclusions are dubious (Jules Verne's *Around the World in Eighty Days* is listed among the detective novels), the catalogue is exemplary as a bibliography. Its descriptions are full and helpful, and its indexing is excellent. Despite its age, the catalogue has enduring reference value.

Note: The first appendix of R. F. Stewart's . . . *And Always a Detective: Chapters on the History of Detective Fiction* (q.v.) provides "some notes, corrections, and comments on *Victorian Detective Fiction*" and should be used in conjunction with this volume.

204. [Randall, David A.?]. **The First Hundred Years of Detective Fiction. 1841–1941. By One Hundred Authors on the Hundred Thirtieth Anniversary of the First Publication in Book Form of Edgar Allan Poe's "The Murders in the Rue Morgue" Philadelphia, 1843.** Lilly Library Publication No. XVIII. Bloomington, Ind.: Lilly Library, 1973. 64 p. Indexes. Paperback.

The First Hundred Years is the catalogue of an exhibition held at Indiana University's Lilly Library from July through September 1973; Randall's name does not appear on its title page but at the end of the foreword. The catalogue contains: (A) foreword; (B) authorities quoted [the exhibition]; (C) Edgar Allan Poe; (D) Sherlock Holmes; (E) Gaboriau to Simenon—France; (F) England to 1914; (G) England since 1914; (H) America to 1920; (I) America since 1920; (J) index of authors; (K) index of titles. Sections C through H are arranged chronologically. The first item described is the April 1841 issue of *Graham's Lady's and Gentleman's Magazine* in which Edgar Allan Poe's "The Murders in the Rue Morgue" was published.

Although the display was probably fascinating, its catalogue leaves something to be desired. Not only is the title inaccurate (the last work described is the 1943 edition of Raymond Chandler's *The Lady in the Lake*), but it is inconsistent in its presentation of citations. Moreover, the annotations often leave something to be desired: in several instances, they commit the unpardonable sin of revealing the identity of the criminal, and even more seriously, they reveal that they were written by somebody unfamiliar with both the history of the detective story and the book's contents. R. Austin Freeman's *The Red Thumb Mark,* for example, is described as "the first to use the new science of fingerprints," effectively ignoring the earlier contributions of Mark Twain and that Freeman's point in writing *The Red Thumb Mark* was to show that fingerprints alone are not sufficient evidence to convict a person. Similarly, the book version of "Maxwell Grant"'s *The Living Shadow* is dated to 1931 (it was in fact published in 1934), and the annotation states (in its entirety) that it was "the first of the long-lasting adventures, in print and on radio, of *The Shadow,*" a statement that is completely and demonstrably inaccurate.

The concluding author and title indexes are capably done.

205. Smith, Wilbur J. **The Boys in the Black Mask: An Exhibit in the UCLA Library, January 6–February 10, 1961.** Preface by Philip Durham. Los Angeles: University of California Library, 1961. 12 p. Paperback. OCLC 7715258.

Perhaps not a reference item, but nevertheless a significant work, this may be the first separately issued catalogue of a display of mystery and detective works. As its title indicates, the exhibit focused on the writers for *Black Mask,* with a particular concentration on the writers who appeared under the editorship of Captain Joseph Shaw. Arrangement is alphabetical, the first items in the catalogue being three works by W. T. Ballard, the last being three works by Cornell Woolrich.

In the display were typescripts and manuscripts from Raymond Chandler, Lester Dent, Dashiell Hammett, Frederick Nebel, and Horace McCoy; and works by Shaw are well represented. It is worth noting that Chandler contributed significantly to this display; Smith's foreword states, "Raymond Chandler, a *Black Mask* contributor, gave us, along with his manuscripts, the issues in which his stories appeared." Annotations are provided for the majority of items displayed, and the bibliographic citations remain helpful.

206.   Sutherland, Michael C. **Landmark Publications in Mystery and Detective Fiction.** Los Angeles: Occidental College Library, 1987. 8 p. Paperback. OCLC 16006457.

This is the catalogue of an exhibition of books from the Guymon Detective and Mystery Fiction Collection held at the Occidental College Library from March through May 1987. The exhibition contained some 24 separate sections, and the catalogue is arranged chronologically, the first item being the 1770 edition of *The Lamentable and True Tragedie of M. Arden of Feversham, in Kent: Who Was Most Wickedlye Murdered, by the Means of His Disloyal and Wanton Wyfe, Who for the Love She Bare to One Mosbie, Hyred Two Desperat Ruffins, Blackwill and Shagbag, to Kill Him,* a work originally published in 1592. Additional works in the exhibition include a first English edition of *The Castle of Otranto,* the 1841 appearance in *Graham's Lady's and Gentleman's Magazine* of Poe's "The Murders in the Rue Morgue," a first edition of *The Mystery of Edwin Drood,* various dime novels, several works by Doyle including the 1887 *Beeton's Christmas Annual* containing *A Study in Scarlet,* and a first edition of Hammett's *The Thin Man* accompanied by its typescript.

This would have been an exhibition worth seeing.

4

National Bibliographies

Scope note: This section lists the monographs and Web sites that attempt to document all mystery and detective fiction published in a specific country.

AUSTRALIA

207. Loder, John. **Australian Crime Fiction: A Bibliography 1857–1993.** Victoria, Australia: D. W. Thorpe, in association with the National Center for Australian Studies, 1994. xiv, 287 p. Indexes. Cloth. ISBN 1-875589-51-1.

Drawing partly from a vast private collection, bibliographer and bibliophile Loder has assembled a bibliography of the crime and mystery fiction published in Australia from 1857 until 1993. Although his focus is on the separately published book, he also has noted a few serializations that were not published as books, and he also has provided data on a number of Australian pulp magazines. In all, more than 2,600 books by more than 500 authors have been recorded, many for the first time. As Loder's introduction states, "It came as a surprise, when the impressive crime fiction bibliography of Hubin was published, to find he had missed a third of the Australian titles. On analysis it was apparent he had missed authors who had not published in America or Great Britain."

The body of Loder's bibliography is alphabetical by the author's last name; magazines are listed alphabetically by their title. A typical author entry provides the author's name (in boldface type), indicating pseudonyms and providing significant biographical data. The title of the book is given in smaller boldface. The place, publisher, and year of publication are provided in regular type, as are the pagination and a physical description of the book, including the existence and placements of plates. The existence of a dust wrapper is noted, as is whether the volume has been recorded by Hubin. Title changes are noted, and a significant number of entries conclude with a brief description of the volume's contents. Cross-references are plentiful. Successive sections provide a title index; an index to the book's illustrators, jacket artists, designers, and photographers; and the volume concludes with an index to the investigators and criminals.

Australian Crime Fiction is in all respects an exemplary bibliography. Loder's biographical data are frequently inaccessible elsewhere, and his bibliographic data are, so far as can be ascertained, gratifyingly accurate and thorough. Indeed, Loder has noted when he has verified the existence of the work through other sources but has been unable to examine it himself. This is a difficult volume to obtain in the United States, but it is worth the effort.

BELGIUM

208. Hermans, Willy. **Petit Dictionnaire des Auteurs Belges de Littérature Policière.** Liege: Librairie Version Originale, 1989. [iv], 93 p. Paperback. ISBN 2-87287-000-8.

Despite the implications of the title, no larger or more comprehensive dictionary to the mystery and detective stories written by Belgian writers seems to exist. This slim volume is arranged alphabetically by the writer's last name, given in boldface capitals. A brief biographical statement is provided; pseudonyms are identified, birth and death dates are given, and the first Belgian (or French) editions of the author's significant mystery and detective works are listed chronologically at the bottom of each entry. Citations include the year of publication and often the publisher and the place of publication. An index to the names given in the biographical statement concludes the book.

CANADA

209. Skene-Melvin, L. David St. C., with Norbert Spehner. **Canadian Crime Fiction: An Annotated Comprehensive Bibliography of Canadian Crime Fiction from 1817 to 1996 and Biographical Dictionary of Canadian Crime Writers, with an Introductory Essay on the History and Development of Canadian Crime Writings.** Shelburne, Ontario: Battered Silicon Dispatch Box, 1996. xxxi, 440 p. Indexes. Cloth. C96-930488-9. ISBN 1-896648-60-6.

Some 11 years in the compilation, this comprehensive bibliography of Canadian crime fiction is vast in its coverage, citing the adventure, crime, detective, espionage, mystery, suspense, and thriller books written by Canadians, by non-Canadians and set in Canada, or somehow connected to Canada that were published between 1817 and 1966. Also included, when relevant, are citations to published dramas; tales of intrigue, violence, and investigation; and juvenile novels having a criminous connection. The cited publications may be in English or French.

The volume begins with a lengthy history of the detective story and Canadian crime fiction; the bibliography opens with "Crime Fiction by Canadians." Author's names are given in boldface, the last name in capital letters. A typical entry includes the author's birth and death dates, a sometimes lengthy biographical profile, and a list of the author's criminous publications giving the title, place of publication, publisher, year of publication, series, and setting. Often the protagonist's name is given, and frequently there is an annotation describing the importance of the work; lists of the author's other publications are often provided. Cross-references abound. Furthermore, every criminous work is keyed to a series of symbols (repeated on the bottom of each page): + (plus) indicates it is by a Canadian writer and set in Canada; * (asterisk) indicates it is by a Canadian writer and set elsewhere; ! (exclamation point) indicates it is fiction by a non-Canadian writer but set in Canada; ? (question mark, rarely used) indicates the work is unidentified; and # (hash mark) indicates that there is a "Canadian connexion" (i.e., a criminous novel with a Canadian protagonist written by a non-Canadian and set outside of Canada; novel that has a portion set in Canada, or that touches peripherally upon Canada with either a Canadian character or a mention of Canada or Canadians; or "authors that passed this way but once, but didn't use Canada as a setting for their work"). It should be mentioned that an enormous number of these data are completely unobtainable through any other reference work.

The bibliography is followed by two appendixes also containing bibliographical data. The first cites the criminous works set in Canada but written by non-Canadians, the second cites the works that have the aforementioned "Canadian connexions." Both of these appendixes follow the format established in "Crime Fiction by Canadians," and the data in these sections are frequently lengthy and unobtainable elsewhere.

Eighteen useful indexes and a bibliography conclude the volume. The indexes offer access to titles of crime fiction by Canadians, to titles by non-Canadians, to titles having a Canadian connection. There are also chronological indexes to the crime fiction by Canadians and to the titles by non-Canadians set in Canada; the characters of Canadian authors are indexed, as are the settings used by the Canadian authors. Juvenile works (for children and young adults) are indexed, as are mysteries about Canada, Mountie novels, short story collections of crime fiction by Canadians, criminous plays, series, Canadian criminal *romans à clef*, cross-genre criminous titles by Canadians, and pseudonyms used by Canadian crime writers. The indexes conclude with lists of the winners of the Crime Writers of Canada's Arthur Ellis Awards, and the Canadian winners of a Mystery Writers of America Edgar.

Unlikely ever to be superseded, *Canadian Crime Fiction* is a monumental achievement; it belongs in all academic libraries.

210.   Spehner, Norbert. **Le Roman Policier en Amérique Français: Essay Critique et Guide de Lecture Analytique du Roman Policier, d'Espionnage, d'Aventures et de Politique-Fiction Francophone.** Quebec: Éditions Alire, 2000. 418 p. Index. Paperback. C00-941604-8. ISBN 2-922145-45-X.

Spehner's guide surveys the mystery and detective works published between 1837 and June 2000 by Canadian authors writing in French; the majority of these authors was Québécois. In all, Spehner lists 606 novels for adults, 350 novels for children, and the contents of 34 series, as well as nearly 1,000 secondary studies of the genre.

Prior to the bibliographies, Spehner provides a number of definitions and genre histories. These are useful, but, perhaps because of their brevity, they contain occasional errors and omissions: the discussion of "Le roman noir ou 'hard-boiled,' " for example, neglects to mention the work of Carroll John Daly and the role of the pulp magazine in popularizing the genre.

Successive sections list the mystery and detective novels for an adult readership and the espionage novels, after which follow lists for the works intended for a younger audience, the secondary bibliography, lists of relevant works translated into French, and indexes for the primary and secondary material. Material in the primary bibliographies is arranged by the author's last name, given in boldface capital letters, after which are given the first name in boldface regular letters and the dates of birth and death. The author's relevant works are listed chronologically: the title is given in boldface letters, followed by the place of publication, publisher, publication date, and number of pages. Each title is annotated, and if the work was reviewed or received critical study, the citations are listed beneath the work in smaller type.

Though Spehner's format and arrangement are occasionally confusing, *Le Roman Policier en Amérique Français* will be welcome in research libraries.

DENMARK

211. Nielsen, Bjarne. **Hvem Begik Hvad? Dansk Kriminalliteratur indtil 1979: En Bibliografi.** København [i.e., Copenhagen]: Antikvariat Pinkerton, 1981. 131 p. Indexes. Paperback. LC 82-112686. OCLC 9918644.

Offset from typed copy, this bibliography of Danish detective fiction published in book form prior to 1979 begins with an introduction providing the bibliography's principles and a brief history of the detective story in Denmark. Only Danish writers or writers of Danish extraction are cited: this is not the place to find the Danish publishing histories of Agatha Christie, Arthur Conan Doyle, and Edgar Wallace.

The first portion of the bibliography is arranged alphabetically by author. The author's name is given in capital letters, underlined, and often is accompanied by biographical dates; brief signed biographies of significant authors occasionally are provided. The titles of books are given in capital letters and are followed by the publisher, the year of publication, and the pagination. Pseudonyms are indicated and numerous cross-references are provided.

The bibliography's second section cites collective and anonymous books using the same procedures as in the first section. The third section indexes anonymous series books: series names are given in capital letters and underlined, the publisher and year in which the series started are given, and each title in the series is numbered; the titles are given in regular type. As in the earlier sections, numerous cross-references are provided. The bibliography concludes with a title index. Very capably done.

FINLAND

212a. Sjöblom, Simo. **Rikoskirjallisuuden Bibliografia, 1864–1984: Eli 120 Vuoden Aikana Suomeksi Limestyneet Jännitysromaanit.** Helsinki: Antikvaarinen Kirjakauppa Simo Sjöblom, 1985. 375 p. Cloth. LC 87-117925. ISBN 951-99692-0-9.

212b. Sjöblom, Simo. **Suomenkielisen Rikoskirjallisuuden ja sen Reuna-Alueiden Bibliografia 1857–1989.** Helsinki: Seaflower Oy, 1990. 1,133 p. Cloth. ISBN 952-666-001-3. 2,000 copies printed.

Unlike Nielsen's bibliography of Danish detective and mystery fiction (q.v.), Sjöblom has concentrated on all mystery and detective fiction published in Finland between 1857 and 1959, and not only the fiction written by authors from Finland or of Finnish extraction. The author's name is given in capital letters, accompanied by his or her birth and death dates; these data at times include the day and month as well as the year. Following is a brief statement of the author's nationality (i.e., "Amerikkalainen" or "Irlantilainen"), and the titles of books are listed alphabetically (in Finnish, of course) beneath this information. (The contents of short story collections are also listed.) They are followed by the original title, accompanied by the date of publication. These are followed by the name of the translator, the publisher, the place of publication, the year of publication, the pagination, and the name of the Finnish series in which the book appeared; ISBNs are given when they exist. There are indexes for titles, the contents of books, the original title and the translator, series, and the translators and the works translated. The book is very capably done but very fragile, falling apart after only minimal use.

GERMANY

213.   Hillich, Reinhard, and Wolfgang Mittmann. **Die Kriminalliteratur der DDR 1949–1990: Bibliografie.** Berlin: Akademie Verlag, 1991. 240 p. Index. Cloth. ISBN 3-05-001856-9.

Research on this bibliography began in 1988, when the two authors—Hillich, a literary historian, and Mittmann, a writer and collector of mysteries—realized the need for a work that documented the detective and mystery books and uncollected stories written by German authors. Following the introduction, a section entitled "Reihen" describes the major series by significant hardcover and pocketbook publishers. Entries provide the publisher's location, its founder, the years during which the publisher remained in business, the typical publication size, the date of the first (and, when relevant, last) publication, and significant additional series. The two successive sections list the bibliographic sources used by Hillich and Mittmann and list their abbreviations.

The first portion of the bibliography is a two-column author list. Names are given in boldface type, followed by the title in regular type; pseudonyms are indicated. Entries for books provide an abbreviated note indicating the nature of the book's contents (i.e., *KR* for Kriminalroman; *KERz[n]* for Kriminalerzählungen; *KNov[n]* for Kriminalnovellen) and list the place of publication, the publisher, and the year of publication. Pagination is given, series numbers are recorded, and the contents of short story collections are listed. Entries for periodical publications give the periodical's title, volume, year, and issue number.

The second section is a two-column chronological list that reprints the data given in the first section. Despite the limitations implied by the title, the list includes some publications from the first part of 1991. The bibliography concludes with a list of authors. Birth and death dates are given when available, as are pseudonyms.

The bibliography lacks a title index, but apart from this, it contains an enormous amount of original research. It is superior to the earlier effort of Klaus-Dieter Walkhoff-Jordan (q.v.) and will be welcome in research libraries.

214.   Walkhoff-Jordan, Klaus-Dieter. **Bibliographie der Kriminalliteratur 1945–1984 im deutschen Sprachraum.** Ullstein Krimi. Mit einem Vorwort von Friedhelm Werremeier. Frankfurt/M: Ullstein, 1985. 547 p. Paperback. LC 86-141552. ISBN 3-548-10325-1.

The first bibliography of mystery and detective fiction published in Germany, this lists works by authors of other nationalities as well as those by German authors. Arrangement is alphabetical by author; names are given in boldface capitals. When employed, pseudonyms are listed beneath the name, as are (in small capital letters) the German titles of their books; when the work is not by a German author, the original title and its publication date are provided in parentheses. Entries conclude with the name of the German publisher given in abbreviated form and keyed to a list of abbreviations at the beginning, the work's series number, and the dates of the work's German editions.

A second section lists the German editions of detective and mystery series. The arrangement is slightly different: entries are alphabetical by series title and given in boldface capitals. Beneath this is the name of the author, after which come the publisher and years it published the series. Next are individually numbered entries that give the German title of the book in small capital letters followed by the year of its first German publication; beneath these in parentheses are the English title and the year of its first publication.

Although a lot of effort has clearly gone into the compilation of the *Bibliographie der Kriminalliteratur 1945–1984*, it lacks a title index, has an occasional error, and is not as comprehensive as the later work compiled by Reinhard Hillich and Wolfgang Mittmann (q.v.). Walkhoff-Jordan has published a supplement extending coverage to 1990 (q.v.).

215.   Walkhoff-Jordan, Klaus-Dieter. **Bibliographie der Kriminalliteratur 1985– 1990 im deutschen Sprachraum.** Ullstein Sachbuch. Mit einem Vorwort von Friedhelm Werremeier. Frankfurt/M: Ullstein, 1991. 228 p. Paperback. LC 92-180642. ISBN 3-548-34813-0.

As its title indicates, this bibliography is a continuation of Walkhoff-Jordan's earlier effort (q.v), listing the detective and mystery fiction published in Germany from 1985 to 1990. The introduction notes that there are 4,684 entries, 1,805 of which are by foreign authors first published in Germany, 718 of which are German originals, 1,658 are reprints from foreign authors, and 503 are reprints from German authors. The bibliography's arrangement is alphabetical by author (given in boldface capital letters), often accompanied by dates of birth and death; pseudonyms are frequently provided. In small capital letters beneath each name are the German titles of the books; these are followed by parentheses containing the English title and the date of first English-language publication. This in turn is followed by the name of the publisher (in highly abbreviated form), the book's series number, and the date of the German edition of the book. A brief concluding section lists the contents of anonymous detective and mystery series published between 1985 and 1990.

This bibliography lacks a title index, and more seriously, Walkhoff-Jordan has included a number of books solely on the strengths of their titles and the fact that characters are killed in them. Thus, references are made to the German editions of works by such authors as Clive Barker, Stephen King, Tabitha King, and Somtow Sucharitikul. Furthermore, this volume is simply not as comprehensive as the effort of Reinhard Hillich and Wolfgang Mittmann (q.v.).

IRELAND

216.   Ingravallo, Ciccio. **Irish Mystery.**

This appears to be the only separately published bibliography on its subject. It is available as part of the archives maintained by the DorothyL listserv. To obtain: send an e-mail message to listserv@listserv.kent.edu; type "get irish.mystery" in the subject line.

JAPAN

217. Nakajima, Kawataro. **Nihon Suiri Shosetsu Jiten.** Tokyo: Tokyo Shuppan, 1985. 422 p. Index. Cloth. LC 86-217532. ISBN 4-490-10204-6.

Apparently the most comprehensive bibliography of Japanese detective stories available, this dictionary includes only Japanese writers, arranged in alphabetical order by author's last name. For each writer, a biography is provided, as are a list of books and a brief description of each. A title index concludes the bibliography.

Note: Katsuo Jinka's *Gendai Kaigai Misuteri Besuto 100* (Tokyo: Shakai Shisosha, 1991) lists 100 "best" detective and mystery stories, but these are not by Japanese writers, and the 100 titles include *Blue Belle, Tinker, Tailor, Soldier, Spy,* and *Presumed Innocent.* The same is true of *Sekai no Suiri Shosetsu Sokaisetsu* by Nakajima and Manji Gonda (Tokyo: Jiyu Kokuminsha, 1982). Nakajima's *Sengo Suiri Shosetsu Somokuroku* (Tokyo: Nippon Suiri Sakka Kyokai, 1970–1980), entry A202 in the second edition of Walter Albert's *Detective and Mystery Fiction* (q.v.), is described as "an index of mystery stories published in Japan since 1945 through 1979. It focuses on the stories which first appeared in magazines, and includes only the novels that were originally written in book form." It has not been seen.

SCANDINAVIA

218. Steffensen, Jan B. **Scandinavian Mysteries in English.**

Compiled by Steffensen, and accessible through his Mysterious Homepage (q.v.), as well being accessible through the archives maintained by the DorothyL listserv. To obtain: send an e-mail message to listserv@listserv.kent.edu; type "get scanmyst.listing" in the subject line.

SOUTH AFRICA

219. Miller, Anita. **Afrikaanse speurverhale uitgegee tot die einde van 1950: 'n Bibliografie.** Johannesburg: Universiteit van die Witwatersrand Departement van Bibliografie, Biblioteekwese en Tipografie, 1967. iv, 23 p. Indexes. Cloth.

Generally, I have not included dissertations in this book, but Miller's bibliography of Afrikaans detective and mystery writers is the first and only bibliography on its subject, and one would be remiss not to acknowledge its existence and the existence of Susan Friedland's continuation (q.v.). Both dissertations were compiled as a partial fulfillment for the requirements for the Diploma in Librarianship at the University of the Witwatersrand, Johannesburg. Miller's, however, is entirely in Afrikaans.

Miller's two-page foreword gives no theoretical discussions or definitions of her subject, but she does provide four criteria she used for determining inclusions in her bibliography: "Die Bibliografie sluit die volgende in: 1. Ooorspronklike [*sic*] Afrikaanse speurromans, en wel slegs dié; 2. wat in die Africana-versameling van die Johannesburgee Openbare biblioteek aanwesig is; 3. wat in boekvorm uitgegee is; and 4. en wat voor en tot die einde van 1950 verskyn hat." (In English, these translate roughly to a statement that the bibliography includes bibliographic information about original Afrikaans detective novels, with specific references only to those novels; what was available in the Afrikaaner collections of the Johannesburg Public Library; what was published in book form; and that they were published before the end of 1950.)

The first section lists the books alphabetically, giving the authors' names in capital letters; book titles are not underlined. In addition, each citation provides the book's place of publication, publisher, date of publication, pagination, and size. Series characters are identified, as are pseudonyms. In all, approximately 300 books are referenced. A one-page section lists the Afrikaans articles published on the subject; and the third and concluding section is a title index to the works cited in the bibliography.

The information in this volume is utterly unique, but the bibliography is not without its share of misspellings, and several of these include names: Petrus J. Nienaber's name is given as "Bienaber," and additional typos are not difficult to find. Probably only specialists will need this and Susan Friedland's continuation.

220.   Friedland, Susan. **South African Detective Stories in English and Afrikaans from 1951–1971.** Johannesburg: University of the Witwatersrand Department of Bibliography, Librarianship and Typography, 1972. ii, 46 p. Indexes. Cloth.

This volume is a direct continuation and expansion of Anita Miller's *Afrikaanse speurverhale uitgegee tot die einde van 1950: 'n bibliografie* (q.v.), and as its title indicates, it documents the South African detective stories published in English and Afrikaans from 1951 to 1971. Like Miller's work, this was compiled as partial fulfillment for the requirements for the Diploma in Librarianship at the University of the Witwatersrand, Johannesburg, but whereas Miller wrote in Afrikaans, Friedland uses English for her prefatory material.

Friedland begins her bibliography with a reasonable caveat: "Since South Africa is still a young country and its population fairly mobile, it is difficult [*sic*] to define as South Africans only those writers who were born here. Writers have therefore been included who spent a considerable part of their lives in South Africa and wrote at least some of their novels while being citizens or residents here." Successive sections list English authors, Afrikaans authors, English titles, Afrikaans titles, English series, and Afrikaans series. The citations·in the sections devoted to the English and Afrikaans authors are numbered; in all, 451 works are listed. Each entry provides the author's name, the title, publication data for the first edition, and the volume's pagination; a brief annotation concerning the volume's contents concludes each entry. The volume concludes with a highly selective bibliography of journal articles on the detective story.

Although lists of the writings of the English authors have been reprinted in *Mysteries of Africa,* edited by Eugene Schleh (Bowling Green, Ohio: Bowling Green State University Popular Press, 1991), the listing of the Afrikaans mystery and detective story writers is apparently unique to this volume. Nevertheless, this work is likely to interest only specialists.

SWEDEN

221.   Hedman-Morelius, Iwan. **Kriminallitteratur på Svenska 1749–1985.** Göteborg: Dast Förlag, 1986. 473 p. Cloth. ISBN 91-85208-07-8.

This is apparently an expansion of Hedman-Morelius's (1974) *Dekare och Thrillers på Svenska, 1864–1973* (not seen). The present volume lists the detective and fiction books that were published in Sweden and Swedish between 1749 and 1985, regardless of the author's initial origins: a number of entries are for the translations of works originally published in English.

The entries in *Kriminallitteratur på Svenska* are arranged alphabetically, but unlike the other national bibliographies herein considered, this volume does not contain a separate index to titles; rather, the title index is incorporated into the volume as part of the main sequence. Each author's entries give his or her name in bolded capital letters; birth and death dates are occasionally provided, as are pseudonyms and the names of significant series characters. The books are listed chronologically by the date of the first Swedish publication, each entry providing in truncated form the citation to the first Swedish edition of that volume; the key to the abbreviations occurs at the beginning of the book. When the referenced book has been reprinted from an English source, the publication data of the first British or American edition are given, also in highly abbreviated form.

In addition, motion picture and dramatic adaptations are listed beneath the relevant author, the reference to these providing only the years of the adaptations. Also cited are significant works of nonfiction: Raymond Chandler's letters are referenced, as are such volumes as Bo Lundin's *Salongsbödlarna* and *The Swedish Crime Story*. Finally, the volume contains numerous photographs, not all of them credited, and concludes with a list of the awards given by the Swedish Academy of Detection.

An enormous amount of effort obviously went into the creation of this book, and like the work of Allen Hubin (q.v.), this is likely to be superseded only by the author's updating of his earlier efforts.

222.   Hedman-Morelius, Iwan. **Kriminallitteratur på Svenska 1986–1990.** DAST Dossier No. 9. Huskvarna: DAST, 1992. 475–580 p. ISBN 91-85208-08-6.

This is apparently a direct continuation of Hedman-Morelius's *Kriminallitteratur på Svenska 1749–1985* (preceding). It has not been seen.

223.   Lingblom, Hans E. **1257 Förteckning över Deckare, Thrillers, Faktaböcker, Memoarer, Kolportageromaner.** Ostersund: Berntssons, 1979.

Not seen.

224.   Tullberg, Sigurd. **O och A. Detektivromaner på Svenska under 1900–talet.** Stockholm: Bibliotekens Bokformedling, 1954. 95 p.

Not seen.

5

Maps and Atlases

Scope note: This chapter cites publications that relate mysteries to specific locations. Many of the indexes and reader's guides also provide indexes for locations.

GENERAL REGIONAL GUIDES

225. Demko, G. J. **G. J. Demko's Landscapes of Crime.** http://www.dartmouth. edu/~gjdemko/uscolumns.html

Demko's site provides columns about five kinds of regional mysteries: mid-Atlantic mysteries, south Atlantic mysteries, New England mysteries, Florida and Louisiana mysteries, and campus mysteries. Lists are not given, but the elements comprising the genres are discussed and defined.

226. King, Nina, with Robin Winks. **Crimes of the Scene: A Mystery Novel Guide for the International Traveler.** New York: St. Martin's, 1997. xi, 291 p. Index. Cloth. LC 96-44225. ISBN 0-312-15174-8.

Crimes of the Scene offers lists and reviews of mystery novels set in countries or regions other than Great Britain and the United States. The book contains 21 chapters, each devoted to the mysteries of a country or a region, each using the same structure. There is a general introduction to the mysteries of that region, followed by an annotated bibliography of the region's mysteries that have been translated into English, and the chapters conclude with a list of works that have been "noted but not reviewed." An author index concludes the work.

There is much to praise in *Crimes of the Scene,* but it is also a work with idiosyncrasies. The authors have made no attempts at distinguishing between genres; in addition to citations to mysteries, there are numerous references to thrillers and adventure novels. One finds here entries for nonmysteries written by Eric Ambler, Ian Fleming, Ken Follett, Frederick Forsyth, Thomas Harris, Jack Higgins, and Donald Westlake, to name but a few. Significant mysteries have nevertheless been omitted. For example, Jonathan

Kellerman's best-selling *Butcher's Theater* has not been included although it is set almost entirely in a meticulously described Jerusalem. Equally seriously, some of the annotations are erroneous: A. E. W. Mason's *The Four Feathers* (another dubious inclusion) is described as "the kitsch classic where the Brits storm Khartoum in 1882 and avenge the slaughter of Chinese Gordon by the 'fuzzie-wuzzies,' " which is only peripherally the plot of Mason's 1902 novel. The indexing, too, is not comprehensive.

Crimes of the Scene is the only work devoted entirely to its subject; it is a book for the armchair traveler. One hopes for a revised, corrected, and expanded edition.

227.   Lachman, Marvin. **The American Regional Mystery.** Minneapolis and San Francisco: Crossover Press, 2000. ix, 542 p. Index. LC 2001-525744. ISBN 0-9628870-3-X.

The American Regional Mystery reviews and lists mystery novels (and some short stories) by their location in the United States. The arrangement is geographical by region, starting with mysteries set on the East Coast (New England, New York, the Middle Atlantic states, and the South), then moving west across the continental United States, going through the Midwest, the Rocky Mountain states, the Pacific Northwest, California, and concluding with works set in Alaska and Hawaii. Bibliographic essays discuss the mysteries set in each state, providing the publication date of each mystery. Special subsections discuss the works set in the major cities and areas within the state (i.e., there is a discussion of the mysteries set in Massachusetts, with separate sections for the works set in Boston, Cape Cod, Martha's Vineyard, and Nantucket). Each essay—state as well as city/region—concludes with an alphabetical list of additional mysteries set in that region; as before, date of publication is given. The volume concludes with a well-done cumulative author and title index.

Although it is not exhaustive—no work could be—more 2,700 works are discussed and more than 3,000 are listed, and Lachman's work is magisterial, exemplary, and scholarly yet readable. *The American Regional Mystery* deserves its praise, and that it was not awarded the Edgar Award for best nonfiction work remains the source of some contention.

228.   Lawson, Janet, and Cynthia Orr. **Mystery by Region.** http://www.barnesandnoble. com/bookbrowser/welcome.asp?

Once an independent site and now part of the Barnes and Noble site, Mystery by Region allows readers to pick a geographical location—Canada, Europe, Scandinavia, the United Kingdom, the United States, and so forth—and to find mysteries set in that region. Clickable maps are provided, as are the names of countries and all of the states. The search leads to the authors who have used that area for their settings and the titles of their works. Minimal bibliographic data are provided, but updates are promised.

229.   Literate Traveller. **Around the World in 80 Mysteries.** http://www. literatetraveller.com/mystery1.html

Very pleasantly laid out and nicely annotated.

230.   Northwest Crime Scene. **Northwest Mystery Authors.** http://www. nwlink.com/~massucco/NW-Myst-Auth/NWAuth.html

Links to information about 30 genre authors resident in the Northwest. The site indicates whether the link possesses an e-mail link, a Web site link, or a sound file of the author's voice.

231. Reader's Advice. **Regional Mysteries.** http://www.readersadvice.com/readadv/000193.html

A lengthy and elaborate list of authors and titles, with links providing access by state and region. Very useful and accessible.

SPECIFIC AREAS

American States and Their Cities

California

232. Derie, Kate. **SanFran Sleuths: San Francisco Bay Area Mysteries.**

This list of mysteries set in the San Francisco Bay area is available through the archives maintained by DorothyL listserv. To obtain: send an e-mail message to listserv@listserv.kent.edu; type "get sanfran.sleuths" in the subject line.

233. Duychak, Linda. **Mysteries: 2001: An LA Odyssey. ARLIS/NA 29th Annual Conference.** http://arlis2001.ucsd.edu/mysteries.html

List of Los Angeles and southern California mystery writers.

234. Herron, Don. **Dashiell Hammett Tour.** Heron's Literary Walks in San Francisco, no. 1. San Francisco, Calif.: Dawn Heron Press, 1982. 95 p. Paperback. ISBN 0-939790-02-5.

From 1921 until 1930, Dashiell Hammett lived in San Francisco, a city he used as background in "The Whosis Kid," "Fly Paper," *The Dain Curse,* and *The Maltese Falcon.* Hammett's locations have been identified in a number of articles, but Heron's is the first separate publication to provide readers with a walking tour of them. Furthermore, Heron identifies (and provides numerous pictures of) the buildings in which Hammett is known to have lived.

Heron begins his 27-stop tour at the San Francisco Library (in which Hammett did research and work) and concludes it with Samuels Jewelers, at which Hammett worked as an advertising writer. (Albert S. Samuels was also the person to whom *The Dain Curse* was dedicated.) Notable sites visited include all of Hammett's rooms, Burritt Street (in which the body of Miles Archer is found), John's Grill (in which Sam Spade ate), and 891 Post (the apartment lived in by Hammett and—probably—by Sam Spade).

The volume contains five maps but lacks scales, distances, and (unfortunately) indexing. It is nevertheless lively, informative, and quite enjoyable.

235. Stone, Carolyn K. **A Reading List for Mystery Lovers! Mysteries on Location. Scene of the Crimes.** Beverly Hills, Calif.; Montpelier, Conn.: Literate Traveller; Stone and Stone Travel Research Services, 1996. 6 leaves.

These guides to regional mysteries have not been formally published, but they have been advertised on the World Wide Web and through the DorothyL discussion group, and they are available through the Web site of the Literate Traveller (http://www. literatetraveller.com). All guides are reproduced from laser-printed copy and were published in 1996; all cleave to the same format. The first five leaves of each are arranged alphabetically by author and provide title, place of publication, publisher, and first publication date for between 13 and 21 mystery novels set in that region. The authors of these mysteries tend to be among the living. Each novel is capably annotated; often, other works by the author are referenced. The sixth leaf provides a bibliography of bibliographies listing mysteries set in that region.

Lists cover mysteries set in Los Angeles, Hollywood, San Francisco, and southern California.

236.   Sunnyvale Public Library Booklists. **California Crime.** http://www.ci. sunnyvale.ca.us/library/booklists/calmyst.htm

237.   Ward, Elizabeth, and Alain Silver. **Raymond Chandler's Los Angeles.** Woodstock, N.Y.: Overlook Press, 1987. 234 p. Cloth. LC 86-18007. ISBN 0-87951-266-0.

Raymond Chandler's Los Angeles is not a walking tour or a guide to the city of Los Angeles in the way that Don Herron's *Dashiell Hammett Tour* (q.v.) offers a guide to San Francisco. It nevertheless deserves mention here because Ward and Silver identify the locations that Chandler used in his short stories and novels and pair Chandler's descriptions with a black-and-white photograph or photographs of the site. In all, more than 100 black-and-white photographs are provided. Although the photographs are contemporary, Ward and Silver manage to make them look timeless and, occasionally, eerie and disturbing. On the debit side, there are no maps, making this "armchair tour of Raymond Chandler's Los Angeles" less than ideal.

Overlook Press reissued this book in 1997, and a selection of the images can be found at http://members.aol.com/chandlerla/index.htm.

Illinois

238.   Dale, Alzina Stone. **Mystery Reader's Walking Guide: Chicago.** Maps by Ben Stone. Lincolnwood, Ill.: Passport Books, 1995. xii, 385 p. Index. Cloth. LC 94-33414. ISBN 0-8442-9607-4.

Mystery Reader's Walking Guide: Chicago follows the same format as Dale's other books, identifying 10 walks that will take the reader through Chicago sites that have been featured in crime and mystery novels. Each walk is accorded a separate chapter. Each chapter begins with a historical introduction, a statement as to the length of the walk, and a list of the places of interest and the places to eat that can be seen and visited during the walk. The descriptions of the walks are agreeably informal, mixing descriptions of sites with discussions of the mysteries set in them. Each chapter is provided with a map drawn specifically for this volume; no distance keys are provided.

The book's second section, "Special Helps," lists the authors, books, and sleuths mentioned in each walk, although restaurants, places of interest, theaters and concert halls, and shops that are given in the body of the book are not repeated. A brief bibliography and very well done indexes conclude the book.

239.   Northbrook Public Library. **Illinois Mysteries and Mystery Authors.** http://
        www.northbrook.info/lib_illinois_mysteries.php

        A very useful list of all Illinois mysteries, arranged alphabetically by author.

Louisiana

240.   Louisiana State University Law School. **Buried on the Bayou: The Louisiana
        Mystery and Detective Page.** http://faculty.law.lsu.edu/ccorcos/louisian/
        bayou.htm

        A lengthy and thorough list, with a special section for New Orleans mysteries.

Maine

241.   Colby Bookstore. **Mysterious Maine.** http://www.colby.edu/bookstore/maine_
        mysteries.html

        Currently available Maine mysteries.

242.   Portland Public Library. **PPL Reader's Corner.** http://www.portlandlibrary.
        com/research/mysteries.htm

        A list of a dozen authors whose mysteries are available through the Portland
Public Library.

Massachusetts

243.   Boston Public Library. **Mysteries That Take Place in Massachusetts.**
        http://www.bpl.org.research/AdultBooklists/massmysteries.htm

        As the title indicates.

244.   Northeast Massachusetts Regional Library System. **Mass Murder Returns . . .
        to the Scene of the Crime Again.** http://www.nmrls.org/resources/mysbkl.
        shtml

245.   Parker, Robert B. **Spenser's Boston.** Photographs by Kasho Kumagai. New
        York: Otto Penzler Books, 1994. 199 p. Cloth. LC 94-17814. ISBN
        1-883402-50-6.

        Although it contains a map of Boston and surrounding areas, *Spenser's Boston*
is not a walking tour of those parts of Boston that appear in Parker's Spenser series. Instead, the book begins with a short story in which Spenser, Susan, and Rachel Wallace
walk around Boston and comment upon the city. Chapters titled "Summer," "Autumn,"
and "Winter" provide seasonal pictures of Boston, New England, and Parker. A chapter
titled "Crossing Mystic River Bridge" provides photographs of some of the sights—
small towns, autumn trees, harbors—that can be seen after crossing the Mystic River
Bridge, and "108 Miles to Cape Cod" provides photographs of Cape Cod, Hyannis, and
Provincetown. Kumagai provides an appreciative afterword, and the concluding "Guide
to Boston" lists 12 places of interest in Boston. Lovers of Spenser and Boston will appreciate Parker's prose and Kumagai's beautifully composed and rendered photographs.

246. Reader's Advisory. **Spotlight on . . . Massachusetts Mysteries.** http://users. rcn.com/hansonpl/page2.html

New Mexico

247. Santa Fe Public Library. **New Mexico Mysteries, Series and Single Titles, and Mysteries Set in the Wider West.** http://www.ci.santa-fe.nm.us/sfpl/ nmmystery.html

A very useful list of the "series set in New Mexico or very close by," with an additional series of linkages that take one directly into the catalogue.

New York

248. Dale, Alzina Stone. **Mystery Reader's Walking Guide: New York.** Maps by Kenneth Herrick Dale. Lincolnwood, Ill.: Passport Books, 1993. xvi, 361 p. Indexes. Cloth. LC 92-60398. ISBN 0-8442-9481-0.

In this enjoyable walking guide to a few of the hundreds of New York City sites that have been used in mysteries, the introduction is weak, managing to put three factual errors into its two opening sentences. Writes Dale: "New York City has been the center of the mystery novel since its inventor, Edgar Allan Poe, borrowed a NYC crime for his chilling tale, *The Mystery of Marie Rogèt,* published in 1841. A generation later, in 1878, New Yorker Anna Katherine Green's *The Leavenworth Case* was the first detective story written by a woman." Apart from the fact that Poe neither wrote mystery novels nor invented New York City, "The Mystery of Marie Rogèt" was first published in Snowden's *Ladies' Companion* in 1842, and to credit Anna Katherine Green with the first detective story is to ignore Metta Victor's 1867 *The Dead Letter.*

This guide concentrates on Manhattan mystery sites, providing 11 walks through such neighborhoods as Wall Street, the Lower East Side, Greenwich Village, Midtown West, Upper East Side, and Central Park. Although each walk covers one neighborhood, some of the walks are split into two or three parts because so many sites have been used.

As in the other volumes in this series, each walk is accorded a separate chapter. Each chapter begins with a historical introduction, a statement as to the length of the walk, and lists of the places of interest and the places to eat that can be seen and visited during the walk. The descriptions of the walks are chatty and lively, mixing descriptions of New York sites with discussions of the mysteries set in them. A map drawn specifically for this volume is provided for each walk; however, no distance keys are provided, and the writing on the map tends toward the microscopic.

The book's second section, "Special Helps," lists the authors, books, and sleuths mentioned in each walk and does not repeat the lists of the restaurants, places of interest, theaters and concert halls, and shops that are given in the body of the book. Concluding the volume are a brief bibliography and a well-done index.

Texas

249. San Antonio Public Library. **San Antonio Community Portal. SAPL: Fiction— Texas Mysteries and Thrillers.** http://www.sanantonio.gov/library/fiction/ fic_TX-Mystery.asp?res=1024&ver=true

Washington, D.C.

250. Dale, Alzina Stone. **Mystery Reader's Walking Guide: Washington, D.C.** Chicago: Passport Books, 1998. xiii, 306 p. Index. Paperback. LC 97-34072. ISBN 0-8442-9480-2.

This enjoyable walking guide provides eight walking tours through the nation's "power capital of the world," covering such sites as the White House and downtown Washington, the East Mall, the West Mall, Capitol Hill, Dupont Circle/Embassy Row, Foggy Bottom, Georgetown, and Arlington Cemetery and Alexandria.

As in the other volumes in this series, each walk is accorded a separate chapter. Each chapter begins with a historical introduction, a statement as to the length of the walk, and lists of the places of interest and the places to eat that can be seen and visited during the walk. The descriptions of the walks are chatty and lively, mixing descriptions of Washington sites with discussions of the mysteries set in them. Each of the walks mentioned is accompanied by a map drawn specifically for this volume; however, no distance keys are provided, and the writing on the map tends toward the microscopic.

The book's second section, "Special Helps," lists the authors, books, and sleuths mentioned in each walk, although it does not repeat the lists of the restaurants, places of interest, theaters and concert halls, and shops that are given in the body of the book. Concluding the volume are a brief bibliography and a well-done index.

There are some small errors—Dale persistently dates Poe's "The Murders in the Rue Morgue" to 1842 (it was 1841)—but the guide remains valid and the walks enjoyable.

England

251. Dale, Alzina Stone, and Barbara Sloan Hendershott. **Mystery Reader's Walking Guide: England.** Maps by Alisa Mueller Burkey. Lincolnwood, Ill.: Passport Books, 1988. xv, 416 p. Indexes. Cloth. LC 88-60300.

Significantly larger in scope than their earlier *Mystery Reader's Walking Guide: London* (q.v.), this walking guide to England nevertheless shares the same premise and arrangement. In the first section, Dale and Hendershott identify 14 towns and regions that can be associated with mysteries, and they plot walks ranging in length from 2.5 to 8.8 miles through them. All towns are accessible by British Rail, and each walk starts and ends at the British Railway Station. As in the earlier volume, each walk is accorded a separate chapter, and the information provided includes not only the authors and works who made use of the area but also the ancillary places of interest (and their hours of operation) and recommended places to eat. Helpful details abound: "Serves pub lunches and dinners to nonresidents." As before, each walk includes a clearly drawn map plotted specifically for this volume, and each map identifies the locations on the walk but does not include a distance key.

The book's second section, "Special Helps," lists the authors, books, and sleuths by walk; the separate lists of restaurants and pubs, the places of interest, the shops, the theaters, and the concert halls are not repeated. The volume concludes with a brief bibliography and a very capable index.

252. Dale, Alzina Stone, and Barbara Sloan Hendershott. **Mystery Reader's Walking Guide: London.** Maps by John Babcock. Lincolnwood, Ill.: Passport Books, 1987. xx, 294 p. Indexes. Cloth. LC 86-60564.

As its title indicates, this is a guide for those whose love of mysteries extends to visiting the places used as their settings. In the first section, Dale and Hendershott identify the London locales used by more than 50 mystery and detective writers and plot 11 walks—ranging in length from 3 to 6.2 miles—that take one through these areas. Each walk is accorded a separate chapter. The information given includes not only the authors and works making use of the area but also ancillary places of interest (and their hours of operation) and recommended places to eat; helpful details abound: "Eating places and pubs within the walk are open Monday–Friday during lunch hours only. (Toilet facilities are also limited.)" Finally, each walk includes a clearly presented map drawn specifically for this volume; each map identifies the locations on the walk but does not include a distance key.

The volume's second section is called "Special Helps" and consists of lists recapitulating the data given in the first section: the places to eat, the places of interest, the theaters and concert halls, the shops mentioned, and the authors, books, and sleuths associated with each walk. Although redundant in content, this section nevertheless provides a convenient checklist of the highlights of each walking tour. A bibliography and an index of the persons, places, and books concludes the book. It is not only well done but also a browser's delight.

253.   Earwaker, Julian, and Kathleen Becker. **Scene of the Crime: A Guide to the Landscapes of British Detective Fiction.** Introduction by P. D. James. London: Aurum Press, 2002. 256 p. Indexes. Paperback. ISBN 1-85410-821-2.

This delightful and well-illustrated volume is a guide to the landscapes of Great Britain that have inspired more than 250 writers of mystery and detective stories, particularly those writers "whose sense of place is strongest, and whose series detectives provide a continuity and deeper attachment to particular locations."

The arrangement of the 13 chapters of *Scene of the Crime* is geographical, from north to south. The volume thus begins with a description of the mystery writers and works of Scotland, and following chapters are for the writers and works of Northumbria, Yorkshire, the North-West, Wales and the Marches [*sic*], the Midlands, Cambridge and the Fens, East Anglia, London (Central and Outer), the South-East and Home Counties, Oxford and the Cotswolds, the South, and Devon and Cornwall. Arrangement in each chapter is broadly chronological; primary locations are referenced in boldface capital letters and other key locations are given in boldface. Biographical data include birth and death dates of authors and the real names when applicable. Works that have won a Crime Writers' Association award are indicated with an asterisk (*), and apart from first book publication date, bibliographic data are deliberately kept to a minimum. The volume concludes with indexes for authors and places and a selected bibliography.

Livelier and more comprehensive and current than the works by Alzina Stone Dale (q.q.v.), *Scene of the Crime* will be appreciated by all lovers of the British regional mystery.

254.   Stone, Carolyn K. **A Reading List for Mystery Lovers! Mysteries on Location. Scene of the Crimes.** Beverly Hills, Calif.; Montpelier, Conn.: Literate Traveller; Stone and Stone Travel Research Services, 1996. 6 leaves.

This is a Literate Traveller guide to the mysteries set in England. See the entry under "California" for a brief description of this set of guides.

Other Countries

255.   Stone, Carolyn K. **A Reading List for Mystery Lovers! Mysteries on Location. Scene of the Crimes.** Beverly Hills, Calif.; Montpelier, Conn.: Literate Traveller; Stone and Stone Travel Research Services, 1996. 6 leaves.

This is a Literate Traveller guide to the mysteries set in Africa, France, and Asia and the Pacific Rim. See the entry under "California" for a brief description of this set of guides.

6

Writer's Associations and Awards

Scope note: This section lists the separately published lists of the genre awards. Many of these awards also are listed in the encyclopedias and the reader's guides sections.

GENERAL WORKS

256. Pearsall, Jay. **Mystery & Crime: The New York Public Library Book of Answers. Intriguing and Entertaining Questions and Answers about the Who's Who and What's What of Whodunits.** New York, London, Toronto: Simon & Schuster, 1995. 175 p. Index. Paperback. LC 94-25127. ISBN 0-671-87237-0.

The New York Public Library sponsored this book of questions and answers about mysteries, and Jay Pearsall, the proprietor of Murder, Ink., compiled the book. According to the introduction, Pearsall intended it as a "gathering together of what is interesting, clever, astounding, and hilarious in the mystery genre. It's the kind of information that you have to share with someone." Its contents are Sherlock Holmes and Forerunners; The Golden Age; Schools and Rules; The Amateur Detective; Agatha; Private Eyes, Grifters, and Dames; Sisters in Crime; Rogues and Scoundrels; Candlesticks and Curare; On the Beat; Murder by Quotation; Questions of Character; The Writers; Pseudonyms; Espionage and Thrillers; Politics and Murder; First, Lasts, and Onlies; The Subject Is Murder; Exotic Locales; Murderous Miscellanea; Killer Titles; Now a Major Motion Picture; Mystery Writers of America Edgar Allan Poe Awards; Bibliography; and Index.

Pearsall has attempted to provide something for everybody, and this is simultaneously one of the book's strengths and weaknesses; it may be something of what one is looking for, but most of the time it is not comprehensive. Also, Pearsall presents his material in what seems to be a lighthearted manner, giving his information in a question and answer format. Thus, although the volume can be browsed with pleasure, it has no uses apart from providing instant fodder to the players of trivia games. Users of the New York Public Library and visitors to Murder, Ink., may indeed have wanted to know the name of the espionage novel in which a fourteen-year-old boy with total recall is recruited by the British Intelligence as a spy, but will anybody else care? A smattering of factual errors makes this work less than completely reliable. Choose instead the lists of Strosser and Stine (q.q.v.).

257a. Strosser, Edward, ed. **The Armchair Detective Book of Lists: A Complete Guide to the Best Mystery, Crime & Suspense Fiction.** New York: Armchair Detective, 1989. 266 p. Paperback. LC 90-105981. ISBN 0-89296-423-5.

257b. Stine, Kate, ed. **The Armchair Detective Book of Lists: A Complete Guide to the Best Mystery, Crime, and Suspense Fiction.** 2nd ed. New York: Otto Penzler Books, 1995. xv, 267 p. Paperback. LC 94-41794. ISBN 1-883402-98-0.

This annotation describes the second edition. Although a daunting 34 chapters are listed in the table of contents, this most useful compilation contains in essence only three sections. The first section provides information about genre awards; the second consists of lists; and the third provides information about mystery organizations, conventions, and publications. There are illustrations throughout.

The material in the first section occupies nearly half the book and begins with lists of the winners of the awards given by the Mystery Writers of America (MWA). The winners of the MWA's Grand Master Award are listed, followed by lists of the winners of the MWA's Edgar Allan Poe Award for best novel, best first novel by an American author, best paperback original, best short story, best fact crime, best critical/biographical work, best young adult mystery, best juvenile mystery, best episode in a television series, best motion picture, best foreign film, best play, best radio drama, outstanding mystery criticism, the winners of the special Edgar, the Ellery Queen Awards, the Robert L. Fish Memorial Awards, and the Raven Awards. When relevant, the lists include the finalists, with the winner's name(s) in boldface type. The list of MWA winners is followed by lists of the Crime Writers' Association of Great Britain Award, the Crime Writers of Canada's Arthur Ellis Awards, the Independent Mystery Booksellers Association's Dilys Winn Award, the International Association of Crime Writers' Hammett Awards, the Wolfe Pack's Nero Wolfe Awards, the Bouchercon World Mystery Convention Anthony Awards, the Private Eye Writers of America Shamus Awards, the Mystery Readers International's Macavity Awards, and the Malice Domestic Agatha Awards. The most recent data are from 1994.

The lists include the Haycraft-Queen definitive library of detective-crime-mystery fiction, the Queen's Quorum (125 titles), Otto Penzler's top 100 Sherlock Holmes books, Robin W. Wink's personal favorites, *The Armchair Detective* Reader's Survey, the *Drood Review*'s Editor's Choice, the *Sunday Times* 100 best crime stories selected by Julian Symons in 1957–1958, Sandoe's *The Hard-Boiled Dick: A Personal Checklist*, H. R. F. Keating's 100 best crime and mystery books, Jon L. Breen's list of the 10 best mystery reference works, Marvin Lachman's list of the 10 best first mystery novels, William Deeck's list of James Corbett's 10 greatest lines, Douglas Greene's list of the most ingenious locked room and impossible crime novels of all time, *Firsts* magazine's list of 25 rapidly appreciating mystery books, Ric Meyer's lists of 10 top mystery movies and television serials, and lists from various authors of their favorite mystery writers and novels.

The third section is the briefest, but it provides useful contact information and data on mystery organizations, author fan clubs and newsletters, mystery fan conventions, and mystery periodicals. As before, data are current as of 1994.

Much of this information is available through other sources, but these sources can be difficult to obtain. Although this book is a treasure trove for the browser as well as an essential reference work, it would have benefited enormously from an index.

SPECIFIC AWARDS

257.5a. Agatha Awards

Given by the Malice Domestic attendees for best traditional mysteries of the previous year. http://www.malicedomestic.org

257.5b. Alexei Tolstoi Awards

Given by the International Association of Crime Writers for the best thrilling novel of the previous year.

International Association of Crime Writers (IACW)
Benjamin Hill 242-244
Colonia Condesa
Mexico City, DF, Mexico

257.5c. Anthony Awards

Given by the attendees of the annual Bouchercon World Mystery Convention. http://www.hycyber.com/MYST/anthonys.html

257.5d. Arthur Ellis Awards

Given by the Crime Writers of Canada to honor the best works published by Canadian authors during the previous year.

Crime Writers of Canada (CWC)
3007 Kingston Road, Box 113
Scarborough, ON Canada M1M 1P1
http://www.swifty.com/cwc/cwchome.htm
http://www.crimewriterscanada.com

257.5e. Barry Awards

Awarded by the readers of *Deadly Pleasures*. http://www.deadlypleasures.com/Barry.htm

257.5f. Chester Himes Award

Awarded at the annual Chester Himes Mystery Writers Conference, in Oakland, California. http://www.cluelass.com/DDO/action.lasso?

257.5g. Dagger Awards

Given by the Crime Writers' Association (of Great Britain). Sometimes called Macallan Daggers because the awards are sponsored by The Macallan, distillers of Highland Malt Whisky, in association with the Crime Writers' Association.

Crime Writers' Association (CWA)
c/o Richard Grayson
5 Highgate Close
London N6 4SD England
http://thecwa.co.uk/awards/2002/index.html

The individual awards include the following.

Cartier Diamond Dagger Award

Given for outstanding contributions to the genre.

The CWA Dagger in the Library

Sponsored by the Random House Group and judged by librarians, this is awarded to the author "whose work has given most pleasure to readers."

The CWA Ellis Peters Historical Dagger

Sponsored by the estate of Ellis Peters and the publishers Headline and Little, Brown, this award is given to the best historical crime novel.

The CWA John Creasey Memorial Dagger

Sponsored by Chivers Press and awarded to first-time novelists writing crime fiction.

The CWA Macallan Short Story Dagger

Given for best short story.

The Debut Dagger

Given to a (thus far) unpublished crime writer.

Ian Fleming Steel Dagger

Given for best thriller, suggested and sponsored by Ian Fleming (Gildrose) Publications, Ltd., to celebrate the best of contemporary thriller writing.

Macallan Gold and Silver Daggers

Given for fiction and nonfiction.

257.5h. Davitt Award

Given by Sisters in Crime Australia for the best crime novel by an Australian woman. http://home.vicnet.net.au/~sincoz/scarlet.htm

257.5i. Derrick Murdoch Award

Awarded by the Crime Writers of Canada to recognize an outstanding contribution to the genre of crime writing in Canada. http://www.crimewriterscanada.com

257.5j. Derringer Awards

Given by members of the Short Mystery Fiction Society for various lengths of short fiction. http://www.thewindjammer.com/smfs/html/derringers.html

257.5k. Deutsche Krimi Preis

Germany's oldest mystery award, given by the BKA: Bochumer Krimi Archiv. http://www.kaliber38.de/preise/dkp.htm

BKA: Bochumer Krimi Archiv
Reinhard Jahn
P.O. Box 10 18 13
D-45018 Essen Germany

257.5l. Dilys Award

Named for Dilys Winn, founder of Murder, Ink bookstore, and awarded by the Independent Mystery Booksellers Association. http://mysterybooksellers.com/dilys.html

257.5m. Edgar Awards

Judged and awarded by the Mystery Writers of America.

Mystery Writers of America (MWA)
17 E. 47th Street, 6th Floor
New York, NY 10017
http://www.bookwire.com/mwa/about
http://www.mysterywriters.org/awards/edgars.html
http://www.hycyber.com/MYST/edgars.html

257.5n. Ellen Nehr Award

Given by the American Crime Writers League for excellence in mystery reviewing. http://acwl.org/nehr.htm

257.5o. Ellery Queen Award

Awarded by the Mystery Writers of America "to honor writing teams and outstanding people in the mystery-publishing industry." http://www.mysterywriters.org/awards/ellery.html

257.5p. Falcon

Given by the Maltese Falcon Society of Japan. http://www.asahi-net.or.jp/~AP9T-AMN/falcon/faward1.html

257.5q. Glass Key

Awarded by the Crime Writers of Scandinavia (the Skandinavisk Kriminalselskap) for the best Scandinavian mystery. http://www.webfic.com/nmn/sks/sks.htm

Crime Writers of Scandinavia
Kirsten Holst, President
Stouby Skovvej 7
DK-7140 Stouby Denmark
Kirsten.holst@get2net.dk

257.5r. Glauser and Ehrenglauser

Two awards given by Das Syndikat, the German Crime Writers Association. The Glauser is given for best novel; the Ehrenglauser is given for lifetime achievement. http://www.das-syndikat.com/glauser.htm

257.5s. Gouden Strop

The Golden Noose is awarded by the Genootschap Nederlandstalige Misdaadauteurs (Dutch Crime Writers Association). http://www.crime.nl/goudenstrop

257.5t. Grand Master Award

Awarded yearly by the Mystery Writers of America and representing "the pinnacle of achievement in the mystery field." http://www.mysterywriters.org.awards/grand.html

257.5u. La Grand Prix de Littérateur Policière

France's highest award for crime writing, awarded annually since 1948 in recognition of the best French crime novel of the year and the best foreign novel translated into French. The administrators of this award do not appear to have either a Web site or an address to which inquiries may be made.

257.5v. Hammett Prize

Given by the North American Branch of the International Association of Crime Writers for a work of literary excellence in the field of crime writing by a U.S. or a Canadian author. http://www.thrillingdetective.com/trivia/triv18.html

257.5w. Herodotus Awards

Awarded by the Historical Mystery Appreciation Society for best historical writing in six categories. http://members.home.net/monkshould/herodotus.html

257.5x. Lambda Literary Awards for Mystery

Given by the Lambda Literary Foundation for best gay men's mystery and best lesbian mystery. http:///lamdalit.org/lammy

257.5y. Lefty Award

Given by the Left Coast Crime Convention for the most humorous book of the previous year. http://www.leftcoastcrime.com

Macallan Daggers. *See* Dagger Awards

257.5z. Marlowe Award

Awarded by the Raymond Chandler Gesellschaft for the best German and International crime novels.

Raymond Chandler Gesellschaft
William R. Adamson
Heidenheimrer Str. 106
D-89075 Ulm Germany

257.5aa. Martin Beck Awards

Given by the Swedish Crime and Mystery Academy for best Swedish original and for translation. http://susning.nu/Svenska_Deckarakademin

Svenska Deckarakademin
Göran Bengtson, President
Bryggargatan 6 B, 1 tr
S-111 21 Stockholm Sweden

257.5bb. Mary Higgins Clark Award

Sponsored by Simon and Schuster and awarded by the Mystery Writers of America for "the book written most closely in the Mary Higgins Clark tradition of romantic suspense." http://www.mysterywriters.org/awards/clark.html

257.5cc. Macavity Awards

Named for Macavity, the mystery cat in T. S. Eliot's *Old Possum's Book of Practical Cats,* the awards are given by the Mystery Readers International. http://www.mysteryreaders.org

257.5dd. Ned Kelly Awards

Awarded by the Crime Writers' Association of Australia. http://members.optusnet.com.au/~honey007/NKNMainy.htm

257.5ee. Nero Wolfe Awards

Given by the Wolfe Pack for the novel that best captures the spirit and "fair play aspects" of Rex Stout's Nero Wolfe novels. http://www.nerowolfe.org

257.5ff. Palle Rosenkrantz Award

Given by the Det Danske Kriminalakademi for the best Danish crime novel of the year. http://www.webfic.com/nmn/dka/prp.htm

257.5gg. Raven Awards

Awarded by the Mystery Writers of America for outstanding achievement in the mystery field "outside the realm of creative writing." http://www.mysterywriters. org/awards/raven.html

257.5hh. Robert L. Fish Memorial Award

Sponsored by the Robert L. Fish estate and administered by the Mystery Writers of America, this award is given to the best first short story by an American author. http://www.mysterywriters.org/awards/fish.html

257.5ii. Romantic Times Reviewers' Choice Awards

Awarded by *Romantic Times Magazine* for mystery and suspense fiction in six categories. http://www.romantictimes.com/b_books/awards.shtml

257.5jj. Scarlet Stiletto Award

Awarded by the Sisters in Crime Australia to the winner of a short story competition open to women resident in Australia or Australian women citizens resident overseas. http://home.vicnet.au/~sincoz/scarlet.htm

257.5kk. Shamus Awards

Awarded in several categories by the Private Eye Writers of America. http://members.aol.com/_ht_a/rrandisi/myhomepage/writing.html

257.5ll. Sherlock Awards

Given by *Sherlock Holmes, the Detective Magazine* for "distinctive detectives in several categories." http://www.pmh.uk.com/sherlock/sherlock.htm

257.5mm. Spotted Owl Award

Awarded by Friends of Mystery for the best mystery book written by a writer from the Pacific Northwest (Alaska, Idaho, Oregon, Washington, and British Columbia). http://www.friendsofmystery.org/award.html

257.5nn. Suomen Dekkariseura/Clue of the Year

Given by the Finnish Whodunnit Society. http://www.dekkariseura.fi

257.5oo. The Thrillies

A readership poll conducted by *The Thrilling Detective*, a Web site magazine; it is done monthly on various topics and compiled annually. "There are no real winners, or even actual physical awards. The honour (or possibly embarrassment) lies in being nominated." http://www.thrillingdetective.com/trivia/poll.html

7

Publisher Bibliographies

Scope note: Included here are the checklists, indexes, and encyclopedic guides to the publications of specific publishing houses. The arrangement is alphabetical by the name of the publishing house or, occasionally, by series put out by a publishing house if the book annotated focuses exclusively on that series.

ACE BOOKS

258. Jaffery, Sheldon. **Double Trouble: A Bibliographic Chronicle of Ace Mystery Doubles.** Starmont Reference Guide no. 12. Mercer Island, Wash.: Starmont House, 1992. xvi, 150 p. Indexes. ISBN 1-55742-119-6 (hc); 1-55742-118-8 (pb).

In the early 1950s, publisher A. A. Wyn of Ace Books hit upon the idea of marketing paperback "doubles," two books bound back to back, each with its own cover art. The formula proved successful, and Ace issued Mystery Doubles, Science Fiction Doubles, Western Doubles, and Romance Doubles. There are at least five indexes and checklists to the Science Fiction Doubles, but relatively little attention has been paid to the other Ace Doubles, and well-known popular culture scholar (and lawyer) Jaffery's annotated bibliography of the Ace Mystery Doubles was overdue as a publication. In all, Jaffery describes approximately 130 books, from the first of the 1952 "D" series (D-1: *Too Hot for Hell* by Keith Vining and *The Grinning Gismo* by Samuel Taylor) through the "F" and "G" series, the last of which appeared in 1963.

A typical entry includes the Ace Double number, the title (in boldface italics), the author's name (pseudonyms are revealed when known), year of publication, and pagination; prices are given at the beginning of each section. Because Ace Doubles typically reprinted a novel, data are provided to earlier publications, as are references to the bibliographical sources used for locating this information; abridgments are noted, but cover artists, alas, are not. Jaffery's annotations range from lighthearted descriptions of the covers—"nice cover of a blonde holding a smoking gun in her right hand and wearing a backless, strapless gown cut down to bikini level in the rear and held up God-knows-how by a perky pair of whatchacallums. (Thank you, Robert Leslie

Bellem.)"—to reprinting the teasers from inside the front covers and excerpts from the critical praise received by the first editions. The result is a delightful guide to a disposable form of entertainment. As Jaffery's introduction puts it: "I don't agree that Ace Mystery Doubles were, on the whole, trashy, though some may be so classified. Many just weren't very good." Well-done author/title and title indexes conclude the volume.

ALBATROSS MODERN CONTINENTAL LIBRARY

259.   Williams, Richard, and Alastair Jollans. **Albatross Modern Continental Library 1932–1949.** British Paperback Checklist, no. 48. Scunthorpe, England: Dragonby Press, 1996. 20 p. Index. Stapled sheets.

Founded in 1931 by a coalition of English and German publishers and businesspeople, the Albatross Modern Continental Library purchased copyright for areas outside the British Empire and the United States and sold their paperbacks throughout Europe. Their books all bore a notice that they were "NOT TO BE INTRODUCED INTO THE BRITISH EMPIRE OR THE U.S.A." The Albatross Crime Club was introduced in 1933, reprinting books—initially published in hardcover by the Collins Crime Club—by such authors as Herbert Adams, Nicholas Blake, Miles Burton, Agatha Christie, G. D. H. Cole, E. C. R. Lorac, Ngaio Marsh, and Edgar Wallace. In all, the Albatross Modern Continental Library published more than 500 titles before going out of business in 1949.

Williams and Jollans's checklist lists the Albatross volumes in the order in which they appeared. Each citation provides the book's series number, its author and title (as given on the title page), the publication date, and dust wrapper (when such existed); pagination and printer are given for some volumes. Because Albatross initially had a different color for each of its series, a key listing the meaning of the color scheme is provided, and each citation also lists the volume's color. The checklist concludes with a cumulative author/title index.

The checklist lacks a separate title index, but it is clearly reproduced from word-processed copy and is easy to use.

ARMED SERVICES EDITIONS

260.   **Books Go to War: The Armed Services Editions in World War Two.** http://www.lib.virginia.edu/speccol/exhibits/ase/

A prefatory note states that "this is the virtual catalog of an exhibition held between 20 April and 10 September 1996 in the Dome Room of the Rotunda at the University of Virginia." The catalogue contains 10 elaborate and well-illustrated chapters providing the history of the Armed Services Editions. Some of this information is derived from Cole (which follows), but some of it is original to *Books Go to War,* for the volumes in their collection were originally the property of Philip Van Doren Stern, an editor at Pocket Books who also served as the general manager of the Armed Services Editions. This would have been an exhibition worth seeing.

261.   Cole, John Y., ed. **Books in Action: The Armed Services Editions.** Washington, D.C.: Center for the Book, Library of Congress, 1984. ix, 78 p. Paperback. LC 84-600198. Supt. of Docs. No. LC 1.2:B64/6. ISBN 0-8444-0466-7.

Between 1943 and 1947, nearly 123 million copies of 1,322 paperbacks were distributed to soldiers in the United States Armed Forces. Despite these astounding numbers, the Armed Services Editions have become surprisingly rare, and but a few research libraries hold complete sets. Furthermore, surprisingly little has been written on these volumes although they published the first editions of William Faulkner and Ernest Hemingway, a number of books "made" particularly for the Armed Services program, and detective and mystery fiction by such notable authors as Earl Derr Biggers, Nicholas Blake, W. R. Burnett, James M. Cain, John Dickson Carr, Dorothy Cameron Disney, Daphne Du Maurier, Hulbert Footner, Erle Stanley Gardner (and "A. A. Fair"), Cornell Woolrich (as "William Irish"), Richard and Frances Lockridge, Ellery Queen, and Patrick Quentin, to name but a few.

The first chapters of *Books in Action* recount the history of the Armed Services Editions. Cole introduces the Armed Services Editions and the meaning of their serial numbers; Michael Hackenberg provides their publishing history; Matthew Bruccoli provides an anecdotal account of his discovery of the volumes and his attempt at collecting them; and Hackenberg provides a two-page bibliography of the literature discussing the Armed Services Editions. The majority of the book, however, is the appendix, which provides a comprehensive list of the Armed Services Editions, correcting and expanding John Jamieson's *Editions for the Armed Services, Inc.: A History with the Complete List of the 1324 Books Published for American Armed Forces* (New York: Armed Services Editions, 1948). The books are listed alphabetically by the author's or editor's last name, given in capital letters. To the left of each name is the book's serial number; to the right of each name is the book's title, given in italics.

More data would have been welcome, but collectors and those curious about the Armed Services Editions will find *Books in Action* a fascinating account. The volume belongs in academic research libraries.

262. Maier, Mark. **Collecting Armed Services Editions: An Annotated Web Guide.** http://www.markmaier.com/ase_webguide.htm

Apparently created as part of a class project, Maier's guide provides a brief history of the Armed Services Editions. Much of this information is derived from Cole (profiled earlier), but making this page particularly useful are its links to the research libraries that have significant collections of Armed Services Editions.

263. **Warletters.com.** http://www.warletters.com/book/asedition.html

This site contains information on the new Armed Services Editions that, starting in December 2002, were distributed by publishers Hyperion, Simon and Schuster, and Dover Publications. The new Armed Services Editions resemble those printed during the Second World War but are thematically repetitious: Allan Mikaelian's *Medal of Honor: Profiles of America's Military Heroes from the Civil War to the Present;* William Shakespeare's *Henry V;* Sun Tzu's *The Art of War;* and *War Letters: Extraordinary Correspondence from American Wars,* edited by Andrew Carroll. One feels sorry for the members of the armed forces who might want to read something escapist.

AVON

264. Cox, J. Randolph. **Avon Mystery.**

Available as part of the archives maintained by the DorothyL listserv, this list of the 38 paperback mysteries published by Avon between 1969 and 1971 is arranged in the order of the books' publication. It should be noted that after the tenth volume in the series, the publisher ceased using series numbers, making this list particularly useful. Each citation provides the book's author and title. To obtain: send an e-mail message to listserv@listserv.kent.edu; type "get avon.mystery" in the subject line.

BIG LITTLE BOOKS

265. Lowery, Lawrence F. **Lowery's the Collector's Guide to Big Little Books and Similar Books.** Danville, Calif.: Educational Research and Applications Corporation, 1981. viii, 378 p. Index. Paperback. LC 81-65771.

One may argue with some justification that a guide to the Big Little Books—the generic term now applied to an oddly sized juvenile series that began in the 1930s—does not belong in this guide. Nevertheless, Lowery's *Collector's Guide* has been included because a number of the Big Little Books adapted the writings of well-known authors. The Big Little Books also adapted stories from motion pictures and pulp magazines, and the curious can find adaptations of the works of such well-known writers as Chester Gould and Edgar Wallace and such lesser-known writers as Isaac McAnally, Thorpe McClusky (as Thorp McCluskey), and Norman Marsh.

Lowery's *Collector's Guide* contains three sections. The first, the introduction, should be read by all unfamiliar with the arcane world of the Big Little Books, for he explains how to use his volume, provides information on collecting and caring for the books, and offers suggestions on the valuing and pricing of titles.

The second section, the entries, is divided into three major historical divisions: publications of the golden age (1932–mid-1938), silver age (mid-1938–1949), and modern age (1950–1981). This section is the longest and most comprehensive, for each of these divisions is further broken down, this next division listing the relevant output of the publishers of the Big Little Books; these include the Whitman Publishing Company, Saalfield Publishing Company, Dell Publishing Company, Goldsmith Publishing Company, World Syndicate Publishing Company, Engel-van Wiseman Book Corporation, Lynn Publishing Company, Fawcett Publishing Company, Waldman and Son Publishing Company, and Ottenheimer Publishers, as well as Blue Ribbon, Cupples and Leon, and McLoughlin, whose small output is listed in a section titled "Miscellaneous Publishers." In each section, the titles in each series are listed. Each entry provides the series number, the book's title in capital boldface type, the size (in inches), whether it was hardcover, the pagination, the artist, the author, the publication year, and a thumbnail reproduction of the cover. Variant editions are listed, as are peripheral books and premium giveaways.

An index by titles concludes the *Collector's Guide*. One regrets that no separate index by authors is provided, but this complaint aside, the *Collector's Guide* offers an apparently comprehensive and a thoroughly fascinating assessment of a small and consistently interesting series. The official Web site of the Big Little Book collectors—http://www.biglittlebooks.com—offers information about the Big Little Books and ways in which they should be graded and cared for, plus items for sale, links, and opportunities to join the club.

BOARDMAN

266. Greenslade, Lyndsey, Tom Lesser, and Richard Williams. **Boardman Crime and Science Fiction 1942–1967, a Checklist of the First Editions, with a Guide to Their Value by Ralph Spurrier.** Dragonby Bibliographies, no. 8. Scunthorpe, England: Dragonby Press, 1991. 44 p. Paperback. ISBN 1-871122-08-2. 300 copies printed.

The English publishing firm of T. V. Boardman lasted from 1942 until 1967, during which time it published 679 crime novels and author short story collections; only 18 of Boardman's titles were science fiction. The Boardman books were published in series, the Boardman Bloodhound being the most popular, appearing on 533 of the firm's titles. Among the authors who appeared under the Boardman imprint were Fredric Brown, Bruno Fischer, Robert L. Fish, William Campbell Gault, Brett Halliday, Ed McBain, Lawrence Treat, Donald E. Westlake, and Cornell Woolrich.

Boardman Crime and Science Fiction is similar in appearance to the previous books in the Dragonby Bibliographies series, reproduced from reduced laser-printed copy. After a foreword giving a brief history of the firm and a discussion of artist Denis McLoughlin (who drew most if not all of the Boardman covers), the majority of the bibliography is devoted to an author/title index of the Boardman authors. Each citation provides the author's byline as it appeared on the title page. On the same line are listed the number of books appearing under that byline in Boardman hardback and the approximate number of books published in England in hardback under that byline. If a pseudonym was employed, the author's real name is given in italics. Beneath each name are listed the books that appeared under that byline; they are listed chronologically by the official publication date, which is given. All titles are capitalized, and all citations include the series in which the book was published, the book's pagination, and its original publication price. Changes in title and whether the book appeared first in the United States are indicated, and citations conclude with Spurrier's assessment of the value. Additional indexes list the books by the Boardman series in which they were published; separate indexes for the Boardman hardcovers and the Boardman paperbacks are included.

Apart from Spurrier's (now-dated) prices, *Boardman Crime and Science Fiction* contains much that is unobtainable elsewhere. It does not, however, include any cross-references; users of the bibliography must know in advance that Evan Hunter also wrote as Hunt Collins, Ed McBain, and Richard Marsten and that Kendell Foster Crossen wrote as M. E. Chaber and Christopher Monig. In addition, it lacks a title index. These shortcomings aside, it remains the only comprehensive attempt at documenting this publisher's output.

267. Williams, Richard. **T. V. Boardman 1942–1957.** British Paperback Checklist, no. 37. Scunthorpe, England: Dragonby Press, 1988. 10 p. Index. Stapled sheets.

T. V. Boardman and Company appears to have started as the British publisher of American crime stories, but as the company grew, it began to issue hardback first editions by British authors, and it issued numerous separate series: Bloodhound Books, TVB Books, TVB Pocket Reader, TVB Red Arrow, TVB Red Arrow Romance, TVB Red Arrow Western, and so forth. Among the authors to appear under this imprint were Fredric Brown, Norbert Davis, Bruno Fischer, William Campbell Gault, and Harold Q. Masur. In all, approximately 220 paperbacks appeared during the first 15 years of the company's existence, and it continued publishing until 1968 or 1969.

Williams has grouped his publications by the T. V. Boardman series in which they appeared. Each entry includes the book's series, its author, title, date of publication, pagination, printer, and cover artist. An alphabetical code (C for crime, R for romance, W for western, etc.) indicates the book's genre. A cumulative author index concludes the checklist.

The checklist appears to have been reproduced from word-processed copy. It lacks a title index and an index for cover artists, but it is nevertheless the only record of this publisher's output.

BROWN, WATSON

268.   Holland, Stephen. **Brown, Watson 1945–1957.** British Paperback Checklists, no. 28. Scunthorpe, England: Richard Williams, n.d. 8 p. Stapled sheets.

The firm of Brown, Watson, Limited, published Digit Books (q.v.) and currently survives as Brown, Watson (Leicester), publishing only children's books. From 1945 until 1957 it published more than 260 paperback books, the majority of which was westerns, although a percentage was crime and mystery. Among the authors published by Brown, Watson were G. D. H. Cole, Bruno Fischer, Sam Merwin, and Walter Standish.

Holland's checklist is an author index to the Brown, Watson publications. Each entry provides the volume's title, date of publication, pagination, and printer. The cover artist is noted when available, and an alphabetical code (B for battle, Bf for foreign legion, C for crime, etc.) concludes each entry.

As with the other bibliographies in this series, this appears to have been reproduced from typescript rather than word-processed copy, and it is typographically cramped and unattractive. It contains neither title index nor cover artist index. It is, however, the only separately published record of this publisher's output.

CHELSEA HOUSE

269.   Huber, Gordon W. **Chelsea House/Street and Smith: A Bibliography.** Cuyahoga Falls, Ohio: [Gordon W. Huber], 2001. Different paginations. Spiral bound.

Between 1921 and 1937 Chelsea House published 414 books, almost all reprinting serials that had appeared in Street and Smith magazines but that had not previously appeared in book form. (There were two exceptions, both published in 1925: Laura Alston Brown's *The Book of Etiquette* and Georgette MacMillan's *The Marvel Cook Book*.) Although the material published in the western and adventure series frequently contained crimes and mysteries, some 90 volumes were marketed as mystery and detective fiction.

The first section of Huber's gratifyingly thorough bibliography describes the Chelsea House $1.00 to $2.00 novels; the second, the Chelsea House 75¢ novels. In both sections, subsections list the books by number and publication date sequence, by author and type sequence, and by title and magazine source sequence.

The entries in these first two sections concentrate on the book at a monographic level. The third section, however, cumulates the contents of the first two sections and puts all the names into one alphabetical sequence. The exact publication date is given (mm/dd/year), followed by the name of the serializing periodical. Dates of serialization are given, as are title changes (if any). The sequence number is listed, as are the story type (i.e., western, love, adventure, and detective). When such can be provided, the dust jacket artist is named.

Concluding sections list the pen names and real names of Chelsea House authors and provide a summation of the annual output.

This bibliography was self-published and can be somewhat difficult to obtain, but Huber's thoroughness warrants the extra effort.

CHERRY TREE BOOKS

270. Williams, Richard. **Cherry Tree Books 1937–1953.** British Paperback Check-lists, no. 35. Scunthorpe, England: Dragonby Press, 1987. 12 p. Index. Stapled sheets.

In the 16 years of its existence, Cherry Tree Books published slightly more than 400 paperback books, a sizable percentage of which was crime and mystery. Among the authors to appear under the Cherry Tree imprint were Herbert Adams, John G. Brandon, Leo Bruce, J. S. Fletcher, Craig Rice, Arthur Somers Roche, and Edgar Wallace. The majority of these publications was reprints.

Williams has arranged his checklist by the order in which the volumes were issued. Each entry provides the book's series number, its author, its title (indicating previous title when such existed), its publication date, its pagination, its printer, and whether the rear cover provides a list or an advertisement. An alphabetical code (BN for war nonfiction, C for crime fiction, F for fiction, etc.) indicates the book's genre, and an author index that identifies pseudonyms (when known) concludes the checklist.

The checklist appears to have been reproduced from word-processed copy. It lacks a title index and is typographically cramped, although the copy is legible. This appears to be the only separately issued record of this publisher's output.

COLLINS CRIME CLUB

271. Foord, Peter, and Richard Williams. **Collins Crime Club: A Checklist of the First Editions, with a Guide to Their Value, by Ralph Spurrier.** Dragonby Bibliographies, no. 1. Scunthorpe, England: Dragonby Press, 1987. 40 p. Paperback. 500 copies printed.

The Collins Crime Club began in 1930 and by the end of 1986 had published approximately 1,700 books by authors as varied as "Anthony Abbott," Agatha Christie, Jonathan Gash, Reginald Hill, Ngaio Marsh, Ellis Peters, and Julian Symons. *Collins Crime Club,* which lists the books published under this imprint, appears to have been reproduced from reduced laser-printed copy. It also appears to have been the work of people intent upon supplying as much information as possible but uncertain as to the way in which they should provide it and unfamiliar in the compilation of bibliographies.

The volume begins with an introduction explaining the book's organizational principles. The checklist is arranged alphabetically by the name under which the book was published, with this name given in boldface. On the same line are listed the number of books appearing under that byline in the Collins Crime Club and the approximate number of books that were published under that byline. If a pseudonym was employed, the author's real name is given in italics. Beneath each name are listed the books that appeared under that byline; they are listed chronologically by the official publication date, which is given. All titles are capitalized, and all citations include the book's pagination and its publication price; changes in title and whether the book appeared first in the United States are indicated, and recent titles provide a truncated version of the ISBN. Each entry concludes with Spurrier's selling price for that volume.

Apart from Spurrier's now-dated prices, *Collins Crime Club* contains much that is unobtainable elsewhere. It does not, however, include any cross-references; users of the bibliography must know in advance that Edith Caroline Rivett used the pseudonyms Carol Carnac and E. C. R. Lorac and that Phoebe Atwood Taylor wrote as Alice Tilton. In addition, the work lacks a title index and provides no information on dust wrapper artists. These shortcomings aside, it remains the only comprehensive attempt at documenting this important series.

COLLINS DETECTIVE STORY CLUB

272. Williams, Richard. **Detective Story Club (Collins).** British Hardback Checklists, no. 4. Scunthorpe, England: Dragonby Press, 2000. 4 leaves. Index. Stapled sheets. ISBN 1-87122-17-1.

The 74 volumes in the Detective Story Club were published from 1929 until 1934. With the exception of the first volume in the series—Edgar Wallace's *The Terror*—and two titles connected with British motion pictures, the entire series reprinted earlier works; one can find such authors as William Harrison Ainsworth, Frank Froest, Anna Katharine Green, Fergus Hume, and Robert Louis Stevenson—as well as three titles by Agatha Christie—offered as part of the Detective Story Club.

Williams's bibliography has two sections. The first lists the books in series order. The author's name is given (last name and first name) followed by the title in capital letters, the month and year of publication, the initial cost, the dust wrapper artist (when known), and a reasonable contemporary price. The second section indexes these works by author. The bibliography lacks indexes for title and artist but will be useful to collectors of this series.

COLLINS WHITE CIRCLE

273. Williams, Richard. **Collins White Circle Books 1936–1959.** 3rd ed. British Paperback Checklists, no. 1. Scunthorpe, England: Dragonby Press, 1995. 24 p. Index. Stapled sheets.

The Collins White Circle paperback books were published from April 1936 until September 1959. In all, approximately 720 books appeared under this imprint. Although Collins White Circle published westerns, romance novels, nonfiction, and newsbooks, nearly 500 of its paperbacks were crime or mystery. The Collins White Circle paperbacks distinguished their different series by color: the nearly 200 paperbacks appearing in the Crime Club series were green, whereas the nearly 200 volumes appearing in the Mystery series were mauve. Among the crime and mystery authors to appear in the White Circle Paperbacks were Anthony Abbott, Peter Cheyney, Agatha Christie, Mignon Eberhart, Elizabeth Ferrars, Sydney Horler, Hammond Innes, Philip Macdonald,

Hugh Pendexter, Rex Stout, and Edgar Wallace. So far as is known, all of these paperbacks had prior publication, often by the Collins Crime Club (q.v.).

Like the other bibliographies in the Dragonby Press's series devoted to British paperbacks, this publication consists of stapled sheets. After a brief introduction containing statistical information about the press, the bibliography begins by arranging the paperbacks into the series in which they appeared, then listing the volumes by series number. Each entry provides the author's name, identifying pseudonyms when possible. The title is provided, with previous and additional titles noted. The date of publication is given, as are the pagination, the printer, and the price. The paperbacks having dust wrappers are identified; cover artists are noted, as are the existence of advertisements on the rear cover. An author index concludes the bibliography.

The bibliography lacks indexes for title and artist, but it nevertheless succeeds admirably in recording this significant British paperback series. *Note:* The prior editions of this publication have not been seen.

CORGI

274.   Williams, Richard. **Corgi and Scottie Books 1951–1960.** British Paperback Checklists, no. 26. Scunthorpe, England: Richard Williams, 1986. 30 p. Index. Stapled sheets.

Until it published the British paperback edition of Vladimir Nabokov's *Lolita* in 1961, the publishing house of Corgi had not been terribly successful, for its competitors for British paperback rights were the well-established firms of Penguin and Pan. Nevertheless, in the years prior to 1960, Corgi—a subsidiary of the American publishing house of Bantam Books—provided the English paperback editions of crime and mystery books by such notable authors as Leigh Brackett, Fredric Brown, John Dickson Carr, and Erle Stanley Gardner.

Williams's bibliography begins by listing the books in the various series appearing under the Corgi imprint: the Corgi Main series, the Corgi Bantam series, the Corgi Pennant series, the Scottie series, and the Scottie Special series. Each entry provides the series number, author's name (identifying the pseudonym when known), title (indicating whether the volume appeared under a previous title), first edition status, publication date, pagination date, and printer. Cover artists are noted, and an alphabetical code (B for battle fiction; BN for battle nonfiction; Bio for biography; C for crime fiction, etc.) indicates the genre in which the book was marketed. An author index concludes the bibliography.

Like the other bibliographies in this most useful series, this appears to have been reproduced from typed rather than word-processed copy. It is cramped and typographically unattractive, and it lacks an index for titles and cover artists. It is, however, apparently the only separately published index to this significant publisher's output.

CURTIS WARREN/GRANT HUGHES

275.   Holland, Stephen. **Curtis Warren and Grant Hughes.** British Paperback Checklists, no. 21. Scunthorpe, England: Richard Williams, n.d. 16 p. Stapled sheets.

The publishing firm of Curtis Warren—which ended its days as the publishing firm of Grant Hughes—was one of the many paperback publishers that flourished briefly in postwar England. During the eight years of its existence (1946–1954), it published just over 500 books, more than 100 of which were crime stories. Like many other paperback publishers documented in this series, its line was written primarily by a small number of hacks. Among these were William Henry, Fleming Bird, Brian Holloway, Dennis Hughes, Norman Lazenby, and John Russell Fearn.

Holland's index is arranged alphabetically by the author's name; when possible, he reveals pseudonyms. Each entry provides the book's title, copyright date (if such is given in the book), price, and total pagination. When known, the printer is listed, as is the cover artist; and the book's genre is indicated by a letter or letters (i.e., A for adventure, B for boxing, C for crime, and so forth).

As with the majority of the British paperbacks published during this time, the history of the publishing firm is probably more interesting than the books that were published. This aside, this bibliography is typographically cramped and unattractive; it appears to have been reproduced from typescript rather than word-processed copy. There is no index to titles or cover artists. On the other hand, this appears to be the only separately published record of the output of this publisher.

DELL

276.   Cox, J. Randolph. **The Dell Great Mystery Library.**

Available as part of the archives maintained by the DorothyL listserv. To obtain: send an e-mail message to listserv@listserv.kent.edu; type "get dell" in the subject line. Cox has compiled a list of the 29 Dell Great Mystery books published between 1957 and 1960, prefacing his discussion with a clear explanation of the differences between first and later printings and a description of the editorial board responsible for selection of titles. The list arranges the books in order of their publication and provides author and title indexes. Much more information on the Dell Great Mystery Library is available in the catalogue-index to Dell Paperbacks compiled by William Lyles (q.v.), but it is accessible through the catalogue-index only with the greatest of difficulty, for the Dell Great Mystery Library was a subseries, and Lyles does not separately index it.

277.   Lyles, William H. **Dell Paperbacks 1942 to Mid-1962: A Catalog-Index.** Westport, Conn.: Greenwood, 1983. xxxv, 471 p. Indexes. Cloth. LC 82-25505. ISBN 0-313-23668-2.

A sizable percentage of Dell Publishing's paperbacks published between 1943 and mid-1962—971 of 2,168 books—was mysteries, and in any given year between 1943 and mid-1962, the Dell Publishing Company published more mysteries than it did westerns, romances, science fiction and fantasy, and nonfiction and humor titles. Crime and mystery fiction was Dell's mainstay; the first Dell paperback was Phillip Ketchum's *Death in the Library,* and George Harmon Coxe's *Four Frightened Women* was the first of the enormously popular Dell "map back" series (paperbacks whose back covers provided a map or architectural re-creation of the crime scene).

Dell Paperbacks 1942 to Mid-1962 is an extraordinarily comprehensive and thorough catalogue-index to the paperbacks published by the Dell Publishing Company during this time span. The volume begins with a series of statistical tables surveying the Dell paperbacks followed by a brief but informative history of the Dell Publishing Company and a lengthy explanation of how to use the catalogue-index and what to expect from it. The catalogue-index is broadly arranged by Dell series, with separate sections listing the Dell reprints, Dell first editions, Dell Laurel editions, and the volumes that were not part of these series: the Dell Visual Books, the Dell Special Student Editions, and the Dell Digest-Sized books. Each series is further divided by Dell's series letter and the accompanying changes in cover price.

Each entry provides the paperback's issue number and its author, title, subtitle, and pagination. Also given are the front and back cover artist, cover blurbs, printing date, publication date (when it differed from the printing date), print run, and number of books that were sent to Canada. Reprints are listed chronologically, each entry including printing date, publication date, and print run. Abridgments are noted, changes in title are provided, ghost writers and ghost editors are identified, and the "head-of-title" notes contained in the Dell paperbacks published prior to 1952 are included. Concluding the volume are indexes for authors, anonymous titles, book subjects, cover artists, maps, special series, the advance blurbs featured on the Dell first editions, and the motion picture, television, and play "tie-ins." So detailed are these latter indexes that they list the actors and actresses featured in the motion picture, television, and play tie-ins.

Dell Paperbacks 1942 to Mid-1962 is reproduced from what appears to be reduced laser-printed copy. Its bibliographical data are frequently cramped, and the uninitiated must make constant reference to the explanatory section at the beginning of the book. Physical flaws aside, the book is by any standard a monumental achievement, an example of what a dedicated and scholarly researcher can do. It has a companion volume, *Putting Dell on the Map: A History of the Dell Paperbacks* (also 1983). Both volumes belong in all academic libraries.

DETECTIVE-CLUB

278.   Baudou, Jacques, and Jean Jacques Schleret. **Les Metamorphoses de la Chouette.** Paris: Futuropolis, 1986. 192 p. Indexes. Paperback. ISBN 2-7376-5488-2.

Although French publications are generally beyond the scope of this work, one would be remiss not to mention this annotated bibliography of the Detective-Club, whose logo, an owl, was the *Chouette* of the title. The majority of the writers published by the Detective-Club was English and American, and the first section of this volume consists of bio-bibliographical data on them. Each entry begins with a sometimes lengthy biography of the writer, followed by a description of the works that were published in the Detective-Club series. The series number is given, as are the French title, the original English title (and significant retitlings); the name of the translator is also provided, as are data on reprintings. Following this, the work is annotated; Baudou and Schleret are careful not to reveal solutions. Successive (and significantly briefer) sections provide lists of the Detective-Club books in series order, information on additional publications and series published under the *chouette* logo. The volume concludes with a filmography providing data on the *chouette* publications that were filmed.

DIGIT BOOKS

279.   Holland, Stephen, and Richard Williams. **Digit Books 1956–1966.** British Paperback Checklists, no. 27. Scunthorpe, England: Richard Williams, 1986. 28 p. Index. Stapled sheets.

Digit Books was not a separate publishing firm but, rather, a series published by Brown, Watson, Limited (q.v.), a company that still exists as Brown, Watson (Leicester), although it is currently a publisher of children's books. Until 1966, when Brown, Watson discontinued Digit Books, the series published crime and mystery fiction by authors including Michael Avallone, Gil Brewer, "Nick Carter," and Edgar Wallace.

Because Digit Books initially published books in an unnumbered series, Holland and Williams's bibliography begins with an alphabetical listing of these volumes. Each entry includes the author, identifying pseudonym when known, the title, the price on the book, and the month and year in which the book was published. An alphabetical code (B for battle, C for crime, E for esoteric, etc.) indicates the book's genre. Printer and cover artist are identified when possible.

The next section lists the books by the Digit series in which they appeared. The information provided is the same as the preceding, with the addition of the Digit series number. An author index concludes the checklist.

As with the other bibliographies in this series, this appears to have been reproduced from typescript rather than word-processed copy. It is typographically cramped and unattractive. It is, however, the only separately published record of this publisher's output.

DOUBLEDAY CRIME CLUB

280.   Nehr, Ellen. **Doubleday Crime Club Compendium 1928–1991.** Martinez, Calif.: Offspring Press, 1992. xxi, 682 p. Index. ISBN 0-9634420-0-7.

During its 62 years, the Doubleday Crime Club published more than 2,000 crime and mystery volumes by authors as diverse as Margery Allingham, Isaac Asimov, George Bagby, H. C. Bailey, Anthony Berkeley, Leslie Charteris, Doris Miles Disney, E. X. Ferrars, Frank L. Packard, Ruth Rendell, Georges Simenon, Arthur Upfield, and Edgar Wallace. In addition, during the early 1930s, the *Crime Club Radio Show* offered radio dramatizations and adaptations of the volumes being published by the Doubleday Crime Club.

Doubleday Crime Club Compendium is a year-by-year listing of the books published by the Doubleday Crime Club. Within each year, the titles are listed alphabetically by author's last name. Nehr prefaces each year's entries with a description of the significant Doubleday Crime Club events of that year; taken cumulatively, they present a reasonably detailed history of the series. Following her history are the citations, each of which provides (at the very least) the author's name in boldface, title of the book, name of its series or lead characters, setting, pagination, and a broad subject description (i.e., "murder of a playboy," "illegal sale of liquor during Prohibition," "werewolf in swamps—or *is* it a werewolf? Locked Room," "army life pre-World War II"). Reprint editions are documented in a note that also lists changes in titles and the form of the author's name. When the dust wrapper and the original binding have been available, Nehr describes the binding's salient features and reprints the dust wrapper's complete blurb. (A doubtless unanticipated result of the latter is that the *Compendium*'s user is intrigued, teased—and all too often frustrated.) Also included, as an unpaginated slick-paper insert, are 24 pages of color reproductions of the more interesting Crime Club dust wrappers. Concluding the volume is a list of the *Crime Club Radio Programs.*

Doubleday Crime Club Compendium contains so much that is unavailable else-where and is so obviously a labor of love that it is almost ungrateful to complain about its shortcomings. Nevertheless, although there is a well-done author index, there are no indexes for titles, series characters, settings, or dust wrapper artists. Given Nehr's thoroughness in mentioning these in the body of the volume, it seems probable that the publisher decided to save money by omitting these indexes, a shortsighted and mercenary decision. One hopes for a second edition that includes these features.

FOUR SQUARE BOOKS

281.   Williams, Richard. **Four Square Books 1–322 (1957–1960).** British Paperback Checklists, no. 39. Scunthorpe, England: Dragonby Press, 1993. 12 p. Index. Stapled sheets.

Although it was a reprint house and never a major publisher of crime and mystery books, the authors appearing under the imprint of Four Square Books included Dorothy L. Sayers and Georges Simenon. Williams's checklist lists the books by their series number. Each entry provides the author, title (indicating previous title when applicable), publication date, pagination, printer, and cover artist. An alphabetical code (C for crime fiction, F for fiction, N for nonfiction, etc.) indicates the book's genre, and an author index concludes the checklist.

The checklist lacks a title index and an index for cover artists, and like the other checklists in this series, appears to have been reproduced from word-processed copy. It is the only record of this publisher's output.

GOLLANCZ

282.   Williams, Richard, and Ralph Spurrier. **Gollancz Crime Fiction 1928–1988, a Checklist of the First Editions, with a Guide to Their Value.** Dragonby Bibliographies, no. 4. Scunthorpe, England: Dragonby Press, 1989. 42 p. Paperback. ISBN 1-871122-04-X. 400 copies printed.

Victor Gollancz began publishing detective and mystery fiction in 1928, categorizing its books as "Detective Stories and Thrillers." By the end of 1988, nearly 1,300 such volumes had appeared, and the categorization had changed to "Thrillers and Crime." The authors appearing under the Gollancz imprint included Joan Aiken, H. C. Bailey, "Tucker Coe" (Donald Westlake), Edmund Crispin, Amanda Cross, Ellery Queen, Dorothy L. Sayers, Dell Shannon, Hillary Waugh, and Charles Willeford. Like the previous volumes in this series, *Gollancz Crime Fiction* appears to have been reproduced from reduced laser-printed copy and to have been the work of people intent upon giving as much information as possible but uncertain as to the way in which they should provide it and unfamiliar in the compilation of bibliographies.

The volume begins with an introduction explaining the book's organizational principles, and a two-page foreword by Spurrier provides a brief history of Gollancz. The checklist is arranged alphabetically by the name under which the book was published, with this name given in boldface type. On the same line are listed the number of books published under that byline by Gollancz and the estimated total number of books published in Great Britain under that byline. If a pseudonym was employed, the real name is given in italics. Beneath each name are listed the books that appeared under that byline; they are listed chronologically by the official publication date, which is given. All titles are capitalized, and all citations include the book's pagination and its publication price. Changes in title and whether the book appeared first in the United States are indicated, and recent titles provide a truncated version of the ISBN. Each entry concludes with Spurrier's selling price for that volume.

The references to the values are out-of-date, but *Gollancz Crime Fiction* contains much that is unobtainable elsewhere. It does not, however, include any cross-references, and it lacks a title index. It nevertheless remains the only comprehensive attempt at documenting the output of this important publisher.

GRAMOL GROUP

283. Holland, Stephen, and Richard Williams. **The Gramol Group 1932–1937.** British Paperback Checklists, no. 44. Scunthorpe, England: Dragonby Press, 1990. 20 p. Index. Stapled sheets.

One of the first British publishers of paperbacks, the Gramol Group appears to have been started by Arthur Gray and F. A. Mowl in 1927. Although the Gramol Group initially published a numbered series of "sexy" books, in 1931 it began to publish a series of thriller novels; in 1933, it expanded its line to include the Gramol Mystery Novels. By the time it went out of business in 1937, approximately a sixth of the Gramol Group's roughly 600 paperbacks were crime and mystery novels.

Holland and Williams have arranged their bibliography by the name of the Gramol series, although the names are listed neither alphabetically nor chronologically. Each entry provides the book's series number, author, title, date of publication, and pagination. Cover artists are listed when available. The checklist concludes with a cumulative author index and a separate index of the anonymously published books.

In addition to lacking a title index and an index for artists, the checklist is confusingly arranged, and its title is belied by the inclusion of data from years prior to 1932. Like other checklists in this series, it appears to have been reproduced from word-processed copies. It is the only record of this publisher's output.

HAMILTON AND PANTHER

284. Holland, Stephen, and Richard Williams. **Hamilton and Panther Books 1945–1956.** British Paperback Checklists, no. 31. Scunthorpe, England: Dragonby Press, 1987. 18 p. Index. Stapled sheets.

In the 11 years of its existence, Hamilton and Panther published slightly more than 500 paperbacks, about a fifth of which were crime and mystery. The majority of these books was published under such house names as Jeff Bogar, Ross Carni, and Duff Johnson.

Holland and Williams have divided their checklist into two sections. The first is an author list of the titles appearing under the Hamilton imprint, and the second is an author list of the titles appearing under the Panther imprint. Each entry provides the series number, the title of the book (indicating simultaneous hardback publication and an original title if such existed), date of publication, pagination, printer, cover artist, and price. An alphabetical code (B for battle, C for crime, E for erotic, etc.) indicates the book's genre. A cumulative author index that identifies known pseudonyms concludes the index.

As are many of the later publications in this series, this checklist appears to have been reproduced from word-processed copy and is rather clear. It lacks indexes for title and cover artist, but it is nevertheless the only separately issued record of this publisher's output.

HODDER AND STOUGHTON

285.   Williams, Richard. **Hodder and Stoughton 1926–1960.** Rev. ed. British Paperback Checklists, no. 6. Scunthorpe, England: Dragonby Press, 1990. 22 p. Index. Stapled sheets.

Between 1926 and 1960, Hodder and Stoughton published approximately 600 paperbacks, all except a few appearing in two major series: the ninepenny Yellow Jackets and the postwar two-shilling Yellow Jackets, which later were renamed Hodder Pocket Books. A sizable percentage of these publications was crime fiction, and the authors published included Francis Beeding, Leslie Charteris, Gerard Fairlie, J. S. Fletcher, Sydney Horler, William Le Queux, E. Phillips Oppenheim, the Baroness Orczy, and Edgar Wallace.

Like the other separately published bibliographies in Dragonby Press's series devoted to British paperbacks, *Hodder and Stoughton 1926–1960* consists of stapled-together sheets. After a brief introduction, the bibliography begins with an author index to the Hodder and Stoughton ninepenny Yellow Jackets; the titles are listed alphabetically beneath the author. In parentheses beside each title is the month and year of publication. Author lists of the books appearing in the short-lived Hodder and Stoughton New at Ninepence and the Crown Octavo series occur next; in their content, they duplicate the earlier section, although pagination of the books is occasionally given.

The following sections list the volumes appearing in Hodder and Stoughton's Two-Shilling Yellow Jackets and the Hodder Pocket Books. These volumes, however, are listed by their series, each entry providing author's name, title, month and year of publication, pagination, printer, price, and cover artist; a "valuation" is given for many of the later volumes. An author index to these sections concludes the publication.

The bibliography lacks index to title and cover artists, and as the preceding description implies, its arrangement can be frustrating. It nevertheless succeeds in documenting the paperbacks published by Hodder and Stoughton, and collectors and libraries will need it. *Note:* The first edition has not been seen.

HUTCHINSON GROUP

286.   Williams, Richard. **Hutchinson Group Post-War Numbered Series, later Arrow Books 1949–1960.** British Paperback Checklists, no. 38. Scunthorpe, England: Dragonby Press, 1988. 18 p. Index. Stapled sheets.

Before becoming Arrow Books in 1953, the Hutchinson Group included the publishers of Hurst and Blackett, Hutchinson, Jarrolds, Leisure Library, John Long, Melrose, Stanley Paul, Rich and Cowan, and Skeffington. Frequently, these publishers had their own series devoted to racing, romance, and westerns, and a sizable percentage of the books published by the Hutchinson Group was crime and detective fiction. Among the authors appearing under the Hutchinson Group's/Arrow Books imprint were James Hadley Chase, John Creasey, Brett Halliday, F. Van Wyck Mason, and Edgar Wallace.

In attempting to list the Hutchinson Group, Williams had a daunting task, for numbering was not used for the first three years of the imprint and was highly erratic when it was instituted; some books were reissued with lower numbers than the original. Nevertheless, his bibliography is arranged in series number, when such exists. Each entry includes the author's name, the title (identifying previous titles when such exist), the publication date, the pagination, the printer, and the publisher. A cumulative author index that identifies known pseudonyms concludes the checklist.

The checklist lacks a title index and the genre code used in so many of the other checklists in this series. Like these other checklists, this one appears to have been reproduced from word-processed copy. It is nevertheless the only record of this publisher's output.

LION BOOKS

287.   Stephens, Christopher P. **Lion Books and the Lion Library: A Checklist.** Hastings-on-Hudson, N.Y.: Ultramarine Publishing, 1991. 62 p. Paperback. ISBN 0-89366-173-2.

Between 1949 and 1957, some 402 paperbacks appeared under the imprints of Lion Books, the Lion Library, and Red Circle Books. Relatively few of these books were detective and mystery stories, but the authors with early work published by these imprints included David Goodis, Harold Q. Masur, and Jim Thompson, and one would be remiss to ignore this publisher and this publication.

The checklist begins with a numerical list of the publications of Lion Books and the Lion Library. It lists the book's series number, author's name, and book's title. The second section uses this format to list the few publications of Red Circle Books.

The majority of the checklist consists of a cumulative alphabetical list of the books appearing under the three imprints. Each citation gives the author's last name in capital letters, underlines the title, and lists the book's series number, publication year, cover price, and pagination. A note indicates the book's content (western, mystery, a novel, humor, etc.) and the name of the cover artist. When the book was a reprint, the original publication data are provided. The publishers of Lion Books and the Lion Library obviously wished to appeal to an audience interested in sex and sensationalism, and whenever possible, they changed the titles on their reprints, making them more risqué: Ralph Ingersoll's *Wine of Violence* became *The Naked and the Guilty;* Anthony Scott's *Mardi Gras Madness* became *Carnival of Love;* Victor Wolfson's *The Lonely Steeple* became *The Passionate Season;* and so forth.

Stephens's checklist would have benefited from the addition of indexes to titles and illustrators, but his is the only separate publication on its subject. It should be noted that the publications of Lion Books, Lion Library, and Red Circle Books have been indexed in Robert Reginald and M. R. Burgess's *Cumulative Paperback Index, 1939–1959,* which also includes a title index, but Reginald and Burgess unfortunately do not provide a checklist of books by publisher, nor do they include data on content, title changes, and reprints. Collectors of early paperbacks should have both books; specialists will be satisfied with Stephens's work.

R & L LOCKER/HARBOROUGH
PUBLISHING/ARCHER PRESS

288.   Holland, Stephen. **R. & L. Locker/Harborough Publishing Co. Ltd./Archer Press (1944–1954).** British Paperback Checklists, no. 29. Scunthorpe, England: Richard Williams, n.d. 10 p. Stapled sheets.

The British paperback publisher R. and L. Locker was established in 1944 by Raymond and Lilian Locker. In 1948, the Lockers acquired the Harborough Publishing Co., Ltd.; also in 1948, the Lockers established the Archer Press. From 1944 to 1954, the three presses published nearly 300 books, the majority of which were soft-core erotica but approximately 17 percent of which were crime and mysteries. Only Harborough Publishing survived, starting publication (in 1957) of Ace Books.

Holland's checklist is an author index to the volumes issued by Locker, Harborough, and Archer. Each entry provides the volume's title, date of publication, pagination, printer, and cover price. The cover artist is noted when available, and an alphabetical code (C for crime, E for esoteric, R for romance, etc.) concludes each entry.

As with the other bibliographies in this series, this appears to have been reproduced from typescript rather than word-processed copy, and it is typographically cramped and unattractive. It contains neither a title index nor a cover artist index. It is, however, the only separately published record of this publisher's output.

DENNIS McMILLAN

289.   Stephens, Christopher P. **A Checklist of the Publications of Dennis McMillan.** Hastings-on-Hudson, N.Y.: Ultramarine Publishing, 1992. 19 p. Index. Paperback. ISBN 0-89366-202-X.

Dennis McMillan is a specialty publisher, perhaps best known for his multivolume reprinting of the works of Fredric Brown. He began publishing in 1983 with the original publication of Brian Hodel's *The Brazilian Guitar* and reprints of Arthur Upfield's *The House of Cain* and Philip Josè Farmer's *Love Song*. This bibliography of McMillan's publications was reproduced from laser-printed copy. The arrangement is chronological, concluding its coverage with the 1991 publication of Brown's *The Gibbering Night* and *The Pickled Punks*. The author's last name is given in capital letters, the title is underlined, and the number of copies and pagination are listed, as are data on original publications and the names of the writers of introductions. An index to the titles concludes the pamphlet.

The contents of McMillan's publications and a history of the press can be found in the third edition of *The Science-Fantasy Publishers: A Critical and Bibliographic History* by Jack L. Chalker and Mark Owings (Westminster, Md.: Mirage Press, 1991), and additional publications are listed on Chalker's elaborate Web site (www.miragepress.com). Collectors of McMillan's publications will probably be satisfied with Stephens's inexpensive checklist, but McMillan has continued to produce excellent work, and an updated bibliography is needed.

MODERN FICTION

290. Holland, Stephen. **Modern Fiction 1945–1958.** British Paperback Checklists, no. 20. Scunthorpe, England: R. A. H. Williams, n.d. 8 p. Stapled sheets.

Although a few of its titles might have been reprints, Modern Fiction Limited published primarily original paperbacks written by a variety of generally pseudonymous authors. Among the writers known to have contributed to this series are Raymond Buxton, Frank Dubrez Fawcett, Ernest L. McKeag, and Alistair Paterson. The names under which these authors contributed American Gangster books included "Griff" (underworld slang for an informant or a newspaper reporter), Hava Gordon, Spike Gordon, Don Rogan, and Ben Sarto. The ownership rights to this last pseudonym were the subject of a lawsuit between Modern Fiction and Fawcett, and although Fawcett won, Modern Fiction continued to issue books under the Sarto name, probably paying Fawcett.

Holland has compiled an author index to the paperbacks appearing under the Modern Fiction imprint. When possible, pseudonyms are revealed. Titles and pagination are provided, as are data on original publication. The cost of the book is given, as are the month and year of publication. The printer is frequently identified.

Although Holland's introduction does not say so, it seems probable that the history of the Modern Fiction company is substantially more interesting than the books it published. In any event, the bibliography lacks a title index and is typographically cramped, appearing to have been reproduced from typescript rather than word-processed copy. It is nevertheless the only record of this publisher; and fly-by-night though it was, Modern Fiction nevertheless lasted nearly 13 years.

MYSTERY BOOK CLUBS

291a. Described in **Mystery, Detective, and Espionage Magazines,** ed. by Michael L. Cook (Westport, Conn.: Greenwood, 1983), pp. 677–85.

291b. Cook, Michael L. **Murder by Mail: Inside the Mystery Book Clubs—With Complete Checklist.** Evansville, Ind.: Cook, 1979. 109 p. Index. LC 79-106640. 25 hardbound copies, the rest paperbound.

291c. Cook, Michael L. **Murder by Mail: Inside the Mystery Book Clubs with Complete Checklist.** Revised, expanded, and updated edition. Bowling Green, Ohio: Bowling Green University Popular Press, 1983. viii, 222 p. Index. LC 83-82013. ISBN 0-87972-265-7 (hc); 0-87972-264-9 (pb).

The self-published first edition of this checklist lists the publications of the three most important mystery book clubs, the Detective Book Club, the Mystery Guild, and the Unicorn Mystery Book Club. A brief history of each book club is provided, and the publications of each club are listed chronologically, concluding with material published in early 1979. Titles are listed in capital letters, and regular type is used for all other information. An intriguing point of this checklist is that Cook's citations are not uniform in appearance and content; each section presents different data. The entries for the Detective Book Club are separately numbered and present their information in three columns: the first column lists the date of publication; the second, book titles; and the third, authors' names. The citations for the Mystery Guild are divided into years and use six columns. The first column lists the month of release by the club; the second, title; the third, author; the fourth, original publisher; the fifth, original date of publication; and the sixth, price of the original publication. The Unicorn Mystery Book Club's data are also grouped by years but present data in four columns. The first lists the month of publication and number of the book in order of its appearance; the second, title; the third, author; and the fourth, original publisher. An author index concludes the volume.

The second edition documents the publications of the three clubs described previously and adds data on the publications of Ellery Queen's Mystery Club, the Masterpieces of Mystery Library, the Mystery Library, and the Raven House Mystery Book Club. As before, Cook provides a brief history of each book club and lists its publications chronologically; in this volume, the citations extend well into 1983. Also as before, the content of Cook's citations differs from club to club. The entries for Ellery Queen's Mystery Club, the Masterpieces of Mystery Library, and the Raven House Mystery Book Club merely list the book titles and authors, whereas the contents of the 12 books published in the Mystery Library are completely described, with Cook including the names of the editors, bibliographers, illustrators; descriptions of maps and essays that were included; obituary notices; and information on the book's first edition. Because the second edition of this checklist is substantially smaller than its predecessor, Cook abandoned his use of columns and listed his bibliographic data beneath the titles of the books. This change is not necessarily an improvement, for it frequently makes information harder to locate. New to this volume is a list of the current addresses of the two extant mystery/detective book clubs. The book concludes with an author index.

Researchers and collectors will want this checklist, but it is very specialized.

PAN BOOKS

292.   Williams, Richard. **Pan Books 1945–1966. A Bibliographical Checklist with a Guide to Their Value.** Dragonby Bibliographies, no. 6. Scunthorpe, England: Dragonby Press, 1990. 72 p. Index. Paperback. ISBN 1-871122-06-6. 200 copies printed.

Pan Books was registered as a corporation in 1944, published three books in 1945 and 1946, and then found its niche as a publisher of mass-market paperbacks. By the end of 1966, Pan Books had issued nearly 1,700 different titles, approximately 750 of which were mystery and detective stories. The authors appearing under the Pan Books imprint included Leslie Charteris, Peter Cheney, Agatha Christie, John Creasey, Erle Stanley Gardner, John D. MacDonald, Ellery Queen, Georges Simenon, Arthur Upfield, and Edgar Wallace.

Pan Books 1945–1966 is similar in appearance to the previous books in the Dragonby Bibliographies series, being reproduced from what appears to be reduced laser-printed copy. Its arrangement, however, differs radically. Williams arranges his bibliography by the series given previously, then lists his citations by their serial number, a largely chronological listing. Each citation provides the author, title, publication date, pagination, printer, whether a dust wrapper was used, book's price, and the cover artist. Pseudonyms are identified when they are known; changes in title are given; and differences between announced and actual publication date are recorded. Each citation concludes with a price that "a collector would pay for a Very Good copy (complete with Very Good dustwrapper where called for)," and the bibliography concludes with an author index that lists the titles, the Pan series in which they appeared, and the year of publication.

The prices listed by Williams are probably dated, but the information contained in *Pan Books 1945–1966* is largely unobtainable elsewhere. The volume lacks a title index, but it successfully documents the output of this significant British publisher.

PENGUIN BOOKS

293.   Williams, Richard, with others. **Penguin Crime Fiction 1935–1990: A Bibliographical Checklist with a Guide to Their Value.** British Paperback Checklists, no. 22; Dragonby Bibliographies, no. 5. Scunthorpe, England: Dragonby Press, 1991. 66 p. Index. Stapled sheets.

By the end of 1990 the redoubtable Penguin Books had published approximately 13,000 titles, approximately 2,000 of which were crime fiction. The authors whose detective and mystery fiction appeared under the Penguin imprint were as varied as Margery Allingham, E. C. Bentley, Anthony Berkeley, John Dickson Carr, Agatha Christie, Erle Stanley Gardner, Elmore Leonard, Oriana Papazoglou, Robert Parker, Georges Simenon, and Donald Westlake.

Although it was separately published and sold, *Penguin Crime Fiction 1935–1990* differs from the earlier bibliographies in the Dragonby Bibliographies series by being stapled-together sheets rather than a pamphlet. In its thoroughness, however, it is every bit the equal of the earlier volumes. Following an introductory key, the body of the bibliography is arranged chronologically by the Penguin Books sequence number. Each entry provides author, title, date of publication, total number of pages, and printer; also recorded are the existence of the dust wrapper, book's price, dust wrapper's color, book's format, a statement about the advertisements appearing on the rear cover (plain covers are so noted), and cover artist. Retitlings are noted, as are the names of translators, and each entry concludes with Williams's (now somewhat dated) appraisal of their value.

Successive sections provide an author/title index, an index to the cover artists, and a list of simultaneous publications by specific authors. However, no separate index to the titles is provided, and the ISBNs are not noted. These shortcomings aside, this publication belongs in academic libraries with the other volumes in the series.

PICADILLY NOVELS/FICTION HOUSE

294.   Holland, Stephen. **Piccadilly Novels.** British Paperback Checklists, no. 25. Scunthorpe, England: Richard Williams, n.d. 8 p. Stapled sheets.

The Piccadilly Novels, an English paperback series, were published by Fiction House Limited from approximately 1935 through 1950. In all, nearly 300 Piccadilly Novels were published, with two of the more notable authors being John Creasy (under the name of Margaret Cooke) and Arlton Eadie. The majority of the Piccadilly Novels was originals rather than reprints; most of them were undated.

Holland's checklist contains two sections. The first is an author index to the Piccadilly Novels. Each entry lists the title, the book's Piccadilly number, and the year in which it was published; when possible, Holland reveals pseudonyms. The second section lists the Piccadilly Novels in the order in which they appeared; each entry provides author's name, title, pagination, and probable date of publication.

The bibliography appears to have been reproduced from typed rather than word-processed copy; it is typographically cramped, unattractive, and contains neither a title index nor an index to cover artists. It is, nevertheless, apparently the only separately published record of this publisher's output, and Holland has obviously demonstrated considerable resourcefulness in obtaining the dates of publication.

SÉRIE NOIRE/GALLIMARD

295. Mesplède, Claude. **Les Années "Série Noire." Bibliographie, Critique, d'Une Collection Policière.** Vol. 1: 1945–1959; Vol. 2: 1959–1966; Vol. 3: 1966–1972; Vol. 4: 1972–1982. Amiens: Editions Encrage, 1992–1995. Index. LC 92-228124. ISBN vol. 1: 2-906389-34-X; vol. 2: 2-906389-43-9; vol. 3: 2-906389-53-6; vol. 4: 2-906389-63-3. 299 copies printed.

Publications in French are generally beyond the scope of this work, but one would be remiss not to mention this monumental bibliography of the Série Noire, a paperback series published by Gallimard that was devoted primarily to reprinting in French the works of British and American detective and mystery writers. Conceived of by mystery lover Marcel Archard in 1945, and edited by Archard's friend Marcel Duhamel, the Série Noire by 1982 contained some 1,866 books, providing the first French edition of works by authors as diverse as Raymond Chandler, Peter Cheyney, Harold Q. Masur, John D. MacDonald, Dick Francis, Ed McBain, Carter Brown, Donald E. Westlake, "K. R. Dwyer," Robert B. Parker, and Stuart Kaminsky.

Mesplède has arranged his bibliography chronologically, the first entry being the October 1945 publication of Peter Cheyney's *La Môme Vert-de-Gris [Poison Ivy];* the last entry is the April 1982 publication of Stuart Kaminsky's *Pour qui Sonne le Clap [High Midnight].* All citations are numbered and provide the author's name and French title in boldface. Immediately following these are parentheses containing the original title in small capital letters and the year of the first publication. The name of the French translator is given, and separate paragraphs provide the book's setting, year in which the action occurs, and name of the principal character. A lengthy annotation describes the action of the novel, placing it in context with other works featuring that character. Each entry concludes with separate sections providing information on later editions and reissuings of the title, data on film and theater adaptations, and a quote from the teaser on the book.

Each volume is separately indexed and contains indexes for the authors, the French titles, the original titles, the themes, the main characters, the settings, and the translators. Furthermore, each volume reproduces archival material that includes unique pictures and letters from the authors. The first volume, for example, contains letters from David Goodis and Raymond Chandler; the former describes being badly beaten while doing research on the Philadelphia waterfront, while Chandler begins in French, lapses into English, mentions the death of his wife, and states, "I have been having a rather wild time with certain lovely ladies who seem, enormously to my surprise, to be willing to be fondled. By me, why? I am neither young nor beautiful."

Future bibliographers will be thoroughly indebted to Mesplède for this splendid achievement.

SEXTON BLAKE

296. Holland, Steve. **The Case of the Perplexing Pen-Names: An Index to the 3rd and 5th Series of the Sexton Blake Library and a Guide to Their Authors, Together with an Index of the Press Editorial Syndicate Titles.** CADS Supplement, no. 3. South Benfleet, Essex, England: CADS, 1994. 58 p. Paperback. ISSN 0965-6561.

This cleanly done volume begins a history of Sexton Blake written by W. O. G. Lofts and Derek Adley and adapted from that first published in *Book and Magazine Collector 16* (June 1985). There are three following sections. The first, "The Riddle of the Perplexing Pen Names," provides a history of the problems associated with the pseudonyms used in the third and fifth series of the Sexton Blake Library.

The second section consists of the author index to the third and fifth series of the Sexton Blake Library: entries give the author's name in capital letters, followed by the author's birth and death dates (when known); the next line states whether the name is a pseudonym, after which the titles of the Sexton Blake Library are given in boldface type. Each title is followed by a bracketed series of numbers that indicates whether the work appeared in the third or fifth series, its series number, and its dates of publication. Numerous helpful cross-references are included.

The third section consists of an index to the Press Editorial Syndicate publications. These are listed by author (given in capital letters), beneath which, in alphabetical order and in boldface type, are given the publication followed by the place of publication, publisher, and date of publication. The first British and first American editions are listed for all titles, as are title changes and byline variations.

This volume and Holland's *The Sexton Blake Library (Third and Fifth Series)* (q.v.) belong together and offer excellent access to a popular series.

297. Holland, Stephen, and Richard Williams. **The Sexton Blake Library (Third and Fifth Series).** British Paperback Checklists, no. 40. Scunthorpe, England: Dragonby Press, 1988. 18 p. Index. Stapled sheets.

The enormously popular Sexton Blake first appeared in a story titled "The Missing Millionaire" that was written by Harry Blyth (under the name of Hal Meredith) and published in the 20 December 1893 issue of *The Halfpenny Marvel.* Since then, more than 200 different authors have written more than 3,500 Sexton Blake stories. The first issue of the Sexton Blake Library appeared in 1915 and ran for more than 380 issues; the second series contained more than 744 issues. The third and fifth series contained 526 and 45 titles, respectively; they were published from 1941 to 1963 and 1965 to 1968, respectively.

Holland and Williams's checklist lists the books in their series order. Each entry provides the book's series number, author, title, and date of publication; pagination is not given because the majority of the books was 64 pages in length. A cumulative author index reveals many of the pseudonyms.

One wishes that the apparently indefatigable Holland and Williams had provided a comprehensive index to the Sexton Blake series, but although aspects of the series have been discussed in numerous publications and at some length in such books as *Boys Will Be Boys,* a separately published bibliography does not seem to exist. As it is, the checklist lacks a title index but is clearly arranged and easy to use.

VIKING/WORLD DISTRIBUTORS/CONSUL

298. Holland, Stephen, and Richard Williams. **Viking/W[orld] D[istributors] L[td.]/Consul 1949–1966.** British Paperback Checklists, no. 30. Scunthorpe, England: Dragonby Press, 1987. 36 p. Indexes. Stapled sheets.

The nature of the relationship between the English paperback publishers of Viking, World Distributors, and Consul is not known, but from 1949 until 1966 the three firms published nearly 1,500 books, many of which were the reprints of works first appearing in hardcover. Among the crime and mystery writers appearing under these three imprints were "Dale Bogard," George Harmon Coxe, Erle Stanley Gardner, Brett Halliday, Evan Hunter, Sax Rohmer, and Charles Willeford.

Holland and Williams have arranged their bibliography by series, beginning with the World Distributors and continuing with Viking, although a new series listing is provided with each change of publisher's address. Each entry provides the series number; author's name (identifying pseudonyms when possible); title (listing previous titles); whether the book was a first edition, issued simultaneously in hardback, or a reissue; copyright date; pagination; printer; cover artist; and price. An alphabetical code (B for battle, C for crime, E for erotic, etc.) provides an indication of the book's genre, and a cumulative author index concludes the checklist.

In its internal arrangement, this bibliography is most frustrating, for it is impossible to determine the books published under a single imprint without a tremendous amount of work. This aside, this bibliography appears to have been reproduced from word-processed copy, and although it is typographically cramped, its data are reasonably accessible.

8

Magazine and Anthology Indexes

Scope note: Included here are checklists of, indexes to, and encyclopedic guides for mystery and detective fiction anthologies and fiction and nonfiction magazines. Monographs referencing anthologies are listed first, after which indexes to magazines are listed. Indexes to individual magazines are listed in alphabetical order by magazine name. When more than one magazine has the same name, an additional identifier—usually the publisher's name—is used to distinguish them. The words *British* and *American* next to a title are used to distinguish between British and American editions of the same magazine.

GENERAL

299. Contento, William G., and Martin H. Greenberg. **Index to Crime and Mystery Anthologies.** Boston: G. K. Hall, 1991. xvi, 736 p. Cloth. LC 90-43578. ISBN 0-8161-8629-4.

This enormous volume indexes more than 1,000 different crime and mystery anthologies published from 1875 through 1990. More than 12,500 different short stories, 3,700 novelettes, 500 novellas, 70 novels, and 300 articles by more than 3,600 different authors are accessible through this massive index. Definitions of terms and explanations of indexing procedures are provided in a helpful user guide, after which the volume contains the following sections: author list: books; title list: books; author list: stories; title list: stories; and book contents. The first brief section lists the books alphabetically by their author, editor, or (if published anonymously) their title; publisher and publication date are given, as are the Library of Congress number, ISBN, price, pagination, and binding. Cross-references are provided to coauthors, coeditors, and pseudonyms; data on changes in title and alterations in the contents of different editions also are given. In addition to listing the books by their titles, the second section includes the names of the editor or compiler and whether the book is an anthology, an original anthology, or a novel.

The third section is the core of the book, listing the contents of the anthologies alphabetically beneath author name or by title if the stories were published anonymously. The original publication data are listed beneath each story, indicated by an asterisk (*), followed by a list of the books and major genre magazines that have reprinted the story. This information includes the book's author and/or editor, publisher, and its date of publication. Coauthors and coeditors are indicated by a plus sign (+), and links to pseudonyms and notes on title changes are provided.

The concluding sections are reasonably brief. The fourth lists the contents of all the anthologies, each entry providing the work's author, its type (i.e., short story, novelette, novella, novel, or article), and original source of publication. As before, notes on title changes are provided, as is the identification of pseudonymous material. The fifth section lists the complete contents of the anthologies alphabetically by their author and/or editor, after which are given the volume's title, publisher, publication date, its Library of Congress number, ISBN, price, pagination, and binding. The author or authors, title, and original publication are given; the story's pagination is frequently provided. Notes on title changes are provided, and an asterisk (*) beside a story's title indicates that it is original to the book. Concluding the volume are a combination errata/addenda sheet that lists one error and the contents of five anthologies that arrived too late to be indexed.

The *Index* is in all respects an exemplary reference work: friendly, accessible, and containing a wealth of data. It is the definitive index to crime and mystery anthologies and belongs in all libraries. CD-ROM updates are available from the Locus Press.

300. Denton, William. **Anthology Listings.** http://www.vex.net/~buff/rara-avis/biblio/anthologies.html

This Web site lists the contents of six significant anthologies of hard-boiled fiction. The site is arranged alphabetically by editor. Titles are italicized; publisher and year of publication are given. Paginations are not provided, but the short stories are listed in the order in which they appeared in the anthology. More would be welcome.

301. Holland, Steve. **British Story Paper Encyclopedia.** Published and produced by Steve Holland, 105 Lexden Road, Colchester, Essex CO3 3RB, United Kingdom, 2002. (Version 1.1.) E-mail: steve@uworldst.demon.co.uk

The British Story Papers were not limited to mystery and detective fiction and included school stories, adventure stories, romance stories, factual publications, games, news, puzzles, and even a science fiction series (*Scoops*). Nevertheless, a reasonable percentage of the story papers was mystery and detective fiction—they included the Sexton Blake series (q.v.)—and one would be remiss not to mention Holland's impressive *British Story Paper Encyclopedia,* the only comprehensive effort at documenting and surveying a fascinating genre.

The *British Story Paper Encyclopedia* is forthright in declaring itself very much a work in progress, but even this earliest version offers a remarkable amount of data. Holland begins by providing a lengthy history of Bear Alley, the place from which many of the story papers originated. This is followed by a checklist of the publishers, a checklist of the British Story Papers, juvenile magazines and pocket libraries, a checklist of the British annuals, biographical information on the authors and artists, and a dictionary of the characters. This information is frequently very detailed: the checklist of the story papers provides the publisher, the run (with exact dates when possible), and the frequency; title changes and mergers are given, as are occasional notes about the contents of the magazine. Frequently, cross-references permit hyperlinkage between different sections. It should be stressed, however, that not all of these checklists are active: in the version being described, only the authors and artists whose last names start with *A* are documented, but at the same time, these provide a wealth of information: biographies with photographs and bibliographies of writings.

This first disk includes bonus material: some articles about the papers and those who wrote for them. According to Holland, this material will not necessarily be on each release.

One hopes that Holland will be able to finish this remarkable work. One also would be remiss not to state that this CD-ROM is probably the most affordable publication listed in this reference guide: in 2002, Holland was selling it for $10, making it a terrific bargain.

302.   Kästner, Dieter. **Bibliographie der Kriminalerzählungen, 1948–2000**. Köln: Baskerville Bücher, 2001. 627 p. Paperback. ISBN 0-930932-51.2.

One does not need to read German to recognize and appreciate Kästner's accomplishment. He has provided the German equivalent of Contento and Greenberg's index to crime and mystery anthologies (q.v.). Kästner's *Bibliographie* is more deliberately limited—it indexes only those anthologies published from 1948 to 2000—but it is otherwise very similar in structure and format.

The *Bibliographie* begins with an introduction in which Kästner explains his methodology and provides a list of the abbreviations. These are followed by the *Autorenalphabet,* which lists the author in boldface type. Titles are listed alphabetically beneath in italic type, set off with a bullet (•); the original date of publication is given. Beneath each are the German appearances of the work. Each German appearance is separately numbered; the German title is given in quotation marks. When available, the name of the translator is given, followed by (in italic type) the title of the anthology in which the story appeared and the anthology's publication date. In all, this section indexes 11,611 stories.

The second section of the *Bibliographie* (the *Anthologienverzeichnis*) is an alphabetical list of the 1,109 anthologies from which the contents of the *Autorenalphabet* were derived. Each anthology is separately numbered (A1–A1109). The title of the anthology is given in boldface italic type followed by the place of publication, publisher, and publication year. Pagination and series number are given, as are the original title and variant titles. These are followed by numbers keyed to the *Autorenalphabet* that indicate the anthology's contents.

A *Detektivregister* lists the detectives appearing in the stories, after which a comprehensive *Titelregister* concludes the volume.

It should be stressed that the *Bibliographie* does not limit itself; it lists the German publications of many English and American writers, and one can see that the Germans are fond of (or at least exposed to) quite a few names likely to be familiar to American audiences: Lilian Jackson Braun, Raymond Chandler, Agatha Christie, Michael Collins, Wilkie Collins, Roald Dahl, and Dashiell Hammett, to name but a few. Like the work of Contento and Greenberg, Kästner's *Bibliographie* is a monumental accomplishment.

303.   la Cour, Tage. **The Short Detective Story 1925–1982: A Personal Checklist.** Copenhagen: Pinkertons Antikvariat, 1983. 200 copies printed.

Not seen.

304. Mundell, E. H. **A Checklist of Detective Short Stories.** Portage, Ind.: N.p., 1968. xiv, 337 p. Indexes. Cloth. LC 68-3329.

As its title indicates, this is a checklist of the detective short stories that appeared in collections of stories and anthologies. The stories in these collections and anthologies that do not feature detectives or detection are not mentioned. In arrangement, the *Check-list* is a thoroughly idiosyncratic work; it does not use alphabetical headings and does not number its approximately 1,100 citations. The contents include "Detective Short Stories," "Detective Experiences," "Secret Service Stories," "Problems," "Addenda," indexes, and book sizes.

The section on detective short stories contains two sections, one listing single-author collections of short stories, the other listing the contents of anthologies. Each entry in the single-author collections provides the author's name in regular letters, the book's title in capital letters, and bibliographic data on the first American and English editions; a code is used to identify the volume's size. If a series detective is featured in the stories, his or her name is given, and the story titles are listed. The listings of the contents of detective story anthologies are selective; only stories not included in author collections are listed, and only the story's first appearance is noted. Furthermore, listings under an anthology's title do not indicate whether the stories are reprints. Additionally complicating this section is the arrangement of entries: anonymous titles are listed first, after which books are listed by their editor's name. Entries provide the author's last name (in italics), the title of the story, and the name of the detective.

"Detective Experiences" references English yellow backs and American dime novels whose titles indicate that they include autobiographical reminiscences. The entries in "Secret Service Stories" provide the author's name in regular letters, the book's title in capitals, and bibliographic data on the first American and British editions; a code is used to identify the volume's size. If a recurrent or series detective is featured in the stories, his or her name is given, and the story titles are listed. "Secret Service" anthologies are listed using the same system used in listing the detective story anthologies.

"Problems" lists collections of solve-it-yourself crimes; "Addenda" lists the volumes Mundell was unable to examine or those that were examined too late for inclusion. The indexes offer access by authors and detective, and the volume concludes with the key to Mundell's code for book sizes. There is no index to titles.

In many respects, this bibliography appears to be a rough draft for Mundell's later collaboration with Rausch (q.v.). Neither this volume nor its separately published supplement (which follows) are necessary for locating detective and mystery short stories.

305. Mundell, E. H. **A Checklist of Detective Short Stories: Supplement One.** Portage, Ind.: N.p., 1968. 34 p. Indexes. Cloth.

A continuation of Mundell's 1968 *A Checklist of Detective Short Stories,* this volume lists 58 titles that supplement the earlier volume. There is no table of contents, and the arrangement is as thoroughly idiosyncratic as that in the first volume. The first section lists detective and spy stories, with each entry providing the author's name in regular letters, the book's title in capital letters, and bibliographic data on the first American and English editions; a code is used to identify the volume's size. If a recurrent detective is featured in the stories, his or her name is given, and the story titles are listed.

The section titled "Experiences" is one page in length; the section titled "Addenda" is three pages; and the volume concludes with separate indexes for authors and detectives. The key listing the explanation of the size codes is not provided, thus necessitating reference to the earlier volume.

As with the previous volume, this is not a necessary adjunct for research.

306.   Mundell, E. H., Jr., and G. Jay Rausch. **The Detective Short Story: A Bibliography and Index.** Bibliography Series, no. 14. Manhattan: Kansas State University Library, 1974. v, 493 p. Index. Cloth. LC 74-181860.

According to its preface, this sizable volume began as separate projects, with the authors merging their manuscripts in 1972. The resulting volume, clearly reproduced from typed copy, is an impressive but somewhat eccentric listing of more than 1,400 mystery and detective fiction collections and approximately 7,500 mystery and detective short stories. The contents include detective stories—author collections, Sherlockiana and Poeiana, detective story anthologies, secret service stories—author collections; secret service anthologies; problems—puzzles, detective experiences, and titles not examined. An index of detectives and agents and an author index are provided. The sections are not clearly delimited, and without constant recourse to the table of contents, locating a specific section can be difficult.

The arrangement and format of each section are similar. The overall arrangement is alphabetical by author or editor, when such is listed on the title page; works with no editor listed on the title page are listed alphabetically by title under "anonymous." Every work is given a unique number, and each entry provides on separate lines the author's (or editor's) name and dates, the book's title in capital letters, and bibliographic data for the first American and English editions. The detective's name is given, and the individual story titles are listed. The first index references only the author of the story, necessitating reference to the second index, which lists book titles in capitals, story titles in lowercase letters, and is keyed to the unique number given by each citation.

Despite its difficult arrangement and some factual errors, this index remains occasionally useful.

307.   **The Pulp.Net.** http://thepulp.net

With a strong focus on the three major hero pulps—*The Shadow, Doc Savage,* and *The Spider*—and its thousands of links to the resources available on these pulp characters as well as on general information about the pulps, this Web site is a superb resource.

308a.   Queen, Ellery. **The Detective Short Story: A Bibliography.** Boston: Little, Brown, 1942. 146 p. Cloth. LC 42-23794.

308b.   Queen, Ellery. **The Detective Short Story: A Bibliography.** With a new introduction by the author. New York: Biblo and Tannen, 1969. 146 p. Cloth. LC 73-79517.

Despite its title, this is not a bibliography of detective short stories but a bibliography of the anthologies in which the short stories appeared. It is a thoroughly idiosyncratic work, lacking table of contents and numbering for its citations, which amount to approximately 600. A brief explanatory note provides Queen's basis for selection: "a detective story is a tale of ratiocination, complete with crime and/or mystery, suspects, investigation, clues, deduction, and solution; in its purest form, the chief character should be a detective, amateur or professional, who devotes most of his (or her) time to the problems of detection" and (more dubiously) " 'crook' stories have been considered eligible for the logical reason that whenever a story is concerned primarily with a criminal, it is concerned also, openly or by implication, with the forces of law operating against the criminal."

The bibliography records books published in Great Britain and the United States between 1841 and 1941. Single-author collections and anthologies are listed in separate sections. The collections are arranged alphabetically by author's name; when the author published more than one collection, the arrangement becomes chronological. The author's name is in boldface type, the title is in small capital letters, and the place of publication and the publisher are treated routinely. The presentation of the publication date, however, takes into consideration the placement of the date on the title page and the copyright page. In addition, the first edition's paper size is given (e.g., 8vo, 12mo, 16mo, 18mo), as is a description of its binding. Occasionally lengthy notes discuss publication histories of landmark collections and comment on the differences between British and American editions. If the collection features a single detective or a recurrent criminal, the name is given. Finally, there are two subsections: "Chinese Detective Stories" (compiled by Vincent Starrett) and "Incunables" (detective stories published prior to 1841) are listed under their respective letters.

The citations to anthologies are essentially similar to those of the single-author collections, although the anthologies are listed chronologically and the notes tend to comment upon unique aspects of the contents. Each entry concludes by listing the name of the editor or editors.

The bibliography contains two indexes. The "Index of Detectives and Criminals" lists the names of detectives in upper- and lowercase and the names of the criminals in italics; characters who are both (e.g., Arsene Lupin) have their names given in large and small capital letters. The "Index of Anthology Editors" is routine. There is no title index.

Although their work occasionally is frustrating, the Queens deserve commendation for compiling the first bibliography of its kind. Furthermore and more important, the citations tend to be accurate, and they often contain substantially more detail than do the citations of later bibliographers. Despite its age and some errors, this book remains useful.

309. Stephenson-Payne, Phil. **The Big List.** http://www.pulpgen.com/pulp/biglist

This is one of the wonderful sites. Stephenson-Payne attempts to provide data on and a guide to all known fiction magazines. More than 4,000 magazines are thus listed, with information about frequency, length of run, publisher, format, and paginations. In addition, frequently representative cover scans are provided, and when the magazine has been indexed by the members of Fictionmags, there are links.

310. Thom, William. **Hero Pulp Reprint Index.** Seymour, Tex.: Fading Shadows, 1997. 62 p. Paperback.

This bibliography lists the book appearances of the characters originally featured in the single-character ("hero pulp") magazines. Its contents include a hero pulp reprint index, an index of previously unpublished stories, and an index of new stories in the pulp tradition. Also, appendixes list magazine title abbreviations, publisher name abbreviations, format abbreviations, artist name abbreviation, and notes.

The majority of the work consists of the hero pulp reprint index, which for each hero provides the title of the work and the name of the book that republished it; abbreviations list the name of the republisher, size (format) of the book, publication date, and cover artist. Also given are the original date and title of the story's publication, and entries conclude with the volume and number of the work's original publication. Similar information is given in the successive sections, although (of course) original publication data are not given.

The arrangement of the entries is idiosyncratic and can be frustrating, for Thom has listed his entries alphabetically by the first part of the fullest name under which the hero is known: the Phantom Detective is listed under *p,* but so too are Phil Towne, Philip Strange, Prester John, Prince Raynor, and Purple Scar; similarly, Mr. Chang, Mr. Death, and Mr. Wong are all listed under the letter *m.* Cross-references have not been provided.

The majority of the data in the *Hero Pulp Reprint Index* cannot be located through any reference sources, and Thom deserves commendation for his efforts, which are accurate and will assist not only the fans of the hero pulps but also the scholars of popular culture.

Note: Earlier versions of this index were serialized in *Echoes* 58, 59, 60, and 85; all entries have been updated and corrected for this edition.

MAGAZINE INDEXES, GENERAL

311.   Contento, William G. **Mystery Magazine Index: 1990–2002: An Index to Mystery Magazines, Anthologies, and Single-Author Collections.** http://users.ev1.net/~homeville/msf/0start.htm

The goal of this remarkable Web site is to list all mystery short fiction published in English since 1990. The books and magazines that are indexed are listed, and one can locate their contents by author and title; chronological lists are available, as are lists of material by series. This index, combined with the magnificent *Index to Crime and Mystery Anthologies* (q.v.), is available on CD-ROM from the Locus Press under the title *Mystery Short Fiction Miscellany: An Index.*

312.   Cook, Michael L. **Monthly Murders: A Checklist and Chronological Listing of Fiction in the Digest-Size Mystery Magazines in the United States and Canada.** Westport, Conn.: Greenwood, 1982. xviii, 1,147 p. Index. Cloth. LC 81-6986. ISBN 0-313-23126-5.

The first digest-sized mystery magazine was the Fall 1941 issue of *Ellery Queen's Mystery Magazine.* Dozens of digest-sized mystery magazines have since been published, most lasting but a few issues. Until recently, very few of these magazines have been collected by academic libraries, and even private collectors have tended to shun them. As Cook states in his introduction, "Digest-size mystery magazines have not been as popular among collectors as the pulp-magazines, digest-size mystery novels, or the paperback books for some reason. They are collected even less in England, yet many of these are far more scarce than is realized. It is estimated by several avid collectors that less than 25 copies of some still exist."

Monthly Murders is not a comprehensive index to the contents of digest-sized mystery magazines; it does not cumulate in the way that other indexes do, nor does it index nonfiction. Rather, it is a listing of the stories appearing in more than 100 English and American digest-sized mystery magazines, the best-known being *Alfred Hitchcock's Mystery Magazine, Ellery Queen's Mystery Magazine,* and *The Saint Detective Magazine;* less familiar titles include *All Mystery* (one issue, 1950), *Bizarre! Mystery Magazine* (three issues, 1965–1966), *The Craig Rice Mystery Digest* (one issue, 1945), *Strange* (three issues, 1952), *Sleuth Mystery Magazine* (two issues, 1958), *Verdict Crime Detection Magazine* (two issues, 1956), and *Whodunit* (one issue, 1967). Chronologically, coverage of *Monthly Murders* begins with the Fall 1941 issue of *Ellery Queen's Mystery Magazine* and concludes with the contents of the digest-sized mystery magazines being published at the end of 1980.

Cook begins each magazine's entry by providing the publisher's name and address, citing changes when they can be documented, although introductory prose is kept to a minimum. The arrangement is issue-by-issue chronological, each entry citing the magazine's publication date, volume and issue numbers, and newsstand cost. Only the fictional contents of the magazines are given; they are listed in no particular order, and their pagination is not included. An alphabetical list of magazines is followed by an author index that reveals occasional pseudonyms, provides some cross-references, and lists the stories alphabetically.

Apart from being somewhat mistitled—several of the digest-sized mystery magazines appeared bimonthly, and at least one was quarterly—*Monthly Murders* is an ambitious achievement with some curious and all too readily noticeable flaws. One cannot fault Cook for being unable to obtain certain issues, nor for neglecting to indicate reprints and stories that were reprinted under different titles, but why, for example, did Cook choose to alphabetize his magazines by an arbitrarily chosen system of abbreviations rather than by the magazines' names? In just the first letter of the alphabet, the reliance on abbreviations leads to the following apparently idiosyncratic arrangement of magazines: *American Agent, Alfred Hitchcock's Mystery Magazine* (British edition), *Accused Detective Story Magazine, Alfred Hitchcock's Mystery Magazine* (American edition), *All Mystery, Avon Modern Short Story Monthly,* and *Avon Detective Mysteries.* Even more seriously, the lack of a title index means that the contents of *Monthly Murders* are effectively inaccessible to those who know neither magazine nor author.

Like Cook's *Mystery Fanfare* and his *Mystery, Detective and Espionage Magazines* (q.q.v.), *Monthly Murders* is a flawed monument. It deserves revising, correcting, expanding, and updating.

313.   Cook, Michael L. **Mystery, Detective, and Espionage Magazines.** Historical Guides to the World's Periodicals and Newspapers. Westport, Conn.: Greenwood, 1983. xxiv, 795 p. Index. Cloth. LC 82-20977. ISBN 0-313-23310-1.

A companion of sorts to Cook's *Mystery, Detective, and Espionage Fiction* (q.v.), this monumental book has a somewhat larger focus than the other volume. Not only does it describe the pulp magazines indexed in the previous volume, but it also describes numerous fan publications and foreign, academic, and nonfiction magazines, and it provides lengthy appendices and a first-rate index.

The first and largest section of the volume focuses on the magazines published in the United States and provides histories that describe the significant events and personalities in the publication's lifetime. These profiles are at times lengthy and are generally proportionate to the magazine's significance. The longest profile is received by *Ellery Queen's Mystery Magazine* (10 pages), but it is followed closely by *Black Mask* (7 pages), *The Spider* (6 pages), and *The Shadow* and *Doc Savage* (5 ½ apiece).

The profiles are by such experts as Walter Albert, J. Randolph Cox, Bernard Drew, E. R. Hagemann, Will Murray, Robert Sampson, and Albert Tonik, and their prose is lively, informative, and very often superior to the stories and publications being described. Sampson in particular appears to have relished his writing assignments, lavishing the trashiest of pulp magazines with the most exuberant of prose. His essay on *Scarlet Adventuress* opens by stating, "The annals of unrepentant trash contain few examples more sleazy than *Scarlet Adventuress*," and continues by stating that "the story was usually told from what passed for the woman's point of view. The prose is unbelievable. The word *exotic* appears about six times per page, never correctly used. *Alluring* is used once per paragraph. The story lines, such as they are, support descriptions of feminine undressing and sly mention of other various mysteries."

Each entry has two concluding sections. A bibliography references the articles and books that discuss the magazine, cites indexes to the magazine (if any), and lists libraries in which the magazine can be found. The second section provides bibliographical information on the publication: its official title and title changes (if any), volume and issue data, publisher, editor, price per issue, size and pagination, and publication status as of 1983.

Successive sections use the same format to provide overviews of foreign magazines and to profile mystery book clubs. These are followed by appendixes listing the magazines by category for the United States, Canada, and Great Britain; certain key writers in the golden age, their most common pseudonyms, and the magazines with which they were commonly associated; a year-by-year chronology of the magazines; lists of American and Canadian true-detective magazines; lists of Sherlock Holmes Scion Society Periodicals; and a list of other periodicals of interest to the collector. A two-page bibliography and a thorough index conclude the volume.

Mystery, Detective, and Espionage Magazines is deservedly acclaimed as a landmark volume, and complaints about it tend to the trivial: Fredric Brown's name is given once as "Frederick," E. Hoffmann Price's middle name is given consistently as "Hoffman," and a ghost is inadvertently created when Lawrence G. Blochman is cited as Lawrence Blackman.

This volume belongs in all academic libraries.

314.   Cook, Michael L. **Mystery Fanfare: A Composite Annotated Index to Mystery and Related Fanzines 1963–1981.** Bowling Green, Ohio: Bowling Green State University Popular Press, 1983. 441 p. Index. LC 82-73848. ISBN 0-87972-229-0 (hc); 0-87972-230-4 (pb).

Although science fiction fanzines have been published since the early 1930s, it is Michael Cook's contention that the first regularly published mystery and detective fanzines not solely devoted to Sherlock Holmes did not appear until the 1960s. Fifty-two of these fanzines are indexed in *Mystery Fanfare,* the chronologically oldest being the Winter 1963 (vol. 60) issue of *Pulp Era.* Other fanzines indexed by Cook include *Armchair Detective, August Derleth Society Newsletter, Bony Bulletin, Clues, Gazette: The Journal of the Wolfe Pack, Mystery Fancier, Mystery Lover's Newsletter, Mystery Readers Newsletter, Poisoned Pen,* and *Thorndyke File.* In all, nearly 600 different issues and approximately 2,400 articles are indexed by author, title, and subject, with a concluding appendix listing the reviews of films, stage productions, and television programs published in these fanzines. Book reviews are included in the major indexing sequence; unless they contained something significant, letters published in the fanzines are indexed by only the name of their writer. Especially useful is the introductory "Guide and Chronology of Magazines Indexed," which provides not only a brief prose history of each magazine but includes such data as the publication history of the issues indexed, the fanzine's usual size and pagination, its status, editor, publisher, and frequency of publication. Each bibliographic citation provides the article's author and title and, in abbreviated form, the fanzine's name, volume, issue, and relevant pages.

The fanzines indexed in *Mystery Fanfare* frequently contained original and significant information, and Cook's ambition to make their contents more widely known is a laudable one. Nevertheless, Cook's desire too often outweighed his indexing skills, for *Mystery Fanfare* has severe methodological problems. Because it is a composite index, Cook assigned each fanzine a one- or two-letter code that is not intuitively obvious; users must constantly check the "alphabetical list of code designations" at the beginning of the volume. More seriously, it is apparent that Cook failed to maintain adequate intellectual control over his material; he used a computer to compile and sort his data without examining and questioning the integrity of the output. Because of this, articles whose titles begin with "A" and "An" are indexed under the letter "A," which leads to separate sections for titles beginning with "An interview with . . ." and "Interview with . . ."; makes such titles as "A John Creasey Bibliography," "A John Dickson Carr Checklist," and "A Simon Ark Bibliography" virtually inaccessible; and splits such series as "A Report on Bouchercon":the title for Report IV apparently did not possess the initial article and is thus listed under "R." Furthermore, because Cook occasionally miskeyed his data, the computer sorted according to its own internal logic: the entries titled "A. D." (an article on August Derleth) and "A. Merritt's Mysteries" occur out of alphabetical sequence because (in Cook's typing) the "A" in the former is followed by a period and no space and in the latter the "A" is (erroneously) followed by a comma. Titles beginning with "The," however, occur in their correct alphabetical sequence, for the initial article is transposed to the end of each title entry. Cook's usage of subject headings is equally idiosyncratic (e.g., different entries occur under "bibliography" and "checklist").

None of this is to say that *Mystery Fanfare* cannot be used. If one is willing to endure the frustrating arrangement, *Mystery Fanfare* can be considered a monumental achievement. It preserves the contents of publications that have been too often discarded as ephemeral, and it has something to offer virtually all researchers on detective and mystery literature. It is clearly reproduced from legible copy, and it exemplifies the concept of "labor of love." A revised, corrected, and updated edition of *Mystery Fanfare* is badly needed.

315. Cook, Michael L., and Stephen T. Miller. **Mystery, Detective, and Espionage Fiction: A Checklist of Fiction in U.S. Pulp Magazines, 1915–1974.** Garland Reference Library of the Humanities, vol. 838. New York: Garland Publishing, 1988. 2 vols. xvi, 1,183 p. Index. Cloth. LC 88-7190. ISBN 0-8240-7539-0.

In a project that took more than four years, Cook and Miller indexed the fiction that appeared in every mystery, detective, and espionage pulp magazine published between 1915 and 1974. An incredible 58,000 stories appearing in nearly 9,000 issues of more than 360 different magazine titles are indexed in these two volumes.

Both volumes contain two columns per page. The first volume lists the magazines alphabetically, then lists the contents in chronological order, by volume and issue number. The authors' names are given in capital letters, titles are given in regular type, and joint authors are listed separately. In addition, each magazine is assigned a two-letter code, and to this code are added numbers signifying the magazine's volume and issue number. *The Illustrated Detective Magazine,* for example, is HJ, and volume 3, no. 4 of the magazine is 3HJ4. The first volume concludes with an alphabetical index providing publication data for the magazines and an index listing the magazines by their commencement dates.

The second volume indexes the stories by author. As before, the author's name is given in capital letters, and the story's title is given in regular type. Each story title is keyed to the coding system described previously.

In intended scope, this index is awe-inspiring; in execution, it is thoroughly frustrating. At its most basic, the index is badly laid out, for approximately a quarter of each page is blank, and had correct formatting been used, this could have been a one-volume work. Layout aside, the author index has severe problems. First, it would appear that Cook and Miller's computer made all of the indexing decisions, and several of its sort routines were inadequately defined: a sorting problem has put some of the names beginning with "Mac" and "Mc" at the beginning of the letter "M," but (in a break with tradition), the majority of the "Mac" and "Mc" entries occurs at the *conclusion* of the letter "M"; stories by Alan MacDonald, William B. MacHarg, and Donald MacGregor (among others) appear in both locations. Other entries—as in the case of Frank Gruber—occur out of their proper alphabetical sequence and are thus inaccessible except by chance.

As if these problems were not enough, Cook and Miller appear to have made no attempts at establishing a consistent or standardized spelling for any of the author's names or even to verify that the author's name does not repeat itself on the page. E. Hoffmann Price's name occurs 18 times on two pages, and beneath each occurrence is a (different) alphabetical list of stories. Nor are any of these lists of titles particularly accessible, for although they are alphabetical, initial articles have been used in their indexing. Researchers must not only look under each variant and repetition of author's name, they must then look to see if a particular title has been given as "A Night for Murder," "The Night for Murder," or "Night for Murder." As if this were not enough, the index contains no separate index to story titles, and the entries do not provide pagination.

None of this is to say that this index cannot be used. If one is willing and able to ignore the preceding problems, enormous amounts of information can sometimes be located. No other index does what this one attempts to: the indexed publications are frequently surpassingly rare, surviving only on microfilm or in the hands of private collectors. Thus, however defective this index is, it provides a means to locate the original magazine work by many of the writers who have since become significant. A thoroughly revised, corrected, and expanded edition of this index is badly needed.

Note: There is some overlap with the indexes compiled by Leonard Robbins (q.v.), but Robbins's work does not supersede that of Cook and Miller.

316. Gunnison, John P. **Street & Smith's Hero Pulp Checklist.** Pulp Collector Press Checklist Series, no. 1. Upper Marlboro, Md.: Pulp Collector Press, 1991. Unpaged. Paperback.

In 1931, Street and Smith, the largest publisher of pulp magazines, started a pulp magazine called *The Shadow* to capitalize on the success of *Detective Story Magazine,* a radio program narrated by a mysterious voice known as the Shadow. Written by Walter Gibson, *The Shadow* became the first of the hero pulps, the pulp magazines devoted to describing heroic activities of one recurrent series character.

Gunnison's checklist is arranged alphabetically by the name of the pulp hero. Illustrations occur throughout and each entry is prefaced by a brief discussion of the character and authors known to have written about the character. Entries for specific magazines are chronologically arranged and list the volume and issue number, date of publication, story's title (in capital letters), and the house name assigned to the work. When the hero was no longer featured in a separate magazine named for him but remained active—as happened with the Avenger, Bill Barnes, Pete Rice, the Skipper, and the Wizard—a separate entry lists the magazine issues in which the stories were published.

Collectors of Street and Smith's hero pulps will find this a useful publication.

317a.   McKinstry, Lohr, and Robert Weinberg. **The Hero Pulp Index.** Hillside Park, N.J.: Robert Weinberg, 1970. 54 p. Index. Paperback. LC 70-24788. 250 copies printed.

317b.   Weinberg, Robert, and Lohr McKinstry. **The Hero Pulp Index.** 2nd rev. ed. Evergreen, Colo.: Opar Press, 1971. 48 p. Index. Paperback.

The Hero Pulp Index attempts to index every major hero pulp magazine published, as well as the heroic series characters who never had pulp magazines devoted to their activities but who were prominently featured in other magazines; pulp antiheroes and supervillains also are described. This description concentrates on the revised (second) edition, which is reproduced from typed copy.

The first section of the *Index* is an issue-by-issue listing of the contents of the hero pulp magazines. The contents are arranged alphabetically by the hero's crime-fighting name, although cross-references to and from the hero's ordinary names are not provided. Citations list the hero's name and the magazine in which he appeared; also given are the house name under which the stories were published. Many pseudonyms are revealed. The arrangement of citations is chronological, and each entry is separately numbered and lists the story title, its volume, issue, month and year of publication. Entries indicate when the hero no longer warranted a pulp of his own but became resident in another pulp (i.e., "Kenneth Robeson" 's the Avenger).

The second section of the *Index* lists some of the noted authors of hero pulp stories and some of the pen names and house names they were known to have used. Listed after each name are the magazines for which the author wrote and the number of stories written for that magazine.

A third section provides information on the book appearances and reprints of the pulp characters. The concluding section, "A Guide to the Pulp Heroes," provides a biographical description of the hero or villain; for example, for *Doctor Yen Sin,* Weinberg and McKinstry write, "Attempting to imitate Sax Rohmer's Fu Manchu, Popular Publications presented Dr. Yen Sin, an Oriental genius who plotted to become emperor of the world. Yen Sin fought the usual group of troubleshooters in the Rohmer pattern. The Doctor, who used super forces, was known as 'The Invisible Peril.' The series was written by pulpster [*sic*] Donald Keyhoe, who was going to gain notoriety many years later with the flying saucer craze."

Though some entries have errors, and the *Index* needs a title index, this remains one of the more useful indexes to a specialized genre of pulp magazine. It has not been indexed because the focus is on characters rather than magazines. A far more comprehensive version—*The Ultimate Pulp Superhero Index*—has been done by Will Murray and is described later (q.v.).

318.   Mundell, E. H. **Detective Mystery Crime Magazines.** Portage, Ind.: N.p., 1971. 47 p. Cloth.

Mundell has compiled an alphabetical list of all of the detective, mystery, and crime magazines in his personal collection or whose titles he found listed in the copyright registers issued by the Library of Congress during the years from 1915 until 1953. Each citation gives the magazine's title, publisher, and date of its first issue; terminal dates are occasionally given, as are changes in title and publisher. The titles of magazines not seen by Mundell are in italics. In all, basic bibliographic information is given for nearly 300 magazines, many of which are not accorded mention in either the works of Michael Cook or Leonard Robbins (q.q.v.).

According to Mundell's brief introduction, this is the third such list he has compiled. One regrets that none of these lists appears to have been widely distributed.

319.   Murray, Will. **The Ultimate Pulp Superhero Index.** http://www.adventurehouse. com/pulpdata/pulp_superhero.htm

More than twice the size of any previous reference work, Murray's index describes heroic pulp magazine characters using a variety of criteria to determine whether they warranted inclusion. The list focuses primarily on the characters who appeared during the Depression era—a time Murray refers to as "The Heroic Age"—and provides data about the magazine(s) (volume and date) in which the character appeared, the story title, and the author (when known). Although Murray excludes certain characters this writer would have included, his list is gratifyingly long and thorough.

320a.   Robbins, Leonard A. **The Pulp Magazine Index: First Series.** Mercer Island, Wash.: Starmont House, 1989. 3 vols. x, 467, 882, 810 p. Index. Cloth. LC 88-20056. ISBN 1-55742-111-0 (set).

320b.   Robbins, Leonard A. **The Pulp Magazine Index: Second Series.** Mercer Island, Wash.: Starmont House, 1989. viii, 583 p. Index. Cloth. LC 89-34752. ISBN 1-55742-162-5.

320c.   Robbins, Leonard A. **The Pulp Magazine Index: Third Series.** Mercer Island, Wash.: Starmont House, 1990. Index. Cloth. xii, 639 p. Index. Cloth. ISBN 1-55742-204-4.

320d.   Robbins, Leonard A. **The Pulp Magazine Index: Fourth Series.** Mercer Island, Wash.: Starmont House, 1991. xi, 567 p. Index. Cloth. ISBN 1-55742-241-9.

A monumental achievement that is largely unknown outside the relatively insular world of pulp magazine collectors, these enormous books cumulatively index several hundred pulp magazines from all genres. Thousands of issues of mystery and detective, romance, western, adventure, aviation, war, hero, science fiction, sports, and shudder pulps are listed issue by issue, then indexed by their authors, titles, illustrators, and various forms of the characters' names. Most of these data do not exist in any other source.

Although individual volumes have a similar arrangement, *The Pulp Magazine Index* is not always an easy work to use, perhaps because of the unique nature of its content. Each series begins with a section titled "Special Remarks" that offers commentary on numbering and table of contents errors or particularly desirable data in the magazines.

These comments will convey nothing to the uninitiated and are arranged by the one- or two-letter code that Robbins has assigned each magazine to facilitate computer sorting. Unfortunately, these codes are not intuitively obvious and follow no discernible order: AO is *Air Trails,* AP is *Triple Detective,* AQ is the *Angel Detective,* and AR is *Captain Hazzard Magazine;* conversely, *Thrilling Mysteries* is BD, *Thrilling Spy Stories* is DW, and the *Thrill Book* is GS.

The following sections are titled "Magazine File Report: Listed by Magazine" and "Magazine File Report: Listed by Code." The former is an alphabetical listing of the magazines by title; accompanying data provide the magazine's price, size, pagination, frequency, publisher, editor(s), and the letter code Robbins has assigned the magazine. The latter contains the same data as the previous section, but the magazines are arranged alphabetically by the letter code rather than alphabetically by title. Users of the index must make constant reference to these sections.

Successive divisions are confusingly titled "Magazine Data File Report: Listed by Code," "Magazine Data File Report: Listed by Title," "Magazine Data File Report: Listed by Author," "Artists File Report: Listed by Artist," "Character File Report: Listed by Character," "Special Zero Character Data," and "Character File Report: Special Zero Code Data." These are, respectively, the issue-by-issue indexes to the magazines arranged by their assigned code, the title index to the stories in magazines, the author index to the stories in the magazines, the artist index to the magazines, and the indexes to various forms of the characters' names. Entries in the issue-by-issue index provide the magazine's publication date (in the form of 08-1935 for August 1935), volume and issue numbers, story's page number, title, and author; these data are rearranged to create the title and author indexes. Entries in the "Artists File Report" list the artists by last name, the code for the magazine to which the artwork was done, the magazine's volume and issue number, and note whether the artwork was a cover or an "int" they [interior illustration]. If the artist contributed more than one interior illustration, the number is given.

Entries in the "Character File Report: Listed by Character" list the names of the characters in the story, the code for the magazine, volume and issue numbers, and title of the story in which the character appeared. The "Special Zero Character Data" provide three symbols—an asterisk (*) is used to signify the hero character aides; a hash mark (#) is used to signify the hero's antagonists; and a plus sign (+) is used to signify aliases and nicknames. These symbols appear after the names in the "Character File Report: Listed by Character" and the "Character File Report: Special Zero Code Data." Entries in this last section list the names of the aliases, nicknames, and antagonists and cross-reference them to the character's name. "Ham+," for example, is linked as the nickname of Theodore Marley Brooks.

Apart from the frustrating use of codes to identify magazines, *The Pulp Magazine Index* has only one serious shortcoming: Robbins depended upon a computer to sort his data, and in this index, all titles that have numbers and symbols as the first word are listed separately at the beginning of their section. Similarly, humans alphabetizing titles beginning with "A," "An," or "The" would know to disregard them and index using the first significant word; in this index the listings have not been integrated, and the titles beginning with "A" and "An" appear alphabetically in section A, and the titles beginning with "The" are listed alphabetically in the T section.

Because of the magnitude of Robbins's accomplishment, the preceding shortcomings can be dismissed as idiosyncrasies. The indexes are clearly reproduced from computer-generated copy, and they belong in all research libraries. Robbins was preparing indexes to the long-lasting *Short Stories* and to a number of additional pulp magazines when the owner of Starmont House died, effectively leaving Robbins without a publisher willing to assume a project of this magnitude. Given the specialized nature of these indexes, it is improbable that additional volumes will be published in paper. The loss will not be noticed by most, but it will be enormous nevertheless.

MAGAZINE HISTORIES AND INDEXES, SPECIFIC TITLES

Accused Detective Story Magazine

321a. Described in **Mystery, Detective, and Espionage Magazines**, ed. by Michael L. Cook (Westport, Conn.: Greenwood, 1983), pp. 3–4.

321b. Indexed in Michael Cook, **Monthly Murders: A Checklist and Chronological Listing of Fiction in the Digest-Size Mystery Magazines in the United States and England** (Westport, Conn.: Greenwood, 1982), pp. 9–10.

Ace Detective

322a. Described in **Mystery, Detective, and Espionage Magazines**, ed. by Michael L. Cook (Westport, Conn.: Greenwood, 1983), pp. 4–5.

322b. Indexed in **Mystery, Detective, and Espionage Fiction,** ed. by Michael L. Cook and Stephen T. Miller (New York: Garland, 1988), pp. 1, 367.

322c. Indexed in **The Pulp Magazine Index: First Series,** by Leonard A. Robbins (Mercer Island, Wash.: Starmont House, 1989).

Ace Detective Magazine. See Ace Detective

Ace G-Man Stories

323a. Described in **Mystery, Detective, and Espionage Magazines,** ed. by Michael L. Cook (Westport, Conn.: Greenwood, 1983), pp. 6–9.

323b. Indexed in **Mystery, Detective, and Espionage Fiction,** ed. by Michael L. Cook and Stephen T. Miller (New York: Garland, 1988), pp. 1–4.

323c. Indexed in **The Pulp Magazine Index: First Series,** by Leonard A. Robbins (Mercer Island, Wash.: Starmont House, 1989).

Ace-High Detective Magazine

324a. Described in **Mystery, Detective, and Espionage Magazines,** ed. by Michael L. Cook (Westport, Conn.: Greenwood, 1983), pp. 9–10.

324b. Indexed in **Mystery, Detective, and Espionage Fiction,** ed. by Michael L. Cook and Stephen T. Miller (New York: Garland, 1988), p. 4.

324c. Indexed in **The Pulp Magazine Index: First Series,** by Leonard A. Robbins (Mercer Island, Wash.: Starmont House, 1989).

Ace Mystery

325a. Described in **Mystery, Detective, and Espionage Magazines,** ed. by Michael L. Cook (Westport, Conn.: Greenwood, 1983), pp. 10–11.

325b. Indexed in **Mystery, Detective, and Espionage Fiction,** ed. by Michael L. Cook and Stephen T. Miller (New York: Garland, 1988), pp. 4, 177.

325c. Indexed in **The Pulp Magazine Index: First Series,** by Leonard A. Robbins (Mercer Island, Wash.: Starmont House, 1989).

Ace Mystery Magazine. See Ace Mystery

Age of the Unicorn

326a. Contents indexed in Michael L. Cook, **Mystery Fanfare: A Composite Annotated Index to Mystery and Related Fanzines 1963–1981** (Bowling Green, Ohio: Bowling Green State University Popular Press, 1983).

326b. Described in **Mystery, Detective, and Espionage Magazines,** ed. by Michael L. Cook (Westport, Conn.: Greenwood, 1983), pp. 12–13.

Air Trails

327a. Checklist to title stories given in John P. Gunnison, **Street & Smith's Hero Pulp Checklist** (Upper Marlboro, Md.: Pulp Collector Press, 1991).

327b. Indexed in **Mystery, Detective, and Espionage Fiction,** ed. by Michael L. Cook and Stephen T. Miller (New York: Garland, 1988), pp. 4–5.

327c. Indexed in **The Pulp Magazine Index: First Series,** by Leonard A. Robbins (Mercer Island, Wash.: Starmont House, 1989).

327d. Indexed in **The Pulp Magazine Index: Fourth Series**, by Leonard A. Robbins (Mercer Island, Wash.: Starmont House, 1991).

Air War

328a. Indexed in **Mystery, Detective, and Espionage Fiction,** ed. by Michael L. Cook and Stephen T. Miller (New York: Garland, 1988), pp. 6–7.

328b. Indexed in **The Pulp Magazine Index: Second Series,** by Leonard A. Robbins (Mercer Island, Wash.: Starmont House, 1989).

The Aldine Celebrated Detective Tales (British). See *Detective Tales* (Aldine Publishing) (British)

Aldine Detective Tales (British). See *Detective Tales* (Aldine Publishing) (British)

Aldine Mystery Novels (British)

329. Described in **Mystery, Detective, and Espionage Magazines,** ed. by Michael L. Cook (Westport, Conn.: Greenwood, 1983), pp. 14–15.

Aldine Thrillers

330. Described in **Mystery, Detective, and Espionage Magazines,** ed. by Michael L. Cook (Westport, Conn.: Greenwood, 1983), p. 15.

Alfred Hitchcock's Mystery Magazine

331a. Described in **Mystery, Detective, and Espionage Magazines,** ed. by Michael L. Cook (Westport, Conn.: Greenwood, 1983), pp. 15–20.

331b. American edition indexed in Michael Cook, **Monthly Murders: A Checklist and Chronological Listing of Fiction in the Digest-Size Mystery Magazines in the United States and England** (Westport, Conn.: Greenwood, 1982), pp. 11–95.

331c. British edition indexed in Michael Cook, **Monthly Murders: A Checklist and Chronological Listing of Fiction in the Digest-Size Mystery Magazines in the United States and England** (Westport, Conn.: Greenwood, 1982), pp. 4–8.

Alibi

332a. Described in **Mystery, Detective, and Espionage Magazines,** ed. by Michael L. Cook (Westport, Conn.: Greenwood, 1983), p. 20.

332b. Indexed in **Mystery, Detective, and Espionage Fiction,** ed. by Michael L. Cook and Stephen T. Miller (New York: Garland, 1988), p. 7.

All Aces Magazine

333a. Indexed in **Mystery, Detective, and Espionage Fiction,** ed. by Michael L. Cook and Stephen T. Miller (New York: Garland, 1988), p. 7.

333b. Indexed in **The Pulp Magazine Index: First Series,** by Leonard A. Robbins (Mercer Island, Wash.: Starmont House, 1989).

All Detective Magazine

334a. Described in **Mystery, Detective, and Espionage Magazines,** ed. by Michael L. Cook (Westport, Conn.: Greenwood, 1983), p. 21.

334b. Indexed in **Mystery, Detective, and Espionage Fiction,** ed. by Michael L. Cook and Stephen T. Miller (New York: Garland, 1988), pp. 8–10.

334c. Indexed in **The Pulp Magazine Index: Second Series,** by Leonard A. Robbins (Mercer Island, Wash.: Starmont House, 1989).

All Fiction Detective Anthology. See *All Fiction Detective Stories*

All Fiction Detective Stories

335a. Described in **Mystery, Detective, and Espionage Magazines,** ed. by Michael L. Cook (Westport, Conn.: Greenwood, 1983), pp. 22–23.

335b. Indexed in **Mystery, Detective, and Espionage Fiction,** ed. by Michael L. Cook and Stephen T. Miller (New York: Garland, 1988), pp. 10, 665.

All Mystery

336a. Described in **Mystery, Detective, and Espionage Magazines,** ed. by Michael L. Cook (Westport, Conn.: Greenwood, 1983), p. 23.

336b. Indexed in Michael Cook, **Monthly Murders: A Checklist and Chronological Listing of Fiction in the Digest-Size Mystery Magazines in the United States and England** (Westport, Conn.: Greenwood, 1982), p. 96.

All Star Detective

337a. Described in **Mystery, Detective, and Espionage Magazines,** ed. by Michael L. Cook (Westport, Conn.: Greenwood, 1983), pp. 23–24.

337b. Indexed in **Mystery, Detective, and Espionage Fiction,** ed. by Michael L. Cook and Stephen T. Miller (New York: Garland, 1988), p. 10.

All Star Detective Stories

338a. Described in **Mystery, Detective, and Espionage Magazines,** ed. by Michael L. Cook (Westport, Conn.: Greenwood, 1983), p. 24.

338b. Indexed in **Mystery, Detective, and Espionage Fiction,** ed. by Michael L. Cook and Stephen T. Miller (New York: Garland, 1988), pp. 11–12.

338c. Indexed in **The Pulp Magazine Index: Fourth Series**, by Leonard A. Robbins (Mercer Island, Wash.: Starmont House, 1991).

All-Story Detective

339a.   Described in **Mystery, Detective, and Espionage Magazines,** ed. by Michael L. Cook (Westport, Conn.: Greenwood, 1983), pp. 24–25.

339b.   Indexed in **Mystery, Detective, and Espionage Fiction,** ed. by Michael L. Cook and Stephen T. Miller (New York: Garland, 1988), pp. 12–13, 328.

339c.   Indexed in **The Pulp Magazine Index: First Series,** by Leonard A. Robbins (Mercer Island, Wash.: Starmont House, 1989).

Amazing Detective Mystery Stories (British)

340.   Described in **Mystery, Detective, and Espionage Magazines,** ed. by Michael L. Cook (Westport, Conn.: Greenwood, 1983), p. 26.

Amazing Detective Stories

341.   Indexed in **Mystery, Detective, and Espionage Fiction,** ed. by Michael L. Cook and Stephen T. Miller (New York: Garland, 1988), p. 13.

Amazing Detective Tales. See *Scientific Detective Monthly*

American Agent

342a.   Described in **Mystery, Detective, and Espionage Magazines,** ed. by Michael L. Cook (Westport, Conn.: Greenwood, 1983), pp. 26–27.

342b.   Indexed in Michael Cook, **Monthly Murders: A Checklist and Chronological Listing of Fiction in the Digest-Size Mystery Magazines in the United States and England** (Westport, Conn.: Greenwood, 1982), p. 3.

The American Eagle. See *The Lone Eagle*

The Angel Detective

343a.   Described in **Mystery, Detective, and Espionage Magazines,** ed. by Michael L. Cook (Westport, Conn.: Greenwood, 1983), pp. 27–29.

343b.   Indexed in **Mystery, Detective, and Espionage Fiction,** ed. by Michael L. Cook and Stephen T. Miller (New York: Garland, 1988), p. 14.

343c.   Indexed in **The Pulp Magazine Index: First Series,** by Leonard A. Robbins (Mercer Island, Wash.: Starmont House, 1989).

The Armchair Detective

344a. Contents indexed in Michael L. Cook, **Mystery Fanfare: A Composite Anno-tated Index to Mystery and Related Fanzines 1963–1981** (Bowling Green, Ohio: Bowling Green State University Popular Press, 1983).

344b. Described in **Mystery, Detective, and Espionage Magazines,** ed. by Michael L. Cook (Westport, Conn.: Greenwood, 1983), pp. 29–33.

344c. Stilwell, Steven A. **The Armchair Detective Index, Volumes 1–10, 1967–1977.** New York: Armchair Detective, 1979. 64 p. Paperback. LC 79-90556. ISBN 0-89296-051-X.

Although indexes to the early issues of the *Armchair Detective* were published in the even-numbered volumes, this is the first separately published index to this long-running and influential magazine. The index has been clearly reproduced from word-processed copy. It is alphabetical by author, title, and subject, listing in one alpha-betic sequence all of the articles, reviews, and letters that were published in the *Armchair Detective* between October 1967 and October 1977. Titles of books, plays, and films are capitalized; subjects are underlined and are in regular type; and titles of short stories are given in quote marks. Symbols and abbreviations have been kept to a minimum: (R) af-ter the title means "reviewed," (MN) means "movie note," and (L) means "letter." Each entry concludes with the volume, issue number, and page upon which the piece ap-peared; the format in which these data are presented is initially unclear—a typical entry looks like 8/4/303—but this is merely an inconvenience. There are occasional problems in alphabetization, the index being derived from a computer sort that puts articles about *Pulps* before a discussion of *Pulp Tradition in Mystery Novels.* Nevertheless, this index offers far greater access to the *Armchair Detective* than does Michael Cook's *Mystery Fanfare* (q.v.). Now, however, it has been completely superseded by the index compiled by Deeck and Stilwell (q.v.).

344d. Deeck, William F., and Steven A. Stilwell. **The Armchair Detective Index, Volumes 1–20, 1967–1987.** New York: Armchair Detective, 1992. iii, 178 p. LC 92-54768. ISBN 1-56287-043-2 (hc); 1-56287-044-0 (pb).

Although Stilwell assisted in the compilation of this volume, it is here considered a separate publication rather than merely a second edition because there have been signifi-cant changes made to the original publication. Many of these changes have to do with im-proved computer technology. The first edition placed *Coxe, George Harmon* prior to *Cox, J. Randolph* and interfiled compound names such as *Van Dine* and *Van Gulik* with such words as *Vance* and *Vanishers.* These and other errors have been silently corrected.

The *Index* is alphabetical by author, title, and subject, listing in one alphabetic sequence all of the articles, reviews, and letters published in the *Armchair Detective* be-tween October 1967 and October 1987. Titles of books, plays, television shows, and films are capitalized; subjects are italicized; and titles of short stories are given in quote marks. Individual reviews of books, short stories, and plays are indexed under the author of the work, the title of the work, the subject, and the author for the review, but movie and television reviews are listed under the title alone. Reviews in columns are listed only under the author and title of the review, the exception being the contents of Charles Shibuk's "The Paperback Revolution," which have not been separately indexed.

Symbols and abbreviations are the same as those in Stilwell's solo effort: (R) after the title means "reviewed," (MN) means "movie note," and (L) means "letter." Letters from individuals are listed in their alphabetical sequence, and those letters related to a subject also are grouped at the conclusion of each subject entry.

Entries conclude with the volume, issue number, and page upon which the piece appeared. As in the other index, the format in which these data are presented is initially unclear—a typical entry looks like 12/3/203—but this is at best a minor inconvenience.

An essential index for all academic and research libraries.

The August Derleth Society Newsletter

345a. Contents indexed in Michael L. Cook, **Mystery Fanfare: A Composite Annotated Index to Mystery and Related Fanzines 1963–1981** (Bowling Green, Ohio: Bowling Green State University Popular Press, 1983).

345b. Described in **Mystery, Detective, and Espionage Magazines,** ed. by Michael L. Cook (Westport, Conn.: Greenwood, 1983), pp. 33–36.

The Avenger

346a. Checklist to title stories given in John P. Gunnison, **Street & Smith's Hero Pulp Checklist** (Upper Marlboro, Md.: Pulp Collector Press, 1991).

346b. Described in **Mystery, Detective, and Espionage Magazines,** ed. by Michael L. Cook (Westport, Conn.: Greenwood, 1983), pp. 36–39.

346c. Indexed in **Mystery, Detective, and Espionage Fiction,** ed. by Michael L. Cook and Stephen T. Miller (New York: Garland, 1988), pp. 14–15.

346d. Indexed in **The Pulp Magazine Index: First Series,** by Leonard A. Robbins (Mercer Island, Wash.: Starmont House, 1989).

346e. Finnan, Robert W. **The Avenger.** http://users.arczip.com/fwdixon/seriesbookcentral/avenger.html

This Web site provides a history and list of the *Avenger* stories, indicating the titles and issues of the magazines in which they appeared as well as their reprint status. Information on authors of specific stories is briefly given. Some cover reproductions of the paperbacks are provided. A complete list of the titles in the *Avenger* on radio is also given.

346f. Hopkins, Howard. **The Gray Nemesis.** Scarboro, Maine: Golden Perils Press, 1992. 148 p. Paperback.

Introduced in 1939, the *Avenger* was one of Street and Smith's last attempts at creating a major pulp hero. Protagonist Richard Henry Benson was intriguingly presented—he was an adventurer whose wife and daughter vanished mysteriously on an airplane trip, so shocking him that his hair turned white and his features became a motionless mask, thereby enabling him to become a master of disguise—but the magazine lasted a mere 24 issues, dying in 1942. In 1974, the Warner Paperback Library reprinted the magazines in paperback form and reintroduced the character in a series of original paperbacks that failed.

Clearly reproduced from word-processed copy, *The Gray Nemesis* is a loving tribute to one of the less successful pulp magazines. The first part of the book consists of descriptions of the world of Benson and descriptions of his assistants. Although most of the latter were standard pulp types, two of them—Joshua Elijah and Rosabel Newton— are reasonably sympathetic portraits of African Americans, and the early magazines contain hints that another character was also intended to be a minority. This section concludes with lists of the radio dramatizations of the *Avenger,* summarizes all of the *Avenger* stories (pulp magazines as well as paperback), and concludes with a chronological list of all of the *Avenger* stories that provides the title under which the story was published, the date the story was submitted, the story's original title, and the date the story was published. This material occupies less than half of the volume; the rest of the book consists of reproductions of illustrations from the magazines.

346g. Kalb, Dave. **The Avenger Archives.** http://members.aol.com/macmurdie

One of several very nicely done sites devoted to the character and his adventures. Bibliographic data are helpful and thorough.

346h. Vaisala, Tomi. **The Avenger/Justice, Inc**. http://www.cs.uku.fi/~vaisala/ AVENGER/Avenger.htm

This Web site provides a complete index to the *Avenger,* using much of the information appearing in Hopkins's *The Gray Nemesis* (q.v.). The title of each issue is given, as are the author, the date of publication, and the series number. When the *Avenger* was forced to appear in other magazines, their titles are also indicated. Lists of the comic book issues of the *Avenger* are given, as are the radio shows in which the *Avenger* was featured. Finally, cover reproductions of the paperback reprints of the *Avenger* are given. A very nicely done site.

Avon Detective Mysteries

347a. Described in **Mystery, Detective, and Espionage Magazines,** ed. by Michael L. Cook (Westport, Conn.: Greenwood, 1983), pp. 39–40.

347b. Indexed in Michael Cook, **Monthly Murders: A Checklist and Chronological Listing of Fiction in the Digest-Size Mystery Magazines in the United States and England** (Westport, Conn.: Greenwood, 1982), p. 98.

Avon Modern Short Story Monthly

348. Indexed in Michael Cook, **Monthly Murders: A Checklist and Chronological Listing of Fiction in the Digest-Size Mystery Magazines in the United States and England** (Westport, Conn.: Greenwood, 1982), p. 97.

Avon Murder Mystery Monthly

349. Described in **Mystery, Detective, and Espionage Magazines**, ed. by Michael L. Cook (Westport, Conn.: Greenwood, 1983), pp. 40–41.

Baffling Detective Mysteries

350a. Described in **Mystery, Detective, and Espionage Magazines,** ed. by Michael L. Cook (Westport, Conn.: Greenwood, 1983), p. 43.

350b. Indexed in **Mystery, Detective, and Espionage Fiction,** ed. by Michael L. Cook and Stephen T. Miller (New York: Garland, 1988), pp. 15–16.

The Baker Street Journal

351. Described in **Mystery, Detective, and Espionage Magazines,** ed. by Michael L. Cook (Westport, Conn.: Greenwood, 1983), pp. 43–45.

Baker Street Miscellanea

352. Described in **Mystery, Detective, and Espionage Magazines,** ed. by Michael L. Cook (Westport, Conn.: Greenwood, 1983), pp. 45–47.

Battle Aces. See *G-8 and His Battle Aces*

Battle Birds. See *Dusty Ayres and His Battle Birds*

Best Detective

353a. Described in **Mystery, Detective, and Espionage Magazines,** ed. by Michael L. Cook (Westport, Conn.: Greenwood, 1983), p. 48.

353b. Indexed in **Mystery, Detective, and Espionage Fiction,** ed. by Michael L. Cook and Stephen T. Miller (New York: Garland, 1988), p. 21.

353c. Indexed in **The Pulp Magazine Index: First Series,** by Leonard A. Robbins (Mercer Island, Wash.: Starmont House, 1989).

Best Detective Magazine

354a. Described in **Mystery, Detective, and Espionage Magazines,** ed. by Michael L. Cook (Westport, Conn.: Greenwood, 1983), pp. 48–52.

354b. Indexed in **Mystery, Detective, and Espionage Fiction,** ed. by Michael L. Cook and Stephen T. Miller (New York: Garland, 1988), pp. 21–31, 665.

Bestseller Mystery Magazine

355a. Described in **Mystery, Detective, and Espionage Magazines,** ed. by Michael L. Cook (Westport, Conn.: Greenwood, 1983), pp. 52–53.

355b. Indexed in Michael Cook, **Monthly Murders: A Checklist and Chronological Listing of Fiction in the Digest-Size Mystery Magazines in the United States and England** (Westport, Conn.: Greenwood, 1982), pp. 104–6.

Big-Book Detective Magazine

356a. Described in **Mystery, Detective, and Espionage Magazines,** ed. by Michael L. Cook (Westport, Conn.: Greenwood, 1983), p. 53.

356b. Indexed in **Mystery, Detective, and Espionage Fiction,** ed. by Michael L. Cook and Stephen T. Miller (New York: Garland, 1988), p. 31.

Big Double Feature Magazine

357. Indexed in **Mystery, Detective, and Espionage Fiction,** ed. by Michael L. Cook and Stephen T. Miller (New York: Garland, 1988), p. 32.

Bill Barnes Air Adventurer. See *Bill Barnes Air Adventures*

Bill Barnes Air Adventures

358a. Checklist to title stories given in John P. Gunnison, **Street & Smith's Hero Pulp Checklist** (Upper Marlboro, Md.: Pulp Collector Press, 1991).

358b. Indexed in **Mystery, Detective, and Espionage Fiction,** ed. by Michael L. Cook and Stephen T. Miller (New York: Garland, 1988), p. 32.

358c. Indexed in **The Pulp Magazine Index: First Series,** by Leonard A. Robbins (Mercer Island, Wash.: Starmont House, 1989).

Bill Barnes Air Trails

359a. Checklist to title stories given in John P. Gunnison, **Street & Smith's Hero Pulp Checklist** (Upper Marlboro, Md.: Pulp Collector Press, 1991).

359b. Indexed in **Mystery, Detective, and Espionage Fiction,** ed. by Michael L. Cook and Stephen T. Miller (New York: Garland, 1988), pp. 32–33.

359c. Indexed in **The Pulp Magazine Index: First Series,** by Leonard A. Robbins (Mercer Island, Wash.: Starmont House, 1989).

Bizarre! Mystery Magazine

360a. Described in **Mystery, Detective, and Espionage Magazines,** ed. by Michael L. Cook (Westport, Conn.: Greenwood, 1983), p. 54.

360b. Indexed in Michael Cook, **Monthly Murders: A Checklist and Chronological Listing of Fiction in the Digest-Size Mystery Magazines in the United States and England** (Westport, Conn.: Greenwood, 1982), pp. 107–8.

Black Aces

361a. Described in **Mystery, Detective, and Espionage Magazines,** ed. by Michael L. Cook (Westport, Conn.: Greenwood, 1983), pp. 54–56.

361b. Indexed in **Mystery, Detective, and Espionage Fiction,** ed. by Michael L. Cook and Stephen T. Miller (New York: Garland, 1988), pp. 33–34.

Black Bat Detective Mysteries

362a. Described in **Mystery, Detective, and Espionage Magazines,** ed. by Michael L. Cook (Westport, Conn.: Greenwood, 1983), p. 56.

362b. Indexed in **Mystery, Detective, and Espionage Fiction,** ed. by Michael L. Cook and Stephen T. Miller (New York: Garland, 1988), p. 34.

362c. Indexed in **The Pulp Magazine Index: Fourth Series,** by Leonard A. Robbins (Mercer Island, Wash.: Starmont House, 1991).

Black Book Detective (Better Publications)

363. Indexed in **The Pulp Magazine Index: First Series,** by Leonard A. Robbins (Mercer Island, Wash.: Starmont House, 1989).

Black Book Detective Magazine (Newsstand Publications)

364a. Described in **Mystery, Detective, and Espionage Magazines,** ed. by Michael L. Cook (Westport, Conn.: Greenwood, 1983), pp. 56–59.

364b. Indexed in Michael Cook, **Monthly Murders: A Checklist and Chronological Listing of Fiction in the Digest-Size Mystery Magazines in the United States and England** (Westport, Conn.: Greenwood, 1982), p. 99.

364c. Indexed in **Mystery, Detective, and Espionage Fiction,** ed. by Michael L. Cook and Stephen T. Miller (New York: Garland, 1988), pp. 34–39.

364d. Indexed in **The Pulp Magazine Index: First Series,** by Leonard A. Robbins (Mercer Island, Wash.: Starmont House, 1989).

Black Box Mystery Magazine (Canadian)

365. Described in **Mystery, Detective, and Espionage Magazines,** ed. by Michael L. Cook (Westport, Conn.: Greenwood, 1983), pp. 59–60.

Black Cat Mystery Magazine (Canadian)

366. Described in **Mystery, Detective, and Espionage Magazines,** ed. by Michael L. Cook (Westport, Conn.: Greenwood, 1983), pp. 60–61.

Black Cat Mystery Quarterly (Canadian). See *Black Cat Mystery Magazine* (Canadian)

Black Hood Detective. See *Hooded Detective*

The Black Mask

367a. Described in **Mystery, Detective, and Espionage Magazines,** ed. by Michael L. Cook (Westport, Conn.: Greenwood, 1983), pp. 62–68.

367b. Indexed in **Mystery, Detective, and Espionage Fiction,** ed. by Michael L. Cook and Stephen T. Miller (New York: Garland, 1988), pp. 39–67.

367c. Hagemann, E. R. **A Comprehensive Index to *Black Mask*, 1920–1951: With Brief Annotations, Preface, and Editorial Apparatus.** Bowling Green, Ohio: Bowling Green State University Popular Press, 1982. 236 p. LC 82-81824. ISBN 0-87972-201-0 (hc); 0-87972-202-9 (pb).

For an astoundingly long time, *Black Mask* set the standard. Other pulp magazines could try to emulate it, but only rarely could they beat it, and it remains a legend, lasting for some 31 years and publishing in its 340 issues approximately 2,500 stories by approximately 640 authors. Although numerous anthologies have been drawn from its pages, surprisingly few indexes to *Black Mask* have been compiled. Hagemann's is but one of two known. Others are rumored to exist but cannot be confirmed.

Despite its title, this is not so much a comprehensive index as it is an author index. The volume opens with "Register of *Black Mask*" that lists the holdings of the British Library, UCLA, the Library of Congress, the University of Louisville, and private collectors. This is followed by data on the magazine's issuance, the editorship, title, and price and a listing of the editors, writers (arranged by debut), frequency of appearance, and series characters.

These facts occupy only 15 pages; the remainder of the volume is the author index. For each author, Hagemann lists alphabetically the stories contributed, numbering each story and including in each citation the volume, issue number, month and year in which the story was published. The story's pagination is given, as are the names of the major series character appearing in the story and, occasionally, an editorial comment (i.e., "unusually well-plotted"). All of this material is clearly presented and admirably accessible.

Had Hagemann continued in this vein and provided indexes listing the contents of the magazine, the titles of the stories, and the illustrators, he would undoubtedly have produced the definitive index to *Black Mask*. As it is, there is still a need for a truly comprehensive index, but given the rarity of the magazine—two complete sets are known to exist—it is improbable that such will ever be compiled. Hagemann's index thus remains the only viable means for accessing the contents of this most important pulp.

367d.   Mundell, E. H. **An Index of Black Mask.** Portage, Ind.: N.p., 1973. 164 p.

According to Mundell's brief preface, this is the second index of the *Black Mask* that he compiled, the first being an issue-by-issue index. This earlier index has not been seen and cannot be located. The contents include indexes of authors, editors, and cover illustrators.

Arrangement in the first section is alphabetical, but author names are not reversed for alphabetization. The names are given in capital letters; beneath each, in regular type, are two columns. The first lists the titles of the stories, the second the month and year in which the story was published; only the last two digits of the year are given. When the author contributed more than one story, the arrangement is chronological. Not provided are the story's pagination and the volume and issue numbers of the magazine in which the story appeared. Nor are cross-references provided to reveal pseudonyms.

The second section lists the editors of *Black Mask* in chronological order, and the third lists the cover artists alphabetically. The entries for the artists are not separated into columns but, rather, lumped together as a paragraph, the year occurring only at the end of each listing of months.

This is not a discreditable effort, but one nevertheless wishes that Mundell had included with it his issue-by-issue index and had indexed nonfiction and editorial material. This aside, although the author index has been superseded by Hagemann's *A Comprehensive Index to* Black Mask*, 1920–1951* (q.v.), the list of cover artists is unique to this volume.

Black Mask Detective. See *The Black Mask*

Black Mask Detective Magazine. See *The Black Mask*

Bloodhound Detective Story Magazine (British)

368a.   Described in **Mystery, Detective, and Espionage Magazines,** ed. by Michael L. Cook (Westport, Conn.: Greenwood, 1983), pp. 68–70.

368b.   Indexed in Michael Cook, **Monthly Murders: A Checklist and Chronological Listing of Fiction in the Digest-Size Mystery Magazines in the United States and England** (Westport, Conn.: Greenwood, 1982), pp. 100–103.

Blue Steel Magazine

369a.   Described in **Mystery, Detective, and Espionage Magazines,** ed. by Michael L. Cook (Westport, Conn.: Greenwood, 1983), pp. 70–71.

369b.   Indexed in **Mystery, Detective, and Espionage Fiction,** ed. by Michael L. Cook and Stephen T. Miller (New York: Garland, 1988), p. 67.

369c.   Indexed in **The Pulp Magazine Index: Second Series,** by Leonard A. Robbins (Mercer Island, Wash.: Starmont House, 1989).

Bob Brooks Library

370. Described in **Mystery, Detective, and Espionage Magazines,** ed. by Michael L. Cook (Westport, Conn.: Greenwood, 1983), pp. 71–72.

Bondage

371. Described in **Mystery, Detective, and Espionage Magazines,** ed. by Michael L. Cook (Westport, Conn.: Greenwood, 1983), pp. 72–73.

Bondage Quarterly. See Bondage

The Bony Bulletin

372. Contents indexed in Michael L. Cook, **Mystery Fanfare: A Composite Annotated Index to Mystery and Related Fanzines 1963–1981** (Bowling Green, Ohio: Bowling Green State University Popular Press, 1983).

Book of Terror

373. Indexed in **Mystery, Detective, and Espionage Fiction,** ed. by Michael L. Cook and Stephen T. Miller (New York: Garland, 1988), p. 67.

Boy's Adventure Magazine

374. Indexed in **Mystery, Detective, and Espionage Fiction,** ed. by Michael L. Cook and Stephen T. Miller (New York: Garland, 1988), p. 68.

The Boy's Book Buff

375. Contents indexed in Michael L. Cook, **Mystery Fanfare: A Composite Annotated Index to Mystery and Related Fanzines 1963–1981** (Bowling Green, Ohio: Bowling Green State University Popular Press, 1983).

The Boys' Book Collector

376. Contents indexed in Michael L. Cook, **Mystery Fanfare: A Composite Annotated Index to Mystery and Related Fanzines 1963–1981** (Bowling Green, Ohio: Bowling Green State University Popular Press, 1983).

Bronze Shadows

377a. Contents indexed in Michael L. Cook, **Mystery Fanfare: A Composite Annotated Index to Mystery and Related Fanzines 1963–1981** (Bowling Green, Ohio: Bowling Green State University Popular Press, 1983).

377b. Described in **Mystery, Detective, and Espionage Magazines**, ed. by Michael L. Cook (Westport, Conn.: Greenwood, 1983), pp. 73–74.

The Bullseye. See *The Bull's Eye* (British)

The Bull's Eye (British)

378. Described in **Mystery, Detective, and Espionage Magazines,** ed. by Michael L. Cook (Westport, Conn.: Greenwood, 1983), p. 75.

Bull's Eye Detective

379a. Described in **Mystery, Detective, and Espionage Magazines,** ed. by Michael L. Cook (Westport, Conn.: Greenwood, 1983), pp. 75–76.

379b. Indexed in **Mystery, Detective, and Espionage Fiction,** ed. by Michael L. Cook and Stephen T. Miller (New York: Garland, 1988), p. 68.

379c. Indexed in **The Pulp Magazine Index: First Series,** by Leonard A. Robbins (Mercer Island, Wash.: Starmont House, 1989).

Burnt Gumshoe. See *Fatal Kiss*

Cabaret Stories

380. Indexed in **Mystery, Detective, and Espionage Fiction,** ed. by Michael L. Cook and Stephen T. Miller (New York: Garland, 1988), p. 68.

CADS: Crime and Detective Stories

381a. Deeck, William F. **CADS: An Index to Issues 1–30.** CADS Supplement, no. 6. South Benfleet, Essex, England: CADS, 1997. 72 p. Paperback. ISSN 0965-6561.

381b. Deeck, William F. **CADS: Index to Issues 31–39.** N.p., n.d. Paperback. 41 p. [ISSN 0965-6561?]

These two publications provide clear and comprehensive author/title indexes to the first 39 issues of *CADS,* one of the preeminent amateur publications. Entries in italic type indicate when the reference is to a subject; plain type indexes a primary work. Book titles are given in capital letters, with subtitles and in upper- and lowercase; references to media are also in capital letters and are so identified. Reviews are indicated by the letter *R* in parentheses. The letters and obituaries appearing in *CADS* also have been indexed, although when the letters have discussed an article, they are listed under the article rather than separately.

Much useful material appears in *CADS,* and it is not indexed elsewhere. Libraries subscribing to it should acquire these publications.

Candid Detective

382a. Indexed in **Mystery, Detective, and Espionage Fiction,** ed. by Michael L. Cook and Stephen T. Miller (New York: Garland, 1988), pp. 68–69.

382b. Indexed in **The Pulp Magazine Index: Third Series,** by Leonard A. Robbins (Mercer Island, Wash.: Starmont House, 1990).

Captain Combat

383a. Described in **Mystery, Detective, and Espionage Magazines,** ed. by Michael L. Cook (Westport, Conn.: Greenwood, 1983), pp. 77–78.

383b. Indexed in **Mystery, Detective, and Espionage Fiction,** ed. by Michael L. Cook and Stephen T. Miller (New York: Garland, 1988), p. 69.

Captain Hazzard

384a. Described in **Mystery, Detective, and Espionage Magazines,** ed. by Michael L. Cook (Westport, Conn.: Greenwood, 1983), pp. 78–79.

384b. Indexed in **Mystery, Detective, and Espionage Fiction,** ed. by Michael L. Cook and Stephen T. Miller (New York: Garland, 1988), p. 69.

384c. Indexed in **The Pulp Magazine Index: First Series,** by Leonard A. Robbins (Mercer Island, Wash.: Starmont House, 1989).

Captain Hazzard Magazine. See Captain Hazzard

Captain Satan

385a. Described in **Mystery, Detective, and Espionage Magazines,** ed. by Michael L. Cook (Westport, Conn.: Greenwood, 1983), pp. 79–83.

385b. Indexed in **Mystery, Detective, and Espionage Fiction,** ed. by Michael L. Cook and Stephen T. Miller (New York: Garland, 1988), p. 69.

385c. Indexed in **The Pulp Magazine Index: First Series,** by Leonard A. Robbins (Mercer Island, Wash.: Starmont House, 1989).

Captain Satan Magazine. See Captain Satan

Captain Zero

386a. Described in **Mystery, Detective, and Espionage Magazines,** ed. by Michael L. Cook (Westport, Conn.: Greenwood, 1983), pp. 83–87.

386b. Indexed in **Mystery, Detective, and Espionage Fiction,** ed. by Michael L. Cook and Stephen T. Miller (New York: Garland, 1988), p. 69.

386c. Indexed in **The Pulp Magazine Index: First Series,** by Leonard A. Robbins (Mercer Island, Wash.: Starmont House, 1989).

Cash Gorman. See The Wizard

Castle Dracula Quarterly

387a. Contents indexed in Michael L. Cook, **Mystery Fanfare: A Composite Annotated Index to Mystery and Related Fanzines 1963–1981** (Bowling Green, Ohio: Bowling Green State University Popular Press, 1983).

387b. Described in **Mystery, Detective, and Espionage Magazines,** ed. by Michael L. Cook (Westport, Conn.: Greenwood, 1983), p. 87.

Celebrated Detective Tales (British). See Detective Tales (Aldine Publishing) (British)

Charlie Chan Mystery Magazine

388a. Described in **Mystery, Detective, and Espionage Magazines,** ed. by Michael L. Cook (Westport, Conn.: Greenwood, 1983), pp. 87–89.

388b. Indexed in Michael Cook, **Monthly Murders: A Checklist and Chronological Listing of Fiction in the Digest-Size Mystery Magazines in the United States and England** (Westport, Conn.: Greenwood, 1982), pp. 109–10.

Chase

389a. Described in **Mystery, Detective, and Espionage Magazines,** ed. by Michael L. Cook (Westport, Conn.: Greenwood, 1983), pp. 89–91.

389b. Indexed in Michael Cook, **Monthly Murders: A Checklist and Chronological Listing of Fiction in the Digest-Size Mystery Magazines in the United States and England** (Westport, Conn.: Greenwood, 1982), p. 113.

Chief Detective

390a. Indexed in **Mystery, Detective, and Espionage Fiction,** ed. by Michael L. Cook and Stephen T. Miller (New York: Garland, 1988), p. 70.

390b. Indexed in **The Pulp Magazine Index: Third Series,** by Leonard A. Robbins (Mercer Island, Wash.: Starmont House, 1990).

Ching Ching Yarns (British)

391. Described in **Mystery, Detective, and Espionage Magazines,** ed. by Michael L. Cook (Westport, Conn.: Greenwood, 1983), pp. 91–92.

C.I.D. Library (British)

392. Described in **Mystery, Detective, and Espionage Magazines,** ed. by Michael L. Cook (Westport, Conn.: Greenwood, 1983), pp. 92–93.

Cloak and Dagger

393a. Contents indexed in Michael L. Cook, **Mystery Fanfare: A Composite Annotated Index to Mystery and Related Fanzines 1963–1981** (Bowling Green, Ohio: Bowling Green State University Popular Press, 1983).

393b. Described in **Mystery, Detective, and Espionage Magazines,** ed. by Michael L. Cook (Westport, Conn.: Greenwood, 1983), pp. 93–95.

Cloak and Pistol

394. Described in **Mystery, Detective, and Espionage Magazines,** ed. by Michael L. Cook (Westport, Conn.: Greenwood, 1983), p. 95.

Clues

395a. Described in **Mystery, Detective, and Espionage Magazines,** ed. by Michael L. Cook (Westport, Conn.: Greenwood, 1983), pp. 96–100.

395b. Indexed in **Mystery, Detective, and Espionage Fiction,** ed. by Michael L. Cook and Stephen T. Miller (New York: Garland, 1988), pp. 70–88, 665.

Clues: A Journal of Detection

396a. Contents indexed in Michael L. Cook, **Mystery Fanfare: A Composite Annotated Index to Mystery and Related Fanzines 1963–1981** (Bowling Green, Ohio: Bowling Green State University Popular Press, 1983).

396b. Described in **Mystery, Detective, and Espionage Magazines,** ed. by Michael L. Cook (Westport, Conn.: Greenwood, 1983), pp. 100–102.

Clues: All Star Detective Stories. See Clues

Clues: A Magazine of Detective Stories. See Clues

Clues (Mystery Writers of America). See The Third Degree

Clues Detective Stories. See Clues

Collecting Paperbacks?

397. Contents indexed in Michael L. Cook, **Mystery Fanfare: A Composite Annotated Index to Mystery and Related Fanzines 1963–1981** (Bowling Green, Ohio: Bowling Green State University Popular Press, 1983).

Complete Detective

398a. Described in **Mystery, Detective, and Espionage Magazines,** ed. by Michael L. Cook (Westport, Conn.: Greenwood, 1983), p. 102.

398b. Indexed in **Mystery, Detective, and Espionage Fiction,** ed. by Michael L. Cook and Stephen T. Miller (New York: Garland, 1988), pp. 88–89.

398c. Indexed in **The Pulp Magazine Index: Second Series,** by Leonard A. Robbins (Mercer Island, Wash.: Starmont House, 1989).

Complete Detective Novel Magazine

399a. Described in **Mystery, Detective, and Espionage Magazines,** ed. by Michael L. Cook (Westport, Conn.: Greenwood, 1983), p. 103.

399b. Indexed in **Mystery, Detective, and Espionage Fiction,** ed. by Michael L. Cook and Stephen T. Miller (New York: Garland, 1988), pp. 89–92, 665.

399c. Indexed in **The Pulp Magazine Index: Third Series,** by Leonard A. Robbins (Mercer Island, Wash.: Starmont House, 1990).

Complete Gang Novel Magazine

400a. Described in **Mystery, Detective, and Espionage Magazines,** ed. by Michael L. Cook (Westport, Conn.: Greenwood, 1983), pp. 103–4.

400b. Indexed in **Mystery, Detective, and Espionage Fiction,** ed. by Michael L. Cook and Stephen T. Miller (New York: Garland, 1988), p. 93.

Complete Mystery Novelettes

401a. Described in **Mystery, Detective, and Espionage Magazines,** ed. by Michael L. Cook (Westport, Conn.: Greenwood, 1983), p. 104.

401b. Indexed in **Mystery, Detective, and Espionage Fiction,** ed. by Michael L. Cook and Stephen T. Miller (New York: Garland, 1988), p. 93.

Complete Underworld Novelettes

402a. Described in **Mystery, Detective, and Espionage Magazines,** ed. by Michael L. Cook (Westport, Conn.: Greenwood, 1983), pp. 104–5.

402b. Indexed in **Mystery, Detective, and Espionage Fiction,** ed. by Michael L. Cook and Stephen T. Miller (New York: Garland, 1988), pp. 93–94.

Confessions of a Federal Dick

403. Indexed in **Mystery, Detective, and Espionage Fiction,** ed. by Michael L. Cook and Stephen T. Miller (New York: Garland, 1988), p. 94.

Confessions of a Stool Pigeon

404. Mentioned in **Mystery, Detective, and Espionage Fiction,** ed. by Michael L. Cook and Stephen T. Miller (New York: Garland, 1988), p. 94.

Conflict

405a. Described in **Mystery, Detective, and Espionage Magazines,** ed. by Michael L. Cook (Westport, Conn.: Greenwood, 1983), p. 105.

405b. Indexed in Michael Cook, **Monthly Murders: A Checklist and Chronological Listing of Fiction in the Digest-Size Mystery Magazines in the United States and England** (Westport, Conn.: Greenwood, 1982), p. 116.

405c. Indexed in **Mystery, Detective, and Espionage Fiction,** ed. by Michael L. Cook and Stephen T. Miller (New York: Garland, 1988), p. 94.

405d. Indexed in **The Pulp Magazine Index: First Series,** by Leonard A. Robbins (Mercer Island, Wash.: Starmont House, 1989).

Conflict—Stories of Suspense. See Conflict

Conflict: Tales of Fighting Adventurers

406. Described in **Mystery, Detective, and Espionage Magazines,** ed. by Michael L. Cook (Westport, Conn.: Greenwood, 1983), p. 106.

Courtroom Stories

407a. Described in **Mystery, Detective, and Espionage Magazines,** ed. by Michael L. Cook (Westport, Conn.: Greenwood, 1983), p. 106.

407b. Indexed in **Mystery, Detective, and Espionage Fiction,** ed. by Michael L. Cook and Stephen T. Miller (New York: Garland, 1988), p. 95.

Coven 13

408a. Described in **Mystery, Detective, and Espionage Magazines,** ed. by Michael L. Cook (Westport, Conn.: Greenwood, 1983), p. 107.

408b. Indexed in Michael Cook, **Monthly Murders: A Checklist and Chronological Listing of Fiction in the Digest-Size Mystery Magazines in the United States and England** (Westport, Conn.: Greenwood, 1982), pp. 117–18.

Crack Detective

409a. Described in **Mystery, Detective, and Espionage Magazines,** ed. by Michael L. Cook (Westport, Conn.: Greenwood, 1983), pp. 108–11.

409b.   Indexed in **Mystery, Detective, and Espionage Fiction,** ed. by Michael L. Cook and Stephen T. Miller (New York: Garland, 1988), pp. 39, 95–98, 271–72, 321–23, 377, 665.

409c.   Indexed in **The Pulp Magazine Index: First Series,** by Leonard A. Robbins (Mercer Island, Wash.: Starmont House, 1989).

409d.   Indexed in **The Pulp Magazine Index: Second Series,** by Leonard A. Robbins (Mercer Island, Wash.: Starmont House, 1989).

409e.   Indexed in **The Pulp Magazine Index: Third Series,** by Leonard A. Robbins (Mercer Island, Wash.: Starmont House, 1990).

409f.   Indexed in **The Pulp Magazine Index: Fourth Series,** by Leonard A. Robbins (Mercer Island, Wash.: Starmont House, 1991).

Crack Detective and Mystery Stories. **See** *Crack Detective*

Crack Detective Stories **(British). See** *Crack Detective*

Crack Detective Stories **(American). See** *Crack Detective*

Craig Rice Crime Casebook. **See** *Detective Files*

Craig Rice Crime Digest

410a.   Described in **Mystery, Detective, and Espionage Magazines,** ed. by Michael L. Cook (Westport, Conn.: Greenwood, 1983), pp. 111–13.

410b.   Indexed in Michael Cook, **Monthly Murders: A Checklist and Chronological Listing of Fiction in the Digest-Size Mystery Magazines in the United States and England** (Westport, Conn.: Greenwood, 1982), p. 111.

Craig Rice Mystery Digest

411a.   Described in **Mystery, Detective, and Espionage Magazines,** ed. by Michael L. Cook (Westport, Conn.: Greenwood, 1983), p. 113.

411b.   Indexed in Michael Cook, **Monthly Murders: A Checklist and Chronological Listing of Fiction in the Digest-Size Mystery Magazines in the United States and England** (Westport, Conn.: Greenwood, 1982), p. 112.

The Creasey Mystery Magazine **(British). See** *John Creasey Mystery Magazine* **(British)**

Crime and Justice Detective Story Magazine

412a.   Described in **Mystery, Detective, and Espionage Magazines,** ed. by Michael L. Cook (Westport, Conn.: Greenwood, 1983), pp. 113–15.

412b. Indexed in Michael Cook, **Monthly Murders: A Checklist and Chronological Listing of Fiction in the Digest-Size Mystery Magazines in the United States and England** (Westport, Conn.: Greenwood, 1982), pp. 114–15.

Crime Busters

413a. Described in **Mystery, Detective, and Espionage Magazines,** ed. by Michael L. Cook (Westport, Conn.: Greenwood, 1983), pp. 115–18.

413b. Indexed in **Mystery, Detective, and Espionage Fiction,** ed. by Michael L. Cook and Stephen T. Miller (New York: Garland, 1988), pp. 99–100, 423–25.

413c. Indexed in **The Pulp Magazine Index: First Series,** by Leonard A. Robbins (Mercer Island, Wash.: Starmont House, 1989).

Crime Detective (British)

414. Described in **Mystery, Detective, and Espionage Magazines,** ed. by Michael L. Cook (Westport, Conn.: Greenwood, 1983), p. 118.

Crime Digest

415. Described in **Mystery, Detective, and Espionage Magazines,** ed. by Michael L. Cook (Westport, Conn.: Greenwood, 1983), pp. 118–19.

Crime Fiction Stories

416. Indexed in **Mystery, Detective, and Espionage Fiction,** ed. by Michael L. Cook and Stephen T. Miller (New York: Garland, 1988), p. 100.

Crime Investigator (British)

417. Described in **Mystery, Detective, and Espionage Magazines**, ed. by Michael L. Cook (Westport, Conn.: Greenwood, 1983), pp. 119–20.

Crime Mysteries

418a. Described in **Mystery, Detective, and Espionage Magazines,** ed. by Michael L. Cook (Westport, Conn.: Greenwood, 1983), p. 120.

418b. Indexed in **Mystery, Detective, and Espionage Fiction,** ed. by Michael L. Cook and Stephen T. Miller (New York: Garland, 1988), p. 101.

Crime Writing (British). See Red Herrings (British)

Current Crime (British)

419. Described in **Mystery, Detective, and Espionage Magazines,** ed. by Michael L. Cook (Westport, Conn.: Greenwood, 1983), pp. 120–21.

Dan Dunn Detective Magazine

420a. Described in **Mystery, Detective, and Espionage Magazines,** ed. by Michael L. Cook (Westport, Conn.: Greenwood, 1983), p. 123.

420b. Indexed in **Mystery, Detective, and Espionage Fiction,** ed. by Michael L. Cook and Stephen T. Miller (New York: Garland, 1988), p. 101.

420c. Indexed in **The Pulp Magazine Index: First Series,** by Leonard A. Robbins (Mercer Island, Wash.: Starmont House, 1989).

Dan Turner, Hollywood Detective

421a. Described in **Mystery, Detective, and Espionage Magazines,** ed. by Michael L. Cook (Westport, Conn.: Greenwood, 1983), pp. 123–25.

421b. Indexed in **Mystery, Detective, and Espionage Fiction,** ed. by Michael L. Cook and Stephen T. Miller (New York: Garland, 1988), pp. 101–2, 373–76.

421c. Indexed in **The Pulp Magazine Index: First Series,** by Leonard A. Robbins (Mercer Island, Wash.: Starmont House, 1989).

Dapa-Em. See Elementary, My Dear Apa

Dare-Devil Aces

422a. Indexed in **Mystery, Detective, and Espionage Fiction,** ed. by Michael L. Cook and Stephen T. Miller (New York: Garland, 1988), pp. 102–11.

422b. Indexed in **The Pulp Magazine Index: First Series,** by Leonard A. Robbins (Mercer Island, Wash.: Starmont House, 1989).

Daredevil Detective Stories

423. Indexed in **Mystery, Detective, and Espionage Fiction,** ed. by Michael L. Cook and Stephen T. Miller (New York: Garland, 1988), p. 663.

Dell Mystery Novels Magazine

424a. Described in **Mystery, Detective, and Espionage Magazines,** ed. by Michael L. Cook (Westport, Conn.: Greenwood, 1983), pp. 125–27.

424b. Indexed in Michael Cook, **Monthly Murders: A Checklist and Chronological Listing of Fiction in the Digest-Size Mystery Magazines in the United States and England** (Westport, Conn.: Greenwood, 1982), p. 153.

Detective (American)

425. Indexed in **Mystery, Detective, and Espionage Fiction,** ed. by Michael L. Cook and Stephen T. Miller (New York: Garland, 1988), p. 112.

Detective (British)

426. Described in **Mystery, Detective, and Espionage Magazines,** ed. by Michael L. Cook (Westport, Conn.: Greenwood, 1983), p. 127.

Detective Aces (British). See *The Dragnet*

Detective Action Stories

427a. Described in **Mystery, Detective, and Espionage Magazines,** ed. by Michael L. Cook (Westport, Conn.: Greenwood, 1983), pp. 127–29.

427b. Indexed in **Mystery, Detective, and Espionage Fiction,** ed. by Michael L. Cook and Stephen T. Miller (New York: Garland, 1988), pp. 112–14.

427c. Indexed in **The Pulp Magazine Index: First Series,** by Leonard A. Robbins (Mercer Island, Wash.: Starmont House, 1989).

427d. Indexed in **The Pulp Magazine Index: Third Series,** by Leonard A. Robbins (Mercer Island, Wash.: Starmont House, 1990).

Detective Adventures

428a. Described in **Mystery, Detective, and Espionage Magazines,** ed. by Michael L. Cook (Westport, Conn.: Greenwood, 1983), pp. 129–30.

428b. Mentioned in **Mystery, Detective, and Espionage Fiction,** ed. by Michael L. Cook and Stephen T. Miller (New York: Garland, 1988), p. 114.

Detective and Murder Mysteries (1935)

429a. Described in **Mystery, Detective, and Espionage Magazines,** ed. by Michael L. Cook (Westport, Conn.: Greenwood, 1983), p. 130.

429b. Indexed in **Mystery, Detective, and Espionage Fiction,** ed. by Michael L. Cook and Stephen T. Miller (New York: Garland, 1988), pp. 114, 401.

Detective and Murder Mysteries (1939–1941)

430a. Described in **Mystery, Detective, and Espionage Magazines,** ed. by Michael L. Cook (Westport, Conn.: Greenwood, 1983), pp. 130–31.

430b. Indexed in **The Pulp Magazine Index: Third Series,** by Leonard A. Robbins (Mercer Island, Wash.: Starmont House, 1990).

Detective Book Magazine

431a. Described in **Mystery, Detective, and Espionage Magazines,** ed. by Michael L. Cook (Westport, Conn.: Greenwood, 1983), pp. 131–32.

431b. Indexed in **Mystery, Detective, and Espionage Fiction,** ed. by Michael L. Cook and Stephen T. Miller (New York: Garland, 1988), pp. 115–18.

431c. Indexed in **The Pulp Magazine Index: Fourth Series,** by Leonard A. Robbins (Mercer Island, Wash.: Starmont House, 1991).

Detective Classics

432a. Described in **Mystery, Detective, and Espionage Magazines**, ed. by Michael L. Cook (Westport, Conn.: Greenwood, 1983), p. 132.

432b. Indexed in **Mystery, Detective, and Espionage Fiction,** ed. by Michael L. Cook and Stephen T. Miller (New York: Garland, 1988), pp. 118–19, 665.

Detective Digest

433a. Described in **Mystery, Detective, and Espionage Magazines,** ed. by Michael L. Cook (Westport, Conn.: Greenwood, 1983), p. 133.

433b. Mentioned in **Mystery, Detective, and Espionage Fiction,** ed. by Michael L. Cook and Stephen T. Miller (New York: Garland, 1988), p. 119.

Detective Dime Novels

434a. Described in **Mystery, Detective, and Espionage Magazines,** ed. by Michael L. Cook (Westport, Conn.: Greenwood, 1983), pp. 133–35.

434b. Indexed in **Mystery, Detective, and Espionage Fiction,** ed. by Michael L. Cook and Stephen T. Miller (New York: Garland, 1988), pp. 119, 481.

434c. Indexed in **The Pulp Magazine Index: First Series,** by Leonard A. Robbins (Mercer Island, Wash.: Starmont House, 1989).

Detective-Dragnet Magazine. See *The Dragnet*

Detective Fiction. See *Detective Fiction Weekly*

Detective Fiction Weekly

435a. Described in **Mystery, Detective, and Espionage Magazines,** ed. by Michael L. Cook (Westport, Conn.: Greenwood, 1983), pp. 135–37.

435b. Indexed in Michael Cook, **Monthly Murders: A Checklist and Chronological Listing of Fiction in the Digest-Size Mystery Magazines in the United States and England** (Westport, Conn.: Greenwood, 1982), pp. 150–51.

435c. Indexed in **Mystery, Detective, and Espionage Fiction,** ed. by Michael L. Cook and Stephen T. Miller (New York: Garland, 1988), pp. 121–72, 331–48.

Detective Files

436a. Described in **Mystery, Detective, and Espionage Magazines,** ed. by Michael L. Cook (Westport, Conn.: Greenwood, 1983), pp. 137–38.

436b. Indexed in Michael Cook, **Monthly Murders: A Checklist and Chronological Listing of Fiction in the Digest-Size Mystery Magazines in the United States and England** (Westport, Conn.: Greenwood, 1982), p. 152.

Detective Library (1895) (British)

437. Described in **Mystery, Detective, and Espionage Magazines,** ed. by Michael L. Cook (Westport, Conn.: Greenwood, 1983), p. 138.

Detective Library (1919–1920) (British)

438. Described in **Mystery, Detective, and Espionage Magazines,** ed. by Michael L. Cook (Westport, Conn.: Greenwood, 1983), pp. 138–39.

Detective Library (American). See New York Detective Library

The Detective Library

439a. Described in **Mystery, Detective, and Espionage Magazines,** ed. by Michael L. Cook (Westport, Conn.: Greenwood, 1983), p. 140.

439b. Indexed in **Mystery, Detective, and Espionage Fiction,** ed. by Michael L. Cook and Stephen T. Miller (New York: Garland, 1988), p. 173.

Detective Magazine (British). See Detective Fiction Weekly

Detective Mysteries

440a. Described in **Mystery, Detective, and Espionage Magazines,** ed. by Michael L. Cook (Westport, Conn.: Greenwood, 1983), pp. 140–41.

440b. Indexed in **Mystery, Detective, and Espionage Fiction,** ed. by Michael L. Cook and Stephen T. Miller (New York: Garland, 1988), p. 173.

440c. Indexed in **The Pulp Magazine Index: First Series,** by Leonard A. Robbins (Mercer Island, Wash.: Starmont House, 1989).

Detective Mystery Novel Magazine

441a. Described in **Mystery, Detective, and Espionage Magazines,** ed. by Michael L. Cook (Westport, Conn.: Greenwood, 1983), p. 141.

441b. Indexed in **Mystery, Detective, and Espionage Fiction,** ed. by Michael L. Cook and Stephen T. Miller (New York: Garland, 1988), pp. 173, 632–38.

441c. Indexed in **The Pulp Magazine Index: First Series,** by Leonard A. Robbins (Mercer Island, Wash.: Starmont House, 1989).

Detective Novel Magazine. **See** *Detective Novels Magazine*

Detective Novels Magazine

442a. Described in **Mystery, Detective, and Espionage Magazines,** ed. by Michael L. Cook (Westport, Conn.: Greenwood, 1983), pp. 142–44.

442b. Indexed in **Mystery, Detective, and Espionage Fiction,** ed. by Michael L. Cook and Stephen T. Miller (New York: Garland, 1988), pp. 173–77.

442c. Indexed in **The Pulp Magazine Index: First Series,** by Leonard A. Robbins (Mercer Island, Wash.: Starmont House, 1989).

Detective Parade

443. Indexed in **Mystery, Detective, and Espionage Fiction,** ed. by Michael L. Cook and Stephen T. Miller (New York: Garland, 1988), p. 177.

Detective Reporter

444a. Described in **Mystery, Detective, and Espionage Magazines,** ed. by Michael L. Cook (Westport, Conn.: Greenwood, 1983), p. 144.

444b. Indexed in **Mystery, Detective, and Espionage Fiction,** ed. by Michael L. Cook and Stephen T. Miller (New York: Garland, 1988), p. 177.

Detective Romances

445a. Described in **Mystery, Detective, and Espionage Magazines,** ed. by Michael L. Cook (Westport, Conn.: Greenwood, 1983), pp. 144–45.

445b. Indexed in **Mystery, Detective, and Espionage Fiction,** ed. by Michael L. Cook and Stephen T. Miller (New York: Garland, 1988), pp. 4, 177.

445c. Indexed in **The Pulp Magazine Index: Fourth Series,** by Leonard A. Robbins (Mercer Island, Wash.: Starmont House, 1991).

Detective Short Stories

446a. Described in **Mystery, Detective, and Espionage Magazines,** ed. by Michael L. Cook (Westport, Conn.: Greenwood, 1983), pp. 145–47.

446b. Indexed in **Mystery, Detective, and Espionage Fiction,** ed. by Michael L. Cook and Stephen T. Miller (New York: Garland, 1988), pp. 178–80.

446c. Indexed in **The Pulp Magazine Index: Fourth Series,** by Leonard A. Robbins (Mercer Island, Wash.: Starmont House, 1991).

Detective Shorts (British)

447. Described in **Mystery, Detective, and Espionage Magazines,** ed. by Michael L. Cook (Westport, Conn.: Greenwood, 1983), p. 145.

Detective Story Annual

448a. Described in **Mystery, Detective, and Espionage Magazines,** ed. by Michael L. Cook (Westport, Conn.: Greenwood, 1983), pp. 147–48.

448b. Indexed in **Mystery, Detective, and Espionage Fiction,** ed. by Michael L. Cook and Stephen T. Miller (New York: Garland, 1988), pp. 180–81.

Detective Story Magazine (British). See *Detective Story Magazine* (Street & Smith)

Detective Story Magazine (New Publications)

449a. Indexed in **Mystery, Detective, and Espionage Fiction,** ed. by Michael L. Cook and Stephen T. Miller (New York: Garland, 1988), p. 249.

449b. Indexed in **The Pulp Magazine Index: Fourth Series,** by Leonard A. Robbins (Mercer Island, Wash.: Starmont House, 1991).

Detective Story Magazine (Popular Publications). See *Detective Story Magazine* (Street & Smith)

Detective Story Magazine (Street & Smith)

450a. Described in **Mystery, Detective, and Espionage Magazines,** ed. by Michael L. Cook (Westport, Conn.: Greenwood, 1983), pp. 148–50.

450b. Indexed in Michael Cook, **Monthly Murders: A Checklist and Chronological Listing of Fiction in the Digest-Size Mystery Magazines in the United States and England** (Westport, Conn.: Greenwood, 1982), pp. 723–35.

450c. Indexed in **Mystery, Detective, and Espionage Fiction,** ed. by Michael L. Cook and Stephen T. Miller (New York: Garland, 1988), pp. 181–249, 558–82, 665.

Detective Tales (Aldine Publishing) (British)

451. Described in **Mystery, Detective, and Espionage Magazines,** ed. by Michael L. Cook (Westport, Conn.: Greenwood, 1983), pp. 150–51.

Detective Tales (Atlas) (British)

452a. Described in **Mystery, Detective, and Espionage Magazines,** ed. by Michael L. Cook (Westport, Conn.: Greenwood, 1983), pp. 151–52.

452b. Indexed in Michael Cook, **Monthly Murders: A Checklist and Chronological Listing of Fiction in the Digest-Size Mystery Magazines in the United States and England** (Westport, Conn.: Greenwood, 1982), pp. 162–65.

Detective Tales (Boardman) (British). See *New Detective Tales* (British)

Detective Tales (Popular Publications)

453a. Described in **Mystery, Detective, and Espionage Magazines,** ed. by Michael L. Cook (Westport, Conn.: Greenwood, 1983), pp. 153–57.

453b. Indexed in **Mystery, Detective, and Espionage Fiction,** ed. by Michael L. Cook and Stephen T. Miller (New York: Garland, 1988), pp. 251–70.

453c. Indexed in **The Pulp Magazine Index: First Series,** by Leonard A. Robbins (Mercer Island, Wash.: Starmont House, 1989).

Detective Tales (Rural Publications)

454a. Described in **Mystery, Detective, and Espionage Magazines,** ed. by Michael L. Cook (Westport, Conn.: Greenwood, 1983), pp. 157–58.

454b. Indexed in **Mystery, Detective, and Espionage Fiction,** ed. by Michael L. Cook and Stephen T. Miller (New York: Garland, 1988), pp. 249–51, 475–80.

Detective Tales-Pocket (British)

455a. Described in **Mystery, Detective, and Espionage Magazines,** ed. by Michael L. Cook (Westport, Conn.: Greenwood, 1983), p. 159.

455b. Indexed in Michael Cook, **Monthly Murders: A Checklist and Chronological Listing of Fiction in the Digest-Size Mystery Magazines in the United States and England** (Westport, Conn.: Greenwood, 1982), pp. 148–49.

Detective Tales—Pocket Reader Series. See *Detective Tales-Pocket* (British)

Detective Thrillers

456a. Described in **Mystery, Detective, and Espionage Magazines,** ed. by Michael L. Cook (Westport, Conn.: Greenwood, 1983), pp. 159–60.

456b. Mentioned in **Mystery, Detective, and Espionage Fiction**, ed. by Michael L. Cook and Stephen T. Miller (New York: Garland, 1988), p. 270.

Detective Trails

457a. Described in **Mystery, Detective, and Espionage Magazines,** ed. by Michael L. Cook (Westport, Conn.: Greenwood, 1983), p. 160.

457b. Indexed in **Mystery, Detective, and Espionage Fiction,** ed. by Michael L. Cook and Stephen T. Miller (New York: Garland, 1988), p. 271.

457c. Indexed in **The Pulp Magazine Index: Third Series,** by Leonard A. Robbins (Mercer Island, Wash.: Starmont House, 1990).

Detective Weekly (British)

458. Described in **Mystery, Detective, and Espionage Magazines,** ed. by Michael L. Cook (Westport, Conn.: Greenwood, 1983), pp. 161–63.

Detective Yarns

459a. Described in **Mystery, Detective, and Espionage Magazines,** ed. by Michael L. Cook (Westport, Conn.: Greenwood, 1983), pp. 163–64.

459b. Indexed in **Mystery, Detective, and Espionage Fiction,** ed. by Michael L. Cook and Stephen T. Miller (New York: Garland, 1988), pp. 39, 95–98, 271–72, 377.

459c. Indexed in **The Pulp Magazine Index: First Series,** by Leonard A. Robbins (Mercer Island, Wash.: Starmont House, 1989).

Dick Dobbs Detective Weekly

460. Described in **Mystery, Detective, and Espionage Magazines,** ed. by Michael L. Cook (Westport, Conn.: Greenwood, 1983), pp. 164–65.

Dick Turpin Library (Aldine Publishing) (British)

461. Described in **Mystery, Detective, and Espionage Magazines,** ed. by Michael L. Cook (Westport, Conn.: Greenwood, 1983), pp. 165–66.

Dick Turpin Library (Newnes) (British)

462. Described in **Mystery, Detective, and Espionage Magazines,** ed. by Michael L. Cook (Westport, Conn.: Greenwood, 1983), pp. 166–67.

Dick Turpin Novels (British)

463. Described in **Mystery, Detective, and Espionage Magazines,** ed. by Michael L. Cook (Westport, Conn.: Greenwood, 1983), p. 167.

Dime Detective

464a. Described in **Mystery, Detective, and Espionage Magazines,** ed. by Michael L. Cook (Westport, Conn.: Greenwood, 1983), pp. 168–70.

464b. Indexed in **Mystery, Detective, and Espionage Fiction,** ed. by Michael L. Cook and Stephen T. Miller (New York: Garland, 1988), pp. 272–89.

464c. Indexed in **The Pulp Magazine Index: Third Series,** by Leonard A. Robbins (Mercer Island, Wash.: Starmont House, 1990).

464d. Traylor, James L. **Dime Detective Index.** New Carrollton, Md.: Pulp Collector Press, 1986. 124 p. Paperback.

Dime Detective Magazine was Popular Publication's imitation of *Black Mask,* but it never captured *Black Mask*'s readership. Indeed, it would probably not be included in most lists of the most important pulp mystery and detective magazines; its stories were frequently tinged with horror, and the covers tended toward the (delightfully) lurid. It nevertheless proved to be Popular Publication's most durable mystery title, lasting from November 1931 until August 1953, a total of 273 issues. Among its more notable authors were Cornell Woolrich (31 stories), Carroll John Daly (53 stories), and John D. MacDonald (35 stories). Raymond Chandler is present with 7 stories, including "The Lady in the Lake."

Traylor's index begins with a brief history of the magazine that discusses its contents, authors, series characters, and artists and their artwork. Following are an issue-by-issue index, an author index, an index to the author profiles and pictures that appeared in the magazine, and an alphabetical list of the story characters, their authors, and the number of stories in which they appeared. Concluding the volume are indexes ranking the frequency of the character's appearance and a brief discussion of two magazine features, "Crossroads of Crime" (a crossword puzzle) and "Ready for the Rackets" (a factual discussion of confidence games). Not included in the table of contents or the pagination are two sections providing black-and-white reproductions of magazine covers.

The *Dime Detective Index* is clearly reproduced from word-processed copy and does much to make accessible the contents of a largely overlooked pulp magazine. It lacks a title index, however, and its entries do not provide pagination. These oversights make the *Dime Detective Index* less than comprehensive, and researchers interested in only the fiction published in *Dime Detective Magazine* should remember that the magazine is also indexed in Leonard Robbins's *Pulp Magazine Index: Third Series* (q.v.). Traylor's introduction, tabular data, and indexes to the author profiles and pictures are, however, unique to his index.

Dime Detective Magazine. See *Dime Detective*

Dime Mystery Book

465a. Described in **Mystery, Detective, and Espionage Magazines,** ed. by Michael L. Cook (Westport, Conn.: Greenwood, 1983), pp. 170–73.

465b. Indexed in **Mystery, Detective, and Espionage Fiction,** ed. by Michael L. Cook and Stephen T. Miller (New York: Garland, 1988), pp. 290–300, 327.

465c. Indexed in **The Pulp Magazine Index: First Series,** by Leonard A. Robbins (Mercer Island, Wash.: Starmont House, 1989).

465d. Indexed in **The Pulp Magazine Index: Fourth Series,** by Leonard A. Robbins (Mercer Island, Wash.: Starmont House, 1991).

Dime Mystery Magazine (British). See Dime Mystery Book

Dime Mystery Magazine (U.S.). See Dime Mystery Book

Dime Novel Roundup

466a. Described in **Mystery, Detective, and Espionage Magazines,** ed. by Michael L. Cook (Westport, Conn.: Greenwood, 1983), pp. 174–75.

466b. Indexed in Michael L. Cook, **Dime Novel Roundup: Annotated Index 1931–1981.** Bowling Green, Ohio: Bowling Green University Popular Press, 1983. 105 p. LC 82-73847. ISBN 0-87972-227-4 (cl); 0-87972-228-2 (pb).

Dimebooks Detective Stories (Canadian)

467. Described in **Mystery, Detective, and Espionage Magazines,** ed. by Michael L. Cook (Westport, Conn.: Greenwood, 1983), pp. 167–68.

Dixon Brett Detective Library

468. Described in **Mystery, Detective, and Espionage Magazines,** ed. by Michael L. Cook (Westport, Conn.: Greenwood, 1983), pp. 175–76.

Dixon Hawke Library (British)

469. Described in **Mystery, Detective, and Espionage Magazines,** ed. by Michael L. Cook (Westport, Conn.: Greenwood, 1983), p. 176.

Doc Savage

470a. Checklist to title stories given in John P. Gunnison, **Street & Smith's Hero Pulp Checklist** (Upper Marlboro, Md.: Pulp Collector Press, 1991).

470b. Described in **Mystery, Detective, and Espionage Magazines,** ed. by Michael L. Cook (Westport, Conn.: Greenwood, 1983), pp. 177–82.

470c. Indexed in Michael Cook, **Monthly Murders: A Checklist and Chronological Listing of Fiction in the Digest-Size Mystery Magazines in the United States and England** (Westport, Conn.: Greenwood, 1982), pp. 154–61.

470d. Indexed in **Mystery, Detective, and Espionage Fiction,** ed. by Michael L. Cook and Stephen T. Miller (New York: Garland, 1988), pp. 301–10.

470e. Indexed in **The Pulp Magazine Index: First Series,** by Leonard A. Robbins (Mercer Island, Wash.: Starmont House, 1989).

470f. Brown, Michael Rogero. **Doc Savage.** http://sflovers.rutgers.edu/archive/bibliographies/doc-savage.txt

Doc Savage is sometimes classified as a science fiction magazine, but the majority of its stories was structured and plotted as traditional mysteries, the last chapter revealing the identity of the villain responsible for all of the misdeeds and misdirections. The first section of Brown's index is an issue-by-issue of the story's title, followed by the initials of its author, date of its publication, volume and number of the magazine, and Bantam reprint number. These are followed by a key to the authors' full names, textual information on the reprints, and Doc Savage's appearances in comic books, radio shows, motion pictures, television, newspaper syndication, and works by other authors. More information and additional indexing would have been welcome, but this is very well done.

470g. Clark, William J. **The Author Index to the Doc Savage Magazine.** Los Angeles: M & B Publications, 1971. 21 p. Paperback. [*Note:* On the cover is "An Author Index to the Doc Savage Magazine."]

Clark's index to the 181 issues published between March 1933 and Summer 1949 is alphabetical by author; within each author, the stories are listed chronologically. Each entry also provides the story's publication date and its page count within the magazine (not its pagination). Stories featuring series characters have the series character's name given in parentheses, and when they are known, pseudonyms and house names are listed in italics. In all, this is an exemplary author index to an important pulp magazine. One wishes that Clark's energies had extended to providing issue-by-issue, title, and illustrator indexes as well.

Note: Lengthy discussions of the character of Doc Savage may be found in Philip Josè Farmer's *Doc Savage: His Apocalyptic Life,* Rick Lai's *The Bronze Age: An Alternate Doc Savage Chronology,* and Rob Smalley's *Doc Savage: The Supreme Adventurer* (q.q.v.).

470h. Kalb, Chris. **The 86th Floor**. http://members.aol.com/the86floor/

A thorough and comprehensive labor of love: illustrations, texts, links, histories, and a general wealth of information.

470i. ThePulp.net. **Doc Savage**. http://thepulp.net/docsavage.html

The history of Doc Savage and his associates and hundreds of links.

470j. Sines, Jeff. **Doc Savage Unchained!** http://users.aol.com/jsines233/private/DocSavage.htm

An enjoyable labor of love with illustrations, texts, links, histories, and a very pleasant abundance of information.

470k. Smalley, Rob. **Doc Savage: The Supreme Adventurer.** http://members. netvalue.net/robsmalley/page1.htm

The last site considered here, this is by no means the least. Although it contains the usual illustrations, links, texts, and histories, its information is sometimes unique: Smalley reproduces letters from illustrator James Bama, offers information about foreign editions, and even provides a Doc Savage quiz.

Doc Savage and Associates

471. Contents indexed in Michael L. Cook, **Mystery Fanfare: A Composite Annotated Index to Mystery and Related Fanzines 1963–1981** (Bowling Green, Ohio: Bowling Green State University Popular Press, 1983).

The Doc Savage Club Reader

472a. Contents indexed in Michael L. Cook, **Mystery Fanfare: A Composite Annotated Index to Mystery and Related Fanzines 1963–1981** (Bowling Green, Ohio: Bowling Green State University Popular Press, 1983).

472b. Described in **Mystery, Detective, and Espionage Magazines,** ed. by Michael L. Cook (Westport, Conn.: Greenwood, 1983), pp. 182–83.

Doc Savage Magazine. **See** *Doc Savage*

Doc Savage Quarterly

473a. Contents indexed in Michael L. Cook, **Mystery Fanfare: A Composite Annotated Index to Mystery and Related Fanzines 1963–1981** (Bowling Green, Ohio: Bowling Green State University Popular Press, 1983).

473b. Described in **Mystery, Detective, and Espionage Magazines,** ed. by Michael L. Cook (Westport, Conn.: Greenwood, 1983), pp. 183–84.

The Doc Savage Reader

474a. Contents indexed in Michael L. Cook, **Mystery Fanfare: A Composite Annotated Index to Mystery and Related Fanzines 1963–1981** (Bowling Green, Ohio: Bowling Green State University Popular Press, 1983).

474b. Described in **Mystery, Detective, and Espionage Magazines,** ed. by Michael L. Cook (Westport, Conn.: Greenwood, 1983), pp. 184–85.

Doc Savage, Science Detective. **See** *Doc Savage*

Doc Savage, Scientific Detective. **See** *Doc Savage*

Doctor Death

475a. Described in **Mystery, Detective, and Espionage Magazines,** ed. by Michael L. Cook (Westport, Conn.: Greenwood, 1983), pp. 185–89.

475b. Indexed in **Mystery, Detective, and Espionage Fiction,** ed. by Michael L. Cook and Stephen T. Miller (New York: Garland, 1988), p. 310.

475c. Indexed in **The Pulp Magazine Index: First Series,** by Leonard A. Robbins (Mercer Island, Wash.: Starmont House, 1989).

Dr. Yen Sin

476a. Described in **Mystery, Detective, and Espionage Magazines,** ed. by Michael L. Cook (Westport, Conn.: Greenwood, 1983), pp. 200–203.

476b. Indexed in **Mystery, Detective, and Espionage Fiction,** ed. by Michael L. Cook and Stephen T. Miller (New York: Garland, 1988), p. 316.

476c. Indexed in **The Pulp Magazine Index: First Series,** by Leonard A. Robbins (Mercer Island, Wash.: Starmont House, 1989).

Don Pendleton's The Executioner Mystery Magazine. See The Executioner Mystery Magazine

Don Winslow of the Navy

477a. Indexed in **Mystery, Detective, and Espionage Fiction,** ed. by Michael L. Cook and Stephen T. Miller (New York: Garland, 1988), p. 310.

477b. Indexed in **The Pulp Magazine Index: First Series,** by Leonard A. Robbins (Mercer Island, Wash.: Starmont House, 1989).

The Dossier

478. Described in **Mystery, Detective, and Espionage Magazines,** ed. by Michael L. Cook (Westport, Conn.: Greenwood, 1983), pp. 189–90.

Double-Action Detective

479a. Described in **Mystery, Detective, and Espionage Magazines,** ed. by Michael L. Cook (Westport, Conn.: Greenwood, 1983), pp. 190–91.

479b. Indexed in **Mystery, Detective, and Espionage Fiction,** ed. by Michael L. Cook and Stephen T. Miller (New York: Garland, 1988), pp. 310–11.

Double-Action Detective and Mystery Stories. See Double-Action Detective Stories

Double-Action Detective Stories

480a. Described in **Mystery, Detective, and Espionage Magazines,** ed. by Michael L. Cook (Westport, Conn.: Greenwood, 1983), pp. 191–93.

480b. Indexed in Michael Cook, **Monthly Murders: A Checklist and Chronological Listing of Fiction in the Digest-Size Mystery Magazines in the United States and England** (Westport, Conn.: Greenwood, 1982), pp. 143–47.

Double-Action Gang Magazine

481a. Described in **Mystery, Detective, and Espionage Magazines,** ed. by Michael L. Cook (Westport, Conn.: Greenwood, 1983), p. 193.

481b. Indexed in **Mystery, Detective, and Espionage Fiction,** ed. by Michael L. Cook and Stephen T. Miller (New York: Garland, 1988), pp. 311–12.

481c. Indexed in **The Pulp Magazine Index: Third Series,** by Leonard A. Robbins (Mercer Island, Wash.: Starmont House, 1990).

Double Detective

482a. Described in **Mystery, Detective, and Espionage Magazines,** ed. by Michael L. Cook (Westport, Conn.: Greenwood, 1983), pp. 194–96.

482b. Indexed in **Mystery, Detective, and Espionage Fiction,** ed. by Michael L. Cook and Stephen T. Miller (New York: Garland, 1988), pp. 312–15.

482c. Indexed in **The Pulp Magazine Index: First Series,** by Leonard A. Robbins (Mercer Island, Wash.: Starmont House, 1989).

The Dracula Journals

483. Described in **Mystery, Detective, and Espionage Magazines,** ed. by Michael L. Cook (Westport, Conn.: Greenwood, 1983), pp. 196–97.

The Dragnet

484a. Described in **Mystery, Detective, and Espionage Magazines,** ed. by Michael L. Cook (Westport, Conn.: Greenwood, 1983), pp. 198–200.

484b. Indexed in **Mystery, Detective, and Espionage Fiction,** ed. by Michael L. Cook and Stephen T. Miller (New York: Garland, 1988), pp. 119, 316–17, 589–605, 666.

484c. Indexed in **The Pulp Magazine Index: First Series,** by Leonard A. Robbins (Mercer Island, Wash.: Starmont House, 1989).

484d. Indexed in **The Pulp Magazine Index: Third Series,** by Leonard A. Robbins (Mercer Island, Wash.: Starmont House, 1990).

Duende

485a. Contents indexed in Michael L. Cook, **Mystery Fanfare: A Composite Annotated Index to Mystery and Related Fanzines 1963–1981** (Bowling Green, Ohio: Bowling Green State University Popular Press, 1983).

485b. Described in **Mystery, Detective, and Espionage Magazines,** ed. by Michael L. Cook (Westport, Conn.: Greenwood, 1983), pp. 203–4.

Dusty Ayres and His Battle Birds

486a. Described in **Mystery, Detective, and Espionage Magazines,** ed. by Michael L. Cook (Westport, Conn.: Greenwood, 1983), pp. 204–5.

486b. Indexed in **Mystery, Detective, and Espionage Fiction,** ed. by Michael L. Cook and Stephen T. Miller (New York: Garland, 1988), pp. 18–21, 317–18.

486c. Indexed in **The Pulp Magazine Index: First Series,** by Leonard A. Robbins (Mercer Island, Wash.: Starmont House, 1989).

Echoes from the Pulps

487. Described in **Mystery, Detective, and Espionage Magazines,** ed. by Michael L. Cook (Westport, Conn.: Greenwood, 1983), p. 207.

Edgar Wallace Club Newsletter. See *Edgar Wallace Society Newsletter*

Edgar Wallace Mystery Magazine (British)

488a. Described in **Mystery, Detective, and Espionage Magazines,** ed. by Michael L. Cook (Westport, Conn.: Greenwood, 1983), pp. 208–9.

488b. Indexed in Michael Cook, **Monthly Murders: A Checklist and Chronological Listing of Fiction in the Digest-Size Mystery Magazines in the United States and England** (Westport, Conn.: Greenwood, 1982), pp. 343–50.

Edgar Wallace Mystery Magazine (U.S.)

489a. Described in **Mystery, Detective, and Espionage Magazines,** ed. by Michael L. Cook (Westport, Conn.: Greenwood, 1983), pp. 209–10.

489b. Indexed in Michael Cook, **Monthly Murders: A Checklist and Chronological Listing of Fiction in the Digest-Size Mystery Magazines in the United States and England** (Westport, Conn.: Greenwood, 1982), p. 203.

Edgar Wallace Society Newsletter

490. Described in **Mystery, Detective, and Espionage Magazines,** ed. by Michael L. Cook (Westport, Conn.: Greenwood, 1983), p. 210.

Ed McBain's 87th Precinct Mystery Magazine

491a. Described in **Mystery, Detective, and Espionage Magazines,** ed. by Michael L. Cook (Westport, Conn.: Greenwood, 1983), pp. 210–11.

491b. Indexed in Michael Cook, **Monthly Murders: A Checklist and Chronological Listing of Fiction in the Digest-Size Mystery Magazines in the United States and England** (Westport, Conn.: Greenwood, 1982), pp. 204–5.

Ed McBain's Mystery Book

492a. Described in **Mystery, Detective, and Espionage Magazines,** ed. by Michael L. Cook (Westport, Conn.: Greenwood, 1983), pp. 211–13.

492b. Indexed in Michael Cook, **Monthly Murders: A Checklist and Chronological Listing of Fiction in the Digest-Size Mystery Magazines in the United States and England** (Westport, Conn.: Greenwood, 1982), pp. 201–2.

Eerie Mysteries

493a. Described in **Mystery, Detective, and Espionage Magazines,** ed. by Michael L. Cook (Westport, Conn.: Greenwood, 1983), pp. 213–14.

493b. Indexed in **Mystery, Detective, and Espionage Fiction,** ed. by Michael L. Cook and Stephen T. Miller (New York: Garland, 1988), p. 318.

493c. Indexed in **The Pulp Magazine Index: First Series,** by Leonard A. Robbins (Mercer Island, Wash.: Starmont House, 1989).

Eerie Stories

494a. Described in **Mystery, Detective, and Espionage Magazines,** ed. by Michael L. Cook (Westport, Conn.: Greenwood, 1983), p. 214.

494b. Indexed in **Mystery, Detective, and Espionage Fiction,** ed. by Michael L. Cook and Stephen T. Miller (New York: Garland, 1988), p. 318.

494c. Indexed in **The Pulp Magazine Index: First Series,** by Leonard A. Robbins (Mercer Island, Wash.: Starmont House, 1989).

Elementary, My Dear Apa

495. Described in **Mystery, Detective, and Espionage Magazines,** ed. by Michael L. Cook (Westport, Conn.: Greenwood, 1983), pp. 215–17.

The Ellery Queen Review. See *The Queen Canon Bibliophile*

Ellery Queen's Mystery Magazine

496a. Described in **Mystery, Detective, and Espionage Magazines,** ed. by Michael L. Cook (Westport, Conn.: Greenwood, 1983), pp. 217–26.

496b. American edition indexed in Michael Cook, **Monthly Murders: A Checklist and Chronological Listing of Fiction in the Digest-Size Mystery Magazines in the United States and England** (Westport, Conn.: Greenwood, 1982), pp. 206–342.

496c. British edition indexed in Michael Cook, **Monthly Murders: A Checklist and Chronological Listing of Fiction in the Digest-Size Mystery Magazines in the United States and England** (Westport, Conn.: Greenwood, 1982), pp. 166–200.

496d. American and British editions indexed in **Mystery Short Fiction Miscellany: An Index,** a CD-ROM available from Locus Press.

496e. Nieminski, John. **EQMM 350: An Author/Title Index to Ellery Queen's Mystery Magazine Fall 1941 through January 1973.** White Bear Lake, Minn.: Armchair Detective Press, 1974. 116 p. Index. Paperback.

As its title indicates, this is an index to the contents of the first 350 issues of the American newsstand edition of *Ellery Queen's Mystery Magazine.* Nieminski has omitted only newspaper item fillers and what his introduction describes as "a few short 'guest' story introductions" and has indexed all the stories, poems, articles, and features that appeared in this popular and long-running digest-sized magazine. The publication is reproduced from clearly typed copy. The contents include a user's guide, a checklist of issues indexed, an author index, a title index, and appendixes.

The user's guide provides explanations of Nieminski's methodology, and the checklist of the issues indexed lists the magazine's volume, number, whole number, date of publication, and overall pagination. The author index lists all names in capital letters (except for such compound names as de la Torre and de Ford) and arranges the titles alphabetically beneath it, providing each with a unique number; the citation provides the story's publication date and pagination within that issue, and frequent headnotes link stories by their series characters and locale and reveal pseudonyms. The title index lists the titles and their unique numbers (thus necessitating reference to the first section). Eleven appendixes list title changes; series characters and their creators; articles, essays, and features; true crime essays; book reviews; poems and verse; quizzes and puzzles; cartoons; translations; Sherlockiana, and "non-Sherlockian parodies, pastiches, burlesques, satires, take-offs and other genre-related narrative fiction."

Although *EQMM 350* lacks an issue-by-issue index, Nieminski's index is an exemplary job. It is accessible, thorough, and provides an enormous amount of data. It is the definitive work on its subject and deserves to be updated.

Note: An index to the fiction in *Ellery Queen's Mystery Magazine* appears in Michael Cook's *Monthly Murders* (q.v.).

Exciting Detective

497a. Described in **Mystery, Detective, and Espionage Magazines,** ed. by Michael L. Cook (Westport, Conn.: Greenwood, 1983), pp. 226–27.

497b. Indexed in **Mystery, Detective, and Espionage Fiction,** ed. by Michael L. Cook and Stephen T. Miller (New York: Garland, 1988), p. 319.

497c. Indexed in **The Pulp Magazine Index: Third Series,** by Leonard A. Robbins (Mercer Island, Wash.: Starmont House, 1990).

Exciting Mystery

498a. Described in **Mystery, Detective, and Espionage Magazines,** ed. by Michael L. Cook (Westport, Conn.: Greenwood, 1983), pp. 227–28.

498b. Indexed in **Mystery, Detective, and Espionage Fiction,** ed. by Michael L. Cook and Stephen T. Miller (New York: Garland, 1988), p. 320.

498c. Indexed in **The Pulp Magazine Index: Third Series,** by Leonard A. Robbins (Mercer Island, Wash.: Starmont House, 1990).

The Executioner Mystery Magazine

499a. Described in **Mystery, Detective, and Espionage Magazines,** ed. by Michael L. Cook (Westport, Conn.: Greenwood, 1983), pp. 228–29.

499b. Indexed in Michael Cook, **Monthly Murders: A Checklist and Chronological Listing of Fiction in the Digest-Size Mystery Magazines in the United States and England** (Westport, Conn.: Greenwood, 1982), pp. 351–52.

F. P. Detective Stories

500. Indexed in **Mystery, Detective, and Espionage Fiction,** ed. by Michael L. Cook and Stephen T. Miller (New York: Garland, 1988), p. 663.

Famous Detective (British). See Crack Detective

Famous Detective (U.S.). See Crack Detective

Famous Detective Stories (U.S.). See Crack Detective

Famous Spy Stories

501a. Described in **Mystery, Detective, and Espionage Magazines,** ed. by Michael L. Cook (Westport, Conn.: Greenwood, 1983), pp. 213–34.

501b. Indexed in **Mystery, Detective, and Espionage Fiction,** ed. by Michael L. Cook and Stephen T. Miller (New York: Garland, 1988), p. 324.

Fantasy Mongers

502. Contents indexed in Michael L. Cook, **Mystery Fanfare: A Composite Annotated Index to Mystery and Related Fanzines 1963–1981** (Bowling Green, Ohio: Bowling Green State University Popular Press, 1983).

Fast Action Detective and Mystery Stories. **See** *Smashing Detective*

Fatal Kiss

503. Described in **Mystery, Detective, and Espionage Magazines,** ed. by Michael L. Cook (Westport, Conn.: Greenwood, 1983), pp. 234–35.

The Faust Collector

504a. Contents indexed in Michael L. Cook, **Mystery Fanfare: A Composite Annotated Index to Mystery and Related Fanzines 1963–1981** (Bowling Green, Ohio: Bowling Green State University Popular Press, 1983).

504b. Described in **Mystery, Detective, and Espionage Magazines,** ed. by Michael L. Cook (Westport, Conn.: Greenwood, 1983), pp. 235–36.

F.B.I. Detective Stories **(British). See** *F.B.I. Detective Stories*

F.B.I. Detective Stories

505a. Described in **Mystery, Detective, and Espionage Magazines,** ed. by Michael L. Cook (Westport, Conn.: Greenwood, 1983), pp. 236–37.

505b. Indexed in **Mystery, Detective, and Espionage Fiction,** ed. by Michael L. Cook and Stephen T. Miller (New York: Garland, 1988), pp. 320–21.

505c. Indexed in **The Pulp Magazine Index: First Series,** by Leonard A. Robbins (Mercer Island, Wash.: Starmont House, 1989).

Fear!

506a. Described in **Mystery, Detective, and Espionage Magazines,** ed. by Michael L. Cook (Westport, Conn.: Greenwood, 1983), p. 237.

506b. Indexed in Michael Cook, **Monthly Murders: A Checklist and Chronological Listing of Fiction in the Digest-Size Mystery Magazines in the United States and England** (Westport, Conn.: Greenwood, 1982), p. 355.

Federal Agent. See Public Enemy

The Feds

507a. Described in **Mystery, Detective, and Espionage Magazines,** ed. by Michael L. Cook (Westport, Conn.: Greenwood, 1983), pp. 237–39.

507b. Indexed in **Mystery, Detective, and Espionage Fiction,** ed. by Michael L. Cook and Stephen T. Miller (New York: Garland, 1988), pp. 325–26.

507c. Indexed in **The Pulp Magazine Index: First Series,** by Leonard A. Robbins (Mercer Island, Wash.: Starmont House, 1989).

Fifteen Detective Stories

508a. Described in **Mystery, Detective, and Espionage Magazines,** ed. by Michael L. Cook (Westport, Conn.: Greenwood, 1983), pp. 239–40.

508b. Indexed in **Mystery, Detective, and Espionage Fiction,** ed. by Michael L. Cook and Stephen T. Miller (New York: Garland, 1988), pp. 326–27, 430–35.

15 Mystery Stories. See Dime Mystery Book

15 Story Detective. See All-Story Detective

Fifth Column Stories

509a. Described in **Mystery, Detective, and Espionage Magazines,** ed. by Michael L. Cook (Westport, Conn.: Greenwood, 1983), p. 241.

509b. Indexed in **Mystery, Detective, and Espionage Fiction,** ed. by Michael L. Cook and Stephen T. Miller (New York: Garland, 1988), pp. 328–29.

Fingerprints Detective

510. Described in **Mystery, Detective, and Espionage Magazines,** ed. by Michael L. Cook (Westport, Conn.: Greenwood, 1983), pp. 241–42.

Fire Fighters

511. Indexed in **Mystery, Detective, and Espionage Fiction,** ed. by Michael L. Cook and Stephen T. Miller (New York: Garland, 1988), p. 329.

Fireside Companion

512. LeBlanc, Edward T. **Bibliography of Fireside Companion** [*sic*]. Fall River, Mass.: Edward T. LeBlanc, 1990. 98 p. Paperback.

The dime novel publisher George Munro published the *Fireside Companion* weekly from 2 November 1867 until 18 July 1903; it lasted for 1,864 issues, the majority of which contained detective and romance serials. The word *old* often was used in the titles of the detective stories, leading to such wonderfully evocative titles as *Old Puritan, the Old Time Yankee Detective; or, the Mystery of a Winter's Night* and *Old Ironsides among the Cowboys; or, the Weird Narrative of a Lost Man. An Exciting Story of Detective Adventure in the Far West.*

LeBlanc's bibliography begins with an introduction that provides a history of the *Fireside Companion,* after which he provides a lengthy list of the abbreviations used in his bibliography, a "statistical summary" of the magazine which includes its size, typical pagination, price, and frequency. These are followed by a three-column chronological listing of the contents of the magazine: the left column lists the magazine numbers, the middle column lists the author, indicating pseudonyms when necessary, and the right column provides the title of the serial, indicating the dates it appeared. Following these data are a brief supplement that supplies data on the few issues LeBlanc had previously been unable to obtain, and indexes list the materials by author and by "principal localities, historical personalities and type of story." Both list the names in capital letters, list the titles alphabetically beneath them, and indicate the issue numbers in which the author appeared.

Although it can be difficult to obtain, LeBlanc's is the only index available to this important publication. It is clearly reproduced from typed copy.

Fireside Detective Casebook (British)

513. Described in **Mystery, Detective, and Espionage Magazines,** ed. by Michael L. Cook (Westport, Conn.: Greenwood, 1983), p. 242.

Five-Cent Detective

514a. Described in **Mystery, Detective, and Espionage Magazines,** ed. by Michael L. Cook (Westport, Conn.: Greenwood, 1983), pp. 242–43.

514b. Indexed in **Mystery, Detective, and Espionage Fiction,** ed. by Michael L. Cook and Stephen T. Miller (New York: Garland, 1988), p. 329.

Five-Detective Mysteries

515a. Described in **Mystery, Detective, and Espionage Magazines,** ed. by Michael L. Cook (Westport, Conn.: Greenwood, 1983), p. 243.

515b. Indexed in **Mystery, Detective, and Espionage Fiction,** ed. by Michael L. Cook and Stephen T. Miller (New York: Garland, 1988), p. 329.

Five Detective Novels

516a. Described in **Mystery, Detective, and Espionage Magazines,** ed. by Michael L. Cook (Westport, Conn.: Greenwood, 1983), pp. 243–45.

516b. Indexed in **Mystery, Detective, and Espionage Fiction,** ed. by Michael L. Cook and Stephen T. Miller (New York: Garland, 1988), pp. 329–30.

516c. Indexed in **The Pulp Magazine Index: First Series,** by Leonard A. Robbins (Mercer Island, Wash.: Starmont House, 1989).

Five Detective Novels Magazine. **See** *Five Detective Novels*

Flynn's. **See** *Detective Fiction Weekly*

Flynn's Detective Fiction Magazine. **See** *Detective Fiction Weekly*

Flynn's Detective Fiction Weekly. **See** *Detective Fiction Weekly*

Flynn's Weekly. **See** *Detective Fiction Weekly*

Flynn's Weekly Detective Fiction. **See** *Detective Fiction Weekly*

Foreign Service

517. Described in **Mystery, Detective, and Espionage Magazines,** ed. by Michael L. Cook (Westport, Conn.: Greenwood, 1983), p. 245.

Four Star Mystery

518. Indexed in **Mystery, Detective, and Espionage Fiction,** ed. by Michael L. Cook and Stephen T. Miller (New York: Garland, 1988), p. 349.

Front Page Stories

519. Indexed in **Mystery, Detective, and Espionage Fiction,** ed. by Michael L. Cook and Stephen T. Miller (New York: Garland, 1988), p. 349.

G-8 and His Battle Aces

520a. Described in **Mystery, Detective, and Espionage Magazines,** ed. by Michael L. Cook (Westport, Conn.: Greenwood, 1983), pp. 253–55.

520b. Indexed in **Mystery, Detective, and Espionage Fiction,** ed. by Michael L. Cook and Stephen T. Miller (New York: Garland, 1988), pp. 16–17, 349–52.

520c. Indexed in **The Pulp Magazine Index: First Series,** by Leonard A. Robbins (Mercer Island, Wash.: Starmont House, 1989).

520d. Carr, Nick. **The Flying Spy: A History of G-8.** Pulp Classic No. 18. Introduction by Jack Deveny. Biography of Robert Jasper Hogan by Sid Bradd. Oak Lawn, Ill.: Robert Weinberg, 1978. 160 p. Paperback. Also: Mercer Island, Wash.: Starmont House, 1989. Starmont Pulp and Dime Novel Studies, no. 3.

160 p. Paperback. LC 75-26231. ISBN 0-930261-72-0 (hc); 0-930261-75-5 (pb). ISSN 0885-0658.

G-8 and His Battle Aces was a hero pulp, its predominant focus being descriptions of the aeronautical deeds of derring-do that repelled a series of increasingly baroque invaders determined to conquer the world. Because reference to the magazine often is made in the standard checklists of detective and mystery magazines, one would be remiss to ignore Carr's account and index to it.

Reproduced from typed copy and heavily illustrated with cover reproductions, *The Flying Spy* is written from the perspective of a believer in the reality of G-8. Different chapters describe the author of the 110 issues of the magazine (Robert J. Hogan), the character of G-8, his three stalwart companions, the recurrent villains, and the frequently incredible inventions employed by the villains. A chronological list gives the year and month of publication and the title of the G-8 novel. Although written with affection, this remains an item for completists.

G-Men. See G-Men Detective

G-Men Detective

521a. Described in **Mystery, Detective, and Espionage Magazines,** ed. by Michael L. Cook (Westport, Conn.: Greenwood, 1983), pp. 263–64.

521b. Indexed in **Mystery, Detective, and Espionage Fiction,** ed. by Michael L. Cook and Stephen T. Miller (New York: Garland, 1988), pp. 352–59.

521c. Indexed in **The Pulp Magazine Index: First Series,** by Leonard A. Robbins (Mercer Island, Wash.: Starmont House, 1989).

The Gang Magazine

522a. Described in **Mystery, Detective, and Espionage Magazines,** ed. by Michael L. Cook (Westport, Conn.: Greenwood, 1983), p. 249.

522b. Indexed in **Mystery, Detective, and Espionage Fiction,** ed. by Michael L. Cook and Stephen T. Miller (New York: Garland, 1988), p. 359.

Gang Shorts (British)

523. Described in **Mystery, Detective, and Espionage Magazines,** ed. by Michael L. Cook (Westport, Conn.: Greenwood, 1983), p. 249.

Gang World (Popular Publications)

524a. Described in **Mystery, Detective, and Espionage Magazines**, ed. by Michael L. Cook (Westport, Conn.: Greenwood, 1983), pp. 251–52.

524b. Indexed in **Mystery, Detective, and Espionage Fiction,** ed. by Michael L. Cook and Stephen T. Miller (New York: Garland, 1988), pp. 359–61.

Gang World (Spencer Publications, Inc.)

525. Indexed in **Mystery, Detective, and Espionage Fiction,** ed. by Michael L. Cook and Stephen T. Miller (New York: Garland, 1988), pp. 361–62.

Gangland Detective Stories

526a. Described in **Mystery, Detective, and Espionage Magazines,** ed. by Michael L. Cook (Westport, Conn.: Greenwood, 1983), p. 247.

526b. Indexed in **Mystery, Detective, and Espionage Fiction,** ed. by Michael L. Cook and Stephen T. Miller (New York: Garland, 1988), pp. 362, 611–12.

Gangland-Racketeer Stories

527. Described in **Mystery, Detective, and Espionage Magazines,** ed. by Michael L. Cook (Westport, Conn.: Greenwood, 1983), p. 248.

Gangland Stories

528a. Described in **Mystery, Detective, and Espionage Magazines,** ed. by Michael L. Cook (Westport, Conn.: Greenwood, 1983), p. 248.

528b. Indexed in **Mystery, Detective, and Espionage Fiction,** ed. by Michael L. Cook and Stephen T. Miller (New York: Garland, 1988), pp. 362–63.

Gangster Stories

529a. Described in **Mystery, Detective, and Espionage Magazines,** ed. by Michael L. Cook (Westport, Conn.: Greenwood, 1983), pp. 250–51.

529b. Indexed in **Mystery, Detective, and Espionage Fiction,** ed. by Michael L. Cook and Stephen T. Miller (New York: Garland, 1988), pp. 363–65, 369–70.

The Gazette (The Journal of the Wolfe Pack)

530a. Contents indexed in Michael L. Cook, **Mystery Fanfare: A Composite Annotated Index to Mystery and Related Fanzines 1963–1981** (Bowling Green, Ohio: Bowling Green State University Popular Press, 1983).

530b. Described in **Mystery, Detective, and Espionage Magazines,** ed. by Michael L. Cook (Westport, Conn.: Greenwood, 1983), pp. 252–53.

Gem Detective

531. Indexed in **Mystery, Detective, and Espionage Fiction,** ed. by Michael L. Cook and Stephen T. Miller (New York: Garland, 1988), p. 366.

The Ghost Detective. See *The Ghost, Super-Detective*

The Ghost, Super-Detective

532a. Described in **Mystery, Detective, and Espionage Magazines,** ed. by Michael L. Cook (Westport, Conn.: Greenwood, 1983), pp. 255–59.

532b. Indexed in **Mystery, Detective, and Espionage Fiction,** ed. by Michael L. Cook and Stephen T. Miller (New York: Garland, 1988), pp. 366–70.

532c. Indexed in **The Pulp Magazine Index: First Series,** by Leonard A. Robbins (Mercer Island, Wash.: Starmont House, 1989).

Giant Detective. See *Mystery Book Magazine*

Giant Detective Annual

533a. Described in **Mystery, Detective, and Espionage Magazines,** ed. by Michael L. Cook (Westport, Conn.: Greenwood, 1983), p. 260.

533b. Indexed in **Mystery, Detective, and Espionage Fiction,** ed. by Michael L. Cook and Stephen T. Miller (New York: Garland, 1988), p. 366.

533c. Indexed in **The Pulp Magazine Index: Fourth Series,** by Leonard A. Robbins (Mercer Island, Wash.: Starmont House, 1991).

Giant Manhunt. See *Manhunt*

The Girl from U.N.C.L.E. Magazine

534a. Described in **Mystery, Detective, and Espionage Magazines,** ed. by Michael L. Cook (Westport, Conn.: Greenwood, 1983), pp. 260–62.

534b. Indexed in Michael Cook, **Monthly Murders: A Checklist and Chronological Listing of Fiction in the Digest-Size Mystery Magazines in the United States and England** (Westport, Conn.: Greenwood, 1982), pp. 356–57.

Girl Rackets

535. Indexed in **Mystery, Detective, and Espionage Fiction,** ed. by Michael L. Cook and Stephen T. Miller (New York: Garland, 1988), p. 366.

Girl's Detective Mysteries

536a. Described in **Mystery, Detective, and Espionage Magazines,** ed. by Michael L. Cook (Westport, Conn.: Greenwood, 1983), p. 262.

536b. Indexed in **Mystery, Detective, and Espionage Fiction,** ed. by Michael L. Cook and Stephen T. Miller (New York: Garland, 1988), p. 367.

Gold Seal Detective

537a. Described in **Mystery, Detective, and Espionage Magazines,** ed. by Michael L. Cook (Westport, Conn.: Greenwood, 1983), pp. 265–66.

537b. Indexed in **Mystery, Detective, and Espionage Fiction,** ed. by Michael L. Cook and Stephen T. Miller (New York: Garland, 1988), pp. 1, 367.

537c. Indexed in **The Pulp Magazine Index: First Series,** by Leonard A. Robbins (Mercer Island, Wash.: Starmont House, 1989).

Golden Fleece

538a. Indexed in **Mystery, Detective, and Espionage Fiction,** ed. by Michael L. Cook and Stephen T. Miller (New York: Garland, 1988), pp. 367–68.

538b. Indexed in **The Pulp Magazine Index: First Series,** by Leonard A. Robbins (Mercer Island, Wash.: Starmont House, 1989).

The Golden Library of Indian and Detective Adventures (British)

539. Described in **Mystery, Detective, and Espionage Magazines,** ed. by Michael L. Cook (Westport, Conn.: Greenwood, 1983), pp. 264–65.

Gramol Thrillers (British)

540. Described in **Mystery, Detective, and Espionage Magazines,** ed. by Michael L. Cook (Westport, Conn.: Greenwood, 1983), pp. 266–67.

Great Detective

541a. Described in **Mystery, Detective, and Espionage Magazines,** ed. by Michael L. Cook (Westport, Conn.: Greenwood, 1983), pp. 267–68.

541b. Indexed in **Mystery, Detective, and Espionage Fiction,** ed. by Michael L. Cook and Stephen T. Miller (New York: Garland, 1988), pp. 368–69.

541c. Indexed in **The Pulp Magazine Index: Third Series,** by Leonard A. Robbins (Mercer Island, Wash.: Starmont House, 1990).

Greater Gangster Stories

542a. Described in **Mystery, Detective, and Espionage Magazines,** ed. by Michael L. Cook (Westport, Conn.: Greenwood, 1983), pp. 268–69.

542b.   Indexed in **Mystery, Detective, and Espionage Fiction,** ed. by Michael L. Cook and Stephen T. Miller (New York: Garland, 1988), pp. 363–65, 369–70.

The Green Ghost Detective. **See** *The Ghost, Super-Detective*

Gripping Terror

543.   Indexed in **Mystery, Detective, and Espionage Fiction,** ed. by Michael L. Cook and Stephen T. Miller (New York: Garland, 1988), p. 663.

Guilty. **See** *Guilty Detective Story Magazine*

Guilty Detective Story Magazine

544a.   Described in **Mystery, Detective, and Espionage Magazines,** ed. by Michael L. Cook (Westport, Conn.: Greenwood, 1983), pp. 269–71.

544b.   Indexed in Michael Cook, **Monthly Murders: A Checklist and Chronological Listing of Fiction in the Digest-Size Mystery Magazines in the United States and England** (Westport, Conn.: Greenwood, 1982), pp. 358–64.

Gun Molls

545a.   Described in **Mystery, Detective, and Espionage Magazines,** ed. by Michael L. Cook (Westport, Conn.: Greenwood, 1983), p. 271.

545b.   Indexed in **Mystery, Detective, and Espionage Fiction,** ed. by Michael L. Cook and Stephen T. Miller (New York: Garland, 1988), pp. 370–71.

Gun Molls Magazine. **See** *Gun Molls*

Hamilton T. Caine's Short Story Newsletter

546.   Described in **Mystery, Detective, and Espionage Magazines,** ed. by Michael L. Cook (Westport, Conn.: Greenwood, 1983), p. 273.

Happy Hours Magazine. **See** *Dime Novel Roundup*

Hardboiled

547a.   Described in **Mystery, Detective, and Espionage Magazines,** ed. by Michael L. Cook (Westport, Conn.: Greenwood, 1983), p. 274.

547b.   Indexed in **Mystery, Detective, and Espionage Fiction,** ed. by Michael L. Cook and Stephen T. Miller (New York: Garland, 1988), pp. 371–72.

Haunt of Horror

548a. Described in **Mystery, Detective, and Espionage Magazines,** ed. by Michael L. Cook (Westport, Conn.: Greenwood, 1983), pp. 274–75.

548b. Indexed in Michael Cook, **Monthly Murders: A Checklist and Chronological Listing of Fiction in the Digest-Size Mystery Magazines in the United States and England** (Westport, Conn.: Greenwood, 1982), p. 365.

Headquarters Detective

549a. Described in **Mystery, Detective, and Espionage Magazines,** ed. by Michael L. Cook (Westport, Conn.: Greenwood, 1983), pp. 275–76.

549b. Indexed in **Mystery, Detective, and Espionage Fiction,** ed. by Michael L. Cook and Stephen T. Miller (New York: Garland, 1988), p. 373.

Headquarters Stories

550a. Described in **Mystery, Detective, and Espionage Magazines,** ed. by Michael L. Cook (Westport, Conn.: Greenwood, 1983), p. 276.

550b. Indexed in **Mystery, Detective, and Espionage Fiction,** ed. by Michael L. Cook and Stephen T. Miller (New York: Garland, 1988), p. 373.

Hollywood Detective. **See** *Dan Turner, Hollywood Detective*

Hollywood Detective **(British). See** *Dan Turner, Hollywood Detective*

Hollywood Detective Magazine. **See** *Dan Turner, Hollywood Detective*

Hollywood Mystery

551a. Described in **Mystery, Detective, and Espionage Magazines,** ed. by Michael L. Cook (Westport, Conn.: Greenwood, 1983), pp. 276–77.

551b. Mentioned in **Mystery, Detective, and Espionage Fiction,** ed. by Michael L. Cook and Stephen T. Miller (New York: Garland, 1988), p. 376.

The Holmesian Federation

552. Described in **Mystery, Detective, and Espionage Magazines,** ed. by Michael L. Cook (Westport, Conn.: Greenwood, 1983), pp. 277–79.

Homicide Detective Story Magazine

553a. Described in **Mystery, Detective, and Espionage Magazines,** ed. by Michael L. Cook (Westport, Conn.: Greenwood, 1983), pp. 279–80.

553b. Indexed in Michael Cook, **Monthly Murders: A Checklist and Chronological Listing of Fiction in the Digest-Size Mystery Magazines in the United States and England** (Westport, Conn.: Greenwood, 1982), pp. 366, 377.

Hooded Detective

554a. Described in **Mystery, Detective, and Espionage Magazines,** ed. by Michael L. Cook (Westport, Conn.: Greenwood, 1983), pp. 280–81.

554b. Indexed in **Mystery, Detective, and Espionage Fiction,** ed. by Michael L. Cook and Stephen T. Miller (New York: Garland, 1988), pp. 39, 95–98, 271–72, 321–23, 377.

554c. Indexed in **The Pulp Magazine Index: Second Series,** by Leonard A. Robbins (Mercer Island, Wash.: Starmont House, 1989).

Hooded Detective (British). See Hooded Detective

Horror Stories

555a. Described in **Mystery, Detective, and Espionage Magazines,** ed. by Michael L. Cook (Westport, Conn.: Greenwood, 1983), pp. 281–85.

555b. Indexed in **Mystery, Detective, and Espionage Fiction,** ed. by Michael L. Cook and Stephen T. Miller (New York: Garland, 1988), pp. 377–80, 613–16.

555c. Indexed in **The Pulp Magazine Index: First Series,** by Leonard A. Robbins (Mercer Island, Wash.: Starmont House, 1989).

555d. Indexed in **The Pulp Magazine Index: Second Series,** by Leonard A. Robbins (Mercer Island, Wash.: Starmont House, 1989).

Hunted Detective Story Magazine

556a. Described in **Mystery, Detective, and Espionage Magazines,** ed. by Michael L. Cook (Westport, Conn.: Greenwood, 1983), pp. 285–86.

556b. Indexed in Michael Cook, **Monthly Murders: A Checklist and Chronological Listing of Fiction in the Digest-Size Mystery Magazines in the United States and England** (Westport, Conn.: Greenwood, 1982), pp. 367–69.

The Illustrated Detective Magazine

557a. Described in **Mystery, Detective, and Espionage Magazines,** ed. by Michael L. Cook (Westport, Conn.: Greenwood, 1983), pp. 287–90.

557b. Indexed in **Mystery, Detective, and Espionage Fiction,** ed. by Michael L. Cook and Stephen T. Miller (New York: Garland, 1988), pp. 380–83, 402–6.

Inspector Malone's Mystery Magazine

558a. Described in **Mystery, Detective, and Espionage Magazines,** ed. by Michael L. Cook (Westport, Conn.: Greenwood, 1983), pp. 290–91.

558b. Indexed in Michael Cook, **Monthly Murders: A Checklist and Chronological Listing of Fiction in the Digest-Size Mystery Magazines in the United States and England** (Westport, Conn.: Greenwood, 1982), p. 370.

International Detective Magazine

559. Indexed in **Mystery, Detective, and Espionage Fiction,** ed. by Michael L. Cook and Stephen T. Miller (New York: Garland, 1988), pp. 383, 666.

Intrigue

560a. Described in **Mystery, Detective, and Espionage Magazines,** ed. by Michael L. Cook (Westport, Conn.: Greenwood, 1983), pp. 291–92.

560b. Indexed in Michael Cook, **Monthly Murders: A Checklist and Chronological Listing of Fiction in the Digest-Size Mystery Magazines in the United States and England** (Westport, Conn.: Greenwood, 1982), p. 371.

Intrigue Magazine. See *Intrigue*

Intrigue Mystery Magazine. See *Intrigue*

JD-Argassy. See *The Pulp Era*

JDM Bibliophile

561a. Contents indexed in Michael L. Cook, **Mystery Fanfare: A Composite Annotated Index to Mystery and Related Fanzines 1963–1981** (Bowling Green, Ohio: Bowling Green State University Popular Press, 1983).

561b. Described in **Mystery, Detective, and Espionage Magazines,** ed. by Michael L. Cook (Westport, Conn.: Greenwood, 1983), pp. 293–95.

561c. Shine, Walter, and Jean Shine. **An Index to the JDM Bibliophile.** 1982. 33 p. Not seen.

John Creasey Mystery Magazine (British)

562a. Described in **Mystery, Detective, and Espionage Magazines,** ed. by Michael L. Cook (Westport, Conn.: Greenwood, 1983), pp. 295–97.

562b. Indexed in Michael Cook, **Monthly Murders: A Checklist and Chronological Listing of Fiction in the Digest-Size Mystery Magazines in the United States and England** (Westport, Conn.: Greenwood, 1982), pp. 119–42.

Journal of the H. P. Lovecraft Society

563. Contents indexed in Michael L. Cook, **Mystery Fanfare: A Composite Annotated Index to Mystery and Related Fanzines 1963–1981** (Bowling Green, Ohio: Bowling Green State University Popular Press, 1983).

Jungle Stories (Clayton)

564a. Indexed in **Mystery, Detective, and Espionage Fiction,** ed. by Michael L. Cook and Stephen T. Miller (New York: Garland, 1988), pp. 383–84.

564b. Indexed in **The Pulp Magazine Index: First Series,** by Leonard A. Robbins (Mercer Island, Wash.: Starmont House, 1989).

Jungle Stories (Glen-Kel Publishing)

565a. Indexed in **Mystery, Detective, and Espionage Fiction,** ed. by Michael L. Cook and Stephen T. Miller (New York: Garland, 1988), pp. 384–88.

565b. Indexed in **The Pulp Magazine Index: First Series,** by Leonard A. Robbins (Mercer Island, Wash.: Starmont House, 1989).

Justice

566a. Described in **Mystery, Detective, and Espionage Magazines,** ed. by Michael L. Cook (Westport, Conn.: Greenwood, 1983), pp. 297–98.

566b. Indexed in Michael Cook, **Monthly Murders: A Checklist and Chronological Listing of Fiction in the Digest-Size Mystery Magazines in the United States and England** (Westport, Conn.: Greenwood, 1982), pp. 372–73.

Keyhole Detective Story Magazine. See *Keyhole Mystery Magazine*

Keyhole Mystery Magazine

567a. Described in **Mystery, Detective, and Espionage Magazines,** ed. by Michael L. Cook (Westport, Conn.: Greenwood, 1983), pp. 299–301.

567b. Indexed in Michael Cook, **Monthly Murders: A Checklist and Chronological Listing of Fiction in the Digest-Size Mystery Magazines in the United States and England** (Westport, Conn.: Greenwood, 1982), pp. 374–76.

Killers Mystery Story Magazine. **See** *Homicide Detective Story Magazine*

Lloyds Detective Series (British)

568.   Described in **Mystery, Detective, and Espionage Magazines,** ed. by Michael L. Cook (Westport, Conn.: Greenwood, 1983), p. 303.

The Locked Room

569.   Contents indexed in Michael L. Cook, **Mystery Fanfare: A Composite Annotated Index to Mystery and Related Fanzines 1963–1981** (Bowling Green, Ohio: Bowling Green State University Popular Press, 1983).

London Mystery Magazine (British). **See** *London Mystery Selection* (British)

London Mystery Selection (British)

570a.   Described in **Mystery, Detective, and Espionage Magazines,** ed. by Michael L. Cook (Westport, Conn.: Greenwood, 1983), pp. 304–5.

570b.   Indexed in Michael Cook, **Monthly Murders: A Checklist and Chronological Listing of Fiction in the Digest-Size Mystery Magazines in the United States and England** (Westport, Conn.: Greenwood, 1982), pp. 378–422.

The Lone Eagle

571a.   Indexed in **Mystery, Detective, and Espionage Fiction,** ed. by Michael L. Cook and Stephen T. Miller (New York: Garland, 1988), pp. 14, 388–91.

571b.   Indexed in **The Pulp Magazine Index: First Series,** by Leonard A. Robbins (Mercer Island, Wash.: Starmont House, 1989).

Lone Wolf Detective

572a.   Described in **Mystery, Detective, and Espionage Magazines,** ed. by Michael L. Cook (Westport, Conn.: Greenwood, 1983), p. 306.

572b.   Indexed in **Mystery, Detective, and Espionage Fiction,** ed. by Michael L. Cook and Stephen T. Miller (New York: Garland, 1988), pp. 392, 658–59.

572c.   Indexed in **The Pulp Magazine Index: Second Series,** by Leonard A. Robbins (Mercer Island, Wash.: Starmont House, 1989).

Lone Wolfe

573a.   Contents indexed in Michael L. Cook, **Mystery Fanfare: A Composite Annotated Index to Mystery and Related Fanzines 1963–1981** (Bowling Green, Ohio: Bowling Green State University Popular Press, 1983).

573b. Described in **Mystery, Detective, and Espionage Magazines,** ed. by Michael L. Cook (Westport, Conn.: Greenwood, 1983), pp. 306–7.

Love-Crime Detective

574a. Described in **Mystery, Detective, and Espionage Magazines,** ed. by Michael L. Cook (Westport, Conn.: Greenwood, 1983), pp. 307–8.

574b. Indexed in **Mystery, Detective, and Espionage Fiction,** ed. by Michael L. Cook and Stephen T. Miller (New York: Garland, 1988), p. 392.

Macabre

575. Described in **Mystery, Detective, and Espionage Magazines,** ed. by Michael L. Cook (Westport, Conn.: Greenwood, 1983), pp. 309–10.

Mack's Pocket Detective Stories Magazine

576. Indexed in **Mystery, Detective, and Espionage Fiction,** ed. by Michael L. Cook and Stephen T. Miller (New York: Garland, 1988), p. 392.

MacKill's Mystery Magazine (British)

577a. Described in **Mystery, Detective, and Espionage Magazines,** ed. by Michael L. Cook (Westport, Conn.: Greenwood, 1983), pp. 310–11.

577b. Indexed in Michael Cook, **Monthly Murders: A Checklist and Chronological Listing of Fiction in the Digest-Size Mystery Magazines in the United States and England** (Westport, Conn.: Greenwood, 1982), pp. 473–76.

Magazine of Horror

578a. Described in **Mystery, Detective, and Espionage Magazines,** ed. by Michael L. Cook (Westport, Conn.: Greenwood, 1983), pp. 312–13.

578b. Indexed in Michael Cook, **Monthly Murders: A Checklist and Chronological Listing of Fiction in the Digest-Size Mystery Magazines in the United States and England** (Westport, Conn.: Greenwood, 1982), pp. 568–75.

Magazine of Horror and Strange Stories. See Magazine of Horror

Magazine of Horror, Strange Tales and Science Fiction. See Magazine of Horror

Magnet Detective Library

579. Cox, J. Randolph. **Magnet Detective Library.** Dime Novel Round-Up: Bibliographic Listing. Supplement no. 51, vol. 54, no. 6, December 1985. Fall River, Mass.: Edward T. LeBlanc, 1985. 48 p. Index. Paperback.

Although not the first paper-covered crime novel series, Street & Smith's *Magnet Detective Library* was one of the most successful. It began life in 1897 and lasted for 483 issues until 1907, at which point it was retitled *New Magnet Library*. This index concentrates on the 483 volumes of the *Magnet Detective Library;* an index to the *New Magnet Library* was separately published and is described in its alphabetical sequence (q.v.).

The arrangement of the index is simple and effective: the books are listed in the order in which they were published. Each entry is numbered and includes the author's name as it appears on the book, author's real name (if known), title, subtitle (if known), pagination, publication date, reprint data, and notes on points of interest. The exception to this rule is for books signed "Nicholas Carter"; for these, only the real author's name is given, in parentheses.

An author index concludes the volume and deserves mention, for it indexes not only the stories in the *Magnet Detective Library* but also the stories in the *Nick Carter Library, Nick Carter Weekly,* and *Nick Carter Stories.* The authors whose names appeared on the title page or covers of the *Magnet Detective Library* have their names given in capital letters.

A title index would have been helpful, as would an index to the numerous retitlings in this series, but this is in all respects an exemplary work.

Malcolm's

580a. Described in **Mystery, Detective, and Espionage Magazines,** ed. by Michael L. Cook (Westport, Conn.: Greenwood, 1983), pp. 313–14.

580b. Indexed in Michael Cook, **Monthly Murders: A Checklist and Chronological Listing of Fiction in the Digest-Size Mystery Magazines in the United States and England** (Westport, Conn.: Greenwood, 1982), pp. 423–24.

Mammoth Detective

581a. Described in **Mystery, Detective, and Espionage Magazines,** ed. by Michael L. Cook (Westport, Conn.: Greenwood, 1983), pp. 314–15.

581b. Indexed in **Mystery, Detective, and Espionage Fiction,** ed. by Michael L. Cook and Stephen T. Miller (New York: Garland, 1988), pp. 393–95.

581c. Indexed in **The Pulp Magazine Index: First Series,** by Leonard A. Robbins (Mercer Island, Wash.: Starmont House, 1989).

Mammoth Detective Stories. **See** *Mammoth Detective*

Mammoth Mystery

582a. Described in **Mystery, Detective, and Espionage Magazines,** ed. by Michael L. Cook (Westport, Conn.: Greenwood, 1983), pp. 315–17.

582b. Indexed in **Mystery, Detective, and Espionage Fiction,** ed. by Michael L. Cook and Stephen T. Miller (New York: Garland, 1988), p. 396.

582c. Indexed in **The Pulp Magazine Index: First Series,** by Leonard A. Robbins (Mercer Island, Wash.: Starmont House, 1989).

Man from U.N.C.L.E. Magazine

583a. Described in **Mystery, Detective, and Espionage Magazines,** ed. by Michael L. Cook (Westport, Conn.: Greenwood, 1983), pp. 317–19.

583b. Indexed in Michael Cook, **Monthly Murders: A Checklist and Chronological Listing of Fiction in the Digest-Size Mystery Magazines in the United States and England** (Westport, Conn.: Greenwood, 1982), pp. 554–59.

Man-Hunters

584. Described in **Mystery, Detective, and Espionage Magazines,** ed. by Michael L. Cook (Westport, Conn.: Greenwood, 1983), p. 322.

The Man of Bronze

585. Contents indexed in Michael L. Cook, **Mystery Fanfare: A Composite Annotated Index to Mystery and Related Fanzines 1963–1981** (Bowling Green, Ohio: Bowling Green State University Popular Press, 1983).

Manhunt

586a. Described in **Mystery, Detective, and Espionage Magazines,** ed. by Michael L. Cook (Westport, Conn.: Greenwood, 1983), pp. 320–21.

586b. American edition indexed in Michael Cook, **Monthly Murders: A Checklist and Chronological Listing of Fiction in the Digest-Size Mystery Magazines in the United States and England** (Westport, Conn.: Greenwood, 1982), pp. 443–72.

586c. British edition indexed in Michael Cook, **Monthly Murders: A Checklist and Chronological Listing of Fiction in the Digest-Size Mystery Magazines in the United States and England** (Westport, Conn.: Greenwood, 1982), pp. 484–87.

Manhunt Detective Story Monthly. **See** *Manhunt*

Mantrap

587a. Described in **Mystery, Detective, and Espionage Magazines,** ed. by Michael L. Cook (Westport, Conn.: Greenwood, 1983), pp. 322–23.

587b. Indexed in Michael Cook, **Monthly Murders: A Checklist and Chronological Listing of Fiction in the Digest-Size Mystery Magazines in the United States and England** (Westport, Conn.: Greenwood, 1982), p. 553.

March of Crime. See *The Third Degree*

Martin Speed, Detective

588. Described in **Mystery, Detective, and Espionage Magazines,** ed. by Michael L. Cook (Westport, Conn.: Greenwood, 1983), pp. 323–24.

The Masked Detective

589a. Described in **Mystery, Detective, and Espionage Magazines,** ed. by Michael L. Cook (Westport, Conn.: Greenwood, 1983), pp. 324–25.

589b. Indexed in **Mystery, Detective, and Espionage Fiction,** ed. by Michael L. Cook and Stephen T. Miller (New York: Garland, 1988), pp. 396–97.

589c. Indexed in **The Pulp Magazine Index: First Series,** by Leonard A. Robbins (Mercer Island, Wash.: Starmont House, 1989).

The Master Detective

590. Indexed in **Mystery, Detective, and Espionage Fiction,** ed. by Michael L. Cook and Stephen T. Miller (New York: Garland, 1988), p. 397.

Master Mysteries Magazine

591. Indexed in **Mystery, Detective, and Espionage Fiction,** ed. by Michael L. Cook and Stephen T. Miller (New York: Garland, 1988), p. 397.

Medical Horrors

592. Indexed in **Mystery, Detective, and Espionage Fiction,** ed. by Michael L. Cook and Stephen T. Miller (New York: Garland, 1988), p. 398.

Megavore **(Canadian)**

593a. Contents indexed in Michael L. Cook, **Mystery Fanfare: A Composite Annotated Index to Mystery and Related Fanzines 1963–1981** (Bowling Green, Ohio: Bowling Green State University Popular Press, 1983).

593b. Described in **Mystery, Detective, and Espionage Magazines,** ed. by Michael L. Cook (Westport, Conn.: Greenwood, 1983), pp. 325–26.

Menace

594a. Described in **Mystery, Detective, and Espionage Magazines,** ed. by Michael L. Cook (Westport, Conn.: Greenwood, 1983), pp. 326–27.

594b. Indexed in Michael Cook, **Monthly Murders: A Checklist and Chronological Listing of Fiction in the Digest-Size Mystery Magazines in the United States and England** (Westport, Conn.: Greenwood, 1982), p. 428.

Mercury Mystery-Book Magazine [also *Mercury Mystery Book-Magazine*]

595a. Described in **Mystery, Detective, and Espionage Magazines,** ed. by Michael L. Cook (Westport, Conn.: Greenwood, 1983), pp. 327–28.

595b. Indexed in Michael Cook, **Monthly Murders: A Checklist and Chronological Listing of Fiction in the Digest-Size Mystery Magazines in the United States and England** (Westport, Conn.: Greenwood, 1982), pp. 479–83.

Mercury Mystery Magazine (British)

596a. Described in **Mystery, Detective, and Espionage Magazines,** ed. by Michael L. Cook (Westport, Conn.: Greenwood, 1983), pp. 328–29.

596b. Indexed in Michael Cook, **Monthly Murders: A Checklist and Chronological Listing of Fiction in the Digest-Size Mystery Magazines in the United States and England** (Westport, Conn.: Greenwood, 1982), pp. 439–40.

Mercury Mystery Magazine (U.S.). See *Mercury Mystery-Book Magazine*

Michael Shayne Mystery Magazine. See *Mike Shayne Mystery Magazine*

Midnight

597. Indexed in **Mystery, Detective, and Espionage Fiction,** ed. by Michael L. Cook and Stephen T. Miller (New York: Garland, 1988), p. 398.

Midnight Mysteries. See *Midnight*

Mike Shayne Mystery Magazine

598a. Described in **Mystery, Detective, and Espionage Magazines,** ed. by Michael L. Cook (Westport, Conn.: Greenwood, 1983), pp. 329–32.

598b. American edition indexed in Michael Cook, **Monthly Murders: A Checklist and Chronological Listing of Fiction in the Digest-Size Mystery Magazines in the United States and England** (Westport, Conn.: Greenwood, 1982), pp. 493–552.

598c. British edition indexed in Michael Cook, **Monthly Murders: A Checklist and Chronological Listing of Fiction in the Digest-Size Mystery Magazines in the United States and England** (Westport, Conn.: Greenwood, 1982), pp. 560–64.

Mind Magic

599. Indexed in **Mystery, Detective, and Espionage Fiction,** ed. by Michael L. Cook and Stephen T. Miller (New York: Garland, 1988), pp. 398–99.

Mobs

600a. Described in **Mystery, Detective, and Espionage Magazines,** ed. by Michael L. Cook (Westport, Conn.: Greenwood, 1983), pp. 332–33.

600b. Indexed in **Mystery, Detective, and Espionage Fiction,** ed. by Michael L. Cook and Stephen T. Miller (New York: Garland, 1988), p. 399.

Mobsters

601a. Described in **Mystery, Detective, and Espionage Magazines,** ed. by Michael L. Cook (Westport, Conn.: Greenwood, 1983), p. 333.

601b. Indexed in **Mystery, Detective, and Espionage Fiction,** ed. by Michael L. Cook and Stephen T. Miller (New York: Garland, 1988), p. 399.

Modern Adventures. **See** *Scarlet Adventuress*

Movie Detective

602a. Described in **Mystery, Detective, and Espionage Magazines,** ed. by Michael L. Cook (Westport, Conn.: Greenwood, 1983), p. 334.

602b. Indexed in **Mystery, Detective, and Espionage Fiction,** ed. by Michael L. Cook and Stephen T. Miller (New York: Garland, 1988), p. 400.

Movie Mystery Magazine [also *Movie-Mystery Magazine*]

603a. Described in **Mystery, Detective, and Espionage Magazines,** ed. by Michael L. Cook (Westport, Conn.: Greenwood, 1983), pp. 334–35.

603b. Indexed in Michael Cook, **Monthly Murders: A Checklist and Chronological Listing of Fiction in the Digest-Size Mystery Magazines in the United States and England** (Westport, Conn.: Greenwood, 1982), p. 565.

603c. Indexed in **Mystery, Detective, and Espionage Fiction,** ed. by Michael L. Cook and Stephen T. Miller (New York: Garland, 1988), p. 400.

Murder

604a. Described in **Mystery, Detective, and Espionage Magazines,** ed. by Michael L. Cook (Westport, Conn.: Greenwood, 1983), pp. 335–36.

604b. Indexed in Michael Cook, **Monthly Murders: A Checklist and Chronological Listing of Fiction in the Digest-Size Mystery Magazines in the United States and England** (Westport, Conn.: Greenwood, 1982), pp. 491–92.

604c. Indexed in **Mystery, Detective, and Espionage Fiction,** ed. by Michael L. Cook and Stephen T. Miller (New York: Garland, 1988), pp. 400–401.

Murder Mysteries Magazine **(1929)**

605a. Described in **Mystery, Detective, and Espionage Magazines,** ed. by Michael L. Cook (Westport, Conn.: Greenwood, 1983), p. 336.

605b. Indexed in **Mystery, Detective, and Espionage Fiction,** ed. by Michael L. Cook and Stephen T. Miller (New York: Garland, 1988), p. 401.

Murder Mysteries Magazine **(1935)**

606a. Described in **Mystery, Detective, and Espionage Magazines,** ed. by Michael L. Cook (Westport, Conn.: Greenwood, 1983), p. 337.

606b. Indexed in **Mystery, Detective, and Espionage Fiction,** ed. by Michael L. Cook and Stephen T. Miller (New York: Garland, 1988), p. 401.

Murder Stories

607a. Described in **Mystery, Detective, and Espionage Magazines,** ed. by Michael L. Cook (Westport, Conn.: Greenwood, 1983), p. 337.

607b. Indexed in **Mystery, Detective, and Espionage Fiction,** ed. by Michael L. Cook and Stephen T. Miller (New York: Garland, 1988), pp. 401–2.

My Life in a Love Cult

608. Indexed in **Mystery, Detective, and Espionage Fiction,** ed. by Michael L. Cook and Stephen T. Miller (New York: Garland, 1988), p. 402.

My Pocket Detective Stories Library **(British)**

609. Described in **Mystery, Detective, and Espionage Magazines,** ed. by Michael L. Cook (Westport, Conn.: Greenwood, 1983), p. 338.

My Pocket Mystery Stories Library **(British)**

610. Described in **Mystery, Detective, and Espionage Magazines,** ed. by Michael L. Cook (Westport, Conn.: Greenwood, 1983), p. 338.

Mysterious Times

611a. Contents indexed in Michael L. Cook, **Mystery Fanfare: A Composite Annotated Index to Mystery and Related Fanzines 1963–1981** (Bowling Green, Ohio: Bowling Green State University Popular Press, 1983).

611b. Described in **Mystery, Detective, and Espionage Magazines,** ed. by Michael L. Cook (Westport, Conn.: Greenwood, 1983), pp. 338–40.

The Mysterious Traveler Magazine

612a. Described in **Mystery, Detective, and Espionage Magazines,** ed. by Michael L. Cook (Westport, Conn.: Greenwood, 1983), pp. 340–41.

612b. Indexed in Michael Cook, **Monthly Murders: A Checklist and Chronological Listing of Fiction in the Digest-Size Mystery Magazines in the United States and England** (Westport, Conn.: Greenwood, 1982), pp. 566–67.

The Mysterious Wu Fang

613a. Described in **Mystery, Detective, and Espionage Magazines,** ed. by Michael L. Cook (Westport, Conn.: Greenwood, 1983), pp. 341–43.

613b. Indexed in **Mystery, Detective, and Espionage Fiction,** ed. by Michael L. Cook and Stephen T. Miller (New York: Garland, 1988), p. 402.

613c. Indexed in **The Pulp Magazine Index: First Series,** by Leonard A. Robbins (Mercer Island, Wash.: Starmont House, 1989).

Mystery (Mystery Magazine, Inc.)

614a. Contents indexed in Michael L. Cook, **Mystery Fanfare: A Composite Annotated Index to Mystery and Related Fanzines 1963–1981** (Bowling Green, Ohio: Bowling Green State University Popular Press, 1983).

614b. Described in **Mystery, Detective, and Espionage Magazines,** ed. by Michael L. Cook (Westport, Conn.: Greenwood, 1983), pp. 343–44.

Mystery (Street & Smith). See Crime Busters

Mystery (Tower Magazines). See The Illustrated Detective Magazine

Mystery Adventure. See New Mystery Adventure

Mystery Adventure Magazine. See New Mystery Adventure

Mystery Adventures Magazine. See New Mystery Adventure

The Mystery and Adventure Series Review

615a. Contents indexed in Michael L. Cook, **Mystery Fanfare: A Composite Annotated Index to Mystery and Related Fanzines 1963–1981** (Bowling Green, Ohio: Bowling Green State University Popular Press, 1983).

615b. Described in **Mystery, Detective, and Espionage Magazines,** ed. by Michael L. Cook (Westport, Conn.: Greenwood, 1983), pp. 344–46.

Mystery Book Magazine

616a. Described in **Mystery, Detective, and Espionage Magazines,** ed. by Michael L. Cook (Westport, Conn.: Greenwood, 1983), pp. 347–48.

616b. Indexed in Michael Cook, **Monthly Murders: A Checklist and Chronological Listing of Fiction in the Digest-Size Mystery Magazines in the United States and England** (Westport, Conn.: Greenwood, 1982), pp. 425–27.

616c. Indexed in **Mystery, Detective, and Espionage Fiction,** ed. by Michael L. Cook and Stephen T. Miller (New York: Garland, 1988), pp. 366, 407–9.

616d. Indexed in **The Pulp Magazine Index: Second Series,** by Leonard A. Robbins (Mercer Island, Wash.: Starmont House, 1989).

Mystery Digest

617a. Described in **Mystery, Detective, and Espionage Magazines,** ed. by Michael L. Cook (Westport, Conn.: Greenwood, 1983), pp. 349–50.

617b. Indexed in Michael Cook, **Monthly Murders: A Checklist and Chronological Listing of Fiction in the Digest-Size Mystery Magazines in the United States and England** (Westport, Conn.: Greenwood, 1982), pp. 429–38.

The Mystery Fancier

618a. Contents indexed in Michael L. Cook, **Mystery Fanfare: A Composite Annotated Index to Mystery and Related Fanzines 1963–1981** (Bowling Green, Ohio: Bowling Green State University Popular Press, 1983).

618b. Described in **Mystery, Detective, and Espionage Magazines,** ed. by Michael L. Cook (Westport, Conn.: Greenwood, 1983), pp. 350–52.

618c. Deeck, William F. **The Mystery Fancier: An Index to Volumes I–XIII, November, 1976–Fall, 1992**. Brownstone Mystery Guides, vol. 9. San Bernardino, Calif.: Brownstone Books, 1993. ix, 169 p. LC 93-341. ISBN 0-941028-11-9 (hc); 0-941028-12-7 (pb).

Edited and published by writer and critic Guy M. Townsend, the *Mystery Fancier* lasted for some 70 issues over 16 years. Each issue was a lively blend of fannish and academic criticism, with often pungent reviews of books, conventions, movies, and television programs. Although the *Mystery Fancier* never achieved the success of the *Armchair Detective,* it had a readership that was equally loyal and vociferous.

Deeck's index to the *Mystery Fancier* begins with a checklist of the issues indexed and a small section listing the cover artists (when known). The body of the book lists the authors and titles of every article featured in the magazine; the names and titles of all of the books, movies, and television programs that were reviewed; and the authors of the letters and (frequently) the contents of their letters. Many reviews also are indexed by subject; biographies of Agatha Christie, for example, are listed under her entry as well as being accessible under the names of their authors by the titles of their works. Book titles are given in capital letters, as are the titles of films and television programs; short story titles are given in quote marks. Eleven abbreviations—(L:) for letters, (IAC) for It's About Crime; (TAR) for the Armchair Reviewer, (TCITC) for the Curmudgeon in the Corner, and so forth—provide the name of the department in which the item appeared, with the rest of the citation providing volume number, issue number, and page numbers on which the item began and ended. Numerous cross-references are provided.

This is an exemplary index to an important small publication. It is accessible and thorough and presents its data concisely and accurately. Although specialized, this index belongs in research libraries, as of course do the 70 issues of the *Mystery Fancier*.

*Mystery*File

619.   Contents indexed in Michael L. Cook, **Mystery Fanfare: A Composite Annotated Index to Mystery and Related Fanzines 1963–1981** (Bowling Green, Ohio: Bowling Green State University Popular Press, 1983).

The Mystery League

620a.   Described in **Mystery, Detective, and Espionage Magazines,** ed. by Michael L. Cook (Westport, Conn.: Greenwood, 1983), pp. 353–55.

620b.   Indexed in Michael Cook, **Monthly Murders: A Checklist and Chronological Listing of Fiction in the Digest-Size Mystery Magazines in the United States and England** (Westport, Conn.: Greenwood, 1982), pp. 477–78.

620c.   Indexed in **Mystery, Detective, and Espionage Fiction,** ed. by Michael L. Cook and Stephen T. Miller (New York: Garland, 1988), p. 409.

The Mystery League Magazine. See *The Mystery League*

The Mystery Lovers' Newsletter. See *The Mystery Reader's Newsletter*

Mystery Magazine (Frank Tousey/Harry E. Wolff/Priscilla Company)

621a.   Described in **Mystery, Detective, and Espionage Magazines,** ed. by Michael L. Cook (Westport, Conn.: Greenwood, 1983), pp. 355–57.

621b.   Indexed in **Mystery, Detective, and Espionage Fiction,** ed. by Michael L. Cook and Stephen T. Miller (New York: Garland, 1988), pp. 409–23, 427–29.

Mystery Magazine (Street & Smith). See *Crime Busters*

The Mystery Magazine (Tower Magazines). See *The Illustrated Detective Magazine*

The Mystery Mentor

622.   Described in **Mystery, Detective, and Espionage Magazines,** ed. by Michael L. Cook (Westport, Conn.: Greenwood, 1983), p. 358.

The Mystery Monitor

623.   Contents indexed in Michael L. Cook, **Mystery Fanfare: A Composite Annotated Index to Mystery and Related Fanzines 1963–1981** (Bowling Green, Ohio: Bowling Green State University Popular Press, 1983).

Mystery Monthly

624a.   Described in **Mystery, Detective, and Espionage Magazines,** ed. by Michael L. Cook (Westport, Conn.: Greenwood, 1983), pp. 358–59.

624b.   Indexed in Michael Cook, **Monthly Murders: A Checklist and Chronological Listing of Fiction in the Digest-Size Mystery Magazines in the United States and England** (Westport, Conn.: Greenwood, 1982), pp. 488–90.

Mystery News

625.   Described in **Mystery, Detective, and Espionage Magazines,** ed. by Michael L. Cook (Westport, Conn.: Greenwood, 1983), pp. 359–60.

The Mystery Nook

626a.   Contents indexed in Michael L. Cook, **Mystery Fanfare: A Composite Annotated Index to Mystery and Related Fanzines 1963–1981** (Bowling Green, Ohio: Bowling Green State University Popular Press, 1983).

626b.   Described in **Mystery, Detective, and Espionage Magazines,** ed. by Michael L. Cook (Westport, Conn.: Greenwood, 1983), pp. 360–61.

Mystery Novels and Short Stories

627a.   Described in **Mystery, Detective, and Espionage Magazines,** ed. by Michael L. Cook (Westport, Conn.: Greenwood, 1983), p. 362.

627b.   Indexed in **Mystery, Detective, and Espionage Fiction,** ed. by Michael L. Cook and Stephen T. Miller (New York: Garland, 1988), pp. 425–26.

Mystery Novels Magazine (Doubleday, Doran)

628a.   Described in **Mystery, Detective, and Espionage Magazines,** ed. by Michael L. Cook (Westport, Conn.: Greenwood, 1983), p. 362.

628b. Indexed in **Mystery, Detective, and Espionage Fiction,** ed. by Michael L. Cook and Stephen T. Miller (New York: Garland, 1988), p. 426.

628c. Indexed in **The Pulp Magazine Index: First Series,** by Leonard A. Robbins (Mercer Island, Wash.: Starmont House, 1989).

Mystery Novels Magazine (Winford Publications)

629a. Described in **Mystery, Detective, and Espionage Magazines,** ed. by Michael L. Cook (Westport, Conn.: Greenwood, 1983), p. 363.

629b. Indexed in **Mystery, Detective, and Espionage Fiction,** ed. by Michael L. Cook and Stephen T. Miller (New York: Garland, 1988), p. 426.

Mystery Novels Magazine Quarterly. **See** *Mystery Novels Magazine* (Doubleday, Doran)

The Mystery Reader's Newsletter

630a. Contents indexed in Michael L. Cook, **Mystery Fanfare: A Composite Annotated Index to Mystery and Related Fanzines 1963–1981** (Bowling Green, Ohio: Bowling Green State University Popular Press, 1983).

630b. Described in **Mystery, Detective, and Espionage Magazines,** ed. by Michael L. Cook (Westport, Conn.: Greenwood, 1983), pp. 363–65.

Mystery Stories (Frank Tousey/Harry E. Wolff/Priscilla Company). See *Mystery Magazine* (Frank Tousey/Harry E. Wolff/ Priscilla Company)

Mystery Stories (The World's Work)

631. Indexed in **Mystery, Detective, and Espionage Fiction,** ed. by Michael L. Cook and Stephen T. Miller (New York: Garland, 1988), p. 663.

Mystery Tales (Atlas Magazines)

632a. Described in **Mystery, Detective, and Espionage Magazines,** ed. by Michael L. Cook (Westport, Conn.: Greenwood, 1983), p. 366.

632b. Indexed in Michael Cook, **Monthly Murders: A Checklist and Chronological Listing of Fiction in the Digest-Size Mystery Magazines in the United States and England** (Westport, Conn.: Greenwood, 1982), pp. 441–42.

Mystery Tales (Western Fiction Publishing). See *Uncanny Tales*

Mystery Thrillers (British)

633. Described in **Mystery, Detective, and Espionage Magazines,** ed. by Michael L. Cook (Westport, Conn.: Greenwood, 1983), pp. 366–67.

The Mystery Trader (British)

634. Described in **Mystery, Detective, and Espionage Magazines,** ed. by Michael L. Cook (Westport, Conn.: Greenwood, 1983), pp. 367–68.

Mystery Writers Annual. See *The Third Degree*

Mystic Agent Double X

635. Described in **Mystery, Detective, and Espionage Magazines,** ed. by Michael L. Cook (Westport, Conn.: Greenwood, 1983), pp. 368–69.

Nemesis, Inc. See *The Doc Savage Club Reader*

Nero Wolfe and Archie Goodwin Fans Newsletter. See *Lone Wolfe*

Nero Wolfe Mystery Magazine

636a. Described in **Mystery, Detective, and Espionage Magazines,** ed. by Michael L. Cook (Westport, Conn.: Greenwood, 1983), pp. 371–72.

636b. Indexed in Michael Cook, **Monthly Murders: A Checklist and Chronological Listing of Fiction in the Digest-Size Mystery Magazines in the United States and England** (Westport, Conn.: Greenwood, 1982), pp. 577–78.

New Detective Magazine (Two-Books Magazines)

637a. Described in **Mystery, Detective, and Espionage Magazines,** ed. by Michael L. Cook (Westport, Conn.: Greenwood, 1983), pp. 372–73.

637b. Indexed in **Mystery, Detective, and Espionage Fiction,** ed. by Michael L. Cook and Stephen T. Miller (New York: Garland, 1988), pp. 430, 645.

637c. Indexed in **The Pulp Magazine Index: Third Series,** by Leonard A. Robbins (Mercer Island, Wash.: Starmont House, 1990).

New Detective Magazine (Fictioneers)

638a. Described in **Mystery, Detective, and Espionage Magazines,** ed. by Michael L. Cook (Westport, Conn.: Greenwood, 1983), pp. 373–74.

638b. Indexed in Michael Cook, **Monthly Murders: A Checklist and Chronological Listing of Fiction in the Digest-Size Mystery Magazines in the United States and England** (Westport, Conn.: Greenwood, 1982), p. 576.

638c. Indexed in **Mystery, Detective, and Espionage Fiction,** ed. by Michael L. Cook and Stephen T. Miller (New York: Garland, 1988), pp. 326–27, 430–35.

New Detective Tales (British)

639. Described in **Mystery, Detective, and Espionage Magazines,** ed. by Michael L. Cook (Westport, Conn.: Greenwood, 1983), p. 374.

New Magnet Library

640. Cox, J. Randolph. **New Magnet Library.** Supplemental notes on *Magnet Detective Library,* by Victor A. Berch. Fall River, Mass.: [Dime Novel Round-Up/Edward T. LeBlanc], 1991. xiv, 115 leaves. Index. Paperback.

New Magnet Library lasted from 1907 until 1932 and published nearly 900 paperbound novels, many of them featuring Nick Carter. It is the continuation of the *Magnet Library* (q.v.), which lasted 483 issues, and its numbering thus begins with issue number 484.

The index to the *New Magnet Library* lists the stories by the order in which they appeared. Entries appear only on the rectos of the sheets; versos are blank. Each citation includes the name of the author as it appears on the book, the real name of the author (if known) in parentheses, title, and subtitle (underlined); pagination, publication date, reprint information, and notes on points of interest conclude the entries. Victor Berch's "Supplemental Notes on *Magnet Detective Library*" follows the major index and contains information that updates the entries in the 1985 index to the *Magnet Detective Library.* An author/detective index to the *New Magnet Library* concludes the volume.

As in the index to the *Magnet Library,* a title index would have helped trace the retitlings, but this is an exemplary work.

New Mystery Adventure

641a. Described in **Mystery, Detective, and Espionage Magazines,** ed. by Michael L. Cook (Westport, Conn.: Greenwood, 1983), pp. 374–75.

641b. Indexed in **Mystery, Detective, and Espionage Fiction,** ed. by Michael L. Cook and Stephen T. Miller (New York: Garland, 1988), pp. 406–7, 436–37.

641c. Indexed in **The Pulp Magazine Index: First Series,** by Leonard A. Robbins (Mercer Island, Wash.: Starmont House, 1989).

New Mystery Adventures. **See** *New Mystery Adventure*

New Nick Carter Weekly

642. Cox, J. Randolph. **New Nick Carter Weekly.** Dime Novel Round-Up: Bibliographic Listing. Supplement vol. 44, no. 9 (December 1975), whole no. 516. Fall River, Mass.: Edward T. LeBlanc, 1975. 64 p. Paperback.

New Nick Carter Weekly was one of the most popular dime-novel detective weeklies, with 819 issues published from 2 January 1897 until 7 September 1912. After a lengthy introduction to the character of Nick Carter and the publications in which he appeared, Cox provides a chronological list of the publications. Each entry is numbered and includes the author's real name (if known) in parentheses, the title and subtitle, the date of publication, and reprint information. Some of the stories were printed in book form prior to being printed in the *New Nick Carter Weekly;* these are noted. A title index would have been useful, as would an index to the retitlings and reprintings, but as with the other volumes in this series, this is an exemplary publication.

New York Detective Library

643.   Described in **Mystery, Detective, and Espionage Magazines,** ed. by Michael L. Cook (Westport, Conn.: Greenwood, 1983), pp. 376–77.

New York Stories

644.   Indexed in **Mystery, Detective, and Espionage Fiction,** ed. by Michael L. Cook and Stephen T. Miller (New York: Garland, 1988), p. 437.

Newnes' "Nick Carter" Series (British). See Nick Carter Weekly

Newspaper Adventure Stories

645.   Indexed in **Mystery, Detective, and Espionage Fiction,** ed. by Michael L. Cook and Stephen T. Miller (New York: Garland, 1988), p. 437.

Nick Carter Detective Library. See Nick Carter Library

Nick Carter Detective Magazine. See Nick Carter Magazine

Nick Carter Library

646a.   Described in **Mystery, Detective, and Espionage Magazines,** ed. by Michael L. Cook (Westport, Conn.: Greenwood, 1983), pp. 377–79.

646b.   Cox, J. Randolph. **The Nick Carter Library (with Notes and Commentary on the Rest of the Saga).** Dime Novel Round-Up: Bibliographic Listing. Supplement vol. 43, no. 7 (15 July 1984), whole no. 502. Fall River, Mass.: Edward T. LeBlanc, 1974. 40 p. Paperback.

The first issue of the *Nick Carter Library* appeared on 8 August 1891, and it continued as a weekly publication for 282 issues, the last issue being dated 26 December 1896. The index to this series comprises slightly less than half the volume, the majority of which is devoted to Cox's history of the series and an account of the other publications in which the character of Nick Carter appeared. The index lists the publications chronologically, with each entry being numbered and including the author's real name (if known) in parentheses, title and subtitle, publication date, and reprint data. A title index would have been helpful, as would an index to the retitlings and reprintings, but in all, this is an exemplary publication.

Nick Carter Magazine. See also *Nick Carter Stories*

647a. Checklist to title stories given in John P. Gunnison, **Street & Smith's Hero Pulp Checklist** (Upper Marlboro, Md.: Pulp Collector Press, 1991).

647b. Described in **Mystery, Detective, and Espionage Magazines,** ed. by Michael L. Cook (Westport, Conn.: Greenwood, 1983), pp. 379–81.

647c. Indexed in **Mystery, Detective, and Espionage Fiction,** ed. by Michael L. Cook and Stephen T. Miller (New York: Garland, 1988), pp. 437–39.

647d. Indexed in **The Pulp Magazine Index: First Series,** by Leonard A. Robbins (Mercer Island, Wash.: Starmont House, 1989).

Nick Carter Stories

648a. Described in **Mystery, Detective, and Espionage Magazines,** ed. by Michael L. Cook (Westport, Conn.: Greenwood, 1983), pp. 381–82.

648b. Cox, J. Randolph. **Nick Carter Stories and Other Series Containing Stories about Nick Carter: Part I: Nick Carter Stories.** Dime Novel Round-Up: Bibliographic Listing. Supplement vol. 46, no. 4 (August 1977), whole no. 526. Fall River, Mass.: Edward T. LeBlanc, 1977. 20 p. Index. Paperback.

648c. Cox, J. Randolph. **Nick Carter Stories and Other Series Containing Stories about Nick Carter. Part II: Nick Carter Magazine, Detective Story Magazine, New York Weekly, and Others.** Dime Novel Round-Up: Bibliographic Listing. Supplement vol. 49, no. 2 (April 1980), whole no. 542. Fall River, Mass.: Edward T. LeBlanc, 1980. 56 p. Paperback.

Although they were published some years apart, the two volumes constitute one work, Cox's documentation of the dime novels that published stories about Nick Carter. The first volume provides a chronological listing of *Nick Carter Stories,* which lasted for some 160 issues published from 1912 through 1915. Each entry is numbered and includes the author's real name (if known) in parentheses, story title and subtitle, date of publication, and reprint information; separate indexes list the serial stories and the known authors.

The second volume provides a chronological index to the dime novels and pulp magazines that published Nick Carter stories. These include the *Nick Carter Magazine, Detective Story Magazine, New York Weekly, Ainselee's, Shield Weekly, Old Broadbrim Weekly, Rough Rider Weekly, New Medal Library, Clues—Detective, Crime Busters,* and the *Shadow.* For each publication, Cox provides the author's name (when known) in parentheses and lists the story's title and subtitle, date of publication, and reprint information. Separate indexes list the issues of dime novels that were eventually rewritten as Nick Carter adventures. As with the other volumes in this series, title indexes would have been useful, but these two publications represent a monumental achievement.

Nick Carter Weekly

649. Described in **Mystery, Detective, and Espionage Magazines,** ed. by Michael L. Cook (Westport, Conn.: Greenwood, 1983), pp. 382–85.

Nickel Detective

650a. Described in **Mystery, Detective, and Espionage Magazines,** ed. by Michael L. Cook (Westport, Conn.: Greenwood, 1983), pp. 385–86.

650b. Indexed in **Mystery, Detective, and Espionage Fiction,** ed. by Michael L. Cook and Stephen T. Miller (New York: Garland, 1988), pp. 439–40, 555–56.

19 Tales of Intrigue, Mystery and Adventure

651a. Described in **Mystery, Detective, and Espionage Magazines,** ed. by Michael L. Cook (Westport, Conn.: Greenwood, 1983), p. 386.

651b. Indexed in **Mystery, Detective, and Espionage Fiction,** ed. by Michael L. Cook and Stephen T. Miller (New York: Garland, 1988), p. 440.

Notes for the Curious

The Not So Private Eye

653a. Contents indexed in Michael L. Cook, **Mystery Fanfare: A Composite Annotated Index to Mystery and Related Fanzines 1963–1981** (Bowling Green, Ohio: Bowling Green State University Popular Press, 1983).

653b. Described in **Mystery, Detective, and Espionage Magazines,** ed. by Michael L. Cook (Westport, Conn.: Greenwood, 1983), pp. 387–89.

Notes for the Curious

654a. Contents indexed in Michael L. Cook, **Mystery Fanfare: A Composite Annotated Index to Mystery and Related Fanzines 1963–1981** (Bowling Green, Ohio: Bowling Green State University Popular Press, 1983).

654b. Described in **Mystery, Detective, and Espionage Magazines,** ed. by Michael L. Cook (Westport, Conn.: Greenwood, 1983), pp. 386–87.

The Octopus

655a. Described in **Mystery, Detective, and Espionage Magazines,** ed. by Michael L. Cook (Westport, Conn.: Greenwood, 1983), pp. 391–94.

655b. Indexed in **Mystery, Detective, and Espionage Fiction,** ed. by Michael L. Cook and Stephen T. Miller (New York: Garland, 1988), pp. 440, 486.

655c. Indexed in **The Pulp Magazine Index: First Series,** by Leonard A. Robbins (Mercer Island, Wash.: Starmont House, 1989).

Off Beat Detective Stories

656a. Described in **Mystery, Detective, and Espionage Magazines,** ed. by Michael L. Cook (Westport, Conn.: Greenwood, 1983), pp. 394–96.

656b. Indexed in Michael Cook, **Monthly Murders: A Checklist and Chronological Listing of Fiction in the Digest-Size Mystery Magazines in the United States and England** (Westport, Conn.: Greenwood, 1982), pp. 579–84.

Official Journal of the International Spy Society. See The Dossier

Old Broadbrim Weekly

657. Described in **Mystery, Detective, and Espionage Magazines,** ed. by Michael L. Cook (Westport, Conn.: Greenwood, 1983), pp. 396–97.

Old Cap. Collier Library

658. Described in **Mystery, Detective, and Espionage Magazines**, ed. by Michael L. Cook (Westport, Conn.: Greenwood, 1983), pp. 397–99.

Old Sleuth Library

659. Described in **Mystery, Detective, and Espionage Magazines,** ed. by Michael L. Cook (Westport, Conn.: Greenwood, 1983), pp. 399–400.

Old Sleuth Weekly

660. Described in **Mystery, Detective, and Espionage Magazines,** ed. by Michael L. Cook (Westport, Conn.: Greenwood, 1983), pp. 400–402.

Operator #5

661a. Described in **Mystery, Detective, and Espionage Magazines,** ed. by Michael L. Cook (Westport, Conn.: Greenwood, 1983), pp. 402–5.

661b. Indexed in **Mystery, Detective, and Espionage Fiction,** ed. by Michael L. Cook and Stephen T. Miller (New York: Garland, 1988), pp. 490–92.

661c. Indexed in **The Pulp Magazine Index: First Series,** by Leonard A. Robbins (Mercer Island, Wash.: Starmont House, 1989).

661d. Brown, Michael R. **Operator #5.** http://sflovers.rutgers.edu/archive/bibliographies/operator%235.txt

The 48 issues of *Operator #5* are sometimes classed as detective and mystery fiction, but it would be more apt to consider them a hero pulp, for in each issue, Operator #5—proclaimed by the majority of the covers to be "America's Undercover Ace"—single-handedly, or almost single-handedly, saved the United States from invasion and destruction by increasingly bizarre agents of foreign powers. Nevertheless, the magazine is occasionally referenced in the standard checklists of detective and mystery magazines, and one would be remiss to ignore this index.

The arrangement is chronological, by magazine issue. Each entry provides the title of the lead story, initials of the author, date of publication, magazine's volume and number, and a note as to reprint. Following the list are the authors' full names and notes. Given the magazine's general rarity, one would have hoped for more comprehensive information about its contents, but Brown's list is very well done.

661e. Carr, Nick. **America's Secret Service Ace: The Operator #5 Story.** Oak Lawn, Ill.: Robert Weinberg, 1974. 63 p. Also: Mercer Island, Wash.: Starmont House, 1985. Starmont Pulp and Dime Novel Studies, no. 2. 63 p. LC 85-26269. ISBN 0-930261-70-4 (hc); 0-930261-73-9 (pb). ISSN 0885-0658. Also: San Bernardino, Calif.: Borgo Press, 1985. 63 p. Paperback. LC 85-31413. ISBN 0-89370-564-0.

Reproduced from typed copy and heavily illustrated with cover reproductions, *America's Secret Service Ace* is written as though Operator #5 (real name: Jimmy Christopher) and his associates existed. Different chapters describe major characters, villains, supporting characters, invasions, inventions, and authors of the magazine. A chronological list gives the month and year of publication and the title of the novel.

As with all of Carr's work on the pulps, this one is written with affection. Nevertheless, as a reference work, this remains an item for completists.

661f. Kalb, Chris. **Operator #5.** http://members.aol.com/opnumber5

This site provides a very readable history of the magazine and the titular character, a description of his paraphernalia and friends, and—of course—cover reproductions and an index. Very nicely done.

Paperback Parade

662. McMillan, Brian. **An Author & Title Index to *Paperback Parade*, Issues 1–54, 1986–2000.** Introduction by Gary Lovisi. Traer, Iowa: Brian McMillan, 2000. 37 p. Paperback.

It is arguable whether *Paperback Parade* should be included in this section, for its focus is on paperbacks as a whole, and only some of these published mystery and detective fiction. Nevertheless, not to mention *Paperback Parade* and this index might do researchers a disservice.

McMillan's index contains two sections, both apparently reproduced from laser-print output. The first section is the author index. Names are given in upper- and lower-case letters, and beneath them, arranged alphabetically, are the titles, given entirely in capital letters, followed by the volume and page numbers connected by hyphens (i.e., 17-28 refers to an article on page 28 in volume 17). Anonymous works are listed under "Anonymous/Other." An additional idiosyncrasy is that titles whose first significant words are numbers ("The 11 Best Private Eye Novels" and "The 1947 Jonas Cover," for example) are listed at the head of their alphabetical sequence.

The title index lists contents by title (in capital letters), followed by the author's last and first names (in upper- and lowercase letters), followed by the hyphenated numbers indicating volume and page number. The titles beginning with numbers are listed before the main sequence.

Libraries holding *Paperback Parade* (OCLC 16186218) may find McMillan's index of assistance.

Paperback Quarterly

663. Contents indexed in Michael L. Cook, **Mystery Fanfare: A Composite Annotated Index to Mystery and Related Fanzines 1963–1981** (Bowling Green, Ohio: Bowling Green State University Popular Press, 1983).

Pete Rice Magazine

664a. Checklist to title stories given in John P. Gunnison, **Street & Smith's Hero Pulp Checklist** (Upper Marlboro, Md.: Pulp Collector Press, 1991).

664b. Indexed in **The Pulp Magazine Index: First Series,** by Leonard A. Robbins (Mercer Island, Wash.: Starmont House, 1989).

Phantom (British)

665a. Described in **Mystery, Detective, and Espionage Magazines,** ed. by Michael L. Cook (Westport, Conn.: Greenwood, 1983), pp. 407–8.

665b. Indexed in Michael Cook, **Monthly Murders: A Checklist and Chronological Listing of Fiction in the Digest-Size Mystery Magazines in the United States and England** (Westport, Conn.: Greenwood, 1982), pp. 585–87.

The Phantom Detective

666a. Described in **Mystery, Detective, and Espionage Magazines,** ed. by Michael L. Cook (Westport, Conn.: Greenwood, 1983), pp. 408–14.

666b. Indexed in **Mystery, Detective, and Espionage Fiction,** ed. by Michael L. Cook and Stephen T. Miller (New York: Garland, 1988), pp. 440–49, 666.

666c. Indexed in **The Pulp Magazine Index: First Series,** by Leonard A. Robbins (Mercer Island, Wash.: Starmont House, 1989).

666d. Halegua, Mark. **The Phantom Detective.** http://www.mindspring.com/~phantom21/phantom.htm

The *Phantom Detective* was one of the more popular pulp magazines, with 170 issues published between 1933 and 1953. Halegua provides a history of the magazine, an index, and a gallery of cover reproductions. As with Sauer and Brown, Halegua indexes only the title story in each magazine, and more comprehensive indexes are to be found in Robbins.

666e. Sauer, Nicholas, and Michael R. Brown. **The Phantom Detective.** http://sflovers.org/pub/sf-lovers/books/misc/phantom-detective.txt

Sauer and Brown's plain-text list is chronological by issue. Each entry provides the lead story's title, initials of its author, date of its publication, volume number, and reprint information. Following the list are the authors' full names and notes and information on the comic book appearance of the Phantom Detective. Information on the rest of the magazine's contents would have been welcome, but this list is well done.

Note: Fuller indexes can be found in the sources listed previously. A lengthy discussion of the character of the Phantom Detective can be found in Tom Johnson's *Phantom Detective: The Original Masked Marvel* (q.v.).

Phantom Detective Cases (British)

667. Described in **Mystery, Detective, and Espionage Magazines,** ed. by Michael L. Cook (Westport, Conn.: Greenwood, 1983), p. 414.

Phantom Mystery Magazine (British)

668a. Described in **Mystery, Detective, and Espionage Magazines,** ed. by Michael L. Cook (Westport, Conn.: Greenwood, 1983), pp. 414–15.

668b. Indexed in Michael Cook, **Monthly Murders: A Checklist and Chronological Listing of Fiction in the Digest-Size Mystery Magazines in the United States and England** (Westport, Conn.: Greenwood, 1982), pp. 592–93.

Phoenix Mystery Novels (British)

669. Described in **Mystery, Detective, and Espionage Magazines,** ed. by Michael L. Cook (Westport, Conn.: Greenwood, 1983), pp. 415–16.

Pocket Detective Magazine (Street & Smith)

670a. Described in **Mystery, Detective, and Espionage Magazines,** ed. by Michael L. Cook (Westport, Conn.: Greenwood, 1983), pp. 416–17.

670b. Indexed in Michael Cook, **Monthly Murders: A Checklist and Chronological Listing of Fiction in the Digest-Size Mystery Magazines in the United States and England** (Westport, Conn.: Greenwood, 1982), pp. 588–90.

670c. Indexed in **Mystery, Detective, and Espionage Fiction,** ed. by Michael L. Cook and Stephen T. Miller (New York: Garland, 1988), pp. 449–50.

Pocket Detective Magazine (Trojan)

671a. Described in **Mystery, Detective, and Espionage Magazines,** ed. by Michael L. Cook (Westport, Conn.: Greenwood, 1983), pp. 417–18.

671b. Indexed in Michael Cook, **Monthly Murders: A Checklist and Chronological Listing of Fiction in the Digest-Size Mystery Magazines in the United States and England** (Westport, Conn.: Greenwood, 1982), p. 594.

671c. Indexed in **Mystery, Detective, and Espionage Fiction,** ed. by Michael L. Cook and Stephen T. Miller (New York: Garland, 1988), p. 450.

The Poisoned Pen

672a. Contents indexed in Michael L. Cook, **Mystery Fanfare: A Composite Annotated Index to Mystery and Related Fanzines 1963–1981** (Bowling Green, Ohio: Bowling Green State University Popular Press, 1983).

672b. Described in **Mystery, Detective, and Espionage Magazines,** ed. by Michael L. Cook (Westport, Conn.: Greenwood, 1983), pp. 418–20.

672c. Deeck, William F. **Index to the Poisoned Pen, Volume 1, Number 1, to Volume 7, Number 1 (January 1978 to Fall/Winter 1987).** N.p., n.d. 70 p. OCLC 42918473.

Not seen.

The Pontine Dossier

673a. Contents indexed in Michael L. Cook, **Mystery Fanfare: A Composite Annotated Index to Mystery and Related Fanzines 1963–1981** (Bowling Green, Ohio: Bowling Green State University Popular Press, 1983).

673b. Described in **Mystery, Detective, and Espionage Magazines,** ed. by Michael L. Cook (Westport, Conn.: Greenwood, 1983), pp. 420–21.

The Pontine Dossier Annual. See The Pontine Dossier

Popular Detective

674a. Described in **Mystery, Detective, and Espionage Magazines,** ed. by Michael L. Cook (Westport, Conn.: Greenwood, 1983), pp. 422–23.

674b. Indexed in **Mystery, Detective, and Espionage Fiction,** ed. by Michael L. Cook and Stephen T. Miller (New York: Garland, 1988), pp. 450–61.

674c. Indexed in **The Pulp Magazine Index: First Series,** by Leonard A. Robbins (Mercer Island, Wash.: Starmont House, 1989).

Prison Life Stories

675a. Described in **Mystery, Detective, and Espionage Magazines,** ed. by Michael L. Cook (Westport, Conn.: Greenwood, 1983), p. 423.

675b.   Indexed in **Mystery, Detective, and Espionage Fiction,** ed. by Michael L. Cook and Stephen T. Miller (New York: Garland, 1988), p. 461.

Prison Stories

676a.   Described in **Mystery, Detective, and Espionage Magazines,** ed. by Michael L. Cook (Westport, Conn.: Greenwood, 1983), pp. 423–25.

676b.   Indexed in **Mystery, Detective, and Espionage Fiction,** ed. by Michael L. Cook and Stephen T. Miller (New York: Garland, 1988), p. 462.

676c.   Indexed in **The Pulp Magazine Index: First Series,** by Leonard A. Robbins (Mercer Island, Wash.: Starmont House, 1989).

Private Detective **(Canadian)**

677.   Described in **Mystery, Detective, and Espionage Magazines,** ed. by Michael L. Cook (Westport, Conn.: Greenwood, 1983), pp. 425–26.

Private Detective. **See** *Private Detective Stories* **(U.S.)**

Private Detective Stories **(U.S.)**

678a.   Described in **Mystery, Detective, and Espionage Magazines,** ed. by Michael L. Cook (Westport, Conn.: Greenwood, 1983), pp. 426–28.

678b.   Indexed in **Mystery, Detective, and Espionage Fiction,** ed. by Michael L. Cook and Stephen T. Miller (New York: Garland, 1988), pp. 462–71.

678c.   Indexed in **The Pulp Magazine Index: First Series,** by Leonard A. Robbins (Mercer Island, Wash.: Starmont House, 1989).

Private Eye

679a.   Described in **Mystery, Detective, and Espionage Magazines,** ed. by Michael L. Cook (Westport, Conn.: Greenwood, 1983), pp. 428–29.

679b.   Indexed in Michael Cook, **Monthly Murders: A Checklist and Chronological Listing of Fiction in the Digest-Size Mystery Magazines in the United States and England** (Westport, Conn.: Greenwood, 1982), p. 591.

Private Investigator Detective Magazine

680a.   Described in **Mystery, Detective, and Espionage Magazines,** ed. by Michael L. Cook (Westport, Conn.: Greenwood, 1983), pp. 429–30.

680b.   Indexed in **Mystery, Detective, and Espionage Fiction,** ed. by Michael L. Cook and Stephen T. Miller (New York: Garland, 1988), p. 471.

Prize Detective Magazine

681. Indexed in **Mystery, Detective, and Espionage Fiction,** ed. by Michael L. Cook and Stephen T. Miller (New York: Garland, 1988), p. 471.

Public Enemy

682a. Described in **Mystery, Detective, and Espionage Magazines,** ed. by Michael L. Cook (Westport, Conn.: Greenwood, 1983), pp. 430–32.

682b. Indexed in **Mystery, Detective, and Espionage Fiction,** ed. by Michael L. Cook and Stephen T. Miller (New York: Garland, 1988), pp. 324–25, 472.

682c. Indexed in **The Pulp Magazine Index: First Series,** by Leonard A. Robbins (Mercer Island, Wash.: Starmont House, 1989).

Pulp

683. Contents indexed in Michael L. Cook, **Mystery Fanfare: A Composite Annotated Index to Mystery and Related Fanzines 1963–1981** (Bowling Green, Ohio: Bowling Green State University Popular Press, 1983).

684. Described in **Mystery, Detective, and Espionage Magazines,** ed. by Michael L. Cook (Westport, Conn.: Greenwood, 1983), pp. 432–34.

The Pulp Era

685a. Contents indexed in Michael L. Cook, **Mystery Fanfare: A Composite Annotated Index to Mystery and Related Fanzines 1963–1981** (Bowling Green, Ohio: Bowling Green State University Popular Press, 1983).

685b. Described in **Mystery, Detective, and Espionage Magazines,** ed. by Michael L. Cook (Westport, Conn.: Greenwood, 1983), pp. 434–35.

Pulpette

686. Described in **Mystery, Detective, and Espionage Magazines,** ed. by Michael L. Cook (Westport, Conn.: Greenwood, 1983), p. 435.

Pulpwoody

687. Contents indexed in Michael L. Cook, **Mystery Fanfare: A Composite Annotated Index to Mystery and Related Fanzines 1963–1981** (Bowling Green, Ohio: Bowling Green State University Popular Press, 1983).

Pursued

688. Indexed in **Mystery, Detective, and Espionage Fiction,** ed. by Michael L. Cook and Stephen T. Miller (New York: Garland, 1988), p. 472.

Pursuit Detective Story Magazine

689a. Described in **Mystery, Detective, and Espionage Magazines,** ed. by Michael L. Cook (Westport, Conn.: Greenwood, 1983), pp. 435–37.

689b. Indexed in Michael Cook, **Monthly Murders: A Checklist and Chronological Listing of Fiction in the Digest-Size Mystery Magazines in the United States and England** (Westport, Conn.: Greenwood, 1982), pp. 595–99.

The Queen Canon Bibliophile

690a. Contents indexed in Michael L. Cook, **Mystery Fanfare: A Composite Annotated Index to Mystery and Related Fanzines 1963–1981** (Bowling Green, Ohio: Bowling Green State University Popular Press, 1983).

690b. Described in **Mystery, Detective, and Espionage Magazines,** ed. by Michael L. Cook (Westport, Conn.: Greenwood, 1983), pp. 439–40.

Queen of the Jungle. See Stories of Sheena, Queen of the Jungle

Racket Stories

691a. Described in **Mystery, Detective, and Espionage Magazines,** ed. by Michael L. Cook (Westport, Conn.: Greenwood, 1983), p. 443.

691b. Mentioned in **Mystery, Detective, and Espionage Fiction,** ed. by Michael L. Cook and Stephen T. Miller (New York: Garland, 1988), p. 472.

Racketeer and Gangland Stories

692a. Described in **Mystery, Detective, and Espionage Magazines,** ed. by Michael L. Cook (Westport, Conn.: Greenwood, 1983), p. 441.

692b. Indexed in **Mystery, Detective, and Espionage Fiction,** ed. by Michael L. Cook and Stephen T. Miller (New York: Garland, 1988), p. 472.

Racketeer Stories

693a. Described in **Mystery, Detective, and Espionage Magazines,** ed. by Michael L. Cook (Westport, Conn.: Greenwood, 1983), pp. 441–43.

693b. Indexed in **Mystery, Detective, and Espionage Fiction,** ed. by Michael L. Cook and Stephen T. Miller (New York: Garland, 1988), pp. 473–74.

Railroad Detective Stories

694a. Described in **Mystery, Detective, and Espionage Magazines,** ed. by Michael L. Cook (Westport, Conn.: Greenwood, 1983), pp. 443–44.

694b. Mentioned in **Mystery, Detective, and Espionage Fiction,** ed. by Michael L. Cook and Stephen T. Miller (New York: Garland, 1988), p. 474.

Rapid-Fire Detective Stories

695a. Described in **Mystery, Detective, and Espionage Magazines,** ed. by Michael L. Cook (Westport, Conn.: Greenwood, 1983), p. 444.

695b. Indexed in **Mystery, Detective, and Espionage Fiction,** ed. by Michael L. Cook and Stephen T. Miller (New York: Garland, 1988), pp. 475–76.

695c. Indexed in **The Pulp Magazine Index: Third Series,** by Leonard A. Robbins (Mercer Island, Wash.: Starmont House, 1990).

Real Detective. See Detective Tales (Rural Publications)

Real Detective Tales. See Detective Tales (Rural Publications)

Real Detective Tales and Mystery Stories. See Detective Tales (Rural Publications)

Real Mystery. See Uncanny Tales

Real Mystery Magazine. See Uncanny Tales

Real Western Mystery Novels

696. Described in **Mystery, Detective, and Espionage Magazines,** ed. by Michael L. Cook (Westport, Conn.: Greenwood, 1983), p. 445.

Red Herrings (British)

697. Described in **Mystery, Detective, and Espionage Magazines,** ed. by Michael L. Cook (Westport, Conn.: Greenwood, 1983), pp. 445–47.

Red Hood Detective Stories. See Red Mask Detective Stories

Red Mask Detective Stories

698a. Described in **Mystery, Detective, and Espionage Magazines,** ed. by Michael L. Cook (Westport, Conn.: Greenwood, 1983), pp. 447–48.

698b. Indexed in **Mystery, Detective, and Espionage Fiction,** ed. by Michael L. Cook and Stephen T. Miller (New York: Garland, 1988), p. 480.

698c. Indexed in **The Pulp Magazine Index: First Series,** by Leonard A. Robbins (Mercer Island, Wash.: Starmont House, 1989).

Red Seal Detective Stories

699a. Described in **Mystery, Detective, and Espionage Magazines,** ed. by Michael L. Cook (Westport, Conn.: Greenwood, 1983), p. 449.

699b. Mentioned in **Mystery, Detective, and Espionage Fiction**, ed. by Michael L. Cook and Stephen T. Miller (New York: Garland, 1988), p. 481.

Red Seal Mystery

700a. Described in **Mystery, Detective, and Espionage Magazines,** ed. by Michael L. Cook (Westport, Conn.: Greenwood, 1983), pp. 449–50.

700b. Mentioned in **Mystery, Detective, and Espionage Fiction,** ed. by Michael L. Cook and Stephen T. Miller (New York: Garland, 1988), p. 481.

Red Seal Mystery Magazine. See Red Seal Mystery

Red Star Detective. See Detective Dime Novels

Red Star Mystery

701a. Described in **Mystery, Detective, and Espionage Magazines,** ed. by Michael L. Cook (Westport, Conn.: Greenwood, 1983), pp. 450–51.

701b. Indexed in **Mystery, Detective, and Espionage Fiction,** ed. by Michael L. Cook and Stephen T. Miller (New York: Garland, 1988), p. 481.

701c. Indexed in **The Pulp Magazine Index: First Series,** by Leonard A. Robbins (Mercer Island, Wash.: Starmont House, 1989).

Rex Stout Mystery Magazine. See Rex Stout's Mystery Monthly

Rex Stout Mystery Quarterly. See Rex Stout's Mystery Monthly

Rex Stout's Mystery Monthly

702a. Described in **Mystery, Detective, and Espionage Magazines,** ed. by Michael L. Cook (Westport, Conn.: Greenwood, 1983), pp. 451–53.

702b. Indexed in Michael Cook, **Monthly Murders: A Checklist and Chronological Listing of Fiction in the Digest-Size Mystery Magazines in the United States and England** (Westport, Conn.: Greenwood, 1982), pp. 600–602.

The Rohmer Review

703a. Contents indexed in Michael L. Cook, **Mystery Fanfare: A Composite Annotated Index to Mystery and Related Fanzines 1963–1981** (Bowling Green, Ohio: Bowling Green State University Popular Press, 1983).

703b. Described in **Mystery, Detective, and Espionage Magazines,** ed. by Michael L. Cook (Westport, Conn.: Greenwood, 1983), pp. 453–54.

Romantic Detective

704a. Described in **Mystery, Detective, and Espionage Magazines,** ed. by Michael L. Cook (Westport, Conn.: Greenwood, 1983), pp. 454–55.

704b. Indexed in **Mystery, Detective, and Espionage Fiction,** ed. by Michael L. Cook and Stephen T. Miller (New York: Garland, 1988), pp. 481–82.

The Saint Detective Magazine

705a. Described in **Mystery, Detective, and Espionage Magazines,** ed. by Michael L. Cook (Westport, Conn.: Greenwood, 1983), pp. 457–59.

705b. American edition indexed in Michael Cook, **Monthly Murders: A Checklist and Chronological Listing of Fiction in the Digest-Size Mystery Magazines in the United States and England** (Westport, Conn.: Greenwood, 1982), pp. 603–36.

705c. British edition indexed in Michael Cook, **Monthly Murders: A Checklist and Chronological Listing of Fiction in the Digest-Size Mystery Magazines in the United States and England** (Westport, Conn.: Greenwood, 1982), pp. 637–67.

705d. Nieminski, John. **The Saint Magazine Index, Authors and Titles, Spring 1953–October 1967**. Unicorn Indexes to the Mystery/Detective Magazines. Evansville, Ind.: Cook & McDowell, 1980. 68 p. Paperback.

Omitting only the purely editorial matter and fillers, this index lists the authors and titles of all material published in the 141 issues of the *Saint Magazine* published from spring 1953 until October 1967. All stories, articles, quizzes, and features are clearly indicated. The index includes a "user's guide," which explains the layout and arrangement of this index, and a checklist of issues indexed; the index contains an author index, a title index, and a series of eight appendixes.

The names of the authors are given in capital letters, and minor variations (e.g., George H. Coxe and George Harmon Coxe) are ignored and interfiled. Joint authors are listed once, by the first name on the byline, with appropriate cross-referencing. All titles are listed alphabetically beneath the author's name and are through numbered; each title is followed by its date of appearance expressed in numbers (i.e., 7/59 for July 1959) and its pagination. Series characters are identified by the code "SC" and the name of the character underlined; reprints are indicated by the letter "R," and "OT" and "BT" identify, respectively, other titles (i.e., retitlings) and book titles.

The title index links the story titles to their unique numbers, and the appendixes list the title changes; series characters; articles, essays, and features; true crime features; book reviews; quizzes and puzzles; translators; and Sherlockiana published in the *Saint Magazine*.

Note: A partial index to the *Saint* is provided by Michael Cook in his *Monthly Murders* (q.v.).

The Saint Magazine. See *The Saint Detective Magazine*

Saint Mystery Library

706a. Described in **Mystery, Detective, and Espionage Magazines,** ed. by Michael L. Cook (Westport, Conn.: Greenwood, 1983), pp. 459–61.

706b. Indexed in Michael Cook, **Monthly Murders: A Checklist and Chronological Listing of Fiction in the Digest-Size Mystery Magazines in the United States and England** (Westport, Conn.: Greenwood, 1982), pp. 689–91.

The Saint Mystery Magazine. See *The Saint Detective Magazine*

The Saint's Choice

707a. Described in **Mystery, Detective, and Espionage Magazines,** ed. by Michael L. Cook (Westport, Conn.: Greenwood, 1983), pp. 461–62.

707b. Indexed in Michael Cook, **Monthly Murders: A Checklist and Chronological Listing of Fiction in the Digest-Size Mystery Magazines in the United States and England** (Westport, Conn.: Greenwood, 1982), pp. 668–69.

Saint's Mystery Library. See *Saint Mystery Library*

Saturn Web. See *Saturn Web Magazine of Detective Stories*

Saturn Web Detective Stories. See *Saturn Web Magazine of Detective Stories*

Saturn Web Magazine of Detective Stories

708a. Described in **Mystery, Detective, and Espionage Magazines,** ed. by Michael L. Cook (Westport, Conn.: Greenwood, 1983), pp. 462–63.

708b. Indexed in Michael Cook, **Monthly Murders: A Checklist and Chronological Listing of Fiction in the Digest-Size Mystery Magazines in the United States and England** (Westport, Conn.: Greenwood, 1982), pp. 714–19.

Saucy Detective

709a. Described in **Mystery, Detective, and Espionage Magazines,** ed. by Michael L. Cook (Westport, Conn.: Greenwood, 1983), pp. 463–64.

709b. Indexed in **Mystery, Detective, and Espionage Fiction,** ed. by Michael L. Cook and Stephen T. Miller (New York: Garland, 1988), p. 482.

Saucy Detective Stories. See *Saucy Detective*

Saucy Movie Tales

710. Indexed in **Mystery, Detective, and Espionage Fiction,** ed. by Michael L. Cook and Stephen T. Miller (New York: Garland, 1988), pp. 482–84.

Saucy Romantic Adventures

711. Indexed in **Mystery, Detective, and Espionage Fiction,** ed. by Michael L. Cook and Stephen T. Miller (New York: Garland, 1988), pp. 484, 666.

Scarab Mystery Magazine

712a. Described in **Mystery, Detective, and Espionage Magazines,** ed. by Michael L. Cook (Westport, Conn.: Greenwood, 1983), p. 464.

712b. Indexed in Michael Cook, **Monthly Murders: A Checklist and Chronological Listing of Fiction in the Digest-Size Mystery Magazines in the United States and England** (Westport, Conn.: Greenwood, 1982), p. 703.

Scarlet Adventuress

713a. Described in **Mystery, Detective, and Espionage Magazines,** ed. by Michael L. Cook (Westport, Conn.: Greenwood, 1983), pp. 464–66.

713b. Indexed in **Mystery, Detective, and Espionage Fiction,** ed. by Michael L. Cook and Stephen T. Miller (New York: Garland, 1988), pp. 399–400, 485, 666.

Scarlet Gang Smashers

714. Indexed in **Mystery, Detective, and Espionage Fiction,** ed. by Michael L. Cook and Stephen T. Miller (New York: Garland, 1988), pp. 485–86.

Scarlet Gang Stories. See *Scarlet Gang Smashers*

The Science Fiction Collector. See *Megavore* (Canadian)

Scientific Detective

715. Described in **Mystery, Detective, and Espionage Magazines,** ed. by Michael L. Cook (Westport, Conn.: Greenwood, 1983), pp. 466–67.

Scientific Detective Annual. See *Scientific Detective*

Scientific Detective Monthly

716a. Described in **Mystery, Detective, and Espionage Magazines,** ed. by Michael L. Cook (Westport, Conn.: Greenwood, 1983), pp. 467–70.

716b. Indexed in **Mystery, Detective, and Espionage Fiction,** ed. by Michael L. Cook and Stephen T. Miller (New York: Garland, 1988), pp. 13–14, 486.

716c. Indexed in **The Pulp Magazine Index: Fourth Series,** by Leonard A. Robbins (Mercer Island, Wash.: Starmont House, 1991).

The Scorpion. See *The Octopus*

Scotland Yard

717a. Described in **Mystery, Detective, and Espionage Magazines,** ed. by Michael L. Cook (Westport, Conn.: Greenwood, 1983), pp. 470–73.

717b. Indexed in **Mystery, Detective, and Espionage Fiction,** ed. by Michael L. Cook and Stephen T. Miller (New York: Garland, 1988), pp. 486–87.

717c. Indexed in **The Pulp Magazine Index: First Series,** by Leonard A. Robbins (Mercer Island, Wash.: Starmont House, 1989).

Scotland Yard Detective Stories. See *Scotland Yard*

Scotland Yard Series of Detective Novels (British)

718. Described in **Mystery, Detective, and Espionage Magazines,** ed. by Michael L. Cook (Westport, Conn.: Greenwood, 1983), pp. 474–75.

Secret Agent 'X'

719a. Described in **Mystery, Detective, and Espionage Magazines,** ed. by Michael L. Cook (Westport, Conn.: Greenwood, 1983), pp. 475–76.

719b. Indexed in **Mystery, Detective, and Espionage Fiction,** ed. by Michael L. Cook and Stephen T. Miller (New York: Garland, 1988), pp. 488–90.

719c. Indexed in **The Pulp Magazine Index: First Series,** by Leonard A. Robbins (Mercer Island, Wash.: Starmont House, 1989).

719d. Brown, Michael Rogero. **Secret Agent 'X.'** http://sflovers.rutgers.edu/archive/bibliographies/secret-agent-x.txt

Brown's index lists the lead stories of 41 issues of *Secret Agent 'X'* in chronological order. Each entry gives the magazine's issue number, story's title, initials of the author, date of publication, magazine's volume and number, and information on reprints. Following the list, the authors' full names are given. Information on contents of the rest of the magazine would have been welcome, but this list is well done.

Note: Fuller indexes to *Secret Agent 'X'* can be found in Michael Cook and Stephen T. Miller's *Mystery, Detective, and Espionage Fiction* and the first series of Leonard Robbins's *The Pulp Magazine Index* (q.q.v.).

Secret Agent 'X' Detective Stories. See Secret Agent 'X'

Secret Service Detective Stories

720a. Described in **Mystery, Detective, and Espionage Magazines,** ed. by Michael L. Cook (Westport, Conn.: Greenwood, 1983), p. 477.

720b. Indexed in **Mystery, Detective, and Espionage Fiction,** ed. by Michael L. Cook and Stephen T. Miller (New York: Garland, 1988), p. 490.

Secret Service: Old and Young King Brady, Detectives

721. Described in **Mystery, Detective, and Espionage Magazines,** ed. by Michael L. Cook (Westport, Conn.: Greenwood, 1983), pp. 477–79.

Secret Service Operator #5. See Operator #5

Secret Service Stories

722. Indexed in **Mystery, Detective, and Espionage Fiction,** ed. by Michael L. Cook and Stephen T. Miller (New York: Garland, 1988), pp. 492–93.

The Secret 6

723a. Described in **Mystery, Detective, and Espionage Magazines,** ed. by Michael L. Cook (Westport, Conn.: Greenwood, 1983), pp. 479–81.

723b. Indexed in **Mystery, Detective, and Espionage Fiction,** ed. by Michael L. Cook and Stephen T. Miller (New York: Garland, 1988), p. 493.

723c. Indexed in **The Pulp Magazine Index: First Series,** by Leonard A. Robbins (Mercer Island, Wash.: Starmont House, 1989).

Secrets of the Secret Service

724a. Described in **Mystery, Detective, and Espionage Magazines,** ed. by Michael L. Cook (Westport, Conn.: Greenwood, 1983), p. 481.

724b. Indexed in **Mystery, Detective, and Espionage Fiction,** ed. by Michael L. Cook and Stephen T. Miller (New York: Garland, 1988), p. 493.

Sensational Startling Stories

725. Indexed in **Mystery, Detective, and Espionage Fiction,** ed. by Michael L. Cook and Stephen T. Miller (New York: Garland, 1988), p. 494.

77 Sunset Strip

726a. Described in **Mystery, Detective, and Espionage Magazines,** ed. by Michael L. Cook (Westport, Conn.: Greenwood, 1983), pp. 481–82.

726b. Indexed in Michael Cook, **Monthly Murders: A Checklist and Chronological Listing of Fiction in the Digest-Size Mystery Magazines in the United States and England** (Westport, Conn.: Greenwood, 1982), p. 722.

726c. Indexed in **Mystery, Detective, and Espionage Fiction,** ed. by Michael L. Cook and Stephen T. Miller (New York: Garland, 1988), p. 494.

The Sexton Blake Library (British)

727. Described in **Mystery, Detective, and Espionage Magazines,** ed. by Michael L. Cook (Westport, Conn.: Greenwood, 1983), pp. 482–84.

The Shadow

728a. Checklist to title stories given in John P. Gunnison, **Street & Smith's Hero Pulp Checklist** (Upper Marlboro, Md.: Pulp Collector Press, 1991).

728b. Described in **Mystery, Detective, and Espionage Magazines,** ed. by Michael L. Cook (Westport, Conn.: Greenwood, 1983), pp. 486–91.

728c. Indexed in Michael Cook, **Monthly Murders: A Checklist and Chronological Listing of Fiction in the Digest-Size Mystery Magazines in the United States and England** (Westport, Conn.: Greenwood, 1982), pp. 670–77.

728d. Indexed in **Mystery, Detective, and Espionage Fiction,** ed. by Michael L. Cook and Stephen T. Miller (New York: Garland, 1988), pp. 494–511.

728e. Indexed in **The Pulp Magazine Index: First Series,** by Leonard A. Robbins (Mercer Island, Wash.: Starmont House, 1989).

728f. Brown, Michael Rogero. **The Shadow.** http://sflovers.rutgers.edu/archive/bibliographies/shadow.txt

Brown's index to *The Shadow* lists only the lead story of each issue. Its arrangement is chronological: the story's title is given, followed by the initials of the author, date of publication, magazine's volume and number, and reprint information. Following the list are the authors' full names, information on reprints, and the appearances of The Shadow in comic books, radio shows, newspaper syndication, and motion pictures. This is a very capable index, but one wishes Brown had provided information on the contents in the rest of the magazine.

Note: A fuller index to the *Shadow* can be found in Michael Cook and Stephen T. Miller's *Mystery, Detective, and Espionage Fiction* and the first series of Leonard Robbins's *The Pulp Magazine Index* (q.q.v.).

728g. Eisgruber, Frank, Jr. **Gangland's Doom.** Preface by Robert Weinberg. Oak Lawn, Ill.: Robert Weinberg, 1974. 64 p. Paperback. Also: Mercer Island, Wash.: Starmont House, 1985. Starmont Pulp & Dime Novel Studies, no. 1. 64 p. Paperback. LC 85-26069. ISBN 0-930261-71-2 (hc); 0-930261-74-7 (pb). ISSN 0885-0658. Also: San Bernardino, Calif.: Borgo Press, 1985. 64 p. Paperback. LC 85-31407. ISBN 0-89370-563-2.

728h. Gibson, Walter B. **The Shadow Scrapbook.** Preface by Chris Steinbrunner. New York: Harcourt Brace Jovanovich, 1979. v, 162 p. Paperback. LC 78-22277. ISBN 0-15-681475-7.

728i. Murray, Will. **The Duende History of** *The Shadow* **Magazine.** Greenwood, Mass.: Odyssey, 1980. 128 p. Paperback. ISBN 0-933752-21-0.

728j. Sampson, Robert. **The Night Master.** Chicago: Pulp Press, 1982. 216 p. Cloth. LC 81-82237. ISBN 0-934498-08-3.

None of these books about the Shadow, supremely lethal hero of the long-lasting the *Shadow* magazine, is, strictly speaking, a reference book. Each nevertheless contains lists of Shadow novels and illustrations and offers additional critical material.

Gangland's Doom is the weakest of the volumes. Reproduced from typed copy and intended primarily for a fannish audience, it is written from the conceit that The Shadow and his assistants were real. Different chapters describe the Shadow's identities, his agents and allies, notable and recurrent villains, The Shadow's sanctums, and The Shadow's travels. Appendixes discuss The Shadow in light of theories put forth by Philip José Farmer, describe the writers of *The Shadow,* and provide a chronological list of the issues of the magazines, indicating when the writer was Theodore Tinsley or Bruce Elliott rather than Walter Gibson.

The Shadow Scrapbook is not a scrapbook but a history by Walter B. Gibson, the man who wrote the majority of the *The Shadow* novels. It begins with "Introducing the Shadow," a historical essay in which Gibson discusses the origin and gradual development of The Shadow and which contains a chronological list of Shadow novels. Gibson explains his use of plot outlines and provides his outline for "The Mask of Mephisto" (published in *The Shadow Magazine* in July 1945), and he discusses the evolution of *The Shadow Magazine*'s covers, agents of the Shadow, and codes used by The Shadow. Anthony Tollin provides an article on the illustrations of *The Shadow Magazine* and a lengthy discussion of the Shadow on radio. A chronology of broadcasts is given (including the date of the broadcast, names of the readers, sponsor's name, and names of individual episodes during the various seasons), and the script for "The Death House Rescue" (broadcast 26 September 1937) is reprinted in virtually its entirety (the conclusion was lost and Gibson wrote another). Also provided are accounts of treatments of The Shadow in motion pictures and comic books and the various collectibles associated with the magazine.

The Duende History of The Shadow is slightly mistitled. In addition to providing the history of the magazine, it contains lengthy biographies of all connected with the creation and writing of *The Shadow Magazine,* and an excellent chronological index to the magazine. Will Murray and Robert Sampson provide a history and description of Lester Dent's "The Golden Vulture," which, written in 1932, appeared in *The Shadow Magazine* in 1938 only after being rewritten by Walter Gibson. Sampson discusses the character of The Shadow as written by Theodore Tinsley and by Bruce Elliott, and there are lengthy interviews with Tinsley and Gibson. Finally, Gibson provides a short account of The Shadow's Girasol and a short story ("Blackmail Bay") written especially for this volume.

The Night Master is a lengthy and affectionate study of the Shadow, with a lively history connecting the pulp series to the events of the real world as well as to the world of publishing. Eleven lists (here referred to as "Tables") provide descriptions of the characters in The Shadow series by time period; a chronology of "certain major events" in the career of Kent Allard, the Living Shadow; lists of the editors of *The Shadow Magazine;* variations in the magazine's title between 1931 and 1949; approximate word counts in Shadow novels; descriptions of the magazine's major departments; and lists of the artists and illustrators for *The Shadow Magazine.* Appendixes describe variations in the magazine's size, pagination, and cost; list reprint appearances of the Shadow; and provide a chronological list of all of *The Shadow Magazines* magazines (reprinted from *The Duende History of The Shadow*). Although unfortunately unindexed (stated Sampson, "I squalled and howled for an index and got overruled because of the extra expense") and oddly laid out (Sampson: "The printer was the one who laid it out. That's the reason the type floods over the illustrations and wanders so about the page in an innocent and simple way, like a little country girl gathering posies"), this remains one of the finest books done on an influential pulp magazine and its series character.

Libraries fortunate enough to be able to purchase *The Shadow Scrapbook, The Duende History of The Shadow,* and *The Night Master* should acquire all; they provide insight into the creation and actions of one of the most durable characters of the pulp magazines.

Note: The bibliography documenting Walter Gibson's enormous output is described in the section devoted to the authors of detective and mystery stories, and a lengthy discussion of the character of the Shadow may be found in Rick Lai's *Chronology of Shadows* (q.q.v.).

728k. ThePulp.net. http://thepulp.net/theshadow.html

A wonderful history of the Shadow, with hundreds of useful links.

728l. The Shadow Magazine. http://www.spaceports.com/~deshadow

This phenomenal site provides a history and description of the series, cover reproductions, hundreds of links, and a list of the entire series—from 1931 until the 1980 paperback originals. Furthermore, the works from the pulp magazines are available for downloading as .txt files.

The Shadow, a Detective Monthly. See *The Shadow*

The Shadow Annual

729a. Checklist to title stories given in John P. Gunnison, **Street & Smith's Hero Pulp Checklist** (Upper Marlboro, Md.: Pulp Collector Press, 1991).

729b. Described in **Mystery, Detective, and Espionage Magazines,** ed. by Michael L. Cook (Westport, Conn.: Greenwood, 1983), pp. 484–86.

729c. Indexed in **Mystery, Detective, and Espionage Fiction,** ed. by Michael L. Cook and Stephen T. Miller (New York: Garland, 1988), p. 503.

729d. Indexed in **The Pulp Magazine Index: Second Series,** by Leonard A. Robbins (Mercer Island, Wash.: Starmont House, 1989).

The Shadow Detective Monthly. See *The Shadow*

The Shadow Magazine. See *The Shadow*

The Shadow Mystery Magazine. See *The Shadow*

Sheena, Queen of the Jungle. See *Stories of Sheena, Queen of the Jungle*

Shell Scott Mystery Magazine

730a. Described in **Mystery, Detective, and Espionage Magazines,** ed. by Michael L. Cook (Westport, Conn.: Greenwood, 1983), pp. 492–93.

730b. Indexed in Michael Cook, **Monthly Murders: A Checklist and Chronological Listing of Fiction in the Digest-Size Mystery Magazines in the United States and England** (Westport, Conn.: Greenwood, 1982), pp. 696–98.

The Sherlock Holmes Journal (British)

731. Described in **Mystery, Detective, and Espionage Magazines,** ed. by Michael L. Cook (Westport, Conn.: Greenwood, 1983), pp. 493–94.

Shield Weekly

732. Described in **Mystery, Detective, and Espionage Magazines,** ed. by Michael L. Cook (Westport, Conn.: Greenwood, 1983), pp. 495–96.

Shock

733a. Described in **Mystery, Detective, and Espionage Magazines,** ed. by Michael L. Cook (Westport, Conn.: Greenwood, 1983), pp. 496–98.

733b. Indexed in **Mystery, Detective, and Espionage Fiction,** ed. by Michael L. Cook and Stephen T. Miller (New York: Garland, 1988), p. 511.

733c. Indexed in **The Pulp Magazine Index: Second Series,** by Leonard A. Robbins (Mercer Island, Wash.: Starmont House, 1989).

Shock Mystery Tales

734a. Described in **Mystery, Detective, and Espionage Magazines,** ed. by Michael L. Cook (Westport, Conn.: Greenwood, 1983), p. 499.

734b. Indexed in Michael Cook, **Monthly Murders: A Checklist and Chronological Listing of Fiction in the Digest-Size Mystery Magazines in the United States and England** (Westport, Conn.: Greenwood, 1982), pp. 684–85.

Shock Mystery Tales Magazine. See *Shock Mystery Tales*

Shock—The Magazine of Terrifying Tales

735a. Described in **Mystery, Detective, and Espionage Magazines,** ed. by Michael L. Cook (Westport, Conn.: Greenwood, 1983), pp. 499–500.

735b. Indexed in Michael Cook, **Monthly Murders: A Checklist and Chronological Listing of Fiction in the Digest-Size Mystery Magazines in the United States and England** (Westport, Conn.: Greenwood, 1982), pp. 682–83.

A Shot Rang Out

736. Described in **Mystery, Detective, and Espionage Magazines,** ed. by Michael L. Cook (Westport, Conn.: Greenwood, 1983), pp. 500–501.

Sinister Stories

737a. Described in **Mystery, Detective, and Espionage Magazines,** ed. by Michael L. Cook (Westport, Conn.: Greenwood, 1983), pp. 501–2.

737b. Indexed in **The Pulp Magazine Index: First Series,** by Leonard A. Robbins (Mercer Island, Wash.: Starmont House, 1989).

Sizzling Detective Mysteries. See *Snappy Detective Mysteries*

The Skipper

738a. Checklist to title stories given in John P. Gunnison, **Street & Smith's Hero Pulp Checklist** (Upper Marlboro, Md.: Pulp Collector Press, 1991).

738b. Described in **Mystery, Detective, and Espionage Magazines,** ed. by Michael L. Cook (Westport, Conn.: Greenwood, 1983), pp. 502–5.

738c. Indexed in **Mystery, Detective, and Espionage Fiction,** ed. by Michael L. Cook and Stephen T. Miller (New York: Garland, 1988), p. 512.

738d. Indexed in **The Pulp Magazine Index: First Series,** by Leonard A. Robbins (Mercer Island, Wash.: Starmont House, 1989).

Skullduggery

739a. Described in **Mystery, Detective, and Espionage Magazines,** ed. by Michael L. Cook (Westport, Conn.: Greenwood, 1983), pp. 505–7.

739b. Indexed in Michael Cook, **Monthly Murders: A Checklist and Chronological Listing of Fiction in the Digest-Size Mystery Magazines in the United States and England** (Westport, Conn.: Greenwood, 1982), pp. 686–87.

Sleuth Mystery Magazine

740a. Described in **Mystery, Detective, and Espionage Magazines,** ed. by Michael L. Cook (Westport, Conn.: Greenwood, 1983), pp. 507–9.

740b. Indexed in Michael Cook, **Monthly Murders: A Checklist and Chronological Listing of Fiction in the Digest-Size Mystery Magazines in the United States and England** (Westport, Conn.: Greenwood, 1982), p. 688.

Slick Detective Yarns (British)

741. Described in **Mystery, Detective, and Espionage Magazines,** ed. by Michael L. Cook (Westport, Conn.: Greenwood, 1983), p. 509.

Smashing Detective

742a. Described in **Mystery, Detective, and Espionage Magazines,** ed. by Michael L. Cook (Westport, Conn.: Greenwood, 1983), pp. 510–11.

742b. Indexed in Michael Cook, **Monthly Murders: A Checklist and Chronological Listing of Fiction in the Digest-Size Mystery Magazines in the United States and England** (Westport, Conn.: Greenwood, 1982), pp. 353–54.

742c. Indexed in **Mystery, Detective, and Espionage Fiction,** ed. by Michael L. Cook and Stephen T. Miller (New York: Garland, 1988), pp. 324, 512–51.

742d. Indexed in **The Pulp Magazine Index: First Series,** by Leonard A. Robbins (Mercer Island, Wash.: Starmont House, 1989).

Smashing Detective Stories. See Smashing Detective

Snappy Adventure Stories

743. Indexed in **Mystery, Detective, and Espionage Fiction,** ed. by Michael L. Cook and Stephen T. Miller (New York: Garland, 1988), p. 515.

Snappy Detective Mysteries

744a. Described in **Mystery, Detective, and Espionage Magazines,** ed. by Michael L. Cook (Westport, Conn.: Greenwood, 1983), p. 512.

744b. Indexed in **Mystery, Detective, and Espionage Fiction,** ed. by Michael L. Cook and Stephen T. Miller (New York: Garland, 1988), pp. 511–12, 515.

Snappy Detective Stories

745a. Described in **Mystery, Detective, and Espionage Magazines,** ed. by Michael L. Cook (Westport, Conn.: Greenwood, 1983), pp. 512–13.

745b. Indexed in **Mystery, Detective, and Espionage Fiction,** ed. by Michael L. Cook and Stephen T. Miller (New York: Garland, 1988), p. 515.

Snappy Mystery Stories

746a. Described in **Mystery, Detective, and Espionage Magazines,** ed. by Michael L. Cook (Westport, Conn.: Greenwood, 1983), pp. 513–14.

746b. Indexed in **Mystery, Detective, and Espionage Fiction,** ed. by Michael L. Cook and Stephen T. Miller (New York: Garland, 1988), p. 515.

Soldier Stories

747. Indexed in **Mystery, Detective, and Espionage Fiction,** ed. by Michael L. Cook and Stephen T. Miller (New York: Garland, 1988), p. 515.

Speakeasy Stories

748a. Described in **Mystery, Detective, and Espionage Magazines,** ed. by Michael L. Cook (Westport, Conn.: Greenwood, 1983), p. 514.

748b. Indexed in **Mystery, Detective, and Espionage Fiction,** ed. by Michael L. Cook and Stephen T. Miller (New York: Garland, 1988), p. 516.

Special Detective

749. Indexed in **Mystery, Detective, and Espionage Fiction,** ed. by Michael L. Cook and Stephen T. Miller (New York: Garland, 1988), p. 516.

Speed Adventure Stories

750a. Indexed in **Mystery, Detective, and Espionage Fiction,** ed. by Michael L. Cook and Stephen T. Miller (New York: Garland, 1988), pp. 516–17.

750b. Indexed in **The Pulp Magazine Index: Second Series,** by Leonard A. Robbins (Mercer Island, Wash.: Starmont House, 1989).

Speed Detective. See Spicy Detective

Speed Stories

751. Indexed in **Mystery, Detective, and Espionage Fiction,** ed. by Michael L. Cook and Stephen T. Miller (New York: Garland, 1988), p. 521.

Spicy Adventure

752. Indexed in **Mystery, Detective, and Espionage Fiction,** ed. by Michael L. Cook and Stephen T. Miller (New York: Garland, 1988), pp. 521–28, 666.

Spicy Adventure Stories. See *Spicy Adventure*

Spicy Detective

753a. Described in **Mystery, Detective, and Espionage Magazines,** ed. by Michael L. Cook (Westport, Conn.: Greenwood, 1983), pp. 515–18.

753b. Indexed in **Mystery, Detective, and Espionage Fiction,** ed. by Michael L. Cook and Stephen T. Miller (New York: Garland, 1988), pp. 517–19, 528–36.

753c. Indexed in **The Pulp Magazine Index: Second Series,** by Leonard A. Robbins (Mercer Island, Wash.: Starmont House, 1989).

Spicy Detective Stories. See *Spicy Detective*

Spicy Movie Tales. See *Saucy Movie Tales*

Spicy Mystery. See *Spicy Mystery Stories*

Spicy Mystery Stories

754a. Described in **Mystery, Detective, and Espionage Magazines,** ed. by Michael L. Cook (Westport, Conn.: Greenwood, 1983), pp. 518–21.

754b. Indexed in **Mystery, Detective, and Espionage Fiction,** ed. by Michael L. Cook and Stephen T. Miller (New York: Garland, 1988), pp. 519–21, 537–42.

754c. Indexed in **The Pulp Magazine Index: Second Series,** by Leonard A. Robbins (Mercer Island, Wash.: Starmont House, 1989).

The Spider

755a. Described in **Mystery, Detective, and Espionage Magazines,** ed. by Michael L. Cook (Westport, Conn.: Greenwood, 1983), pp. 521–27.

755b. Indexed in **Mystery, Detective, and Espionage Fiction,** ed. by Michael L. Cook and Stephen T. Miller (New York: Garland, 1988), pp. 543–48.

755c.   Indexed in **The Pulp Magazine Index: First Series,** by Leonard A. Robbins (Mercer Island, Wash.: Starmont House, 1989).

755d.   Brown, Michael Rogero. **The Spider.** http://sflovers.rutgers.edu/archive/bibliographies.spider.txt

Brown's index to *The Spider* is arranged by issue. The title of the lead story featuring the Spider is given, followed by the initials of its author, the date of its publication, the issue's volume number, and its reprint availability. At the conclusion of the list, the authors' full names are given, and Brown provides information on the Spider's appearance in comic books and movie serials. Information on the other works appearing in the magazine and additional indexes would have been welcome, but this is a very usable index.

Note: A fuller index to *The Spider* can be found in Michael Cook and Stephen T. Miller's *Mystery, Detective, and Espionage Fiction* (q.v.). Robert Sampson's *Spider* (Bowling Green, Ohio: Bowling Green State University Popular Press, 1987) contains appendixes providing a checklist of *The Spider* novels, a checklist of short fiction appearing in the magazine, and a checklist of the writers publishing short fiction in the magazine.

755e.   Kalb, Chris. **The Spider: Master of Men!** http://members.aol.com/spiderpage/

Another excellent site by Kalb, with illustrations, texts, and a general wealth of information.

755f.   Sampson, Robert D. **Spider**. Bowling Green, Ohio: Bowling Green State University Popular Press, 1987. 250 p. Index. LC 87-71412. ISBN 0-87972-398-X (pb); 0-87972-397-1.

Though this is a lengthy and affectionate history of the magazine and not a reference book, it nevertheless contains a lengthy bibliography and appendixes giving checklists of the *Spider* novels, the short fiction appearing in the *Spider,* and the writers who published the short fiction. It is well indexed.

755g.   **ThePulp.net.** http://thepulp.net/thespider.html

An excellent history of the *Spider*, with hundreds of links.

Spiderweb

756.   Described in **Mystery, Detective, and Espionage Magazines,** ed. by Michael L. Cook (Westport, Conn.: Greenwood, 1983), p. 527.

Springheeled Jack (**British**)

757.   Described in **Mystery, Detective, and Espionage Magazines,** ed. by Michael L. Cook (Westport, Conn.: Greenwood, 1983), pp. 527–28.

Spy Novels Magazine

758a.   Described in **Mystery, Detective, and Espionage Magazines,** ed. by Michael L. Cook (Westport, Conn.: Greenwood, 1983), pp. 528–30.

758b. Indexed in **Mystery, Detective, and Espionage Fiction,** ed. by Michael L. Cook and Stephen T. Miller (New York: Garland, 1988), p. 548.

758c. Indexed in **The Pulp Magazine Index: First Series,** by Leonard A. Robbins (Mercer Island, Wash.: Starmont House, 1989).

Spy Secrets

759. Indexed in **Mystery, Detective, and Espionage Fiction,** ed. by Michael L. Cook and Stephen T. Miller (New York: Garland, 1988), p. 548.

Spy Stories (Albert Publishing)

760a. Described in **Mystery, Detective, and Espionage Magazines,** ed. by Michael L. Cook (Westport, Conn.: Greenwood, 1983), pp. 530–31.

760b. Indexed in **Mystery, Detective, and Espionage Fiction,** ed. by Michael L. Cook and Stephen T. Miller (New York: Garland, 1988), p. 548.

760c. Indexed in **The Pulp Magazine Index: Second Series,** by Leonard A. Robbins (Mercer Island, Wash.: Starmont House, 1989).

Spy Stories (Magazine Publishers)

761a. Described in **Mystery, Detective, and Espionage Magazines,** ed. by Michael L. Cook (Westport, Conn.: Greenwood, 1983), p. 531.

761b. Indexed in **The Pulp Magazine Index: Second Series,** by Leonard A. Robbins (Mercer Island, Wash.: Starmont House, 1989).

Spy Stories (Monthly Magazine Publishers)

762a. Described in **Mystery, Detective, and Espionage Magazines,** ed. by Michael L. Cook (Westport, Conn.: Greenwood, 1983), pp. 531–32.

762b. Indexed in **Mystery, Detective, and Espionage Fiction,** ed. by Michael L. Cook and Stephen T. Miller (New York: Garland, 1988), pp. 548–50.

Star Detective

763a. Described in **Mystery, Detective, and Espionage Magazines,** ed. by Michael L. Cook (Westport, Conn.: Greenwood, 1983), p. 532.

763b. Indexed in **The Pulp Magazine Index: First Series,** by Leonard A. Robbins (Mercer Island, Wash.: Starmont House, 1989).

Star Detective Magazine. See *Star Detective*

Star Novels. **See** *Star Novels Magazine*

Star Novels Magazine

764. Indexed in **Mystery, Detective, and Espionage Fiction,** ed. by Michael L. Cook and Stephen T. Miller (New York: Garland, 1988), pp. 550–52.

Star Novels Quarterly

765. Indexed in **Mystery, Detective, and Espionage Fiction,** ed. by Michael L. Cook and Stephen T. Miller (New York: Garland, 1988), p. 552.

Startling Detective Adventures

766a. Described in **Mystery, Detective, and Espionage Magazines,** ed. by Michael L. Cook (Westport, Conn.: Greenwood, 1983), p. 533.

766b. Indexed in **Mystery, Detective, and Espionage Fiction,** ed. by Michael L. Cook and Stephen T. Miller (New York: Garland, 1988), p. 552.

Startling Mystery

767a. Described in **Mystery, Detective, and Espionage Magazines,** ed. by Michael L. Cook (Westport, Conn.: Greenwood, 1983), pp. 533–34.

767b. Indexed in **Mystery, Detective, and Espionage Fiction,** ed. by Michael L. Cook and Stephen T. Miller (New York: Garland, 1988), p. 553.

767c. Indexed in **The Pulp Magazine Index: First Series,** by Leonard A. Robbins (Mercer Island, Wash.: Starmont House, 1989).

Startling Mystery Magazine. **See** *Startling Mystery*

Startling Mystery Stories

768a. Described in **Mystery, Detective, and Espionage Magazines,** ed. by Michael L. Cook (Westport, Conn.: Greenwood, 1983), pp. 534–36.

768b. Indexed in Michael Cook, **Monthly Murders: A Checklist and Chronological Listing of Fiction in the Digest-Size Mystery Magazines in the United States and England** (Westport, Conn.: Greenwood, 1982), pp. 692–95.

Stirring Adventures

769. Indexed in **Mystery, Detective, and Espionage Fiction,** ed. by Michael L. Cook and Stephen T. Miller (New York: Garland, 1988), p. 553.

Stirring Detective and Western Stories

770a. Described in **Mystery, Detective, and Espionage Magazines,** ed. by Michael L. Cook (Westport, Conn.: Greenwood, 1983), p. 536.

770b. Indexed in **Mystery, Detective, and Espionage Fiction,** ed. by Michael L. Cook and Stephen T. Miller (New York: Garland, 1988), p. 553.

Stirring Detective Cases

771. Indexed in **Mystery, Detective, and Espionage Fiction,** ed. by Michael L. Cook and Stephen T. Miller (New York: Garland, 1988), pp. 663–64.

Stirring Detective Stories (British)

772. Described in **Mystery, Detective, and Espionage Magazines,** ed. by Michael L. Cook (Westport, Conn.: Greenwood, 1983), p. 537.

Stories of Sheena, Queen of the Jungle

773. Indexed in **Mystery, Detective, and Espionage Fiction,** ed. by Michael L. Cook and Stephen T. Miller (New York: Garland, 1988), p. 553.

Story Digest Magazine

774a. Described in **Mystery, Detective, and Espionage Magazines,** ed. by Michael L. Cook (Westport, Conn.: Greenwood, 1983), p. 537.

774b. Indexed in Michael Cook, **Monthly Murders: A Checklist and Chronological Listing of Fiction in the Digest-Size Mystery Magazines in the United States and England** (Westport, Conn.: Greenwood, 1982), p. 736.

The Strand

775. Whitt, J. F. **The Strand Magazine, 1891–1950: A Selective Checklist, Listing All Material Relating to Arthur Conan Doyle, All Stories by P. G. Wodehouse, and a Selection of Other Contributions, Mainly by Writers of Detective, Mystery, or Fantasy Fiction.** London: J. F. Whitt, 1979. 48 p. Index. Paperback. ISBN 0-95067000-0-6.

Although it is renowned for publishing the Sherlock Holmes of Arthur Conan Doyle, the *Strand* published dozens of other noted writers, including such luminaries as H. G. Wells, P. G. Wodehouse, Algernon Blackwood, Nicholas Blake, John Dickson Carr, G. K. Chesterton, Agatha Christie, and Robert Graves. A separately published index to the *Strand* does exist, *Index to the Strand Magazine, 1891–1950* (Westport, Conn.: Greenwood, 1982) compiled by Geraldine Beare, but Whitt's self-published *Selective Checklist* is the only known index to the genre writers published in the magazine. It is cleanly offset from what appears to be computer copy.

The pamphlet contains three parts. The first is an issue-by-issue list of the 711 issues of the *Strand,* a chronological list that contains works by the writers named earlier as well as "by writers outside the mystery field, who are intrinsically important or have a special relation with the magazine." Each volume of the magazine is given in capital letters followed by the publication year and the months in which the volume was published. Beneath these data, each issue is numbered and followed by a three-letter abbreviation for the month, after which the author's name is given, with the last name in capital letters. The story title is also given in capital letters, with the name of its illustrator (if any) listed in parentheses. Works published anonymously are so indicated.

The second part contains an alphabetical list of all of the material by Arthur Conan Doyle and all the related Holmesiana that were listed in the first section. The titles are given in capital letters, followed by the issue number. This section also contains a note on Doyle and "The Chronicles of the *Strand* Club," published from 1905 and 1907.

The third section is a full index to the contributors listed in the first section as well as the contributions of a lengthy list of additional authors Whitt found important, although it must be emphasized that it does not necessarily list all of the contributions of these authors. The last names of the authors are given in capital letters followed by the issue number(s) in which they appeared; if they were cited in the chronological list, the issue number is underlined.

The *Checklist* is an eccentric work, and although no statement of limitations is given, it is doubtful that more than a few hundred copies were printed. Furthermore, Whitt does not distinguish between the English and American editions of the *Strand,* and there were often differences. The *Checklist* is nevertheless a work with some uses, and it is to be regretted that it never received wide circulation. Most researchers, however, will be content with Beare's work, which offers author, illustrator, and subject indexes, as well as appendixes providing access to authors and their illustrators, single-author series, multiauthor series, anonymous articles and stories, anonymous cartoons, symposia, illustrated interviews, and series and nonseries stories for children.

Strange

776a.   Described in **Mystery, Detective, and Espionage Magazines,** ed. by Michael L. Cook (Westport, Conn.: Greenwood, 1983), pp. 538–39.

776b.   Indexed in Michael Cook, **Monthly Murders: A Checklist and Chronological Listing of Fiction in the Digest-Size Mystery Magazines in the United States and England** (Westport, Conn.: Greenwood, 1982), pp. 680–81.

Strange Detective Mysteries

777a.   Described in **Mystery, Detective, and Espionage Magazines,** ed. by Michael L. Cook (Westport, Conn.: Greenwood, 1983), p. 539.

777b.   Indexed in **Mystery, Detective, and Espionage Fiction,** ed. by Michael L. Cook and Stephen T. Miller (New York: Garland, 1988), pp. 553–55.

777c.   Indexed in **The Pulp Magazine Index: First Series,** by Leonard A. Robbins (Mercer Island, Wash.: Starmont House, 1989).

Strange Detective Stories

778a. Described in **Mystery, Detective, and Espionage Magazines,** ed. by Michael L. Cook (Westport, Conn.: Greenwood, 1983), p. 540.

778b. Indexed in **Mystery, Detective, and Espionage Fiction,** ed. by Michael L. Cook and Stephen T. Miller (New York: Garland, 1988), pp. 439–40, 555–56.

778c. Indexed in **The Pulp Magazine Index: First Series,** by Leonard A. Robbins (Mercer Island, Wash.: Starmont House, 1989).

Strange Stories

779a. Described in **Mystery, Detective, and Espionage Magazines,** ed. by Michael L. Cook (Westport, Conn.: Greenwood, 1983), pp. 540–41.

779b. Indexed in **Mystery, Detective, and Espionage Fiction,** ed. by Michael L. Cook and Stephen T. Miller (New York: Garland, 1988), pp. 556–57.

779c. Indexed in **The Pulp Magazine Index: First Series,** by Leonard A. Robbins (Mercer Island, Wash.: Starmont House, 1989).

Strange Suicides

780. Mentioned in **Mystery, Detective, and Espionage Fiction,** ed. by Michael L. Cook and Stephen T. Miller (New York: Garland, 1988), p. 557.

Strange Tales of Mystery and Terror

781a. Described in **Mystery, Detective, and Espionage Magazines,** ed. by Michael L. Cook (Westport, Conn.: Greenwood, 1983), p. 541.

781b. Indexed in **Mystery, Detective, and Espionage Fiction,** ed. by Michael L. Cook and Stephen T. Miller (New York: Garland, 1988), pp. 557–58.

781c. Indexed in **The Pulp Magazine Index: First Series,** by Leonard A. Robbins (Mercer Island, Wash.: Starmont House, 1989).

Street & Smith Sampler

782. Indexed in **Mystery, Detective, and Espionage Fiction,** ed. by Michael L. Cook and Stephen T. Miller (New York: Garland, 1988), p. 558.

Street & Smith's Clues Detective Stories. See Clues

Street & Smith's Detective Monthly (British)

783. Described in **Mystery, Detective, and Espionage Magazines,** ed. by Michael L. Cook (Westport, Conn.: Greenwood, 1983), pp. 541–42.

Street & Smith's Detective Stories (British). See *Street & Smith's Detective Monthly* (British)

Street & Smith's Detective Story Magazine. See *Detective Story Magazine* (Street & Smith)

Street & Smith's Mystery Detective (British)

784. Described in **Mystery, Detective, and Espionage Magazines,** ed. by Michael L. Cook (Westport, Conn.: Greenwood, 1983), pp. 542–43.

Street & Smith's Mystery Magazine. See *Crime Busters*

Super-Detective

785a. Described in **Mystery, Detective, and Espionage Magazines,** ed. by Michael L. Cook (Westport, Conn.: Greenwood, 1983), pp. 543–45.

785b. Indexed in **Mystery, Detective, and Espionage Fiction,** ed. by Michael L. Cook and Stephen T. Miller (New York: Garland, 1988), pp. 583–87.

785c. Indexed in **The Pulp Magazine Index: First Series,** by Leonard A. Robbins (Mercer Island, Wash.: Starmont House, 1989).

Super Detective Library (British)

786. Described in **Mystery, Detective, and Espionage Magazines,** ed. by Michael L. Cook (Westport, Conn.: Greenwood, 1983), pp. 545–46.

Super-Detective Stories

787. Indexed in **Mystery, Detective, and Espionage Fiction,** ed. by Michael L. Cook and Stephen T. Miller (New York: Garland, 1988), pp. 587–88.

Sure-Fire Detective Magazine

788a. Described in **Mystery, Detective, and Espionage Magazines,** ed. by Michael L. Cook (Westport, Conn.: Greenwood, 1983), pp. 546–47.

788b. Indexed in **Mystery, Detective, and Espionage Fiction,** ed. by Michael L. Cook and Stephen T. Miller (New York: Garland, 1988), p. 588.

788c. Indexed in **The Pulp Magazine Index: Third Series,** by Leonard A. Robbins (Mercer Island, Wash.: Starmont House, 1990).

Sure-Fire Detective Stories (Duchess Printing and Publishing Co.)

789. Indexed in **Mystery, Detective, and Espionage Fiction,** ed. by Michael L. Cook and Stephen T. Miller (New York: Garland, 1988), p. 664.

Sure Fire Detective Stories (Pontiac Publishing Corporation)

790a. Described in **Mystery, Detective, and Espionage Magazines,** ed. by Michael L. Cook (Westport, Conn.: Greenwood, 1983), pp. 547–48.

790b. Indexed in Michael Cook, **Monthly Murders: A Checklist and Chronological Listing of Fiction in the Digest-Size Mystery Magazines in the United States and England** (Westport, Conn.: Greenwood, 1982), pp. 678–79.

Suspect Detective Stories

791a. Described in **Mystery, Detective, and Espionage Magazines,** ed. by Michael L. Cook (Westport, Conn.: Greenwood, 1983), pp. 548–50.

791b. Indexed in Michael Cook, **Monthly Murders: A Checklist and Chronological Listing of Fiction in the Digest-Size Mystery Magazines in the United States and England** (Westport, Conn.: Greenwood, 1982), pp. 699–700.

Suspense

792a. Described in **Mystery, Detective, and Espionage Magazines,** ed. by Michael L. Cook (Westport, Conn.: Greenwood, 1983), pp. 550–52.

792b. Indexed in Michael Cook, **Monthly Murders: A Checklist and Chronological Listing of Fiction in the Digest-Size Mystery Magazines in the United States and England** (Westport, Conn.: Greenwood, 1982), pp. 720–21.

Suspense (British)

793a. Described in **Mystery, Detective, and Espionage Magazines,** ed. by Michael L. Cook (Westport, Conn.: Greenwood, 1983), pp. 552–53.

793b. Indexed in Michael Cook, **Monthly Murders: A Checklist and Chronological Listing of Fiction in the Digest-Size Mystery Magazines in the United States and England** (Westport, Conn.: Greenwood, 1982), pp. 704–13.

Suspense Novels

794. Described in **Mystery, Detective, and Espionage Magazines,** ed. by Michael L. Cook (Westport, Conn.: Greenwood, 1983), pp. 553–54.

Suspense Stories (British)

795. Described in **Mystery, Detective, and Espionage Magazines,** ed. by Michael L. Cook (Westport, Conn.: Greenwood, 1983), pp. 554–55.

Suspense—The Mystery Magazine [also *Suspense, the Mystery Magazine*]

796a. Described in **Mystery, Detective, and Espionage Magazines,** ed. by Michael L. Cook (Westport, Conn.: Greenwood, 1983), pp. 555–56.

796b. Indexed in Michael Cook, **Monthly Murders: A Checklist and Chronological Listing of Fiction in the Digest-Size Mystery Magazines in the United States and England** (Westport, Conn.: Greenwood, 1982), pp. 701–2.

Swift Story Magazine

797. Indexed in **Mystery, Detective, and Espionage Fiction,** ed. by Michael L. Cook and Stephen T. Miller (New York: Garland, 1988), p. 588.

Tailspin Tommy Air Adventure Magazine

798a. Indexed in **Mystery, Detective, and Espionage Fiction,** ed. by Michael L. Cook and Stephen T. Miller (New York: Garland, 1988), p. 588.

798b. Indexed in **The Pulp Magazine Index: First Series,** by Leonard A. Robbins (Mercer Island, Wash.: Starmont House, 1989).

Tales of Crime and Punishment

799. Indexed in **Mystery, Detective, and Espionage Fiction,** ed. by Michael L. Cook and Stephen T. Miller (New York: Garland, 1988), p. 664.

Tales of Magic and Mystery

800a. Described in **Mystery, Detective, and Espionage Magazines,** ed. by Michael L. Cook (Westport, Conn.: Greenwood, 1983), p. 557.

800b. Indexed in **Mystery, Detective, and Espionage Fiction,** ed. by Michael L. Cook and Stephen T. Miller (New York: Garland, 1988), pp. 588–89.

800c. Indexed in **The Pulp Magazine Index: Second Series,** by Leonard A. Robbins (Mercer Island, Wash.: Starmont House, 1989).

Tales of Mystery and Detection

801. Indexed in **Mystery, Detective, and Espionage Fiction,** ed. by Michael L. Cook and Stephen T. Miller (New York: Garland, 1988), p. 664.

Tales of Terror

802. Indexed in **Mystery, Detective, and Espionage Fiction,** ed. by Michael L. Cook and Stephen T. Miller (New York: Garland, 1988), p. 664.

Tales of the Frightened

803a. Described in **Mystery, Detective, and Espionage Magazines,** ed. by Michael L. Cook (Westport, Conn.: Greenwood, 1983), pp. 557–58.

803b. Indexed in Michael Cook, **Monthly Murders: A Checklist and Chronological Listing of Fiction in the Digest-Size Mystery Magazines in the United States and England** (Westport, Conn.: Greenwood, 1982), pp. 740–41.

Ten Detective Aces. See *The Dragnet*

10 Detective Mysteries

804. Described in **Mystery, Detective, and Espionage Magazines,** ed. by Michael L. Cook (Westport, Conn.: Greenwood, 1983), pp. 558–59.

10-Story Detective

805a. Described in **Mystery, Detective, and Espionage Magazines,** ed. by Michael L. Cook (Westport, Conn.: Greenwood, 1983), pp. 559–60.

805b. Indexed in **Mystery, Detective, and Espionage Fiction,** ed. by Michael L. Cook and Stephen T. Miller (New York: Garland, 1988), pp. 605–11.

10-Story Detective Magazine. See *10-Story Detective*

Ten Story Gang

806a. Described in **Mystery, Detective, and Espionage Magazines,** ed. by Michael L. Cook (Westport, Conn.: Greenwood, 1983), p. 561.

806b. Indexed in **Mystery, Detective, and Espionage Fiction,** ed. by Michael L. Cook and Stephen T. Miller (New York: Garland, 1988), pp. 362, 611–12.

Ten Story Mystery

807a. Described in **Mystery, Detective, and Espionage Magazines,** ed. by Michael L. Cook (Westport, Conn.: Greenwood, 1983), pp. 561–62.

807b. Indexed in **Mystery, Detective, and Espionage Fiction,** ed. by Michael L. Cook and Stephen T. Miller (New York: Garland, 1988), pp. 612–13.

Ten Story Mystery Magazine. See *Ten Story Mystery*

Terror Detective Story Magazine

808a. Described in **Mystery, Detective, and Espionage Magazines,** ed. by Michael L. Cook (Westport, Conn.: Greenwood, 1983), pp. 562–63.

808b. Indexed in Michael Cook, **Monthly Murders: A Checklist and Chronological Listing of Fiction in the Digest-Size Mystery Magazines in the United States and England** (Westport, Conn.: Greenwood, 1982), pp. 738–39.

Terror Tales. See *Horror Stories*

The Third Degree

809. Described in **Mystery, Detective, and Espionage Magazines,** ed. by Michael L. Cook (Westport, Conn.: Greenwood, 1983), p. 564.

The Thorndyke File

810a. Contents indexed in Michael L. Cook, **Mystery Fanfare: A Composite Annotated Index to Mystery and Related Fanzines 1963–1981** (Bowling Green, Ohio: Bowling Green State University Popular Press, 1983).

810b. Described in **Mystery, Detective, and Espionage Magazines,** ed. by Michael L. Cook (Westport, Conn.: Greenwood, 1983), pp. 564–66.

The Thriller (British)

811. Described in **Mystery, Detective, and Espionage Magazines,** ed. by Michael L. Cook (Westport, Conn.: Greenwood, 1983), pp. 566–69.

Thrilling Detective

812a. Described in **Mystery, Detective, and Espionage Magazines,** ed. by Michael L. Cook (Westport, Conn.: Greenwood, 1983), pp. 569–71.

812b. Indexed in **Mystery, Detective, and Espionage Fiction,** ed. by Michael L. Cook and Stephen T. Miller (New York: Garland, 1988), pp. 616–32.

812c. Indexed in **The Pulp Magazine Index: Third Series,** by Leonard A. Robbins (Mercer Island, Wash.: Starmont House, 1990).

Thrilling Mysteries

813a. Described in **Mystery, Detective, and Espionage Magazines,** ed. by Michael L. Cook (Westport, Conn.: Greenwood, 1983), pp. 572–73.

813b. Indexed in **Mystery, Detective, and Espionage Fiction,** ed. by Michael L. Cook and Stephen T. Miller (New York: Garland, 1988), p. 632.

813c. Indexed in **The Pulp Magazine Index: First Series,** by Leonard A. Robbins (Mercer Island, Wash.: Starmont House, 1989).

Thrilling Mystery

814a. Described in **Mystery, Detective, and Espionage Magazines,** ed. by Michael L. Cook (Westport, Conn.: Greenwood, 1983), pp. 573–75.

814b. Indexed in **Mystery, Detective, and Espionage Fiction,** ed. by Michael L. Cook and Stephen T. Miller (New York: Garland, 1988), pp. 173, 632–38.

814c. Indexed in **The Pulp Magazine Index: First Series,** by Leonard A. Robbins (Mercer Island, Wash.: Starmont House, 1989).

Thrilling Mystery Novel

815a. Described in **Mystery, Detective, and Espionage Magazines,** ed. by Michael L. Cook (Westport, Conn.: Greenwood, 1983), pp. 575–76.

815b. Indexed in **The Pulp Magazine Index: First Series,** by Leonard A. Robbins (Mercer Island, Wash.: Starmont House, 1989).

Thrilling Mystery Novel Magazine. See Thrilling Mystery Novel

Thrilling Spy Stories

816a. Described in **Mystery, Detective, and Espionage Magazines,** ed. by Michael L. Cook (Westport, Conn.: Greenwood, 1983), pp. 576–78.

816b. Indexed in **Mystery, Detective, and Espionage Fiction,** ed. by Michael L. Cook and Stephen T. Miller (New York: Garland, 1988), p. 638.

816c. Indexed in **The Pulp Magazine Index: First Series,** by Leonard A. Robbins (Mercer Island, Wash.: Starmont House, 1989).

Thrilling Tales

817. Indexed in **Mystery, Detective, and Espionage Fiction,** ed. by Michael L. Cook and Stephen T. Miller (New York: Garland, 1988), p. 638.

Thrills of the Jungle

818a. Indexed in **Mystery, Detective, and Espionage Fiction,** ed. by Michael L. Cook and Stephen T. Miller (New York: Garland, 1988), p. 639.

818b. Indexed in **The Pulp Magazine Index: First Series,** by Leonard A. Robbins (Mercer Island, Wash.: Starmont House, 1989).

Tightrope!

819a. Described in **Mystery, Detective, and Espionage Magazines,** ed. by Michael L. Cook (Westport, Conn.: Greenwood, 1983), pp. 578–79.

819b. Indexed in Michael Cook, **Monthly Murders: A Checklist and Chronological Listing of Fiction in the Digest-Size Mystery Magazines in the United States and England** (Westport, Conn.: Greenwood, 1982), p. 742.

819c. Indexed in **Mystery, Detective, and Espionage Fiction,** ed. by Michael L. Cook and Stephen T. Miller (New York: Garland, 1988), p. 639.

Tip Top Detective Tales (British)

820. Described in **Mystery, Detective, and Espionage Magazines,** ed. by Michael L. Cook (Westport, Conn.: Greenwood, 1983), p. 579.

Top Detective Annual

821a. Described in **Mystery, Detective, and Espionage Magazines,** ed. by Michael L. Cook (Westport, Conn.: Greenwood, 1983), p. 580.

821b. Indexed in **Mystery, Detective, and Espionage Fiction,** ed. by Michael L. Cook and Stephen T. Miller (New York: Garland, 1988), p. 639.

821c. Indexed in **The Pulp Magazine Index: Second Series,** by Leonard A. Robbins (Mercer Island, Wash.: Starmont House, 1989).

Top-Notch Detective

822a. Described in **Mystery, Detective, and Espionage Magazines,** ed. by Michael L. Cook (Westport, Conn.: Greenwood, 1983), pp. 580–81.

822b. Indexed in **Mystery, Detective, and Espionage Fiction,** ed. by Michael L. Cook and Stephen T. Miller (New York: Garland, 1988), pp. 639–40.

Trapped. See Trapped Detective Story Magazine

Trapped Detective Story Magazine

823a. Described in **Mystery, Detective, and Espionage Magazines,** ed. by Michael L. Cook (Westport, Conn.: Greenwood, 1983), pp. 581–82.

823b. Indexed in Michael Cook, **Monthly Murders: A Checklist and Chronological Listing of Fiction in the Digest-Size Mystery Magazines in the United States and England** (Westport, Conn.: Greenwood, 1982), pp. 743–48.

Triple Detective

824a. Described in **Mystery, Detective, and Espionage Magazines,** ed. by Michael L. Cook (Westport, Conn.: Greenwood, 1983), pp. 582–83.

824b. Indexed in **Mystery, Detective, and Espionage Fiction,** ed. by Michael L. Cook and Stephen T. Miller (New York: Garland, 1988), pp. 640–42.

824c. Indexed in **The Pulp Magazine Index: First Series,** by Leonard A. Robbins (Mercer Island, Wash.: Starmont House, 1989).

Tropical Adventures

825a. Indexed in **Mystery, Detective, and Espionage Fiction,** ed. by Michael L. Cook and Stephen T. Miller (New York: Garland, 1988), pp. 642–43.

825b. Indexed in **The Pulp Magazine Index: Second Series,** by Leonard A. Robbins (Mercer Island, Wash.: Starmont House, 1989).

True Gang Life

826. Indexed in **Mystery, Detective, and Espionage Fiction**, ed. by Michael L. Cook and Stephen T. Miller (New York: Garland, 1988), pp. 643–44.

True Gangster Stories **(Columbia Publications, Inc.)**

827.1. Indexed in **Mystery, Detective, and Espionage Fiction**, ed. by Michael L. Cook and Stephen T. Miller (New York: Garland, 1988), pp. 644–45.

True Gangster Stories **(Winford Publications, Inc.)**

827.2. Indexed in **Mystery, Detective, and Espionage Fiction**, ed. by Michael L. Cook and Stephen T. Miller (New York: Garland, 1988), p. 644.

The Tutter Bugle

828a. Contents indexed in Michael L. Cook, **Mystery Fanfare: A Composite Annotated Index to Mystery and Related Fanzines 1963–1981** (Bowling Green, Ohio: Bowling Green State University Popular Press, 1983).

828b. Described in **Mystery, Detective, and Espionage Magazines,** ed. by Michael L. Cook (Westport, Conn.: Greenwood, 1983), pp. 583–84.

Twelve Stories Detective Tales

829a. Described in **Mystery, Detective, and Espionage Magazines,** ed. by Michael L. Cook (Westport, Conn.: Greenwood, 1983), pp. 584–85.

829b. Mentioned in **Mystery, Detective, and Espionage Fiction,** ed. by Michael L. Cook and Stephen T. Miller (New York: Garland, 1988), p. 645.

Two-Book Detective Magazine. See *Two-Books Detective Magazine*

Two-Books Detective Magazine

830a. Described in **Mystery, Detective, and Espionage Magazines,** ed. by Michael L. Cook (Westport, Conn.: Greenwood, 1983), p. 585.

830b. Indexed in **Mystery, Detective, and Espionage Fiction,** ed. by Michael L. Cook and Stephen T. Miller (New York: Garland, 1988), pp. 430, 645.

830c. Indexed in **The Pulp Magazine Index: Third Series,** by Leonard A. Robbins (Mercer Island, Wash.: Starmont House, 1990).

2-Book Mystery Magazine

831a. Described in **Mystery, Detective, and Espionage Magazines,** ed. by Michael L. Cook (Westport, Conn.: Greenwood, 1983), pp. 585–86.

831b. Indexed in Michael Cook, **Monthly Murders: A Checklist and Chronological Listing of Fiction in the Digest-Size Mystery Magazines in the United States and England** (Westport, Conn.: Greenwood, 1982), p. 737.

Two Complete Detective Books

832a. Described in **Mystery, Detective, and Espionage Magazines,** ed. by Michael L. Cook (Westport, Conn.: Greenwood, 1983), pp. 586–88.

832b. Indexed in **Mystery, Detective, and Espionage Fiction,** ed. by Michael L. Cook and Stephen T. Miller (New York: Garland, 1988), pp. 645–48.

832c. Indexed in **The Pulp Magazine Index: First Series,** by Leonard A. Robbins (Mercer Island, Wash.: Starmont House, 1989).

2 Detective Mystery Novels

833a. Described in **Mystery, Detective, and Espionage Magazines,** ed. by Michael L. Cook (Westport, Conn.: Greenwood, 1983), pp. 588–89.

833b. Indexed in **Mystery, Detective, and Espionage Fiction,** ed. by Michael L. Cook and Stephen T. Miller (New York: Garland, 1988), pp. 173, 648–49.

833c. Indexed in **The Pulp Magazine Index: First Series,** by Leonard A. Robbins (Mercer Island, Wash.: Starmont House, 1989).

Two Detective Mystery Novels Magazine. See *2 Detective Mystery Novels*

Two-Fisted Detective Stories

834a. Described in **Mystery, Detective, and Espionage Magazines,** ed. by Michael L. Cook (Westport, Conn.: Greenwood, 1983), pp. 589–90.

834b. Indexed in Michael Cook, **Monthly Murders: A Checklist and Chronological Listing of Fiction in the Digest-Size Mystery Magazines in the United States and England** (Westport, Conn.: Greenwood, 1982), pp. 749–51.

Uncanny Stories

835. Indexed in **Mystery, Detective, and Espionage Fiction,** ed. by Michael L. Cook and Stephen T. Miller (New York: Garland, 1988), p. 649.

Uncanny Tales

836a. Described in **Mystery, Detective, and Espionage Magazines,** ed. by Michael L. Cook (Westport, Conn.: Greenwood, 1983), pp. 591–94.

836b. Indexed in **Mystery, Detective, and Espionage Fiction,** ed. by Michael L. Cook and Stephen T. Miller (New York: Garland, 1988), pp. 429–30, 480, 649.

836c. Indexed in **The Pulp Magazine Index: First Series,** by Leonard A. Robbins (Mercer Island, Wash.: Starmont House, 1989).

Undercover Detective

837a. Described in **Mystery, Detective, and Espionage Magazines,** ed. by Michael L. Cook (Westport, Conn.: Greenwood, 1983), p. 595.

837b. Indexed in **Mystery, Detective, and Espionage Fiction,** ed. by Michael L. Cook and Stephen T. Miller (New York: Garland, 1988), p. 649.

837c. Indexed in **The Pulp Magazine Index: Second Series,** by Leonard A. Robbins (Mercer Island, Wash.: Starmont House, 1989).

The Underworld

838a. Described in **Mystery, Detective, and Espionage Magazines,** ed. by Michael L. Cook (Westport, Conn.: Greenwood, 1983), pp. 595–96.

838b. Indexed in **Mystery, Detective, and Espionage Fiction,** ed. by Michael L. Cook and Stephen T. Miller (New York: Garland, 1988), pp. 650–58.

The Underworld Detective. See *The Underworld*

The Underworld Detective Magazine. See *The Underworld*

Underworld Love Stories. See *Underworld Romances*

The Underworld Magazine. See *The Underworld*

Underworld Romances

839. Indexed in **Mystery, Detective, and Espionage Fiction,** ed. by Michael L. Cook and Stephen T. Miller (New York: Garland, 1988), pp. 653, 658.

Union Jack. See Detective Weekly (British)

Up-to-Date Boys' Library

840. Described in **Mystery, Detective, and Espionage Magazines,** ed. by Michael L. Cook (Westport, Conn.: Greenwood, 1983), pp. 597–98.

Vampire Tales. See Haunt of Horror

Variety Detective Magazine

841a. Described in **Mystery, Detective, and Espionage Magazines,** ed. by Michael L. Cook (Westport, Conn.: Greenwood, 1983), p. 599.

841b. Indexed in **Mystery, Detective, and Espionage Fiction,** ed. by Michael L. Cook and Stephen T. Miller (New York: Garland, 1988), pp. 392, 658–59.

841c. Indexed in **The Pulp Magazine Index: Third Series,** by Leonard A. Robbins (Mercer Island, Wash.: Starmont House, 1990).

Venture Action Stories

842. Indexed in **Mystery, Detective, and Espionage Fiction,** ed. by Michael L. Cook and Stephen T. Miller (New York: Garland, 1988), p. 659.

Verdict

843a. Described in **Mystery, Detective, and Espionage Magazines,** ed. by Michael L. Cook (Westport, Conn.: Greenwood, 1983), pp. 600–601.

843b. American edition indexed in Michael Cook, **Monthly Murders: A Checklist and Chronological Listing of Fiction in the Digest-Size Mystery Magazines in the United States and England** (Westport, Conn.: Greenwood, 1982), pp. 754–55.

843c. English edition indexed in Michael Cook, **Monthly Murders: A Checklist and Chronological Listing of Fiction in the Digest-Size Mystery Magazines in the United States and England** (Westport, Conn.: Greenwood, 1982), pp. 752–53.

Verdict Crime Detection Magazine

844a. Described in **Mystery, Detective, and Espionage Magazines,** ed. by Michael L. Cook (Westport, Conn.: Greenwood, 1983), pp. 601–2.

844b. Indexed in Michael Cook, **Monthly Murders: A Checklist and Chronological Listing of Fiction in the Digest-Size Mystery Magazines in the United States and England** (Westport, Conn.: Greenwood, 1982), p. 756.

Vice Squad Detective

845a. Described in **Mystery, Detective, and Espionage Magazines,** ed. by Michael L. Cook (Westport, Conn.: Greenwood, 1983), p. 602.

845b. Indexed in **Mystery, Detective, and Espionage Fiction,** ed. by Michael L. Cook and Stephen T. Miller (New York: Garland, 1988), p. 659.

845c. Indexed in **The Pulp Magazine Index: Fourth Series,** by Leonard A. Robbins (Mercer Island, Wash.: Starmont House, 1991).

War Thriller. See The Thriller (British)

Web Detective Stories. See Saturn Web Magazine of Detective Stories

Web Terror Stories. See Saturn Web Magazine of Detective Stories

Weird Mystery

846a. Described in **Mystery, Detective, and Espionage Magazines,** ed. by Michael L. Cook (Westport, Conn.: Greenwood, 1983), pp. 603–4.

846b. Indexed in Michael Cook, **Monthly Murders: A Checklist and Chronological Listing of Fiction in the Digest-Size Mystery Magazines in the United States and England** (Westport, Conn.: Greenwood, 1982), p. 758.

The Weird Tale Collector

847. Contents indexed in Michael L. Cook, **Mystery Fanfare: A Composite Annotated Index to Mystery and Related Fanzines 1963–1981** (Bowling Green, Ohio: Bowling Green State University Popular Press, 1983).

Weird Tales

848a. Described in **Mystery, Detective, and Espionage Magazines,** ed. by Michael L. Cook (Westport, Conn.: Greenwood, 1983), pp. 604–5.

It is debatable whether *Weird Tales* had any direct influence on the development of the mystery and detective story. It published a number of psychic detective stories by writers such as Seabury Quinn, but the psychic detective appeared first in England. Nevertheless, *Weird Tales* published works by writers such as Robert Bloch, Ray Bradbury, Frederic Brown, August Derleth, Frank Gruber, Henry Kuttner, and John D. MacDonald, and it reprinted work by writers such as Arthur Conan Doyle and Edgar Allan Poe. Although these stories tended to be weird fiction rather than traditional (genre) mystery and detective fiction, they nevertheless exposed readers to these writers and, perhaps, aroused curiosity about their work in other genres.

The history and development of *Weird Tales* are discussed at length in the following resources:

848b. Tymn, Marshall B., and Mike Ashley, eds. **Science Fiction, Fantasy, and Weird Fiction Magazines.** Westport, Conn.: Greenwood, 1985. xxx, 970 p. Indexes. LC 84-11523. ISBN 0-313-21221-X.

848c. Weinberg, Robert. **The Weird Tales Story.** West Linn, Ore.: FAX Collector's Editions, 1977. ix, 134 p. LC 77-73602. ISBN 0-913960-16-0.
Weird Tales is perhaps the most heavily indexed of pulp magazines, with perhaps as many as a dozen separate indexes to it in existence. The following indexes are readily accessible and are recommended:

848d. Jaffery, Sheldon, and Fred Cook. The Collector's Index to **Weird Tales.** Bowling Green, Ohio: Bowling Green State University Popular Press, 1985. 162 p. LC 85-71020. ISBN 0-87972-293-5 (cl); 0-87972-284-3. Indexes *Weird Tales* by issue, author, author and poem, and cover artist. An appendix provides indexes to *Oriental Stories* and *Magic Carpet Magazine*.

848e. Parnell, Frank, with the assistance of Mike Ashley. **Monthly Terrors: An Index to the Weird Fantasy Magazines Published in the United States and Great Britain.** Westport, Conn.: Greenwood, 1985. xxvii, 602 p. LC 84-19225. ISBN 0-313-23989-4. An issue-by-issue index to *Weird Tales* appears on pages 247–287; the volume contains an author index.

Weird Terror Tales

849a. Described in **Mystery, Detective, and Espionage Magazines,** ed. by Michael L. Cook (Westport, Conn.: Greenwood, 1983), pp. 605–7.

849b. Indexed in Michael Cook, **Monthly Murders: A Checklist and Chronological Listing of Fiction in the Digest-Size Mystery Magazines in the United States and England** (Westport, Conn.: Greenwood, 1982), p. 759.

The Whisperer

850a. Checklist to title stories given in John P. Gunnison, **Street & Smith's Hero Pulp Checklist** (Upper Marlboro, Md.: Pulp Collector Press, 1991).

850b. Described in **Mystery, Detective, and Espionage Magazines,** ed. by Michael L. Cook (Westport, Conn.: Greenwood, 1983), pp. 607–11.

850c. Indexed in **Mystery, Detective, and Espionage Fiction,** ed. by Michael L. Cook and Stephen T. Miller (New York: Garland, 1988), pp. 660–61.

850d. Indexed in **The Pulp Magazine Index: First Series,** by Leonard A. Robbins (Mercer Island, Wash.: Starmont House, 1989).

Whodunit?

851a. Described in **Mystery, Detective, and Espionage Magazines,** ed. by Michael L. Cook (Westport, Conn.: Greenwood, 1983), pp. 611–12.

851b. Indexed in Michael Cook, **Monthly Murders: A Checklist and Chronological Listing of Fiction in the Digest-Size Mystery Magazines in the United States and England** (Westport, Conn.: Greenwood, 1982), p. 757.

Witchcraft & Sorcery

852. Described in **Mystery, Detective, and Espionage Magazines,** ed. by Michael L. Cook (Westport, Conn.: Greenwood, 1983), pp. 612–13.

The Wizard

853a. Checklist to title stories given in John P. Gunnison, **Street & Smith's Hero Pulp Checklist** (Upper Marlboro, Md.: Pulp Collector Press, 1991).

853b. Described in **Mystery, Detective, and Espionage Magazines,** ed. by Michael L. Cook (Westport, Conn.: Greenwood, 1983), pp. 613–15.

853c. Indexed in **Mystery, Detective, and Espionage Fiction,** ed. by Michael L. Cook and Stephen T. Miller (New York: Garland, 1988), pp. 70, 661.

853d. Indexed in **The Pulp Magazine Index: First Series,** by Leonard A. Robbins (Mercer Island, Wash.: Starmont House, 1989).

The Wold Atlas

854. Contents indexed in Michael L. Cook, **Mystery Fanfare: A Composite Annotated Index to Mystery and Related Fanzines 1963–1981** (Bowling Green, Ohio: Bowling Green State University Popular Press, 1983).

World Man Hunters

855a. Indexed in **Mystery, Detective, and Espionage Fiction,** ed. by Michael L. Cook and Stephen T. Miller (New York: Garland, 1988), pp. 661–62.

855b. Indexed in **The Pulp Magazine Index: Second Series,** by Leonard A. Robbins (Mercer Island, Wash.: Starmont House, 1989).

Xenophile

856a. Contents indexed in Michael L. Cook, **Mystery Fanfare: A Composite Annotated Index to Mystery and Related Fanzines 1963–1981** (Bowling Green, Ohio: Bowling Green State University Popular Press, 1983).

856b. Described in **Mystery, Detective, and Espionage Magazines,** ed. by Michael L. Cook (Westport, Conn.: Greenwood, 1983), pp. 617–19.

Yankee Gang Shorts (British)

857. Described in **Mystery, Detective, and Espionage Magazines,** ed. by Michael L. Cook (Westport, Conn.: Greenwood, 1983), p. 621.

Yankee Mystery Shorts (British)

858. Described in **Mystery, Detective, and Espionage Magazines,** ed. by Michael L. Cook (Westport, Conn.: Greenwood, 1983), pp. 621–22.

Yellowback Library

859a. Contents indexed in Michael L. Cook, **Mystery Fanfare: A Composite Annotated Index to Mystery and Related Fanzines 1963–1981** (Bowling Green, Ohio: Bowling Green State University Popular Press, 1983).

859b. Described in **Mystery, Detective, and Espionage Magazines,** ed. by Michael L. Cook (Westport, Conn.: Greenwood, 1983), pp. 622–24.

Young Broadbrim Weekly. See *Old Broadbrim Weekly*

Young Sleuth Library

860. Described in **Mystery, Detective, and Espionage Magazines,** ed. by Michael L. Cook (Westport, Conn.: Greenwood, 1983), pp. 624–25.

Zeppelin Stories

861a. Described in **Mystery, Detective, and Espionage Magazines,** ed. by Michael L. Cook (Westport, Conn.: Greenwood, 1983), p. 627.

861b. Indexed in **Mystery, Detective, and Espionage Fiction,** ed. by Michael L. Cook and Stephen T. Miller (New York: Garland, 1988), p. 662.

861c. Indexed in **The Pulp Magazine Index: Second Series**, by Leonard A. Robbins (Mercer Island, Wash.: Starmont House, 1989).

9

Biographies and Pseudonyms

Scope note: Included here are the who's whos, bio-bibliographical directories, and literary dictionaries. Additional biographical data that can be found in many different sources, including encyclopedias and reader's guides, are covered in the appendix.

BIOGRAPHICAL COLLECTIONS

862. Anderson, George Parker, and Julie B. Anderson, eds. **American Hard-Boiled Crime Writers.** Dictionary of Literary Biography, vol. 226. Detroit: Gale, 2000. xviii, 437 p. Index. LC 00-028761. ISBN 0-7876-3135-3.

American Hard-Boiled Crime Writers provides bio-bibliographical and biocritical data on 31 writers of the twentieth century, 19 of whom are dead. Entries are arranged alphabetically by the subject's surname; the name and affiliation of the critic are given at the top of the article. Each entry begins with a chronologically arranged primary bibliography listing the first British and American editions of the subject's works; these are followed by selective lists of the subject's uncollected prose. The essays that follow the bibliography range in length from 2,000 to 5,000 words; frequently, they are illustrated with photographs of the subject and the subject's works. Concluding each essay is a selective bibliography of secondary sources; concluding each of these volumes is a bibliography listing additional sources for reading, a list of the contributors' affiliations, and a cumulative index to the other volumes in the Dictionary of Literary Biography series.

The subjects of the essay range alphabetically from Lawrence Block to Cornell Woolrich and include such writers as James Lee Burke, W. R. Burnett, James M. Cain, Raymond Chandler, Carroll John Daly, Davis Dresser, James Ellroy, Sue Grafton, Dashiell Hammett, Chester Himes, Elmore Leonard, Ross Macdonald, Marcia Muller, Bill Pronzin, Mickey Spillane, and Jim Thompson. The essays are solid assessments of their subjects, although one senses that a number of the critics surveying the writers who began in the pulp magazines are not overly familiar with the magazines whereof they write. The essay on Raoul Whitfield, for example, states that "in the late 1920s Whitfield moved to Los Angeles and began publishing in *Adventure, Air Trails,* and *Triple-X.*"

This is so, but in the late 1920s *Adventure* was probably the finest pulp magazine extant, and *Air Trails* and *Triple-X* were significantly less prestigious—an aviation pulp and a western pulp, respectively—and to lump them together does readers a disservice. This complaint aside, *American Hard-Boiled Writers* offers an excellent introduction to its subject.

863. Bakerman, Jane S., ed. **And Then There Were Nine … More Women of Mystery.** Bowling Green, Ohio: Bowling Green State University Popular Press, 1985. 218 p. LC 84-72822. ISBN 0-87972-319-x (hc); 0-87972-320-3 (pb).

A successor to *10 Women of Mystery* (profiled later), *And Then There Were Nine* contains biocritical essays on Daphne du Maurier (by Jane S. Bakerman), Margery Allingham (by Rex W. Gaskill), Anne Morice (by Martha Alderson and Neysa Chouteau), Dorothy Uhnak (by George N. Dove), Lillian O'Donnell (by Neysa Chouteau and Martha Alderson), Craig Rice (by Peggy Moran), E. X. Ferrars (by Susan Baker), Patricia Highsmith (by Kathleen Gregory Klein), and Shirley Jackson (by Carol Cleveland). As in the earlier volume, bibliographic data are minimal and are presented in notes concluding each chapter. Also as before, the essays vary in length and quality, and in some cases they reveal conclusions. There are no indexes.

864. Bargainnier, Earl F., ed. **10 Women of Mystery.** Bowling Green, Ohio: Bowling Green State University Popular Press, 1981. 304 p. Indexes. LC 80-86393. ISBN 0-87972-172-3 (hc); 0-87972-173-1 (pb).

This volume and its sequel (*And Then There Were Nine* [preceding]) are included because their biographical essays are significant. Essays are included for Dorothy Sayers (by Kathleen Gregory Klein), Josephine Tey (by Nancy Ellen Talburt), Ngaio Marsh (by Earl F. Bargainnier), P. D. James (by Nancy C. Joyner), Ruth Rendell (by Jane S. Bakerman), Anna Katharine Green (by Barrie Hayne), Mary Roberts Rinehart (by Jan Cohn), Margaret Millar (by John M. Reilly), Emma Lathen (by Jeanne F. Bedell), and Amanda Cross (by Steven F. Carter). Each essay provides a photograph of its subject, and each chapter is followed by brief and selective bibliographies of the subject's works. The volume concludes with indexes listing the names of the characters and the names of the titles mentioned in the body of the book.

Several of the essays warrant updating, but the writers are generally successful in providing an understanding of the lives and prose of their subjects.

865. Bargainnier, Earl F., ed. **Twelve Englishmen of Mystery.** Bowling Green, Ohio: Bowling Green State University Popular Press, 1984. 325 p. LC 83-72499. ISBN 0-87972-249-5 (hc); 0-87972-250-9 (pb).

Although it is similar in format and approach to Bargainnier's *10 Women of Mystery* (q.v.), the contents of this volume are more idiosyncratic. Essays are included for Wilkie Collins (by Jeanne F. Bedell), A. E. W. Mason (by Barrie Hayne), G. K. Chesterton (by Thomas E. Porter), H. C. Bailey (by Nancy Ellen Talbot), Anthony Berkeley Cox (by William Bradley Strickland), Nicholas Blake (by Earl F. Bargainnier), Michael Gilbert (by George N. Dove), Julian Symons (by Larry E. Grimes), Dick Francis (by Marty Knepper), Edmund Crispin (by Mary Jean DeMarr), H. R. F. Keating (by Meera T. Clark), and Simon Brett (by Earl F. Bargainnier). Each essay begins with a picture and a brief chronology of its subject; each concludes with brief and selective bibliographies of its subject's works. No indexes are provided.

In addition to the somewhat puzzling choice of subjects, the quality of the essays varies. The weakest is probably Knepper's discussion of Dick Francis. Not only are conclusions occasionally revealed, but statements such as "even persons who are not enamored of the hard-boiled mystery genre are reading and enjoying Francis's novels" reveal very little awareness of either Francis's writings or the world of mysteries.

Choose instead the vastly more comprehensive work of Benstock and Pederson (profiled later).

866.   Benstock, Bernard, and Thomas F. Staley, eds. **British Mystery Writers, 1860–1919.** Dictionary of Literary Biography, vol. 70. Detroit: Gale, 1988. xi, 389 p. Index. Cloth. LC 88-11465. ISBN 0-8103-1748-6.

867.   Benstock, Bernard, and Thomas F. Staley, eds. **British Mystery Writers, 1920–1939.** Dictionary of Literary Biography, vol. 77. Detroit: Gale, 1989. xi, 414 p. Index. Cloth. LC 88-30048. ISBN 0-8103-4555-2.

868.   Benstock, Bernard, and Thomas F. Staley, eds. **British Mystery and Thriller Writers Since 1940, First Series.** Dictionary of Literary Biography, vol. 87. Detroit: Gale, 1989. xi, 419 p. Index. Cloth. LC 89-12021. ISBN 0-8103-4565-X.

The three volumes of the Dictionary of Literary Biography provide bio-bibliographical and biocritical information on 105 British writers of mystery and detective fiction. Each volume follows the pattern of the series as a whole: entries are arranged alphabetically by subject's surname; the name and affiliation of the critic is given at the top of the article. Entries begin with a chronologically arranged bibliography listing the first separate British and American editions of the subject's published works; these are followed by selective lists of the subject's uncollected short prose. The essays that follow are biocritical surveys ranging in length from 1,000 to 5,000 words; they are frequently illustrated with photographs of the subject and the subject's works. Concluding each essay is a selective bibliography of secondary sources; concluding each of these volumes is a bibliography listing additional sources for reading, a list of the contributors' affiliations, and a cumulative index to the other volumes in the series. There are 35 entries in *British Mystery Writers, 1860–1919,* 45 in *British Mystery Writers, 1920–1939,* and 25 in *British Mystery and Thriller Writers since 1940, First Series.*

The first two volumes are particularly useful because major and minor writers for each time period are profiled. The first volume, for example, contains entries on such writers as Mary Elizabeth Braddon, John Buchan, Wilkie Collins, Charles Dickens, Sir Arthur Conan Doyle, and Edgar Wallace, and also included are entries for such lesser luminaries as M. McDonnell Bodkin, J. S. Fletcher, Fergus Hume, Angus Reach, and Victor L. Whitechurch. The second volume has entries for Margery Allingham, Eric Ambler, Agatha Christie, John Creasey, Ngaio Marsh, Dorothy L. Sayers, and Josephine Tey, and there are entries for Winston Graham, Richard Hull, C. B. Kitchen, Gladys Mitchell, Helen Simpson, and Henry Wade. The expanded focus of the third volume allows the inclusion of essays on Ian Fleming, Ken Follett, Geoffrey Household, John le Carré, and Peter O'Donnell, all of whom are known for their thrillers and espionage fiction.

The three volumes edited by Benstock and Staley can be compared to *The St. James Guide to Crime and Mystery Writers* (q.v.), which contains the same primary bibliographies and, in return for offering significantly less biographical data, provides entries on many more writers. Nevertheless, such a comparison does neither series justice; the volumes are intended for different audiences. The volumes of the Dictionary of Literary Biography offer structured and organized criticism that the *St. James Guide* cannot, whereas the latter offers what are essentially brief encyclopedic entries on a wider variety of contemporary writers. Neither series is inexpensive, but both should be held by academic and public libraries.

869.   Breen, Jon L., and Martin Harry Greenberg, eds. **Murder off the Rack: Critical Studies of Ten Paperback Masters.** Metuchen, N.J.: Scarecrow, 1989. x, 178 p. Cloth. LC 89-33085. ISBN 0-8108-2232-6.

Murder off the Rack provides extensive bio-bibliographical discussion of 10 significant crime and mystery writers whose fate it was to have their work appear primarily (or entirely) in paperbacks. In alphabetical order, these authors are Marvin Albert (by George Kelley), Donald Hamilton (by Loren D. Estleman), Ed Lacy (by Marvin Lachman), Warren Murphy (by Dick Lochte), Vin Packer (by Jon L. Breen), Don Pendleton (by Will Murray), Peter Rabe (by Donald E. Westlake), Jim Thompson (by Max Allan Collins), Harry Whittington (by Bill Crider), and Charles Williams (by Ed Gorman). Each chapter concludes with a partial bibliography of the author's works, and the volume concludes with separate indexes listing the book titles and the personal names mentioned in the essays.

As with the rest of Breen's works, this is a well-conceived and generally well-executed volume. The 10 essays are critical, but the criticism is tempered by affection and compassion. The indexing is well done. The volume's greatest flaws lie in the bibliographies, which are deliberately incomplete, concentrating only on the crime and mystery fiction written by the subject. This is thoroughly understandable, but it is nevertheless frustrating to learn that Vin Packer's first story appeared under the name Laura Winston in a 1951 *Ladies' Home Journal,* but the story's title and the issue in which it appeared are never given.

Murder off the Rack presents its subject admirably. One wishes that Breen and his fellow contributors had included additional profiles.

870a.   Bruccoli, Matthew Joseph, and Richard Layman, eds. **Hardboiled Mystery Writers: Raymond Chandler, Dashiell Hammett, Ross Macdonald.** Dictionary of Literary Biography Documentary Series; no. 6. Detroit, Mich.: Gale, 1989. xi, 383 p. LC 82-1105. ISBN 0-8103-1112-7.

870b.   Bruccoli, Matthew Joseph, and Richard Layman, eds. **Hardboiled Mystery Writers: Raymond Chandler, Dashiell Hammett, Ross Macdonald.** 2nd ed. A Bruccoli Clark Layman Book. New York: Carroll & Graf, 2002. xii, 326 p. Index. ISBN 0-7867-1029-2.

The second edition of this work is largely identical to the first edition, with the exception of the bibliographies, which have been updated.

It is debatable whether a book that discusses only three writers can be considered a reference work in the way that the other volumes in this section are, but *Hardboiled Mystery Writers* provides an excellent introduction to three major figures, each of whom is discussed in a separate chapter. Each chapter begins with a chronologically arranged bibliography of its subject; major books are listed, as are biographies, bibliographies, edited works, collections of letters, publications of notebooks, and the location of the subject's archives. Following are autobiographical statements, biographical statements, reprints of obscure writings, and reviews and critical assessments culled from the author's writings and the writings of others. Each chapter is heavily illustrated with pictures of the subject, his works, and his friends and relatives.

Hardboiled Mystery Writers is not without fault. Its notes are occasionally insensitive, as when it states that "by the mid 1960s, the suppression of Hammett's works that had occurred after his imprisonment ended, and his reputation was restored," but Hammett had died in 1961, so his reputation received posthumous restoration. There are also occasional paste-up problems—pages from *Red Harvest* are given out of order—and rather surprisingly, Hammett's first name—Samuel—is not given at the head of the article but only in the body. The indexing is inadequate.

These complaints aside, *Hardboiled Mystery Writers* belongs in academic and public libraries.

871.   Budd, Elaine. **13 Mistresses of Murder.** New York: Ungar, 1986. xiii, 144 p. LC 86-1459. ISBN 0-8044-2086-6.

During the first part of the 1980s, Budd interviewed 13 notable women writers of mystery and detective fiction: Mary Higgins Clark, Amanda Cross, Dorothy Salisbury Davis, Lady Antonia Fraser, Lucy Freeman, Dorothy B. Hughes, P. D. James, Emma Lathen, Margaret Millar, Shannon OCork, Ruth Rendell, Dorothy Uhnak, and Phyllis A. Whitney. The results of these interviews became *13 Mistresses of Murder,* and it is mentioned here as a thematic companion to the works of Bakerman, Bargainnier, and Breen (q.q.v.).

Budd provides the edited interview in each chapter, then a lengthy summary of the author's best-known works. Occasional criticism occurs in the summaries; plot holes are mentioned, as are weaknesses in the presentation of characters. The volume concludes with notes and brief selective primary bibliographies. Still occasionally useful.

872.   Carr, John C. **The Craft of Crime: Conversations with Crime Writers.** Boston: Houghton Mifflin, 1983. 349 p. LC 83-133. ISBN 0-395-33120-X (hc); 0-395-33121-8 (pb).

In the words of Carr's introduction, "This book brings together conversations with thirteen practitioners—eight male and five female . . . seven American, four English, one South African, and one Dutch—of the novels of detection and pursuit, mystery, and police procedure." These writers are Ruth Rendell, Peter Lovesey, Ed McBain, Dick Francis, Jane Langton, Gregory Mcdonald, Mark Smith, Robert B. Parker, Janwillem van de Wetering, June Thomson, James McClure, and "Emma Lathen." Each conversation is prefaced with an introduction by Carr in which he provides some biographical data and an appreciation of the author, and the conversations themselves are occasionally quite informative and are enjoyably freewheeling, for while Carr is well informed and unafraid of asking questions, he is not conducting formal interviews. On the debit side, there are no bibliographic lists or photographs.

873.   Cooper-Clark, Diana. **Designs of Darkness: Interviews with Detective Novelists.** Bowling Green, Ohio: Bowling Green State University Popular Press, 1983. 239 p. LC 82-74452. ISBN 0-87972-223-1 (cl); 0-87972-224-X (pb).

Designs of Darkness contains interviews with 13 mystery and detective writers: P. D. James, Jean Stubbs, Peter Lovesey, Margaret Millar, Ross Macdonald, Howard Engel, Ruth Rendell, Janwillem van de Wetering, Patricia Highsmith, Julian Symons, Amanda Cross (i.e., Carolyn Heilbrun), Anne Perry, and Dick Francis. With the exception of the interview with Amanda Cross, each interview is prefaced with a picture of its subject. The volume contains neither bibliographies nor index.

Cooper-Clark's interviews show that she is well read and intelligent but unfortunately, not a particularly good interviewer. She tends to ask her subjects leading questions, as in the following, asked of P. D. James: "Would you say that formula writing is limited in a way that other writing isn't, and for the worse?" James is thus obligated to say, "Well, I think for the worse," whereas a more indirect questioner might have elicited a different kind of response. The interview with Dick Francis is equally unperceptive. Cooper-Clark tells Francis, "Julian Symons has said that, 'the detective story reduces the unruly shape of life to an ideal order.' Marjorie Nicholson has added that, 'The detective story is a revolt . . . from a smart and easy pessimism, which interprets men and the universe in terms of unmoral purposelessness, to a re-belief in a universe governed by cause and effect.' Do you think that this is what your novels do?" Francis's response in toto—and one wonders whether he was bewildered by this droppage of names, or merely bemused, is, "No, I don't think they do."

A sense of personality does occasionally emerge from some of the interviews. Patricia Highsmith shows herself to be surprisingly wary, Ross Macdonald emerges as thoughtful and somehow weary, Howard Engel shows himself to be patient and ambivalent about what he is doing, and the interviews with Rendell, Perry, and Symons are likewise informative. Nevertheless, this is not the book it could have been.

874.   Dubose, Martha Hailey, and Margaret Caldwell Thomas. **Women of Mystery: The Lives and Works of Notable Women Crime Novelists.** New York: Thomas Dunne Books, St. Martin's Minotaur, 2000. xi, 467 p. LC 00-040240. ISBN 0-312-20942-8.

Women of Mystery is not a large biographical dictionary akin to Kathleen Gregory Klein's *Great Women Mystery Writers* (q.v.). It is, instead, 18 chronologically arranged essays on the lives and works of notable women mystery writers; 13 of these essays were written by Dubose, and Thomas's solo contributions are signed. The volume contains three sections: "In the Beginning" discusses the history of the mystery and two "Mothers of Detection," Anna Katharine Green and Mary Roberts Rinehart. "A Golden Era" discusses Agatha Christie, Dorothy L. Sayers, Ngaio Marsh, Josephine Tey, and Margery Allingham. "Modern Motives" discusses Patricia Highsmith, P. D. James, Ruth Rendell, Mary Higgins Clark, Sue Grafton, Patricia Cornwell, Minette Walters, Emma Lathen, Margaret Millar, Lilian Jackson Braun, and Anne Perry. Each essay concludes with a selective primary bibliography, and the volume includes a chapter ("Some of the Best of the Rest") that briefly describes the works of 17 additional contemporary women writers. Included are three chronologies of crime and mystery fiction, a lengthy bibliography that lists the secondary material on the writers profiled earlier, and an index.

Although one may object to some of the choices of Dubose and Thomas, and their writing is occasionally unnecessarily flippant, their presentations and discussions are frequently first rate.

875a. Gorman, Ed, and Martin H. Greenberg, eds. **Speaking of Murder: Interviews with the Masters of Mystery and Suspense.** New York: Berkley Prime Crime, 1998. x, 245 p. Unindexed. Paperback. LC 98-165924. ISBN 0-425-16145-5.

875b. Gorman, Ed, and Martin H. Greenberg, eds. **Speaking of Murder: Interviews with the Masters of Mystery and Suspense.** Vol. II. New York: Berkley Prime Crime, 1999. x, 242 p. Unindexed. Paperback. ISBN 0-425-16547-7.

The first of these volumes contains interviews with 21 contemporary writers; the second, with 22 writers. The writers include such genre figures as Lawrence Block, Edna Buchanan, Patricia Cornwell, Sue Grafton, Carl Hiaasen, Tony Hillerman, and Donald E. Westlake, but there are some surprises: Stephen King and Dean Koontz are among the subjects interviewed, although neither is particular significant to mystery and detective fiction. Interviews include no photographs and only sporadically provide brief bibliographies of their subjects, and neither volume lists its contents in any recognizable order or contains any indexing. It is thus debatable whether these volumes are reference books in the sense of the other volumes in this section, but they have been listed and indexed because of the currency of their contents and because some of the interviews are very skillfully conducted and offer insights into their subjects: for example, Minette Walters reveals that prior to writing mysteries she wrote a number of pseudonymous romances. It should be mentioned that Charles L. P. Silet conducted a number of the interviews, and although some of these writers are also interviewed in Silet's *Talking Murder* (q.v.), the interviews were conducted at different times.

876. Heising, Willetta L. **Detecting Men: A Reader's Guide and Checklist for Mystery Series Written by Men.** Dearborn, Mich.: Purple Moon Press, 1998. 448 p. Index. Paperback. ISBN 0-9644593-3-7.

After the success of the first edition of *Detecting Women* (q.v.), Heising turned her efforts to the mystery series written by men. Using the format of the earlier book, she describes 813 mystery series—4,531 titles—written by more than 600 men. *Detecting Men* thus contains the following chapters: (1) Master List; (2) Mystery Types; (3) Series Characters; (4) Settings; (5) Title Chronology; (6) Alphabetical List of Titles; (7) Pseudonyms; and (8) Mystery Book Awards. The "Master List" is arranged alphabetically by author's last name, given in boldface. A biographical profile is provided for each author, and beneath the profile, in boldface, is listed the name of the series character, accompanied by a brief description of the character. The titles in which the series character appears are numbered and listed chronologically; the date of first publication is given. When a book is known by more than one title, both are listed, with a note indicating whether the second title is American, English, or a paperback retitling. When a book was nominated for or received a major mystery award, its title is boldfaced and marked with a star and the name of the award. When the author has more than one series detective, the characters are listed in alphabetical order by first name.

Chapters 2 through 7 rearrange the data presented in the first chapter. "Mystery Types" separates the books into four categories: police procedurals, private eye novels, espionage novels, and "traditional mysteries featuring amateur detectives." These mysteries are further classified using 69 subject categories to indicate their backgrounds; these include "academic," "animals," "art and antiques," "ecclesiastical and religious," "gay and lesbian," "humor," "medical," "theatre and performing arts," and "travel." Beneath each of these categories, the books are listed alphabetically by author, and the publication year, volumes in the series, series character name, series character occupation, and setting are given. "Series Characters" lists the characters alphabetically by first name; each entry provides the author's name, the book's publication year, the volumes in the series, the character's occupation, and the setting. The fourth chapter rearranges these data to provide a settings index, with geographically arranged entries listing the book's setting, author, publication year, number of volumes in the series, and the character's name and occupation.

Chapter 5, the "Title Chronology," groups the books chronologically, listing title and author; when more than one series was published in a year, the list becomes alphabetical by author. First books in series are marked with a number 1. Chapter 6 lists the titles alphabetically, also indicating the first book in a series with the number 1. Chapter 7 lists the pseudonym, the series character, the year the series began, the number of volumes in the series, the autonym, and other pseudonyms known. "Mystery Book Awards" lists only those awards and nominations given to series mysteries written by women; it contains three lists. The first shows winners and nominees in alphabetical order by the awarding agency and the name of the award; the second rearranges these data and lists them by year, then award; and the third lists the authors' names alphabetically, after which the awards are listed.

Like *Detecting Women, Detecting Men* is a monumental accomplishment, and it has the same idiosyncrasies, chief among which is that it is inadequately cross-referenced. This aside, it belongs in all libraries. One hopes for a second edition.

877a.   Heising, Willetta L. **Detecting Women: A Reader's Guide and Checklist for Mystery Series Written by Women.** Dearborn, Mich.: Purple Moon Press, 1995. 256 p. Index. Paperback. LC 95-221452. ISBN 0-9644593-0-2.

877b.   Heising, Willetta L. **Detecting Women 2: A Reader's Guide and Checklist for Mystery Series Written by Women.** Dearborn, Mich.: Purple Moon Press, 1996. 384 p. Index. Paperback. ISBN 0-9644593-1-0.

877c.   Heising, Willetta L. **Detecting Women: A Reader's Guide and Checklist for Mystery Series Written by Women.** 3rd ed. Dearborn, Mich.: Purple Moon Press, 1999. 478 p. Index. ISBN 0-9644593-5-3 (hc); 0-9644593-6-1 (pb).

Like so many reference books, *Detecting Women* began as a labor of love. Heising wanted to document the mystery series being written by women writers and began compiling lists. She received assistance from mystery lovers, making her lists increasingly lengthy and elaborate. At the time the first volume was published, Heising had recorded information on the authors of more than 2,340 titles in 479 mystery series published between 1900 and 1995. The second volume expanded these data, offering information on nearly 600 women authors of 681 series—nearly 3,600 titles—published between 1878 and 1996. The third edition is expanded again, although its focus is now primarily on those women series writers who were alive in 1998. The volume provides data on 690 authors of more than 3,700 titles in 815 series, published between 1944 and 1998, although lists of titles are projected for publication in 1999, 2000, 2001, and 2002.

The third edition of *Detecting Women* contains 8 chapters: (1) Master List; (2) Mystery Types; (3) Series Characters; (4) Settings; (5) Title Chronology; (6) Alphabetical List of Titles; (7) Pseudonyms; and (8) Mystery Book Awards. The "Master List" is arranged alphabetically by author's last name, given in boldface. A biographical profile is provided for each author, and beneath the profile, in boldface, is listed the name of her series character, accompanied by a brief description of the character. The titles in which the series character appears are numbered and listed chronologically; the date of first publication is given. When a book is known by more than one title, both are listed, with a note indicating whether the second title is American, English, or a paperback retitling. When a book was nominated for or received a major mystery award, its title is boldfaced and marked with a star and the name of the award. When the author has more than one series detective, the characters are listed in alphabetical order by first name.

Chapters 2 through 7 rearrange the data presented in the first chapter. "Mystery Types" separates the books into four categories: police procedurals, private eye novels, espionage novels, and "traditional mysteries featuring amateur detectives." These mysteries are further classified using 78 subject categories to indicate their backgrounds; these include "academic," "animals," "art and antiques," "ecclesiastical and religious," "gay and lesbian," "humor," "medical," "theatre and performing arts," and "travel." Beneath each of these categories, the books are listed alphabetically by author, and the publication year, volumes in the series, series character name, series character occupation, and setting are given. "Series Characters" lists the characters alphabetically by first name; each entry provides the author's name, the book's publication year, the volumes in the series, the character's occupation, and the setting. The fourth chapter rearranges these data to provide a settings index, with entries listing the book's setting, author, publication year, number of volumes in the series, and the character's name and occupation.

Chapter 5, the "Title Chronology," groups the books chronologically, listing title and author; when more than one series was published in a year, the list becomes alphabetical by author. First books in series are marked with a number 1. Chapter 6 lists the titles alphabetically, also indicating the first book in a series with the number 1. Chapter 7 lists the pseudonym, the series character, the year the series began, the number of volumes in the series, the autonym, and other pseudonyms known. "Mystery Book Awards" lists only those awards and nominations given to series mysteries written by women; it contains three lists. The first shows winners and nominees in alphabetical order by the awarding agency and the name of the award; the second rearranges these data and lists them by year, then award; and the third lists the authors' names alphabetically, after which the awards are listed.

There are four appendixes. The first lists the dead authors who appeared in *Detecting Women 2* and who have been dropped from the third edition. The second lists additional authors and titles that were dropped from the third edition, along with a reason why they were dropped. The third is an addendum of 60 titles that should have been added to the body of the third edition, and the fourth is an addendum for the *Pocket Guide* (q.v.), deleting 28 titles. The volume concludes with a bibliography and a lengthy index listing the authors, characters, and names mentioned in the biographical descriptions in the first section.

Detecting Women is a monumental achievement albeit one with some idiosyncrasies. First, only series authors are included, and those seeking information on such excellent writers as Minette Walters will find nothing in any of these volumes, for Walters does not work in series. Next, one wishes Heising had cross-referenced her entries more elaborately: the entry for Elizabeth Peters, for example, reveals that this is the pseudonym for Dr. Barbara Mertz and mentions the Barbara Michaels series. Similarly, the entry for Barbara Michaels reveals the pseudonym and mentions the Elizabeth Peters series. Neither a separate entry for Mertz nor anything in either entry indicates that the other entries exist.

Detecting Women should be held by all.

878. Herbert, Rosemary. **The Fatal Art of Entertainment: Interviews with Mystery Writers.** Foreword by Antonia Fraser. New York: G. K. Hall, 1994. xx, 351 p. Cloth. LC 93-22862. ISBN 0-8161-7279-X.

During the early 1990s, Herbert talked with 13 notable English and American mystery and detective writers: Julian Symons, Sue Grafton, P. D. James, Tony Hillerman, John Mortimer, Patricia Cornwell, Jonathan Gash, Reginald Hill, Jane Langton, Robert Barnard, Jeremiah Healy, Catherine Aird, and Barbara Neely. The transcripts of these conversations became *The Fatal Art of Entertainment.*

Herbert begins each chapter with a photograph and a brief discussion of her subject's writing, and then provides the transcripts of her conversation; the dates of these conversations are not provided. The transcripts do not appear to have been edited, and the conversations thus appear unstructured and spontaneous. This is simultaneously the book's greatest strength and weakness, for asking each writer a structured same series of questions might have eliminated the spontaneity but led to a greater depth in responses. As it is, the authors discuss their lives, families, and works, occasionally with introspection, often with the pride of creation. Solutions occasionally are revealed: Reginald Hill, for example, reveals that the death in *A Clubbable Woman* was inspired by a childhood memory. John Mortimer discusses his father, and Sue Grafton mentions her parents, stating that her father wrote; Herbert does not follow up on this, and readers must be aware that Grafton's father, C. W. Grafton, was a well-regarded mystery novelist in his own right.

Rather frustratingly, the volume contains neither bibliographies nor index.

879. Herman, Linda, and Beth Stiel. **Corpus Delicti of Mystery Fiction: A Guide to the Body of the Case.** Metuchen, N.J.: Scarecrow, 1974. viii, 180 p. Cloth. LC 74-16319. ISBN 0-8108-0770-X.

Although this volume begins with a series of brief chapters offering a brief history and a defense of mystery fiction and definitions of various terms, the majority of the book consists of bio-bibliographic sketches of "fifty representative authors and their works" chosen "because their writings form a balanced collection within our present scope." These authors range alphabetically from Margery Allingham and Eric Ambler to Arthur Upfield and S. S. Van Dine, and they include such stalwarts as Raymond Chandler, Agatha Christie, Dashiell Hammett, John D. MacDonald, Ngaio Marsh, Ellery Queen, and Dorothy L. Sayers. Each author's entry provides a brief biographical profile, cites a few secondary sources, and concludes with a chronological list of titles. The book has name and title indexes.

Nothing in this book cannot be readily obtained elsewhere. Herman and Stiel's choice of authors is weak, including many espionage and thriller writers while neglecting such significant talents as Fredric Brown and R. Austin Freeman. International writers are particularly neglected and are represented by only Robert van Gulik (whose last name is indexed under "G"), Maurice Leblanc, and Georges Simenon. Finally, Herman and Stiel fail to provide even the publishers of the books in their bibliographic citations.

880. Klein, Kathleen Gregory, ed. **Great Women Mystery Writers: Classic to Contemporary.** Westport, Conn.: Greenwood, 1994. xxi, 432 p. Cloth. LC 94-16123. ISBN 0-313-28770-8.

In arrangement, this guide is similar to the various editions of the *Twentieth Century Crime and Mystery Writers* (q.v.), consisting of alphabetically arranged signed bio-bibliographical essays. In content, however, the focus is tighter, for *Great Women Mystery Writers* surveys 117 (predominantly) Anglo-American women writers. These essays range in length from 500 to 1,500 words, provide excellent introductions to the totality of the writer's output, discuss her series and series characters, attempt to put her into a greater literary context, and conclude with a primary bibliography and, when relevant, a secondary bibliography.

Following the biocritical discussions are seven appendixes: (A) lists the Edgar Awards won by women writers; (B) lists the Agatha Awards and their winners; (C) discusses the organization Sisters in Crime; (D) discusses activities for mystery fans; (E) discusses DorothyL, the electronic discussion group for fans of mysteries; (F) lists the names, addresses, and telephone numbers of approximately a hundred North American booksellers specializing in crime and mystery fiction; and (G) offers 14 categories of mystery fiction into which the 117 writers discussed may be classified. The volume concludes with an author/pseudonym index and a title index to the works discussed in the essays.

On the debit side, the discussion of historically important women writers is lacking. Mary Elizabeth Braddon is the only woman writer from the nineteenth century to be discussed; and the discussion of twentieth-century women writers is not all that it could be; one looks in vain for such figures as Leigh Brackett, Lillian de la Torre, Mignon Eberhart, and Carolyn Wells. Among the moderns, Sandra Scoppettone and Janice Law have been overlooked. In addition, one wishes that the editor had included more international writers, for apart from discussions of one South African and two Japanese writers, all subjects profiled are Anglo-American. Finally, one wonders whether the editor should have unilaterally excluded discussion of collaborations; collaborative partnerships such as Frances and Richard Lockridge, Maj Sjöwall and Per Wahlöö, or Sarah and Peter Dunant probably warrant discussion.

The preceding criticisms in no way detract from the usability and importance of Klein's efforts, she deserves nothing but praise for this book. Not only is it almost everything that a reference book should be (but rarely is), its contents are timely and of enormous importance.

881. Lockhart, Darrell B., ed. **Latin American Mystery Writers: An A to Z Guide.** Westport, Conn.: Greenwood, 2004. ISBN 0-313-30554-4.

Not yet published as of this writing, the description of the book on the Greenwood Web site (www.greenwood.com/books) states that it includes "alphabetically arranged entries on 53 writers, most of whom are from Argentina, Mexico, and Cuba. . . . Each entry is written by an expert contributor and includes a brief biography, a critical discussion of the writer's works, and primary and secondary bibliographies. The volume closes with a general bibliography of anthologies and criticism."

In addition, an unedited copy of the preface was seen. It states that there is an introduction by Argentine detective author Mempo Giardianelli and that "entries on the individual practitioners of detective fiction are arranged alphabetically by the author's actual surname, or the pseudonym by which he/she is best known. The country listed in each heading is not necessarily the author's country of birth, rather the country with which he/she is associated as a writer."

882a. Reilly, John M., ed. **Twentieth-Century Crime and Mystery Writers.** Twentieth-Century Writers of the English Language. New York: St. Martin's, 1980. xxiv, 1,568 p. Cloth. LC 79-92844. ISBN 0-312-82417-3.

882b. Reilly, John M., ed. **Twentieth-Century Crime and Mystery Writers.** 2nd ed. Twentieth-Century Writers Series. Chicago: St. James, 1985. xx, 1,094 p. Index. Cloth. LC 87-37779. ISBN 0-912289-17-1.

882c. Henderson, Lesley, ed. **Twentieth-Century Crime and Mystery Writers.** 3rd ed. Twentieth-Century Writers Series. Chicago: St. James, 1991. xxxi, 1,294 p. Index. Cloth. LC 90-63662. ISBN 1-55862-031-1.

882d. Pederson, Jay P., and Taryn Benbow-Pfalzgraf, eds. **St. James Guide to Crime & Mystery Writers.** 4th ed. Detroit: St. James, 1996. xiv, 1,264 p. Index. Cloth. LC 96-18661. ISBN 1-55862-178-4.

The four editions of this work are part of a larger series that provides bio-bibliographical information on significant twentieth-century writers whose work can be readily classified into a genre. Companion volumes are devoted to science fiction writers, western writers, children's writers, and romance and historical writers. Each volume in each of these series has had multiple editions and often multiple publishers and title changes. Each edition is more comprehensive in content and physically larger than its predecessor; each is in its own right a monumental achievement and essential as a reference; and each contains crucial flaws that a firmer editorial hand and greater bibliographic control would not have permitted. The following description concentrates on the fourth (1996) edition, which profiles approximately 650 authors.

A typical entry begins with "who's who" biographical information. At its fullest, this includes pseudonyms, the place and date of the author's birth, his or her education, military service, marriage date(s), spouse's name(s), number of children, significant place(s) of employment, and notable awards. Entries for the dead conclude with the death date, whereas entries for the living tend to conclude by providing the subject's literary agent's name and address and the subject's address.

Often lengthy bibliographies follow the biographical information. Mystery and detective novels are listed first; the principal series character(s) (if any) is named at the head of the list, and entries indicate the works in which that character appears. Citations to mystery and detective short story collections follow; these do not indicate the presence of the series character. If the subject has written in multiple genres, a section devoted to "other publications" lists the author's novels, short story collections, plays, screenplays, radio plays, nonfiction, and edited works. If the subject used more than one name, the works are listed beneath the respective names. Citations in all sections are arranged chronologically and provide the publication data for the first British and American editions; retitlings are indicated, and first edition publication data are provided for them. After the bibliography are selective references to uncollected short stories and media adaptations.

After the bibliography comes a listing for the location of the author's manuscripts, and selective references to significant biocritical studies are included. If the author has chosen to provide a brief biographical comment, it is given; the comment is dated if the author made it for an earlier edition and has chosen not to revise it or has since died. Finally, a signed article provides a biocritical statement of the author's major works and themes. The volume concludes with separate indexes to the nationalities of the subjects and to the titles of the publications that were cited in the bibliographies, and it offers a lengthy reading list that does not distinguish between criticism, bibliographies, and coffee-table books.

The fourth edition has corrected a number of the typographical errors found in the earlier editions, and its bibliographies have been updated and compressed (the previous editions in this series tended to provide exhaustive lists of uncollected short works). A number of errors introduced in the earlier volumes nevertheless remain, as in the case of Gil Brewer. Although Brewer's birth date is given, the bibliographer has confused his output with that of a (probably pseudonymous) pulp writer. (Common sense should dictate that Brewer was not writing for *Zeppelin Stories* at age seven!) Additional complaints may be made with regard to the biocritical statements, which tend to the adulatory rather than the acute, and to the volume's editorial balance. The entries for Agatha Christie and Dashiell Hammett are barely one column in length, Arthur Conan Doyle is discussed in one and a half columns, and Raymond Chandler and Dorothy L. Sayers merit but two columns; the thrillers of Tom Clancy, on the other hand, have been accorded four full columns of space. Furthermore, why have thriller writers such as Clancy and Ian Fleming been accorded entries, when such talented crime and mystery writers as Thomas Cook and Sandra Scoppettone (to name but two) have not?

It must be stressed that no other one-volume work attempts to do so much, and the strengths of this book far outweigh its weaknesses. This series is indispensable for research, and its editors deserve commendation rather than censure. All editions of this book should be held by academic and public libraries.

882.5. Reynolds, Moira Davison. **Women Authors of Detective Series: Twenty-One American and British Writers, 1900– 2000.** Jefferson, NC: McFarland, 2001. vii, 182 p. Paperback. Index. LC 2001-30515. ISBN 0-7864-0982-7.

Reynolds provides biographical descriptions and assessments of 21 women writers from the 20th century who wrote (or write) mystery series. These authors are listed chronologically, beginning with Dora Turnbull (1879–1961) and concluding with Megan Rust (1957–); the list includes 10 British writers, 10 American writers, and 1 New Zealand writer (Ngaio Marsh). The essays are readable, but they are neither particularly insightful nor as strong as they might be, relying occasionally on too much uninspired plot summary. Each essay is followed by a chronological list of the author's works; retitlings are provided and, when the author was highly productive, the list becomes selective. Although there is nothing intrinsically wrong with this volume, it is not the work it might have been. This is not Reynolds's fault: one would need a volume much longer than this to begin to do justice to the subject. Nevertheless, other works in this section, particularly Dubose and Thomas's *Women of Mystery,* Klein's *Great Women Mystery Writers,* and Swanson and James's *By a Woman's Hand* (q.q.v.) are superior.

883. Silet, Charles L. P. **Talking Murder: Interviews with 20 Mystery Writers.** Princeton, N.J.: Ontario Review Press; New York: Distributed by W. W. Norton, 1999. xii, 267 p. LC 99-18501. ISBN 0-86538-096-1.

As its title indicates, this volume contains interviews with 20 contemporary mystery writers, ranging alphabetically from Thomas Adcock to Donald E. Westlake. The interviews, the majority of which first appeared in the *Armchair Detective* and *Mystery Scene,* are prefaced by a brief introduction and contain a picture of their subject but no bibliographies. Like *Speaking of Murder* (q.v.), it is debatable whether this is a reference book, but Silet is a skilled interviewer, and his profiles are lively and interesting. It should be mentioned that some of these writers are also interviewed in *Speaking of Murder,* but the interviews were conducted at different times.

884a. Swanson, Jean, and Dean James. **By a Woman's Hand: A Guide to Mystery Fiction by Women.** New York: Berkley Books, 1994. 254 p. Index. Paperback. ISBN 0-425-14143-8.

884b. Swanson, Jean, and Dean James. **By a Woman's Hand: A Guide to Mystery Fiction by Women.** 2nd. ed. New York: Berkley Prime Crime, 1996. Index. Paperback. ISBN 0-425-15472-6.

Unlike the other guides considered in this section, these books include minimal biographical data. Instead, they serve as reader's advisers, with brief essays discussing and describing the series characters and recurrent themes in the best-known works written by the Anglo-American women mystery writers of the late twentieth century. The first edition profiles the work of approximately 200 such writers; the second edition revises and expands the entries in the first and profiles nearly 300 women writers.

The introductory material is largely reprinted from the first edition, and the volume begins with an alphabetical listing of the authors whose works have been profiled. The essays are listed alphabetically by the name of the profiled authors and are typically between 200 and 400 words in length. More important, these essays are selective in their presentation of data: only two of Patricia Highsmith's five "Tom Ripley" novels are listed, for example. Furthermore, these essays tend toward the appreciative rather than the critical, and their arrangement is occasionally questionable: Oriana Papazoglou's entry can be found under her "Jane Haddam" pseudonym, although the majority of the entries is given under the author's real name. Each essay concludes with the advisory tips that on occasion are surprising but effective.

A brief list of important short story anthologies of women mystery writers follows, and indexes pair the series character with the author, list authors by the geographical setting of their books, and offer access by the detective's profession.

By a Woman's Hand contains significantly fewer entries than does Willetta L. Heising's *Detecting Women* (q.v.), but the entries are longer, and mystery lovers are likely to welcome its concluding advisories.

884.1. Winks, Robin W., ed. **Colloquium on Crime: Eleven Renowned Mystery Writers Discuss Their Work.** New York: Charles Scribner's Sons, 1986. viii, 216 p. Paperback. Index. LC 85-25195. ISBN 0-684-18428-1.

This volume had its genesis when Winks decided to write to his 15 favorite mystery writers and ask them to answer some questions. In Winks's words, "it turned out that four of my favorites didn't like being interrogated this way, and so they are not here, but eleven of those writers found it amusing, perhaps even productive, to think about themselves, their work habits, and the words they use as authors." These 11 are really 12, for although there essays by Robert Barnard, Rex Burns, K. C. Constantine, Dorothy Salisbury Davis, Michael Gilbert, Donald Hamilton, Joseph Hansen, Tony Hillerman, Reginald Hill, and James McClure, the concluding essay is by Robert B. Parker and Anne Ponder. Each author discusses his or her life and writing in an original essay (the Parker and Ponder essay is an expansion of one first published in *The Armchair Detective* in 1984), and although there is a sameness to some of their accounts, all essays are lively and worth reading. Winks contributes a lively introduction and a brief afterward, and it includes basic bibliographic data on the writers, and a capable index. Although the contents are now somewhat dated, this volume should be held by academic libraries.

884.2. Winks, Robin, and Maureen Corrigan, editors. **Mystery and Suspense Writers: The Literature of Crime, Detection, and Espionage.** New York: Scribner's Sons, 1998. xiv, 1296 p. 2 vols. Index. ISBN 0-684-80492-1. LC 98-36812.

The two volumes of *Mystery and Suspense Writers*—big, red, and black—are physically impressive and intellectually stimulating, combining 67 biocritical essays with 15 thematic essays. The authors profiled range alphabetically from Margery Allingham to Cornell Woolrich, and include such historically important figures as Edgar Allan Poe, Arthur Conan Doyle, Agatha Christie, Anna Katherine Green, Edgar Wallace, Sax Rohmer, and Dorothy L. Sayers, as well as such contemporary writers as Amanda Cross, Dick Francis, Sue Grafton, P. D. James, Robert B. Parker, Ruth Rendell, and Donald E. Westlake. The thematic essays include discussions of the Nick Carter Stories, the Armchair Detective, Black Detective Fiction, Gay and Lesbian Mystery Fiction, Religious Mysteries, the Romantic Suspense Mystery, and the Spy Thriller. Each essay concludes with a lengthy bibliography of primary and secondary works, and there are three appendixes: lists of pseudonyms and series characters, an index to the authors by genre, and a list of the major prizewinning authors.

There is much to praise about *Mystery and Suspense Writers.* The essays are solid, magisterial, and withstand repeated readings; indeed, the volumes deservedly won the 1999 Edgar Award for Best Critical/Biographical Work. At the same time, and perhaps inevitably given a work of this size, questions can be asked about its contents. Wilkie Collins is profiled, but his friend and colleague Charles Dickens is not. Why were Fredric Brown and R. Austin Freeman not accorded entries? Similarly, although Winks obviously attempted to profile writers who were not Anglo American—there are entries for Jorge Luis Borges, Émile Gaboriau, Maj Sjöwall and Per Wahlöö, and Robert van Gulik—the important Arthur Upfield is relegated to a section in the discussion of the Ethnic Detective.

Mystery and Suspense Writers is an essential work. It should be held by all academic and public libraries.

PSEUDONYMS

Scope note: The following section lists only the works that are discrete lists of pseudonyms and real names of mystery writers. Partial lists can be found in many of the readers' guides and biographical dictionaries listed earlier.

885. Bates, Susannah. **The Pendex: An Index of Pen Names and House Names in Fantastic, Thriller, and Series Literature.** Garland Reference Library of the Humanities, vol. 227. New York: Garland, 1981. xii, 233 p. Index. LC 80-8486. ISBN 0-8240-9501-4.

Although her focus is on the literature of the fantastic, a sizable percentage of the approximately 950 authors and their 1,700 pseudonyms listed in this volume belong to mystery and detective writers. There are five sections and two appendixes: (I) Real Names; (II) Pen Names; (III) Collaborative Pen Names; (IV) House Names; (5)

Stratemeyer Syndicate Names; Appendix A, "Pulps and Digests: Some Working Definitions"; and Appendix B, "Round Robin Serials."

The contents of the sections and appendixes are as one would expect. The first section lists in capital letters the author's name and beneath it, indented two spaces and in regular type, the pseudonyms he or she has used; birth and death dates often are given, as are whether the name is a collaborative pen name (CPN), a house name (HN), or a name used in the Stratemeyer Syndicate (SSN). The second section lists the pseudonym in capital letters and, beneath it, indented two spaces, in regular type and prefaced with RN:, the real name of the writer(s) who used it. The third section lists collaborative pseudonyms, providing the pseudonym in capital letters and beneath it, in regular type, the names of the writers who used it. The fourth section lists house names in capital letters, provides a brief description of the type of publication in which the name was used, and concludes with a list of the names of the writers who are known to have used the house names. The fifth section lists the names of the writers known to have worked in the Stratemeyer Syndicate, an organization whose thousands of juvenile and young adult titles appeared under hundreds of pseudonyms.

A number of sources have pilloried Bates. First, the book is rife with misspellings: "Frank Aubray" instead of Frank Aubrey, "Algerdas Budrys" instead of Algirdas Jonas Budrys, "Greya La Spina" instead of Greye La Spina, and so forth. Next, the volume contains such errors as "Catherine Louise Moore" instead of Catherine Lucille Moore, and such misattributions as Julian Chain being May Dikty. Worst of all, it is incomplete: when Bates does list a name, her lists of pseudonyms are grossly inadequate: Harlan Ellison is known to have used in excess of 20 pseudonyms; Bates lists but three. Similarly, Hugh Cave's famous "Justin Case" and Dashiell Hammett's "Peter Collinson" are not mentioned.

In the fields of science fiction, fantasy, and horror fiction, superior pseudonym indexes exist, and Bates's work is considered negligible. In the field of detective and mystery fiction, however, such is not the case; although works such as Hubin's and Contento's (q.q.v.) reveal many pseudonyms, such is not their primary purpose. Users of Bates are cautioned to verify her data elsewhere.

886. Directories of Pseudonyms (Working Names) of Mystery and Suspense Writers. http://www.hcyber.com/MYST/pseudo_dir.htm

Offers access by writer and by pseudonym.

887. Hawk, Pat. Hawk's Author's Pseudonyms for Book Collectors: A Collector's Reference of Modern Author's Pseudonyms. Southlake, Tex.: Pat Hawk, 1992+.

Although it does not limit itself to mystery and detective fiction, each edition of *Hawk's* lists hundreds of pseudonyms and the names behind them. The book's first section provides access by author name, permitting researchers to see the pseudonyms used; the second section lists the pseudonyms and those who have used them. As of this writing, there have been three editions of *Hawk's,* each more comprehensive and error-free than the previous, and more are anticipated. The third edition is also available on CD-ROM.

888. Kenner, Pat. File of Mystery Authors and Their Pseudonyms.

Available in the archives maintained by the DorothyL listserv. To obtain: send an e-mail message to listserv@listserv.kent.edu; type "get writer.noms" in the subject line.

10

Individual Biographies

ALLEN, GRANT; I.E., CHARLES GRANT BLAIRFINDIE ALLEN

889. Stephensen-Payne, Phil, and Virgil Utter. **Grant Allen: Hill-Top Philosopher. A Working Bibliography.** Galactic Central Bibliographies for the Avid Reader, vol. 52. Leeds, West Yorkshire, England: Galactic Central Publications, 1999. vii, 106 p. Paperback. ISBN 1-871133-51-1.

Like many late-Victorian writers, Grant Allen wrote widely, and detective and mystery fiction—and thrillers—are a significant part of his output. The introduction to this volume states that it contains the following 18 sections: (0) "Awards and Pseudonymns"; (1) "Prose Fiction"; (2) "Prose Fiction Books"; (3) "Series"; (4) "Poetry and Drama"; (5) "Poetry and Drama Books"; (6) "Articles"; (7) "Miscellaneous"; (8) "Non-fiction Books"; (9) "Edited Books"; (10) "Other Media"; (11) "Articles on the Author"; (12) "Reviews"; (13) "Books about the Author"; (14) "Phantom and Forthcoming Titles"; (15) "Related Items by Other Authors"; (16) "Textual Variations"; and (17) "Chronological Listing of Fiction." All of these sections contain material.

The contents of the first three sections are alphabetically arranged, each citation being separately lettered and numbered. In the first section, beneath each story's title are the places in which it has seen print. Book titles are capitalized and often accompanied by the names of the editors. Journal titles are given in regular type and the original publication date is given in abbreviated form (i.e., 5-1899 for May 1899), as is the pseudonym under which it appeared, if any. An abbreviation indicates whether the piece is a short-short story or vignette, short story, novelette, novella, short novel, or novel. Cross-references are provided for retitlings and alternative titles. The titles for Allen's books are given in capital letters. All known English editions are cited, and each citation lists publisher, series number, pagination, original price, and cover artist. If a translation is cited, the translated title is given as is the name of the translator.

Less needs to be said about the other sections, whose titles indicate their contents and reveal that Grant could (and did) write almost anything as well as that he was attracting significant attention. Had he not died young he might be better remembered.

Stephensen-Payne and Utter are to be commended for this very useful volume.

ANDERSON, FREDERICK IRVING

890.   Fisher, Benjamin Franklin, IV. **Frederic Irving Anderson (1877–1947): A Biobibliography.** Brownstone Chapbook Series, vol. 4. Madison, Ind.: Brownstone Books, 1987. 43 p. LC 88-34112. ISBN 0-8095-6403-3 (hc); 0-941028-07-0 (pb).

Today remembered only by specialists, Frederick Irving Anderson (1877–1947) created a versatile conman (the Infallible Godahl), vividly described a queen of crooks (in *The Notorious Sophie Lang*), and wrote a number of detective short stories noted for their craftsmanship, style, and local color. Although his work appeared in a number of magazines, particularly the *Saturday Evening Post,* Anderson apparently left few personal records, and he would probably be entirely forgotten were it not for Ellery Queen, whose *Queen's Quorum* (q.v.) cites Anderson's *The Book of Murder* (1930) as item 82 on its list of the 125 most important books of detective-crime-mystery short stories. Fisher's biography presents the few known facts of Anderson's life, corrects a few erroneous beliefs about Anderson, and discusses Anderson's works.

The bibliography begins by listing Anderson's works. The first citations are for Anderson's nonfiction and "semi-fiction;" these are followed by citations listing Anderson's books and his short fiction. Each section is arranged chronologically; all citations are consecutively numbered. Citations to publications in periodicals provide the title in quotations, list the periodical title in italics, and give its month and volume, and the story's pagination. Reprints are cited in the same fashion. The citations to Anderson's five books list their titles in italics, and their place, publisher, and year of publication; reprints are noted by listing the year of the reprint edition, and the collections of Anderson's short fiction include cross-references to the story's original appearance. Pagination is not provided. All citations are annotated.

The secondary bibliography begins by citing contemporary reviews of Anderson's books. These are followed by a lengthy listing of "additional secondary material" that in some way discusses or describes Anderson and his work. These citations are arranged alphabetically by author and are documented using the formats described earlier. As before, all citations are annotated.

Indexes to titles and periodical names would have benefited researchers, but apart from this lack, this belongs in collections with an historical focus.

BEDFORD-JONES, H.; I.E., HENRY JAMES O'BRIEN

891.   Ruber, Peter, Darrell C. Richardson, and Victor A. Berch. **"King of the Pulps": The Life & Writings of H. Bedford-Jones.** Shelburne, Ontario, Canada: Battered Silicon Dispatch Box, 2003. 316 p. Paperback. ISBN 1-55246-464-4. C2002-902765-9.

Although the title has been carelessly bestowed, Henry James O'Brien Bedford-Jones was certainly one of the kings of the pulp magazines. In a writing career that lasted almost exactly 40 years, he wrote some 25 million publishable words under a variety of pseudonyms; his total output includes some 231 novels and 1,141 shorter works. He was also a translator and operated a small press that published a number of his works. Despite this incredible output—much of which is intelligent, exciting, and compulsively readable—he is today largely unknown.

Ruber's biobibliography begins with a series of essays providing (for the first time) an extensive life of Bedford-Jones, complete with pictures of his parents. The second section—the bibliography—contains the following sections: fiction (novels and short stories) as H. Bedford-Jones; poetry; nonfiction; translations; fiction as Allan Hawkwood; fiction as Gordon Keyne; fiction as Capt. Bedford Foran; fiction as John Wycliffe; fiction as Montague Brisard; fiction as Donald Bedford; fiction as Emerson Baker; fiction as Margaret Love Sanderson; fiction as Gordon Stuart; fiction as Elliot Whitney; ephemera; anthology appearances. This section is followed by a bibliography of Bedford-Jones's magazine writings: the works that appeared under his name and under such names as Allan Hawkwood, Gordon Keyne, Capt. Michael Gallister, David Seabrooke, Torquay Trevision, H. E. Twinells, Bedford Rohmer, Rodney Blake, Capt. L. B. Williams, H. E. Williamson, and Burt L. Standish. Bedford-Jones's nonfiction is listed, as are radio shows, film adaptations, and articles and obituaries about him. These are followed by a reprint of an autobiographical statement initially printed in an edition of 86 copies, a discussion (by Ruber) of Bedford-Jones's John Solomon and Sherlock Holmes, and the reprinting of two obscure works: the newly discovered "The Wisdom of Solomon," and "The Affair of the Aluminium Crutch."

King of the Pulps is a fine work with some small faults: the self-published 30-copy *Bigfoot Joe and Others* (1920), for example, isn't strictly a book of poetry, for although it contains verse, the majority of the volume is prose. These faults are trivial, and *King of the Pulps* is an incredible work that—like its subject—deserves to be widely known.

BERKELEY, ANTHONY: PSEUDONYM FOR ANTHONY BERKELEY COX

892.   Johns, Ayresome [George Locke]. **The Anthony Berkeley Cox Files: Notes Towards a Bibliography.** London, England: Ferret Fantasy, 1993. 32 p. Paperback. 300 copies printed.

The only separately published bibliography of the works of Anthony Berkley Cox (1893–1971), this volume is cleanly offset from word-processed copy and contains the following sections: (A) "English First Editions"; (D) "Dust Jackets of English First Editions"; (B) "Contributions to Books"; (C) "Contributions to Periodicals"; (CB) "Contributions to Periodicals: 'Brenda' Stories"; (CD) "Contributions to Periodicals: 'Down Our Road' Stories"; (M) "Catalogue of Manuscripts"; (MB) "Catalogue of Manuscripts: 'Brenda' Stories"; (MD) "Catalogue of Manuscripts: 'Down Our Road" stories; "(P) "Plays, Radio, Films, and Other Media"; and an unlettered section titled "Who Was Francis Iles?—The Debate." The entries in each section are separately numbered and lettered; in sections A and D, the book's title is given in boldface capital letters. The contents of all sections are chronologically arranged.

Descriptions of the British first editions provide a transcription of the title page of the book, a collation of its pagination and contents, a description of its binding, a reference to the description of its dust jacket, the date upon which the British Museum

Library's copy was accessioned, and notes about the contents of the work. If the book had an American edition, it is cited. The description of the dust jackets of the English editions is equally thorough, with each citation transcribing the contents of the spine, the front panel, the rear panel, the front flap, and the rear flap.

The majority of the contents of this bibliography are devoted to describing Cox's contributions to periodicals and his numerous extant manuscripts. The former provide the name of the work, title of the periodical that published it, date of publication, and include a cross-reference to its publication in book form or the existence of its manuscript or both. The descriptions of the manuscripts provide the title of the work, its length, whether it is a carbon or a ribbon copy, and include a cross-reference to its original publication.

Although the contents often are cramped, and a title index would have been helpful, the bibliography is reasonably easy to use and thorough. Each of the 300 copies of this bibliography has the typescript of one of Cox's manuscripts tipped into it.

BIGGERS, EARL DERR

893.   Penzler, Otto. **Earl Derr Biggers' Charlie Chan.** Collection Mystery Fiction 2. New York: Mysterious Bookshop, 1999. 23 p. Paperback. 250 copies printed.

Reprinted from material first published in the *Armchair Detective* (vol. 15, no. 2 [1984], and vol. 15, no. 4 [1984]), this provides bibliographic descriptions of the six Charlie Chan books written by Earl Derr Biggers, after which Penzler discusses a few of the many ephemeral items related to Biggers and Chan. Penzler's descriptions focus on the first American edition and provide its place of publication, publisher, publication year, and a brief prose description of the color of the binding and its lettering. Following these data are relevant notes about later editions (i.e., "there is no other indication of printing history, the publisher merely having removed the bow-and-arrow symbol from later printings") and a black-and-white reproduction of the book's dust wrapper. Each entry concludes by providing an estimated value of the book in a variety of conditions.

BLAKE, NICHOLAS:
PSEUDONYM FOR CECIL DAY LEWIS

894.   Handley-Taylor, Geoffrey, and Timothy D'Arch Smith. **Day-Lewis, the Poet Laureate: A Bibliography.** With a Letter of Introduction by W. H. Auden. Chicago and London: St. James, 1968. xii, 42 p. Index. LC 73-1604. ISBN 0-900997-00-1.

From 1968 until his death in 1972, Cecil Day-Lewis was the Poet Laureate of England. In addition, from 1935 until 1968, using the pseudonym of Nicholas Blake, Day-Lewis wrote some 20 detective novels featuring as detective Oxford graduate Nigel Strangeways, apparently modeled on Day-Lewis's friend, the poet W. H. Auden. This bibliography of the works of C. Day-Lewis begins with a delightful letter from W. H. Auden, whose penultimate sentence states that the bibliography "does, however, make reference to that secretive character N****** B****, who has given more pleasure to more people than, in our age, any writer of verses can ever hope to give." This is followed by acknowledgments, a "bibliographical note," which explains the bibliographical principles used for compiling the body of the volume, and a poem by Day-Lewis, "Sunday Afternoon," which is original to this book.

The bibliography contains three sections: books and pamphlets by C. Day-Lewis; books and pamphlets with contributions by C. Day-Lewis; and detective stories by C. Day-Lewis under the pseudonym of Nicholas Blake. The data in the first two section are very thorough. Each item is separately numbered. Titles are given in capital letters; in smaller capitals are given the place of publication and the publisher, and the publisher's address is given in italics. The paper size is given, as are pagination and a description of the book's binding. The exact publication date is given, and references are made to American editions and to locations of the manuscripts of the poems. References to periodical publications are not included.

The final section, however, is merely a chronological list of the titles of Day-Lewis's mysteries, accompanied only by the date of their first publications. Day-Lewis's most popular and enduring writings are thus marginalized and dismissed, an indefensible action on the part of the bibliographers.

This is the only book-length bibliography of Day-Lewis. A comprehensive and sympathetic bibliography remains to be done.

BLOCH, ROBERT [ALBERT]

895a. Flanagan, Graeme. **Robert Bloch: A Bio-Bibliography.** Canberra, Australia: Graeme Flanagan, 1979. 64 p. Paperback.

Although he is probably better known for his cheerfully macabre fantasies and horror fiction, Robert Bloch wrote a number of detective and mystery stories and warrants inclusion here. This bio-bibliography was compiled with Bloch's assistance and with the assistance of Randall D. Larson, who was later to compile his own Bloch bibliography (q.v.). It contains the following sections: an introduction; "Robert Bloch: A Few Words of Friendship" by Harlan Ellison; a biography; the Robert Bloch collection; "Mr. Weird Tales" by Robert Weinberg; Interview One: Mostly Concerning *Weird Tales*; "When Screwballs Meet . . ." by Fritz Leiber; Interview Two; a bibliography; radio, television and motion pictures; "My Weird Little Brother, Bob," by Mary Elizabeth Counselman. In addition, numerous photographs are included.

The biography is a reprint from that appearing in the summer 1949 issue of the *Fanscient*. The bibliography contains the following sections: short stories—first magazine printings; nonfiction published in magazines; novels; collections—short stories; collections—nonfiction; short stories and nonfiction published in anthologies; short stories and nonfiction reprinted in magazines; foreign translations; and miscellanea. The entries in the first two sections are arranged chronologically; the title is given, followed by the pseudonym (if any), the magazine in which it appeared, and the month and year of publication. The citations in the third, fourth, and fifth sections are arranged alphabetically; the book's title is given in capital letters and underlined, and listed beneath the book title are the publisher, place of publication, year of publication, pagination, and original cost of all known printings of the book. The contents of collections are provided. The anthology citations are listed chronologically; the magazine citations are listed alphabetically. The translation section is an alphabetical listing of titles followed by the language into which the work has been translated; full publication data are not provided. The section devoted to miscellanea references Bloch's introductions and afterwords, printed speeches, interviews, and sources of biographical data.

The bibliography of Bloch's radio, television, and motion pictures lists the titles of Bloch's radio series, with a subsection listing the titles, stations, and air dates of those pieces for which Bloch provided only the story. The section devoted to Bloch's television writing lists the teleplays, the show for which they were written, and the year in which they appeared; casts are occasionally provided. The section on Bloch's motion pictures lists the studio, the year of release, the producer's name, and the cast.

Although this work is a very worthy effort, Bloch's fan writings are not cited, and Flanagan's accomplishment has been superseded by Larson's (profiled later).

895b. Hall, Graham M. **Robert Bloch Bibliography.** Tewksbury, England: Graham M. Hall, 1965. 32 p. Paperback.

Not seen. Referenced in Michael Burgess, *Reference Guide to Science Fiction, Fantasy, and Horror* (Littleton, Colo.: Libraries Unlimited, 1992).

895c. Larson, Randall D. **The Complete Robert Bloch: An Illustrated, International Bibliography.** Sunnyvale, Calif.: Fandom Unlimited Enterprises, 1986. x, 126 p. Paperback. LC 85-82410. ISBN 0-96071-81-1. Also: San Bernardino, Calif.: Borgo Press, 1987. x, 126 p. Index. LC 87-20858. ISBN 0-8095-6106-9.

Like the earlier Bloch bibliography compiled by Graeme Flanagan (profiled earlier), this bibliography was compiled with Bloch's assistance; Bloch even provides a brief introduction. This heavily illustrated bibliography, however, largely eschews the biographical data offered by Flanagan and concentrates on providing what Larson's brief preface describes as the "first *complete* and comprehensive bibliography of all the work of Robert Bloch, including international appearances in print, radio, television and film, both professional and amateur." It contains the following sections: a preface; an introduction by Robert Bloch; "Robert Bloch: The Man with the Heart of a Small Boy," by Larson; the main bibliography; the fanzine bibliography; supplemental bibliographies; and "Themes and Variations: A Categorical Guide to the Short Stories and Novels of Robert Bloch." The main bibliography contains the following sections: short stories; novels; collections; nonfiction; introductions and forewords; verse; radio, television and motion pictures; bibliographic and biographic material; and miscellany. The supplemental bibliographies are a series of indexes: selected story index by magazine; chronology of first appearances; unanthologized stories; Lefty Feep stories; collaborative stories; and pseudonymous stories.

The entries in the first six sections are alphabetical by title. Entries for short stories provide the title in boldface, the story's wordage, the title and date (month and year) of the magazine in which it first appeared, and all known subsequent appearances, including international publications and anthologizations. Magazine titles are underlined; book titles are in capitals. Retitlings are cross-referenced to the original title, stories that appeared under pseudonyms are indicated, and stories that were adapted for television and motion pictures are also indicated. Finally, Bloch's popular Lefty Feep stories are marked with an [LF] by their title. The sections devoted to Bloch's books provide the place of publication, publisher and year of publication, and translated title for all known editions; wordage is provided for Bloch's novels, and the contents of Bloch's collections are listed. In no section are paginations provided. The sections devoted to the media adaptations are arranged chronologically. The title or program titles are given in boldface, accompanied by the date of broadcast or release, the production company or broadcasting network, and the director (for motion pictures). International rebroadcasts of television shows also are indicated, though the data are sketchier.

The indexes in the "Supplemental Bibliographies" rearrange much of the data presented in the earlier sections. In addition to listing the stories by the magazine in which they appeared, the first index provides a series of abbreviations indicating whether the work is a cover story [c], a reprinted story [r], a nonfiction article [n], a Lefty Feep story [LF], or a story that appeared under a pseudonym. The chronology of the second index indicates whether the piece is nonfiction or is a Lefty Feep story. The entries in the unanthologized stories are listed alphabetically, with a note indicating whether the piece was anthologized only in a foreign publication, reprinted only in an American magazine, or reprinted only in a fan magazine.

Although still the most comprehensive bibliography of Bloch available, this is now outdated. Bloch has since died, and a comprehensive bibliography of works published during his life is possible. One hopes that Larson manages to do this, adding paginations and, perhaps, references to the increasing body of literature about Bloch.

BLOCK, LAWRENCE

896. Seels, James T., ed. **Lawrence Block: Bibliography 1958–1993.** Introduction by Wendy Hornsby. "Pen Names and Other Subterfuge" and "One Thousand Dollars a Word" by Lawrence Block. An Appreciation by Charles Ardai. Afterword by Philip Friedman. Royal Oak, Mich.; Mission Viejo, Calif.: ASAP/Airtight-Seels Allied Production, 1993. 103 p. Paperback. Indexes. 30 copies in cloth slipcases; 50 copies in acrylic slipcases; 420 trade copies.

Despite being compiled with the assistance of Block, this bibliography is less than satisfactory; it is certainly less than comprehensive. Block's introduction states forthrightly that "there are other pseudonymous books that I feel more kindly towards. Some thought and care went into their composition, and I remain pleased with the way they turned out. I thought about allowing some of them to be listed in this bibliography, and I decided against it." What is present is awkwardly designed, difficult to use, and does not follow a known form of bibliographic citation.

Following an introduction by Wendy Hornsby and Block's history of his use of pseudonyms, the first section of the bibliography is a chronological list of the books appearing under Block's name. Titles are listed in bold capital letters; beneath each title is a statement indicating whether the work is a short story, a novel, or a nonfiction work. The bibliographic information includes the book's place of publication, its publisher, its publication year, its stock number, its format (paperback or hardcover). Statements of printing are provided for each edition, as are information on later publications and retitlings. Occasional notes on the series to which the book belongs are also given. Following this section and using the same format are lists of Block's works as Chip Harrison and Paul Kavanagh. Concluding this section are alphabetical lists of Block's works and a list of his works by series: these do not include the year in which the work was published, making them useless except as lists.

The bibliography's second section is a chronological list of the short stories written by Block. Titles are set in quotation marks in bold capital letters, and the citation lists the magazine's place of publication, its title (in italics), and the month and year of publication. If the story was collected or anthologized, the citation includes the place of publication, the title (in small bold capital letters), and the year of publication. Notes indicate title changes and occasionally the series character featured in the story. An alphabetical list of the short stories concludes the bibliography, and the volume concludes with publication of Block's short story, "One Thousand Dollars a Word" and an afterword by Philip Friedman.

Seels's edition of Block's *Ehrengraf for the Defense* is a beautiful piece of fine printing, and this bibliography is likewise very attractive. Nevertheless, a comprehensive bibliography, one that lists all of Block's work, provides information on pagination and dust wrappers, contains indexes, and uses a recognizable system of bibliographical citation, remains to be done.

BRACKETT, LEIGH

897.   Arbur, Rosemarie. **Leigh Brackett, Marion Zimmer Bradley, Anne McCaffrey: A Primary and Secondary Bibliography.** Boston: G. K. Hall, 1982. xlviii, 277 p. Indexes. LC 81-4216. ISBN 0-8161-8120-9.

Although all three authors are best-known science fiction and fantasy writers, all also have written detective and mystery stories, but only Brackett's work achieved any fame. Arbur provides lengthy introductions to the writers, providing general biographical data on them and simple comparisons and contrasts of the themes found in their writing (e.g., "both Bradley and McCaffrey chose for the science part of their science fictions the relatively soft science of psychology") . Following the introduction, the bibliography is tripartite, with separate sections for each writer. Each of these sections uses a similar arrangement in its presentation of material: fiction, miscellaneous media, nonfiction, and critical studies. Furthermore, the data in each section are similarly numbered; for example, Brackett, Bradley, and McCaffrey each have sections beginning A1, A2, and A3. Each section is chronologically arranged.

In the fiction section, book titles are underlined, and the place of publication and publisher are given. Titles of short stories are in quotations, and the publication data include periodical name, volume, issue number, month, and story's pagination. Beneath each citation are lists giving additional appearances of the work; also, these reprints are numbered separately and cited in their chronological sequence, with cross-references to their first appearance. Paginations of books are not provided.

The material listed in the miscellaneous media section includes lengthy lists of Brackett's screenplays, short poems by Bradley, and spoken recordings by McCaffrey. The citations for the majority of Brackett's materials are based on materials in the Brackett Collection at Eastern New Mexico University Golden Library. Entries provide the title of the piece (underlined), the name of the production company, the date of original broadcast, whether the screenplay was original or based on somebody's work, and a note as to the format of the screenplay (e.g., "original and carbon typescript of final draft, 500 leaves") .

The material listed in the other sections is very capably annotated and follows the arrangement of the first section. The volume concludes with six separate indexes, offering author and title access to the works by and the works about the author.

Brackett died in 1978 and her section is essentially complete. Bradley and McCaffery had their greatest successes in the years following the publication of Arbur's book, and Bradley wrote a number of best-sellers before her death in 1999. This nevertheless remains a useful bibliography. It has an unnecessarily redundant system of documenting primary publications, and the six indexes are unnecessarily cumbersome, but these problems aside, it offers data that cannot be found elsewhere. There is now academic interest in all three authors, and significant work has been produced on each. One hopes that this bibliography can be expanded and updated.

898a. Benson, Gordon, Jr. **Leigh Douglas Brackett and Edmond Hamilton: A Working Bibliography.** Galactic Central Bibliographies for the Avid Reader, vol. 20. Leeds, England; Albuquerque, N. Mex.: Galactic Central, 1988. i, 25 p. Paperback. ISBN 0-912613-05-X.

898b. Benson, Gordon, Jr. **Leigh Brackett & Edmond Hamilton: The Enchantress & the World Wrecker: A Working Bibliography.** Galactic Central Bibliographies for the Avid Reader, vol. 20. Polk City, Iowa; Leeds, England: Galactic Central, 1988. 25 p. Paperback. ISBN 0-912613-05-X.

Leigh Brackett is generally remembered as a writer of science fiction and fantasy, but she worked on the screenplay of *The Big Sleep* and wrote several fine detective novels, including the noir classic *No Good from a Corpse.* (Although several of his short stories appeared in the mystery and detective pulp magazines, her husband Edmond Hamilton was predominantly a science fiction writer.) Pages 1 to 9 in this bibliography list Brackett's work; the remainder (pages 10 to 25) list Hamilton's. Each section begins with the subject's name in capital letters and a double underline, followed by the dates of birth and death. Their awards are listed, as are citations to biographical data appearing in specialized publications. The data for both authors are arranged by subject, with separate sections for stories, books, and series. Entries in each section are separately numbered and arranged alphabetically; the titles of all books and magazines are capitalized. Each citation lists all known appearances and publications of that work. For stories, Benson lists the magazine's name and provides the date of publication in abbreviated form (7-41 for July 1941); reprints are listed beneath. Paginations for short stories are not provided. For books, Benson lists the publisher, the series number, the year of publication, the pagination, the initial price, and the cover artist of all known editions. Title changes are indicated and cross-referenced.

The bibliographic data in Hamilton's section are preceded by a lengthy list of the abbreviations used to reference the magazines in which he was published. The references to Hamilton's short stories exclude Hamilton's work for *Captain Future,* and the 27 Captain Future tales are listed in chronological order in the section devoted to Hamilton's series followed by separate sections listing the Captain Future books and the "other" books.

The arrangement of Hamilton's work is unnecessarily baroque, the bibliography lacks a title index, and its periodical citations fail to provide paginations. Worse, it is incomplete, lacking the data on screenplays provided by Arbur (q.v.). Nevertheless, this remains an inexpensive and useful introduction to a pair of significant and too often neglected writers. One hopes for a revised and expanded edition.

BRAUN, LILIAN JACKSON

899a. Feaster, Sharon. **The Cat Who—Companion.** New York: Berkley Prime Crime Books, 1998. xvi, 312 p. Paperback. LC 99-160213. ISBN 0-425-16540-X.

899b. Feaster, Sharon. **The Cat Who—Companion.** Rev. ed. New York: Berkley Prime Crime Books, 1999. xvi, 345 p. Paperback. LC 00-265618. ISBN 0-425-16425-5.

The revised edition is described here.

Following maps of Moose County and downtown Pickax, the *Companion* contains 13 chapters, 11 of which discuss Braun's writing. The first 10 of these 11 describe Koko and Yum Yum and James Mackintosh Qwilleran and the world they inhabit: their games, geography, houses, food, friends, the characters who also inhabit their world, and the crimes they encounter and solve. The majority of the chapters discusses these subjects in chronological order, from *The Cat Who Could Read Backwards* (1966) to *The Cat Who Sang for the Birds* (1998), although the lists of characters are given in alphabetical order. The eleventh chapter discusses Braun's short story collection, *The Cat Who Had 14 Tales* (1988), the twelfth discusses Braun, and the volume concludes with a quiz.

Fans of Braun will perhaps want this volume—and it appears to be written for fans rather than the researcher—for it contains no bibliographic data, offers very little about Braun, and is unindexed.

BROWN, FREDRIC

900a.   Ahearn, Allen, and Patricia Ahearn. **Author Price Guides: Fredric Brown.** Rockville, Md.: Quill & Brush, 1996. 7 leaves. APG 153.

This Author Price Guide lists the writings of Fredric Brown from the 1947 publication of the uncorrected proof of *The Fabulous Clipjoint* to the 1991 appearance of *The Pickled Punks*.

The Author Price Guides include a facsimile of the author's signature, a brief biographical sketch, a list of the author's first English and American editions with separate entries for limited and trade editions, the number of copies printed, how to identify the first edition, and estimated value. Each guide presents the bibliographical information chronologically; each separate publication is separately numbered, with different editions indicated by lowercase letters.

The first entry in each citation is the title, given in capital letters. The second is the publisher's name as it appears on the title page; if the name does not appear there, it is enclosed in parentheses. The third entry is the place of publication, and the fourth is the date of publication; as before, parentheses enclose these data if they are not listed on the title page. The fifth entry is a code providing information on how to identify the first printing (first edition) of the particular book. Notes indicate when more than one issue of a particular first edition exists; page and line numbers are provided if it is necessary to identify issues; first editions appearing in paper are so indicated.

The Author Price Guides are inexpensive and useful bibliographies for those collecting separate publications. On the debit side, separately published pieces in anthologies are not identified, published letters are not traced, dramatic works are only sporadically recorded, and the contents of short story collections are not noted.

900b.   Baird, Newton. **A Key to Fredric Brown's Wonderland: A Study and an Annotated Bibliographical Checklist with Reminiscences by Elizabeth Brown and Harry Altshuler and "It's Only Everything" by Fredric Brown.** Georgetown, Calif.: Talisman Literary Research, 1981. 63 p. Index. LC 81-52422. 275 copies paperbound; 85 copies hardcover.

One of the few authors equally adept at short stories and novels, and noted for detective and mystery fiction as well as science fiction, fantasy, and weird fiction, Fredric Brown unfortunately remains largely unstudied. Baird's introduction to this excellent bibliography acknowledges Brown's originality, linking him to writers as diverse as Ayn Rand, Mickey Spillane, William Campbell Gault, and Lewis Carroll: "His 'wonderland,' like Carroll's, is full of wonder and curiosity, created from what he saw in reality, and he shared Carroll's sense of the fantastic and delight with word inventions and puzzles. But no other author, including Lewis Carroll, became a prototype for Fredric Brown. He is one of the most original writers of all time."

Prior to the bibliography, the *Key* contains separate sections providing a chronology of Fredric Brown and two reminiscences of Brown from *Les Amis du Crime:* "Fredric Brown, My Husband," by Elizabeth Brown and "The Early Career of Fredric Brown" by Harry Altshuler; and "It's Only Everything" by Fredric Brown. Elizabeth Brown was Fredric's wife; Altshuler was his first literary agent and his friend; and "It's Only Everything" is a brief, thought-provoking essay discussing atheism, Christianity, and the need for conviction.

The bibliography contains the following sections: (A) books; (B) foreign anthologies not published in the United States; (C) parts of books; (D) short stories; (E) poetry: books and periodicals; (F) other contributions to periodicals; (G) radio adaptations of short stories; (H) television adaptations of fiction; (I) film adaptations of fiction (other than films made for television); (J) phonograph recordings of fiction; (K) parts of books; and (L) articles, parts of articles, and published letters about Fredric Brown. An appendix titled "A Few Supplemental Matters" is included, and an index to the entire *Key*—prefatory material, biographical reminiscences, as well as the bibliography— concludes the volume.

With the exception of the material in sections 11 and 12, which are listed alphabetically, the citations in each section are arranged chronologically. The book citations list the book's title in italics and provide publication data—publisher, place and year of publication, and pagination—for all known editions of the work. The annotation provides the names of the character and a clear statement of the plot without revealing the climax and includes a note on Brown's narrative style (i.e., "third person narration with nine points-of-view, including 'Death' "). Each citation concludes with a list of the contemporary reviews.

The citations in the other sections vary in their comprehensiveness. The listing for Brown's short stories provides the name, month, and year of the periodical in which the piece appeared, as well as the titles of the books in which they were reprinted. Oddly, the story's original pagination is not given. Furthermore, Baird's data were undoubtedly as complete as could be hoped for in 1981, but additional short stories by Brown have since been discovered, and an error in the citation for "Jaycee" has recently been discovered.

Although it is not recent nor as comprehensive in its listings of short stories as Christopher Stephens's *A Checklist of Fredric Brown* (q.v.), this nevertheless contains much that cannot be obtained elsewhere, and it presents its material well. Baird should revise and update his *Key* and print a larger quantity of copies.

900c. Stephens, Christopher P. **A Checklist of Fredric Brown.** Hastings-on-Hudson, N.Y.: Ultramarine Publishing, 1992. 83 p. Paperback. Index. ISBN 0-89366-225-9.

One of the longest of the Ultramarine bibliographies, this is also one of the more thorough. It contains three chronologically arranged sections: books written by Fredric Brown, books edited by him, and short stories written by him. In the first section, each citation is numbered, and publication data are provided on the first American and first English edition and the first paperback edition of each. Titles are underlined; retitlings are indicated; and data on paginations, dust wrapper artists, prices, and identifying points also are given. The citations for the short stories are arranged chronologically also. Story titles are given in quote marks, magazine names are underlined, publication date is provided, and reprint information is also given. Original paginations, however, are not given. An index to all works concludes the checklist.

Stephens lists far more short stories by Brown than does Baird (q.v.), and his entries are significantly more recent than Baird's. On the debit side, Stephens's format for listing his citations is thoroughly unattractive, to the point of impeding rather than enhancing access. Flaws of appearance aside, this is the most comprehensive bibliography of Fredric Brown's short works available, and most researchers will find its listings of Brown's novels quite adequate.

900d.   Williams, Richard, ed. **Fredric Brown: British and American Books and Films: A Checklist.** British Author Checklists, no. 2. Scunthorpe, England: Dragonby Press, 1991. 4 p. Collated sheets.

This brief bibliography contains almost no information on Brown's films and is an alphabetical listing of his books. Each title is given in boldface capitals. A note indicates whether the book is short stories or a novel, and a list provides data on all of the American and English editions of the book. These data are presented in abbreviated form but usually include the publisher's name and the date of publication; pagination is sometimes provided, as is the artist for the paperback editions of the book. Despite its brevity, this bibliography cites some English paperback editions that are not listed in Baird's or Stephens's bibliographies of Fredric Brown (q.q.v.), but it contains little else that is not readily accessible elsewhere.

BUCHAN, JOHN, FIRST BARON TWEEDSMUIR OF ELSFIELD

Scope note: Although Buchan wrote excellent thrillers and adventure stories, he did not write traditional mystery and detective fiction. He is included here because he is well represented in the appendix, and not to mention the works on him would be to do him a disservice.

901a.   Blanchard, Robert G. **The First Editions of John Buchan: A Collector's Bibliography.** Hamden, Conn.: Archon Books, 1981. xi, 284 p. Index. LC 81-10902. ISBN 0-20801-905-7.

Blanchard's bibliography contains five sections: Buchan's books and pamphlets; his edited works; his contributions to books; his uncollected contributions to periodicals and public documents; and his contributions to the *Spectator*.

In the first section, 136 English and American editions of Buchan's works are listed chronologically and described bibliographically. Each citation gives the title in capital letters followed by the book's collation, pagination, printing, physical description, publication price, dedication, and contents; each concludes with detailed notes about the book, including whether the item had periodical serialization prior to its publication. Perhaps the only fault with this section lies in Blanchard's definition of "book and pamphlet," which permits him to include such works as a 1936 address at an alumni dinner: at nine typed pages, is this either a book or a pamphlet, or does it warrant inclusion in another section?

The material in the other sections is equally thoroughly described: the second section references the first publication of 14 books; the third, contains 141 citations; the fourth, 235; and the fifth, 805. The index is thorough and comprehensive.

Although Blanchard's work occasionally raises questions, and one would have liked more information about Buchan's life, his *Collector's Bibliography* thoroughly supersedes the work of Hanna (q.v.).

901b.   Hanna, Archibald, Jr. **John Buchan, 1875–1940, a Bibliography.** Introduction by Robert F. Metzdorf. Hamden, Conn.: Shoe String Press, 1953. xi, 135 p. Index. LC 53-12764.

The first separately published bibliography devoted to Buchan—Hanna's brief preface hints intriguingly of consulting an "unpublished bibliography of Buchan" compiled by Mr. James Mack, librarian of Lehigh University—this volume contains four sections: books and pamphlets; contributions to books; contributions to periodicals; and writings about John Buchan.

The first section is arranged chronologically and references 115 editions of Buchan's works. Each citation gives the title in capital letters followed by the book's place of publication, publisher, publication year, and pagination. When relevant, these are followed by a description of the half title, a note as to the illustrations and illustrator, and a list of the contents. Beneath this information, Hanna lists the different editions of each work, including editions published in such languages as Czech, Dutch, French, and Danish, but it would seem he has equated *edition* with *printing,* leading to significant repetition of otherwise identical citations. (There are five references to the Hodder and Stoughton publication of *John McNab,* for example; apart from differences in publication date, the citations are identical, although Hanna states that each is "another edition"). Also, as mentioned in the description of Blanchard (profiled previously), some of Hanna's references are to works that are neither book nor pamphlet: *The Battlefield of Bannockburn Appeal: A Message from John Buchan* (1918) is but one page in length. Surely it belongs elsewhere.

Hanna's second section references the first editions of 63 books; the third contains 287 periodical citations; and the fourth, 40 chronologically listed citations to books and periodicals. The volume's index is comprehensive. Hanna's pioneering effort is not discreditable, but it has been thoroughly superseded by Blanchard's work.

901c.   Webb, Paul. **A Buchan Companion: A Guide to the Novels and Short Stories.** Far Thrupp, Stroud, Gloucestershire; Dover, N.H.: Alan Sutton, 1994. xxii, 126 p. LC 95-204040. ISBN 0-86299-870-0.

In the words of Webb's introduction, "This guide is an alphabetical record of characters and places having a significant role in the novels and stories, in many cases described in Buchan's own words." Forty-one works by Buchan are thus indexed, with Webb presenting his entries in alphabetical order, intermixing descriptions of people with those of places and plots. Also included are statements as to how the books were received upon publication and identifications of the people Buchan used as models for his characters. Although the *Companion*'s entries are unnumbered, there are approximately 500 in all, most in the 100- to 200-word range, though some are much longer. The volume includes an unpaginated section of black-and-white plates and concludes with a bibliography listing the works that were indexed; this is followed by a very selective secondary bibliography.

A *Buchan Companion* contains no cross-references and no indexing and should have included more secondary characters, but it is not a discreditable effort. Webb possesses sufficient critical acumen to provide a realistic assessment of Buchan's oeuvre, and he is not averse to observing when Buchan's plots and prose flag and fail, as when Koré Arabin of *The Dancing Floor* "of course . . . remained pure as snow throughout a childhood spent in a house where the guests routinely indulged in the wildest of orgies." (It is hard to imagine another single-author dictionary having the audacity to state that "the most successful thing about [fictional character Richard] Hannay is his ability as a social climber, and in this he resembles his creator").

Researchers interested in Buchan will enjoy the *Companion,* but it remains a work for specialists.

901d. [Wilmot, B. C.] **Checklist of Works by and about John Buchan in the John Buchan Collection, Douglas Library, Queen's University, Kingston, Ontario.** Boston: G. K. Hall, 1961. 38 plus unnumbered pages. Index. LC 62-1196.

This checklist began life as a mimeographed work first issued in 1958, which has not been seen.

Buchan's personal archive—his manuscripts and his books—were given to the Douglas Library upon his death, and the *Checklist,* offset from typescript, is a comprehensive catalogue of this collection. It contains the following sections: Buchan's manuscripts and typescripts, including a list of manuscripts not intended for publication; selections, anthologies, extracts; fiction; major prose other than fiction; minor prose, with subsections for collections and separate works; poetry; works compiled and edited by Buchan, with sections listing collections and individual authors; and works with minor contributions by Buchan. A separate section lists the works about Buchan, with citing bibliographies; periodicals, societies, and collections; autobiographies; letters; biographies and criticism; miscellaneous biography and criticism; and books dedicated to Buchan. An addenda section is included, and the volume concludes with a lengthy but unpaginated index listing titles and personal names.

The information presented can be quite thorough: the descriptions are lengthy, providing in addition to the usual publication data (place of publication, publisher, publication year) pagination, illustrative material, a note as to the contents, and a note as to Buchan's involvement with the particular work (i.e., "author's marginal corrections in ms"). Nevertheless, the arrangement of the material is idiosyncratic at best, and although Buchan scholars will need to use this volume, others will be more than satisfied with the work of Blanchard (q.v.).

CARR, JOHN DICKSON

902. Keirans, James E. **Poison and Poisoners in the Mysteries of John Dickson Carr: An Aficionado's Vademecum.** CADS Supplement, no. 5. South Benfleet, Essex, England: CADS, 1996. 57 p. Paperbound. ISSN 0965-6561.

This fascinating and informative work lists all the references to poison and poisoners in the works of John Dickson Carr. The list is arranged alphabetically, with [R] before an entry indicating whether it is a reference to a real-life person (a "victim or villain"). The entries discuss the person or the poison, listing in boldface type the book(s) in which the reference is given; fictitious books references by Carr are listed in boldface italic type, magazine titles are given in italics, and the titles of short radio play scripts and short stories are printed within quotation marks. The entries are occasionally lengthy and are always enjoyable; included are numerous cross-references. The work concludes with a list of Carr's works that have been cited in the text; separate sections exist for the novels he wrote as John Dickson Carr and Carter Dickson, as well as for Carr's true crime, his collaborations and collections, and his radio scripts and short stories.

CHANDLER, RAYMOND [THORNTON]

903a.   Ahearn, Allen, and Patricia Ahearn. **Author Price Guides: Raymond Chandler.** Rockville, Md.: Quill & Brush, 1992. 5 leaves. APG 124.

This Author's Price Guide to Raymond Chandler lists his work from the 1939 advance publication copy of *The Big Sleep* to the 1990 publication of *Poodle Springs*.

For a more thorough description of the format of Author Price Guides, see the entry under Fredric Brown.

903b.   Bruccoli, Matthew J. **Raymond Chandler: A Checklist.** Serif Series: Bibliographies and Checklists. Kent, Ohio: Kent State University Press, 1968. ix, 35 p. LC 68-16892.

Bruccoli's introduction begins by stating that this slim volume is not a bibliography but a checklist. Nevertheless, the book lists "all editions of the books, first periodical appearances only, and first book appearances only of short pieces. For the first printing of the first edition of a Chandler book, it supplies a short form title-page transcription, pagination, and signature collation." That these do not make the work a bibliography are because (in Bruccoli's words), it "fails to provide the detailed descriptive and analytical information about paper, type, binding, printing, and text—especially text—that a true bibliography, no matter how digressive, must provide."

The checklist begins with a chronological list of Chandler's books. Separate sections provide chronological lists of Chandler's first book appearances, stories, articles, reviews, columns, letters, poems, and blurbs. Other sections contain an interview with Chandler, a statement by Chandler, and a brief list of references (three items cited).

Although Bruccoli is accurate in his presentation of its material, Chandler wrote far more than he is here given credit for, and this volume has been thoroughly superseded by Bruccoli's later work on the subject (q.v.).

903c.   Bruccoli, Matthew J. **Raymond Chandler: A Descriptive Bibliography.** Pittsburgh Series in Bibliography. Pittsburgh, Pa.: University of Pittsburgh, 1979. xv, 146 p. Index. LC 78-4280. ISBN 0-8229-3382-9.

As if to make amends for his earlier *Raymond Chandler: A Checklist* (q.v.), Bruccoli here presents a comprehensive bibliography of the works of Raymond Chandler. The bibliography contains six lettered sections: (A) "Separate Publications"; (B) "First-Appearance Contributions to Books"; (C) "First Appearances in Magazines and Newspapers"; (D) "Keepsake"; (E) "Dust-Jacket Blurbs"; (F) "Motion-Picture Work."

The citations in each of these sections are arranged chronologically and are separately lettered and numbered.

Section A, the longest section in the book, consists of the first 106 pages. Each citation reproduces the title page of the first edition of all English and American hardcovers and paperbacks. Each entry provides an exhaustive analytical bibliographical description of the first edition, with the collation, pagination, contents, typography and paper, binding, dust jacket, publication, and printing noted and described at length. A section called "Notes" provides additional information and cross-references to other sections, and a section for "Locations" provides not only a list of the holdings of libraries but also the dates on which the major copyright libraries received the volume. Additional printings and editions are also noted and described, although the descriptions of these are of necessity terser; the title and copyright pages are described at length. A supplement (section AA) lists collections of Chandler's writings using the same principles of bibliographical description.

The concluding sections provide similarly detailed bibliographical data. Retitlings of short stories are indicated, as are unsigned works. Section D contains one citation; Section E contains two citations. Section F lists the motion pictures written by Chandler as well as those based on his work: it contains 17 citations. Appendixes list the compiler's notes and provide a brief list of the principal works about Chandler, and the volume concludes with a comprehensive index.

Although the concluding sections could well have been compressed, this remains the definitive bibliography of Chandler.

903d. Lovisi, Gary. **Dashiell Hammett and Raymond Chandler: A Checklist and Bibliography of Their Paperback Appearances.** Brooklyn, N.Y.: Gryphon Books, 1994. 82 p. Paperback. LC 96-134119. ISBN 0-936071-36-2. 500 copies printed.

After an appreciation of the two authors and the section devoted to the paperbacks of Dashiell Hammett, the paperback appearances of Raymond Chandler are listed. The citations are arranged alphabetically by title and then listed alphabetically by publisher, a reasonable arrangement that quickly develops problems when Lovisi cites international editions without any familiarity with the language; the paperback editions of Ullstein Verlag's publication of *The Big Sleep,* for example, are listed under the words "Allgemeine Reihe." The citations include the book's series and the year of publication; often included is a note on the cover artist, the cover price, and the pagination. The section concludes with the following disturbing statement: "There are also various German editions, mostly from Ullstein Verlag in the 1970's and 1980's that collect Chandler stories under titles usually not used in the English language editions. These I've omitted as some combine stories from different collections and only serve to complicate matters bibliographically. Besides, as I don't know German it's impossible to decipher these editions."

Separate sections discuss paperbacks on and about Hammett and Chandler, collecting Hammett and Chandler in paperback, and collecting the foreign editions of their works. Lovisi includes significantly more listings of Chandler's paperback appearances than does Bruccoli, but this remains a discreditable bibliography.

903e. Widdicombe, Toby. **A Reader's Guide to Raymond Chandler.** Westport, Conn.: Greenwood, 2001. xix, 211 p. Index. LC 00-049058. ISBN 0-313-30767-9.

Widdicombe has provided a detailed guide to the prose fiction of Raymond Chandler. His volume begins with a detailed chronology and biography, following which the book is dominated by "Chandler's World," an alphabetical dictionary of all of the characters and places in Chandler's 7 novels and 25 short stories. Each work is summarized, and making this *Guide* especially useful are a series of insightful essays on a variety of subjects such as those titled "Chandler and Cars," "Chandler and Drink," "Chandler and Homosexuality," and "Chandler and Racism." The volume concludes with three appendixes: "Marlowe on Film, TV, and Radio" describes the way in which Chandler's detectives have been presented by the media; cast, credits, release dates, and a brief assessment of the work are given. "Chandler as Screenwriter" discusses the five films to which Chandler contributed between September 1944 and 1951 as well as his unproduced and incomplete work. "Appendix C" discusses other writers' versions of Chandler, provides a bibliography of Chandler's novels (citing first American and British publications), the first magazine and book appearances of Chandler's short stories, and a list of secondary materials. The volume concludes with a very good index.

There is much to praise about *A Reader's Guide to Raymond Chandler.* It is well written, insightful, thorough, and generally sympathetic toward its subject. At the same time, there are some odd omissions. First, the contents of short story collections published during Chandler's life are not listed, and readers curious about the contents of such works as *Five Sinister Characters* or *The Finger Man* will have to look elsewhere. Next, Widdicombe addresses only Chandler's published fiction, not his poetry, letters, or nonfiction, and although the first is ephemeral, the second is lively, acerbic, and witty, and the third includes what might be Chandler's most widely read work, "The Simple Art of Murder."

One looks forward to an expanded edition of the *Reader's Guide to Raymond Chandler.*

CHARTERIS, LESLIE: NAME CHANGE FROM LESLIE CHARLES BOWYER YIN

904a. Ahearn, Allen, and Patricia Ahearn. **Author Price Guides: Leslie Charteris.** Rockville, Md.: Quill & Brush, 1993. 10 leaves. APG 135.

This Author's Price Guide lists the publications of Leslie Charteris from the 1927 *X Esquire* to the 1983 collection *The Saint: Five Complete Novels.*
For a more thorough description of the format of Author Price Guides, see the entry under Fredric Brown.

904b. Alexandersson, Jan, and Iwan Hedman. **Leslie Charteris och Helgonet under 5 Decennier en Bio-Bibliographi.** DAST Dossier, no. 2. Stockholm, Sweden: Strängnäs, 1973. 124 p. Paperback. Index. ISBN 91-85208-01-9.

A reading knowledge of Swedish is not necessary to appreciate this bio-bibliography of Leslie Charteris. Following a brief biography of Charteris, a lengthy seven-column bibliography lists the English, American, and Swedish editions of Charteris's publications. Each citation is numbered, followed by the publication date in reverse order (i.e., 2 February 1929 is listed as 29.03.02). The following column lists the title of Charteris's work; short stories are listed in regular type, whereas book titles are in capital letters. The first appearance of a work is underlined. Retitlings are indicated in this column, as are media adaptations. Successive columns list the publisher's or magazine's name in highly abbreviated form, the nature of the work, its pagination (given only for books), and the price (also given only for books). Publications through 1971 are covered, although one 1972 publication is listed.

The following section provides significantly greater bibliographic data on the first editions of Charteris's English-language and Swedish books. Each citation is separately numbered and cross-referenced to the bibliography in the first section. Arrangement is chronological. There are two columns: the left describes the first English-language edition, and the right describes the first Swedish edition. Each citation lists the book's title in underlined capital letters. The publisher of the first edition is given, as are the place of publication, year of publication, printer, book's size, the number of chapters in the book, pagination, a description of the binding, price, and dedication.

The third section provides publication data on Charteris's short fiction. Each citation is separately numbered and cross-referenced to the bibliography in the first section. The publication date is given in the same format as the first section; the title is underlined, and the place of publication is given. Magazine titles are listed in regular type, whereas book titles are in capital letters. A list at the conclusion of this section provides retitlings and original titles for Charteris's short fiction.

The fourth section lists Charteris's Swedish publications. As before, citations are arranged chronologically, separately numbered, and cross-referenced to the bibliography in the first section. The Swedish title is given followed by the original English title, and the publication data lists magazine titles in regular type and capitalizes the names of book titles.

A fifth section selectively lists Charteris's nonfiction, and lengthy lists of the cast and credits of motion picture and television adaptations follow. Included are the names of the actors and actresses and the characters they portray, the production company, producer, distributor, distribution company, director, author of the screenplay, camera operator, music director, running time, and name of the work by Charteris from which the work is adapted. A well-done index concludes the book.

Although dated, this work is superior to the effort by W. O. G. Lofts and Derek Adley (q.v.), but fans of the Saint will be more satisfied with Burl Barer's 1993 *The Saint* (q.v.).

904c.   Barer, Burl. **The Saint: A Complete History in Print, Radio, Film and Television of Leslie Charteris's Robin Hood of Modern Crime, Simon Templar, 1928–1992.** Jefferson, N.C.: McFarland, 1993. xii, 419 p. Index. LC 92-53509. ISBN 0-89950-723-9.

Like the bio-bibliography compiled by Lofts and Adley (q.v.), the first part of this book describes Leslie Charteris's life and career. The bibliography is contained in seven appendixes: (I) *The Saint* Radio Script Synopses; (II) Episode and Players Guide to *The Saint,* starring Roger Moore; (III) *Return of The Saint* Script Synopses and Credits; (IV) "Mystery Wheel of Adventure" Press Releases and Feature Stories; (V) the Saint's Automotive Icon; (VI) Chronology of *The Saint* Writings; and (VII) The Saint Club. In the case of the radio scripts, each script is numbered by the week in which it aired, with air dates, and (in most cases) the name of the writer. Although the actors playing the Saint are identified at the beginning of the appendix, the casts are not given. Gimmicks are revealed, although not the names of the villains.

The episodes of *The Saint* starring Roger Moore provide the episodes' original promotional "log lines," written by ITC for newspaper listings, the production numbers; the acting credits for principal actors and actresses; and the opening lines spoken by the Saint. The section concludes with a lengthy list of the actors and actresses from the Roger Moore series and the episodes of *The Saint* in which they appeared. This list is not keyed to the production numbers, necessitating use of the index.

The synopses in *The Return of the Saint,* 24 television films that starred Ian Ogilvy, are longer than those in the previous sections, provide lengthy lists of casts and credits, and are listed in the order in which they were sold for syndication.

The material surveying "The Mystery Wheel of Adventure," six television films that starred Simon Dutton as Simon Templar, were drawn largely from the promotional material released by one of the co-producers, DLT Entertainment Limited. The annotations are lengthy but do not provide separate lists of casts and credits.

The appendix devoted to the Saint's automobile provides its history in its various incarnations, from the 5,000-pound Hirondel of the early novels to the Volvo P1800 used by Roger Moore to the white Jaguar XJ-S piloted by Ian Ogilvy.

The "Chronology of *The Saint* Writings" contains three sections. The first section lists original publication information for all short stories and novels. The second section provides publication histories on the books about the Saint and also is arranged chronologically. The book data in these sections provides the title in italics, publisher, and month and year of publication. The short story information lists the title in quotation marks, the publishing periodical in italics, and gives the date of publication and (when relevant) the original title. Contents of short story collections are given. Data on Charteris's numerous collaborators and ghostwriters are provided in each entry. The third section is devoted to the French printing of Charteris's books, several of which were not published in English. Citations are listed chronologically and follow the same format as described previously. However, they give the original (English) title when one exists and include series number, date of the French copyright, and contents of short story collections.

The volume concludes with information on contacting the fan club devoted to the Saint and a well-done index. The bibliography of Charteris's writings leaves a bit to be desired, but the book is up-to-date and reasonably comprehensive. Nevertheless, Charteris wrote about more than the Saint, and this bibliography does not list these works.

904d.   Bodenheimer, Daniel. **The Saint and Leslie Charteris: A Collection.** [Santa Cruz, Calif.?]: [University of California, Santa Cruz?], 1993. 4 vols. OCLC 28155273.

Although this work is unobtainable in its entirety, photocopies indicate that this is a bibliography of commendable complexity and comprehensiveness. "The Saint Books" lists in boldface the titles and retitlings of Charteris's works, and elaborate publication data are provided beneath each title, including the publisher of the first English and American editions, publishers of serializations and condensations, and publishers of retitlings and paperback editions. The contents of collections are given, as are the authors of the ghostwritten volumes; all citations are separately numbered. Paginations, however, do not appear to be provided.

904e. Lofts, W. O. G., and Derek Adley. **The Saint and Leslie Charteris.** London: Hutchinson Library Services, 1971. 134 p. ISBN 0-09-304800-9.

The first half of this book (pages 11–67) consists of biographical data on Charteris and appreciations of Charteris's writings. The bibliography begins with a list of "Leslie Charteris in Book Form." This chronologically arranged list provides the book's title in italics, publisher, and year of publication; data are current as of 1969. Entries in "Leslie Charteris in Book Form" are cross-referenced to a section titled "The Books of Leslie Charteris," but before this section is reached, two sections intervene. A section titled "The Saint's Travels" lists chronologically the novels featuring the Saint and provides setting and year of publication; an asterisk indicates whether the story was adopted for television. In the chronologically arranged section titled "The Saint Films," titles are listed in italics, followed by issuing studio, film's director, length, time, and major cast.

Entries in "The Books of Leslie Charteris" are arranged alphabetically. Each entry provides the book's title in italics, followed by the publisher's name, the location of the copyright date (e.g., dated reverse to the title page), and the copyright date. A brief physical description is given (e.g., *Cr. 8vo* for *crown octavo*), as are the pagination and the color of the cover. The dedication is reprinted, and the rest of each citation indicates serialization and reprint data; these are linked to the bibliography's concluding section, "Stories by Leslie Charteris Appearing in Magazines and Newspapers." First sentences are provided for all separately published sections; alternate titles and retitlings are also given.

"Leslie Charteris Stories Included in Collections of Short Stories" gives publication data for two titles. It is followed by "Books about The Saint by Other Authors," which contains data (in the form of the citations in "The Books of Leslie Charteris") on three titles.

"Stories by Leslie Charteris Appearing in Magazines and Newspapers" is arranged by the title of the publication, beneath which, listed chronologically, are the title of the story, first sentence, and successive reprintings, also listed chronologically. Cross-references indicate when the story received book publication.

Although compiled with the assistance of Charteris, this bibliography is virtually impossible to use and lacks that most basic of bibliographical necessities, an index to titles. Choose Andersson and Hedman and Barer (q.q.v.) for superior treatments of a similar subject.

904f. Mechele, Tony, and Dick Fiddy. **The Saint.** London: Boxtree, 1989. 176 p. Index. Paperback. ISBN 1-85283-259-2.

This bibliography contains separate chapters on the Saint's adventures in and on radio, film, television, and comic books. Also included is a chronological list of Charteris's books. Place of publication, publisher, and date of publication are indicated, as are retitlings and reissuings. Most chapters begin with a prose history of the Saint in that medium and contain numerous stills.

The section devoted to radio lists broadcasting station, actors and actresses, director, script writers, producer, adaptor of Charteris's stories, title of the play, date on which it was first broadcast, and a brief annotation that is probably superior to the original broadcast. One would be hard put to improve upon "The Saint crosses swords with a mad scientist and his giant ant."

The sections on the Saint in the visual media list the year of release and the title of the production in a grey box; entries for motion pictures also include the issuing studio. Each entry lists cast, screenplay writers, director, and producer. Annotations range from 250 to 500 words and include the running time and the book or story upon which the adventure was based.

The chapter on the comic book adaptations of the Saint contains virtually no data and consists primarily of reproductions of the covers of the U.S. and British versions. Those interested in the thespians who appeared in the various adaptations of the Saint will find the index dismal, for it indexes only the material in the prose histories. Completists interested in the media versions of the Saint will find similar annotations and better indexing—but far fewer illustrations—in Burl Barer's *The Saint* (q.v.).

CHESTERTON, G. K.; I.E., GILBERT KEITH

905a.   Chesterton, G. K. **The Mask of Midas, with a Father Brown Bibliography by John Peterson.** Edited and with a preface by Geir Hasnes. Illustrated by Noralf Husby. Trondheim, Norway: Classica Forlag AS, 1991. 62 p. ISBN 82-7610-000-7 (leather edition); 82-7610-001-5 (standard edition). 1,000 copies printed.

The first half of *The Mask of Midas* consists of the first publication of a previously unpublished Father Brown story; Hasne's introduction provides its complex history. The latter half of the volume is a three-part bibliography listing Chesterton's Father Brown stories, Chesterton's writings on crime and mystery fiction and Father Brown, and a secondary bibliography of studies of Father Brown and Chesterton's crime and mystery fiction.

The first section lists the Father Brown stories in chronological order. Each citation is numbered and lists the story title in boldface; its first publication date is given, as is the name of the periodical in which it was first published. Entries indicate in which Chesterton collections the story was published and whether it was retitled for book publication.

The second section is alphabetical by the title of the article, printed in boldface type. Names of the periodicals and books are given in italics. Periodical publication data include the page on which the article appeared; book publication data include the place of publication, publisher, date of publication, and page on which the article appeared. Reprints and retitlings also are indicated.

The third section of the bibliography is alphabetical by author and references books, chapters in books, articles, and miscellaneous materials. It includes a number of references that are not listed in either of Sullivan's three volumes of Chesterton bibliography (q.v.) or the standard indexes to literary criticism.

Although *The Mask of Midas* is difficult to obtain, it repays the effort, for the material is well presented, accurate, and helpful. Serious scholars of Chesterton's mystery fiction will wish to examine it, and fans of Chesterton's Father Brown will rejoice in the volume's first part.

905b. Sullivan, John. **G. K. Chesterton: A Bibliography, with an Essay, on Books, by G. K. Chesterton.** Epitaph by Walter de la Mare. London: University of London Press, 1958. 208 p. Also: New York: Barnes & Noble, 1958.

Only a small percentage of G. K. Chesterton's enormous output was mystery and detective stories, but that percentage remains historically significant and justifies the inclusion of these bibliographies.

The first volume of Johnson's comprehensive Chesterton bibliography contains eight sections: (A) books and pamphlets by Chesterton; (B) contributions to books and pamphlets; (C) contributions to periodicals; (D) books and periodicals containing illustrations by Chesterton; (E) books and articles about Chesterton; (F) collections and selections; (G) translations into foreign languages; and (H) a G. K. C. miscellany. Except in the cases of sections C and G, the entries in each section are chronologically arranged and separately numbered. In section C, the entries are alphabetically ordered by periodical title and then listed chronologically beneath each title. In section G, the entries are alphabetically ordered by the language into which they were translated, then listed chronologically. The 954 citations are continuously numbered and are current as of 1957.

The citations in section A provide a full description of the first English editions of all works by Chesterton and of his works published in the United States that contained material not in the English editions. The title page of each work is transcribed in the quasi-facsimile method, a collation statement is provided, the contents are given, illustrations are detailed, the binding is described, and dust jackets or wrappers are described. The first publication date is given, as is the date of the copy held in the British Museum, and notes indicate the source of original publication (if any). Later editions are referenced if their contents are different.

The citations in sections B through G are equally thorough, although paginations are not provided for the secondary materials listed in section E, and section G does not always provide the translated titles. A thorough index concludes the volume.

905c. Sullivan, John. **Chesterton Continued: A Bibliographical Supplement, Together with Some Uncollected Prose and Verse by G. K. Chesterton.** London: University of London Press, 1968. xiv, 120 p. Index. LC 72-370814. ISBN 0-340-09457-5.

The second volume of Johnson's G. K. Chesterton bibliography uses the same arrangement as the first for its citations, and its citations are numbered and keyed to the entries in the first volume. It corrects errors and expands upon the data presented in the first volume and continues its documentation of material by and about Chesterton. Section 7 is lengthy, bespeaking international interest in and awareness of the writings of Chesterton. Entries are current as of 1966.

905d. Sullivan, John. **Chesterton Three: A Bibliographical Postscript.** Bedford, England: Vintage Publications, 1980. 46 p. Paperback.

Reprinted from articles appearing in the *Chesterton Review,* this slim volume corrects and updates the data published in Sullivan's 1958 and 1968 bibliographies of Chesterton (q.q.v.). The notes follow the arrangement and numbering system introduced in the previous two volumes. The section containing the most citations is 7, which lists the translations into foreign languages of books by G. K. Chesterton. The data in all sections are complete as of 1978. Owners of the first two volumes of Sullivan's Chesterton bibliography will want *Chesterton Three,* but it does not stand on its own.

CHRISTIE, [DAME] AGATHA; I.E., AGATHA MARY CLARISSA MILLER CHRISTIE MALLOWAN

906a. Ahearn, Allen, and Patricia Ahearn. **Author Price Guides: Agatha Christie.** Rockville, Md.: Quill and Brush, 1995. 14 leaves. APG 082.2.

This Author's Price Guide to Agatha Christie documents her work from the 1920 publication of *The Mysterious Affair at Styles* to the 1991 publication of *Problems at Pollensa Bay*.

For a thorough description of the format of Author Price Guides, see the entry under Fredric Brown.

906b. Bunson, Matthew. **The Complete Christie: An Agatha Christie Encyclopedia.** New York: Pocket Books, 2000. viii, 454 p. LC 00-42793. ISBN 0-7434-0785-7 (hc); 0-671-02831-6 (pb).

Although it strives for encyclopedic comprehensiveness, *The Complete Christie* has an unusual and occasionally frustrating arrangement, for it is not a unified volume akin to Dawn Sova's *Agatha Christie A to Z* (q.v.). Instead, Bunson's volume contains different sections, each discussing a facet of Christie's life and accomplishments. The volume begins with relatively brief sections providing a biography of Christie and an alphabetical list of Christie's writings that contains separate sections for novels and story collections and short stories. Much lengthier sections are devoted to an alphabetically arranged description of all of the writings: publication data are provided, as are a plot summary and descriptions of the characters and the works in which they appeared. A separate section, arranged alphabetically, provides information about the adaptations of Christie's work for motion pictures, television, and the stage, including also biographical information on 10 thespians who excelled in productions of Christie's works and providing information about the motion pictures loosely based on Christie's life. Appendixes list Christie's detectives and the novels and short stories in which they appeared and provide chronological lists of the motion picture, television, and dramatic adaptations. The volume also contains a number of photographs and concludes with a lengthy bibliography.

The Complete Christie contains much, but it is also a frustrating work. A unified presentation of the data would have been better, for the present arrangement hampers access to the material. Furthermore, those looking for bibliographic comprehensiveness will find Bunson's data only sporadically offer information about first periodical publication—and often these data are incomplete—and concentrate instead on first book appearances. Similarly, those looking for information on Christie's writings as "Mary Westmacott" will find it only by accident, for there is no separate entry for Westmacott, and those seeking information on important people in Christie's life—Eden Philpotts, for example—will find nothing whatsoever. Finally, the majority of the photographs is not adequately captioned.

As with Sova's work, one hopes for an expanded and revised second edition.

906c. Campbell, Mark. **Agatha Christie.** Foreword by Simon Brett. Harpenden, Herts, England: Pocket Essentials, 2001; North Pomfret, Vt.: Trafalgar Square, 2001. 96 p. Paperback. ISBN 1-903047-77-3.

Although published without fanfare and apparently ignored by reviewers because of its small size, *Agatha Christie* offers a first-rate introduction to its subject and should not be overlooked. Following Simon Brett's brief foreword, the volume contains 19 sections: a rationale for the volume titled "The Puppet Master"; a biography; a chronologically arranged checklist of Christie's separately published works that is current as of 1997 and that indicates whether the volume was written by Christie or "Mary Westmacott," which series detective it features, and whether it is a novel or a short story collection; descriptions of the books by detective, with separate chapters for Hercule Poirot, Jane Marple, Tommy and Tuppence Beresford, Mr. Parker Pyne, and Mr. Harley Quin; miscellaneous thrillers, mysteries, and collaborative mysteries; supernatural works, romances, poems and children's stories, memoirs, stage plays, radio plays, and adaptations for various media. Concluding the volume is an annotated bibliography of reference material about Christie that includes Internet resources.

When relevant, each section begins with a description of how many of Christie's novels and short stories used that detective or theme. The detectives are described, as are the other series characters. The individual works are discussed in chronological order, with "case" describing the work, "context" providing a brief history of its composition or publication, and "conclusion" appraising the work's success and ranking it on a scale of 1 to 5. The descriptions of the stage plays, radio plays, and adaptations provide the premiere date or the first broadcast date, the cast, crew, observations, and a "verdict" ranking the success of the work.

Campbell presents his subject clearly and with understanding and verve, and *The Pocket Essential* is a fine work, showing that great things can come in small packages.

906d. Fitzgibbon, Russell H. **The Agatha Christie Companion.** Bowling Green, Ohio: Bowling Green State University Popular Press, 1980. ix, 178 p. LC 78-61075. ISBN 0-8792-137-5 (hc); 0-8792-138-3 (pb).

Despite its title, this is not a companion to the works of Agatha Christie in the way that the books with similar titles by Saunders and Lovallo and Riley and McAllister are (q.q.v.). The first half of the book contains essays in which Fitzgibbon discusses the history of the detective story, Christie's life and accomplishments, and her detectives.

The second half of the book begins with a lengthy bibliography of Christie's work. Only the first British publications are included, and the emphasis and arrangement concentrates on Christie's detective and mystery stories. Each citation is separately numbered. Bibliographic information includes the title (in italics), place of publication, publisher, and year of publication for each known edition. Contents of short story collections are listed; title changes are noted.

The next section provides a comprehensive list of all detective and mystery book and short story titles. Entries in italics refer to books; entries in roman type refer to short stories. All entries are keyed to the imprint of first publication listed in the previous bibliography.

A list of alternate Christie book titles follows, after which a grid lists the contents of Christie's short story collections. Collections of short stories are listed chronologically from left to right at the top of the grid, with each keyed to its entry in the bibliography. Story titles are listed at the left side of each page; in parentheses following each title are the initials of what Fitzgibbon describes as Christie's "central detective." An *X* indicates whether the story appeared in the collection listed at the top of the page.

A selective but lengthy list of Christie's characters concludes the book. Each character's function is defined, and his or her appearance is keyed to the bibliography. The lists do not include the appearances of Christie's detectives.

This contains nothing that cannot be found elsewhere.

906e.   Haining, Peter. **Agatha Christie: Murder in Four Acts. A Centenary Celebration of "The Queen of Crime" on Stage, Film, Radio, and Television.** London: Virgin Books, 1990. 159 p. GB 90-24438. ISBN 1-85227-273-2.

Although occasionally described as a reference book, this heavily illustrated work is an amiable prose survey of Christie's works that have been adapted for the stage, film, radio, and television. Separate chapters survey the works that appeared in each medium and describe 10 actors who have played Hercule Poirot, 6 actresses who have played Miss Jane Marple, and 4 couples who have played Tuppence and Tommy Beresford. The volume contains no lists, no documentation, and is unindexed, effectively preventing researchers from using it.

906f.   Hart, Anne. **The Life and Times of Hercule Poirot: Agatha Christie's Poirot.** London: Pavilion Books, 1990. 263 p. ISBN 1-85145-400-4.

906g.   Hart, Anne. **The Life and Times of Hercule Poirot.** New York: Putnam, 1990. 286 p. LC 89-39051. ISBN 0-3-9913848-4-0.

906h.   Hart, Anne. **The Life and Times of Miss Jane Marple.** New York: Dodd, Mead, 1985. x, 161 p. LC 85-12946. ISBN 0-396-0874-8-5.

It may reasonably be argued that these volumes are not reference books, but they nevertheless deserve a brief mention here. Each volume is a biography, offering the characters' life story from their earliest appearance to their last days. The sometimes inconsistent details provided in Christie's works are reconciled, lists of cases and media adaptations are given, secondary characters are discussed, and the curious reader reaches a greater understanding of the character as well as a greater awareness of Christie's remarkable accomplishments. Both volumes are lively reading, enjoyable, and affectionate toward their subjects in a way that many biographies are not. Alas, neither volume is indexed.

906i.   Morselt, Ben. **An A to Z of the Novels and Short Stories of Agatha Christie.** Hertfordshire, England: Phoenix Publishing, 1985. 255 p. Indexes. LC 86-16678. ISBN 0-9465-7649-1 (hc); 0-9465-7643-2 (pb).

Morselt provides plot summaries for Christie's work, with separate chronologically arranged sections for summarizing the 66 novels and 143 short stories. Virtually no bibliographical data are provided. Entries in both sections list the work's title in boldface capital letters, provide a summary of rarely more than one page, and conclude with an entry number and the year of publication. An occasional section titled "Remarks" lists alternative titles and title changes without indicating preferences.

Following the summaries, a section titled "Whodunits" provides the names of Christie's criminals (when such exist), keyed to the entries in the first two sections. The book contains numerical and alphabetical lists of all of the works summarized, a list of Christie's short story collections whose contents are keyed to the numerical lists (but whose titles are not revealed), and numerical lists of the works in which Miss Jane

Marple, Hercule Poirot, Tommy and Tuppence, Parker Pyne, Colonel Race, and Super-intendent Battle appear as characters.

Lacking in significant detail (Poirot's nonexistent brother Achille surely merits mention but is accorded none), by no means free from typos (*N or M?* is cited as *N of M?*), poorly arranged, and occasionally missing the point of the story (Morselt fails at providing a solution to *The Murder on the Orient Express*), this is a work only completists will want.

906j.   Riley, Dick, and Pam McAllister, eds. **The Bedside, Bathtub & Armchair Companion to Agatha Christie.** Introduction by Julian Symons. New York: Frederick Ungar, 1979. xviii, 330 p. Index. LC 79-4822. ISBN 0-8044-5971-3 (hc); 0-8044-6733-1 (pb).

906k.   Riley, Dick, and Pam McAllister, eds. **The New Bedside, Bathtub & Arm-chair Companion to Agatha Christie.** Foreword by Julian Symons. Additional material edited by Pam McAllister and Bruce Cassiday. New York: Ungar Pub-lishing, 1986. xviii, 362 p. Index. LC 86-6960. ISBN 0-8044-5803-0 (hc); 0-8044-6725-0 (pb).

The expanded and revised second edition is described.

This heavily illustrated and highly frustrating guide provides signed synopses of every Christie novel and original play and many of the short stories, occasionally in con-junction with Christie's comments from her autobiographical writings. The arrangement is chronological by British book publication date. Each entry is prefaced with symbols indicating whether the work is a novel, play, or short story collection, and whether it fea-tures Hercule Poirot, Jane Marple, Ariadne Oliver, and Tuppence and Tommy Beresford. The entries provide the book's year of publication and a lengthy summary in which situations, characters, and motivations are described, but the solution is left unrevealed. Retitlings also are indicated.

If the *Companion* had contained only synopses, the book would be usable, though by no means as comprehensive as Saunders and Lovallo's work on the same subject (q.v.), but making this work unique are several dozen original essays on Christie-related topics. Murder weapons and victims are described; the history of the British po-lice is expounded; motion picture adaptations are detailed; and English dishes are listed. A map shows key crime locations in Christie's fiction set in southern England, and in-cluded are crossword puzzles and double-crostics featuring the names of Christie's char-acters. Bruce Cassiday describes being murdered at an Agatha Christie weekend; descriptions of the events in the Detective Club that led to Christie contributing to "round robin" novels are provided; and the filming of *Agatha*, the movie, is discussed.

Most of this material is unfortunately inaccessible, for the essays are in no dis-cernible order. Summaries of *Death in the Air* and *The A.B. C. Murders* are interrupted by an appreciation of the movie version of *Murder on the Orient Express* and a "word-find" using the names of Christie's characters. Similarly, between the summaries of *N or M?* and *The Body in the Library* are a lengthy essay on Christie's writings as Mary Westmacott and a discussion of the history of the title and the motion picture adap-tations of the work now known as *And Then There Were None*.

The volume concludes with lists of Christie on video, Christie editions in print, Christie's books arranged by detective, Christie's plays and short story collections, and a title index. (And interrupting these is a verse about Agatha Christie.) Devout fans and desperate researchers may want to use the *Bedside, Bathtub, and Armchair Companion,* but its value as a reference work is unfortunately low, and it contains little that is not better presented elsewhere.

906l. Ryan, Richard T. **Agatha Christie Trivia.** Boston: Quinlan Press, 1987. Reprint: New York: Bell Publishing Company, 1990. 185 p. Paperback. LC 89-18165. ISBN 0-517-69917-6.

Although sometimes listed as a reference book, this collection of trivia questions about Christie's writings has no research value. Its 12 sections each contain two parts; the first asks the questions, the second provides the answers. The book is superior to Andy East's *Agatha Christie Quizbook* (New York: Drake Publishers, 1975) in that there are more multiple-choice questions, but it contains no lists, no index, and nothing to benefit the student or researcher.

906m. Saunders, Dennis, and Len Lovallo. **The Agatha Christie Companion: The Complete Guide to Agatha Christie's Life and Work.** New York: Delacorte, 1984. xxvii, 523 p. Index. LC 83-5167. ISBN 0-38529285-6.

906n. Saunders, Dennis, and Len Lovallo. **The Agatha Christie Companion: The Complete Guide to Agatha Christie's Life and Work.** Rev. ed. New York: Berkley Books, 1989. xxviii, 498 p. Paperback. Index. LC 89-218325. ISBN 0-425-11845-2.

With thorough descriptions and evaluations of virtually all of Christie's prose, as well as equally thorough descriptions and evaluations of the dramatic adaptations of those works, *The Agatha Christie Companion* is one of the most comprehensive guides to Agatha Christie's works currently available.

Following a biographical sketch of Christie, the first section of the *Companion* contains a chronologically arranged list of Christie's books. Each book is accorded a separate chapter and given a number that reflects its publication order. The first British title is then listed, followed by any additional titles the book might have been given. The contents of each chapter describe the role the book occupied in Christie's career and the circumstances surrounding its composition and reception. Poems and songs that inspired Christie are quoted at length, as are numerous contemporary reviews. A separate section describes the plot of the book, providing situations without revealing solutions; another section lists the names of the characters who play a role in the work. Data on the first English and American editions are provided, each entry listing the place of publication, publisher's name, year of publication, pagination, retitling (if any), and original cost. Each book's entry concludes with a section listing the dramatic adaptations of the work; cast and credits are not provided, but enough details are to locate the adaptation in the *Companion*'s second section, which provides data on the stage, motion picture, and television adaptations of Christie's works. Each medium is treated separately, but all entries provide the year in which the work first was performed, the circumstances behind the adaptation, contemporary reviews, and the casts of the first British and American performances. Numerical cross-references are provided, linking the title of the work to the description given in the first section of the *Companion*.

The third section of the *Companion* contains lists: alphabetical lists of Christie's books and short stories and lists of books and short stories featuring Hercule Poirot, Jane Marple, Tommy and Tuppence Beresford, Mrs. Ariadne Oliver, Captain Arthur

Hastings, Chief Inspector James Japp, Superintendent Battle, Colonel Johnny Race, Mr. Parker Pyne, and Mr. Harley Quin. A select bibliography and a Christie chronology follow. The *Companion* concludes with an excellent index to the names and works.

The *Companion* is generally an exemplary achievement, but it is not without a few typographical errors. For some reason, it omits discussion of the work Christie wrote as a member of the Detection Club. More seriously, Sanders and Lovallo occasionally express critical judgments that are undeservedly harsh, assigning to the author sentiments that are expressed by her characters. In their discussion of *Cards on the Table,* for example, they assume that certain references to a "damned dago" are expressions of Christie's attitudes and state, "It is not unusual while reading the early Christie novels to come across some racial and ethnic slurs. Christie was a product of her times, reflecting the middle- and upper-middle class English attitude towards foreigners."

These objections aside, the *Companion* is a superb achievement.

906o. Sova, Dawn B. **Agatha Christie A to Z: The Essential Reference to Her Life and Writings.** Foreword by David Suchet. Introduction by Mathew Prichard. New York: Facts on File, 1996. xv, 400 p. Index. LC 95-48326. ISBN 0-8160-3018-9.

A volume that unfortunately delivers less than its title promises, *Agatha Christie A to Z* contains more than 2,500 encyclopedic entries, a majority of which consists of descriptions of Christie's characters and the works in which they appear. In addition, included are entries for significant people in Christie's life, a description of the facts known of Christie's disappearance in 1926, chapter-by-chapter synopses of all her mystery novels, summaries of all her stories, and references to the stage, screen, and television adaptations of Christie's works. Furthermore, a number of illustrations are provided, and the volume includes a separate list of Christie's works, a chronological list of the works, a bibliography of suggested readings, a "categorical appendix" that lists the works by their detective(s) and by their murder method(s). An excellent index concludes the volume.

Agatha Christie A to Z is a work with significant flaws, and it is especially weak in providing adequate bibliographical data; the list of Christie's works is merely an alphabetically arranged hodgepodge whose purpose here is pointless. Similarly, only minimal first-edition information is provided for the books, original publication data are not provided for the short stories, and retitlings are inadequately indicated. Only through careful reading of the entry for *And Then There Were None* can one learn Christie's original title, for Sova does not even include a cross-reference from Christie's original title. The references to the stage, screen, and television adaptations provide neither casts nor credits, and the entries provide none of the data routinely given by Saunders and Lovallo in *The Agatha Christie Companion* (q.v.). Finally, Sova's prose occasionally leaves something to be desired. She states that "The Blue Geranium" appeared "under the title, *The Tuesday Club Murders*, by Dodd, Mead and Company in New York," but this is simply not so; it was merely one story in the collection.

One hopes for an expanded and corrected second edition.

906p. Toye, Randall. **The Agatha Christie Who's Who.** New York: Holt, Rinehart and Winston, 1980. 264 p. Indexes. LC 80-14148. ISBN 0-03-057588-5.

Undoubtedly a labor of love, this most enjoyable guide provides biographical and identifying data on more than 2,000 of the memorable and significant characters created by Agatha Christie in her 66 novels and 147 short stories. Toye's delightful introduction explains that his initial catalogue contained over 7,000 listings, but that he pared them down, eliminating "such miscellaneous characters as cousins and aunts, postmistresses and innkeepers, and chauffeurs and cooks." Toye thus refrained from citing Jane Marple's "village parallels," the people "who have experienced situations similar to the one Miss Marple is currently investigating and who indirectly help her find the solution to the problem," but he has cited the victims "who have died before the action of the story begins and who, though they do not actually appear, are important to the plot and therefore warrant an entry."

The names of the characters are in boldface and are listed alphabetically by surname, followed by their first name. Nicknames are cited in parentheses, and if the character was also known by another name, an "also known as" note (AKA) and a cross-reference are provided. The function and identifying features of the character are then provided, and each entry concludes with the name of the work in which the character appeared, the exception being Christie's most famous series characters. The works in which Arthur Hastings, Jane Marple, Ariadne Oliver, and Hercule Poirot appeared are listed in Appendix A.

The book concludes with a chronological listing of Christie's mystery novels and short stories. Differences between British and American titles are indicated, and the stories in collections not published in the United States are cross-referenced to their subsequent appearances in U.S. collections. A separate index provides a title index to the bibliography, and Appendix B lists the works by Agatha Christie—her plays, her romantic novels as Mary Westmacott, her autobiographies, and her children's work—that have not been indexed.

In all, this is an exemplary work, enlivened by a number of illustrations and by Toye's obvious affection for his subject. Jon Breen's comment, "There is at least one glaring omission: there is no entry on Mr. Parker Pyne, just a 'see' reference to a criminal who once disguised himself as Pyne" (*What About Murder*, p. 137), is in error: Parker Pyne's entry is to be found under "Parker Pyne, Christopher."

906q. Underwood, Lynn, ed. **Agatha Christie: Official Centenary Edition, 1890–1990.** England: Belgrave Publishing for Agatha Christie Centenary Trust. 1990. 98 p. Paperback. LC 90-51017. ISBN 0-006-37675-4. Also: New York: HarperCollins, 1990. 98 p. Paperback. ISBN 0-06-100126-0.

Not a reference book, this glossy, heavily illustrated work deserves to be mentioned for several reasons. It contains a chronological list of Christie's novels and short story collections; a complete list of Christie's plays that includes details of directors, casts, and premiere dates; a complete list of Christie's films that includes details about the directors and stars; and information about Christie's characters. Although this information is engagingly presented, none of this information is unique to this volume. Nevertheless, a surprising depth is achieved through brief essays on the world in which Christie matured, examinations of Christie's notebooks that reveal the writer's mind at work, and an account of her only child Rosalind. Reprinted in this volume is "Trap for the Unwary," a short story previously published in 1923 in a short-lived periodical titled the *Novel,* and published for the first time is an article by Christie on her relationship with her paperback publisher Allen Lane. Although predictions of Christie's grandson end the book, the volume effectively concludes with the moving funeral speech delivered by Sir William Collins, Christie's publisher for 50 years.

906r. Wynne, Nancy Blue. **An Agatha Christie Chronology.** New York: Ace Books, 1976. 266 p. Paperback.

The first reference book devoted to Agatha Christie, the *Chronology* has obviously been assembled as a labor of love by a passionate devotee whose knowledge of the history of mystery and detective stories is minimal. The first page of the first entry states that "prior to 1920, the detective story was almost purely a short story form," revealing the author is ignorant of the presence of hundreds if not thousands of novels. Soon thereafter comes a comment that R. Austin Freeman "wrote only in the short story form," which will come as a surprise to those who love his many novels.

The first section of the *Chronology* consists of chronologically arranged appreciations of Christie's work, each book accorded a separate chapter. Titlings and retitlings are not consistently applied. Unpleasant though it is to modern sensibilities, there is no denying that one of Christie's finest novels was first titled *Ten Little Niggers,* and to list the book first as *And Then There Were None* is to evade bibliographic responsibility. Wynne's appreciations are virtually uniform in praise for Christie's work, are chatty and filled with exclamation points, and demonstrate no critical acumen. Worse, they occasionally reveal the gimmick or solution.

Following sections link Christie's short stories to their first book publication; list her short stories published in anthologies between 1928 and 1973; list all of her titles in chronological order; list the books in which Poirot, Marple, Tuppence and Tommy, Ariadne Oliver, and Superintendent Battle appear; list her nonmystery books, omnibus volumes, plays; and provide a bibliography of her works. The latter is arranged alphabetically and provides place of publication, publisher, year of publication, and pagination for all English-language hardcover editions known to exist; determining first edition and/or priorities is impossible. The *Chronology* concludes with a brief biography of Christie.

Dated and worthless to researchers.

COLLINS, WILKIE; I.E., WILLIAM WILKIE

907a. Andrew, R. V. **Wilkie Collins: A Critical Survey of His Prose Fiction with a Bibliography.** Fiction of Popular Culture. New York: Garland, 1979. 358 p. LC 78-60801. ISBN 0-8240-9667-3.

Sometimes cited as a reference book, this work began its life in 1959 as a thesis presented at the Potchefstroom University for C. H. E. in South Africa; the Garland edition is the offset typed thesis. The vast majority of the book is Andrew's observations about Collins, and the bibliography does not commence until page 338. The first part of the bibliography lists its citations alphabetically, the second chronologically. In both sections titles of books, short stories, and journals are given in capital letters, making locating a reference quite difficult; neither are paginations provided. Furthermore, Andrew's typing was not of the highest quality, and the bibliography contains a number of overstrikes. Although Andrew's work was once significant, the full-length bibliographies compiled by Beetz and Parrish and Miller (q.q.v.) are better.

907b. Beetz, Kirk H. **Wilkie Collins: An Annotated Bibliography, 1889–1976.** Scarecrow Author Bibliographies, no. 35. Metuchen, N.J.: Scarecrow, 1978. viii, 167 p. Index. LC 77-26609. ISBN 0-8108-1103-0.

Beetz's contribution to Collins studies begins with a capable 21-page bibliographical essay; each of its 82 paragraphs is numbered and separately indexed. The bibliography contains three sections, the first citing Collins's works; the second listing the criticism and scholarship about Collins; and the third, selective book reviews. Primary and secondary citations are continuously numbered; in all, 688 articles, books, chapters, dissertations, and selective book reviews are cited. Book citations are underlined and provide the place of publication, the publisher, the year of publication, the series, and the pagination. Citations to articles are generally by author, with the title of the article in quotations, the journal name underlined, and the volume, month, publication year, and pagination given; anonymous articles are listed under the journal's name. The volume concludes with separate indexes for authors, editors, illustrators, and subjects.

Although its contents are as thorough as can be reasonably hoped, the arrangement and layout of this book can be frustrating. The primary bibliography starts by listing different editions of Collins's collected works. This list is followed by an alphabetical list of the different editions of his novels and other book-length works, a list of his plays, a list of his short works and correspondence (with books devoted solely to Collins and works in collections not devoted solely to Collins separated), and lists of his collaborations with Charles Dickens. The arrangement of the secondary bibliography is even more cumbersome, with separate sections for books, periodical articles, and dissertations. The section for books arranges its citations into the following sections: biographical, bibliographical, assessments of Collins's life and works, discussions of individual works, influences on Collins, Collins's reputation and influence, correspondence (written by and to Collins), and other scholarship.

The primary bibliographies provided by M. L. Parrish and Elizabeth V. Miller in their *Wilkie Collins and Charles Reade: First Editions Described with Notes* (q.v.), as well as that of Michael Sadleir in his *Excursions in Victorian Bibliography* (London: Chaundy & Cox, 1922) and his *XIX Century Fiction: A Bibliographic Record Based on His Own Collection* (London: Constable; Berkeley: University of California Press, 1951), are significantly clearer than those provided by Beetz, and they have the added blessing of being chronologically arranged. Nevertheless, Beetz offers comprehensiveness in his citations, whereas Parrish and Miller and Sadleir do not. In addition, Beetz's secondary bibliography and annotations make this a useful acquisition. It is to be preferred to the work of R. V. Andrew (q.v.).

907c.   Gasson, Andrew. **Wilkie Collins: An Illustrated Guide.** Oxford and New York: Oxford University Press, 1998. xviii, 189 p. LC 98-216552. ISBN 0-19-866215-7.

Wilkie Collins: An Illustrated Guide does not limit itself to Collins's mystery and detective fiction writing and is, instead, an encyclopedic dictionary of Collins's life. Opening the volume are a chronological list of Collins's main works, including their first publisher, and a detailed chronology of Collins's life that concludes with the 1998 publication of *Ioláni*. The *Wilkie Collins* describes every one of Collins's works, including essays and plays. Also described are his family, friends, publishers, correspondents, dedicatees, and parodists. Included are entries discussing the periodicals to which Collins contributed accompanied by bibliographic data listing Collins's contributions, and entries describe Collins's illustrators, the actors and actresses who had roles in his plays, his clubs, vacation homes, walking tours, and banks. Accompanying these entries—which number in the thousands—are more than 200 striking black-and-white images, and five appendixes are provided: a reproduction of a page of the manuscript of *After Dark;* an alphabetical list of the characters in Collins's novels which also provides the character's role; the Collins family tree; a map of Marylebone indicating Collins's residences; and a select bibliography.

Gasson is cofounder and chairman of the Wilkie Collins Society, and his knowledge of his subject is formidable, albeit conveyed with grace and skill. *Wilkie Collins* belongs in all libraries in which there is any interest in Collins and the world he inhabited.

907d. Parrish, M. L., with the assistance of Elizabeth V. Miller. **Wilkie Collins and Charles Reade: First Editions (with a Few Exceptions) in the Library of Dormy House, Pine Valley, New Jersey.** London: Constable, 1940. x, 355 p. Index. LC 41-19254. 150 copies printed. Reprinted as **Wilkie Collins and Charles Reade: First Editions Described with Notes.** New York: Burt Franklin, 1968. x, 355 p. Index. LC 68-4143.

The first 161 pages of this well-done bibliography describe Collins's writings with exemplary thoroughness, the majority of the citations being derived from the Wilkie Collins collection privately held in Dormy House, New Jersey. The citations in the bibliography are not numbered, but this in no way impedes its usefulness.

The bibliography is divided into four lettered sections, the first of which provides Collins's biography; it reprints several letters by Collins that contain extensive biographical data. The bibliography is a chronological list of all separately published first English-language editions in the collection. Each entry provides an exhaustive analytical bibliographical description of these books, transcribing their title pages, noting the number of volumes, the size of their paper, and giving the books' collation, pagination, contents, illustrations, binding, publication, and printing. Variant editions are noted, and a section called "notes" provides additional information about the publication histories and contents of the books. Letters inlaid in these books are transcribed in full, and reproductions of title pages are provided in several instances.

The third section is titled "Errata in Works of Wilkie Collins" and contains lengthy lists of all of the typographical errors in the editions described in the first section. The concluding section is titled "Posters and Programmes of the Plays of Wilkie Collins" and describes the posters and theater programs that advertised Collins's dramatic works. Reproductions of several of these posters and programs are provided.

A very thorough index concludes the volume. Although somewhat dated, this remains the most thorough monographic Collins bibliography extant.

CORNWELL, PATRICIA DANIELS

908. Beahm, George. **The Unofficial Patricia Cornwell Companion.** New York: St. Martin's Minotaur, 2002. xvii, 300 p. Index. Paperback. LC 2002-069834. ISBN 0-312-30732-2.

Beahm, who has previously assembled companions to Michael Jordan, Stephen King, and Anne Rice, states forthrightly in his introduction that "much of what is in this book is common knowledge, collected for the first time under one set of covers." The *Companion* contains three sections, the first of which concentrates on Cornwell's life. A chronology is provided, as are descriptions of her life before the 1990 publication of *Postmortem,* her college days and days as a reporter, an "a to z" of her life, excerpts from Cornwell's interviews, and an interview with Cornwell reprinted from *Deadly Women* (q.v.).

The second section, "The Fiction," offers a largely chronological look at Cornwell's monographs. Basic publication data for each work are provided, as are its approximate value, the dedication (and the story behind it), the setting, a descriptive summary, excerpts from reviews, and an alphabetical list of the characters, settings, and major plot devices. It should be mentioned that this section also includes discussion of Cornwell's 1983 (revised, 1997) biography of her friend and inspiration Ruth Bell Graham, wife of evangelist Billy Graham.

The third section is the briefest, describing Cornwell's forthcoming projects, after which there are three lengthy appendixes: "A Technical Key to the World of Kay Scarpetta," "Scarpetta's Home Turf: Virginia," and "A Guide to Collecting Patricia Cornwell." The first describes the world of the forensic detective; the second, Virginia settings in the Scarpetta novels; and the third offers book-collecting tips and minimal bibliographic data that repeat the values listed earlier. The volume concludes with an elaborate index.

Researchers hoping to learn about Cornwell will find nothing substantial in this calculatedly lightweight guide.

CRUMLEY, JAMES

909.   Ahearn, Allen, and Patricia Ahearn. **Author Price Guides: James Crumley.** Rockville, Md.: Quill & Brush, 1995. 3 leaves. APG 023.3.

This Author's Price Guide to James Crumley documents his work from the 1969 appearance of *One to Count Cadence* to the 1995 publication of *The Mexican Tree Duck*.

For a thorough description of the format of Author Price Guides, see the entry under Fredric Brown.

CUMBERLAND, MARTEN

910.   Sargeant, William A. S. **A Policeman in Post-War Paris: The Saturnin Dax Novels of Marten Cumberland.** CADS Supplement, no. 8. South Benfleet, Essex, England: CADS, 2000. 42 p. Paperback. ISSN 0965-6561.

This slim volume is arguably not a reference book, but it deserves mention as an engaging account of Saturnin Dax, the protagonist of 34 novels written by Marten Cumberland and published between 1940 and 1966. Paris—as presented in the novels—is described, as is Dax, along with his varied (and mouthwatering) diet, technical aids, abilities, and perceptions. The last two pages provide a chronological list of the Dax novels. The titles are given in boldface, followed by the place of publication, publisher, and publication date of the first English edition; when the work received an American edition, it also is cited.

CUMMINGS, RAYMOND KING

911.   Utter, Virgil, and Gordon Benson Jr. **Raymond King Cummings: Explorer of the Infinite. A Working Bibliography.** Galactic Central Bibliographies for the Avid Reader, vol. 50. Leeds, West Yorkshire, England: Galactic Central Publications, 1999. ix, 85 p. Paperback. ISBN 1-871133-53-X.

Raymond King Cummings—who wrote as Ray Cummings and used a variety of pseudonyms—often is, and with some justification, dismissed as one of the more egregious hacks working for the pulp magazines. When he is remembered, it is for his science fiction—one of his novels opened by defining *time* as what prevents everything from happening at once, a definition that has moved into popular culture—but as Utter and Benson's bibliography shows, Cummings wrote far more mystery and detective fiction than he did science fiction. Cummings routinely published stories in magazines as varied as *Black Book Detective Magazine, Crack Detective Stories, Detective Fiction Weekly, Detective Tales, Dime Mystery Magazine, Flynn's, Popular Detective, Private Detective Stories, Thrilling Detective,* and *Thrilling Mystery.*

The introduction to this volume states that it contains the following 18 sections: (0) Awards and Pseudonyms; (1) "Prose Fiction"; (2) "Prose Fiction Books"; (3) "Series"; (4) "Poetry and Drama"; (5) "Poetry and Drama Books"; (6) "Articles"; (7) "Miscellaneous"; (8) "Non-fiction Books"; (9) "Edited Books"; (10) "Other Media"; (11) "Articles on the Author"; (12) "Reviews"; (13) "Books about the Author"; (14) "Phantom and Forthcoming Titles"; (15) "Related Items by Other Authors"; (16) "Textual Variations"; and (17) "Chronological Listing of Fiction." Several of these sections contain no material.

The contents of the first three sections are alphabetically arranged, each citation being separately lettered and numbered. In the first section, beneath each story's title are the places in which it has seen print. Book titles are capitalized and often accompanied by the names of the editors. Journal titles are given in regular type and the original publication date is given in abbreviated form (i.e., 5-40 for May 1940), as is the pseudonym under which it appeared, if any. An abbreviation indicates whether the piece is a short-short story or vignette, short story, novelette, novella, short novel, or novel. Cross-references are provided for retitlings and alternative titles. The titles for Cummings's books are given in capital letters. All known English editions are cited, and each citation lists publisher, series number, pagination, original price, and cover artist. If a translation is cited, the translated title is given as is the name of the translator.

Less needs to be said about the other sections, whose titles indicate their contents; sections 4, 5, 8, 9, and 15 are empty.

This is the only substantial work on Cummings, and although it is doubtful he will ever be rediscovered or receive critical adulation, the bibliography remains as comprehensive as can be hoped.

DEIGHTON, LEN; I.E., LEONARD CYRIL

912a. Milward-Oliver, Edward. **Len Deighton: An Annotated Bibliography 1954–1985.** With a foreword by Julian Symons. Maidstone, Kent: Sammler Press, 1985. 64 p. ISBN 0-948368-00-4.

This slim bibliography surveys Deighton's output for the first 31 years of his career. Following an introduction, Symons's foreword, a brief biography, and an interview with Deighton, the volume contains a chronological list of British and American first editions, then separate lists of Deighton's fiction, nonfiction, miscellaneous work, articles, and screenplays. The chronological list gives the month in which the book was published, and the genre lists provide the significant information about the first edition of the book: publisher, publication place, date of publication, cost, size, pagination, word count, dust wrapper and designer, binding, print run, proof copies, and first serialization.

Because all but two of Deighton's novels and two of his nonfiction works were first published in England, greater attention is consistently paid to the British editions.

Collectors interested in Deighton's early works will welcome the detail provided by this volume, but it contains fewer overall data than the lists given in such reference books as *The St. James Guide to Crime and Mystery Writers*.

912b. Milward-Oliver, Edward. **The Len Deighton Companion.** London: Grafton Books, 1987. 332 p. ISBN 0-246-13231-0.

The Len Deighton Companion is an enjoyable labor of love, an encyclopedic description of all of the plots and characters in Len Deighton's work, from the 1954 publication of "Abroad in London," first published in *Ark,* the journal of London's Royal College of Art, to the 1987 appearance of *Winter.* The volume opens with a key to abbreviations and acronyms, then provides an interview with Deighton and a 25-year chronology of British and American first editions of Deighton's work; a portion of the interview was first published in Milward-Oliver's *Len Deighton: An Annotated Bibliography* (q.v.), as was the chronology. The annotations in the *Companion* are informative, helpful, and enjoyable, although no cross-references are provided and the volume contains no index. (This is deliberate: Milward-Oliver's brief preface notes reasonably enough that "there's no index, since the whole book is one vast index.") Particularly useful are thematic annotations that discuss subjects such as Deighton's abandoned novels and Deighton's use of subjects as diverse as computers, cover names, cryptonyms, laundered money, masers, music, railway stations, spy satellites, trains, underwater sequences, warfare, and zeppelins.

The volume concludes with two useful appendixes: an alphabetical list of themes explored and a register of characters by nationality, and a primary and secondary bibliography. The section for *Q* in the companion consists of a 50-question quiz; the answers are given in the penultimate section of the conclusion, and the volume closes with a brief bibliography.

DENT, LESTER

913a. Cannaday, Marilyn. **Bigger than Life: The Creator of Doc Savage.** Bowling Green, Ohio: Bowling Green State University Popular Press, 1990. 201 p. Index. LC 89-085739. ISBN 0-87972-471-4 (hc); 0-87972-472-2 (pb).

913b. McCarey-Laird, M. Martin. **Lester Dent: The Man, His Craft and His Market.** West Des Moines, Iowa: Hidalgo Publishing Company, 1994. 104 p. Paperback. Index. LC 94-076268. ISBN 0-961004-9-5.

913c. Weinberg, Robert, ed. **Lester Dent: The Man behind Doc Savage.** Cover Title: **The Man behind Doc Savage: A Tribute to Lester Dent.** Oak Lawn, Ill.: Robert Weinberg, 1974. 127 p. Paperback.

Lester Dent wrote the majority of the 181 *Doc Savage* novels, a number of lively mysteries, and numerous short stories published in pulp magazines ranging from *Argosy* and *Black Mask* to *Nation's Business* and the *Saturday Evening Post*. It is thus surprising that, as of this writing, no comprehensive and separately published bibliography of his writings exists. The three books discussed here are among the most widely accessible studies of Dent, but others exist, in particular a series of booklets written by Will Murray and published by Odyssey Publications of Massachusetts.

Marilyn Cannaday's biography of Dent is a lengthy and affectionate tribute. It contains illustrations, although these tend to be of Dent and his relations, and it reprints "The Pulp Paper Master Fiction Plot" (also in Weinberg) and an article by Dent ("Wave Those Tags") first published in the 1940 *Writer's Digest Yearbook*. Particularly useful is a partial checklist of Dent's published fiction. Arranged chronologically, it lists the title of the work and the place of publication. Titles of stories appearing in *Doc Savage* are capitalized. On the debit side, it is not without error: Dent did not write boys' series books for Grossett and Dunlop under the name John Baine. Furthermore, Cannaday's discussion of Dent's "Oscar Sail" stories is surprisingly (and perhaps uncomfortably) reminiscent of the discussion by Robert Sampson first published in *Lester Dent: The Man behind Doc Savage*.

Lester Dent: The Man, His Craft and His Market began its life as a 1979 master's thesis written by Margaret Gwinn at Northeast Missouri State University in Kirksville. It was revised for publication, but the revisions did not redress numerous factual errors, and McCarey-Laird's writing is distressingly poor. Dent's vital personality occasionally reveals itself through quoted interviews, letters, and articles, but he would have been hard put to praise this amateurish effort.

Lester Dent: The Man behind Doc Savage is reproduced from typed copy and is heavily illustrated with black-and-white reproductions of the covers of magazines in which Dent appeared. It contains eight chapters of criticism: three by Will Murray discuss aspects of Doc Savage; three by Robert Sampson discuss Dent's writings apart from Doc Savage; one by Robert Weinberg provides a biographical profile of Dent; and one by Philip Josè Farmer provides an account of Farmer's *Doc Savage: His Apocalyptic Life*. Also, chapters reprint Dent's formula for plotting ("The Pulp Paper Master Fiction Plot") and two of Dent's lesser-known short stories. Although riddled with typos and unfortunately amateurish in appearance, the work is not without its uses, for its contents are valuable and not readily accessible elsewhere.

DERLETH, AUGUST [WILLIAM]

914a. Boulden, Daniel J.-P. **Pocket Price Guide to August W. Derleth.** Greensboro, N.C.: Daniel J-P Boulden, 2000. Unpaged. Paper.

Boulden lists Derleth's monographic and edited publications in chronological order. Beneath each title he lists the publisher of the first edition, its year of publication, and the high and low prices for the book. Boulden's bibliographic data leave much to be desired—he does not distinguish between Derleth's work and those works edited by him, he confuses place of publication with the publisher for several of Derleth's titles—and the way in which the low and high prices were derived is never revealed. The guide contains a prose preface and a conclusion that are riddled with typographical errors. This was certainly a labor of love, but it is only for completists.

914b. Derleth, August. **August Derleth: Twenty Years of Writing, 1926–1946.** Sauk City, Wisc.: Arkham House, 1946. 20 p. Paperback.

914c. Derleth, August. **August Derleth: Twenty-Five Years of Writing, 1926–1951.** 2nd ed. Sauk City, Wisc.: Arkham House, 1951. 24 p. Paperback.

914d.   Derleth, August. **August Derleth: Thirty Years of Writing, 1926–1956.** 3rd ed. Sauk City, Wisc.: Arkham House, 1956. 30 p. Paperback.

914e.   Derleth, August. **100 Books by August Derleth.** [4th ed.] Foreword by Donald Wandrei. Sauk City, Wisc.: Arkham House, 1962. 121 p. LC 63-4567. 1,225 copies: 200 hardbound, 1,025 paperbound.

During his lifetime, Derleth was noted as a regionalist writer and acclaimed for his mysteries and weird fiction. Today his mysteries are all but forgotten, and he is remembered for his posthumous collaborations with H. P. Lovecraft and for establishing Arkham House, the oldest and finest specialty publisher of weird fiction, in 1939. Because the first three versions of this bibliography were never advertised for sale but were given gratis to the regular customers of Derleth's Arkham House, it is debatable whether they were formally published; in any event, they have not been seen. There is no doubt, however, that the fourth edition was formally published; indeed, the 200 hardbound copies were intended primarily for the library market.

Following a foreword by Donald Wandrei (cofounder of Arkham House and a talented writer in his own right), *100 Books by August Derleth* contains the following sections: "Biographical" (autobiographical as well as excerpts from reference books); "Bibliographical" (a listing of the titles of the publications that have published Derleth's short stories, essays, reviews, poetry, and miscellaneous prose since 1 April 1926); "A Checklist of Published Books" (a chronological listing of 102 of Derleth's cloth or board-bound volumes, with the exception of hardcover reprints); "Awaiting Publication" (14 books); "Work in Progress" (9 books); "Summary" (Derleth's books listed by series [e.g., the Judge Peck mysteries] and broad subject [e.g., "Books for younger readers"]); "Recordings" (2 recordings are cited; the contents of one are given); "Compilations" (lists of the works compiled by Derleth or which have Derleth introductions or both); "Anthologies/Textbooks" (citations to the anthologies and textbooks that have published Derleth's short stories, poems, and miscellaneous prose); "Publications" (a list of the Arkham House books that have not been cited in the preceding sections of this bibliography); "Films" (the titles of 15 of Derleth's short stories that were adapted for television); "Lectures" (titles of the 9 subjects upon which Derleth delivered occasional lectures); "Appraisals" (excerpts from the favorable criticism of notable writers); "From the Reviews" (excerpts from the favorable reviews); "Self-Appraisal" (Derleth's list of his 10 best works). A reproduction of a diploma from "Miskatonic University" concludes the publication.

The "Checklist of Published Books" occupies the majority of this bibliography and contains the fullest data. Each citation is numbered. The titles are given in capital letters and provide publisher, place, and year of publication, pagination, and initial cost. Title changes are indicated, as are the names of illustrators and dust wrapper designers and data on international editions known to Derleth. The contents of Derleth-edited anthologies also are given, an invaluable list. Oddly enough, Derleth neglected to number his original paperback appearances, and such works as Derleth's *Some Notes on H. P. Lovecraft* (Sauk City, Wisc.: Arkham House, 1959) appear in their chronological sequence but without being counted. (A more accurate title for this publication would be *105 Books by August Derleth*.)

The other sections contain far less data and, more often than not, are mere lists of titles, arousing curiosity without satisfying it. The section titled "Bibliographical," for example, lists only the title of the publication in which Derleth's work appeared, not the publication data for Derleth's appearance, and it is prefaced with a headnote that speaks of "the byline of August Derleth or one of his pen names." The pen names, however, are given nowhere.

Lacking a title index, incomplete (Derleth continued producing virtually until his death in 1971), and reminiscent of a vanity publication, *100 Books by August Derleth* is nevertheless more than the product of an oversized ego. Derleth's remarkable achievements and versatility make him a significant figure in several distinct areas, and that he was not a trained bibliographer in no way invalidates his importance and the importance of this work.

Note: 100 Books by August Derleth was also reprinted in 1974 by E. V. A. Publishers of Sauk City, Wisconsin (LC 74-162941), but this is a facsimile of the 1962 edition and contains no new data.

914f.   Dutch, William, James P. Roberts, George A. Vanderburgh, Alison M. Wilson, Joseph Wrzos. **August Derleth (1909–1971): A Bibliographical Checklist of His Works.** Shelburne, Ontario, Canada: Battered Silicon Dispatch Box/George A. Vanderburgh, 1996. 76 p. Index. Paperback. LC 96-86124. ISBN 1-896648-14-2.

The cover of this book has as its subtitle "A Selective Checklist of His Books and Assorted Commentary by Many Hands," an assessment of the book's contents more accurate than that found on the title page, for this is not intended to serve as a comprehensive bibliography of Derleth's works. It contains the following sections: "An Autobiography" by August Derleth; "August Derleth: Storyteller of the Sac Prairie" by Norbert Blei; "A Bibliographical Checklist of the Books of August Derleth"; "Addenda: Derleth Bibliography" by Alison M. Wilson; "About August Derleth: The Writings about the Writings"; "The August Derleth Society Newsletters"; and "August Derleth Society Newsletters [New Series]." In addition, included are two appendixes: "Abbreviations for the Solar Pons Canon" by Peter Ruber, Ronald B. De Waal, and George A. Vanderburg, and "August Derleth: The Writings by Genre." An index to titles is provided.

Derleth's autobiography was written in 1961. Norbert Blei's chatty account was originally published in the 15 August 1971 issue of the *Chicago Tribune Sunday Magazine,* and the chronologically arranged "Bibliographical Checklist" cites the books written by and edited by Derleth. Titles are listed in italicized boldface type, and the place of publication, publisher, and year of publication are provided for all known editions. Data are current into 1997, and each citation concludes with a one- or two-word description of the book's contents. Alison Wilson's addendum to her bibliography (q.v.) is alphabetical in arrangement and provides reprint data for more than 100 of Derleth's writings. Each citation provides the title in boldface type, gives its original publication, and lists beneath it the sources in which the reprint appeared. Book titles are given in italics; editors' names are listed, and the publisher, place of publication, and year of publication are given. The titles of periodicals also are italicized, and the month and year of publication are given.

"The Writings about the Writings" cites 11 books about Derleth; articles are not listed. The sections devoted to the different series of the August Derleth Society's *Newsletter* consist of an issue-by-issue listing of the contents of the 65 issues published to date (52 issues in the first series, 13 issues in the new series).

Researchers interested in Derleth and the areas in which he worked and published will want this publication, but it is an item for specialists.

914g. Wilson, Alison M. **August Derleth: A Bibliography.** Scarecrow Author Bibliographies, no. 59. Metuchen, N.J.: Scarecrow, 1983. xxvi, 229 p. Index. LC 82-24020. ISBN 0-8108-1606-7.

Wilson conceived of this bibliography while writing an entry on Derleth for Gale's *Dictionary of Literary Biography* and initially planned to annotate all of Derleth's published work. The size of Derleth's published output made her reconsider her goal, but she has nevertheless annotated virtually everything cited in this volume. After providing an introduction and a chronology to Derleth, Wilson divides his output into two broad sections: "The Fantasy World: Mystery, Science Fiction, and Horror"; and "Sac Prairie and the Real World." Each of these sections is in turn subdivided. The first contains the following sections: "Short Stories," "Anthologies of Derleth's Own Work," " 'Posthumous Collaborations' with H. P. Lovecraft," "Collaboration with Mark Schorer," "Collaborations: Books," "The Pontine Canon," "Judge Peck," "Miscellaneous Mysteries," "Books Edited by Derleth;" and "Derleth Introductions." The contents of "Sac Prairie and the Real World" are "Sac Prairie Saga: Short Stories," "Sac Prairie Saga: Collections," "Sac Prairie Saga: Novels," "Sac Prairie Saga: Miscellaneous Prose," "Sac Prairie Saga: Steve-Sim Juvenile Mysteries," "Wisconsin Saga," "Other Juvenile Literature," "Poetry," "Nonfiction: Books," "Nonfiction: Articles, Reviews, Introductions," and "Representative Published Letters." An index to titles concludes the bibliography.

Despite the plethora of sections, the 736 citations are numbered consecutively, but additional problems are caused by the individual arrangement of each section. Wilson has arranged her entries alphabetically rather than chronologically, and chronological lists are nowhere given. Derleth wrote 10 Judge Peck novels, but the first citation is to the last one, and it is up to the reader to put the works into the order in which they appeared. This problem is exacerbated in the sections devoted to Derleth's mainstream fiction.

Apart from the arrangement of the work, the contents are accurate but occasionally lacking in necessary data. Entries for short stories have the title of the story in quotations, an annotation, and the publication. Periodical titles are underlined, and the volume and numbering are given, as are the month, year, and pagination. When the story was anthologized in one of Derleth's own works, the book's title is given in capital letters and the story's pagination is listed. When a story was reprinted elsewhere, the book's title is given in roman type and underlined, and the publisher, date and place of publication, and pagination are given. Retitlings are noted. Citations for books underline the book's title, and (on a separate line) provide the publisher and the date and place of publication. Each citation is annotated and concludes with citations to the major reviews. Reprints and title changes are noted, and the contents of Derleth's collections and collaborations are listed. The contents of the Derleth-edited anthologies are not listed, and paginations for novels, collections, collaborations, and anthologies are nowhere provided.

Researchers interested in Derleth will get a better sense of Derleth's achievements from his own publications (q.v.), but Wilson's bibliography provides a foundation upon which scholars can build. A comprehensive and accessible Derleth bibliography nevertheless remains to be done.

For the curious: Wilson's biographical article appeared in *American Novelists, 1910–1945* (Dictionary of Literary Biography, vol. 9), ed. by James J. Martine (Detroit: Gale Research Co., 1981). A supplement appears in Dutch (profiled earlier).

DICKENS, CHARLES [JOHN HUFFAM]

915a.   Cox, Don Richard. **Charles Dickens's "The Mystery of Edwin Drood": An Annotated Bibliography.** AMS Studies in the Nineteenth Century, no. 19. New York: AMS Press, 1998. xxxvi, 669 p. LC 97-36302. ISBN 0-404-61497-3. ISSN 0196-657X.

With more than 1,900 citations, Cox's *Annotated Bibliography* is the lengthiest work on its subject to date, longer and more current than the bibliography compiled by E. F. Bleiler that was published in Walter Albert's *Mystery and Detective Fiction* (q.v.).

Cox's citations are divided into three broad groupings: those that offer commentary on textual issues, the studies and secondary materials discussing the work, and biographies and bibliographies. Each section is further divided. Part I has seven sections: manuscripts, letters, original materials; textual issues, illustrations, editing problems; related writings of Dickens; editions from 1870 to the present; dramatizations, films, television, radio, recordings; commentaries upon dramatizations; continuations, conclusions, sequels, and alternate versions. Part II has six sections: contemporary reactions, reviews, announcements; appreciations, topographical studies, ephemera; literary criticism and analysis, 1871–1939; literary criticism and analysis, 1940–1997; possible sources and influences, background information, works influenced by the novel; indices, guides, and encyclopedias. The third section has but two parts: biographical information and bibliographies.

Each section is arranged in alphabetical order by author (except for the list of editions from 1870 to the present). Entries are numbered continuously in boldface type. The author's last name is given, followed by the first or first initial. Citations to chapters provide the section (or chapter) in quotations, followed by the book's title in italics, the place of publication, publisher, year of publication, and relevant pagination. Citations to articles put the article title in capitals, followed by the italicized journal title, the volume, month and year, and pagination. The annotations are full and informative and contain numerous cross-references, and the volume concludes with an index that lists authors, characters, and themes.

Cox's preface estimates that he has listed and annotated at least 90 percent of the extant *Drood* commentary, "perhaps as much as 95% of this material." Bleiler's bibliography (profiled earlier) has been neglected and thus falls into the 5 percent extant. This aside, it is a monumental accomplishment, one that should be held by all research libraries.

915b.   Jacobson, Wendy S. **The Companion to "The Mystery of Edwin Drood."** Dickens Companions. London: Allen & Unwin, 1986. xvii, 209 p. Index. LC 85-22855. ISBN 0-04-800063-9.

Charles Dickens's *The Mystery of Edwin Drood* is probably the most famous unfinished work in the English language, and Jacobson's *Companion* deserves mention here because it explicates *The Mystery of Edwin Drood* in the same way that Jack Tracy's *Encyclopaedia Sherlockiana* or Christopher Redmond's *The Sherlock Holmes Handbook* (q.q.v.) explicate their sources.

Using as text the 1972 Clarendon Dickens edited by Margaret Cardwell, the *Companion* presents a chapter-by-chapter explication of the novel. (Jacobson also has consulted Dickens's manuscripts and has discovered a number of significant variants not mentioned by Cardwell.) As the general preface notes, each annotation identifies Dickens's "allusions to current events and intellectual and religious issues, and supplies information on topography, social customs, costume, furniture, transportation, and so on. Identifications are provided for allusions to plays, poems, songs, the Bible, the Book of Common Prayer, and other literary sources." Similarly, Dickens's illustrators are discussed, as are those texts that represent Dickens's experiences and those texts that directly influenced the works of other writers. An appendix discusses and annotates the "Sapsea Fragment." A lengthy bibliography and an index are included.

An encyclopedic format might have made many of Dickens's references more accessible, but *The Companion* can be used with no trouble. It will assist all readers not intimately versed in Victorian culture and Dickens's life and habits.

DOYLE, [SIR] ARTHUR CONAN

Scope note: More has been written about Arthur Conan Doyle's Sherlock Holmes than about any other detective. This section is highly selective in its contents, listing only a few of the many reference sources available. The entries have been chosen for their comprehensiveness, significance, provision of unique material, and probable availability in most libraries.

Primary Bibliographies

916a. Goldscheider, Gaby. **Conan Doyle Bibliography: A Bibliography of the Works of Sir Arthur Conan Doyle, M.D., LL.D. (1859–1930).** Windsor, England: Gaby Goldscheider, 1977. 40 p. Paperback.

Prior to Goldscheider's bibliography, the most comprehensive listing of the works of Sir Arthur Conan Doyle was H. Locke's *A Bibliographical Catalogue of the Writings of Sir Arthur Conan Doyle, 1879–1928* (Tunbridge Wells, England: D. Webster, 1928). Enterprising individuals such as Reece (q.v.) had updated Locke's effort, but it remained for Goldscheider to prepare a comprehensive catalogue of the writings of Doyle, incorporating the additions of the other bibliographers into the effort. Its contents: "The Works of the Master"; "Biographies and Critical Writings"; "Holmesiana"; and "What the Press Said." The entries in the first three sections are consecutively numbered; there are 1,158 citations.

The first section dominates the book and contains 1,063 citations. It is divided into three sections: Doyle's works, his contributions to the works of others, and his collected works. The entries in each section are arranged alphabetically by title; short story titles are in boldface type, book titles are in capitals. Beneath each, the citations provide the date (in boldface type) and list in chronological order the work's appearances. Citations to periodical publications are uniformly inadequate, only occasionally providing the month of the periodical and never providing the story's pagination. Citations to books are more thorough, providing the publisher, place and date of publication, illustrator, pagination, binding color, and paper size; the contents of books are not given.

The second and third sections primarily list monographs and are alphabetical by the author's name; the concluding section provides snippets of praise culled from contemporary reviews. Apart from the name of the periodical in which the review appeared, no bibliographic data are provided.

The more comprehensive bibliography of Green and Gibson (which follows) is preferable.

916b. Green, Richard Lancelyn, and John Michael Gibson. **A Bibliography of A. Conan Doyle.** Soho Bibliographies, XXIII. Foreword by Graham Greene. Oxford: Clarendon, 1983. xvi, 712 p. Indexes. LC 82-3541. ISBN 0-19-818190-6.

916c. Green, Richard Lancelyn, and John Michael Gibson. **A Bibliography of A. Conan Doyle.** Foreword by Graham Greene. Boston: Hudson House, 2000. New revised and expanded edition with addenda and corrigenda. xvi, 726 p. Indexes. ISBN 0-9677500-0-8.

The first edition of this volume was compiled with the intention of listing all of the works of Arthur Conan Doyle published in English during his lifetime. Translations are not listed, and citations to reprints are confined to listing the colonial, Canadian, American, and copyright editions that appeared during Doyle's life. The resulting bibliography was astoundingly thorough.

The bibliography is divided into five lettered sections, the first of which lists all known English, Canadian, American, and continental editions; copyright pamphlets; plays; belles lettres; poetry; collected editions; sets; and omnibus volumes. Each citation is numbered, and many are accompanied by an illustration of the cover of the first edition. Each entry provides an exhaustive analytical bibliographical description of the various editions of the book, starting with a transcription of the title page and followed by the book's collation and pagination and descriptions of its contents, typography, paper, binding, dust jacket, printing, and publication. The date of publication is given, as are the initial cost and data on the serialization of the text. A section titled "Notes" provides additional information about the composition of the book and comments on the texts. The last work cited in this section is *The Crowborough Edition,* a 24-volume set of 760 copies, published in 1930, that was intended to be a complete and definitive edition of Doyle's works; Doyle died before he could revise his texts, write new prefaces, and arrange the stories in a meaningful order.

Section B, "Miscellaneous Works," lists Doyle's histories, speeches, offprints, propaganda, autobiography, psychic books, pamphlets, and open letters. As in the first section, the bibliographical data are thorough: citations are numbered, and many are accompanied by an illustration reproducing the cover of the first edition. Entries provide exhaustive analytical bibliographical description of the various editions of the work, beginning with a transcription of the title page and followed by the book's collation, pagination, contents, typography, paper, binding, dust jacket, printing, and publication. The date of publication is given, as are the initial cost and data on the serialization of the text. As before, "Notes" contains additional information about the composition of the book and comments on the texts. The last citation in this section is to the 1963 *Strange Studies from Life,* a reprinting of three uncollected studies that first appeared in the *Strand Magazine* in 1901.

Section C, "Minor Contributions," documents Doyle's prefaces, forewords, collaborations, translations, and appearances in symposia; special anthologies of Doyle's work, a selective list of important anthologies, and ephemera also are cited. Although posthumous reprints are occasionally included (i.e., the 60-copy edition of "How Watson Learned the Trick" published in 1947), the majority of the citations is to materials published during Doyle's life.

Section D, "Periodical and Newspaper Contributions," lists Doyle's uncollected fiction and poetry and his miscellaneous fiction and poetry. It includes also a chronological list of Doyle's fiction with information on the first serial publication of each item, and it concludes with a section listing Doyle's miscellaneous writings: medical, photography, and travel articles; his published letters; contribution to symposia; and his translations.

Section E, "Biographical Sources," provides a lengthy but selective list of the important interviews, reports of speeches, biographical references, and articles on Doyle's life, work, and opinions that were published in newspapers and periodicals during Doyle's life. The section concludes with the 1978 publication of an article in *Blackwood's Magazine*. A special section lists the different editions of the book-length biographies of Doyle and the books and other publications of biographical, bibliographical, and critical interest.

An appendix contains publisher listings for Doyle's British, colonial, continental, Canadian, and American publications, including references to the "unauthorized and cheap American editions." In addition, included are references to a vocal score and Doyle's poetry set to music, information on Doyle's dramas (first performances, unpublished, and unfinished plays), misattributions to Doyle, the dedications of Doyle, bibliographies, checklists, and other material of bibliographical interest, and shorthand editions of Doyle's works. The index is thorough, referencing all books, periodicals, short stories, articles, and letters, and providing access by page and citation number.

The second edition is identical to the first except that it adds a section—"Addenda and Corrigenda"—following the index. This section uses the same arrangement as the first edition; the numbering of the citations matches those of the first editions. Bibliographic data are added and typos are corrected.

This bibliography belongs in all academic libraries.

916d. Lovisi, Gary. **Sherlock Holmes: The Great Detective in Paperback.** Introduction by John Bennett Shaw. Brooklyn, N.Y.: Gryphon Books, 1990. 151 p. Index. ISBN 0-936071-15-x (hc); 0-936071-14-1 (pb).

Reproduced from clearly typed copy, this extended bibliographic essay on the paperback editions of Sherlock Holmes had its origins in a booklet published in 1983 titled *Sherlock Holmes; Fifty Years of the Great Detective in Paperback* (New York: Fantasia Books). The present work begins with an appreciative essay by Baker Street Irregular John Bennett Shaw and contains the following unnumbered chapters: "Collecting Sherlockian Paperbacks"; "British and Other Foreign Paperbacks"; "Before the Mass-Market: Dime Novels and Proto Paperbacks"; "The Doyle Tales: The Official Books"; "The Doyle Tales: Publishers Compliations [*sic*]"; "Sherlock Holmes: The Pastiches and Others"; "Books Yet to Appear"; "The Solar Pons Series"; "Small Press Items"; "Specialty Items"; "Some Juvenile Paperbacks"; and "Afterword." Included are separate indexes to the works by Doyle and to those by other authors.

Lovisi's citations tend to provide the title of the work and list beneath it all known printings of all known paperback houses. Series numbers tend to be provided; so too are paginations and cover prices. Reproductions of numerous rare covers often are given, and often there are useful annotations differentiating between editions. On the debit side, misspellings are rife (*separate* is apparently consistently misspelled), and Lovisi's arrangement occasionally makes it difficult to locate specific references. A title index would be welcome.

916e. Redmond, Donald A. **Sherlock Holmes among the Pirates: Copyright and Conan Doyle in America 1890–1930.** Westport, Conn.: Greenwood, 1990. Contributions to the Study of World Literature, no 36. xviii, 286 p. Index. LC 89-27280. ISBN 0-313-27230-1. ISSN 0738-9345.

Not intended to be as comprehensive as the work of Green and Gibson (q.v.), this monograph contains two sections. The first provides a prose history of the appearances of Arthur Conan Doyle's earliest American editions, which (because of the absence of an international copyright law) were pirated by dozens of publishers. The second section is a publishing history of the different printings and editions of *A Study in Scarlet* and *The Sign of the Four* published between 1890 and 1930. The various plates from which the texts were printed are described, and successive publications from these plates are described in thorough bibliographical detail. The title page is transcribed: measurements, pagination, and signature markings are given; the bindings are described, with variants noted; and textual variations and individualities likewise are noted and described at length. Entries conclude by indicating whether the copy has been cited in the bibliographies of Green and Gibson or De Waal (q.v.). The book contains an appendix reprinting Jay Finley Christ's 1952 bibliographic study, "Sherlock Comes to America," and it concludes with tables listing the appearances of the different editions of *A Study in Scarlet* and *The Sign of the Four.*

Although intended for a very specialized audience, this nevertheless remains an exemplary textual bibliography and is also an excellent publishing history. It should be noted that in 1991 this book won the Crime Writers of Canada Arthur Ellis Award for Best Genre Criticism/Reference Book.

916f. Reece, Benny R. **A Bibliography of First Appearances of the Writings by A. Conan Doyle.** Greenville, S.C.: Furman University, 1975. 48 p. Paperback. LC 75-35398.

Reece's brief preface states that this bibliography is "necessarily an extension and correction of Harold Locke, *A Bibliographical Catalogue of the Writings of Sir Arthur Conan Doyle.*" The bibliography is reproduced from typescript—its cover reproduces handwriting—and is an alphabetical list of Doyle's works, from the magazine article "About Cricket" to the poem "Ypres." Citations to material published in journals frequently provide a statement as to the nature of the item (i.e., "chapter 6 of 'The Uncharted Coast' in serial form," "poem," "interview"); the journal title is underlined, and the volume, month, year, and pagination are given. Citations to books underline the book titles, provide first-edition publication data, pagination, and a table of contents. Illustrators are given for both journals and books, and cross-references are provided for such elements as title changes and to link a periodical publication to its later appearance in a book.

Although not a discreditable effort, Reece's *Bibliography* lacks indexes and has been superseded.

Secondary Bibliographies

916g.   De Waal, Ronald Burt. **The World Bibliography of Sherlock Holmes and Dr. Watson: A Classified and Annotated List of Materials Relating to Their Lives and Adventures.** New York: New York Graphic Society, 1974. xvi, 526 p. Indexes. LC 72-80900. ISBN 0-821204-20-3.

916h.   De Waal, Ronald Burt. **The International Sherlock Holmes: A Companion Volume to the World Bibliography of Sherlock Holmes and Dr. Watson.** Hamden, Conn.: Archon Books, 1980. 621 p. Indexes. LC 79-24533. ISBN 0-208-01777-1.

916i.   De Waal, Ronald Burt. **The Universal Sherlock Holmes.** Foreword by John Bennett Shaw. Edited by George A. Vanderburgh. Illustrated by Betty Wells and George Wells. Shelburne, Ontario, Canada: Metropolitan Toronto Reference Library, 1994–1995. 5 vols. Index. c93-095453-X. ISBN 1-896032-00-1 (Cerlox bound); 1-896032-01-X (not yet bound set). Volume 5 is titled: **The Indexes to "The Universal Sherlock Holmes."**

The first volume of this monumental set records every known publication of the Sacred Writings (i.e., the 56 short stories and four novels featuring Sherlock Holmes) and of the Apocrypha (works that do not feature Holmes but otherwise resemble the Sacred Writings), together with citations to the translations of these tales into 50 languages. In addition, all critical writings about Sherlock Holmes are cited, as are the films, musicals, plays, radio and television programs, recordings, parodies, pastiches, and miscellaneous usages of Holmes in popular culture (i.e., Christmas cards). Despite the enormity of this undertaking, the volume contains only 10 sections: (1) "The Sacred Writings"; (2) "The Apocrypha"; (3) "Manuscripts"; (4) "Foreign-Language Editions (Translations, English Readers, Parodies and Pastiches)"; (5) "The Writings About the Writings"; (6) "Sherlockians and the Societies"; (7) "Memorials and Mementos"; (8) "Games and Competitions"; (9) "Criticism"; and (10) "Parodies, Pastiches, Burlesques, Travesties, Satires." Each of these sections contains numerous subdivisions; in all, there are 6,221 citations to materials published between 1887 and 1971. De Waal's bibliographical data are gratifyingly thorough, and many of his citations are annotated. An appendix provides abbreviations, a directory of the collections used for compiling the volume, and contact information for Sherlock Holmes societies. Finally, separate indexes for names and titles are included.

The International Sherlock Holmes contains a list of Sherlockiana published between 1971 and 1979, as well as references to earlier publications that De Waal missed in his first volume. The section devoted to manuscripts has been dropped; sections 7 and 8 have been retitled as "Memorials and Memorabilia" and "Games, Puzzles, and Quizzes"; and lengthy sections devoted to actors, performances, and recordings and to cartoons, comic strips, and comic books have been added. In all, 6,135 citations are given; and as before, De Waal's bibliographic data are thorough, and many of his citations are annotated. A directory of Sherlock Holmes societies is provided, and the volume concludes with separate indexes for names and titles.

The Universal Sherlock Holmes was conceived as a four-volume work that cumulated the two preceding editions, added references to earlier publications that had been missed, and listed the materials published up through 7 January 1994. Despite its size, its arrangement is essentially similar to the earlier volumes; a section titled "The Literary Agent" has been added, and several sections have changed titles. Furthermore, the fourth volume contains a "selective concordance," a list of some 55,000 words that effectively indexes the keywords appearing in the set's 24,703 citations. As before, many of these citations are annotated.

The separately published fifth volume of *The Universal Sherlock Holmes* provides indexes to the names and titles appearing in the four volumes. Included are separate indexes for headings and classifications, pseudonyms, personal names, titles, thespians appearing in Sherlock Holmes adaptations, and the reviewers of the books and dramas. In addition, an index of the "imposters" of Holmes is provided. The volume concludes with conversion tables that permit the entries in *The World Bibliography of Sherlock Holmes* and *The International Bibliography of Sherlock Holmes* to be matched with the entries in *The Universal Sherlock Holmes*.

Superlatives do not do justice to this obsessively comprehensive labor of love. Sherlock Holmes is one of a very few literary figures to have achieved global recognition, and de Waal documents his every known appearance, in every known venue, with unparalleled thoroughness. *The Universal Sherlock Holmes* was produced in a very short print run, but it belongs in all academic libraries. One hopes that an electronic version becomes available.

Encyclopedias and Dictionaries

916j.   Bigelow, Sherburne Tupper. **An Irregular Anglo-American Glossary of More or Less Unfamiliar Words, Terms and Phrases in the Sherlock Holmes Saga.** Toronto: Castalotte & Zamba, 1959. 47 p. Spiral binding.

916k.   Bigelow, Sherburne Tupper. **An Irregular Anglo-American Glossary of More or Less Unfamiliar Words, Terms and Phrases in the Sherlock Holmes Saga.** 2nd ed. with additional writings by the author. Revised and extended by Donald A. Redmond and Peter Calamai. Shelburne, Ontario, Canada: Battered Silicon Dispatch Box, 1998. 130 p. C 94-932617. ISBN 0-896032-31-1 (hc); 0-896032-30-3 (pb).

The first edition has not been seen; its bibliographic data are taken from De Waal (q.v.).

The majority of this brief but most enjoyable dictionary is ably described by the "irregular" in its title: it is an arbitrary selection of the words, terms, and phrases that contemporary readers of Doyle might find unfamiliar. The definitions are brief and reasonable, often combining a dry wit with information, as in this definition of the problematic swamp adder: "The Writings Upon the Writings are abundant in their treatment of this reptile and its possible identity. This deponent knoweth not."

Following the glossary are essays upon matters Sherlockian written by Bigelow (1901–1993), an early and ardent member of the Baker Street Irregulars, and a brief account of Bigelow by George A. Vanderburgh, the owner of the Battered Silicon Dispatch Box. Readers of De Waal will know that additional writings by Bigelow remain uncollected.

916l. Bullard, Scott R., and Michael Leo Collins. **Who's Who in Sherlock Holmes.** New York: Taplinger, 1980. 251 p. LC 79-66638. ISBN 0-8008-8281-4 (hc); 0-8008-8281-4 (pb).

Who's Who in Sherlock Holmes has references to places and significant objects in the short stories and novels and contains significantly more than its title implies. The entries begin with "Abbas Parva" and conclude with a reference to a Signor Zamba from "The Adventure of the Red Circle." In all, approximately 1,600 definitions are given, all keyed to the two volumes of Baring-Gould's *The Annotated Sherlock Holmes*. No illustrations are included, and media adaptations are not discussed.

As a reference work, *Who's Who in Sherlock Holmes* is inferior. Bullard and Collins's definitions are frequently self-referential and utterly useless. For example, the definition for "Crimean War" states in its entirety that "the ill-fated *Gloria Scott* left England from Falmouth, bound for Australia with her cargo of criminals, at the height of the Crimean War," forcing those who would know anything of the Crimean War to look elsewhere. Internal cross-references are not provided, and definitions are often oddly placed (the references to the hotels Cosmopolitan, Dulong, Escurial, and National are listed under "H" with no corresponding entries under their respective letters of the alphabet) or are missing: no entries are included for the stories (indeed, no separate list of the works is ever given) or for such significant creatures as "swamp adder."

The encyclopedic works of Tracy and Bunson (q.q.v.) are superior.

916m. Bunson, Matthew E. **Encyclopedia Sherlockiana: An A-to-Z Guide to the World of the Great Detective.** New York: Macmillan, 1994. xxi, 326 p. LC 94-10714. ISBN 0-671-79826-X.

The *Encyclopedia Sherlockiana* contains approximately 1,500 articles and more than 100 illustrations relating to the life, achievements, and world in which the Sherlock Holmes stories take place. The book begins with "A Chronology of Sherlockiana," which chronicles events in the lives of Holmes and Watson; lists the works in "The Canon"; and presents the results of a 1927 poll by the *Strand Magazine* in which readers and Doyle answered the question, "Which Sherlock Holmes stories are the best?" This is followed by the a list of the "Unchronicled Cases of the Canon," which provides the names of cases referenced but not described in the texts.

The *Encyclopedia*'s entries begin with "Abbas Parva" (a small village in Berkshire mentioned in "The Adventure of the Veiled Lodger") and conclude with a reference to "Zucco, George," who acted in some of the early motion pictures. Significant characters, places, and incidents are described; all of the stories and a number of the notable pastiches are summarized; notable actors and actresses who have played in adaptations of the works are profiled; the appearances of Holmes on screen and television are listed; and aliases, codes, and disguises used by Holmes are given. Included are entries for subjects as varied as "Dog-Cart" and "Dogs of the Canon," for the titles of the books carried by Holmes while he was disguised as an old bibliophile in "The Adventure of the Empty House," and for people who figured notably in Doyle's life (i.e., George Edalji).

The *Encyclopedia* concludes with a list of the writings of Holmes, the names of the noted artists who portrayed Holmes in the early publications and the works for which their illustrations were made, a lengthy list of Sherlock Holmes in film, and an even lengthier list of the names and addresses of more than 300 of the Sherlock Holmes societies around the world. A biographical account of Doyle reproduces his bookplate, but (somewhat surprisingly) the book nowhere contains a picture of Doyle.

One can always complain about depth and balance in a work such as this—is there a need for so many references to actors and actresses when the fine pastiches of John Dickson Carr and Adrian Conan Doyle are mentioned but in passing? when cross-references are not always adequate?—but the *Encyclopedia Sherlockiana* is enjoyable and generally useful.

916n. Park, Orlando. **Sherlock Holmes, Esq., and John H. Watson, M.D.: An Encyclopaedia of Their Affairs.** Evanston, Ill.: Northwestern University Press, 1962. viii, 205 p. LC 62-17805. Reprinted as: **The Sherlock Holmes Encyclopedia [A Complete Guide to the People, Towns, Streets, Estates, Railway Stations, Objects—in Fact, Everything].** New York: Carol Publishing, 1994. 205 p. LC 93-42779. ISBN 0-8065-0764-0.

The oldest of the Sherlock Holmes encyclopedias considered here, this is also the weakest. It is unillustrated, and its approximately 2,000 entries are unexceptional and frequently contain less information than the corresponding entries in the other volumes. Like Bullard and Collins's *Who's Who in Sherlock Holmes* and Matthew E. Bunson's *Encyclopedia Sherlockiana* (q.q.v.), Park begins his entries with "Abbas Parva," but although Park correctly cites the significance of the place, he provides no explanation of meaning. Similarly, although Park concludes his entries with "Zoo," his definition mentions only the story in which the word was used; Jack Tracy's *Encyclopaedia Sherlockiana* (q.v.) gives a significantly superior definition, citing not only the story but also the Zoological Gardens in Regent's Park in London.

Park provides no separate list of the stories and no chronologies, fails to comment upon such animals as "swamp adder," and provides cross-references at the end of each article that are meaningless unless one has internalized the full title of the story. For example, *vampire* refers to "The Adventure of the Sussex Vampire," which is listed under the letter *S,* but there is no cross-reference under the letter *V.* Choose Tracy or Bunson instead.

916o. Riley, Dick, and Pam McAllister. **The Bedside, Bathtub and Armchair Companion to Sherlock Holmes.** New York: Continuum, 1999. xii, 216 p. Paperback. LC 98-23376. ISBN 0-8264-1140-1.

Like Riley and McAllister's earlier *Bedside, Bathtub and Armchair Companion to Agatha Christie* (q.v.), this is a highly illustrated guide to the cases and world of Sherlock Holmes. Chapters discuss the illustrators of Holmes, the Victorian life, Arthur Conan Doyle, Dr. Joseph Bell, actors who played Holmes, English coinage, London, and so forth. Interspersed among these chapters are discussions of the stories and novels in the canon. These are presented in chronological order; each discussion provides data on first publication, a statement of the predicament, "notable features" of the story, and, when relevant, "quotable quotes" and "oddities and discrepancies" of the story. Interspersed among these are quizzes, games, and a crossword puzzle. The book concludes with a useful list of the "official" story abbreviations and the solution to the crossword puzzle.

916p. Ross, Thomas W. **Good Old Index: The Sherlock Holmes Handbook. A Guide to the Sherlock Holmes Stories of Sir Arthur Conan Doyle: Persons, Places, Themes, Summaries of All of the Tales, with Commentary on the Style of the Author.** Columbia, S.C.: Camden House, 1997. 171 p. Paperback. LC 96-749. ISBN 1-57113-049-7.

As its title implies, this is a guide to the people, places, and notable themes in the works featuring Sherlock Holmes. The volume begins with a lively introduction, after which there is a list containing the abbreviations, dramatis personae, and thumbnail synopses of the tales. The index begins with "Abbas Parva" and concludes with "Zeppelin, Count Ferdinand von (1838–1917)," who was mentioned in "His Last Bow." In all, there are approximately 2,000 entries.

The *Good Old Index* is obviously a labor of love, and it can be useful. At the same time, it is less useful than the works of Tracy, Park, and Bunson (q.q.v.), for unlike those works, Ross lists without explaining. His entry for "Les Huguenots" states in its entirety "opera by Giacomo Meyerbeer, German composer (1791–1864) HOUN." Tracy's definitions, on the other hand, are two: he defines "Huguenots" ("the persecuted French Protestants of the sixteenth and seventeenth centuries, finally expelled from France in 1685. Charles Gorot was of Huguenot extraction (NAVA), and Holmes attended a performance of 'Les Huguenots' [HOUN]") as well as defining "Les Huguenots" ("an opera composed in 1836 by the German composer Giacomo Meyerbeer [1791–1864]. Holmes had a box for a performance [HOUN]") .

Given the ready availability of the other Sherlock Holmes reference works, one wonders why *Good Old Index* was published.

916q. Tracy, Jack. **The Encyclopaedia Sherlockiana; or, a Universal Dictionary of the State of Knowledge of Sherlock Holmes and His Biographer John H. Watson, M.D.** Garden City, N.Y.: Doubleday, 1977. xv, 411 p. LC 75-13394.

The most comprehensive of the Sherlock Holmes encyclopedias examined here, *The Encyclopaedia Sherlockiana* contains more than 3,500 entries and 8,000 story citations, as well as nearly 200 period illustrations. Where it differs from such works as Matthew Bunsons's *Encyclopedia Sherlockiana* and Orlando Park's *The Sherlock Holmes Encyclopedia* (q.q.v.) is that its references and entries are limited to Doyle's world and background; no lists of media adaptations and no entries for the actors and actresses who have performed in motion picture adaptations of Doyle are included.

Tracy begins his *Encyclopaedia* with an entry for the letter *A,* the volume of the *Encyclopaedia Britannica* out of which Jabez Wilson spent eight weeks copying entries ("The Red-Headed League"), and concludes with an entry for "Zoology" (which figures in *The Hound of the Baskervilles* and "The Adventure of the Creeping Man"). All characters, places, and incidents are described. Included are entries for subjects as varied as the names of the newspapers that figure in the canon; historical figures as varied as Charles Darwin, Edgar Allan Poe, Brigham Young, and Count Ferdinand von Zeppelin; regions and locations in which the stories are set; principal railway stations of London; and references that might have meant something to one of Doyle's readers but whose meanings are today largely lost: crystal palace, dark lantern, doctor's commons, Sepoy, and student lamp. The illustrations are well chosen, support the text, and include one of Doyle. A lengthy bibliography concludes the book.

The Encyclopaedia Sherlockiania has its faults. Although the story titles are listed, the list does not provide the complete names and neglects to distinguish the collections from the short stories. In addition, definitions are occasionally dubious: it is most improbable that the sheet of royal cream paper received by Mycroft Holmes measured 19 inches by 24 inches. And why are no entries included for the periodicals in which the canon was first published?—contemporary readers would benefit from knowing the significance of a Christmas Annual or the general editorial approach of the

Strand Magazine. Furthermore, the volume is so prodigiously cross-referenced that the user must often check four or five entries before finding the complete data. Nevertheless, Tracy successfully gives a sense of the world in which the Sherlock Holmes stories take place, and his *Encyclopaedia* is thoroughly useful.

Handbooks, Companions, and Text Explications

916r. Doyle, Arthur Conan. **The Annotated Sherlock Holmes: The Four Novels and Fifty-Six Short Stories Complete, with an Introduction, Notes, and Bibliography by William S. Baring-Gould; Lavishly Illustrated with Maps, Diagrams, Photographs, and Drawings.** New York: Crown for Clarkson Potter, 1967. 2 vols. 688 p., 824 p. Indexes. LC 67-22406. Many later editions.

The contents of the two volumes of *The Annotated Sherlock Holmes* are arranged chronologically. Accompanying the text of each work are explanations of Doyle's references, frequently accompanied by illustrations from period publications. Baring-Gould's annotations are useful and will benefit readers new to Doyle and the world in which Holmes operated, but as Barzun's *A Catalogue of Crime* (q.v.) notes, they are "marred by many misprints, errors of fact, and errors of judgment." A corrected and expanded edition of this work would be welcome.

916s. Redmond, Christopher. **A Sherlock Holmes Handbook.** Toronto: Simon & Pierre, 1993. 251 p. Index. C93-094437-2. ISBN 0-88924-246-1.

Redmond's brief introduction explains that he intended *The Sherlock Holmes Handbook* to be used by two kinds of people: those curious about Holmes, and those who know a lot about Holmes. It is possible that the second group will not need a work such as this, but a novice to the worlds of Arthur Conan Doyle and Sherlock Holmes will more than likely find something of use in the nine lively chapters in the *Handbook*.

Redmond—son of the Donald Redmond whose works are also discussed in this chapter (q.v.)—begins by explaining the concept of the canon, a discussion that presents in "Canonical order" (the order in which the pieces are usually published in collected editions) concise summaries of the stories; first publication data also are provided. The successive chapters survey and discuss the characters and adventures, Sherlock Holmes in print, Sir Arthur Conan Doyle, the Victorian backgrounds of the stories, crime and punishment, modern media adaptations of Holmes, the fans and followers of Holmes, and the influence of Holmes. An appendix lists the 60 tales and provides the commonly used abbreviations for them, along with its date of first publication and the volume and page of the 1967 *The Annotated Sherlock Holmes* on which it is discussed. An excellent index concludes the book.

All chapters contain an enormous amount of information, and on occasion strange juxtapositions occur. The chapter on crime and punishment discusses British law of the late nineteenth and early twentieth centuries, policing and detection in the late nineteenth and early twentieth centuries; it also has statements on the history of the detective story, including a number of stories that owe debts to Doyle. Redmond's opinions in this latter section are occasionally waspish and highly debatable. For example, R. Austin Freeman's Dr. Thorndyke is dismissed as a "humourless polymath," Agatha Christie's output consists of "dozens of enjoyable but forgettable novels," and for Redmond to state that "there is detection in such books [as Chandler's *The Big Sleep* and

Hammett's *Red Harvest* and *The Maltese Falcon*], but primarily there is violence, usually accompanied by sex" is simply incorrect. Furthermore, his discussion of electronic resources has dated badly.

Nevertheless, in all sections Redmond's writing is admirably clear, and his enthusiasm for the character of Holmes and the writings of Doyle is infectious. An audience that has somehow missed reading Doyle or that wants to know about the world in which Doyle lived and worked will find the *Handbook* extraordinarily helpful.

Names and Sources

916t. Redmond, Donald A. **Sherlock Holmes: A Study in Sources.** Kingston and Montreal: McGill-Queen's University Press, 1982. xviii, 357 p. Index. C82-094628-1. ISBN 0-7735-0391-9.

A somewhat mistitled volume, *Sherlock Holmes: A Study in Sources* does not concentrate on the sources used by Doyle but on the names in Sherlock Holmes, focusing on the probable significance and derivation of each name. Although the names are not discussed in a single alphabetical sequence but instead are organized by the stories in which they first appeared, this nevertheless remains a "who's who" to the characters, of whom (states Redmond) "there are 763 named characters of whom 269 are allusions or 'mentioned characters' who are named but do not appear in person or in eyewitness narration. Add to these forty-nine aliases, maiden names and subordinate titles of nobility, at least twenty-one real persons, and forty-eight firm names compounded of personal names; ships, real firms, etcetera, and the total appears to be over 890."

Redmond has devoted an enormous amount of effort to identifying sources likely to have inspired Doyle, working through contemporary newspapers, histories of banks and banking, clerical directories, biographical dictionaries, library catalogues, military lists, registries of ships, alumni directories, regional directories, place-name indexes, obituary indexes, and cricketing yearbooks, to name but a few. His derivations and accounts of origins are generally reasonable and acceptable, although taken collectively they have the (probably unintentional) effect of diminishing Doyle's achievements by making him appear to have been entirely derivative rather than creative.

On the debit side, Redmond does not indicate pronunciations, and in the case of a name such as "Lestrade," this would be helpful: is it "Lestrahd" or "Lestrayed"? Furthermore, Redmond's discussion of Lestrade mentions "Bleiler, speculating on its pronunciation," an apparent reference to critic E. F. Bleiler's "Marmelahd or Marmelade" (*Armchair Detective* vol. 13, no. 4 [Fall 1980]: 334–35), but nowhere is this article referenced in Redmond's bibliography. Apart from the questions of pronunciation and documentation, this remains a thoroughly useful work, on the level of Christopher Redmond's helpful *A Sherlock Holmes Handbook* (q.v.). It belongs in academic libraries.

Television and Motion Picture Adaptations

916u. Barnes, Alan. **Sherlock Holmes on Screen: The Complete Film and TV History.** London: Reynolds & Hearn, 2002. 240 p. Paperback. ISBN 1-903111-04-08.

This A to Z listing provides data on all known film and television adaptations, parodies, and pastiches of Sherlock Holmes, from the early parody *Sherlock Holmes*

Baffled (here dated 1900) to the 2001 adaptation of *The Sign of the Four*. Each entry provides the title in bold letters, followed by country of origin, year of first release, type (i.e., adaptation, parody, pastiche), production company, length, whether it is color or black and white, writer, producer, director, and the cast. When relevant, a literal English translation of the title is given, as are alternate titles. Television adaptations are differentiated by TVM (stand-alone movies), and entries for television serials provide the number of episodes and their approximate length. At their fullest, the entries provide a statement of the mystery, the nature of the investigation, the solution, and an acute and sometimes lengthy discussion of the adaptation. The book is illustrated with stills and concludes with an appendix describing "the lost Detektivfilms" of the second decade of the twentieth century and a useful chronology.

Although the discussions are not as lengthy as those in Pohle and Hart's volume (q.v.), its inclusion of pastiches, parodies, and television shows is superior, and it has more current data. It is pleasurable browsing and contains much to commend it. At the same time, its usefulness is severely compromised by the lack of any index.

916v. Haining, Peter. **The Television Sherlock Holmes.** London: W. H. Allen, 1986. 224 p. Paperback. LC 86-235166. ISBN 0-49103055-X.

916w. Haining, Peter. **The Television Sherlock Holmes.** 2nd ed. London: Virgin Publishing, 1991. 238 p. Paperback. GB 92-20231. ISBN 0-86369-537-X.

916x. Haining, Peter. **The Television Sherlock Holmes.** 3rd ed. London: Virgin Books, 1994. 255 p. Paperback. LC 93-44613. ISBN 0-86369-793-3.

The third edition is described here.

This elaborately illustrated volume provides a history of all the known television adaptations of Sherlock Holmes, although many of the earlier motion picture adaptations also are described. Sherlock Holmes first appeared on television in 1937, and Haining provides stills from and an account of the first production, an adaptation of "The Three Garridebs," which starred Louis Hector as Holmes and William Podmore as Doctor Watson. Dozens of additional adaptations are described, often accompanied by photographs of the actors playing Holmes (these have been as physically diverse as Peter Cushing, John Cleese, Christopher Lee, Stewart Granger, Peter Cook, and Frank Langella). A sizable percentage of the book is devoted to describing the Granada Television adaptations of the stories starring Jeremy Brett as Holmes and having either David Burke or Edward Hardwicke as Watson. Casts and credits of all television shows are provided, although the lengthiest descriptions are accorded to those starring Brett et al. This is an enjoyable book to browse, but alas, it is unindexed.

916y. Kelley, Gordon E. **Sherlock Holmes: Screen and Sound Guide.** Metuchen, N.J.: Scarecrow, 1994. xiv, 317 p. LC 94-4386. ISBN 0-8108-2859-6.

Sherlock Holmes: Screen and Sound Guide contains 13 chapters describing the motion picture, television, radio, recorded performances, and computer games in which Sherlock Holmes is featured or named; entries for pastiches, parodies, serious adaptations, and television advertisements are given. The citations in each chapter are separately numbered, and each chapter is arranged chronologically. Those describing motion pictures provide the title in italics followed by the production company, copyright year, writer and director, cast, alternate titles, length, whether the production is color and available on videotape, and (often) a brief summary. Descriptions for television and radio programs also provide the initial broadcast date and discuss Japanese television programs; entries for animated programs give the actors providing the voices; and entries for television advertisements tend to list the product being advertised, the year in which the advertisement aired, and the corporation. The entries for computer games list the vendor and its location, the year of release, and provide a description of the game. The volume concludes with two appendixes. The lengthy first lists and describes the Sherlock Holmes stories in order of their publication: publication data are provided, as are the name of the illustrator(s) and a summary of the work. The brief second appendix offers a list of some of the sources from which the broadcasts of Sherlock Holmes may be obtained. The volume concludes with an annotated bibliography and a very capable index.

Much is listed in Kelley's bibliography that is not listed in the thematically similar volumes by Barnes, Haining, and Pohle and Hart (q.q.v.). It remains useful.

916z. Pohle, Robert W., and Douglas C. Hart. **Sherlock Holmes on the Screen: The Motion Picture Adventures of the World's Most Popular Detective.** South Brunswick and New York: A. S. Barnes; London: Thomas Yoseloff, 1977. 260 p. Indexed. LC 76-10887. ISBN 0-498-01889-X.

This excellent and enjoyable volume provides a chronological list of all known motion picture adaptations of Sherlock Holmes, from *Sherlock Holmes Baffled* (here dated 24 February 1903, though "perhaps filmed as early as April 1900") to the 1975 parody *The Adventure of Sherlock Holmes' Smarter Brother*. Unlike the other volume discussing media adaptations, this volume generally eschews discussion of parodies and pastiches, relegating them to a separate chapter, and focuses on the serious adaptations.

Pohle and Hart arrange their material primarily by the actor playing Holmes, although chapters discuss the early silent films, the Nordisk (Danish) series, the German series, and the Franco-British series. A typical chapter surveys the motion pictures in the order in which they were filmed and released, with a typical entry providing the title in boldface capital letters; alternate titles are indicated. The dates of release in Britain and the United States are given, as are length and running time, production company, producer, director, director of photography, author of the screenplay, the work(s) on which the motion picture was based, the people responsible for the design, the country and locations in which the motion picture was filmed, and the cast. A sometimes lengthy and always informative synopsis discusses the motion picture, its cast, and the other works they made. The book is heavily illustrated with stills, many of which are here first published. It concludes with discussions of "The Apocryphal Adventures of Sherlock Holmes (Parodies, Pastiches, and Near-Misses)," and "The Televised Adventures of Sherlock Holmes," followed by appendixes listing the Sherlock Holmes stories, an asterisk (*) indicating the stories never filmed, and explaining the British Film Censors Certificate ratings. A lengthy bibliography and a very capable index are provided.

Pohle and Hart provide what is unquestionably the best discussion of the motion picture adaptations of Sherlock Holmes, although this discussion now needs updating and expansion. One longs for such a volume.

Web Sites

916aa. Newbury, Jenny. **Sherlock Holmes International.** http://www.sherlock-holmes. org/

Available in English, French, German, Spanish, Italian, Danish, and Japanese versions, this monumental site contains sections for and links to major Sherlockian resources, the canon online, useful information, multimedia Holmes, specialized sites, Granada's TV series with Jeremy Brett, Sherlockian publications, Holmesian societies, Sherlockians' Holmes pages, essays and scholarly ramblings, pastiches and fan fiction, museums and restaurants, and Sherlockian items for sale. Numerous subdivisions exist.

The layout is clear, accessible, and facilitates access to the information. One can only wish that other detectives were so beloved.

916bb. Redmond, Chris. **A Sherlockian.Net.** http://www.sherlockian.net

Noted Sherlockian scholar Redmond's Web site is unquestionably the best Sherlock Holmes Web site available. One can find on it the original Sherlock Holmes stories; information about the world of Holmes and Watson; biographical data on Arthur Conan Doyle; links to Sherlockian resources on the Web; pictures, sounds and games; bibliographical information on books and journals; and much, much more, all clearly and intelligently presented and accessible. An exemplary achievement.

916cc. Sherlock Holmes Fan Clubs and Societies

Hundreds of fan clubs and Holmes societies exist, and contact information for many of these can be found in the different editions of Ronald de Waal's bibliographies or through the Web sites cited previously, in particular http://www.sherlock-holmes.org/ and http://www.sherlock-holmes.org.uk/. Nevertheless, one would be remiss not to mention the Baker Street Irregulars, established in 1934 and still flourishing:

Baker Street Irregulars
P.O. Box 2189
Easton, MO 21601
745-5553

The address of their "irregular quarterly of Sherlockiana" is as follows:

Baker Street Journal
c/o Sheridan Press
Box 465
Hanover, PA 17331-5172
ISSN 0005-4070

Numerous additional periodicals exist, and the following is nothing more than a selective list. Additional names can be found in the different editions of Ronald de Waal's bibliographies or through the Web sites cited earlier.

A C D: The Journal of the Arthur Conan Doyle Society
c/o Christopher Roden
Ashcroft
2 Abbotsford Drive
Penyfford, Ches. CH4 0JG
England ·
ISSN 0966-0763

The Battered Silicon Dispatch Box
P.O. Box 204
Shelburne, Ontario, LON ISO
Canada
ISSN 1188-0449

The Musgrave Papers
c/o Northern Musgraves Sherlock Holmes Society
69 Greenhead Road
Huddersfield, W. York, HD1 4ER
England
ISSN 1351-1890

Sherlock Holmes Gazette
46 Purfield Drive
Wargrave, Berks RG10 8AR
England
ISSN 0965-5549

Sherlock Holmes Journal
c/o R. J. Ellis
13 Crofton Avenue
Orpington, Kent BR6 8DU
England
0037-3621

The Sherlock Holmes Museum
221b Baker Street
London, England
http://www.sherlock-holmes.co.uk

Sherlockian Tidbits
42 Melrose Place
Montclair, NJ 07042-2028
ISSN 1040-4937

ESTLEMAN, LOREN D.

917. Stephens, Christopher P. **A Checklist of Loren D. Estleman.** Hastings-on-Hudson, N.Y.: Ultramarine Publishing Company, 1991. 16 p. Index. Paperbound. ISBN 0-89366-176-7.

Apparently offset from typed copy, this bibliography lists the books written by Loren Estleman from the 1976 *Oklahoma Punk* until the 1991 publication of *Motown;* the 1992 *King of the Corner* and the 1993 *The Witchfinder* are listed as forthcoming. Each numbered citation provides publication data on the first American and first English edition of the book. Titles are underlined; retitlings are indicated; and information on dust wrapper artists, prices, and identifying points occasionally are given also. Following the bibliography of primary texts, a section lists the works edited by Estleman;

as before, titles are underlined, although because two of the three books in this section are listed as forthcoming, data are minimal. An index to the titles and retitlings concludes the pamphlet. Although this pamphlet is a useful starting point for collectors, it does not list Estleman's nonbook writings, and he has of course been active since 1991. An updated edition is needed.

FISCHER, BRUNO

918. Williams, Richard. **Bruno Fischer.** British Author Checklists, no. 1. Scunthorpe, England: Dragonby Press, 1990. 4 p. Stapled sheets.

Despite the implications of the series title, Bruno Fischer (1908–1992) was an American, one of many who began his writing career in the pulp magazines. This brief checklist cites only Fischer's books. The first section is a chronological listing of the American first editions; the entries provide the year of publication, the book's title (in capital letters), and the publisher's name. The second section lists Fischer's American paperback editions. Arranged alphabetically by publisher, it provides series number, title (in capital letters), and the year of publication (in parentheses). The third section lists Fischer's British first editions. The entries in this section are arranged chronologically, with the year and month of publication given, the title (in capital letters), the pagination, the price, and the name of the publisher. The fourth section lists Fischer's British paperback editions; arranged alphabetically by publisher, it lists the book's series number, the title (in capital letters), the date of publication, pagination, and price. An index lists the books and, beneath them, their publishers. A comprehensive Fischer bibliography remains to be done.

FLEMING, IAN L[ANCASTER].

919. Penzler, Otto. **Ian Fleming's James Bond.** Collecting Mystery Fiction, no. 1. New York: Mysterious Bookshop, 1999. 34 p. Paperback. 250 copies printed.

Reprinted from material first published in the *Armchair Detective* (vol. 17, no. 4 [1984] and vol. 29, no. 1 [1995]), this booklet provides bibliographic data on the monographic appearances of Ian Fleming's famous spy. The arrangement is chronological, the first work described being *Casino Royale* (1953) and the last being the posthumous *Octopussy* and *The Living Daylights*. A reproduction of the dust wrapper for each book is given. The publication data are minimal and include only the publisher of the first English and American editions, a prose description of the volume (i.e., "pale gray cloth, lettered on black on front cover and spine; rear cover blank"), and the book's initial cover price. The number of copies printed also is given, as are descriptions of the proof copies (when they exist) and the estimated retail value of the first editions in various conditions, with and without dust wrapper. A reproduction of Fleming's signature appears on the booklet's cover.

FORTUNE, MARY HELENA

920. Sussex, Lucy, and Elizabeth Gibson. **Mary Helena Fortune ("Waif Wander"/"W. W.") c. 1833–1910.** Queensland, Australia: Department of English, University of Queensland, [1998]. Victorian Fiction Research Guide, no. 27. iv, 48 p. Paperback. LC 99-209699. ISBN 1-86499-004-X. ISSN 0158-3921.

The still mysterious Mrs. Mary Helena Fortune, who wrote as Waif Wander, "W. W.," and "M. H. F.," was not only the first Australian to author a book of detective stories but was also one of the first women—if not the first woman—to write detective stories.

Following Sussex's introduction, which summarizes the poorly documented life of Fortune, *Mary Helena Fortune* contains eight sections: books; serialized novels; series of crime short stories; other series; other short fiction; autobiographical writings and journalism; poems; miscellaneous writings. A list of secondary material is included and an appendix lists lost works. The bibliography is clearly offset from what appears to be last-print copy. Each citation is numbered: there are 737 in all, although reprints comprise a number of these.

The three citations for the books give the book's title in italics, the place of publication, publisher, and publication year. The contents are listed, cross-referenced to the citations for the original publication. The seven entries for the serialized novels provide the serialization date and the story's pagination. The entries for Fortune's short work are arranged chronologically, with the title in quotation marks followed by the name under which the work was published, the title of the publishing periodical (generally the *Australian Journal*) given in italics, followed by the date of publication and the pagination.

This is an important bibliography and admirably documents much of the output of an otherwise forgotten writer, but it nevertheless remains an item for specialists and completists. *Note:* The bibliography is undated, but the date has been verified by the primary author.

FRANCIS, DICK; I.E., RICHARD STANLEY

921a.　Ahearn, Allen, and Patricia Ahearn. **Author Price Guides: Dick Francis.** Rockville, Md.: Quill & Brush, 1997. 8 leaves. APG 096.2.

This Author's Price Guide to Dick Francis lists his work from the 1957 publication of *The Sport of Queens* to the 1996 appearance of *To the Hilt*.

For a thorough description of the format of Author Price Guides, see the entry under Fredric Brown.

921b.　Swanson, Jean, and Dean James. **The Dick Francis Companion.** New York: Berkley Prime Crime, 2003. xiii, 210 p. Paperback. LC 2003-051954. ISBN 0-425-18187-1.

Swanson and James have compiled a companion to the 38 novels of Dick Francis. The *Companion* opens with a brief biography and an interview with Francis, after which " 'Tell Me a Story, and Tell It Strong and Quick': The Novels of Dick Francis" lists Francis's novels in chronological order. No publication data are provided in this section, and the reader must know that the dates given are for Francis's English editions, which were occasionally published a year prior to the American editions.

The next chapter in the *Companion,* "Field of Thirteen," lists and describes the contents of Francis's one short story collection, *Field of Thirteen* (London: Joseph; New York: Putnam, 1998). Although Swanson and James open their discussion by stating that "eight of the stories were previously published elsewhere; five were written expressly for this book," they do not indicate original publication data, which were sometimes decades prior to being collected: "Carrot for a Chestnut" first appeared in 1970, "The Gift" was first published in 1973, "Nightmare" appeared in 1974, and "The Raid at

Kingdom Hill" not only appeared in 1975, it was titled "The Rape of Kingdom Hill." None of these data are indicated by Swanson and James.

"Cast of Characters" is an alphabetical list of Francis's major characters and the works in which they appear; "A Dick Francis Gazetteer" and "Racing Links" describe and discuss Francis's locations and the race courses used by Francis. These are followed by a list of the horses used by Francis, a list of Francis's opening lines, and some nicely written excerpts; and the volume concludes with a bibliography that provides bibliographic data on the novels and a reasonably thorough list of secondary resources.

The Dick Francis Companion is nicely written and may appeal to Francis's many fans, but it is not the work it could be. One hopes for an expanded and corrected second edition.

FREEMAN, R. AUSTIN; I.E., RICHARD AUSTIN

922.   Chapman, David Ian. **R. Austin Freeman: A Bibliography.** Shelburne, Ontario, Canada: Battered Silicon Dispatch Box, 2000. 84 p. Paperback. C00-930260-3. ISBN 1-55246-282-X.

Although such books as Norman Donaldson's *In Search of Dr. Thorndyke* (Bowling Green, Ohio: Bowling Green State University Popular Press, 1971) document and discuss Freeman's writings, Chapman's is apparently the first separately published bibliography of its subject. It has separate sections for books and periodicals, each arranged chronologically. Books list the title in bold letters at the top of the page. Beneath are the month and year of publication, the place of publication, the publisher, and (a repetition) the date of publication. Beneath these are a transcription of the title page: the title is given in capital letters, with lines indicating line breaks. Collation, pagination, contents, binding color, dust wrapper, and printer are noted, as are prior serialization. Additional printings, editions, and retitlings also are noted, although they are not described at any length.

Freeman's periodical publications are separated into fiction and nonfiction. Each is arranged chronologically, giving the title of the work in capital letters, the periodical title in italics, the month, year, pagination, and illustrator (if any). Separate sections list Freeman's lost and untraced publications, after which are a bibliography of secondary sources, a list of Freeman's *Eugenics Review* book reviews, a list of the works of Jack Wylde (occasionally and probably erroneously considered a Freeman pseudonym), a list of miscellaneous material, and a list of lost and untraced material.

Too many lists are included, but the bibliography as a whole is an excellent work.

GARDNER, ERLE STANLEY

923a.   Miller, John Anthony. **The Erle Stanley Gardner Home Page.** http://www. phantoms.com/~phantom/gardner/

Miller operates the Phantom Bookshop in Ventura, California, across the street from the place where Gardner wrote his first Perry Mason mysteries. His Web site provides information on Gardner and his use of Ventura sites in his writings, information on the Temecula group that is trying to get the library's name changed to reflect Gardner's influence, Gardner's recipe for Podunk Candy, a Gardner quiz, and information on a

Gold Coast Virtual Bus tour, wherein one can visit some of the places Gardner visited. Also included is a comprehensive list of Gardner's book publications; the fiction is arranged by series, the titles are listed chronologically. In addition, illustrations of the covers of Gardner's books are provided, as well as advertisements for Richard L. Senate's *Erle Stanley Gardner's Ventura: The Birthplace of Perry Mason* (Ventura, Calif.: Charon Press, 1996), a paperback account of Gardner and Ventura, whose contents do not quite justify giving it a separate entry. One hopes Miller continues to maintain this site.

923b. Moore, Ruth. **Bibliography of Erle Stanley Gardner.** N.p., 1970. 115 leaves. LC 79-23856.

Not seen. Moore was one of three sisters who worked with Gardner and was with him at his death in 1970. It would appear that the *Bibliography of Erle Stanley Gardner* is the copied manuscript of the Gardner bibliography by Moore that appeared on pages 311–341 of *Erle Stanley Gardner: The Case of the Real Perry Mason* by Dorothy B. Hughes (New York: William Morrow, 1978). This bibliography is arranged chronologically. Titles of all pieces are given in boldface capitals. Data included are a note indicating whether the work was a letter, short story, article, pamphlet, television adaptation, or novel; whether it featured one of Gardner's series characters (i.e., Speed Dash, Paul Pry, Fish Mouth McGinnis, the Patent Leather Kid, Mr. Manse, Lester Leith, and, of course, Perry Mason); and whether it appeared under one of Gardner's pseudonyms. Serialization data are provided. Periodical titles are given in italics and are followed by the date of publication. Book publications provide the publisher's name and the month and year of publication for the first hardcover and the first paperback editions. Data are reasonably comprehensive until 1970. Lacking are indexes to title, publication, and series character, but as far as listing most of Gardner's output, this remains the most comprehensive Gardner bibliography currently available.

923c. Mundell, E. H. **Erle Stanley Gardner: A Checklist.** Portage, Ind.: N.p., 1968. 80 p. Indexes. LC 78-111.

Apparently only the second book-length work on Erle Stanley Gardner, this self-published and often frustrating checklist contains five sections: short fiction; book fiction; magazine nonfiction; book nonfiction; and miscellaneous print appearances. Each section is arranged chronologically.

Coverage of the short fiction starts with the appearance of "Chas. M. Green" 's "The Shrieking Skeleton" in the 15 December 1923 *Black Mask* and concludes with a publication from 1965; also included is a list of seven stories (including a 1921 *Breezy Stories*) about which publication data are uncertain. Story pagination and volume and issue numbers are not given, and magazine names are not typographically distinguished. Title changes are not acknowledged, and a number of stories are listed twice, with no indication that they are reprints.

The citations for the books provide the book's title and an indication of the number of foreign editions it had. Because all of the volumes were first published by William Morrow and Company of New York, none of the book citations lists the publisher's name. Paperback editions are not included. This section concludes with a list of the titles that were condensed in Canadian periodical publication; publication dates are not provided.

The section devoted to Gardner's magazine nonfiction provides neither pagination nor volume and issue numbers for the magazines that published Gardner's prose, and the titles of the magazines are not distinguishable from their surroundings.

The section for book-length nonfiction lists the title of the book and provides an indication of the number of foreign editions the publication went through. The name of the publisher is not provided (presumably it was William Morrow). Finally, the miscellaneous section mentions the television adaptation of Perry Mason ("Perry Mason appeared in 270–80 television plays") and mentions syndicated comic adaptations of Gardner's work. A series of indexes provides title keyword access to Gardner's fiction, a subject index to Gardner's nonfiction, and a selective list of Gardner's series characters (exclusive of Perry Mason, Bertha Cool, and Donald Lam) and the titles of some of the stories in which they appeared.

A somewhat revised edition of this book is described later.

923d. Mundell, E. H. **Erle Stanley Gardner: A Checklist.** Kent, Ohio: Kent State University Press, 1970. 91 p. Indexes. LC 70-97619. ISBN 0-87338-034-7.

Although this bibliography is in a great many ways defective, it is nevertheless a substantial improvement over the first edition. The arrangement is essentially the same as the first edition, with five chronologically arranged sections listing Gardner's short fiction, book fiction, short nonfiction, book nonfiction, and miscellanea.

Coverage of the short fiction starts with two appearances in *Breezy Stories* of 1921 and concludes with a publication from 1965. Volume and issue numbers are not given, paginations are not provided, magazine titles are not typographically distinguished, and stories that were retitled and reprinted are listed without any indication of their status.

Apart from some typographical changes, the data in the first four sections are essentially unchanged from their earlier appearances. Publishers are not provided; paperback editions are not cited; publication dates of periodical appearances have not been given; magazine names are not distinguished; and pertinent publication data are not provided.

The section devoted to miscellanea has been expanded to include the selective list of Gardner's series characters (exclusive of Perry Mason, Bertha Cool, and Donald Lam) and the titles of some of the stories in which they appeared. The indexes still include the keyword listing of title words from Gardner's fiction, and it now offers access to Gardner's series characters and his pseudonymous work. An index to Gardner's nonfiction concludes the book.

GIBSON, WALTER B[ROWN].

924. Cox, J. Randolph. **Man of Magic and Mystery: A Guide to the Works of Walter B. Gibson.** Metuchen, N.J.: Scarecrow, 1988. xxiv, 382 p. Indexes. LC 88-31917. ISBN 0-8108-2192-3.

Although he is today largely unknown, Walter B. Gibson (1897–1985) wrote at least 20 million words for the pulp magazines, including (as "Maxwell Grant") some 283 pulp novels, two short stories, and one paperback original featuring the Shadow. Gibson was also a noted magician, a friend to magicians including Houdini and Blackstone, an astrologer, a pioneer in the history of comic books, a lover of mysteries, and an enthusiastic games player, and in all these areas he had numerous publications. Finally, he was a professional ghost, responsible for the novelization (as "Harry Hershfield") of the script of Preston Sturges's *The Sin of Harold Diddlebock,* for the historical novel (as "Douglas Brown") *Anne Bonny, Pirate Queen* ("She could fight like the devil and love like an angel" reads the cover), for books on yoga, the martial arts, and true crime, and for numerous articles, one of which—"A Million Words a Year for Ten Straight Years"— appeared in 1941, when Gibson's writing career was barely 20 years old and had another 44 years to run.

Librarian and scholar Cox was a friend of Walter Gibson, and his *Guide* is an account of Gibson as well as a documentation of Gibson's prodigious output. It contains the following sections: books and pamphlets by Walter B. Gibson; contributions to periodicals; contributions to books and pamphlets by other writers; syndicated features; comic books and newspaper strips; radio scripts; and miscellaneous works. Each of these sections contains biographical data on Gibson and citations to Gibson's publications. Citations are arranged chronologically, each entry having a section letter and a separate number. Book titles are given in boldface, followed (on a separate line) by the place of publication, publisher, year of publication, pagination, whether it was illustrated, and whether it appeared in paperback. Periodical publications give the title in quotation marks, the publication's name in boldface type, volume, date of publication, and pagination of Gibson's story. When the title of an entry does not explain its contents, Cox provides an annotation ranging from one to several dozen words.

Five appendixes provide a list of Walter Gibson's pseudonyms, a list of the magazines in which Gibson was published, information on the other writers and writings to appear under the Maxwell Grant name, three comic book series and six movies adapted from Gibson's writings, and a list of secondary sources about Gibson and his works. The *Guide* concludes with a checklist of the 187 books written by Gibson, an index to the titles mentioned in *The Guide* that indicates whether the piece is an independent unit or part of a larger unit, and a list of the names, including Gibson's pseudonyms, found in the first section, and the appendixes involving the other Maxwell Grants and the comic book and motion picture adaptations of Gibson's work.

This is an exemplary bio-bibliography about a fascinating figure.

GILBERT, MICHAEL

925.   Pike, B. A. **The Short Stories of Michael Gilbert: An Annotated Checklist 1948–1997.** CADS Supplement, no. 7. South Benfleet, Essex, England: CADS, 1998. 60 p. Paperbound.

Not seen. Described by William Contento (http://users.ev1.net/~homeville/msf/0start.htm) as "a comprehensive index to Michael Gilbert's short stories, listing original publication, reprints, and title changes. Sections include Collected Stories, Uncollected Stories, Title Index, and Series Characters."

GOODIS, DAVID

926.   Stephens, Christopher P. **A Checklist of David Goodis.** Hastings-on-Hudson, N.Y.: Ultramarine Publishing Company, 1992. 16 p. Index. Paperbound. ISBN 0-89366-233-X.

Like many authors, David Goodis (1917–1967) got his start in the pulp magazines and moved into producing paperback originals, with an occasional hardcover. Offset from laser-printed copy, this bibliography contains separate sections listing Goodis's books and short stories. The overall arrangement in each section is chronological. Book citations are numbered and provide publication data on the first American and first British edition. Titles are underlined; retitlings are indicated; and information on paginations, dust wrapper artists, prices, and identifying points is also given. The citations for the short stories also are arranged chronologically; story titles are given in quote marks, pulp magazine names are underlined, volume and issue numbers are given, publication date is provided. Pagination, however, is not given. An index to the titles and retitlings concludes the pamphlet. The data on Goodis's books are accurate, but less than half of his short fiction has been cited, and an occasional typo (*Crace Detective* instead of *Crack Detective*) does not help its credibility. A new and updated edition is badly needed.

GRAFTON, SUE

927. Ahearn, Allen, and Patricia Ahearn. **Author Price Guides: Sue Grafton.** Rockville, Md.: Quill & Brush, 1993. 3 leaves. APG 140.

This Author's Price Guide lists Sue Grafton's works from the 1967 appearance of *Keziah Dane* to the 1993 publication of *J Is for Judgment*.

For a thorough description of the format of Author Price Guides, see the entry under Fredric Brown.

GREELEY, ANDREW M.

928. Harrison, Elizabeth. **Andrew M. Greeley: An Annotated Bibliography.** Scarecrow Author Bibliographies, no. 92. Metuchen, N.J.: Scarecrow, 1994. xvii, 390 p. LC 94-25619. ISBN 0-8108-2931-2.

Only a fraction of the Reverend Andrew M. Greeley's impressively large output is fiction, and only a fraction of the fiction is mystery and detective fiction. That latter fraction nevertheless consists of nearly two dozen novels, a majority featuring Msgr. Blackwood ("Blackie") Ryan.

Harrison begins her bibliography by providing a chronology of Greeley's life, a list of his awards and honors, and a useful key to the abbreviations she uses throughout the volume. The bibliography's 3,715 citations are divided into two groups: primary and secondary sources. The section devoted to primary sources has nine chapters: books (with separate lists for nonfiction, novels, short stories, and poems); contributions to books (with separate lists for essays, introductions, and short stories); contributions to periodicals (articles, interviews, letters, and short stories); newspaper columns (Catholic); newspaper columns (secular); book and film reviews; unpublished papers and theses; newsletters; and miscellanea. The citations in each section are brief but adequate: those for books give the book's title in boldface italic type and provide the place of publication, publisher, and publication date of the first edition, stating whether it is paperbound but not whether it is hardcover and indicating whether it contains illustrations, notes, and a bibliography. The citations to periodicals provide the article title in quotation marks, the periodical title in italic type, the volume, month, year, and pagination.

The citations to newspaper columns reference those seen in the *Catholic Messenger* and the *Chicago Tribune,* but because Greeley was widely syndicated, other references are certainly available. In each section, the arrangement is chronological, and Harrison uses an asterisk (*) to indicate those few items she has not personally inspected.

The section devoted to secondary sources lists books; essays, parts of books, and directories; periodical articles; news reports; and selected reviews of Greeley's books. The citation styles used are those described previously.

Included are indexes for author and title, and the appendixes serve as subject indexes, offering access to works on American Catholicism; catechisms, meditations, prayers; education; ethnicity; the Irish; the priesthood; the religious imagination; social and political commentary; sociology of religion; and the youth ministry.

Harrison's annotations are of necessity brief but helpful, concentrating on Greeley's books, his contributions to books, and a selection of the secondary material. This is a fine volume on a productive figure. One hopes for an updated edition.

GREENE, GRAHAM

Note: Although Greene wrote excellent thrillers and espionage stories, he did not write traditional mystery and detective fiction. He is nevertheless included here because he is well represented in the appendix, and not to mention the many works on him would be to do him a disservice.

929a. Cassis, A. F. **Graham Greene: An Annotated Bibliography of Criticism.** Scarecrow Author Bibliographies, no. 55. Metuchen, N.J.: Scarecrow, 1981. xx, 401 p. Index. LC 81-770. ISBN 0-8108-1418-8.

Recognizing that Greene is perhaps "the leading man of letters on the English literary scene," Cassis compiled a bibliography of Greene criticism, excluding the criticism in the popular Catholic press but including material in languages other than English.

Cassis's bibliography is arranged chronologically. Apart from two reviews of Greene's *Babbling April* (one in 1925, the other in 1926), coverage effectively begins in 1929 and concludes in 1979. Cassis annotates and indexes books and portions thereof; articles, including select review articles; reviews of books and performances of plays; dissertations and theses; and miscellaneous material. In all, well in excess of a thousand citations are given. Citations to books give the author, underline the title, and give the place of publication and publisher; chapter paginations are given. Journal and review citations give the author, put the title in quotation marks, abbreviate the journal name, and provide pagination; the key to the journal abbreviations is at the beginning of the volume. Dissertation and theses citations underline the title, give whether the degree is an M.A. or a Ph.D. and list the institution that awarded the degree; they are not annotated. Included are indexes to critics and selected topics and themes.

Graham Greene: An Annotated Bibliography of Criticism is a supremely frustrating work, not because of Cassis's citations and annotations, which are generally accurate and perceptive, but because of its remarkably baroque internal arrangement. First, within each year Cassis separates the citations by category, grouping citations to books, articles, reviews, dissertations, and the miscellaneous material. (Anonymous articles and reviews are, however, listed separately at the end of each category and are arranged alphabetically by the *journal's* title.) Furthermore, every citation is numbered, but the numbering system is unique to this volume, for it is intended to indicate the category, the publication year, and the number within the category; for example, A6910 indicates that the reference is an article (A) published in 1969 (69), the tenth such listed (10). Furthermore, the index of topics and themes is wholly inadequate.

929b. (Henry) Graham Greene. http://www.kirjasto.sci.fi/greene.htm

Part of an enormous Finnish site devoted to authors and their works, this very well done entry provides a lengthy biocritical discussion of Greene and concludes with a chronological list of Greene's works, including screenplays, travel books, poetry, and short stories. Alas, publication data are not provided, nor as of this writing is there any indication as to the genre of the book.

929c.   Hoskins, Robert. **Graham Greene: A Character Index and Guide.** Garland Reference Library of the Humanities, no. 923. New York: Garland, 1991. xiii, 512 p. Index. LC 91-2714. ISBN 0-8240-4111-9.

Compiled shortly after Greene's death, this volume is what Hoskins describes as "a character index and guide to Graham Greene's fiction and drama," listing the characters, allusions (historical and literary), place names, and foreign phrases found in all of Greene's fiction and dramas. Essentially, four sections comprise the volume: novels, short stories, dramas, and *The Last Word* (Greene's final work, published in 1990).

The ultimate arrangement in each section is chronological: Hoskins lists the title of the work, its date of publication, and beneath—in alphabetical order—an explanation of the character's role, allusion, place name, or foreign phrase. Appendixes list the editions used in preparation of the guide, provide a selected bibliography and a list of abbreviations, and the book concludes with a "General Index" listing alphabetically all of the characters, allusions, places, and foreign phrases given in the body of the book.

Although not free from typographical errors—H. Rider Haggard's *Allan Quatermain* is misspelled (offering an odd connection to Wobbe's work, which follows)—Hoskins's efforts are generally helpful and will undoubtedly assist students and researchers.

929d.   Vann, J. Don. **Graham Greene: A Checklist of Criticism.** Serif Series: Bibliographies and Checklists, no. 14. Kent, Ohio: Kent State University Press, 1970. vii, 69 p. LC 70-113763. ISBN 0-87338-101-7.

Graham Greene: A Checklist of Criticism contains five sections and citations to books and chapters, journal articles, book reviews, and a few dissertations, the majority of which were published prior to 1966 (a few entries are more current). In general, material in each section is listed alphabetically by the critic's last name, but there is one exception: anonymous publications are listed at the conclusion of each section. Material in languages other than English is cited.

The first section, "Bibliographies," lists eight other bibliographies of Greene criticism; six of these appeared in journals, one as a chapter, and one as a full-length book. The second section lists the books about Greene; beneath each title are citations to book reviews. The third section lists chapters about Greene and references to him in books. The fourth and longest section lists the critical articles about Greene, and the concluding fifth section is a chronological list of Greene's novels and references to the publications that reviewed them. No indexing is provided.

Greene wrote travel books, plays, and motion picture screenplays; he edited a number of books; and several collections of his short stories had been published at the time this *Checklist* was compiled. The *Checklist* references none of these except for the 1963 *A Sense of Reality*. It is an alarmingly inadequate work.

929e.   Wobbe, R. A. **Graham Greene: A Bibliography and Guide to Research.** Garland Reference Library of the Humanities, no. 173. New York: Garland, 1979. xvi, 440 p. Index. LC 78-68307. ISBN 0-8240-9760-2.

This engagingly thorough bibliography lists all known material by and about Graham Greene published prior to December 1977, although a few publications from 1978 are included. It contains seven sections: books and pamphlets by Greene; books with contributions by Greene; Greene's contributions to newspapers and periodicals; miscellanea; works about Greene; Greene's radio and television broadcasts and film appearances; and published or broadcast interviews with Greene. Each item is individually numbered.

The first section comprises nearly half of the volume. First English and American editions of Greene's works are listed chronologically and described bibliographically. Each citation gives the title in capital letters followed by the book's collation, pagination, printing, physical description, publication price, dedication, and contents; each concludes with detailed notes about the book, including where the copies Wobbe examined are located and differences between editions.

The second section indicates only the first publications of Greene's contributions, which are given in quotation marks followed by the book's title in italic type, the editor (if any), the place of publication, publisher, publication year, and pages on which Greene's contribution may be found. An item preceded by a single asterisk indicates that the item is fiction; two asterisks indicate that the item is poetry.

Greene's contributions to newspapers and periodicals are arranged chronologically. Greene's contributions are given in quotation marks, followed by the periodical or newspaper title in italic type, its publication date, and the pages on which Greene appeared. Title changes are noted, and because they have some bibliographic complexities, Greene's film criticisms are listed separately, in a separate subsection. As earlier, an item preceded by a single asterisk indicates that the item is fiction; two asterisks indicate that the item is poetry.

The section for miscellanea lists and describes manuscripts, typescripts, galley proofs, letters, cards, and annotated print copies held in research collections (i.e., the Humanities Research Center at the University of Texas at Austin, the Library at Indiana University, the New York Public Library, and the Library of the British Film Institute).

The works about Greene section lists, in separate sections, the books, theses and dissertations, bibliographies, and articles. Each section is arranged alphabetically, and it should be stressed that Wobbe has made every effort to locate and cite non-English material.

Greene's media broadcasts and film appearances are listed chronologically, whereas Greene's interviews are listed alphabetically by the last name of the interviewer.

The *Bibliography* concludes with a series of indexes: an alphabetical list of Greene's books and pamphlets, a title list of Greene's periodical and newspaper contributions, and indexes to the works and dramas reviewed by Greene.

Wobbe's bibliography is not quite perfect—it contains the occasional minor typo, as when H. Rider Haggard's *Nada the Lily* is misspelled—but such faults are trivial, and his effort is first-rate. One longs for a second edition covering Greene's output until his death.

929f. Yiu, Melody. **Greeneland: The World of Graham Greene.** http://members. tripod.com/~greeneland

This well-designed site provides a biography, a bibliography, and a lengthy discussion of selected individual works by Greene.

GRIMES, MARTHA

930. Ahearn, Allen, and Patricia Ahearn. **Author Price Guides: Martha Grimes.** Rockville, Md.: Quill & Brush, 1997. 4 leaves. APG 097.2.

This Author's Price Guide to Martha Grimes lists her works from the 1981 publication of *The Man with a Load of Mischief* to the 1996 publication of *Hotel Paradise.*

For a thorough description of the format of Author Price Guides, see the entry under Fredric Brown.

GRUBER, FRANK

931. Clark, William J. **The Frank Gruber Index.** Los Angeles: William J. Clark, 1969. 18 p. Stapled sheets.

Compiled largely from the information contained in Frank Gruber's own files, this index contains three sections. The first lists the books by Gruber; the second lists his fiction; the third, his nonfiction. It is reproduced from typed copy.

The first section is chronological. The book's publication date is given, followed by the title and the name of the publisher. Although this section is but one page in length, it contains a few surprises: Gruber's first book, *The Dillinger Book,* was published in 1934, but *The Pulp Jungle,* Gruber's 1967 autobiography, makes no mention of it, and Gruber describing the events of 1934 largely in terms of his rejected short stories and his acceptance by *Operator #5.*

The second and third sections are arranged alphabetically by the title of the publication in which Gruber appeared, with Gruber's appearances listed chronologically. Publication titles are given in capital letters and are underlined. Gruber's titles are listed in regular type followed by a parenthetical note giving the number of pages in the story or the number of columns in the piece; serializations are indicated by (S) followed by the number of parts in the serialization. The series character's name appears in parentheses. A (+) indicates that the work appeared in book form. Entries conclude by providing additional reprint information, including whether the work appeared under a pseudonym.

Although Gruber died in 1969, this is the only separate list of his work, and it is incomplete, failing to mention Gruber's writing for motion pictures and television. Gruber is now largely forgotten except for devotees of the pulp magazines, but a full bibliography of the man once dubbed "The American Edgar Wallace" would be helpful.

HAMMETT, [SAMUEL] DASHIELL

932a. Gale, Robert L. **A Dashiell Hammett Companion.** Westport, Conn.: Greenwood, 2000. xviii, 317 p. Index. LC 99-046037. ISBN 0-313-31095-5.

Dashiell Hammett's professional career was brief—he published primarily between 1922 and 1934—but it was nevertheless productive, for during these 12 years he published 5 novels, 60 short stories, a number of incisive book reviews, and some miscellaneous verse and prose. His life and these accomplishments are described in *A Dashiell Hammett Companion,* whose approximately 1,200 alphabetical entries profile and describe the major people and events in Hammett's life, summarize Hammett's fiction, and provide entries for all named characters in Hammett's fiction. In addition, the *Companion* offers a useful Hammett chronology and concludes with a bibliography and a capably done index.

It is unfortunate that *A Dashiell Hammett Companion* is far from being the work it could be. On a bibliographical level, the *Companion* is frustrating, for the short story citations provide only the year in which the work was first published, never listing the periodical in which the story appeared. (It does no good to be told only that a story appeared in 1925, for in 1925, Hammett appeared in periodicals as diverse as *Sunset Magazine, Smart Set, The Lariat, The Editor, The Forum,* and *Black Mask.*) Neither is the *Companion* comprehensive: Hammett published "The Crusader" using his daughter's name as his pseudonym; there is no entry for this story, although it is mentioned in Mary Jane Hammett's entry. There is no mention of *Creeps by Night,* the 1931 collection of short stories edited by Hammett, and there is likewise no entry for "Immortality," Gale stating it is "unlocated," although this is far from the case: Richard Layman's excellent *Dashiell Hammett: A Descriptive Bibliography* (q.v.) states that "Immortality" appeared in the November 1922 *10 Story Book*—but then, Gale's bibliography does not cite Layman's work. Gale's annotations often are incomplete: the entry for "Collinson, Peter"— one of Hammett's pseudonyms—mentions only "The Road Home," although Hammett used the pseudonym on a number of short stories, and Gale's entries for these short stories tend to indicate the Collinson attribution. Similarly, interesting and intriguing details provided by Hammett—the Continental Op's reading matter in "The Gutting of Couffignal," for example—are unmentioned by Gale.

The *Companion* is definitely not the work it could be, although it might assist the curious and those interested in Hammett's too-brief career and sad life. One awaits a revised and expanded second edition.

932b. Layman, Richard. **Dashiell Hammett: A Descriptive Bibliography.** Pittsburgh Series in Bibliography. Pittsburgh, Pa.: University of Pittsburgh Press, 1979. xiii, 185 p. Index. LC 78-53600. ISBN 0-8229-3394-2.

This fine volume is without doubt the most comprehensive bibliography of the writings of Dashiell Hammett likely to appear. Oddly, its compiler does not seem to have been aware of Mundell's earlier effort (q.v.), or he would not have opened his acknowledgments by stating that "Hammett bibliography started with William F. Nolan. His *Dashiell Hammett: A Casebook* (Santa Barbara: McNally & Loftin, 1969) has been the sole book-length study of Hammett." Apart from this oversight, Laymon's work is exemplary.

The bibliography contains six lettered sections: (A) "Separate Publications"; (B) "First-Appearance Contributions to Books"; (C) "First-Appearances in Periodicals"; (D) "First Appearances in Newspapers"; (E) "Movies"; (F) "Miscellanea." Each of these sections is arranged chronologically, and the citations in each are separately lettered and numbered.

Section A is 112 pages in length. Each citation reproduces the title page of the first edition of all British and American hardcovers and paperbacks. Each entry then provides an extensive analytical bibliographical description of the first edition, describing the collation, pagination, contents, typography and paper, binding, dust jacket, publication, and printing. A section called "Notes" provides additional information and cross-references to other sections. A section titled "Locations" provides not only a list of the holdings of libraries but also the dates on which the major copyright libraries received the volume. Additional printings and editions also are noted and described; although the descriptions of these are of necessity brief, the title and copyright pages are described at length. A supplement (section AA) lists collections of Hammett's writings using the same principles of bibliographical description.

Sections B, C, D, and E are equally thorough, the citations referencing pseudonymous works, public letters or petitions signed by Hammett, and the movies for which Hammett provided the original story or script material. (Only six movies are cited, but a footnote makes intriguing reference to four unpublished typescripts at the MGM studios in Culver City, California.)

Section F contains only two citations, one referencing a dust-jacked blurb Hammett provided for Nathanael West's *The Day of the Locust* and the other describing a copy of a typed form letter in the F. Scott Fitzgerald archives at Princeton University Library.

Six appendixes list the advertising copy that Hammett might have written for the Albert S. Samuels Jewelry Company in San Francisco between 1922 and 1926, radio plays based on Hammett's work, the television plays, movies, and stage plays based on Hammett's work, the syndication of previously published work by Hammett, notes by the compiler, and a brief bibliography. A comprehensive index lists all titles and names mentioned in the book.

932c. Lovisi, Gary. **Dashiell Hammett and Raymond Chandler: A Checklist and Bibliography of Their Paperback Appearances.** Brooklyn, N.Y.: Gryphon Books, 1994. 82 p. Paperback. LC 96-134119. ISBN 0-936071-36-2. 500 copies printed.

See the entry under Raymond Chandler for a description of this book.

932d. Mundell, E. H. **A List of the Original Appearances of Dashiell Hammett's Magazine Work.** Portage, Ind.: N.p., 1968. 52 p. Index. LC 71-41.

Not seen, but presumably the first edition of the work that follows (q.v.). Mundell was a printer and owned his own press. He frequently published very limited editions of his works that were later published by commercial presses.

932e. Mundell, E. H. **A List of the Original Appearances of Dashiell Hammett's Magazine Work.** Serif Series: Bibliographies and Checklists, no. 13. Kent, Ohio: Kent State University Press, 1968. 52 p. Index. LC 75-97620. ISBN 0-87338-033-9.

As its title indicates, this is a list of the first magazine appearances of Dashiell Hammett's short stories, poetry, and letters; Hammett's nonfiction, which included numerous book reviews, is not treated. The list is arranged chronologically. Each citation provides the story's title and the issue of the magazine in which the piece appeared; often the opening sentence is quoted. Mundell indicates when he has been unable to obtain the original publication data. A number at the bottom of each citation indicates when the material has been collected and/or reprinted; these numbers are keyed to a section near the book's conclusion. Indexes list the stories by title, Hammett's books, verse, letters to *Black Mask,* pseudonyms, magazines in which he published, and the names of Hammett's detectives and the cases in which they appeared.

The opening sentences are unique to this bibliography, but the publication has been effectively superseded by Richard Layman's *Dashiell Hammett: A Descriptive Bibliography* (q.v.).

932f. Nolan, William F. **Dashiell Hammett: A Casebook.** Introduction by Philip Durham. Santa Barbara, Calif.: McNally & Loftin, 1969. xvi, 189 p. Index. LC 68-8393.

Although cited by Layman (q.v.) as the first bibliography of Hammett, it would be more accurate to refer to this pioneering work as the first book-length study of Hammett. Nolan's life of Hammett comprises pages 1 to 127; the bibliography does not begin until page 132. Called "A Dashiell Hammett Checklist," the bibliography has separate sections for books, magazine fiction, articles, introductions, poetry, reviews, letters, newspaper work, radio work, motion pictures (written by Hammett), and Hammett's anthology appearances. Unlike the other bibliographies in this section, Nolan documents secondary literature, and the checklist concludes with a bibliographic essay describing books relating to the hard-boiled school of literature.

The checklist is not as comprehensive as either Mundell's or Layman's work, but Nolan's life of Chandler, apparently written without the assistance of Lillian Hellman, is sympathetic and worth reading.

HILLERMAN, TONY; I.E., ANTHONY GROVE

933a. Ahearn, Allen, and Patricia Ahearn. **Author Price Guides: Tony Hillerman.** Rockville, Md.: Quill & Brush, 1996. 7 leaves. APG 158.

This Author's Price Guide lists the works of Tony Hillerman from the 1970 appearance of *The Blessing Way* to the 1996 appearance of *Finding Moon.*

For a thorough description of the format of Author Price Guides, see the entry under Fredric Brown.

933b. Greenberg, Martin, ed. **The Tony Hillerman Companion: A Comprehensive Guide to His Life and Work.** New York: HarperCollins, 1994. viii, 375 p. LC 93-49507. ISBN 0-06-017034-4.

Despite the title, this is not a comprehensive guide to Hillerman's life and works but is instead a seven-chapter miscellany, the last two chapters of which print three of Hillerman's short stories and six of his articles. The book contains maps of the Southwest as its endpapers and opens with a two-page chronology of Hillerman's life and career. The first five chapters focus on Hillerman's writing, and the first two of these are by Jon L. Breen. In "The Detective Fiction of Tony Hillerman: A Book-by-Book Guide," Breen provides lengthy, appreciative, and intelligent descriptions of Hillerman's novels (as of 1993), and Breen's "Interview with Tony Hillerman" is exactly as its title indicates and has not had prior publication.

The third chapter, George Hardeen's "The Navajo Nation," is reprinted from APA Publication's 1991 *Insight Guide: Native America*. It was recommended by Hillerman as being the finest account by a Navajo available, and it vividly describes "Navajoland," the physical area in which the Navajo live. The fourth chapter, "Native American Clans in Tony Hillerman's Fiction: A Guide" is coauthored by Elizabeth A. Gaines and Diane Hammer. The clans are arranged alphabetically within tribes, and under each clan are listed the names of the characters belonging to it. Each name is followed by "p" (indicating paternal clan) or "m" (indicating maternal clan), and an abbreviation indicates the name of the book in which the relationship is revealed. Clans that are named but for which no characters are identified are listed at the conclusion of this section.

The fifth chapter, also by Gaines and Hammer, lists and describes all of the people who have appeared as characters or who are mentioned in Hillerman's 13 novels and 3 short stories. Each entry provides the character's name, works in which he or she appeared, clan, history, and function within the work. Characters known only by a descriptive name (e.g., Blue Policeman or Fly on the Wall) are listed under the first letter of that name.

Hillerman has continued to write, and a comprehensive guide to Hillerman's life and works still remains to be done. Nevertheless, this solidly written and pioneering effort will be welcome to those wanting information about a significant, popular, and deservedly honored writer.

933c. Hieb, Louis A. **Collecting Tony Hillerman: A Checklist of the First Editions of Tony Hillerman, with Approximate Value and Commentary.** Santa Fe, N. Mex.: Vinegar Tom Press, 1992. Unpaged. 275 copies printed.

Not seen.

933d. Hieb, Louis A. **Fifty Foreign Firsts: A Tony Hillerman Checklist.** Santa Fe, N. Mex.: Parker Books of the West, 1991. 16 p. 50 copies printed.

Not seen but apparently superseded by *Tony Hillerman Abroad* (q.v.).

933e. Hieb, Louis A. **On Collecting Hillerman.** Tucson: University of Arizona, 1990. Unpaginated [5 p.].

Although occasionally cited as a reference publication, this pamphlet consists of prose discussions of Hillerman's works. Hieb discusses Hillerman's first editions, nonfiction, juvenile fiction, advance reading copies, paperback reprints, British editions, other challenges, foreign-language editions, and reading and collecting. Each of those subjects is accorded one paragraph. The Hillerman completist may want this, but it has been thoroughly superseded by Hieb's book-length bibliography (q.v.).

933f. Hieb, Louis A. **Tony Hillerman: A Bibliography.** Gigantic Hound Keepsake. Tucson, Ariz.: Gigantic Hound, 1988. 18 p. 100 copies printed.

Not seen.

933g. Hieb, Louis A. **Tony Hillerman: From "The Blessing Way" to "Talking God": A Bibliography.** Tucson, Ariz.: Giant Hound, 1990. 88 p. Cloth. 1,000 copies printed.

Tony Hillerman: From "The Blessing Way" to "Talking God" is apparently an expansion of Hieb's 1988 *Tony Hillerman: A Bibliography*. Following a biographical introduction and a two-page chronology of Hillerman's life, this well-done bibliography contains seven lettered sections: (A) "Novels"; (B) "Short Fiction"; (C) "Non-fiction"; (D) "Contributions to Books"; (E) "Contributions to Periodicals"; (F) "Works about Hillerman"; and (G) "Audio Recordings." The arrangement of citations in each section is chronological, with each entry separately lettered and numbered.

Section A describes the first American and British editions of all printings of Hillerman's novels; illustrations are provided for many of these books. Each entry provides a title page transcription; a description of the content; a description of the binding using the Inter-Society Color Council of the National Bureau of Standards method of designating colors; notes about publication and the novel's first price; and notes regarding the novel's setting, awards it has won, and unusual features of the book. Although the focus is on the American and British first editions, later editions and translations are nevertheless listed, but extensive bibliographic data are not provided for them. Although they are briefer, sections B through G are equally thorough.

Hieb's citations are clear and well presented. At this writing, this is the most accessible and comprehensive bibliography of Hillerman. One hopes for updated editions that maintain the thoroughness of this edition but have wider distribution.

933h.   Hieb, Louis A. **Tony Hillerman Abroad: An Annotated Checklist of Foreign Language Editions.** Santa Fe, N. Mex.: Parker Books of the World, 1993. 45 p. 75 copies printed.

Not seen, but apparently an expansion of the material first presented in *Fifty Foreign Firsts: A Tony Hillerman Checklist* (q.v.).

933i.   Linford, Laurance D. **Tony Hillerman's Navajoland: Hideouts, Haunts, and Havens in the Joe Leaphorn and Jim Chee Mysteries.** Foreword by Tony Hillerman. Salt Lake City: University of Utah Press, 2001. xvi, 272 p. Index. Paperback. LC 2001-2731. ISBN 0-8748-0698-4.

As its title indicates, this is a guide to the locations—geographical as well as social—used in Tony Hillerman's 14 novels featuring Joe Leaphorn and Jim Chee. Linford—who compiled the well-received *Navajo Places: History, Legend, Landscape* (Salt Lake City: University of Utah Press, 2000)—arranged his guide alphabetically, the first entry being "Abajo Mountains" and the last being "Zuni Wash." Entries for geographical regions locate them, provide their physical characteristics and their Navajo and Hopi names, and give a brief history; entries for the towns provide the previous information as well as population and elevation. Beneath all entries are the words "Role in Hillerman Fiction," following which are the novel's title and an explanation of the way in which the location is used. When the location is used in more than one novel, the discussions are listed alphabetically by title. Following the discussions of the place names are a bibliography, a key to Navajo pronunciation, and an index of places by title. Finally, the book provides a map of Navajoland, and scattered throughout are some 50 black-and-white photographs.

Linford is thorough and presents his subject with affection. Hillerman enthusiasts will delight in this volume.

933j. Thorpe, Peter, Tony Hillerman, and Florence Cline Lister. **Tony Hillerman's Indian Country.** Mancos, Colo.: Time Traveler Maps, 1999. Map. ISBN 1-892040-01-8.

Maps are not generally included in this volume, but *Tony Hillerman's Indian Country* is mentioned because it is attractive and offers a sense of the large geographic regions covered in Hillerman's work. Fully unfolded, the map measures 24 inches by 36 inches. The back of the map lists Hillerman's novels, from *The Blessing Way* to *Hunting Badger*. Beneath each title (and separately numbered) are listed up to five of the locations in the novel, with text clarifying and defining the location. These locations are plotted onto the front of the map. Also included on the map are a brief introduction by Hillerman and information about the Native Americans in the region and the sacred mountains of the cardinal directions. A small section headed "Travelers Etiquette" begins with the warning that "reservations in Indian Country are sovereign nations, and therefore private property. Please obtain permission from tribal members and authorities to venture off main roads, photograph individuals, or otherwise invade the individual privacy of local Native Americans."

HIMES, CHESTER [BOMAR]

934a. Ahearn, Allen, and Patricia Ahearn. **Author Price Guides: Chester Himes.** Rockville, Md.: Quill & Brush, 1995. APG 059.3.

This Author's Price Guide to Chester Himes documents his work from the 1945 publication of *If He Hollers Let Him Go* to the 1995 publication of *Conversations with Chester Himes*.

For a thorough description of the format of Author Price Guides, see the entry under Fredric Brown.

934b. Fabre, Michel, Robert E. Skinner, and Lester Sullivan. **Chester Himes: An Annotated Primary and Secondary Bibliography.** Bibliographies and Indexes in Afro-American and African Studies, no. 30. Westport, Conn.: Greenwood, 1992. xxvi, 216 p. Index. LC 92-18316. ISBN 0-313-28396-6.

This solid bibliography begins by providing an introduction and a chronology to the life and career of Chester Himes, a man worthy of study. A precocious child from Ohio's African American middle class, Himes entered The Ohio State University at age 16; was soon expelled for a prank; and, following an abortive armed robbery, was sentenced to 20 years at hard labor in the Ohio State Penitentiary. He began to write while in prison, and like Richard Wright and James Baldwin, explored in his work the problems of racial identity. After his release, Himes worked for the Works Progress Administration (WPA) and labor organizations and became an expatriate; he did not start his career as a writer of crime fiction until 1953. When he died in 1983, his work was out of print in the United States but was enormously popular in Europe, in particular France.

The publications in all sections are listed in chronological order. The primary bibliography contains separate sections for Himes's fiction, nonfiction, manuscript materials, and a filmography. Citations to the fiction and nonfiction are continuously numbered, entries beginning with letter *P* and a number, and the manuscripts and filmography are designated with letters *M* and *F*, respectively. Novel titles are given in italics, followed by the place of publication, publisher, publication year, pagination, and (when relevant) paperback series number for all known English, French, and British editions; names of translators are provided. Data on titles first appearing in French are listed ahead of the subsequent printings in England and America, and because most of Himes's French publications appeared in a designated series, the series title appears in italics between the publisher's name and the publication date.

The section describing Himes's short fiction has two parts. The first lists first periodical appearances and gives story titles in quotation marks, publication title in italics, and the magazine's month, year, volume number, and pagination. The second gives the contents of short story collections; it uses the same citation format as the section listing Himes's novels, but the contents are listed and cross-referenced to their previous appearances as short fiction and nonfiction.

Himes's nonfiction is listed according to the principles described previously. Entries for his manuscripts are to those that are documented in OCLC and the *National Union Catalog of Manuscript Collections,* and the filmography provides the cast and credits of the three motion pictures that have (thus far) been made of Himes's writings.

The citations in the secondary bibliography are continuously ordered with the letter *S* and a number and reference French publications as well as American and British criticism. In all, some 680 reviews, articles, chapters, and full-length books are cited using the citation formats and principles described previously. Anonymous works are listed at the start of the chronological sequence, and all citations are annotated helpfully. Indexes to critics and to the titles of Himes's works conclude the volume.

Although alternative arrangements might have made the secondary bibliography less cumbersome, this remains a solid and usable work.

HOCH, EDWARD D[ENTINGER].

935. Moffatt, June M., and Francis M. Nevins Jr. **Edward D. Hoch Bibliography, 1955–1991.** Introduction by Marvin Lachman. Van Nuys: Southern California Institute for Fan Interests, 1991. xii, 112 p.

Hoch has published at least one short story in every issue of *Ellery Queen's Mystery Magazine* since May 1973, and he is perhaps the most prolific writer of mystery short stories currently alive. This bibliography documents an impressive output that rarely disappoints. Compiled for the Bouchercon .22 [*sic*], the 22nd Annual Anthony Boucher Memorial Mystery Convention held in Pasadena, California, in 1991, this bibliography begins with an appreciative introduction by fellow crime writer Marvin Lachman. This is followed by a guide to abbreviations which explains the abbreviations used in the bibliography and defines the attributes of Hoch's 24 series characters. The bibliography contains the following sections: novels, story collections and anthologies; short fiction as Edward D. Hoch; short fiction as Anthony Circus; short fiction as Stephen Dentinger; short fiction as R. L. Stevens; short fiction as Mr. X; short fiction as Pat McMahon; short fiction as Irwin Booth; novels and short stories as Ellery Queen; contest novels under pseudonyms; nonfiction as Edward D. Hoch; nonfiction as Stephen Dentinger; nonfiction as Irwin Booth; nonfiction as R. E. Porter; stories on audiotape; and film adaptations of stories by Hoch. Following this listing are 24 indexes providing access to Hoch's works by series character.

In all sections, titles of books are given in italic capital letters, and magazine titles are given in italics; titles of short stories are given in regular type. Citations to Hoch's books provide the publisher and year of publication. When relevant, the contents are given, with cross-references to the original magazine publications. Citations to Hoch's magazine appearances are arranged chronologically within each magazine; story titles are cross-referenced to their later book appearances. Paginations are not provided for either books or magazine publications, and citations to magazine publications do not include the magazine's volume number.

In addition to the preceding shortcomings, the volume does not include a comprehensive chronological list of Hoch's works, and it lacks a title index. It remains, nevertheless, a useful publication:

HUXLEY, ELSPETH [JOSCELINE GRANT]

936.   Cross, Robert S., and Michael Perkin. **Elspeth Huxley: A Bibliography.** Winchester Bibliographies of 20th Century Writers. Foreword by Elspeth Huxley. New Castle, Del.: Oak Knoll Press; Winchester, England: St. Paul's Bibliographies, 1996. xix, 187 p. Index. LC 95-26301. ISBN 1-8847-1817-5.

Compiled with the assistance of Huxley and current as of 1995, this fine bibliography uses a format reminiscent of the Pittsburgh Series in Bibliography. The bibliographical citations are arranged into five sections, each separately lettered, with each citation separately numbered: (A) books and pamphlets by Elspeth Huxley including translations; (B) books edited or with contributions by Elspeth Huxley; (C) contributions to newspapers and periodicals; (D) radio and television appearances; and (E) miscellanea. Also included are a chronology of Huxley's life, numerous reproductions of dust wrappers and bindings, and a fine index.

The data in each section are gratifyingly thorough. In section A, the title page is transcribed in the quasi-facsimile method, and there is a collation statement. Each book's contents are given, illustrations are detailed, binding cases and their colors are described, dust jackets or wrappers are described, as is also the paper on which the book was printed. The bibliographer's notes also indicate which copy or copies were used for the description, provides notes on the printing history (the number of copies printed, the prices, the textual changes, cancellations, author's agreements, etc.), and each entry concludes by citing the contemporary reviews received by the book. Corrected editions and the first American editions also are accorded this bibliographical treatment.

The citations to Huxley's material in the other sections are equally thorough and detailed, although (oddly) paginations are only sporadically provided for Huxley's contributions to newspapers and periodicals. The index thoroughly covers sections A, B, and E; sections C and D are indexed only by the name of the periodical or the radio or television station. These minor lacunae in no way invalidate the usefulness of this bibliography, which remains comprehensive and accessible.

JAMES, P. D.; I.E., PHYLLIS DOROTHY JAMES WHITE, BARONESS JAMES

937.   Ahearn, Allen, and Patricia Ahearn. **Author Price Guides: P. D. James.** Rockville, Md.: Quill & Brush, 1992. 2 leaves. APG 116.

This Author's Price Guide lists the works of P. D. James from the 1962 publication of *Cover Her Face* to the 1990 publication of *Devices and Desires*.

For a thorough description of the format of Author Price Guides, see the entry under Fredric Brown.

JANSON, HANK

938. Williams, Richard, and Stephen Holland. **Hank Janson Books: A Checklist.** British Author Checklists, no. 3. [Scunthorpe, England: Dragonby Press, 2001.] 8 leaves. Index. Stapled sheets. ISBN 1-871122-18-X.

Hank Janson was a house name used by English publishers. According to Philip Harbottle and Stephen Holland's *British Science Fiction Paperbacks and Magazines, 1949–1956* (San Bernardino, Calif.: Borgo, 1994), "The name that started the boom in American gangster novels, *Janson* was the creation of *Stephen D. Frances,* who wrote the first novel, *When Dames Get Tough* (Ward & Hitchon) in 1946. Two years later, *Frances* began to produce them for his own company and the series rapidly became a smash success. By the time the first science fiction title was published, Janson sales were topping eight million copies" (88).

The first section of Williams and Holland's *Hank Janson Books: A Checklist* is arranged by publisher. Within the publisher, the books are listed by series, in the order in which they were published. Each title is given in capital letters followed by the month of publication, the pagination, the cost, and the cover artist. A second section lists the books alphabetically by title, indicating retitlings and the author when known.

Though "Janson" is discussed in works surveying the British postwar paperback boom, this remains the only separate publication on its subject. It is clearly offset from laser-generated copy.

KEELER, HARRY STEPHEN

939. Tucker, Fender, ed. **"A to Izzard": A Harry Stephen Keeler Companion.** Shreveport, La.: Ramble House, 2003. vi, 11–311 p. Hardcover and paperback.

The first book devoted to the marvelously eccentric Keeler, the *Companion* begins with 10 essays surveying Keeler's life and works. The essays have been reprinted from various sources and are thus sometimes repetitive, but the writers include such critics as Francis M. Nevins and Bill Pronzini, and all are worth reading. The *Companion*'s next section reprints seven short pieces by Keeler, including what may be his best-known work, "The Strange Story of John Jones's Dollar" (*The Black Cat,* 1915), after which there are four pieces of original fiction in a style "sort of like Harry." A series of color plates reproduces the Ramble House covers for their reprints of Keeler, after which there is an alphabetical bibliography of Keeler's work. It contains three sections, the first of which provides bibliographic data on the first editions of Keeler's American and English publications; the second, on Keeler's original publications in Spanish; the third, on Keeler's original publications in Portuguese. This is followed by a list of Keeler's series, after which is a list (chronological) giving Keeler's opening lines. The volume concludes with a list (surprisingly lengthy) of Keeler's works that as yet remain unpublished in English.

The *Companion* is enjoyable, yet one cannot help wishing for more depth and comprehensiveness. Keeler's editorship of *10-Story Book* is mentioned but in passing, yet it is not unreasonable to wonder about his editorial practices, whether they influenced the stories appearing in the magazine and directed his own fiction. One wishes the bibliography were more thorough. It is known that "The Strange Adventures of the Twelve Coins of Confucius" was serialized in *Great Detective* in 1933, but it is not cited in the bibliography: does this piece remain unreprinted, or has it appeared under yet another title? What of Keeler's many short pieces?—they are virtually unmentioned and are uncited in the bibliography.

After ending his life in obscurity, Keeler is now finding an American audience, and the *Companion* is must reading for anybody interested in him.

KELLERMAN, FAYE [MARDER], AND KELLERMAN, JONATHAN

940. Seels, James T., ed. **Jonathan and Faye Kellerman: American and English Publications, 1972–1996.** Foreword and short story "Malibu Dog" by Faye Kellerman. Afterword by Jonathan Kellerman. Royal Oak, Mich.; Mission Viejo, Calif.: ASAP/Airtight-Seels Allied Publication, 1994. 54 p. Indexes. Paperback. 60 copies in acrylic slipcases and 240 limited copies.

Despite being compiled with assistance from the Kellermans, this bibliography manages to be quite disappointing. Following an introduction by Faye Kellerman (in which she discusses Jonathan), the bibliography provides a chronologically arranged list of her publications, the first citation being the 1986 *The Ritual Bath*. Titles of books and short stories are listed in capital letters, the latter being in quotations; beneath each title is a statement indicating whether the work is a short story or a novel. The publication data list the place of publication, publisher's name, and year of publication. When the publisher identified works with the words "first edition" or with numbers indicating printing, these too are listed; the data are current through 1995. Pagination, paperback reprints, dust wrapper information, and commentary about texts are not provided. An index to titles concludes this section.

The second section is also chronological in arrangement, the citations beginning with the statement that between 1972 and 1985 "Jonathan Kellerman wrote and edited numerous articles in peer-review psychology and medical journals. He also wrote articles in newspapers and magazines." None of these are listed, the first complete citation being to Kellerman's 1977 short story "The Questioner." As in the previous section, titles of books and short stories are listed in capital letters, the latter distinguished by quotations. A statement indicates whether the work is a short story, a novel, a children's book, or nonfiction, and the publication data list the place of publication, publisher's name, and year of publication. When the publisher identified works with the words "first edition" or with numbers indicating printing, these are listed. International and limited editions are listed, although paperback reprints are not; data extend through 1996. Pagination, dust wrapper information, and commentary about texts are not provided. A title index lists the cited works.

An afterword by Jonathan Kellerman (in which he discusses Faye), and the reprinting of Faye Kellerman's 1990 short story "Malibu Dog" conclude the book. The Kellermans are talented, versatile, and enormously popular writers, and a comprehensive and thorough bibliography of them remains to be done.

HUTTNER, HENRY. *SEE* MOORE, CATHERINE LUCILLE AND HENRY RUTTNER

LEONARD, ELMORE [JOHN]

941a. Ahearn, Allen, and Patricia Ahearn. **Author Price Guides: Elmore Leonard.** Rockville, Md.: Quill & Brush, 1995. 7 leaves. APG 036.4.

This Author's Price Guide to Elmore Leonard begins with a brief bibliography citing secondary references. It documents Leonard's work from the 1954 publication of *The Bounty Hunters* to the 1995 appearance of *Riding the Rap*.

For a thorough description of the format of Author Price Guides, see the entry under Fredric Brown.

941b. Stephens, Christopher P. **A Checklist of Elmore Leonard.** Hastings-on-Hudson, N.Y.: Ultramarine Publishing, 1991. 17 p. Paperback. Index. ISBN 0-89366-215-1.

Apparently offset from laser-printed copy, this bibliography lists the books written by Elmore Leonard, from his earliest days as a western writer until the 1992 publication of *Rum Punch*. Each numbered citation provides publication data on the first American and first British editions. Titles are underlined; retitlings are indicated; and information on dust wrapper artists, prices, and identifying points occasionally are given also. An index to the titles and retitlings concludes the bibliography. Although this pamphlet is a useful starting point for collectors, it lists neither Leonard's nonbook writings nor his short fiction, and he has of course remained active beyond 1992. A comprehensive bibliography of the writings of Elmore Leonard is desirable.

MACDONALD, JOHN D[ANN].

942a. Ahearn, Allen, and Patricia Ahearn. **Author Price Guides: John D. MacDonald.** Rockville, Md.: Quill & Brush, 1993. 14 leaves. APG 143.

This Author Price Guide lists John D. MacDonald's works from the 1950 appearance of *The Brass Cupcake* to the 1987 publication of *Reading for Survival*.

For a thorough description of the format of Author Price Guides, see the entry under Fredric Brown.

942b. Campbell, Frank D., Jr. **John D. MacDonald and the Colorful World of Travis McGee.** Milford series, Popular Writers of Today, vol. 5. San Bernardino, Calif.: Borgo Press, 1977. 64 p. Paperback. LC 77-773. ISBN 0-89370-208-0.

Arguably not a reference book, this slim volume contains virtually nothing about MacDonald but provides chatty plot summaries of 16 of MacDonald's Travis McGee novels, from the 1964 *Deep Blue Good-By* to the 1975 *The Dreadful Lemon Sky*. The arrangement of the summaries is chronological, and each chapter has as its title the color used in MacDonald's title. The book concludes with a one-page bio-bibliography that lists the Travis McGee books. No table of contents is provided, and users not intimate with MacDonald's bibliography must either consult the bibliography for the publication year and then endeavor to locate the summary by its relative position in the bibliography or page through the book in the hopes of finding the essay. Neither approach is satisfactory, and Campbell's often facetious comments make it difficult to take this publication seriously.

942c. MacLean, David C. **John D. MacDonald: A Checklist of Collectible Editions and Translations with Notes on Prices.** Decatur, Ind.: Americana Books, 1987. 32 p. Index. Paperback. ISBN 0-917902-06-8.

Concerned only with those works of John D. MacDonald that appeared in book form under his own name—the one exception is so noted—this bibliography is arranged chronologically. Titles are listed in capital letters and are separately numbered. Beneath each title are listed the editions known to MacLean. English-language editions are listed first followed by references to editions in French, Swedish, German, and so forth. Each citation provides place of publication, publisher, year of publication, height (in centimeters), pagination, and series and stock number. Reprint editions and large-type editions also are referenced. A note by the title indicates whether the book was part of MacDonald's Travis McGee series. A guide to the price cross-references the citation number to the price offered by various dealers. The bibliography concludes with a title index.

MacLean forthrightly states that many of his entries are "from catalog card entries and not from books actually seen," and his citations contain far fewer data than the bibliographies done by Walter Shine and Jean Shine (q.v.). Nevertheless, this checklist is capably done—portable, lean, and well arranged. One wishes that MacLean had found the energies to document MacDonald's short stories.

942d. Moffatt, Len, June Moffatt, and William J. Clark. **The JDM Master Checklist: A Bibliography of the Published Writings of John D. MacDonald.** Downey, Calif.: Moffatt House, 1969. xii, 42 p. Index. Paperback. LC 71-7688.

Based upon a bibliography serialized in the *JDM Bibliophile,* the *JDM Master Checklist* is apparently the first separately published bibliography devoted to John D. MacDonald; it is reproduced from clearly photocopied material and printed on blue paper. The *Master Checklist* begins with an introduction to MacDonald's life and works and contains the following sections: (1) "Magazine Stories and Articles (American)"; (2) "Stories in Anthologies"; (3) "Books: U.S.A. Editions"; (4) "A Special List of Fawcett Editions"; (5) "Books: British Editions"; (6) "Stories Reprinted in British Magazines"; (7) "Books (International Editions)"; and (8) "Stories Reprinted in Japanese Magazines." The data in each section are complete until 1968, although titles projected for 1969 are listed.

The first section is arranged alphabetically by magazine. Beneath each magazine's title is a chronologically arranged list of MacDonald's appearances that includes the publication date, story's title, word count or number of pages, and name under which the title was published. Reprints, retitlings, and stories that were part of a series are indicated. This format is also used in the sixth section.

Sections 2 through 5 are chronological in arrangement, although not consistent in format. In the second section, book titles are capitalized; year of publication, publisher, and names of editors are given; and MacDonald's contribution is in quotations and capital letters. In the third section, titles are in capital letters, beneath which are given the publisher and the year of first publication. Reprint data are provided as are lists of the contents of MacDonald's short story collections. In the fourth section, the data include the book's stock number, title, price, and original publication date. Those books that were out of print when this list was compiled have an *X* listed in the column for the price. In the fifth section, the title, publication date, and name of the publisher are given.

The section on MacDonald's international publications is alphabetical by language. Within each language, titles are listed chronologically, accompanied by the publisher's name and date of publication; the translated title is followed by parentheses containing the original title. In the case of MacDonald's Japanese translations, the original title is given in parentheses, followed by a romanized version of the title, Japanese title in Japanese characters, magazine's name, and date of publication. The bibliography concludes with a comprehensive title index.

The title has been superseded by the work of Walter Shine and Jean Shine, in particular *A Bibliography of the Published Works of John D. MacDonald, with Selected Biographical Materials and Critical Essays* (q.v.). However, the appearance of Japanese characters is unique to this bibliography.

942e. Shine, Walter, and Jean Shine. **A Bibliography of the Published Works of John D. MacDonald, with Selected Biographical Materials and Critical Essays.** Gainesville, Fla.: Patrons of the Libraries, 1980. xiv, 209 p. Index. Spiralbound. LC 80-22673.

Unlike the Shines' 1988 *A MacDonald Potpourri* (q.v.), which concentrates exclusively on MacDonald's book publications, this bibliography lists all the published works by John D. MacDonald, from the January 1946 appearance of "Conversation on Deck" through November of 1980, although the 1981 *Free Fall in Crimson* is listed. The bibliography is heavily illustrated, provides enormous amounts of data, and is far too long. It is nevertheless described here in some detail, for its data are important and often are unique to this volume.

The bibliography begins by listing MacDonald's publications chronologically, each entry providing the month and year in which the piece was published, title, and word/page count. Titles of books are given in uppercase letters; titles of short publications are in quotation marks; and nonfiction, science fiction, and sports stories are indicated by (nf), (sf), and (sp). References to MacDonald's letters, speeches, and nonprofessional writings are not included in this section.

The second section documents MacDonald's books, starting with a chronological checklist. Seventy titles are numbered and listed in capital letters, an asterisk indicating whether the first printing was in hardcover. This material is followed by lists of the Travis McGee series, an alphabetical checklist of MacDonald's books, and the contents of MacDonald's short story collections. Book titles are given in capital letters, followed by place of publication, publisher, year of publication, and a list of the stories; an asterisk indicates whether the story had no prior publication. Next comes a lengthy list of the publishing histories of MacDonald's American editions. Books are arranged alphabetically, with the first line beneath each title providing the original place of publication, publisher, and year of the first printing. Each entry then repeats the year of the first printing, lists the number of interim paperback printings or the number of hardcover printings with the date of the most recent printing as of November 1980; publisher's stock number, ISBN, or Library of Congress card number; and prices of the first and latest printings. Paperback publishers are indicated by lowercase; hardcover publishers, by uppercase. The section concludes with data on MacDonald's Braille and books on cassettes and discs and a list (with addresses) of MacDonald's U.S. publishers.

Similar publication data for MacDonald's British editions are provided; this section concludes with a list (with addresses) for MacDonald's British publishers. These data are followed by a list of MacDonald's translations into other languages. The titles are listed alphabetically; the languages into which the work was translated are listed beneath. The foreign title is underlined, the translator's name, country of publication, publisher, year of publication, and series (if any) in which the book appeared are given. Titles appearing in non-Romance languages are romanized. This section concludes with a list of the translations of MacDonald's magazine stories published as books and the addresses of MacDonald's international publishers.

The next section lists MacDonald's appearances in magazines and newspapers. The publications in which MacDonald appeared are arranged alphabetically, their titles capitalized. Beneath each title is a chronologically arranged list of MacDonald's contributions that includes the publication date, MacDonald's title (in quotation marks), the magazine's volume and issue numbers, and the page upon which the item was published.

The following section records MacDonald's appearances in anthologies and collections. MacDonald's stories are listed alphabetically, titles underlined and in quotation marks. The titles of the collections are capitalized, and the citations include editor, place of publication, publisher, and year of publication.

Listings for MacDonald's nonfiction "et al." come next. Citations reference MacDonald's articles on the art and business of writing and on the environment, articles of general interest, published letters to the editor, speeches, interviews and public appearances, and early, nonprofessional writings.

Next are data on the adaptations of MacDonald's writings for motion picture, television, and radio. The section begins with a chronological checklist of MacDonald's adaptations for television and motion pictures. This is followed by more thorough data on the television adaptations. Entries provide the show's air date, title of MacDonald's story, television sponsor and show's name, and cast and credits. Data on MacDonald's motion picture adaptations provide the year in which the movie was released, title of MacDonald's work, producing studio, and cast and credits.

The next section provides a biographical sketch of MacDonald; a chronological list of various biographical and autobiographical articles; honors, awards, and prizes given to (or won by) MacDonald; his professional and civic activities; and summary data on his education, military service, and employment.

The final section lists critical articles about MacDonald, cites book reviews, and concludes with information about the *JDM Bibliophile*. These listings form the core of the material documented at much greater length in Shine and Shine's 1993 *Rave or Rage* (q.v.). The bibliography concludes with indexes listing MacDonald's titles in English and in translation.

As stated previously, this work is too long, but it is the only comprehensive bibliography of the works of John D. MacDonald. It thoroughly supersedes the earlier checklist produced by Len Moffat, June Moffatt, and William J. Clark (q.v.). A revised edition citing the publications from MacDonald's last years is rumored to be forthcoming and would be most welcome.

942f. Shine, Walter, and Jean Shine. **John D. MacDonald: A True Bibliophile.** North Palm Beach, Fla.: Walter and Jean Shine, 1985. ix, 54 p. Paperback.

Reproduced from typed copy, this semiannotated list examines the books that John D. MacDonald is known to have read and, in many cases, reviewed. MacDonald's reading and comments are described in chapters titled "Fiction in the Early Years" and "Non-Fiction Reading," but much of the volume consists of excerpts from MacDonald's reviews. In "Recent Reading and Reviews," the books read and reviewed by MacDonald are listed alphabetically by title, and an annotation provides an indicative excerpt from MacDonald's assessment. "Caustic, Critical Comments" provides excerpts from MacDonald's often mordant reviews, but these (unfortunately) are not matched to the work, although a list of the works that MacDonald reviewed negatively (and from which the reviews are taken) is given at the end of the section. "Detective & Mystery Fiction—and Views" provides further indication of MacDonald's views on writing, and this work concludes with a list of MacDonald's reviews and introductions.

MacDonald may have been a perceptive reviewer, but this volume does him a disservice. It is amateurish in presentation, riddled with typographical errors, and because it contains nothing in the way of bibliographic citations, it is utterly useless for research purposes.

942g. Shine, Walter, and Jean Shine. **A MacDonald Potpourri . . . Being a Miscellany of Post-Perusal Pleasures of the John D. MacDonald Books for Bibliophiles, Bibliographers and Bibliomaniacs.** Gainesville: University of Florida Libraries, 1988. xii, 219 p. LC 88-14419. ISBN 0-929595-00-9.

Far from being the potpourri promised by the title, this lengthy bibliography is a comprehensive list of all MacDonald books published in the United States, Great Britain, and internationally. Sprawling, often frustrating to use, and extraordinarily thorough at times, this is the only bibliography in this section that provides comparative charts of its subject's appearance on the best-seller lists compiled by *Time, Publisher's Weekly,* and the *New York Times.*

After an introduction, the volume distinguishes between "printing" and "edition," and then describes the various symbols used by MacDonald's publishers to distinguish first printings of first editions from later printings and later editions. Publisher in-house numbers are detailed, as are Fawcett's "dot device," the end print number, Library of Congress numbers, the Standard Book Number System, the International Standard Book Number System, the printing key, and other features that can be (and are) used to identify different editions.

The bibliography begins with two checklists of MacDonald's work, one chronological, the other alphabetical. The chronological checklist indicates whether the book appeared first in hardcover, whether it was a short story collection, whether it contained Captain John Kilpack, whether it was part of the Travis McGee series, and whether it was edited and introduced (or merely introduced) by MacDonald. The posthumously published *Reading for Survival* is identified as such.

The next checklist is an alphabetical list of MacDonald's first printings in paperback. The publishers are listed, as are the books' in-house number and date of publication. Next comes a list of MacDonald's U.S. publishers and those of his books they published. Included are separate sections for paperback publishers, hardcover publishers, book club publishers, and large-print editions.

Following are sections describing the contents of MacDonald's trilogies and omnibus editions and the contents of his short story collections. The former provides the book's title and standard bibliographical data—place of publication, publisher, year of publication—and its Library of Congress number, pagination, book club number, and ISBN. The section on his short story collections merely lists the contents of the books.

A lengthy list of the total copies of MacDonald's books printed or sold by publishers in the United States is provided. The list is arranged alphabetically. Each entry provides publisher, number of printings the book received, and total number printed or sold. Columns permit comparison of the sales of paperback and hardcover printings. These are followed by lists of MacDonald's foreign editions arranged by language. Citations provide only the English title of MacDonald's work and an English translation of the foreign title—in the German publications, *The Deceivers* becomes *Adultery, The Dreadful Lemon Sky* becomes *Death Casts Yellow Shadows,* and the like.

The next section is an alphabetical list of MacDonald's typographical errors and inappropriate word choices. Entries provide the page and line number for the paperback and hardcover editions, the word or phrase in question, how MacDonald wanted it to be, and how many printings this error appeared in before it was corrected. (It is perhaps worth noting that, like many of us, MacDonald occasionally confused "infer" and "imply.")

An alphabetical reprinting of the epigraphs in MacDonald's books is followed by a list of MacDonald's original working titles and the published title, a reprinting of MacDonald's dedications, a list of the photographers of MacDonald and the books in which their photographs appeared, reproductions of the photographs, lists of the cover artists and jacket designers of MacDonald's books and the books they illustrated, and reproductions of all English-language covers of each edition.

The bibliography concludes with a lengthy list of every printing of every one of MacDonald's books. Arranged alphabetically, each entry provides printing number, book number, cost, photographer responsible for MacDonald's picture, cover artist, end print number, dot device, or printing key, pagination, issue date, and miscellaneous data on the mail ads, lists, and colors of back covers.

A must for MacDonald collectors and dealers, but the unnecessarily baroque arrangement does not facilitate access to the data.

942h. Shine, Walter, and Jean Shine. **Rave or Rage: The Critics & John D. MacDonald.** Gainesville: University of Florida, George A. Smathers Libraries, 1993. xv, 261 p. Index. LC 93-19930. ISBN 0-929595-02-5.

This comprehensive annotated bibliography of the criticism of John D. MacDonald begins with a statement of the necessity for such a bibliography, acknowledgments, an explanation of the style and abbreviations used, and contains the following sections: (A) critical essays and articles and awards (with a special section listing obituaries and posthumous tributes); (B) book reviews; (C) books about John D. MacDonald or his work; (D) miscellaneous articles and parodies; (E) a selected list of essays and reviews of particular merit; and (F) an afterword by John D. MacDonald.

The material in sections A and B is arranged chronologically, the coverage ending with publications in late 1992. Citations provide the author's name in regular type, title of the article or book review in quotation marks, publication's name in boldface capital letters, issue number and/or date of publication, and (often) pagination. Annotations are printed in smaller type and are pithy, informative, and full of surprises. For example, Pablo Neruda praised MacDonald, as did figures as diverse as Kingsley Amis, Anthony Boucher, Harry Reasoner, Charles Willeford, and Carl Sagan.

The third section cites only eight items, five of which are by the Shines. Arranged chronologically, all citations give the author's name in regular type, title of the publication in boldface capital letters and quotations, place of publication, publisher, year of publication, ISBN, pagination, and arrangement of contents. Reviews of the publications are listed, and the Shines provide comments on the publications of others.

Sections D and E contain few citations and probably could have been integrated into the previous sections with no loss. MacDonald's "afterword" is a reprint from a

1945 publication. The book concludes with an index of the books and a numerical list of the reviews received by each book.

Essential for MacDonald scholars, and given the overall quality of MacDonald's writing, their number is bound to increase.

942i. Shine, Walter, and Jean Shine. **The Special Confidential Report.** Tampa, Fla.: JDM Bibliophile, 1979. 34 p. Paperback.

942j. Shine, Walter, and Jean Shine. **Special Confidential Report: Subject: Travis McGee.** 2nd ed. Fort Lauderdale: Florida Center for the Book and Literary Landmarks Association, 1987. 32 p. Paperback.

942k. Shine, Walter, and Jean Shine. **Special Confidential Report: Subject: Travis McGee.** Fort Lauderdale and North Palm Beach, Fla.: Bahia Mar Resort and Yachting Center and the Shines' Cottage Industry, 1992. 66 p. Paperback.

The first two editions have not been seen.

Written as a confidential report from a series of private detectives who have been shadowing MacDonald's Travis McGee, the character's life, friends, possessions, and personality are described at length through quotations from MacDonald's publications. Each "detective" has been assigned a code name based on the color used in the title of MacDonald's novel from which the "evidence" has been derived. Descriptions of McGee and his military record, criminal record, education, background, Bahia Mar Friends, longtime friends, and other acquaintances are provided as lists, with page references indicating the source of the data. McGee's personality is described at some length in a separate section, with subsections profiling his special and professional talents; hobbies; cultural interests; clothing, food, restaurant, and drink preferences; personal effects; sexual experiences; travel records; and adversaries. Separate exhibits prepared by the detectives describe Meyer, *The Busted Flush,* the *Muñequita,* and "Miss Agnes."

A labor of love but necessary only for MacDonald obsessives.

MACDONALD, ROSS: PSEUDONYM FOR KENNETH MILLAR

943a. Ahearn, Allen, and Patricia Ahearn. **Author Price Guides: Ross Macdonald [Kenneth Millar].** Rockville, Md.: Quill & Brush, 1993. 7 leaves. APG 144.

This Author's Price Guide lists Ross Macdonald's writings from the 1944 appearance of *The Dark Tunnel* (written as Kenneth Millar) to the 1982 publication of *Early Millar; the First Stories of Ross Macdonald & Margaret Millar.*

For a thorough description of the format of Author Price Guides, see the entry under Fredric Brown.

943b. Bruccoli, Matthew J. **Kenneth Millar/Ross Macdonald: A Checklist.** Detroit: Gale, 1971. xvii, 86 p.

A compiler's note by Bruccoli introduces this slim volume and states that it is a checklist and not a bibliography of the works of Kenneth Millar/Ross Macdonald. Those who would know the difference are referenced in a footnote to Bruccoli's 1968 *Raymond Chandler: A Checklist* (q.v.), in which Bruccoli states that a checklist "fails to provide the detailed descriptive and analytical information about paper, type, binding, printing, and text—especially text—that a true bibliography, no matter how digressive, must provide."

Questions of nomenclature aside, this book lacks a table of contents and any sense of organization, but it has been compiled with Millar's assistance and contains a fine autobiographical essay by Millar. It lists all editions of Millar's books; his contributions to books; his stories, articles, verse, reviews, letters, blurbs, interviews, references, "ana," apocrypha; and the sketches, reviews, and verse in the Toronto *Saturday Night* between 1939 and 1942. (Reproductions of pages from Millar's notebooks and from term papers are also provided.)

The bibliographic data in this checklist tend to be given on the right (even-numbered) pages, and the left (odd-numbered) pages tend to be reserved for reproductions of the title pages of Millar's books. Citations for books are arranged chronologically and give the title in boldface capital letters next to which, in parentheses, is the publication year. Following are a statement of edition from the copyright page, pagination, collation, and exact date of first publication. Separately numbered citations list each known printing and paperback edition, including stock number; retitlings are indicated, as are periodical appearances.

Citations for first book appearance list the title of the book in italics and provide the editor, place of publication, publisher, and year of publication; Millar's contributions are listed in quotation marks. The citations for Millar's stories and verse provide the title of his contribution in quotation marks; periodical title in italics; volume, month, and year of publication; and pagination. In some cases, as in the publications from the Toronto *Saturday Night,* a majority of the data is not available, and the citations are only to the title of the work.

Frustrating in arrangement and poorly laid out, this checklist has been thoroughly superseded by Bruccoli's 1983 *Ross Macdonald/Kenneth Millar: A Descriptive Bibliography* (q.v.).

943c. Bruccoli, Matthew J. **Ross Macdonald/Kenneth Millar: A Descriptive Bibliography.** Pittsburgh Series in Bibliography. Pittsburgh, Pa.: University of Pittsburgh Press, 1983. xv, 259 p. Index. LC 83-1398. ISBN 0-8229-3482-5.

A completely new work rather than a revision of Bruccoli's earlier checklist, this descriptive bibliography is a comprehensive and analytical list of all English-language editions of all works in which Kenneth Millar has in some way been involved. Millar, whose early books are signed John Macdonald and John Ross Macdonald, dropped the "John" in order to avoid being confused with John D. MacDonald.

The bibliography contains four lettered sections: (A) "Separate Publications"; (B) "First-Appearance Contributions to Books"; (C) "First Appearances in Magazines and Newspapers"; and (D) "Blurbs." The citations in each of these sections are arranged chronologically and are separately lettered and numbered.

Section A, the longest section, occupies the first 204 pages of the book. Each citation reproduces the title page of the first edition of all British and American hardcovers and paperbacks. Each entry provides an exhaustive analytical bibliographical description of the first edition, with collation, pagination, contents, typography and paper, binding, dust jacket, publication, and printing noted and described at length. A section called "Locations" lists whether the book may be found in the holdings of six research libraries and/or Bruccoli's own collections; the entry for the Library of Congress lists the books' deposit date. Additional printings and editions also are noted and described, although the data given are briefer, the title and copyright pages are described at length. Section AA lists the collections of Millar/Macdonald's novels using the same principles of bibliographical description.

Sections B, C, and D are equally thorough, referencing previously unpublished material, unsigned works, and retitled works. Two appendixes—the compiler's notes, and a highly selective and very brief list of books and articles about Millar/Macdonald— follow; an excellent index concludes the book. Because Millar/Macdonald is now dead, an updated edition would be useful.

943d. Gale, Robert L. **A Ross Macdonald Companion.** Westport, Conn.: Greenwood, 2002. xv, 363 p. Index. LC 2001-58645. ISBN 0-313-32057-8.

Gale, who has compiled companions to Nathaniel Hawthorne and Dashiell Hammett (q.v.), here turns his attentions to the works of Ross Macdonald, describing the plots and characters in Macdonald's "twenty-four novels and twelve short stories, and also about the major nonfictional aspects of his life, including his family members." The resulting volume contains nearly 1,200 alphabetically arranged entries, some of which— the summaries of the novels—are quite detailed. Included are numerous cross-references, a selective bibliography, and a thorough index.

It is unfortunate, but *A Ross Macdonald Companion* is far from being the work it could be. Its contents are incomplete: Macdonald wrote far in excess of 12 short stories. Its contents are bibliographically frustrating, for Gale fails to follow any known citation standard, and the original publication sources of the majority of those short stories that are described—such as "Midnight Blue"—are not given. Gale's summaries are verbose: the description of *The Blue Hammer* occupies nearly eight wearisome pages and manages to mention every single plot element; other plot summaries are equally and unnecessarily lengthy. Finally, such recent publications as *Strangers in Town: Three Newly Discovered Mysteries by Ross Macdonald* (Norfolk, Va.: Crippen and Landru, 2001)—and the accompanying booklet *Winnipeg, 1929*—have rendered *A Ross Macdonald Companion* out of date before it was even published. If the volume receives a second edition, one hopes that it will deal with the problems mentioned here.

MARQUAND, JOHN P[HILLIPS].

944. Penzler, Otto. **John P. Marquand's Mr. Moto.** Collecting Mystery Fiction, no. 7. New York: Mysterious Bookshop, 2000. 20 p. Paperback. 250 copies printed.

Reprinted from material first published in the *Armchair Detective,* this pamphlet begins with a brief biography of John P. Marquand, then describes the first American edition of the six Mr. Moto books Marquand wrote between 1935 and 1957. The bibliographic data include the publisher and the publication place and date. Also included are a prose description of the work (e.g., "bright teal blue cloth, front cover and spine printed in red; rear cover blank") and the specific publication date; if the work was made into a motion picture, the adaptation is so noted. Each entry concludes with an estimated value for the book in various states and a reproduction of the dust wrapper. No facsimile of Marquand's signature appears on the cover; there is instead a picture of Marquand looking somewhat amused.

MARSH, [DAME EDITH] NGAIO

945. Gibbs, Rowan, and Richard Williams. **Ngaio Marsh: A Bibliography of English Language Publications in Hardback and Paperback, with a Guide to the Value of the First Editions.** Dragonby Bibliographies, no. 7. Scunthorpe, England: Dragonby Press, 1990. 51 p. Paperback. ISBN 1-871122-07-4. 300 copies printed.

As its title indicates, this bibliography lists the English-language book publications of New Zealand writer Ngaio Marsh. In all, she wrote some 32 detective novels, 8 short stories (6 of which were criminous), a number of play scripts, much incidental material, and her autobiography. The bibliography is reproduced from what appears to be dot-matrix printout and is surprisingly complex in its arrangement. It begins with a "main index," an alphabetical listing of all of the books by Marsh. Each title is given in boldface capital letters; beneath it are listed the first editions of all hardbacks and paperbacks in the approximate order of their publication. Data in this list include country of publication, publisher's name, book's series number, and year and month of publication.

The second section describes Marsh's British hardbacks. This list is arranged chronologically, and as before, titles are given in bold capital letters. The data include the book's pagination, a description of the binding and dust wrapper, size, dedication, and original price and value as of 1990. Later editions and their distinguishing points also are listed. This section concludes with listings of British book club editions, British large-print editions, and British audio editions.

The third, fourth, and fifth sections are arranged by publishers. The third section lists the British paperback editions of Marsh's work. Beneath each publisher's name is a chronological list of the paperbacks. Each citation gives the book's title in capital letters, series number, date of publication, pagination, cover artist (when available), and ISBN (when available). The fourth section lists the American hardbacks of Marsh's work; when the title is a first American edition, the citation provides publication data, book's pagination, a description of the binding and the dust wrapper, size, original price, and value as of 1990. Later editions and their distinguishing points also are listed. This section concludes with listings of the American book club editions and the American large-print editions. The fifth section lists Marsh's American paperback editions. Beneath each publisher's name is a chronological list of the paperbacks; each citation gives the book's title in capital letters, series number, date of publication, pagination, original price, and ISBN (when available).

Significantly briefer sections list Marsh's Australian, Canadian, New Zealand, and European editions. A separate section lists her short stories alphabetically and provides data on their original publication and subsequent anthologization. Another section lists Marsh's plays and films, providing information on the production and the director.

The primary bibliography concludes with a section listing the articles and pamphlets by Marsh. The list is alphabetical; titles are in capital letters, and publication data are provided. The volume concludes with a lengthy selected bibliography of sources used in the compilation of this bibliography.

Although the volume lacks a cumulative index and has an unnecessarily baroque and convoluted arrangement, Gibbs and Williams deserve commendation. One hopes for a revised and simplified edition.

MOORE, CATHERINE LUCILLE, AND HENRY KUTTNER

946.   Utter, Virgil, Gordon Benson, Jr., and Phil Stephensen-Payne. **Catherine Lucille Moore and Henry Kuttner: A Marriage of Souls and Talent.** 4th ed. Galactic Central Bibliographies for the Avid Reader, vol. 21. Leeds, England: Galactic Central, 1996. x, 142 p. Paperback. ISBN 1-871133-44-0.

C. L. Moore and Henry Kuttner had separate careers writing for the pulp magazines, but they began to collaborate after their 1940 marriage, producing not only the science fiction, fantasy, and weird fiction for which they are renowned but also a number of well-crafted detective and mystery stories. This collaboration lasted until Kuttner's untimely death in 1958, after which Moore turned her attention to television writing. She died in Hollywood, California, in 1987. The very demanding Jacques Barzun stated that it was "a pity the author [Kuttner] did not live to write more, for he was fully aware of the demands of physical objects, time, and space."

An explanatory introduction and a list of bibliographical sources used begin the bibliography, following which it contains three major sections: (1) C. L. Moore solo; (2) Henry Kuttner solo and with C. L. Moore; and (3) secondary material. Each section is further divided, the first two sections containing the date and place of the author's birth and death, a list of the awards and pseudonyms used, and the following divisions: (A) prose fiction; (B) prose fiction books; (C) series; (D) poetry and drama; (E) poetry and drama books; (F) articles; (G) miscellaneous; (H) nonfiction books; and (I) publications edited. The third section contains the following: (J) other media; (K) articles on Henry Kuttner and C. L. Moore; (L) reviews; (M) books about Henry Kuttner and C. L. Moore; (N) phantom and forthcoming titles; (O) related items by other authors; (P) textual variations and other notes; and (Q) a chronological index of prose fiction.

The sections citing the primary literature are arranged alphabetically, with each citation in each section given a separate letter and a number. Entries for the prose fiction provide the story's title and the name of the publication in regular type; month and year of publication are given, and if the story was accompanied by an internal illustration or featured on the cover, the artist's name is provided. A brief note indicates whether the story was a short-short story (sss), short story (ss), novelette (NT), novella (NA), or short novel (SN). Paginations are not given. Reprints of the stories are listed alphabetically beneath the initial citations. The titles of the books are given in capital letters, the editor's name is listed, and the publication data cite the publisher and year of publication. Book prices and translations also are referenced, but the names of translators are given only sporadically.

The sections listing books are comparable to the sections listing the prose fiction. Entries list the book's contents by referencing the citation letters and numbers given in the section for prose fiction. Titles are given in capital letters; editor's names, stock numbers, and prices are given; and the publication data cite the publisher and year of publication. Reprints and republications are noted, as are translations, and the names of translators are given sometimes. As before, pagination is not given.

The data in other sections tend to be less thorough. The listing for series lists the series by title, then lists beneath each title the works comprising the series, but contains no cross-references to the section for short fiction. The sections listing the poetry and drama books known by Moore and Kuttner are empty; no such works are known. (One wonders why Utter et al. did not simply note the absence of these works in the introduction to this bibliography.)

The listing of secondary sources is arranged alphabetically and references fan publications as well as a number of international publications. The section called "Textual Variations and Other Notes" is somewhat mistitled, for it has nothing to do with textual variations but lists sometimes intriguing background data on the stories. Did Kuttner use the name "Leslie Charteris" for some radio plays? (A section devoted to correcting and acknowledging misspellings and variant titles is buried in "Phantom and Forthcoming Titles.")

Although lacking an index to titles and unfortunately incomplete in documenting Moore's writing career following Kuttner's death, this is one of the best of the Galactic Central bibliographies. It is clearly reproduced from word-processed copy, and its data are current through 1995. Researchers interested in two of the finest pulp writers will need this book.

O'CALLAGHAN, [HELEN] MAXINE

947. Seels, James T., ed. **Maxine O'Callaghan: Bibliography 1974–1995.** Introduction by Maxine O'Callaghan. Appreciation by Marcia Muller. Short Stories "A Change of Clients" and "Deal with the Devil" by Maxine O'Callaghan. Afterword by Wendy Hornsby. Royal Oaks, Mich.; Mission Viejo, Calif.: ASAP/Airtight-Seels Publication, 1994. 51 p. Paperback. 50 collectors copies in acrylic slipcase and 200 limited copies.

In 1974 Maxine O'Callaghan created Delilah West, one of the first female private investigators created by an American woman author. O'Callaghan has since written half a dozen mystery novels, four horror/dark suspense novels, one pseudonymous romance novel, and a handful of short stories. O'Callaghan's output is thus relatively brief; only six pages of this bibliography are necessary to document it. The rest of the book consists of an introduction by O'Callaghan, two of O'Callaghan's short stories (one first published here), an appreciation by Marcia Muller, and an afterword by Wendy Hornsby.

The bibliography lists O'Callaghan's works in chronological order, with separate sections listing her mystery novels, her horror/dark suspense novels, and her short fiction. Beneath each year, the book's title is listed in boldface capital letters and a note indicates whether the work is a novel or a short story. The publication data list the place of publication, publisher, and year of publication; when the publisher identified works with the words "first edition" or with numbers indicating printing, these too are listed. The data are current through 1994, although information on some 1995 titles is provided. Pagination, paperback reprints, dust wrapper information, and commentary about texts are not provided. No index to titles is provided.

A disappointment as a bibliography.

PETERS, ELLIS:
PSEUDONYM FOR EDITH MARY PARGETER

948a. Whiteman, Robin. **The Cadfael Companion: The World of Brother Cadfael.** Introduction by Ellis Peters. London: MacDonald, 1991. 288 p. GB 91-91175. ISBN 0356200523.

948b. Whiteman, Robin. **The Cadfael Companion: The World of Brother Cadfael.** Rev. ed. Introduction by Ellis Peters. New York: Mysterious Press/Warner Books, 1995. 412 p. LC 95-15435. ISBN 0-89296-513-4.

This large, well-illustrated volume is a guide to the characters and locations appearing in the 20 novels and 1 short story collection chronicling the cases of Brother Cadfael, the twelfth-century merchant/warrior/lover turned Benedictine monk and herbalist who remains one of "Ellis Peter"'s (Edith Pargeter's) finest creations. Approximately 1,200 entries are provided, and the volume is thoroughly cross-referenced, indicating such with small capital letters. Headings and entry names are given in boldface Gothic. Pronunciation keys are not provided.

Entries for geographical locations provide a brief history of the location, its significance in the twelfth century, and excerpts from Peters's fiction in which the location is mentioned. Location entries conclude with a key to Peters's works that indicates the page upon which the location is mentioned. Entries for historical characters provide the character's birth and death dates (when known), their significance in the twelfth century, excerpts from the fiction in which they appear or are mentioned, and a key to Peters's works that indicates the page upon which the character is mentioned or appears. Entries for fictional characters are indicated with (fict.) but are otherwise identical in format to the entries of historical characters, although roles of the fictional characters are described in some detail.

The volume concludes with four appendixes. The first lists the plants and herbs mentioned in *The Chronicles of Brother Cadfael* and provides the plant's Latin name and references the works in which it appeared. The second appendix provides a list of the brothers and sisters of Cadfael's Shrewsbury Abbey; the third appendix provides a list of the eleventh- and twelfth-century kings of England, France, and Jerusalem, the emperors of the Holy Roman Empire and the Byzantine Empire, the popes (excluding Antipopes), and the archbishops of Canterbury. The fourth appendix is a glossary to words that have special meaning in *The Chronicles of Brother Cadfael* (i.e., "banker" is "a stone bench used by masons to cut stone").

Enthusiasts of the Cadfael novels will delight in this book.

POE, EDGAR ALLAN

Scope note: With but three works—"The Murders in the Rue Morgue" (*Graham's Magazine,* April 1841), "The Mystery of Marie Rogét: A Sequel to 'The Murders in the Rue Morgue' " (*Snowden's Ladies' Companion,* November 1842–February 1843), and "The Purloined Letter" (*The Gift: A Christmas, New Year, and Birthday Present, MDCCCXLV* published September/October 1844)—Edgar Allan Poe can be said to have established the recognizable forms of the mystery and detective story. (Two additional stories, "The Gold-Bug" [the Philadelphia *Dollar Newspaper,* 21 and 28 June 1843] and "Thou Art the Man" [*Godey's Lady's Book,* November 1844] are of less genre importance.)

Prior writers—notably William Godwin, William Leggett, and William Gilmore Simms—wrote works that are unquestionably mysteries, but the times were not right for them to be seen as establishing new forms. They are best regarded as anticipations, sparks that helped ignite the inferno. Histories of the mystery and detective story very rightly tend to date the creation of the field to Poe's advent in April 1841.

Because of Poe's monumental importance this section describes a number of the works that discuss his life, works, and accomplishments.

949a. Dameron, J. Lasley, and Irby B. Cauthen. **Edgar Allan Poe: A Bibliography of Criticism, 1827–1967.** A John Cook Wyllie Memorial Publication. Charlottesville: Published for the Bibliographical Society of the University of Virginia by the University Press of Virginia, 1974. xvi, 386 p. LC 73-89824. ISBN 0-8139-0498-6.

Dameron and Cauthen annotate approximately 3,000 criticisms of Poe published from 1827 (the year in which *Tamerlane* appeared) until 1967. The arrangement of the citations is chronological, with entries for books, articles, chapters, and dissertations; works in languages other than English also are cited. The annotations are brief but informative, the arrangement often frustrating, and the volume concludes with a comprehensive name and title index and a somewhat less comprehensive subject index.

Dameron and Cauthen reference much that can be difficult to locate. In comparison with other similar bibliographies—particularly Esther F. Hyneman's *Edgar Allan Poe: An Annotated Bibliography of Books and Articles in English, 1827–1973* (Boston: G. K. Hall, 1974)—Dameron and Cauthen contains more material and more substantial annotations. Hyneman's work, on the other hand, does contain an additional six years' worth of citations, although the majority of these can be readily located using the *MLA Bibliography.*

949b. Frank, Frederick S., and Anthony Magistrale. **The Poe Encyclopedia.** Westport, Conn.: Greenwood, 1997. xxii, 453 p. Index. LC 96-22005. ISBN 0-313-27768-0.

Although Frank and Magistrale concentrate on Poe's life and oeuvre rather than on Poe as a pioneering writer of mystery and detective fiction, their volume is included here for several reasons, the first of which is that it is an excellent work that does not appear to have attracted the attention it deserves.

The *Encyclopedia* begins with a discussion of Poe criticism, lists the abbreviations used in the text, and provides a thorough chronology of Poe's life and major publications. These are followed by approximately 2,500 entries on subjects as disparate as the people known by Poe in person or as correspondents, the addresses of the houses in which Poe lived, the magazines in which Poe published, the books Poe reviewed, and the names of the characters in Poe's works. Each work of fiction is discussed, with entries providing the original publication data and references to key works of critical analysis. Entries also discuss Poe's military service, his noted critics and translators, his publishers, and even provide the name of the cemetery in which he is interred. A select bibliography of primary and secondary works follows the *Encyclopedia*'s articles, after which are indexes to Poe's critics, editors, and acquaintances; to authors, artists, and titles; and to themes, subjects, and characters.

Clearly written, insightful, authoritative, and thorough, this work belongs in all libraries.

949c. Gale, Robert L. **Plots and Characters in the Fiction and Poetry of Edgar Allan Poe.** Hamden, Conn.: Archon Books, 1970. xxiii, 191 p. LC 76-113809. ISBN 0-208-00974-4.

It is important to realize that *Plots and Characters in the Fiction and Poetry of Edgar Allan Poe* is described by its title. It does not concern itself with bio-bibliographic questions or with describing Poe's life and acquaintances; for those, one should use the works of Frank and Magistrale, Sova, or Thomas and Jackson (q.q.v.).

Gale thus identifies 523 named characters (including about 30 nicknames) in the works of Poe, which he states comprise "one novel (*The Narrative of Arthur Gordon Pym*), one nouvelle (*The Journal of Julius Rodman*), sixty-eight short stories, sixty-four poems, one fragmentary blank-verse play ("Scenes from 'Politian' ") , and *Eureka,* which is so poetic and moreover so intriguing for space-age readers that I have treated it in this handbook."

He opens this volume by providing a chronology of Poe's life, followed by a chronological list of Poe's fiction and poetry. These are followed by summaries ("Plots") of each of Poe's works, sometimes at great length: although most works receive a paragraph or page, *Eureka* is described in 8 pages, and *The Narrative of Arthur Gordon Pym* receives 11. Each summary concludes with a list of the characters named in the work. When the narrator is unidentified, Gale describes it as "Persona." The next section, "Characters," lists alphabetically all of the characters identified in "Plots," plus the salient points of each character are described; the characters of the Personas are also described. Included are two appendixes, one listing the variant titles of Poe's works, the other listing the titles of 10 poems that have been attributed to Poe.

Despite its age, this volume remains useful.

949d. Hammond, J. R. **An Edgar Allan Poe Companion: A Guide to the Short Stories, Romances and Essays.** Totowa, N.J.: Barnes & Noble, 1981. xii, 205 p. Index. LC 81-167695. ISBN 0-389-20172-3.

Hammond's *Edgar Allan Poe Companion* is an odd work, part dictionary, part encyclopedia, part biography, and part critical essay. The volume contains seven sections, the first of which is a reasonably detailed account of Poe's life and an assessment of his literary reputation.

The second part, described as an Edgar Allan Poe dictionary, is an alphabetical list of the titles of Poe's short stories, essays, and poems, with first publication data, a brief description, a list of Poe's major book reviews, and the contents of the collections published in Poe's lifetime.

The third part is a critical discussion and assessment of Poe's short stories, which Hammond numbers as 40 (see Gale, earlier). Hammond's discussions are brief but acute and intelligent; his judgments remain relevant.

The fourth part is a critical discussion and assessment of Poe's romances; that is, what Hammond (quoting William Rose Benet) describes as "a work of prose fiction in which the scenes and incidents are more or less removed from common life and are surrounded by a halo of mystery, an atmosphere of strangeness and adventure." Significant attention is paid to *The Narrative of Arthur Gordon Pym* and "The Balloon Hoax."

The fifth part discusses Poe's essays and criticism, and the sixth part discusses Poe's poetry. The seventh part is an alphabetical list and description of the characters and locations in Poe's fiction. Because Hammond limits himself to listing the characters and places "occupying a significant role in the short stories and romances," the list is not as comprehensive as it might be.

An appendix lists film versions of Poe's stories and works using Poe as a character. The lists are chronological. The first generally provides the studio, director, and major actors; the second gives the author and some publication data that are at best dubious (i.e., Robert Bloch's "The Man Who Collected Poe" is dated 1967, presumably because it can be connected to the 1968 motion picture *Torture Garden,* but the story was first published in *Famous Fantastic Mysteries* in October 1951). A selective bibliography and an inadequate index conclude the volume.

Although *An Edgar Allan Poe Companion* is not a bad job, it is not as good as it could be, and it is inadequate when compared with the work of Frank and Magistrale, Gale, Sova, and Thomas and Jackson (q.q.v).

949e.   Hayes, Kevin J., ed. **The Cambridge Companion to Edgar Allan Poe.** Cambridge Companions to Literature. New York: Cambridge University Press, 2002. xx, 266 p. Index. LC 2001-43972. ISBN 0-521-79326-2 (hc); 0-521-79727-6 (pb).

Despite its title, this *Companion* is neither a Poe encyclopedia nor a Poe dictionary. It is, instead, a collection of frequently lengthy scholarly articles of many subjects such as those titled "Poe and the Gothic Tradition," "Poe's Humor," "Poe, Sensationalism, and Slavery," "A Confused Beginning: *The Narrative of Arthur Gordon Pym of Nantucket,*" and "Extra! Extra! Poe Invents Science Fiction!" (by, respectively, Benjamin Franklin Fisher IV, Daniel Royot, Teresa A. Goddu, Geoffrey Sanborn, and John Tresch). In all, there are 14 articles, and Peter Thoms's "Poe's Dupin and the Power of Detection" should be mentioned as being germane to the subject of this volume. The *Companion* does not belong in reference collections, but it will undoubtedly benefit scholars and those seeking to see Poe's role in various literary traditions.

949f.   Heartman, Charles F., and Kenneth Rede. **A Census of First Editions and Source Materials by Edgar Allan Poe in American Collections.** Metuchen, N.J.: Privately Printed, 1932–1933. 3 vols. Vol. 1: 240 copies printed; vol. 2: 202 copies printed; vol. 3: 100 copies printed.

949g.   Heartman, Charles F., and James R. Canny. **A Bibliography of First Printings of the Writings of Edgar Allan Poe: Together with a Record of First and Contemporary Later Printings of His Contributions to Annuals, Anthologies, Periodicals and Newspapers Issued during His Lifetime: Also Some Spurious Poeana and Fakes.** Heartman's Historical Series, no. 53. Hattiesburg, Miss.: Book Farm, 1943. Rev. ed. x, 294 p. LC 44-7988.

The first edition of this bibliography is sometimes referred to as the *Poe Census.*

The contents of Heartman and Canny's volume are well described by the title. The volume is a chronological listing of Poe's works. Separate publications are thoroughly described; their title pages are transcribed and their publishing histories are given. The volume is thoroughly indexed.

Although Heartman and Canny's work is no longer current or comprehensive, it was at one time fairly widely held and still may be found in many academic libraries. A revised and expanded third edition, dated 1977, is said to exist, but it has not been seen. More accessible, more current, and more comprehensive is the extensive bibliography given in volume 7 of Jacob Blanck's *Bibliography of American Literature,* edited by Virginia L. Smyers and Michael Winship (New Haven, Conn.: Yale University Press, 1983), pages 115 to 154. This bibliography, however, does not cite Poe's periodical appearances.

949h. [Miller, John Carl.] **John Henry Ingram's Poe Collection at the University of Virginia: A Calendar and Index of Letters and Other Manuscripts, Photographs, Printed Matter, and Biographical Source Materials Concerning Edgar Allan Poe Assembled by John Henry Ingram, with Prefatory Essay by John Carl Miller on Ingram as a Poe Editor and Biographer and as a Collector of Poe Materials.** 2nd ed. Charlottesville: University of Virginia Library, 1994. xii, 220 p. Index. Paperbound. ISBN 0-8139-1552-x.

The first edition of this catalogue was published in 1960 and has not been seen.

John Henry Ingram (1842–1916) was an obsessive collector of material by and about Poe; he ultimately published two biographies, more than 50 articles, and variety of prefaces and introductions about Poe, to say nothing of publishing eight separate editions of Poe's works. This catalogue of his collection at the University of Virginia begins with a biography of Ingram and a description of his collecting habits. The description of the collection arranges its material into five sections: letters, manuscripts, and other documents; photographs; miscellaneous undated photographs; printed matter from newspapers and magazines; and miscellaneous undated items. But for the sections listing undatable material, each section is chronologically arranged. The annotations are full and informative, fascinating, and will assist researchers enormously.

Although others have provided fuller accounts of Poe's life and writings, as well as the writings about him, this work should not be discounted, particularly since the John Henry Ingram Collection is available on microfilm and this guide can serve as an index to the various reels.

949i. Sova, Dawn B. **Edgar Allan Poe A to Z: The Essential Reference to His Life and Work.** New York: Checkmark Books, 2001. x, 310 p. Index. LC 00-061039. ISBN 0-8160-4161-x (hc); 0-8160-3850-3 (pb).

Edgar Allan Poe A to Z won the 2002 Edgar Award for best nonfiction book. Like the *Poe Encyclopedia* of Frank and Magistrale (q.v.), it offers encyclopedic access to Poe's life and oeuvre. Sova's introduction states that the volume "is a comprehensive examination of Poe's writings that presents a complete portrait of a complicated and brilliant thinker and writer."

The entries in *Edgar Allan Poe A to Z* are in general longer and more elaborate than those in Frank and Magistrale's *Encyclopedia*. Furthermore, Sova's volume contains a number of uncommon illustrations: reproductions of title pages, manuscripts, Poe's dwellings, and portraits of the people Poe knew. Sova's discussions of Poe's creative writings are frequently lengthy; each work is accorded up to four sections that discuss its role in Poe's life and accomplishments, its publication and dramatization history, its characters, and a formal synopsis of its plot. The characters, publishers, and adapters of Poe also are accorded separate entries. Other entries discuss the periodicals in which Poe published; Poe's friends, acquaintances, and correspondents; Poe's dwellings; and the books Poe reviewed. Following the entries are four appendixes. The first, described as a time line, is a chronology of Poe's life and accomplishments; the second is a chronology of Poe's works (creative and selected nonfiction); the third provides contact information for research libraries containing Poe research collections; and the fourth is a lengthy selected bibliography. The volume concludes with a capable index.

Although exact numbers are unavailable, *Edgar Allan Poe A to Z* contains fewer entries than Frank and Magistrale's *Encyclopedia*. Examination shows that section *Fr* in the *Encyclopedia* contains 15 relevant entries, beginning with "Fragment of a Campaign

Song" and concluding with "Frost, Robert"; the same section in Sova's work contains but 6 relevant entries, though one of these is devoted to French critics and criticism and contains 4 cross-references. Furthermore, Sova is not as graceful a writer as she might be; her discussion of "The Oval Portrait" states that "the tale appears to adapt ideas contained in *The Picture of Dorian Gray,* an 1891 novel written by Oscar Wilde," although the opposite can only be true. Finally, Sova's bibliography neglects to mention the *Encyclopedia* of Frank and Magistrale, an odd omission in that at least a percentage of her entries appear to open with the identical words used by Frank and Magistrale. (In section *Fr,* for example, the entries for "Francis, John Wakefield"; "Fricassee"; "Frogpondians"; and "Froissart, Monsieur" have identical beginnings, although this might be mere coincidence, there being only so many ways to describe certain things.)

The preceding criticisms aside, *Edgar Allan Poe A to Z* should be held by all libraries.

949j. Thomas, Dwight, and David K. Jackson. **The Poe Log: A Documentary Life of Edgar Allan Poe, 1809–1849.** American Authors Log Series. Boston: G. K. Hall, 1987. l, 919 p. Index. LC 86-19319. ISBN 0-8161-8734-7.

This splendid guide provides a complete chronology of Poe's life "as revealed in excerpts from contemporary documents: the letters he wrote or received, newspaper reports, magazine articles, reminiscences, and legal records." Many of the sources cited were accessible prior to this volume.

The Poe Log has a very simple arrangement. It begins with "Biographical Notes on Persons Mentioned in the Text," an alphabetically arranged section that provides birth and death dates and the person's connection with Poe. Some hundreds of names are listed in this section, including Poe's parents and relations, those who reviewed or published Poe, and those who were mentioned or noticed by Poe. The *Log* has 11 chapters, covering Poe's life from 1809–1825 (chapter 1), 1826–1830 (chapter 2), 1831–1834 (chapter 3), 1835–1837 (chapter 4), 1838–1840 (chapter 5), 1841–1842 (chapter 6), 1843–1844 (chapter 7), 1845 (chapter 8), 1846–1847 (chapter 9), 1848 (chapter 10), and 1849 (chapter 11). Each chapter quotes from and references contemporary material— the letters, newspaper reports, magazine articles, reminiscences, and legal records—and enables researchers to determine what Poe was doing, and what was being said about him or his writing, at virtually any point in his life.

A lengthy bibliography and an excellent index conclude this volume. It belongs in all libraries.

PRAED, ROSA [CAROLINE MURRAY-PRIOR PRAED]

950. Tiffin, Chris. **Rosa Praed (Mrs. Campbell Praed) 1851–1935: A Bibliography.** Victorian Fiction Research Guides, no. XV. Queensland, Australia: Victorian Fiction Research Unit, Department of English, University of Queensland, 1989. 66 p. Paperback. ISBN 0-86776-234-9. ISSN: 0 15 3921 [*sic*].

Rosa Praed was by birth Australian and by genre a late-Victorian sensationalistic novelist whose works were occasionally mysteries. Tiffin's excellent bibliography provides a lengthy life of Praed, followed by the primary bibliography, which contains different sections for fiction, collaborative fiction, nonfiction books, collaborative nonfiction, edited books, fiction in anthologies and periodicals, nonfiction and journalism, and surviving manuscript material. All items are numbered, with 753 citations in all; each section is arranged chronologically. The sections for books gives the title in boldface type. Listed beneath, in chronological order, are the various editions, with the place of publication, publisher, publication date, series, and pagination; a note indicates when the item has not been seen. If the work was serialized prior to book publication, serialization information (periodical, date, and pagination) is given. The list of fiction in anthologies and periodicals and the nonfiction and journalism also are arranged chronologically and reference all known appearances of Praed's fiction, not only those occurring during her lifetime. A secondary bibliography lists reviews and has sections for contemporary biography, interviews, and assessments and later biographical, critical, and general assessments of Praed and her work. The section for reviews is arranged chronologically and includes journals and newspapers. The title of the novel is listed, and beneath it are given the citations to the reviews: the place of publication, date of publication, and page on which the review appeared; if the review was signed, the reviewer's name is given also. The first biographical and critical section is arranged chronologically; the second is alphabetically by author. Both cite books, journal articles, and chapters in books; the latter also includes references to radio programs and theses and dissertations. A specialized work, but well done.

QUEEN, ELLERY:
PSEUDONYM FOR MANFRED BENNINGTON LEE
AND FREDERIC DANNAY AND OTHERS

Those curious about the others who used this pseudonym are referred to Francis M. Nevins, "Death and Ghosts: The Ellery Queen Paperback Originals," *Dime Novel Round-Up* 67, no. 1 (1998): 3–17.

951. Sullivan, Eleanor. **Whodunit: A Biblio-Bio-Anecdotal Memoir of Frederic Dannay, "Ellery Queen."** New York: Targ Editions, 1984. 45 p. LC 85-134154. 150 copies printed.

Containing no table of contents or index, this slim volume has a first section that provides a biographical account of the two writers who wrote as Ellery Queen, beginning with the 12-year-old Frederic Dannay's discovery of Sherlock Holmes and continuing with a brief account of his cousin Manfred Lee's childhood. The bibliographical section begins on page 40 and contains sections listing the novels, short story collections, and short story anthologies edited by Queen. Each section is arranged chronologically; book titles are italicized and accompanied by the year of first publication. Additional publication data are not given for books, and publication data for individual short stories are not provided. Dannay and Lee were important as writers, editors, and publishers, and although Sullivan's tribute is affectionate, it does not do them full justice, nor is it complete. A comprehensive bibliography of the works of Ellery Queen is needed.

RANKIN, IAN

952. Plain, Gill. **Ian Rankin's Black and Blue: A Reader's Guide.** Continuum Contemporaries. New York: Continuum, 2002. 95 p. Paperbound. LC 2001-407752. ISBN 0-8264-5244-2.

Despite its title, this is not a reader's guide to Ian Rankin's *Black and Blue* (London: Orion; New York: St. Martin's Paperbacks, 1997) but, rather, a critical assessment of it. The volume opens with a discussion of Rankin's life, after which *Black and Blue*—the eighth of Rankin's Inspector John Rebus novels—is discussed, as are its reception and the motion picture adaptations of the Rebus novels. The volume closes with suggestions for further reading, a bulleted list of discussion questions, and a brief bibliography citing Web sites as well as more traditional resources.

Whether one novel of Ian Rankin deserves an extended summation and a mildly theoretical explication is one question. Whether it needs this particular effort is another question entirely. Plain's prose tends toward the pedestrian. The volume contains its share of errors, as when Moose Malloy is erroneously identified as "the mythical big man hunted by Philip Marlowe throughout *Farewell, My Lovely.*" Worse yet, the theoretical assessments are too often unconvincing, as when Rebus breaks down and cries, and Plain assesses this as meaning that "Rebus's hard masculine exterior has metamorphosed into a leaky, feminized body." Rankin's novels deserve reading; the same cannot be said for this reader's guide.

RAWSON, CLAYTON

953a. Canick, Michael. **Clayton Rawson: Magic and Mystery.** New York: Volcanick Press, 1999. Unpaginated. Side-stapled paper.

Canick's *Clayton Rawson* begins with a brief biography of Rawson, after which the first part contains six largely prose sections: Rawson as artist; Rawson as magician; Rawson as writer; Rawson as editor; Rawson as master of ceremonies; and references. These sections frequently are illustrated, however, and reproduce such curiosities as the cover for the one issue of *Clue* edited by Rawson and an illustration Rawson did for Al Baker's *Pet Secrets*.

This second section is "An Annotated Bibliography of the Works of Clayton Rawson," which opens by describing the novels featuring the magician/detective the Great Merlini; each edition is described, and the covers of many are reproduced. The next section is a chronological list of Rawson's short stories featuring the Great Merlini: first periodical appearances are listed, as are anthologizations. Publication data on the four novelettes and short stories Rawson wrote as Stuart Towne are provided, as are data on Rawson's one-act plays, his nonfiction, his magic books, his articles in *Hugard's Magic Monthly* and the *Jinx*. The final two sections provide information about the films based on Rawson's books and miscellaneous works by or related to Rawson. An appendix is devoted to Rawson's artwork and images.

Although apparently self-published by Canick—a professional magician who also deals in books devoted to magic and by magicians—this bibliography is unquestionably the most thorough extant. Fans of Rawson's work—and there are many—will find it a fascinating accomplishment.

953b. Penzler, Otto. **Clayton Rawson.** Collection Mystery Fiction, no. 8. New York: Mysterious Bookshop, 2001. 31 p. Paperback. 250 copies printed.

Reprinted from material originally published in the *Armchair Detective,* this work begins with a brief biography of Rawson, after which Penzler provides bibliographical descriptions of Rawson's books from the 1938 appearance of *Death from a Top Hat* to the 1979 *The Great Merlini*. A reproduction of the dust wrapper for each book is given. The publication data are minimal and include only the publisher of the first American editions, a prose description of the volume (i.e., "blue cloth, lettered in black on front cover and spine, with a vignette, also in black, on front cover") ; the placement of the plates, and notes as to whether the book was filmed, and its original periodical serialization. The estimated retail value of the first editions in various conditions with and without dust wrapper are given, and the volume concludes by listing the uncollected stories Rawson published as "Stuart Towne," the data on Rawson's comic one-act plays written for the annual Mystery Writers of America banquet, and information about miscellaneous short fiction. A reproduction of Rawson's signature appears on the booklet's cover. Although nicely done, Canick's work (profiled earlier) is more comprehensive.

RENDELL, RUTH [BARBARA]

954. Tallett, Dennis. **The Ruth Rendell Companion: "From Doon with Death" to "The Crocodile Bird."** Santa Barbara, Calif.: CB/Companion Books, 1995. iv, 285 p. Index. Paperback. OCLC 37049872.

The Ruth Rendell Companion is a labor of love, a transplanted Californian's desire to find "a project to see me through the brisk chilliness of the Ohio winter." After a brief introduction, Tallett provides a chronology and profile of Rendell, a Polestead–Rendell connection, and a comparison of Rendell and Anthony Trollope. The *Companion* contains three major sections, with portions devoted to the Wexford material, the psychological thrillers, and the material Rendell has written as Barbara Vine. The Wexford section provides a description and map of Kingsmarkham and its police station, a statement about the ways in which Rendell's murders have been committed, and a chronological discussion of Rendell's works, starting with *From Doon with Death* (1964) and concluding with *Kissing the Gunner's Daughter* (1992). Each discussion provides the novel's plot, lists of its characters, names, places, and useful details, and a comment about the book; also included are publication data for the first English and American editions and name changes, if any. The Wexford section concludes with descriptions of the short stories featuring Wexford.

The other two sections are likewise arranged chronologically and contain the same data. Appendixes (not labeled as such) list book reviews, articles, and media adaptations and provide a "miscellany and afterword." The index lists titles and, occasionally, subjects and character names.

Tallett writes well and offers sound judgments. At the same time the specialized nature of this volume—and that it has become increasingly dated—do not make it a necessary acquisition.

RENIN, PAUL

955. Holland, Stephen, and Richard Williams. **Paul Renin: A Bibliographical Checklist.** British Paperback Checklists, no. 43. Scunthorpe, England: Dragonby Press, 1990. 8 p. Stapled sheets. Index.

Under the names of "Paul Renin," "John Courage," and his own name, Richard Goyne (1902–1957) wrote at least 40 mysteries. This checklist concentrates on the books written under the name of Renin, works that predominantly concerned what Holland and Williams describe in their brief foreword as "naughty ladies."

The checklist begins with the index, an alphabetical listing that gives the title of the book in capital letters; beneath each title are the publishers of the work and the year in which it was published. Following the index is an alphabetical list of the publishers. Beneath each publisher are the titles of the books in capital letters, the year of publication in parentheses, and pagination.

A comprehensive bibliography of the works of Richard Goyne remains to be done.

SAPPER: PSEUDONYM USED FIRST BY HERMAN CYRIL MCNEILE, LATER BY GERARD FAIRLIE (Q.V.)

956. Treadwell, Lawrence P., Jr. **The Bulldog Drummond Encyclopedia.** Forewords by Andrew Drummond Calthrop McNeile and F. I. ("Jock") Fairlie. Jefferson, N.C.: McFarland & Company, 2001. x, 213 p. Index. LC 00-68704. ISBN 0-7864-0769-7.

Captain Hugh "Bulldog" Drummond is among the nastiest of the popular literary figures created following the First World War. An enormous demobilized Englishman, Drummond finds peace boring and, with a gang of like-minded cronies, battles all those who would threaten the English way of life, particularly the trade unionists, anarchists, foreigners, communists, and Jews. Created by Herman Cyril McNeile writing as "Sapper," Drummond appears as the protagonist in 17 novels and more than 20 motion pictures, stage plays, and radio programs; after McNeile's death in 1937, the novels were continued until 1961 by Gerard Fairlie (1899–1983).

The introduction to *The Bulldog Drummond Encyclopedia* states that it describes the characters "as well as significant places, hotels, restaurants, landmarks, gadgets, techniques, expressions and systems" (1–2) in the novels written by McNeile. Also included are entries for such secondary studies as Richard Usborne's *Clubland Heroes* (1953), and the volume concludes with the transcript of a 1936 British Broadcasting Company (BBC) dialogue between McNeile and Fairlie, a stage bill for the 8 November 1932 special matinee performance of *Bull-dog Drummond* [*sic*] starring Gerald du Maurier, charts of the characters and settings, maps, bibliographies, and an index.

It must be emphasized that the *Encyclopedia*'s entries are consistently disingenuous (or dishonest) in their presentation. The author does not admit when his subject is unpalatable but instead sees Drummond as "the likable, demobilized officer, with his fine sense of sportsmanship and the camaraderie of his band of brothers" as providing "the best of adventure reading to the public" (1). This misdirection is serious: *The Black Gang* (1922), for example, concludes with the revelation that Drummond has been kidnapping undesirables (communists) and "reeducating" them at hard labor on a private penal island. The *Encyclopedia* ignores Drummond's activities and merely states that the police find "some 50 rabid anarchists presided over by 20 demobilized soldiers." Other entries are similarly and consistently misleading: Drummond's brutal fascistic activities are ignored or whitewashed, to the detriment of accuracy.

Libraries specializing in the best-forgotten popular literature of the early twentieth century may want *The Bulldog Drummond Encyclopedia,* but it is not reliable.

SAYERS, DOROTHY L[EIGH].

957a. Clarke, Stephan P. **The Lord Peter Wimsey Companion.** New York: Mysterious Press, 1985. [ix], 563 p. Indexes. LC 85-060072. ISBN 0-89296-850-8.

957b. Clarke, Stephan P. **The Lord Peter Wimsey Companion: A New Edition, Completely Revised and Incorporating Thrones, Dominations, Papers Relating to the Family of Wimsey, an Account of Lord Mortimer Wimsey, the Hermit of the Wash, and the Wimsey Papers.** 2nd ed. Hurstpierpoint, West Sussex, England: Dorothy L. Sayers Society, 2002. xxvi, 773 p. Indexes. ISBN 0-9518000-8-6.

The second edition is described.

Unlike the first edition, which contained some 7,509 numbered entries, the entries in the enormous second edition are not numbered, although rough calculations show that there must be approximately 10,000. Nevertheless, the goal of the volume remains simple and is, in Clarke's words, "to make the Peter Wimsey stories accessible to more readers who choose to participate in the stories at some level beyond that of simple entertainment."

Following prefatory material, the *Companion* begins with calendars for the canonical years 1920 to 1941 and period maps of England and Wales, Scotland, and central, northern, and western London in the early twentieth century. For the body of the *Companion,* Clarke has combed Sayers's stories for names, events, references, and allusions that readers of a later generation might not necessarily recognize. For each reference, he provides an explanatory definition as well as a citation (in abbreviated form) to the work in which the reference is to be found. The names and roles of all characters are given, as are numerous illustrated references to subjects as diverse as "cathedral close," "cricket," "Milford Hill," "Roland," the "Tower of London," and the "Underground." An appendix provides "The Rosemonde," a short story by Julian [Julien] Sermet, a translation of which appeared in the *Strand* (vol. 8 [1894]: 450–54) and is referenced in *The Nine Tailors.* A section for "agenda and corrigenda" is blank, but it is followed by "information still being sought," which provides an alphabetical list of references that "have eluded adequate identification." A lengthy bibliography of books, articles, and Web sites follows, and the *Companion* concludes with an elaborate series of indexes: sources referenced in passing, sources for which general information is given, and work-by-work listing that indexes the described references.

Like Jack Tracy, whose *Encyclopaedia Sherlockiana* (q.v.) similarly explicates the works and world of Doyle, Clarke has explained much that is obscure and clarified references that largely would be lost on a contemporary audience. His writing is clear, and the book is easy to use and remarkably helpful. Clarke is to be commended for what surely must have been a more than arduous labor of love. If he is to be faulted, it is on the grounds of overspecialization, but each year enables a specialized work such as this to grow in usefulness.

957c. Gilbert, Colleen B. **A Bibliography of the Works of Dorothy L. Sayers.** Hamden, Conn.: Archon Books, 1978. 263 p. Indexes. LC 78-18795. ISBN 0-2080-1755-0.

Five years in the compilation and unquestionably the definitive bibliography of the works of Dorothy L. Sayers, this volume is an exemplary achievement. Intended as a comprehensive description of Sayers's works, it contains seven sections: books, pamphlets, cards and ephemera by Dorothy L. Sayers alone or in collaboration; contributions to books, pamphlets, and miscellanea; contributions to newspapers and periodicals; book reviews; broadcasts, play productions, films, and records; lectures; and manuscript collections. Entries in all the sections are chronologically arranged and separately numbered.

In the first and second sections, descriptions begin with a quasi-facsimile transcription of the title page and are followed by a statement of collation, pagination, book's length and width (in centimeters), and bulk of the sheets and endpapers with and without the binding (in centimeters). Paper, endpapers, binding, original price, print run, and official date of publication are given, as are any textual variants or typographic idiosyncrasies that distinguish the first state of a first edition from later states. Finally, the first section provides numerous reproductions of title pages and book bindings.

Entries in the third and fourth sections provide complete citations to the periodicals that published Sayers's original work and her reviews. Periodical titles are italicized, and bibliographic data include volume, issue number, month, year, and page upon which the work was published. In the third section, a concluding note indicates whether Sayers's piece was a poem, a letter to the editor, an essay; reprint data are provided, as are occasional notes on the nature of Sayers's contribution. In the fourth section, a note provides authors' names and titles of the books reviewed by Sayers.

The entries in the fifth and sixth sections provide the exact date and the title of the play or lecture. A note indicates the nature of the broadcast or lecture; a star by an item indicates that it was published as well as broadcast.

The entries in the last section are grouped by repository. Each citation provides the title of the work, its number of pages (or leaves), and indicates whether it is an AMS (autograph manuscript), a TMS (typed manuscript), a TCC (typed carbon copy), an ALS (autograph letter signed), a TLS (typed letter signed). As in the preceding two sections, a star by an item indicates that it was published.

An excellent index concludes the volume, which belongs in all academic libraries.

957d. Harmon, Robert B., and Margaret A. Burger. **An Annotated Guide to the Work of Dorothy L. Sayers.** Garland Reference Library of the Humanities, vol. 80. New York: Garland, 1977. x, 286 p. Index. LC 76-57952. ISBN 0-8240-9896-X.

The introduction to this, one of two book-length Sayers bibliographies published in 1977, reveals a bias toward Sayers akin to hero worship. This might not be objectionable if Harmon and Burger expressed their adulation without cliché and with some recognition of literary history. Instead, readers get such sentences as "in the 1920's and 1930's, Miss Sayers established herself as one of the few who could give a new look to the detective novel. Her recipe was to deftly mix [sic] a plot that kept readers guessing with inside information, told without tears, about some fascinating subject." The conclusion to the introduction begins "Dorothy L. Sayers was definitely no fly-by-night writer of thrillers" and is lifted word-for-word (and without acknowledgment!) from the writings of Carolyn Heilbrun.

The bibliography contains the following sections: novels, short stories, essays, dramatic works, poetry, translations, miscellaneous works, criticism, sources, and adaptations. Each section contains numerous subdivisions; the first section, for example, has listings for the novels written by Sayers, the novels written in collaboration with others, and the novels collected in omnibus editions. Miscellaneous works section lists addresses, lectures, speeches, bibliographies in which Sayers's name appears, book reviews of her works, children's books by her, series edited by her, published letters, and pamphlets by her. Entries in all sections and subsections are arranged alphabetically and are separately numbered. The titles of novels are underlined. Beneath each title are bibliographical data for all known Anglo-American editions: place of publication, publisher, year of publication, and pagination. A lengthy (and adulatory) annotation concludes each entry. Entries for short stories underline the title, provide an annotation, and list all known appearances of the story, cross-referencing titles to collections. Entries in other sections are similarly arranged.

The sections presenting the secondary sources also contain numerous subdivisions; sources, for example, lists bibliographies, biographies, indexes, obituaries, portraits, and reviews in which Sayers's name or image appears. As before, annotations tend to be adulatory, downplaying the work of those critics who have not been enchanted by Sayers's prose. Their entry for Edmund Wilson states in its entirety that "on pages 339 to 341, Mr. Wilson criticizes Miss Sayers' ability as a detective fiction writer as exemplified in her novel *The Nine Tailors*." In actuality, Wilson was far more caustic, stating in part, "I have heard people say that Dorothy Sayers wrote well, and I felt that my correspondents had been playing her as their literary ace. But, really, she does not write very well: it is simply that she is more consciously literary than most of the other detective-story writers and that she thus attracts attention in a field which is mostly on a sub-literary level. In any serious department of fiction, her writing would not appear to have any distinction at all." (Wilson dismisses *The Nine Tailors* as "one of the dullest books I have ever encountered in any field. The first part of it is all about bell-ringing as it is practised in English churches and contains a lot of information of the kind that you might expect to find in an encyclopedia article on campanology.")

A Sayers chronology, a checklist of Sayers's papers at Wheaton College, and a capable author/title index conclude the *Guide*. As a primary bibliography, this is inferior to Colleen B. Gilbert's *A Bibliography of the Works of Dorothy L. Sayers* (profiled earlier). As a secondary bibliography, it is inferior to Ruth Youngberg's *Dorothy L. Sayers: A Reference Guide* (profiled later).

957e. Youngberg, Ruth Tanis. **Dorothy L. Sayers: A Reference Guide.** Boston: G. K. Hall, 1982. xxii, 178 p. Index. LC 81-6992. ISBN 0-8161-8198-5.

This "reference guide" is in fact a well-done annotated bibliography of the literature studying Dorothy L. Sayers. Following a lively and well-written introduction, Youngberg provides a selective bibliography of Sayers's writings, listing only the works by Sayers that have received critical attention. This is nevertheless quite a sizable number, and different sections list Sayers's novels, collaborative novels, short stories, collected short stories, collected novels and short stories, the short story collections edited by Sayers, Sayers's poems, plays, collected plays, films, miscellaneous essays and nonfiction, collected essays, translations by Sayers, biographies by Sayers, children's books by Sayers, and books reprinting selections of Sayers's writings. Each section provides the title of the work (underlined), the place of publication, publisher, and year of publication for the first English and the first American editions. Retitlings are clearly indicated.

The secondary bibliography is chronologically arranged; each year's entries are separately numbered and alphabetically arranged. Citations are given for the books, chapters, journal articles, significant newspaper articles, speeches, and dissertations written in English and published in the United States and England. All entries list the critic's name in capital letters and are otherwise consistent and clear; anonymous works are listed under "ANON" rather than by title. Youngberg's annotations are pithy and accurate; her description of Edmund Wilson's famous dismissal of Sayers's work is a model of abstraction: "Following a series of letters in response to his article 'Why Do People Read Detective Stories?' in the 14 October 1944 issue [of the *New Yorker*], tells of his attempt to give detective fiction another trial. Since Sayers's *The Nine Tailors* was urged on him, he skimmed it, picking up the thread of the story. Criticizes her writing adversely on the strength of this incomplete reading." (Compare with the milquetoast annotation given by Harmon and Burger previously) Although three publications from 1981 are cited, the bibliography effectively ceases its coverage as of September 1980.

A nicely done author/title index concludes the bibliography, which is clearly reproduced from typed copy. An updated edition would be welcome.

SIMENON, GEORGES [JOSEPH CHRISTIAN]

958a.   Georges Simenon. http://www.ulg.ac.be/libnet/simenon.htm

This site offers access to exhaustive and comprehensive bibliographic data compiled by Claude Menguy (discussed subsequently) and Pierre Deligny. The list of Simenon's pseudonymous works, for example, comprises four full pages and lists the books by publisher, providing also the name under which they were published, the series and series number, the title, and the year of publication.

958b.   Arens, Arnold. Das phänomen Simenon: Einführung in das Werk: Bibliographie (Verzeichnis der Werke und der Sekundärliteratur). Stuttgart, Germany: Franz Steiner Verlag Wiesbaden, 1988. 166 p. Indexes. ISBN 3-515-05243-7.

German-language publications are generally beyond the scope of this work, but the elaborate secondary bibliography makes *Das phänomen Simenon* deserving of mention. Following an introduction, the first section of this bibliography lists Simenon's pseudonymous works, grouped alphabetically by the pseudonym under which Simenon wrote them. Each of the 16 sections contains chronologically arranged but unnumbered citations. Titles are given in italics, and place of publication, publisher, and year of publication are listed. The second section lists Simenon's Maigret novels; the third, the non-Maigret novels; the fourth, Simenon's autobiographical works; the fifth, the novellas and short stories; the sixth, Simenon's introductions; the seventh, Simenon's theatrical works; the eighth, Simenon's published letters, and the ninth, collected editions of Simenon. Data in these sections also are arranged chronologically. Citations are not numbered, titles are given in italics, and place of publication, publisher, and year of publication are provided. The first German and Swiss editions are also cited in this format.

The primary bibliography occupies the first 70 pages of this volume. The remainder is occupied by an extensive bibliography of secondary literature on Simenon. Arranged chronologically, then listed alphabetically by author's last name, the entries begin with publications from 1932 and conclude with publications of 1985. In all, some 815 separately numbered citations to books, chapters in books, journal articles, and dissertations are given. Furthermore, although a few of these citations are to works published in English, the majority are from European publications unindexed by standard reference sources.

Research libraries supporting serious studies in the twentieth-century French novel and scholars doing research on Simenon will find that Arens's secondary bibliography justifies purchasing this book.

958c. Foord, Peter. **Georges Simenon: A Bibliography of the British First Editions in Hardback and Paperback and of the Principal French and American Editions, with a Guide to Their Value, edited by Richard Williams and Sally Swan.** Dragonby Bibliographies, no. 3. Scunthorpe, England: Dragonby Press, 1988. 85 p. Index. Paperback. ISBN 1-871122-03-1.

As its title indicates, this bibliography lists the British first editions and many of the French and American editions of the books of the prolific Georges Simenon. The French section of the bibliography cites some 371 works, of which 240 were translated into English editions. The bibliography is reproduced from what appears to be dot-matrix printout and is quite elaborate in its arrangement, containing the following sections: main index: Maigret titles in English, alphabetically; main index: non-Maigret titles in English, alphabetically; French first editions: Maigret, in order of publication; French first editions: non-Maigret, in order of publication; French title index: Maigret alphabetically (with subsections listing translated works with original English titles and short stories and collections not translated); French title index: non-Maigret alphabetically (with subsections listing translated works with original English titles and short stories, other works, and collections not translated); British first editions: Maigret, in order of publication; British first editions: non-Maigret, in order publication; British paperback editions: serially by imprint; other British editions: by publisher and date; American first editions: Maigret, in order of publication; American first editions: non-Maigret, in order of publication; American paperback editions: serially by imprint; other American editions: by publisher and date; British and American anthologies in which Simenon short stories appear; British, American, and French magazines in which Simenon short stories appear. Finally, included are lists of printer abbreviations and the translators of Simenon and a selected bibliography.

The data provided differ from section to section. At their fullest, however, entries include the book's title (in capital letters), the exact date of publication, publisher, pagination, binding, dust wrapper, and the name of its artist. Translated editions provide the translator's name and the book's original title. The 1988 value of the book (in English pounds) is provided.

Although it is overly complex in its arrangement and thus occasionally frustrating, this is more substantial than Trudee Young's earlier bibliography (q.v.) and is the most comprehensive English-language bibliography of Georges Simenon available.

958d. Haining, Peter. **The Complete Maigret: From Simenon's Original Novels to Granada's Much Acclaimed TV Series.** London: Boxtree Limited, 1994. 128 p. Index. Paperback. LC: 94-20780. ISBN 1-85283-447-1.

Although not a reference book, this heavily illustrated appreciation of the media adaptations of Simenon's Maigret novels nevertheless deserves mention. The book opens with a description of Maigret and provides surveys of the adaptations of Maigret in the cinema and on television; the films that were made with Budapest serving as Paris are described and praised at some length. The book concludes with a chronological listing of the films and television series in which Chief Inspector Jules Maigret appeared. The principal entry, however, is the name (capitalized and in boldface type) of the actor who portrayed Maigret. This is followed by the adaptation's title in italics; non-English titles are followed by a parenthetical translation into English. The names of the production company, producer, the director, scriptwriter, release/transmission date, and leading co-stars also are given.

958e. Lemoine, Michel. **Index des Personnages de Georges Simenon.** Bruxelles: Editions Labor, 1985. 695 p. Index. ISBN 2-8040-0119-9.

Although French-language publications are generally beyond the scope of this work, one would be remiss to ignore Lemoine's monumental index to and description of all of the named characters (and a few of the unnamed but readily identifiable characters) appearing in the collected works of Georges Simenon.

The first section of the index lists the characters. Each name is given in small capital letters; the name of the work or works in which the character appears is given in italics. A few keywords and occasionally a sentence or two identify the character's gender and describe his or her role in the novel. In the case of enormously important characters (e.g., Paul, Lucas, and Henriette and Louise Maigret), the descriptions are substantially longer.

The index to character names is followed by three appendixes, both using the format of the first section. The first lists the named animals in Simenon's collected works; the second, the named boats. The third indexes the cited works.

Maigret lovers will delight in this well-done index, but it is unlikely to be used in most American libraries.

958f. Menguy, C. **Bibliographie des Éditions Originales de Georges Simenon y Compris les Oeuvres Publiées sous des Pseudonymes.** Brussels: Le Livre et l'estampe, 1967. Extrait de la revue "Le Livre et L'Estampe." Numéro 49–50, Premier numéro, double, de 1967. 100 p. Index. Paperbound.

The first section of this separately published fascicle of *Le Livre et L'Estampe,* "Oeuvres publiees sous des pseudonymes," contains a thorough and accessible bibliography of Simenon's early pseudonymous publications. The arrangement of this section is alphabetical by the pseudonym. Citations then are numbered separately and listed chronologically. Each entry lists the title in italics and provides the place of publisher, publisher name, and date of publication. Series titles and series numbers are given, as are pagination, book size, a description of the cover, and original price. Retitlings and re-issues are listed and cross-referenced to the original work. In all, more than 100 publications under 18 pseudonyms are documented.

The second section, "Oeuvres publiees sous son patronyme," lists Simenon's works under his own name. It is chronological in arrangement, with the 1967 *Le Voleur de Maigret* being the last title cited. The data included are the same as in the first section. Separate title indexes to the pseudonymous and acknowledged work conclude the bibliography.

Although the list of acknowledged publications is superseded by Menguy's later work (q.v.), the thoroughly documented and easily accessible list of Simenon's pseudonymous works makes this quite a useful bibliography.

958g. **Le nouvelisste et le conteur.** Cahiers Simenon, no. 6. Bruxelles: Les Amis de Georges Simenon, 1993. 133 p. Index. Paperback.

The first section of this volume consists of appreciations and discussions of Simenon, but the last 50 pages are Claude Menguy's "Inventaire raisonné des nouvelles de Georges Simenon." French publications are largely beyond the scope of this work, but Menguy's bibliography deserves mention for the currency of his citations and the clarity of his presentation.

Like Piron before him, Menguy divides Simenon's output into two chronologically arranged sections: the "Séries Policières" and the "Nouvelles Diverses." Although the content for individual entries varies, at their fullest both sections list the story's title in boldface type, date of composition, date of first periodical publication, first book publication, later French publications, position it holds in Simenon's *Oeuvres Complètes* (Éditions Rencontre, 1967–1973), and position it holds in the *Tout Simenon* (Presses de la Cité, 1988–1992). For book publications, Menguy provides publisher's name, location, date of publication, and pagination. For the periodical publications, he provides the volume, month, and year. The index is by title.

Researchers and collectors of the French editions of Simenon will find Menguy's data are clearly presented and accessible.

958h. Piron, Maurice. **L'Univers de Simenon: Guide des Romans et Nouvelles (1931–1972) de Georges Simenon.** Paris: Presses de la Cité, 1983. 490 p. Index. Paperback. LC 83-147085. ISBN 2-258-01152-3.

French publications are generally beyond the scope of this work, but one would be remiss to ignore this comprehensive annotated bibliography of the works of Georges Simenon. The volume is dominated by two sections: "Les romans de la destinée" and "Les romans de Maigret." Each of these is arranged chronologically, and all citations are separately numbered and occupy two facing pages. The book's title is given on the top of the right page; at the top of the left page are the date of composition and minimal publication data (publisher's name and date of publication). Each entry begins with a statement of the time and place of the work in a section titled "Cadre spatio-temporel." This is followed by a section describing the protagonists: the description in "Les romans de la destinée" is titled "Statut du héros" and provides the protagonist's full name, profession, marital status, and age. The description in "Les romans de Maigret" is essentially the same, with "Status de Maigret, héros du roman" providing Maigret's name, rank, and marital status, and "Statut du héros" providing the full name, profession, marital status, and age of other significant characters. Each entry has a section titled "Autres personnages principaux," which lists the names, marital status, profession, and age of the other principal characters. This is followed by "Aspects particuliers du roman," a statement of the noteworthy incidents in the work, and each citation concludes with a lengthy summary of the contents ("Résumé").

Following the descriptions of the novels are descriptions of Simenon's shorter works. As before, information is split into two sections, each arranged chronologically. The first concentrates on Simenon's non-Maigret works. Each citation occupies one page; provides periodical title, date of the initial publication, including month, and title of its first book appearance; and concludes with a summarization of the story. The second section concentrates on Simenon's Maigret stories and uses the same arrangement. None of these citations in either section is numbered.

Indexes to the titles, side-by-side chronological lists of non-Maigret and Maigret publications, and indexes to the settings conclude this volume. Although not comprehensive in presenting bibliographical data, readers of French will find the annotations thorough and helpful. An English edition of this book would be welcome.

958i.   Trussel, Steve. **Simenon's Maigret.** http://www.trussel.com/f_maig.htm

Although not as elaborate as the site compiled by Menguy and Deligny (see earlier), this English site is nevertheless excellent. It provides thorough bibliographies, statistical data about Maigret, access to online texts by and about Simenon, a Maigret/Simenon gallery, and information about media adaptations of Maigret.

958j.   Young, Trudee. **Georges Simenon: A Checklist of His "Maigret" and Other Mystery Novels and Short Stories in French and English Translation.** Scarecrow Author Bibliographies, no. 29. Metuchen, N.J.: Scarecrow, 1976. iii, 153 p. Index. LC 76-14410. ISBN 0-8108-0964-8.

Despite the limitations apparently imposed by its title, this bibliography does not restrict itself to Simenon's "Maigret" and other mystery novels and short stories, although it does refrain from documenting his juvenilia, pseudonymously published hackwork, and uncollected publications.

In arrangement, this bibliography is roughly chronological, with Young having arranged Simenon's output by the decade in which it was first published. These data are presented in sections titled "Titles First Published in the 1930s," "Titles First Published in the 1940s," and so forth; the last section is "Titles First Published in the 1970s." Within each of these sections, however, the citations are arranged alphabetically. Each citation is separately numbered and begins by listing the title of the first French edition (in capital letters), followed by the place of publication, publisher, year of publication, and pagination. Additional French editions are listed beneath this entry using the same format. They are followed by the English translations, the data on the British editions preceding that of the American editions. The format is essentially the same as that used for citing the first French edition, although the translator's name is provided. The contents of Simenon's anthologies and collections are not distinguished by a separate section and also are listed in this format. Concluding the bibliography are separate indexes for the French titles and the English translations. In all, some 222 works are listed.

Although typographically much clearer than Foord's later work (q.v.), Young's bibliography is substantially more frustrating. There is no reason to divide Simenon's work by decade other than convenience, but then to list the output of each decade alphabetically rather than chronologically prevents access to the work and necessitates constant use of the indexes. Researchers wanting comprehensiveness in a Simenon bibliography will prefer Foord.

SPILLANE, MICKEY: I.E., FRANK MORRISON SPILLANE

959a.   Gale, Robert L. **A Mickey Spillane Companion.** Westport, Conn.: Greenwood, 2003. xvii, 338 p. Index. LC 2002-035339. ISBN 0-313-32334-8.

Gale has compiled a guide to his life and works of Mickey Spillane, justifying this endeavor by stating that Spillane "may well be the most widely read author in the world" and that "at one point, he wrote seven of the ten best-sellers of all time." The approximately seven hundred alphabetical entries in the *Companion* profile and describe the major people and events in Spillane's life, summarize Spillane's fiction, and provide descriptions for all the named characters in Spillane's works. In addition, the *Companion* offers a useful Spillane chronology and concludes with a bibliography and a capably done index.

The volume is unfortunately far from being the work it could be. Its contents are bibliographically frustrating, for Gale fails to follow any known citation standard, and the original publication sources of neither Spillane's novels nor his short stories are given. Gale's summaries are verbose: the description of *The Killing Man* occupies nearly five wearisome pages and manages to mention every single plot element, relevant or not; other plot summaries are equally and unnecessarily lengthy. Gale's entries conceal information: users must use either the index or know to look under "Movies" to find information about films made of Spillane's works, for there are no cross-references. Finally, there are a smattering of typographical errors ("The Girl Behind the Hedge" was not published in 1853) and several outright errors: although "The Veiled Woman" (1952) was published under Spillane's name, it is fairly common knowledge that this story was ghosted by Howard Browne, who had acquired Spillane's "The Woman with Green Skin" for *Fantastic* but been unable to use it because portions were published in *Life*. Gale mentions neither Browne nor "The Woman with Green Skin."

Gale has compiled companions to the works of Dashiell Hammett, Nathaniel Hawthorne, and Ross Macdonald. All are flawed in one way or another, but all will have to stand until something better comes along. So it is with *A Mickey Spillane Companion.*

959b.   Penzler, Otto. **Mickey Spillane.** Collection Mystery Fiction, no. 4. New York: Mysterious Bookshop, 1999. 35 p. Paperback. 250 copies printed.

Reprinted from material first published in the *Armchair Detective,* Penzler begins his bibliography by observing that Spillane "has been dramatically underestimated and unfairly ignored." He ultimately quotes Ayn Rand, whose *Romantic Manifesto* observes approvingly that Spillane's style is "reality-oriented and addressed to an objective psycho-epistemology." Following this, Penzler presents a bibliography of Spillane's output, the first section describing Spillane's Mike Hammer novels, the section describing the non–Mike Hammer mysteries. Each section is arranged chronologically. Citations describe the first American edition, providing for each the place of publication, publisher, publication year, a prose description of the volume, and a description of the dust wrapper. Notes describe bibliographic points and indicate media adaptations. The estimated value of the book in a variety of conditions is given, and the bibliography concludes with a partial list of Spillane's short fiction.

STARRETT, [CHARLES] VINCENT [EMERSON]

960a.   Honce, Charles. **A Vincent Starrett Library: The Astonishing Result of Twenty-Three Years of Library Activity.** Mount Vernon, N.Y.: Golden Eagle Press, 1941. 81 p. LC 41-15879. 100 copies printed.

Not seen.

960b.   Norfolk-Hall. **A Vincent Starrett Catalogue: First Editions, Books by and About, Fine Association Copies & Ephemera.** Oakville, Mo.: Norfolk-Hall, 1979. 38 p.

Dealer's catalogues generally are not included here, but like the work of Enola Stewart (which follows), this dealer's catalogue must be mentioned. Items in it are separately numbered and arranged chronologically; items published prior to 1941 have their number in Honce's bibliography given. References to books list the place of publication, publisher, year of publication, and significant features; references to fascicles also are provided. More is listed in this catalogue than in Stewart's, but its arrangement is less felicitous.

960c. Ruber, Peter. **The Last Bookman.** New York: Candlelight Press, 1968. 115 p. LC 72-44.

960d. Ruber, Peter. **The Last Bookman.** 2nd ed. Vincent Starrett Memorial Library, vol. 3. Toronto: Metropolitan Toronto Reference Library, 1995. 172 p. CN 95-931571. ISBN 1-896032-66-4.

This tribute to Starrett contains a partial bibliography compiled by Esther Longfellow. The bibliography contains the following sections: novels; short stories; juveniles; poetry; critical studies and essays by Starrett; books edited; and a section titled "About Vincent Starrett." Citations in each section are arranged chronologically, and bibliographic data for each citation include place of publication, publisher, year of publication, pagination, paper size (i.e., 16mo.), and, when relevant, notes on the size of the edition.

A comprehensive Starrett bibliography remains to be compiled, but given Starrett's prolixity, it is unlikely such will ever be attempted.

960e. Stewart, Enola. **Vincent Starrett: A Catalogue of First and Variant Editions of His Work, Including Books Edited by Him and Those with Introductions, Prefaces, Afterwords, or Anthologized Contributions.** Pocono Pines, Pa.: Gravesend Books, 1975. 26 leaves. 300 copies printed.

Although dealer's catalogues generally are not included here, this one must be mentioned. Reproduced from typed copy and compiled by the owner of Gravesend Books, it offers a cover illustration by Mathew Zimmer and contains 10 sections: first and variant editions of books and pamphlets written by Starrett; books edited by Starrett; books and pamphlets containing introductions, prefaces, forewords, and afterwords by Vincent Starrett; books and pamphlets containing contributions by Vincent Starrett; books and pamphlets containing information pertaining to Vincent Starrett and his books; magazines and journals containing stories and articles written by Vincent Starrett; books once in the possession of Vincent Starrett; ephemera; reference books used in preparing the catalogue; and terms. Citations are numbered continuously and are arranged chronologically in each section; in all, 139 items are listed. In every citation, the publication's title, publisher, and place of publication are given in capital letters and are followed by the date of publication.

As Stewart's foreword explains, Starrett wrote far more than is listed in the bibliography, and "the catalogue . . . although by no means complete, is a representative sampling of his work." Affectionate though Stewart's sampling is, it is inadequate as a bibliography, and one regrets that Starrett, who died in 1974, was unable to assist in its compilation.

STEVENS, SHANE

961. Legg, John. **Collecting Shane Stevens a.k.a. J. W. Rider.** Charleston, W. Va.: Black Diamond Books, 1995. 88 p. Paperback. LC 94-96663. ISBN 0-9644069-0-X.

Though he is hardly well known, Shane Stevens has a devoted core of fans, and no less a writer than Stephen King has appropriated and used the names of Shane Stevens's characters. This affectionate tribute to the elusive thriller/mystery writer Shane Stevens/J. W. Rider contains nine chapters, the first of which is a biographical recounting of the few facts known about the reclusive Stevens. Chapter 2 describes Stevens's magazine and newspaper contributions; chapter 3 describes the Shane Stevens novels. Chapter 4 discusses the two pseudonymous novels Stevens has written as J. W. Rider, chapter 5 discusses book-collecting basics; chapter 6 provides a checklist of Shane Stevens, and chapter 7, a J. W. Rider checklist. Chapter 8 presents illustrations of letters written by and books inscribed by Stevens. Chapter 9 lists booksellers specializing in modern first editions. The book concludes with a glossary of bookselling terms and a quick reference checklist of Stevens's/Rider's works. Numerous illustrations are included throughout.

The largest sections in the book are chapters 6 and 7, which describe all known English-language editions of Steven's books. The arrangement in these chapters is chronological, and each edition is separately numbered. The distinguishing features of each edition are described; bibliographic data include place of publication, publisher, and month of publication. When relevant, ISBNs also are provided, as are the name of the dust jacket artist, pagination, and measurements of the book. Finally, changes in printings and covers are detailed, and the approximate worth of the book (as of late 1995) is given.

The bibliographic data in the other chapters are less comprehensive, and in the case of chapter 2, they would appear to be incomplete, for Stevens's autobiographical accounts mention publications that are not referenced by Legg. This aside, the volume's organization is occasionally frustrating, for it follows no pattern and mixes chapters containing useful book-collecting hints with chapters documenting publications. Nevertheless, *Collecting Shane Stevens* can be used with ease, and it is the only significant publication on an intriguing and quietly influential writer.

STOUT, REX [TODHUNTER]

962a. Ahearn, Allen, and Patricia Ahearn. **Author Price Guides: Rex Stout.** Rockville, Md.: Quill & Brush, 1995. 9 leaves. APG 076.2.

This Author's Price Guide to Rex Stout documents his work from the 1929 publication of *How Like a God* to the 1987 publication of *Under the Andes;* the Nero Wolfe pastiches by Robert Goldsborough also are listed.

For a thorough description of the format of Author Price Guides, see the entry under Fredric Brown.

962b. Gotwald, Frederick G. **The Nero Wolfe Companion.** Salisbury, N.C.: Rev. Frederick G. Gotwald, 1996–. 9 vols. Paperback.

Inspired by William S. Baring-Gould's annotations to Sherlock Holmes (q.v.), the introduction to each volume of this nine-volume guide to the Nero Wolfe novels of Rex Stout states that "it is the conclusion of the author that the setting of the Wolfe adventures were in real time. Over four hundred and thirty names of real persons are name-dropped. Events of the day are noted and even become the topic of an adventure. Rex Stout's attitudes about social and political issues of the time are revealed through his primary characters Nero Wolfe and Archie." To provide biographical data on these names, explanations of these events, and explications of these attitudes is the purpose of these self-published guides.

The volumes and the works they annotate are as follows:

Volume 1: *Fer-de-Lance, The League of Frightened Men, The Rubber Band, The Red Box, Too Many Cooks*

Volume 2: *Some Buried Caesar, Over My Dead Body, Where There's a Will; Bitter End, Black Orchids, Not Quite Dead Enough*

Volume 3: *The Silent Speaker, Too Many Women, And Be a Villain, The Second Confession, In the Best Families*

Volume 4: *Trouble in Triplicate, Three Doors to Death, Curtains for Three, Triple Jeopardy, Murder by the Book*

Volume 5: *Three Men Out, Prisoner's Base, The Golden Spiders, The Black Mountain, Three Witnesses*

Volume 6: *Before Midnight, Three for the Chair, And Four to Go, Might as Well Be Dead, If Death Ever Slept*

Volume 7: *Champagne for One, Three at Wolfe's Door, Homicide Trinity, Plot It Yourself, Too Many Clients*

Volume 8: *Trio for Blunt Instruments, The Final Deduction, Gambit, The Mother Hunt, A Right to Die, The Doorbell Rang*

Volume 9: *Death of a Doxy, The Father Hunt, Death of a Dude, Please Pass the Guilt, A Family Affair*

Each volume is reproduced from typed copy. Each entry begins with a reproduction of the cover or title page (or both) of the first edition and an account of its publication. Stout's references are explicated in the order in which they occur, with Gotwald's left column listing the chapter in which the reference is located and the right column providing the explanatory data. The majority of the explications are accompanied by (occasionally grainy) illustrations; concluding each chapter are reprints of contemporary reviews.

Gotwald has performed yeoman service in his explications, which are concise and generally helpful. On the debit side, he has not indicated the sources from which he has derived his data; occasional misspellings occur (including Hemingway's name); and the lack of a cumulative index prohibits researchers from locating similar references in different novels. Readers new to Stout and Nero Wolfe may nevertheless find these volumes quite helpful.

962c. Townsend, Guy M., ed., with John J. McAleer, Judson C. Sapp, and Arriean Schemer. **Rex Stout: An Annotated Primary and Secondary Bibliography.** Garland Reference Library of the Humanities, vol. 239. New York: Garland, 1980. xxvi, 199 p. Index. LC 80-8507. ISBN 0-8240-9479-4.

This excellent bibliography lists every available item by or about Rex Stout written in English and published in the United States, Great Britain, and Canada, with the exception of newspaper stories: in these, it is selective. The volume begins with a lively biography of Stout, who can be said to have had three writing careers but who did not start seriously writing detective and mystery stories until 1934, when he was in his late forties—and who then wrote some 72 novels and novellas before his death at age 89 in 1975. Near the conclusion of this section, Townsend (et al.) offers a statement that simultaneously explains Stout's technique, rationalizes his popularity, and justifies his enormous importance: "One of the chief reasons why the Nero Wolfe stories command so extraordinary a following is that in them Stout reconciled the formal detective story with the hard-boiled detective story at a time when the steadily widening breach separating them threatened the dissolution of the genre." To this one might add that despite occasional deficiencies in plot, Stout's stories were lively and witty, his characterizations and settings were vivid and exact; and his sense of the rights of the individual and the importance of humanity was pervasive and appealing.

The bibliography contains the following sections: novels; short stories; short story collections; omnibus volumes; articles; forewords, introductions, prefaces, afterwords, and jacket essays; reviews; jacket blurbs; edited volumes; poetry; broadcasts in print; movies; Nero Wolfe radio broadcasts; pastiches; interviews; criticism. The contents of each of the sections are arranged chronologically and are exemplary in their presentation of data. The section devoted to novels contains separately numbered citations, each of which provides information on all known appearances of the work, starting with the original serialization of the piece. Data presented for serializations include the magazine's date of publication, volume, and pagination. Citations for books list place of publication, publisher, date of publication, pagination, and all known reprint editions. The annotations are lively, providing plot elements without revealing the conclusion. Finally, each entry concludes with a list of the significant reviews received by the book upon original publication.

The citations for Stout's short stories also are numbered individually. Each lists every appearance of the story, from its first periodical publication to its later appearance in Stout's collections and its eventual anthologization. As before, the data are gratifyingly comprehensive. Periodical publication data include the magazine's name, volume, and story's pagination, and the references to the story's anthologization provide the book's editor, anthology's title, publisher, place of publication, year of publication, series number, and pagination. As in the earlier section, the annotations are models at stimulating interest in the story. Furthermore, cross-references are provided throughout this section, linking the story to its appearances in the short story collections and omnibus volumes. The successive sections of the primary bibliography are equally comprehensive and well done, revealing a man of extraordinary energies and versatility.

The secondary bibliography indexes and annotates some 112 articles, chapters in books, and books. Although many of these publications appeared in (virtually inaccessible) fan magazines, a gratifying number are from sources as varied and accessible as the London *Times, Nation, English Studies,* and the *Practitioner.* An excellent author/title index concludes the volume, which belongs in all academic libraries.

962d. Van Dover, J. Kenneth. **At Wolfe's Door: The Nero Wolfe Novels of Rex Stout.** Milford Series Popular Writers of Today, vol. 52. San Bernardino, Calif.: Borgo Press, 1991. 120 p. Index. LC 88-34363. ISBN 0-89370-189-0 (hc); 0-89370-289-7 (pb). ISSN 0163-2469.

At Wolfe's Door provides a synopsis of every mystery novel and each short story published by Stout between 1934 and 1975; such posthumously published works as *Death Times Three* (1985) also are summarized. Because Nero Wolfe is by far Stout's best-known creation, the first section of the volume surveys those works in which Wolfe appears, and the volume's second section surveys the rest of Stout's writings. Both sections are arranged chronologically; when more than one work appeared in a particular year, the arrangement is alphabetical. Each entry is numbered, with the title of the work appearing in boldface type with the date of publication beside it; when the work is a short story, its first book appearance is indicated. Each entry lists the name and identifying activity of the victim(s), the client(s), and the principal(s). A synopsis of the plot follows, although the murderer's identity is never revealed, and each entry concludes with a critical comment on the merits of the work; in all, 85 works are summarized. An essay comparing Stout with Erle Stanley Gardner follows the summaries, and the volume concludes with an index.

Apart from their titles and dates of publication, Van Dover provides no bibliographic data, and in summarizing only the mysteries, Van Dover deliberately neglects Stout's early novels and much ephemeral work, including poetry and articles which occasionally contain themes that prefigure his later work. Nevertheless, Van Dover should not be faulted for limiting his focus to Stout's criminous work; the 85 annotations are well written and clear, and his concluding essay is insightful.

STRAUB, PETER

963. Collings, Michael R. **Hauntings: The Official Peter Straub Bibliography.** Biblio Series. Interview with Peter Straub conducted by Stanley Wiater. Woodstock, Ga.: Overlook Connection Press, 2000 [title page erroneously states 1999]. 193 p. Index. ISBN 1-892950-16-2 (hc); 1-892950-16-2 (pb).

Peter Straub is rarely considered a writer of mystery and detective fiction, but anybody familiar with his works will recognize that *mystery* is central to almost all of them. In addition, Straub has written the Blue Rose series, which among other things concerns a serial killer, and among his works is the eponymous *Mystery*.

Hauntings begins with a lengthy six-part interview with Straub conducted by Stanley Wiater. The bibliography contains seven lettered sections, the first six of which (A–F) concentrate on material by Straub: book-length publications: fiction and poetry; short fiction: short story, novella; nonfiction: introductions, essays, reviews, afterwords; poetry; liner note: jazz records and CDs; and miscellaneous. Each separate item in these sections is numbered. The seventh section documents selected secondary sources: interviews, reviews, articles, biographical sketches, and so forth.

The material in each section except the seventh is arranged chronologically and includes data through 1999. The data in the book section (A) provide a reproduction of the book's cover, and the book's title in bold capital letters is followed by the place of publication, publisher, publication year, pagination, original cover price, edition size, and ISBN. Reprints, later and international editions are listed beneath and provide information but for edition size; title changes are indicated, as are translators. A chronological list of selected articles and reviews about the book follows. The contents of short story collections are listed, as are individual reprints and the awards they have won. Section E, the listing of Straub's liner notes for jazz records and CDs provides the work's title, its main performer, place of publication, publisher, date of imprint, and CD serial number.

The material in the seventh section is arranged alphabetically and references books, chapters, articles, and Web sites. The index does not provide pagination but references section and item numbers, making it sometimes difficult to locate individual citations.

Although now somewhat out of date, this remains the best list of material by and about Straub.

SYMONS, JULIAN [GUSTAVE]

964. Walsdorf, John J., and Bonnie J. Allen. **Julian Symons: A Bibliography with Commentaries and a Personal Memoir by Julian Symons and a Preface by H. R. F. Keating.** Winchester Bibliographies of 20th Century Writers. New Castle, Del.: Oak Knoll Press; Winchester, England: St. Paul's Bibliographies, 1996. xliii, 296 p. Index. LC 96-12092. ISBN 1-8847-1822-1.

Compiled with the assistance of Symons, who died two years prior to its publication, this fine bibliography uses a format reminiscent of the Pittsburgh Series in Bibliography. The contents: (A) "Fiction"; (B) "Poetry"; (C) "Nonfiction"; (D) "Works Edited"; (E) "Contributions to Books"; (F) "Contributions to Anthologies"; (G) "Selected Contributions to Periodicals"; and (H) "Contributions to *Ellery Queen's Mystery Magazine.*" Entries in the all sections are chronologically arranged and separately numbered. In addition, a lengthy autobiographical statement by Symons (reprinted from the Contemporary Authors Autobiography series from Gale) is included, as well as introductions by H. R. F. Keating and John Walsdorf, and a brief reminiscence by Kathleen Symons (reprinted from the *Mystery Writers Annual,* 1987). Finally, a chronology of Symons's life is provided, as are numerous reproductions of title pages, an appendix, and an epilogue. The volume concludes with well-done indexes.

The data in each section are gratifyingly thorough. In sections A through C, the title page of each work is transcribed in the quasi-facsimile method; a collation statement is provided; the contents are given; any illustrations are detailed; the binding cases and their colors are described; the dust jackets or wrappers are described; and the paper on which the book was printed is detailed. The bibliographer's notes provides statements on the printing history (the number of copies printed, prices, textual changes, author's agreements, etc.). Corrected editions and the first American editions also are accorded this bibliographical treatment. Furthermore, Symons has provided notes on many of the titles.

The citations to Symons's material in the other sections are equally thorough and detailed. The appendix lists selected biographical and critical material about Symons, and the epilogue lists the dates on which obituaries of Symons appeared in major publications. The indexes contain separate sections listing titles, publishers, printers, designer/illustrators, photographers, poems (by title), and short fiction (by title); they conclude with a listing of the names and titles not listed in the previous sections.

THOMAS, ROSS [ELMORE]

965a. Ahearn, Allen, and Patricia Ahearn. **Author Price Guides: Ross Thomas.** Rockville, Md.: Quill & Brush, 1995. 4 leaves. APG 022.3.

This Author's Price Guide to Ross Thomas documents his work from the 1966 appearance of *The Cold War Swap* to the 1994 publication of *Ah, Treachery!*

For a thorough description of the format of Author Price Guides, see the entry under Fredric Brown.

965b. Stephens, Christopher P. **A Checklist of Ross Thomas.** Hastings-on-Hudson, N.Y.: Ultramarine Publishing, 1992. 13 p. Paperback. Index. ISBN 0-89366-228-3.

Apparently offset from typed copy, this brief checklist lists the books written by Ross Thomas under his own name as well as those he wrote under the pseudonym Oliver Bleeck. Each numbered citation provides publication data on the first American and first British editions. Titles are underlined; retitlings are indicated; and information on dust wrapper artists, prices, and identifying points is given. An index to the titles and retitlings is included, and pagination is inconsistently provided. Although this pamphlet is a useful starting point for collectors, it does not list Thomas's nonbook writings, and a comprehensive bibliography remains needed.

TUCKER, [ARTHUR] WILSON

966a. Stephens, Christopher P. **A Checklist of Wilson Tucker.** Hastings-on-Hudson, N.Y.: Ultramarine Publishing, 1991. 18 p. Paperback. Index. ISBN 0-89366-211-9.

Wilson Tucker is traditionally considered a writer of science fiction, but more of his work is detective and mystery stories than it is science fiction. This checklist of Tucker's output begins with a chronologically arranged listing of Tucker's books, from the 1946 *The Chinese Doll* to the 1982 *The Best of Wilson Tucker*. Each of the citations is separately numbered and provides data on the first American and the first British editions. Titles are underlined, and information is given on pagination, retitlings, dust wrapper artists, prices, and identifying points. The second section lists Tucker's short stories, from the 1941 publication of "Interstellar Way-Station" in *Super Science Stories* to the 1978 publication of "The Near Zero Crime Rate on JJ Avenue" in *Analog;* the citations provide only the month and year of the magazine. An index to the books and short stories concludes the bibliography.

In science fiction circles, Tucker is something of a legend, and stories about his youthful behavior still circulate. Unfortunately for his fans and collectors, this checklist is far from comprehensive. Not only does it neglect to provide Tucker's full name (Arthur Wilson Tucker), it neglects to cite his semiprofessionally published works in fanzines. The bibliography of Phil Stephensen-Payne and Gordon Benson Jr. (q.v.) is a superior work.

966b. Stephensen-Payne, Phil, and Gordon Benson Jr. **Wilson "Bob" Tucker: Wild Talent.** 4th rev. ed. Galactic Central Bibliographies for the Avid Reader, vol. 8. Leeds, England; Albuquerque, N. Mex.: Galactic Central, 1994. 29 p. Paperback. LC 94-51091. ISBN 1-871133-41-6.

The earlier editions have not been seen.

This bibliography attempts to cite all the published works in English by or about Wilson Tucker and as many foreign-language items as can be located. It contains the following sections: "Stories"; "Books"; "Series"; "Poems and Songs"; "Poem and Song Collections"; "Articles"; "Miscellaneous"; "Nonfiction Books"; "Edited Books"; "Media Presentations"; "Articles on the Author"; "Reviews"; "Books about the Author"; "Phantom and Forthcoming Titles"; "Related Works by Other Authors"; "Textual Variations"; and a chronological listing of fiction. Several of these sections contain no data, making the bibliography less formidable than it appears in description.

In each section entries tend to follow a chronological order, with each section having its own numbering. Entries in "Stories" reference all professionally published fiction that appeared as part of a larger publication (i.e., a magazine or a collection). An abbreviation (*sss* for short-short story or vignette; *NT* for novelette; *N* for novel, etc.) indicates the approximate length of the item, and serialization is indicated. Paginations are not given.

The entries for books list all separate publications, excluding poetry. Each entry provides title, publisher, ISBN, date of publication, pagination, original price, and artist. Reprints and reissues by the same publisher are listed chronologically beneath the first edition. When ISBNs were not available, the publisher's stock number, the number given by the Library of Congress, or the British Library General Catalogue—or some combination of these three—is listed. The contents of collections are given, and editions in languages other than English are cited when they are known.

"Articles on the Author" references all known articles that relate to the author and his work, excluding book reviews. In the case of Tucker, who has been enormously visible in fan circles, the secondary literature concentrates primarily on the professionally published material, and Stephensen-Payne and Benson's introduction states forthrightly (and optimistically) that "there are bound to have been many secondary items (particularly in fanzines) that have been omitted. These omissions will hopefully be corrected in future editions of this bibliography."

Despite the somewhat cumbersome arrangement, this is the most comprehensive bibliography of Wilson Tucker available.

UPFIELD, ARTHUR W[ILLIAM].

967a.   Asdell, Philip T. **A Revised Descriptive Bibliography of First Editions of Arthur W. Upfield: Australian, British, and U.S.** Frederick, Md.: P. T. Asdell, 1988. 32 p. Paperback. LC 88-165213.

Not seen. Apparently a revision of an earlier publication, the 1984 *Provisional Descriptive Bibliography of First Editions of the Works of Arthur W. Upfield.*

967b.   Burnet, Ross. **An Upfield Bibliography: A Guide to Identification and Value of the Books Written by Arthur William Upfield (1.9.1890–12.2.1964).** Uralla, New South Wales, Australia: Australian Book Collector, 1998. [ii, 19 p.] Index. Paperback. OCLC 40791887.

Burnet's bibliography of Arthur Upfield does not appear to have received U.S. distribution, but although it is somewhat crudely produced—it appears to be photocopied from laser-print copy—it is a very capable work, full of useful data. It begins with a checklist of major works that lists Upfield's books in chronological order; each is numbered, titles are given in boldface type, followed by the dates of the first editions in the United Kingdom, the United States, and Australia. Retitlings are indicated.

The second section, "Major Works," expands on the information presented in the checklist. The books are listed in chronological order. Each citation is numbered, and fuller bibliographic data are given for each work: place of publication, publisher, year of publication, pagination, binding type. Retitlings are indicated as are later printings, different editions, cover prices, ISBNs, and height (in centimeters). Cover reproductions occasionally are given.

A brief third section provides a chronological list of minor works, biography, and commentary, and the bibliography concludes with an index to names and titles.

967c. Stephens, Christopher P. **A Checklist of Arthur Upfield.** Hastings-on-Hudson, N.Y.: Ultramarine Publishing, 1991. 18 p. Paperback. Index. ISBN 0-89366-135-X.

Arthur Upfield was born in England, thrice failed to pass his examinations for professional advancement, and was sent to Australia by his father. Following a stint in the armed forces, he returned to Australia and, in his second novel, created the character of Inspector Napoleon Bonaparte (Bony to his friends), a half-caste educated at Brisbane University and employed by the Queensland Police Department. Stephens's bibliography, apparently offset from typed copy, lists chronologically the books by Upfield. Each citation is numbered; the title is underlined; and publication data on first English, American, Canadian, and Australian editions are given. Retitlings are documented, and pagination is provided (when available), as is information on the dust wrapper artist. An index to the titles (including the retitlings) concludes the pamphlet. Although not complete—Upfield wrote a fair amount of incidental material, including numerous articles, none of which have been reprinted—and containing an occasional typo (*Wings above the Diamantina* has become *Wings above the Diamantia* in the index)—this is nevertheless a helpful listing.

VANCE, JOHN HOLBROOK; I.E., JACK

968a. Cockrum, Kurt, Daniel J. H. Levack, and Tim Underwood. **Fantasms II: A Bibliography of the Works of Jack Vance.** Canoga Park, Calif.: Kurt Cockrum, 1979. xiii, 83 p. Approximately 100 copies issued.

Not seen.

968b. Cunningham, A. E., ed. **Jack Vance: Critical Appreciations and a Bibliography.** Boston Spa and London: British Library, 2000. 232 p. ISBN 0-7123-1103-3 (signed); 0-7123-1102-5 (trade). 1,000 copies printed, 250 signed.

More than half of this volume consists of essays about Jack Vance and his work. These essays, by scholars, professional writers, and Vance's publisher Charles F. Miller, are uniformly enjoyable, insightful, and worth reading. Cunningham's bibliography is forthright about the work of Hewett and Mallett (q.v.) being "a monument of research which is unlikely to be surpassed and is absolutely indispensable to the serious student or researcher." Nevertheless, Cunningham compiled his bibliography, in part "to provide a handy point of reference for the citations given by the various authors in this volume," and as such it is a very useful accomplishment. It contains 13 sections, though the last 3—Internet resources, and lists arranged chronologically and alphabetically—are lists, and the latter two lists could serve as an index to the sections described later.

The first section, "Fiction First Published in Magazines or Anthologies," numbers its citations, then lists them alphabetically by title, given in bold type; periodical titles are listed in italics; volume, issue, month, year, and pagination are given, as is a note about the story's publication history. "Novels and Short Story Collections" likewise numbers its citations, lists them alphabetically by title, given in bold type, and lists the

English and American editions: place of publication, publisher, publication year, pagination, original price, and ISBN are given, as are a note when the work first appeared in paperback and information about Vance's numerous limited editions. The third and fourth sections are devoted to adaptations of Vance and ephemera by Vance and contain one citation each; the fifth section lists bibliographies of Vance: in this case, the works of Levack and Underwood and Hewett and Mallett (q.v.) are described. The sixth section lists and describes three critical works about Vance, including this one; the seventh, the booklets of three conventions in which Vance was the guest of honor; the eighth, two fanzines devoted to Vance. The ninth section lists "associational" items, which in this case are an artist's portfolio, a guide to Vance's use of space, and a Vance dictionary (not seen by the present writer); and the tenth lists and describes Michael Shea's *A Quest for Simbilis,* which is set in Vance's universe and uses one of his best-known characters.

Additional lists would have been welcome, but Cunningham's bibliography is useful and very attractively presented.

968c. Hewett, Jerry, and Daryl F. Mallett. **The Work of Jack Vance: An Annotated Bibliography & Guide.** Bibliographies of Modern Authors, no. 29. Introduction by Robert Silverberg. San Bernadino, Calif.: Borgo Press; Penn Valley, Calif.; and Lancaster, Pa.: Underwood-Miller, 1994. xxiv, 293 p. Indexes. LC 92-28056. ISBN 0-8095-0509-6 (hc); 0-8095-15-9-1 (pb); 0-88733-165-3 (trade cloth); 0-88733-166-1 (limited edition).

Although he is best known as a science fiction author, Jack Vance has written a number of mysteries under his full name, John Holbrook Vance, and under several pseudonyms, including that of Ellery Queen, as whom he ghostwrote several novels. This gratifyingly comprehensive and elaborate bibliography of Vance was compiled with the assistance of Jack and Norma Vance and with the compilers' desire to rectify the inadequacies of the previously published bibliographies. The volume begins with Robert Silverberg's introduction, "The World of Jack Vance." This appreciation is followed by a lengthy Vance chronology, whose contents were assembled by Norma Vance using information derived from personal journals.

The bibliography contains the following sections: (A) "Books"; (B) "Short Fiction"; (C) "Verse and Poetry"; (D) "Nonfiction"; (E) "Other Media"; (F) "Interviews"; (G) "Maps and Drawings"; (H) "Phantom Editions and Works"; (I) "Unpublished Manuscripts"; (J) "Honors and Awards"; (K) "Guest of Honor Appearances"; (L) "Interviews with Vance"; (M) "Secondary Sources"; (N) "Miscellanea"; "The Genesee Slough Murders: Outline for a Novel" by Jack Vance; Afterword: "Jack Vance: The Man and the Myth" by Tim Underwood; and the index. The contents of the first six sections are chronologically arranged, with each citation being separately lettered and numbered.

The first section is the longest and dominates the bibliography. The title of each work is given in boldface type, followed by the place of publication, publisher, year of publication, pagination, and publisher's series number. The book's contents are itemized. Short story paginations are provided and cross-referenced to the contents of the other sections. The collation, binding measurements (in centimeters), notes about the contents, cover illustrator, original price, and ISBN are given. Similar data are provided for all English-language reprint editions and for the international editions; the titles of international editions are also in boldface type, and the name of the translator is given. When relevant, retitlings are indicated. Following the bibliographic descriptions of each work is an alphabetical list of the secondary sources and the reviews that the discuss the work.

In "Short Fiction," the title of each story is given in boldface and quotation marks. The publication data italicizes periodical titles and provides the periodical's volume, publication date, and story's pagination. Book titles also are italicized. The publication data include name of the editor, place of publication, publisher, date of publication, and pagination. All reprints of every story are listed. When relevant, retitlings are indicated and cross-references link these items to other sections.

Less needs to be said about the other sections, whose titles indicate their contents. The section documenting Vance's nonfiction begins by listing the editorials Vance wrote while a student at the University of California, Berkeley. "Other Media" provides production data on Vance's radio and television adaptations that include broadcast date, cast, and notes on the availability of the work. "Phantom Editions and Works" lists titles that appear to have been published. "Interviews with Jack Vance" cites radio interviews as well as those that have been published.

The bibliography concludes with eight separate indexes. The first indexes Vance's works by their title; book titles are italicized. The second lists the artists who have illustrated Vance's work; the third, the editors of works in which Vance has appeared or has been discussed; the fourth, Vance's translators; the fifth, the titles of the magazines and anthologies in which Vance has appeared; the sixth, Vance's publishers; the seventh, the titles of the secondary works that have discussed Vance; and the eighth, the names of the critics and reviewers of Vance.

A table listing the retitlings of Vance's publications would have been useful, but apart from this minor lacuna, *The Work of Jack Vance* is a thoroughly impressive achievement.

968d. Levack, Daniel J. H., and Tim Underwood. **Fantasms: A Bibliography of the Literature of Jack Vance.** San Francisco, Calif.; Columbia, Pa.: Underwood-Miller, 1978. 91 p. 1,000 copies printed, 100 clothbound.

Fantasms attempts to provide a complete listing of Vance's English-language publications, including a complete printing history of Vance's books and a list of all Vance's English-language periodical, anthology, and collection appearances through early 1978. It is heavily illustrated with numerous black-and-white reproductions of Vance's works.

The first section lists Vance's book publications in alphabetical order, separately numbering each citation. Titles are given in boldface capital letters; prior periodical publication data are listed on the next lines, as are the contents of short story collections and the name of the series (if any) to which the work belongs. Separate lines provide a chronological list of the book's different editions. Publication data include publisher, stock number (for paperbacks), year of publication, and whether the work appeared in paperback or cloth.

The second section is an alphabetical list of Vance's short stories. It, too, is arranged alphabetically, with its entries separately numbered. Each citation contains a chronological list of the story's appearance in periodicals and books; series names are indicated, as is occasionally the story's length (in number of words).

The next sections list Vance's works by series, his pseudonyms (and the works written under each name), his works chronologically, and his works that have been adapted for television.

In many respects, *Fantasms* appears to be an early draft that was rushed to print. It lacks such minimal data as the publisher's location and pagination; the names of cover illustrators are not provided; the television adaptations provide no data about the shows; and worst of all, the bibliography provides no sense of the author's varied accomplishments. It is now outdated and has been thoroughly superseded by the work of Hewett and Mallett (q.v.).

968e. Mead, David G. **Encyclopedia of Jack Vance, 20th Century Science Fiction Writer.** 3 vols. Studies in American Literature, vol. 50A. Lewiston, Maine: Edwin Mellen, 2002. 460 + 164 + 381 p. LC 2001-44206. ISBN 0-7734-7313-0 (vol. 1); 0-7734-7222-3 (vol. 2); 0-7734-7224-x (vol. 3).

Not seen. Volume 1 is described as covering Vance's work from A to J; volume 2, from K to N; and volume 3 from "numericals through Z." A review of the first volume may be found in *Extrapolation* (vol. 43, no. 2 [2002]: 241–42).

968f. Stephensen-Payne, Phil, and Gordon Benson Jr. **Jack Vance: A Fantasmic Imagination.** Galactic Central Bibliographies for the Avid Reader, vol. 28. Albuquerque, N. Mex.: Galactic Central, 1988. 46 p. Paperback.

968g. Stephensen-Payne, Phil, and Gordon Benson Jr. **Jack Vance: A Fantasmic Imagination, a Working Bibliography.** 2nd rev. ed. Galactic Central Bibliographies for the Avid Reader, vol. 28. Leeds, England; Polk City, Iowa: Galactic Central, 1990. 61 p. Paperback. ISBN 1-871133-02-5.

Although not as comprehensive as the Vance bibliography compiled by Hewett and Mallett (q.v.), *Jack Vance: A Fantasmic Imagination* is nevertheless a reasonably thorough list of the English editions of Vance's work. Like most of the publications of Galactic Central, its introduction states that it contains the following sections: (A) "Stories"; (B) "Books"; (C) "Series"; (D) "Poems, Songs and Plays"; (E) "Poem, Song and Play Volumes"; (F) "Articles"; (G) "Miscellaneous"; (H) "Non-fiction Books"; (I) "Edited Books"; (J) "Media Presentations"; (K) "Articles on the Author"; (L) "Reviews"; (M) "Books about the Author"; (N) "Phantom and Forthcoming Titles"; (O) "Related Works by Other Authors"; (P) "Textual Variations"; and (Q) "Chronological Listing of Fiction." And, as in rather too many publications of Galactic Central, several of these sections contain no material whatsoever.

The contents of the first three sections are alphabetically arranged; each citation is lettered and numbered separately. In the first section, beneath each story's title are the places in which it has seen print. Book titles are capitalized and accompanied often by the names of the editors. Journal titles are given in regular type and the original publication date is given in abbreviated form (i.e., 8-52 for August 1952). An abbreviation indicates whether the piece is a short-short story or vignette, short story, novelette, novella, short novel, or novel. Cross-references are provided for retitlings and alternative titles. The titles for Vance's books are given in capital letters. Each citation lists publisher, series number, pagination, ISBN, original price, and cover artist. All known English editions are cited.

Less needs to be said about the other sections, whose titles indicate their contents; sections E, H, I, and O are empty. The section on media presentations provides only the title and year in which the work appeared, and Vance's radio interviews are not listed. No indexes are provided.

A useful introduction, but no more.

VAN DINE, S. S.:
PSEUDONYM FOR WILLARD HUNTINGTON WRIGHT

969. Penzler, Otto. **S. S. Van Dine.** Collecting Mystery Fiction, no. 3. New York: Mysterious Bookshop, 1999. 36 p. 250 copies printed.

Reprinted from material published first in the *Armchair Detective* (vol. 15, no. 4 [1982]), the first half of this booklet discusses Van Dine's output and significance, after which three sections follow. The first describes the 12 Philo Vance novels; the second, other Vance and mystery fiction written by Van Dine; and the third, related material by other writers. Data in the first section are arranged in chronological order and include the place of publication, publisher, publication year, a prose description of the volume, and a note, which includes bibliographic data. Each entry provides an illustration of the book's dust wrapper and concludes with an estimated retail value of the book in a variety of conditions. The second and third sections are of necessity briefer, but they, too, are in chronological order, and the entries indicate Van Dine's contribution or connection. Of particular interest is a reproduction of the cover of the salesman's dummy of the only known copy of *The Powwow Murder Case.*

VAN GULIK, ROBERT H[ANS].

970. **Bibliography of Dr. R. H. van Gulik (D. Litt).** N.p., n.d. Compiled for the Benefit of the Boston University Libraries, Mugar Memorial Library "Robert van Gulik Collection." 82 p. Paperback.

Although undated, this pamphlet almost certainly was compiled shortly after van Gulik's death in 1967, perhaps in early 1968. It is not merely a bibliography but an account of the life of an extraordinarily versatile man. The volume begins with a curriculum vitae for van Gulik. Separate sections list data on his education and career, family background, marriage and children, decorations, memberships, pen names, and theses. Chinese characters are given when applicable, as are romanizations of Chinese names.

The bibliography contains sections for van Gulik's books, pamphlets, essays, articles, book reviews, vocabularies, encyclopedia entries, lectures, necrologies, and translations of Chinese and Japanese poems. The data include the book's title (with an English translation as necessary), the language in which the book was written, the printer, and publisher. Paginations occasionally are given, as are citations to reviews.

The documentation of van Gulik's own work follows and begins with citations to his poetry, each reference listing the poem's title, the English equivalent, year in which the poem was published, language in which the poem was written, and place of its publication; unpublished (typescript) poems also are listed. This material is followed by citations to the justly famous Judge Dee stories; separate sections list all first editions of the works in all languages. Lists of the comic strip syndication in the Dutch and Scandinavian newspapers and lengthy series of miscellaneous notes conclude the pamphlet.

The bibliography appears to have been offset from photocopied typescript and would have benefited immensely from better printing. Moreover, it lacks a table of contents and a title index. These complaints aside, the bibliography is quite usable and seemingly comprehensive. It remains a substantial achievement and deserves to be better known.

WALLACE, [RICHARD HORATIO] EDGAR

971a. Kiddle, Charles. **A Guide to the First Editions of Edgar Wallace.** Morcombe, England: Ivory Head Press, 1981. 88 p. Index. Paperback. LC 82-100973. ISBN 0-903639-05-X .

This bibliography describes the first editions of Edgar Wallace published in the United Kingdom and the United States. Wallace's plays, poems issued as broadsides, and U.K. collections of stories are not included, nor are the data on original periodical publications of the contents of Wallace's books that occupy so much space in the Wallace bibliography done by Lofts and Adley (q.v.). In all, Kiddle describes 183 books. (A laid-in errata sheet describes a 184th book and corrects some small typographical errors.)

The bibliography is arranged alphabetically by English title. Citations begin with a "first edition reference number" and the book's title in boldface type. A second line provides publisher, date of publication, initial cost, size of the book (in inches), color of the binding, and its "rarity factor." The rarity factor allows comparison between different first editions: for example, Wallace's extremely rare *Smithy and the Hun* and *The Tomb of Ts'in* have rarity factors of 400 and 275, respectively, whereas his *Again the Ringer* and *The Frightened Lady* have rarity factors of 2 and 5. A section titled "Identification" provides the points used to identify a first edition; these include pagination and descriptions of the advertisements and contents. A section called "Notes" lists retitlings and title changes, mentions variant bindings, and contains such comments as "a book at 7/6d dated 1925 without a catalogue is not a First Edition." Each entry concludes with a citation to the first U.S. edition that includes publisher and year of publication, binding color, pagination, and other data allowing for the identification of a first edition.

A chronological index provides the year and month in which the book appeared, title, and the publisher. (Wallace's busiest year appears to have been 1929: 25 titles appeared, including 5 in April.) Separate section lists the titles of the first U.K. editions and the titles under which they were later reprinted, American collections of Wallace that have no English equivalent, and American retitlings listed next to their U.K. originals.

This bibliography would have been easier to use had the title cross-references been within the body of the book rather than separately listed at the conclusion. Furthermore, the relatively recent discovery of Wallace's *The Real Shell-Man: The Story of Chetwynd of Chilwell* (London: John Waddington, 1919) means that Kiddle is not complete. This lacuna does not mar the bibliography's usability, and it belongs in all libraries, next to the earlier effort of Lofts and Adley (q.v.).

971b. Kiddle, Charles, and Richard Williams. **Edgar Wallace: First American Editions.** Edgar Wallace Monographs, no. 4. Scunthorpe, England: Dragonby Press, 1992. 4 p. Stapled sheets.

Some 91 titles are listed in this bibliography of the first American editions of Edgar Wallace. The data are arranged chronologically by date of publication and provide the title (as given on the title page), the position of the publication dates in the book ("t" indicates the date appeared on the title page; "v," that it appeared on the verso of the title page), color of the cloth binding, publisher's name, highest numbered page, original price, a valuation price, and (when relevant) the original British title in italics and a note indicating that the American edition preceded the first British edition. Finally, an alphabetical list of publishers' names states the number of Wallace titles they published and provides notes on their indications of first editions.

Reproduced from word-processed copy and cramped, little is here that cannot be extracted from Kiddle's earlier *A Guide to the First Editions of Edgar Wallace* (q.v.).

971c. Lofts, W. O. G., and Derek Adley. **The British Bibliography of Edgar Wallace.** London: Howard Baker, 1969. [xv], 246 p. LC 74-426863. ISBN 0-09-394760-6.

In his introduction, Lofts states that he and Adley decided to compile a bibliography of the works of Edgar Wallace published in the United Kingdom thinking that "the task would not be too difficult." Soon after, Lofts states, "I could not have been more wrong. It has proved to be a most laborious business. For Wallace's output was truly prodigious, and he himself kept few records, and of the few that he did keep none is anywhere close to being complete." Worse: writes Lofts, the "favoured recourse of the British bibliographer, the British Museum, has been unable to assist authoritatively in this instance either, since many of its files of the popular magazines of the Twenties, which contained the bulk of first publications of Wallace's work, were destroyed in the Blitz." Worse yet: "Unfailing sources of irritation along the way have been the erroneous, and often downright misleading, brief bibliographies contained in all too many of the multitudinous books about Edgar Wallace. A little more care on the part of their authors would have saved Derek Adley and I [*sic*] many hours of fruitless research."

Thus plaintively introduced, the resulting bibliography contains the following sections: (A) "Books by Year of Publication"; (B) "Short Stories"; (C) "Rare Editions"; (D) "First Editions"; (E) "Works Published in Book Form"; (F) "Autobiographies and Biographies"; (G) "Collections of Stories"; (H) "Stories in Short Story Collections"; (I) "Plays"; (J) "True Crime Articles"; (K) "Miscellanea"; (L) "Works Contained in Magazines and Newspapers"; and (L) "First London Magazine Stories."

"Books by Year of Publication" lists chronologically the 172 books by Wallace that are documented in this bibliography. Each entry provides the year of publication, a boldface reference number keyed to sections D and E, the title of the book in capital letters, and the publisher's name. "Short Stories" lists titles of short stories known to exist but "they did not appear in book form—nor have they been traced in magazines." "Rare Editions" is an essay mentioning the rarest Wallace items.

"First Editions" begins with a lively essay detailing the frustrations involved in documenting Wallace. A lengthy "classification of first editions" follows: books are listed alphabetically, each one assigned a boldface reference number. Titles are listed in capital letters, and book's publisher and year of publication, paper size (i.e., Cr 8vo for "Crown Octavo"), pagination, and dedication are included. Cover designs and interior illustrations are so noted.

"Works Published in Book Form" expands the data presented in "First Editions." One hundred seventy-two of Wallace's books are listed alphabetically, each entry prefaced with a note that indicates whether the work is V (verse), HF (historical fiction), NF (nonfiction), SS (short stories with central character), CSS (collected miscellaneous short stories), LSS (long short stories), BK (book), MG (magazine), N (newspaper), and/or published in the *EWMM* (*Edgar Wallace Mystery Magazine*). The reference number and title are given in boldface type and are followed by the publisher and publication date, dates of later editions, and series. The contents of collections are listed; when previously published, citations provide the title under which the story was published, name of the publishing magazine and its volume, and date of original publication. The opening words of short stories and novels are given.

The sections titled "Autobiographies and Biographies," "Collections of Short Stories," "Stories in Short Story Collections," "Plays," "True Crime Articles," and "Miscellanea" are brief, generally making reference to the material documented in the previous sections. The listings of Wallace's appearances in magazines and newspapers, however, are quite lengthy. This section begins with an alphabetical list of the periodicals containing Wallace's work and a note as to whether the work is a serial, short story, article, poem, or true crime publication. It is followed by a list of Wallace's periodical contributions arranged by periodical title. Entries are arranged chronologically and provide the periodical's number, date in which Wallace's contribution appeared, and title and opening words of Wallace's contribution. A note indicates whether the contribution appeared in book form and whether Wallace used a pseudonym.

More Wallace titles have since surfaced, but despite this volume's sometimes baroque arrangement and the lack of a cumulative title index, it remains the most accessible list of Wallace's books available.

971d.   Williams, Richard. **Edgar Wallace: A Filmography.** 2nd ed. Edgar Wallace Monographs, no. 1. Scunthorpe, England: Dragonby Press, 1990. 21 leaves. Stapled sheets.

This filmography lists all the films based on Edgar Wallace's writings or on characters created by Wallace, as well as those films in which Wallace played a role in the production. In all, some 176 films and 5 variants are listed and described, the most recent being from 1976. The filmography is international in scope, referencing films made in Great Britain, Germany, and the United States.

The first section of the filmography arranges the films by their titles, using as the principal entry the title given the film in the country of its production. Where two or more countries were involved in production, the British title is given preference, then the American, then the German.

All alternate titles are indicated, and cross-references are provided when the film was shown in another country under a different title. The film script's source is given, as well as a note indicating whether it was one of Wallace's novels, short stories, or whether the film was adapted "freely from Wallace." Additional data list the name of the production company, country of production, whether the film was in color or black and white, year of release, and running time. The names of the scriptwriters and directors are given, and a list of the sources from which data were derived is given at the bottom of each entry.

The filmography's second section is a chronological index to the films. Release date, title, production company, and country in which the film was made are listed. The third section of the filmography lists the production and distribution companies responsible and an abbreviation indicating the company's nationality.

Although easy to use and containing a wealth of data not readily available elsewhere, this is likely to be too specialized for all but the most comprehensive of academic libraries or the most determined of Edgar Wallace collectors.

971e.   Williams, Richard. **Edgar Wallace British Magazine Appearances (Fiction).** Edgar Wallace Monographs, no. 2. Scunthorpe, England: Dragonby Press, 1988. 18 p. Stapled sheets.

A revision of the data first published in Lofts and Adley's *British Bibliography of Edgar Wallace* (q.v.), this bibliography lists all the fiction written by Edgar Wallace that appeared in British magazines, newspapers, and periodicals. The contents are arranged alphabetically by publication name, and under each publication stories are listed in chronological order. Numeration and/or volume and issue number are given, as is the story's title. An abbreviation indicates the work's category ("n" for novels, "sn" for serialized novel with the number of episodes in the serial, "s" for short story, and "ss" for short story collection with the number of stories given in the collection), and entries conclude with the date of publication.

Reproduced from word-processed copy, the bibliography is cramped and would have benefited enormously from a title index. It nevertheless remains the most comprehensive list of Wallace's English periodical publications currently available.

971f.   Williams, Richard. **Edgar Wallace Index.** 2nd ed. British Paperback Checklists, no. 17. Scunthorpe, England: Dragonby Press, 1986. 8 p. Stapled sheets.

This list of Edgar Wallace titles appearing in paperback is clearly reproduced from typed copy. The citations are arranged alphabetically by book title. The data presented include the previous title (when such exists), date and publisher of the original hardback edition (when such exist), an abbreviation indicating the genre of the book (i.e., "NF" for nonfiction; "Poe" for poetry), another abbreviation indicating whether the book is short stories (ss), stories and novelettes (s), and whether the work appeared in more than one volume. Finally, the paperback's publishers are listed chronologically, with the publisher's name abbreviated and keyed to a note on the first sheet and accompanied by the date of publication.

Collectors of Edgar Wallace paperbacks will find this well arranged and useful, but all save the most comprehensive research libraries will be able to do without it.

Note: This publication also serves as the title index to the later *Edgar Wallace Paperbacks* (which follows).

971g.   Williams, Richard. **The Edgar Wallace Index (Books and Fiction).** Edgar Wallace Monographs, no. 5. Scunthorpe, England: Dragonby Press, 1996. 76 p. Stapled sheets.

Containing data cumulated from the Dragonby Press's monograph series devoted to Edgar Wallace, and reproduced from word-processed copy, *The Edgar Wallace Index (Books and Fiction)* uses a single alphabetical index to provide citations to all of Wallace's books and short stories. References to Wallace's uncollected articles, verse, and other nonfiction are not included.

All titles are listed in capital letters, and a category note indicates whether the work is an anthology, novel, twosome (two novels in one binding), omnibus (three or more novels in one binding), nonfiction, short story collection, play, short story, soldier-oriented short story, or verse. Additional notes indicate whether Wallace's piece was based on work by somebody else and whether the work was announced for publication under a different title. The opening words for all pieces are provided. Citations for books provide the publisher and date of the first English edition. Citations to the first British hardcovers often are followed by citations to additional British hardcovers, British paperback editions and citations to the first American and Tauchnitz editions. The contents of short story collections are listed.

Citations to short stories give periodical, volume, issue, month, day, and year and list the books by Wallace in which the story was published; the name of the illustrator is provided if the periodical was illustrated. Additional notes indicate abridgments, revisions, and whether the work was filmed.

Indexes to periodical titles, pagination, and a citation numbering system would have strengthened the bibliography, but it is easy to use and does a very good job in making an enormous amount of data readily accessible. Academic libraries holding Lofts and Adley and Kiddle (q.q.v.) will find this a very useful addendum.

971h.   Williams, Richard, and Charles Kiddle. **Edgar Wallace Paperbacks: A Bibliographic Checklist by Imprint. With Valuations.** Edgar Wallace Monographs, no. 3. Scunthorpe, England: Dragonby Press, 1990. 17 p. Stapled sheets.

As its title indicates, this is a bibliography of all Edgar Wallace books issued in paperback or in light card covers. The bibliography is arranged alphabetically by the publisher's series name. The beginning of each series entry provides the publisher's name and address, size of the books in the series (in millimeters), a brief description of the cover, price, and notes about the series. Individual citations provide the book's series number, title (indicating retitling), edition status (whether first book publication or first paperback appearance), date of publication, number of copies printed, pagination, printer (in abbreviated form), price, dust wrapper (if such existed), cover artist, and price a collector would pay for a very good copy.

The checklist is clearly reproduced from word-processed copy, but it lacks a title index. Those wishing to learn whether a Wallace title has appeared in paperback must consult the separately published *Edgar Wallace Index* (profiled earlier).

Wallace completists will want this, but unless it is used in conjunction with other publications, it is unlikely to be of significant use to libraries or researchers.

WOOLRICH, CORNELL [GEORGE HOPLEY]

972a.   Nilsen, Bjarne. **Bibliography in Black: The Works of Cornell Woolrich.** Copenhagen, Denmark: Antikvariat Pinkerton, 1988. 40 p. ISBN 8-7884691-0-7.

Not seen.

972b.   Penzler, Otto. **Cornell Woolrich, Part I: A Descriptive Bibliography and Price Guide.** Collecting Mystery Fiction, no. 5. New York: Mysterious Bookshop, 1999. 36 p. Paperbound. 250 copies printed.

972c.   Penzler, Otto. **Cornell Woolrich, Part II: A Descriptive Bibliography and Price Guide.** Collecting Mystery Fiction, no. 6. New York: Mysterious Bookshop, 1999. 36 p. Paperbound. 250 copies printed.

The first of these pamphlets discusses the monographs published under Woolrich's name; the second, under the William Irish and George Hopley bylines. Contents of both bibliographies are derived from material first published in the *Armchair Detective*. The arrangement of material is chronological. For each book, a reproduction of the dust wrapper is given, when one is available. Publication data include the publisher of the American hardcover and paperback editions, a prose description of the volume (i.e., "brick colored cloth stamped with the publisher's logo and the numerals '923'"), and the book's initial cover price. The contents and original publication data for collections are given, as are the estimated retail value of the book in various states and conditions. A facsimile of Woolrich's signature appears on the covers.

972d. Spindel, Howard. [**Cornell Woolrich**]. 2000. Separately numbered sheets. [6 + 28 + 29 + 32 p.]

In March 2000, Spindel was offering a Cornell Woolrich bibliography on eBay. It consisted of unbound separately numbered pages that provided a list of Woolrich's publications; Woolrich's stories grouped by publication; Woolrich's stories grouped by original title; and Woolrich's stories grouped by their published title. These data are arranged clearly, although they occasionally are incomplete. The list of stories grouped by publication, for example, merely states that the work appeared in the publication in a certain year; it does not provide the month of publication. In 2002, I chanced to speak with Francis Nevins about Spindel's work. His assessment was that it was a very good bibliography, for Spindel had extracted it (with permission) from the appendix of Nevin's *First You Dream, Then You Die.*

972e. Stewart, Enola. **Cornell Woolrich (William Irish, George Hopley). A Catalogue of First and Variant Editions of His Work, Including Anthology and Magazine Appearances.** Pocono Pines, Pa.: Gravesend Books, [1975?]. v, 30 leaves. Paperback. 250 copies printed.

Although dealers' catalogues have not been included here, this sale catalogue, compiled by the owner of Gravesend Books, must be mentioned, because it is the only separately published bibliography of Cornell Woolrich issued to date. Reproduced from typed copy, it contains five sections: first and variant editions of books written by Cornell Woolrich; magazines containing stories written by Cornell Woolrich; anthologies containing stories written by Cornell Woolrich; miscellaneous works containing information pertaining to Cornell Woolrich and his books; and reference books used in preparing this catalogue. Entries in all sections are numbered and are chronologically arranged; data are provided on only one side of each sheet. An unnumbered sheet reprints Jack Gaughan's illustration of Woolrich.

The entries in the first section give the book's title, publisher, place of publication, and publication date in capital letters. A note on the book's condition follows. Entries conclude with pagination and the asking price. Paperback, variant, and reprint editions are cited; stock numbers are given for the former, and occasionally lengthy notes are provided on Woolrich's significant novels: for example, the entries for the different editions of *The Bride Wore Black* describe the dedication, title page quote, dust wrapper of the first hardcover edition and the appearance of the first Dell edition at some length.

Citations to Woolrich's short fiction have the story's title in parentheses, and the title, publication, and date are in capital letters. Entries describe the magazine's condition and conclude with the pagination of Woolrich's contribution and Stewart's asking price. Citations to Woolrich's anthology appearances have the book's title, editor, publisher, and place of publication in capital letters. Entries describe the book's condition, list the title of Woolrich's contribution in capital letters and its pagination, and conclude with Stewart's asking price.

The final two sections are perhaps unduly brief, occupying one leaf apiece.

Despite containing some typos and omissions, this is not a wholly discreditable attempt, but it is a work necessary only to completists. A more recent and accessible bibliography may be found at the conclusion of Francis Nevins's *First You Dream, Then You Die* (New York: Mysterious Press, 1988), which updates Nevins's 1985 bibliography published in *Darkness at Dawn* (Carbondale: Southern Illinois University Press), which is in turn an updating of Nevins's bibliography first published in *Nightwebs* (New York: Harper and Row, 1971).

The primary bibliography in *First You Dream, Then You Die* contains sections devoted to Woolrich's novels, separately published short novels, collections of short stories, short fiction (listed chronologically by the magazine in which it was published), short stories first published in collections of Woolrich's short fiction, short stories first published in anthologies, and articles. Successive sections provide full cast and credit information on Woolrich adaptations for movies, U.S. radio, and television. The bibliography concludes with a lengthy list of secondary sources, each annotated. As bibliographies go, it is well done, although more data in citations would be helpful. A separately published and comprehensive bibliography of Woolrich is still desirable.

WREN, P. C.

973. Stephens, Christopher P. **A Checklist of Percival Christopher Wren.** Hastings-on-Hudson, N.Y.: Ultramarine Publishing, 1991. 18 p. Paperback. ISBN 0-89366-178-3.

Best known for writing *Beau Geste* and other stirring stories of the French Foreign Legion, P. C. Wren wrote a number of works in which crime and mystery figured in the background and motivated the characters. This checklist of Wren's books is chronologically arranged, beginning with the 1912 *Dew and Mildew* and concluding with the 1949 *Dead Men's Boots*. Each citation is separately numbered and provides data on the first American and the first British editions. Titles are underlined and include information on pagination, retitlings, dust wrappers, original prices, and identifying points, although not always consistently. A title index concludes the checklist.

Although Wren's books are documented, data on his short stories and other publications have not been provided. A revised and expanded edition of this bibliography is to be hoped for, but given the general lack of interest in Wren, it will not be surprising if such never materializes. Researchers determined to find a more thorough bibliography of Wren's works are referenced to H. C. Arbuckle III, "Bibliography, Chronological Listing, and Comments on the Works of Major Percival Christopher Wren, I.A.R.," *Taius* (December 1972), n.p. It is difficult to obtain and also is far from complete, but Arbuckle provides more data and a useful biographical sketch of Wren.

11

Character Indexes

Scope note: This chapter references only general works, works surveying the characters of more than one author, and works documenting series characters. Indexes to and discussions of the characters created by specific writers—as in the characters created by Christie, Doyle, and Simenon—will be found under their respective authors.

GENERAL WORKS

974a. Amos, William. **The Originals: An A–Z of Fiction's Real-Life Characters.** Boston: Little, Brown, 1985. xx, 614 p. Index. Cloth. LC 85-81298. ISBN 0-316-03741-9.

974b. Amos, William. **The Originals: Who's Really Who in Fiction.** London: Jonathan Cape, 1985. xx, 614 p. Index. Cloth. LC 86-191609. ISBN 0-2240-2419-5.

This entertaining collection identifies nearly 3,000 people who inspired the creation of fictional characters. Irene Adler, the Baskervilles, Dr. Gideon Fell, Sherlock Holmes, Miss Marple, Nigel Strangeways, and Lord Peter Wimsey are but a few of the fictional detectives who have been linked to human models.

The book's arrangement is alphabetical by the character's full name or the name by which the character is commonly known, given in boldface type; the Continental Op, for example, is profiled under the letter *C*. The entry identifies the author who created the character, names the work in which the character first appeared, and provides the identity of and basic biographical data on the person (or people) on whom the character was based. The book concludes with a selective bibliography of the sources Amos used to identify the originals and an index to the people who were named in the volume. Included are several sections of black-and-white photographs of the people who were turned into characters. Although this is a specialized volume, it is well written and presents its data well; it remains consistently helpful.

975a. Barnett, Colleen. **Mystery Women: An Encyclopedia of Leading Women Characters in Mystery Fiction**. Vol. 1: 1860–1979. South Bend, Ind.: Ravenstone/E. B. Houchin, 1997. ii, 299 p. Indexes. Paperback. LC 97-67554. ISBN 0-9383132-9-0.

975b. Barnett, Colleen. **Mystery Women: An Encyclopedia of Leading Women Characters in Mystery Fiction. Vol. 1 (1860–1979).** Rev. ed. Scottsdale, Ariz.: Poisoned Pen Press, 2001. xiv, 384 p. Indexes. Paperback. LC 2001-86357. ISBN 1-890208-61-2.

975c. Barnett, Colleen. **Mystery Women: An Encyclopedia of Leading Women Characters in Mystery Fiction. Vol. 2: 1980–1989.** Scottsdale, Ariz.: Poisoned Pen Press, 2002. xi, 397 p. Indexes. Paperback. ISBN 1-890208-69-8.

The revised edition and its second volume are described. Some 25 years in the compilation, the two volumes of *Mystery Women* list and describe more than titles published between 1860 and 1989 in which a woman had a dominant role in solving the crime. The arrangement of the first volume is chronological, with sections listing the women sleuths appearing between 1860 and 1899, 1900 and 1919, 1920 and 1939, 1940 and 1959, and 1960 and 1979; the second volume concentrates on the sleuths appearing between 1980 and 1989. Within each section, arrangement is alphabetical by the sleuth's last name. A typical entry gives the sleuth's name in large boldface letters, the author's name in italics, and a description of the sleuth's cases. The publisher and publication year of the books in which the sleuth appears are listed in the body of the description. The first volume concludes with three indexes: an author/character index lists the author, character, and volumes in which the character appeared, and the page in *Mystery Women* on which the character is discussed. The character index merely lists the page on which the character is discussed, but the book titles index lists the books by title, providing for each the name of the author and the character. An author/character index and a book title index appear in the second volume, as do a character index and a chronology of characters, the latter two of which index the contents of both volumes.

Mystery Women is an idiosyncratic work. It contains a gratifyingly large amount of original material, and readers interested in the role of women characters in the history of mystery and detective fiction will find this volume absolutely essential. At the same time, Barnett never defines her subject, stating in the first volume only that "defining the mystery itself was a personal task as there were crossovers with science fiction, romance, westerns, and horror series. Other far more noteworthy researchers have defined mystery series differently than I did." Perhaps because of this diffidence, Barnett describes such works as L. T. Meade's *The Sorceress of the Strand* and Edgar Wallace's *Four Square Jane:* the former features a male detective and a female criminal, the latter describes a female criminal achieving vengeance for past mistreatments. Oddly enough, more relevant titles, such as Wallace's *Barbara on Her Own,* are not mentioned, nor are the writings of such authors as Janice Law. Equally important, Barnett's focus on books has led to the exclusion of enormous numbers of magazine serials, and it should be mentioned that if data on serializations were provided and given primacy, some of her titles would need to be placed into earlier decades.

A third volume is intended to cover relevant fiction published from 1990 to 1999.

976. Brown, Michael Rogero, and Nicholas Sauer. **Index of Small Hero Pulps from Dell [and Others].** http://sflovers.rutgers.edu/archive/bibliographies/small-hero-pulps.txt

The title of this Web site refers not to the size of the heroes but to their importance and duration: few of the pulps listed by Brown and Sauer appeared for more than a few issues, and their heroes often were equally short-lived. The pulps listed include *Doctor Death, Terence X. O'Leary's War Birds, Public Enemy, Captain Satan, Doctor Yen Sin, Dusty Ayers and His Battle Birds, The Octopus, The Scorpion, The Secret Six, The Mysterious Wu Fang, The Ghost—Super Detective*, and *The Masked Detective*. The characters listed include Anthony Hamilton, Doc Harker, Don Diavolo, the Green Lama, Matalaa, Captain V, the Crimson Mask, the Domino Lady, and Captain Danger.

The arrangement is by issue of appearance. For each, Brown lists the title of the lead story, author initials, publication date, volume and issue numbers, and reprint information. These are followed by the authors' full names and information on the characters' appearances in other venues. Although fuller indexes to these pulps can be found in Michael Cook and Stephen T. Miller's *Mystery, Detective, and Espionage Fiction* and the first series of Leonard Robbins's *The Pulp Magazine Index* (q.q.v.), these works are increasingly difficult to find. Brown and Sauer's Web site is useful and well done.

977. Carr, Wooda Nick. **The Other Detective Pulp Heroes.** Pulp Vault Pulp Study, no. 1. Chicago: Tattered Pages Press, 1992. 96 p. Index. Paperback.

A comprehensive description of the detectives that appeared in series in the pulp magazines would be lengthy, so Carr has limited himself to describing just 40 of them. These 40 include policemen, secret agents, private eyes, lawyers, millionaire playboys with secret identities, and encyclopedia salesmen with quick memories and quicker fists. The volume is illustrated with numerous illustrations reprinted from the pulp magazines showing these characters in action.

Carr's list is arranged alphabetically by author, starting with Seven Anderton's Edna Pender and Steve Ware and concluding with Jean Francis Webb's Kimo. Additional authors having their detectives described include Robert Leslie Bellem's Dan Turner, Carroll John Daly's Satan Hall, John Dickson Carr's Dr. Gideon Fell, Erle Stanley Gardner's Edward Jenkins and Barney Killigen, Frank Gruber's Oliver Quade, Louis L'Amour's Kip Morgan, and Theodore Tinsley's Terry "Bulldog" Black and Major John T. Lacy.

A checklist of pulp appearances follows Carr's descriptions. It, too, is alphabetical by author, listing the pulp magazine(s) in which the character appeared and giving the magazine's date and the story's title. Reprints and book appearances of these stories are not noted.

One can cavil that some of the more interesting pulp detectives (including some mentioned in Carr's introduction) are not described. Furthermore, Carr's enthusiasm is often stronger than the stories would seem to warrant. Nevertheless, by describing several dozen detectives who are rarely considered in genre surveys, Carr has performed a considerable achievement.

978. Conquest, John. **Trouble Is Their Business: Private Eyes in Fiction, Film and Television, 1927–1988.** Garland Reference Library of the Humanities, vol. 1151. New York: Garland, 1990. liii, 497 p. Index. Cloth. LC 89-33039. ISBN 0-8240-5947-6.

In 1985 the Bowling Green State University Popular Press published Robert A. Baker and Michael T. Nietzel's *Private Eyes: One Hundred and One Knights, a Survey of American Detective Fiction 1922–1984* (q.v.), a prose study dealt with elsewhere in this volume and mentioned here because it stands directly behind Conquest's monumental achievement. Baker and Nietzel provided generally appreciative surveys of private investigators, but it was Conquest's more ambitious goal to document "all private eye writers and their creations published in English since 1927 plus films and television and radio shows in which PIs are the main characters; nine hundred fifty-two authors, one hundred seventy-six feature films, one hundred sixty-four television series, pilots and films, fifty six radio programs and a grand total of 1563 PIs are listed." In general, Conquest's 952 authors are novelists; short stories, unless somehow notable, are not listed.

A lengthy, excellent introduction defines and discusses the private investigator, providing a lively history of the genre and a survey of some of the more notable subgenres of private eye: homosexual detectives, ethnic detectives, the unbaptized private investigator, wounded heroes, animal private eyes, science fiction private eye, and so forth.

The next section of the volume is devoted to the 952 authors and their creations. It is arranged alphabetically by the author's last name, given in boldface capitals, and the private investigator's name, given in boldface upper- and lowercase. Entries for the private investigators reference users to the author's entry, which describe the investigator. These descriptions do not mince words and are witty and accurate; one author's works are described as "aspiring to mediocrity, they never quite achieve it," while the private investigator of another "keeps reminding the reader how confusing everything is and wanders around dark houses at night." Entries conclude with references to media adaptations (given in boldface capitals) and a brief bibliography listing the titles in which the investigator appeared and the year in which the book was published. A date by itself is always for a first American edition, and dates prefaced by "UK," "Aus," and "Can" are for the first British, Australian, and Canadian editions, respectively. In the case of certain important writers (e.g., Raymond Chandler), bibliographic data are provided not only for Chandler's novels but also for his short stories, the entries listing each story's original publication and (when relevant) the novel it later became. Finally, a section devoted to private-eye anthologies lists their contents, providing details under the author's heading.

Successive sections list television, motion picture, and radio shows featuring private investigators. The entries list the shows' years, the premise, the actors playing the private investigator, authors and titles of novelizations, and the names of notable scriptwriters. A "Yellow Pages" provides a geographic index to the investigators; a "Check List of Authors and Titles" recapitulates the contents of the first section. The volume concludes with a capably done title index and a section titled "Stop Press" that lists late additions.

It is possible to fault Conquest for being too catholic in his contents, for he includes references to a number of works in which the private investigator is actually an amateur detective, but this criticism is readily dismissed, for the comprehensiveness of this book is one of its strengths. Conquest's data are accurate, and his arrangement and organization are exemplary. Its physical appearance is unprepossessing, however, for Conquest uses so much boldface that he occasionally inhibits access to the data. This aside, the volume is a monumental achievement and belongs in all libraries.

979. DellaCava, Frances A., and Madeline H. Engel. **Female Detectives in American Novels: A Bibliography and Analysis of Serialized Female Sleuths.** Garland Reference Library of the Humanities, vol. 1685. New York: Garland, 1993. xiv, 157 p. Index. Cloth. LC 93-30644. ISBN 0-8153-1264-4.

The first 50 pages of this guide discuss the series character heroine, analyzing similarities and differences, and surveying such social issues as sexism, gay and lesbian rights, racism, anti-Semitism, homelessness, illegal aliens, substance abuse, crimes involving women and children, and conservatism as they are addressed in the series novels featuring American female sleuths. In all, 161 American female sleuths in 636 books by 147 authors are analyzed.

The second half of the volume provides bibliographic data and profiles of the works discussed earlier, with the data presented in chronological groupings for the female sleuths of the nineteenth century, the early twentieth century to the mid-1960s, the mid-1960s until 1979, and 1980 until the present. The profiles in each section are arranged alphabetically by author's name. The titles of works in which the character appears are listed chronologically, with the title in italics and the place and year of publication and publisher provided. The profile describes the main character and, often, names her friends, helpers, and the social themes addressed in the mystery. The volume concludes with indexes to the authors, sleuths, and book titles.

Although clearly written and containing original research, *Female Detectives in American Novels* lacks the thoroughness and comprehensiveness of Victoria Nichols and Susan Thompson's *Silk Stalkings* and Willeta Heising's *Detecting Women* (q.q.v.). The authors' *Sleuths in Skirts* (which follows) is intended to supersede this volume.

980. DellaCava, Frances A., and Madeline H. Engel. **Sleuths in Skirts: Analysis and Bibliography of Serialized Female Sleuths.** New York: Routledge, 2002. xii, 315 p. Indexes. LC 2001-048492. ISBN 0-8153-3884-8.

In structure, this volume is somewhat similar to the authors' earlier *Female Detectives in American Novels* (q.v.). The first half of the volume is a thematic discussion of the series character heroine, analyzing such social issues as sexism, gay and lesbian rights, racism, anti-Semitism, homelessness, illegal aliens, substance abuse, religion, minority sleuths, classism, and substance abuse, as they are addressed in the series novels featuring American female sleuths. In all, DellaCava and Engle analyze 2,283 novels, noting that "whereas 45 female sleuths were created between the 1890s and 1979, 477 of the characters in this bibliography have appeared since 1980."

The second half of the volume provides bibliographic data and descriptions of the works discussed earlier. This section is arranged alphabetically by author, given in boldface type. In each entry, the female sleuth is clearly identified, DellaCava and Engel using "S=" to indicate the sleuth's name and follow this with her occupation and the primary location of the mysteries. Beneath this, listed in chronological order, are the mysteries in which the sleuth appeared; also provided are place of publication, publisher, and publication date of the first edition. Each entry concludes with a useful note providing a little more detail about the sleuth and, sometimes, the author. The volume concludes with a series of indexes: pen names of series' authors, sleuths, sleuths' occupations, and book titles.

Sleuths in Skirts is an impressive analysis. It will doubtless assist researchers.

981. **Directories of Fictional Characters in Mystery and Suspense Fiction.**

http://www.hycyber.com/MYST/character_dir.htm.
Offers access by writer and character.

982.   Drew, Bernard A. **Heroines: A Bibliography of Women Series Characters in Mystery, Espionage, Action, Science Fiction, Fantasy, Horror, Western, Romance and Juvenile Novels.** Garland Reference Library of the Humanities, vol. 878. New York: Garland, 1989. 400 p. Index. LC 89-34233. ISBN 0-8240-3047-8.

As its title indicates, this volume lists the women series characters in a number of fictional genres. Nearly 1,200 series are listed, of which approximately 350 are detective and mystery fiction. No attempt has been made to distinguish between women series characters created by men and those created by women, nor does Drew attempt to provide a literary evaluation of these series.

Drew begins his listings with an index to the authors that lists both pseudonyms and real names. Each name is followed by the name of the series that is listed in the main section of the bibliography. The main section is arranged alphabetically by series character's name or by the series name. Each series is separately numbered. The author (or authors) of the series is listed below, followed by an extremely brief annotation and a chronological list of the books in the series. Each title is followed by the name of the first publisher and the year of publication. Retitlings are not indicated. Indexes (here called appendixes) provide access to the series by the genres named in the title as well as by such subjects as "Miscellaneous Domestic, Humor and Literary Titles" and "Comic Book and Comic Strip Reprints and Related Prose Series." A title index concludes the volume.

Drew attempts too much in *Heroines,* and the book is rife with problems. The listings in the main section often are frustrating in their arrangement. For example, the series featuring Nancy Drew can be located without any difficulty, but in the case of the series created by Laura Ingalls Wilder that featured Mary and Laura Ingalls, the entry is under neither Ingalls nor Wilder but under "Little House on the Prairie," with no cross-references. Similarly, Drew's annotations are uninformative and repetitive; one shudders to see how often he has used "this is a girls' book series." Finally, Drew lists a number of women characters who appeared in but one book, thus vitiating his stated purpose of listing women series characters.

Readers and researchers interested in the detective and mystery stories featuring women as series characters would be better served by using Victoria Nichols and Susan Thompson's *Silk Stalkings* (q.v.). Those interested in the subject of mystery series written by women will find Willetta Heising's *Detecting Women* (q.v.) offers superior access to the subject.

983.   Green, Joseph, and Jim Finch. **Sleuths, Sidekicks and Stooges: An Annotated Bibliography of Detectives, Their Assistants and Their Rivals in Crime, Mystery and Adventure Fiction, 1795–1995.** Aldershot, England; Brookfield, Vt.: Scolar Press, 1997. 874 p. Index. Cloth. LC 95-49334. ISBN 1-85928-192-3.

The most thorough work considered in this section, *Sleuths, Sidekicks and Stooges* contains nearly 8,000 entries on the sleuths, their sidekicks, and their rivals appearing in British and American mystery and detective fiction published between 1795 and 1995. It is a monumental work, but it is not always easy to use, and it is unfortunately not always reliable. The contents: a preface; an introduction; a guide to the detectives ; the detectives; the authors; the books; the sidekicks; and the stooges. Included are three appendixes: sources; source discrepancies, and Sherlock Holmes parodies.

The fourth section, on the detectives, constitutes the majority of the volume and is arranged alphabetically by detective. The detective's name is given in boldface with the last name capitalized. The entry for each detective, however, can have up to 18 parts. A prose description of the character is given; this is followed by a line (in italics) providing the detective's nationality, sex, location of operations, and type (i.e., police, professional amateur, private detective, professional investigator, secret agent, amateur, pulp, and sleuth). Following this, the name(s) of the detective's sidekick(s) and stooge(s) are noted as such, their last names printed in capital letters; these are occasionally accompanied by a description providing details of their relationship to the detective. Next, the author's name is given in boldface type, with the last name capitalized, along with a biography of the author. Following this are names and biographies of other authors who have used the same character, also using the preceding format. Other bylines of the primary author are listed, with reference made to other detectives created by the primary author, and the other detectives are listed, with reference given to the bylines under which they appeared. In addition, a "citation record" lists the frequency of the detective's appearances, excluding radio, television, and motion picture appearances. The title, publisher, and year of publication of the first and last book in which the detective appeared are given (and noted as such), occasionally accompanied by an explanatory narrative of their own. Pairs and multiple detectives are listed under the name for which the most biographical information can be given; cross-references are provided.

As can be inferred, the arrangement of the main section is very confusing and repetitive, albeit detailed. Although pages are numbered and letter-tabbed and have the name of the detective given in the upper right corner, the layout of entries is frequently unclear; this is especially so in the case of the stories featuring Sherlock Holmes. Furthermore, perhaps because the authors attempted to do so much, numerous errors have crept in, often in the entries for the older writers. As examples, Jacques Futrelle's *The Diamond Master* does not feature the Thinking Machine as detective; Nevada Alvarado, sidekick to Cleve Adams's Violet McDade, is not a Hispanic male; Chester Himes did not graduate from The Ohio State University; T. S. Stribling's Henry Poggioli is a character in 36 short stories, not 20; Carroll John Daly's Race Williams did not surface in 1927, nor was "he fairly moderate in his activities and not widely imitated"; Doc Savage's full name is not given, nor are the names of any of his sidekicks; the correct identity of The Shadow is not revealed. The cross-referencing system is frequently frustrating. A user looking at James Bond finds an entry for Robert Markham, author of a James Bond pastiche; the user is then referenced to Peter Furneaux, and only then can it be discovered that Markham was a pseudonym for Kingsley Amis. One may also take the authors to task for equating dime novels and pulp magazines and for demonstrating familiarity with neither.

None of this is to say that *Sleuths, Sidekicks, and Stooges* cannot be used, but too often it must be used with caution rather than confidence. One longs for a revised second edition.

984a. Hullar, Link, and Frank Hamilton. **Amazing Pulp Heroes.** Brooklyn, N.Y.: Gryphon Books, 1988. 58 p. Paperback.

984b. Hamilton, Frank, and Link Hullar. **Amazing Pulp Heroes: A Celebration of the Glorious Pulp Magazines.** Brooklyn, N.Y.: Gryphon Books, 1996. 201 p. Paperback. ISBN 0-936071-68-0 (pb); 0-936071-69-9 (limited ed.).

Although its contents are not limited to the detectives appearing in the pulp magazines, a sizable percentage of the entries appearing in *Amazing Pulp Heroes* are either detectives (the Phantom Detective, Nick Carter, Secret Agent X, Operator #5, etc.) or serve a detective's function (Doc Savage, the Shadow, the Avenger, etc.). Approximately 50 characters are described and portrayed, with Hullar providing the prose and Hamilton the illustrations. In addition, the authors comment on subjects as diverse as Doc Savage and American history, the Bama Doc Savage covers, women in the bloody pulps, the men's action/adventure magazines, and so forth.

Unlike such similar works as Wooda Nick Carr's *The Other Detective Pulp Heroes* (q.v.), the contents of *Amazing Pulp Heroes* follow no discernible order. Furthermore, although Hullar writes enthusiastically about the characters, the volume contains occasionally significant typos ("Grant Stickbridge" rather than "Grant Stockbridge" for the entry on *The Spider*), and the entries more often than not fail to provide any bibliographic data. Hamilton's artwork is generally excellent.

985. Jakubowsky [*sic*], Maxim, ed. **100 Great Detectives; or, the Detective Directory.** London: Xanadu, 1991. 255 p. GB 91-16041. ISBN 1-95480025-6. New York: Carroll & Graf, 1991. 255 p. ISBN 1-85480-025-6.

Note: Jakubowski's name is misspelled on the title page, although it is elsewhere spelled correctly.

100 Great Detectives consists of approximately 100 essays of 250 to 500 words on peoples' favorite detectives. The title is slightly erroneous, for one of the essays discusses the detectives of different authors (Anthony Berkeley's Roger Sheringham and Philip Macdonald's Anthony Gethryn), and several essays discuss detectives who operate in teams (e.g., Joe Leaphorn and Jim Chee, Ed and Am Hunter, Dalziel and Pascoe). The volume focuses on the detectives (rather than on the writers), and the essays are thus arranged alphabetically by the name of the detective. Each essay concludes with a brief bibliography listing the books in which the detective appeared. The approaches range from the uncritically appreciative to the acute.

In his *CADS* review of the first edition of the *Reference Guide,* Geoff Bradley took me to task for misrepresenting the intent of *100 Great Detectives,* explaining that the volume was not intended to be a "best" list at all, that it was instead intended to be a list in which 100 contributors could list and describe their favorite detectives. Notes Bradley, "There is a distinct difference between 'favourite' and 'best.' " Bradley is quite correct. Nevertheless, the majority of the original annotations remains valid: this volume strikes me as a marketing ploy, in which the compilers assemble a volume that can be sold to collectors (known for obsessiveness), detective and mystery readers (known for voraciousness), and libraries (known for largely indiscriminate acquisitiveness). There is nothing wrong with this; a list of favorites is a list meant to be enjoyed and discussed, and the enjoyment value of the book lies in its very idiosyncrasies. Jakubowski has assembled a volume replete with surprises. Writer Michael Moorcock writes glowingly of Margery Allingham's Albert Campion ("he's a joy to live with, and so, incidentally are the many recurring characters of the series"), and graphic novelist Neil Gaiman provides a thought-provoking analysis of G. K. Chesterton's Father Brown. Many writers offer discussions of favorite characters that provide insights into their own writings: Reginald Hill, for example, turns out to be a devotee of Anthony Trollope's *Eustace Diamonds*.

On the debit side, the book is unindexed, and its value is as an enjoyable list, not as a research tool.

986. Madden, Cecil, ed. **Meet the Detective.** London: Allen & Unwin, 1935. 142 p. Cloth. New York: Telegraph Press, 1935. 158 p. Cloth. LC 36-533.

Note: Madden's name does not appear on the title page but appears at the conclusion of an introduction.

Like Otto Penzler's *The Great Detectives* (q.v.), *Meet the Detective* traditionally is not considered a reference work but should be. Its title, however, is not strictly accurate, for although this book consists of essays in which the authors describe the genesis and creation of their literary characters, one of the characters we are asked to meet is Sax Rohmer's Dr. Fu Manchu and another is the Baroness Orczy's the Scarlet Pimpernel. These are hardly detectives, and one wonders why Orczy was not asked to discuss her series involving Bill Owen, the Old Man in the Corner.

In all, 15 characters are described, the majority of whom is forgotten except by specialists: Rupert Grayson's Gun Cotton, Sydney Horler's Tiger Standish, Francis D. Grierson's Professor Wells, Andrew Soutar's Phineas Spinnet, G. D. H. Cole and Margaret Cole's Superintendent Wilson, and Anthony Wynne's Dr. Eustace Hailey. A few names might be recognizable to readers of the golden age: Leslie Charteris has a piece describing the genesis of the Saint, Sapper describes the creation of Bull-Dog Drummond, and essays by H. C. Bailey, E. C. Bentley, and R. Austin Freeman describe, respectively, Mr. Fortune, Trent, and Dr. Thorndyke.

Forgotten though the majority of these writers are, their essays tend to remain alive and readable, albeit not particularly deep or insightful, occasionally revealing more than their creators intended: Sapper created Drummond because he could not kill a golfer with an annoying sniff, and Horler, very fond of his Standish, complains about "women's ideas" and states that his character "appeals to the heart of the boy which is in every man—every man who *is* a man," providing a number of excerpts from his fiction that will (more than likely) fail to convince most contemporary readers of Standish's likeability.

Enjoyable, but now a work for completists and specialists.

987. Mattson, E. (Ed) Christian, and Thomas (Tom) B. Davis. **A Collector's Guide to Hardcover Boy's Series Books; or, Tracing the Trail of Harry Hudson.** Newark, Del.: MAD Book, 1997. viii, 578 p. Indexes. Paperback.

The second printing (1997) is described.

This monumental guide lists the boys' series books published in hardcover between 1872 and 1993. Researchers and determined collectors of boys' series books should read section A, "Collecting Information," which contains numerous subsections and includes discussions of the history of boys' series books, collecting boys' series books, book and dust jacket grading, cleaning and repairing books, reference periodicals, hunting for series books, using the MAD (Mattson and Davis) numbering system, logging your collection, rare series and rare books, research on Altemus series books, and additions or corrections for future editions of this book. Important and useful though this material is, it is not necessary to have read section A in order to use the *Guide* at a basic level.

Following the introduction and acknowledgments, the contents are (A) collecting information; (B) author listing (alphabetical—cross-referenced by MAD number);

(C) series listing (alphabetical—cross-referenced by MAD number); (D) publisher listing (alphabetical—cross-referenced by MAD number); (E) artist listing (alphabetical—
cross-referenced by MAD number); (F) subject listing (alphabetical—cross-referenced
by MAD number); (G) miscellaneous series listing (alphabetical, no cross-references);
(H) additional information: nonseries books by popular authors (alphabetical by author)
and a listing of phantom titles (alphabetical—cross-referenced by MAD number); and
(I) illustrators (by publishers—cross-referenced by MAD number).

The entries in section C comprise the majority of the volume. Listings are alphabetical by series name. Within each series, the titles are listed in their publication order,
followed by the artist's name, the author, the publication date; accompanying each reference are checklists for condition, dust wrappers, and plates that can be used by collectors. Numerous notes are provided, as are comments on variants, spin-offs, and
renumberings. Only the first printing of each series is documented, and information is
clearly presented and accessible. The discussions of the individual series in no way approach the bibliographical convolutions of works such as Farah (q.v.).

Collectors of boys' mysteries from the Adventure and Mystery series to the
Young Reporter series will welcome the *Guide*. It belongs next to the University of Minnesota's *Girls Series Books: A Checklist of Hardback Books Published 1900–1975*
(q.v.) in all research libraries.

988.   Nevins, Jess. **Fantastic, Mysterious, and Adventurous Victoriana.** http://www.
geocities.com/jessnevins/vicintro.html

Describing more than 500 notable characters from Victorian-era popular literature, this site is remarkably thorough, although marred by a coy introduction. Nevins
provides information on the characters appearing in the books and magazines written
prior to the 1901 death of Queen Victoria. The data describe the character and provide
the literary source of the character's appearance.

989.   Nevins, Jess. **Pulp and Adventure Heroes of the Pre-War Years.** http://
www.geocities.com/jjnevins/pulpsintro.html

This incredible site provides bio-bibliographic information about 1,770 characters who appeared in the pulp and adventure fiction prior to the Second World War.
Nevins does not restrict himself to the magazines, and one can find information on characters appearing in comic strips, radio shows, and children's fiction, and even from
"respectable" fiction. It is a companion to Nevins's *Fantastic, Mysterious, and Adventurous
Victoriana* (profiled earlier), which describes more than 500 notable characters and creations from Victorian-era popular literature.

990a.   Nichols, Victoria, and Susan Thompson. **Silk Stalkings: When Women Write
of Murder: A Survey of Series Characters Created by Women Authors in
Crime and Mystery Fiction.** Berkeley, Calif.: Black Lizard Books, 1988. xviii,
522 p. Index. Paperback. LC 88-10491. ISBN 0-88739-096-X.

990b.   Nichols, Victoria, and Susan Thompson. **Silk Stalkings: More Women Write
of Murder.** Lanham, Md.: Scarecrow, 1998. xix, 634 p. Index. Cloth. LC
97-24372. ISBN 0-8108-3393-X.

Nichols and Thompson—who between them have more than 60 years of mystery reading experience—have compiled a partially annotated bibliography of the series

characters created by women authors. Nearly 600 characters appearing in more than 3,000 English and American works between 1867 and 1987 are listed in what is described as the "Master List." It is organized alphabetically by autonym, listing the series characters created by each author, the titles featuring the character, the book's year of publication. It also should be noted that the authors appearing in the Master List include not only women but also men writing under female pseudonyms, and writing teams; numerous cross-references are provided.

The Master List does not open the book, however. Instead, the first section of the book consists of 15 chapters in which a selection of series characters is first grouped thematically by profession, vocation, setting, or inclination, and then described in depth. The thematic groupings include detectives who are (or who are involved with) academics, police detectives, aristocrats, religion, medicine, stage, television and motion pictures, business and finance, the law, writers and journalists, curators, bibliophiles, art experts, the visual arts, professional detectives, the military, wives and other significant others, and unexpected detectives. The descriptions list the series character's name, the years in which the character flourished, the number of books in which he or she appeared, the character's nationality, and the author's name. A "biography" of the character is then provided, along with explanations of how the character functions and evolves from novel to novel; often included are relevant quotations from the books.

Sections following the Master List provide a chronology of series characters, a pseudonym to autonym index, and an index that links series characters to their authors.

Nichols and Thompson deserve commendations for compiling an extraordinarily useful reference book. There are, however, some odd omissions (Lillian de la Torre's Dr. Sam: Johnson among them), and more seriously, short stories are sometimes listed as books, and title changes are not always noted. These bibliographic shortcomings do not significantly detract from the virtues of the book, which are many. This belongs in academic and public libraries.

991. Pate, Janet. **The Book of Sleuths.** Chicago: Contemporary Books, 1977. 124 p. LC 77-75843. ISBN 0-8092-7838-3 (hc); 0-8092-7837-5 (pb).

Pate's heavily illustrated guide focuses on the detectives, not on the novels in which they appeared. In order to show the development of the detective novel in relation to the changing social times, she has arranged her 40 entries roughly chronologically, dividing them into three separately titled sections, "Classical Beginnings," "The Heyday," and "Goodbye to the Gentleman." Each detective's entry opens with a quotation (or quotations) describing the detective followed by a lengthier description of the detective's life and achievements. A concluding bibliography lists the first editions of the books in which the detective appeared as well as the films and theater productions featuring the detective. There are some surprises in Pate's choices of detectives, for in addition to the names one would expect (Dupin, Holmes, Poirot, Marlowe, Spade, etc.) she has described such figures as Sexton Blake, Bulldog Drummond, Rin Tin Tin (!), J. G. Reeder, Batman, Inspector Clouseau, and Theo Kojak.

Whimsical choices of detectives aside, Pate's writing occasionally flags, and her entries lack the depth found in such works as Otto Penzler's *The Great Detectives* (q.v.). Nevertheless, Pate's argument about the detective tending to reflect changing social times is valid if obvious, and although it is less than it could be, this work is more than a coffee-table book.

992. Penzler, Otto, ed. **The Great Detectives.** Boston: Little, Brown, 1978. xvii, 281 p. Cloth. LC 77-25487. ISBN 0-316-69883-0.

Although it has not traditionally been listed as a reference book, this collection of 26 essays describing the creation of significant detectives is as important as the *Detectionary, Silk Stalkings,* or such volumes as Maxim Jakubowski's *100 Great Detectives* (q.q.v.). With two arguable exceptions, the essays have been written by the creators of the detectives, who more often than not reveal the processes that went into the creation and development of their characters. The list begins with Ngaio Marsh discussing her Roderick Alleyn; concludes with Nicholas Freeling discussing his Inspector Van der Valk; and includes such joys as Ross Macdonald discussing Lew Archer, Ed McBain revealing his intentions to kill off Carella, H. R. F. Keating providing a somewhat bemused look at his Inspector Ghote through the eyes of a colleague, and "Maxwell Grant" (Walter Gibson) surveying the life and adventures of the Shadow. Donald Hamilton's essay reveals the almost inadvertent creation of Matt Helm; John Ball's essay is written as if he and Virgil Tibbs were sharing a dinner in Pasadena; Brett Halliday's essay explains that Michael Shayne was based on a real person; and Chester Gould's essay surveys the development and evolution of his Dick Tracy. All essays are delightful and the majority contains information useful to researchers; all conclude with a facsimile of their writer's signature. (The arguable exceptions are Gibson's article on the Shadow and "Carolyn Keene"'s [Harriet Stratemeyer Adams's] description of Nancy Drew: although Gibson created the character and wrote 282 novels in the series, 43 books were written by others; and although "Keene" wrote and rewrote many Nancy Drew mysteries, they were created by her father, Edward Stratemeyer, and written by a stable of authors, including Mildred Wirt Benson.)

Concluding the volume are a bibliography and filmography. The former is occasionally incomplete, lists only books, and provides only their year of publication and publisher, whereas the latter merely lists the year in which the film appeared and the studio that released it.

The majority of the authors who contributed essays on their characters is now dead, making the contents of this volume historically valuable and important for the study of some of the more significant detectives of the twentieth century. A follow-up volume would be most useful.

993a. Penzler, Otto, and others. **Detectionary: A Biographical Dictionary of Leading Characters in Detective and Mystery Fiction, Including Famous and Little-Known Sleuths, Their Helpers, Rogues Both Heroic and Sinister, and Some of Their Most Memorable Adventures, as Recounted in Novels, Short Stories, and Films.** Lock Haven, Pa.: Hammermill Paper, Lock Haven Division, 1971. xi, 290 p. Index. Paperback. LC 74-179410.

993b. Penzler, Otto, and others. **Detectionary: A Biographical Dictionary of Leading Characters in Detective and Mystery Fiction, Including Famous and Little-Known Sleuths, Their Helpers, Rogues Both Heroic and Sinister, and Some of Their Most Memorable Adventures, as Recounted in Novels, Short Stories, and Films.** Revised and expanded edition. New York: Overlook Press. 1977. xi, 299 p. LC 75-27326. ISBN 0-87951-041-2.

The first edition of this volume was published as a private limited edition intended by the Hammermill Paper Company to demonstrate its printing capabilities.

Many of this edition were accidentally destroyed, and those copies that survived became collectable rarities. The second edition of the *Detectionary* is physically larger, contains a new preface, and somewhat expands the concluding author index, but the contents are largely similar to the first edition.

The history and monetary value of the various editions aside, Penzler and his colleagues have created a dictionary to the characters and the cases of detective and mystery fiction. These are arranged into four sections: detectives; rogues and companions in crime; cases, and detective and mystery motion pictures. Each section is arranged alphabetically. The first two sections identify the character, name his or her creator, and give his or her background. The third and fourth sections list and describe the cases and the actors and actresses who played the detectives and villains. Symbolic "clues" are used to facilitate cross-reference between sections; a star is used for detectives, a bullet for rogues and helpers, a square for cases, and a triangle for movies. In addition, the volume is illustrated throughout with stills from motion pictures that have nothing to do with the text on the page on which they appear and whose citations provide only the title of the motion picture, the year in which it appeared, and the studio that made it; actors and actresses are not listed. The book concludes with an author index that lists the detectives, rogues and helpers, and the titles in which these characters appeared.

It is obvious that an enormous amount of effort went into compiling the *Detectionary,* and the contents of the first two sections provide data on some obscure characters. The weaker third and fourth sections are not as comprehensive and are less useful. As a reference work, the *Detectionary* is idiosyncratic and occasionally frustrating, but despite its age and eccentricities, it remains useful.

994a. Pringle, David. **Imaginary People: A Who's Who of Modern Fictional Characters.** London and Glasgow: Grafton Books, 1987. x, 515 p. Cloth. GB 87-32384. ISBN 0-246-12968-9. New York: World Almanac, 1988. x, 518 p. Cloth. LC 88-60375. ISBN 0-88687-364-9.

994b. Pringle, David. **Imaginary People: A Who's Who of Fictional Characters from the Eighteenth Century to the Present Day.** 2nd ed. Aldershot, England: Scolar/Ashgate Press, 1996. x, 296 p. Index. Cloth. LC 95-43986. ISBN 1-85928-162-1.

The second edition of *Imaginary People* provides information on more than 1,400 modern fictional characters created between 1719 (Daniel Defoe's Robinson Crusoe) and the early 1990s (Forrest Gump is mentioned); a sizable percentage of these characters appeared in detective and mystery stories. The characters are listed in alphabetical order under the best-known form of his or her name; last names precede first names except when the last name is unknown or rarely used. (The Continental Op, for example, is listed under the letter *C*.) The character's name is given in boldface, after which a biography is provided. The character's creator is named, and the character's attributes are described; the date of the character's first print appearance is given, and later appearances are selectively mentioned. When the character has been adopted for motion pictures, data on these—year of release, director, star—are provided. Coverage of sequels and pastiches written by "other hands" is provided, as well as numerous cross-references, a bibliography of sources, and an index to the characters' creators.

The characters described are well chosen and varied; the first letter of the alphabet contains biographies of Uncle Abner, Hilda Adams, Nick Adams, Roderick Alleyn,

Pepper Anderson, John Appleby, Lew Archer, plus those of a number of characters appearing in the related genres of thrillers and espionage. Although additional bibliographic data would have been welcome, this is a well-done and often useful volume.

995. Rovin, Jeff. **Adventure Heroes: Legendary Characters from Odysseus to James Bond.** New York: Facts on File, 1994. vi, 314 p. Index. LC 93-46603. ISBN 0-8160-288108 (hc); 0-8160-2886-9 (pb).

Rovin's guide is a companion of sorts to his *Encyclopedia of Superheroes,* but in this volume he eschews characters with superpowers to describe more than 500 comic book, television, motion picture, and literary characters who have no super powers but whose behavior is nevertheless heroic. A significant percentage of these characters is detectives.

The arrangement of *Adventure Heroes* is alphabetical by the name of the hero, or by the name of the group in which the hero functioned (e.g., the Impossible Mission Force). Each entry provides a one- or two-letter code indicating whether the hero is found in comic books, comic strips, folklore, literature, mythology, a motion picture, an opera, the radio, the stage, a toy, trading cards, television, or a video game. The first appearance of the hero is noted, followed by a biography of the hero and his sidekicks, cohorts, and cases; a comment on the hero concludes each entry, and a brief bibliography and an index conclude the volume.

Rovin's arrangement is idiosyncratic and occasionally makes locating information on a character time-consuming. Characters are listed by their first names; for example, Philip Marlowe's entry is found under *p* rather than under *m,* and Sam Spade's entry is found in the first part of *s* rather than the later part. Additional confusion is caused by Rovin alphabetizing by titles: Mr. and Mrs. North are listed under *m,* Sergeant Joe Friday is listed under *s,* and cross-references are not provided. Neither are data in Rovin's entries consistently correct.

The worst problem with *Adventure Heroes* is simply that its 500 entries are inadequate, and the book should have been at least three times its present length. Collectors of comic books might want *Adventure Heroes,* but the volume contains little that is not available elsewhere.

996. Thrilling Detective Web Site. **Everything You Ever Wanted to Know about Private Eyes & Other Tough Guys.** http://www.thrillingdetective.com/eyes.html

This very thorough site provides information on hundreds of fictional private eyes and "tough" characters who nominally do detecting. The arrangement is alphabetical by the character's last name. A typical entry provides the creator's name, a description of the character, some biographical data on the author, and a list of the works in which the character appeared. When relevant, links to the creator's home page and other sources are provided. In all, a very useful site.

997a. University of Minnesota, Children's Literature Research Collections. **Girls Series Books: A Checklist of Hardback Books Published 1900–1975.** Minneapolis: Children's Literature Research Collections, University of Minnesota Libraries, 1978. ix, 121 p. Indexes. Paperback. LC 78-623834.

997b. University of Minnesota, Children's Literature Research Collections. **Girls Series Books: A Checklist of Titles Published 1840–1991.** Minneapolis: Children's Literature Research Collections, University of Minnesota Libraries, 1992. x, 347 p. Indexes. Paperback.

The second edition is described.

As its title indicates, the focus is on the hardcover series books published between 1840 and 1991 that were produced (predominantly) for girls; a significant number of these series featured girls solving mysteries. Arrangement is alphabetical by series name. The title of each series is given in boldface capital letters; on separate lines beneath it are the name of the stated series author and the publisher(s); if the author is a known pseudonym, the real name is given in parentheses, and if the book originally appeared in paperback, the publisher's name is accompanied by (PB). Separately numbered beneath these are the titles of the books in their series order, with the date of first publication given. Renumberings are indicated (as in the Wanderer Books reprints of the Bobbsey Twins series); cross-references indicate related titles and spin-offs; and an asterisk indicates that the title is in the Children's Literature Research Collection. Citations do not reference reprint publishers.

Successive sections provide an author index, a publisher index, and a chronological index; this last is arranged alphabetically within decade divisions.

Although more information on the contents of the book would have been welcome, this volume is nicely produced and essential for the collectors of juvenile series ranging from Patricia Giff's Abby Jones, Junior Detective to Hilda Stahl's Wren House. It belongs next to the Mattson and Davis *A Collector's Guide to Hardcover Boys' Series Books* (q.v.) in all research libraries.

SPECIFIC CHARACTERS

Black Bat

998. Brown, Michael Rogero, and Nicholas Sauer. **The Black Bat.** http://sflovers.rutgers.edu/archive/bibliographies/black-bat.txt

Although this file is maintained in the sf-lovers archives at Rutgers University, the Black Bat was a character appearing in 62 issues of *Black Book Detective Magazine* from 1 July 1939 until winter 1953. Brown's index lists the issue number in which the Black Bat appeared, followed by the title of the adventure, the initials of the author's name, the date of publication, the magazine's volume, and the story's number in the Hanos reprint series. The key to the authors' full names is given at the bottom of the file. More data would have been welcome, but what Brown and Sauer provide is very capably presented.

Note: Black Book Detective Magazine is also indexed through the first series of Leonard Robbins's *The Pulp Magazine Index* and through Michael Cook and Steve Miller's *Mystery, Detective, and Espionage Fiction* (q.q.v.).

Cherry Ames

999. Mikucki, Eleanor. **The Cherry Ames Page.** http://www.netwrx1.net/CherryAmes

Devoted to Cherry Ames, the quick-witted nurse-sleuth, this delightful Web site provides links to information about her: her name, her childhood, her family, her friends, her adversaries, her patients, her home, her apartment, her job history, and her birthday. An alphabetical index of characters is given, as are links to scholarly analyses of the Cherry Ames series, summaries of the books, and information about other books written by the authors. Related material—information about the Cherry Ames board game, links to sites featuring nurse-sleuths, biographical information on the authors of the books, and descriptions of the Cherry Ames *Book of First Aid and Home Nursing*—is accessible, and numerous cover reproductions are given. All information is clearly presented and thorough; the site is an affectionate and well-done tribute.

Dan Fowler

1000. Johnson, Tom. **Dan Fowler: Ace of the G-Men.** Seymour, Tex.: Fading Shadows, 1997. 52 p. Paperback.

From 1935 through 1953, Dan Fowler was the lead character in some 112 issues of the pulp magazine *G-Men* (later *G-Men Detective*). Because the stories were published under the house pseudonym "C. K. M. Scanlon," authorship of the individual stories remains in doubt, although George F. Eliot, Edward Churchill, D. L. Champion, Whit Ellsworth, and Manly Wade Wellman all appear to have written Fowler's adventures.

Johnson's self-published annotated bibliography provides extensive story summaries of Fowler's first 53 adventures. Johnson begins with a discussion of the characters, after which there is a chronological list of the stories along with date of issue, volume and issue numbers, and a guess as to the author's identity. These are followed by individual descriptions of the 53 issues. Each issue is numbered, and data given previously are repeated. Each citation lists the story's setting(s) and its characters, provides a detailed synopsis, and concludes with notes. Johnson concludes his list with a list titled "Top Ten and a Stinker," after which is a reprint of "Diamonds across the Atlantic," which first appeared in the winter 1946 *G-Men Detective*. The back page of the book is a chronological checklist of all 112 issues; titles are given, as are the volume and issue number, and the month and year of issue.

Doc Savage

1001a. Farmer, Philip José. **Doc Savage: His Apocalyptic Life as the Archangel of Technopolis, as the Golden-Eyed Hero of 181 Supersagas[,] as the Bronze Knight of the Running Board, Including His Final Battle against the Forces of Hell Itself.** Garden City, N.Y.: Doubleday 1973. 226 p. Cloth. LC 72-96236. ISBN 0-385-08488-9.

Biographies of fictional characters have not been included in this work, but Farmer's life of Doc Savage is mentioned here for its three concluding sections. The first, "The Fabulous Family Tree of Doc Savage (Another Excursion into Creative Mythography)," provides a lengthy history of Doc Savage and all of his ancestors. Farmer's coverage starts in 1795, when a meteor in Wold Newton, Yorkshire, England, irradiated the genes of the inhabitants, enabling their descendants to become such supermen as Captain Blood, Tarzan, Micah Clarke, Solomon Kane, Allan Quatermain, Sherlock Holmes, Wolf Larsen, Mr. Moto, and Doc Savage, and such supervillains as Professor Moriarty and Fu Manchu. This section—which has taken on a life of its own—is essential for anybody desiring to understand what is sometimes referred to as the "Wold Newton" mythology.

The second and third sections are more germane to the subject of this section. Addendum two is a lengthy chronology of the life and career of Doc Savage, as related in the adventures described in *Doc Savage*. Arranged chronologically by adventure, each reference provides the month of publication, the duration of the adventure, and the issue (or issues) in which it was described.

Finally, the "List of Doc Savage Stories" lists all 181 *Doc Savage* stories in order of publication. Clark's *The Author Index to the Doc Savage Magazine* (q.v.) not being generally accessible, this was for many years the closest thing to a readily obtainable index to *Doc Savage* available. Farmer's introductory material to this section is nevertheless not completely reliable, for he was unaware of the contributions of Ryerson Johnson.

1001b. Lai, Rick. **The Bronze Age: An Alternate Doc Savage Chronology.** Seymour, Tex.: Fading Shadows, 1992. 60 p. Paperback. 100 copies printed.

Written partially to expand upon the chronology of Doc Savage's life presented by Farmer in *Doc Savage: His Apocalyptic Life* (q.v.), Lai has proposed an alternative chronology for Doc Savage's life and adventures. Drawing upon the researches of Farmer and such Doc Savage scholars as Will Murray, Lai presents a chronology of Doc Savage's life and adventures from 1918 onward, as recorded in the pulp magazines and books. Each adventure is separately numbered; its date is given, as is the number of days it involved. The title of the magazine or book printing the adventure is given (in capital letters), followed by its author and first publication date. A description of each adventure is given.

This is a worthy alternative to Farmer's work, but the work is for specialists.

1001c. Sines, Jeff. **Doc Savage Unchained!** http://users.aol.com/jsines233/private/DocSavage.htm

The most comprehensive collection of Doc Savage images currently available on the Web, this Web site provides images of the covers of all of the pulp magazines and paperback editions of Doc Savage. The section devoted to paperbacks reprints the material from the books' back covers, gives the date of the first magazine publication, and provides images of the covers of the Bantam editions, the new novels, and the omnibus editions. The section devoted to the pulps provides the cover images, arranged chronologically; images for the early book reprints also are provided. Images of the covers of *Doc Savage* comic books are given, as are the lyrics to the theme song of the 1975 motion picture. Finally, there are numerous links to other Doc Savage sites.

1001d. Smalley, Rob. **Doc Savage: The Supreme Adventurer.** http://members.aol.com/smalleyra/docsvg.html

This Web site provides significant information about the character of Doc Savage and his adventures; in addition, information about Doc Savage's associates and his lairs is given. Especially useful is a comprehensive listing of Doc Savage's adventures. The magazine's original publication date is provided, as are the Bantam paperback reprint number and the title of the adventure. A number of the titles are linked to reproductions of the paperback covers and are accompanied by synopses of the stories. Clark Savage's final message to Doc is provided, and there are links to other Doc Savage

sites, including the Doc Savage WebRing (http://www.webring.org/cgi-bin/webring?
ring=docsavagering&list), a metasite devoted to Doc Savage. Smalley's Web site is obviously a labor of love and is well done.

The Hardy Boys

1002a. Carpentieri, Tony. **Frank and Joe Turn Blue.** Rheem Valley, Calif.: SynSine
Press, 1993. 234 p. Spiral-bound. LC 94-173259. ISBN 0-9639949-2-1.

1002b. Carpentieri, Tony. **Frank and Joe Turn Blue.** 2nd ed. Rheem Valley, Calif.:
SynSine Press, 1994.

1002c. Carpentieri, Tony. **Frank and Joe Turn Blue.** 3rd ed. Rheem Valley, Calif.:
SynSine Press, 1994. 248 p. Spiral-bound. ISBN 0-9639949-9-9.

This description is based on the third edition.

Frank and Joe Turn Blue lists every known printing of the first 58 Hardy Boys
books, from the appearance of *The Tower Treasure* in 1927 until the 1979 publication of
The Sting of the Scorpion. In addition, printings for all known Grosset and Dunlap library bindings are described. Entries for each book provide information on cover/dust
jacket artists, front and back cover styles, material on the endpapers, information on the
spine, and all the relevant data that can be used to differentiate the numerous different
printings of each title.

Thorough though Carpentieri is, his work is almost unusable, for he presents the
data of each citation through a complex series of abbreviations. These abbreviations are
keyed to a lengthy list given only at the book's beginning, and until readers have internalized Carpentieri's system, readers will remain baffled by page after page of entries
akin to 17 (yel)//e-2/eb/blx2/syn/pf/tp3.1/cp(loc,isbnt,isbn1)/tc/bl/c1/176/blx3/BT(48)
of/HB#1-58 of (eb)/e-2//nn.

Like Farah's guide to the Nancy Drew series (q.v.), this volume is a labor of
love. Its coverage is greater than that in Heffelfinger's *The Bayport Companion* (q.v.),
but it is nonetheless very specialized and very difficult to use.

1002d. Finnan, Robert W. **The Hardy Boys Unofficial Home Page.** http://users.arczip.
com/fwdixon

Unofficial, perhaps, but with hundreds of links to other sites including book
sales, discussion groups, and other series.

1002e. Heffelfinger, Charles. **The Bayport Companion.** Tampa, Fla.: Midnight Press,
1992. 93 p. Paperback. OCLC 30750970.

1002f. Heffelfinger, Charles. **The Bayport Companion.** 2nd ed. Tampa, Fla.: Midnight Press, 1994. 102 p. Paperback. OCLC 33364572.

This description is based on the second edition.

The Bayport Companion lists every known printing of the first 40 Hardy Boys
books, from the 1927 appearance of *The Tower Treasure* until the 1961 publication of
The Mystery of the Desert Giant. In addition, Heffelfinger discusses Hardy Boys comics,
record albums, games, and collectibles. Entries for each separate printing of each book
provide the year of its publication and information on cover/dust jacket artists, number

of books listed on the front flap, color of the spine of the dust jacket, frontispiece artists, color of the endpapers, color of the binding, rear flap ad, and back cover ad.

Thorough though Heffelfinger is, he has consciously modeled the format for his citations after those used by Farah (q.v.), and the result is equally unusable to the uninitiated. Page after page of citations appear akin to gf;tp+;cp,HB1-8,TSc1-10;tc;tc(t);; HB1-14,16;WS1-16;HG(9);TOA(7);b1;b1; and the only key is at the beginning of the volume.

Like Farah's guide to the Nancy Drew series and the guide to the Hardy Boys compiled by Carpentieri (q.v.), this volume is an obvious labor of love. Collectors of the Hardy Boys series will probably be satisfied with Carpentieri's effort, but the information provided by this volume should not be discounted.

Judy Bolton

1003. Finnan, Robert W. **Judy Bolton Series Books.** http://users.arczip.com/fwdixon/ seriesbookcentral/bolton.html

Finnan provides a list of the 38 Judy Bolton mysteries written by "Margaret Sutton," from the 1932 *The Vanishing Shadow* to the 1967 *The Secret of the Sand Castle*. Apart from the date of first publication, no bibliographic data are provided, but the list is clearly presented and very well illustrated.

The Moon Man

1004. Brown, Michael Rogero. **The Moon Man.** http://sflovers.rutgers.edu/archive/ bibliographies/moon-man.txt

Created by pulp writer Frederick Davis, the Moon Man was one of the more popular characters to appear in *Ten Detective Aces*. Brown's index to the 39 appearances of the Moon Man is arranged by issue. The story's title is given, followed by Davis's initials, and the date of the story's publication; the volume and issue numbers of the magazine are not known. Separate reprints are noted, and a note makes reference to *The Night Nemesis,* the first of a proposed two-volume reprinting of the collected Moon Man.

Nancy Drew

1005a. Farah, David. **Farah's Guide.** Pasadena, Calif.: Farah's Books, 1985–. Various pagings. Spiral-bound. Numerous editions.

The following annotation describes the tenth (1994) edition.

In what must have been an extraordinary labor of love, Farah describes every known printing of every volume featuring the character of Nancy Drew published between 1930 and 1994. Grosset and Dunlap issued the regular editions of Nancy Drew in some 20 different formats, and Farah's bibliography arranges its contents according to these formats. Each entry provides the print run, the number of printings, the price of the book in good condition in a dust jacket, data on the dust jacket front flap, the cover art, the spine, the back flap, the reverse, the pretext pages, the posttext pages. Furthermore, he provides biographical information on the authors and writers of Nancy Drew.

On the debit side, these data are presented in highly abbreviated form, and the key to these data is given only at the beginning of the volume. Until they have internalized Farah's system, users will remain baffled by page after page of entries akin to 5050,ND#1-19,110-150/1/1f/ML#1-8/DG#1-10 / pwt/pf/tp+/cp,ND#1-18/tc/b1/pwt/b1 (t)//b1.

Devout Nancy Drew fans and collectors will want this book.

1005b. Finnan, Robert W. **The Unofficial Nancy Drew Home Page.** http://users.arczip.com/fwdixon/NancyDrew/nd1.htm

1005c. The Unofficial Nancy Drew Home Page. http://www.geocities.com/SoHo/Nook/3173/nd1.htm

Both these sites provide a phenomenal amount of information on Nancy Drew, with links to (and information on) the original series, media adaptations, the paperback versions, the Hardy Boys cross-overs, the River Heights series, and so forth.

The Phantom Detective (aka the Phantom)

1006a. Halegua, Mark S. **Phantom Detective.** http://www.mindspring.com/~phantom21/phantom.htm

Halegua's site provides information about the character of the Phantom (in the series, nobody ever referred to him as the Phantom Detective). In addition, a subsection titled "The Phantom Detective Index" (http://www.mindspring.com/~phantom21/PD-Index.html) lists the 170 Phantom Detective novels in chronological order, giving for each its title, publication date, and volume and issue number. A nicely done site, although Tom Johnson's *Phantom Detective* (which follows) is more comprehensive.

1006b. Johnson, Tom. **Phantom Detective: The Original Masked Marvel.** Seymour, Tex.: Fading Shadows, 1996. 86 p. Index. Paperback.

From 1933 through 1953, the Phantom Detective—the lethal alter ego of rich playboy, dilettante, and disguise expert Richard Curtis Van Loan—was the lead character in some 170 stories appearing in the pulp magazine the *Phantom Detective*. Because the stories were published under the house pseudonym "G. Wayman Jones," authorship of the individual stories remains in doubt, although D. L. Champion, C. S. Montayne, Emil Tepperman, and Norman Daniels all appear to have written stories about the Phantom Detective.

Johnson's self-published annotated bibliography provides extensive story summaries of all 170 adventures of the Phantom Detective. Johnson begins with a history of the characters, after which there are descriptions of the individual adventures. Each entry is numbered, and the date of the issue and the volume and issue number are given, along with a guess as to the author's identity. Each citation lists the story's setting(s) and its characters, provides a detailed synopsis, and concludes with notes about the story. Concluding the book is a chronological list of the stories that is misidentified as a title index.

The Shadow

1007. Lai, Rick. **Chronology of Shadows.** Seymour, Tex.: Fading Shadows, 1995. 94 p. Paperback. 100 copies printed.

In *Chronology of Shadows,* Lai proposes a chronology for the life and adventures of the Shadow. The contents: (1) "Introduction"; (2) "The Shadow's Early Years"; (3) "Chronology of the Shadow's Early Years"; (4) "Chronology of Recorded Exploits"; (5) "Afterword: Apocryphal Shadows."

Lai's chronology of the Shadow's early years begins in 1892 with the birth of Kent Allard and concludes in 1929, the year in which the Shadow begins to impersonate Lamont Cranston. In the chronology of recorded exploits, publications are separately numbered. The date of the adventure is given, as is the number of days the adventure involved. The title in which the adventure was published is given in italics, followed by the date of its first publication; a note indicates when the adventure was written by an author other than Walter Gibson. A brief description of the adventure follows.

Lovers of the Shadow will appreciate Lai's efforts.

Trixie Belden

1008. It is debatable whether Julie Campbell [Tatham]'s creation belongs in this guide, but the adventures of the irrepressible Trixie Belden remain perennially popular, and the following Web sites offer a gratifying amount of information, often with reproductions.

> http://www.barbln.org/trixie
>
> http://www.geocities.com/Heartland/Shores/6423/trixie.html
>
> ftp://members.aol.com/sharon899/library/TrixieBeldenFAX.txt
>
> http://www.geocities.com/Hollywood/Location/2933/title.html
>
> http://trixie.hypermart.net/index.html
>
> http://members.tripod.com/~Tim_Lisa/trixie.html

12

Secondary Literature

Scope note: Included in this section are the bibliographies of the literature written about mystery and detective fiction. Primary and secondary bibliographies devoted to individual authors are listed in the author section.

1009a. Adams, Donald K., ed. **The Mystery & Detection Annual.** Beverly Hills, Calif.: Donald Adams, 1972–1973. xii, 264 p. Cloth. LC 72-87432. ISBN 0-913288-00-4 (1972).

1009b. Adams, Donald K., ed. **The Mystery and Detection Annual.** Beverly Hills, Calif.: 1973 [i.e., 1974]. xii, 337 p. Cloth. 0-913288-01-2. ISSN 000-0302.

Although it lasted but two years, these annuals nevertheless contain excellent and incisive articles, criticism, and reviews. The volume for 1972 is dedicated to Edgar Allan Poe, and several of its essays discuss aspects of Poe's detective fiction. In addition, articles about detective and mystery fiction written during the nineteenth century and by authors born during the nineteenth century are included. The volume's focus is not limited to the nineteenth century, however, and articles on such writers as Horace McCoy, Dashiell Hammett, and Ross Macdonald are provided. A surprising inclusion is Lawrence D. Stewart's "Gertrude Stein and the Vital Dead." A section devoted to reviews provides informed criticism on several significant mystery and detective studies published from 1969 until 1972. Julian Symons takes the first edition of Barzun and Taylor's *A Catalog of Crime* to task for bibliographical inaccuracy, Wilbur Jordan Smith discusses Ordean Hagen's deficiencies in listing nineteenth-century titles in *Who Done It?* and additional reviews address such significant works as Julian Symons's *Mortal Consequences* and la Cour and Mogensen's *The Murder Book.* In addition, a number of primary works are reviewed.

Although Adams had hoped to dedicate the 1973 volume of *The Mystery and Detection Annual* to Arthur Conan Doyle, his contributors chose to write on different subjects, and the volume has as its theme "The Southern California Scene." Nevertheless, historical subjects are treated. Included are articles on James Hogg's *The Private Memoirs and Confessions of a Justified Sinner,* Poe, and William Godwin. The discussion of the moderns includes an interview with, and an article about, Ross Macdonald;

the first publication of Horace McCoy's "Death in Hollywood"; and a discussion of Raymond Chandler and F. Scott Fitzgerald's *The Great Gatsby;* and articles on Georges Simenon, Paul Bowles, and Dorothy L. Sayers are included. The critical reviews are diverse, discussing books as varied as *Graham Greene on Film: Collected Film Criticism 1935–1940; Chandler Before Marlowe: Raymond Chandler's Early Prose and Poetry, 1908–1912,* and *The Ghost Stories of Edith Wharton.* As before, a number of primary works are reviewed.

It is to be regretted that this series lasted only two years. Its contents are of consistently high quality.

1010a. Albert, Walter. **Detective and Mystery Fiction: An International Bibliography of Secondary Sources.** Madison, Ind.: Brownstone Books, 1985. xii, 781 p. Index. Cloth. ISBN 0-941028-02-X.

1010b. Albert, Walter. **Detective and Mystery Fiction: An International Bibliography of Secondary Sources.** 2nd ed. Brownstone Mystery Guides, vol. 10. San Bernardino, Calif.: Brownstone Books/Borgo Press, 1997. 672 p. Index. LC 95-5335. ISBN 0-941028-15-1 (hc); 0-941028-16-X (pb).

Intended as a comprehensive list of the secondary material in the area of crime, detective, and mystery fiction and suspense and espionage fiction, this volume references more than 7,700 books, chapters, journal and magazine articles, dissertations, dealer catalogues, an occasional newspaper article, an enormous amount of fan literature, and such ephemera as calendars, trade reports, and company publications. The contents include numerous Swedish, German, French, and Spanish publications as well as (romanized) references to Japanese sources. Excluded are materials on Sherlock Holmes and publications dealing solely with film, television, radio, and stage adaptations.

The second edition of *Detective and Mystery Fiction* contains six sections: (A) "Reference Works: Bibliographies, Dictionaries, Encyclopedias, and Checklists" (282 citations); (B) "General Historical and Critical Works: Books" (678 citations); (C) "General Historical and Critical Works: Articles" (1,369 citations); (D) "Dime Novels, Juvenile Series, and the Pulps" (859 citations); (E) "Works on Specific Authors" (4,490 citations); (F) "Magazines" (58 citations). Each section numbers its citations consecutively; all citation numbers and author names are in boldface type. Sections A through C are arranged alphabetically by the critic's last name. Section D contains subsections for materials studying the dime novels and juveniles and the pulps and further divides these contents by offering sections on general works and on works studying specific publications. The general sections are alphabetical by author; the sections dealing with specific publications are alphabetical by publication name. Section E is alphabetical by the subject's name; section F is alphabetical by title. Virtually all entries are annotated, occasionally lengthily, and many are signed, for some 23 experts assisted Albert in the collection of data, including such notables as Robert C. S. Adey, John L. Apostolou, Everett F. Bleiler, Robert E. Briney, J. Randolph Cox, Iwan Hedman, Deidre Johnson, Will Murray, John Nieminski, and Robert Sampson. Internal cross-references are given in parentheses. Data are complete as of 1990.

Detective and Mystery Fiction is almost unbelievably comprehensive, and it is remarkably accurate. The occasional errors and omissions are trivial. All academic libraries and researchers should hold this volume. Although the Borgo Press no longer exists, Albert's work is available on CD-ROM from the Locus Press.

In late 2003 a CD-ROM was obtained from Locus Press containing an advance uncorrected copy of the third edition of *Detective and Mystery Fiction: An International Bibliography of Secondary Sources*. Concentrating on paper rather than electronic resources, it contains 10,715 citations and updates its entries through 2000. There are four sections: Section I references all bibliographies, dictionaries, and checklists; Section II describes critical and historical essays, articles, and books; Section III lists material about the dime novel, juvenile mystery series, and the pulp magazines; and Section IV discusses material about individual authors. There is a lengthy appendix on "limited circulation magazines" that supplements and updates the material provided in Michael Cook's *Mystery, Detective, and Espionage Magazines* (q.v.). A comprehensive index lists the authors of primary and secondary material, series characters, specialty magazines, and publishing houses where those items are the subject of the entry. Albert's knowledge of his material remains unparalleled, and this remains an essential publication.

1011.   Bloom, Harold, ed. **Classic Crime and Suspense Writers.** Writers of English: Lives and Works. New York: Chelsea House, 1995. xii, 188 p. LC 93-22607. ISBN 0-7910-2206-4 (hc); 0-7910-2231-5 (pb).

The first sentence of this book claims that it "provides biographical, critical, and bibliographical information on the thirteen most significant crime and suspense writers of the first half of the twentieth century." It does not. One of the writers (E. W. Hornung) had a career that began prior to the twentieth century, four of the writers (Ian Fleming, John D. MacDonald, Ross Macdonald, and Jim Thompson) did not publish significantly until the latter half of the twentieth century, and although the remaining eight names consist of such notables as Eric Ambler, John Buchan, James M. Cain, Raymond Chandler, Daphne du Maurier, Graham Greene, Dashiell Hammett, and Cornell Woolrich, it would hardly be accurate to state that these few are the "most significant crime and suspense writers."

Prior to the start of the biographical, critical, and bibliographical information is Bloom's essay titled "The Life of the Author." It contains such sentences as "Beckett was perhaps the least egoistic post-Joycean, post-Proustian, post-Kafkan of writers" and has nothing whatsoever to do with detective and mystery fiction.

Each chapter of the book is devoted to one of the named authors and consists of three parts: a biography, a selection of critical extracts about the author, and a bibliography of the author's published books. The biographies often are inadequate; for example, Hammett's Continental Op is erroneously described as "a hired gunman," and Hammett first appeared in *Black Mask* in 1922, not 1923. The critical extracts tend to be brief, in the 250- to 400-word range, and the bibliographies provide only the dates of book publication, with no indication of whether the work is fiction, nonfiction, poetry, play, essay collection, short story collection, or novel.

The thematically similar work compiled by Bruce Cassiday (q.v.) is superior.

1012.   Bloom, Harold, ed. **Classic Mystery Writers.** Writers of English: Lives and Works. New York: Chelsea House, 1995. xii, 188 p. LC 94-5882. ISBN 0-7910-2210-2 (hc); 0-7910-2235-8 (pb).

A companion to Bloom's *Classic Crime and Suspense Writers* (profiled earlier), this volume is only marginally better. Its introduction states that it "provides biographical, critical, and bibliographical information on the thirteen most significant writers of mystery and detective fiction through the 1920s." These 13 include Wilkie Collins, Arthur Conan Doyle, Edgar Allan Poe, and Melville Davisson Post (all of whom were dead or inactive prior to the conclusion of 1920s), but the majority of the book is devoted to Anthony Berkeley, G. K. Chesterton, Agatha Christie, Freeman Wills Crofts, R. Austin Freeman, Mary Roberts Rinehart, Dorothy L. Sayers, S. S. Van Dine, and Edgar Wallace, virtually all of whom were active after the 1920s.

As in the other volume, Bloom's essay titled "The Life of the Author" precedes the biographical, critical, and bibliographical information and has nothing whatsoever to do with classic mystery writers, the ostensible subject of this volume.

Each chapter is devoted to one of the authors and consists of three parts: a biography, a selection of critical extracts about the author, and a bibliography of the author's published books. The biographies are cleanly written and reasonably accurate, although not without errors: to state that Christie's *Murder on the Orient Express* (1934), *The A.B.C. Murders* (1936), and *The Body in the Library* (1942) . . . established the 'cozy' British mystery" is to be unaware of literary history. The critical extracts tend to be brief, in the 250- to 400-word range, and the bibliographies provide only the dates of book publication, with no indication of whether the work is fiction, nonfiction, poetry, play, essay collection, short story collection, or novel.

Again, the thematically similar work compiled by Bruce Cassiday (q.v.) is preferable.

1013. Breen, Jon L. **The Girl in the Pictorial Wrapper: An Index to Reviews of Paperback Original Novels in the New York Times' "Criminals at Large" Column, 1953–1970.** Carson: California State College, Dominguez Hills Library, 1972. 46 leaves.

From 1953 until his death in 1968, Anthony Boucher regularly reviewed paperback original novels in the *New York Times Book Review* in his column "Criminals at Large"; he was succeeded by noted bibliographer Allen J. Hubin. Most of these reviews are not listed in the *New York Times Index,* which until relatively recently did not index "Criminals at Large," and this in turn has made it virtually impossible for researchers to locate contemporary reactions to authors as diverse as Chester Himes, William Bradford Huie, MacKinlay Kantor, John D. MacDonald, Jim Thompson, and Cornell Woolrich.

The index is arranged alphabetically by author's name (given in capital letters); beneath each name (also in capital letters) are the titles of the books that were reviewed. Also provided are the book's publisher, the date of the review in highly abbreviated form (e.g., 7Jul63 or 3Nov57), and the page of the *New York Times Book Review* upon which the review appeared.

Breen's citations are accurate and are models of brevity, and it is unfortunate that this index was not printed in hardcover and made more widely available, for it deserves wider circulation and belongs in all academic libraries.

Note: The bibliographic data provided occur nowhere in the index itself and are extracted from Breen's *What about Murder?* A revised and expanded second edition has remained inaccessible to me.

1014. Breen, Jon L. **What about Murder? A Guide to Books About Mystery and Detective Fiction.** Introduction by Ellery Queen. Metuchen, N.J.: Scarecrow, 1981. xviii, 157 p. Index. Cloth. LC 81-645. ISBN 0-8108-1413-7.

Despite its brevity, *What about Murder?* is a gold mine, an expertly annotated and beautifully arranged bibliography of 239 (predominantly) English-language books about detective and mystery fiction published during the twentieth century. The volume begins with an excellent introduction in which Breen provides the criteria he used to choose his contents. In brief, he opted for comprehensiveness except in the case of Sherlock Holmes materials, books on motion pictures, dealer and exhibition catalogues, publicity materials, and works on individual authors who were significant *outside* the mystery field.

The bibliography contains seven sections: general histories; reference books; special subjects; collected essays and reviews; technical manuals; coffee-table books (not meant pejoratively); and works on individual authors. Each entry provides the book's author, title, and publication data (place of publication, publisher, and date of publication for the first English-language edition and the first American edition if it is different). Pagination of these books is provided, as are the names of others who appear on the title page (e.g., the illustrator, translator, editor, introduction writer), the book's series (if any), and whether the book has illustrations, a bibliography, and an index. Finally, Breen records whether the book's title was changed upon reprinting. All citations are arranged alphabetically by author except for the citations on individual authors, which are grouped alphabetically under the author being studied. An excellent author/title index concludes the volume.

Breen's annotations may be browsed with enormous pleasure, for he is neither afraid to damn nor reluctant to praise, and his tastes are quite reliable. One may occasionally cavil at Breen's choices, for he has referenced such books as Donald McCormick's *Who's Who in Spy Fiction* and James Robert Parish and Michael Pitts's *The Great Spy Pictures,* titles that are completely out of place in a volume such as this. Also, although Geoffrey Household was indeed as fine a stylist as Breen says, he was primarily a thriller writer, writing neither mysteries nor detective stories, and his autobiography really does not need to be referenced in the section devoted to individual authors, especially since Breen references neither the autobiography nor any publication concerning the equally significant thriller writer John Buchan.

These complaints are minor. Although the citations in this volume are included in Walter Albert's work (q.v.), Breen's annotations are of enduring value and are quite reliable. *What about Murder?* and its successor volume *What about Murder? 1981–1991* (which follows) belong in all libraries in which there is an interest in studies of mystery and detective fiction.

1015.   Breen, Jon L. **What About Murder? 1981–1991. A Guide to Books about Mystery and Detective Fiction.** Metuchen. N.J.: Scarecrow, 1993. xi, 376 p. Index. Cloth. LC 92-34547. ISBN 0-8108-2609-7.

Like Breen's earlier *What about Murder?* this edition, *What about Murder? 1981–1991,* is exemplary, an annotated bibliography whose 565 entries survey English-language books about mystery and detective fiction that were published primarily between 1981 and 1991. A few citations, such as number 198, David Madden's *James M. Cain,* were published earlier (1970, in this instance), and number 330, J. Kenneth Van Dover's *Polemical Pulps: The Martin Beck Novels of Maj Sjöwall and Per Wahlöö,* was not published until 1992.

As in the earlier volume, Breen has grouped his material by subject, but he has altered his subject headings, in part to acknowledge the increasing number of publications about mystery and detective fiction. He has dropped the section devoted to coffee-table books, describing it as "a somewhat amorphous and artificial category to begin with and one to which few if any of the new entries would properly belong," and he has expanded his divisions. The present volume thus contains nine sections: general histories; reference books; special subjects; collected essays and reviews; technical manuals; works on individual authors; anthologies whose editorial matter contains material of reference value; new editions and supplements of volumes included in the original *What about Murder?;* and an addendum.

Citations in these sections are arranged alphabetically by their author's name, except in the case of the works on individual authors when they are listed alphabetically under their subject's name. Each citation provides the book's author, title, and publication data (place of publication, publisher, and date of publication for the first English-language edition and the first American edition if it differs). Pagination of these books is provided, as are the names of others who appear on the title page (e.g., the illustrator, translator, editor, introduction writer), the book's series (if any), and whether the book has illustrations, a bibliography, and an index. Title changes are noted, and an excellent author/title index concludes the volume.

As before, the annotations in *What about Murder? 1981–1991* are pithy and knowledgeable, providing clear and cogent commentary. However, as in the previous volume, Breen has referenced a number of titles surveying espionage fiction. This volume belongs next to its predecessor in all libraries in which there is an interest in the study of mystery and detective fiction.

1016. Cassiday, Bruce, ed. **Modern Mystery, Fantasy and Science Fiction Writers.** A Library of Literary Criticism. New York: Continuum/Frederick Ungar, 1993. x, 673 p. Index. Cloth. LC 92-33859. ISBN 0-8264-0583-8.

Modern Mystery, Fantasy and Science Fiction Writers contains approximately 800 critical citations to the works of 88 writers of mysteries, fantasies, and science fiction. Most of these writers are Anglo-Americans active during the twentieth century, but some significant nineteenth-century and international writers have been included. A comprehensive list of the mystery writers included would be lengthy, but there are a few disappointments and some pleasant surprises: Mary Higgins Clark, Friedrich Dürrenmatt, Dick Francis, Sue Grafton, Edward D. Hoch, Elmore Leonard, Ed McBain, Marcia Muller, Bill Pronzini, and Phyllis Whitney rub shoulders with Eric Ambler, E. C. Bentley, Lawrence Block, James M. Cain, John Dickson Carr, Raymond Chandler, Agatha Christie, Sir Arthur Conan Doyle, Dashiell Hammett, and Chester Himes; and criticism is available on Michael Innes, P. D. James, John D. MacDonald, Ross Macdonald, Ngaio Marsh, Ellery Queen, Ruth Rendell, Mary Roberts Rinehart, Dorothy L. Sayers, Rex Stout, Josephine Tey, S. S. Van Dine, and Donald E. Westlake. The volume is arranged alphabetically by the subject's name, and the criticism generally is arranged chronologically.

The annotations are not the work of the compiler but are excerpted from the published criticism itself, and Cassiday has taken pains to ensure that the selections and excerpts lead to a greater understanding of the work. Furthermore, a gratifyingly large percentage of the criticism excerpted by Cassiday has been written by professional authors active within or knowledgeable about the genre whose writers they are criticizing: John Dickson Carr, Julian Symons, Edmund Wilson, W. H. Auden, Jacques Barzun, and Ian Fleming (among others) provide criticism of the works of Raymond Chandler; G. K. Chesterton, Dorothy L. Sayers, Graham Greene, and Rex Stout (among others) provide commentary on the works of Arthur Conan Doyle; and Victoria Nichols and Susan

Thompson, Jacques Barzun and Wendell Taylor, Maureen T. Reddy, Kathleen Klein, Sue Feder, and Carolyn G. Heilbrun (among others) provide criticism on the works of Sara Paretsky. Each citation is documented thoroughly, allowing ready access to the original source.

The volume concludes with a list of works mentioned and an index to the criticism. One can cavil that criticism of more writers should have been provided, and indeed, no entries exist for such notables as R. Austin Freeman, Arthur Upfield, and Robert van Gulik. One also may argue that certain entries should have included more criticism, for Lawrence Block is underrepresented with only two citations. Nevertheless, for providing an excellent assortment of criticism on a significant number of the major writers of the twentieth century, one could hardly ask for more than Cassiday has provided here. This volume belongs in all academic and public libraries.

1017. Cox, J. Randolph. **Masters of Mystery and Detective Fiction: An Annotated Bibliography.** Magill Bibliography. Pasadena, Calif.; Englewood Cliffs, N.J.: Salem Press, 1989. xvi, 281 p. Index. Cloth. LC 89-10987. ISBN 0-89356-652-7.

Compiled by a librarian and noted scholar of mystery and detective fiction, this annotated bibliography lists critical work on 74 important writers of mystery and detective fiction. Despite the limitations implied by the title, a number of women writers are among those included. Following an introduction to the history and development of the genre, the book is arranged alphabetically by subject, beginning with Margery Allingham and concluding with Cornell Woolrich. Three notable writers of the nineteenth century (Edgar Allan Poe, Wilkie Collins, and Charles Dickens) are among those profiled, but the majority of the writers is of the twentieth century and include such contemporaries as Amanda Cross, Tony Hillerman, Harry Kemelman, Elmore Leonard, and Robert Parker, to name but a few. The focus is predominantly on Anglo-American writers, but Arthur Upfield, Maj Sjöwall and Per Wahlöö, Georges Simenon, and Robert van Gulik also are accorded entries.

Each author's entry contains two sections, the first annotating biographical data and the second annotating the critical commentary. Although Cox's preference is to cite books and essays in books, a number of his subjects have never been the recipients of such, and the journals Cox uses range from *Time, Newsweek,* and the *New Republic* to *The Armchair Detective* and *Clues: A Journal of Mystery and Detection.* When even journal articles are lacking or inadequate, Cox cites feature stories from the *New York Times.* Cox's citations are accurate, and his annotations are brief and non-evaluative. The volume concludes with a very good index to the critics.

This bibliography is not intended to be comprehensive, for the Magill Bibliographies are intended for undergraduate and novice audiences. Its contents are now somewhat dated, but the book offers researchers a good starting place.

1018. Hanrahan, Rita M. **Detective Fiction: An Annotated Bibliography of Critical Writings.** San Jose: San Jose State University, 1976. 114 p. A research paper presented to the faculty of the Department of Librarianship[,] San Jose State University[,] in partial fulfillment of the requirements for the degree Master of Arts.

Hanrahan's thesis contains three major sections. The first provides a brief history of English and American detective fiction that is unfortunately not free from errors, some of which are egregious. (Writes Hanrahan, "In 1926 the leading American 'pulp' magazine, *Black Mask,* which had featured traditional puzzle-type detective stories, began to publish the 'hard-boiled' stories of Dashiell Hammett, Erle Stanley Gardner, and Raymond Chandler." In actuality, in 1926 the title of the magazine was still *The Black Mask;* it was far from being the leading American pulp magazine; Hammett had appeared in the magazine since 1922; Gardner, since 1923; and Chandler would not appear in it until 1933.)

In the second section, Hanrahan discusses her research methodology and lists the bibliographies she checked. Rather surprisingly (to this librarian), she lists neither the *MLA International Bibliography* nor its English counterpart, *The Annual Bibliography of English Language and Literature.*

The bibliography comprises the third section. Hanrahan has subsections for books, material in books, material in periodicals, and dissertations; rather surprisingly, her focus is international in scope, and the diligent researcher can find references to material in French, German, Spanish, and Czech. Each section lists its material alphabetically by author. There are 383 citations, each numbered. Titles of books and periodicals are given in capital letters, and when Hanrahan was able to examine the work, she provides an annotation, often acute; citations to unexamined works are indicated with an asterisk (*). Following these are appendixes listing bibliographies of detective fiction and useful references works; and the thesis concludes with an author index.

Although Hanrahan clearly earned her degree, her bibliography has been thoroughly superseded by Walter Albert's work (q.v.).

1019. Johnson, Timothy W., and Julia Johnson. **Crime Fiction Criticism: An Annotated Bibliography.** Garland Reference Library of the Humanities, vol. 233. New York: Garland, 1981. xii, 423 p. Index. Cloth. LC 80-8497. ISBN 0-8240-9490-5.

Crime Fiction Criticism is an annotated bibliography listing (in separate section) 1,810 books, book chapters, dissertations, and periodical articles that offer criticism of detective and mystery fiction as a genre or that study its more influential authors. The first section of the volume surveys general works, with different chapters devoted to describing reference works, full-length books, dissertations, and articles and book chapters. The second section contains the secondary literature on some 250 notable authors, although in the case of such authors as Dickens, Doyle, and Poe the Johnsons were of course selective. Each chapter is arranged alphabetically by author; when the work is anonymous, it is listed by title. Cross-references abound, and a cumulative index to the critics concludes the book.

The Johnsons' effort is more comprehensive than that of the Skene Melvins' (q.v.), but their work has its own lacunae and shortcomings. Apart from indexing materials published in the *Armchair Detective,* they have deliberately ignored all fan materials, and they have similarly ignored most book reviews and all publications about crime fiction for television, radio, and motion pictures. The citations tend to be for Anglo-American publications, although a few foreign-language publications have been included. The contents of essay collections are separately annotated in their respective subjects, but these separately listed annotations are neither numbered nor accessible through the index. In addition, one wonders why the second section contains entries for the criticism on William Hope Hodgson and Arthur Machen, neither of whom wrote significant amounts of crime fiction. Finally, the volume lacks a title index.

With the publication of Walter Albert's bibliography (q.v.), this work has been effectively superseded.

1020. Lindsay, Ethel. **Here Be Mystery and Murder: Reference Books in the Mystery Genre, Excluding Sherlockiana.** Privately published, 1982. Various paginations. Paperback. OCLC 9663628. 100 copies printed.

According to Lindsay's preface, she was inspired to begin her list of mystery works by the work of Derek Adley, but after assembling more than 800 file cards, she obtained copies of *The World Bibliography of Sherlock Holmes* and *The International Sherlock Holmes* (q.q.v.), realized that she was duplicating the efforts of De Waal, and decided to focus her efforts on "all the main classic mystery reference books . . . also . . . books about mystery writers, non-fiction books by mystery writers, biographies and autobiographies. There is also a sampling of books about true crimes . . . the history of the police, forensic medicine, codes, poisons and even a book about comics." In all, Lindsay has referenced 748 titles. The contents are reproduced from typescript.

There are two sections to *Here Be Mystery and Murder*. The first is a title index. Books are listed by title (in capital letters), and citations provide author, publisher, publication year, pagination, and (often) a brief note on the relevant contents; places of publication are occasionally given. The second section is an author index; the author's last name is given in capital letters, and beneath it are the titles of the works cited in the title index.

Although legendarily rare, the lack of focus indicated previously renders the contents of no particular value. Researchers interested in the secondary literature surrounding mystery and detective fiction will do better with the works of Walter Albert, Jon Breen, and Norbert Spehner and Yvon Allard (q.q.v.).

1021. Skene Melvin, David, and Skene Melvin, Ann. **Crime, Detective, Espionage, Mystery, and Thriller Fiction & Film: A Comprehensive Bibliography of Critical Writing through 1979.** Westport, Conn.: Greenwood, 1980. xx, 367 p. Index. Cloth. LC 80-1194. ISBN 0-313-22062-X.

First, despite the promises of the subtitle, this book is not a "comprehensive bibliography." Not included are writers who deal with crime who are accepted literati; Holmesiana; discussions of Buchan and Greene beyond those items that "discuss their thrillers and entertainments"; articles dealing with techniques for writers; picaresque literature; studies of pre-1841 crime, detective, espionage, mystery, and thriller literature; studies of the macabre, fantasy, ghosts, supernatural, gothic, and science fiction; and incidental or casual references to crime literature. Also excluded is fan literature.

Reasonable though these criteria for exclusion are, they appear to have been applied on a wholesale basis rather than selectively. To fail to cite material written about literati is to presume not only that a fixed literary canon exists but also that no new readings of these writers is possible. To exclude the criticism of gothic fiction is to overlook that the gothic frequently involves a crime that must be righted and a mystery (or mysteries) that must be solved, and the criticism of the gothic often has noted this. Similarly, although it can be deplorably written, fan literature also can contain significant material that is not elsewhere accessible.

The issues of its comprehensiveness and philosophical focus aside, *Crime, Detective, Espionage, Mystery, and Thriller Fiction and Film* contains 1,628 numbered citations to books, chapters, and journal articles; dissertations also are referenced. The citations are arranged alphabetically by the author's or editor's last name, and all are numbered; numerous cross-references are provided. Materials published in languages as varied as Norwegian, Afrikaans, Japanese, and Czechoslovakian are present, but none of the citations has been annotated, and it will be the exceptional researcher who is able to judge a book such as Manji Gonda's *Shukumei no Bigaku* by its title. Separate title and subject indexes are included, and the materials published in languages other than English also are accessible through a separate appendix. The volume has been reproduced from clearly typed copy, but the indexes and the appendix are double-spaced and give the book an undeservedly amateurish appearance.

The citations are accurate and valid, and the Skene-Melvins should be commended for being among the first to document the secondary literature dealing with mystery and detective fiction. Nevertheless, with the publication of Walter Albert's *Detective and Mystery Fiction* and Timothy W. Johnson and Julia Johnson's *Crime Fiction Criticism* (q.q.v.), *Crime, Detective, Espionage, Mystery, and Thriller Fiction and Film* effectively has been superseded.

1022. Skinner, Robert E. **The Hard-Boiled Explicator: A Guide to the Study of Dashiell Hammett, Raymond Chandler and Ross Macdonald.** Metuchen, N.J.: Scarecrow, 1985. x, 125 p. Index. Cloth. LC 84-20246. ISBN 0-8108-1749-7.

Intended as "a starting point for those interested in these writers or for those interested in hard-boiled writing in general," this volume begins with an engaging 24-page introduction in which Skinner provides biographical data and a discussion of the importance of his three subjects. The guide is divided into four sections—articles and essays; books and monographs; fugitive material; and book reviews—and contains 646 citations. Each section is arranged alphabetically by the critic's last name, although anonymous works are listed at the beginning of each section under "anonymous" rather than alphabetically by their titles. The citations in the first three sections are briefly annotated, as are some of the book reviews, and the volume concludes with a brief subject index.

Although the citations generally are accurate, Skinner's arrangement and indexing do much to preclude this volume's being used. The alphabetical arrangement hinders rather than enhances access to the material, and researchers interested in the criticism written about a specific author will be unable to locate it without having to work through the wholly inadequate subject index. No index to the critics being cited is provided.

Skinner's citations are duplicated in Walter Albert's substantially more comprehensive work (q.v.). This volume is necessary only for completists.

1023. Spehner, Norbert, and Yvon Allard. **Écrits sur le Roman Policier: Bibliographie Analytique et Critique des Études & Essais sur le Roman et le Film Policiers.** Collection Paralittératures. Sér. Études et Références. Longueuil, PC: Les Éditions du Préambule, 1990. 769 p. Index. Paperback. C 90-096350-6. ISBN 2-81933-121-4.

Although publications in languages other than English have generally not been included in this work, *Écrits sur le Roman Policier* has been described here because a sizable majority of its more than 5,000 citations is in English. Furthermore, the arrangement of this bibliography is such that the contents are very accessible. One need not know French to be able to use this volume profitably.

Écrits sur le Roman Policier is a selectively annotated bibliography of the studies of detective and mystery stories and motion pictures that were published in English and French (and occasionally in other languages) between 1900 and December 1989. Preceding the citations is the transcription of a telephone call, in which the compilers discuss the history and development of the detective and mystery story. This is followed by an introduction that explains the grounds used for selecting material and offers definitions of terms used in discussing the detective and mystery story.

The bibliography contains eight sections and several subsections. Each section and subsection is separately lettered and numbered, and the first element of all citations (the author's last name or the title) is in capital letters. The contents of all sections except the last are in alphabetical order; occasional lists and the volume's last section are in chronological order.

The bibliography's contents (in English): (I) descriptions and citations of the journals and relevant special issues of journals; (II) citations to reference books and bibliographies; (III) citations to the books and articles (and a few of the historically important texts) that discuss the theory, history, themes, and generalities of detective and mystery fiction; (IV) citations to the books and articles that discuss the technique of writing works of detective and mystery; (V) citations to the books and articles studying detective and mystery motion pictures, with descriptions of the special issues of journals; (VI) citations to the books and articles providing comparative studies and analyses of multiple authors; (VII) citations to the books and articles studying individual authors; and (VIII) citations to the lists and studies of the best detective and mystery stories. The volume concludes with separate indexes to authors of the criticism and to the subjects of the studies.

Although many of its entries duplicate those in Walter Albert's *Detective and Mystery Fiction* (q.v.), *Écrits sur le Roman Policier* is more selective in its coverage, and its contents therefore can be more accessible. It belongs in academic libraries.

13

Cataloging Guides

1024. Burgess, Michael. **Mystery and Detective Fiction in the Library of Congress Classification Scheme.** Borgo Cataloging Guides, no. 2. San Bernardino, Calif.: Borgo Press, 1987. 184 p. LC 84-12344. ISBN 0-89370-818-6 (cloth); 0-89370-918-2 (pb).

Noted cataloger and bibliographer Burgess has prepared a guide to the cataloging of mystery and detective novels, espionage fiction, and suspense stories under the classification system used by the Library of Congress. Although the first two sections deal respectively with the application of subject headings and the creation of Library of Congress classification numbers, and the last three sections deal with the creation of Library of Congress main entries and classification numbers for motion pictures, television programs, and comic strips. However, the majority of the volume is devoted to listing the writers of genre fiction and providing the call numbers that would probably be (or have been) assigned to them under the Library of Congress classification system. The list of authors is derived primarily from the second edition of Allen J. Hubin's *Crime Fiction, 1749–1980: A Comprehensive Bibliography* (q.v.).

All too often the Library of Congress does not know the identities behind pseudonymous works or collaborative efforts, and because Burgess derived his material from the Library of Congress, his classification scheme for genre writers has the same problems as its model. "Clifford Ashdown," for example, was a collaborative pseudonym used by R. Austin Freeman and John James Pitcairn, but the Library of Congress does not appear to know this and thus assigns different call numbers to the works of these writers: Freeman's is PR6011.R43; "Ashdown" 's is PR6001.S42; Pitcairn is not accorded a number; and no cross-referencing exists. Gerard Fairlie and Henry Cyril McNeile both wrote as "Sapper," the former continuing the Bulldog Drummond series after McNeile's death in 1937, but despite the continuity of the character, there is no cross-referencing between the two men, whose Library of Congress call numbers are PR6011.A43 and PR6025.A317; no entry for "Sapper" is provided. Similar problems exist with contemporary writers: William DeAndrea occasionally wrote as Philip DeGrave, but the Library of Congress classification numbers do not collocate the works: DeAndrea's are PS3554.E174 and DeGrave's are PS3554.E416.

451

These problems, however, are relatively minor, for despite its occasional lapses, the Library of Congress is generally reliable, as is this presentation of its classification scheme. Nevertheless, with the relative accessibility of online data, this guide is not likely to be particularly useful to most academic libraries, although catalogers working extensively with mystery, detective, espionage, and suspense fiction may occasionally benefit from having it. Mystery aficionados who visit different academic libraries may find the listings of call numbers useful.

14

Artist Studies

1025. Benton, Mike. **The Illustrated History of Crime Comics.** Dallas, Tex.: Taylor Publishing Company, 1993. 166 p. Index. LC 92-37159. ISBN 0-87833-814-4.

The crime comics began publication during the Great Depression, with such detectives as Dick Tracy and Secret Agent X-9 battling a never-ending series of villains. Other comic book heroes and villains emerged, and the crime comics became increasingly sensationalistic and stylized. During the late 1940s and early 1950s, crime comics were the subject of governmental hearings, and they were eventually brought down by the publication of Dr. Fredric Wertham's *Seduction of the Innocent* (1954), a hysterical best-seller that blamed the crime comics for every known instance of juvenile delinquency.

Benton's history of the crime comics is lively, well written, and nicely illustrated with more than 300 color reproductions of covers and interior panels. Making his book particularly useful is the last chapter, "Crime and Detective Comics: A Guide and Checklist." Over 300 comic book titles are listed alphabetically. Each entry gives the publisher, the dates of publication, the number of issues the comic lasted, and a note about the contents. Researchers interested in the history of the crime comics may find Benton is an excellent starting place.

1026. Collins, Max Allan. **The History of Mystery.** Portland, Ore.: Collectors Press, 2001. 196 p. Index. Cloth. LC 2001-001531. ISBN 1-888054-53-0.

As with the similar works of Peter Haining (which follows), it is debatable whether this oversized and profusely illustrated volume is a reference book, but it contains hundreds of uncommon illustrations, a linking text, and a roughly chronological presentation. Chapters present the illustrations used at the beginning of the genre, those used for Arthur Conan Doyle's work, in pulp fiction, in detective comics, for depicting private detectives, and so forth. Although many of the illustrations are of dust wrappers and magazine covers, also included are stills from motion pictures and pictures of authors. The volume concludes with a brief (and, alas, inadequate) bibliography and a capable index. Some small errors creep into *The History of Mystery,* as well as some omissions, but it can be browsed with pleasure, and its illustrations may assist researchers interested in the depiction of genre subjects.

1027. Cooper, John, and B. A. Pike. **Artists in Crime: An Illustrated Survey of Crime Fiction First Edition Dustwrappers, 1920–1970.** Aldershot, England; Brookfield, Vt.: Scolar Press, 1995. xiv, 203 p. plus 12 unnumbered pages of colored plates. Index. Cloth. LC 95-14558. ISBN 1-85928-188-5.

A number of illustrated histories of mystery fiction are available, but this is the only one devoted entirely to the dust wrappers of the older books. As its title indicates, the concentration is on the works published between 1920 and 1970. Following an introduction discussing mystery dust wrappers, Cooper and Pike class the subjects of the dust wrappers into 18 categories: "Damsels in Distress"; "Distraught Men"; "Scene of the Crime"; "Deadly Demesnes"; "The Watchers"; "The Killers"; "The Victims"; "A Variety of Weapons"; "An Inquiry"; "Arm of the Law"; "The Detectives"; "The Clues"; "Murder on the Move"; "Murder in the Past"; "Creatures in Crime"; "Scent of Death"; "Pastimes in Purgatory"; and "Old Bones." Each chapter contains black-and-white illustrations of dust wrappers accompanied by the title of the book, author, publisher of the first English edition, and name of the artist (when known). These data are followed by a brief appreciative description of the contents of the book. In addition, each chapter contains a number of references to the colored plates. A nineteenth chapter provides biographical information on 30 of the more significant artists and lists their works that have been reproduced here, and the book concludes with separate indexes to artists and authors.

In all, approximately 300 black-and-white illustrations of dust wrappers are reproduced and described according to the preceding format. However, it is never explained why these particular dust wrappers were selected. Also, the questions of balance can be raised. Why are Raymond Chandler and Dashiell Hammett represented by one dust wrapper apiece, whereas John Dickson Carr is represented by 19, more even than Agatha Christie, who is represented by 17? Why is Rex Stout represented by 7 dust wrappers and the infinitely less important G. D. H. Cole and M. Cole by 8? Additional problems include no discernible arrangement in the contents of the 18 chapters; no bibliographic measurements or data that can be used for identifying the dust wrappers of first editions; and no references from the color plates to the prose discussions.

In their *Detective Fiction: The Collector's Guide* (q.v.) Cooper and Pike state that they "are amateurs in bibliography, with no training or specialized knowledge of this field," and this lack of bibliographical background is evident here, for this book is more appreciation than scholarship. A bibliographically rigid work on dust wrappers and the artists that produced them remains to be done.

1028. Haining, Peter. **The Classic Era of Crime Fiction.** Chicago: Chicago Review Press, 2002. vii, 213 p. Index. ISBN 1-55652-465-X.

As with Haining's *Mystery!* (profiled later), *The Classic Era of Crime Fiction* is a heavily illustrated volume that may be read as well as browsed, and its illustrations may be used for research into the depiction of genre subjects. Nevertheless, as with the earlier volumes, this one is a work that must be used with caution: some of its conclusions are suspect, and it contains entirely too many errors for comfort.

The Classic Era of Crime Fiction is a historical survey of the crime literature produced between the advent of Poe's "The Murders in the Rue Morgue" (*Graham's Magazine,* April 1841) and the espionage literatures of Graham Greene, Eric Ambler, and Donald Hamilton. Haining's discussion is roughly chronological, with different chapters surveying the notable material published in the Victorian "bloods" and the yellow-back crime novels, the dime novel detectives, the rivals of Sherlock Holmes, the private detectives, the hard-boiled detectives, "the poets of tabloid murder," and the espionage novels. Each chapter is heavily illustrated, although the illustrations for the early material often depict later (more sensationalistic) editions of the works being discussed. Furthermore, the captions are sometimes highly debatable, as when Haining states, "Poe's mystery of *The Purloined Letter* (1844) is regarded as a prototype of spy stories like those of James Bond." Indeed?—by whom? On what basis?

Equally seriously, a number of typographical errors occur that might mislead researchers. In the first chapter alone, there are references to Poe's unfinished drama *Politan* (the title should be *Politian*), to *Recollections of a Detective Police-Officer* by "Walters" (the author should be Waters), and the writer Cecil Henry "Bullivent" (the last name should be Bullivant). Finally, the volume begins with a crashing error—Haining states in the first paragraph that Poe's "tragic life was cut short before he reached the age of 40"—that automatically renders all of Haining's conclusions suspect, whether or not this is justified.

No bibliography of sources discussed is provided, but the indexing is capable.

1029a. Haining, Peter. **Mystery! An Illustrated History of Crime and Detective Fiction.** London: Souvenir Press, 1977. 176 p. LC 78-309192. ISBN 0-28562-218-8.

1029b. Haining, Peter. **Mystery! An Illustrated History of Crime and Detective Fiction.** New York: Stein and Day, 1981. 176 p. LC 80-6170. ISBN 0-81282-805-4.

1029c. Haining, Peter. **The Art of Mystery & Detective Stories: The Best Illustrations from over a Century of Crime Fiction.** Secaucus, N.J.: Chartwell Books, 1986. 176 p. ISBN 1-55521-096-1.

The first two editions have not been seen.

Like the work of Max Allan Collins (profiled earlier), it may be debated whether this profusely illustrated volume is a reference book or should be considered a coffee-table book. Although brief, Haining's linking text is not without interest, and *The Art of Mystery and Detective Stories* may be read as well as browsed. And, of course, its illustrations may be analyzed and can serve to direct researches into the depiction of genre subjects.

The volume contains over 400 uncommon illustrations and presents its material in a roughly chronological order. It begins by discussing the history of crime reporting in England—the Annals of Newgate—after which it discusses Poe, the French writers of "Le roman policier," crime in the Victorian penny bloods, Arthur Conan Doyle and Sherlock Holmes, the rivals of Sherlock Holmes, the American mystery, and hard-boiled mysteries and their detectives. Particularly interesting are chapters discussing and depicting the arch villains, lady detectives, and the works produced during "the Golden Era" (i.e., between World War I and World War II). The illustrations reproduce dust wrappers and the covers and contents of magazines and books; stills from motion pictures and photographs are not included.

For all that it may be browsed with pleasure, *The Art of Mystery and Detective Stories* contains some significant errors and misstatements; that is, in discussing villains,

Haining states, "America had Wu Fang, written by Roland Daniel (1880–1969), who tangled with other criminals as well as the law, and continued to thrive even when the gangsters of the twenties made their appearance," but the Wu Fang stories were written by Robert J. Hogan (1897–1963), and *The Mysterious Wu Fang* pulp magazine was published only in 1935 and 1936, lasting but seven issues. Nevertheless, researchers may find this volume offers material not accessible elsewhere. It is unindexed.

1030. Mori, Hidetoshi. **Mystery Art Gallery: The Illustrated History of Detective Story** [*sic*]. 160 + vii p. Index. ISBN 4-336-03633-0.

Japanese publications are generally beyond the scope of this volume, but one does not need to know Japanese to appreciate the numerous cover illustrations in *Mystery Art Gallery;* indeed, captions are frequently given in English as well as Japanese. The majority of the illustrations is reproduced from English and American publications, but reproductions of the covers of the Hayakawa Pocket Mystery and the Sogen Suiri Bunko series also are given, although these are Japanese editions of English and American books. The index is in both Japanese and English.

1031. Siegel, Jeff. **The American Detective: An Illustrated History.** Dallas, Tex.: Taylor Publishing Company, 1993. vii, 168 p. Index. LC 93-7189. ISBN 0-87833-829-2.

Siegel's introduction provides a definition of detective—"someone who tries to discover some sort of truth, and is around at the end to reflect on his search and his discovery"—and explains that his history focuses on detectives created by American writers. He thus begins with Poe and moves forward, discussing notable detectives. Included in this survey are fictional sheriffs, lawyers, and spies. Many of the discussions are accompanied by a sidebar, "Examining the Clues," that presents interesting points of trivia: the one meeting of Hammett and Chandler, William Campbell Gault's references to Chandler, and Carroll John Daly's strangest character (Vee Brown). Included are numerous lists (the 10 silliest cop shows in television history) and a lengthy list of the winners of the Mystery Writers of America Edgar Allan Poe Award from 1946 until 1993. The volume concludes with a very capable index.

Although heavily illustrated, Siegel's work should not be dismissed as a coffee-table book. It is opinionated, intelligent, and lively; and one wishes for an updated edition.

15

Media Catalogues and Guides

Scope note: Included in this chapter are guides to motion pictures, television programs, and radio shows, as well as the guides to specific programs and series. Additional information on these subjects often can be found in the encyclopedias, reader's guides, and studies of individual authors.

GENERAL

1032. Cox, Jim. **Radio Crime Fighters: Over 300 Programs from the Golden Age.** Jefferson, N.C.: McFarland, 2002. 323 p. Index. LC 2002-12039. ISBN 0-7864-1390-5.

In his brief preface, Cox states that *Radio Crime Fighters* "includes network and syndicated radio mystery and adventure series heard in the United States between 1920 and 1960 in which one or more figures regularly appeared in occupations or avocations that fought against criminal offense." The resulting bibliography contains information on over 300 radio programs, including a number aimed at a juvenile audience.

The annotations are arranged alphabetically by program name (given in boldface italic type); alternative program names and retitlings are given, and cross-references abound. A typical citation provides broadcast information: the date the program first aired, including the day and time of the broadcast as well as the radio network that broadcast the program. If the program's name, broadcast time, or radio network changed, these data also are given. The name of the sponsor(s) is provided, as are the number of extant episodes, after which the cast and credits are listed: the director(s), writer(s), music composer(s), announcer(s), the lead actor(s), and the actors in support roles. A discussion of the radio show, sometimes lengthy, concludes each entry.

The annotations are followed by an appendix that groups the radio series by character and genre types; that is, there are listings for "Amateur Sleuths—Full Time," "Anthologies," and "Audience Participation," as well as for the various kinds of sleuths: journalists, jurists, federal agents, police detectives, private eyes, and so forth. A brief annotated bibliography follows, and a thorough index concludes the volume. A small number of black-and-white photos appear throughout.

457

Scholars, enthusiasts, and those curious about old-time radio will find that *Radio Crime Fighters* offers much that is unavailable elsewhere.

1033. Hardy, Phil, ed. **The BFI Companion to Crime.** London: Cassell/British Film Institute, 1997. 352 p. ISBN 0-34043-321-9 (hc); 0-34043-3215-1 (pb). Also: Berkeley: University of California Press, 1997. 352 p. LC 99-184720. ISBN 0-520-21538-9 (pb).

Although the introduction to this delightful volume states that it attempts "a survey and a classification of the main types and examples of crime fiction in the cinema," the contents of the British Film Institute's *Companion to Crime* are in fact more varied. Crime fiction in the cinema is the volume's focus, but included are significant discussions of the writers of mysteries and detective fiction (i.e., Eric Ambler, Raymond Chandler, Daphne du Maurier, Graham Greene, Dashiell Hammett, Patricia Highsmith, and Edgar Wallace), and notable detectives also are discussed (i.e., Lemmy Caution, Charlie Chan, the Falcon, Sherlock Holmes, Ellery Queen, and the Pink Panther). In all, there are more than 500 well-written and lively assessments of the motion pictures, people, characters, and recurrent genre themes (i.e., children, corpses, the FBI, parodies, poison, and vigilantes) that have some relation to the concept of crime. Although the focus tends to be on Anglo-American motion pictures made from the first decades of the twentieth century until the 1990s, included are numerous entries for international motion pictures. The volume is well illustrated and delightful to browse, with numerous cross-references, but it lacks an index.

1034. Harmon, Jim. **Radio Mystery and Adventure and Its Appearances in Film, Television and Other Media.** Jefferson, N.C.: McFarland, 1992. xvi, 286 p. Index. Cloth. LC 92-54086. ISBN 0-89950-663-1.

Data on the early mystery and adventure radio programs are scarce, and in *Radio Mystery and Adventure,* Harmon provides the histories of 14 notable radio mystery and adventure programs, describing their adaptations by television, motion pictures, and other media. The 14 radio programs described are *The Air Adventures of Jimmie Allen; Captain Midnight; Challenge of the Yukon* (i.e., *Sergeant Preston of the Yukon*); *Dick Tracy; Green Hornet; I Love a Mystery; Jack Armstrong; Little Orphan Annie; The Lone Ranger; The Shadow; Sherlock Holmes; Sky King; Superman;* and *Tom Mix.* Each of these programs is accorded a separate chapter.

Harmon starts each chapter with background information that provides the date of the first and last broadcasts and lists the sponsors and the dates of their coverage. The names of the scriptwriters, producers, directors, and actors are listed. A history of the production is then given, including information on the actors and actresses responsible for defining the character; data on work environments are provided also. This is followed by discussions of the motion picture, television, comic, and (in several cases) the magazine and book adaptations of the character. Each chapter concludes with a list of the various premiums given to those who responded to radio advertisements and their probable values (in 1992 dollars); the book concludes with an index.

Occasional typos occur, and the indexing is unfortunately less than comprehensive, but Harmon's writing is clear, and he provides a wealth of information about each show that is accessible nowhere else. This volume should be held by all academic libraries and fans of old-time radio.

1035. Howard, Tom. **More Movie Thrillers.** Reid's Film Index, no. 10. Sydney, Australia: John Howard Reid, 1993. 218 p. ISBN 0-949149-87-X (cl); 0-949149-86-1 (pb).

The tenth in the heavily illustrated (black-and-white) Australian filmographies, this volume ostensibly examines the thriller movie. Despite the implications of its title, an earlier volume devoted to thrillers does not seem to exist, although Howard's brief introduction makes reference to his earlier *Tom Howard on Mystery Movies* (q.v.), referring to it as *Movie Mysteries*. As in that volume, the salient characteristics of a thriller never are defined, and Howard, in addition to discussing the various film adaptations of Agatha Christie's *And Then There Were None* and a number of detective and mystery movies, discusses such films as Laurel and Hardy's *A-Haunting We Will Go,* James Cagney's *Blonde Crazy,* Charles Laughton's *The Hunchback of Notre Dame,* and Marlon Brando's *Viva Zapata!*

Like the other volumes in this series, *More Movie Thrillers* is arranged alphabetically by movie title; its first entry is the 1942 *Across the Pacific* and its last is the 1963 *The Yellow Canary.* Each entry provides the name of the actors (in boldface type) and the characters they played; credits are provided, with the names of the people responsible for creating the film also given in boldface type. The dates of production and release in the United States, England, and Australia are listed, as are the names of the production and distribution companies, the running time, and the movie's length (in feet). A one- or two-sentence synopsis describes the crux of the movie, and often lengthy notes provide histories, evaluations, and critical commentary on all aspects of the movie, although the solutions are not revealed. Approximately 200 "thrillers" are treated in this volume.

Howard clearly knows his subject and offers occasionally shrewd insights, but the volume is not as useful as the similar work of Parish and Pitts (q.v.). Furthermore, many of the photos are not captioned, and the volume lacks indexes. It is not a necessary acquisition.

1036. Howard, Tom. **Suspense in the Cinema.** Reid's Film Index, no. 13. Wyong, Australia: John Howard Reid, 1995. 219 p. Index. ISBN 0-949149-80-2 (cl); 0-949149-79-9 (pb).

The thirteenth in the heavily illustrated (black-and-white) Australian filmographies, this volume begins with an index to the previous 12 volumes, after which it offers surveys of approximately 100 suspense films. The elements that make up a suspense film are never defined, but in a very brief introduction, Howard states that he has "concentrated on mysteries and thrillers, but . . . have not neglected spies, spoofs, romances, even westerns." The mystery movies discussed thus include *The Adventure of Sherlock Holmes' Smarter Brother, Charlie Chan in Panama, Dial M for Murder,* and *The Lady in the Lake,* although these movies are discussed in conjunction with such films as *The Adventures of Tom Sawyer, Anna Christie, Invaders from Mars,* and *Mummy's Boys* (a 1936 comedy).

As in the other volumes in this series, *Suspense in the Cinema* is arranged alphabetically by movie title. Its first entry is the 1946 *Abilene Town* and its last is the 1945 *The Shanghai Cobra.* Each entry provides the name of the actors (in boldface type) and the characters they played; credits are provided, with the names of the people responsible for creating the film also given in boldface type. The dates of production and release in the United States, England, and Australia are listed, as are the names of the production and distribution companies, the running time, and the movie's length (in feet). A one- or two-sentence synopsis describes the movie, and occasionally lengthy notes provide histories, evaluations, and critical commentary, although the solutions are not revealed.

Howard clearly loves his subject and offers occasionally shrewd insights, but the volume is not as useful as the similar work of Parish and Pitts (q.v.).

1037. Howard, Tom. **Tom Howard on Mystery Movies.** Reid's Film Index, no. 8. Sydney, Australia: John Howard Reid, [1992]. 220 p. ISBN 0-949149-92-6 (hc); 0-949149-91-8 (pb).

This Australian volume is the eighth in a series of heavily illustrated (black-and-white photographs) filmographies. Previous volumes have examined the "Memorable Films of the Forties," "Popular Films of the Forties," "Academy Award-Winning Films of the Thirties," and "Academy Award Winning Films 1940–1947" and have provided such thematic approaches as "A Feast of Films," "Unique Black-and-White," and "Movies as Entertainment."

Tom Howard on Mystery Movies is arranged alphabetically by movie title, the first entry being the 1941 *Among the Living* and the last being the 1959 *The Wreck of the Mary Deare*. Major series discussed include Charlie Chan, Sherlock Holmes, and Mr. Moto. Each entry provides the name of the actors (in boldface type) and the characters they played; credits are provided, with the names of the people responsible for creating the film also given in boldface type. The dates of production and release in the United States, England, and Australia are given, as are the names of the production and distribution companies, the running time, and the movie's length (in feet). A one- or two-sentence synopsis describes the crux of the movie, and often lengthy notes provide histories, evaluations, and critical commentary on all aspects of the movie, although the solutions are not revealed. Approximately 220 mystery movies are treated in this volume, which closes with two title indexes: the first covers volumes 1 to 4 in this series; the second, volumes 5 to 7.

Although Howard clearly knows his subject and offers occasionally shrewd insights, the volume is not as useful as the similar work of Parish and Pitts (q.v.). The means by which Howard chose his movies is not given and appears arbitrary, for he has included espionage movies, thrillers, westerns, and such adventures as the 1954 *Valley of the Kings,* while ignoring such movies as *The Maltese Falcon* (and its earlier incarnations), *Farewell My Lovely,* and all adaptations of the work of Agatha Christie. A substantial number of the photographs are not captioned, and the indexing covers only movie titles. Although an amiable publication, *Tom Howard on Mystery Movies* is not a necessary acquisition.

1038. Lewis, Jon E., and Penny Stempel. **Cult TV: The ... Detectives.** London: Pavilion Books, 1999. 256 p. Index. Paperback. ISBN 1-86205-311-1.

Cult TV: The ... Detectives is part of a series, other volumes of which discuss such subjects as television comedies. In this case, the body of the book consists of descriptions of approximately 200 Anglo-American television shows "which really matter—the shows which have truly handcuffed the viewer to the screen." The entries are arranged alphabetically by the name of the television show (given in boldface capital letters), beneath which are given the country of origin, the years of transmission, the number of episodes, the program length, whether it was color or black and white, original transmission channel in the country of origin, production company/companies, transmission dates in a secondary country, transmission channel in the secondary country, and the creator—the executive producer(s), writer(s), director(s), and music composer(s). Following this are the usual cast, a description of the show's premise, and a list of the notable guest stars, and the volume concludes with an index.

There is much to like in *Cult TV:* it is nicely illustrated with numerous black-and-white stills, and the entries are lively and brash. At the same time, it is a frustrating volume. There are no cross-references, and the indexing is inadequate. American viewers remembering the English import *My Partner the Ghost* will find no entry for it, although it can be found under its English title, *Randall and Hopkirk (Deceased)*. Furthermore, simply listing the guest stars without indicating the specific shows in which they appeared does not help researchers. Although its back cover states that this is an "essential guide," its shortcomings make it anything but.

1039. Martindale, David. **Television Detective Shows of the 1970s: Credits, Storylines and Episode Guides for 109 Series.** Jefferson, N.C.: McFarland, 1991. xii, 563 p. Index. Cloth. LC 90-53508. ISBN 0-89950-557-0.

As its title indicates, this is a lengthy guide to the credits, storylines, and episodes of 109 detective and mystery television series broadcast on American television during the 1970s. As television shows do not conveniently start and conclude with the advent of a new decade, the book's chronological coverage starts with programs from the 1960s and concludes with those from the 1980s; the factor that determined a show's inclusion was (in Martindale's words) "if the series had new network-televised episodes during the 1970s, regardless how many, the series is included." Furthermore, Martindale has defined "detective" broadly, including not only the television shows featuring police and private detectives but also those featuring lawyers and crime-solving reporters (e.g., *Kolchak: The Night Stalker*). Espionage shows, nondetective newspaper dramas, rescue shows, sit-coms, and traditional westerns are not included.

Martindale's list is arranged alphabetically, beginning with *Adam-12* and concluding with *The Young Lawyers*. For each of the series, he provides a brief broadcast history that includes the network responsible, length of the episode, air date (starting and concluding), usual broadcast time, number of episodes produced, cast and credits, and a discussion of the detective and the environment in which he, she, or they functioned. Individual shows are then profiled: the title, air date, guest stars, and a brief (one to three sentences) summary are given. A gratifyingly thorough index lists all names given in the body of the volume (cast, credits, guest stars, series names, and production companies). Numerous stills enhance the volume.

Martindale's discussions of the shows tend to be more enthusiastic than critical, and the volume contains a few factual errors, although these are rarely significant. A chronology and an index to the shows by their network would have been useful. These complaints are minor, however; *Television Detective Shows* is an impressive achievement.

1040. Meyers, Richard. **TV Detectives.** San Diego, Calif.: A. S. Barnes, 1981. xii, 276 p. Index. LC 91-3576. ISBN 0-498-02576-4 (hc); 0-498-02236-6 (pb).

TV Detectives consists of a year-by-year historical survey of the detective series that appeared on American television from 1947–1948 until 1980–1981. Written in essay form rather than as encyclopedia entries, each year's contents describe—in occasionally hilarious detail—the detective series that premiered during the course of the year. Excluded from the history are "one-shot specials," movies, anthology shows, and shows that featured crimes and crime solving but were advertised as something else (e.g., westerns). Also excluded from the history—to its occasional detriment—are significant lists of casts and credits and consistently provided information on guest stars (if any), the show's producer and executive producers, the creator, the person responsible for the music, and the show's play time. The volume concludes with a nicely done index listing names and titles.

TV Detectives is a thoroughly enjoyable volume. It is heavily illustrated, and more important, Meyers is an engaging and witty writer, not afraid to share his opinions. He offers lengthy and occasionally poignant discussions of such shows as *The Man from U.N.C.L.E., Get Smart,* and *Barney Miller,* and he opens his discussion of *The Avengers* by stating, "If a list of the greatest entertainment ever provided to us by Britain were compiled, *The Avengers* would have to rank high—somewhere between The Beatles and *Secret Agent.*" Meyers is equally lavish in his assessment of the ludicrous, and rarely have so many bad detective shows been described so cheerfully and so well: "A mystery show does not have to have violence, but it has to have something besides pretty girls and atrocious dialog. The makers of *Charlie's Angels* did not seem to think so." (A judgment that remains valid for the motion picture version.)

Meyers followed *TV Detectives* with *Murder on the Air: Television's Great Mystery Series* (New York: Mysterious Press, 1989), but rather than attempting to provide a chronological summary of the field, this volume contains essays on only a few mystery series.

1041. Mulay, James J., Daniel Curran, and Jeffrey H. Wallenfeldt, eds. **Spies and Sleuths: Mystery, Spy and Suspense Films on Videocassette.** CineBooks Home Library Series, no. 1. Evanston, Ill.: CineBooks, 1988. xx, 211 p. Index. Paperback. LC 88-71573. ISBN 0-933997-18-3.

Derived in part from the first 12 volumes of CineBooks's *The Motion Picture Guide, Spies and Sleuths* provides descriptions of the approximately 400 mystery, detective, and espionage movies that were available on videocassette as of 1988. It is arranged alphabetically by the film's title (in boldface type), and each entry provides a star rating (from zero to five, with five being a masterpiece), the year the film was made, the producing/releasing company, whether it was black and white (bw) or color (c), whether it had an additional title, a list of the cast and characters, a plot synopsis, and the production credits; entries conclude with the parental recommendation and the film's MPAA rating. Included are indexes listing the films by star rating, parental recommendation, year, and series and offering access through the actors, cinematographers, directors, editors, music composers, producers, screenwriters, and source authors.

The indexing is superb, but this is best considered an historical document, offering far fewer descriptions than Sennett's *Murder on Tape* (q.v.).

1042. Parish, James Robert, and Michael R. Pitts. **The Great Detective Pictures.** Metuchen, N.J.: Scarecrow, 1990. xiii, 616 p. Cloth. LC 90-8551. ISBN 0-8108-2286-5.

This volume is a continuation of an unnumbered series, the Great . . . Pictures, where the ellipses may be replaced by the words "Gangster," "Hollywood Musical," "Spy," "Cop," "Animal," and "Science Fiction." Nevertheless, a recurrent and unanswered question throughout this series involves the use of the word *great* in the titles of the volumes, for a great many of the motion pictures are far from great—in fact, they are mediocre at best. In their introduction to the present volume, Parish and Pitts explain that the word *great* refers to the specific genre being covered, "and *not* to all of the titles included as we continue to run the gamut from the very best to the very worst, with lots of selections in between."

Approximately 400 detective motion pictures and television films are described in this volume. The listings are arranged alphabetically by the picture's title, which is given in capitals and is accompanied by information on the producing studio, year in which the picture was released, and running time. These data are followed by extensive lists of the cast and credits for the picture. In several instances, these lists are longer than the actual descriptions of the pictures, which provide the plot, cross-references to similar films, and critical commentary. In at least one instance, the film described no longer exists, although intriguing stills survive. In the case of significant remakes, the different versions of the movies are compared. A great many obscure films have been resurrected, and effort has been made to describe the films that featured women as detectives.

Included are four appendixes. The first two list radio and television detective programs. Each entry includes the studio that produced the program, the date on which the program premiered, the date on which the last program aired, and the writers; crime and police shows are not included on these lists. The third is a chronology of the described films that starts with the 1905 *Adventures of Sherlock Holmes* and concludes with the 1988 *Without a Clue;* these entries provide only titles. Finally, T. Allan Taylor provides a two-page bibliography of detective fiction sources.

The Great Detective Pictures is not without errors. In discussing the 1940 *The Missing People,* Parrish and Pitts state erroneously that "Edgar Wallace . . . had few continuing characters in his works," a statement that is far from the case. Greater flaws include Dorothy L. Sayers's *Busman's Honeymoon* being misidentified as "Busman's Holiday" in the discussion of the 1940 *Haunted Honeymoon.* Similarly, names of actors and actresses also are misidentified on occasion. The volume's most serious flaw, however, is not in its presentation of data, but, rather, in its lack of indexes to the casts and credits of the pictures being discussed.

Overall, those who know the title of the picture will find this volume full of information not readily accessible elsewhere. It belongs in the libraries of all aficionados of detective and mystery films.

1043. Penzler, Otto. **Stage and Screen: 101 Greatest Movies of Mystery and Suspense.** Garden City, N.Y.: Doubleday Direct, 2000. viii, 304 p. ISBN 0-7394-0939-5. Also: **101 Greatest Films of Mystery and Suspense.** New York: iBooks, 2000. viii, 304 p. Paperback. ISBN 0-7434-0717-2.

This is a personal list of noted authority Penzler describing the 101 motion pictures that he considers the greatest mysteries. His definition of mystery is broad: "Any movie in which a crime, or the threat of a crime, is central to the plot or the theme," and the resulting list is equally broad, encompassing traditional classics (i.e., *The Maltese Falcon, The Hound of the Baskervilles,* and *The Lady Vanishes*) as well as a number of movies that are traditionally classified as thrillers (i.e., *The Night of the Hunter, The 39 Steps,* and *Taxi Driver*), espionage movies (i.e., *The Ipcress File, The Spy Who Came in from the Cold,* and *The Manchurian Candidate*), and crime movies (i.e., *Reservoir Dogs, Little Caesar,* and *The Sting*). Even a few science fiction movies are included: Penzler describes *Who Framed Roger Rabbit?* and *Blade Runner.*

Penzler has arranged his movies in reverse order: the one-hundred-first movie *(Charlie Chan at the Opera)* starts the volume, and the best movie *(The Third Man)* concludes it. Each film is accorded a separate chapter that begins with the film's name and release year. These are followed by a list indicating the type of film (crime, espionage, noir, detective, suspense, gangster, and courtroom), its studio, producer, director, screenwriter, source, running time, and the principal players and the characters they played. Each discussion opens with the question of Penzler asking, *Did you know?* after which he reveals an interesting piece of trivia. The story of the movie is then summarized (conclusions and gimmicks are sometimes revealed), and Penzler offers a commentary, after which the chapter concludes with the line of dialogue that Penzler considers the best line. (He tends to favor wisecracks and snappy comebacks.) No indexes are provided.

Movie buffs will find this a wonderful volume to disagree with: surely *The Big Clock* is more important and *better* than *Freaks*? Why are *Farewell My Lovely* and *Green for Danger* not accorded mention? (The latter is described in Penzler and Steinbrunner's *Encyclopedia of Mystery and Detection* as "among the best mystery films ever.") Questions of content and judgment aside, the lack of indexing seriously detracts from what could otherwise have been a major reference work; at the very least, an alphabetical list of the motion pictures should have been provided.

1044a. Pitts, Michael R. **Famous Movie Detectives.** Metuchen, N.J.: Scarecrow, 1979. ix, 357 p. Cloth. LC 79-17474. ISBN 0-8108-1236-3.

1044b. Pitts, Michael R. **Famous Movie Detectives II.** Metuchen, N.J.: Scarecrow, 1991. viii, 349 p. Cloth. LC 90-9083. ISBN 0-8108-2345-4.

Although Pitts's introduction to the first volume never defines the criteria that constitute a "famous movie detective," his purpose is to trace the celluloid careers of movie detectives, excluding Sir Arthur Conan Doyle's Sherlock Holmes and Raymond Chandler's Philip Marlowe. Seventeen detectives are profiled at length, with Pitts devoting lengthy chapters to the cinematic realizations of Boston Blackie, Bulldog Drummond, Charlie Chan, Crime Doctor, Dick Tracy, Ellery Queen, the Falcon, Hildegard Withers, the Lone Wolf, Michael Shayne, Mr. Moto, Mr. Wong, Philo Vance, the Saint, Sam Spade, the Thin Man, and Torchy Blane. A briefer concluding chapter examines the cinematic realizations of seven additional detectives: Bill Crane, Craig Kennedy, J. G. Reeder, Lemmy Caution, Nancy Drew, Nero Wolfe, and Nick Carter. The entries for all 24 detectives provide sometimes lengthy histories and detail the successes and failures of the various films and their lead characters. Each concludes with a filmography that lists (in chronological order) the title of the film, the studio that made it, its running time, director, screenwriter, and cast. The number of chapters is given when the film is a serial, as are the titles of the individual chapters. A number of stills are included. The volume concludes with a bibliography listing the novels about the fictional detectives listed in the text and a well-done name and title index.

The second volume is similar in arrangement, although it adds a useful chapter titled "Additions and Corrections to the Base Volume," a page-by-page listing of addenda and corrigenda that users of the first volume must consult. In the second volume, 14 chapters provide the cinematic histories and realizations of detectives Arsène Lupin, Hercule Poirot, Inspector Clouseau, Inspector Maigret, Mike Hammer, Miss Jane Marple, Nurse Sarah Keate, Perry Mason, Philip Marlowe, Raffles, Sexton Blake,

Sherlock Holmes, The Shadow, and the Whistler. A briefer concluding chapter discusses the cinematic careers of Bill and Sally Reardon, C. Auguste Dupin, Duncan MacLain, Father Brown, Flashgun Casey, Frank Cannon, Hank Hyer, Inspector Hornleigh, Jack Packard and Doc Long, Joe Dancer, Joel and Garda Sloane, Kitty O'Day, Kojak, Lew Archer, Lord Peter Wimsey, Philip Trent, The Roving Reporters, Russ Ashton, Shaft, Thatcher Colt, Tony Rome, Travis McGee, and Wally Benton. Entries for Philip Marlowe and Sherlock Holmes are not exhaustive but are recountings of the films involving those characters that appeared since the publication of the first volume. Filmographies for all detectives have been expanded and now provide chronological lists that include the title of the film, studio that made it, running time, director, assistant director, technical director, art director, music director, producer, executive producer, associate producer, production manager, photographer, editor, screenwriter, special effects, and number and titles of chapters for serializations; the cast of the movies is listed also. The volume includes a number of stills, and a bibliography lists the novels about the fictional detectives covered in the text. The volume concludes with a name, title, and photograph index.

Despite occasional errors, these volumes are labors of love, well written, and full of information that cannot be readily located elsewhere. They belong in the libraries of all aficionados of detective and mystery films.

1045. Sennett, Ted. **Murder on Tape: A Comprehensive Guide to Murder and Mystery on Video.** New York: Billboard Books, 1997. 238 p. Paperback. LC 97-15711. ISBN 0-8230-8335-7.

Describing itself as "the first comprehensive video guide to movies on crime and punishment," this guide provides annotations to more than 1,000 motion pictures, filmed from the early 1930s until 1997, all of which are available on videotape (as of 1997). Arrangement is alphabetical by movie title. Each movie is rated (from one-half to four stars). Data include the name of the producing or releasing company, "c" or "b/w" if the film is in color or black and white, running time, director's name, screenplay author(s), and principal cast members. The annotations that follow are rarely more than 75 words, but Sennett's succinctness is one of the great strengths of this shrewd and genial guide. In addition, numerous stills, lists of great movie moments, and biographical data on some of the great noir actresses are included.

Some surprising omissions (no *Silence of the Lambs*?) and odd entries (*Death Wish II* is annotated, but not the original *Death Wish*) occur, and a few errors in dates and descriptions creep in, but the biggest problem with this guide is that it has no indexes. This in no way prevents the contents of *Murder on Tape* from being accessible, and one hopes that it receives frequent updates.

1046. Terrace, Vincent. **Crime Fighting Heroes of Television: Over 10,000 Facts from 151 Shows: 1949–2001.** Jefferson, N.C.: McFarland, 2002. 218 p. Index. LC 2002-13181. ISBN 0-7864-1395-6.

Crime Fighting Heroes of Television lists and annotates 151 shows—125 network, cable, and syndicated series, and 26 pilot films—that in some way feature a crime-fighting hero. These range from *Kung Fu* to the *Mighty Morphin Power Rangers* to the *Magician* to *Model by Day* to *Witchblade*. Each annotation gives the name of the show, its network of origin, and the year(s) it appeared and discusses the show's plot and major characters. Appendixes list superheroes by name, mortals by their superhero name, crime-fighting machines and the shows in which they appeared, and the performers mentioned in the annotation.

Crime Fighting Heroes of Television has some odd omissions—no *Get Smart*— and is calculatedly lightweight, particularly when one sees that Terrace is capable of such genuine works of research as *Radio Programs, 1924–1984* (which follows). *Crime Fighting Heroes* can be browsed with enjoyment, but its entries generally are inadequate, and it offers little that cannot be readily obtained elsewhere.

1047. Terrace, Vincent. **Radio Programs, 1924–1984: A Catalog of Over 1800 Shows.** Jefferson, N.C.: McFarland, 1999. 399 p. Index. LC 98-26269. ISBN 0-7864-0351-9.

Only a minority of the radio programs between 1924 and 1984 were crime or mystery, and finding information about them can be difficult. This *Catalog* is listed here because it is readily obtainable and can be useful to researchers. It is arranged alphabetically by the name of the show. Each show is given a one- or two-word subject classification (i.e., "crime drama," "comedy," "game," and "variety") followed by the broadcast length, the station that aired it, and the years in which it was broadcast. Each show is then described, occasionally at some length—openings are occasionally given—and the cast is listed, as are the announcer and producer (when relevant). An appendix lists "lost" programs about which little is known, and the volume concludes with a well-done index. Also, occasional black-and-white photographs are included, but there is, alas, no index by subject classifications. Researchers interested in radio crime and mystery programs must either know the name of the program or one of its cast.

1048. Tibballs, Geoff. **The Boxtree Encyclopedia of TV Detectives.** London: Boxtree, 1992. 458 p. Paperback. ISBN 1-85238-129-4.

Despite its title, this is not an encyclopedia of television detectives. A researcher looking for information on the television careers of "Fletcher, Jessica Beatrice" or "Tibbs, Virgil" will be sorely disappointed. This is instead an alphabetical list of television detective series. Tibballs, who makes no claims for comprehensiveness, documents approximately 500 detective series that have appeared on English and American television since World War II. Miniseries, television movies, and single plays are not included, nor are the majority of the television series that featured animal detectives, secret agents, superheroes, and lawyers and courtrooms. Regarding these criteria, this volume is similar to Richard Meyers's earlier *TV Detectives* (q.v.).

Tibballs's list begins with begins with *Ace Crawford, Private Eye* and concludes with *Zero One*. Each entry describes the detective and his or her methodology and friends; the regular cast are listed, and seasonal changes of cast are noted. Additional information often includes the show's producer and executive producers, creator, person responsible for the music, show's play time, premiere date, and television networks on which it played. A section called "Detective Notes" lists such information as the longest-running detective shows, stars who made it big after playing detectives, and the best- (and worst-) dressed detectives. A chronology listing the major events in the history of television detective series concludes the volume.

It is regrettable that Tibballs did not include indexes for cast and detective and did not provide a full chronology, for without these, this book is accessible only if one wants information on a specific television series. Whatever its shortcomings as a reference book, however, it is a delight to read. Tibballs is a witty writer, and his descriptions of such shows as *The Pursuers* ("the series flopped miserably because not only was the dog more intelligent than the two policeman, it was also a better actor") are probably better than the programs themselves.

SPECIFIC SHOWS AND CHARACTERS

Alfred Hitchcock Presents

1049. McCarty, John, and Brian Kelleher. **Alfred Hitchcock Presents: An Illustrated Guide to the Ten-Year Television of the Master of Suspense.** New York: St. Martin's, 1985. xiv, 338 p. Index. LC 84-22887. ISBN 0-312-01710-3 (hc); 0-312-01711-1 (pb).

For 10 years, from 1955 until 1965, Alfred Hitchcock was the witty host—and occasionally the director—of two television shows, the half-hour *Alfred Hitchcock Presents* (266 shows) and its successor, *The Alfred Hitchcock Hour* (93 shows). The television series adapted some excellent short stories by such authors as Robert Bloch, John Cheever, John Collier, Roald Dahl, Stanley Ellin, Henry Slesar, Talmage Powell, Lawrence Treat, and Roy Vickers, and the stars who appeared in the dramatizations included such notables as Mary Astor, Charles Bronson, Peter Lorre, Steve McQueen, Vincent Price, Claude Rains, Robert Redford, William Shatner, Jessica Tandy, and Fay Wray.

Starting with a discussion of Hitchcock's blackly humorous *The Trouble with Harry* (1955) and Hitchcock's Shamley Production Company's contributions to *Suspicion* (1957–1958), the authors of *Alfred Hitchcock Presents* provide a summary of each of the television shows. Arrangement is chronological by air date; each entry provides the show's title, director, author of the teleplay, and author of the story. The summarization includes the name of the lead actors and/or actresses and concludes with the initial air date. A number of small photographs are sprinkled throughout, and an index offers access to the shows by their titles but not by their cast and credits.

Alfred Hitchcock Presents is an engaging and chatty guide that is delightful to browse. It has a few flaws—McCarty and Kelleher claim that *Alfred Hitchcock's Mystery Magazine* started in 1955, at the same time as the television show, whereas its first issue was in fact dated December 1956—but these do not seriously affect the content of the volume. More data could have been provided, for several descriptions do not even name the cast, and the credits are occasionally incomplete, but this volume is an excellent survey of one of the most influential television series.

Charlie Chan

1050a. Berlin, Howard M. **The Charlie Chan Film Encyclopedia.** Jefferson, N.C.: McFarland, 2000. 375 p. Index. Cloth. LC 99-56163. ISBN 0-7864-0709-3.

Unlike the works of Hanke and Mitchell (q.q.v.), this enjoyable volume offers an encyclopedic survey of its subject. *The Charlie Chan Film Encyclopedia* contains more than 1,900 entries based on the Charlie Chan movies made from 1925 (*The House without a Key,* although some sources date it to 1926) until 1949 (*The Sky Dragon*). (Berlin deliberately eschews the Charlie Chan films and television series from the 1950s, 1970s, and 1980s.) One can thus find information about the motion pictures, their actors, characters, plots, and assorted trivia. Much of this information is likely to interest only

Charlie Chan fans and trivia hunters: included are entries for such numbers as *8251* (prisoner number of convict Jimmy Slade in *Dark Alibi* [1946]) and times mentioned in the motion pictures (e.g., 11:30: the "time that Billie Bronson tells Murdock to meet her in her hotel room so that he can buy a diary in *Charlie Chan on Broadway* [1937]); and there are entries for Jesse Owens (whose footage from the 1936 Olympics was used in *Charlie Chan at the Olympics*); and there is even an entry for and a picture of Nobel Prize–winning physicist Dr. Glenn T. Seaborg, who led the team that discovered element 95, mentioned as the "95th element" in *The Red Dragon* (1945). In addition, there are tables indicating retitlings and the aliases used by Chan, plus a lengthy list (arranged by motion picture) of Chan's more notable aphorisms. Berlin's biographical assessments are capable and sympathetic, and his descriptive data are wonderfully thorough. Berlin's annotations of the motion pictures, including the six "lost" films, are excellent: he provides the source upon which the film was based, the copyright owner(s), the production and release dates, the film length and motion picture time. Production credits are provided, as are the full casts. (But who is Suzanna Kim, on whose bathing suit Keye Luke is painting "Oriental designs"?) The volume concludes with a full index.

1050b. Hanke, Ken. **Charlie Chan at the Movies: History, Filmography, and Criticism.** Jefferson, N.C.: McFarland, 1989. xvi, 270 p. Index. Cloth. LC 89-42718. ISBN 0-89950-427-2.

As its title indicates, this is a filmography devoted to Charlie Chan, the sympathetic Chinese detective and the most durable creation of novelist Earl Derr Biggers. Hanke's arrangement is essentially chronological. Starting with Warner Oland, "the most prestigious Charlie Chan the movies ever had," Hanke lists the cast and credits of each picture and provides commentary and an elaborate summary of the plot (without revealing the solution). The volume is illustrated with black-and-white stills from the pictures under discussion.

Later sections provide the same attention to detail for the Charlie Chans acted by Sidney Toler for Twentieth Century Fox and Monogram, and for the Charlie Chan played by Roland Winters ("the curious thing about much of the criticism of Winters's portrayal lies in the fact that in many ways his characterization is far closer to Earl Derr Biggers' original than either Oland's . . . or Toler's"). A section titled "Imitations and Offshoots" discusses Mr. Moto and Mr. Wong, the latter of whom is one of Boris Karloff's less memorable screen ventures. A well-done index concludes the volume.

1050c. Mitchell, Charles P. **A Guide to Charlie Chan Films.** Bibliographies and Indexes in the Performing Arts, no. 23. Westport, Conn.: Greenwood, 1999. xxx, 260 p. Index. Cloth. LC 99-12472. ISBN 0-313-30985-X. ISSN 0742-6933.

Mitchell's *Guide* is divided into three parts. The first, the introduction, discusses briefly the origins of Charlie Chan, the development of Chan into a film series, the personnel associated with the various series, the aphorisms, the influence of the films, and Asian American criticism of the series. The second is a discussion of the 44 extant Charlie Chan films, presenting them in alphabetical order. Each film is rated from one (*) to five stars (*****), after which basic production data are given, including producer, director, writers, the issuing studio, the work it was based on, and the length. A cast list is provided, after which Mitchell provides a synopsis and appraisal of the work, a discussion of the performances, and a note as to the notable aphorisms. The third section consists of appendixes listing the criminals from the motion pictures, providing a guide to the appearances by Chan's children, describing the six "lost films," providing the text of the 1935 "Pennsylvania Referendum" narrated by Warner Oland, discussing the Mexican adaptations of Charlie Chan, listing Chan's television appearances, and giving brief biographical data on the actors who played Chan. A thorough index concludes the volume, but pleasant though it is, it lacks the depth and comprehensiveness of Berlin's work on the same subject (q.v.).

Columbo

1051. Dawidziak, Mark. **The Columbo Phile: A Casebook.** New York: Mysterious Press, 1989. xiv, 353 p. Index. Paper. LC 88-43479. ISBN 0-89296-984-9.

Dawidziak provides a comprehensive history of *Columbo,* a television program remembered fondly by many. Starring Peter Falk as the titular homicide detective, the rumpled Columbo (his first name was never given) matched wits against those who thought they had committed the perfect murder. The series lasted seven seasons, from 1971 until 1978, and comprises 45 episodes in its original; there was even a short-lived spin-off, *Mrs. Columbo,* featuring the wife Columbo talked about, but who never appeared on any of the shows.

Dawidziak opens his *Casebook* by providing a history of the show's conception, after which different chapters describe the shows of each season. The original broadcast date is given, as are the production staff, the running time, the cast, and a synopsis that describes the situation and discusses its quality; each of these chapters concludes with a discussion of the season's quality. Following these are chapters discussing the spin-offs, those who appeared on multiple *Columbo* episodes, *Columbo* quotes, a description of Mrs. Columbo, a *Columbo* trivia contest, a bibliography, and a surprisingly thorough index. Also included are a number of black-and-white photographs throughout.

Hawaii Five-O

1052. Rhodes, Karen. **Booking Hawaii Five-O: An Episode and Critical History of the 1968–1980 Television Detective Series.** Foreword by Rose Freeman. Jefferson, N.C.: McFarland, 1997. viii, 333 p. Index. Cloth. LC 96-39668. ISBN 0-7864-0171-0.

As its title indicates, this is a comprehensive guide to the once-popular *Hawaii Five-O* television series. The arrangement is chronological, with the first chapter summarizing the pilot movie and listing its cast and credits. Episodes are numbered consecutively, and different chapters provide a season-by-season breakdown of each episode of the show, providing original air date, teleplay author, story author, director, composer, cast, credits, and summary. Appendixes discuss *Hawaii Five-O* collectibles and the show as a cultural icon, provide a glossary of Hawaiian words and phrases used in the television show, and list the episodes in order of filming. The index is thorough, and numerous illustrations are included.

Heartbeat

1053. Tangled Web. **Heartbeat TV Series.** http://www.totalweb.co.uk/tangledweb/autors/heartbeat.html

Heartbeat is a popular British television drama series featuring the activities of a young constable in rural Yorkshire. It is based on a series of novels written by Peter

Walker using the name Nicholas Rhea. This Web site provides a discussion of the series with photographs of the recurrent character. Particular emphasis is given to the books: cover reproductions of five novels are given, accompanied by the material from the back covers and excerpts from positive reviews, and the concluding bibliography lists all of the titles in the Constable series.

Mystery!

1054a. Miller, Ron. **Mystery! A Celebration. Stalking Public Television's Greatest Sleuths.** Foreword by P. D. James. San Francisco, Calif.: KQED Books, 1996. xv, 304 p. Index. Paperback. LC 96-42130. ISBN 0-912333-89-8.

Although the lavishly illustrated *Mystery! A Celebration* is not a filmography akin to the other works in this section, it nevertheless deserves mention, for it is an engaging and affectionate survey of the enormously popular series that has appeared on public television from 1980 until 1997. Initially hosted by Gene Shalit, then by Vincent Price, and currently by Diana Rigg, and featuring wonderfully macabre drawings by Edward Gorey, *Mystery!* presented often first-rate adaptations of the works of, among others, Dornford Yates, Agatha Christie, Arthur Conan Doyle, John Mortimer, Dick Francis, Ellis Peters, Margery Allingham, Ngaio Marsh, and Dorothy L. Sayers.

Miller introduces *Mystery! A Celebration* by providing a brief history of the series and biographical sketches of the hosts. Following this, he takes a broadly thematic approach to his subject, dividing his material into sections titled "The Investigators" and "The Cases for Investigation." The division is unnecessary, for the information in each section is essentially the same. The author is profiled and when possible interviewed; the chief players are described and often interviewed; summarizations occasionally reveal the solutions; and included are photographs, brief bibliographies, and numerous sidebars. In addition, a list of the shows by season is provided, and there is a 100-question trivia quiz; a series of appendixes provide the complete production credits for each show (arranged alphabetically) and a (highly selective) state-by-state list of dealers specializing in crime and mystery fiction. The volume is well indexed.

Fans of the television series—and those who are curious about why the series has such devoted adherents—will find this book a delight.

1054b. Mystery! Home Page. http://www.boston.com/wgbh/pages/mystery/mysteryhome.html

This delightful site makes use of Edward Gorey's artwork to inform viewers about the long-running public television series. It includes links offering information about the season's programming schedule, and more links provide well-illustrated information about the detectives featured in past *Mystery!* series. The curious may browse an enjoyable *Mystery! History!* take a *Mystery! Quiz!* and read a murder story. In addition, one can learn about past programs, purchase *Mystery!* memorabilia, and leave feedback. Although lighthearted, this is a very informative site.

Thriller

1055. Warren, Alan. **This Is a *Thriller*: An Episode Guide, History and Analysis of the Classic 1960s Television Series.** Jefferson, N.C.: McFarland, 1996. viii, 207 p. Index. LC 96-32736. ISBN 0-7864-0256-3.

Unlike *The Twilight Zone,* to which it is often compared, *Thriller* was not particularly consistent in its subject matter. As Warren's preface notes, "Its chief failing was its near schizophrenic attitude toward subject matter: although approximately half of its 67 episodes could be categorized as horror, an equal number were unmistakably crime oriented, leading to an inevitable quandary among viewers confused by the program's apparently random alternation between two distinctly different genres."

Warren's guide opens with a history of *Thriller,* after which is an episode guide, presenting the shows in chronological appearance. Each episode's title is given in bold-face type *and* quotation marks, followed by its air date, its credits, cast, and an annotation that describes and evaluates the show. Appendixes list the ancestors, descendants, and top-25 episodes of *Thriller,* and the volume concludes with a bibliography and an index.

A loving work, but one for specialists.

16

Calendars

Scope note: Although a number of calendars listing anniversaries in mystery and detective fiction have been published, only the following Web site and publication provide these data in a cumulative and nonrestrictive fashion.

1056. Liukkonen, Petri. **Authors' Calendar—Books and Writers.** http://www.kirjasto. sci.fi/kalendar.htm

This Finnish Web site offers calendrical information on thousands of writers. One can search by birthday or by name, and although the results are sometimes brief, they appear to be correct.

1057. Malloy, William. **The Mystery Book of Days.** New York: Mysterious Press, 1990. Unpaged. Index. Cloth. LC 90-43560. ISBN 0-89296-422-7.

Malloy has compiled a day-by-day listing of events that are significant (or amusing) and that are somehow related to detective and mystery literature. The arrangement begins with January 1 and concludes with December 31; events occurring on the same date are listed chronologically. A few days have nothing listed for them, and either the Leap Year has not been taken into consideration or nothing of significance has occurred in a mystery on a February 29. The entries are amusing and informative, and virtually every page contains photographs, illustrations from books and magazines, or stills from motion pictures. The volume concludes with an index listing the names, titles, and illustrations.

A few minor errors occur, but this is generally reliable as a reference book. More significantly, this is a delightful volume to browse. It should be updated every five or six years.

17

Directories and Dealers

Scope note: Here are directories of publishers, bookstores, and booksellers specializing in mysteries and detective fiction. Many reader's guides also provide lists of bookstores and booksellers.

DIRECTORIES

1058. Collingwood, Donna, and Robin Gee, eds. **Mystery Writer's Sourcebook: Where to Sell Your Manuscripts.** Cincinnati, Ohio: Writer's Digest Books, 1993–. ISSN 1081-6747 (2nd ed.)

Published biennially, the *Sourcebook* serves several markets. For the putative mystery writer, the *Sourcebook* offers discussions on trends in crime fiction and ways in which mysteries can be written; lists of reference books (many published by Writer's Digest Books) are provided. For the writer who has completed a manuscript, the *Sourcebook* offers examinations of the markets for short stories and novels, describing the interests and requirements of the publishers that issue mystery lines and the agents who represent authors to these publishers. For the mystery fan, the *Sourcebook* offers information about mystery conventions, book clubs, bookstores, and awards. Finally, included are glossaries of mystery terms, information about the authors who contributed sections to the *Sourcebook,* and indexes to the categories of mystery publishers tend to issue and that agents tend to like.

Although the different editions of the *Sourcebook* contain errors—the glossary persistently states that the "hard-boiled detective" is "a detective character type popularized in the 1940s and 1950s"—it is probable that novice writers will be assisted greatly by the information it offers. Lovers of mysteries should be aware that Kate Derie's *The Deadly Directory* (q.v.) lists significantly more information about bookstores and conventions and provides reference to electronic resources, but the two publications cannot otherwise be compared. The *Sourcebook* belongs in all libraries.

1059. Derie, Kate, ed. **The Deadly Directory.** Tucson, Ariz.: Deadly Serious Press, 1995–. Index. Paperback. ISBN 0-9667534-5-3. ISSN 1521-9690.

The 2002 edition of *The Deadly Directory* contains separate sections listing genre booksellers, organizations, events, periodicals and reviewers, independent publishers, information resources, entertainment and gift retailers, and it provides useful information about the genre awards. Each section is presented in alphabetical sequence; contact information includes telephone and fax numbers, addresses (e-mail and snail mail), and Web site address. Various icons in each section provide additional information on each organization; for example, a small falcon by the name of a bookseller means the seller is a mystery specialist who carries new books, sometimes combines mysteries with other genres, and sometimes offers used and collectible titles, whereas a star in the periodicals and reviewers section means that it is a newsletter or magazine that focuses on a favorite character or author. The contents of *The Deadly Directory* are international: researchers looking for Swedish periodicals, German Sherlock Holmes clubs, Australian booksellers, and French libraries will not be disappointed. The volume concludes with a name, title, and geographical location index.

The Deadly Directory is a wonderful resource. It belongs in all libraries.

PRICE GUIDES

1060. The previous edition annotated two works: Nick Pappas's *Bloody Dagger Reference: A Price Guide to Mystery-Crime-Detection* (San Diego, Calif.: Bloody Dagger Books, 1997) and Marshall Snow's *A Comprehensive Price List of Crime, Mystery, Thriller and Detective Fiction* (South Grafton, Mass.: Mostly Murder, Mystery and Mayhem Publications, 1995). These works remain available, but they have been superseded by the new and used book metasites available on the World Wide Web. Furthermore, the names, addresses, telephone numbers, fax numbers, and Web sites of a gratifying number of specialty dealers are listed in *The Deadly Directory,* edited by Kate Derie (q.v.), which is updated annually.

The Web addresses given in this section are recommended for those seeking information about, and comparative prices of, mystery and detective fiction.

1061. Abebooks. http://www.abebooks.com

One of the oldest antiquarian book sites, Abebooks is also probably the largest online marketplace, and it still has its adherents. In addition to looking for books by author and title (which all the sites mentioned here do), users can search by publisher and date, various keywords, the ISBN, country of publication, binding type, edition type (first, signed, whether it has a dust wrapper), and price range. Retrievals can be sorted by price, author, and title. This is one of the sites searched through Addall (q.v.).

1062. Addall. http://www.addall.com

At this writing, Addall is unquestionably the best Web site for locating new and used books and comparing their prices. Addall is a metasite, searching and returning results from many sites with but one search strategy. The used and out-of-print book search presently examines the contents of Abebooks, Alibris, AntiQbook, Bibliology, Biblion, Bibliophile, Bibliopoly, Biblioroom, Chapitre, ElephantBooks, Half.com, ILAB, Mare Magnum, Powell's Books, and the Strand Book Store. Searches may be customized and saved; cookies may be avoided. In addition, one also can search by ISBN, title, price, edition, and binding type; display results in a variety of orders and currencies; and use fuzzy searching strategies.

1063.   Alibris. http://www.alibris.com

It is hard to categorize and assess Alibris. On the one hand, it offers access to a wealth of titles that no other site lists; on the other hand, because it seems to serve as an intermediary, its prices are always 15 to 20 percent more than those of the original dealer. It nevertheless offers searches by author and title, and users can search by subject, keyword, and publisher and can narrow searches by binding type, currency in the database, language, price, and publication year. This is one of the sites searched through Addall (q.v.).

1064.   AntiQbook. http://www.antiqbook.com

AntiQbook describes itself as "Europe's premier antiquarian booksite." It offers English, French, and Dutch search interfaces. One may limit searches to new and used books; look for first and signed editions; examine recent additions to the database and books from booksellers in specific countries. Searches may be structured to look for binding type, the presence of a dust wrapper, and publication year or century.

1065.   Bibliology. http://www.bibliology.com

Describing itself as "the on-line book fair," Bibliology offers searches by author and title, and users can search by subject, keyword, and publisher and can narrow searches by binding type, currency in the database, language, price, and publication year. This is one of the sites searched through Addall (q.v.).

1066.   Biblion. http://www.biblion.com

Biblion contains approximately 3 million titles. It offers news, permits one to see the database's top 16 searches, and permits searches by author, title, keywords, prices, whether the book is signed or a first edition, and the binding type. Its instructions are useful, although one wonders about the quality of a database whose instructions state "where possible use only author surnames." Results can be arranged by author and title. This is one of the sites searched through Addall (q.v.).

1067.   Bibliophile.net. http://www.bibliophile.net

Bibliophile.net is not a large site, but it is friendly, permitting users to search from English, German, Italian, French, and Spanish interfaces. Its opening page states that "fine press volumes, rare editions, old books, new books, maps, autographs, manuscripts—you'll find them all here at the really user-friendly international bookselling Web Site." This is one of the sites searched through Addall (q.v.).

1068.   Bibliopoly. http://www.bibliopoly.com

Established by noted English bookseller Bernard Quaritch, Bibliopoly is strongest in locating antiquarian books rather than used books. The database can be searched by author, title, "imprint details," publication year(s), language, keyword, price and price range, and date of addition to the database. This is one of the sites searched through Addall (q.v.).

1069. Biblioroom. http://www.biblioroom.com

A European site, Biblioroom permits searches by author, title, editor, keyword, and specific dealer's catalogue. A subject search is offered, but the subjects that may be used are never presented. This is one of the sites searched through Addall (q.v.).

1070. BookFinder. http://www.bookfinder.com

A metasite almost as good as Addall, BookFinder offers its users English, French, German, and Italian interfaces. Searches may be modified to look for new and used books, first editions, signed copies and to display the results in various currencies and orders. Before there was Addall, there was BookFinder. It remains useful.

1071. Books and Collectibles. http://www.booksandcollectibles.com.au

This Australian site does not limit itself to used books, but it permits users to search for new and used books, first editions, signed copies, hardcover editions, and specific publishers. Searchers can eliminate ex-library books from results and display results in a variety of orders. Not yet as useful as it could be is a search that attempts to locate books by subject. This is one of the sites searched through Addall (q.v.).

1072. Chapitre. http://www.chapitre.com

A French site, Chapitre's opening screen states that it contains more than 15 million titles and their reviews. It does not limit itself to books, and users also can look for photographs, music, and DVDs. Books can be searched for by author, title, and keyword. This is one of the sites searched through Addall (q.v.).

1073. ElephantBooks. http://www.elephantbooks.com

Describing itself as "a unique and independent online bookseller in out-of-print, rare, and used books," ElephantBooks is a friendly site, although this user has never found much through it. Books may be located by author, title, publisher, keyword(s), and whether they are first or signed editions. This is one of the sites searched through Addall (q.v.).

1074. Ibooknet. http://www.ibooknet.co.uk

The Independent Booksellers' Network—Ibooknet—is the Web site of a cooperative of independent booksellers in the United Kingdom and permits one to look for collectible, rare, out-of-print, and second-hand books. Searches can be limited to look for first editions, signed copies, and binding types and can be conducted by keyword. Although small, Ibooknet does occasionally offer material that is not available through the other sites, but its contents appear similar to those of the UKBookWorld, which follows. This is one of the sites searched through Addall (q.v.).

1075. ILAB-LILA. http://www.ilab-lila.com/english/main.php

The International League of Antiquarian Booksellers/Ligue Internationale de la Librarie is for the serious collector, not the casual browser. It represents the dealers from 20 nations (the wares of approximately 2,000 booksellers), and collectors can do a "quicksearch," a keyword search through the books, maps, prints, and autographs. The recommended advanced search looks for new and used books, first editions, signed copies, hardcover editions, and specific publishers. Making this site particularly enjoyable is that it contains news of the antiquarian book trade, including information about book fairs and auctions. This is one of the sites searched through Addall (q.v.).

1076. Mare Magnum Librorum. http://www.maremagnum.com

Like Bibliopoly (q.v.), the Italian Mare Magnum Librorum is stronger on offering access to antiquarian books than used books, but users also can look for new titles. Collectors can look for author, title, publisher, publication year, "bibliographical description," subject, bookseller, price, and date of addition to the database. This is one of the sites searched through Addall (q.v.).

1077. Powell's Books. http://www.powells.com

Powell's is a West Coast franchise of used bookstores whose Web site permits all of their contents to be searched. The Web site is chatty and very friendly. Searches can look for books by author, title, keyword, ISBN, publisher, and binding type. Furthermore, "book class" permits one to restrict searches by one of 46 subject categories (i.e., art, architecture, biography, crafts, and—of course—mystery). The prices at Powell's tend to be lower than those at other locations, and the stock is wonderfully idiosyncratic. This is one of the sites searched through Addall (q.v.).

1078. Strand Book Store. http://www.strandbooks.com

New York City's Strand is a landmark, and its eight miles of bookshelves perpetually yield surprises. Like the Powell's Books Web site, the Strand Book Store's Web site is chatty and informative. Researchers can look for books by author, title, keyword(s), ISBN, publisher, catalogue number, binding type, price, and whether the book is signed, rare, or a new arrival. A subject search permits one to restrict searches by one of 20 subject categories (i.e., Americana, art/architecture, military; alas, "mystery" is not one of the categories). With constantly changing stock, the Strand may be strongest on new releases. This is one of the sites searched through Adall (q.v.).

1079. UKBookWorld. http://ukbookworld.com

The contents of the UKBookWorld seems to be quite similar to those of Ibooknet (profiled earlier). In addition to the usual author and title search, users may search for books by publisher and date, subject, and price. The subject search is not yet as useful as it might be. This is one of the sites searched through Adall (q.v.).

1080. WorldBookDealers. http://www.worldbookdealers.com

Describing itself as "the rare book oasis," WorldBookDealers offers links to dealer catalogues and book fairs and provides antiquarian book news. Users can search for books by keyword, publisher, date, and binding. This is one of the sites searched through Adall (q.v.).

18

Quotations

Scope note: Many reference books also include citations to favorite passages from favorite works, and publications whose contents are drawn from the works of such authors as Arthur Conan Doyle exist, but the following is the only work entirely devoted to quotations from the field as a whole rather than a specific author.

1081. Horning, Jane E., compiler and arranger. **The Mystery Lovers' Book of Quotations: A Choice Selection from Murder Mysteries, Detective Stories, Suspense Novels, Spy Thrillers, and Crime Fiction.** New York and London: Mysterious Press, 1988. ix, 277 p. Indexes. Paperback. LC 87-73208. ISBN 0-89296-948-2.

Horning has compiled a list of more than 1,600 quotations arranged alphabetically by author, with the titles from which the quotations have been drawn listed chronologically beneath the author. The authors from whom the quotations have been mined range alphabetically from Peter Ackroyd (represented by three examples) to Israel Zangwill (represented by two examples). The genre greats are of course present—Raymond Chandler is represented by 14 examples; Agatha Christie, by 23 examples; Arthur Conan Doyle, by 48 examples; and Dorothy L. Sayers, by 13 examples—but making the volume a browser's delight is that Horning has not limited her focus to the genre writers. Rather, she has found relevant and significant quotations in such writers as Geoffrey Chaucer ("Mordre wol out, certeyn, it wol nat faille"), William Faulkner ("In my time I have seen truth that was anything under the sun but just, and I have seen justice using tools and instruments I wouldn't want to touch with a ten-foot fence rail"), George Bernard Shaw ("When we want to read of the deeds that are done for love, whither do we turn? To the murder column; and there we are rarely disappointed"), and Edmund Wilson ("The reading of detective stories is simply a kind of vice that, for silliness and minor harmfulness, ranks somewhere between crossword puzzles and smoking").

Two indexes conclude the volume, a title index that lists not only the titles used in the citations but also the alternate titles under which the work was published and a subject/keyword index that permits thematic access to the quotations. The latter index is the weakest part of the volume—the entry under "reading," for example, fails to list Wilson's comment—but this in only slightly harms the usefulness of this volume. In her preface, Horning states that she conceived of the volume as "a delight to the browser, useful to the scholar. The indexes would be impressive, the attributions impeccable." In all of these, she has succeeded, and *The Mystery Lovers' Book of Quotations* belongs in all libraries.

19

Web Resources

Scope note: The number of Web sites concerned with aspects of mystery and detective fiction is enormous and constantly growing. The following list is highly selective. Additional Web pages are cited throughout this guide in appropriate chapters.

1082. Derie, Kate. **ClueLass.com and the Mysterious Home Page.** http://www. cluelass.com

The ClueLass Home Page by itself offers a wide variety of predominantly contemporary information about virtually all aspects of detective and mystery fiction. It offers extensive lists of the nominees and winners of various genre awards, with information provided on the Agathas, the Anthonys, the Arthur Ellis Awards, the CWA Daggers, the Edgars, the Hammett Prize, the Lambda Awards, the Macavity Awards, the Ned Kelly Awards, and the Shamus Awards, among others. In addition, information about conferences, conventions, classes, and other mystery-related events is provided. Included are links to mystery groups for writers and fans, to groups intended to help aspiring writers succeed, to lists of frequently asked questions about detective and mystery fiction, to information about new and forthcoming releases, to lists of the mystery magazines and newsletters (including electronic publications), to dealers in and publishers of mystery fiction, to factual sites about crime and investigation (including law enforcement and forensics), and to other Web sites that are relevant for fans of detective and mystery fiction. Furthermore, it now incorporates Jan Steffensen's Mysterious Home Page, described later, giving it unparalleled depth. Very well designed, with well-chosen icons and helpful colors, this site is recommended for all novices to the Web.

1083. Kimura, Jiro. **Gumshoe Site.** http://www.nsknet.or.jp/~jkimura/

Devoted to news about detective fiction, this attractive Japanese site offers information about recent book and motion picture releases, with numerous graphics accompanied by lengthy reviews. Although no attempt is made at exhaustive comprehensiveness, a gratifying amount of information is present.

1084. Magic Dragon Multimedia. **Ultimate Mystery/Detective Web Guide.** http://www.magicdragon.com/UltimateMystery/Mystery-Index.html

Despite its name, this Web site is not so comprehensive as some of the other Web sites considered in this section, but it is nevertheless an impressively large compilation, offering links to information about detective and mystery authors, book reviews, movies and television shows, magazines, games and software, publishers, bookstores, recent news, and stories and hypertext fiction. The author section references some 1,911 authors not known to be on the Web and has links to 1,174 Web sites of individual authors, although a number of these latter are entries in the reading list compiled by Michael Grost (q.v.). Similarly, the material in the section devoted to book reviews appears to have been based on voluntary submission rather than on any consistent basis, and the lists of movies and television shows appear to have been chosen randomly. This site has data not readily locatable elsewhere, is growing steadily, and cannot be dismissed.

1085. **Mystery Vault.** http://www.mysteryvault.net

Although it is described rather blandly as an archives of "mystery related e-digests and e-newsletters," the Mystery Vault is a massive index to the archives of a number of news and discussion groups, including DorothyL, the Sisters in Crime, Gaslight, I-Love-A-Mystery-Newsletter, Murder on the Internet, the Deadly Web, and many more.

1086. Mystery Writers of America. **Mystery Writers of America.** http://www.mysterywriters.org

The home page of the Mystery Writers of America offers lists of the winners of MWA awards and links to information about the MWA, to lists of MWA presidents, and to information about regional chapters. Included are a calendar of crime and information about membership. A section titled "Mystery Links" provides connections to recommended sites, specific author Web sites, booksellers specializing in mysteries, and mystery review sources. Although not as comprehensive as some of the other Web sites considered in this section, the importance of the MWA as an organization makes its site significant.

1087. Sisters in Crime. **Sisters in Crime Internet Chapter.** http://www.sistersincrime.org

The Web site of the Internet Chapter of the Sisters in Crime explains that Sisters in Crime is not only for women and offers links to information about authors, juvenile and young adult crime fiction, local and international chapters of the organization, membership lists, and upcoming events. Also included is a lengthy list of bookstores offering mystery and detective fiction.

1088. Steffensen, Jan B. **The Mysterious Home Page.** http://www.cluelass.com/MystHome/index.html

A librarian in Aalborg, Denmark, Jan Steffensen created one of the finest detective and mystery Web sites. Its contents are gratifyingly thorough, and its arrangement and layout facilitate access to these contents. Steffensen went on to other projects, but his site remains active, run by Kate Derie as part of the Cluelass.com site (q.v.). Steffensen offers links to general Web sites, mystery events, mystery organizations, mystery awards, publishers, magazines, e-zines, mailing lists and newsgroups, mystery reviews, official Web sites, fan favorites, and media sites. In all areas, Steffensen has striven for comprehensiveness: the section for general guides offers links to more than 50 different sites, and the list of electronic mystery magazines links to numerous different sources.

1089.   Stop You're Killing Me. http://www.stopyourkillingme.com

    This most useful Web site describes itself as "a resource for the lovers of mystery, intrigue and suspense books" and offers links that provide biocritical data on hundreds of authors. Also included are links to characters, permitting one to find the books in which a specific character has appeared.

1090.   Tangled Web UK. http://www.twbooks.co.uk/

    This British site is not limited to mystery and detective fiction, but it nevertheless offers an engaging potpourri of information about all aspects of detective and mystery fiction. It provides links to sections devoted to individual authors, lists of awards, information about motion pictures and television, bookstores specializing in genre fiction, and current news. Although the Tangled Web provides information on events and happenings in the United Kingdom, including information about many writers whose works are not published or readily available in the United States, it lacks the comprehensiveness provided by such Web sites as Steffensen's and ClueLass (q.q.v.). Furthermore, its bibliographies are rarely comprehensive and are often inconsistent in their presentation of data. For all that, the Tangled Web remains a significant and often useful site.

1091.   Thrilling Detective. http://www.thrillingdetective.com

    Thrilling Detective began as a Web site devoted to private eye fiction, and it offers information about hundreds of fictional private detectives. It has expanded, however, and now contains links to home pages, newsletter articles, bibliographic data, and many other sites. It contains much that is unique, including a glossary of English and French bibliographic terms, and it remains a pleasure to browse.

20

Current Periodicals

Scope note: The following lists the publications from the United Kingdom and the United States that are not devoted entirely to one author or subject. Publications devoted to one author or subject may be found under that author or subject.

1092. *Alfred Hitchcock's Mystery Magazine* (1956+)

Editorial address:

c/o Dell Magazines
475 Park Avenue South, 11th Floor
New York, NY 10016

Subscription address:

P.O. Box 54011
Boulder, CO 80322
ISSN: 0002-5224
Web site: www.themysteryplace.com
Publishes: Primarily fiction

1093. *CADS: Crime and Detective Stories*

9 Vicarage Hill
South Benfleet, Essex
SS7 1PA UK
ISSN: 0965-6561
Publishes: Reviews, criticism, and bibliographic supplements

1094. *Crime Factory*

c/o Preston Lower Post Office
3 Gilbert Road
West Preston
Victoria 3072, Australia
ISSN: 1444-5379

Web site: www.crimefactory.net
Publishes: Reviews, interviews, and criticism with a focus on Australia

1095. *Crime Time* (1995+)

Editorial address:

18 Coleswood Road
Harpenden, Herts
AL 5 1EQ UK

Subscription address:

c/o Oldcastle Books, Ltd.
P.O. Box 394
Harpenden, Herts
AL 5 1XJ UK
ISSN: none
Web site: www.crimetime.co.uk
Publishes: Fiction, criticism, and interviews

1096. *CrimeWave* (1998+)

T T A Press
5 Martins Lane
Witchm, Ely, Cambs
CB6 2LB United Kingdom
ISSN: 1463-1350
Web site: www.ttapress.com/publCW.html
Publishes: Fiction

1097. *Deadly Pleasures* (1993+)

P.O. Box 969
Bountiful, UT 84011
ISSN: 1069-6601
Web site: www.deadlypleasures.com
Publishes: Reviews and interviews

1098. *The Drood Review of Mystery* (1982+)

484 E. Carmel Drive, #378
Carmel, IN 46032
ISSN: 0893-0252
Web site: www.droodreview.com
Publishes: Reviews and news

1099. *Ellery Queen's Mystery Magazine* (1941+)

Editorial address:

475 Park Avenue South
New York, NY 10016

Subscription address:

P.O. Box 54052
Boulder, CO 80322
ISSN: 0093-6328
Web site: www.themysteryplace.com
Publishes: Fiction

1100. *Hardboiled* (1990+)

c/o Gryphon Books
P.O. Box 209
Brooklyn, NY 11228
ISSN: 1088-5633
Web site: www.gyphonbooks.com
Publishes: Fiction

1101. *Mostly Murder*

P.O. Box 191207
Dallas, TX 75219
Publishes: News, interviews, and reviews

1102. *Murder Is Academic* (1992+)

c/o English Department
Hunter College
695 Park Avenue
New York, NY 10021
ISSN: 1076-9471

1103. *Mystery Buff Magazine* (1998+)

304 Lovers Lane
Townsend, TN 37882
ISSN: 1524-7899
Web site: www.mysterybuff.com
Publishes: Fiction, nonfiction, and news

1104. *Mystery News*

c/o Black Raven Press
P.O. Box 152
105 East Townline Drive
Vernon Hills, IL 60061
Publishes: Reviews

1105. *Mystery Readers Journal* (1985+)

c/o Mystery Readers International
P.O. Box 8116
Berkeley, CA 94707

ISSN: 1043-3473
Web site: www.mysteryreaders.org/journal.html
Publishes: Criticism, reviews, articles, and news.

1106. *Mystery Review* (1992+)

c/o C. von Hessert & Associates
P.O. Box 233
Colborne, Ontario
K0K 1S0 Canada
ISSN: 1192-8700
Web site: www.themysteryreview.com
Publishes: Reviews focusing on Canadian mystery writers and writing

1107. *Mystery Scene* (1985+)

c/o Fedora, Inc.
P.O. 669
Cedar Rapids, IA 52046
ISSN: 1087-674X
Web site: www.mysteryscenemag.com
Publishes: Trade news, reviews, interviews, and articles

1108. *Mystery Time* (1983+)

c/o Hutton Publications
P.O. Box 2907
Decatur, IL 62524
ISSN: 0886-2958
Publishes: Fiction

1109. *New Mystery* (1989+)

c/o New Mystery, Inc.
101 West 23rd Street, PMB #7
New York, NY 10011
ISSN: 1048-8324
Web site: www. newmystery.com
Publishes: Fiction and articles

1110. *Paperback Parade* (1986+)

c/o Gryphon Books
P.O. Box 209
Brooklyn, NY 11228
ISSN: None
Web site: www.gryphonbooks.com
Publishes: Criticism and articles on those who are involved in paperbacks

1111. *The Strand* (1998+)

P.O. Box 1418
Birmingham, MI 48012

ISSN: 1523-8709
Web site: www.strandmag.com
Publishes: Fiction, reviews, interviews, and articles

1112. *The Third Degree* (1946+)

c/o Mystery Writers of America
17 East 47th Street, 6th Floor
New York, NY 10017
ISSN: 1535-9034
Web site: www.mysterywriters.org
Publishes: Trade and professional news

1113. *Dime Novel Round-up* (1931+)

P.O. Box 226
Dundas, MN 55019
ISSN: 0012-2874
Publishes: Criticism and reviews

1114. Dragonby Books.

Dragonby Books published four series: the British Paperback Checklists, the Dragonby Bibliographies, the British Author Checklists, and the British Hardback Checklists. The series are reproduced from word-processed typescript; their focus is on the bibliography. New publications in the series are no longer published, but back issues are available from the publisher at the following address:

Mr. Richard Williams
c/o Dragonby Books
15 High Street, Dragonby
Scunthorpe, North Lincolnshire
DN15 OBE England

1115. Galactic Central Bibliographies.

Galactic Central Bibliographies are inexpensive and useful checklists. The series tends to concentrate on science fiction and fantasy writers, but many of the subjects also have had significant careers as writers of detective and mystery fiction. In the United States they are available from this address:

Chris Drumm Books
P.O. Box 445
Polk City, IA 50226
E-mail: cdrummbks@aol.com

In England, they are available from this address:

Phil Stephensen-Payne
25 A, Copgrove Road
Leeds, West Yorkshire
LS8 S2P England
E-mail: philsp@compuserve.com

1116. Ahearn, Allen, and Patricia Ahearn. **Quill and Brush Author Price Guides.**

Allen and Patricia Ahearn, owners of Quill and Brush, have published numerous author price guides to contemporary writers, a significant percentage of whom are mystery and detective writers. Their focus is on the bibliography. The price guides are available from the following address:

> Quill and Brush
> P.O. Box 5363
> Rockville, MD 20848

1117. **Ultramarine Publishing Company.**

Ultramarine Publishing Company has published numerous checklists devoted to contemporary authors. Most of their checklists are devoted to science fiction and fantasy authors, but a significant percentage document contemporary mystery and detective authors. The focus is on the bibliography. The checklists are available from the following address:

> Christopher P. Stevens
> c/o Ultramarine Publishing Company, Inc.
> P.O. Box 303
> Hastings-on-Hudson, NY 10706

Appendix

A

Aarons, Edward S[idney].
Bio-bibliographic data:
The Big Book of Noir, p. 188. (24)
Encyclopedia Mysteriosa, p. 1. (2)
The Encyclopedia of Murder and Mystery,
  p. 1 (6)
The Encyclopedia of Mystery and
  Detection, p. 1 (7)
St. James Guide to Crime & Mystery
  Writers, 4th ed., pp. 1–2. (882d)
Twentieth-Century Crime and Mystery
  Writers, 1st ed., pp. 9–12. (882a)
Twentieth-Century Crime and Mystery
  Writers, 2nd ed., pp. 1–2. (882b)
Twentieth-Century Crime and Mystery
  Writers, 3rd ed., pp. 1–3. (882c)
Web site: http://goldmed.virtualave.
  net/aarons.htm; http://www.
  stopyourekillingme.com/
  Edward-S-Aarons.html
Abbey, Kieran. *See* Reilly, Helen
Abbot, Anthony. *Pseud. for* Charles
  Fulton Oursler
Bio-bibliographic data:
Critical Survey of Mystery and Detective
  Fiction, pp. 1–5. (41)
Encyclopedia Mysteriosa, p. 2. (2)
The Encyclopedia of Murder and Mystery,
  p. 1. (6)
The Encyclopedia of Mystery and
  Detection, pp. 1–2. (7)
Twentieth-Century Crime and Mystery
  Writers, 1st ed., pp. 12–15. (882a)
Twentieth-Century Crime and Mystery
  Writers, 2nd ed., pp. 3–4. (882b)
Abbott, Jeff
Bio-bibliographic data:
Detecting Men, 1st ed., p. 17. (876)
The Mammoth Encyclopedia of Modern
  Crime Fiction, p. 24. (1)
Web site: www.jeffabbot.com
Abbott, J. H. C.: i.e., John Henry
  Macartney
Bio-bibliographic data:
Australian Crime Fiction, p. 1. (207)

Abdullah, Achmed. *Pseud. for* Alexander
  Nicholayevitch Romanoff
Bio-bibliographic data:
The Encyclopedia of Mystery and
  Detection, p. 3. (7)
Web site: http://www.
  fantasticfiction.co.uk/authors/
  Achmed_Abdullah.htm
Abel, Dominick
Bio-bibliographic data:
Speaking of Murder, pp. 135–42. (875a)
Abós, Alvaro
Bio-bibliographic data:
Latin American Mystery Writers: An A to
  Z Guide. (881)
Abrahams, Peter
Bio-bibliographic data:
Canadian Crime Fiction, p. 1. (209)
The Mammoth Encyclopedia of Modern
  Crime Fiction, pp. 24–25. (1)
Web site: www.peterabrahams.com
Achard, Eugène and Frédéric Bronner
Bio-bibliographic data:
Canadian Crime Fiction, p. 1. (209)
Ackroyd, Peter
Bio-bibliographic data:
The Encyclopedia of Murder and Mystery,
  p. 2. (6)
Web site: http://lidiavianu.scriptmainia.
  com/peter_ackroyd.htm
Acre, Stephen. *See* Gruber, Frank
Adair, Denis [I]. *See* Cronin, Bernard
  Adair, Denis [II]
Bio-bibliographic data:
Canadian Crime Fiction, pp. 1, 184. (209)
Adams, Bronte
Bio-bibliographic data:
Australian Crime Fiction, p. 1. (207)
Adams, Cleve F[ranklin].
Bio-bibliographic data:
Critical Survey of Mystery and Detective
  Fiction, pp. 6–10. (41)
Encyclopedia Mysteriosa, p. 3. (2)
The Encyclopedia of Mystery and
  Detection, p. 3. (7)
St. James Guide to Crime & Mystery
  Writers, 4th ed., p. 3 (882d)

Twentieth-Century Crime and Mystery Writers, 1st ed., pp. 15–17. (882a)
Twentieth-Century Crime and Mystery Writers, 2nd ed., pp. 4–6. (882b)
Twentieth-Century Crime and Mystery Writers, 3rd ed., pp. 3–5. (882c)

Adams, Deborah
Bio-bibliographic data:
By a Woman's Hand, 1st ed., pp. 23–24. (884a)
By a Woman's Hand, 2nd ed., pp. 17–18. (884b)
Detecting Women 2, p. 19. *(877b)*
Detecting Women, 3rd ed., p. 17. (877c)
The Mammoth Encyclopedia of Modern Crime Fiction, p. 25. (1)
Web site: www.jesuscreek.com

Adams, Francis [William Lauderdale]
Bio-bibliographic data:
Australian Crime Fiction, pp. 1–2. (207)

Adams, Harold
Bio-bibliographic data:
Detecting Men, 1st ed., pp. 17–18. (876)
The Mammoth Encyclopedia of Modern Crime Fiction, p. 26. (1)
St. James Guide to Crime & Mystery Writers, 4th ed., pp. 3–5. (882d)
Twentieth-Century Crime and Mystery Writers, 3rd ed., pp. 5–6. (882c)
Web site: http://www.booksnbytes.com/authors/adams_harold.html; http://www.stopyourekillingme.com/Harold-Adams.html

Adams, Harriet S[tratemeyer]. *See* **Keene, Carolyn**

Adams, Herbert
Bio-bibliographic data:
The Encyclopedia of Murder and Mystery, p. 3. (6)
The Encyclopedia of Mystery and ·Detection, pp. 3–4. (7)
Twentieth-Century Crime and Mystery Writers, 3rd ed., pp. 6–7. (882c)

Adams, Ian
Bio-bibliographic data:
Canadian Crime Fiction, pp. 1–2. (209)

Adams, Jane
Bio-bibliographic data:
Detecting Women, 3rd ed., p. 17. (877c)
The Mammoth Encyclopedia of Modern Crime Fiction, pp. 26–27. (1)
Web site: www.twbooks.co.uk/authors/janeadams.html

Adams, Samuel Hopkins
Bio-bibliographic data:
The Encyclopedia of Murder and Mystery, p. 4. (6)
The Encyclopedia of Mystery and Detection, p. 4. (7)
Web site: http://www.spartacus.schoolnet.co.uk/USAadamsS.htm

Adamson, [George Ernest] Bartlett
Bio-bibliographic data:
Australian Crime Fiction, p. 2. (207)

Adamson, Lydia. *See* **King, Frank**

Adamson, M. J.; i.e., Mary Jo
Bio-bibliographic data:
By a Woman's Hand, 1st ed., p. 24. (884a)
Detecting Women, 1st ed., p. 18. (877a)
Detecting Women 2, p. 19. (877b)
Detecting Women, 3rd ed., p. 18. (877c)
Web site: http://www.myunicorn.com/bibl35/bibl3575.html

Adcock, Thomas
Bio-bibliographic data:
Detecting Men, 1st ed., pp. 18–19. (876)
The Mammoth Encyclopedia of Modern Crime Fiction, pp. 28–29. (1)
Talking Murder, pp. 3–11. (883)
Web site: www.uni.edu/kollasch/darkmaze

Adelaide, Debra [Kim]
Bio-bibliographic data:
Australian Crime Fiction, p. 2. (207)

Adler, Warren
Bio-bibliographic data:
Detecting Men, 1st ed., p. 19. (876)
The Mammoth Encyclopedia of Modern Crime Fiction, p. 29. (1)
Web site: www.warrenadler.com

Aeby, Jacquelyn
Bio-bibliographic data:
Canadian Crime Fiction, p. 245. (209)

Afford, Malcolm [Max]
Bio-bibliographic data:
Australian Crime Fiction, pp. 2–4. (207)

Aiken, Joan [Delano]
Bio-bibliographic data:
Encyclopedia Mysteriosa, p. 4. (2)
Twentieth-Century Crime and Mystery Writers, 1st ed., pp. 18–20. (882a)
Twentieth-Century Crime and Mystery Writers, 2nd ed., pp. 6–7. (882b)
Twentieth-Century Crime and Mystery Writers, 3rd ed., pp. 7–9. (882c)
Web site: http://falcoln.jmu.edu/~ramseyil/aiken.htm; http://webpages.

marshall.edu/~pbostic/author. html;
http://www.fantasticfiction.
co.uk/authors/Joan_Aiken.htm
Ainsworth, Patricia. *Pseud. for* **Patricia Nina Bigg**
Bio-bibliographic data:
Australian Crime Fiction, p. 4. (207)
Aintree. *See* **Wallace, John**
Aird, Catherine. *Pseud. for* **Kinn Hamilton McIntosh**
Bio-bibliographic data:
By a Woman's Hand, 1st ed., p. 25. (884a)
By a Woman's Hand, 2nd ed., p. 18. (884b)
Detecting Women, 1st ed., p. 20. (877a)
Detecting Women 2, p. 20. (877b)
Detecting Women, 3rd ed., p. 18. (877c)
Encyclopedia Mysteriosa, p. 4. (2)
The Encyclopedia of Murder and Mystery, p. 5. (6)
The Encyclopedia of Mystery and Detection, p. 4. (7)
The Fatal Art of Entertainment, pp. 300–325. (878)
Great Women Mystery Writers, pp. 11–13. (880)
The Mammoth Encyclopedia of Modern Crime Fiction, pp. 29–30. (1)
St. James Guide to Crime & Mystery Writers, 4th ed., pp. 5–6. (882d)
Twentieth-Century Crime and Mystery Writers, 1st ed., pp. 20–21. (882a)
Twentieth-Century Crime and Mystery Writers, 2nd ed., pp. 7–8. (882b)
Twentieth-Century Crime and Mystery Writers, 3rd ed., pp. 9–11. (882c)
Whodunit? A Who's Who in Crime and Mystery Writing, pp. 5–6. (5)
Women of Mystery, p. 433. (874)
Web site: http://www.
stopyourekillingme.com/
Catherine_Aird.html; http://www.
booksnbytes.com/authors/
aird_catherine.html;
http://www.fortunecity.com/
millennium/sat/212/aird.htm
Airth, Rennie
Bio-bibliographic data:
The Mammoth Encyclopedia of Modern Crime Fiction, p. 31. (1)
Aisemberg, Isaac
Bio-bibliographic data:
Latin American Mystery Writers: An A to Z Guide. (881)

Alberg, Karl. *See* **Wright, L. R.**
Albert, Marvin H[ubert].
Bio-bibliographic data:
The Big Book of Noir, p. 189. (24)
Detecting Men, 1st ed., pp. 19, 221. (876)
Encyclopedia Mysteriosa, pp. 4–5. (2)
Murder off the Rack: Critical Studies of Ten Paperback Masters, pp. 71–88. (869)
St. James Guide to Crime & Mystery Writers, 4th ed., pp. 6–8. (882d)
Twentieth-Century Crime and Mystery Writers, 2nd ed., pp. 9–10. (882b)
Twentieth-Century Crime and Mystery Writers, 3rd ed., pp. 11–13. (882c)
Web site: http://goldmed.virtualave.net/albert.htm
Albert, Neil
Bio-bibliographic data:
Detecting Men, 1st ed., p. 20. (876)
Albert, Susan Wittig. *See also* **Albert, Susan Wittig and Bill Albert**
Bio-bibliographic data:
By a Woman's Hand, 2nd ed., pp. 18–19. (884b)
Detecting Women, 1st ed., p. 20. (877a)
Detecting Women 2, p. 20. (877b)
Detecting Women, 3rd ed., p. 19. (877c)
Web site: http://www.
mysterypartners.com; http://www.
booksnbytes.com/authors/
albert_susanwittig.html; http://www.
tsar.net/~china/index.html
Albert, Susan Wittig and Bill Albert
Bio-bibliographic data:
Detecting Women, 3rd ed., pp. 112, 152, 215. (877c)
Albrand, Martha. *Pseud. for* **Heidi Huberta Freybe**
Bio-bibliographic data:
Encyclopedia Mysteriosa, p. 5. (2)
The Encyclopedia of Murder and Mystery, p. 5. (6)
The Encyclopedia of Mystery and Detection, pp. 4–5. (7)
Twentieth-Century Crime and Mystery Writers, 1st ed., pp. 21–24. (882a)
Twentieth-Century Crime and Mystery Writers, 2nd ed., pp. 10–12. (882b)
Twentieth-Century Crime and Mystery Writers, 3rd ed., pp. 13–14. (882c)
Personal papers in Mugar Memorial Library, Boston University

Alding, Peter. *See* **Roderic Jeffries**
Aldous, Allan [Charles]
Bio-bibliographic data:
Australian Crime Fiction, p. 5. (207)
Aldrich, Thomas Bailey
Bio-bibliographic data:
*Critical Survey of Mystery and Detective
Fiction,* pp. 11–15. (41)
*The Encyclopedia of Mystery and
Detection,* p. 5. (7)
Web site: http://www.seacostnh.
com/aldrich/bio.html
Aldridge, [Harold Edward] James
Bio-bibliographic data:
Australian Crime Fiction, p. 5. (207)
Aldyne, Nathan. *Pseud. for* **Michael
McDowell and Dennis Schuetz**
Bio-bibliographic data:
Detecting Men, 1st ed., pp. 20–21. (876)
Web site: http://www.stopyourkillingme.
com/Nathan-Aldyne.html
Alexander, Bruce. *Pseud. for* **Bruce Cook**
Bio-bibliographic data:
Detecting Men, 1st ed., p. 21. (876)
Web site: http://www.angelfire.com/ct/
TORTUGA/bruce.html;
http://www.stopyourekillingme.
com/Bruce-Alexander.html
Alexander, David
Bio-bibliographic data:
Encyclopedia Mysteriosa, p. 5. (2)
The Encyclopedia of Murder and Mystery,
pp. 5–6. (6)
*The Encyclopedia of Mystery and
Detection,* p. 5. (7)
*St. James Guide to Crime & Mystery
Writers,* 4th ed., pp. 9–10. (882d)
*Twentieth-Century Crime and Mystery
Writers,* 2nd ed., pp. 12–13. (882b)
*Twentieth-Century Crime and Mystery
Writers,* 3rd ed., pp. 14–15. (882c)
Web site: http://www.booksnbytes.com/
authors/alexander_david.html;
http://www.davidalexanderbooks.
com
Alexander, Gary
Bio-bibliographic data:
Detecting Men, 1st ed., p. 21. (876)
Alexander, Gordon
Bio-bibliographic data:
Australian Crime Fiction, p. 5. (207)
Alexander, Lawrence
Bio-bibliographic data:
Detecting Men, 1st ed., pp. 21–22. (876)

Web site: http://www.stopyourekillingme.
com/Lawrence-Alexander.html
Alexander, Skye
Bio-bibliographic data:
Detecting Women, 3rd ed., p. 19. (877c)
Web site: http://www2.shore.net/~mojo;
http://www.booksnbytes.com/
authors/alexander_skye.html
Algie, James
Bio-bibliographic data:
Canadian Crime Fiction, pp. 2, 132. (209)
Allain, Marcel
Bio-bibliographic data:
The Encyclopedia of Murder and Mystery,
p. 6. (6)
Web site: http://www.sdm.qc.ca/
txtdoc/pol/adu/
SOUVESTREPIERRE.html
Allan, Dennis. *See* **Foley, Rae**
Alan, Iris Constance [Sommerville]
Bio-bibliographic data:
Canadian Crime Fiction, p. 2. (209)
Allan, Luke. *See* **Amy, William Lacey**
**Allbeury, Ted: Theodore Edward le
Bouthillier Allbeury**
Bio-bibliographic data:
Australian Crime Fiction, p. 46. (207)
*British Mystery and Thriller Writers since
1940, First Series,* pp. 3–16. (868)
Detecting Men, 1st ed., pp. 22, 50. (876)
*St. James Guide to Crime & Mystery
Writers,* 4th ed., pp. 10–12. (882d)
*Twentieth-Century Crime and Mystery
Writers,* 1st ed., pp. 25–27. (882a)
*Twentieth-Century Crime and Mystery
Writers,* 2nd ed., pp. 13–14. (882b)
*Twentieth-Century Crime and Mystery
Writers,* 3rd ed., pp. 15–17. (882c)
Personal papers in Mugar Memorial
Library, Boston University
Web site: http://www.myunicorn.
com/bibl0/bibl009.html
Allegretto, Michael
Bio-bibliographic data:
Detecting Men, 1st ed., p. 22. (876)
*The Mammoth Encyclopedia of Modern
Crime Fiction,* pp. 31–32. (1)
*St. James Guide to Crime & Mystery
Writers,* 4th ed., pp. 12–13. (882d)
*Twentieth-Century Crime and Mystery
Writers,* 3rd ed., pp. 17–18. (882c)
Web site: http://www.stopyourekillingme.
com/Michael-Allegretto.html

Allen, Conrad. *See* **Marston, Edward**
Allen, Felicity. *See* **Lewis, Catherine**
Allen, Garrison. *Pseud. for* **Gary Amo**
Bio-bibliographic data:
Detecting Men, 1st ed., pp. 22–23. (876)
Web site: http://www.booksnbytes.com/
authors/allen_garrison.html;
http://www.stopyourekillingme.
com/Garrison-Allen.html
Allen, Grant; i.e., Charles Grant
Blairfindie Allen
Bio-bibliographic data:
British Mystery Writers, 1860–1919, pp.
3–13. (866)
Canadian Crime Fiction, pp. 2–4. (209)
Critical Survey of Mystery and Detective
Fiction, pp. 16–22. (41)
Encyclopedia Mysteriosa, pp. 5–6. (2)
The Encyclopedia of Murder and Mystery,
p. 6. (6)
The Encyclopedia of Mystery and
Detection, pp. 5–6. (7)
Twentieth-Century Crime and Mystery
Writers, 2nd ed., pp. 14–16. (882b)
Web site: http://www.chriswillis.
freeserve.co.uk/grantallen.htm;
http://ehlt.flinders.edu.au/english/GA/
GAHome.htm
Allen, Irene. *Pseud. for* **Elsa Kirsten**
Peters
Bio-bibliographic data:
Detecting Women, 1st ed., p. 20. (877a)
Detecting Women 2, p. 20. (877b)
Detecting Women, 3rd ed., p. 19. (877c)
Web site: http://www.booksnbytes.com/
authors/allen_irene.html;
http://www.stopyourekillingme.
com/Irene-Allen.html
Allen, Kate: unidentified pseud.
Bio-bibliographic data:
Detecting Women 2, pp. 20–21. (877b)
Detecting Women, 3rd ed., p. 20. (877c)
Web site: http://www.users.uswest.net/
~kateallen/
Allen, Robert Thomas
Bio-bibliographic data:
Canadian Crime Fiction, p. 4. (209)
Allen, Steve
Bio-bibliographic data:
Detecting Men, 1st ed., p. 23. (876)
Web site: http://www.
steveallenonline.com/
Allerton, Berridge
Bio-bibliographic data:

Australian Crime Fiction, p. 5. (207)
Allingham, Margery [Louise]
Bio-bibliographic data:
And Then There Were Nine . . . More
Women of Mystery, pp. 30–57. (863)
Women of Mystery, pp. 30–57. (874)
British Mystery Writers, 1920–1939, pp.
3–12. (867)
Corpus Delicti of Mystery Fiction, pp.
31–33. (879)
Critical Survey of Mystery and Detective
Fiction, pp. 23–28. (41)
Detecting Women, 1st ed., p. 21. (877a)
Detecting Women 2, p. 21. (877b)
Encyclopedia Mysteriosa, p. 6. (2)
The Encyclopedia of Murder and Mystery,
pp. 7–8. (6)
The Encyclopedia of Mystery and
Detection, pp. 6–7. (7)
Great Women Mystery Writers, pp. 13–17.
(880)
Mystery and Suspense Writers, pp. 1–12.
(884.2)
100 Masters of Mystery and Detective
Fiction, pp. 1–7. (37)
The Oxford Companion to Crime and
Mystery Writing, pp. 14–15. (4)
St. James Guide to Crime & Mystery
Writers, 4th ed., pp. 13–14. (882d)
Twentieth-Century Crime and Mystery
Writers, 1st ed., pp. 27–30. (882a)
Twentieth-Century Crime and Mystery
Writers, 2nd ed., pp. 16–18. (882b)
Twentieth-Century Crime and Mystery
Writers, 3rd ed., pp. 18–20. (882c)
Whodunit? A Who's Who in Crime and
Mystery Writing, pp. 6–7. (5)
Women Authors of Detective Series, pp.
65–73. (882.5)
Women of Mystery, pp. 280–318. (874)
Web site: http://idir.net/~nedblake/
allingham_01.html;
http://www.margeryallingham.
fsnet.co.uk/home1.html
The Margery Allingham Society
c/o Mrs. Pamela Bruxner
2b Hiham Green
Winchelsea, East Sussex
TN36 4HB United Kingdom
Allinson, Sidney
Bio-bibliographic data:
Canadian Crime Fiction, p. 4. (209)
Allyn, Doug
Bio-bibliographic data:

Detecting Men, 1st ed., p. 23. (876)
The Mammoth Encyclopedia of Modern Crime Fiction, pp. 32–33. (1)
St. James Guide to Crime & Mystery Writers, 4th ed., pp. 14–16. (882d)
Web site: http://www.booksnbytes.com/authors/allyn_doug.html; http://www.crippenlandru.com/allyn.html; http:stopyourekillingme.com/Doug-Allyn.html

Alter, Robert Edmond
Bio-bibliographic data:
The Encyclopedia of Murder and Mystery, pp. 8–9. (6)
Web site: http://goldmed.virtualave.net/alter.htm

Amato, Angela, and Joe Sharkey
Bio-bibliographic data:
Detecting Women, 3rd ed., p. 20. (877c)

Amberhill, Bevan. *Joint pseud. for* **Bruce Aubrey Barber and Virgil Burnett (q.q.v.)**
Bio-bibliographic:
Canadian Crime Fiction, pp. 4–5. (209)

Ambler, Eric
Bio-bibliographic data:
British Mystery Writers, 1920–1939, pp. 13–24. (867)
Corpus Delicti of Mystery Fiction, pp. 33–34. (879)
Critical Survey of Mystery and Detective Fiction, pp. 29–34. (41)
Detecting Men, 1st ed., p. 24. (876)
Encyclopedia Mysteriosa, p. 7. (2)
The Encyclopedia of Murder and Mystery, pp. 9–10. (6)
The Encyclopedia of Mystery and Detection, pp. 7–9. (7)
Mystery and Suspense Writers, pp. 13–30. (884.2)
100 Masters of Mystery and Detective Fiction, pp. 8–14. (37)
The Oxford Companion to Crime and Mystery Writing, p. 17. (4)
St. James Guide to Crime & Mystery Writers, 4th ed., pp. 16–18. (882d)
Twentieth-Century Crime and Mystery Writers, 1st ed., pp. 30–33. (882a)
Twentieth-Century Crime and Mystery Writers, 2nd ed., pp. 18–20. (882b)
Twentieth-Century Crime and Mystery Writers, 3rd ed., pp. 20–22. (882c)
Personal papers in Mugar Memorial Library, Boston University

Web site: http://www.kirjasto.sci.fi/eamber.htm; http://www.booksnbytes.com/authors/ambler_eric.html; http://www. stopyourekillingme.com/Eric-Ambler.html

Ames, Delano
Bio-bibliographic data:
Twentieth-Century Crime and Mystery Writers, 2nd ed., pp. 20–21. (882b)
Twentieth-Century Crime and Mystery Writers, 3rd ed., pp. 22–23. (882c)
Web site: http://www.bol.ucla.edu/~ryoder/mystery/ames.html; http://www. stopyourekillingme.com/Delano-Ames.html

Ames, Leslie. *Joint pseud. for* **Orlando Joseph Rigoni and William Edward Daniel Ross (q.q.v.)**
Bio-bibliographic data:
Canadian Crime Fiction, p. 5. (209)

Amey, Linda
Bio-bibliographic data:
Detecting Women 2, p. 21. (877b)
Detecting Women, 3rd ed., p. 20. (877c)
Web site: http://www.stopyourekillingme.com/Linda-Amey.html

Amis, Kingley
Bio-bibliographic data:
The Encyclopedia of Murder and Mystery, p. 10. (6)
Twentieth-Century Crime and Mystery Writers, 1st ed., pp. 33–35. (882a)
Personal Papers in State University of New York, Buffalo
Web site: http://www.kirjasto.sci.fi/amis.htm; http://www.fantasticfiction.co.uk/authors/Kingsley-Amis.htm; http://books.guardian.co.uk.authors/author0,5917,-5,00.html; http://www.bond.00go.com/biography.amis.htm

Amparán, Francisco José
Bio-bibliographic data:
Latin American Mystery Writers: An A to Z Guide. (881)

Ampuero, Roberto
Bio-bibliographic data:
Latin American Mystery Writers: An A to Z Guide. (881)

Amy, William Lacey
Bio-bibliographic data:
Canadian Crime Fiction, pp. 2, 5–7. (209)

Ananada, Lou
Bio-bibliographic data:
Canadian Crime Fiction, p. 7. (209)
Anaya, Rudolfo
Bio-bibliographic data:
Detecting Men, 1st ed., p. 24. (876)
Anderson, Ann
Bio-bibliographic data:
Canadian Crime Fiction, p. 245. (209)
Anderson, Doug
Bio-bibliographic data:
Canadian Crime Fiction, p. 7. (209)
Anderson, Frederick Irving
Bio-bibliographic data:
Encyclopedia Mysteriosa, p. 8. (2)
*The Encyclopedia of Mystery and
Detection*, pp. 9–10. (7)
*St. James Guide to Crime & Mystery
Writers*, 4th ed., p. 19. (882d)
*Twentieth-Century Crime and Mystery
Writers,* 1st ed., pp. 35–36. (882a)
*Twentieth-Century Crime and Mystery
Writers*, 2nd ed., pp. 21–22. (882b)
*Twentieth-Century Crime and Mystery
Writers*, 3rd ed., p. 24. (882c)
Web site: http://members.aol.com/
MG4273/anderson.htm
Anderson, Hugh A. *See* **Harrower,
Captain Robert Hamilton**
Anderson, Ian
Bio-bibliographic data:
Canadian Crime Fiction, p. 245. (209)
Anderson Imbert, Enrique
Bio-bibliographic data:
*Latin American Mystery Writers: An A to
Z Guide. (881)*
Anderson, James
Bio-bibliographic data:
Encyclopedia Mysteriosa, pp. 8–9. (2)
*The Mammoth Encyclopedia of Modern
Crime Fiction*, pp. 33–34. (1)
*St. James Guide to Crime & Mystery
Writers*, 4th ed., pp. 19–20. (882d)
*Twentieth-Century Crime and Mystery
Writers,* 1st ed., pp. 36–37. (882a)
*Twentieth-Century Crime and Mystery
Writers*, 2nd ed., pp. 22–23. (882b)
*Twentieth-Century Crime and Mystery
Writers*, 3rd ed., pp. 24–25. (882c)
Web site: http://www.
jamesanderson-writer.co.uk
Anderson, Jessica [Margaret Queale]
Bio-bibliographic data:
Australian Crime Fiction, pp. 6–7. (207)

Anderson, Marc
Bio-bibliographic data:
Canadian Crime Fiction, p. 7. (209)
Andreae, Christine
Bio-bibliographic data:
Detecting Women, 1st ed., p. 22. (877a)
Detecting Women 2, p. 22. (877b)
Detecting Women, 3rd ed., p. 21. (877c)
Web site: http://www.christineandreae.
com
Andrew, Meredith
Bio-bibliographic data:
Canadian Crime Fiction, p. 7. (209)
Andrews, John Malcolm. *See* **Malcolm,
John**
Andrews, Sarah
Bio-bibliographic data:
Detecting Women, 1st ed., p. 22. (877a)
Detecting Women 2, p. 22. (877b)
Detecting Women, 3rd ed., p. 21. (877c)
Web site: http://www.sonoma.edu/
geology/andrews.htm; http://www.
booksnbytes.com/authors/
andrews_sarah.html;
Andrus, Jeff
Bio-bibliographic data:
Detecting Men, 1st ed., p. 24. (876)
Web site: http://www.jeffandrus.com
Angers, François-Réal
Bio-bibliographic data:
Canadian Crime Fiction, p. 7. (209)
Anghel, Anton
Bio-bibliographic data:
Canadian Crime Fiction, p. 7. (209)
Angus, Douglas [Ross]
Bio-bibliographic data:
Canadian Crime Fiction, pp. 7–8. (209)
Angus, John
Bio-bibliographic data:
Canadian Crime Fiction, p. 8. (209)
Annand, Alan
Bio-bibliographic data:
Canadian Crime Fiction, pp. 8, 78,
146–47. (209)
Anthony, Evelyn. *Pseud. for* **Evelyn
Bridget Patricia Ward-Thomas**
Bio-bibliographic data:
*St. James Guide to Crime & Mystery
Writers*, 4th ed., pp. 20–22. (882d)
*Twentieth-Century Crime and Mystery
Writers,* 1st ed., pp. 37–39. (882a)
*Twentieth-Century Crime and Mystery
Writers*, 3rd ed., pp. 25–26. (882c)

Anthony, Lew. *Joint pseud. for* **Bill Marshall and Robert Miller (q.q.v.)**
Bio-bibliographic data:
Canadian Crime Fiction, p. 8. (209)

Anthony, Michael David
Bio-bibliographic data:
Detecting Men, 1st ed., pp. 24–25. (876)

Antill, Elizabeth. *Pseud. for* **Elizabeth Middleton**
Bio-bibliographic data:
Australian Crime Fiction, p. 7. (207)

Antony, Peter. *Joint pseud. for* **Anthony Joshua Shaffer and Peter Levin Shaffer**
Bio-bibliographic data:
Encyclopedia Mysteriosa, p. 9. (2)
The Encyclopedia of Mystery and Detection, pp. 10–11. (7)
The Mammoth Encyclopedia of Modern Crime Fiction, pp. 435–36. (1)
Twentieth-Century Crime and Mystery Writers, 1st ed., pp. 39–41. (882a)
Twentieth-Century Crime and Mystery Writers, 2nd ed., pp. 23–24. (882b)
Twentieth-Century Crime and Mystery Writers, 3rd ed., pp. 26–28. (882c)

Apostolou, Anna. *See* **Doherty, Paul C.**

Appel, Benjamin
Bio-bibliographic data:
Canadian Crime Fiction, p. 245. (209)

Apple, A. E.; i.e., Albert E. Apple[baum?]
Bio-bibliographic data:
Canadian Crime Fiction, p. 8. (209)

Aquin, Hubert
Bio-bibliographic data:
Canadian Crime Fiction, p. 8. (209)

Ard, William
Bio-bibliographic data:
Encyclopedia Mysteriosa, p. 10. (2)
The Encyclopedia of Murder and Mystery, p. 15. (6)
St. James Guide to Crime & Mystery Writers, 4th ed., pp. 22–23. (882d)
Twentieth-Century Crime and Mystery Writers, 2nd ed., pp. 25–26. (882b)
Twentieth-Century Crime and Mystery Writers, 3rd ed., pp. 29–29. (882c)
Web site: http://goldmed.virtualave. net/ward. htm

Arden, William. *See* **Lynds, Dennis**

Ardies, Tom
Bio-bibliographic data:
Canadian Crime Fiction, p. 9. (209)
Detecting Men, 1st ed., p. 25. (876)

St. James Guide to Crime & Mystery Writers, 4th ed., p. 23. (882d)
Twentieth-Century Crime and Mystery Writers, 1st ed., pp. 41–42. (882a)
Twentieth-Century Crime and Mystery Writers, 2nd ed., p. 26. (882b)
Twentieth-Century Crime and Mystery Writers, 3rd ed., pp. 29–30. (882c)
Web site: http://www.stopyourekillingme. com/Tom-Ardies.html

Ardin, William
Bio-bibliographic data:
Detecting Men, 1st ed., pp. 25–26. (876)

Arjouni, Jakob
Bio-bibliographic data:
The Mammoth Encyclopedia of Modern Crime Fiction, p. 34. (1)

Arlen, Michael: born Dikran Kouyoumdjian or Kuyumjian
Bio-bibliographic data:
British Mystery Writers, 1920–1939, pp. 25–29. (867)
Encyclopedia Mysteriosa, p. 11. (2)
The Encyclopedia of Murder and Mystery, pp. 15–16. (6)
The Encyclopedia of Mystery and Detection, pp. 12–13. (7)
Web site: http://freepages.pavilion. net/users/tartarus/arlen.htm

Arlt, Roberto
Bio-bibliographic data:
Latin American Mystery Writers: An A to Z Guide. (881)

Armistead, John
Bio-bibliographic data:
Detecting Men, 1st ed., p. 26. (876)

Armitage, Audrey. *See* **McCall, K T.**

Armour, John
Bio-bibliographic data:
Australian Crime Fiction, p. 8. (207)

Armstrong, Anthony. *Pseud. for* **George Anthony Armstrong Willis, O.B.E., M.C.**
Bio-bibliographic data:
Canadian Crime Fiction, pp. 9–10, 233. (209)
The Encyclopedia of Mystery and Detection, p. 13. (7)

Armstrong, Charlotte
Bio-bibliographic data:
Corpus Delicti of Mystery Fiction, pp. 34–36. (879)
Critical Survey of Mystery and Detective Fiction, pp. 35–41. (41)

Detecting Women, 1st ed., p. 22. (877a)
Detecting Women 2, p. 22. (877b)
Encyclopedia Mysteriosa, p. 11. (2)
The Encyclopedia of Murder and Mystery,
    p. 16. (6)
*The Encyclopedia of Mystery and
    Detection,* pp. 13–14. (7)
Great Women Mystery Writers, pp. 18–21.
    (880)
*St. James Guide to Crime & Mystery
    Writers,* 4th ed., pp. 24–25. (882d)
*Twentieth-Century Crime and Mystery
    Writers,* 1st ed., pp. 42–45. (882a)
*Twentieth-Century Crime and Mystery
    Writers,* 2nd ed., pp. 26–28. (882b)
*Twentieth-Century Crime and Mystery
    Writers,* 3rd ed., pp. 30–31. (882c)
*Whodunit? A Who's Who in Crime and
    Mystery Writing,* pp. 12–13. (5)
Personal Papers in Mugar Memorial
    Library, Boston University
Web site: http://www.booksnbytes.
    com/authors/armstrong_charlotte.html
Armstrong, Raymond. *See* **Lee, Norman**
Arnason, David
Bio-bibliographic data:
Canadian Crime Fiction, p. 10. (209)
Arnau, Yves E.
Bio-bibliographic data:
Canadian Crime Fiction, p. 10. (209)
Arncliffe, Andrew. *See* **Rhea, Nicholas**
Arnold, Catherine. *Pseud. for* **Theresa
    Sandberg**
Bio-bibliographic data:
Detecting Women, 3rd ed., p. 21. (877c)
Arnold, Margot. *Pseud. for* **Petronelle
    Marguerite Mary Cook**
Bio-bibliographic data:
By a Woman's Hand, 1st ed., pp. 25–26.
    (884a)
By a Woman's Hand, 2nd ed., pp. 19–20.
    (884b)
Detecting Women, 1st ed., pp. 22–23.
    (877a)
Detecting Women 2, pp. 22–23. (877b)
Detecting Women, 3rd ed., p. 22. (877c)
Great Women Mystery Writers, pp. 21–23.
    (880)
*The Mammoth Encyclopedia of Modern
    Crime Fiction,* pp. 34–35. (1)
Web site: http://www.booksnbytes.
    com/authors/arnold_margot.html;
    http://www.stopyourekillingme.com/
    Margot-Arnold.html

Arnott, Jake
Bio-bibliographic data:
*The Mammoth Encyclopedia of Modern
    Crime Fiction,* p. 35. (1)
Web site: http://www.durhamcityarts.
    demon.co.uk/festivals/a_jake.htm;
    http://www.booksnbytes.com/authors/
    arnott_jake.html
Arouet, François-Marie. *See* **Voltaire**
Arthur, Frank. *Pseud. for* **Arthur Frank
    Ebert**
Bio-bibliographic data:
*Twentieth-Century Crime and Mystery
    Writers,* 1st ed., pp. 45–47. (882a)
Arvonen, Helen
Bio-bibliographic data:
Canadian Crime Fiction, p. 245. (209)
Ascher, Isidore Gordon
Bio-bibliographic data:
Canadian Crime Fiction, pp. 9–10. (209)
Ashby, R. C.; i.e., Rubie Constance
Bio-bibliographic data:
*The Encyclopedia of Mystery and
    Detection,* p. 14. (7)
Ashdown, Clifford. *Pseud. for* **R. Austin
    Freeman (q.v.) and John James
    Pitcairn**
Bio-bibliographic data:
*The Encyclopedia of Mystery and
    Detection,* pp. 14–15. (7)
Ashe, Gordon. *See* **Creasey, John**
Ashford, Jeffery. *See* **Jeffries, Roderic**
Ashlee, Ted
Bio-bibliographic data:
Canadian Crime Fiction, p. 11. (209)
Asimov, Isaac
Bio-bibliographic data:
Encyclopedia Mysteriosa, pp. 11–12. (2)
The Encyclopedia of Murder and Mystery,
    p. 19. (6)
*St. James Guide to Crime & Mystery
    Writers,* 4th ed., pp. 25–28. (882d)
*Twentieth-Century Crime and Mystery
    Writers,* 1st ed., pp. 47–54. (882a)
*Twentieth-Century Crime and Mystery
    Writers,* 2nd ed., pp. 28–33. (882b)
*Twentieth-Century Crime and Mystery
    Writers,* 3rd ed., pp. 32–38. (882c)
Personal Papers in Mugar Memorial Library,
    Boston University
Web site: http://www.asimovonline.com;
    http://www.asimovians.com
Askey, Derek C.
Bio-bibliographic data:

Canadian Crime Fiction, p. 11. (209)

Aspler, Tony
Bio-bibliographic data:
Canadian Crime Fiction, pp. 11, 165.
(209)
Detecting Men, 1st ed., p. 26. (876)
Web site: http://www.tonyaspler.com

Atherton, Nancy
Bio-bibliographic data:
By a Woman's Hand, 2nd ed., p. 20.
(884b)
Detecting Women, 1st ed., p. 23. (877a)
Detecting Women 2, p. 23. (877b)
Detecting Women, 3rd ed., p. 22. (877c)
Web site: http://www.mysteryguide.com/
atherton.html

Atkey, Bertram
Bio-bibliographic data:
Encyclopedia Mysteriosa, p. 12. (2)
The Encyclopedia of Murder and Mystery,
p. 20. (6)
*The Encyclopedia of Mystery and
Detection*, p. 15. (7)

Atkey, Philip. *See* **Perowne, Barry**

Atkey, Ron
Bio-bibliographic data:
Canadian Crime Fiction, p. 11. (209)

Atkinson, Hugh. *See* **Geddes, Hugh**

Atlee, Philip. *Pseud. for* **James Atlee
Phillips**
Bio-bibliographic data:
Australian Crime Fiction, p. 8. (207)
Canadian Crime Fiction, pp. 245, 263.
(209)
*Twentieth-Century Crime and Mystery
Writers,* 1st ed., pp. 54–56. (882a)
*Twentieth-Century Crime and Mystery
Writers*, 2nd ed., pp. 33–34. (882b)
*Twentieth-Century Crime and Mystery
Writers*, 3rd ed., pp. 38–39. (882c)
Web site: http://goldmed.virtualave.
net/atlee.htm

Attema, Martha
Bio-bibliographic data:
Canadian Crime Fiction, p. 11. (209)

Attiwill, Ken; i.e., Kenneth Andrew
Bio-bibliographic data:
Australian Crime Fiction, p. 8. (207)

Atwood, Margaret
Bio-bibliographic data:
Canadian Crime Fiction, p. 12. (209)
Web site: http://www.owtoad.com;
http://www.cariboo.bc.ca/atwood/

**Aubert de Gaspé,
Philippe-Ignace-François**
Bio-bibliographic data:
Canadian Crime Fiction, p. 12. (209)

Aubert, Rosemary
Bio-bibliographic data:
Canadian Crime Fiction, pp. 12–13. (209)
*The Mammoth Encyclopedia of Modern
Crime Fiction*, p. 36. (1)
Web site: www.doortosummer.com/aubert

Aubrey-Fletcher, Henry Lancelot. *See*
Wade, Henry

Audemars, Pierre
Bio-bibliographic data:
The Encyclopedia of Murder and Mystery,
p. 20. (6)
*St. James Guide to Crime & Mystery
Writers*, 4th ed., pp. 28–29. (882d)
*Twentieth-Century Crime and Mystery
Writers,* 1st ed., pp. 56–58. (882a)
*Twentieth-Century Crime and Mystery
Writers*, 2nd ed., pp. 34–35. (882b)
*Twentieth-Century Crime and Mystery
Writers*, 3rd ed., pp. 39–40. (882c)
Web site: http://www.fantomas-lives.com

Auden, W[ystan]. H[ugh].
Bio-bibliographic data:
The Encyclopedia of Murder and Mystery,
pp. 20–21. (6)
Web site: http://www.audensociety.org;
http://www.poets.org/poes/poets.cfm?
prmID=121

Auger, Clément
Bio-bibliographic data:
Canadian Crime Fiction, p. 13. (209)

Aumonier, Stacy
Bio-bibliographic data:
*The Encyclopedia of Mystery and
Detection*, p. 15. (7)

Auspitz, Kate. *See* **Belfort, Sophie**

Auster, Paul
Bio-bibliographic data:
*The Mammoth Encyclopedia of Modern
Crime Fiction*, pp. 36–37. (1)
*St. James Guide to Crime & Mystery
Writers*, 4th ed., pp. 29–39. (882d)
*Twentieth-Century Crime and Mystery
Writers*, 3rd ed., pp. 40–41. (882c)
Web site: http://www.paulaster.co.uk

Austin, Rev. Benjamin Fish
Bio-bibliographic data:
Canadian Crime Fiction, pp. 13, 158.
(209)

Austwick, John. *Pseud. for* **Austin Lee**
Bio-bibliographic data:
*Twentieth-Century Crime and Mystery
Writers,* 1st ed., pp. 58–59. (882a)

Avallone, Michael [Angelo], Jr.
Bio-bibliographic data:
*Critical Survey of Mystery and Detective
Fiction*, pp. 42–47. (41)
Detecting Men, 1st ed., p. 27. (876)
Encyclopedia Mysteriosa, p. 13. (2)
*The Encyclopedia of Mystery and
Detection*, pp. 15–16. (7)
*The Mammoth Encyclopedia of Modern
Crime Fiction*, pp. 37–39. (1)
*St. James Guide to Crime & Mystery
Writers*, 4th ed., pp. 30–33. (882d)
*Twentieth-Century Crime and Mystery
Writers,* 1st ed., pp. 59–64. (882a)
*Twentieth-Century Crime and Mystery
Writers*, 2nd ed., pp. 35–38. (882b)
*Twentieth-Century Crime and Mystery
Writers*, 3rd ed., pp. 41–44. (882c)
Personal papers in Mugar Memorial
Library, Boston University
Web site: http://goldmed.virtualave.net/
avallone.htm; http://www.
thrillingdetective.com/trivia/avallone.
html

Aveling, Ann
Bio-bibliographic data:
Canadian Crime Fiction, p. 13. (209)

Avery, Martin
Bio-bibliographic data:
Canadian Crime Fiction, p. 13. (209)

Axler, Leo. *Pseud. for* **Gene Lazuta**
Bio-bibliographic data:
Detecting Men, 1st ed., p. 28. (876)

Ayala Guana, Velmiro
Bio-bibliographic data:
*Latin American Mystery Writers: An A to
Z Guide. (881)*

**Ayres, E. C.: form of name used by
Eugene C. Ayres**
Bio-bibliographic data:
Detecting Men, 1st ed., p. 28. (876)
Web site: http://members.aol.com/ecayres/
home.htm

Ayres, Noreen
Bio-bibliographic data:
Detecting Women, 1st ed., p. 23. (877a)
Detecting Women 2, p. 23. (877b)
Detecting Women, 3rd ed., pp. 22–23.
(877c)

Web site: http://www.noreenayres.com;
http://www.booksnbytes.com/authors/
ayres_noreen.html

Ayres, Paul. *See* **Aarons, Edward S.**

B

Baantjer, Albert Cornelis
Bio-bibliographic data:
*The Mammoth Encyclopedia of Modern
Crime Fiction*, pp. 39–40. (1)
*The Oxford Companion to Crime and
Mystery Writing*, p. 34. (4)
*Whodunit? A Who's Who in Crime and
Mystery Writing*, p. 15. (5)
Web site: www.baantjer.net

Babbin, Jacqueline
Bio-bibliographic data:
Detecting Women 2, p. 23. (877b)
Detecting Women, 3rd ed., p. 23. (877c)

Babson, Marian. *Pseud. for* **Ruth
Stenstreem**
Bio-bibliographic data:
By a Woman's Hand, 1st ed., pp. 27–28.
(884a)
By a Woman's Hand, 2nd ed., p. 21.
(884b)
*Critical Survey of Mystery and Detective
Fiction*, pp. 48–52. (41)
Deadly Women, pp. 167–71. (26.5)
Detecting Women, 1st ed., pp. 23–24.
(877a)
Detecting Women 2, pp. 23–24. (877b)
Detecting Women, 3rd ed., p. 23. (877c)
Encyclopedia Mysteriosa, p. 15. (2)
Great Women Mystery Writers, pp. 25–28.
(880)
*The Mammoth Encyclopedia of Modern
Crime Fiction*, pp. 40–41. (1)
*St. James Guide to Crime & Mystery
Writers*, 4th ed., pp. 35–36. (882d)
*Twentieth-Century Crime and Mystery
Writers,* 1st ed., pp. 64–65 (882a)
*Twentieth-Century Crime and Mystery
Writers*, 2nd ed., pp. 38–39. (882b)
*Twentieth-Century Crime and Mystery
Writers*, 3rd ed., pp. 45–46. (882c)
*Whodunit? A Who's Who in Crime and
Mystery Writing*, pp. 15–16. (5)
Web site: http://www.
stopyourekillingme.com/marian-babs
on.html; http://www.twbooks.co.uk/
authors/mbabson.html; http://www.
booksnbytes.com/authors/
babson_marian.html

Babula, William
Bio-bibliographic data:
Detecting Men, 1st ed., p. 28. (876)
Web site: http://www.stopyourekillingme.
com/william-babula.html
Backhouse, [Enid] Elizabeth
Bio-bibliographic data:
Australian Crime Fiction, p. 10. (207)
Bacon, Gail. *See* **Kufeld, Mary Pulver,
and Gail Bacon**
Bacon-Smith, Camille
Bio-bibliographic data:
Detecting Women, 3rd ed., p. 24. (877c)
Badcock, T.C.; i.e., Thomas C.
Bio-bibliographic data:
Canadian Crime Fiction, p. 14. (209)
Bagby, George. *See* **Stein, Aaron Marc**
Bagley, Desmond
Bio-bibliographic data:
*British Mystery and Thriller Writers since
1940, First Series,* pp. 17–27. (868)
Canadian Crime Fiction, pp. 245–246,
271. (209)
*Critical Survey of Mystery and Detective
Fiction,* pp. 53–58. (41)
*The Oxford Companion to Crime and
Mystery Writing,* p. 34. (4)
*St. James Guide to Crime & Mystery
Writers,* 4th ed., pp. 36–37. (882d)
*Twentieth-Century Crime and Mystery
Writers,* 1st ed., pp. 65–67. (882a)
*Twentieth-Century Crime and Mystery
Writers,* 2nd ed., pp. 39–40. (882b)
*Twentieth-Century Crime and Mystery
Writers,* 3rd ed., pp. 46–47. (882c)
Web site: http://www.crimetime.
co.uk/profiles/desmondbagley.html;
http://www.kirjasto.sci.fi/
dbagley.htm
Bailey, Don
Bio-bibliographic data:
Canadian Crime Fiction, p. 14. (209)
Bailey, Eric
Bio-bibliographic data:
Canadian Crime Fiction, p. 246. (209)
Bailey, H. C.; i.e., Henry Christopher
Bio-bibliographic data:
British Mystery Writers, 1920–1939, pp.
30–35. (867)
*Critical Survey of Mystery and Detective
Fiction,* pp. 59–66. (41)
Encyclopedia Mysteriosa, pp. 15–16. (2)
The Encyclopedia of Murder and Mystery,
p. 23. (6)

*The Encyclopedia of Mystery and
Detection,* p. 17. (7)
*The Oxford Companion to Crime and
Mystery Writing,* pp. 34–35. (4)
*St. James Guide to Crime & Mystery
Writers,* 4th ed., pp. 37–39. (882d)
Twelve Englishmen of Mystery, pp.
88–118. (865)
*Twentieth-Century Crime and Mystery
Writers,* 1st ed., pp. 67–70. (882a)
*Twentieth-Century Crime and Mystery
Writers,* 2nd ed., pp. 40–42. (882b)
*Twentieth-Century Crime and Mystery
Writers,* 3rd ed., pp. 47–49. (882c)
*Whodunit? A Who's Who in Crime and
Mystery Writing,* p. 16. (5)
Bailey, Jo
Bio-bibliographic data:
Detecting Men, 1st ed., p. 29. (876)
Detecting Women, 1st ed., p. 24. (877a)
Bailey, Linda
Bio-bibliographic data:
Canadian Crime Fiction, p. 14. (209)
Bailey, Michele
Bio-bibliographic data:
Detecting Women, 3rd ed., p. 24. (877c)
Web site: http://www.
stopyourekillingme.com/
michele-bailey.html
Bailey, Robert
Web site: http://www.
stopyourekillingme.com/
robert-bailey.html
Baillie, Allan [Stuart]
Bio-bibliographic data:
Australian Crime Fiction, p. 10. (207)
Bain, Donald. *See* **Fletcher, Jessica, and
Donald Bain**
Bainbridge, Beryl
Bio-bibliographic data:
The Encyclopedia of Murder and Mystery,
p. 23. (6)
Baird, Thomas
Bio-bibliographic data:
Canadian Crime Fiction, p. 246. (209)
Baker, Asa. *See* **Halliday, Brett**
Baker, Elmer Leroy
Bio-bibliographic data:
Canadian Crime Fiction, p. 246. (209)
Baker, John
Bio-bibliographic data:
Detecting Men, 1st ed., p. 29. (876)
Web site: http://www.
stopyourekillingme.com/john-baker.

html; http://www.bakers64.freeserve.
co.uk; http://www.johnbakeronline.
co.uk

Baker, Nancy
Bio-bibliographic data:
Canadian Crime Fiction, pp. 14–15. (209)

Baker, Nikki
Bio-bibliographic data:
By a Woman's Hand, 2nd ed., p. 22.
 (884b)
Detecting Women, 1st ed., p. 24. (877a)
Detecting Women 2, p. 24. (877b)
Detecting Women, 3rd ed., p. 24. (877c)
Great Women Mystery Writers, pp. 28–29.
 (880)
Web site: http://www.
 stopyourekillingme.com/
 nikki-baker.html; http://members.
 fortunecity.com/le10/authors/
 authorsA-G/nikkibaker.htm

Baker, Sidney James
Bio-bibliographic data:
Australian Crime Fiction, pp. 10–11.
 (207)

Ball, Doris Bell Collier. *See* **Bell, Josephine**

Ball, Duncan
Bio-bibliographic data:
Australian Crime Fiction, p. 11. (207)

Ball, John [Dudley], Jr.
Bio-bibliographic data:
Critical Survey of Mystery and Detective Fiction, pp. 67–73. (41)
The Encyclopedia of Murder and Mystery,
 p. 24. (6)
The Encyclopedia of Mystery and Detection, pp. 17–18. (7)
The Mammoth Encyclopedia of Modern Crime Fiction, pp. 41–43. (1)
The Oxford Companion to Crime and Mystery Writing, p. 34. (4)
St. James Guide to Crime & Mystery Writers, 4th ed., pp. 39–41. (882d)
Twentieth-Century Crime and Mystery Writers, 1st ed., pp. 70–73. (882a)
Twentieth-Century Crime and Mystery Writers, 2nd ed., pp. 42–44. (882b)
Twentieth-Century Crime and Mystery Writers, 3rd ed., pp. 49–50. (882c)
Whodunit? A Who's Who in Crime and Mystery Writing, p. 16. (5)
Personal papers in Mugar Memorial
 Library, Boston University

Web site: http://www.
 stopyourekillingme.com/john-ball.
 html

Ballard, K. G. *See* **Roth, Holly**

Ballard, Mignon F.
Bio-bibliographic data:
By a Woman's Hand, 1st ed., p. 28. (884a)
By a Woman's Hand, 2nd ed., pp. 22–23.
 (884b)
Detecting Women, 1st ed., p. 24. (877a)
Detecting Women 2, p. 24. (877b)
Web site: http://www.
 stopyourekillingme.com/
 mignon-ballard.html;
 http://www.mignonballard.com

Ballard, P. D. *See* **Ballard, Willis Todhunter**

Ballard, Willis Todhunter
Bio-bibliographic data:
Encyclopedia Mysteriosa, p. 16. (2)
The Encyclopedia of Murder and Mystery,
 p. 24. (6)
St. James Guide to Crime & Mystery Writers, 4th ed., pp. 41–43. (882d)
Twentieth-Century Crime and Mystery Writers, 1st ed., pp. 74–76. (882a)
Twentieth-Century Crime and Mystery Writers, 2nd ed., pp. 44–48. (882b)
Twentieth-Century Crime and Mystery Writers, 3rd ed., pp. 51–56. (882c)
Personal papers in University of Oregon
 Library, Eugene

Ballem, John [Bishop]
Bio-bibliographic data:
Canadian Crime Fiction, p. 15. (209)

Ballinger, Bill S[anborn].
Bio-bibliographic data:
Encyclopedia Mysteriosa, p. 16. (2)
The Encyclopedia of Mystery and Detection, p. 18. (7)
St. James Guide to Crime & Mystery Writers, 4th ed., pp. 44–45. (882d)
Twentieth-Century Crime and Mystery Writers, 1st ed., pp. 76–78. (882a)
Twentieth-Century Crime and Mystery Writers, 2nd ed., pp. 49–50. (882b)
Twentieth-Century Crime and Mystery Writers, 3rd ed., pp. 56–57. (882c)
Personal papers in Mugar Memorial
 Library, Boston University

Balmer, Edwin
Bio-bibliographic data:
Encyclopedia Mysteriosa, p. 16. (2)

The Encyclopedia of Murder and Mystery,
pp. 24–25. (6)
*The Encyclopedia of Mystery and
Detection,* p. 18. (7)
*Twentieth-Century Crime and Mystery
Writers,* 1st ed., pp. 78–80. (882a)
*Twentieth-Century Crime and Mystery
Writers,* 2nd ed., pp. 50–51. (882b)
*Twentieth-Century Crime and Mystery
Writers,* 3rd ed., pp. 57–59. (882c)

Balzac, Honoré de
Bio-bibliographic data:
*Critical Survey of Mystery and Detective
Fiction,* pp. 74–81. (41)
The Encyclopedia of Murder and Mystery,
p. 25. (6)
*The Encyclopedia of Mystery and
Detection,* pp. 18–19. (7)
*100 Masters of Mystery and Detective
Fiction,* pp. 15–22. (37)
Web site: http://members.aol.com/
balssa/balzac/balzac.html;
http://www. kirjasto.sci.fi/balzac.htm

Bamman, George. *See* **Harrower, Captain
Robert Hamilton**

Bangs, John Kendrick
Bio-bibliographic data:
*The Encyclopedia of Mystery and
Detection,* p. 19. (7)

Bankier, William
Bio-bibliographic data:
Canadian Crime Fiction, p. 15. (209)
*St. James Guide to Crime & Mystery
Writers,* 4th ed., pp. 45–46. (882d)
*Twentieth-Century Crime and Mystery
Writers,* 2nd ed., pp. 51–53. (882b)
*Twentieth-Century Crime and Mystery
Writers,* 3rd ed., pp. 59–61. (882c)

Banks, Carolyn
Bio-bibliographic data:
Detecting Women, 1st ed., p. 24. (877a)
Detecting Women 2, p. 24. (877b)
Detecting Women, 3rd ed., p. 25. (877c)
Web site: http://www.
stopyourekillingme.com/
carolyn-banks.html

Banks, Jacqueline Turner
Bio-bibliographic data:
Detecting Women, 3rd ed., p. 25. (877c)

Banks, John
Bio-bibliographic data:
Canadian Crime Fiction, p. 15. (209)

Bannister, Jo
Bio-bibliographic data:

By a Woman's Hand, 2nd ed., p. 23.
(884b)
Detecting Women, 1st ed., p. 25. (877a)
Detecting Women 2, pp. 24–25. (877b)
Detecting Women, 3rd ed., pp. 25–26.
(877c)
*The Mammoth Encyclopedia of Modern
Crime Fiction,* pp. 43–44. (1)
Web site: http://www.
stopyourekillingme.com/
jo-bannister.html; http://www.
twbooks.co.uk/authors/jbannister.html

Banville, John
Bio-bibliographic data:
The Encyclopedia of Murder and Mystery,
pp. 25–26. (6)

Barber, Bruce Aubrey
Bio-bibliographic data:
Canadian Crime Fiction, pp. 4–5, 15–16.
(209)

Barber, Dulan. *See* **Fletcher, David**

Barber, Willetta Ann
Bio-bibliographic data:
Detecting Women, 1st ed., p. 25. (877a)
Detecting Women 2, p. 25. (877b)

Barden, Robert Andrew
Bio-bibliographic data:
Australian Crime Fiction, p. 9. (207)

Bardin, John Franklin
Bio-bibliographic data:
The Encyclopedia of Murder and Mystery,
p. 26. (6)
*St. James Guide to Crime & Mystery
Writers,* 4th ed., p. 47. (882d)
*Twentieth-Century Crime and Mystery
Writers,* 1st ed., pp. 80–82. (882a)
*Twentieth-Century Crime and Mystery
Writers,* 2nd ed., pp. 53–54. (882b)
*Twentieth-Century Crime and Mystery
Writers,* 3rd ed., pp. 61–62. (882c)
Web site: http://www.
johnfranklinbardin.com

Barer, Burl
Web site: http://www.
stopyourekillingme.com/burl-barer.
html; http://www.burlbarer.com

Baring-Gould, William S[tuart].
Bio-bibliographic data:
The Encyclopedia of Murder and Mystery,
pp. 26–27. (6)

Barker, Dudley. *See* **Black, Lionel**
Barnao, Jack. *See* **Wood, Ted**
Barnard, Elizabeth. *See* **Quinn, Elizabeth**
  Barnard
Barnard, Marjorie Faith. *See* **Eldershaw,**
  M. Barnard
Barnard, Robert
  Bio-bibliographic data:
  Australian Crime Fiction, p. 11. (207)
  Colloquium on Crime, pp. 7–22. (884.1)
  Critical Survey of Mystery and Detective
    Fiction, pp. 82–87. (41)
  Detecting Men, 1st ed., pp. 29–30, 32.
    (876)
  Encyclopedia Mysteriosa, pp. 17–18. (2)
  The Encyclopedia of Murder and Mystery,
    p. 27. (6)
  The Fatal Art of Entertainment, pp.
    250–75. (878)
  The Mammoth Encyclopedia of Modern
    Crime Fiction, pp. 44–46. (1)
  Mystery and Suspense Writers, pp. 31–40.
    (884.2)
  The Oxford Companion to Crime and
    Mystery Writing, p. 36. (4)
  St. James Guide to Crime & Mystery
    Writers, 4th ed., pp. 48–49. (882d)
  Twentieth-Century Crime and Mystery
    Writers, 2nd ed., pp. 54–55. (882b)
  Twentieth-Century Crime and Mystery
    Writers, 3rd ed., pp. 62–64. (882c)
  Whodunit? A Who's Who in Crime and
    Mystery Writing, p. 16. (5)
  Web site: http://www.
    stopyourekillingme.com/robert-barnar
    d. html;
    http://www.poisonedpenpress.
    com/robertbarnard
Barnes, Julian
  Bio-bibliographic data:
  Detecting Men, 1st ed., p. 142. (876)
  The Encyclopedia of Murder and Mystery,
    p. 27. (6)
  The Mammoth Encyclopedia of Modern
    Crime Fiction, pp. 261–62. (1)
  Twentieth-Century Crime and Mystery
    Writers, 3rd ed., pp. 614–15. (882c)
  Web site: http://www.julianbarnes.com
Barnes, Linda
  Bio-bibliographic data:
  By a Woman's Hand, 1st ed., pp. 28–29.
    (884a)
  By a Woman's Hand, 2nd ed., pp. 23–24.
    (884b)

Detecting Women, 1st ed., pp. 25–26.
    (877a)
  Detecting Women 2, pp. 25–26. (877b)
  Detecting Women, 3rd ed., p. 26. (877c)
  Encyclopedia Mysteriosa, p. 18. (2)
  Great Women Mystery Writers, pp. 29–32.
    (880)
  St. James Guide to Crime & Mystery
    Writers, 4th ed., pp. 49–51. (882d)
  Twentieth-Century Crime and Mystery
    Writers, 3rd ed., pp. 64–65. (882c)
  Whodunit? A Who's Who in Crime and
    Mystery Writing, pp. 16–17. (5)
  Women of Mystery, p. 432. (874)
  Web site: http://www.
    stopyourekillingme.com/linda-barnes.
    html; http://www.lindabarnes.com
Barnes, Trevor
  Bio-bibliographic data:
  Detecting Men, 1st ed., p. 30. (876)
Barnett, James
  Bio-bibliographic data:
  Detecting Men, 1st ed., p. 30. (876)
Barr, Nevada
  Bio-bibliographic data:
  By a Woman's Hand, 2nd ed., pp. 24–25.
    (884b)
  Detecting Women, 1st ed., p. 26. (877a)
  Detecting Women 2, p. 26. (877b)
  Detecting Women, 3rd ed., p. 27. (877c)
  The Mammoth Encyclopedia of Modern
    Crime Fiction, pp. 47–48. (1)
  St. James Guide to Crime & Mystery
    Writers, 4th ed., pp. 51–52. (882d)
  Speaking of Murder, vol. II, pp. 78–88.
    (875b)
  Whodunit? A Who's Who in Crime and
    Mystery Writing, p. 17. (5)
  Women Authors of Detective Series, pp.
    145–48. (882.5)
  Web site: http://www.nevadabarr.com;
    http://www.stopyourekillingme.com/
    nevada-barr.html;
Barr, Robert
  Bio-bibliographic data:
  British Mystery Writers, 1860–1919, pp.
    14–22. (866)
  Canadian Crime Fiction, pp. 16–17. (209)
  Critical Survey of Mystery and Detective
    Fiction, pp. 88–93. (41)
  Encyclopedia Mysteriosa, p. 19. (2)
  The Encyclopedia of Murder and Mystery,
    p. 28. (6)

*The Encyclopedia of Mystery and
Detection*, p. 19. (7)
*Twentieth-Century Crime and Mystery
Writers*, 2nd ed., pp. 55–56. (882b)
*Twentieth-Century Crime and Mystery
Writers*, 3rd ed., pp. 65–66. (882c)
Personal papers in Crane Collection,
Butler Library, Columbia University.
Personal papers in Regional History
Department, University of Western
Ontario.

Barre, Richard
Bio-bibliographic data:
Detecting Men, 1st ed., p. 31. (876)
*The Mammoth Encyclopedia of Modern
Crime Fiction*, pp. 48–49. (1)
Web site: http://www.stopyourekillingme.
com/richard-barre. html

Barrett, James
Bio-bibliographic data:
Canadian Crime Fiction, p. 17. (209)

Barrett, Kathleen Anne
Bio-bibliographic data:
Detecting Women, 3rd ed., p. 27. (877c)
Web site: http://www.
stopyourekillingme.com/
kathleen-anne-barrett.html

**Barrett, Margaret [*pseud. for* Anne
Rudman] and Charles Dennis [I]**
Bio-bibliographic data:
Detecting Women, 3rd ed., p. 27. (877c)
Web site: http://www.
stopyourekillingme.com/
margaret-barrett.html

Barrett, Michael [John]
Bio-bibliographic data:
Australian Crime Fiction, p. 11. (207)

Barrett, Neal, Jr.
Bio-bibliographic data:
The Big Book of Noir, pp. 325–26. (24)
Detecting Men, 1st ed., p. 31. (876)
Web site: http://www.
stopyourekillingme.com/
neal-barrett.html; http://www.
nealbarrett.com/

Barrett, Robert G.
Bio-bibliographic data:
Australian Crime Fiction, p. 12. (207)
Detecting Men, 1st ed., p. 31. (876)

**Barron, Stephanie. *Pseud. for* Francine
Stephanie Mathews**
Bio-bibliographic data:
Detecting Women, 3rd ed., p. 28. (877c)

Web site: http://www.
stopyourekillingme.com/
stephanie-barron.html

Barth, Richard
Bio-bibliographic data:
Detecting Men, 1st ed., p. 32. (876)
*Twentieth-Century Crime and Mystery
Writers*, 3rd ed., pp. 66–67. (882c)
Web site: http://www.stopyourekillingme.
com/ richard-barth.html; http://www.
booksnbytes.com/authors/
barth_ richard.html

Bartholomew, Nancy: unidentified pseud.
Bio-bibliographic data:
Detecting Women, 3rd ed., p. 28. (877c)
Web site: http://www.
stopyourekillingme.com/
nancy-barth.html; http://www.
nancybartholomew.com

Barton, Carl
Bio-bibliographic data:
Canadian Crime Fiction, p. 17. (209)

**Barton, Dr. Eustace Robert. *See* Eustace,
Robert**

Barzun, Jacques Martin
Bio-bibliographic data:
Encyclopedia Mysteriosa, p. 19. (2)
The Encyclopedia of Murder and Mystery,
p. 29. (6)
*The Encyclopedia of Mystery and
Detection*, p. 19. (7)

Base, Ron
Bio-bibliographic data:
Canadian Crime Fiction, p. 17. (209)

Bass, Milton R.
Bio-bibliographic data:
Detecting Men, 1st ed., p. 32. (876)

Bass, Walter
Bio-bibliographic data:
Australian Crime Fiction, p. 9. (207)

Bassingthwaite, Don
Bio-bibliographic data:
Canadian Crime Fiction, p. 121. (209)

Bastable, Bernard. *See* Robert Barnard

Batchelor, Denzil [Stanley]
Bio-bibliographic data:
Australian Crime Fiction, pp. 12–13.
(207)

Bates, Walter
Bio-bibliographic data:
Canadian Crime Fiction, p. 17. (209)

Bateson, David
Bio-bibliographic data:
Australian Crime Fiction, p. 13. (207)

Detecting Men, 1st ed., p. 33. (876)
Batt, Leon
Bio-bibliographic data:
Australian Crime Fiction, p. 13. (207)
Batten, Jack
Bio-bibliographic data:
Canadian Crime Fiction, p. 18. (209)
Detecting Men, 1st ed., p. 32. (876)
Web site: http://www.
stopyourekillingme.com/
jack-batten.html
Battista, Vicente
Bio-bibliographic data:
*Latin American Mystery Writers: An A to
Z Guide. (881)*
Bauer, Nancy
Bio-bibliographic data:
Canadian Crime Fiction, p. 18. (209)
Bawden, Nina
Bio-bibliographic data:
*Twentieth-Century Crime and Mystery
Writers,* 1st ed., pp. 82–83. (882a)
Bax, Roger. *See* **Garve, Andrew**
Baxt, George
Bio-bibliographic data:
Detecting Men, 1st ed., pp. 32–33. (876)
Encyclopedia Mysteriosa, pp. 21–22. (2)
The Encyclopedia of Murder and Mystery,
pp. 30–31. (6)
*The Mammoth Encyclopedia of Modern
Crime Fiction*, pp. 49–50. (1)
*The Oxford Companion to Crime and
Mystery Writing*, p. 36. (4)
*St. James Guide to Crime & Mystery
Writers*, 4th ed., pp. 52–53. (882d)
*Twentieth-Century Crime and Mystery
Writers,* 1st ed., pp. 84–85. (882a)
*Twentieth-Century Crime and Mystery
Writers*, 2nd ed., p. 57. (882b)
*Twentieth-Century Crime and Mystery
Writers*, 3rd ed., p. 68. (882c)
*Whodunit? A Who's Who in Crime and
Mystery Writing*, p. 17. (5)
Personal papers in Mugar Memorial
Library, Boston University.
Web site: http://www.stopyourekillingme.
com/george-baxt.html; http://www.
booksnbytes.com/authors/baxt_
george.html
Baxter, George Owen. *See* **Brand, Max**
Baxter, John. *See* **Hunt, E. Howard, Jr.**
Bayer, William
Bio-bibliographic data:
Detecting Men, 1st ed., p. 33. (876)

Encyclopedia Mysteriosa, p. 22. (2)
*The Mammoth Encyclopedia of Modern
Crime Fiction*, pp. 50–51. (1)
*St. James Guide to Crime & Mystery
Writers*, 4th ed., pp. 53–55. (882d)
Web site: http://www.williambayer.com;
http://www.stopyourekillingme.com/
william-bayer.html
Bayle, B. J.
Bio-bibliographic data:
Canadian Crime Fiction, p. 18. (209)
Baylis, Samuel Mathewson
Bio-bibliographic data:
Canadian Crime Fiction, pp. 18–19. (209)
Baynton, Barbara Jane
Bio-bibliographic data:
Australian Crime Fiction, p. 13. (207)
Beach, Rex
Bio-bibliographic data:
Canadian Crime Fiction, p. 246. (209)
Beahan, G.
Bio-bibliographic data:
Canadian Crime Fiction, p. 19. (209)
Bean, Gregory
Bio-bibliographic data:
Detecting Men, 1st ed., p. 34. (876)
Web site: http://www.stopyourekillingme.
com/gregory-bean.html
Beasley, David R.
Bio-bibliographic data:
Canadian Crime Fiction, p. 19. (209)
Beaston, Allen
Bio-bibliographic data:
Australian Crime Fiction, pp. 13–14.
(207)
**Beaton, M. C.; i.e., Marion Chesney
Beaton**
Bio-bibliographic data:
By a Woman's Hand, 1st ed., pp. 29–30.
(884a)
By a Woman's Hand, 2nd ed., pp. 25–26.
(884b)
Detecting Women, 1st ed., p. 26. (877a)
Detecting Women 2, pp. 26–27. (877b)
Detecting Women, 3rd ed., pp. 28–29.
(877c)
*The Mammoth Encyclopedia of Modern
Crime Fiction*, p. 52. (1)
*St. James Guide to Crime & Mystery
Writers*, 4th ed., pp. 55–57. (882d)
Web site: http://www.stopyourekillingme.
com/m-c-beaton.html; http://
members.ozemail.com.au/~blinda/
hmbeaton. htm

Beauchesne, Yves
Bio-bibliographic data:
Canadian Crime Fiction, pp. 19, 193.
(209)
Beaudet, Raymond
Bio-bibliographic data:
Canadian Crime Fiction, p. 19. (209)
Beaudry, Jean
Bio-bibliographic data:
Canadian Crime Fiction, p. 19. (209)
Beauford, Tom. *Pseud. for* **John Sligo**
Bio-bibliographic data:
Australian Crime Fiction, p. 14. (207)
**Beaufort, Simon [*pseud. for* Susanna
Gregory and Beau Riffenburgh].** *See*
Gregory, Susanna
Beaulieu, Victor-Lévy
Bio-bibliographic daa:
Canadian Crime Fiction, pp. 19–20. (209)
Beaulne, Monique
Bio-bibliographic data:
Canadian Crime Fiction, p. 20. (209)
Beck, K. K. *Pseud. for* **Katherine Marris,
name changed to Katherine Beck**
Bio-bibliographic data:
By a Woman's Hand, 1st ed., pp. 30–31.
(884a)
By a Woman's Hand, 2nd ed., p. 26.
(884b)
Canadian Crime Fiction, pp. 246, 260,
271, 283. (209)
Detecting Women, 1st ed., p. 27. (877a)
Detecting Women 2, p. 27. (877b)
Detecting Women, 3rd ed., pp. 29–30.
(877c)
*The Mammoth Encyclopedia of Modern
Crime Fiction*, pp. 52–53. (1)
*St. James Guide to Crime & Mystery
Writers*, 4th ed., pp. 57–58. (882d)
*Twentieth-Century Crime and Mystery
Writers*, 3rd ed., pp. 68–69. (882c)
Web site: http://www.stopyourekillingme.
com/k-k-beck.html
Beck III, Robert Maupin. *See* **Slim,
Iceberg**
Becke, Louis [George Lewis Becke]
Bio-bibliographic data:
Australian Crime Fiction, p. 14. (207)
Becket, Lalie
Bio-bibliographic data:
Canadian Crime Fiction, p. 20. (209)
Bédard, Elaine
Bio-bibliographic data:
Canadian Crime Fiction, p. 20. (209)

Bedford, Jean [Gladys Agnes]
Bio-bibliographic data:
Australian Crime Fiction, pp. 14, 146.
(207)
Detecting Women 2, p. 27. (877b)
Detecting Women, 3rd ed., p. 30. (877c)
Bedford, Randolph
Bio-bibliographic data:
Australian Crime Fiction, pp. 14–15.
(207)
Bedford, Ruth
Bio-bibliographic data:
Australian Crime Fiction, p. 183. (207)
**Bedford-Jones, H.; i.e., Henry James
O'Brien**
Bio-bibliographic data:
Canadian Crime Fiction, pp. 20, 98–99.
(209)
**Bedwell, William LeBreton Harvey
Brisbane.** *See* **Brisbane-Bedwell,
William LeBreton Harvy**
Beeby, G. S.; i.e., Sir George Stephenson
Bio-bibliographic data:
Australian Crime Fiction, p. 15. (207)
Beeby, Otto
Bio-bibliographic data:
Australian Crime Fiction, p. 15. (207)
Beecham, Rose: unidentified pseud.
Bio-bibliographic data:
Detecting Women 2, p. 27. (877b)
Detecting Women, 3rd ed., p. 30. (877c)
Beeck, Christopher. *See* **Bridges, T. C.**
Beede, John
Bio-bibliographic data:
Australian Crime Fiction, p. 16. (207)
Beeding, Francis. *Pseud. for* **John Leslie
Palmer and Hilary Aidan. St. George
Saunders**
Bio-bibliographic data:
*Critical Survey of Mystery and Detective
Fiction*, pp. 94–98. (41)
Encyclopedia Mysteriosa, pp. 22–23. (2)
The Encyclopedia of Murder and Mystery,
p. 33. (6)
*The Encyclopedia of Mystery and
Detection*, p. 22. (7)
*St. James Guide to Crime & Mystery
Writers*, 4th ed., pp. 58–60. (882d)
*Twentieth-Century Crime and Mystery
Writers,* 1st ed., pp. 85–88. (882a)
*Twentieth-Century Crime and Mystery
Writers*, 2nd ed., pp. 58–59. (882b)
*Twentieth-Century Crime and Mystery
Writers*, 3rd ed., pp. 69–71. (882c)

Beeman, Herbert
Bio-bibliographic data:
Canadian Crime Fiction, p. 20. (209)
Beetham-Endersby, Beverley
Bio-bibliographic data:
Canadian Crime Fiction, p. 21. (209)
Behn, Noel
Bio-bibliographic data:
Twentieth-Century Crime and Mystery Writers, 1st ed., p. 89. (882a)
Twentieth-Century Crime and Mystery Writers, 2nd ed., p. 60. (882b)
Twentieth-Century Crime and Mystery Writers, 3rd ed., pp. 71–72. (882c)
Personal papers in Green Library, Stanford University
Web site: http://www-sul.stanford. edu/depts/hasrg/ablit/amerlit/ Noelbehn.html
Beinhart, Larry
Bio-bibliographic data:
Detecting Men, 1st ed., p. 35. (876)
The Mammoth Encyclopedia of Modern Crime Fiction, pp. 53–54. (1)
Web site: http://www.stopyourekillingme. com/larry-beinhart.html
Bélanger, Jean-Pierre
Bio-bibliographic data:
Canadian Crime Fiction, p. 21. (209)
Belcourt, Claude
Bio-bibliographic data:
Canadian Crime Fiction, p. 21. (209)
Belfort, Sophie. *Pseud. for* **Kate Auspitz**
Bio-bibliographic data:
By a Woman's Hand, 1st ed., pp. 31–32. (884a)
By a Woman's Hand, 2nd ed., pp. 26–27. (884b)
Detecting Women, 1st ed., p. 27. (877a)
Detecting Women 2, p. 28. (877b)
Detecting Women, 3rd ed., pp. 30–31. (877c)
Belkom, Edo van. *See* **van Belkom, Edo**
Bell, Eleanor
Bio-bibliographic data:
Canadian Crime Fiction, p. 21. (209)
Bell, Josephine. *Pseud. for* **Doris Bell Collier Ball**
Bio-bibliographic data:
Critical Survey of Mystery and Detective Fiction, pp. 99–106. (41)
Detecting Women, 1st ed., p. 27. (877a)
Detecting Women 2, p. 28. (877b)
Encyclopedia Mysteriosa, p. 23. (2)

The Encyclopedia of Mystery and Detection, p. 22. (7)
St. James Guide to Crime & Mystery Writers, 4th ed., pp. 60–62. (882d)
Twentieth-Century Crime and Mystery Writers, 1st ed., pp. 90–93. (882a)
Twentieth-Century Crime and Mystery Writers, 2nd ed., pp. 60–62. (882b)
Twentieth-Century Crime and Mystery Writers, 3rd ed., pp. 72–74. (882c)
Web site: http://www.xsfall.nl/ ~embden11/Engels/bell.htm
Bell, Nancy
Bio-bibliographic data:
Detecting Women, 3rd ed., p. 31. (877c)
Web site: http://www.stopyourekillingme. com/nancy-bell.html
Bell, Pauline
Bio-bibliographic data:
Detecting Women, 3rd ed., p. 31. (877c)
The Mammoth Encyclopedia of Modern Crime Fiction, p. 54. (1)
Web site: http://www.stopyourekillingme. com/pauline-bell.html; http://www. twbooks.co.uk/authors/pbell.html
Bellairs, George. *Pseud. for* **Harold Blundell**
Bio-bibliographic data:
The Encyclopedia of Murder and Mystery, pp. 34–35. (6)
The Encyclopedia of Mystery and Detection, pp. 22–23. (7)
St. James Guide to Crime & Mystery Writers, 4th ed., pp. 62–63. (882d)
Twentieth-Century Crime and Mystery Writers, 1st ed., pp. 93–95. (882a)
Twentieth-Century Crime and Mystery Writers, 3rd ed., pp. 74–75. (882c)
Web site: http://www.xs4all.nl/ ~embden11/Engels3/bellairs.htm
Bellem, Robert Leslie
Bio-bibliographic data:
Encyclopedia Mysteriosa, pp. 23–24. (2)
The Encyclopedia of Murder and Mystery, pp. 35. (6)
St. James Guide to Crime & Mystery Writers, 4th ed., pp. 63–64. (882d)
Twentieth-Century Crime and Mystery Writers, 1st ed., pp. 95–96. (882a)
Twentieth-Century Crime and Mystery Writers, 2nd ed., pp. 62–63. (882b)
Twentieth-Century Crime and Mystery Writers, 3rd ed., pp. 75–85. (882c)

Personal papers in the University of
California at Los Angeles.
Web site: http://www.bleekerbooks.com/
Books/Authors/RobertLeslieBellem.
asp

Bellemare, Pauline Vanier. *See*
Vanier-Bellemare, Pauline

Belloc Lowndes, Mrs. Marie. *See*
Lowndes, Mrs. Marie Belloc

Belsky, Dick
Bio-bibliographic data:
Detecting Men, 1st ed., p. 35. (876)

Bending, Frederick J.
Bio-bibliographic data:
Canadian Crime Fiction, p. 21. (209)

Benison, C. C. *Pseud. for* **Douglas**
Whiteway
Bio-bibliographic data:
Detecting Men, 1st ed., p. 35. (876)
Web site: http://www.stopyourekillingme.
com/c-c-benison.html

Benjamin, Carole Lea
Bio-bibliographic data:
Detecting Women, 3rd ed., p. 32. (877c)
The Mammoth Encyclopedia of Modern
Crime Fiction, pp. 54–55. (1)
Web site: http://www.carolleabenjamin.
com; http://www.stopyourekillingme.
com/carole-lea-benjamin.html

Benjamin, Pierre. *Pseud. for*
Joseph-Alphonse Bourdon
Bio-bibliographic data:
Canadian Crime Fiction, p. 21. (209)

Benke, Patricia D.
Bio-bibliographic data:
Detecting Women, 3rd ed., p. 32. (877c)

Bennett, [Enoch] Arnold
Bio-bibliographic data:
Critical Survey of Mystery and Detective
Fiction, pp. 107–11. (41)
The Encyclopedia of Mystery and
Detection, p. 23. (7)

Bennett, Billy L.
Bio-bibliographic data:
Canadian Crime Fiction, p. 246. (209)

Bennett, Liza
Bio-bibliographic data:
Detecting Women, 1st ed., p. 28. (877a)
Detecting Women 2, p. 29. (877b)
Detecting Women, 3rd ed., p. 32. (877c)

Bennett, Margot
Bio-bibliographic data:
Australian Crime Fiction, p. 16. (207)

St. James Guide to Crime & Mystery
Writers, 4th ed., pp. 64–65. (882d)
Twentieth-Century Crime and Mystery
Writers, 1st ed., pp. 97–98. (882a)
Twentieth-Century Crime and Mystery
Writers, 2nd ed., pp. 63–64. (882b)
Twentieth-Century Crime and Mystery
Writers, 3rd ed., pp. 85–86. (882c)
Web site: http://www.stopyourekillingme.
com/margot-bennett.html; http://
www. xs4all.nl/~embden11/
Engels/bennett.htm

Bennett, Robert D[onald].
Bio-bibliographic data:
Canadian Crime Fiction, p. 246. (209)

Benson, Benjamin
Bio-bibliographic data:
The Encyclopedia of Mystery and
Detection, pp. 23–24. (7)
St. James Guide to Crime & Mystery
Writers, 4th ed., pp. 65–66. (882d)
Twentieth-Century Crime and Mystery
Writers, 1st ed., pp. 99–100. (882a)
Twentieth-Century Crime and Mystery
Writers, 2nd ed., pp. 64–65. (882b)
Twentieth-Century Crime and Mystery
Writers, 3rd ed., pp. 86–87. (882c)

Benson, E. F.; i.e., Edward Frederick
Bio-bibliographic data:
Twentieth-Century Crime and Mystery
Writers, 1st ed., pp. 100–104. (882a)
Web site: http://www.geocities.com/
SoHo/Nook/7665; http://www.
efbenson.co.uk
E. F. Benson Society
c/o Allan Downend
The Old Coach House
Rye TN31 7JF
United Kingdom

Benson, Eugene Patrick
Bio-bibliographic data:
Canadian Crime Fiction, p. 21. (209)

Benson, Godfrey [Rathbone]
Bio-bibliographic data:
The Encyclopedia of Mystery and
Detection, p. 24. (7)

Bentley, E. C.; i.e., Edmund Clerihew
Bio-bibliographic data:
British Mystery Writers, 1860–1919, pp.
23–29. (866)
Critical Survey of Mystery and Detective
Fiction, pp. 112–17. (41)
Encyclopedia Mysteriosa, pp. 24–25. (2)

The Encyclopedia of Murder and Mystery, p. 36. (6)
The Encyclopedia of Mystery and Detection, p. 24. (7)
Mystery and Suspense Writers, pp. 41–49. (884.2)
100 Masters of Mystery and Detective Fiction, pp. 23–28. (37)
The Oxford Companion to Crime and Mystery Writing, p. 37. (4)
St. James Guide to Crime & Mystery Writers, 4th ed., pp. 66–67. (882d)
Twentieth-Century Crime and Mystery Writers, 1st ed., pp. 104–6. (882a)
Twentieth-Century Crime and Mystery Writers, 2nd ed., pp. 65–66. (882b)
Twentieth-Century Crime and Mystery Writers, 3rd ed., pp. 87–88. (882c)
Whodunit? A Who's Who in Crime and Mystery Writing, p. 18. (5)
Web site: http://www.stopyourekillingme. com/e-c-bentley.html
Bentley, Nicolas
Bio-bibliographic data:
Twentieth-Century Crime and Mystery Writers, 1st ed., pp. 106–8. (882a)
Bentley, Phyllis
Bio-bibliographic data:
The Encyclopedia of Mystery and Detection, pp. 24–25. (7)
Twentieth-Century Crime and Mystery Writers, 1st ed., pp. 108–11. (882a)
Bentley, Robert
Bio-bibliographic data:
Canadian Crime Fiction, p. 21. (209)
Benton, Kenneth
Bio-bibliographic data:
Twentieth-Century Crime and Mystery Writers, 1st ed., pp. 111–12. (882a)
Twentieth-Century Crime and Mystery Writers, 2nd ed., pp. 66–67. (882b)
Ber, André
Bio-bibliographic data:
Canadian Crime Fiction, p. 21. (209)
Berckman, Evelyn
Bio-bibliographic data:
The Encyclopedia of Mystery and Detection, p. 25. (7)
Twentieth-Century Crime and Mystery Writers, 1st ed., pp. 112–14. (882a)
Twentieth-Century Crime and Mystery Writers, 2nd ed., pp. 67–68. (882b)
Twentieth-Century Crime and Mystery Writers, 3rd ed., pp. 88–89. (882c)

Personal papers in Mugar Memorial Library, Boston University
Berenson, Laurien
Bio-bibliographic data:
Detecting Women, 1st ed., p. 28. (877a)
Detecting Women 2, p. 29. (877b)
Detecting Women, 3rd ed., p. 33. (877c)
Web site: http://www.stopyourekillingme. com/ laurien-berenson.html; http:// www. aurienberenson.com
Berger, Bob
Bio-bibliographic data:
Detecting Men, 1st ed., p. 36. (876)
Berger, Thomas
Bio-bibliographic data:
The Encyclopedia of Murder and Mystery, p. 37. (6)
Bergeron, Jean-Marc
Bio-bibliographic data:
Canadian Crime Fiction, p. 21. (209)
Bergman, Andrew
Bio-bibliographic data:
Twentieth-Century Crime and Mystery Writers, 1st ed., pp. 114–15. (882a)
Berkeley, Anthony. *Pseud. for* Anthony Berkeley Cox
Bio-bibliographic data:
British Mystery Writers, 1920–1939, pp. 36–43. (867)
Critical Survey of Mystery and Detective Fiction, pp. 118–23. (41)
Encyclopedia Mysteriosa, pp. 25–26. (2)
The Encyclopedia of Murder and Mystery, p. 37. (6)
The Encyclopedia of Mystery and Detection, pp. 25–27. (7)
100 Masters of Mystery and Detective Fiction, pp. 29–35. (37)
The Oxford Companion to Crime and Mystery Writing, pp. 37–38. (4)
St. James Guide to Crime & Mystery Writers, 4th ed., pp. 67–69. (882d)
Twelve Englishmen of Mystery, pp. 120–41. (865)
Twentieth-Century Crime and Mystery Writers, 1st ed., pp. 115–18. (882a)
Twentieth-Century Crime and Mystery Writers, 2nd ed., pp. 68–70. (882b)
Twentieth-Century Crime and Mystery Writers, 3rd cd., pp. 89–91. (882c)
Whodunit? A Who's Who in Crime and Mystery Writing, pp. 18–19. (5)
Web site: http://www.stopyourekillingme. com/anthony-berkley.html

Berlinski, David
Bio-bibliographic data:
Detecting Men, 1st ed., p. 36. (876)
Bermúdez, María Elvira
Bio-bibliographic data:
Latin American Mystery Writers: An A to Z Guide. (881)
Bernal, Rafael
Bio-bibliographic data:
Latin American Mystery Writers: An A to Z Guide. (881)
Bernard, Evelyne
Bio-bibliographic data:
Canadian Crime Fiction, p. 21. (209)
Bernard, Patricia Scot. *See* **Scot-Bernard, P.**
Bernard, Pierre
Bio-bibliographic data:
Canadian Crime Fiction, p. 21. (209)
Berne, Karin. *Pseud. for* **Sue Bernell and Michaela Karni**
Bio-bibliographic data:
Detecting Women, 3rd ed., p. 33. (877c)
Web site: http://www.stopyourekillingme. com/karin-berne.html
Bernell, Sue. *See* **Berne, Karin**
Bernhardt, William
Bio-bibliographic data:
Detecting Men, 1st ed., p. 36. (876)
The Mammoth Encyclopedia of Modern Crime Fiction, pp. 55–56. (1)
Web site: http://www.williambernhardt. com; http://www.stopyourekillingme.com/ william-bernhardt.html
Bernier, Gaston
Bio-bibliographic data:
Canadian Crime Fiction, p. 22. (209)
Berrow, N.; i.e., Cyril Norman
Bio-bibliographic data:
Australian Crime Fiction, p. 17. (207)
Berry, Carole
Bio-bibliographic data:
By a Woman's Hand, 1st ed., p. 32. (884a)
By a Woman's Hand, 2nd ed., pp. 27–28. (884b)
Detecting Women, 1st ed., p. 28. (877a)
Detecting Women 2, p. 29. (877b)
Detecting Women, 3rd ed., pp. 33–34. (877c)
Web site: http://www.stopyourekillingme. com/carole-berry.html
Berthelot, Hector
Bio-bibliographic data:

Canadian Crime Fiction, p. 22. (209)
Bertie, Charles Henry
Bio-bibliographic data:
Australian Crime Fiction, pp. 17, 183. (207)
Berton, Dick. *Joint pseud. for* **Robert Laroque de Roquebrune and de Fernand Préfontaine**
Bio-bibliographic data:
Canadian Crime Fiction, p. 22. (209)
Betcherman, Barbara
Bio-bibliographic data:
Canadian Crime Fiction, p. 22. (209)
Bettany, George [Kernaham Gwynne]
Bio-bibliographic data:
Canadian Crime Fiction, p. 22. (209)
Betz, Ingrid
Bio-bibliographic data:
Canadian Crime Fiction, p. 22. (209)
Bhabra, H. S.; i.e., Hargurchet Singh
Bio-bibliographic data:
Canadian Crime Fiction, pp. 22, 117. (209)
Bice, Clare
Bio-bibliographic data:
Canadian Crime Fiction, p. 22. (209)
Bickham, Jack
Bio-bibliographic data:
Detecting Men, 1st ed., pp. 37, 181. (876)
Web site: http://www.stopyourekillingme. com/jack-bickham.html
Biderman, Bob
Bio-bibliographic data:
Detecting Men, 1st ed., p. 37. (876)
Bidmead, Charles
Bio-bibliographic data:
Australian Crime Fiction, p. 17. (207)
Bierce, Ambrose [Gwinett]
Bio-bibliographic data:
Critical Survey of Mystery and Detective Fiction, pp. 124–29. (41)
The Encyclopedia of Mystery and Detection, p. 27. (7)
Bigg, Patricia Nina. *See* **Ainsworth, Patricia**
Biggers, Earl Derr
Bio-bibliographic data:
Corpus Delicti of Mystery Fiction, pp. 36–37. (879)
Critical Survey of Mystery and Detective Fiction, pp. 130–35. (41)
Encyclopedia Mysteriosa, p. 26. (2)
The Encyclopedia of Murder and Mystery, p. 40. (6)

The Encyclopedia of Mystery and Detection, pp. 27–28. (7)
100 Masters of Mystery and Detective Fiction, pp. 36–41. (37)
The Oxford Companion to Crime and Mystery Writing, p. 38. (4)
St. James Guide to Crime & Mystery Writers, 4th ed., pp. 69–70. (882d)
Twentieth-Century Crime and Mystery Writers, 1st ed., pp. 118–20. (882a)
Twentieth-Century Crime and Mystery Writers, 2nd ed., pp. 70–71. (882b)
Twentieth-Century Crime and Mystery Writers, 3rd ed., pp. 91–92. (882c)
Whodunit? A Who's Who in Crime and Mystery Writing, p. 19. (5)
Web site: http://www.stopyourekillingme. com/ earl-derr-biggers.html; http:// members.aol.com/meow103476/ biobiggers.html; http://charliechanfamily. tripod.com/thecharliechanfamilyhome / id74.html; http://members.aol.com/ meow103476/charliechan.html; http://www.charliechan.net

Biggle, Lloyd
Bio-bibliographic data:
Detecting Men, 1st ed., p. 37. (876)

Billett, Mrs. Mabel Broughton
Bio-bibliographic data:
Canadian Crime Fiction, p. 22. (209)

Billon, Pierre
Bio-bibliographic data:
Canadian Crime Fiction, p. 22. (209)

Bindloss, Harold [Edward]
Bio-bibliographic data:
Canadian Crime Fiction, pp. 246–47, 271. (209)

Bingham, John
Bio-bibliographic data:
St. James Guide to Crime & Mystery Writers, 4th ed., pp. 70–72. (882d)
Twentieth-Century Crime and Mystery Writers, 1st ed., pp. 120–23. (882a)
Twentieth-Century Crime and Mystery Writers, 2nd ed., pp. 71–72. (882b)
Twentieth-Century Crime and Mystery Writers, 3rd ed., pp. 92–94. (882c)

Binns, Otwell
Bio-bibliographic data:
Canadian Crime Fiction, p. 247. (209)

Bioy Casares, Adolfo
Bio-bibliographic data:

Latin American Mystery Writers: An A to Z Guide. (881)

Bird, Delys
Bio-bibliographic data:
Australian Crime Fiction, p. 17. (207)

Birkett, John
Bio-bibliographic data:
Detecting Men, 1st ed., p. 38. (876)

Biro, Frederick
Bio-bibliographic data:
Canadian Crime Fiction, p. 22. (209)

Bishop, Claudia. *Pseud. for* **Mary Stanton**
Bio-bibliographic data:
By a Woman's Hand, 2nd ed., p. 28. (884b)
Detecting Women, 1st ed., p. 28. (877a)
Detecting Women 2, pp. 29–30. (877b)
Detecting Women, 3rd ed., p. 34. (877c)
Web site: http://www.stopyourekillingme. com/claudia-bishop.html

Bishop, Ernest Franklin
Bio-bibliographic data:
Canadian Crime Fiction, p. 247. (209)

Bishop, Paul
Bio-bibliographic data:
Detecting Men, 1st ed., p. 38. (876)
The Mammoth Encyclopedia of Modern Crime Fiction, pp. 56–57. (1)
Web site: http://www.bookradio.com/ Bishop; http://www.stopyourekillingme. com/paul-bishop.html

Bissonnette, Jacques
Bio-bibliographic data:
Canadian Crime Fiction, p. 23. (209)

Black, Cara
Bio-bibliographic data:
Detecting Women, 3rd ed., p. 34. (877c)
Web site: http://www.stopyourekillingme. com/cara-black.html; http://www. carablack.com

Black, Gavin. *Pseud. for* **Oswald Morris Wynd**
Bio-bibliographic data:
Encyclopedia Mysteriosa, p. 27. (2)
The Encyclopedia of Murder and Mystery, p. 41. (6)
St. James Guide to Crime & Mystery Writers, 4th ed., pp. 72–73. (882d)
Twentieth-Century Crime and Mystery Writers, 1st ed., pp. 123–25. (882a)
Twentieth-Century Crime and Mystery Writers, 2nd ed., pp. 73–74. (882b)

Twentieth-Century Crime and Mystery Writers, 3rd ed., pp. 94–95. (882c)
Personal papers in Mugar Memorial Library, Boston University
Web site: http://www.stopyourekillingme. com/gavin-black.html
Black, Laura. *See* **Longrigg, Roger**
Black, Lionel. *Pseud. for* **Dudley Barker**
Bio-bibliographic data:
Encyclopedia Mysteriosa, p. 27. (2)
The Encyclopedia of Murder and Mystery, p. 41. (6)
St. James Guide to Crime & Mystery Writers, 4th ed., pp. 73–74. (882d)
Twentieth-Century Crime and Mystery Writers, 1st ed., pp. 125–27. (882a)
Twentieth-Century Crime and Mystery Writers, 2nd ed., pp. 74–75. (882b)
Twentieth-Century Crime and Mystery Writers, 3rd ed., pp. 95–96. (882c)
Web site: http://www.stopyourekillingme. com/lionel-black.html
Black, Malacai. *See* **D'Amato, Barbara**
Black, Veronica. *Pseud. for* **Maureen Peters**
Bio-bibliographic data:
By a Woman's Hand, 1st ed., pp. 32–33. (884a)
By a Woman's Hand, 2nd ed., pp. 28–29. (884b)
Detecting Women, 1st ed., p. 28. (877a)
Detecting Women 2, p. 30. (877b)
Detecting Women, 3rd ed., pp. 34–35. (877c)
Web site: http://www.stopyourekillingme. com/ veronica-black.html; http:// www.xs4all.nl/~embden11/ Engels3/black.htm
Black, William
Bio-bibliographic data:
Canadian Crime Fiction, p. 247. (209)
Blackburn, John
Bio-bibliographic data:
St. James Guide to Crime & Mystery Writers, 4th ed., pp. 75–76. (882d)
Twentieth-Century Crime and Mystery Writers, 1st ed., pp. 127–29. (882a)
Twentieth-Century Crime and Mystery Writers, 2nd ed., pp. 75–76. (882b)
Twentieth-Century Crime and Mystery Writers, 3rd ed., pp. 96–97. (882c)
Personal papers in Mugar Memorial Library, Boston University

Blackledge, Leonard. *See* **Knox, Alexander**
Blackmur, L. L. *Pseud. for* **Lydia Long**
Bio-bibliographic data:
Detecting Women, 1st ed., p. 29. (877a)
Blackstock, Charity. *Pseud. for* **Ursula Torday**
Bio-bibliographic data:
The Encyclopedia of Murder and Mystery, p. 44. (6)
St. James Guide to Crime & Mystery Writers, 4th ed., pp. 76–77. (882d)
Twentieth-Century Crime and Mystery Writers, 1st ed., pp. 129–32. (882a)
Twentieth-Century Crime and Mystery Writers, 2nd ed., pp. 76–77. (882b)
Twentieth-Century Crime and Mystery Writers, 3rd ed., pp. 97–99. (882c)
Web site: http://www.stopyourekillingme. com/charity-blackstock.html
Blackwood, Algernon
Bio-bibliographic data:
Canadian Crime Fiction, p. 247. (209)
The Encyclopedia of Murder and Mystery, p. 45. (6)
The Encyclopedia of Mystery and Detection, p. 28. (7)
St. James Guide to Crime & Mystery Writers, 4th ed., pp. 77–79. (882d)
Twentieth-Century Crime and Mystery Writers, 1st ed., pp. 132–34. (882a)
Twentieth-Century Crime and Mystery Writers, 2nd ed., pp. 77–79. (882b)
Twentieth-Century Crime and Mystery Writers, 3rd ed., pp. 99–100. (882c)
Personal papers in BBC Written Archives at Caversham, Reading in Berkshire.
Personal papers in British Library, Manuscripts Division.
Web site: http://www.stopyourekillingme. com/algernon-blackwood.html; http://www.geocities.com/Area51/ Corridor/5582/blakwood.html
Blague, Frank
Bio-bibliographic data:
Australian Crime Fiction, p. 17. (207)
Blais, Marie-Claire
Bio-bibliographic data:
Canadian Crime Fiction, pp. 23–24. (209)
Blaisdell, Anne. *See* **Linington, Elizabeth**
Blake, Margaret. *See* **Gill, B. M.**
Blake, Nicholas. *Pseud. for* **Cecil Day Lewis**
Bio-bibliographic data:

British Mystery Writers, 1920–1939, pp. 44–51. (867)

Corpus Delicti of Mystery Fiction, pp. 37–38. (879)

Critical Survey of Mystery and Detective Fiction, pp. 136–43. (41)

Encyclopedia Mysteriosa, p. 29. (2)

The Encyclopedia of Murder and Mystery, pp. 45–46. (6)

The Encyclopedia of Mystery and Detection, pp. 29–30. (7)

Mystery and Suspense Writers, pp. 51–62.(884.2)

The Oxford Companion to Crime and Mystery Writing, pp. 40–41. (4)

St. James Guide to Crime & Mystery Writers, 4th ed., pp. 79–82. (882d)

Twelve Englishmen of Mystery, pp. 142–69. (865)

Twentieth-Century Crime and Mystery Writers, 1st ed., pp. 135–39. (882a)

Twentieth-Century Crime and Mystery Writers, 2nd ed., pp. 79–82. (882b)

Twentieth-Century Crime and Mystery Writers, 3rd ed., pp. 100–103. (882c)

Whodunit? A Who's Who in Crime and Mystery Writing, pp. 19–20. (5)

Personal papers in New York Public Library.

Personal papers in State University of New York at Buffalo.

Personal papers in British Library.

Personal papers in University of Liverpool.

Web site: http://www.stopyourekillingme. com/nicholas-blake.html; http://www. kirjasto.sci.fi/nblake.htm; http://www. t wbooks.co.uk/authors.blaken.html

Blake, Norman. *Joint pseud. for* **Robert Kay Gordon and Heber Carss Jamieson (q.q.v.)**
Bio-bibliographic data:
Canadian Crime Fiction, p. 24. (209)

Blake, Terry
Bio-bibliographic data:
Australian Crime Fiction, pp. 17–18. (207)

Blakeslee, Mary
Bio-bibliographic data:
Canadian Crime Fiction, p. 23. (209)

Blanc, Suzanne
Bio-bibliographic data:
Detecting Women, 3rd ed., p. 35. (877c)

Twentieth-Century Crime and Mystery Writers, 1st ed., pp. 139–40. (882a)

Twentieth-Century Crime and Mystery Writers, 2nd ed., p. 82. (882b)

Blanchard, André. *See* **JAB**

Bland, Eleanor Taylor
Bio-bibliographic data:
By a Woman's Hand, 2nd ed., pp. 29–30. (884b)

Detecting Women, 1st ed., p. 29. (877a)

Detecting Women 2, p. 30. (877b)

Detecting Women, 3rd ed., p. 35. (877c)

The Mammoth Encyclopedia of Modern Crime Fiction, p. 57. (1)

Web site: http://home.earthlink.net/ ~etbland; http://www. stopyourekillingme.com/eleanor -taylor-bland.html

Blankenship, William [Douglas]
Bio-bibliographic data:
Canadian Crime Fiction, p. 247. (209)

Blatty, William Peter
Bio-bibliographic data:
Detecting Men, 1st ed., p. 38. (876)

Blechta, Rick; i.e., Richard
Bio-bibliographic data:
Canadian Crime Fiction, p. 24. (209)

Bleeck, G. C.
Bio-bibliographic data:
Australian Crime Fiction, p. 18. (207)

Bleeck, Oliver. *See* **Thomas, Ross**

Bleiler, Everett F[ranklin].
Bio-bibliographic data:
The Encyclopedia of Murder and Mystery, p. 46. (6)

Blincoe, Nicholas
Web site: twbooks.co.uk/authors/ nicholasblincoe.html
Bio-bibliographic data:
The Mammoth Encyclopedia of Modern Crime Fiction, p. 58. (1)

Bliss, J. Michael
Bio-bibliographic data:
Canadian Crime Fiction, p. 24. (209)

Bloch, Robert [Albert]
Bio-bibliographic data:
Critical Survey of Mystery and Detective Fiction, pp. 144–48. (41)

Encyclopedia Mysteriosa, p. 29. (2)

The Encyclopedia of Mystery and Detection, pp. 31–32. (7)

The Mammoth Encyclopedia of Modern Crime Fiction, pp. 58–60. (1)

100 Masters of Mystery and Detective Fiction, pp. 42–47. (37)
St. James Guide to Crime & Mystery Writers, 4th ed., pp. 82–84. (882d)
Twentieth-Century Crime and Mystery Writers, 1st ed., pp. 141–44. (882a)
Twentieth-Century Crime and Mystery Writers, 2nd ed., pp. 83–84. (882b)
Twentieth-Century Crime and Mystery Writers, 3rd ed., pp. 103–5. (882c)
Personal papers in University of Wyoming Library, Laramie.
Web site: http://www.stopyourekillingme. com/ robert-bloch.html; http:// mgpfeff.home.sprynet.com/ bloch.html

Bloch-Hansen, Peter
Bio-bibliographic data:
Canadian Crime Fiction, pp. 24–25. (209)

Blochman, Lawrence G[oldtree].
Bio-bibliographic data:
Encyclopedia Mysteriosa, pp. 29–30. (2)
The Encyclopedia of Mystery and Detection, pp. 32–33. (7)
St. James Guide to Crime & Mystery Writers, 4th ed., pp. 84–85. (882d)
Twentieth-Century Crime and Mystery Writers, 1st ed., pp. 144–146. (882a)
Twentieth-Century Crime and Mystery Writers, 2nd ed., pp. 84–85. (882b)
Twentieth-Century Crime and Mystery Writers, 3rd ed., pp. 105–6. (882c)
Personal papers in University of Wyoming Library, Laramie

Block, Barbara
Bio-bibliographic data:
Detecting Women, 1st ed., p. 29. (877a)
Detecting Women 2, p. 30. (877b)
Detecting Women, 3rd ed., p. 36. (877c)
Web site: http://www.stopyourekillingme. com/barbara-block.html

Block, Lawrence
Bio-bibliographic data:
American Hard-Boiled Crime Writers, pp. 3–10. (862)
The Big Book of Noir, pp. 323–24, 329. (24)
Canadian Crime Fiction, p. 247. (209)
Critical Survey of Mystery and Detective Fiction, pp. 149–54. (41)
Detecting Men, 1st ed., p. 39. (876)
Encyclopedia Mysteriosa, p. 30. (2)
The Encyclopedia of Murder and Mystery, p. 47. (6)

The Mammoth Encyclopedia of Modern Crime Fiction, pp. 60–63. (1)
Mystery and Suspense Writers, pp. 63–81. (884.2)
100 Masters of Mystery and Detective Fiction, pp. 48–54. (37)
The Oxford Companion to Crime and Mystery Writing, p. 41. (4)
St. James Guide to Crime & Mystery Writers, 4th ed., pp. 86–88. (882d)
Speaking of Murder, vol. II, pp. 202–10. (875b)
Twentieth-Century Crime and Mystery Writers, 1st ed., pp. 146–49. (882a)
Twentieth-Century Crime and Mystery Writers, 2nd ed., pp. 86–87. (882b)
Twentieth-Century Crime and Mystery Writers, 3rd ed., pp. 106–8. (882c)
Whodunit? A Who's Who in Crime and Mystery Writing, p. 20. (5)
Personal papers in University of Oregon, Eugene.
Web site: http://www.lawrenceblock.com; http://www.stopyourekillingme.com/ lawrence-block.html; http://www. thrillingdetective.com/trivia/block. html

Blood, Matthew. *See* **Halliday, Brett**
Blundell, Harold. *See* **Bellairs, George**
Blunt, Giles
Bio-bibliographic data:
Canadian Crime Fiction, p. 25. (209)

Board, J.
Bio-bibliographic data:
Canadian Crime Fiction, p. 25. (209)

Bodington, Nancy Hermione. *See* **Smith, Shelley**
Bodkin, Matthias M'Donnell; i.e., McDonnell
Bio-bibliographic data:
British Mystery Writers, 1860–1919, pp. 30–33. (866)
The Encyclopedia of Murder and Mystery, p. 49. (6)
The Encyclopedia of Mystery and Detection, p. 34. (7)
Twentieth-Century Crime and Mystery Writers, 1st ed., pp. 149–50. (882a)

Boenhardt, Patricia. *See* **Hart, Ellen**
Bogart, Stephen Humphrey
Bio-bibliographic data:
Detecting Men, 1st ed., p. 40. (876)

Boileau, Pierre and Thomas Narcejac
Bio-bibliographic data:

Critical Survey of Mystery and Detective Fiction, pp. 155–60. (41)
St. James Guide to Crime & Mystery Writers, 4th ed., pp. 88–89. (882d)
Twentieth-Century Crime and Mystery Writers, 2nd ed., pp. 939–40. (882b)
Twentieth-Century Crime and Mystery Writers, 3rd ed., pp. 1129–30. (882c)

Boisjolie, Charlotte
Bio-bibliographic data:
Canadian Crime Fiction, p. 25. (209)

Boisvert, Nicole-M.
Bio-bibliographic data:
Canadian Crime Fiction, p. 25. (209)

Boland, Bertram John
Bio-bibliographic data:
Twentieth-Century Crime and Mystery Writers, 1st ed., pp. 150–53. (882a)
Twentieth-Century Crime and Mystery Writers, 2nd ed., pp. 87–89. (882b)

Boland, John C.
Bio-bibliographic data:
Detecting Men, 1st ed., p. 40. (876)

Bolen, Dennis E[dward].
Bio-bibliographic data:
Canadian Crime Fiction, p. 25. (209)

Boldrewood, Rolf. *Pseud. for* Thomas Alexander Brown
Bio-bibliographic data:
Australian Crime Fiction, p. 18. (207)

Bolitho, Janie
Bio-bibliographic data:
Detecting Women, 3rd ed., p. 36. (877c)

Bolton, Melvin
Bio-bibliographic data:
Detecting Men, 1st ed., p. 40. (876)

Bond, Michael
Bio-bibliographic data:
Detecting Men, 1st ed., pp. 40–41. (876)
The Encyclopedia of Murder and Mystery, p. 51. (6)
Web site: http://www.stopyourekillingme.com/michael-bond.html

Bonenfant, Alain
Bio-bibliographic data:
Canadian Crime Fiction, p. 25. (209)

Bonfiglioli, Kyril
Bio-bibliographic data:
The Encyclopedia of Murder and Mystery, pp. 51–52. (6)
The Mammoth Encyclopedia of Modern Crime Fiction, p. 63. (1)

Bonnamy, Francis. *Pseud. for* Audrey Walz
Bio-bibliographic data:
Canadian Crime Fiction, pp. 247, 269. (209)
The Encyclopedia of Murder and Mystery, p. 52. (6)

Bonner, Hilary
Bio-bibliographic data:
The Mammoth Encyclopedia of Modern Crime Fiction, p. 64. (1)

Bonner, Margerie
Bio-bibliographic data:
Canadian Crime Fiction, p. 25. (209)

Bonnett, John and Emery. *Pseud. for* John Hubert Arthur Coulson and Felicity Winifred Carter
Bio-bibliographic data:
The Encyclopedia of Mystery and Detection, p. 39. (7)
Twentieth-Century Crime and Mystery Writers, 1st ed., pp. 153–54. (882a)
Twentieth-Century Crime and Mystery Writers, 2nd ed., pp. 89–90. (882b)
Twentieth-Century Crime and Mystery Writers, 3rd ed., pp. 108–9. (882c)

Bookluck, Laurie. *See* Adelaide, Debra

Booth, Charles G[ordon].
Bio-bibliographic data:
Canadian Crime Fiction, p. 271. (209)

Boothby, Guy [Newell]
Bio-bibliographic data:
Australian Crime Fiction, pp. 18–25. (207)
The Encyclopedia of Murder and Mystery, pp. 53–54. (6)
The Encyclopedia of Mystery and Detection, pp. 39–40. (7)

Borgenicht, Miriam
Bio-bibliographic data:
Twentieth-Century Crime and Mystery Writers, 1st ed., pp. 154–55. (882a)

Borges, Jorge Luis
Bio-bibliographic data:
Critical Survey of Mystery and Detective Fiction, pp. 161–67. (41)
The Encyclopedia of Murder and Mystery, pp. 54–55. (6)
Latin American Mystery Writers: An A to Z Guide. (881)
Mystery and Suspense Writers, pp. 83–96. (884.2)
St. James Guide to Crime & Mystery Writers, 4th ed., pp. 89–91. (882d)

Twentieth-Century Crime and Mystery Writers, 1st ed., p. 1537. (882a)
Twentieth-Century Crime and Mystery Writers, 2nd ed., p. 940. (882b)
Twentieth-Century Crime and Mystery Writers, 3rd ed., p. 1130. (882c)
Personal papers in University of Virginia Library.

Borlase, James Skipp
Bio-bibliographic data:
Australian Crime Fiction, p. 25. (207)
Borneham, Ernest [William Julius]. *See* **Borneman, Ernest [William Julius]**
Bio-bibliographic data:
Canadian Crime Fiction, pp. 271–72, 282. (209)
Borthwick, J. S. *Pseud. for* **Joan Scott Creighton**
Bio-bibliographic data:
By a Woman's Hand, 1st ed., pp. 33–34. (884a)
By a Woman's Hand, 2nd ed., p. 30. (884b)
Detecting Women, 1st ed., p. 29. (877a)
Detecting Women 2, p. 31. (877b)
Detecting Women, 3rd ed., pp. 36–37. (877c)
Great Women Mystery Writers, pp. 32–35. (880)
The Mammoth Encyclopedia of Modern Crime Fiction, pp. 64–65. (1)
St. James Guide to Crime & Mystery Writers, 4th ed., pp. 91–92. (882d)
Twentieth-Century Crime and Mystery Writers, 3rd ed., p. 110. (882c)
Web site: http://www.stopyourekillingme. com/j-s-borthwick.html
Borton, Della B. *Pseud. for* **Lynette Carpenter**
Bio-bibliographic data:
By a Woman's Hand, 2nd ed., pp. 30–31. (884b)
Detecting Women, 1st ed., p. 30. (877a)
Detecting Women 2, p. 31. (877b)
Detecting Women, 3rd ed., p. 37. (877c)
Web site: http://www.stopyourekillingme. com/d-b-borton.html; http://www. dbborton.com
Bosco, María Angélica
Bio-bibliographic data:
Latin American Mystery Writers: An A to Z Guide. (881)

Boston, Charles K. *See* **Gruber, Frank**
Boswell, John
Bio-bibliographic data:
Australian Crime Fiction, p. 25. (207)
Bothuri, Alexandre de
Bio-bibliographic data:
Canadian Crime Fiction, p. 25. (209)
Bouchard, Camille
Bio-bibliographic data:
Canadian Crime Fiction, p. 25. (209)
Boucher, Anthony. *Pseud. for* **William Anthony Parker White.**
Bio-bibliographic data:
Critical Survey of Mystery and Detective Fiction, pp. 168–72. (41)
Encyclopedia Mysteriosa, pp. 35–36. (2)
The Encyclopedia of Murder and Mystery, pp. 55–56. (6)
The Encyclopedia of Mystery and Detection, pp. 42–43. (7)
100 Masters of Mystery and Detective Fiction, pp. 55–60. (37)
The Oxford Companion to Crime and Mystery Writing, p. 45. (4)
St. James Guide to Crime & Mystery Writers, 4th ed., pp. 92–93. (882d)
Twentieth-Century Crime and Mystery Writers, 1st ed., pp. 155–59. (882a)
Twentieth-Century Crime and Mystery Writers, 2nd ed., pp. 90–91. (882b)
Twentieth-Century Crime and Mystery Writers, 3rd ed., pp. 110–12. (882c)
Whodunit? A Who's Who in Crime and Mystery Writing, pp. 21–22. (5)
Personal papers in Lilly Library, Indiana University.
Web site: http://www.stopyourekillingme. com/anthony-boucher.html
Boucher, Bernard [Cyril]
Bio-bibliographic data:
Australian Crime Fiction, pp. 25–26. (207)
Boucher, Denis
Bio-bibliographic data:
Canadian Crime Fiction, p. 25. (209)
Boucher, Jacqueline
Bio-bibliographic data:
Canadian Crime Fiction, p. 26. (209)
Boucher de Boucherville, [Pierre] Georges [-Prevost]
Bio-bibliographic data:
Canadian Crime Fiction, p. 26. (209)
Boulle, Pierre
Bio-bibliographic data:

Twentieth-Century Crime and Mystery Writers, 1st ed., pp. 1537–38. (882a)
Bourdon, Joseph-Alphonse. *See* **Benjamin, Pierre**
Bourgeau, Art
Bio-bibliographic data:
Detecting Men, 1st ed., p. 41. (876)
Encyclopedia Mysteriosa, p. 36. (2)
Bourne, Peter. *See* **Graeme, Bruce**
Boussard, Robert
Bio-bibliographic data:
Canadian Crime Fiction, p. 26. (209)
Bouyoucas, Pan
Bio-bibliographic data:
Canadian Crime Fiction, p. 26. (209)
Bow, Jane R.
Bio-bibliographic data:
Canadian Crime Fiction, p. 26. (209)
Bowen, Gail
Bio-bibliographic data:
By a Woman's Hand, 2nd ed., pp. 31–32. (884b)
Canadian Crime Fiction, pp. 26–27. (209)
Detecting Women 2, p. 31. (877b)
Detecting Women, 3rd ed., pp. 37–38. (877c)
The Mammoth Encyclopedia of Modern Crime Fiction, p. 65. (1)
Web site: http://www.stopyourekillingme. com/gail-bowen.html; http://www. writersunion.ca/b/bowen_g.htm
Bowen, Michael
Bio-bibliographic data:
Detecting Men, 1st ed., p. 41. (876)
Bowen, Peter
Bio-bibliographic data:
Detecting Men, 1st ed., p. 42. (876)
Web site: http://www.stopyourekillingme. com/peter-bowen.html
Bowen, Rhys. *Pseud. for* **Janet Quin-Harkin**
Bio-bibliographic data:
Detecting Women, 3rd ed., p. 38. (877c)
Web site: http://www.stopyourekillingme. com/ rhys-bowen.html; http://jqh. home.netcom.com; http://www. rhysbowen.com
Bowen-Judd, Sara Hutton
Bio-bibliographic data:
By a Woman's Hand, 1st ed., pp. 223–24. (884a)
By a Woman's Hand, 2nd ed., pp. 237–38. (884b)

Canadian Crime Fiction, pp. 27, 33, 40, 130, 236–37. (209)
Detecting Women, 1st ed., pp. 150–51. (877a)
Detecting Women 2, pp. 35–36, 38, 116, 198–200. (877b)
Encyclopedia Mysteriosa, p. 383. (2)
The Encyclopedia of Mystery and Detection, p. 535. (7)
The Encyclopedia of Mystery and Detection, p. 429. (7)
Great Women Mystery Writers, pp. 357–61. (880)
St. James Guide to Crime & Mystery Writers, 4th ed., pp. 1073–75. (882d)
Twentieth-Century Crime and Mystery Writers, 1st ed., pp. 1507–8. (882a)
Twentieth-Century Crime and Mystery Writers, 2nd ed., pp. 918–19. (882b)
Twentieth-Century Crime and Mystery Writers, 3rd ed., pp. 1104–6. (882c)
Web site: http://stopyourekillingme.com/ sara-woods.html
Bower, Lindsay Q.
Bio-bibliographic data:
Australian Crime Fiction, p. 26. (207)
Bowering, Geroge
Bio-bibliographic data:
Canadian Crime Fiction, p. 27. (209)
Bowers, Elisabeth
Bio-bibliographic data:
Canadian Crime Fiction, p. 27. (209)
Detecting Women, 1st ed., p. 30. (877a)
Detecting Women 2, p. 31. (877b)
Detecting Women, 3rd ed., p. 38. (877c)
Great Women Mystery Writers, pp. 35–36. (880)
Web site: http://www.stopyourekillingme. com/elisabeth-bowers.html
Bowles, Colin. *See* **Falconer, Colin**
Bowser, Jim. *See* **Carter, Nick**
Box, Edgar. *Pseud. for* **Gore Vidal**
Bio-bibliographic data:
Critical Survey of Mystery and Detective Fiction, pp. 173–78. (41)
Detecting Men, 1st ed., p. 42. (876)
Encyclopedia Mysteriosa, pp. 36–37. (2)
The Encyclopedia of Murder and Mystery, p. 56. (6)
The Encyclopedia of Mystery and Detection, pp. 43–44. (7)
St. James Guide to Crime & Mystery Writers, 4th ed., pp. 93–95. (882d)

Twentieth-Century Crime and Mystery Writers, 1st ed., pp. 159–61. (882a)
Twentieth-Century Crime and Mystery Writers, 2nd ed., pp. 91–93. (882b)
Twentieth-Century Crime and Mystery Writers, 3rd ed., pp. 112–13. (882c)
Personal papers in University of Wisconsin, Madison.
Web site: http://www.stopyourekillingme. com/edgar-box.html; http://www.pitt. edu/~kloman/vidalindex.html

Boyarsky, Andrew
Bio-bibliographic data:
Canadian Crime Fiction, p. 28. (209)

Boyd, Aubrey
Bio-bibliographic data:
Canadian Crime Fiction, p. 247. (209)

Boyd, Hamish
Bio-bibliographic data:
Canadian Crime Fiction, p. 248. (209)

Boyer, Rick
Bio-bibliographic data:
Detecting Men, 1st ed., p. 42. (876)
The Encyclopedia of Murder and Mystery, pp. 56–57. (6)
St. James Guide to Crime & Mystery Writers, 4th ed., pp. 95–97. (882d)
Twentieth-Century Crime and Mystery Writers, 3rd ed., pp. 113–15. (882c)
Web site: http://www.stopyourekillingme. com/rick-boyer.html; http://www3. wcu.edu/~boyer

Boylan, Eleanor
Bio-bibliographic data:
By a Woman's Hand, 1st ed., pp. 34–35. (884a)
By a Woman's Hand, 2nd ed., p. 32. (884b)
Detecting Women, 1st ed., p. 30. (877a)
Detecting Women 2, p. 32. (877b)
Detecting Women, 3rd ed., pp. 38–39. (877c)
Web site: http://www.stopyourekillingme. com/eleanor-boylan.html

Boyle, Gerry
Bio-bibliographic data:
Detecting Men, 1st ed., p. 43. (876)
Web site: http://www.stopyourekillingme. com/gerry.boyle.html

Boyle, Jack
Bio-bibliographic data:
Canadian Crime Fiction, p. 28. (209)
Twentieth-Century Crime and Mystery Writers, 1st ed., p. 162. (882a)

Boyle, John B.
Bio-bibliographic data:
Canadian Crime Fiction, p. 28. (209)

Boyle, [Emily] Joyce
Bio-bibliographic data:
Canadian Crime Fiction, p. 28. (209)

Boyle, Kay
Bio-bibliographic data:
The Encyclopedia of Murder and Mystery, p. 57. (6)

Brackett, Leigh
Bio-bibliographic data:
St. James Guide to Crime & Mystery Writers, 4th ed., pp. 97–98. (882d)
Twentieth-Century Crime and Mystery Writers, 2nd ed., pp. 93–94. (882b)
Twentieth-Century Crime and Mystery Writers, 3rd ed., pp. 115–16. (882c)
Web site: http://www.thrillingdetective. com/trivia/brackett.html
Personal papers in Special Collections, Eastern New Mexico University Library, Portales.

Bradberry, James
Bio-bibliographic data:
Detecting Men, 1st ed., p. 43. (876)

Bradbury, Ray [Douglas]
Bio-bibliographic data:
The Encyclopedia of Murder and Mystery, p. 57. (6)
Twentieth-Century Crime and Mystery Writers, 1st ed., pp. 162–65. (882a)
Web site: http://www.raybradbury.com

Braddon, Mary Elizabeth [Maxwell]
Bio-bibliographic data:
British Mystery Writers, 1860–1919, pp. 34–44. (866)
Critical Survey of Mystery and Detective Fiction, pp. 179–85. (41)
The Encyclopedia of Murder and Mystery, pp. 57–58. (6)
The Encyclopedia of Mystery and Detection, p. 44. (7)
Great Women Mystery Writers, pp. 37–40. (880)
The Oxford Companion to Crime and Mystery Writing, pp. 45–46. (4)
St. James Guide to Crime & Mystery Writers, 4th ed., pp. 98–99. (882d)
Twentieth-Century Crime and Mystery Writers, 1st ed., p. 1525. (882a)
Twentieth-Century Crime and Mystery Writers, 2nd ed., p. 931. (882b)

*Twentieth-Century Crime and Mystery
  Writers,* 3rd ed., p. 1121. (882c)
*Whodunit? A Who's Who in Crime and
  Mystery Writing,* p. 22. (5)
Braddon, Russell [Reading]
Bio-bibliographic data:
Australian Crime Fiction, pp. 26–27.
  (207)
Bradley, Charles
Bio-bibliographic data:
Australian Crime Fiction, p. 27. (207)
Bradley, J. J. G. *See* **Borlase, James Skipp**
Bradley, Lynn
Bio-bibliographic data:
Detecting Women, 1st ed., p. 30. (877a)
Detecting Women 2, p. 32. (877b)
Bradley, Michael [Anderson]
Bio-bibliographic data:
Canadian Crime Fiction, p. 28. (209)
Brady, John
Bio-bibliographic data:
Canadian Crime Fiction, pp. 28–29. (209)
Detecting Men, 1st ed., p. 43. (876)
*The Mammoth Encyclopedia of Modern
  Crime Fiction,* pp. 65–66. (1)
Web site: http://www.stopyourekillingme.
  com/john.brady.html
Brady, Tess [Mariwyn Nelson]
Bio-bibliographic data:
Australian Crime Fiction, p. 27. (207)
Brahms, Caryl. *Pseud. for* **Doris Caroline
  Abrahams**
Bio-bibliographic data:
*Twentieth-Century Crime and Mystery
  Writers,* 1st ed., pp. 165–68. (882a)
*Twentieth-Century Crime and Mystery
  Writers,* 2nd ed., pp. 94–95. (882b)
Brainard, Dulcy
Bio-bibliographic data:
Speaking of Murder, vol. II, pp. 233–38.
  (875b)
Braithwaite, Lawrence
Bio-bibliographic data:
Canadian Crime Fiction, p. 29. (209)
Braithwaite, Max
Bio-bibliographic data:
Canadian Crime Fiction, pp. 29–30. (209)
Braley, Malcolm
The Big Book of Noir, p. 184. (24)
Bramah, Ernest. *Pseud. for* **Ernest
  Bramah Smith**
Bio-bibliographic data:
British Mystery Writers, 1860–1919, pp.
  45–50. (866)

*Critical Survey of Mystery and Detective
  Fiction,* pp. 186–91. (41)
Encyclopedia Mysteriosa, p. 37. (2)
The Encyclopedia of Murder and Mystery,
  p. 59. (6)
*The Encyclopedia of Mystery and
  Detection,* p. 44. (7)
*The Oxford Companion to Crime and
  Mystery Writing,* p. 46. (4)
*St. James Guide to Crime & Mystery
  Writers,* 4th ed., pp. 99–100. (882d)
*Twentieth-Century Crime and Mystery
  Writers,* 1st ed., pp. 168–70. (882a)
*Twentieth-Century Crime and Mystery
  Writers,* 2nd ed., pp. 96–97. (882b)
*Twentieth-Century Crime and Mystery
  Writers,* 3rd ed., pp. 116–17. (882c)
*Whodunit? A Who's Who in Crime and
  Mystery Writing,* p. 22. (5)
Personal papers held in Humanities
  Research Center, University of Texas
  at Austin.
Web site: http://www.massmedia.com/
  ~mikeb/ bramah/home.html;
  http://www. ernestbramah.com
Bramlette, Paula. *See* **Yates, Margaret
  [Polk]**
Branch, Pamela
Bio-bibliographic data:
*The Encyclopedia of Mystery and
  Detection,* p. 45. (7)
*Twentieth-Century Crime and Mystery
  Writers,* 3rd ed., pp. 117–18.
Brand, Christianna. *Pseud. for* **Mary
  Christianna Lewis**
Bio-bibliographic data:
*Critical Survey of Mystery and Detective
  Fiction,* pp. 192–97. (41)
Detecting Women, 1st ed., p. 31. (877a)
Detecting Women 2, p. 32. (877b)
Encyclopedia Mysteriosa, pp. 37–38. (2)
The Encyclopedia of Murder and Mystery,
  pp. 59–60. (6)
*The Encyclopedia of Mystery and
  Detection,* p. 45. (7)
Great Women Mystery Writers, pp. 41–43.
  (880)
*100 Masters of Mystery and Detective
  Fiction,* pp. 61–66. (37)
*The Oxford Companion to Crime and
  Mystery Writing,* p. 46. (4)
*St. James Guide to Crime & Mystery
  Writers,* 4th ed., pp. 100–102. (882d)

*Twentieth-Century Crime and Mystery
  Writers,* 1st ed., pp. 170–72. (882a)
*Twentieth-Century Crime and Mystery
  Writers,* 2nd ed., pp. 97–98. (882b)
*Twentieth-Century Crime and Mystery
  Writers,* 3rd ed., pp. 118–19. (882c)
*Whodunit? A Who's Who in Crime and
  Mystery Writing,* pp. 22–23. (5)
Web site: http://www.stopyourekillingme.
  com/christianna-brand.html;
  http://www.bastulli.com/Brand/
  Brand.htm
**Brand, Max. *Pseud. for* Frederick Schiller
  Faust**
  Bio-bibliographic data:
  Canadian Crime Fiction, pp. 248, 254.
    (209)
  *The Encyclopedia of Mystery and
    Detection,* p. 146. (7)
  *Twentieth-Century Crime and Mystery
    Writers,* 1st ed., pp. 172–79. (882a)
Brandon, Jay
  Bio-bibliographic data:
  *The Mammoth Encyclopedia of Modern
    Crime Fiction,* pp. 66–67. (1)
  Web site: http://www.jaybrandon.com;
    http://www.stopyourekillingme.com/
    jay-brandon.html
Brandon, John Gordon
  Bio-bibliographic data:
  Australian Crime Fiction, pp. 27–28.
    (207)
  *Twentieth-Century Crime and Mystery
    Writers,* 1st ed., pp. 179–82. (882a)
Brandt, Tom. *See* Dewey, Thomas B.
Branson, H. C.; i.e., Henry C.
  Bio-bibliographic data:
  *The Encyclopedia of Mystery and
    Detection,* pp. 45–46. (7)
  *St. James Guide to Crime & Mystery
    Writers,* 4th ed., p. 102. (882d)
  *Twentieth-Century Crime and Mystery
    Writers,* 1st ed., pp. 182–83. (882a)
  *Twentieth-Century Crime and Mystery
    Writers,* 2nd ed., p. 98. (882b)
  *Twentieth-Century Crime and Mystery
    Writers,* 3rd ed., pp. 119–20. (882c)
Brashler, William. *See* Evers, Crabbe
Braun, Lilian Jackson
  Bio-bibliographic data:
  By a Woman's Hand, 1st ed., pp. 35–36.
    (884a)
  By a Woman's Hand, 2nd ed., pp. 32–33.
    (884b)

Canadian Crime Fiction, p. 272. (209)
Detecting Women, 1st ed., p. 31. (877a)
Detecting Women 2, pp. 32–33. (877b)
Detecting Women, 3rd ed., p. 39. (877c)
Encyclopedia Mysteriosa, p. 38. (2)
Great Women Mystery Writers, pp. 43–46.
  (880)
*The Mammoth Encyclopedia of Modern
  Crime Fiction,* pp. 67–68. (1)
*St. James Guide to Crime & Mystery
  Writers,* 4th ed., pp. 102–4. (882d)
*Twentieth-Century Crime and Mystery
  Writers,* 1st ed., pp. 183–84. (882a)
*Twentieth-Century Crime and Mystery
  Writers,* 3rd ed., pp. 120–21. (882c)
*Whodunit? A Who's Who in Crime and
  Mystery Writing,* p. 23. (5)
Women of Mystery, pp. 419–24. (874)
Web site: http://www.stopyourekillingme.
  com/lilian-jackson-braun.html; http://
  www.expage.com/page/thecatwho;
  http://www.geocities.com/Heartland/
  Estates/6371/lillian.htm; http://home.
  att.net/~RACapowski
  Fan newsletter:
    Helen McCarthy
    4 Tamarack Road
    Natick, MA 01760
Brean, Herbert
  Bio-bibliographic data:
  Encyclopedia Mysteriosa, p. 38. (2)
  The Encyclopedia of Murder and Mystery,
    p. 60. (6)
  *The Encyclopedia of Mystery and
    Detection,* p. 46. (7)
  *St. James Guide to Crime & Mystery
    Writers,* 4th ed., pp. 104–5. (882d)
  *Twentieth-Century Crime and Mystery
    Writers,* 1st ed., pp. 184–86. (882a)
  *Twentieth-Century Crime and Mystery
    Writers,* 2nd ed., pp. 99–100. (882b)
  *Twentieth-Century Crime and Mystery
    Writers,* 3rd ed., pp. 121–22. (882c)
  Personal papers in Mugar Memorial
    Library, Boston University.
Breen, Jon L[inn].
  Bio-bibliographic data:
  *Critical Survey of Mystery and Detective
    Fiction,* pp. 198–202. (41)
  Detecting Men, 1st ed., p. 44. (876)
  Encyclopedia Mysteriosa, p. 39. (2)
  The Encyclopedia of Murder and Mystery,
    pp. 61–62. (6)

*The Encyclopedia of Mystery and
    Detection*, pp. 46–47. (7)
*The Mammoth Encyclopedia of Modern
    Crime Fiction*, pp. 68–69. (1)
*St. James Guide to Crime & Mystery
    Writers*, 4th ed., pp. 105–6. (882d)
*Twentieth-Century Crime and Mystery
    Writers*, 2nd ed., pp. 100–101. (882b)
*Twentieth-Century Crime and Mystery
    Writers*, 3rd ed., pp. 122–24. (882c)
*Whodunit? A Who's Who in Crime and
    Mystery Writing*, pp. 23–24. (5)
Web site: http://www.stopyourekillingme.
    com/jon-breen.html

Brennan, Anthony
Bio-bibliographic data:
Canadian Crime Fiction, p. 30. (209)

Brennan, Carol
Bio-bibliographic data:
By a Woman's Hand, 2nd ed., pp. 33–34.
    (884b)
Detecting Women, 1st ed., p. 32. (877a)
Detecting Women 2, p. 33. (877b)
Detecting Women, 3rd ed., pp. 39–40.
    (877c)

Brennan, Joseph Payne
Bio-bibliographic data:
*The Encyclopedia of Mystery and
    Detection*, p. 47. (7)

Brennan, Noelle
Bio-bibliographic data:
Australian Crime Fiction, p. 183. (207)

Brent, Peter Ludwig. See Peters, Ludovic

Brereton, F. S.
Bio-bibliographic data:
Canadian Crime Fiction, p. 248. (209)

**Breton, William. See Gurr, David Hugh
    Courtney**

**Brett, John Michael. See Tripp, Miles
    Barton**

**Brett, Martin. See Sanderson, [Ronald]
    Douglas**

Brett, Michael
Bio-bibliographic data:
Detecting Men, 1st ed., pp. 44–45. (876)
The Encyclopedia of Murder and Mystery,
    p. 62. (6)
*Twentieth-Century Crime and Mystery
    Writers*, 2nd ed., pp. 101–2. (882b)

Brett, Simon [Anthony Lee]
Bio-bibliographic data:
*Critical Survey of Mystery and Detective
    Fiction*, pp. 203–9. (41)
Detecting Men, 1st ed., p. 45. (876)

Encyclopedia Mysteriosa, p. 39. (2)
The Encyclopedia of Murder and Mystery,
    p. 62. (6)
*The Mammoth Encyclopedia of Modern
    Crime Fiction*, pp. 69–71. (1)
Speaking of Murder, pp. 55–64. (875a)
*St. James Guide to Crime & Mystery
    Writers*, 4th ed., pp. 106–8. (882d)
Twelve Englishmen of Mystery, pp.
    302–25. (865)
*Twentieth-Century Crime and Mystery
    Writers*, 1st ed., pp. 186–87. (882a)
*Twentieth-Century Crime and Mystery
    Writers*, 2nd ed., pp. 102–3. (882b)
*Twentieth-Century Crime and Mystery
    Writers*, 3rd ed., pp. 124–26. (882c)
*Whodunit? A Who's Who in Crime and
    Mystery Writing*, p. 24. (5)
Personal papers in Mugar Memorial
    Library, Boston University.
Web site: http://www.stopyourekillingme.
    com/simon-brett.html; http://www.
    twbooks.co.uk/authors/simonbrett.
    html

Brewer, Gil
Bio-bibliographic data:
The Big Book of Noir, pp. 186–87,
    191–200. (24)
*St. James Guide to Crime & Mystery
    Writers*, 4th ed., pp. 108–9. (882d)
*Twentieth-Century Crime and Mystery
    Writers*, 1st ed., pp. 188–89. (882a)
*Twentieth-Century Crime and Mystery
    Writers*, 2nd ed., pp. 103–5. (882b)
*Twentieth-Century Crime and Mystery
    Writers*, 3rd ed., pp. 126–27. (882c)

Brewer, James D.
Bio-bibliographic data:
Detecting Men, 1st ed., p. 46. (876)

Brewer, Steve
Bio-bibliographic data:
Detecting Men, 1st ed., p. 46. (876)
Web site: http://www.stopyourekillingme.
    com/steve-brewer.html

Brickhill, Paul [Chester Jerome]
Bio-bibliographic data:
Australian Crime Fiction, p. 28. (207)

**Bridge, Ann. *Pseud. for* Lady Mary
    Dolling Saunders O'Malley**
Bio-bibliographic data:
Detecting Women 2, p. 33. (877b)
*Twentieth-Century Crime and Mystery
    Writers*, 1st ed., pp. 190–91. (882a)

Bridges, Hilda [Maggie]
Bio-bibliographic data:
Australian Crime Fiction, pp. 28–29.
(207)
Bridges, Roy; i.e., Royal
Bio-bibliographic data:
Australian Crime Fiction, p. 29. (207)
Bridges, T. C.; i.e., Thomas Charles
Bio-bibliographic data:
Canadian Crime Fiction, p. 248. (209)
Bridges, Tom. *See* **Bridges, T. C.**
Bridges, Victor
Bio-bibliographic data:
*Twentieth-Century Crime and Mystery
Writers,* 1st ed., pp. 191–93. (882a)
Brightwell, Emily. *Pseud. for* **Cheryl
Arguile**
Bio-bibliographic data:
By a Woman's Hand, 2nd ed., p. 34.
(884b)
Detecting Women, 1st ed., p. 32. (877a)
Detecting Women 2, pp. 33–34. (877b)
Detecting Women, 3rd ed., p. 40. (877c)
Web site: http://www.stopyourekillingme.
com/emily-brightwell.html; http://
www.emilybrightwell.com
Brill, Toni. *Pseud. for* **Anthony Olcott and
Martha Olcott**
Bio-bibliographic data:
Detecting Women, 1st ed., p. 32. (877a)
Detecting Women 2, p. 34. (877b)
Detecting Women, 3rd ed., p. 40. (877c)
Web site: http://www.stopyourekillingme.
com/toni-brill.html
Brillant, J. Maurice
Bio-bibliographic data:
Canadian Crime Fiction, p. 30. (209)
Briody, Thomas Gately
Bio-bibliographic data:
Detecting Men, 1st ed., p. 46. (876)
Web site: http://www.stopyourekillingme.
com/thomas-gately-briody.html;
http://www.thomasgatelybriody.html
**Brisbane-Bedwell, William LeBreton
Harvey.** *See* **Gurr, David Hugh
Courtney**
Brissenden, R. F.; i.e., Robert Francis
Bio-bibliographic data:
Australian Crime Fiction, pp. 29–30.
(207)
Bristow, Gwen
Bio-bibliographic data:
*The Encyclopedia of Mystery and
Detection*, p. 47. (7)

Brittain, William
Bio-bibliographic data:
*Twentieth-Century Crime and Mystery
Writers,* 1st ed., pp. 193–97. (882a)
*Twentieth-Century Crime and Mystery
Writers,* 2nd ed., pp. 105–6. (882b)
*Twentieth-Century Crime and Mystery
Writers,* 3rd ed., pp. 127–29. (882c)
Personal papers in University of
Wyoming, Laramie.
Brochu, Yvon
Bio-bibliographic data:
Canadian Crime Fiction, p. 30. (209)
Brock, Leon
Bio-bibliographic data:
Australian Crime Fiction, p. 30. (207)
Brock, Lynn. *Pseud. for* **Alister McAllister**
Bio-bibliographic data:
*The Encyclopedia of Mystery and
Detection*, p. 47. (7)
*Twentieth-Century Crime and Mystery
Writers,* 1st ed., pp. 197–98. (882a)
*Twentieth-Century Crime and Mystery
Writers,* 2nd ed., pp. 106–7. (882b)
Brockie, William: unidentified pseud.
Bio-bibliographic data:
Canadian Crime Fiction, p. 30. (209)
Brod, D. C.; i.e., Deborah Cobban
Bio-bibliographic data:
By a Woman's Hand, 1st ed., p. 36. (884a)
By a Woman's Hand, 2nd ed., p. 35.
(884b)
Detecting Women, 1st ed., p. 32. (877a)
Detecting Women 2, p. 34. (877b)
Detecting Women, 3rd ed., p. 41. (877c)
Web site: http://www.stopyourekillingme.
com/d-c-brod.html
Brodeur, Michel
Bio-bibliographic data:
Canadian Crime Fiction, p. 30. (209)
Brody, Marc. *Pseud. for* **W. H. [Bill]
Williams**
Bio-bibliographic data:
Australian Crime Fiction, pp. 30–32.
(207)
Bronner, Frédéric. *See* **Achard, Eugène
and Frédéric Bronner**
Bronson-Howard, George [Fitzalan]
Bio-bibliographic data:
*The Encyclopedia of Mystery and
Detection*, p. 47. (7)
Brooker, Bertram
Bio-bibliographic data:

Canadian Crime Fiction, pp. 30–31, 102.
(209)
Brookmyre, Christopher
Bio-bibliographic data:
*The Mammoth Encyclopedia of Modern
Crime Fiction*, p. 71. (1)
Web site: http://www.brookmyre.
clara.net; http://www.brookmyre.
co.uk
Brooks, Edwy Searles
Bio-bibliographic data:
Canadian Crime Fiction, pp. 272, 277–78.
(209)
*The Encyclopedia of Mystery and
Detection*, pp. 47–48. (7)
*Twentieth-Century Crime and Mystery
Writers,* 1st ed., pp. 688–91. (882a)
*Twentieth-Century Crime and Mystery
Writers,* 2nd ed., pp. 397–99. (882b)
Brooks, Janice Young. *See* **Churchill, Jill**
Brooks, Laura Francis. *See* **Ross, William
Edward Daniel**
Brouillet, Chrystine
Bio-bibliographic data:
Canadian Crime Fiction, pp. 31–32. (209)
Brouwer, Sigmund
Bio-bibliographic data:
Canadian Crime Fiction, p. 32. (209)
Brown, Carter. *Pseud. for* **Alan Geoffrey
Yates**
Bio-bibliographic data:
Australian Crime Fiction, pp. 33–44,
256–57. (207)
Canadian Crime Fiction, pp. 248, 254,
270. (209)
Encyclopedia Mysteriosa, p. 39. (2)
*The Oxford Companion to Crime and
Mystery Writing*, p. 47. (4)
*St. James Guide to Crime & Mystery
Writers*, 4th ed., pp. 109–14. (882d)
*Twentieth-Century Crime and Mystery
Writers,* 1st ed., pp. 199–205. (882a)
*Twentieth-Century Crime and Mystery
Writers,* 2nd ed., pp. 107–12. (882b)
*Twentieth-Century Crime and Mystery
Writers,* 3rd ed., pp. 129–34. (882c)
Brown, Charles Brockden
Bio-bibliographic data:
Encyclopedia Mysteriosa, pp. 39–40. (2)
The Encyclopedia of Murder and Mystery,
p. 64. (6)
*The Encyclopedia of Mystery and
Detection*, p. 48. (7)

Brown, Fredric
Bio-bibliographic data:
The Big Book of Noir, pp. 171–75. (24)
*Critical Survey of Mystery and Detective
Fiction*, pp. 210–14. (41)
Encyclopedia Mysteriosa, pp. 40–41. (2)
The Encyclopedia of Murder and Mystery,
pp. 65–66. (6)
*The Encyclopedia of Mystery and
Detection*, pp. 49–50. (7)
*The Oxford Companion to Crime and
Mystery Writing*, p. 48. (4)
*St. James Guide to Crime & Mystery
Writers*, 4th ed., pp. 114–16. (882d)
*Twentieth-Century Crime and Mystery
Writers,* 1st ed., pp. 206–8. (882a)
*Twentieth-Century Crime and Mystery
Writers,* 2nd ed., pp. 112–13. (882b)
*Twentieth-Century Crime and Mystery
Writers,* 3rd ed., pp. 134–36. (882c)
*Whodunit? A Who's Who in Crime and
Mystery Writing*, pp. 24–25. (5)
Web site: http://www.stopyourekillingme.
com/fredric-brown.html; http://www.
thrillingdetective.com/trivia/brown.ht
ml;
http://www.kirjasto.sci.fi/brown.htm
Brown, Hosanna. *Pseud. for* **Robert
Malcolm Ward Dixon**
Bio-bibliographic data:
Australian Crime Fiction, p. 44. (207)
Brown, Lizbie. *Pseud. for* **Mary Marriott**
Bio-bibliographic data:
Detecting Women 2, p. 34. (877b)
Detecting Women, 3rd ed., p. 41. (877c)
Web site: http://www.stopyourekillingme.
com/lizbie-brown.html
Brown, Molly
Bio-bibliographic data:
Detecting Women, 3rd ed., p. 41. (877c)
Web site: http://www.stopyourekillingme.
com/molly-brown.html; http://www.
okima.com/book/index.html
Brown, Morna Doris. *See* **Ferrars, E. X.**
Brown, Rita Mae
Bio-bibliographic data:
By a Woman's Hand, 1st ed., pp. 36–37.
(884a)
By a Woman's Hand, 2nd ed., pp. 35–36.
(884b)
Detecting Women, 1st ed., pp. 32–33.
(877a)
Detecting Women 2, p. 34. (877b)
Detecting Women, 3rd ed., p. 42. (877c)

Web site: http://www.stopyourekillingme.
com/rita-mae-brown.html;
http://www.ritamaebrown.com

Brown, Roderick L[angmere]. Haig. *See*
Haig-Brown, Roderick L[angmere].

Brown, Susan
Bio-bibliographic data:
Canadian Crime Fiction, pp. 32, 212.
(209)

Brown, Zenith Jones
Bio-bibliographic data:
Canadian Crime Fiction, pp. 272, 276–77.
(209)
Detecting Women 2, pp. 69, 72. (877b)
Encyclopedia Mysteriosa, pp. 123–24. (2)
The Encyclopedia of Murder and Mystery,
pp. 182–83. (6)
*The Encyclopedia of Mystery and
Detection*, pp. 153–54. (7)
Great Women Mystery Writers, pp.
108–12. (880)
*St. James Guide to Crime & Mystery
Writers*, 4th ed., pp. 368–69. (882d)
*Twentieth-Century Crime and Mystery
Writers,* 1st ed., pp. 595–98. (882a)
*Twentieth-Century Crime and Mystery
Writers*, 2nd ed., pp. 335–37. (882b)
*Twentieth-Century Crime and Mystery
Writers*, 3rd ed., pp. 388–90. (882c)
Personal papers in St. John's College
Library, Annapolis, Maryland.

Browne, Gerald A.
Bio-bibliographic data:
*Twentieth-Century Crime and Mystery
Writers*, 3rd ed., pp. 136–37. (882c)

Browne, Howard
Bio-bibliographic data:
American Hard-Boiled Crime Writers, pp.
11–18. (862)
Encyclopedia Mysteriosa, p. 41. (2)
The Encyclopedia of Murder and Mystery,
p. 66. (6)
*The Encyclopedia of Mystery and
Detection*, pp. 50–51. (7)
*St. James Guide to Crime & Mystery
Writers*, 4th ed., pp. 116–17. (882d)
*Twentieth-Century Crime and Mystery
Writers*, 2nd ed., p. 114. (882b)
*Twentieth-Century Crime and Mystery
Writers*, 3rd ed., pp. 137–38. (882c)
Personal papers in University of
Wyoming, Laramie.
Personal papers in Mugar Memorial
Library, Boston University.

Browne, Marshall Leigh
Bio-bibliographic data:
Australian Crime Fiction, p. 45. (207)
Web site: http://www.stopyourekillingme.
com/marshall-browne.html

Browne, Thomas Alexander. *See*
Boldrewood, Rolf

Browning, Sherry. *See* **Gribble, Leonard
R.**

Broxholme, John Franklin. *See* **Kyle,
Duncan**

Bruce, Leo. *Pseud. for* **Rupert
Croft-Cooke**
Bio-bibliographic data:
British Mystery Writers, 1920–1939, pp.
52–57. (867)
*Critical Survey of Mystery and Detective
Fiction*, pp. 215–22. (41)
Encyclopedia Mysteriosa, p. 41. (2)
The Encyclopedia of Murder and Mystery,
p. 67. (6)
*The Oxford Companion to Crime and
Mystery Writing*, p. 48. (4)
*St. James Guide to Crime & Mystery
Writers*, 4th ed., pp. 117–20. (882d)
*Twentieth-Century Crime and Mystery
Writers,* 1st ed., pp. 209–13. (882a)
*Twentieth-Century Crime and Mystery
Writers*, 2nd ed., pp. 114–16. (882b)
*Twentieth-Century Crime and Mystery
Writers*, 3rd ed., pp. 138–41. (882c)
Personal papers in Humanities Research
Center, University of Texas at Austin.
Web site: http://www.stopyourekillingme.
com/leo-bruce.html

Brûlé, Michel
Bio-bibliographic data:
Canadian Crime Fiction, p. 32. (209)

Brulls, Christian. *See* **Simenon, Georges**

Bruno, Anthony
Bio-bibliographic data:
Detecting Men, 1st ed., p. 47. (876)
Web site: http://www.anthony-bruno.com

Bruton, Eric
Bio-bibliographic data:
*Twentieth-Century Crime and Mystery
Writers,* 1st ed., pp. 213–14. (882a)
*Twentieth-Century Crime and Mystery
Writers*, 2nd ed., pp. 117–18. (882b)
*Twentieth-Century Crime and Mystery
Writers*, 3rd ed., pp. 141–42. (882c)

Bryan, Kate. *Pseud. for* **Ellen Recknor**
Bio-bibliographic data:
Detecting Women, 3rd ed., p. 42. (877c)

Web site: http://www.stopyourekillingme.
com/kate-bryan.html
Bryan, Michael. *See* **Moore, Brian**
**Buchan, John, 1st Baron Tweedsmuir of
Elsfield**
Bio-bibliographic data:
British Mystery Writers, 1860–1919, pp.
51–61. (866)
Canadian Crime Fiction, pp. 248, 272.
(209)
Corpus Delicti of Mystery Fiction, pp.
38–39. (879)
*Critical Survey of Mystery and Detective
Fiction*, pp. 223–30. (41)
Encyclopedia Mysteriosa, pp. 41–42. (2)
The Encyclopedia of Murder and Mystery,
pp. 67–68. (6)
*The Encyclopedia of Mystery and
Detection*, pp. 51–52. (7)
Mystery and Suspense Writers, pp.
97–111.(884.2)
*100 Masters of Mystery and Detective
Fiction*, pp. 67–74. (37)
*The Oxford Companion to Crime and
Mystery Writing*, pp. 48–49. (4)
*St. James Guide to Crime & Mystery
Writers*, 4th ed., pp. 120–23. (882d)
*Twentieth-Century Crime and Mystery
Writers,* 1st ed., pp. 214–19. (882a)
*Twentieth-Century Crime and Mystery
Writers,* 2nd ed., pp. 118–20. (882b)
*Twentieth-Century Crime and Mystery
Writers,* 3rd ed., pp. 142–45. (882c)
Personal papers in National Library of
Scotland, Edinburgh.
Personal papers in Edinburgh University
Library.
Personal papers in Douglas Library,
Queen's University, Kingston,
Ontario.
Web site: http://www.stopyourekillingme.
com/john-buchan.html
The John Buchan Society
c/o Kenneth Hillier
Greenmantle, Main Street
Kings Newton
Melbourne, Derbyshire
DE73 1BX United Kingdom
Buchanan, Edna [Rydzik]
Bio-bibliographic data:
By a Woman's Hand, 2nd ed., pp. 36–37.
(884b)
Detecting Women, 1st ed., p. 33. (877a)
Detecting Women 2, p. 35. (877b)

Detecting Women, 3rd ed., p. 42. (877c)
*The Mammoth Encyclopedia of Modern
Crime Fiction*, pp. 71–72. (1)
*St. James Guide to Crime & Mystery
Writers*, 4th ed., pp. 123–24. (882d)
Speaking of Murder, vol. II, pp. 133–39.
(875b)
Talking Murder, pp. 12–23. (883)
*Whodunit? A Who's Who in Crime and
Mystery Writing*, p. 25. (5)
Women Authors of Detective Series, pp.
119–27. (882.5)
Web site: http://www.stopyourekillingme.
com/edna-buchanan.html
Buchanan, Marie. *See* **Curzon, Clare**
Buckley, Fiona: unidentified pseud.
Bio-bibliographic data:
Detecting Women, 3rd ed., p. 43. (877c)
Web site: http://www.stopyourekillingme.
com/fiona-buckley.html
Buckley, William F[rank].
Bio-bibliographic data:
*Critical Survey of Mystery and Detective
Fiction*, pp. 231–37. (41)
Detecting Men, 1st ed., p. 47. (876)
Encyclopedia Mysteriosa, p. 42. (2)
*St. James Guide to Crime & Mystery
Writers*, 4th ed., pp. 124–26. (882d)
*Twentieth-Century Crime and Mystery
Writers,* 2nd ed., pp. 120–22. (882b)
*Twentieth-Century Crime and Mystery
Writers,* 3rd ed., pp. 145–46. (882c)
Web site: http://www.stopyourekillingme.
com/william-f-buckley.html
Buckstaff, Kathryn
Bio-bibliographic data:
Detecting Women 2, p. 35. (877b)
Detecting Women, 3rd ed., p. 43. (877c)
Bude, John. *Pseud. for* **Ernest Carpenter
Elmore**
Bio-bibliographic data:
*Twentieth-Century Crime and Mystery
Writers,* 1st ed., pp. 219–20. (882a)
*Twentieth-Century Crime and Mystery
Writers,* 2nd ed., pp. 122–23. (882b)
Buell, John [Edward]
Bio-bibliographic data:
Canadian Crime Fiction, pp. 32–33. (209)
Bueno, Lillian de la Torre. *See* **de la
Torre, Lillian**
Buffie, Margaret
Bio-bibliographic data:
Canadian Crime Fiction, p. 33. (209)

Buggé, Carole
Bio-bibliographic data:
Detecting Women, 3rd ed., p. 43. (877c)
Web site: http://www.stopyourekillingme.
com/carole-bugge.html
Bugnet, Georges. *See* **Doutremont, Henri**
Bullivant, Cecil Henry
Bio-bibliographic data:
*The Encyclopedia of Mystery and
Detection,* pp. 52–53. (7)
Bunce, Sydney [George]
Bio-bibliographic data:
Australian Crime Fiction, p. 45. (207)
Bunker, Edward
Bio-bibliographic data:
The Encyclopedia of Murder and Mystery,
pp. 68–69. (6)
*The Mammoth Encyclopedia of Modern
Crime Fiction,* pp. 72–73. (1)
Burbidge, Dighton William
Bio-bibliographic data:
Australian Crime Fiction, p. 45. (207)
Burbidge, E. R.; i.e., Enid [Ethel] Ruyton.
See **Burbidge, Dighton William**
Burden, Pat
Bio-bibliographic data:
By a Woman's Hand, 1st ed., pp. 37–38.
(884a)
By a Woman's Hand, 2nd ed., p. 37.
(884b)
Detecting Women, 1st ed., p. 33. (877a)
Detecting Women 2, p. 35. (877b)
Detecting Women, 3rd ed., p. 44. (877c)
Burdett, Charles
Bio-bibliographic data:
*The Encyclopedia of Mystery and
Detection,* p. 53. (7)
Burford, Eleanor. *See* **Holt, Victoria**
Burge, Milward Rodon Kennedy. *See*
Kennedy, Milward
Burgess, [Frank] Gelett
Bio-bibliographic data:
*The Encyclopedia of Mystery and
Detection,* pp. 53–54. (7)
*Twentieth-Century Crime and Mystery
Writers,* 1st ed., pp. 220–22. (882a)
Burke, James
Bio-bibliographic data:
Canadian Crime Fiction, p. 33. (209)
Burke, James Lee
Bio-bibliographic data:
American Hard-Boiled Crime Writers, pp.
19–30. (862)
Detecting Men, 1st ed., p. 48. (876)

Encyclopedia Mysteriosa, p. 42. (2)
The Encyclopedia of Murder and Mystery,
pp. 70–71. (6)
*The Mammoth Encyclopedia of Modern
Crime Fiction,* pp. 73–74. (1)
*St. James Guide to Crime & Mystery
Writers,* 4th ed., pp. 126–28. (882d)
*Twentieth-Century Crime and Mystery
Writers,* 3rd ed., pp. 146–48. (882c)
*Whodunit? A Who's Who in Crime and
Mystery Writing,* pp. 25–26. (5)
Web site: http://www.stopyourekillingme.
com/james-lee-burke.html;
http://www.jamesleeburke.com;
http://www.webfic.dk/jlb/jlb.asp
Burke, Jan
Bio-bibliographic data:
By a Woman's Hand, 2nd ed., pp. 37–38.
(884b)
Detecting Women, 1st ed., p. 33, (877a)
Detecting Women 2, p. 35. (877b)
Detecting Women, 3rd ed., p. 44. (877c)
*The Mammoth Encyclopedia of Modern
Crime Fiction,* pp. 74–75. (1)
Web site: http://www.janburke.com;
http://www.stopyourekillingme.com/
jan-burke.html
Burke, John
Bio-bibliographic data:
*Twentieth-Century Crime and Mystery
Writers,* 1st ed., pp. 223–27. (882a)
*Twentieth-Century Crime and Mystery
Writers,* 2nd ed., pp. 123–25. (882b)
*Twentieth-Century Crime and Mystery
Writers,* 3rd ed., pp. 148–50. (882c)
Burke, Martin
Bio-bibliographic data:
Canadian Crime Fiction, p. 33. (209)
Burke, Thomas
Bio-bibliographic data:
Encyclopedia Mysteriosa, p. 43. (2)
*The Encyclopedia of Mystery and
Detection,* p. 54. (7)
*St. James Guide to Crime & Mystery
Writers,* 4th ed., pp. 129–30. (882d)
*Twentieth-Century Crime and Mystery
Writers,* 1st ed., pp. 227–30. (882a)
*Twentieth-Century Crime and Mystery
Writers,* 2nd ed., pp. 125–27. (882b)
*Twentieth-Century Crime and Mystery
Writers,* 3rd ed., pp. 150–52. (882c)
Burkhardt, Eve
Bio-bibliographic data:
Canadian Crime Fiction, p. 248. (209)

Burkhardt, Robert Ferdinand
Bio-bibliographic data:
Canadian Crime Fiction, p. 249. (209)
Burley, W. J.; i.e., William John
Bio-bibliographic data:
Critical Survey of Mystery and Detective Fiction, pp. 238–41. (41)
Detecting Men, 1st ed., pp. 48–49. (876)
The Encyclopedia of Murder and Mystery, p. 71. (6)
The Mammoth Encyclopedia of Modern Crime Fiction, pp. 75–76. (1)
St. James Guide to Crime & Mystery Writers, 4th ed., pp. 130–132. (882d)
Twentieth-Century Crime and Mystery Writers, 1st ed., pp. 230–31. (882a)
Twentieth-Century Crime and Mystery Writers, 2nd ed., pp. 127–28. (882b)
Twentieth-Century Crime and Mystery Writers, 3rd ed., pp. 152–53. (882c)
Web site: http://www.stopyourekillingme.com/w-j-burley.html
Burnett, Virgil
Bio-bibliographic data:
Canadian Crime Fiction, pp. 4–5, 33. (209)
Burnett, W. R.; i.e., William Riley
Bio-bibliographic data:
American Hard-Boiled Crime Writers, pp. 31–47. (862)
Critical Survey of Mystery and Detective Fiction, pp. 242–48. (41)
Encyclopedia Mysteriosa, p. 43. (2)
The Encyclopedia of Murder and Mystery, p. 72. (6)
The Encyclopedia of Mystery and Detection, pp. 55–57. (7)
100 Masters of Mystery and Detective Fiction, pp. 75–82. (37)
St. James Guide to Crime & Mystery Writers, 4th ed., pp. 132–34. (882d)
Twentieth-Century Crime and Mystery Writers, 1st ed., pp. 231–34. (882a)
Twentieth-Century Crime and Mystery Writers, 2nd ed., pp. 128–29. (882b)
Twentieth-Century Crime and Mystery Writers, 3rd ed., pp. 153–55. (882c)
Personal papers in the Humanities Research Center, University of Texas at Austin.
Personal papers in the Columbia University.
Personal papers in the Firestone Library, Princeton University.

Personal papers in the Library of Congress.
Web site: http://www.miskatonic.org/rara-avis/biblio/burnett.html
Burns, Rex [*pseud.*]. Real name given variously as Rex Raoul Stephen Sehler Burns and Raoul Stephen Sehler
Bio-bibliographic data:
Colloquium on Crime, pp. 23–40. (884.1)
Critical Survey of Mystery and Detective Fiction, pp. 249–54. (41)
Detecting Men, 1st ed., p. 49. (876)
Encyclopedia Mysteriosa, p. 43. (2)
The Mammoth Encyclopedia of Modern Crime Fiction, pp. 76–77. (1)
St. James Guide to Crime & Mystery Writers, 4th ed., pp. 134–35. (882d)
Twentieth-Century Crime and Mystery Writers, 1st ed., pp. 234–35. (882a)
Twentieth-Century Crime and Mystery Writers, 2nd ed., pp. 129–30. (882b)
Twentieth-Century Crime and Mystery Writers, 3rd ed., pp. 155–56. (882c)
Web site: http://www.stopyourekillingme.com/rex-burns.html; http://rexburns.com
Burns, Ron
Bio-bibliographic data:
Detecting Men, 1st ed., p. 49. (876)
Burton, Anne. *See* **Bowen-Judd, Sara Hutton**
Burton, Miles. *See* **Street, Cecil John Charles**
Burton, Sarah. *See* **Wakefield, Hannah**
Busby, Roger
Bio-bibliographic data:
Detecting Men, 1st ed., p. 50. (876)
The Mammoth Encyclopedia of Modern Crime Fiction, pp. 77–78. (1)
St. James Guide to Crime & Mystery Writers, 4th ed., p. 135. (882d)
Twentieth-Century Crime and Mystery Writers, 1st ed., p. 236. (882a)
Twentieth-Century Crime and Mystery Writers, 2nd ed., pp. 130–31. (882b)
Twentieth-Century Crime and Mystery Writers, 3rd ed., pp. 156–57. (882c)
Web site: http://www.stopyourekillingme.com/roger-busby-html

Bush, Charlie Christopher. *See* **Bush, Christopher**
Bush, Christopher. *Pseud. for* **Charlie Christmas Bush**
Bio-bibliographic data:
Encyclopedia Mysteriosa, p. 43. (2)
The Encyclopedia of Murder and Mystery, p. 73. (6)
The Encyclopedia of Mystery and Detection, p. 57. (7)
St. James Guide to Crime & Mystery Writers, 4th ed., pp. 135–38. (882d)
Twentieth-Century Crime and Mystery Writers, 1st ed., pp. 237–40. (882a)
Twentieth-Century Crime and Mystery Writers, 3rd ed., pp. 157–59. (882c)
Bushell, Agnes
Bio-bibliographic data:
Detecting Women 2, p. 36. (877b)
Detecting Women, 3rd ed., pp. 44–45. (877c)
Butler, Ellis Parker
Bio-bibliographic data:
The Encyclopedia of Mystery and Detection, p. 57. (7)
Web site: http://www.ellisparkerbutler. info
Butler, Gwendoline
Bio-bibliographic data:
By a Woman's Hand, 1st ed., pp. 38–39. (884a)
By a Woman's Hand, 2nd ed., pp. 38–39. (884b)
Detecting Women, 1st ed., pp. 34, 99. (877a)
Detecting Women 2, pp. 36, 134–35. (877b)
Detecting Women, 3rd ed., pp. 45, 189. (877c)
Encyclopedia Mysteriosa, p. 44. (2)
The Encyclopedia of Murder and Mystery, p. 73. (6)
Great Women Mystery Writers, pp. 46–50. (880)
The Mammoth Encyclopedia of Modern Crime Fiction, pp. 78–80. (1)
St. James Guide to Crime & Mystery Writers, 4th ed., pp. 138–39. (882d)
Twentieth-Century Crime and Mystery Writers, 1st ed., pp. 240–42. (882a)
Twentieth-Century Crime and Mystery Writers, 2nd ed., pp. 131–32. (882b)
Twentieth-Century Crime and Mystery Writers, 3rd ed., pp. 159–60. (882c)

Whodunit? A Who's Who in Crime and Mystery Writing, p. 26. (5)
Women Authors of Detective Series, pp. 91–97. (882.5)
Women of Mystery, pp. 433–34. (874)
Web site: http://www.stopyourekillingme. com/gwendoline-butler.html; http:// www.twbooks.co.uk/authors/gbutler. html
Butler, Juan
Bio-bibliographic data:
Canadian Crime Fiction, p. 34. (209)
Butler, K. R.; i.e., Katherine Rosemary
Bio-bibliographic data:
Australian Crime Fiction, p. 46. (207)
Butler, Richard. *See* **Allbeury, Ted**
Butler, Walter C. *See* **Brand, Max**
Butor, Michel
Bio-bibliographic data:
Twentieth-Century Crime and Mystery Writers, 1st ed., pp. 1538–39. (882a)
Twentieth-Century Crime and Mystery Writers, 2nd ed., p. 940. (882b)
Butters, Dorothy Gilman. *See* **Gilman, Dorothy**
Butterworth, Michael
Bio-bibliographic data:
Canadian Crime Fiction, p. 273. (209)
Byfield, Barbara Ninde
Bio-bibliographic data:
Detecting Women, 3rd ed., p. 46. (877c)
Byrd, Max
Bio-bibliographic data:
Detecting Men, 1st ed., p. 50. (876)
The Encyclopedia of Murder and Mystery, p. 74. (6)
St. James Guide to Crime & Mystery Writers, 4th ed., pp. 139–41. (882d)
Twentieth-Century Crime and Mystery Writers, 3rd ed., pp. 160–61. (882c)
Byrne, David. *See* **Peterson, Gary and David Byrne**

C

Cade, Paul
Bio-bibliographic data:
Canadian Crime Fiction, p. 34. (209)
Cadieux, Pauline
Bio-bibliographic data:
Canadian Crime Fiction, p. 34. (209)
Cadwell, Dorothy
Bio-bibliographic data:
Canadian Crime Fiction, p. 34. (209)

Cahill, James
Bio-bibliographic data:
Canadian Crime Fiction, p. 34. (209)
Cail, Carol
Bio-bibliographic data:
Detecting Women 2, p. 36. (877b)
Web site: http://www.stopyourekillingme.
com/carol-cail.html
**Caillou, Alan. *Pseud. for* Alan
Lyle-Smythe**
Bio-bibliographic data:
*Twentieth-Century Crime and Mystery
Writers,* 1st ed., pp. 242–45. (882a)
*Twentieth-Century Crime and Mystery
Writers,* 2nd ed., pp. 132–34. (882b)
*Twentieth-Century Crime and Mystery
Writers,* 3rd ed., pp. 162–63. (882c)
Cain, James M[allahan].
Bio-bibliographic data:
American Hard-Boiled Crime Writers, pp.
48–69. (862)
Corpus Delicti of Mystery Fiction, pp.
39–40. (879)
*Critical Survey of Mystery and Detective
Fiction*, pp. 255–61. (41)
Encyclopedia Mysteriosa, p. 46. (2)
The Encyclopedia of Murder and Mystery,
pp. 75–76. (6)
*The Encyclopedia of Mystery and
Detection*, pp. 58–60. (7)
*100 Masters of Mystery and Detective
Fiction*, pp. 83–89. (37)
*The Oxford Companion to Crime and
Mystery Writing*, pp. 51–52. (4)
*St. James Guide to Crime & Mystery
Writers*, 4th ed., pp. 143–44. (882d)
*Twentieth-Century Crime and Mystery
Writers,* 1st ed., pp. 245–47. (882a)
*Twentieth-Century Crime and Mystery
Writers,* 2nd ed., pp. 134–35. (882b)
*Twentieth-Century Crime and Mystery
Writers,* 3rd ed., pp. 163–65. (882c)
*Whodunit? A Who's Who in Crime and
Mystery Writing*, pp. 27–28. (5)
Personal papers in the Library of
Congress.
Personal papers in the New York Public
Library.
Personal papers in the Firestone Library,
Princeton University.
Web site: http://www.stopyourekillingme.
com/james-m-cain.html; http://www.
eskimo.com/~noir/btitles/cain/index.

shtml; http://www.miskatonic.org/
rara-avis/biblio/jmcain.html
**Cain, Paul. *Pseud. for* George Carroll
Sims; occasionally misidentified as the
pseud. for Peter Ruric**
Bio-bibliographic data:
The Encyclopedia of Murder and Mystery,
pp. 76–77. (6)
*St. James Guide to Crime & Mystery
Writers*, 4th ed., pp. 144–45. (882d)
*Twentieth-Century Crime and Mystery
Writers,* 2nd ed., pp. 135–36. (882b)
*Twentieth-Century Crime and Mystery
Writers,* 3rd ed., pp. 165–66. (882c)
Web site: http://www.stopyourekillingme.
com/paul-cain.html
**Caine, Hamilton. *Pseud. for* Stephen (Lee)
Smoke**
Bio-bibliographic data:
Detecting Men, 1st ed., p. 51. (876)
Caird, Janet
Bio-bibliographic data:
*Twentieth-Century Crime and Mystery
Writers,* 1st ed., pp. 248–49. (882a)
Personal papers in Mugar Memorial
Library, Boston University
Cairncross, C. J.
Bio-bibliographic data:
Australian Crime Fiction, p. 47. (207)
Callaghan, Morley [Edward]
Bio-bibliographic data:
Canadian Crime Fiction, pp. 34–35. (209)
Callahan, Rod
Bio-bibliographic data:
Australian Crime Fiction, p. 47. (207)
Calloway, Kate
Bio-bibliographic data:
Detecting Women, 3rd ed., pp. 46–47.
(877c)
Web site: http://www.stopyourekillingme.
com/kate-calloway.html
**Cambridge, Ada. *Pseud. for* Ada
Cambridge Cross**
Bio-bibliographic data:
Australian Crime Fiction, p. 47. (207)
Cameron, Donald [Allan]
Bio-bibliographic data:
Canadian Crime Fiction, pp. 35–36. (209)
Cameron, Lou
Bio-bibliographic data:
Canadian Crime Fiction, pp. 249, 254.
(209)

Cameron, Miranda. *See* Kahnykevych, Tania Maria

Cameron, Silver Donald. *See* Cameron, Donald [Allan]

Cameron, Scott. *See* Coreman, Jay S.

Cameron, Vicki; i.e., Victoria
Bio-bibliographic data:
Canadian Crime Fiction, p. 36. (209)

Campbell, Arthur
Bio-bibliographic data:
Canadian Crime Fiction, p. 36. (209)

Campbell, D[onald]. Frederick
Bio-bibliographic data:
Canadian Crime Fiction, p. 118. (209)

Campbell, Gabrielle Margaret Vere. *See* Shearing, Joseph

Campbell, Harlen
Bio-bibliographic data:
Detecting Men, 1st ed., p. 51. (876)

Campbell, R. W.; i.e., Reginald Wilfred
Bio-bibliographic data:
Canadian Crime Fiction, p. 249. (209)

Campbell, Robert [Wright]
Bio-bibliographic data:
Detecting Men, 1st ed., pp. 51–52. (876)
Encyclopedia Mysteriosa, p. 47. (2)
The Mammoth Encyclopedia of Modern Crime Fiction, pp. 80–81. (1)
St. James Guide to Crime & Mystery Writers, 4th ed., pp. 146–47. (882d)
Twentieth-Century Crime and Mystery Writers, 3rd ed., pp. 166–67. (882c)
Web site: http://www.stopyourekillingme. com/robert-campbell.html; http://www.hycyber.com/MYST/ campbell_robert.html

Campbell, Ronald [Grayson]
Bio-bibliographic data:
Australian Crime Fiction, p. 47. (207)

Campbell, William [Archibald]
Bio-bibliographic data:
Canadian Crime Fiction, p. 36. (209)

Canaday, John. *See* Head, Matthew

Candy, Edward. *Pseud. for* Barbara Alison Neville
Bio-bibliographic data:
Twentieth-Century Crime and Mystery Writers, 1st ed., pp. 249–50. (882a)

Cannan, Joanna
Bio-bibliographic data:
Twentieth-Century Crime and Mystery Writers, 1st ed., pp. 250–52. (882a)
Twentieth-Century Crime and Mystery Writers, 2nd ed., pp. 136–37. (882b)

Twentieth-Century Crime and Mystery Writers, 3rd ed., pp. 167–68. (882c)

Cannell, Dorothy [Reddish]
Bio-bibliographic data:
By a Woman's Hand, 1st ed., pp. 40–41. (884a)
By a Woman's Hand, 2nd ed., p. 40. (884b)
Deadly Women, pp. 57–59. (26.5)
Detecting Women, 1st ed., p. 34. (877a)
Detecting Women 2, p. 37. (877b)
Detecting Women, 3rd ed., p. 47. (877c)
Encyclopedia Mysteriosa, p. 48. (2)
The Mammoth Encyclopedia of Modern Crime Fiction, pp. 81–82. (1)
St. James Guide to Crime & Mystery Writers, 4th ed., pp. 147–48. (882d)
Web site: http://www.stopyourekillingme. com/dorothy-cannell.html

Cannell, Stephen J.; i.e., Joseph
Bio-bibliographic data:
Encyclopedia Mysteriosa, p. 48. (2)
The Mammoth Encyclopedia of Modern Crime Fiction, pp. 82–83. (1)
Web site: http://www.cannell.com; http://www.stopyourekillingme.com/ stephen-j-cannell.html; http:// thrillingdetective.com/trivia/sjc.html

Canning, Victor
Bio-bibliographic data:
Encyclopedia Mysteriosa, pp. 48–49. (2)
The Encyclopedia of Murder and Mystery, pp. 79–80. (6)
The Encyclopedia of Mystery and Detection, pp. 61–62. (7)
St. James Guide to Crime & Mystery Writers, 4th ed., pp. 148–50. (882d)
Twentieth-Century Crime and Mystery Writers, 1st ed., pp. 252–55. (882a)
Twentieth-Century Crime and Mystery Writers, 2nd ed., pp. 137–39. (882b)
Twentieth-Century Crime and Mystery Writers, 3rd ed., pp. 168–69. (882c)
Web site: http://www.xs4all.nl/ ~embden11/Engels3/canning.htm

Cannon, Curt. *See* Hunter, Evan

Cannon, Taffy; i.e., Eileen E. Cannon
Bio-bibliographic data:
Detecting Women, 1st ed., p. 35. (877a)
Detecting Women 2, p. 37. (877b)
Detecting Women, 3rd ed., p. 47. (877c)
Web site: http://www.stopyourekillingme. com/taffy-cannon.html; http://www. taffycannon.com

Cantin, Roger
Bio-bibliographic data:
Canadian Crime Fiction, p. 36. (209)
Caparrós, Martín
Bio-bibliographic data:
Latin American Mystery Writers: An A to Z Guide. (881)
Capistran, Michel
Bio-bibliographic data:
Canadian Crime Fiction, p. 36. (209)
Capote, Truman
Bio-bibliographic data:
The Encyclopedia of Murder and Mystery, p. 81. (6)
Personal papers at the New York Public Library.
Web site: http://www.levity.com/corduroy/capote.htm; http://www.ansoniadesign.com/capote; http://www.kirjasto.sci.fi/capote.htm
Cardwell, Ann. *See* **Powley, Jean [Makins]**
Carette, Marcel
Bio-bibliographic data:
Canadian Crime Fiction, p. 37. (209)
Carew, Jack. *See* **Walsh, J. M.**
Carey, Douglas
Bio-bibliographic data:
Canadian Crime Fiction, p. 37. (209)
Carin, Michael
Bio-bibliographic data:
Canadian Crime Fiction, p. 37. (209)
Carleton, Cousin May. *See* **Fleming, Mrs. May Agnes [Early]**
Carleton, Hal
Bio-bibliographic data:
Australian Crime Fiction, p. 48. (207)
Carleton, S. *See* **Jones, Susan Carleton [Morrow]**
Carlon, Patricia [Bernadette]
Bio-bibliographic data:
Australian Crime Fiction, pp. 48–49. (207)
Whodunit? A Who's Who in Crime and Mystery Writing, p. 28. (5)
Carlshon, John
Bio-bibliographic data:
Australian Crime Fiction, p. 49. (207)
Carlson, P. M.: name used by Patricia McElroy Carlson
Bio-bibliographic data:
By a Woman's Hand, 1st ed., pp. 41–42. (884a)
By a Woman's Hand, 2nd ed., p. 41. (884b)

Detecting Women, 1st ed., p. 35. (877a)
Detecting Women 2, p. 37. (877b)
Detecting Women, 3rd ed., pp. 47–48. (877c)
Encyclopedia Mysteriosa, p. 50. (2)
Great Women Mystery Writers, pp. 51–53. (880)
The Mammoth Encyclopedia of Modern Crime Fiction, pp. 83–84 (1)
St. James Guide to Crime & Mystery Writers, 4th ed., pp. 150–52. (882d)
Web site: http://www.stopyourekillingme.com/p-m-carlson.html; http://www.booksnbytes.com/authors/carlson_pm.html
Carmichael, Claire. *See* **McNab, Claire**
Carmichael, Harry. *See* **Ognall, Leopold Horace**
Carnac, Carol. *Pseud. for* **Edith Caroline Rivett-Carnac**
Bio-bibliographic data:
Encyclopedia Mysteriosa, p. 209. (2)
The Encyclopedia of Mystery and Detection, pp. 251–52. (7)
St. James Guide to Crime & Mystery Writers, 4th ed., pp. 153–55. (882d)
Twentieth-Century Crime and Mystery Writers, 1st ed., pp. 259–61. (882a)
Twentieth-Century Crime and Mystery Writers, 2nd ed., pp. 140–42. (882b)
Twentieth-Century Crime and Mystery Writers, 3rd ed., pp. 172–73. (882c)
Web site: http://www.xs4all.nl/~embden11/Engels/lorac.htm
Caron, J. R.
Bio-bibliographic data:
Canadian Crime Fiction, p. 37. (209)
Caron, Roger
Bio-bibliographic data:
Canadian Crime Fiction, pp. 37–38. (209)
Carpenter, Chris. *See* **Daniel, David, and Chris Carpenter**
Carpenter, David [C.]
Bio-bibliographic data:
Canadian Crime Fiction, p. 38. (209)
Carpenter, Lynette. *See* **Borton, D. B.**
Carr, A. H. Z. *Pseud. for* **Albert Z. Carr**
Bio-bibliographic data:
The Encyclopedia of Murder and Mystery, p. 82. (6)
The Encyclopedia of Mystery and Detection, p. 62. (7)
Twentieth-Century Crime and Mystery Writers, 1st ed., pp. 262–63. (882a)

Carr, Caleb
Bio-bibliographic data:
The Encyclopedia of Murder and Mystery, p. 82. (6)
The Mammoth Encyclopedia of Modern Crime Fiction, p. 84. (1)
Web site: http://www.stopyourekillingme. com/caleb-carr.html; http://www.bdd. com/features/calebcarr/carr/frame.htm l

Carr, Glyn. *Pseud. for* Frank Showell Styles
Bio-bibliographic data:
St. James Guide to Crime & Mystery Writers, 4th ed., pp. 155–57. (882d)
Twentieth-Century Crime and Mystery Writers, 1st ed., pp. 263–67. (882a)
Twentieth-Century Crime and Mystery Writers, 2nd ed., pp. 142–44. (882b)
Twentieth-Century Crime and Mystery Writers, 3rd ed., pp. 173–75. (882c)

Carr, John Dickson
Bio-bibliographic data:
Corpus Delicti of Mystery Fiction, pp. 40–44. (879)
Critical Survey of Mystery and Detective Fiction, pp. 267–74. (41)
Encyclopedia Mysteriosa, p. 50–51. (2)
The Encyclopedia of Murder and Mystery, pp. 82–83. (6)
The Encyclopedia of Mystery and Detection, pp. 62–64. (7)
Mystery and Suspense Writers, pp. 113–29. (884.2)
100 Masters of Mystery and Detective Fiction, pp. 90–97. (37)
The Oxford Companion to Crime and Mystery Writing, pp. 56–57. (4)
St. James Guide to Crime & Mystery Writers, 4th ed., pp. 157–60. (882d)
Twentieth-Century Crime and Mystery Writers, 1st ed., pp. 267–72. (882a)
Twentieth-Century Crime and Mystery Writers, 2nd ed., pp. 144–46. (882b)
Twentieth-Century Crime and Mystery Writers, 3rd ed., pp. 175–78. (882c)
Whodunit? A Who's Who in Crime and Mystery Writing, pp. 28–29. (5)
Web site: http://www.stopyourekillingme. com/ john-dickson-carr.html; http:// www.jdcarr.com; http://www.scifi. demon.co.uk/carr.htm; http:// members.aol.com/_ht_a/grobius/

carr.htm; http:// www.twbooks.co.uk/ authors/jdcarr.html

Carr, Joylon. *See* Peters, Ellis
Carr, Margaret
Bio-bibliographic data:
Twentieth-Century Crime and Mystery Writers, 1st ed., pp. 272–73. (882a)

Carrier, Roch
Bio-bibliographic data:
Canadian Crime Fiction, pp. 38–39. (209)

Carroll, John Richard
Bio-bibliographic data:
Australian Crime Fiction, pp. 49–50. (207)

Carroll, Joy
Bio-bibliographic data:
Canadian Crime Fiction, p. 39 (209)

Carroll, Terry
Bio-bibliographic data:
Canadian Crime Fiction, p. 39. (209)

Carroll, W. J.; i.e., William Joseph
Bio-bibliographic data:
Australian Crime Fiction, p. 50. (207)

Carson, Sylvia. *See* Halliday, Brett
Carter, Ace
Bio-bibliographic data:
Australian Crime Fiction, p. 50. (207)

Carter, Alixe
Bio-bibliographic data:
Canadian Crime Fiction, p. 39. (209)

Carter, Charlotte
Bio-bibliographic data:
Detecting Women, 3rd ed., p. 48. (877c)
Web site: http://www.stopyourekillingme. com/charlotte-carter.html

Carter, Felicity Winifred. *See* Bonett, John, and Emery
Carter, John Franklin. *See* "Diplomat"
Carter, Nick (I): House name first used by John Coryell (1851–1924) for dime novels and pulp magazines but also used by such writers as Frederick Van Rensselaer Dey (q.v.). It was resurrected for a paperback series written by a variety of writers including Jim Bowser.
Critical Survey of Mystery and Detective Fiction, pp. 275–88. (41)
100 Masters of Mystery and Detective Fiction, pp. 98–110. (37)

Carter, Nick (II)
Bio-bibliographic data:
Australian Crime Fiction, p. 50. (207)

Web site: http://www.stopyourekillingme.
com/nick-carter.html
Cartier, Georges
Bio-bibliographic data:
Canadian Crime Fiction, p. 39. (209)
Carvic, Heron
Bio-bibliographic data:
*The Mammoth Encyclopedia of Modern
Crime Fiction*, pp. 84–85. (1)
*Twentieth-Century Crime and Mystery
Writers*, 1st ed., pp. 274–75. (882a)
Web site: http://www.stopyourekillingme.
com/heron-carvic.html
Case, David
Bio-bibliographic data:
Canadian Crime Fiction, p. 249. (209)
Case, Robert Ormond
Bio-bibliographic data:
Canadian Crime Fiction, p. 249. (209)
Caseleyr, Camille Auguste Marie. *See*
Danvers, Jack
Casley, Dennis
Bio-bibliographic data:
Detecting Men, 1st ed., p. 52. (876)
Caspary, Vera
Bio-bibliographic data:
*Critical Survey of Mystery and Detective
Fiction*, pp. 289–94. (41)
Encyclopedia Mysteriosa, pp. 53–54. (2)
The Encyclopedia of Murder and Mystery,
pp. 87–88. (6)
*The Encyclopedia of Mystery and
Detection*, pp. 68–70. (7)
Great Women Mystery Writers, pp. 53–56.
(880)
*100 Masters of Mystery and Detective
Fiction*, pp. 111–16. (37)
*St. James Guide to Crime & Mystery
Writers*, 4th ed., pp. 160–61. (882d)
*Twentieth-Century Crime and Mystery
Writers*, 1st ed., pp. 275–77. (882a)
*Twentieth-Century Crime and Mystery
Writers*, 2nd ed., pp. 146–48. (882b)
*Twentieth-Century Crime and Mystery
Writers*, 3rd ed., pp. 178–79. (882c)
Cassells, John. *See* **Duncan, W[illiam].
Murdoch**
Cassidy, Richard [Edward Lloyd]
Bio-bibliographic data:
Australian Crime Fiction, p. 51. (207)
Cassou, Jean-Claude Lalanne. *See*
Lalanne-Cassou, Jean-Claude
Castellani, Leonardo
Bio-bibliographic data:

*Latin American Mystery Writers: An A to
Z Guide. (881)*
Castle, Jayne. *Pseud. for* **Jayne Ann
Krentz**
Bio-bibliographic data:
Detecting Women, 3rd ed., pp. 48–49.
(877c)
Web site: http://www.krentz-quick.com
Castle, John. *Joint pseud. for* **John
William Garrod and Ronald Charles
Payne (q.q.v.)**
Bio-bibliographic data:
Canadian Crime Fiction, pp. 39–40. (209)
Castro, Brian [Albert]
Bio-bibliographic data:
Australian Crime Fiction, pp. 51, 146.
(207)
Catton, C. M.; i.e., C. Marie
Bio-bibliographic data:
Australian Crime Fiction, p. 51. (207)
Caudwell, Christopher. *See* **Sprigg, C. St.
John**
Caudwell, Sarah. *Pseud. for* **Sarah
Cockburn**
Bio-bibliographic data:
By a Woman's Hand, 1st ed., p. 42. (884a)
By a Woman's Hand, 2nd ed., pp. 41–42.
(884b)
Detecting Women, 1st ed., p. 35. (877a)
Detecting Women 2, p. 38. (877b)
Detecting Women, 3rd ed., p. 49. (877c)
Encyclopedia Mysteriosa, p. 54. (2)
The Encyclopedia of Murder and Mystery,
p. 89. (6)
Great Women Mystery Writers, pp. 56–58.
(880)
*The Mammoth Encyclopedia of Modern
Crime Fiction*, pp. 85–86. (1)
*St. James Guide to Crime & Mystery
Writers*, 4th ed., pp. 162–63. (882d)
*Twentieth-Century Crime and Mystery
Writers*, 2nd ed., p. 148. (882b)
*Twentieth-Century Crime and Mystery
Writers*, 3rd ed., pp. 179–80. (882c)
*Whodunit? A Who's Who in Crime and
Mystery Writing*, pp. 29–30. (5)
Women of Mystery, p. 434. (874)
Web site: http://www.stopyourekillingme.
com/sara-caudwell.html; http://www.
jduquette.com/authors/scaudwell.html
Caverly, Carol
Bio-bibliographic data:
Detecting Women, 3rd ed., p. 49. (877c)

Web site: http://www.stopyourekillingme.
com/carol-caverly.html; http://www.
writeawaypub.com/frogskin.html

Cavenne, Alain
Bio-bibliographic data:
Canadian Crime Fiction, p. 40. (209)

Cecil, Henry. *Pseud. for* **Henry Cecil Leon**
Bio-bibliographic data:
Canadian Crime Fiction, pp. 281–82.
(209)
Encyclopedia Mysteriosa, p. 54. (2)
The Encyclopedia of Murder and Mystery,
p. 89. (6)
*The Encyclopedia of Mystery and
Detection*, p. 70. (7)
*St. James Guide to Crime & Mystery
Writers*, 4th ed., pp. 163–64. (882d)
*Twentieth-Century Crime and Mystery
Writers,* 1st ed., pp. 277–80. (882a)
*Twentieth-Century Crime and Mystery
Writers*, 2nd ed., pp. 148–50. (882b)
*Twentieth-Century Crime and Mystery
Writers*, 3rd ed., pp. 180–82. (882c)
Personal papers at McMaster University,
Hamilton, Ontario
Web site: http://www.crimetime.co.
uk/profiles/henrycecil.html

Cercone, Karen Rose
Bio-bibliographic data:
Detecting Women, 3rd ed., pp. 49–50.
(877c)
Web site: http://www.stopyourekillingme.
com/karen-rose-cercone.html

Cederberg, Fred
Bio-bibliographic data:
Canadian Crime Fiction, p. 40. (209)

Chabrillan, [Elizabeth] Céleste [Venard] de
Bio-bibliographic data:
Australian Crime Fiction, p. 51. (207)

Chadwick, Vivienne Charlton
Bio-bibliographic data:
Canadian Crime Fiction, p. 40. (209)

Chaffer, Frederic[k?]
Bio-bibliographic data:
Australian Crime Fiction, pp. 51–52.
(207)

Challis, Mary. *See* **Bowen-Judd, Sara
Hutton**
Challis, Simon. *See* **Daniels, Philip**
Chalmers, John W.
Bio-bibliographic data:
Canadian Crime Fiction, p. 40. (209)

Chalmers, Stephen
Bio-bibliographic data:

Canadian Crime Fiction, p. 249. (209)

Chambers, Jack
Bio-bibliographic data:
Canadian Crime Fiction, p. 249. (209)

Chambers, Peter. *See* **Daniels, Philip**
Champagne, Paul M.
Bio-bibliographic data:
Canadian Crime Fiction, p. 40. (209)

Champetier, Joël
Bio-bibliographic data:
Canadian Crime Fiction, p. 40. (209)

Champion, D. L.
Bio-bibliographic data:
Australian Crime Fiction, p. 52. (207)

Champion, David
Bio-bibliographic data:
Detecting Men, 1st ed., p. 53. (876)

Champlin, Caroline [Llewellyn]. *See*
Llewelly, Caroline
Chan, Melissa. *Pseud. for* **Jocelynne
Annette Scutt**
Bio-bibliographic data:
Australian Crime Fiction, p. 52. (207)

Chance, John Newton
Bio-bibliographic data:
*Critical Survey of Mystery and Detective
Fiction*, pp. 295–302. (41)
*St. James Guide to Crime & Mystery
Writers*, 4th ed., pp. 166–68. (882d)
*Twentieth-Century Crime and Mystery
Writers,* 1st ed., pp. 280–84. (882a)
*Twentieth-Century Crime and Mystery
Writers*, 2nd ed., pp. 150–52. (882b)
*Twentieth-Century Crime and Mystery
Writers*, 3rd ed., pp. 183–86. (882c)

Chandler, Raymond [Thornton]
Bio-bibliographic data:
American Hard-Boiled Crime Writers, pp.
70–91. (862)
Canadian Crime Fiction, p. 273. (209)
Corpus Delicti of Mystery Fiction, pp.
44–46. (879)
*Critical Survey of Mystery and Detective
Fiction*, pp. 303–11. (41)
Encyclopedia Mysteriosa, pp. 57–58. (2)
The Encyclopedia of Murder and Mystery,
pp. 92–93. (6)
*The Encyclopedia of Mystery and
Detection*, pp. 77–78. (7)
Hardboiled Mystery Writers, pp. 3–83.
(870a)
Mystery and Suspense Writers, pp.
143–68.(884.2)

100 Masters of Mystery and Detective Fiction, pp. 117–26. (37)
The Oxford Companion to Crime and Mystery Writing, pp. 60–61. (4)
St. James Guide to Crime & Mystery Writers, 4th ed., pp. 168–70. (882d)
Twentieth-Century Crime and Mystery Writers, 1st ed., pp. 284–86. (882a)
Twentieth-Century Crime and Mystery Writers, 2nd ed., pp. 152–53. (882b)
Twentieth-Century Crime and Mystery Writers, 3rd ed., pp. 186–88. (882c)
Whodunit? A Who's Who in Crime and Mystery Writing, pp. 30–31. (5)
Personal papers in Department of Special Collections, University of California, Los Angeles.
Personal papers in the Bodleian Library, Oxford.
Web site: http://www.stopyourekillingme. com/raymond-chandler.html; http:// home.usit.net/~mossr; http://www. miskatonic.org/rara-avis/biblio/ chandler.html; http://www. thrillingdetective.com/trivia/chandler. html
　　Raymond Chandler Gesellschaft
　　c/o William R. Adamson
　　Heindenheimer Strasse 106
　　D89075 Germany
Chaplin, Elizabeth. *See* **McGown, Jill**
Chapman, Maurice D.
Bio-bibliographic data:
Australian Crime Fiction, pp. 52–53. (207)
Chapman, Sally
Bio-bibliographic data:
Detecting Women, 1st ed., p. 36. (877a)
Detecting Women 2, p. 38. (877b)
Detecting Women, 3rd ed., pp. 50, 115. (877c)
Web site: http://www.stopyourekillingme. com/sally-chapman.html; http://www. booksnbytes.com/authors/chapman_ sally.html
Chappell, Helen
Bio-bibliographic data:
Detecting Women, 3rd ed., p. 50. (877c)
Web site: http://www.stopyourekillingme. com/helen-chappell.html
Chaput, W. J.
Bio-bibliographic data:
Canadian Crime Fiction, p. 249. (209)

Charbonneau, Marie-Josée
Bio-bibliographic data:
Canadian Crime Fiction, p. 40. (209)
Charland, Jean-Pierre
Bio-bibliographic data:
Canadian Crime Fiction, p. 40. (209)
Charles, Hampton. *See* **Melville, James**
Charles, Kate. *Pseud. for* **Carol Chase**
Bio-bibliographic data:
By a Woman's Hand, 1st ed., pp. 42–43. (884a)
By a Woman's Hand, 2nd ed., pp. 42–43. (884b)
Detecting Women, 1st ed., p. 36. (877a)
Detecting Women 2, p. 38. (877b)
Detecting Women, 3rd ed., pp. 50–51. (877c)
The Mammoth Encyclopedia of Modern Crime Fiction, pp. 86–87. (1)
Web site: http://www.stopyourekillingme. com/kate-charles.html; http://www. twbooks.co.uk/authors/katecharles.ht ml; http://www.bastulli.com/Charles/ CHARLES.htm
Charnwood, Lord. *See* **Benson, Godfrey**
Charteris, Leslie: name change from Leslie Charles Bowyer Yin
Bio-bibliographic data:
British Mystery Writers, 1920–1939, pp. 58–67. (867)
Corpus Delicti of Mystery Fiction, pp. 46–49. (879)
Critical Survey of Mystery and Detective Fiction, pp. 312–18. (41)
The Encyclopedia of Murder and Mystery, p. 94. (6)
The Encyclopedia of Mystery and Detection, pp. 80–81. (7)
Mystery and Suspense Writers, pp. 169–80. (884.2)
100 Masters of Mystery and Detective Fiction, pp. 127–34. (37)
The Oxford Companion to Crime and Mystery Writing, pp. 62–63. (4)
St. James Guide to Crime & Mystery Writers, 4th ed., pp. 171–73. (882d)
Twentieth-Century Crime and Mystery Writers, 1st ed., pp. 286–90. (882a)
Twentieth-Century Crime and Mystery Writers, 2nd ed., pp. 153–55. (882b)
Twentieth-Century Crime and Mystery Writers, 3rd ed., pp. 188–90. (882c)
Whodunit? A Who's Who in Crime and Mystery Writing, p. 32. (5)

Personal papers in Mugar Memorial
Library, Boston University.
Web site: http://www.stopyourekillingme.
com/ leslie-charteris.html; http://
www.saint.org; http://www.
kirjasto.sci.fi/ charteri.htm
The Saint Club
c/o Ian Dickerson
Shandy St., Stepney
London E1 4ST United
Kingdom

Chartrand, Richard
Bio-bibliographic data:
Canadian Crime Fiction, p. 41. (209)

Charyn, Jerome
Bio-bibliographic data:
Detecting Men, 1st ed., p. 53. (876)
The Encyclopedia of Murder and Mystery,
p. 94. (6)
*The Mammoth Encyclopedia of Modern
Crime Fiction*, pp. 87–88. (1)
*St. James Guide to Crime & Mystery
Writers*, 4th ed., pp. 173–75. (882d)
*Twentieth-Century Crime and Mystery
Writers*, 3rd ed., pp. 190–91. (882c)
Personal papers in Fales Collection, Elmer
Holmes Bobst Library, New York
University.
Web site: http://www.twbookmark.
com/authors/63/261

Chase, Elaine Raco
Bio-bibliographic data:
Detecting Women 2, p. 39. (877b)
Detecting Women, 3rd ed., p. 51. (877c)

Chase, James Hadley. *Pseud. for* René
Brabazon Raymond
Bio-bibliographic data:
*Critical Survey of Mystery and Detective
Fiction*, pp. 319–24. (41)
Encyclopedia Mysteriosa, p. 60. (2)
The Encyclopedia of Murder and Mystery,
p. 94. (6)
*The Encyclopedia of Mystery and
Detection*, pp. 81–82. (7)
*100 Masters of Mystery and Detective
Fiction*, pp. 135–40. (37)
*The Oxford Companion to Crime and
Mystery Writing*, p. 63. (4)
*St. James Guide to Crime & Mystery
Writers*, 4th ed., pp. 175–77. (882d)
*Twentieth-Century Crime and Mystery
Writers,* 1st ed., pp. 290–93. (882a)
*Twentieth-Century Crime and Mystery
Writers*, 2nd ed., pp. 155–57. (882b)

*Twentieth-Century Crime and Mystery
Writers*, 3rd ed., pp. 191–93. (882c)
*Whodunit? A Who's Who in Crime and
Mystery Writing*, p. 32. (5)
Web site: http://www.kirjasto.sci.fi/
jhchase.htm; http://www.twbooks.co.
uk/authors/jameshadleychase.html

Chase, Nicholas. *Joint pseud. for* Anthony
Hyde and Christopher Hyde (q.q.v.)

Chastain, Thomas
Bio-bibliographic data:
Encyclopedia Mysteriosa, pp. 60–61. (2)
*The Mammoth Encyclopedia of Modern
Crime Fiction*, pp. 88–89. (1)
*St. James Guide to Crime & Mystery
Writers*, 4th ed., pp. 177–78. (882d)
*Twentieth-Century Crime and Mystery
Writers*, 2nd ed., pp. 157–58. (882b)
*Twentieth-Century Crime and Mystery
Writers*, 3rd ed., pp. 193–94. (882c)
Web site: http://www.stopyourekillingme.
com/thomas-chastain.html

Chavarie, Robert
Bio-bibliographic data:
Canadian Crime Fiction, p. 41. (209)

Chesbro, George C[lark].
Bio-bibliographic data:
Detecting Men, 1st ed., pp. 54, 69. (876)
Encyclopedia Mysteriosa, p. 61. (2)
*St. James Guide to Crime & Mystery
Writers*, 4th ed., pp. 178–79. (882d)
*Twentieth-Century Crime and Mystery
Writers*, 3rd ed., pp. 194–96. (882c)
Web site: http://www.stopyourekillingme.
com/george-c-chesbro.html; http://
www.dangerousdwarf.com

Chester, George Randolph
Bio-bibliographic data:
*The Encyclopedia of Mystery and
Detection*, p. 82. (7)

Chester, Peter. *See* Daniels, Philip

Chesterton, G. K.; i.e., Gilbert Keith
Bio-bibliographic data:
British Mystery Writers, 1860–1919, pp.
62–79. (866)
Corpus Delicti of Mystery Fiction, pp.
49–51. (879)
*Critical Survey of Mystery and Detective
Fiction*, pp. 325–32. (41)
Encyclopedia Mysteriosa, p. 62. (2)
The Encyclopedia of Murder and Mystery,
p. 95. (6)
*The Encyclopedia of Mystery and
Detection*, pp. 82–83. (7)

Mystery and Suspense Writers, pp.
181–94. (884.2)
*100 Masters of Mystery and Detective
Fiction,* pp. 141–48. (37)
*The Oxford Companion to Crime and
Mystery Writing,* pp. 63–64. (4)
*St. James Guide to Crime & Mystery
Writers,* 4th ed., pp. 180–83. (882d)
Twelve Englishmen of Mystery, pp. 64–87.
(865)
*Twentieth-Century Crime and Mystery
Writers,* 1st ed., pp. 293–99. (882a)
*Twentieth-Century Crime and Mystery
Writers,* 2nd ed., pp. 158–61. (882b)
*Twentieth-Century Crime and Mystery
Writers,* 3rd ed., pp. 196–99. (882c)
*Whodunit? A Who's Who in Crime and
Mystery Writing,* p. 33. (5)
Personal papers in Humanities Research
Center, University of Texas, Austin.
Personal papers in John Carroll University
Library, Cleveland, Ohio.
Web site: http://www.stopyourekillingme.
com/g-k-chesterton.html; http://www.
chesterton. org; http://www.
gilbertmagazine.com
    American Chesterton Society
    Dale Ahlquist, Pres.
    4117 Pebblebrook Circle
    Minneapolis, MN 55437
Chetcuti, Paul
Bio-bibliographic data:
Canadian Crime Fiction, p. 41. (209)
**Chevrette, Christiane, and Danielle
Sylvestre**
Bio-bibliographic data:
Canadian Crime Fiction, p. 41. (209)
**Cheyney, Peter; i.e., Reginald Evelyn
Peter Southouse**
Bio-bibliographic data:
*Critical Survey of Mystery and Detective
Fiction,* pp. 333–39. (41)
Encyclopedia Mysteriosa, pp. 62–63. (2)
The Encyclopedia of Murder and Mystery,
pp. 95–96. (6)
*The Encyclopedia of Mystery and
Detection,* pp. 83–84. (7)
*Twentieth-Century Crime and Mystery
Writers,* 1st ed., pp. 299–303. (882a)
*Twentieth-Century Crime and Mystery
Writers,* 2nd ed., pp. 161–63. (882b)
*Twentieth-Century Crime and Mystery
Writers,* 3rd ed., pp. 199–201. (882c)

*St. James Guide to Crime & Mystery
Writers,* 4th ed., pp. 183–85. (882d)
Web site: http://www.stopyourekillingme.
com/peter-cheyney.html; http://www.
thrillingdetective.com/trivia/cheyney.
html; http://eng-wdixon.unl.edu/
cheyney.html; http://www.xs4all.nl/
~embden11/Engels/cheyney.htm
Chicoine, René
Bio-bibliographic data:
Canadian Crime Fiction, p. 41. (209)
**Child, Charles B. *Pseud. for* C. Vernon
Frost**
Bio-bibliographic data:
*The Encyclopedia of Mystery and
Detection,* p. 84. (7)
Child, Lee
Bio-bibliographic data:
*The Mammoth Encyclopedia of Modern
Crime Fiction,* pp. 89–90. (1)
Web site: http://www.leechild.com;
http://www.stopyourekillingme.com/
lee-child.html
Child, Richard Washburn
Bio-bibliographic data:
*The Encyclopedia of Mystery and
Detection,* p. 84. (7)
Childerhose, R. J.; i.e., Robert James
Bio-bibliographic data:
Canadian Crime Fiction, p. 41. (209)
Childers, [Robert] Erskine
Bio-bibliographic data:
British Mystery Writers, 1860–1919, pp.
80–84. (866)
*Critical Survey of Mystery and Detective
Fiction,* pp. 340–44. (41)
Encyclopedia Mysteriosa, p. 63. (2)
The Encyclopedia of Murder and Mystery,
p. 96. (6)
*The Encyclopedia of Mystery and
Detection,* p. 84. (7)
*100 Masters of Mystery and Detective
Fiction,* pp. 149–53. (37)
*The Oxford Companion to Crime and
Mystery Writing,* p. 64. (4)
*Twentieth-Century Crime and Mystery
Writers,* 1st ed., pp. 303–4. (882a)
*Twentieth-Century Crime and Mystery
Writers,* 2nd ed., pp. 163–64. (882b)
*Twentieth-Century Crime and Mystery
Writers,* 3rd ed., pp. 201–2. (882c)
Personal papers in Trinity College
Library, Cambridge.

Personal papers in Trinity College
Library, Dublin.
Web site: http://209.11.144.65/
eldritchpress/rec/rs.html; http://
www.firstworldwar. com/
poetsandprose/childers.htm
Childers, James S[axon].
Bio-bibliographic data:
Canadian Crime Fiction, p. 249. (209)
Chisholm, P. F. *See* **Finney, Patricia**
Chittenden, Margaret
Bio-bibliographic data:
Detecting Women, 3rd ed., p. 52. (877c)
Web site: http://www.stopyourekillingme.
com/margaret-chittenden.html; http://
users.techline.com/megc; http://www.
mchittenden.com
Chittenden, Meg. *See* **Chittenden,
Margaret**
Choyce, Lesley
Bio-bibliographic data:
Canadian Crime Fiction, pp. 41–42. (209)
**Christie, Dame Agatha; i.e., Agatha Mary
Clarissa Miller Christie Mallowan**
Bio-bibliographic data:
British Mystery Writers, 1920–1939, pp.
68–82. (867)
Canadian Crime Fiction, p. 273. (209)
Corpus Delicti of Mystery Fiction, pp.
51–55. (879)
*Critical Survey of Mystery and Detective
Fiction*, pp. 345–53. (41)
Detecting Women, 1st ed., pp. 36–37.
(877a)
Detecting Women 2, pp. 39–40. (877b)
Encyclopedia Mysteriosa, pp. 63–65. (2)
The Encyclopedia of Murder and Mystery,
pp. 97–98. (6)
*The Encyclopedia of Mystery and
Detection*, pp. 84–88. (7)
Great Women Mystery Writers, pp. 58–66.
(880)
Mystery and Suspense Writers, pp.
195–216. (884.2)
*100 Masters of Mystery and Detective
Fiction*, pp. 154–63. (37)
*The Oxford Companion to Crime and
Mystery Writing*, pp. 68–69. (4)
*St. James Guide to Crime & Mystery
Writers*, 4th ed., pp. 185–89. (882d)
*Twentieth-Century Crime and Mystery
Writers,* 1st ed., pp. 304–10. (882a)
*Twentieth-Century Crime and Mystery
Writers*, 2nd ed., pp. 164–67. (882b)

*Twentieth-Century Crime and Mystery
Writers*, 3rd ed., pp. 202–6. (882c)
*Whodunit? A Who's Who in Crime and
Mystery Writing*, pp. 33–36. (5)
Women Authors of Detective Series, pp.
16–32. (882.5)
Women of Mystery, pp. 86–160. (874)
Web site: www.agathachristie.com;
http://www.stopyourekillingme.com/
agatha-christie.html; http://www.
nd.edu/~rwoodbur/christie/christie.
html; http://www.stmarysmead.com
Agatha Christie Society
P.O. Box 985
London, SW1X 9XA
United Kingdom
Agatha Christie Limited
40 Shaftesbury Avenue
London W1D 7ER
United Kingdom
Christmas, Joyce
Bio-bibliographic data:
By a Woman's Hand, 1st ed., pp. 43–44.
(884a)
By a Woman's Hand, 2nd ed., p. 43.
(884b)
Detecting Women, 1st ed., p. 38. (877a)
Detecting Women 2, p. 41. (877b)
Detecting Women, 3rd ed., p. 52. (877c)
Web site: http://www.stopyourekillingme.
com/ joyce-christmas.html; http://
www.writerwrite.com/authors/
joycechristmas
Christopher, Ben
Bio-bibliographic data:
Australian Crime Fiction, p. 53. (207)
Chudley, Ron; i.e., Ronald Alexander
Bio-bibliographic data:
Canadian Crime Fiction, p. 42. (209)
Churchill, Jill. *Pseud. for* **Janice Young
Brooks**
Bio-bibliographic data:
By a Woman's Hand, 1st ed., pp. 44–45.
(884a)
By a Woman's Hand, 2nd ed., p. 44.
(884b)
Detecting Women, 1st ed., p. 38. (877a)
Detecting Women 2, p. 41. (877b)
Detecting Women, 3rd ed., p. 53. (877c)
*The Mammoth Encyclopedia of Modern
Crime Fiction*, pp. 90–91. (1)
Web site: http://www.jillchurchill.com;
http://www.stopyourekillingme.com/
jill-churchill.html

Claire, Edie
Bio-bibliographic data:
Detecting Women, 3rd ed., p. 53. (877c)
Web site: http://www.stopyourekillingme.
com/edie-claire.html; http://
sleuths2die4. thewriters.com

Clancy, Tom
Bio-bibliographic data:
Detecting Men, 1st ed., p. 54. (876)
Encyclopedia Mysteriosa, p. 66. (2)
*St. James Guide to Crime & Mystery
Writers,* 4th ed., pp. 189–92. (882d)
*Twentieth-Century Crime and Mystery
Writers,* 3rd ed., pp. 206–8. (882c)
Web site: http://www.stopyourekillingme.
com/tom-clancy.html; http://www.
clancyfaq.com; http://users.cybercity.
dk/~buu2619

Clapperton, Richard
Bio-bibliographic data:
Australian Crime Fiction, p. 53. (207)

Clare, Evelyn [Kathleen]. *See* **Clare,
Lynne**

Clare, John
Bio-bibliographic data:
Canadian Crime Fiction, p. 42. (209)

Clare, Lynne: i.e., Evelyn [Kathleen]
Bio-bibliographic data:
Canadian Crime Fiction, p. 42. (209)

Clarement, Ruth. *Pseud. for* **Rosemary
Creswell and Carol Manners**
Bio-bibliographic data:
Australian Crime Fiction, p. 53. (207)

Clark, Alfred Alexander Gordon. *See*
Hare, Cyril

Clark, Carol Higgins
Bio-bibliographic data:
By a Woman's Hand, 1st ed., pp. 45–46.
(884a)
By a Woman's Hand, 2nd ed., pp. 44–45.
(884b)
Detecting Women, 1st ed., p. 38. (877a)
Detecting Women 2, p. 41. (877b)
Detecting Women, 3rd ed., p. 54. (877c)
*The Mammoth Encyclopedia of Modern
Crime Fiction,* p. 91. (1)
Women Authors of Detective Series, pp.
155–59. (882.5)
Web site: http://www.stopyourekillingme.
com/carol-higgins-clark.html;
http://www.booksnbytes.com/
authors/clark_carolhiggins.html;
http://www.twbookmark.com/
authors/54/450

Clark, Carolyn Chambers
Bio-bibliographic data:
Detecting Women, 1st ed., pp. 38–39.
(877a)
Detecting Women 2, p. 42. (877b)

Clark, Douglas [Malcolm Jackson]
Bio-bibliographic data:
Detecting Men, 1st ed., p. 55. (876)
Encyclopedia Mysteriosa, p. 66. (2)
The Encyclopedia of Murder and Mystery,
pp. 99–100. (6)
*The Mammoth Encyclopedia of Modern
Crime Fiction,* pp. 91–92. (1)
*St. James Guide to Crime & Mystery
Writers,* 4th ed., pp.192–93. (882d)
*Twentieth-Century Crime and Mystery
Writers,* 2nd ed., pp. 167–68. (882b)
*Twentieth-Century Crime and Mystery
Writers,* 3rd ed., pp. 208–10. (882c)

Clark, Joan
Bio-bibliographic data:
Canadian Crime Fiction, p. 42. (209)

Clark, Larry
Bio-bibliographic data:
Canadian Crime Fiction, pp. 42–43. (209)

Clark, Mark. *Pseud. for* **Ken Clarke**
Bio-bibliographic data:
Canadian Crime Fiction, p. 43. (209)

Clark, Mary Higgins
Bio-bibliographic data:
By a Woman's Hand, 2nd ed., p. 45.
(884b)
Deadly Women, pp. 47–54. (26.5)
Encyclopedia Mysteriosa, p. 66. (2)
The Encyclopedia of Murder and Mystery,
p. 100. (6)
Great Women Mystery Writers, pp. 66–69.
(880)
*The Mammoth Encyclopedia of Modern
Crime Fiction,* pp. 92–94. (1)
*The Oxford Companion to Crime and
Mystery Writing*, p. 73. (4)
*St. James Guide to Crime & Mystery
Writers,* 4th ed., pp. 194–95. (882d)
Speaking of Murder, pp. 15–28. (875a)
13 Mistresses of Murder, pp. 1–11. (871)
*Twentieth-Century Crime and Mystery
Writers,* 2nd ed., p. 168. (882b)
*Twentieth-Century Crime and Mystery
Writers,* 3rd ed., pp. 210–11. (882c)
*Whodunit? A Who's Who in Crime and
Mystery Writing*, pp. 34–35. (5)
Women of Mystery, pp. 374–85. (874)

Web site: http://www.simonsays.com/
MHClark; http://www.
stopyourekillingme.com/
mary-higgins-clark.html

Clarke, Anna
Bio-bibliographic data:
By a Woman's Hand, 1st ed., p. 46. (884a)
By a Woman's Hand, 2nd ed., p. 46.
(884b)
*Critical Survey of Mystery and Detective
Fiction*, pp. 354–59. (41)
Detecting Women, 1st ed., p. 39. (877a)
Detecting Women 2, p. 42. (877b)
Detecting Women, 3rd ed., p. 54. (877b)
Great Women Mystery Writers, pp. 69–71.
(880)
*The Mammoth Encyclopedia of Modern
Crime Fiction*, pp. 94–95. (1)
*St. James Guide to Crime & Mystery
Writers*, 4th ed., pp. 195–97. (882d)
*Twentieth-Century Crime and Mystery
Writers*, 1st ed., pp. 310–12. (882a)
*Twentieth-Century Crime and Mystery
Writers*, 2nd ed., pp. 169–71. (882b)
*Twentieth-Century Crime and Mystery
Writers*, 3rd ed., pp. 211–13. (882c)
Personal papers in Mugar Memorial
Library, Boston University.
Web site: http://www.stopyourekillingme.
com/anna-clarke.html; http://
members.fortunecity.com/le10/author
s/ authorsA-G/annaclarke.htm

**Clarke, Brenda Margaret Lilian
Honeyman.** *See* **Sedley, Kate**

Clarke, Jay
Bio-bibliographic data:
Canadian Crime Fiction, p. 43. (209)

Clarke, Ken. *See* **Clark, Mark**

Clarke, Marcus [Andrew Hislop]
Bio-bibliographic data:
Australian Crime Fiction, pp. 53–54.
(207)

Clarkston, Geoffrey
Bio-bibliographic data:
Canadian Crime Fiction, p. 273. (209)

Clarkson, John
Bio-bibliographic data:
Detecting Men, 1st ed., pp. 55–56. (876)

Clason, Clyde B.
Bio-bibliographic data:
*St. James Guide to Crime & Mystery
Writers*, 4th ed., pp. 197–98. (882d)
*Twentieth-Century Crime and Mystery
Writers*, 2nd ed., p. 171. (882b)

*Twentieth-Century Crime and Mystery
Writers*, 3rd ed., p. 213. (882c)

Clay, Charles
Bio-bibliographic data:
Canadian Crime Fiction, p. 43. (209)

Clay, E. Hamilton
Bio-bibliographic data:
Australian Crime Fiction, p. 54. (207)

Clayton, Mary
Bio-bibliographic data:
Detecting Women, 3rd ed., pp. 54–55.
(877c)

Clayton, Richard Henry Michael. *See*
Haggard, William

Cleary, Jon [Stephen]
Bio-bibliographic data:
Australian Crime Fiction, pp. 54–56.
(207)
*Critical Survey of Mystery and Detective
Fiction*, pp. 360–64. (41)
Detecting Men, 1st ed., p. 56. (876)
*The Mammoth Encyclopedia of Modern
Crime Fiction*, pp. 95–96. (1)
*St. James Guide to Crime & Mystery
Writers*, 4th ed., pp. 198–200. (882d)
*Twentieth-Century Crime and Mystery
Writers*, 1st ed., pp. 312–14. (882a)
*Twentieth-Century Crime and Mystery
Writers*, 2nd ed., pp. 171–73. (882b)
*Twentieth-Century Crime and Mystery
Writers*, 3rd ed., pp. 213–15. (882c)
Web site: http://www.stopyourekillingme.
com/jon-cleary.html; http://www.
kirjasto.sci.fi/jcleary.htm; http://
www.crimefactory.net/CF004–02.htm

Cleary, Melissa: unidentified pseud.
Bio-bibliographic data:
By a Woman's Hand, 1st ed., pp. 46–47.
(884a)
By a Woman's Hand, 2nd ed., pp. 46–47.
(884b)
Detecting Women, 1st ed., p. 39. (877a)
Detecting Women 2, p. 42. (877b)
Web site: http://www.stopyourekillingme.
com/melissa-cleary.html; http://www.
booksnbytes.com/authors/cleary_
melissa.html

Cleeve, Brian
Bio-bibliographic data:
Detecting Men, 1st ed., p. 56. (876)
*St. James Guide to Crime & Mystery
Writers*, 4th ed., pp. 200–201. (882d)

Twentieth-Century Crime and Mystery Writers, 1st ed., pp. 314–16. (882a)
Twentieth-Century Crime and Mystery Writers, 2nd ed., pp. 173–74. (882b)
Twentieth-Century Crime and Mystery Writers, 3rd ed., pp. 215–16. (882c)
Personal papers in Mugar Memorial Library, Boston University

Cleeves, Ann
Bio-bibliographic data:
By a Woman's Hand, 1st ed., pp. 47–48. (884a)
By a Woman's Hand, 2nd ed., p. 47. (884b)
Detecting Women, 1st ed., pp. 39–40. (877a)
Detecting Women 2, pp. 42–43. (877b)
Detecting Women, 3rd ed., pp. 55–56. (877c)
The Mammoth Encyclopedia of Modern Crime Fiction, pp. 96–97. (1)
St. James Guide to Crime & Mystery Writers, 4th ed., pp. 201–3. (882d)
Twentieth-Century Crime and Mystery Writers, 3rd ed., pp. 216–17. (882c)
Web site: http://www.twbooks.co.uk/authors/anncleaves.html; http://www.stopyourekillingme.com/ann-cleeves.html; http://www.crimetime.co.uk/profiles/anncleeves.html

Clémence: unidentified pseud.
Bio-bibliographic data:
Canadian Crime Fiction, p. 41. (209)

Clemens, Samuel Langhorne
Bio-bibliographic data:
Critical Survey of Mystery and Detective Fiction, pp. 1609–15. (41)
Encyclopedia Mysteriosa, p. 358. (2)
The Encyclopedia of Murder and Mystery, pp. 496–97. (6)
The Encyclopedia of Mystery and Detection, p. 90. (7)
Mark Twain Association
c/o Salwen Business Communications
156 5th Ave., Suite 517
New York, NY 10010
Mark Twain Home Foundation
c/o Henry H. Sweets III
208 Hill Street
Hannibal, MO 63401
Mark Twain House
c/o John V. Boyer
351 Farmington Avenue

Hartford, CT 06105
Mark Twain Research Foundation
c/o Mark Twain Birthplace
37352 Shrine Road
Stoutsville, MO 65283

Clifford, Francis. *Pseud. for* **Arthur Leonard Bell Thompson**
Bio-bibliographic data:
Twentieth-Century Crime and Mystery Writers, 1st ed., pp. 316–18. (882a)
Twentieth-Century Crime and Mystery Writers, 2nd ed., pp. 174–75. (882b)
Twentieth-Century Crime and Mystery Writers, 3rd ed., pp. 217–18. (882c)

Clinton-Baddeley, V. C.
Bio-bibliographic data:
St. James Guide to Crime & Mystery Writers, 4th ed., pp. 203–4. (882d)
Twentieth-Century Crime and Mystery Writers, 1st ed., pp. 318–20. (882a)
Twentieth-Century Crime and Mystery Writers, 2nd ed., pp. 175–76. (882b)
Twentieth-Century Crime and Mystery Writers, 3rd ed., pp. 218–19. (882c)

Clive, John
Bio-bibliographic data:
Australian Crime Fiction, p. 56. (207)

Cloutier, Eugène
Bio-bibliographic data:
Canadian Crime Fiction, p. 43. (209)

Clune, Frank; i.e., Francis Patrick
Bio-bibliographic data:
Australian Crime Fiction, pp. 56–57. (207)

Cluster, Dick
Bio-bibliographic data:
Detecting Men, 1st ed., p. 57. (876)

Clynes, Michael. *See* **Doherty, P. C.**

Cobb, G. Belton
Bio-bibliographic data:
Twentieth-Century Crime and Mystery Writers, 1st ed., pp. 320–22. (882a)

Cobb, Irvin S[hrewsbury].
Bio-bibliographic data:
The Encyclopedia of Mystery and Detection, p. 91. (7)

Cobb, Sylvanus, Jr.
Bio-bibliographic data:
The Encyclopedia of Mystery and Detection, p. 91. (7)

Coben, Harlan
Bio-bibliographic data:
Detecting Men, 1st ed., p. 57. (876)

*The Mammoth Encyclopedia of Modern
      Crime Fiction*, pp. 97–98. (1)
Web site: http://www.harlancoben.com;
      http://www.stopyourekillingme.com/
      harlan-coben.html
Coburn, Andrew
Bio-bibliographic data:
Detecting Men, 1st ed., p. 58. (876)
*St. James Guide to Crime & Mystery
      Writers,* 4th ed., pp. 204–5. (882d)
*Twentieth-Century Crime and Mystery
      Writers,* 2nd ed., pp. 176–77. (882b)
*Twentieth-Century Crime and Mystery
      Writers,* 3rd ed., p. 220. (882c)
Coburn, Laura
Bio-bibliographic data:
Detecting Women, 3rd ed., p. 56. (877c)
Cockburn, Sarah. *See* **Caudwell, Sarah**
Cocke, Emmanuel
Bio-bibliographic data:
Canadian Crime Fiction, p. 43. (209)
Cocking, Ronald
Bio-bibliographic data:
Canadian Crime Fiction, p. 43. (209)
Cody, Rev. Hiram Alfred
Bio-bibliographic data:
Canadian Crime Fiction, pp. 43–44. (209)
Cody, Liza. *Pseud. for* **Liza Nassim**
Bio-bibliographic data:
By a Woman's Hand, 1st ed., pp. 48–49.
      (884a)
By a Woman's Hand, 2nd ed., pp. 47–48.
      (884b)
Detecting Women, 1st ed., p. 40. (877a)
Detecting Women 2, p. 43. (877b)
Detecting Women, 3rd ed., pp. 56–57.
      (877c)
Encyclopedia Mysteriosa, p. 68. (2)
Great Women Mystery Writers, pp. 71–75.
      (880)
*The Mammoth Encyclopedia of Modern
      Crime Fiction,* pp. 98–99. (1)
*St. James Guide to Crime & Mystery
      Writers,* 4th ed., pp. 205–6. (882d)
Talking Murder, pp. 24–38. (883)
*Twentieth-Century Crime and Mystery
      Writers,* 3rd ed., pp. 220–21. (882c)
*Whodunit? A Who's Who in Crime and
      Mystery Writing,* p. 36. (5)
Web site: http://www.twbooks.co.uk/
      authors/lcody.html; http://www.
      stopyourekillingme.com/liza-cody.ht
      ml

Coe, Charles Francis
Bio-bibliographic data:
*The Encyclopedia of Mystery and
      Detection,* p. 92. (7)
Coe, Tucker. *See* **Westlake, Donald E.**
Coel, Margaret
Bio-bibliographic data:
Detecting Women 2, p. 43. (877b)
Detecting Women, 3rd ed., p. 57. (877c)
Web site: http://www.stopyourekillingme.
      com/margaret-coel.html
Coelho, Luiz Lopes
Bio-bibliographic data:
*Latin American Mystery Writers: An A to
      Z Guide. (881)*
Coffin, Geoffrey. *See* **Mason, F. van Wyck**
Cogan, Priscilla
Bio-bibliographic data:
Detecting Women, 3rd ed., p. 57. (877c)
Cohen, Anthea. *Pseud. for* **Doris Simpson**
Bio-bibliographic data:
Detecting Women 2, pp. 43–44. (877b)
Detecting Women, 3rd ed., pp. 57–58.
      (877c)
*St. James Guide to Crime & Mystery
      Writers,* 4th ed., pp. 206–7. (882d)
*Twentieth-Century Crime and Mystery
      Writers,* 3rd ed., pp. 222–23. (882c)
Web site: http://www.stopyourekillingme.
      com/anthea-cohen.html
Cohen, Janet. *See* **Neel, Janet**
Cohen, Martin S[amuel].
Bio-bibliographic data:
Canadian Crime Fiction, p. 44. (209)
Cohen, Matt
Bio-bibliographic data:
Canadian Crime Fiction, p. 44. (209)
Cohen, Octavus Roy
Bio-bibliographic data:
*Critical Survey of Mystery and Detective
      Fiction,* pp. 365–69. (41)
Encyclopedia Mysteriosa, pp. 68–69. (2)
The Encyclopedia of Murder and Mystery,
      p. 104. (6)
*The Encyclopedia of Mystery and
      Detection,* pp. 92–93. (7)
*St. James Guide to Crime & Mystery
      Writers,* 4th ed., pp. 208–9. (882d)
*Twentieth-Century Crime and Mystery
      Writers,* 1st ed., pp. 322–25. (882a)
*Twentieth-Century Crime and Mystery
      Writers,* 2nd ed., pp. 177–78. (882b)
*Twentieth-Century Crime and Mystery
      Writers,* 3rd ed., pp. 223–24. (882c)

Coker, Carolyn
Bio-bibliographic data:
By a Woman's Hand, 2nd ed., pp. 48–49. (884b)
Detecting Women, 1st ed., p. 40. (877a)
Detecting Women 2, p. 44. (877b)
Detecting Women, 3rd ed., p. 58. (877c)
Web site: http://www.stopyourekillingme. com/carolyn-coker.html
Colby, Lydia. *See* **W. E. D. Ross**
Colby, Robert
Bio-bibliographic data:
The Big Book of Noir, p. 189. (24)
Cole, Derek
Bio-bibliographic data:
Australian Crime Fiction, p. 57. (207)
Cole, G. D. H. and Cole, M.; i.e., Gordon Douglas Howard Cole and Margaret Isabel Postgate Cole
Bio-bibliographic data:
Critical Survey of Mystery and Detective Fiction, pp. 370–78. (41)
Encyclopedia Mysteriosa, p. 69. (2)
The Encyclopedia of Murder and Mystery, p. 104. (6)
The Encyclopedia of Mystery and Detection, p. 93. (7)
The Oxford Companion to Crime and Mystery Writing, p. 81. (4)
St. James Guide to Crime & Mystery Writers, 4th ed., pp. 209–14. (882d)
Twentieth-Century Crime and Mystery Writers, 1st ed., pp. 325–34. (882a)
Twentieth-Century Crime and Mystery Writers, 2nd ed., pp. 178–83. (882b)
Twentieth-Century Crime and Mystery Writers, 3rd ed., pp. 224–29. (882c)
Cole, Trevor
Bio-bibliographic data:
Canadian Crime Fiction, p. 45. (209)
Coleman, Evelyn
Bio-bibliographic data:
Detecting Women, 3rd ed., pp. 58–59. (877c)
Web site: http://www.stopyourekillingme. com/evelny-coleman.html
Coles, Cyril Henry. *See* **Coles, Manning**
Coles, Manning. *Pseud. for* **Cyril Henry Coles and Adelaide Francis Oke Manning**
Bio-bibliographic data:
Canadian Crime Fiction, p. 274. (209)
Encyclopedia Mysteriosa, p. 69. (2)

The Encyclopedia of Murder and Mystery, pp. 104–5. (6)
The Encyclopedia of Mystery and Detection, pp. 93–94. (7)
St. James Guide to Crime & Mystery Writers, 4th ed., pp. 214–16. (882d)
Twentieth-Century Crime and Mystery Writers, 1st ed., pp. 334–37. (882a)
Twentieth-Century Crime and Mystery Writers, 2nd ed., pp. 183–84. (882b)
Twentieth-Century Crime and Mystery Writers, 3rd ed., pp. 229–30. (882c)
Web site: http://www.stopyourekillingme. com/manning-coles.html
Colley, Peter
Bio-bibliographic data:
Canadian Crime Fiction, p. 45. (209)
Collier, John
Bio-bibliographic data:
British Mystery Writers, 1920–1939, pp. 83–86. (867)
The Encyclopedia of Mystery and Detection, p. 96. (7)
Twentieth-Century Crime and Mystery Writers, 1st ed., pp. 337–39. (882a)
Twentieth-Century Crime and Mystery Writers, 2nd ed., pp. 184–85. (882b)
Twentieth-Century Crime and Mystery Writers, 3rd ed., pp. 230–31. (882c)
Collins, Anna Ashwood
Bio-bibliographic data:
Detecting Women, 1st ed., p. 40. (877a)
Detecting Women 2, p. 44. (877b)
Collins, [Cuthbert] Dale
Bio-bibliographic data:
Australian Crime Fiction, pp. 57–58. (207)
Collins, Hunt. *See* **Hunter, Evan**
Collins, Joseph Edmund
Bio-bibliographic data:
Canadian Crime Fiction, p. 45. (209)
Collins, Mary [Garden]
Bio-bibliographic data:
Canadian Crime Fiction, pp. 45–46. (209)
Collins, Max Allan
Bio-bibliographic data:
The Big Book of Noir, pp. 327–28. (24)
Detecting Men, 1st ed., pp. 58–59. (876)
Encyclopedia Mysteriosa, pp. 69–70. (2)
The Encyclopedia of Murder and Mystery, p. 105. (6)
The Mammoth Encyclopedia of Modern Crime Fiction, pp. 99–102. (1)

St. James Guide to Crime & Mystery Writers, 4th ed., pp. 216–18. (882d)
Twentieth-Century Crime and Mystery Writers, 2nd ed., pp. 185–87. (882b)
Twentieth-Century Crime and Mystery Writers, 3rd ed., pp. 231–33. (882c)
Whodunit? A Who's Who in Crime and Mystery Writing, p. 36. (5)
Personal papers in Center for the Study of Popular Culture, Bowling Green State University, Bowling Green, Ohio.
Web site: http://www.muscanet.com/~phoenix/main.html; http://www.stopyourekillingme.com/max-allan-collins.html; http://www.thrillingdetective.com/trivia/mac.html; http://www.muscanet.com/~phoenix
Max Allan Collins Newsletter
301 Fairview Ave.
Muscatine, IA 52761
http://www.maxallancollins.com

Collins, Maynard
Bio-bibliographic data:
Canadian Crime Fiction, p. 46. (209)

Collins, Michael. *See* Lynds, Dennis

Collins, Robert G.
Bio-bibliographic data:
Canadian Crime Fiction, p. 46. (209)

Collins, Robert J.
Bio-bibliographic data:
Canadian Crime Fiction, pp. 46–47. (209)

Collins, Wilkie; i.e., William Wilkie
Bio-bibliographic data:
British Mystery Writers, 1860–1919, pp. 85–101. (866)
Critical Survey of Mystery and Detective Fiction, pp. 387–93. (41)
Encyclopedia Mysteriosa, pp. 70–71. (2)
The Encyclopedia of Murder and Mystery, pp. 105–6. (6)
The Encyclopedia of Mystery and Detection, pp. 97–99. (7)
Mystery and Suspense Writers, pp. 217–31. (884.2)
100 Masters of Mystery and Detective Fiction, pp. 164–70. (37)
The Oxford Companion to Crime and Mystery Writing, pp. 81–82. (4)
St. James Guide to Crime & Mystery Writers, 4th ed., pp. 221–23. (882d)
Twelve Englishmen of Mystery, pp. 8–32. (865)
Twentieth-Century Crime and Mystery Writers, 1st ed., pp. 1525–26. (882a)
Twentieth-Century Crime and Mystery Writers, 2nd ed., pp. 931–932. (882b)
Twentieth-Century Crime and Mystery Writers, 3rd ed., pp. 1121–22. (882c)
Whodunit? A Who's Who in Crime and Mystery Writing, pp. 36–37. (5)
Personal papers in Columbia University Library.
Personal papers in Princeton University Library.
Web site: http://www.deadline.demon.co.uk/ wilkie.wilkie.htm; http://www.rightword.com/au/writers/wilkie; http://www. gasson.demon.co.uk
Wilkie Collins Society
c/o Andrew Gasson
3 Merton House
36 Belsize Park
London, NW 3 4EA
United Kingdom
http://www.gasson.demon.co.uk/wcs.html

Collinson, Peter. *See* Hammett, Dashiell
Comfort, B.; i.e., Barbara Comfort
Bio-bibliographic data:
By a Woman's Hand, 2nd ed., pp. 49–50. (884b)
Detecting Women, 1st ed., p. 41. (877a)
Detecting Women 2, p. 44. (877b)
Detecting Women, 3rd ed., p. 59. (877c)
Web site: http://www.stopyourekillingme.com/b-comfort.html

Conan Doyle, Arthur. *See* Doyle, Arthur Conan
Conant, Susan
Bio-bibliographic data:
By a Woman's Hand, 1st ed., pp. 49–50. (884a)
By a Woman's Hand, 2nd ed., p. 50. (884b)
Detecting Women, 1st ed., p. 41. (877a)
Detecting Women 2, pp. 44–45. (877b)
Detecting Women, 3rd ed., p. 59. (877c)
Great Women Mystery Writers, pp. 75–77. (880)
The Mammoth Encyclopedia of Modern Crime Fiction, p. 105. (1)
Web site: http://www.stopyourekillingme.com/susan-conant.html

Condon, Richard
Bio-bibliographic data:
St. James Guide to Crime & Mystery Writers, 4th ed., pp. 223–24. (882d)

Twentieth-Century Crime and Mystery Writers, 1st ed., pp. 344–46. (882a)
Twentieth-Century Crime and Mystery Writers, 2nd ed., pp. 190–91. (882b)
Twentieth-Century Crime and Mystery Writers, 3rd ed., pp. 237–38. (882c)
Personal papers in Mugar Memorial Library, Boston University

Cone, Tom
Bio-bibliographic data:
Canadian Crime Fiction, p. 47. (209)

Connell, Richard [Edward]
Bio-bibliographic data:
The Encyclopedia of Murder and Mystery, p. 108. (6)
The Encyclopedia of Mystery and Detection, p. 104. (7)

Connelly, Michael [Joseph]
Bio-bibliographic data:
Detecting Men, 1st ed., p. 60. (876)
The Encyclopedia of Murder and Mystery, pp. 108–9. (6)
The Mammoth Encyclopedia of Modern Crime Fiction, pp. 105–6. (1)
St. James Guide to Crime & Mystery Writers, 4th ed., pp. 224–26. (882d)
Speaking of Murder, vol. II, pp. 196–201. (875b)
Talking Murder, pp. 39–57. (883)
Whodunit? A Who's Who in Crime and Mystery Writing, p. 38. (5)
Web site: http://www.michaelconnelly.com; http://www.stopyourekillingme.com/michael-connelly.html; http://www.danfortune.com

Connington, J. J. *Pseud. for* **Alfred Walter Stewart**
Bio-bibliographic data:
The Encyclopedia of Murder and Mystery, p. 109. (6)
The Encyclopedia of Mystery and Detection, pp. 104–5. (7)
St. James Guide to Crime & Mystery Writers, 4th ed., pp. 226–27. (882d)
Twentieth-Century Crime and Mystery Writers, 1st ed., pp. 346–48. (882a)
Twentieth-Century Crime and Mystery Writers, 2nd ed., pp. 191–92. (882b)
Twentieth-Century Crime and Mystery Writers, 3rd ed., pp. 238–39. (882c)

Connolly, John
Bio-bibliographic data:
The Mammoth Encyclopedia of Modern Crime Fiction, pp. 106–7. (1)

Web site: http://www.twbooks.co.uk/authors/ johnconnolly.html; http://www.stopyourekillingme.com/john-connolly.html; http://www.johnconnolly.co.uk

Connor, Beverly
Bio-bibliographic data:
Detecting Women, 3rd ed., p. 60. (877c)
The Mammoth Encyclopedia of Modern Crime Fiction, p. 107. (1)
Web site: www.athens.net/~bconnor/index.html; http://www.stopyourekillingme.com/beverly-connor.html

Connor, Ralph. *See* **Gordon, Rev. Charles William**

Conrad, Brenda. *See* **Ford, Leslie**

Conrad, Joseph: born Józef Teodor Konrad Korzeniowski
Bio-bibliographic data:
The Encyclopedia of Murder and Mystery, p. 109. (6)
The Encyclopedia of Mystery and Detection, p. 105. (7)

Conrad, Tod. *See* **Hunter, Richard Wilkes**

Conroy, Richard Timothy
Bio-bibliographic data:
Detecting Men, 1st ed., p. 60. (876)

Constantine, K. C. *Pseud. for* **Carl Constantine Kosak**
Bio-bibliographic data:
Colloquium on Crime, pp. 41–61. (884.1)
Detecting Men, 1st ed., pp. 60–61. (876)
Encyclopedia Mysteriosa, p. 74. (2)
The Encyclopedia of Murder and Mystery, pp. 109–10. (6)
The Mammoth Encyclopedia of Modern Crime Fiction, p. 108. (1)
Mystery and Suspense Writers, pp. 233–41. (884.2)
St. James Guide to Crime & Mystery Writers, 4th ed., pp. 227–28. (882d)
Twentieth-Century Crime and Mystery Writers, 2nd ed., p. 193. (882b)
Twentieth-Century Crime and Mystery Writers, 3rd ed., pp. 239–40. (882c)
Whodunit? A Who's Who in Crime and Mystery Writing, pp. 38–39. (5)
Web site: http://www.stopyourekillingme.com/ k-c-constantine.html; http://www.badattitudes.com/Constantine.html

Contant, Alain
Bio-bibliographic data:

Canadian Crime Fiction, p. 48. (209)
Conteris, Híber
Bio-bibliographic data:
Latin American Mystery Writers: An A to Z Guide. (881)
Conway, Peter. *Pseud. for* **Peter Claudius Gautier Smith**
Bio-bibliographic data:
Detecting Men, 1st ed., p. 61. (876)
Conyn, Cornelius, and John Chisholm Marten
Bio-bibliographic data:
Australian Crime Fiction, p. 59. (207)
Coo-ee. *See* **Walker, William Sylvester**
Cook, Bob
Bio-bibliographic data:
Detecting Men, 1st ed., p. 61. (876)
Cook, Bruce
Bio-bibliographic data:
Detecting Men, 1st ed., p. 62. (876)
The Mammoth Encyclopedia of Modern Crime Fiction, pp. 108–9. (1)
Web site: www.angelfire.com/ct/tortuga/bruce.html; http://www.stopyourekillingme.com/bruce-cook.html
Cook, Glen
Bio-bibliographic data:
Detecting Men, 1st ed., p. 62. (876)
Web site: http://www.stopyourekillingme.com/glen-cook.html; http://www.xmission.com/~shpshftr/GC/GC-Home.html
Cook, Judith [Anne]
Bio-bibliographic data:
Detecting Women, 3rd ed., p. 60. (877c)
The Mammoth Encyclopedia of Modern Crime Fiction, pp. 109–10. (1)
Cook, Kenneth
Bio-bibliographic data:
Australian Crime Fiction, pp. 59–60. (207)
Cook, Petronelle. *See* **Arnold, Margot**
Cook, Robert William Arthur. *See* **Raymond, Derek**
Cook, Robin. *See* **Raymond, Derek**
Cook, Ronald J.
Bio-bibliographic data:
Canadian Crime Fiction, p. 48. (209)
Cook, Stephen
Bio-bibliographic data:
Detecting Men, 1st ed., p. 62. (876)
Cook, Thomas H.
Bio-bibliographic data:

Detecting Men, 1st ed., p. 63. (876)
The Encyclopedia of Murder and Mystery, pp. 110–11. (6)
The Mammoth Encyclopedia of Modern Crime Fiction, pp. 110–11. (1)
Web site: http://www.stopyourekillingme.com/thomas-cook.html
Cooke, M. E. *See* **Creasey, John**
Cooper, Brian
Bio-bibliographic data:
Detecting Men, 1st ed., p. 63. (876)
Twentieth-Century Crime and Mystery Writers, 1st ed., pp. 349–50. (882a)
Twentieth-Century Crime and Mystery Writers, 2nd ed., p. 194. (882b)
Twentieth-Century Crime and Mystery Writers, 3rd ed., pp. 240–41. (882c)
Web site: http://www.stopyourekillingme.com/brian-cooper.html
Cooper, Charles. *Pseud. for* **Arnold Charles Cooper Lock**
Bio-bibliographic data:
Australian Crime Fiction, p. 60. (207)
Cooper, Clarence Lavaugn, Jr.
Bio-bibliographic data:
The Mammoth Encyclopedia of Modern Crime Fiction, pp. 111–12. (1)
Cooper, James Fenimore
Bio-bibliographic data:
The Encyclopedia of Murder and Mystery, p. 112. (6)
Cooper, Natasha. *Pseud. for* **Daphne Wright**
Bio-bibliographic data:
By a Woman's Hand, 1st ed., p. 50. (884a)
By a Woman's Hand, 2nd ed., pp. 50–51. (884b)
Detecting Women, 1st ed., p. 41. (877a)
Detecting Women 2, p. 45. (877b)
Detecting Women, 3rd ed., pp. 60–61. (877c)
The Mammoth Encyclopedia of Modern Crime Fiction, pp. 112–13. (1)
Web site: http://www.twbooks.co.uk/authors/ncooper.html; http://www.stopyourekillingme.com/natasha-cooper.html
Cooper, Susan Rogers
Bio-bibliographic data:
By a Woman's Hand, 1st ed., pp. 50–51. (884a)
By a Woman's Hand, 2nd ed., pp. 51–52. (884b)
Detecting Women, 1st ed., p. 42. (877a)

Corris, Peter [Robert]
Bio-bibliographic data:
Australian Crime Fiction, pp. 62–64, 145,
146. (207)
Detecting Men, 1st ed., pp. 65–66. (876)
*The Mammoth Encyclopedia of Modern
Crime Fiction*, pp. 114–16. (1)
*St. James Guide to Crime & Mystery
Writers*, 4th ed., pp. 233–34. (882d)
*Twentieth-Century Crime and Mystery
Writers*, 3rd ed., pp. 242–44. (882c)
Web site: http://www.stopyourekillingme.
com/peter-corris.html
Corriveau, Mrs. Monique Chouinard
Bio-bibliographic data:
Canadian Crime Fiction, p. 48. (209)
**Cory, Desmond. *Pseud. for* Shaun Lloyd
McCarthy**
Bio-bibliographic data:
Detecting Men, 1st ed., pp. 66–67. (876)
*St. James Guide to Crime & Mystery
Writers*, 4th ed., pp. 234–36. (882d)
*Twentieth-Century Crime and Mystery
Writers*, 1st ed., pp. 358–61. (882a)
*Twentieth-Century Crime and Mystery
Writers*, 2nd ed., pp. 197–98. (882b)
*Twentieth-Century Crime and Mystery
Writers*, 3rd ed., pp. 244–45. (882c)
Personal papers in Mugar Memorial
Library, Boston University
Cosgrave, Patrick
Bio-bibliographic data:
*Twentieth-Century Crime and Mystery
Writers*, 2nd ed., p. 199.
Cosgrove, Edmund [Carew]
Bio-bibliographic data:
Canadian Crime Fiction, p. 48. (209)
Costa-Gavras, Constantin
Bio-bibliographic data:
The Encyclopedia of Murder and Mystery,
pp. 112–13. (6)
Côté, Denis
Bio-bibliographic data:
Canadian Crime Fiction, pp. 48–49. (209)
Coté, Jean
Bio-bibliographic data:
Canadian Crime Fiction, p. 49. (209)
Côté, Laurier
Bio-bibliographic data:
Canadian Crime Fiction, p. 49. (209)
Côté, Maryse
Bio-bibliographic data:
Canadian Crime Fiction, p. 49. (209)

Cotton, Marie. *See* Catton, C. M.
Coughlin, William Jeremiah
Bio-bibliographic data:
*The Mammoth Encyclopedia of Modern
Crime Fiction*, pp. 116–17. (1)
Web site: http://www.stopyourekillingme.
com/william-j-coughlin.html
**Coulson, John Hubert Arthur. *See* Bonett,
John, and Emery**
**Coulson, Robert [Stratten]. *See* De Weese,
Gene**
Coulter, John [William]
Bio-bibliographic data:
Canadian Crime Fiction, p. 49. (209)
Coulter, Stephen
Bio-bibliographic data:
*Twentieth-Century Crime and Mystery
Writers,* 1st ed., pp. 361–62. (882a)
*Twentieth-Century Crime and Mystery
Writers*, 2nd ed., pp. 199–200. (882b)
*Twentieth-Century Crime and Mystery
Writers*, 3rd ed., pp. 245–46. (882c)
Coupe, Stuart, and Julie Ogden
Bio-bibliographic data:
Australian Crime Fiction, p. 64. (207)
Courtier, S. H.; i.e., Sidney Hobson
Bio-bibliographic data:
Australian Crime Fiction, pp. 65–69.
(207)
*The Encyclopedia of Mystery and
Detection*, p. 107. (7)
*Twentieth-Century Crime and Mystery
Writers,* 1st ed., pp. 362–64. (882a)
*Twentieth-Century Crime and Mystery
Writers*, 2nd ed., pp. 200–201. (882b)
*Twentieth-Century Crime and Mystery
Writers*, 3rd ed., pp. 246–47. (882c)
Courtney, D. G. *See* Gurr, David
Covell, Richard
Bio-bibliographic data:
Canadian Crime Fiction, p. 49. (209)
Cowan, James [Granville]
Bio-bibliographic data:
Australian Crime Fiction, p. 69. (207)
Cowan, Janice
Bio-bibliographic data:
Canadian Crime Fiction, p. 49. (209)
Cowen, Frances
Bio-bibliographic data:
*Twentieth-Century Crime and Mystery
Writers,* 1st ed., pp. 364–66. (882a)

Cox, A. B. *See* Berkeley, Anthony
Cox, Anthony Berkeley. *See* Berkeley,
Anthony
Cox, William R.
Bio-bibliographic data:
*St. James Guide to Crime & Mystery
Writers*, 4th ed., pp. 236–38. (882d)
*Twentieth-Century Crime and Mystery
Writers*, 2nd ed., pp. 201–4. (882b)
*Twentieth-Century Crime and Mystery
Writers*, 3rd ed., pp. 247–50. (882c)
Personal papers in University of Oregon,
Eugene, Oregon.
Personal papers in University of
Wyoming, Laramie, Wyoming.
Coxe, George Harmon
Bio-bibliographic data:
*Critical Survey of Mystery and Detective
Fiction*, pp. 394–99. (41)
Encyclopedia Mysteriosa, pp. 76–77. (2)
The Encyclopedia of Murder and Mystery,
p. 114. (6)
*The Encyclopedia of Mystery and
Detection*, pp. 107–8. (7)
*The Oxford Companion to Crime and
Mystery Writing*, p. 97. (4)
*St. James Guide to Crime & Mystery
Writers*, 4th ed., pp. 238–40. (882d)
*Twentieth-Century Crime and Mystery
Writers*, 1st ed., pp. 366–72. (882a)
*Twentieth-Century Crime and Mystery
Writers*, 2nd ed., pp. 204–7. (882b)
*Twentieth-Century Crime and Mystery
Writers*, 3rd ed., pp. 250–54. (882c)
*Whodunit? A Who's Who in Crime and
Mystery Writing*, p. 43. (5)
Personal papers in Beinecke Rare Book
and Manuscript Library, Yale
University, New Haven, Connecticut
Web site: http://members.aol.com/
MG4273/hardboil.htm
Craig, Alisa. *See* MacLeod, Charlotte
Craig, David. *Pseud. for* Allan James
Tucker
Bio-bibliographic data:
Detecting Men, 1st ed., p. 67. (876)
Web site: http://www.stopyourekillingme.
com/david-craig.html
Craig, Georgiana Ann Randolph. *See*
Rice, Craig
Craig, James. *Pseud. for* Roy Judson Snell
Bio-bibliographic data:
Canadian Crime Fiction, pp. 249, 267.
(209)

Craig, John [Ernest]
Bio-bibliographic data:
Canadian Crime Fiction, p. 50. (209)
Craig, Jonathan. *Pseud. for* Frank E.
Smith
Bio-bibliographic data:
*St. James Guide to Crime & Mystery
Writers*, 4th ed., pp. 240–41. (882d)
*Twentieth-Century Crime and Mystery
Writers*, 2nd ed., pp. 207–9. (882b)
*Twentieth-Century Crime and Mystery
Writers*, 3rd ed., pp. 254–56. (882c)
Craig, Philip [R.]
Bio-bibliographic data:
Detecting Men, 1st ed., p. 68. (876)
Web site: http://www.stopyourekillingme.
com/ philip-craig.html; http://
philiprcraig. com
Crais, Robert
Bio-bibliographic data:
Detecting Men, 1st ed., p. 68. (876)
*The Mammoth Encyclopedia of Modern
Crime Fiction*, pp. 117–18. (1)
*St. James Guide to Crime & Mystery
Writers*, 4th ed., pp. 241–42. (882d)
Speaking of Murder, vol. II, pp. 140–52.
(875b)
Web site: http://www.robertcrais.com;
http://www.stopyourekillingme.com/
robert-crais.html
Cramer, Rebecca
Bio-bibliographic data:
Detecting Women, 3rd ed., p. 63. (877c)
Crane, Alex. *See* Hunter, Richard Wilkes
Crane, Caroline
Bio-bibliographic data:
By a Woman's Hand, 1st ed., pp. 52–53.
(884a)
By a Woman's Hand, 2nd ed., p. 53.
(884b)
Crane, Frances
Bio-bibliographic data:
Detecting Women, 1st ed., p. 43. (877a)
Detecting Women 2, pp. 46–47. (877b)
Encyclopedia Mysteriosa, p. 77. (2)
The Encyclopedia of Murder and Mystery,
p. 115. (6)
*The Encyclopedia of Mystery and
Detection*, p. 109. (7)
*St. James Guide to Crime & Mystery
Writers*, 4th ed., pp. 242–43. (882d)
*Twentieth-Century Crime and Mystery
Writers*, 1st ed., pp. 372–74. (882a)

Twentieth-Century Crime and Mystery Writers, 2nd ed., pp. 209–10. (882b)
Twentieth-Century Crime and Mystery Writers, 3rd ed., pp. 256–57. (882c)
Web site: http://www.xs4all.nl/
~embden11/Engels2/crane.htm
Crane, Hamilton. *See* **Mason, Sarah J.**
Creasey, John
Bio-bibliographic data:
Australian Crime Fiction, p. 69. (207)
Corpus Delicti of Mystery Fiction, pp. 58–64. (879)
Critical Survey of Mystery and Detective Fiction, pp. 400–411. (41)
Encyclopedia Mysteriosa, pp. 77–78. (2)
The Encyclopedia of Murder and Mystery, pp. 115–16. (6)
The Encyclopedia of Mystery and Detection, pp. 109–10. (7)
100 Masters of Mystery and Detective Fiction, pp. 171–82. (37)
The Oxford Companion to Crime and Mystery Writing, p. 100. (4)
St. James Guide to Crime & Mystery Writers, 4th ed., pp. 243–53. (882d)
Twentieth-Century Crime and Mystery Writers, 1st ed., pp. 374–91. (882a)
Twentieth-Century Crime and Mystery Writers, 2nd ed., pp. 210–19. (882b)
Twentieth-Century Crime and Mystery Writers, 3rd ed., pp. 257–66. (882c)
Whodunit? A Who's Who in Crime and Mystery Writing, p. 43. (5)
Web site: http://www.stopyourekilling me.com/ john-creasey.html; http://www. kirjasto.sci.fi/creasey.htm; http:// www.bbc.co.uk/dna/h2g2/ alabaster/a613289
Creighton, Donald Grant
Bio-bibliographic data:
Canadian Crime Fiction, pp. 50–51. (209)
Crespi, Camilla T., i.e., Trella
Bio-bibliographic data:
By a Woman's Hand, 1st ed., pp. 53–54. (884a)
By a Woman's Hand, 2nd ed., pp. 53–54. (884b)
Detecting Women, 1st ed., p. 44. (877a)
Detecting Women 2, pp. 47–48. (877b)
Detecting Women, 3rd ed., p. 64. (877c)
Web site: http://www.stopyourekilling me. com/camilla-t-crespi.html; http:// members.aol.com/camcrespi/ index.html

Crespi, Trella. *See* **Crespi, Camilla T.**
Creswell, Maurice
Bio-bibliographic data:
Canadian Crime Fiction, p. 51. (209)
Creswell, Rosemary. *See* **Clarement, Ruth**
Crichton, Michael
Bio-bibliographic data:
St. James Guide to Crime & Mystery Writers, 4th ed., pp. 253–54. (882d)
Twentieth-Century Crime and Mystery Writers, 1st ed., pp. 391–93. (882a)
Twentieth-Century Crime and Mystery Writers, 2nd ed., pp. 219–20. (882b)
Twentieth-Century Crime and Mystery Writers, 3rd ed., pp. 266–67. (882c)
Web site: http://www.michaelcrichton.net;
http://www.stopyourekillingme.com/
michael-crichton.html
Crichton, William
Bio-bibliographic data:
Canadian Crime Fiction, p. 51. (209)
Crider, Bill; i.e., Allen Billy
Bio-bibliographic data:
Detecting Men, 1st ed., pp. 68–69. (876)
Encyclopedia Mysteriosa, p. 78. (2)
The Encyclopedia of Murder and Mystery, p. 116. (6)
The Mammoth Encyclopedia of Modern Crime Fiction, pp. 118–19. (1)
St. James Guide to Crime & Mystery Writers, 4th ed., pp. 254–55. (882d)
Twentieth-Century Crime and Mystery Writers, 3rd ed., pp. 267–68. (882c)
Whodunit? A Who's Who in Crime and Mystery Writing, pp. 43–44. (5)
Web site: http://www.readthewest.com/
billcrider.htm; http://www.
stopyourekillingme.com/bill-crider.ht
ml
Crisp, Jack H.
Bio-bibliographic data:
Canadian Crime Fiction, p. 51. (209)
Crispin, Edmund. *Pseud. for* **Robert Bruce Montgomery**
Bio-bibliographic data:
British Mystery and Thriller Writers since 1940, First Series, pp. 28–35. (868)
Critical Survey of Mystery and Detective Fiction, pp. 412–17. (41)
Encyclopedia Mysteriosa, p. 79. (2)
The Encyclopedia of Murder and Mystery, p. 118. (6)
The Encyclopedia of Mystery and Detection, pp. 111–12. (7)

Mystery and Suspense Writers, pp. 251–58. (884.2)

St. James Guide to Crime & Mystery Writers, 4th ed., pp. 255–57. (882d)

Twelve Englishmen of Mystery, pp. 250–75. (865)

Twentieth-Century Crime and Mystery Writers, 1st ed., pp. 393–95. (882a)

Twentieth-Century Crime and Mystery Writers, 2nd ed., pp. 220–21. (882b)

Twentieth-Century Crime and Mystery Writers, 3rd ed., pp. 268–70. (882c)

Whodunit? A Who's Who in Crime and Mystery Writing, p. 44. (5)

Web site: http://www.stopyourekillingme. com/edmund-crispin.html

Crocker, Arthur

Bio-bibliographic data:

Australian Crime Fiction, p. 69. (207)

Croft-Cooke, Rupert. *See* **Bruce, Leo**

Crofts, Freeman Wills

Bio-bibliographic data:

British Mystery Writers, 1920–1939, pp. 105–9. (867)

Critical Survey of Mystery and Detective Fiction, pp. 418–24. (41)

Encyclopedia Mysteriosa, p. 79. (2)

The Encyclopedia of Murder and Mystery, p. 119. (6)

The Encyclopedia of Mystery and Detection, p. 112. (7)

Mystery and Suspense Writers, pp. 259–69. (884.2)

The Oxford Companion to Crime and Mystery Writing, p. 111. (4)

St. James Guide to Crime & Mystery Writers, 4th ed., pp. 257–59. (882d)

Twentieth-Century Crime and Mystery Writers, 1st ed., pp. 395–99. (882a)

Twentieth-Century Crime and Mystery Writers, 2nd ed., pp. 221–23. (882b)

Twentieth-Century Crime and Mystery Writers, 3rd ed., pp. 270–71. (882c)

Whodunit? A Who's Who in Crime and Mystery Writing, pp. 44–45. (5)

Web site: http://members.aol.com/ MG4273/ crofts.htm

Crombie, Deborah [Darden]

Bio-bibliographic data:

By a Woman's Hand, 1st ed., p. 54. (884a)

By a Woman's Hand, 2nd ed., pp. 54–55. (884b)

Detecting Women, 1st ed., p. 45. (877a)

Detecting Women 2, p. 48. (877b)

Detecting Women, 3rd ed., pp. 64–65. (877c)

The Mammoth Encyclopedia of Modern Crime Fiction, p. 120. (1)

Women of Mystery, p. 434. (874)

Web site: http://www.deborahcrombie. com; http://www.stopyourekillingme. com/deborah-crombie.html; http:// 64.70.139.77/welcome/welcome.html

Cronin, A. J.: i.e., Archibald Joseph

Bio-bibliographic data:

The Encyclopedia of Murder and Mystery, pp. 119–20. (6)

Cronin, Bernard [Charles]

Bio-bibliographic data:

Australian Crime Fiction, pp. 70–71. (207)

Crook, Marion. *Pseud. for* **Marion Crook McKinnon**

Bio-bibliographic data:

Canadian Crime Fiction, pp. 51–52, 141. (209)

Cross, Ada Cambridge. *See* **Cambridge, Ada**

Cross, Amanda. *Pseud. for* **Carolyn Gold Heilbrun**

Bio-bibliographic data:

By a Woman's Hand, 1st ed., pp. 54–55. (884a)

By a Woman's Hand, 2nd ed., p. 55. (884b)

Critical Survey of Mystery and Detective Fiction, pp. 425–30. (41)

Designs of Darkness, pp. 187–202. (873)

Detecting Women, 1st ed., p. 45. (877a)

Detecting Women 2, p. 48. (877b)

Detecting Women, 3rd ed., p. 65. (877c)

Encyclopedia Mysteriosa, p. 80. (2)

The Encyclopedia of Murder and Mystery, pp. 120–21. (6)

Great Women Mystery Writers, pp. 79–83. (880)

The Mammoth Encyclopedia of Modern Crime Fiction, pp. 120–21. (1)

Mystery and Suspense Writers, pp. 271–80. (884.2)

100 Masters of Mystery and Detective Fiction, pp. 183–90. (37)

The Oxford Companion to Crime and Mystery Writing, pp. 111–12. (4)

St. James Guide to Crime & Mystery Writers, 4th ed., pp. 259–60. (882d)

10 Women of Mystery, pp. 269–96. (864, 865)

13 Mistresses of Murder, pp. 13–19. (871)
Twentieth-Century Crime and Mystery Writers, 1st ed., pp. 399–401. (882a)
Twentieth-Century Crime and Mystery Writers, 2nd ed., pp. 223–25. (882b)
Twentieth-Century Crime and Mystery Writers, 3rd ed., pp. 271–73. (882c)
Whodunit? A Who's Who in Crime and Mystery Writing, p. 45. (5)
Women Authors of Detective Series, pp. 104–10. (882.5)
Personal papers in Smith College, Northampton, Massachusetts.
Web site: http://www.stopyourekillingme. com/amanda-cross.html; http://www. hycyber.com/MYST/cross_amanda. html
Cross, David. *See* **Chesbro, George C.**
Crossen, Ken
Bio-bibliographic data:
St. James Guide to Crime & Mystery Writers, 4th ed., pp. 261–62. (882d)
Twentieth-Century Crime and Mystery Writers, 1st ed., pp. 401–5. (882a)
Twentieth-Century Crime and Mystery Writers, 2nd ed., pp. 225–27. (882b)
Twentieth-Century Crime and Mystery Writers, 3rd ed., pp. 273–75. (882c)
Personal papers in Mugar Memorial Library, Boston University
Crowe, John. *See* **Lynds, Dennis**
Crowleigh, Ann. *Pseud. for* **Barbara Cummings and Jo-Ann Power**
Bio-bibliographic data:
Detecting Women, 1st ed., p. 45. (877a)
Detecting Women 2, p. 48. (877b)
Detecting Women, 3rd ed., pp. 65–66. (877c)
Crozier, John. *See* **Knox, [William] Alexander**
Crum, Laura
Bio-bibliographic data:
Detecting Women, 1st ed., p. 45. (877a)
Detecting Women 2, pp. 48–49. (877b)
Detecting Women, 3rd ed., p. 66. (877c)
Web site: http://www.stopyourekillingme. com/laura-crum.html; http://members. cruzio.com/~absnow
Crumley, James
Bio-bibliographic data:
American Hard-Boiled Crime Writers, pp. 92–99. (862)
Critical Survey of Mystery and Detective Fiction, pp. 431–36. (41)

Detecting Men, 1st ed., p. 70. (876)
Encyclopedia Mysteriosa, p. 80. (2)
The Encyclopedia of Murder and Mystery, p. 121. (6)
The Mammoth Encyclopedia of Modern Crime Fiction, pp. 121–22. (1)
St. James Guide to Crime & Mystery Writers, 4th ed., pp. 262–63. (882d)
Talking Murder, pp. 58–70. (883)
Twentieth-Century Crime and Mystery Writers, 2nd ed., pp. 227–28. (882b)
Twentieth-Century Crime and Mystery Writers, 3rd ed., p. 276. (882c)
Whodunit? A Who's Who in Crime and Mystery Writing, p. 45. (5)
Web site: http://www.stopyourekillingme. com/james-crumley.html; http://www. geocities.com/Athens/6384/crumley. html
Csonka, Louis
Bio-bibliographic data:
Canadian Crime Fiction, p. 52. (209)
Cullingford, Guy. *Pseud. for* **Constance Lindsay Taylor**
Bio-bibliographic data:
Twentieth-Century Crime and Mystery Writers, 1st ed., pp. 405–7. (882a)
Twentieth-Century Crime and Mystery Writers, 2nd ed., pp. 228–29. (882b)
Twentieth-Century Crime and Mystery Writers, 3rd ed., pp. 276–77. (882c)
Cullum, Ridgwell
Bio-bibliographic data:
Canadian Crime Fiction, pp. 249–50, 274. (209)
Culver, Kathryn. *See* **Halliday, Brett**
Cumberland, Marten
Bio-bibliographic data:
Twentieth-Century Crime and Mystery Writers, 1st ed., pp. 407–0. (882a)
Twentieth-Century Crime and Mystery Writers, 2nd ed., pp. 229–30. (882b)
Cunningham, Chet
Bio-bibliographic data:
Canadian Crime Fiction, pp. 250, 252. (209)
Cunningham, E. V. *See* **Fast, Howard [Melvin]**
Curran, Colleen
Bio-bibliographic data:
Canadian Crime Fiction, p. 52. (209)
Currie, Harry
Bio-bibliographic data:
Canadian Crime Fiction, p. 52. (209)

Curry, Gene. *Pseud. for* **Peter McCurtin**
Bio-bibliographic data:
Canadian Crime Fiction, p. 250. (209)
Curtis, Richard
Bio-bibliographic data:
Canadian Crime Fiction, p. 250. (209)
Curtiss, Ursula
Bio-bibliographic data:
Encyclopedia Mysteriosa, p. 81 (2)
The Encyclopedia of Mystery and Detection, p. 114. (7)
St. James Guide to Crime & Mystery Writers, 4th ed., pp. 266–67. (882d)
Twentieth-Century Crime and Mystery Writers, 1st ed., pp.413–15. (882a)
Twentieth-Century Crime and Mystery Writers, 2nd ed., pp. 232–34. (882b)
Twentieth-Century Crime and Mystery Writers, 3rd ed., pp. 280–81. (882c)
Personal papers in Mugar Memorial Library, Boston University
Curwood, James Oliver
Bio-bibliographic data:
Canadian Crime Fiction, pp. 250–51. (209)
Curzon, Clare. *Pseud. for* **Eileen-Marie Duell Buchanan**
Bio-bibliographic data:
By a Woman's Hand, 1st ed., pp. 55–56. (884a)
By a Woman's Hand, 2nd ed., pp. 55–56. (884b)
Detecting Women, 1st ed., p. 46. (877a)
Detecting Women 2, pp. 49, 157. (877b)
Detecting Women, 3rd ed., pp. 66, 221–22. (877c)
The Mammoth Encyclopedia of Modern Crime Fiction, pp. 122–23. (1)
St. James Guide to Crime & Mystery Writers, 4th ed., pp. 267–69. (882d)
Twentieth-Century Crime and Mystery Writers, 1st ed., pp. 1178–79. (882a)
Twentieth-Century Crime and Mystery Writers, 2nd ed., p. 711. (882b)
Twentieth-Century Crime and Mystery Writers, 3rd ed., pp. 281–82. (882c)
Web site: http://www.stopyourekillingme. com/clare-curzon.html
Cusack, [Ellen] Dymphna
Bio-bibliographic data:
Australian Crime Fiction, p. 71. (207)
Cushing, E. Louise; i.e., Enid
Bio-bibliographic data:
Canadian Crime Fiction, pp. 52–53. (209)

Cussler, Clive
Bio-bibliographic data:
Canadian Crime Fiction, p. 251. (209)
Detecting Men, 1st ed., pp. 70–71. (876)
St. James Guide to Crime & Mystery Writers, 4th ed., pp. 269–70. (882d)
Twentieth-Century Crime and Mystery Writers, 3rd ed., pp. 282–83. (882c)
Web site: http://www.stopyourekillingme. com/clive-cussler.html; http://www. simonsays.com/CCussler; http://www.bradland.com/cussler
Custer, Tex: unidentified pseud.
Bio-bibliographic data:
Australian Crime Fiction, pp. 71, 221–22. (207)
Cutcheon, Edgar
Bio-bibliographic data:
Australian Crime Fiction, p. 71. (207)
Cutler, Judith
Bio-bibliographic data:
Detecting Women, 3rd ed., p. 67. (877c)
Web site: http://www.stopyourekillingme. com/judith-cutler.html; http://www. judithcutler.co.uk
Cutler, Stan
Bio-bibliographic data:
Detecting Men, 1st ed., p. 71. (876)
Cyr, Céline
Bio-bibliographic data:
Canadian Crime Fiction, p. 53. (209)

D
Daeninckx, Didier
Bio-bibliographic data:
The Encyclopedia of Murder and Mystery, p. 123. (6)
Daheim, Mary
Bio-bibliographic data:
By a Woman's Hand, 1st ed., pp. 57–58. (884a)
By a Woman's Hand, 2nd ed., pp. 57–58. (884b)
Detecting Women, 1st ed., p. 47. (877a)
Detecting Women 2, p. 50. (877b)
Detecting Women, 3rd ed., pp. 67–68. (877c)
Web site: http://www.stopyourekillingme. com/mary-daheim.html; http:// members.aol.com/ktbooks/daheim. htm
Dahl, Roald
Bio-bibliographic data:

The Encyclopedia of Murder and Mystery,
   p. 123. (6)
Twentieth-Century Crime and Mystery
   Writers, 1st ed., pp. 416–18. (882a)
Daigle, France
   Bio-bibliographic data:
   Canadian Crime Fiction, p. 53. (209)
Daignault, Claire
   Bio-bibliographic data:
   Canadian Crime Fiction, p. 53. (209)
Daigneault, Pierre
   Bio-bibliographic data:
   Canadian Crime Fiction, p. 53. (209)
Dain, Catherine. *Pseud. for* **Judith**
   Garwood
   Bio-bibliographic data:
   By a Woman's Hand, 1st ed., p. 58. (884a)
   By a Woman's Hand, 2nd ed., p. 58.
     (884b)
   Detecting Women, 1st ed., p. 47. (877a)
   Detecting Women 2, p. 50. (877b)
   Detecting Women, 3rd ed., p. 68. (877c)
   Web site: http://www.stopyourekillingme.
     com/catherine-dain.html
Dakin, Professor W. J.
   Bio-bibliographic data:
   Australian Crime Fiction, p. 183. (207)
Dale, Brian
   Bio-bibliographic data:
   Australian Crime Fiction, p. 72. (207)
Daley, Robert [Blake]
   Bio-bibliographic data:
   Canadian Crime Fiction, p. 275. (209)
Dallas, John. *See* **Duncan, W. Murdoch**
Daly, Carroll John
   Bio-bibliographic data:
   American Hard-Boiled Crime Writers, pp.
     100–5. (862)
   Critical Survey of Mystery and Detective
     Fiction, pp. 445–49. (41)
   Encyclopedia Mysteriosa, p. 83. (2)
   The Encyclopedia of Murder and Mystery,
     p. 124. (6)
   The Encyclopedia of Mystery and
     Detection, pp. 115–16. (7)
   Mystery and Suspense Writers, pp.
     281–89. (884.2)
   The Oxford Companion to Crime and
     Mystery Writing, p. 114. (4)
   St. James Guide to Crime & Mystery
     Writers, 4th ed., pp. 271–72. (882d)
   Twentieth-Century Crime and Mystery
     Writers, 1st ed., pp. 418–22. (882a)

Twentieth-Century Crime and Mystery
   Writers, 2nd ed., pp. 234–36. (882b)
Twentieth-Century Crime and Mystery
   Writers, 3rd ed., pp. 284–86. (882c)
Whodunit? A Who's Who in Crime and
   Mystery Writing, p. 49. (5)
Daly, Conor
   Bio-bibliographic data:
   Detecting Men, 1st ed., p. 71. (876)
Daly, Elizabeth
   Bio-bibliographic data:
   Critical Survey of Mystery and Detective
     Fiction, pp. 450–54. (41)
   Detecting Women, 1st ed., pp. 47–48.
     (877a)
   Detecting Women 2, p. 51. (877b)
   Encyclopedia Mysteriosa, p. 83. (2)
   The Encyclopedia of Murder and Mystery,
     pp. 124–25. (6)
   The Encyclopedia of Mystery and
     Detection, p. 116. (7)
   Great Women Mystery Writers, pp. 85–88.
     (880)
   The Oxford Companion to Crime and
     Mystery Writing, p. 114. (4)
   St. James Guide to Crime & Mystery
     Writers, 4th ed., pp. 272–73. (882d)
   Twentieth-Century Crime and Mystery
     Writers, 1st ed., pp. 422–24. (882a)
   Twentieth-Century Crime and Mystery
     Writers, 2nd ed., pp. 236–37. (882b)
   Twentieth-Century Crime and Mystery
     Writers, 3rd ed., pp. 286–87. (882c)
   Whodunit? A Who's Who in Crime and
     Mystery Writing, p. 49. (5)
   Web site: http://www.stopyourekillingme.
     com/elizabeth-daly.html
D'Amato, Barbara [Steketee]
   Bio-bibliographic data:
   By a Woman's Hand, 1st ed., p. 59. (884a)
   By a Woman's Hand, 2nd ed., pp. 58–59.
     (884b)
   Detecting Women, 1st ed., p. 46. (877a)
   Detecting Women 2, p. 49. (877b)
   Detecting Women, 3rd ed., pp. 68–69.
     (877c)
   Encyclopedia Mysteriosa, pp. 83–84. (2)
   Great Women Mystery Writers, pp. 88–90.
     (880)
   The Mammoth Encyclopedia of Modern
     Crime Fiction, pp. 123–24. (1)
   St. James Guide to Crime & Mystery
     Writers, 4th ed., pp. 273–74. (882d)
   Talking Murder, pp. 71–86. (883)

Whodunit? A Who's Who in Crime and Mystery Writing, pp. 49–50. (5)
Web site: http://www.barbaradamato.com;
http://www.stopyourekillingme.com/
barbara-damato.html

Dams, Jeanne M.
Bio-bibliographic data:
Detecting Women, 3rd ed., p. 69. (877c)
Web site: http://www.stopyourekillingme.
com/jeanne-m-dams.html

Dana, Rose. *See* **Ross, W. E. D.**

Danberg, Norman A. *See* **Daniels, Norman A.**

Dandenault, Roch
Bio-bibliographic data:
Canadian Crime Fiction, p. 53. (209)

Dandurand, Anne
Bio-bibliographic data:
Canadian Crime Fiction, p. 53. (209)

Dane, Alan. *See* **Goodchild, George**

Dane, Clemence. *Pseud. for* **Winifred Ashton**
Bio-bibliographic data:
Twentieth-Century Crime and Mystery Writers, 1st ed., pp. 424–27. (882a)

Daniel, David
Bio-bibliographic data:
Detecting Men, 1st ed., p. 72. (876)

Daniel, David, and Chris Carpenter
Bio-bibliographic data:
Detecting Men, 1st ed., p. 72 (876)

Daniel, Glyn Edmund
Bio-bibliographic data:
The Encyclopedia of Mystery and Detection, p. 116. (7)
Twentieth-Century Crime and Mystery Writers, 1st ed., pp. 427–29. (882a)

Daniel, William Roland
Bio-bibliographic data:
Canadian Crime Fiction, p. 275. (209)
Twentieth-Century Crime and Mystery Writers, 1st ed., pp. 429–33. (882a)
Twentieth-Century Crime and Mystery Writers, 2nd ed., pp. 237–39. (882b)

Daniels, Dorothy
Bio-bibliographic data:
Canadian Crime Fiction, p. 251. (209)

Daniels, Harold R.
Bio-bibliographic data:
The Big Book of Noir, p. 264. (24)

Daniels, Jan. *See* **Ross, W. E. D.**

Daniels, Norman A. *Pseud. for* **Norman A. Danberg**
Bio-bibliographic data:

Australian Crime Fiction, p. 72. (207)
Twentieth-Century Crime and Mystery Writers, 2nd ed., pp. 239–42. (882b)
Twentieth-Century Crime and Mystery Writers, 3rd ed., pp. 287–90. (882c)
Personal papers in Center for the Study of Popular Culture, Bowling Green State University, Bowling Green, Ohio.

Daniels, Philip; i.e., Dennis John Andrew Phillips
Bio-bibliographic data:
Detecting Men, 1st ed., pp. 52–53. (876)
The Mammoth Encyclopedia of Modern Crime Fiction, pp. 125–26. (1)
St. James Guide to Crime & Mystery Writers, 4th ed., pp. 164–66. (882d)
Twentieth-Century Crime and Mystery Writers, 3rd ed., pp. 182–83. (882c)

Dank, Gloria
Bio-bibliographic data:
By a Woman's Hand, 1st ed., pp. 59–60. (884a)
Detecting Women 2, p. 51. (877b)
Detecting Women, 3rd ed., p. 69. (877c)

Danks, Denise
Bio-bibliographic data:
Detecting Women, 1st ed., p. 48. (877a)
Detecting Women 2, p. 51. (877b)
Detecting Women, 3rd ed., p. 70. (877c)
Web site: http://www.stopyourekillingme.
com/denise-danks.html

Dannay, Frederic. *See* **Queen, Ellery**

Danvers, Jack. *Pseud. for* **Camille August Marie Caselyr**
Bio-bibliographic data:
Australian Crime Fiction, p. 72. (207)

Dark, James. *See* **Macdonnell, J. E.**

Darrell, George Frederick Price
Bio-bibliographic data:
Australian Crime Fiction, p. 72. (207)

Darrigo, David
Bio-bibliographic data:
Canadian Crime Fiction, pp. 217, 554. (209)

Daunais, Jean
Bio-bibliographic data:
Canadian Crime Fiction, p. 54. (209)

Davey, Jocelyn. *Pseud. for* **Chaim Raphael**
Bio-bibliographic data:
St. James Guide to Crime & Mystery Writers, 4th ed., pp. 275–76. (882d)
Twentieth-Century Crime and Mystery Writers, 1st ed., pp. 433–35. (882a)

Twentieth-Century Crime and Mystery Writers, 2nd ed., pp. 242–43. (882b)
Twentieth-Century Crime and Mystery Writers, 3rd ed., pp. 290–91. (882c)
Daviault, Pierre. *See* **Hartex, Pierre**
Davidson, Avram
Web site: http://www.avramdavidson.org
Davidson, Diane Mott
Bio-bibliographic data:
By a Woman's Hand, 1st ed., pp. 60–61. (884a)
By a Woman's Hand, 2nd ed., pp. 59–60. (884b)
Detecting Women, 1st ed., p. 48. (877a)
Detecting Women 2, p. 52. (877b)
Detecting Women, 3rd ed., p. 70. (877c)
The Mammoth Encyclopedia of Modern Crime Fiction, p. 126. (1)
Web site: http://members.aol.com/ biblioholc/ goldy.html; http:// mysterybooks.about.com/library/ mad/blad_ davidsonm.htm; http://www. stopyourekillingme.com/ diane-mott-davidson.html
Davidson, Lionel
Bio-bibliographic data:
Canadian Crime Fiction, p. 251. (209)
Critical Survey of Mystery and Detective Fiction, pp. 455–60. (41)
Encyclopedia Mysteriosa, p. 84. (2)
The Encyclopedia of Murder and Mystery, p. 128. (6)
The Mammoth Encyclopedia of Modern Crime Fiction, p. 127. (1)
St. James Guide to Crime & Mystery Writers, 4th ed., pp. 276–77. (882d)
Twentieth-Century Crime and Mystery Writers, 1st ed., pp. 435–36. (882a)
Twentieth-Century Crime and Mystery Writers, 2nd ed., pp. 243–44. (882b)
Twentieth-Century Crime and Mystery Writers, 3rd ed., p. 292. (882c)
Web site: http://www.stopyourekillingme. com/lionel-davidson.html
Davidson, T. L. *See* **Thomson, David Landsborough**
Davidts, Robert
Bio-bibliographic data:
Canadian Crime Fiction, p. 54. (209)
Davies, John Evan Weston. *See* **Mather, Berkley**
Davies, L. P.; i.e., Leslie Purnell
Bio-bibliographic data:

Critical Survey of Mystery and Detective Fiction, pp. 461–65. (41)
St. James Guide to Crime & Mystery Writers, 4th ed., pp. 277–78. (882d)
Twentieth-Century Crime and Mystery Writers, 1st ed., pp. 436–38. (882a)
Twentieth-Century Crime and Mystery Writers, 2nd ed., pp. 244–46. (882b)
Twentieth-Century Crime and Mystery Writers, 3rd ed., pp. 292–94. (882c)
Davies, [William] Robertson
Bio-bibliographic data:
Canadian Crime Fiction, pp. 54–56. (209)
Daviot, Gordon. *See* **Tey, Josephine**
Davis, Don. *See* **Halliday, Brett**
Davis, Dorothy Salisbury
Bio-bibliographic data:
By a Woman's Hand, 1st ed., pp. 61–62. (884a)
By a Woman's Hand, 2nd ed., p. 60. (884b)
Colloquium on Crime, pp. 63–78. (884.1)
Detecting Women, 1st ed., pp. 48–49. (877a)
Detecting Women 2, p. 52. (877b)
Detecting Women, 3rd ed., pp. 70–71. (877c)
Encyclopedia Mysteriosa, pp. 84–85. (2)
The Encyclopedia of Murder and Mystery, p. 129. (6)
The Encyclopedia of Mystery and Detection, p. 117. (7)
Great Women Mystery Writers, pp. 90–93. (880)
The Mammoth Encyclopedia of Modern Crime Fiction, pp. 127–29. (1)
The Oxford Companion to Crime and Mystery Writing, p. 115. (4)
St. James Guide to Crime & Mystery Writers, 4th ed., pp. 278–80. (882d)
13 Mistresses of Murder, pp. 21–32. (871)
Twentieth-Century Crime and Mystery Writers, 1st ed., pp. 439–41. (882a)
Twentieth-Century Crime and Mystery Writers, 2nd ed., pp. 246–47. (882b)
Twentieth-Century Crime and Mystery Writers, 3rd ed., pp. 294–96. (882c)
Whodunit? A Who's Who in Crime and Mystery Writing, p. 50. (5)
Personal papers in Brooklyn College Library, City of New York.
Personal papers in Mugar Memorial Library, Boston University.

Davis, Francis Louise. *See* **Lockridge, Richard, and Frances Lockridge**
Davis, Frederick C.
Bio-bibliographic data:
St. James Guide to Crime & Mystery Writers, 4th ed., pp. 280–81. (882d)
Twentieth-Century Crime and Mystery Writers, 1st ed., pp. 441–44. (882a)
Twentieth-Century Crime and Mystery Writers, 2nd ed., pp. 247–49. (882b)
Twentieth-Century Crime and Mystery Writers, 3rd ed., pp. 296–98. (882c)
Davis, Gordon. *See* **Hunt, E. Howard, Jr.**
Davis, Helen
Bio-bibliographic data:
Australian Crime Fiction, p. 73. (207)
Davis, J. Madison
Bio-bibliographic data:
Detecting Men, 1st ed., p. 72. (876)
Davis, Kaye
Bio-bibliographic data:
Detecting Women, 3rd ed., p. 71. (877c)
Davis, Kenn
Bio-bibliographic data:
Detecting Men, 1st ed., pp. 72–73. (876)
St. James Guide to Crime & Mystery Writers, 4th ed., pp. 281–82. (882d)
Twentieth-Century Crime and Mystery Writers, 3rd ed., pp. 298–99. (882c)
Davis, Lindsey
Bio-bibliographic data:
By a Woman's Hand, 1st ed., p. 62. (884a)
By a Woman's Hand, 2nd ed., p. 61. (884b)
Detecting Women, 1st ed., p. 49. (877a)
Detecting Women 2, pp. 52–53. (877b)
Detecting Women, 3rd ed., pp. 71–72. (877c)
The Mammoth Encyclopedia of Modern Crime Fiction, pp. 129–30. (1)
St. James Guide to Crime & Mystery Writers, 4th ed., pp. 283–84. (882d)
874.*Women of Mystery*, p. 434.
Web site: http://www.lindseydavis.co.uk; http://www.stopyourekillingme.com/lindsey-davis.html; http://www.geocities.com/Athens/Oracle/7330
Davis, Mildred
Bio-bibliographic data:
Twentieth-Century Crime and Mystery Writers, 2nd ed., pp. 249–50. (882b)
Personal papers in Mugar Memorial Library, Boston University.

Davis, Norbert
Bio-bibliographic data:
The Encyclopedia of Murder and Mystery, p. 129. (6)
Web site: http://www.thrillingdetective.com/trivia/davis.html
Davis, Richard Harding
Bio-bibliographic data:
Canadian Crime Fiction, pp. 251–52. (209)
The Encyclopedia of Murder and Mystery, pp. 129–30. (6)
The Encyclopedia of Mystery and Detection, p. 117. (7)
Davis, Thomas D.
Bio-bibliographic data:
Detecting Men, 1st ed., p. 73. (876)
Davis, Val. *Pseud. for* **Angela Irvine and Robert Irvine**
Bio-bibliographic data:
Detecting Women, 3rd ed., p. 72. (877c)
Web site: http://www.stopyourekillingme.com/val-davis.html
Davitt, Ellen Heseltine
Bio-bibliographic data:
Australian Crime Fiction, p. 73. (207)
Dawe, [William] Carlton [Lanyon]
Bio-bibliographic data:
Australian Crime Fiction, p. 73. (207)
Dawkins, Cecil
Bio-bibliographic data:
Detecting Women, 3rd ed., p. 72. (877c)
Dawson, A. J.; i.e., Alec John
Bio-bibliographic data:
Australian Crime Fiction, p. 74. (207)
Canadian Crime Fiction, p. 252. (209)
Dawson, Coningsby [William]
Bio-bibliographic data:
Canadian Crime Fiction, pp. 56–57. (209)
Dawson, David [F.] Laing
Bio-bibliographic data:
Canadian Crime Fiction, p. 57. (209)
Dawson, Janet
Bio-bibliographic data:
By a Woman's Hand, 1st ed., p. 63. (884a)
By a Woman's Hand, 2nd ed., pp. 61–62. (884b)
Detecting Women, 1st ed., p. 49. (877a)
Detecting Women 2, p. 53. (877b)
Detecting Women, 3rd ed., pp. 72–73. (877c)
The Mammoth Encyclopedia of Modern Crime Fiction, pp. 130–31. (1)

St. James Guide to Crime & Mystery Writers, 4th ed., pp. 284–86. (882d)
Web site: http://www.janetdawson.com; http://www.stopyourekillingme.com/janet-dawson.html

Dawson, MacKenzie [hoax]
Bio-bibliographic data:
Canadian Crime Fiction, p. 57. (209)

Day, Dianne
Bio-bibliographic data:
Detecting Women 2, p. 53. (877b)
Detecting Women, 3rd ed., p. 73. (877c)
Web site: http://www.stopyourekillingme.com/dianne-day.html

Day, Marele [Lorraine]
Bio-bibliographic data:
Australian Crime Fiction, pp. 74, 145, 146. (207)
By a Woman's Hand, 2nd ed., pp. 62–63. (884b)
Detecting Women, 1st ed., p. 49. (877a)
Detecting Women 2, p. 53. (877b)
Detecting Women, 3rd ed., p. 73. (877c)
The Mammoth Encyclopedia of Modern Crime Fiction, pp. 131–32. (1)
Web site: http://www.twbooks.co.uk/authors.mareled.html; http://www.stopyourekillingme.com/marele-day.html

Day Lewis, C. *See* **Blake, Nicholas**

Deacon, William Frederick
Bio-bibliographic data:
Canadian Crime Fiction, p. 57. (209)

Dean, Amber. *Pseud. for* **Amber Dean Getzin**
Bio-bibliographic data:
Canadian Crime Fiction, pp. 252, 254. (209)
Twentieth-Century Crime and Mystery Writers, 1st ed., pp. 445–46. (882a)
Personal papers in University of Rochester Library, New York

Dean, S. F. X. *Pseud. for* **Francis Smith**
Bio-bibliographic data:
Twentieth-Century Crime and Mystery Writers, 3rd ed., pp. 299–300. (882c)

DeAndrea, William L[ouis].
Bio-bibliographic data:
Critical Survey of Mystery and Detective Fiction, pp. 466–70. (41)
Detecting Men, 1st ed., pp. 73–74. (876)
Encyclopedia Mysteriosa, pp. 85–86. (2)
The Encyclopedia of Murder and Mystery, pp. 130–31. (6)

The Mammoth Encyclopedia of Modern Crime Fiction, pp. 132–33. (1)
St. James Guide to Crime & Mystery Writers, 4th ed., pp. 286–87. (882d)
Twentieth-Century Crime and Mystery Writers, 2nd ed., pp. 250–51. (882b)
Twentieth-Century Crime and Mystery Writers, 3rd ed., pp. 300–301. (882c)
Personal papers in Mugar Memorial Library, Boston University.
Web site: http://www.stopyourekillingme.com/william-deandrea.html

Deane, Aubrey
Bio-bibliographic data:
Canadian Crime Fiction, p. 57. (209)

Deane, Norman. *See* **Creasey, John**

Deaver, Jeffery [Wilds]
Bio-bibliographic data:
Detecting Men, 1st ed., p. 74. (876)
The Mammoth Encyclopedia of Modern Crime Fiction, pp. 133–34. (1)
Talking Murder, pp. 87–97. (883)
Web site: http://www.jeffreydeaver.com; http://www.stopyourekillingme.com/jeffrey-deaver.html

De Bothuri, Alexandre. *See* **Bothuri, Alexandre de**

De Boucherville, Georges Boucher. *See* **Boucher de Boucherville, Georges**

DeBrett, Hal. *See* **Halliday, Brett**

DeBrosse, Jim
Bio-bibliographic data:
Detecting Men, 1st ed., p. 74. (876)

De Brune, [Charles Francis] Aidan
Bio-bibliographic data:
Australian Crime Fiction, pp. 74–75. (207)

Decolta, Ramon. *See* **Whitfield, Raoul**

Decotret, Claude
Bio-bibliographic data:
Canadian Crime Fiction, p. 57. (209)

Dee, Ed
Bio-bibliographic data:
Detecting Men, 1st ed., p. 74. (876)
The Encyclopedia of Murder and Mystery, p. 134. (6)
Web site: http://www.stopyourekillingme.com/ed-dee.html; http://www.edwarddee.com; http://www.edDee.net

Defoe, Daniel
Bio-bibliographic data:
The Encyclopedia of Murder and Mystery, pp. 135–36. (6)

deFord, Miriam Allen
Bio-bibliographic data:
The Encyclopedia of Mystery and Detection, pp. 119–20. (7)
Twentieth-Century Crime and Mystery Writers, 1st ed., pp. 446–48. (882a)
de Forest, John William
Bio-bibliographic data:
The Encyclopedia of Mystery and Detection, p. 120. (7)
De Fraga, Geoff
Bio-bibliographic data:
Australian Crime Fiction, p. 75. (207)
De Franchesi, Marisa
Bio-bibliographic data:
Canadian Crime Fiction, p. 57. (209)
De Gaspé, Philippe-Ignace-François Aubert. *See* **Aubert de Gaspé, Philippe-Ignace-François**
De Gramont, Monique. *See* **Gramont, Monique de**
DeGrave, Philip. *See* **DeAndrea, William L.**
De Grosbois, Paul. *See* **Grosbois Paul de**
De Hamel, Herbert
Bio-bibliographic data:
Australian Crime Fiction, p. 75. (207)
Deighton, Len; i.e., Leonard Cyril
Bio-bibliographic data:
British Mystery and Thriller Writers since 1940, First Series, pp. 36–54. (868)
Canadian Crime Fiction, p. 275. (209)
Corpus Delicti of Mystery Fiction, pp. 64–65. (879)
Critical Survey of Mystery and Detective Fiction, pp. 471–76. (41)
Detecting Men, 1st ed., p. 75. (876)
Encyclopedia Mysteriosa, p. 87. (2)
The Encyclopedia of Murder and Mystery, pp. 136–37. (6)
The Encyclopedia of Mystery and Detection, pp. 120–21. (7)
100 Masters of Mystery and Detective Fiction, pp. 191–98. (37)
The Oxford Companion to Crime and Mystery Writing, p. 115. (4)
St. James Guide to Crime & Mystery Writers, 4th ed., pp. 288–90. (882d)
Twentieth-Century Crime and Mystery Writers, 1st ed., pp. 448–51. (882a)
Twentieth-Century Crime and Mystery Writers, 2nd ed., pp. 252–53. (882b)
Twentieth-Century Crime and Mystery Writers, 3rd ed., pp. 301–3. (882c)

Web site: http://www.stopyourekillingme.com/len-deighton.html; http://www.geocities.com/Colosseum/1767/deighton.htm
Dekker, Carl. *See* **Lafflin, John**
Delacorta. *See* **Odier, Daniel**
De Lamirande, Claire. *See* **Lamirande, Claire de**
de la Torre, Lillian. *Pseud. for* **Lillian McCue**
Bio-bibliographic data:
Critical Survey of Mystery and Detective Fiction, pp. 477–82. (41)
Detecting Women 2, p. 54. (877b)
The Encyclopedia of Murder and Mystery, p. 137. (6)
The Encyclopedia of Mystery and Detection, p. 121. (7)
St. James Guide to Crime & Mystery Writers, 4th ed., pp. 290–91. (882d)
Twentieth-Century Crime and Mystery Writers, 1st ed., pp. 451–53. (882a)
Twentieth-Century Crime and Mystery Writers, 2nd ed., pp. 253–54. (882b)
Twentieth-Century Crime and Mystery Writers, 3rd ed., pp. 303–4. (882c)
Personal papers in Harold B. Lee Collection, Brigham Young University, Provo, Utah.
Web site: http://www.stopyourekillingme.com/lillian-de-la-torre.html
Delisle, Roger
Bio-bibliographic data:
Canadian Crime Fiction, p. 58. (209)
DeLoach, Nora
Bio-bibliographic data:
Detecting Women, 3rd ed., p. 74. (877c)
Web site: http://www.stopyourekillingme.com/nora-deloach.html; http://members.aol.com/atlsinc/ndeloach
Delving, Michael. *Pseud. for* **Jay Williams**
Bio-bibliographic data:
The Encyclopedia of Murder and Mystery, pp. 137–38. (6)
Twentieth-Century Crime and Mystery Writers, 1st ed., pp. 453–56 (882a)
Twentieth-Century Crime and Mystery Writers, 2nd ed., pp. 254–56. (882b)
Personal papers in Mugar Memorial Library, Boston University
De Mar, Paul. *See* **Foley, Pearl Beatrix**
Demaris, Ovid
Bio-bibliographic data:

Twentieth-Century Crime and Mystery Writers, 1st ed., pp. 456–57. (882a)

De Mille, James
Bio-bibliographic data:
Canadian Crime Fiction, p. 58. (209)

Demille, Nelson
Bio-bibliographic data:
Detecting Men, 1st ed., p. 75. (876)
St. James Guide to Crime & Mystery Writers, 4th ed., pp. 291–92. (882d)
Twentieth-Century Crime and Mystery Writers, 3rd ed., pp. 304–6. (882c)
Web site: http://www.stopyourekillingme. com/nelson-demille.html

Deming, Richard
Bio-bibliographic data:
Twentieth-Century Crime and Mystery Writers, 1st ed., pp. 458–61. (882a)
Twentieth-Century Crime and Mystery Writers, 2nd ed., pp. 256–59. (882b)
Twentieth-Century Crime and Mystery Writers, 3rd ed., pp. 306–9. (882c)

Denevi, Marco
Bio-bibliographic data:
Latin American Mystery Writers: An A to Z Guide. (881)

Dengler, Sandy
Bio-bibliographic data:
Detecting Women 2, p. 54. (877b)
Detecting Women, 3rd ed., p. 74. (877c)
The Mammoth Encyclopedia of Modern Crime Fiction, pp. 134–35. (1)

Denison, Muriel [Goggin]; Mrs. Merrill
Bio-bibliographic data:
Canadian Crime Fiction, pp. 58–59. (209)

Denison, Winifred Catherine. *See* **Gray, Dulcie**

Dennis, Charles [I]. *See* **Barrett, Margaret, and Charles Dennis**

Dennis, Charles [II]
Bio-bibliographic data:
Canadian Crime Fiction, p. 59. (209)
Web site: http://www.stopyourekillingme. com/charles-dennis.html

Dennis, Ralph
Bio-bibliographic data:
Canadian Crime Fiction, p. 252. (209)

Dent, John Charles
Bio-bibliographic data:
Canadian Crime Fiction, p. 59. (209)

Dent, Lester
Bio-bibliographic data:
Canadian Crime Fiction, p. 252. (209)

Corpus Delicti of Mystery Fiction, pp. 109–11. (879)
Critical Survey of Mystery and Detective Fiction, pp. 483–88. (41)
The Encyclopedia of Murder and Mystery, p. 138. (6)
St. James Guide to Crime & Mystery Writers, 4th ed., pp. 292–95. (882d)
Twentieth-Century Crime and Mystery Writers, 1st ed., pp. 461–67. (882a)
Twentieth-Century Crime and Mystery Writers, 2nd ed., pp. 260–63. (882b)
Twentieth-Century Crime and Mystery Writers, 3rd ed., pp. 309–12. (882c)
Personal papers in University of Missouri, Columbia.
Web site:
http://www.miskatonic.org/dent.html; http://www.mindspiring.com/~sheba/ dent.html; http://www.fantasticfiction. co.uk/authors/Lester_Dent.htm

Dentinger, Jane
Bio-bibliographic data:
By a Woman's Hand, 1st ed., pp. 63–64. (884a)
By a Woman's Hand, 2nd ed., p. 63. (884b)
Detecting Women, 1st ed., p. 50. (877a)
Detecting Women 2, p. 54. (877b)
Detecting Women, 3rd ed., p. 75. (877c)
The Mammoth Encyclopedia of Modern Crime Fiction, pp. 135–36. (1)
St. James Guide to Crime & Mystery Writers, 4th ed., pp. 295–96. (882d)
Web site: http://www.stopyourekillingme. com/jane-dentinger.html

Denton, Kit [Arnold Christopher]
Bio-bibliographic data:
Australian Crime Fiction, p. 75. (207)

Dentry, Robert: unidentified pseud.
Bio-bibliographic data:
Australian Crime Fiction, pp. 75–76. (207)

Dereske, Jo
Bio-bibliographic data:
Detecting Women, 1st ed., p. 50. (877a)
Detecting Women 2, p. 55. (877b)
Detecting Women, 3rd ed., p. 75. (877c)
Web site: http://www.stopyourekillingme. com/jo-dreske.html; http://www. nwlink.com/~massucco/NW-Mys t-Auth/Dereske.html

Derleth, August [William]
Bio-bibliographic data:

Critical Survey of Mystery and Detective Fiction, pp. 489–96. (41)
Encyclopedia Mysteriosa, p. 89. (2)
The Encyclopedia of Murder and Mystery, p. 139. (6)
The Encyclopedia of Mystery and Detection, pp. 121–22. (7)
St. James Guide to Crime & Mystery Writers, 4th ed., pp. 296–300. (882d)
Twentieth-Century Crime and Mystery Writers, 1st ed., pp. 467–73. (882a)
Twentieth-Century Crime and Mystery Writers, 2nd ed., pp. 263–66. (882b)
Twentieth-Century Crime and Mystery Writers, 3rd ed., pp. 312–16. (882c)
Personal papers at State Historical Society of Wisconsin Library, Madison, Wisconsin.
Web site: http://www.derleth.org
    August Derleth Societies
        Kay Price, Executive Secretary
        c/o The August Derleth Society
        P.O. Box 481
        Sauk City, WI 53583
        Praed Street Irregulars
        c/o Dr. George A. Vanderburgh
        P.O. Box 204
        Shelburne, ON
        Canada L0N 1S0
De Roquebrune, Robert Laroque. *See* **Roquebrune, Robert Laroque de**
Derrick, Lionel: alternating pseud. of Mark K. Roberts and Chet Cunningham (q.q.v.)
Desaulniers, Diane
Bio-bibliographic data:
Canadian Crime Fiction, p. 60. (209)
Descarries, Michel, et Thérèse Descarries
Bio-bibliographic data:
Canadian Crime Fiction, p. 60. (209)
Descarries, Thérèse. *See* **Descarries, Michel, et Thérèse Descarries**
Descheneaux, Norman
Bio-bibliographic data:
Canadian Crime Fiction, p. 60. (209)
Deschênes, Jean Milville. *See* **Miville-DeschLnes, Jean**
Desgent, Jean-Marc
Bio-bibliographic data:
Canadian Crime Fiction, p. 60. (209)
Desgranges, Jean
Bio-bibliographic data:
Canadian Crime Fiction, p. 60. (209)

Desjardins, Denis
Bio-bibliographic data:
Canadian Crime Fiction, p. 60. (209)
Desmarins, Paul: unidentified pseud.
Bio-bibliographic data:
Canadian Crime Fiction, p. 60. (209)
Desmond, Hugh
Bio-bibliographic data:
Twentieth-Century Crime and Mystery Writers, 1st ed., pp. 473–75. (882a)
Twentieth-Century Crime and Mystery Writers, 2nd ed., pp. 266–67. (882b)
Desrosiers, Danièle
Bio-bibliographic data:
Canadian Crime Fiction, p. 60. (209)
Desrosiers, Sylvie
Bio-bibliographic data:
Canadian Crime Fiction, p. 60. (209)
De Vaubert, Michelle. *See* **Vaubert, Michelle de**
Deverell, William [Herbert]
Bio-bibliographic data:
Canadian Crime Fiction, pp. 60–61. (209)
The Mammoth Encyclopedia of Modern Crime Fiction, pp. 136–37. (1)
Web site: http://www.deverell.com
De Vernal, François. *See* **Vernal, François de**
De Villers, Jean-Pierre
Bio-bibliographic data:
Canadian Crime Fiction, p. 61, (209)
Devine, D. M.; i.e., David McDonald
Bio-bibliographic data:
The Encyclopedia of Murder and Mystery, p. 140. (6)
The Encyclopedia of Mystery and Detection, p. 122. (7)
Twentieth-Century Crime and Mystery Writers, 1st ed., pp. 475–76. (882a)
Twentieth-Century Crime and Mystery Writers, 2nd ed., pp. 267–68. (882b)
Devine, Dominic. *See* **Devine, D. M.**
Devine, Llew; i.e., [J.] Llewellyn
Bio-bibliographic data:
Canadian Crime Fiction, p. 61. (209)
De Weese, Gene; i.e., Thomas Eugene
Bio-bibliographic data:
Australian Crime Fiction, p. 76. (207)
Dewey, Thomas B[lanchard].
Bio-bibliographic data:
American Hard-Boiled Crime Writers, pp. 106–11. (862)
The Big Book of Noir, p. 264. (24)
Encyclopedia Mysteriosa, p. 90. (2)

The Encyclopedia of Murder and Mystery,
pp. 140–41. (6)
*The Encyclopedia of Mystery and
Detection*, pp. 122–13. (7)
*St. James Guide to Crime & Mystery
Writers*, 4th ed., pp. 300–301. (882d)
*Twentieth-Century Crime and Mystery
Writers,* 1st ed., pp. 477–79. (882a)
*Twentieth-Century Crime and Mystery
Writers*, 2nd ed., pp. 268–70. (882b)
*Twentieth-Century Crime and Mystery
Writers*, 3rd ed., pp. 316–17. (882c)
Personal papers in Mugar Memorial
Library, Boston University.
Dewhurst, Eileen
Bio-bibliographic data:
By a Woman's Hand, 2nd ed., pp. 63–64.
(884b)
Detecting Women, 3rd ed., p. 76. (877c)
*St. James Guide to Crime & Mystery
Writers*, 4th ed., pp. 301–2. (882d)
*Twentieth-Century Crime and Mystery
Writers*, 3rd ed., pp. 317–18. (882c)
Personal papers in Mugar Memorial
Library, Boston University.
Web site: http://www.stopyourekillingme.
com/eileen-dewhurst.html
Dewhurst, Keith
Bio-bibliographic data:
Australian Crime Fiction, p. 76. (207)
Dexter, [Norman] Colin
Bio-bibliographic data:
*British Mystery and Thriller Writers since
1940, First Series*, pp. 55–64. (868)
*Critical Survey of Mystery and Detective
Fiction*, pp. 497–501. (41)
Detecting Men, 1st ed., p. 76. (876)
Encyclopedia Mysteriosa, p. 90. (2)
The Encyclopedia of Murder and Mystery,
p. 141. (6)
*The Mammoth Encyclopedia of Modern
Crime Fiction*, p. 137. (1)
Mystery and Suspense Writers, pp.
291–99. (884.2)
*The Oxford Companion to Crime and
Mystery Writing*, p. 118. (4)
*St. James Guide to Crime & Mystery
Writers*, 4th ed., pp. 303–4. (882d)
*Twentieth-Century Crime and Mystery
Writers*, 2nd ed., pp. 270–71. (882b)
*Twentieth-Century Crime and Mystery
Writers*, 3rd ed., pp. 318–20. (882c)
*Whodunit? A Who's Who in Crime and
Mystery Writing*, pp. 50–51. (5)

Web site: http://www.stopyourekillingme.
com/colin-dexter.html; http://www.
inspectormorse.co.uk
Dexter, Ted
Bio-bibliographic data:
Australian Crime Fiction, pp. 76–77.
(207)
Dey, Frederic Van Rensselaer
Bio-bibliographic data:
Canadian Crime Fiction, pp. 252, 268.
(209)
*Twentieth-Century Crime and Mystery
Writers,* 1st ed., pp. 479–85. (882a)
*Twentieth-Century Crime and Mystery
Writers*, 2nd ed., pp. 271–73. (882b)
Deyglun, Henry
Bio-bibliographic data:
Canadian Crime Fiction, p. 61. (209)
Dibdin, Michael
Bio-bibliographic data:
Canadian Crime Fiction, p. 275. (209)
Detecting Men, 1st ed., p. 76. (876)
The Encyclopedia of Murder and Mystery,
pp. 141–42. (6)
*The Mammoth Encyclopedia of Modern
Crime Fiction*, pp. 137–39. (1)
*St. James Guide to Crime & Mystery
Writers*, 4th ed., pp. 304–5. (882d)
*Twentieth-Century Crime and Mystery
Writers*, 3rd ed., pp. 320–21. (882c)
*Whodunit? A Who's Who in Crime and
Mystery Writing*, p. 51. (5)
Web site: http://www.stopyourekillingme.
com/michael-dibdin.html
Dick, George
Bio-bibliographic data:
Canadian Crime Fiction, p. 61. (209)
Dick, Philip K[indred].
Bio-bibliographic data:
The Encyclopedia of Murder and Mystery,
p. 142. (6)
Dick, T. *Pseud. for* **Eric Richard Osler**
Dickens, Charles [John Huffam]
Bio-bibliographic data:
British Mystery Writers, 1860–1919, pp.
102–11. (866)
*Critical Survey of Mystery and Detective
Fiction*, pp. 502–507. (41)
The Encyclopedia of Murder and Mystery,
pp. 142–43. (6)
*The Encyclopedia of Mystery and
Detection*, pp. 123–24. (7)
*The Oxford Companion to Crime and
Mystery Writing*, pp. 118–19. (4)

*St. James Guide to Crime & Mystery
Writers*, 4th ed., pp. 305–6. (882d)
*Twentieth-Century Crime and Mystery
Writers,* 1st ed., p. 1527. (882a)
*Twentieth-Century Crime and Mystery
Writers*, 2nd ed., p. 932. (882b)
*Twentieth-Century Crime and Mystery
Writers*, 3rd ed., p. 1122. (882c)
*Whodunit? A Who's Who in Crime and
Mystery Writing*, p. 51. (5)
Personal papers in Beinecke Rare Book
and Manuscript Library, Yale
University.
Personal papers in Berg Collection, New
York Public Library.
Personal papers in Dickens House,
London.
Personal papers in Free Library of
Philadelphia, Pennsylvania.
Personal papers in Huntington Library,
San Marino, California.
Personal papers in Pierpont Morgan
Library, New York.
   Dickens Society
    Robert J. Heaman,
     Secretary-Treasurer
    School of Liberal Arts and
     Sciences
    Wilkes University
    Wilkes-Barre, PA 18766

Dickens, Francis Jeffrey
Bio-bibliographic data:
Canadian Crime Fiction, pp. 61–62. (209)
Dickie, Francis [Joseph]
Bio-bibliographic data:
Canadian Crime Fiction, p. 62. (209)
Dickinson, Peter [Malcolm de Brissac]
Bio-bibliographic data:
*British Mystery and Thriller Writers since
1940, First Series*, pp. 65–72. (868)
*Critical Survey of Mystery and Detective
Fiction*, pp. 508–14. (41)
Detecting Men, 1st ed., pp. 76–77. (876)
Encyclopedia Mysteriosa, p. 91. (2)
The Encyclopedia of Murder and Mystery,
pp. 143–44. (6)
*The Encyclopedia of Mystery and
Detection*, pp. 124–25. (7)
*The Mammoth Encyclopedia of Modern
Crime Fiction*, pp. 139–40. (1)
*St. James Guide to Crime & Mystery
Writers*, 4th ed., p.306–8. (882d)
*Twentieth-Century Crime and Mystery
Writers,* 1st ed., pp. 485–87. (882a)

*Twentieth-Century Crime and Mystery
Writers*, 2nd ed., pp. 274–75. (882b)
*Twentieth-Century Crime and Mystery
Writers*, 3rd ed., pp. 321–22. (882c)
*Whodunit? A Who's Who in Crime and
Mystery Writing*, pp. 51–52. (5)
Web site: http://www.stopyourekillingme.
com/peter-dickinson.html
Dicks, Terrance
Bio-bibliographic data:
Canadian Crime Fiction, p. 252. (209)
Dickson, Carr. *See* **Carr, John Dickson**
Dickson, Carter. *See* **Carr, John Dickson**
Dickson, Helen. *See* **Reynolds, Helen
Mary Greenwood [Campbell Dickson]**
Dietrich, Robert. *See* **Hunt, E. Howard,
Jr.**
Dietz, Denise
Bio-bibliographic data:
Detecting Women, 1st ed., p. 50. (877a)
Detecting Women 2, p. 55. (877b)
Detecting Women, 3rd ed., p. 76. (877c)
Web site: http://www.stopyourekillingme.
com/denise-dietz.html; http://www.
eclectics.com/denise
Diment, Adam
Bio-bibliographic data:
*Twentieth-Century Crime and Mystery
Writers,* 1st ed., p. 488. (882a)
Di Michele, Mary
Bio-bibliographic data:
Canadian Crime Fiction, p. 62. (209)
Dimmock, F. H.; i.e., Frederick Haydn
Bio-bibliographic data:
Canadian Crime Fiction, p. 252. (209)
Dion, Germain
Bio-bibliographic data:
Canadian Crime Fiction, p. 62. (209)
**"Diplomat." *Pseud. for* John Franklin
Carter**
Bio-bibliographic data:
Encyclopedia Mysteriosa, p. 94. (2)
*The Encyclopedia of Mystery and
Detection*, p. 126. (7)
Disher, Garry [Donald]
Bio-bibliographic data:
Australian Crime Fiction, pp. 77, 145,
146. (207)
Detecting Men, 1st ed., p. 77. (876)
Disney, Doris Miles
Bio-bibliographic data:
Detecting Women, 1st ed., p. 50. (877a)
Detecting Women 2, p. 55. (877b)
Encyclopedia Mysteriosa, p. 95. (2)

The Encyclopedia of Murder and Mystery, pp. 144–45. (6)
The Encyclopedia of Mystery and Detection, p. 127. (7)
Great Women Mystery Writers, pp. 94–97. (880)
St. James Guide to Crime & Mystery Writers, 4th ed., pp. 308–10. (882d)
Twentieth-Century Crime and Mystery Writers, 1st ed., pp. 488–91. (882a)
Twentieth-Century Crime and Mystery Writers, 2nd ed., pp. 275–77. (882b)
Twentieth-Century Crime and Mystery Writers, 3rd ed., pp. 322–24. (882c)
Personal papers in Mugar Memorial Library, Boston University.
Web site: http://www.stopyourekillingme. com/doris-miles-disney.html

Disney, Dorothy Cameron
Bio-bibliographic data:
Canadian Crime Fiction, pp. 252–53. (209)
Encyclopedia Mysteriosa, p. 95. (2)
The Encyclopedia of Mystery and Detection, p. 127. (7)
Twentieth-Century Crime and Mystery Writers, 1st ed., pp. 491–92. (882a)
Twentieth-Century Crime and Mystery Writers, 2nd ed., p. 277. (882b)
Twentieth-Century Crime and Mystery Writers, 3rd ed., pp. 324–25. (882c)

Ditton, James. *See* **Clark, Douglas**

Dix, Maurice Buxton
Bio-bibliographic data:
Canadian Crime Fiction, p. 62. (209)

Dixon, Franklin W.: house pseud. *See* **Hardy Boys in section devoted to series characters. The following references the titles written by Canadian writer Leslie McFarlane:**
Bio-bibliographic data:
Canadian Crime Fiction, p. 63. (209)

Dixon, Jean [Clarence]
Bio-bibliographic data:
Australian Crime Fiction, pp. 77–78. (207)

Dixon, Louisa
Bio-bibliographic data:
Detecting Women, 3rd ed., p. 77. (877c)
Web site: http://www.stopyourekillingme. com/louisa-dixon.html; http://www. louisadixon.com/index.htm

Dixon, Robert Malcolm Ward. *See* **Brown, Hosanna**

Dobey, Pat
Bio-bibliographic data:
Canadian Crime Fiction, p. 63. (209)

Dobson, Joanne
Bio-bibliographic data:
Detecting Women, 3rd ed., p. 77. (877c)
Web site: http://www.stopyourekillingme. com/joanne-dobson.html

Dobyns, Stephen
Bio-bibliographic data:
Detecting Men, 1st ed., p. 77. (876)
Encyclopedia Mysteriosa, p. 95. (2)
The Encyclopedia of Murder and Mystery, p. 145. (6)
The Mammoth Encyclopedia of Modern Crime Fiction, pp. 140–41. (1)
St. James Guide to Crime & Mystery Writers, 4th ed., pp. 310–11. (882d)
Twentieth-Century Crime and Mystery Writers, 3rd ed., pp. 325–26. (882c)
Whodunit? A Who's Who in Crime and Mystery Writing, p. 53. (5)
Web site: http://www.stopyourekillingme. com/stephen-dobyns.html;

Docherty, James L. *See* **Chase, James Hadley**

Doctorow, E. L.; i.e., Edgar Lawrence
Bio-bibliographic data:
The Encyclopedia of Murder and Mystery, pp. 145–46. (6)

Doderer, Heimito von
Bio-bibliographic data:
Critical Survey of Mystery and Detective Fiction, pp. 515–21. (41)

Dodge, David
Bio-bibliographic data:
Twentieth-Century Crime and Mystery Writers, 1st ed., pp. 493–94. (882a)
Twentieth-Century Crime and Mystery Writers, 2nd ed., pp. 277–78. (882b)
Twentieth-Century Crime and Mystery Writers, 3rd ed., pp. 326–27. (882c)
Web site: http://www.thrillingdetective. com/trivia/dodge.html

Doherty, P. C.; i.e., Paul Charles
Bio-bibliographic data:
Detecting Men, 1st ed., pp. 57, 78, 82, 104–5, 115. (876)
The Mammoth Encyclopedia of Modern Crime Fiction, pp. 141–43. (1)
Speaking of Murder, vol. II, pp. 162–72. (875b)

Web site: http://www.stopyourekillingme.
com/p-c-doherty.html
Dold, Gaylord
Bio-bibliographic data:
Detecting Men, 1st ed., pp. 78–79. (876)
Dolson, Hildegarde
Bio-bibliographic data:
Detecting Women, 1st ed., p. 51. (877a)
Detecting Women 2, p. 56. (877b)
*Twentieth-Century Crime and Mystery
Writers,* 1st ed., pp. 494–95. (882a)
*Twentieth-Century Crime and Mystery
Writers,* 2nd ed., pp. 278–79. (882b)
Web site: http://www.stopyourekillingme.
com/hildegarde-dolson.html
Dominic, R. B. *See* **Lathen, Emma**
Donald, Anabel
Bio-bibliographic data:
By a Woman's Hand, 2nd ed., pp. 64–65.
(884b)
Detecting Women 2, p. 56. (877b)
Detecting Women, 3rd ed., p. 78. (877c)
*The Mammoth Encyclopedia of Modern
Crime Fiction,* p. 143. (1)
Donaldson, D. J. [Donald J.]
Bio-bibliographic data:
Detecting Men, 1st ed., p. 79. (876)
Web site: http://www.stopyourekillingme.
com/d-j-donaldson.html; http://
dondonaldson.com
Donaldson, Stephen R. *See* **Stephens, Reed**
Donoghue, P. S. *See* **Hunt, E. Howard, Jr.**
Donovan, Dick. *Pseud. for* **Joyce
Emmerson Preston Muddock**
Bio-bibliographic data:
Australian Crime Fiction, p. 78. (207)
Encyclopedia Mysteriosa, pp. 95–96. (2)
The Encyclopedia of Murder and Mystery,
p. 146. (6)
*The Encyclopedia of Mystery and
Detection,* pp. 127–28. (7)
*Twentieth-Century Crime and Mystery
Writers,* 1st ed., pp. 496–99. (882a)
*Twentieth-Century Crime and Mystery
Writers,* 2nd ed., pp. 279–81. (882b)
*Twentieth-Century Crime and Mystery
Writers,* 3rd ed., pp. 327–28. (882c)
Donovan, Laurence
Bio-bibliographic data:
Canadian Crime Fiction, p. 253. (209)
Doody, Margaret [Anne]
Bio-bibliographic data:
Canadian Crime Fiction, p. 63. (209)

Dooley, Anne M.
Bio-bibliographic data:
Canadian Crime Fiction, p. 63. (209)
Doolittle, Jerome
Bio-bibliographic data:
Detecting Men, 1st ed., p. 79. (876)
Web site: http://www.stopyourekillingme.
com/jerome-doolittle.html; http://
www.badattitudes.com/Doolittle.html
Doran, Jeff
Bio-bibliographic data:
Canadian Crime Fiction, p. 63. (209)
Dorland, Michael
Bio-bibliographic data:
Canadian Crime Fiction, p. 63. (209)
Dorman, Sparkle Vera Lynette [Hayter].
See **Hayter, Sparkle Vera Lynette**
Dorrance, Ethel [Arnold Smith]
Bio-bibliographic data:
Canadian Crime Fiction, p. 253. (209)
Dorrance, James [French]
Bio-bibliographic data:
Canadian Crime Fiction, p. 253. (209)
Dorrington, Albert
Bio-bibliographic data:
Australian Crime Fiction, p. 78. (207)
Doss, James D.
Bio-bibliographic data:
Detecting Men, 1st ed., p. 80. (876)
Web site: http://www.stopyourekillingme.
com/james-d-doss.html
Dostoevski, Fyodor Mikhailovich. *See*
Dostoyevsky, Fyodor Mikhaylovich
Dostoyevsky, Fyodor Mikhaylovich
Bio-bibliographic data:
*Critical Survey of Mystery and Detective
Fiction,* pp. 522–28. (41)
Encyclopedia Mysteriosa, p. 97. (2)
The Encyclopedia of Murder and Mystery,
pp. 147–48. (6)
*The Encyclopedia of Mystery and
Detection,* p. 128. (7)
*100 Masters of Mystery and Detective
Fiction,* pp. 199–206. (37)
*The Oxford Companion to Crime and
Mystery Writing,* pp. 122–23. (4)
*Whodunit? A Who's Who in Crime and
Mystery Writing,* p. 53. (5)
International Dostoevsky Society
Dr. Deborah Martinson,
Treasurer
c/o Professor Nadine Natov
Office of the Core Curriculum,
Hamilton Hall

New York, NY 10027

Douglas, Arthur. *See* **Hammond, Gerald**

Douglas, Carole Nelson
Bio-bibliographic data:
By a Woman's Hand, 1st ed., pp. 64–65.
(884a)
By a Woman's Hand, 2nd ed., pp. 65–66.
(884b)
Detecting Women, 1st ed., pp. 51–52.
(877a)
Detecting Women 2, pp. 56–57. (877b)
Detecting Women, 3rd ed., pp. 78–79.
(877c)
*The Mammoth Encyclopedia of Modern
Crime Fiction*, pp. 144–45. (1)
*St. James Guide to Crime & Mystery
Writers*, 4th ed., pp. 311–13. (882d)
*Whodunit? A Who's Who in Crime and
Mystery Writing*, pp. 53–54. (5)
Web site: http://www.stopyourekillingme.
com/carole-nelson-douglas.html
Midnight Louie's Scratching
Post-Intelligencer
c/o Carole Nelson Douglas
P.O. Box 331555
Fort Worth, TX 76163
http://www.catwriter.com

Douglas, John: undisclosed pseud.
Bio-bibliographic data:
Detecting Men, 1st ed., p. 80. (876)
Web site: http://www.stopyourekillingme.
com/john-douglas.html

Douglas, Lauren Wright
Bio-bibliographic data:
By a Woman's Hand, 1st ed., p. 65. (884a)
By a Woman's Hand, 2nd ed., p. 66.
(884b)
Canadian Crime Fiction, pp. 63–64, (209)
Detecting Women, 1st ed., p. 52. (877a)
Detecting Women 2, p. 57. (877b)
Detecting Women, 3rd ed., p. 79. (877c)

Douglas, Malcolm. *See* **Sanderson,
[Ronald] Douglas**

Douthwaite, L. C.; i.e., Louis Charles
Bio-bibliographic data:
Canadian Crime Fiction, p. 64. (209)

Doutremont, Henri. *Pseud. for* **Georges
Bugnet**
Bio-bibliographic data:
Canadian Crime Fiction, pp. 64–65. (209)

Dowd, John
Bio-bibliographic data:
Canadian Crime Fiction, p. 65. (209)

Dowling, Gregory
Bio-bibliographic data:
Detecting Men, 1st ed., pp. 80–81. (876)

Downes, Quentin. *See* **Harrison, Michael**

Downing, Warwick
Bio-bibliographic data:
Detecting Men, 1st ed., p. 81. (876)

Doyle, [Sir] Arthur Conan
Bio-bibliographic data:
Australian Crime Fiction, pp. 78–79.
(207)
British Mystery Writers, 1860–1919, pp.
112–34. (866)
Canadian Crime Fiction, p. 274. (209)
Corpus Delicti of Mystery Fiction, pp.
55–58. (879)
*Critical Survey of Mystery and Detective
Fiction*, pp. 529–37. (41)
Encyclopedia Mysteriosa, pp. 98–99. (2)
The Encyclopedia of Murder and Mystery,
pp. 149–51. (6)
*The Encyclopedia of Mystery and
Detection*, pp. 102–4. (7)
Mystery and Suspense Writers, pp.
301–30. (884.2)
*100 Masters of Mystery and Detective
Fiction*, pp. 207–16. (37)
*The Oxford Companion to Crime and
Mystery Writing*, pp. 124–25. (4)
*St. James Guide to Crime & Mystery
Writers*, 4th ed., pp. 314–18. (882d)
*Twentieth-Century Crime and Mystery
Writers*, 1st ed., pp. 499–504. (882a)
*Twentieth-Century Crime and Mystery
Writers*, 2nd ed., pp. 281–84. (882b)
*Twentieth-Century Crime and Mystery
Writers*, 3rd ed., pp. 329–32. (882c)
*Whodunit? A Who's Who in Crime and
Mystery Writing*, pp. 54–55 (5)
Personal papers in Humanities Research
Center, University of Texas, Austin
Web site: Sherlock Holmes International.
http://www.sherlock-holmes.org/;
Chris Redmond, A Sherlockian.Net,
http://www.sherlockian.net
Sherlock Holmes Fan Clubs and
Societies
Baker Street Irregulars
P.O. Box 2189
Easton, MO 21601
(410) 745–5553

Their "irregular quarterly of
Sherlockiana" is at the following
address:
Baker Street Journal
c/o Sheridan Press
Box 465
Hanover, PA 17331–5172
ISSN 0005–4070
Numerous additional periodicals exist, and
the following is nothing more than a
selective list. Additional names can be
found in the different editions of
Ronald De Waal's bibliographies or
through the Web sites cited earlier.
A C D The Journal of the Arthur
Conan Doyle Society
c/o Christopher Roden
Ashcroft
2 Abbotsford Drive
Penyfford, Ches. CH4 0JG
England
ISSN 0966–0763
The Battered Silicon Dispatch Box
P.O. Box 204
Shelburne, Ontario, LON ISO
Canada
ISSN 1188–0449
The Musgrave Papers
c/o Northern Musgraves
Sherlock Holmes Society
69 Greenhead Road
Huddersfield, W. York, HD1
4ER
England
ISSN 1351–1890
Sherlock Holmes Gazette
46 Purfield Drive
Wargrave, Berks RG10 8AR
England
ISSN 0965–5549
Sherlock Holmes Journal
c/o R. J. Ellis
13 Crofton Avenue
Orpington, Kent BR6 8DU
England
0037–3621
The Sherlock Holmes Museum
221b Baker Street
London, England
http://www.sherlock-holmes.
co.uk
Sherlockian Tidbits
42 Melrose Place
Montclair, NJ 07042–2028

ISSN 1040–4937
Doyle, Peter
Bio-bibliographic data:
*The Mammoth Encyclopedia of Modern
Crime Fiction*, p. 145. (1)
Drábek, Jan
Bio-bibliographic data:
Canadian Crime Fiction, p. 65. (209)
Drago, [Harry] Sinclair
Bio-bibliographic data:
Canadian Crime Fiction, p. 253. (209)
Drake, Alison. *See* MacGregor, T. J.
Drake, Mary
Bio-bibliographic data:
Australian Crime Fiction, p. 79. (207)
Draper, Hastings. *See* Jeffries, Roderic
Dreux, Albert. *Pseud. for* Albert Maillé
Bio-bibliographic data:
Canadian Crime Fiction, p. 65. (209)
Dreher, Sarah
Bio-bibliographic data:
By a Woman's Hand, 1st ed., p. 66. (884a)
By a Woman's Hand, 2nd ed., pp. 66–67.
(884b)
Detecting Women 2, pp. 57–58. (877b)
Detecting Women, 3rd ed., p. 80. (877c)
Dreiser, Theodore [Herman Albert]
Bio-bibliographic data:
The Encyclopedia of Murder and Mystery,
pp. 151–52. (6)
*The Encyclopedia of Mystery and
Detection*, p. 130. (7)
Dresser, Davis. *See* Halliday, Brett
Drew, Con; i.e., Conway
Bio-bibliographic data:
Australian Crime Fiction, p. 79. (207)
Dreyer, Eileen
Bio-bibliographic data:
Detecting Women, 3rd ed., p. 80. (877c)
Web site: http://www.stopyourekillingme.
com/eileen-dreyer.html;
http://walden.
mo.net/~kdreyer/dreyer.html
Driscoll, Peter
Bio-bibliographic data:
*St. James Guide to Crime & Mystery
Writers*, 4th ed., pp. 318–19. (882d)
*Twentieth-Century Crime and Mystery
Writers*, 1st ed., pp. 504–6. (882a)
*Twentieth-Century Crime and Mystery
Writers*, 2nd ed., pp. 284–85. (882b)
*Twentieth-Century Crime and Mystery
Writers*, 3rd ed., pp. 332–34. (882c)

Personal papers in Mugar Memorial
  Library, Boston University
Dropaott, Papartchu: unidentified pseud.
  Bio-bibliographic data:
  Canadian Crime Fiction, p. 65. (209)
Droste-Hülshoff, Annette von
  Bio-bibliographic data:
  *Critical Survey of Mystery and Detective
    Fiction*, pp. 538–42. (41)
Drummond, Ivor. *See* **Longrigg, Roger
  Erskine**
Drummond, June
  Bio-bibliographic data:
  *St. James Guide to Crime & Mystery
    Writers*, 4th ed., pp. 319–21. (882d)
  *Twentieth-Century Crime and Mystery
    Writers*, 1st ed., pp. 508–10. (882a)
  *Twentieth-Century Crime and Mystery
    Writers*, 2nd ed., pp. 286–87. (882b)
  *Twentieth-Century Crime and Mystery
    Writers*, 3rd ed., pp. 334–445. (882c)
Drury, Joan M.
  Bio-bibliographic data:
  Detecting Women, 3rd ed., pp. 80–81.
    (877c)
Dubois, Brendan
  Bio-bibliographic data:
  Detecting Men, 1st ed., p. 82. (876)
  Web site: http://www.stopyourekillingme.
    com/brendan-dubois.html; http://
    www.resurrectionday.com
Du Bois, Leon. *See* **Batt, Leon**
**Du Boisgobey, Fortuné [Hippolyte
  Auguste]**
  Bio-bibliographic data:
  *The Encyclopedia of Mystery and
    Detection*, pp. 134–35. (7)
Duckworth, Colin [Ryder]
  Bio-bibliographic data:
  Australian Crime Fiction, p. 79. (207)
Dudgeon, Robert
  Bio-bibliographic data:
  Australian Crime Fiction, p. 80. (207)
Dudley-Smith, Trevor. *See* **Trevor,
  Elleston**
Duell, Marie. *See* **Curzon, Clare**
Duffy, Margaret
  Bio-bibliographic data:
  Detecting Women, 1st ed., p. 52. (877a)
  Detecting Women 2, p. 58. (877b)
  Detecting Women, 3rd ed., p. 81. (877c)
  Web site: http://www.stopyourekillingme.
    com/mararet-duffy.html

Duffy, Stella
  Bio-bibliographic data:
  Detecting Women, 3rd ed., p. 81. (877c)
  *The Mammoth Encyclopedia of Modern
    Crime Fiction*, pp. 145–46. (1)
  Web site: http://www.twbooks.co.uk/
    authors/sduffy.html
Dufour, Josée
  Bio-bibliographic data:
  Canadian Crime Fiction, p. 65. (209)
Duke, Madelaine
  Bio-bibliographic data:
  *Twentieth-Century Crime and Mystery
    Writers*, 2nd ed., pp. 288–89.
Duke, Winifred
  Bio-bibliographic data:
  *The Encyclopedia of Mystery and
    Detection*, pp. 135. (7)
Dukthas, Ann. *See* **Doherty, P. C.**
Dumas, Alexandre (Dumas pPre)
  Bio-bibliographic data:
  *Critical Survey of Mystery and Detective
    Fiction*, pp. 543–50. (41)
  The Encyclopedia of Murder and Mystery,
    p. 153. (6)
Dumas, Jacqueline
  Bio-bibliographic data:
  Canadian Crime Fiction, p. 65. (209)
du Maurier, Daphne
  Bio-bibliographic data:
  *And Then There Were Nine . . . More
    Women of Mystery*, pp. 10–29. (863)
  *Critical Survey of Mystery and Detective
    Fiction*, pp. 551–56. (41)
  Encyclopedia Mysteriosa, p. 103. (2)
  The Encyclopedia of Murder and Mystery,
    pp. 153–54. (6)
  *The Encyclopedia of Mystery and
    Detection*, pp. 135–36. (7)
  Mystery and Suspense Writers, pp.
    331–43. (884.2)
  *100 Masters of Mystery and Detective
    Fiction*, pp. 217–23. (37)
  *The Oxford Companion to Crime and
    Mystery Writing*, p. 126. (4)
  *St. James Guide to Crime & Mystery
    Writers*, 4th ed., pp. 321–23. (882d)
  *Twentieth-Century Crime and Mystery
    Writers*, 1st ed., pp. 510–513. (882a)
  *Twentieth-Century Crime and Mystery
    Writers*, 2nd ed., pp. 289–90. (882b)
  *Twentieth-Century Crime and Mystery
    Writers*, 3rd ed., pp. 335–37. (882c)

Whodunit? A Who's Who in Crime and Mystery Writing, pp. 55–56. (5)
Web site: http://www.stopyourekillingme.com/daphne-dumaurier.html
Dumouchel, Ernestine
Bio-bibliographic data:
Canadian Crime Fiction, p. 66. (209)
Dunant, Peter. *See* **Dunant, Sarah**
Dunant, Sarah
Bio-bibliographic data:
By a Woman's Hand, 1st ed., pp. 66–67. (884a)
By a Woman's Hand, 2nd ed., pp. 67–68. (884b)
Detecting Women, 1st ed., p. 53. (877a)
Detecting Women 2, p. 58. (877b)
Detecting Women, 3rd ed., p. 82. (877c)
The Mammoth Encyclopedia of Modern Crime Fiction, pp. 146–47. (1)
Web site: http://www.stopyourekillingme.com/sarah-dunant.html
Dunbar, Sophie: unidentified pseud.
Bio-bibliographic data:
Detecting Women 2, p. 59. (877b)
Detecting Women, 3rd ed., p. 82. (877c)
Web site: http://www.stopyourekillingme.com/sophie-dunbar.html
Dunbar, Tony
Bio-bibliographic data:
Detecting Men, 1st ed., p. 82. (876)
Web site: http://www.stopyourekillingme.com/tony-dunbar.html
Duncan, Helen [Harger Bodwell Brown]
Bio-bibliographic data:
Canadian Crime Fiction, p. 66. (209)
Duncan, W. Glenn
Bio-bibliographic data:
Detecting Men, 1st ed., p. 83. (876)
Duncan, W[illiam]. Murdoch
Bio-bibliographic data:
Canadian Crime Fiction, pp. 249, 251, 253, 260. (209)
Twentieth-Century Crime and Mystery Writers, 1st ed., pp. 513–18. (882a)
Twentieth-Century Crime and Mystery Writers, 2nd ed., pp. 290–93. (882b)
Dundee, Wayne
Bio-bibliographic data:
Detecting Men, 1st ed., p. 83. (876)
Dunlap, Susan [Sullivan]
Bio-bibliographic data:
Australian Crime Fiction, p. 81. (207)
By a Woman's Hand, 1st ed., pp. 67–68. (884a)

By a Woman's Hand, 2nd ed., pp. 68–69. (884b)
Detecting Women, 1st ed., p. 53. (877a)
Detecting Women 2, p. 59. (877b)
Detecting Women, 3rd ed., pp. 82–83. (877c)
Encyclopedia Mysteriosa, p. 104. (2)
Great Women Mystery Writers, pp. 97–100. (880)
The Mammoth Encyclopedia of Modern Crime Fiction, pp. 147–48. (1)
St. James Guide to Crime & Mystery Writers, 4th ed., pp. 323–24. (882d)
Twentieth-Century Crime and Mystery Writers, 3rd ed., pp. 337–38. (882c)
Whodunit? A Who's Who in Crime and Mystery Writing, p. 56. (5)
Web site: http://www.stopyourekillingme.com/susan-dunlap.html
Dunmore, Spencer [Sambrook]
Bio-bibliographic data:
Canadian Crime Fiction, p. 66. (209)
Dunn, Carola
Bio-bibliographic data:
Detecting Women 2, pp. 59–60. (877b)
Detecting Women, 3rd ed., p. 83. (877c)
Web site: http://www.stopyourekillingme.com/carola-dunn.html; http://www.geocities.com/CarolaDunn
Dunn, Des R.
Bio-bibliographic data:
Australian Crime Fiction, p. 81. (207)
Dunne, John Gregory
Bio-bibliographic data:
The Encyclopedia of Murder and Mystery, p. 154. (6)
Twentieth-Century Crime and Mystery Writers, 1st ed., pp. 518–19. (882a)
Dunnett, Dorothy
Bio-bibliographic data:
By a Woman's Hand, 1st ed., pp. 68–69. (884a)
By a Woman's Hand, 2nd ed., pp. 69–70. (884b)
Detecting Women 2, p. 60. (877b)
Detecting Women, 3rd ed., pp. 83–84. (877c)
St. James Guide to Crime & Mystery Writers, 4th ed., pp. 324–25. (882d)
Twentieth-Century Crime and Mystery Writers, 1st ed., pp. 519–20. (882a)
Twentieth-Century Crime and Mystery Writers, 2nd ed., p. 293. (882b)

Twentieth-Century Crime and Mystery Writers, 3rd ed., pp. 338–39. (882c)
Web site: http://www.stopyourekillingme.com/dorothy-dunnett.html

Dunning, John
Bio-bibliographic data:
Detecting Men, 1st ed., p. 83. (876)
Talking Murder, pp. 98–114. (883)
Web site: http://www.stopyourekillingme.com/john-dunning.html

Dunsany, Lord; i.e., Edward John Moreton Drax Plunkett, Eighteenth Baron Dunsany
Bio-bibliographic data:
British Mystery Writers, 1920–1939, pp. 110–16. (867)
The Encyclopedia of Murder and Mystery, p. 154. (6)
The Encyclopedia of Mystery and Detection, pp. 136–37. (7)

Durbridge, Francis [Henry]
Bio-bibliographic data:
Encyclopedia Mysteriosa, pp. 104–5. (2)
The Encyclopedia of Mystery and Detection, p. 139. (7)
St. James Guide to Crime & Mystery Writers, 4th ed., pp. 325–27. (882d)
Twentieth-Century Crime and Mystery Writers, 1st ed., pp. 521–23. (882a)
Twentieth-Century Crime and Mystery Writers, 2nd ed., pp. 293–95. (882b)
Twentieth-Century Crime and Mystery Writers, 3rd ed., pp. 339–40. (882c)

Durham, David. *See* **Vickers, Roy**
Durkin, Douglas Leader
Bio-bibliographic data:
Canadian Crime Fiction, p. 66. (209)

Dürrenmatt, Friedrich
Bio-bibliographic data:
Critical Survey of Mystery and Detective Fiction, pp. 557–61. (41)
The Encyclopedia of Murder and Mystery, pp. 155–56. (6)
The Oxford Companion to Crime and Mystery Writing, p. 127. (4)
St. James Guide to Crime & Mystery Writers, 4th ed., pp. 327–28. (882d)
Twentieth-Century Crime and Mystery Writers, 1st ed., pp. 1539–40. (882a)
Twentieth-Century Crime and Mystery Writers, 2nd ed., pp. 940–41. (882b)
Twentieth-Century Crime and Mystery Writers, 3rd ed., pp. 1130–31. (882c)

Whodunit? A Who's Who in Crime and Mystery Writing, p. 57. (5)
Personal papers in Schwizerische Literaturarchiv, Bern.

Dutrisac, Billy Bob
Bio-bibliographic data:
Canadian Crime Fiction, p. 66. (209)

Dutrizac, Benoît
Bio-bibliographic data:
Canadian Crime Fiction, pp. 66–67. (209)

Dutton, James S., Jr.
Bio-bibliographic data:
Canadian Crime Fiction, p. 67. (209)

Duvert, Tony
Bio-bibliographic data:
Canadian Crime Fiction, p. 67. (209)

Dwyer, James Francis
Bio-bibliographic data:
Australian Crime Fiction, p. 81. (207)

Dymmoch, Michael Allen. *Pseud. for* **E. M. Grant**
Bio-bibliographic data:
Detecting Women 2, p. 60. (877b)
Detecting Women, 3rd ed., p. 84. (877c)
Web site: http://www.stopyourekillingme.com/michael-allen-dymmoch.html

E

Earl, Lawrence
Bio-bibliographic data:
Canadian Crime Fiction, p. 67. (209)

Early, Jack. *See* **Scoppettone, Sandra**
East, F. Llewellyn
Bio-bibliographic data:
Australian Crime Fiction, p. 82. (207)

East, Michael. *See* **West, Morris**
Eberhart, Mignon G[ood].
Bio-bibliographic data:
Corpus Delicti of Mystery Fiction, pp. 65–67. (879)
Critical Survey of Mystery and Detective Fiction, pp. 562–67. (41)
Detecting Women, 1st ed., p. 54. (877a)
Detecting Women 2, pp. 60–61. (877b)
Encyclopedia Mysteriosa, p. 106. (2)
The Encyclopedia of Murder and Mystery, p. 157. (6)
The Encyclopedia of Mystery and Detection, pp. 140–41. (7)
Mystery and Suspense Writers, pp. 345–56. (884.2)
100 Masters of Mystery and Detective Fiction, pp. 224–29. (37)

*The Oxford Companion to Crime and
  Mystery Writing*, p. 129. (4)
*St. James Guide to Crime & Mystery
  Writers*, 4th ed., pp. 331–33. (882d)
*Twentieth-Century Crime and Mystery
  Writers*, 1st ed., pp. 523–26. (882a)
*Twentieth-Century Crime and Mystery
  Writers*, 2nd ed., pp. 295–97. (882b)
*Twentieth-Century Crime and Mystery
  Writers*, 3rd ed., pp. 341–43. (882c)
*Whodunit? A Who's Who in Crime and
  Mystery Writing*, p. 59. (5)
Personal papers in Mugar Memorial
  Library, Boston University.
Web site: http://www.stopyourekillingme.
  com/mignon-g-eberhart.html

Ebersohn, Wessel [Schalk]
Bio-bibliographic data:
The Encyclopedia of Murder and Mystery,
  pp. 157–58. (6)
*Twentieth-Century Crime and Mystery
  Writers*, 2nd ed., pp. 297–98.

Ebert, Arthur Frank. *See* **Arthur, Frank**

Eccles, Marjorie
Bio-bibliographic data:
By a Woman's Hand, 1st ed., pp. 70–71.
  (884a)
By a Woman's Hand, 2nd ed., p. 71.
  (884b)
Detecting Women, 1st ed., p. 54. (877a)
Detecting Women 2, p. 61. (877b)
Detecting Women, 3rd ed., pp. 84–85.
  (877c)

Eco, Umberto
Bio-bibliographic data:
*Critical Survey of Mystery and Detective
  Fiction*, pp. 568–73. (41)
The Encyclopedia of Murder and Mystery,
  p. 158. (6)
*The Mammoth Encyclopedia of Modern
  Crime Fiction*, p. 148. (1)
*Whodunit? A Who's Who in Crime and
  Mystery Writing*, p. 60. (5)
Web site:
  http://www.dsc.unibo.it/dipartimento/
  people/eco; http://www.
  stopyourekillingme.com/
  umberto-eco.html

Eddenden, A. E.; i.e., Arthur Edward
Bio-bibliographic data:
Canadian Crime Fiction, p. 67. (209)
Detecting Men, 1st ed., p. 84. (876)
Web site: http://www.stopyourekillingme.
  com/a-e-eddenden.html

Eden, Dorothy [Enid]
Bio-bibliographic data:
Australian Crime Fiction, p. 82. (207)
Corpus Delicti of Mystery Fiction, pp.
  67–68. (879)
*Twentieth-Century Crime and Mystery
  Writers*, 1st ed., pp. 526–28. (882a)
Personal papers in Mugar Memorial
  Library, Boston University.

Eden, Matthew
Bio-bibliographic data:
Canadian Crime Fiction, p. 67. (209)

Edgar, Keith
Bio-bibliographic data:
Canadian Crime Fiction, p. 67. (209)

**Edghill, Rosemary. Pseud. for eluki bes
  shahar**
Bio-bibliographic data:
Detecting Women, 1st ed., p. 54. (877a)
Detecting Women 2, p. 61. (877b)
Detecting Women, 3rd ed., p. 85. (877c)
Web site: http://www.stopyourekillingme.
  com/rosemary-edghill.html; http://
  www.sff.net/people/eluki/index2.htp

Edwards, Alberto
Bio-bibliographic data:
*Latin American Mystery Writers: An A to
  Z Guide. (881)*

Edwards, Grace F.
Bio-bibliographic data:
Detecting Women, 3rd ed., p. 85. (877c)
Web site: http://www.stopyourekillingme.
  com/grace-f-edwards.html; http://
  members.aol.com/malmystery/
  index.html

Edwards, [Kenneth] Martin
Bio-bibliographic data:
Detecting Men, 1st ed., p. 84. (876)
*The Mammoth Encyclopedia of Modern
  Crime Fiction*, pp. 148–49. (1)
*Whodunit? A Who's Who in Crime and
  Mystery Writing*, p. 60. (5)
Web site:
  www.twbooks.co.uk/authors/medwar
  ds.html;

Edwards, Ralph
Bio-bibliographic data:
Australian Crime Fiction, p. 82. (207)

Edwards, Ruth Dudley
Bio-bibliographic data:
By a Woman's Hand, 1st ed., p. 71. (884a)
By a Woman's Hand, 2nd ed., pp. 71–72.
  (884b)
Detecting Women 2, pp. 61–62. (877b)

Detecting Women, 3rd ed., p. 86. (877c)
*The Mammoth Encyclopedia of Modern
    Crime Fiction,* pp. 149–50. (1)
Web site: http://www.ruthdudleyedwards.
    co.uk; http://www.twbooks.co.uk/
    authors/redwards.html; http://www.
    stopyourekillingme.com/
    ruth-dudley-edwards.html
Egan, Lesley. *See* **Linington, Elizabeth**
Egleton, Clive
Bio-bibliographic data:
Detecting Men, 1st ed., p. 84. (876)
Encyclopedia Mysteriosa, pp. 106–7. (2)
*St. James Guide to Crime & Mystery
    Writers,* 4th ed., pp. 333–35. (882d)
*Twentieth-Century Crime and Mystery
    Writers,* 1st ed., pp. 529–30. (882a)
*Twentieth-Century Crime and Mystery
    Writers,* 2nd ed., pp. 298–99. (882b)
*Twentieth-Century Crime and Mystery
    Writers,* 3rd ed., pp. 343–44. (882c)
Personal papers in Mugar Memorial
    Library, Boston University.
Egremont, Michael. *See* **Harrison,
    Michael**
Ehrlich, Jack
Bio-bibliographic data:
The Big Book of Noir, p. 264. (24)
Eichler, Selma
Bio-bibliographic data:
Detecting Women 2, pp. 62–63. (877b)
Detecting Women, 3rd ed., p. 86. (877c)
Web site: http://www.stopyourekillingme.
    com/selma-eichler.html
Eiffe, Patrick
Bio-bibliographic data:
Australian Crime Fiction, p. 82. (207)
Eipper, Christopher [McCallum]
Bio-bibliographic data:
Australian Crime Fiction, pp. 82–83.
    (207)
Ekman, Kerstin
Bio-bibliographic data:
The Encyclopedia of Murder and Mystery,
    p. 162. (6)
Eldershaw, Flora Sydney Patricia. *See*
    Eldershaw, M. Barnard
Eldershaw, M. Barnard. *Pseud. for* **Flora
    Sydney Patricia Eldershaw and
    Marjorie Faith Barnard**
Bio-bibliographic data:
Australian Crime Fiction, pp. 83, 183.
    (207)

Elkins, Aaron J. *See also:* **Elkins,
    Charlotte and Aaron Elkins**
Bio-bibliographic data:
Detecting Men, 1st ed., p. 85. (876)
Encyclopedia Mysteriosa, p. 108. (2)
The Encyclopedia of Murder and Mystery,
    p. 162. (6)
*The Mammoth Encyclopedia of Modern
    Crime Fiction,* pp. 150–51. (1)
*St. James Guide to Crime & Mystery
    Writers,* 4th ed., pp. 335–37. (882d)
*Twentieth-Century Crime and Mystery
    Writers,* 3rd ed., pp. 344–45. (882c)
*Whodunit? A Who's Who in Crime and
    Mystery Writing,* p. 62. (5)
Web site: http://www.stopyourekillingme.
    com/aaron-elkins.html
Elkins, Charlotte. *See also* **Elkins,
    Charlotte, and Aaron Elkins**
Bio-bibliographic data:
Detecting Women 2, p. 63. (877b)
Elkins, Charlotte, and Aaron Elkins
Bio-bibliographic data:
Detecting Women, 3rd ed., pp. 86–87.
    (877c)
Ellin, Stanley [Bernard]
Bio-bibliographic data:
*Critical Survey of Mystery and Detective
    Fiction,* pp. 574–78. (41)
Encyclopedia Mysteriosa, pp. 108–9. (2)
The Encyclopedia of Murder and Mystery,
    pp. 162–63. (6)
*The Encyclopedia of Mystery and
    Detection,* pp. 141–43. (7)
*The Mammoth Encyclopedia of Modern
    Crime Fiction,* pp. 151–52. (1)
Mystery and Suspense Writers, pp.
    357–66. (884.2)
*100 Masters of Mystery and Detective
    Fiction,* pp. 230–34. (37)
*The Oxford Companion to Crime and
    Mystery Writing,* p. 132. (4)
*St. James Guide to Crime & Mystery
    Writers,* 4th ed., pp. 337–38. (882d)
*Twentieth-Century Crime and Mystery
    Writers,* 1st ed., pp. 530–32. (882a)
*Twentieth-Century Crime and Mystery
    Writers,* 2nd ed., pp. 299–300. (882b)
*Twentieth-Century Crime and Mystery
    Writers,* 3rd ed., pp. 345–47. (882c)
*Whodunit? A Who's Who in Crime and
    Mystery Writing,* p. 62. (5)
Personal papers in Mugar Memorial
    Library, Boston University.

Elliott, Peers
Bio-bibliographic data:
Australian Crime Fiction, p. 83. (207)
Elliott, Sumner Locke
Bio-bibliographic data:
Australian Crime Fiction, p. 83. (207)
Ellis, Bret Easton
Bio-bibliographic data:
*The Mammoth Encyclopedia of Modern
Crime Fiction*, pp. 152–53. (1)
Web site: http://www.stopyourekillingme.
com/bret-easton-ellis.html; http://
www.geocities.com/Athens/Forum/
8506/index.html
Ellis, Julie [M.]
Bio-bibliographic data:
Canadian Crime Fiction, pp. 253, 260,
264. (209)
Ellis, Kate
Bio-bibliographic data:
*The Mammoth Encyclopedia of Modern
Crime Fiction*, p. 153. (1)
Web site: http://www.kateellis.co.uk;
http://www.stopyourekillingme.com/
kate-ellis.html
Ellis, Peter [John Philip] Berresford. *See*
Tremayne, Peter
Ellis, Wesley: unidentified house pseud.
Bio-bibliographic data:
Canadian Crime Fiction, p. 253. (209)
Ellroy, James
Bio-bibliographic data:
American Hard-Boiled Crime Writers, pp.
120–30. (862)
The Big Book of Noir, p. 328. (24)
Detecting Men, 1st ed., p. 85. (876)
Encyclopedia Mysteriosa, p. 109. (2)
The Encyclopedia of Murder and Mystery,
pp. 163–64. (6)
*The Mammoth Encyclopedia of Modern
Crime Fiction*, pp. 153–55. (1)
*The Oxford Companion to Crime and
Mystery Writing*, p. 132. (4)
*St. James Guide to Crime & Mystery
Writers*, 4th ed., pp. 339–40. (882d)
Talking Murder, pp. 115–28. (883)
*Twentieth-Century Crime and Mystery
Writers*, 3rd ed., pp. 347–48. (882c)
*Whodunit? A Who's Who in Crime and
Mystery Writing*, p. 62. (5)
Web site: http://www.ellroy.com; http://
www.stopyourekillingme.com/
james-ellroy.html

Elrod, P. N.; i.e., Patricia Nead
Bio-bibliographic data:
By a Woman's Hand, 2nd ed., pp. 72–73.
(884b)
Detecting Women 2, p. 63. (877b)
Detecting Women, 3rd ed., p. 87. (877c)
Web site: http://www.stopyourekillingme.
com/p-n-elrod.html
Ely, Ron
Bio-bibliographic data:
Detecting Men, 1st ed., p. 85. (876)
Web site: http://www.stopyourekillingme.
com/on-ely.html
Emerson, Earl W.
Bio-bibliographic data:
Detecting Men, 1st ed., p. 86. (876)
*The Mammoth Encyclopedia of Modern
Crime Fiction*, pp. 155–56. (1)
*St. James Guide to Crime & Mystery
Writers*, 4th ed., pp. 340–41. (882d)
*Twentieth-Century Crime and Mystery
Writers*, 3rd ed., p. 348. (882c)
Web site: http://www.stopyourekillingme.
com/earl-emerson.html; http://
earlemerson.com
Emerson, Kathy Lynn
Bio-bibliographic data:
Detecting Women, 3rd ed., p. 87. (877c)
Web site: http://www.stopyourekillingme.
com/kathy-lynn-emerson.html; http://
www.kathylynnemerson.com
Émond, Louis
Bio-bibliographic data:
Canadian Crime Fiction, pp. 67–68. (209)
Endersby, Beverley Beetham. *See*
Beetham-Endersby, Beverly
Engel, Howard
Bio-bibliographic data:
Canadian Crime Fiction, pp. 68–69, 237,
238. (209)
Designs of Darkness, pp. 102–22. (873)
Detecting Men, 1st ed., p. 86. (876)
Encyclopedia Mysteriosa, pp. 109–10. (2)
*The Mammoth Encyclopedia of Modern
Crime Fiction*, pp. 156–67. (1)
*St. James Guide to Crime & Mystery
Writers*, 4th ed., pp. 341–42. (882d)
*Twentieth-Century Crime and Mystery
Writers*, 3rd ed., pp. 348–50. (882c)
*Whodunit? A Who's Who in Crime and
Mystery Writing*, pp. 62–63. (5)
Personal papers in National Public
Archives, Ottawa.

Web site: http://www.stopyourekillingme.
com/howard-engel.html

Engleman, Paul
Bio-bibliographic data:
Detecting Men, 1st ed., p. 87. (876)

English, Brenda
Bio-bibliographic data:
Detecting Women, 3rd ed., p. 88. (877c)
Web site: http://www.stopyourekillingme.
com/brenda-english.html

English, Robert
Bio-bibliographic data:
Australian Crime Fiction, pp. 83–84.
(207)

Ennis, Catherine
Bio-bibliographic data:
Detecting Women 2, p. 63. (877b)
Detecting Women, 3rd ed., p. 88. (877c)

Epstein, Carole
Bio-bibliographic data:
Canadian Crime Fiction, p. 69. (209)
Detecting Women, 3rd ed., p. 88. (877c)

Erdman, Paul E[mil].
Bio-bibliographic data:
Canadian Crime Fiction, p. 69. (209)
*Twentieth-Century Crime and Mystery
Writers,* 1st ed., pp. 532–33. (882a)
*Twentieth-Century Crime and Mystery
Writers,* 2nd ed., p. 300. (882b)
*Twentieth-Century Crime and Mystery
Writers,* 3rd ed., pp. 350–51. (882c)

Ericson, Walter. *See* **Fast, Howard**
Ermine, Will. *See* **Drago, [Harry] Sinclair**
Erskine, Laurie York
Bio-bibliographic data:
Canadian Crime Fiction, pp. 253–54, 275.
(209)

Erskine, Margaret. *Pseud. for* **Margaret
Wetherby Williams**
Bio-bibliographic data:
Canadian Crime Fiction, pp. 69–70, 233.
(209)
Detecting Women 2, pp. 63–64. (877b)
*Twentieth-Century Crime and Mystery
Writers,* 1st ed., pp. 533–35. (882a)
*Twentieth-Century Crime and Mystery
Writers,* 2nd ed., pp. 300–301. (882b)
*Twentieth-Century Crime and Mystery
Writers,* 3rd ed., pp. 351–52. (882c)

Escott, Jonathan. *See* **Scott, Jack S.**
Escott-Inman, H. *See* **Inman, H. Escott**
Estabrook, Barry
Bio-bibliographic data:
Canadian Crime Fiction, p. 70. (209)

Detecting Men, 1st ed., p. 87. (876)
Estey, Dale
Bio-bibliographic data:
Canadian Crime Fiction, p. 70. (209)

Estleman, Loren D.
Bio-bibliographic data:
American Hard-Boiled Crime Writers, pp.
131–39. (862)
Detecting Men, 1st ed., pp. 87–88. (876)
Encyclopedia Mysteriosa, p. 110. (2)
The Encyclopedia of Murder and Mystery,
pp. 165–66. (6)
*The Mammoth Encyclopedia of Modern
Crime Fiction,* pp. 157–58. (1)
*St. James Guide to Crime & Mystery
Writers,* 4th ed., pp. 342–44. (882d)
Speaking of Murder, vol. II, pp. 184–95.
(875b)
*Twentieth-Century Crime and Mystery
Writers,* 2nd ed., pp. 301–3. (882b)
*Twentieth-Century Crime and Mystery
Writers,* 3rd ed., pp. 352–54. (882c)
*Whodunit? A Who's Who in Crime and
Mystery Writing,* p. 63. (5)
Personal papers in Eastern Michigan
University, Ypsilanti, Michigan.
Web site: http://www.lorenestleman.com;
http://www.stopyourekillingme.com/
loren-d-estleman.html; http://www.
thrillingdetective.com/trivia/estleman.
html; http://www.lorenestleman.com

Estrada, Patricia Wallace. *See* **Wallace,
Patricia**
Etienne, Gérard
Bio-bibliographic data:
Canadian Crime Fiction, p. 70. (209)

Ettridge, William
Bio-bibliographic data:
Canadian Crime Fiction, p. 70. (209)

**Eustace, Robert. Pseud. used by several
independent collaborators including
Eustace Rawlins and L. T. Meade
(q.v.), and Dr. Eustace Robert Barton
and Dorothy L. Sayers (q.v.)**
Bio-bibliographic data:
Australian Crime Fiction, p. 84. (207)

Eustace, Robert [Barton]
Bio-bibliographic data:
The Encyclopedia of Murder and Mystery,
p. 166. (6)
*Twentieth-Century Crime and Mystery
Writers,* 1st ed., pp. 535–37. (882a)

Eustis, Helen
Bio-bibliographic data:

Critical Survey of Mystery and Detective Fiction, pp. 579–84. (41)
The Encyclopedia of Murder and Mystery, pp. 166–67. (6)
The Encyclopedia of Mystery and Detection, p. 143. (7)
Twentieth-Century Crime and Mystery Writers, 1st ed., pp. 537–38. (882a)
Twentieth-Century Crime and Mystery Writers, 2nd ed., pp. 303–4. (882b)
Twentieth-Century Crime and Mystery Writers, 3rd ed., p. 354. (882c)
Evanovich, Janet
Bio-bibliographic data:
Deadly Women, pp. 227–31. (26.5)
Detecting Women, 1st ed., p. 54. (877a)
Detecting Women 2, p. 64. (877b)
Detecting Women, 3rd ed., p. 89. (877c)
The Encyclopedia of Murder and Mystery, p. 167. (6)
The Mammoth Encyclopedia of Modern Crime Fiction, pp. 158–59. (1)
Speaking of Murder, vol. II, pp. 38–43. (875b)
Whodunit? A Who's Who in Crime and Mystery Writing, pp. 64–65. (5)
Web site: http://www.evanovich.com; http://www.stopyourekillingme.com/janet-evanovich.html
Evans, Geraldine
Bio-bibliographic data:
Detecting Women, 3rd ed., p. 89. (877c)
Evans, John. *See* **Browne, Howard**
Evans, Stan
Bio-bibliographic data:
Canadian Crime Fiction, p. 70. (209)
Evans, Tabor: house pseud. used by Lou Cameron, Will C. Knott, Harry Whittington, and Mel Marshall (q.q.v.)
Evelyn, John Michael. *See* **Underwood, Michael**
Evers, Crabbe. *Pseud. for* **William Brashler and Reinder Van Til**
Bio-bibliographic data:
Detecting Men, 1st ed., p. 88. (876)
Web site: http://www.stopyourekillingme.com/crabbe-evers.html
Everson, David H.
Bio-bibliographic data:
Detecting Men, 1st ed., p. 88. (876)
Everton, Frank. *See* **Meares, Leonard**
Eversz, Robert
Bio-bibliographic data:

Detecting Men, 1st ed., p. 89. (876)
Eyre, Elizabeth. *See* **Staynes, Jill, and Margaret Storey**

F
Faherty, Terence
Bio-bibliographic data:
Detecting Men, 1st ed., p. 89. (876)
The Encyclopedia of Murder and Mystery, p. 169. (6)
The Mammoth Encyclopedia of Modern Crime Fiction, pp. 159–60. (1)
Web site: www.terencefaherty.com
Fair, A. A. *See* **Gardner, Erle Stanley**
Fairbanks, Cassie
Bio-bibliographic data:
Canadian Crime Fiction, p. 71. (209)
Fairburn, Laura
Bio-bibliographic data:
Canadian Crime Fiction, p. 71. (209)
Fairleigh, Runa. *See* **Morse, Larry**
Fairlie, Gerard. *See also* **Sapper** for a list of the works providing data on Herman C. McNeile, the first writer to use this pseud.
Bio-bibliographic data:
British Mystery Writers, 1920–1939, pp. 117–21. (867)
Encyclopedia Mysteriosa, p. 112. (2)
The Encyclopedia of Murder and Mystery, p. 169. (6)
Twentieth-Century Crime and Mystery Writers, 1st ed., pp. 538–40. (882a)
Twentieth-Century Crime and Mystery Writers, 2nd ed., pp. 304–5. (882b)
Twentieth-Century Crime and Mystery Writers, 3rd ed., pp. 355–56. (882c)
Fairlie Fuentes, Enrique
Bio-bibliographic data:
Latin American Mystery Writers: An A to Z Guide. (881)
Fairstein, Linda
Bio-bibliographic data:
Detecting Women, 3rd ed., p. 90. (877c)
874.*Women of Mystery*, pp. 434–35.
Web site: http://www.stopyourekillingme.com/linda-fairstein.html; http://www.lindafairstein.com
Falardeau, Pierre
Bio-bibliographic data:
Canadian Crime Fiction, p. 71. (209)
Falconer, Colin. *Pseud. for* **Colin Richard Bowles**
Bio-bibliographic data:

Australian Crime Fiction, p. 85. (207)
Falk, A. R.
Bio-bibliographic data:
Australian Crime Fiction, p. 85. (207)
Falk, David G.
Bio-bibliographic data:
Australian Crime Fiction, p. 85. (207)
Falkner, Frederick
Bio-bibliographic data:
Canadian Crime Fiction, p. 71. (209)
Falkner, Heather
Bio-bibliographic data:
Australian Crime Fiction, p. 85. (207)
Fallon, Ann C.; i.e., Connerton
Bio-bibliographic data:
By a Woman's Hand, 1st ed., pp. 72–73.
(884a)
By a Woman's Hand, 2nd ed., p. 74.
(884b)
Detecting Women, 1st ed., p. 55. (877a)
Detecting Women 2, p. 65. (877b)
Detecting Women, 3rd ed., p. 90. (877c)
Web site: http://www.stopyourekillingme.
com/ann-c-fallon.html
Fallon, Martin. *See* **Patterson, Harry**
Farjeon, B. L.; i.e., Benjamin Leopold
Bio-bibliographic data:
Australian Crime Fiction, p. 86. (207)
*The Encyclopedia of Mystery and
Detection*, pp. 145–46. (7)
Farkas, Endre
Bio-bibliographic data:
Canadian Crime Fiction, p. 71. (209)
Farmer, Jerrilyn
Bio-bibliographic data:
Detecting Women, 3rd ed., pp. 90–91.
(877c)
Web site: http://www.stopyourekillingme.
com/jerrilyn-farmer.html
**Farr, Caroline: shared pseud. for several
Australian writers, including Richard
Wilkes Hunter (q.v.), Lee Pattinson,
and Carl Ruhen. Also used by Carter
Brown (q.v.).**
Bio-bibliographic data:
Australian Crime Fiction, pp. 86–87.
(207)
Farrell, Gillian B.
Bio-bibliographic data:
Detecting Women, 1st ed., p. 55. (877a)
Detecting Women 2, p. 65. (877b)
Detecting Women, 3rd ed., p. 91. (877c)
Web site: http://www.stopyourekillingme.
com/gillian-b-farrell.html

Farrelly, Gail E.
Bio-bibliographic data:
Detecting Women, 3rd ed., p. 91. (877c)
Farrer, Katharine
Bio-bibliographic data:
*Twentieth-Century Crime and Mystery
Writers*, 1st ed., pp. 541–42. (882a)
*Twentieth-Century Crime and Mystery
Writers*, 3rd ed., pp. 356–57. (882c)
Fast, Howard [Melvin]
Bio-bibliographic data:
*Critical Survey of Mystery and Detective
Fiction*, pp. 437–44. (41)
Detecting Men, 1st ed., p. 70. (876)
Encyclopedia Mysteriosa, p. 81. (2)
The Encyclopedia of Murder and Mystery,
p. 122. (6)
*The Mammoth Encyclopedia of Modern
Crime Fiction*, pp. 160–61. (1)
*St. James Guide to Crime & Mystery
Writers*, 4th ed., pp. 263–66. (882d)
*Twentieth-Century Crime and Mystery
Writers*, 1st ed., pp. 410–13. (882a)
*Twentieth-Century Crime and Mystery
Writers*, 2nd ed., pp. 230–32. (882b)
*Twentieth-Century Crime and Mystery
Writers*, 3rd ed., pp. 277–80. (882c)
Personal papers in University of
Pennsylvania Library, Philadelphia.
Personal papers in University of
Wisconsin, Madison.
Web site: www.trussel.com/f_how.htl;
http://www.stopyourekillingme.com/
howard-fast.html
Faulkner, William [Cuthbert]
Bio-bibliographic data:
*Critical Survey of Mystery and Detective
Fiction*, pp. 585–91. (41)
Encyclopedia Mysteriosa, p. 117. (2)
The Encyclopedia of Murder and Mystery,
p. 172. (6)
*The Encyclopedia of Mystery and
Detection*, p. 146. (7)
*Twentieth-Century Crime and Mystery
Writers*, 1st ed., pp. 542–45. (882a)
*Twentieth-Century Crime and Mystery
Writers*, 2nd ed., pp. 305–7. (882b)
*Whodunit? A Who's Who in Crime and
Mystery Writing*, p. 68. (5)
Faust, Frederick Schiller. *See* **Brand, Max**
Faust, Ron
Bio-bibliographic data:
The Encyclopedia of Murder and Mystery,
pp. 172–73. (6)

Favenc, Ernest
Bio-bibliographic data:
Australian Crime Fiction, pp. 87–88.
(207)
Fawcett, Frank Dubrez
Bio-bibliographic data:
The Big Book of Noir, pp. 213–21. (24)
Fawcett, Quinn. *See* **Yarbro, Chelsea Quinn; Yarbro, Chelsea Quinn, and Bill Fawcett**
Fearing, Kenneth [Flexner]
Bio-bibliographic data:
Critical Survey of Mystery and Detective Fiction, pp. 592–98. (41)
Encyclopedia Mysteriosa, p. 117. (2)
The Encyclopedia of Murder and Mystery,
p. 173. (6)
The Encyclopedia of Mystery and Detection, pp. 146–47. (7)
St. James Guide to Crime & Mystery Writers, 4th ed., pp. 345–46. (882d)
Twentieth-Century Crime and Mystery Writers, 1st ed., pp. 546–47. (882a)
Twentieth-Century Crime and Mystery Writers, 2nd ed., pp. 307–8. (882b)
Twentieth-Century Crime and Mystery Writers, 3rd ed., pp. 357–58. (882c)
Web site: http://www.stopyourekillingme.
com/kenneth-fearing.html
Feddersen, Connie
Bio-bibliographic data:
Detecting Women, 1st ed., p. 56. (877a)
Detecting Women 2, p. 65. (877b)
Detecting Women, 3rd ed., p. 92. (877c)
Web site: http://www.stopyourekillingme.
com/connie-feddersen.html; http://
www.nettrends.com/carolfinch
Feiling, C. E.
Bio-bibliographic data:
Latin American Mystery Writers: An A to Z Guide. (881)
Feinmann, José Pablo
Bio-bibliographic data:
Latin American Mystery Writers: An A to Z Guide. (881)
Feldmeyer, Dean
Bio-bibliographic data:
Detecting Men, 1st ed., p. 90. (876)
Femling, Jean
Bio-bibliographic data:
By a Woman's Hand, 1st ed., p. 73. (884a)
Detecting Women, 1st ed., p. 56. (877a)
Detecting Women 2, pp. 65–66. (877b)
Detecting Women, 3rd ed., p. 92. (877c)

Fenisong, Ruth
Bio-bibliographic data:
Detecting Women 2, p. 66. (877b)
Twentieth-Century Crime and Mystery Writers, 1st ed., pp. 547–48. (882a)
Twentieth-Century Crime and Mystery Writers, 2nd ed., pp. 308–9. (882b)
Fenn, Caroline K.
Bio-bibliographic data:
Canadian Crime Fiction, p. 71. (209)
Fennario, David. *Pseud. for* **David William Wiper**
Bio-bibliographic data:
Canadian Crime Fiction, pp. 71–72, 235.
(209)
Fennelly, Tony
Bio-bibliographic data:
By a Woman's Hand, 2nd ed., p. 74.
(884b)
Detecting Women 2, p. 66. (877b)
Detecting Women, 3rd ed., pp. 92–93.
(877c)
Great Women Mystery Writers, pp. 101–3.
(880)
Web site: http://www.stopyourekillingme.
com/tony-fennelly.html
Fenwick, Elizabeth
Bio-bibliographic data:
Twentieth-Century Crime and Mystery Writers, 1st ed., pp. 548–49. (882a)
Twentieth-Century Crime and Mystery Writers, 2nd ed., p. 309. (882b)
Twentieth-Century Crime and Mystery Writers, 3rd ed., p. 358. (882c)
Personal papers in Mugar Memorial Library, Boston University
Ferguson, Frances. *Pseud. for* **Barbara-Serene Perkins**
Bio-bibliographic data:
Detecting Women, 3rd ed., p. 93. (877c)
Ferguson, James. *See* **Rhea, Nicholas**
Ferguson, Trevor
Bio-bibliographic data:
Canadian Crime Fiction, p. 72. (209)
Ferguson, W. Humer: unidentified pseud.
Bio-bibliographic data:
Australian Crime Fiction, p. 88. (207)
Ferland, Léon-Gérald
Bio-bibliographic data:
Canadian Crime Fiction, p. 72. (209)
Fernd, Arch
Bio-bibliographic data:
Australian Crime Fiction, p. 88. (207)

Fernet, André
Bio-bibliographic data:
Canadian Crime Fiction, p. 72. (209)
Feron, Jean. *Pseud. for*
    Joseph-Marc-Octave-Antoine Lebel
Bio-bibliographic data:
Canadian Crime Fiction, pp. 72, 129.
    (209)
Ferrars, E. X. *See* **Ferrars, Elizabeth**
Ferrars, Elizabeth. *Pseud. for* **Morna**
    Doris Brown, born Morna Doris
    MacTaggart
Bio-bibliographic data:
And Then There Were Nine . . . More
    Women of Mystery, pp. 146–67. (863)
Australian Crime Fiction, p. 88. (207)
British Mystery and Thriller Writers since
    1940, First Series, pp. 73–84. (868)
By a Woman's Hand, 1st ed., pp. 73–74.
    (884a)
By a Woman's Hand, 2nd ed., pp. 75–76.
    (884b)
Critical Survey of Mystery and Detective
    Fiction, pp. 599–604. (41)
Detecting Women, 1st ed., p. 56. (877a)
Detecting Women 2, pp. 66–67. (877b)
Encyclopedia Mysteriosa, p. 119. (2)
The Encyclopedia of Murder and Mystery,
    p. 176. (6)
The Encyclopedia of Mystery and
    Detection, p. 148. (7)
Great Women Mystery Writers, pp. 103–7.
    (880)
The Oxford Companion to Crime and
    Mystery Writing, p. 156. (4)
St. James Guide to Crime & Mystery
    Writers, 4th ed., pp. 346–49. (882d)
Twentieth-Century Crime and Mystery
    Writers, 1st ed., pp. 550–53. (882a)
Twentieth-Century Crime and Mystery
    Writers, 2nd ed., pp. 309–11. (882b)
Twentieth-Century Crime and Mystery
    Writers, 3rd ed., pp. 358–60. (882c)
Whodunit? A Who's Who in Crime and
    Mystery Writing, pp. 70–71. (5)
Web site: http://www.stopyourekillingme.
    com/e-x-ferrars.html
Ferris, James Cody: house pseud. for
    Stratemeyer Syndicate. This reference
    is to a pseudonymous work by Leslie
    McFarlane (q.v.).
Bio-bibliographic data:
Canadian Crime Fiction, p. 72. (209)

Ferris, Monica. *See* **Kuhfeld, Mary Pulver**
Ferris, Tom. *See* **Rhea, Nicholas**
Feuer, Lewis S.
Bio-bibliographic data:
Canadian Crime Fiction, p. 276. (209)
Fickling, Forrest E. *See* **Fickling, G. G.**
Fickling, G. G.: joint pseud. for Gloria
    Gautraud Fickling and Forrest
    Ellison Fickling
Bio-bibliographic data:
Detecting Women 2, pp. 68–69. (877b)
Detecting Women, 3rd ed., pp. 93–94.
    (877c)
Encyclopedia Mysteriosa, p. 119. (2)
Fickling, Gloria G. *See* **Fickling, G. G.**
Fiedler, Jacqueline
Bio-bibliographic data:
Detecting Women, 3rd ed., p. 94. (877c)
Web site: http://www.stopyourekillingme.
    com/jacqueline-fiedler.html
Fielding, A. *Pseud. for* **Dorothy Fielding**
Bio-bibliographic data:
Twentieth-Century Crime and Mystery
    Writers, 1st ed., pp. 553–54. (882a)
Fielding, Henry
Bio-bibliographic data:
The Encyclopedia of Murder and Mystery,
    p. 176. (6)
Fielding, Joy [Tepperman]
Bio-bibliographic data:
Canadian Crime Fiction, pp. 72–73. (209)
Speaking of Murder, vol. II, pp. 115–25.
    (875b)
Web site: http://www.stopyourekillingme.
    com/joy-fielding.html; http://www.
    joyfielding.com
Fields, Bert. *See* **Kincaid, D.**
Findley, Timothy
Bio-bibliographic data:
Canadian Crime Fiction, p. 73. (209)
The Encyclopedia of Murder and Mystery,
    p. 177. (6)
Fink, John
Bio-bibliographic data:
Detecting Men, 1st ed., p. 90. (876)
Finkelstein, Jay
Bio-bibliographic data:
Detecting Men, 1st ed., p. 90. (876)
Finlay, Iain [Murray Mckenzie]
Bio-bibliographic data:
Australian Crime Fiction, pp. 88–89.
    (207)
Finn, Edmund
Bio-bibliographic data:

Australian Crime Fiction, p. 89. (207)
Finnegan, Robert. *Pseud. for* **Paul William Ryan**
Bio-bibliographic data:
Twentieth-Century Crime and Mystery Writers, 1st ed., pp. 554–55. (882a)
Twentieth-Century Crime and Mystery Writers, 2nd ed., pp. 311–12. (882b)
Twentieth-Century Crime and Mystery Writers, 3rd ed., p. 361. (882c)
Finnegan, Sam
Bio-bibliographic data:
Australian Crime Fiction, p. 89. (207)
Finney, Jack. *Pseud. for* **Walter Braden Finney**
Bio-bibliographic data:
The Big Book of Noir, p. 265 (24)
St. James Guide to Crime & Mystery Writers, 4th ed., pp. 349–50. (882d)
Twentieth-Century Crime and Mystery Writers, 1st ed., pp. 555–57. (882a)
Twentieth-Century Crime and Mystery Writers, 2nd ed., p. 312. (882b)
Twentieth-Century Crime and Mystery Writers, 3rd ed., pp. 361–62. (882c)
Finney, Patricia
Bio-bibliographic data:
Detecting Women 2, p. 39. (877b)
Detecting Women, 3rd ed., p. 51. (877c)
The Mammoth Encyclopedia of Modern Crime Fiction, pp. 161–62 (1)
Web site: www.patricia-finney.co.uk
Finton, Reg L.
Bio-bibliographic data:
Australian Crime Fiction, p. 89. (207)
Fischer, Bruno
Bio-bibliographic data:
The Big Book of Noir, p. 188. (24)
Encyclopedia Mysteriosa, p. 120. (2)
The Encyclopedia of Murder and Mystery, pp. 178–79. (6)
St. James Guide to Crime & Mystery Writers, 4th ed., pp. 350–51. (882d)
Twentieth-Century Crime and Mystery Writers, 1st ed., pp. 557–62. (882a)
Twentieth-Century Crime and Mystery Writers, 2nd ed., pp. 312–15. (882b)
Twentieth-Century Crime and Mystery Writers, 3rd ed., pp. 362–65. (882c)
Fish, Robert L[loyd].
Bio-bibliographic data:
Critical Survey of Mystery and Detective Fiction, pp. 605–10. (41)
Encyclopedia Mysteriosa, p. 120. (2)

The Encyclopedia of Murder and Mystery, p. 179. (6)
The Encyclopedia of Mystery and Detection, pp. 148–50. (7)
The Mammoth Encyclopedia of Modern Crime Fiction, pp. 162–63. (1)
100 Masters of Mystery and Detective Fiction, pp. 235–40. (37)
St. James Guide to Crime & Mystery Writers, 4th ed., pp. 351–52. (882d)
Twentieth-Century Crime and Mystery Writers, 1st ed., pp. 562–64. (882a)
Twentieth-Century Crime and Mystery Writers, 2nd ed., pp. 315–17. (882b)
Twentieth-Century Crime and Mystery Writers, 3rd ed., pp. 365–67. (882c)
Personal papers in Mugar Memorial Library, Boston University.
Fisher, Mark. *Pseud. for* **Marc-André Poissant**
Bio-bibliographic data:
Canadian Crime Fiction, pp. 73, 172. (209)
Fisher, Steve; i.e., Stephen Gould Fisher
Bio-bibliographic data:
American Hard-Boiled Crime Writers, pp. 140–48. (862)
Encyclopedia Mysteriosa, p. 121. (2)
The Encyclopedia of Murder and Mystery, p. 179. (6)
The Encyclopedia of Mystery and Detection, pp. 150–51. (7)
St. James Guide to Crime & Mystery Writers, 4th ed., pp. 352–53. (882d)
Twentieth-Century Crime and Mystery Writers, 1st ed., pp. 565–66. (882a)
Twentieth-Century Crime and Mystery Writers, 2nd ed., pp. 317–18. (882b)
Twentieth-Century Crime and Mystery Writers, 3rd ed., pp. 367–71. (882c)
Personal papers in the Margaret Herrick Library of the Center for Motion Picture Study, Beverly Hills, California.
Fitt, Mary. *Pseud. for* **Kathleen Freeman**
Bio-bibliographic data:
St. James Guide to Crime & Mystery Writers, 4th ed., pp. 353–55. (882d)
Twentieth-Century Crime and Mystery Writers, 1st ed., pp. 566–69. (882a)
Twentieth-Century Crime and Mystery Writers, 2nd ed., pp. 312–13. (882b)
Twentieth-Century Crime and Mystery Writers, 3rd ed., pp. 371–72. (882c)

Fitzgerald, F. Scott; i.e., Francis Scott Key
Bio-bibliographic data:
The Encyclopedia of Murder and Mystery,
pp. 179–80. (6)
*The Encyclopedia of Mystery and
Detection*, p. 151. (7)
Fitzgerald, Nigel
Bio-bibliographic data:
*Twentieth-Century Crime and Mystery
Writers*, 1st ed., pp. 569–70. (882a)
*Twentieth-Century Crime and Mystery
Writers*, 2nd ed., p. 320. (882b)
**Fitzpatrick, Peter [Henry] and Barbara
[Ann] Wenzel**
Bio-bibliographic data:
Australian Crime Fiction, p. 89. (207)
Fitzwater, Judy
Bio-bibliographic data:
Detecting Women, 3rd ed., pp. 94–95.
(877c)
Web site: http://www.stopyourekillingme.
com/judy-fitzwater.html; http://
sleuths2die4.thewriters.com/fitzwater/
default.htm
Flanagan, Joan [Evelyn Stewart]
Bio-bibliographic data:
Australian Crime Fiction, pp. 89–90.
(207)
Flanagan, Thomas
Bio-bibliographic data:
*The Encyclopedia of Mystery and
Detection*, p. 151. (7)
Flannery, Sean. *Pseud. for* David Hagberg
Bio-bibliographic data:
Encyclopedia Mysteriosa, p. 121. (2)
Web site: http://www.stopyourekillingme.
com/sean-flannery.html
Fleming, Ian L[ancaster].
Bio-bibliographic data:
*British Mystery and Thriller Writers since
1940, First Series*, pp. 85–112. (868)
Canadian Crime Fiction, p. 276. (209)
Corpus Delicti of Mystery Fiction, pp.
68–70. (879)
*Critical Survey of Mystery and Detective
Fiction*, pp. 611–16. (41)
Encyclopedia Mysteriosa, p. 121. (2)
The Encyclopedia of Murder and Mystery,
pp. 180–81. (6)
*The Encyclopedia of Mystery and
Detection*, pp. 151–52. (7)
Mystery and Suspense Writers, pp.
367–81. (884.2)

*100 Masters of Mystery and Detective
Fiction*, pp. 241–47. (37)
*The Oxford Companion to Crime and
Mystery Writing*, p. 161. (4)
*St. James Guide to Crime & Mystery
Writers*, 4th ed., pp. 355–57. (882d)
*Twentieth-Century Crime and Mystery
Writers*, 1st ed., pp. 570–73. (882a)
*Twentieth-Century Crime and Mystery
Writers*, 2nd ed., pp. 320–21. (882b)
*Twentieth-Century Crime and Mystery
Writers*, 3rd ed., pp. 372–74. (882c)
Web site: http://www.stopyourekillingme.
com/ian-fleming.html
Fleming, Joan [Margaret]
Bio-bibliographic data:
*Critical Survey of Mystery and Detective
Fiction*, pp. 617–20. (41)
Encyclopedia Mysteriosa, pp. 121–22. (2)
*St. James Guide to Crime & Mystery
Writers*, 4th ed., pp. 357–58. (882d)
*Twentieth-Century Crime and Mystery
Writers*, 1st ed., pp. 573–75. (882a)
*Twentieth-Century Crime and Mystery
Writers*, 2nd ed., pp. 322–23. (882b)
*Twentieth-Century Crime and Mystery
Writers*, 3rd ed., pp. 374–75. (882c)
Personal papers in Mugar Memorial
Library, Boston University.
Fleming, Mrs. May Agnes [Early]
Bio-bibliographic data:
Canadian Crime Fiction, pp. 74–75. (209)
Fleming, Oliver. *See* Macdonald, Philip
Fletcher, David. *Pseud. for* Dulan Barber
Bio-bibliographic data:
*St. James Guide to Crime & Mystery
Writers*, 4th ed., pp. 359–60. (882d)
*Twentieth-Century Crime and Mystery
Writers*, 3rd ed., pp. 376–77. (882c)
Fletcher, Henry
Bio-bibliographic data:
Australian Crime Fiction, p. 90. (207)
Fletcher, J. S.; i.e., Joseph Smith
Bio-bibliographic data:
British Mystery Writers, 1860–1919, pp.
135–42. (866)
Canadian Crime Fiction, p. 276. (209)
*Critical Survey of Mystery and Detective
Fiction*, pp. 621–28. (41)
Encyclopedia Mysteriosa, p. 122. (2)
The Encyclopedia of Murder and Mystery,
p. 181. (6)
*The Encyclopedia of Mystery and
Detection*, p. 152. (7)

*St. James Guide to Crime & Mystery
Writers,* 4th ed., pp. 360–63. (882d)
*Twentieth-Century Crime and Mystery
Writers,* 1st ed., pp. 575–81. (882a)
*Twentieth-Century Crime and Mystery
Writers,* 2nd ed., pp. 323–26. (882b)
*Twentieth-Century Crime and Mystery
Writers,* 3rd ed., pp. 377–80. (882c)
Fletcher, James
Bio-bibliographic data:
Australian Crime Fiction, p. 90. (207)
Fletcher, Jessica, and Donald Bain
Bio-bibliographic data:
Detecting Women, 3rd ed., p. 95. (877c)
Web site: http://www.stopyourekillingme.
com/jessica-fletcher.html;
http://www. stopyourekillingme.com/
donald-bain.html
Fletcher, Lucille
Bio-bibliographic data:
*St. James Guide to Crime & Mystery
Writers,* 4th ed., pp. 363–65. (882d)
*Twentieth-Century Crime and Mystery
Writers,* 1st ed., pp. 582–83. (882a)
*Twentieth-Century Crime and Mystery
Writers,* 2nd ed., p. 327. (882b)
*Twentieth-Century Crime and Mystery
Writers,* 3rd ed., pp. 380–81. (882c)
Fliegel, Richard
Bio-bibliographic data:
Detecting Men, 1st ed., pp. 90–91. (876)
Flora, Fletcher
Bio-bibliographic data:
Detecting Women, 3rd ed., p. 95. (877c)
*Twentieth-Century Crime and Mystery
Writers,* 1st ed., pp. 583–86. (882a)
*Twentieth-Century Crime and Mystery
Writers,* 2nd ed., pp. 328–29. (882b)
*Twentieth-Century Crime and Mystery
Writers,* 3rd ed., pp. 381–83. (882c)
Flora, Kate Clark
Bio-bibliographic data:
Detecting Women 2, p. 68. (877b)
Web site: http://www.stopyourekillingme.
com/kate-clark-flora.html; http://
www.kateflora.com
Florian, S. L.
Bio-bibliographic data:
Detecting Women, 1st ed., pp. 56–57.
(877a)
Detecting Women 2, p. 68. (877b)
Flower, Pat[ricia Mary Bryson]
Bio-bibliographic data:

Australian Crime Fiction, pp. 90–91.
(207)
*Critical Survey of Mystery and Detective
Fiction,* pp. 629–33. (41)
*Twentieth-Century Crime and Mystery
Writers,* 1st ed., pp. 586–88. (882a)
*Twentieth-Century Crime and Mystery
Writers,* 2nd ed., pp. 329–30. (882b)
Flynn, Don
Bio-bibliographic data:
Detecting Men, 1st ed., p. 91. (876)
Fodden, Simon R[itchie].
Bio-bibliographic data:
Canadian Crime Fiction, pp. 75, 180.
(209)
Foisy, Michel
Bio-bibliographic data:
Canadian Crime Fiction, p. 75. (209)
Folch-Ribas, Jacques
Bio-bibliographic data:
Canadian Crime Fiction, p. 75. (209)
Foley, Pearl Beatrix
Bio-bibliographic data:
Canadian Crime Fiction, pp. 58, 75. (209)
Foley, Rae. *Pseud. for* **Elinore Denniston**
Bio-bibliographic data:
Detecting Women 2, pp. 68–69. (877b)
*Twentieth-Century Crime and Mystery
Writers,* 1st ed., pp. 588–90. (882a)
*Twentieth-Century Crime and Mystery
Writers,* 2nd ed., pp. 330–31. (882b)
Follett, Ken; i.e., Kenneth Martin
Bio-bibliographic data:
*British Mystery and Thriller Writers since
1940, First Series,* pp. 113–24. (868)
*Critical Survey of Mystery and Detective
Fiction,* pp. 634–39. (41)
Detecting Men, 1st ed., pp. 91, 189. (876)
Encyclopedia Mysteriosa, pp. 122–23. (2)
*St. James Guide to Crime & Mystery
Writers,* 4th ed., pp. 365–66. (882d)
*Twentieth-Century Crime and Mystery
Writers,* 2nd ed., pp. 331–32. (882b)
*Twentieth-Century Crime and Mystery
Writers,* 3rd ed., pp. 383–84. (882c)
Web site: http://www.stopyourekillingme.
com/ken-follett.html
Fonseca, Ruben
Bio-bibliographic data:
*Latin American Mystery Writers: An A to
Z Guide. (881)*
Fontaine, Richard
Bio-bibliographic data:
Canadian Crime Fiction, p. 75. (209)

Fontana, James A.
Bio-bibliographic data:
Canadian Crime Fiction, p. 75. (209)
Foon, Dennis
Bio-bibliographic data:
Canadian Crime Fiction, p. 75. (209)
Footner, [William] Hulbert
Bio-bibliographic data:
Canadian Crime Fiction, pp. 75–77. (209)
The Encyclopedia of Mystery and Detection, p. 153. (7)
Twentieth-Century Crime and Mystery Writers, 1st ed., pp. 590–92. (882a)
Twentieth-Century Crime and Mystery Writers, 2nd ed., pp. 332–34. (882b)
Twentieth-Century Crime and Mystery Writers, 3rd ed., pp. 384–85. (882c)
Forbes, Colin. *Pseud. for* Raymond Harold Sawkins
Bio-bibliographic data:
Canadian Crime Fiction, pp. 276. (209)
Detecting Men, 1st ed., pp. 91–92. (876)
St. James Guide to Crime & Mystery Writers, 4th ed., pp. 366–67. (882d)
Twentieth-Century Crime and Mystery Writers, 3rd ed., pp. 385–86. (882c)
Web site: http://www.stopyourekillingme.com/colin-forbes.html
Forbes, George
Bio-bibliographic data:
Australian Crime Fiction, pp. 91–92. (207)
Forbes, [DeLoris Florine] Stanton
Bio-bibliographic data:
Detecting Women 2, pp. 192–93. (877b)
Detecting Women, 3rd ed., p. 281. (877c)
Encyclopedia Mysteriosa, p. 123. (2)
The Encyclopedia of Murder and Mystery, p. 182. (6)
The Encyclopedia of Mystery and Detection, p. 153. (7)
Twentieth-Century Crime and Mystery Writers, 1st ed., pp. 592–94. (882a)
Twentieth-Century Crime and Mystery Writers, 2nd ed., pp. 334–35. (882b)
Twentieth-Century Crime and Mystery Writers, 3rd ed., pp. 387–88. (882c)
Personal papers in Mugar Memorial Library, Boston University.
Ford, Elbur. *See* Holt, Victoria
Ford, G. M.
Bio-bibliographic data:
Detecting Men, 1st ed., p. 92. (876)

Web site: http://www.stopyourekillingme.com/g-m-ford.html; http://www.nwlink.com/~massucco/NW-Myst-Auth/GMFord.html
Ford, Harriet
Bio-bibliographic data:
Canadian Crime Fiction, p. 77. (209)
Ford, Leslie. *See* Brown, Zenith Jones
Ford, M. *Pseud. for* Jon Lewis
Bio-bibliographic data:
Australian Crime Fiction, pp. 92, 153. (207)
Forester, C. S.; i.e., Cecil Scott, born Cecil Lewis Troughton Smith
Bio-bibliographic data:
Critical Survey of Mystery and Detective Fiction, pp. 640–645. (41)
The Encyclopedia of Murder and Mystery, p. 183. (6)
The Encyclopedia of Mystery and Detection, p. 154. (7)
Forrest, A. E.; Alfred Edgar
Bio-bibliographic data:
Canadian Crime Fiction, p. 254. (209)
Forrest, Katherine V[irgnia].
Bio-bibliographic data:
By a Woman's Hand, 1st ed., pp. 74–75. (884a)
By a Woman's Hand, 2nd ed., pp. 76–77. (884b)
Canadian Crime Fiction, p. 77. (209)
Detecting Women, 1st ed., p. 57. (877a)
Detecting Women 2, pp. 69–70. (877b)
Detecting Women, 3rd ed., p. 96. (877c)
Great Women Mystery Writers, pp. 112–14. (880)
The Mammoth Encyclopedia of Modern Crime Fiction, pp. 163–64. (1)
St. James Guide to Crime & Mystery Writers, 4th ed., pp. 369–71. (882d)
Twentieth-Century Crime and Mystery Writers, 3rd ed., pp. 390–91. (882c)
Web site:
http://www.art-with-attitude.com/forrest; http://www.geocities.com/WestHollywood/Heights/9558/KVForrest.htm;
http://stopyourekillingme.com/katherine-v-forrest.html
Forrest, Richard [Stockton]
Bio-bibliographic data:
Detecting Men, 1st ed., p. 92. (876)
Encyclopedia Mysteriosa, p. 124. (2)

*Twentieth-Century Crime and Mystery
Writers*, 2nd ed., pp. 337–38. (882b)
*Twentieth-Century Crime and Mystery
Writers*, 3rd ed., pp. 391–92. (882c)
Personal papers in Mugar Memorial
Library, Boston University.
Web site:
http://stopyourekillingme.com/richard
-forrest.html
Forrester, Andrew, Jr.
Bio-bibliographic data:
The Encyclopedia of Murder and Mystery,
p. 183. (6)
Forrester, E. *See* **Batt, Leon**
Forsyth, Frederick
Bio-bibliographic data:
*British Mystery and Thriller Writers since
1940, First Series*, pp. 125–35. (868)
*Critical Survey of Mystery and Detective
Fiction*, pp. 646–50. (41)
Encyclopedia Mysteriosa, p. 124. (2)
The Encyclopedia of Murder and Mystery,
p. 184. (6)
*100 Masters of Mystery and Detective
Fiction*, pp. 248–52. (37)
*St. James Guide to Crime & Mystery
Writers*, 4th ed., pp. 371–73. (882d)
*Twentieth-Century Crime and Mystery
Writers,* 1st ed., pp. 598–600. (882a)
*Twentieth-Century Crime and Mystery
Writers*, 2nd ed., p. 339. (882b)
*Twentieth-Century Crime and Mystery
Writers*, 3rd ed., pp. 393–94. (882c)
Web site: http://stopyourekillingme.com/
frederick-forsyth.html
Fortune, Mrs. Mary Helena
Bio-bibliographic data:
Australian Crime Fiction, p. 239. (207)
Canadian Crime Fiction, p. 276. (209)
Foster, David [Manning]
Bio-bibliographic data:
Australian Crime Fiction, p. 92. (207)
Foster, J. A.; i.e., James Anthony
Bio-bibliographic data:
Canadian Crime Fiction, p. 78. (209)
Foster, Marion. *See* **Shea, Shirley**
Foucher, Jacques
Bio-bibliographic data:
Canadian Crime Fiction, p. 78. (209)
Fournier, Pierre-Sylvain
Bio-bibliographic data:
Canadian Crime Fiction, p. 78. (209)
Fowler, Earlene
Bio-bibliographic data:

By a Woman's Hand, 2nd ed., pp. 77–78.
(884b)
Detecting Women, 1st ed., p. 57. (877a)
Detecting Women 2, p. 70. (877b)
Detecting Women, 3rd ed., p. 96. (877c)
Web site: http://stopyourekillingme.com/
earlene-fowler.html; http://www.
earlenefowler.com
Fowler, Sydney. *Pseud. for* **Sydney Fowler
Wright**
Bio-bibliographic data:
*Twentieth-Century Crime and Mystery
Writers,* 1st ed., pp. 600–603. (882a)
*Twentieth-Century Crime and Mystery
Writers*, 2nd ed., pp. 339–41. (882b)
Fox, James M. *Pseud. for* **Johannes
Mattijis Willem Knipscheer**
Bio-bibliographic data:
*Twentieth-Century Crime and Mystery
Writers*, 2nd ed., pp. 341–42. (882b)
*Twentieth-Century Crime and Mystery
Writers*, 3rd ed., pp. 394–95. (882c)
Fox, Tom. *Pseud. for* **John Bennett**
Bio-bibliographic data:
The Encyclopedia of Murder and Mystery,
p. 185. (6)
Foxx, Aleister. *Pseud. for* **Alan Annand**
Foxx, Jack. *See* **Pronzini, Bill**
Francis, Clare [Mary]
Bio-bibliographic data:
*The Mammoth Encyclopedia of Modern
Crime Fiction*, pp. 164–65. (1)
Francis, Dick; i.e., Richard Stanley
Bio-bibliographic data:
Australian Crime Fiction, pp. 92–93.
(207)
*British Mystery and Thriller Writers since
1940, First Series*, pp. 136–55. (868)
Canadian Crime Fiction, p. 254. (209)
Corpus Delicti of Mystery Fiction, pp.
70–71. (879)
*The Craft of Crime: Conversations with
Crime Writers*, pp. 202–21. (872)
*Critical Survey of Mystery and Detective
Fiction*, pp. 651–55. (41)
Designs of Darkness, pp. 224–39. (873)
Detecting Men, 1st ed., p. 93. (876)
Encyclopedia Mysteriosa, p. 126. (2)
The Encyclopedia of Murder and Mystery,
pp. 186–87. (6)
*The Encyclopedia of Mystery and
Detection*, pp. 155–56. (7)
*The Mammoth Encyclopedia of Modern
Crime Fiction*, pp. 165–66. (1)

Mystery and Suspense Writers, pp.
383–98. (884.2)
*100 Masters of Mystery and Detective
Fiction*, pp. 253–57. (37)
*The Oxford Companion to Crime and
Mystery Writing*, p. 168. (4)
*St. James Guide to Crime & Mystery
Writers*, 4th ed., pp. 373–75. (882d)
Twelve Englishmen of Mystery, pp.
222–49. (865)
*Twentieth-Century Crime and Mystery
Writers,* 1st ed., pp. 603–5. (882a)
*Twentieth-Century Crime and Mystery
Writers*, 2nd ed., pp. 342–44. (882b)
*Twentieth-Century Crime and Mystery
Writers*, 3rd ed., pp. 395–97. (882c)
*Whodunit? A Who's Who in Crime and
Mystery Writing*, p. 74. (5)
Web site: http://stopyourekillingme.com/
dick-francis.html; http://www.
thrillingdetective.com/trivia/
francis.html

Francis, Maurice
Bio-bibliographic data:
Australian Crime Fiction, p. 93. (207)

Francome, John
Bio-bibliographic data:
*The Mammoth Encyclopedia of Modern
Crime Fiction*, pp. 166–67. (1)

Frank, Sophie
Bio-bibliographic data:
Australian Crime Fiction, p. 93. (207)

Frankau, Gilbert
Bio-bibliographic data:
*The Encyclopedia of Mystery and
Detection*, p. 156. (7)

Franke, Wolfgang E.
Bio-bibliographic data:
Canadian Crime Fiction, p. 78. (209)

Frankel, Neville
Bio-bibliographic data:
Canadian Crime Fiction, pp. 78–79. (209)

Frankel, Valerie
Bio-bibliographic data:
By a Woman's Hand, 2nd ed., pp. 78–79.
(884b)
Detecting Women, 1st ed., p. 57. (877a)
Detecting Women 2, p. 70. (877b)
Detecting Women, 3rd ed., pp. 96–97.
(877c)

Franklin, [Stella Maria Sarah] Miles
Bio-bibliographic data:
Australian Crime Fiction, p. 93. (207)

Fraser, Anthea [Mary]
Bio-bibliographic data:
By a Woman's Hand, 1st ed., p. 75. (884a)
By a Woman's Hand, 2nd ed., p. 79.
(884b)
Detecting Women, 1st ed., p. 57. (877a)
Detecting Women 2, pp. 70–71. (877b)
Detecting Women, 3rd ed., p. 97. (877c)
*The Mammoth Encyclopedia of Modern
Crime Fiction*, p. 167. (1)
*St. James Guide to Crime & Mystery
Writers*, 4th ed., pp. 375–77. (882d)
*Twentieth-Century Crime and Mystery
Writers*, 3rd ed., pp. 397–98. (882c)
*Whodunit? A Who's Who in Crime and
Mystery Writing*, p. 74. (5)
Web site: http://stopyourekillingme.com/
anthea-fraser.html

Fraser, [Lady] Antonia Pakenham
Bio-bibliographic data:
By a Woman's Hand, 1st ed., p. 76. (884a)
By a Woman's Hand, 2nd ed., pp. 79–80.
(884b)
*Critical Survey of Mystery and Detective
Fiction*, p. 656–61. (41)
Detecting Women, 1st ed., pp. 58. (877a)
Detecting Women 2, pp. 71. (877b)
Detecting Women, 3rd ed., p. 97–98.
(877c)
Encyclopedia Mysteriosa, pp. 126. (2)
The Encyclopedia of Murder and Mystery,
p. 187. (6)
Great Women Mystery Writers, pp.
114–17. (880)
*The Mammoth Encyclopedia of Modern
Crime Fiction*, pp. 168–69. (1)
*St. James Guide to Crime & Mystery
Writers*, 4th ed., pp. 377–79. (882d)
13 Mistresses of Murder, pp. 33–44. (871)
*Twentieth-Century Crime and Mystery
Writers,* 1st ed., pp. 606–7. (882a)
*Twentieth-Century Crime and Mystery
Writers*, 2nd ed., pp. 344–45. (882b)
*Twentieth-Century Crime and Mystery
Writers*, 3rd ed., pp. 398–400. (882c)
*Whodunit? A Who's Who in Crime and
Mystery Writing*, p. 74–75. (5)
Web site: http://stopyourekillingme.com/
antonia-fraser.html

Fraser, James. *Pseud. for* Alan White
Bio-bibliographic data:
Detecting Men, 1st ed., p. 93. (876)
*St. James Guide to Crime & Mystery
Writers*, 4th ed., pp. 379–80. (882d)

Twentieth-Century Crime and Mystery Writers, 3rd ed., pp. 400–401.
Fraser, Sylvia
Bio-bibliographic data:
Canadian Crime Fiction, p. 79. (209)
Fraser, William Alexander
Bio-bibliographic data:
Canadian Crime Fiction, p. 79. (209)
Fray, Al
Bio-bibliographic data:
The Big Book of Noir, p. 265. (24)
Frazer, Margaret. *See* **Kuhfeld, Mary Pulver and Gail Bacon**
Frazer, Robert Caine. *See* **Creasey, John**
Freedgood, Morton. *See* **Godey, John**
Freedman, Benedict
Bio-bibliographic data:
Canadian Crime Fiction, p. 254. (209)
Freedman, Nancy. *See* **Freedman, Benedict**
Freeling, Nicolas
Bio-bibliographic data:
British Mystery and Thriller Writers since 1940, First Series, pp. 156–76. (868)
Critical Survey of Mystery and Detective Fiction, pp. 661–66. (41)
Detecting Men, 1st ed., p. 94. (876)
Encyclopedia Mysteriosa, p. 126. (2)
The Encyclopedia of Murder and Mystery, pp. 187–88. (6)
The Encyclopedia of Mystery and Detection, p. 157. (7)
The Mammoth Encyclopedia of Modern Crime Fiction, pp. 169–71. (1)
100 Masters of Mystery and Detective Fiction, pp. 258–63. (37)
The Oxford Companion to Crime and Mystery Writing, p. 168. (4)
St. James Guide to Crime & Mystery Writers, 4th ed., pp. 381–82. (882d)
Twentieth-Century Crime and Mystery Writers, 1st ed., pp. 608–10. (882a)
Twentieth-Century Crime and Mystery Writers, 2nd ed., pp. 345–47. (882b)
Twentieth-Century Crime and Mystery Writers, 3rd ed., pp. 401–3. (882c)
Whodunit? A Who's Who in Crime and Mystery Writing, p. 75. (5)
Web site: http://stopyourekillingme.com/nicholas-freeling.html
Freeman, Lucy
Bio-bibliographic data:
13 Mistresses of Murder, pp. 45–52. (871)

Freeman, R. Austin; i.e., Richard Austin
Bio-bibliographic data:
British Mystery Writers, 1860–1919, pp. 143–53. (866)
Critical Survey of Mystery and Detective Fiction, pp. 667–73. (41)
Encyclopedia Mysteriosa, pp. 126–27. (2)
The Encyclopedia of Murder and Mystery, pp. 188–89. (6)
The Encyclopedia of Mystery and Detection, pp. 157–58. (7)
100 Masters of Mystery and Detective Fiction, pp. 264–70. (37)
The Oxford Companion to Crime and Mystery Writing, pp. 168–69. (4)
St. James Guide to Crime & Mystery Writers, 4th ed., p.383–84. (882d)
Twentieth-Century Crime and Mystery Writers, 1st ed., pp. 611–14. (882a)
Twentieth-Century Crime and Mystery Writers, 2nd ed., pp. 347–48. (882b)
Twentieth-Century Crime and Mystery Writers, 3rd ed., pp. 403–5. (882c)
Whodunit? A Who's Who in Crime and Mystery Writing, pp. 75–76. (5)
Personal papers in Occidental College, Los Angeles.
Web site: http://stopyourekillingme.com/r-austin-freeman.html
John Thorndyke's Journal
c/o David Ian Chapman
55 Highfield Gardens
Aldershot, Hampshire
GU11 3DB United Kingdom
Freemantle, Brian
Bio-bibliographic data:
Detecting Men, 1st ed., p. 95. (876)
Encyclopedia Mysteriosa, p. 127. (2)
The Encyclopedia of Murder and Mystery, pp. 189–90. (6)
St. James Guide to Crime & Mystery Writers, 4th ed., pp. 384–85. (882d)
Twentieth-Century Crime and Mystery Writers, 1st ed., pp. 614–15. (882a)
Twentieth-Century Crime and Mystery Writers, 2nd ed., pp. 348–49. (882b)
Twentieth-Century Crime and Mystery Writers, 3rd ed., pp. 405–6. (882c)
Fremlin, Celia Margaret. *Pseud. for* **Celia Fremlin Goller**
Bio-bibliographic data:
By a Woman's Hand, 1st ed., pp. 76–77. (884a)

By a Woman's Hand, 2nd ed., p. 80.
(884b)
The Encyclopedia of Murder and Mystery,
p. 190. (6)
*St. James Guide to Crime & Mystery
Writers*, 4th ed., pp. 385–86. (882d)
*Twentieth-Century Crime and Mystery
Writers,* 1st ed., pp. 615–17. (882a)
*Twentieth-Century Crime and Mystery
Writers*, 2nd ed., pp. 349–50. (882b)
*Twentieth-Century Crime and Mystery
Writers*, 3rd ed., pp. 406–7. (882c)
Personal papers in Mugar Memorial
Library, Boston University.
Web site: http://stopyourekillingme.com/
celia-fremlin.html
French, David
Bio-bibliographic data:
Canadian Crime Fiction, pp. 79–80. (209)
French, Jackie
Bio-bibliographic data:
Australian Crime Fiction, p. 9. (207)
French, Linda: unidentified pseud.
Bio-bibliographic data:
Detecting Women, 3rd ed., p. 98. (877c)
Web site: http://stopyourekillingme.com/
linda-french.html
French, Nicci. *Pseud. for* Nicci Gerard
Bio-bibliographic data:
*The Mammoth Encyclopedia of Modern
Crime Fiction*, pp. 171–72. (1)
Web site: http://www.niccifrench.com
French, Roy
Bio-bibliographic data:
Canadian Crime Fiction, p. 80. (209)
Freney, Denis
Bio-bibliographic data:
Australian Crime Fiction, p. 93. (207)
Freugon, Ruby. *See* Ashby, R. C.
**Freybe, Heidi Huberta. *See* Albrand,
Martha**
Freyer, Frederic. *See* Ballinger, Bill S.
**Friedman, Kinky. *Pseud. for* Richard
Friedman**
Bio-bibliographic data:
Detecting Men, 1st ed., p. 95 (876)
The Encyclopedia of Murder and Mystery,
pp. 191–92. (6)
*The Mammoth Encyclopedia of Modern
Crime Fiction*, p. 172. (1)
*St. James Guide to Crime & Mystery
Writers*, 4th ed., pp. 387–88. (882d)
*Twentieth-Century Crime and Mystery
Writers*, 3rd ed., pp. 407–8. (882c)

Web site: http://www.kinkyfriedman.com;
http://stopyourekillingme.com/
kinky-friedman.html
**Friedman, Mickey; i.e., Michaele
Thompson**
Bio-bibliographic data:
By a Woman's Hand, 1st ed., pp. 77–78.
(884a)
By a Woman's Hand, 2nd ed., pp. 80–81.
(884b)
Detecting Women, 1st ed., p. 58. (877a)
Detecting Women 2, pp. 71–72. (877b)
Detecting Women, 3rd ed., p. 99. (877c)
Friedman, Richard. *See* Friedman, Kinky
Fritchley, Alma
Bio-bibliographic data:
Detecting Women, 3rd ed., p. 99. (877c)
Frith, Ellen
Bio-bibliographic data:
Canadian Crime Fiction, p. 80. (209)
Froetschel, Susan
Bio-bibliographic data:
Detecting Women 2, p. 72. (877b)
Frome, David. *See* Ford, Leslie
Fromer, Margot J.
Bio-bibliographic data:
Detecting Women, 1st ed., p. 58. (877a)
Detecting Women 2, p. 73. (877b)
Detecting Women, 3rd ed., p. 99. (877c)
Frommer, Sara Hoskinson
Bio-bibliographic data:
Detecting Women 2, p. 73. (877b)
Detecting Women, 3rd ed., p. 100. (877c)
Web site: http://stopyourekillingme.com/
sara-hoskinson-frommer.html;
http://www.sff.net/people/
SaraHoskinsonFrommer
Frost, C. Vernon. *See* Child, Charles S.
Frost, David
Bio-bibliographic data:
Australian Crime Fiction, p. 94. (207)
Frost, Frederick. *See* Brand, Max
Frost, Mark
Bio-bibliographic data:
Detecting Men, 1st ed., p. 96. (876)
Fry, Alan
Bio-bibliographic data:
Canadian Crime Fiction, p. 80. (209)
Fry, Pamela
Bio-bibliographic data:
Canadian Crime Fiction, p. 80. (209)
Fuentes, Carlos
Bio-bibliographic data:

Latin American Mystery Writers: An A to Z Guide. (881)
Fulford, Paul A.
Bio-bibliographic data:
Canadian Crime Fiction, p. 80. (209)
Fuller, Dean
Bio-bibliographic data:
Detecting Men, 1st ed., p. 96. (876)
Fuller, Roy
Bio-bibliographic data:
Twentieth-Century Crime and Mystery Writers, 1st ed., pp. 617–19. (882a)
Twentieth-Century Crime and Mystery Writers, 2nd ed., pp. 350–52. (882b)
Twentieth-Century Crime and Mystery Writers, 3rd ed., pp. 408–10. (882c)
Personal papers in State University of New York, Buffalo.
Personal papers in British Library, London.
Fuller, Samuel
Bio-bibliographic data:
Twentieth-Century Crime and Mystery Writers, 1st ed., pp. 619–21. (882a)
Fuller, Timothy(1). *See* **Marquand, John P.**
Fuller, Timothy(2)
Bio-bibliographic data:
Detecting Men, 1st ed., p. 96. (876)
Fuller, William
Bio-bibliographic data:
The Big Book of Noir, p. 265. (24)
The Encyclopedia of Murder and Mystery, p. 192. (6)
Fullerton, Mary Eliza. *See* **Manners, Gordon**
Furlong, Nicola
Bio-bibliographic data:
Canadian Crime Fiction, p. 80. (209)
Web site: http://stopyourekillingme.com/ nicola-furlong.html
Fulton, Eileen
Bio-bibliographic data:
Detecting Women 2, p. 73. (877b)
Detecting Women, 3rd ed., p. 100. (877c)
Furey, Michael. *See* **Rohmer, Sax**
Furie, Ruthe
Bio-bibliographic data:
Detecting Women 2, p. 73. (877b)
Detecting Women, 3rd ed., p. 100. (877c)
Furutani, Dale
Bio-bibliographic data:
Detecting Men, 1st ed., pp. 96–97. (876)

The Mammoth Encyclopedia of Modern Crime Fiction, p. 173. (1)
Web site:
http://members.aol.com/DFurutani; http://stopyourekillingme.com/ dale-furutani.html
Futrelle, Jacques
Bio-bibliographic data:
Critical Survey of Mystery and Detective Fiction, pp. 674–79. (41)
Encyclopedia Mysteriosa, p. 129. (2)
The Encyclopedia of Murder and Mystery, pp. 193–94. (6)
The Encyclopedia of Mystery and Detection, p. 162. (7)
The Oxford Companion to Crime and Mystery Writing, p. 171. (4)
St. James Guide to Crime & Mystery Writers, 4th ed., pp. 388–89. (882d)
Twentieth-Century Crime and Mystery Writers, 1st ed., pp. 621–22. (882a)
Twentieth-Century Crime and Mystery Writers, 2nd ed., p. 352. (882b)
Twentieth-Century Crime and Mystery Writers, 3rd ed., p. 410. (882c)
Whodunit? A Who's Who in Crime and Mystery Writing, pp. 76–77. (5)
Web site: http://stopyourekillingme.com/ jacques-futrelle.html
Fyffe, Laurie
Bio-bibliographic data:
Canadian Crime Fiction, p. 80. (209)
Fyfield, Frances. *Pseud. for* **Frances Hegarty**
Bio-bibliographic data:
By a Woman's Hand, 1st ed., p. 78. (884a)
By a Woman's Hand, 2nd ed., pp. 81–82. (884b)
Detecting Women, 1st ed., p. 59. (877a)
Detecting Women 2, p. 74. (877b)
Detecting Women, 3rd ed., p. 101. (877c)
The Encyclopedia of Murder and Mystery, p. 194. (6)
Great Women Mystery Writers, pp. 117–19. (880)
The Mammoth Encyclopedia of Modern Crime Fiction, pp. 173–74. (1)
St. James Guide to Crime & Mystery Writers, 4th ed., pp. 389–90. (882d)
Whodunit? A Who's Who in Crime and Mystery Writing, p. 77. (5)
874.*Women of Mystery*, p. 435.
Web site: http://stopyourekillingme.com/ frances-fyfield.html; http://www.

figuresdestyle.com/fyfield/
index_en.html

G

Gaetz, Dale
Bio-bibliographic data:
Canadian Crime Fiction, p. 81. (209)
Gaboriau, Émile
Bio-bibliographic data:
*Critical Survey of Mystery and Detective
Fiction*, pp. 680–86. (41)
Encyclopedia Mysteriosa, p. 130. (2)
The Encyclopedia of Murder and Mystery,
p. 195. (6)
*The Encyclopedia of Mystery and
Detection*, p. 163. (7)
Mystery and Suspense Writers, pp.
399–407. (884.2)
*The Oxford Companion to Crime and
Mystery Writing*, p. 173. (4)
*St. James Guide to Crime & Mystery
Writers*, 4th ed., pp. 391–92. (882d)
*Twentieth-Century Crime and Mystery
Writers*, 1st ed., pp. 1540–41. (882a)
*Twentieth-Century Crime and Mystery
Writers*, 2nd ed., pp. 941–42. (882b)
*Twentieth-Century Crime and Mystery
Writers*, 3rd ed., p. 1131. (882c)
*Whodunit? A Who's Who in Crime and
Mystery Writing*, p. 79. (5)
Web site:
http://authorsdirectory.com/biography
_online_book_portrait_picture/
g_authors_emile_gaboriau.shtml
Gadney, Reg
Bio-bibliographic data:
*St. James Guide to Crime & Mystery
Writers*, 4th ed., pp. 392–93. (882d)
*Twentieth-Century Crime and Mystery
Writers*, 1st ed., pp. 622–23. (882a)
*Twentieth-Century Crime and Mystery
Writers*, 2nd ed., pp. 352–53. (882b)
*Twentieth-Century Crime and Mystery
Writers*, 3rd ed., pp. 411–12. (882c)
Personal papers in Mugar Memorial
Library, Boston University
Gagnon, Cécile
Bio-bibliographic data:
Canadian Crime Fiction, p. 81. (209)
Gagnon, Gérald
Bio-bibliographic data:
Canadian Crime Fiction, p. 81. (209)
Gagnon, Maurice
Bio-bibliographic data:

Canadian Crime Fiction, p. 81. (209)
Gahagan, Marguerite or Margaret
Bio-bibliographic data:
Australian Crime Fiction, p. 95. (207)
Gainham, Sarah. *Pseud. for* [Sarah]
Rachel Ames
Bio-bibliographic data:
*Twentieth-Century Crime and Mystery
Writers*, 1st ed., pp. 624–25. (882a)
*Twentieth-Century Crime and Mystery
Writers*, 2nd ed., pp. 353–54. (882b)
*Twentieth-Century Crime and Mystery
Writers*, 3rd ed., p. 412. (882c)
Gaitano, Nick. *See* **Izzi, Eugene [John]**
Gaite, Francis. *See* **Coles, Manning**
Galbally, Frank; i.e., Francis Eugene
Bio-bibliographic data:
Australian Crime Fiction, p. 95. (207)
Gallico, Paul
Bio-bibliographic data:
The Encyclopedia of Murder and Mystery,
pp. 195– 196. (6)
Gallison, Kate
Bio-bibliographic data:
By a Woman's Hand, 2nd ed., pp. 83–84.
(884b)
Detecting Women 2, p. 74. (877b)
Detecting Women, 3rd ed., p. 101. (877c)
Women Authors of Detective Series, pp.
128–31. (882.5)
Web site: http://stopyourekillingme.com/
kate-gallison.html; http://www.
kategallison.com
Galway, Robert Conington. *See*
McCutchan, [Donald] Philip
Gamble, Henry Elliott
Bio-bibliographic data:
Canadian Crime Fiction, p. 82. (209)
Gammon, David
Bio-bibliographic data:
Canadian Crime Fiction, p. 82. (209)
Gandley, Kenneth Royce. *See* **Royce,
Kenneth**
Gant, James
Bio-bibliographic data:
Australian Crime Fiction, p. 95. (207)
Garand, Edouard. *See* **Riel, Louis**
Garcia-Aguilera, Carolina
Bio-bibliographic data:
Detecting Women, 3rd ed., p. 102. (877c)
Web site: http://stopyourekillingme.com/
carolina-garcia-aguilera.html
Gardiner, Dorothy
Bio-bibliographic data:

Detecting Women 2, p. 74. (877b)
Twentieth-Century Crime and Mystery Writers, 1st ed., pp. 625–26. (882a)
Twentieth-Century Crime and Mystery Writers, 2nd ed., pp. 354–55. (882b)
Gardiner, Heather
Bio-bibliographic data:
Australian Crime Fiction, p. 95. (207)
Gardiner, Joan. *See* **Bridges, Hilda**
Gardner, Erle Stanley
Bio-bibliographic data:
Corpus Delicti of Mystery Fiction, pp. 71–74. (879)
Critical Survey of Mystery and Detective Fiction, pp. 687–93. (41)
Encyclopedia Mysteriosa, pp. 130–31. (2)
The Encyclopedia of Murder and Mystery, pp. 169, 197–98. (6)
The Encyclopedia of Mystery and Detection, pp. 164–66. (7)
Mystery and Suspense Writers, pp. 409–25. (884.2)
100 Masters of Mystery and Detective Fiction, pp. 271–77. (37)
The Oxford Companion to Crime and Mystery Writing, p. 174. (4)
St. James Guide to Crime & Mystery Writers, 4th ed., pp. 393–97. (882d)
Twentieth-Century Crime and Mystery Writers, 1st ed., pp. 626–33. (882a)
Twentieth-Century Crime and Mystery Writers, 2nd ed., pp. 355–59. (882b)
Twentieth-Century Crime and Mystery Writers, 3rd ed., pp. 413–16. (882c)
Whodunit? A Who's Who in Crime and Mystery Writing, pp. 79–80. (5)
Personal papers in Humanities Research Center, University of Texas at Austin.
Web site: http://stopyourekillingme.com/ erle-stanley-gardner.html; http://www. erlestanleygardner.com; http://www. thrillingdetective.com/trivia/ gardner.html; http://www.phantoms.com/ ~phantom/gardner/
Gardner, John [Edmond]
Bio-bibliographic data:
Critical Survey of Mystery and Detective Fiction, pp. 694–699. (41)
Detecting Men, 1st ed., p. 98. (876)
Encyclopedia Mysteriosa, pp. 131–32. (2)
St. James Guide to Crime & Mystery Writers, 4th ed., pp. 397–99. (882d)

Twentieth-Century Crime and Mystery Writers, 1st ed., pp. 633–36. (882a)
Twentieth-Century Crime and Mystery Writers, 2nd ed., pp. 359–60. (882b)
Twentieth-Century Crime and Mystery Writers, 3rd ed., pp. 416–18. (882c)
Web site: http://stopyourekillingme.com/ john-gardner.html; http://www. john-gardner.co.uk
Garfield, Brian [Francis Wynne]
Bio-bibliographic data:
Detecting Men, 1st ed., p. 99. (876)
Encyclopedia Mysteriosa, p. 132. (2)
The Mammoth Encyclopedia of Modern Crime Fiction, pp. 174–76. (1)
St. James Guide to Crime & Mystery Writers, 4th ed., pp. 399–402. (882d)
Twentieth-Century Crime and Mystery Writers, 1st ed., pp. 636–41. (882a)
Twentieth-Century Crime and Mystery Writers, 2nd ed., pp. 360–63. (882b)
Twentieth-Century Crime and Mystery Writers, 3rd ed., pp. 418–21. (882c)
Personal papers in University of Oregon Library, Eugene, Oregon.
Web site: http://stopyourekillingme.com/ brian-garfield.html
Garfield, Henry
Bio-bibliographic data:
Detecting Men, 1st ed., p. 99. (876)
Garner, Bill
Bio-bibliographic data:
Australian Crime Fiction, p. 95. (207)
Garner, Hugh
Bio-bibliographic data:
Canadian Crime Fiction, pp. 82–83. (209)
Garrod, John William. *See* **Castle, John**
Garve, Andrew. *Pseud. for* **Paul Winterton**
Bio-bibliographic data:
Australian Crime Fiction, p. 96. (207)
British Mystery and Thriller Writers since 1940, First Series, pp. 177–84. (868)
Critical Survey of Mystery and Detective Fiction, pp. 700–704. (41)
Encyclopedia Mysteriosa, pp. 132–33. (2)
The Encyclopedia of Murder and Mystery, pp. 198. (6)
The Encyclopedia of Mystery and Detection, pp. 166–67. (7)
The Oxford Companion to Crime and Mystery Writing, p. 175. (4)
St. James Guide to Crime & Mystery Writers, 4th ed., pp. 402–4. (882d)

Twentieth-Century Crime and Mystery Writers, 1st ed., pp. 641–44. (882a)
Twentieth-Century Crime and Mystery Writers, 2nd ed., pp. 363–65. (882b)
Twentieth-Century Crime and Mystery Writers, 3rd ed., pp. 421–23. (882c)
Personal papers in Mugar Memorial Library, Boston University.
Web site: http://stopyourekillingme.com/andrew-garve.html

Garwood, Judith. *See* **Dain, Catherine**
Gash, Joe. *See* **Granger, Bill**
Gash, Jonathan. *Pseud. for* **John Grant**
  Bio-bibliographic data:
  Critical Survey of Mystery and Detective Fiction, pp. 705–10. (41)
  Detecting Men, 1st ed., pp. 99–100. (876)
  Encyclopedia Mysteriosa, p. 133. (2)
  The Encyclopedia of Murder and Mystery, pp. 198–99. (6)
  The Fatal Art of Entertainment, pp. 162–93. (878)
  The Mammoth Encyclopedia of Modern Crime Fiction, pp. 176–77. (1)
  Twentieth-Century Crime and Mystery Writers, 2nd ed., pp. 365–66. (882b)
  Twentieth-Century Crime and Mystery Writers, 3rd ed., pp. 423–24. (882c)
  Whodunit? A Who's Who in Crime and Mystery Writing, p. 80. (5)
  Web site: http://www.frii.com/~saunders/gash.htm; http://stopyourekillingme.com/jonathan-gash.html; http://www.frii.com/~saunders/gash.htm

Gask, Arthur [Cecil]
  Bio-bibliographic data:
  Australian Crime Fiction, pp. 96–99. (207)

Gaskin, Catherine [Majella Sinclair]
  Bio-bibliographic data:
  Australian Crime Fiction, p. 99. (207)
  Twentieth-Century Crime and Mystery Writers, 1st ed., pp. 644–45. (882a)

Gaspé, Phillipe-Ignace-François Aubert de. *See* **Aubert de Gaspé, Phillipe-Ignace-François**

Gat, Dimitri
  Bio-bibliographic data:
  Detecting Men, 1st ed., p. 100. (876)

Gaudreault-Labrecque, Madeleine
  Bio-bibliographic data:
  Canadian Crime Fiction, p. 83. (209)

Gault, William Campbell
  Bio-bibliographic data:

American Hard-Boiled Crime Writers, pp. 149–56. (862)
Critical Survey of Mystery and Detective Fiction, pp. 711–16. (41)
Encyclopedia Mysteriosa, p. 133. (2)
The Encyclopedia of Murder and Mystery, p. 199. (6)
The Encyclopedia of Mystery and Detection, p. 167. (7)
The Oxford Companion to Crime and Mystery Writing, pp. 175–76. (4)
St. James Guide to Crime & Mystery Writers, 4th ed., pp. 405–7. (882d)
Twentieth-Century Crime and Mystery Writers, 1st ed., pp. 646–48. (882a)
Twentieth-Century Crime and Mystery Writers, 2nd ed., pp. 366–68. (882b)
Twentieth-Century Crime and Mystery Writers, 3rd ed., pp. 424–27. (882c)
Whodunit? A Who's Who in Crime and Mystery Writing, pp. 80–81. (5)
Personal papers in University of Oregon, Eugene, Oregon.
Web site:
  http://www.thrillingdetective.com/trivia/gault.html

Gaunt, Graham. *See* **Gash, Jonathan**
Gaunt, M. B. *Pseud. for* **Richard Edward Horsfield**
  Bio-bibliographic data:
  Canadian Crime Fiction, p. 83. (209)
Gaunt, Mary [Eliza Bakewell]
  Bio-bibliographic data:
  Australian Crime Fiction, p. 99. (207)
Gauthier, Gilles
  Bio-bibliographic data:
  Canadian Crime Fiction, p. 83. (209)
Gauthier, Louis
  Bio-bibliographic data:
  Canadian Crime Fiction, p. 83. (209)
Gauvreau, Marguerite
  Bio-bibliographic data:
  Canadian Crime Fiction, p. 83. (209)
Gauveaul, Marguerite-G.
  Bio-bibliographic data:
  Canadian Crime Fiction, p. 83. (209)
Gazounaud: unidentified pseud.
  Bio-bibliographic data:
  Canadian Crime Fiction, p. 83. (209)
Geason, Susan
  Bio-bibliographic data:
  Australian Crime Fiction, pp. 99–100, 146. (207)

By a Woman's Hand, 2nd ed., pp. 84–85.
(884b)
Canadian Crime Fiction, p. 277. (209)
Detecting Women, 1st ed., p. 59. (877a)
Detecting Women 2, p. 75. (877b)
Detecting Women, 3rd ed., p. 102. (877c)
Geddes, Hugh. *Pseud. for* Hugh Atkinson
Bio-bibliographic data:
Australian Crime Fiction, p. 100. (207)
Geddes, Paul
Bio-bibliographic data:
Canadian Crime Fiction, p. 254. (209)
Gedge, Pauline
Bio-bibliographic data:
Canadian Crime Fiction, pp. 83–84. (209)
Gélinas, Gratien
Bio-bibliographic data:
Canadian Crime Fiction, p. 84. (209)
Gellatly, Francis Mephan
Bio-bibliographic data:
Australian Crime Fiction, p. 100. (207)
George, Anne
Bio-bibliographic data:
Detecting Women, 3rd ed., pp. 102–3.
(877c)
*The Mammoth Encyclopedia of Modern
Crime Fiction*, pp. 177–78. (1)
Web site: http://stopyourekillingme.
com/anne-george.html
George, Elizabeth; i.e., [Susan] Elizabeth
Bio-bibliographic data:
By a Woman's Hand, 1st ed., pp. 79–80.
(884a)
By a Woman's Hand, 2nd ed., pp. 85–86.
(884b)
Deadly Women, pp. 199–203. (26.5)
Detecting Women, 1st ed., p. 59. (877a)
Detecting Women 2, p. 75. (877b)
Detecting Women, 3rd ed., p. 103. (877c)
Encyclopedia Mysteriosa, p. 134. (2)
The Encyclopedia of Murder and Mystery,
p. 202. (6)
Great Women Mystery Writers, pp.
121–24. (880)
*The Mammoth Encyclopedia of Modern
Crime Fiction*, pp. 178–79. (1)
*St. James Guide to Crime & Mystery
Writers*, 4th ed., pp. 407–8. (882d)
Speaking of Murder, pp. 65–71. (875a)
*Twentieth-Century Crime and Mystery
Writers*, 3rd ed., pp. 427–28. (882c)
*Whodunit? A Who's Who in Crime and
Mystery Writing*, p. 84. (5)
Women of Mystery, p. 435. (874)

Personal papers in Mugar Memorial
Library, Boston University.
Web site:
http://www.elizabethgeorgeonline.
html; http://stopyourekillingme.com/
elizabeth-george.html
George, Stephen R.
Bio-bibliographic data:
Canadian Crime Fiction, p. 84. (209)
Gerard, Nicci. *See* French, Nicci
Germain, Doric
Bio-bibliographic data:
Canadian Crime Fiction, p. 84. (209)
Getzin, Amber Dean. *See* Dean, Amber
Giardinelli, Mempo
Bio-bibliographic data:
*Latin American Mystery Writers: An A to
Z Guide. (881)*
Gibbon, John Murray
Bio-bibliographic data:
Canadian Crime Fiction, pp. 84–85. (209)
Gibbons, Charles Harrison
Bio-bibliographic data:
Canadian Crime Fiction, p. 85. (209)
**Gibbs, Henry St. John Clair. *See*
Harvester, Simon**
Gibbs, Tony; i.e., Wolcott Gibbs, Jr.
Bio-bibliographic data:
Detecting Men, 1st ed., p. 100. (876)
Web site: http://stopyourekillingme.com/
tony-gibbs.html
Gibson, Judy
Bio-bibliographic data:
Canadian Crime Fiction, p. 85. (209)
Gibson, Walter B[rown].
Bio-bibliographic data:
*Critical Survey of Mystery and Detective
Fiction*, pp. 717–24. (41)
Encyclopedia Mysteriosa, p. 136. (2)
*The Encyclopedia of Mystery and
Detection*, pp. 168–69. (7)
*St. James Guide to Crime & Mystery
Writers*, 4th ed., pp. 408–10. (882d)
*Twentieth-Century Crime and Mystery
Writers*, 1st ed., pp. 648–54. (882a)
*Twentieth-Century Crime and Mystery
Writers*, 2nd ed., pp. 368–72. (882b)
*Twentieth-Century Crime and Mystery
Writers*, 3rd ed., pp. 428–32. (882c)
Gibson, William
Bio-bibliographic data:
Canadian Crime Fiction, p. 85. (209)
Gielgud, Val [Henry]
Bio-bibliographic data:

*The Encyclopedia of Mystery and
Detection*, pp. 169–70. (7)
*Twentieth-Century Crime and Mystery
Writers,* 1st ed., pp. 654–58. (882a)
*Twentieth-Century Crime and Mystery
Writers,* 2nd ed., pp. 372–74. (882b)
*Twentieth-Century Crime and Mystery
Writers,* 3rd ed., pp. 432–34. (882c)

Gieshardt, T. William
Bio-bibliographic data:
Canadian Crime Fiction, p. 85. (209)

Gifford, Thomas
Bio-bibliographic data:
*St. James Guide to Crime & Mystery
Writers,* 4th ed., pp. 410–11. (882d)
*Twentieth-Century Crime and Mystery
Writers,* 1st ed., pp. 658–59. (882a)
*Twentieth-Century Crime and Mystery
Writers,* 2nd ed., p. 374. (882b)
*Twentieth-Century Crime and Mystery
Writers,* 3rd ed., p. 434. (882c)

Gilan: unidentified pseud.
Bio-bibliographic data:
Canadian Crime Fiction, p. 85. (209)

Gilbert, Anthony. *Pseud. for* **Lucy
Beatrice Malleson**
Bio-bibliographic data:
British Mystery Writers, 1920–1939, pp.
122–27. (867)
*Critical Survey of Mystery and Detective
Fiction*, pp. 725–30. (41)
Detecting Women 2, pp. 75–77. (877b)
Encyclopedia Mysteriosa, p. 136. (2)
The Encyclopedia of Murder and Mystery,
p. 204. (6)
*The Encyclopedia of Mystery and
Detection*, p. 10. (7)
*St. James Guide to Crime & Mystery
Writers,* 4th ed., pp. 411–13. (882d)
*Twentieth-Century Crime and Mystery
Writers,* 1st ed., pp. 659–64. (882a)
*Twentieth-Century Crime and Mystery
Writers,* 2nd ed., pp. 374–77. (882b)
*Twentieth-Century Crime and Mystery
Writers,* 3rd ed., pp. 434–37. (882c)

Gilbert, Bernard
Bio-bibliographic data:
Canadian Crime Fiction, p. 85. (209)

Gilbert, Louise
Bio-bibliographic data:
Canadian Crime Fiction, p. 85. (209)

Gilbert, Michael [Francis]
Bio-bibliographic data:

*British Mystery and Thriller Writers since
1940, First Series*, pp. 185–93. (868)
Canadian Crime Fiction, p. 277. (209)
Colloquium on Crime, pp. 79–98. (884.1)
*Critical Survey of Mystery and Detective
Fiction*, pp. 731–38. (41)
Detecting Men, 1st ed., p. 101. (876)
Encyclopedia Mysteriosa, pp. 136–37. (2)
The Encyclopedia of Murder and Mystery,
pp. 204–5. (6)
*The Encyclopedia of Mystery and
Detection*, pp. 170–71. (7)
*The Mammoth Encyclopedia of Modern
Crime Fiction*, pp. 179–81. (1)
Mystery and Suspense Writers, pp.
427–37. (884.2)
*100 Masters of Mystery and Detective
Fiction*, pp. 278–86. (37)
*The Oxford Companion to Crime and
Mystery Writing*, p. 183. (4)
*St. James Guide to Crime & Mystery
Writers,* 4th ed., pp. 413–16. (882d)
Twelve Englishmen of Mystery, pp.
170–95. (865)
*Twentieth-Century Crime and Mystery
Writers,* 1st ed., pp. 664–67. (882a)
*Twentieth-Century Crime and Mystery
Writers,* 2nd ed., pp. 377–79. (882b)
*Twentieth-Century Crime and Mystery
Writers,* 3rd ed., pp. 437–39. (882c)
*Whodunit? A Who's Who in Crime and
Mystery Writing*, p. 85. (5)
Personal papers at University of
California, Berkeley.
Personal papers at Mugar Memorial
Library, Boston University.
Web site: http://stopyourekillingme.com/
michael-gilbert.html

Gilbert, Michael A.
Bio-bibliographic data:
Canadian Crime Fiction, p. 85. (209)

Gilbert, Sky
Bio-bibliographic data:
Canadian Crime Fiction, p. 86. (209)

Gill, B. M. *Pseud. for* **Barbara Margaret
Trimble**
Bio-bibliographic data:
By a Woman's Hand, 1st ed., pp. 80–81.
(884a)
By a Woman's Hand, 2nd ed., p. 86.
(884b)
*Critical Survey of Mystery and Detective
Fiction*, pp. 739–44. (41)
Detecting Women 2, p. 77. (877b)

Detecting Women, 3rd ed., p. 103. (877c)
Great Women Mystery Writers, pp. 124–26. (880)
The Mammoth Encyclopedia of Modern Crime Fiction, pp. 181–82. (1)
St. James Guide to Crime & Mystery Writers, 4th ed., pp. 416–17. (882d)
Twentieth-Century Crime and Mystery Writers, 2nd ed., pp. 379–80. (882b)
Twentieth-Century Crime and Mystery Writers, 3rd ed., pp. 439–40. (882c)
Web site: http://stopyourekillingme.com/ b-m-gill.html

Gill, Bartholomew. *Pseud. for* **Mark McGarrity**
Bio-bibliographic data:
Detecting Men, 1st ed., p. 101. (876)
The Encyclopedia of Murder and Mystery, p. 205. (6)
The Mammoth Encyclopedia of Modern Crime Fiction, pp. 182–83. (1)
St. James Guide to Crime & Mystery Writers, 4th ed., pp. 417–18. (882d)
Twentieth-Century Crime and Mystery Writers, 2nd ed., pp. 380–81. (882b)
Twentieth-Century Crime and Mystery Writers, 3rd ed., pp. 440–41. (882c)
Whodunit? A Who's Who in Crime and Mystery Writing, p. 85. (5)
Web site: http://stopyourekillingme.com/ bartholomew-gill.html

Gill, Max
Bio-bibliographic data:
Australian Crime Fiction, p. 100. (207)

Gilman, Dorothy; i.e., Dorothy Gilman Butters
Bio-bibliographic data:
By a Woman's Hand, 1st ed., pp. 81–82. (884a)
By a Woman's Hand, 2nd ed., pp. 86–87. (884b)
Canadian Crime Fiction, p. 273. (209)
Critical Survey of Mystery and Detective Fiction, pp. 745–49. (41)
Detecting Women, 1st ed., p. 60. (877a)
Detecting Women 2, p. 77. (877b)
Detecting Women, 3rd ed., p. 104. (877c)
Encyclopedia Mysteriosa, p. 137. (2)
Great Women Mystery Writers, pp. 126–29. (880)
St. James Guide to Crime & Mystery Writers, 4th ed., pp. 419–20. (882d)
Twentieth-Century Crime and Mystery Writers, 1st ed., pp. 667–69. (882a)

Twentieth-Century Crime and Mystery Writers, 2nd ed., pp. 381–82. (882b)
Twentieth-Century Crime and Mystery Writers, 3rd ed., pp. 441–43. (882c)
Personal papers at Mugar Memorial Library, Boston University
Web site: http://stopyourekillingme.com/ dorothy-gilman.html

Gilmour, David
Bio-bibliographic data:
Canadian Crime Fiction, p. 86. (209)

Gilpatrick, Noreen
Bio-bibliographic data:
Detecting Women, 1st ed., p. 60. (877a)
Detecting Women 2, pp. 77–78. (877b)
Detecting Women, 3rd ed., p. 104. (877c)

Girdner, Jaqueline
Bio-bibliographic data:
By a Woman's Hand, 1st ed., p. 82. (884a)
By a Woman's Hand, 2nd ed., p. 87. (884b)
Detecting Women, 1st ed., p. 60. (877a)
Detecting Women 2, p. 78. (877b)
Detecting Women, 3rd ed., pp. 104–5. (877c)
Web site: http://stopyourekillingme.com/ jacqueline-girdner.html; http:// members.aol.com/Girdner/index.html

Giroux, E. X. *Pseud. for* **Doris [Giroux] Shannon**
Bio-bibliographic data:
By a Woman's Hand, 1st ed., pp. 82–83. (884a)
By a Woman's Hand, 2nd ed., pp. 87–88. (884b)
Canadian Crime Fiction, pp. 86, 198. (209)
Detecting Women, 1st ed., p. 61. (877a)
Detecting Women 2, p. 78. (877b)
Detecting Women, 3rd ed., p. 105. (877c)
Great Women Mystery Writers, pp. 129–31. (880)
The Mammoth Encyclopedia of Modern Crime Fiction, pp. 183–84. (1)
St. James Guide to Crime & Mystery Writers, 4th ed., pp. 420–21. (882d)
Twentieth-Century Crime and Mystery Writers, 3rd ed., pp. 443–44. (882c)

Glass, Leslie
Bio-bibliographic data:
Detecting Women, 1st ed., p. 61. (877a)
Detecting Women 2, p. 78. (877b)
Detecting Women, 3rd ed., pp. 105–6. (877c)

The Mammoth Encyclopedia of Modern
Crime Fiction, pp. 184–85. (1)
Web site: http://www.aprilwoo.com;
http://stopyourekillingme.com/
leslie-glass.html; http://www.
mystery-book.com
Glaze, Dave
Bio-bibliographic data:
Canadian Crime Fiction, p. 86. (209)
Glazer, Hal
Bio-bibliographic data:
Canadian Crime Fiction, p. 86. (209)
Glazner, Joseph Mark
Bio-bibliographic data:
Canadian Crime Fiction, p. 86. (209)
Glen, Alison. *Pseud. for* **Cheryl Meredith**
Lowry and Louise Vetter
Bio-bibliographic data:
Detecting Women, 1st ed., p. 61. (877a)
Detecting Women 2, p. 79. (877b)
Detecting Women, 3rd ed., p. 106. (877c)
Glenning, Raymond. Pseud. used by
various writers including Carter
Brown (q.v.)
Bio-bibliographic data:
Australian Crime Fiction, pp. 100–101.
(207)
Glover, Douglas [H.]
Bio-bibliographic data:
Canadian Crime Fiction, pp. 86–87. (209)
Gobeil, Pierre
Bio-bibliographic data:
Canadian Crime Fiction, p. 87. (209)
Godard, Marc
Bio-bibliographic data:
Canadian Crime Fiction, p. 87. (209)
Goddard, Ken
Bio-bibliographic data:
Detecting Men, 1st ed., p. 102. (876)
Web site: http://stopyourekillingme.com/
ken-goddard.html; http://members.
aol.com/kengoddard/kenhome.htm
Goddard, Peter
Bio-bibliographic data:
Canadian Crime Fiction, p. 87. (209)
Goddard, Robert
Bio-bibliographic data:
Detecting Men, 1st ed., p. 102. (876)
Web site: http://stopyourekillingme.com/
robert-goddard.html
Godey, John. *Pseud. for* **Morton**
Freedgood
Bio-bibliographic data:

The Encyclopedia of Murder and Mystery,
pp. 206–7. (6)
The Encyclopedia of Mystery and
Detection, pp. 171–72. (7)
The Mammoth Encyclopedia of Modern
Crime Fiction, pp. 185–86. (1)
St. James Guide to Crime & Mystery
Writers, 4th ed., p. 422. (882d)
Twentieth-Century Crime and Mystery
Writers, 1st ed., pp. 669–71. (882a)
Twentieth-Century Crime and Mystery
Writers, 2nd ed., pp. 382–83. (882b)
Twentieth-Century Crime and Mystery
Writers, 3rd ed., pp. 444–45. (882c)
Godfrey, Dave; i.e., David
Bio-bibliographic data:
Canadian Crime Fiction, p. 87. (209)
Godfrey, Ellen
Bio-bibliographic data:
By a Woman's Hand, 2nd ed., pp. 88–89.
(884b)
Canadian Crime Fiction, p. 87. (209)
Detecting Women, 3rd ed., p. 106. (877c)
Web site: http://stopyourekillingme.com/
ellen-godfrey.html
Godin, Gérald
Bio-bibliographic data:
Canadian Crime Fiction, p. 88. (209)
Godin, Marcel
Bio-bibliographic data:
Canadian Crime Fiction, p. 88. (209)
Godwin, John
Bio-bibliographic data:
Australian Crime Fiction, p. 101. (207)
Godwin, William
Bio-bibliographic data:
Critical Survey of Mystery and Detective
Fiction, pp. 750–57. (41)
The Encyclopedia of Mystery and
Detection, p. 172. (7)
The Oxford Companion to Crime and
Mystery Writing, p. 183. (4)
St. James Guide to Crime & Mystery
Writers, 4th ed., pp. 422–23. (882d)
Twentieth-Century Crime and Mystery
Writers, 1st ed., p. 1528. (882a)
Twentieth-Century Crime and Mystery
Writers, 2nd ed., pp. 932–33. (882b)
Twentieth-Century Crime and Mystery
Writers, 3rd ed., p. 1122. (882c)
Whodunit? A Who's Who in Crime and
Mystery Writing, pp. 85–86. (5)
Goines, Donald
Bio-bibliographic data:

St. James Guide to Crime & Mystery Writers, 4th ed., pp. 423–24. (882d)
Twentieth-Century Crime and Mystery Writers, 2nd ed., pp. 383–84. (882b)
Twentieth-Century Crime and Mystery Writers, 3rd ed., p. 445. (882c)

Goldberg, Lee
Bio-bibliographic data:
Detecting Men, 1st ed., p. 102. (876)

Goldberg, Leonard S.
Bio-bibliographic data:
Detecting Men, 1st ed., pp. 102–3. (876)
Web site: http://stopyourekillingme.com/ leonard-s-goldberg.html

Goldfrap, John H. *See* **Payson, Lt. Howard**

Goldman, E. M.; i.e., E. Maureen
Bio-bibliographic data:
Canadian Crime Fiction, p. 88. (209)

Goldman, William
Bio-bibliographic data:
The Mammoth Encyclopedia of Modern Crime Fiction, pp. 186–87. (1)

Goldstein, Arthur D.
Bio-bibliographic data:
Twentieth-Century Crime and Mystery Writers, 1st ed., p. 671. (882a)

Goldstone, Lawrence Arthur. *See* **Treat, Lawrence**

Goldstone, Nancy
Bio-bibliographic data:
Detecting Women, 3rd ed., p. 107. (877c)

Goller, Celia Fremlin. *See* **Fremlin, Celia Margaret**

Gom, Leona
Bio-bibliographic data:
Canadian Crime Fiction, p. 88. (209)
Detecting Women, 3rd ed., p. 107. (877c)

Goodchild, George
Bio-bibliographic data:
Canadian Crime Fiction, pp. 254–55, 264, 268. (209)

Goode, Arthur Russell. *See* **Russell, Arthur**

Goodis, David
Bio-bibliographic data:
American Hard-Boiled Crime Writers, pp. 157–65. (862)
The Big Book of Noir, p. 185. (24)
Encyclopedia Mysteriosa, p. 138. (2)
The Encyclopedia of Murder and Mystery, pp. 210–11. (6)
St. James Guide to Crime & Mystery Writers, 4th ed., pp. 424–25. (882d)

Twentieth-Century Crime and Mystery Writers, 2nd ed., pp. 384–85. (882b)
Twentieth-Century Crime and Mystery Writers, 3rd ed., pp. 446–47. (882c)
Whodunit? A Who's Who in Crime and Mystery Writing, p. 86. (5)
Web site:
http://www.miskatonic.org/rara-avis/ biblio/goodis.html

Goodman, Jonathan
Bio-bibliographic data:
The Encyclopedia of Murder and Mystery, p. 211. (6)

Goodrich, Henry Newton
Bio-bibliographic data:
Australian Crime Fiction, p. 101. (207)

Goodrum, Charles A.
Bio-bibliographic data:
Detecting Men, 1st ed., p. 103. (876)

Goodspeed, Lt-Col. D. J.; i.e., Donald James
Bio-bibliographic data:
Canadian Crime Fiction, pp. 89, 141–42. (209)

Gordon, Alison
Bio-bibliographic data:
By a Woman's Hand, 1st ed., pp. 83–84. (884a)
By a Woman's Hand, 2nd ed., pp. 89–90. (884b)
Canadian Crime Fiction, p. 89. (209)
Detecting Women, 1st ed., pp. 61–62. (877a)
877a. *Detecting Women 2*, p. 79. (877b)
Detecting Women, 3rd ed., pp. 107–8. (877c)
Web site: http://stopyourekillingme.com/ alison-gordon.html

Gordon, Rev. Charles William
Bio-bibliographic data:
Canadian Crime Fiction, pp. 47, 89–90. (209)

Gordon, Robert Kay
Bio-bibliographic data:
Canadian Crime Fiction, p. 90. (209)

The Gordons; i.e., Mildred Gordon and Gordon Gordon
Bio-bibliographic data:
Encyclopedia Mysteriosa, pp. 138–39. (2)
The Encyclopedia of Murder and Mystery, pp. 211–12. (6)
The Encyclopedia of Mystery and Detection, p. 172. (7)

St. James Guide to Crime & Mystery
    Writers, 4th ed., pp. 425–27. (882d)
Twentieth-Century Crime and Mystery
    Writers, 1st ed., pp. 672–74. (882a)
Twentieth-Century Crime and Mystery
    Writers, 2nd ed., pp. 385–86. (882b)
Twentieth-Century Crime and Mystery
    Writers, 3rd ed., pp. 447–49. (882c)
Personal papers in Mugar Memorial
    Library, Boston University.
Gores, Joe; i.e., Joseph Nicholas Gores
Bio-bibliographic data:
American Hard-Boiled Crime Writers, pp.
    166–74. (862)
Critical Survey of Mystery and Detective
    Fiction, pp. 758–63. (41)
Detecting Men, 1st ed., p. 103. (876)
Encyclopedia Mysteriosa, p. 139. (2)
The Encyclopedia of Murder and Mystery,
    pp. 212–13. (6)
The Mammoth Encyclopedia of Modern
    Crime Fiction, pp. 187–88. (1)
St. James Guide to Crime & Mystery
    Writers, 4th ed., pp. 427–29. (882d)
Twentieth-Century Crime and Mystery
    Writers, 1st ed., pp. 674–77. (882a)
Twentieth-Century Crime and Mystery
    Writers, 2nd ed., pp. 386–88. (882b)
Twentieth-Century Crime and Mystery
    Writers, 3rd ed., pp. 449–51. (882c)
Whodunit? A Who's Who in Crime and
    Mystery Writing, p. 86. (5)
Web site: http://stopyourekillingme.com/
    joe-gores.html
Gorman, Carol
Bio-bibliographic data:
Deadly Women, pp. 255–57. (26.5)
Gorman, Ed; i.e., Edward Gorman
Bio-bibliographic data:
The Big Book of Noir, p. 327. (24)
Detecting Men, 1st ed., pp. 103–4. (876)
Encyclopedia Mysteriosa, p. 139. (2)
The Mammoth Encyclopedia of Modern
    Crime Fiction, pp. 188–90. (1)
St. James Guide to Crime & Mystery
    Writers, 4th ed., pp. 429–30. (882d)
Twentieth-Century Crime and Mystery
    Writers, 3rd ed., pp. 451–52. (882c)
Whodunit? A Who's Who in Crime and
    Mystery Writing, p. 86. (5)
Web site: http://www.mysteryscene.
    cjb.net; http://stopyourekillingme.
    com/ed-gorman.html

Gosling, Paula
Bio-bibliographic data:
By a Woman's Hand, 1st ed., pp. 84–85.
    (884a)
By a Woman's Hand, 2nd ed., p. 90.
    (884b)
Detecting Women, 1st ed., p. 62. (877a)
Detecting Women 2, p. 79. (877b)
Detecting Women, 3rd ed., p. 108. (877c)
Great Women Mystery Writers, pp.
    131–34. (880)
The Mammoth Encyclopedia of Modern
    Crime Fiction, pp. 190–91. (1)
St. James Guide to Crime & Mystery
    Writers, 4th ed., pp. 431–32. (882d)
Twentieth-Century Crime and Mystery
    Writers, 2nd ed., pp. 388–89. (882b)
Twentieth-Century Crime and Mystery
    Writers, 3rd ed., pp. 452–53. (882c)
Personal papers in Mugar Memorial
    Library, Boston University.
Web site: http: www/twbooks.co.uk/
    authors/pgosling.html;
    www.geocities.
    com/WestHollywood/Heights/9558/
    paulagosling.htm; http://
    stopyourekillingme.com/
    paula-gosling.html
Gosselin, André
Bio-bibliographic data:
Canadian Crime Fiction, p. 90. (209)
Gough, Bill; i.e., William [John]
Bio-bibliographic data:
Canadian Crime Fiction, p. 91. (209)
Gough, Laurence [Gordon John]
Bio-bibliographic data:
Canadian Crime Fiction, pp. 90–91. (209)
Detecting Men, 1st ed., p. 104. (876)
The Mammoth Encyclopedia of Modern
    Crime Fiction, p. 192. (1)
Web site: http://stopyourekillingme.com/
    laurence-gough.html
Goulart, Ron; i.e., Ronald Joseph
Bio-bibliographic data:
Critical Survey of Mystery and Detective
    Fiction, pp. 764–768. (41)
Encyclopedia Mysteriosa, pp. 139–40. (2)
The Encyclopedia of Murder and Mystery,
    pp. 213. (6)
The Mammoth Encyclopedia of Modern
    Crime Fiction, pp. 192–93. (1)
St. James Guide to Crime & Mystery
    Writers, 4th ed., pp. 432–34. (882d)

Twentieth-Century Crime and Mystery Writers, 1st ed., pp. 677–681. (882a)
Twentieth-Century Crime and Mystery Writers, 2nd ed., pp. 389–92. (882b)
Twentieth-Century Crime and Mystery Writers, 3rd ed., pp. 453–56. (882c)
Whodunit? A Who's Who in Crime and Mystery Writing, pp. 86–87. (5)
Web site: http://stopyourekillingme.com/ron-goulart.html
Gould, Chester. *See* **Canning, Victor**
Gould, Chester
Bio-bibliographic data:
The Encyclopedia of Mystery and Detection, pp. 172–73. (7)
Gould, Nat; i.e., Nathaniel
Bio-bibliographic data:
Australian Crime Fiction, pp. 101–2. (207)
Gould, Stephen. *See* **Fisher, Steve**
Goyder, Margot. *See* **Neville, Margot**
Grace, C. L. *See* **Doherty, P. C.**
Grady, James
Bio-bibliographic data:
Detecting Men, 1st ed., p. 105. (876)
Web site: http://stopyourekillingme.com/james-grady.html
Graeme, Bruce. *Pseud. for* **Graham Montague Jeffries**
Bio-bibliographic data:
Critical Survey of Mystery and Detective Fiction, pp. 769–73. (41)
Encyclopedia Mysteriosa, p. 140. (2)
The Encyclopedia of Murder and Mystery, pp. 213–14. (6)
The Encyclopedia of Mystery and Detection, p. 173. (7)
St. James Guide to Crime & Mystery Writers, 4th ed., pp. 434–36. (882d)
Twentieth-Century Crime and Mystery Writers, 1st ed., pp. 681–85. (882a)
Twentieth-Century Crime and Mystery Writers, 2nd ed., pp. 392–94. (882b)
Twentieth-Century Crime and Mystery Writers, 3rd ed., pp. 456–58. (882c)
Web site: http://stopyourekillingme.com/bruce-graeme.html
Graeme, David. *See* **Graeme, Bruce**
Graeme, Roderic. *See* **Jeffries, Roderic**
Grafton, C. W.; i.e., Cornelius Warren
Bio-bibliographic data:
Encyclopedia Mysteriosa, p. 140. (2)
The Encyclopedia of Murder and Mystery, p. 214. (6)

St. James Guide to Crime & Mystery Writers, 4th ed., p. 437. (882d)
Twentieth-Century Crime and Mystery Writers, 2nd ed., pp. 394–95. (882b)
Twentieth-Century Crime and Mystery Writers, 3rd ed., pp. 458–59. (882c)
Grafton, Sue
Bio-bibliographic data:
American Hard-Boiled Crime Writers, pp. 175–87. (862)
By a Woman's Hand, 1st ed., pp. 85–86. (884a)
By a Woman's Hand, 2nd ed., pp. 90–91. (884b)
Detecting Women, 1st ed., pp. 62–63. (877a)
Detecting Women 2, p. 80. (877b)
Detecting Women, 3rd ed., pp. 108–9. (877c)
Encyclopedia Mysteriosa, pp. 140–41. (2)
The Encyclopedia of Murder and Mystery, pp. 214–15. (6)
The Fatal Art of Entertainment, pp. 28–53. (878)
Great Women Mystery Writers, pp. 134–37. (880)
The Mammoth Encyclopedia of Modern Crime Fiction, pp. 194–95. (1)
Mystery and Suspense Writers, pp. 439–48. (884.2)
The Oxford Companion to Crime and Mystery Writing, p. 190. (4)
St. James Guide to Crime & Mystery Writers, 4th ed., pp. 437–39. (882d)
Speaking of Murder, pp. 205–21. (875a)
Twentieth-Century Crime and Mystery Writers, 3rd ed., pp. 459–60. (882c)
Whodunit? A Who's Who in Crime and Mystery Writing, p. 87. (5)
Women Authors of Detective Series, pp. 132–38. (882.5)
874.*Women of Mystery,* pp. 386–92.
Personal papers in Mugar Memorial Library, Boston University.
Web site: http://www.suegrafton.com; http://stopyourekillingme.com/sue-grafton.html
Graham, Caroline
Bio-bibliographic data:
By a Woman's Hand, 1st ed., p. 86. (884a)
By a Woman's Hand, 2nd ed., pp. 91–92. (884b)
Detecting Women, 1st ed., p. 63. (877a)
Detecting Women 2, p. 80. (877b)

Detecting Women, 3rd ed., p. 109. (877c)
The Mammoth Encyclopedia of Modern Crime Fiction, pp. 195–96. (1)
St. James Guide to Crime & Mystery Writers, 4th ed., pp. 439–40. (882d)
Twentieth-Century Crime and Mystery Writers, 3rd ed., pp. 460–61. (882c)
Web site: http://stopyourekillingme.com/caroline-graham.html

Graham, Charles R. *See* **Montrose, David**
Graham, Nancy
Bio-bibliographic data:
Australian Crime Fiction, p. 102. (207)

Graham, Winston
Bio-bibliographic data:
British Mystery Writers, 1920–1939, pp. 128–33. (867)
Critical Survey of Mystery and Detective Fiction, pp. 774–79. (41)
Encyclopedia Mysteriosa, p. 141. (2)
The Encyclopedia of Murder and Mystery, p. 215. (6)
St. James Guide to Crime & Mystery Writers, 4th ed., pp. 440–41. (882d)
Twentieth-Century Crime and Mystery Writers, 1st ed., pp. 685–88. (882a)
Twentieth-Century Crime and Mystery Writers, 2nd ed., pp. 395–96. (882b)
Twentieth-Century Crime and Mystery Writers, 3rd ed., pp. 461–62. (882c)

Grahame, Gordon Hill
Bio-bibliographic data:
Canadian Crime Fiction, p. 91. (209)

Grahame, Michael
Bio-bibliographic data:
Australian Crime Fiction, p. 102. (207)

Grainger, Francis Edward. *See* **Hill, Headon**
Gramont, Monque de
Bio-bibliographic data:
Canadian Crime Fiction, p. 91. (209)

Granger, [Patricia] Ann
Bio-bibliographic data:
By a Woman's Hand, 1st ed., pp. 86–87. (884a)
By a Woman's Hand, 2nd ed., p. 92. (884b)
Detecting Women, 1st ed., p. 63. (877a)
Detecting Women 2, pp. 80–81. (877b)
Detecting Women, 3rd ed., pp. 109–10. (877c)
The Mammoth Encyclopedia of Modern Crime Fiction, pp. 196–97. (1)

Web site: http://stopyourekillingme.com/ann-granger.html

Granger, Bill
Bio-bibliographic data:
Canadian Crime Fiction, p. 277. (209)
Detecting Men, 1st ed., p. 106. (876)
The Mammoth Encyclopedia of Modern Crime Fiction, p. 197 (1)
St. James Guide to Crime & Mystery Writers, 4th ed., pp. 444–43. (882d)
Twentieth-Century Crime and Mystery Writers, 2nd ed., pp. 396–97. (882b)
Twentieth-Century Crime and Mystery Writers, 3rd ed., pp. 462–63. (882c)
Web site: http://stopyourekillingme.com/bill-granger.html

Grant, Ambrose. *See* **Chase, James Hadley**
Grant, Anne Underwood
Bio-bibliographic data:
Detecting Women, 3rd ed., p. 110. (877c)
Web site: http://stopyourekillingme.com/ann-underwood-grant.html; http://www.underwoodgrant.com

Grant, John. *See* **Gash, Jonathan**
Grant, [Hilda] Kay
Bio-bibliographic data:
Canadian Crime Fiction, pp. 91–92, 104. (209)

Grant, John. *See* **Gash, Jonathan**
Grant, Jonathan. *See* **Gash, Jonathan**
Grant, Landon. *See* **Gribble Leonard R.**
Grant, Linda. *Pseud. for* **Linda V. Williams**
Bio-bibliographic data:
By a Woman's Hand, 1st ed., pp. 87–88. (884a)
By a Woman's Hand, 2nd ed., pp. 92–93. (884b)
Detecting Women, 1st ed., p. 63. (877a)
Detecting Women 2, p. 81. (877b)
Detecting Women, 3rd ed., p. 110. (877c)
Great Women Mystery Writers, pp. 137–38. (880)
Web site: http://stopyourekillingme.com/linda-grant.html

Grant, Maxwell: "Maxwell Grant" was a house pseud. used by Street & Smith as the byline for *The Shadow*. Behind the pseud. were a number of writers, chief among which was Walter Gibson (q.v.), although Dennis Lynds (q.v.) also used it. *See also* the section

devoted to the discussion of pulp
magazines and their characters.
Bio-bibliographic data:
Australian Crime Fiction, p. 103. (207)
Grant-Adamson, Lesley
Bio-bibliographic data:
By a Woman's Hand, 1st ed., p. 88. (884a)
By a Woman's Hand, 2nd ed., pp. 93–94.
(884b)
Detecting Women, 1st ed., p. 64. (877a)
Detecting Women 2, p. 81. (877b)
Detecting Women, 3rd ed., p. 111. (877c)
Great Women Mystery Writers, pp.
139–41. (880)
*The Mammoth Encyclopedia of Modern
Crime Fiction*, pp. 198–99. (1)
*St. James Guide to Crime & Mystery
Writers*, 4th ed., pp. 444–45. (882d)
*Twentieth-Century Crime and Mystery
Writers*, 3rd ed., pp. 464–65. (882c)
Web site: www.crimefiction.co.uk;
http://stopyourekillingme.com/
lesley-grant-adamson.html
Grantham, Gerald. *See* **Wallace, John**
Gravel, François
Bio-bibliographic data:
Canadian Crime Fiction, p. 92. (209)
Graves, Sarah. *See* **Kittredge, Mary**
Gray, A. W.; i.e., Albert William
Bio-bibliographic data:
Detecting Men, 1st ed., pp. 107, 109. (876)
Gray, Berkeley. *See* **Brooks, Edwy Searles**
Gray, Dulcie. *Pseud. for* **Dulcie Winifred
Catherine Denison**
Bio-bibliographic data:
Australian Crime Fiction, p. 103. (207)
Detecting Women 2, p. 82. (877b)
Detecting Women, 3rd ed., pp. 111–12.
(877c)
*Twentieth-Century Crime and Mystery
Writers,* 1st ed., pp. 692–94. (882a)
*Twentieth-Century Crime and Mystery
Writers*, 2nd ed., pp. 398–400. (882b)
*Twentieth-Century Crime and Mystery
Writers*, 3rd ed., pp. 465–66. (882c)
Gray, Elayne Taylor. *See* **Taylor Gray,
Elayne**
Gray, Gallagher. *Pseud. for* **Katy Munger**
Bio-bibliographic data:
By a Woman's Hand, 1st ed., p. 89. (884a)
By a Woman's Hand, 2nd ed., p. 94.
(884b)
Detecting Women, 1st ed., p. 64. (877a)
Detecting Women 2, p. 82. (877b)

Detecting Women, 3rd ed., pp. 112, 201.
(877c)
Web site: http://stopyourekillingme.
com/gray-gallagher.html; http://www.
katymunger.com
Gray, John Morgan
Bio-bibliographic data:
Canadian Crime Fiction, p. 92. (209)
Grayson, Rex. *See* **Campbell, Ronald
[Grayson]**
Grayson, Richard. *Pseud. for* **Richard
Grindal**
Bio-bibliographic data:
Detecting Men, 1st ed., pp. 107–8. (876)
Greaves, Richard. *See* **Simonds, Peter**
Greber, Judith. *See* **Roberts, Gillian**
Greeley, Andrew M.
Bio-bibliographic data:
Detecting Men, 1st ed., p. 108. (876)
*St. James Guide to Crime & Mystery
Writers*, 4th ed., pp. 445–49. (882d)
*Twentieth-Century Crime and Mystery
Writers*, 3rd ed., pp. 467–69. (882c)
Web site: http://stopyourekillingme.
com/andrew-m-greeley.html
Green, Anna Katharine
Bio-bibliographic data:
*Critical Survey of Mystery and Detective
Fiction*, pp. 780–88. (41)
Detecting Women 2, pp. 82–83. (877b)
Encyclopedia Mysteriosa, p. 142. (2)
The Encyclopedia of Murder and Mystery,
pp. 216–17. (6)
*The Encyclopedia of Mystery and
Detection*, pp. 173–74. (7)
Great Women Mystery Writers, pp.
141–45. (880)
Mystery and Suspense Writers, pp.
449–57. (884.2)
*The Oxford Companion to Crime and
Mystery Writing*, pp. 194–95. (4)
*St. James Guide to Crime & Mystery
Writers*, 4th ed., pp. 449–50. (882d)
10 Women of Mystery, pp. 150–78. (864,
865)
*Twentieth-Century Crime and Mystery
Writers,* 1st ed., pp. 694–97. (882a)
*Twentieth-Century Crime and Mystery
Writers*, 2nd ed., pp. 400–401. (882b)
*Twentieth-Century Crime and Mystery
Writers*, 3rd ed., pp. 469–71. (882c)
*Whodunit? A Who's Who in Crime and
Mystery Writing*, pp. 88–89. (5)
Women of Mystery, pp. 5–17. (874)

Personal papers in the Humanities
Research Center, University of Texas
at Austin.
Web site: http://stopyourekillingme.
com/anna-katherine-green.html
Green, Bill
Bio-bibliographic data:
Australian Crime Fiction, p. 103. (207)
Green, Charles M. *See* **Gardner, Erle
Stanley**
Green, Christine
Bio-bibliographic data:
By a Woman's Hand, 2nd ed., pp. 94–95.
(884b)
Detecting Women, 1st ed., p. 64. (877a)
Detecting Women 2, p. 83. (877b)
Detecting Women, 3rd ed., p. 112. (877c)
*The Mammoth Encyclopedia of Modern
Crime Fiction*, p. 199. (1)
Web site: http://www.christine-green.com;
http://stopyourekillingme.com/
christine-green.html
Green, Edith Pinero
Bio-bibliographic data:
Detecting Women 2, p. 83. (877b)
Detecting Women, 3rd ed., p. 113. (877c)
Green, Kate
Bio-bibliographic data:
By a Woman's Hand, 1st ed., pp. 89–90.
(884a)
By a Woman's Hand, 2nd ed., pp. 95–96.
(884b)
Detecting Women, 1st ed., p. 65. (877a)
Detecting Women 2, pp. 83–84. (877b)
Detecting Women, 3rd ed., p. 113. (877c)
Green, Terence M.
Bio-bibliographic data:
Canadian Crime Fiction, p. 92. (209)
Greene, Graham
Bio-bibliographic data:
British Mystery Writers, 1920–1939, pp.
134–52. (867)
Canadian Crime Fiction, p. 277 (209)
Corpus Delicti of Mystery Fiction, pp.
75–76. (879)
*Critical Survey of Mystery and Detective
Fiction*, pp. 789–94. (41)
Encyclopedia Mysteriosa, pp. 142–43. (2)
The Encyclopedia of Murder and Mystery,
p. 218. (6)
*The Encyclopedia of Mystery and
Detection*, pp. 174–77. (7)
Mystery and Suspense Writers, pp.
459–71. (884.2)

*100 Masters of Mystery and Detective
Fiction*, pp. 287–93. (37)
*The Oxford Companion to Crime and
Mystery Writing*, p. 195. (4)
*St. James Guide to Crime & Mystery
Writers*, 4th ed., pp. 450–54. (882d)
*Twentieth-Century Crime and Mystery
Writers*, 1st ed., pp. 697–701. (882a)
*Twentieth-Century Crime and Mystery
Writers*, 2nd ed., pp. 401–4. (882b)
*Twentieth-Century Crime and Mystery
Writers*, 3rd ed., pp. 471–74. (882c)
*Whodunit? A Who's Who in Crime and
Mystery Writing*, pp. 89–90. (5)
Personal papers in the Humanities
Research Center, University of Texas
at Austin.
Web site: http://members.tripod.com/
~greeneland/; http://www.kirjasto.sci.
fi/greene.htm
Greene, Hugh
Bio-bibliographic data:
The Encyclopedia of Murder and Mystery,
p. 218. (6)
Greenleaf, Stephen [Howell]
Bio-bibliographic data:
Detecting Men, 1st ed., pp. 108–9. (876)
*The Mammoth Encyclopedia of Modern
Crime Fiction*, pp. 199–200. (1)
*St. James Guide to Crime & Mystery
Writers*, 4th ed., pp. 454–56. (882d)
*Twentieth-Century Crime and Mystery
Writers*, 2nd ed., pp. 404–5. (882b)
*Twentieth-Century Crime and Mystery
Writers*, 3rd ed., pp. 474–75. (882c)
Web site: http://stopyourekillingme.com/
stephen-greenleaf.html
Greenwood, D. M.; i.e., Diane M.
Bio-bibliographic data:
By a Woman's Hand, 1st ed., pp. 90–91.
(884a)
By a Woman's Hand, 2nd ed., p. 96.
(884b)
Detecting Women, 1st ed., p. 65. (877a)
Detecting Women 2, p. 84. (877b)
Detecting Women, 3rd ed., pp. 113–14.
(877c)
*The Mammoth Encyclopedia of Modern
Crime Fiction*, p. 200. (1)
Web site: http://stopyourekillingme.com/
d-m-greenwood.html

Greenwood, Diane M. *See* Greenwood, D.
M.
Greenwood, John. *See* Hilton, John
Buxton
Greenwood, Kerry
Bio-bibliographic data:
Australian Crime Fiction, pp. 103–4, 146.
(207)
By a Woman's Hand, 2nd ed., pp. 96–97.
(884b)
Detecting Women, 1st ed., p. 65. (877a)
Detecting Women 2, p. 84. (877b)
Detecting Women, 3rd ed., p. 114. (877c)
Web site: http://stopyourekillingme.com/
kerry-greenwood.html
Greenwood, L. B.; i.e., Lillian Bethal
Bio-bibliographic data:
By a Woman's Hand, 1st ed., p. 91. (884a)
Canadian Crime Fiction, pp. 92–93. (209)
Greer, Robert O.
Bio-bibliographic data:
Detecting Men, 1st ed., p. 109. (876)
Greg, Percy Albert
Bio-bibliographic data:
Australian Crime Fiction, p. 104. (207)
Gregg, Alan. *See* Mallette, Gertrude Ethel
Gregory, Sarah. *See* Gray, A. W.
Gregory, Susanna: unidentified pseud.
Bio-bibliographic data:
Detecting Women, 3rd ed., pp. 29–30, 114.
(877c)
*The Mammoth Encyclopedia of Modern
Crime Fiction*, p. 201. (1)
Web site: http://stopyourekillingme.com/
susanna-gregory.html
Grescoe, Paul
Bio-bibliographic data:
Canadian Crime Fiction, p. 93. (209)
Greth, Roma
Bio-bibliographic data:
Detecting Women 2, pp. 84–85. (877b)
Detecting Women, 3rd ed., p. 115. (877c)
Grex, Leo. *See* Gribble, Leonard R.
Grey, Eve
Bio-bibliographic data:
Canadian Crime Fiction, p. 93. (209)
Grey, Louis. *See* Gribble, Leonard R.
Grey, Zane
Bio-bibliographic data:
Canadian Crime Fiction, p. 255. (209)
Gribble, Leonard R[eginald].
Bio-bibliographic data:
*The Encyclopedia of Mystery and
Detection*, pp. 177–78. (7)

*St. James Guide to Crime & Mystery
Writers*, 4th ed., pp. 456–59. (882d)
*Twentieth-Century Crime and Mystery
Writers*, 1st ed., pp. 702–6. (882a)
*Twentieth-Century Crime and Mystery
Writers*, 2nd ed., pp. 405–8. (882b)
*Twentieth-Century Crime and Mystery
Writers*, 3rd ed., pp. 475–78. (882c)
Grierson, Edward
Bio-bibliographic data:
The Encyclopedia of Murder and Mystery,
p. 220. (6)
*St. James Guide to Crime & Mystery
Writers*, 4th ed., pp. 459–60. (882d)
*Twentieth-Century Crime and Mystery
Writers*, 1st ed., pp. 707–8. (882a)
*Twentieth-Century Crime and Mystery
Writers*, 2nd ed., pp. 408–9. (882b)
*Twentieth-Century Crime and Mystery
Writers*, 3rd ed., pp. 478–79. (882c)
Grierson, Francis D[urham]
Bio-bibliographic data:
The Encyclopedia of Murder and Mystery,
p. 220. (6)
Griff. *See* Fawcett, Frank Dubrez
Griffin, Annie. *See* Chapman, Sally
Griffith, Bill. *See* Granger, Bill
Griffiths, Major Arthur
Bio-bibliographic data:
The Encyclopedia of Murder and Mystery,
p. 220. (6)
Grimes, Martha
Bio-bibliographic data:
By a Woman's Hand, 1st ed., p. 92. (884a)
By a Woman's Hand, 2nd ed., pp. 97–98.
(884b)
*Critical Survey of Mystery and Detective
Fiction*, pp. 795–800. (41)
Detecting Women, 1st ed., pp. 65–66.
(877a)
Detecting Women 2, p. 85. (877b)
Detecting Women, 3rd ed., pp. 115–16.
(877c)
Encyclopedia Mysteriosa, pp. 143–44. (2)
The Encyclopedia of Murder and Mystery,
p. 221. (6)
Great Women Mystery Writers, pp.
145–48. (880)
*The Mammoth Encyclopedia of Modern
Crime Fiction*, pp. 201–3. (1)
*100 Masters of Mystery and Detective
Fiction*, pp. 294–300. (37)
*St. James Guide to Crime & Mystery
Writers*, 4th ed., pp. 460–62. (882d)

Twentieth-Century Crime and Mystery Writers, 3rd ed., pp. 479–81. (882c)
Whodunit? A Who's Who in Crime and Mystery Writing, p. 90. (5)
Web site: http://www.marthagrimes.com; http://stopyourekillingme.com/martha-grimes.html

Grimes, Terris McMahan
Bio-bibliographic data:
Detecting Women, 3rd ed., p. 116. (877c)
The Mammoth Encyclopedia of Modern Crime Fiction, p. 203. (1)
Web site: http://www.vme.net/dvm/sister-sleuth/index2.html; http://stopyourekillingme.com/terris-mcmahan-grimes.html

Grimshaw, Beatrice [Ethel]
Bio-bibliographic data:
Australian Crime Fiction, pp. 104–5. (207)

Grindle, Lucretia
Bio-bibliographic data:
Detecting Women, 1st ed., p. 66. (877a)
Detecting Women 2, p. 85. (877b)
Detecting Women, 3rd ed., p. 116. (877c)

Gripp, [Andreas] Michael
Bio-bibliographic data:
Canadian Crime Fiction, p. 93. (209)

Grisham, John
Bio-bibliographic data:
The Encyclopedia of Murder and Mystery, pp. 221–22. (6)
The Mammoth Encyclopedia of Modern Crime Fiction, pp. 203–4. (1)
St. James Guide to Crime & Mystery Writers, 4th ed., pp. 462–63. (882d)
Whodunit? A Who's Who in Crime and Mystery Writing, p. 90. (5)
Web site: http://www.randomhouse.com/features/grisham; http://stopyourekillingme.com/john-grisham.html

Grissom, Ken
Bio-bibliographic data:
Detecting Men, 1st ed., p. 109. (876)

Grosbois, Paul de
Bio-bibliographic data:
Canadian Crime Fiction, p. 93. (209)

Grove, Frederick Philip
Bio-bibliographic data:
Canadian Crime Fiction, pp. 93–94. (209)

Gruber, Frank
Bio-bibliographic data:

The Encyclopedia of Murder and Mystery, pp. 222–23. (6)
The Encyclopedia of Mystery and Detection, pp. 178–79. (7)
St. James Guide to Crime & Mystery Writers, 4th ed., pp. 463–65. (882d)
Twentieth-Century Crime and Mystery Writers, 1st ed., pp. 709–12. (882a)
Twentieth-Century Crime and Mystery Writers, 2nd ed., pp. 409–11. (882b)
Twentieth-Century Crime and Mystery Writers, 3rd ed., pp. 481–84. (882c)
Web site: http://stopyourekillingme.com/frank-gruber.html; http://www.thrillingdetective.com/trivia/gruber.html

Grover, Marshall. *See* Meares, Leonard
Guerin, Judith. *See* Lewis, Catherine and Judith Guerin
Guillet, Jean-Pierre
Bio-bibliographic data:
Canadian Crime Fiction, p. 94. (209)

Guiver, Patricia
Bio-bibliographic data:
Detecting Women, 3rd ed., pp. 116–17. (877c)
Web site: http://stopyourekillingme.com/patricia-guiver.html

Gulik, Robert Hans van. *See* van Gulik, Robert Hans
Gunn, Elizabeth
Bio-bibliographic data:
Detecting Women, 3rd ed., p. 117. (877c)
Web site: http://stopyourekillingme.com/elizabeth-gunn.html

Gunn, Victor. *See* Brooks, Edwy Searles
Gunning, Sally
Bio-bibliographic data:
By a Woman's Hand, 1st ed., p. 93. (884a)
By a Woman's Hand, 2nd ed., p. 98. (884b)
Detecting Women, 1st ed., p. 66. (877a)
Detecting Women 2, p. 85. (877b)
Detecting Women, 3rd ed., p. 117. (877c)
Web site: http://stopyourekillingme.com/sally-gunning.html

Gunton, Eric
Bio-bibliographic data:
Australian Crime Fiction, p. 105. (207)

Gur, Batya
Bio-bibliographic data:
By a Woman's Hand, 2nd ed., pp. 98–99. (884b)
Detecting Women 2, p. 86. (877b)

Detecting Women, 3rd ed., p. 118. (877c)
The Mammoth Encyclopedia of Modern Crime Fiction, pp. 204–5. (1)
Web site: http://stopyourekillingme.com/batya-gur.html
Gurr, David Hugh Courtney
Bio-bibliographic data:
Canadian Crime Fiction, pp. 30, 49, 94. (209)
Gutteridge, Don; i.e., Donald George
Bio-bibliographic data:
Canadian Crime Fiction, pp. 94–95. (209)
Guttridge, Peter
Bio-bibliographic data:
The Mammoth Encyclopedia of Modern Crime Fiction, p. 205. (1)
Web site: http://www.peterguttridge.com; http://www.twbooks.co.uk/authors/peterguttridge.html; http://stopyourekillingme.com/peter-guttridge.html
Gwynne, A.; i.e., Agnes
Bio-bibliographic data:
Australian Crime Fiction, p. 105. (207)

H
Hackler, Micah S.
Bio-bibliographic data:
Detecting Men, 1st ed., p. 110. (876)
Web site: http://stopyourekillingme.com/micah-s-hackler.html
Haddad, C.A.; i.e., Carolyn A.
Bio-bibliographic data:
Detecting Women, 1st ed., p. 66. (877a)
Detecting Women 2, p. 86. (877b)
Detecting Women, 3rd ed., p. 118. (877c)
Haddam, Jane. *See* Papazoglou, Orania
Haddock, Lisa
Bio-bibliographic data:
Detecting Women, 1st ed., p. 67. (877a)
Detecting Women 2, p. 87. (877b)
Detecting Women, 3rd ed., p. 119. (877c)
Hadley, Joan. *See* Hess, Joan
Haffner, Margaret
Bio-bibliographic data:
Canadian Crime Fiction, p. 95. (209)
Detecting Women, 3rd ed., p. 120. (877c)
Hagarty, Britt
Bio-bibliographic data:
Canadian Crime Fiction, p. 95. (209)
Hagberg, David. *See* Flannery, Sean
Hagen, Miriam-Ann
Bio-bibliographic data:
Canadian Crime Fiction, p. 255. (209)

Hager, [Wilma] Jean
Bio-bibliographic data:
By a Woman's Hand, 1st ed., pp. 95–96. (884a)
By a Woman's Hand, 2nd ed., pp. 101–2. (884b)
Detecting Women, 1st ed., p. 67. (877a)
Detecting Women 2, p. 87. (877b)
Detecting Women, 3rd ed., p. 120. (877c)
The Mammoth Encyclopedia of Modern Crime Fiction, pp. 205–6. (1)
St. James Guide to Crime & Mystery Writers, 4th ed., pp. 467–68. (882d)
Web site: http://stopyourekillingme.com/jean-hager.html
Haggard, Sir Henry Rider
Bio-bibliographic data:
British Mystery Writers, 1860–1919, pp. 154–65. (866)
The Encyclopedia of Murder and Mystery, p. 226. (6)
Haggard, William. *Pseud. for* Richard Henry Michael Clayton
Bio-bibliographic data:
Critical Survey of Mystery and Detective Fiction, pp. 801–7. (41)
Encyclopedia Mysteriosa, p. 146. (2)
The Encyclopedia of Murder and Mystery, pp. 226–27. (6)
The Encyclopedia of Mystery and Detection, p. 180. (7)
St. James Guide to Crime & Mystery Writers, 4th ed., pp. 468–69. (882d)
Twentieth-Century Crime and Mystery Writers, 1st ed., pp. 712–14. (882a)
Twentieth-Century Crime and Mystery Writers, 2nd ed., pp. 411–13. (882b)
Twentieth-Century Crime and Mystery Writers, 3rd ed., pp. 485–86. (882c)
Haig, Irene. *See* Haig, John and Irene Haig
Haig, John and Irene Haig
Bio-bibliographic data:
Canadian Crime Fiction, p. 95. (209)
Haig-Brown, Roderick L[angmere].
Bio-bibliographic data:
Canadian Crime Fiction, pp. 95–96. (209)
Hailey, Arthur
Bio-bibliographic data:
Canadian Crime Fiction, p. 96. (209)
Hailey, J. P. *See* Hall, Parnell
Hails, Ian McAuley
Bio-bibliographic data:
Australian Crime Fiction, p. 106. (207)

Hale, Alan
Bio-bibliographic data:
Australian Crime Fiction, p. 106. (207)
Hales, A. G.; i.e., Alfred [Arthur] Greenwood
Bio-bibliographic data:
Australian Crime Fiction, p. 106. (207)
Hall, Adam. *See* **Trevor, Elleston**
Hall, Douglas
Bio-bibliographic data:
Canadian Crime Fiction, p. 96. (209)
Hall, James W.; i.e., James Wilson
Bio-bibliographic data:
Detecting Men, 1st ed., pp. 110–11. (876)
The Mammoth Encyclopedia of Modern Crime Fiction, p. 207. (1)
Web site: http://www.jameswhall.com;
http://stopyourekillingme.com/
james-w-hall.html
Hall, Linda
Bio-bibliographic data:
Canadian Crime Fiction, p. 96. (209)
Detecting Women, 3rd ed., p. 121. (877c)
Web site: http://stopyourekillingme.com/
linda-hall.html; http://www.
writerhall.com
Hall, M. Helen. *See* **Mace, Helen**
Hall, Mary Bowen
Bio-bibliographic data:
By a Woman's Hand, 1st ed., p. 96. (884a)
Detecting Women, 1st ed., p. 68. (877a)
Detecting Women 2, p. 87. (877b)
Web site: http://stopyourekillingme.com/
mary-bowen-hall.html
Hall, Parnell
Bio-bibliographic data:
Detecting Men, 1st ed., pp. 110, 111. (876)
The Encyclopedia of Murder and Mystery,
p. 227. (6)
The Mammoth Encyclopedia of Modern Crime Fiction, pp. 207–8. (1)
St. James Guide to Crime & Mystery Writers, 4th ed., pp. 472–73. (882d)
Web site: http://www.parnellhall.com;
http://stopyourekillingme.com/
parnell-hall.html
Hall, Patricia. *Pseud. for* **Maureen O'Connor**
Bio-bibliographic data:
By a Woman's Hand, 2nd ed., pp. 102–3.
(884b)
Detecting Women, 1st ed., p. 68. (877a)
Detecting Women 2, p. 88. (877b)
Detecting Women, 3rd ed., p. 121. (877c)

The Mammoth Encyclopedia of Modern Crime Fiction, p. 208. (1)
Web site:
http://www.twbooks.co.uk/authors/
patriciahall.html; http://
stopyourekillingme.com/patricia-hall.
html
Hall, Richard Victor
Bio-bibliographic data:
Australian Crime Fiction, pp. 106–7, 146
(207)
Hall, Robert Lee
Bio-bibliographic data:
Detecting Men, 1st ed., p. 111. (876)
Web site: http://stopyourekillingme.com/
robert-lee-hall.html
Hallahan, William H[enry].
Bio-bibliographic data:
Encyclopedia Mysteriosa, p. 147. (2)
Twentieth-Century Crime and Mystery Writers, 2nd ed., p. 413. (882b)
Twentieth-Century Crime and Mystery Writers, 3rd ed., pp. 488–89. (882c)
Halliday, Brett. *Pseud. for* **Davis Dresser**
Bio-bibliographic data:
American Hard-Boiled Crime Writers, pp.
112–19. (862)
Corpus Delicti of Mystery Fiction, pp.
77–79. (879)
Critical Survey of Mystery and Detective Fiction, pp. 808–14. (41)
Encyclopedia Mysteriosa, p. 147. (2)
The Encyclopedia of Murder and Mystery,
p. 228. (6)
The Encyclopedia of Mystery and Detection, pp. 181–82. (7)
St. James Guide to Crime & Mystery Writers, 4th ed., pp. 474–75. (882d)
Twentieth-Century Crime and Mystery Writers, 1st ed., pp. 714–19. (882a)
Twentieth-Century Crime and Mystery Writers, 2nd ed., pp. 413–15. (882b)
Twentieth-Century Crime and Mystery Writers, 3rd ed., pp. 489–91. (882c)
Personal papers in the Mugar Memorial Library, Boston University.
Web site: http://stopyourekillingme.com/
brett-halliday.html; http://www.
miskatonic.org/rara-avis/biblio/
halliday.html
Halliday, Michael. *See* **Creasey, John**
Halligan, Marion
Bio-bibliographic data:

Australian Crime Fiction, pp. 145, 146. (207)
Hallinan, Timothy
Bio-bibliographic data:
Detecting Men, 1st ed., p. 112. (876)
Web site: http://stopyourekillingme.com/timothy-hallinan.html
Halls, Geraldine [Mary]. *See* **Jay, Charlotte**
Hambly, Barbara
Bio-bibliographic data:
Detecting Women 2, p. 88. (877b)
Detecting Women, 3rd ed., pp. 121–22. (877c)
Web site: http://stopyourekillingme.com/barbara-hambly.html; http://www.barbarahambly.com
Hamel, Cécile Helie. *See* **Helie-Hamel, Cécile**
Hamilton, [Arthur Douglas] Bruce
Bio-bibliographic data:
The Encyclopedia of Murder and Mystery, p. 228. (6)
The Encyclopedia of Mystery and Detection, pp. 182–83. (7)
Hamilton, Donald [Bengtsson]
Bio-bibliographic data:
The Big Book of Noir, pp. 186, 281–90. (24)
Canadian Crime Fiction, p. 255. (209)
Colloquium on Crime, pp. 99–110. (884.1)
Critical Survey of Mystery and Detective Fiction, pp. 815–21. (41)
Detecting Men, 1st ed., pp. 112–13. (876)
Encyclopedia Mysteriosa, p. 148. (2)
The Encyclopedia of Murder and Mystery, p. 229. (6)
The Encyclopedia of Mystery and Detection, p. 183. (7)
Murder off the Rack: Critical Studies of Ten Paperback Masters, pp. 99–111. (869)
St. James Guide to Crime & Mystery Writers, 4th ed., pp. 476–78. (882d)
Twentieth-Century Crime and Mystery Writers, 1st ed., pp. 719–721. (882a)
Twentieth-Century Crime and Mystery Writers, 2nd ed., pp. 416–17. (882b)
Twentieth-Century Crime and Mystery Writers, 3rd ed., pp. 491–93. (882c)
Personal papers in University of California, Los Angeles.
Web site: http://stopyourekillingme.com/donald-hamilton.html; http://www.

miskatonic.org/rara-avis/biblio/hamilton.html
Hamilton, [Lord] Ernest [William]
Bio-bibliographic data:
Canadian Crime Fiction, p. 278. (209)
Hamilton, Ian
Bio-bibliographic data:
Australian Crime Fiction, p. 107. (207)
Hamilton, Janet [Evelyn]
Bio-bibliographic data:
Canadian Crime Fiction, pp. 96–97, 237. (209)
Hamilton, Laurell K.
Bio-bibliographic data:
Detecting Women 2, p. 88. (877b)
Detecting Women, 3rd ed., p. 122. (877c)
Web site: http://stopyourekillingme.com/laurell-k-hamilton.html; http://www.laurellkhamilton.org
Hamilton, Lyn
Bio-bibliographic data:
Detecting Women, 3rd ed., p. 122. (877c)
Web site: http://stopyourekillingme.com/lyn-hamilton.html
Hamilton, [Anthony Walter] Patrick
Bio-bibliographic data:
Encyclopedia Mysteriosa, p. 148. (2)
The Encyclopedia of Murder and Mystery, p. 229. (6)
The Encyclopedia of Mystery and Detection, pp. 183–84. (7)
Twentieth-Century Crime and Mystery Writers, 1st ed., pp. 721–23. (882a)
Twentieth-Century Crime and Mystery Writers, 2nd ed., pp. 417–18. (882b)
Twentieth-Century Crime and Mystery Writers, 3rd ed., pp. 493–94. (882c)
Hamilton, Steve
Bio-bibliographic data:
The Mammoth Encyclopedia of Modern Crime Fiction, pp. 208–9. (1)
Web site: http://www.authorstevehamilton.com; http://stopyourekillingme.com/steve-hamilton.html
Hammett, [Samuel] Dashiell
Bio-bibliographic data:
American Hard-Boiled Crime Writers, pp. 188–208. (862)
Canadian Crime Fiction, p. 278. (209)
Corpus Delicti of Mystery Fiction, pp. 79–82. (879)
Critical Survey of Mystery and Detective Fiction, pp. 822–28. (41)

Twentieth-Century Crime and Mystery Writers, 2nd ed., p. 421. (882b)
Twentieth-Century Crime and Mystery Writers, 3rd ed., p. 500. (882c)

Hanson, Rick
Bio-bibliographic data:
Detecting Men, 1st ed., p. 115. (876)
Web site: http://stopyourekillingme.com/
rick-hanson.html

Harbage, Alfred B. *See* **Kyd, Thomas**

Harbec, Hèléne
Bio-bibliographic data:
Canadian Crime Fiction, p. 97. (209)

Harcourt, Pamela
Bio-bibliographic data:
Canadian Crime Fiction, p. 255. (209)

Harden, E.
Bio-bibliographic data:
Australian Crime Fiction, pp. 107–8.
(207)

Hardin, J. D.: unidentified house pseud.
Bio-bibliographic data:
Canadian Crime Fiction, p. 255. (209)

Hardin, Peter. *See* **Vaczek, Louis Charles**

Harding, Paul. *See* **Doherty, P. C.**

Hardwick, Mollie
Bio-bibliographic data:
By a Woman's Hand, 1st ed., pp. 96–97.
(884a)
By a Woman's Hand, 2nd ed., p. 103.
(884b)
Detecting Women, 1st ed., p. 68. (877a)
Detecting Women 2, pp. 88–89. (877b)
Detecting Women, 3rd ed., p. 123. (877c)

Hardy, Arthur Sherburne
Bio-bibliographic data:
The Encyclopedia of Mystery and Detection, p. 190. (7)

Hardy, Lindsay
Bio-bibliographic data:
Australian Crime Fiction, p. 108. (207)

Hare, Cyril. *Pseud. for* **Alfred Alexander Gordon Clark**
Bio-bibliographic data:
British Mystery Writers, 1920–1939, pp. 153–56. (867)
Critical Survey of Mystery and Detective Fiction, pp. 841–46. (41)
Encyclopedia Mysteriosa, p. 155. (2)
The Encyclopedia of Murder and Mystery, p. 233. (6)
The Encyclopedia of Mystery and Detection, pp. 190–91. (7)

The Oxford Companion to Crime and Mystery Writing, p. 203. (4)
St. James Guide to Crime & Mystery Writers, 4th ed., pp. 485–86. (882d)
Twentieth-Century Crime and Mystery Writers, 1st ed., pp. 730–31. (882a)
Twentieth-Century Crime and Mystery Writers, 2nd ed., pp. 422–23. (882b)
Twentieth-Century Crime and Mystery Writers, 3rd ed., pp. 501–2. (882c)
Whodunit? A Who's Who in Crime and Mystery Writing, p. 94. (5)
Web site: http://stopyourekillingme.com/
cyril-hare.html

Haring, Don
Bio-bibliographic data:
Australian Crime Fiction, p. 108. (207)

Harkness, Clare
Bio-bibliographic data:
Canadian Crime Fiction, p. 97. (209)

Harknett, Terry Williams
Bio-bibliographic data:
Detecting Men, 1st ed., pp. 116, 240. (876)

Harling, Robert
Bio-bibliographic data:
Canadian Crime Fiction, p. 278. (209)
Twentieth-Century Crime and Mystery Writers, 1st ed., pp. 731–34. (882a)
Twentieth-Century Crime and Mystery Writers, 2nd ed., pp. 423–24. (882b)
Twentieth-Century Crime and Mystery Writers, 3rd ed., pp. 502–3. (882c)

Harper, Richard
Bio-bibliographic data:
Detecting Men, 1st ed., p. 116. (876)

Harrington, Joseph
Bio-bibliographic data:
The Encyclopedia of Mystery and Detection, p. 191. (7)
Twentieth-Century Crime and Mystery Writers, 1st ed., pp. 734–35. (882a)

Harrington, Joyce
Bio-bibliographic data:
Encyclopedia Mysteriosa, pp. 155–56. (2)
St. James Guide to Crime & Mystery Writers, 4th ed., pp. 486–87. (882d)
Twentieth-Century Crime and Mystery Writers, 1st ed., pp. 735–36. (882a)
Twentieth-Century Crime and Mystery Writers, 2nd ed., pp. 424–25. (882b)
Twentieth-Century Crime and Mystery Writers, 3rd ed., pp. 503–4. (882c)

Harrington, William
Bio-bibliographic data:

Detecting Men, 1st ed., pp. 116–17. (876)
The Mammoth Encyclopedia of Modern Crime Fiction, pp. 210–11. (1)
St. James Guide to Crime & Mystery Writers, 4th ed., pp. 487–88. (882d)
Twentieth-Century Crime and Mystery Writers, 3rd ed., pp. 504–5. (882c)
Web site: http://stopyourekillingme.com/ william-harrington.html

Harris, Brian [Charles]
Bio-bibliographic data:
Canadian Crime Fiction, p. 97. (209)

Harris, Charlaine
Bio-bibliographic data:
By a Woman's Hand, 1st ed., pp. 97–98. (884a)
By a Woman's Hand, 2nd ed., pp. 103–4. (884b)
Detecting Women, 1st ed., p. 68. (877a)
Detecting Women 2, p. 89. (877b)
Detecting Women, 3rd ed., pp. 123–24. (877c)
Web site: http://stopyourekillingme.com/ charlaine-harris.html; http://members. aol.com/femmesweb/harris.htm

Harris, David
Bio-bibliographic data:
Canadian Crime Fiction, p. 97. (209)

Harris, Herbert
Bio-bibliographic data:
The Encyclopedia of Mystery and Detection, pp. 191–92. (7)
Twentieth-Century Crime and Mystery Writers, 1st ed., pp. 737–39. (882a)
Twentieth-Century Crime and Mystery Writers, 2nd ed., pp. 425–26. (882b)
Twentieth-Century Crime and Mystery Writers, 3rd ed., pp. 505–6. (882c)

Harris, John. *See* **Hebden, Mark**

Harris, John Norman
Bio-bibliographic data:
Canadian Crime Fiction, p. 97. (209)

Harris, Lee. *Pseud. for* **Syrell Rogovin Leahy**
Bio-bibliographic data:
By a Woman's Hand, 2nd ed., p. 104. (884b)
Detecting Women, 1st ed., p. 69. (877a)
Detecting Women 2, p. 89. (877b)
Detecting Women, 3rd ed., p. 124. (877c)
Web site: http://stopyourekillingme.com/ lee-harris.html

Harris, Rosemary
Bio-bibliographic data:

Twentieth-Century Crime and Mystery Writers, 1st ed., pp. 739–41. (882a)
Twentieth-Century Crime and Mystery Writers, 2nd ed., pp. 426–27. (882b)

Harris, Thomas
Bio-bibliographic data:
Encyclopedia Mysteriosa, p. 156. (2)
The Mammoth Encyclopedia of Modern Crime Fiction, pp. 211–12. (1)
St. James Guide to Crime & Mystery Writers, 4th ed., pp. 488–89. (882d)
Twentieth-Century Crime and Mystery Writers, 3rd ed., p. 507. (882c)
Web site: http://www.randomhouse. com/features/thomasharris; http:// stopyourekillingme.com/thomas. harris.html

Harris, Timothy
Bio-bibliographic data:
Twentieth-Century Crime and Mystery Writers, 3rd ed., pp. 507–8. (882c)

Harrison, Chip. *See* **Block, Lawrence**

Harrison, Ernest
Bio-bibliographic data:
Canadian Crime Fiction, p. 98. (209)

Harrison, J. E.
Bio-bibliographic data:
Australian Crime Fiction, p. 108. (207)

Harrison, Jamie
Bio-bibliographic data:
Detecting Women 2, p. 89. (877b)
Detecting Women, 3rd ed., pp. 124–25. (877c)
Web site: http://stopyourekillingme.com/ jamie-harrison.html

Harrison, Michael
Bio-bibliographic data:
The Encyclopedia of Mystery and Detection, p. 192. (7)
St. James Guide to Crime & Mystery Writers, 4th ed., pp. 489–91. (882d)
Twentieth-Century Crime and Mystery Writers, 1st ed., pp. 741–44. (882a)
Twentieth-Century Crime and Mystery Writers, 2nd ed., pp. 427–29. (882b)
Twentieth-Century Crime and Mystery Writers, 3rd ed., pp. 508–10. (882c)
Personal papers in Mugar Memorial Library, Boston University.

Harrison, Ray
Bio-bibliographic data:
Detecting Men, 1st ed., p. 117. (876)
St. James Guide to Crime & Mystery Writers, 4th ed., pp. 491–92. (882d)

Twentieth-Century Crime and Mystery Writers, 3rd ed., pp. 510–11. (882c)

Harrison, Susan Frances. *See* **Seranus**

Harriss, Will
Bio-bibliographic data:
Detecting Men, 1st ed., p. 117. (876)

Harrod-Eagles, Cynthia
Bio-bibliographic data:
By a Woman's Hand, 1st ed., p. 98. (884a)
By a Woman's Hand, 2nd ed., p. 105. (884b)
Detecting Women, 1st ed., p. 69. (877a)
Detecting Women 2, p. 90. (877b)
Detecting Women, 3rd ed., p. 125. (877c)
Web site: http://stopyourekillingme.com/cynthia-harrod-eagles.html; http://www.twbooks.co.uk/authors/cheagles.html

Harrower, Captain Robert Hamilton; i.e., "Hammy"
Bio-bibliographic data:
Canadian Crime Fiction, p. 98. (209)

Hart, Anne
Bio-bibliographic data:
Canadian Crime Fiction, p. 98. (209)

Hart, Carolyn G.; i.e., Carolyn Gimpel
Bio-bibliographic data:
By a Woman's Hand, 1st ed., pp. 98–99. (884a)
By a Woman's Hand, 2nd ed., pp. 105–6. (884b)
Detecting Women, 1st ed., pp. 69–70. (877a)
Detecting Women 2, p. 90. (877b)
Detecting Women, 3rd ed., pp. 125–26. (877c)
Encyclopedia Mysteriosa, p. 156. (2)
The Encyclopedia of Murder and Mystery, p. 234. (6)
Great Women Mystery Writers, pp. 149–52. (880)
The Mammoth Encyclopedia of Modern Crime Fiction, pp. 213–14. (1)
St. James Guide to Crime & Mystery Writers, 4th ed., pp. 492–94. (882d)
Speaking of Murder, pp. 87–101. (875a)
Twentieth-Century Crime and Mystery Writers, 3rd ed., pp. 511–12. (882c)
Whodunit? A Who's Who in Crime and Mystery Writing, p. 94. (5)
Web site: http://www.carolynhart.com; http://stopyourekillingme.com/carolyn-g-hart.html

Hart, Ellen. *Pseud. for* **Patricia Ellen Boenhardt**
Bio-bibliographic data:
By a Woman's Hand, 1st ed., p. 100. (884a)
By a Woman's Hand, 2nd ed., pp. 106–7. (884b)
Detecting Women, 1st ed., p. 70. (877a)
Detecting Women 2, pp. 90–91. (877b)
Detecting Women, 3rd ed., p. 126. (877c)
The Mammoth Encyclopedia of Modern Crime Fiction, pp. 214–15. (1)
Web site: http://www.ellenhart.com; http://stopyourekillingme.com/ellen-hart.html

Hart, Frances [Newbold] Noyes
Bio-bibliographic data:
Encyclopedia Mysteriosa, p. 157. (2)
The Encyclopedia of Mystery and Detection, p. 192. (7)
St. James Guide to Crime & Mystery Writers, 4th ed., p. 494. (882d)
Twentieth-Century Crime and Mystery Writers, 1st ed., pp. 744–45. (882a)
Twentieth-Century Crime and Mystery Writers, 2nd ed., pp. 429–30. (882b)
Twentieth-Century Crime and Mystery Writers, 3rd ed., pp. 512–13. (882c)

Hart, Jeanne
Bio-bibliographic data:
Detecting Women, 1st ed., p. 70. (877a)
Detecting Women 2, p. 91. (877b)

Hart, Roy
Bio-bibliographic data:
Detecting Men, 1st ed., p. 118. (876)
Web site: http://stopyourekillingme.com/roy-hart.html

Harte, Bret. *Pseud. for* **Francis Brett Harte**
Bio-bibliographic data:
The Encyclopedia of Murder and Mystery, p. 234. (6)

Hartex, Pierre. *Pseud. for* **Pierre Daviault**
Bio-bibliographic data:
Canadian Crime Fiction, p. 98. (209)

Hartzmark, Gini
Bio-bibliographic data:
Detecting Women, 1st ed., p. 71. (877a)
Detecting Women 2, p. 91. (877b)
Detecting Women, 3rd ed., pp. 126–27. (877c)
Web site: http://stopyourekillingme.com/gini-hartzmark.html

Harvester, Simon. *Pseud. for* **Henry St.**
John Clair Rumbold-Gibbs
Bio-bibliographic data:
Australian Crime Fiction, p. 109. (207)
Critical Survey of Mystery and Detective
Fiction, pp. 847–51. (41)
Twentieth-Century Crime and Mystery
Writers, 1st ed., pp. 745–48. (882a)
Twentieth-Century Crime and Mystery
Writers, 2nd ed., pp. 430–31.
Twentieth-Century Crime and Mystery
Writers, 3rd ed., pp. 513–14. (882c)
Harvey, Clay
Bio-bibliographic data:
Detecting Men, 1st ed., p. 118. (876)
Web site: http://stopyourekillingme.com/
clay-harvey.html
Harvey, Jack. *See* **Rankin, Ian**
Harvey, James Neal
Bio-bibliographic data:
Detecting Men, 1st ed., pp. 118–19. (876)
Web site: http://stopyourekillingme.com/
james-neal-harvey.html
Harvey, John [Barton]
Bio-bibliographic data:
Detecting Men, 1st ed., p. 119. (876)
The Encyclopedia of Murder and Mystery,
pp. 234–35. (6)
The Mammoth Encyclopedia of Modern
Crime Fiction, pp. 215–16. (1)
St. James Guide to Crime & Mystery
Writers, 4th ed., pp. 495–97. (882d)
Speaking of Murder, pp. 181–89. (875a)
Talking Murder, pp. 129–41. (883)
Whodunit? A Who's Who in Crime and
Mystery Writing, p. 94. (5)
Web site: http://www.mellotone.co.uk;
http://stopyourekillingme.com/
john-harvey.html
Harvey, Ken J.; i.e., Kenneth Joseph
Bio-bibliographic data:
Canadian Crime Fiction, p. 98. (209)
Hashian, James T.
Bio-bibliographic data:
Canadian Crime Fiction, pp. 98, 231.
(209)
Hasse, Henry
Bio-bibliographic data:
Australian Crime Fiction, p. 109. (207)
Hastings, Graham. *See* **Jefferies, Roderic**
Hastings, Macdonald
Bio-bibliographic data:
The Encyclopedia of Mystery and
Detection, p. 192. (7)

Twentieth-Century Crime and Mystery
Writers, 1st ed., pp. 748–50. (882a)
Twentieth-Century Crime and Mystery
Writers, 2nd ed., pp. 431–32. (882b)
Personal papers in Mugar Memorial
Library, Boston University.
Hathaway, Robin
Bio-bibliographic data:
Detecting Women, 3rd ed., p. 127. (877c)
Web site: http://stopyourekillingme.com/
robin-hathaway.html; http://www.
robinhathaway.com
Hausfeld, Russell
Bio-bibliographic data:
Australian Crime Fiction, p. 109. (207)
Hautman, Pete; i.e., Peter Murray
Bio-bibliographic data:
Detecting Men, 1st ed., p. 119. (876)
Web site: http://stopyourekillingme.com/
pete-hautman.html; http://www.
petehautman.com
Havill, Steven F.
Bio-bibliographic data:
Detecting Men, 1st ed., p. 120. (876)
Web site: http://stopyourekillingme.com/
steven-f-havill.html
Hawk, Steve
Bio-bibliographic data:
Australian Crime Fiction, pp. 109–10.
(207)
Hawkshaw. *See* **Bullivant, Cecil Henry**
Hawkwood, Allan. *See* **Bedford-Jones, H,**
Hawthorn, Clyde. *Pseud. for* **Thomas**
David Smith
Bio-bibliographic data:
Canadian Crime Fiction, p. 99. (209)
Hawthorne, Julian
Bio-bibliographic data:
The Encyclopedia of Mystery and
Detection, pp. 192–93. (7)
Hay, William [Gosse]
Bio-bibliographic data:
Australian Crime Fiction, p. 110. (207)
Haycraft, Howard
Bio-bibliographic data:
Encyclopedia Mysteriosa, p. 158. (2)
The Encyclopedia of Murder and Mystery,
p. 236. (6)
The Encyclopedia of Mystery and
Detection, p. 193. (7)
Hayden, G. Miki
Bio-bibliographic data:
Detecting Women, 3rd ed., p. 127. (877c)

Hayes, Clair W.
Bio-bibliographic data:
Canadian Crime Fiction, p. 255. (209)
Hayes, John F[rancis]
Bio-bibliographic data:
Canadian Crime Fiction, p. 99. (209)
Hayes, Joseph
Bio-bibliographic data:
*Twentieth-Century Crime and Mystery
    Writers,* 1st ed., pp. 751–53. (882a)
*Twentieth-Century Crime and Mystery
    Writers,* 2nd ed., pp. 432–34. (882b)
*Twentieth-Century Crime and Mystery
    Writers,* 3rd ed., pp. 514–16. (882c)
Personal papers in Lilly Library, Indiana
    University, Bloomington, Indiana.
Haymon, S. T.; i.e., Sylvia Theresa
Bio-bibliographic data:
By a Woman's Hand, 1st ed., pp. 100–101.
    (884a)
By a Woman's Hand, 2nd ed., p. 107.
    (884b)
Detecting Women, 1st ed., p. 71. (877a)
Detecting Women 2, pp. 91–92. (877b)
Detecting Women, 3rd ed., pp. 127–28.
    (877c)
Encyclopedia Mysteriosa, p. 158. (2)
Great Women Mystery Writers, pp.
    152–54. (880)
*The Mammoth Encyclopedia of Modern
    Crime Fiction*, pp. 216–17. (1)
*St. James Guide to Crime & Mystery
    Writers*, 4th ed., pp. 498–99. (882d)
*Twentieth-Century Crime and Mystery
    Writers*, 3rd ed., pp. 516–17. (882c)
Web site: http://stopyourekillingme.com/
    s-t-haymon.html
Hays, Peter. *See* **Jeffries, Ian**
Hayter, Sparkle [Vera Lynette]
Bio-bibliographic data:
Canadian Crime Fiction, p. 99. (209)
Detecting Women, 1st ed., p. 71. (877a)
Detecting Women 2, p. 92. (877b)
Detecting Women, 3rd ed., p. 128. (877c)
*The Mammoth Encyclopedia of Modern
    Crime Fiction*, pp. 217–18. (1)
Web site: http://members.aol.com/
    SHayter370/index.html; http://
    stopyourekillingme.com/
    sparkle-hayter.html; http://www.
    noexit.co.uk/hayter.htm; http://www.
    januarymagazine.com/profiles.
    hayter.html

Haywood, Gar Anthony
Bio-bibliographic data:
Detecting Men, 1st ed., p. 120. (876)
The Encyclopedia of Murder and Mystery,
    pp. 236–37. (6)
*The Mammoth Encyclopedia of Modern
    Crime Fiction*, p. 218. (1)
Web site: http://stopyourekillingme.com/
    gar-anthony.haywood.html
Head, Matthew. *Pseud. for* **John Edwin
    Canaday**
Bio-bibliographic data:
Encyclopedia Mysteriosa, p. 158. (2)
The Encyclopedia of Murder and Mystery,
    pp. 237–38. (6)
*The Encyclopedia of Mystery and
    Detection*, p. 193. (7)
*St. James Guide to Crime & Mystery
    Writers,* 4th ed., pp. 499–500. (882d)
*Twentieth-Century Crime and Mystery
    Writers,* 1st ed., pp. 753–54. (882a)
*Twentieth-Century Crime and Mystery
    Writers,* 2nd ed., pp. 434–35. (882b)
*Twentieth-Century Crime and Mystery
    Writers,* 3rd ed., pp. 517–18. (882c)
Personal papers in Alderman Library,
    University of Virginia,
    Charlottesville.
Headley, A. C.
Bio-bibliographic data:
Australian Crime Fiction, p. 110. (207)
Headley, Victor
Bio-bibliographic data:
*The Mammoth Encyclopedia of Modern
    Crime Fiction*, pp. 218–19. (1)
Heald, Tim. *See* **Heald, Timothy**
Heald, Timothy [Villiers]
Bio-bibliographic data:
Canadian Crime Fiction, pp. 255–56.
    (209)
Detecting Men, 1st ed., pp. 120–21. (876)
Encyclopedia Mysteriosa, pp. 158–59. (2)
*The Mammoth Encyclopedia of Modern
    Crime Fiction*, pp. 219–20. (1)
*St. James Guide to Crime & Mystery
    Writers*, 4th ed., pp. 500–501. (882d)
*Twentieth-Century Crime and Mystery
    Writers,* 1st ed., pp. 754–56. (882a)
*Twentieth-Century Crime and Mystery
    Writers,* 2nd ed., pp. 435–36. (882b)
*Twentieth-Century Crime and Mystery
    Writers,* 3rd ed., pp. 518–19. (882c)
Personal papers in Mugar Memorial
    Library, Boston University.

Web site: http://stopyourekillingme.com/
tim-heald.html

Healy, Jeremiah
Bio-bibliographic data:
Detecting Men, 1st ed., p. 121. (876)
Encyclopedia Mysteriosa, p. 159. (2)
The Fatal Art of Entertainment, pp.
276–99. (878)
*The Mammoth Encyclopedia of Modern
Crime Fiction,* p. 220. (1)
*St. James Guide to Crime & Mystery
Writers,* 4th ed., pp. 501–3. (882d)
*Twentieth-Century Crime and Mystery
Writers,* 3rd ed., pp. 519–20. (882c)
*Whodunit? A Who's Who in Crime and
Mystery Writing,* pp. 94–95. (5)
Web site: http://stopyourekillingme.com/
jeremiah-healy.html

Healy, R. Austin
Bio-bibliographic data:
Detecting Men, 1st ed., p. 121. (876)

Heaps, Leo [Jack]
Bio-bibliographic data:
Canadian Crime Fiction, pp. 99–100.
(209)

**Heard, H. F.; i.e., Henry Fitz Gerald
Heard; name sometimes given as
Fitzgerald**
Bio-bibliographic data:
Encyclopedia Mysteriosa, p. 159. (2)
*The Encyclopedia of Mystery and
Detection,* pp. 193–94. (7)
*Twentieth-Century Crime and Mystery
Writers,* 1st ed., pp. 756–58. (882a)
*Twentieth-Century Crime and Mystery
Writers,* 2nd ed., pp. 436–37. (882b)
*Twentieth-Century Crime and Mystery
Writers,* 3rd ed., pp. 520–21. (882c)

Hebden, Juliet. *Pseud. for* **Juliet Harris**
Bio-bibliographic data:
Detecting Women, 3rd ed., pp. 128–29.
(877c)
Web site: http://stopyourekillingme.com/
juliet-hebden.html

Hebden, Mark. *Pseud. for* **John Harris**
Bio-bibliographic data:
Encyclopedia Mysteriosa, p. 159. (2)
*The Mammoth Encyclopedia of Modern
Crime Fiction,* pp. 220–21. (1)
*St. James Guide to Crime & Mystery
Writers,* 4th ed., pp. 503–5. (882d)
*Twentieth-Century Crime and Mystery
Writers,* 2nd ed., pp. 437–39. (882b)

*Twentieth-Century Crime and Mystery
Writers,* 3rd ed., pp. 522–24. (882c)
Personal papers in Mugar Memorial
Library, Boston University.
Web site: http://stopyourekillingme.com/
mark-hebden.html

Heberden, M. V.; i.e., Mary Violet
Bio-bibliographic data:
Detecting Women 2, pp. 92–93, 117–18.
(877b)
Encyclopedia Mysteriosa, p. 159. (2)

Hébert, Anne
Bio-bibliographic data:
Canadian Crime Fiction, p. 100. (209)

Hecht, Ben
Bio-bibliographic data:
The Encyclopedia of Murder and Mystery,
p. 238. (6)
*The Encyclopedia of Mystery and
Detection,* p. 194. (7)

Heck, Peter J.
Bio-bibliographic data:
Detecting Men, 1st ed., p. 122. (876)
Web site: http://stopyourekillingme.com/
peter-j-heck.html; http://www.sff.net/
people/peter.heck

Heffernan, William
Bio-bibliographic data:
Detecting Men, 1st ed., p. 122. (876)
*The Mammoth Encyclopedia of Modern
Crime Fiction,* p. 222. (1)
Web site: http://homepages.together.net/
~dsychn; http://stopyourekillingme.
com/william-heffernan.html

Hegarty, Frances. *See* **Fyfield, Frances**
Heilbrun, Carolyn G. *See* **Cross, Amanda**
**Heinkel, Stanford: house pseud. also used
by Stanford Hennell**
Bio-bibliographic data:
Australian Crime Fiction, p. 110. (207)

Held, Peter. *See* **Vance, John Holbrook**
Heldmann, Bernard. *See* **Marsh, Richard**
Helie-Hamel, Cécile
Bio-bibliographic data:
Canadian Crime Fiction, p. 100. (209)

Heller, Keith
Bio-bibliographic data:
Detecting Men, 1st ed., p. 122. (876)
Web site: http://stopyourekillingme.com/
keith-heller.html

Helú, Antonio
Bio-bibliographic data:
*Latin American Mystery Writers: An A to
Z Guide. (881)*

Helwig, David [Gordon]
Bio-bibliographic data:
Canadian Crime Fiction, p. 100. (209)
Heming, Eileen
Bio-bibliographic data:
Canadian Crime Fiction, p. 100. (209)
Heming, John Winton
Bio-bibliographic data:
Australian Crime Fiction, pp. 110–11.
(207)
Hemingway, Ernest
Bio-bibliographic data:
The Encyclopedia of Murder and Mystery,
p. 240. (6)
Hemlin, Tim
Bio-bibliographic data:
Detecting Men, 1st ed., p. 123. (876)
Web site: http://stopyourekillingme.com/
tim-hemlin.html
Hemming, N. K.; i.e., Norma Kathleen
Bio-bibliographic data:
Australian Crime Fiction, p. 111. (207)
Hemyng, [Samuel] Bracebridge
Bio-bibliographic data:
*The Encyclopedia of Mystery and
Detection*, pp. 195–96. (7)
Henderson, Bob
Bio-bibliographic data:
Australian Crime Fiction, p. 111. (207)
Henderson, James
Bio-bibliographic data:
Canadian Crime Fiction, pp. 100–101.
(209)
Henderson, Lauren
Bio-bibliographic data:
Detecting Women, 3rd ed., p. 129. (877c)
*The Mammoth Encyclopedia of Modern
Crime Fiction*, pp. 222–23. (1)
Web site: http://www.tartcity.html; www.
twbooks.co.uk/authors/lhenderson.
html; http://stopyourekillingme.com/
laren-henderson.html
Henderson, Laurence
Bio-bibliographic data:
Detecting Men, 1st ed., p. 123. (876)
Henderson, Walter Gordon
Bio-bibliographic data:
Australian Crime Fiction, p. 111. (207)
Hendrickson, Louise
Bio-bibliographic data:
Detecting Women, 1st ed., p. 71. (877a)
Detecting Women 2, p. 93. (877b)
Detecting Women, 3rd ed., p. 129. (877c)

Hendryx, James B[eardsley]
Bio-bibliographic data:
Canadian Crime Fiction, pp. 101–2. (209)
Heneghan, James
Bio-bibliographic data:
Canadian Crime Fiction, p. 102. (209)
Hennell, Stanford. *See* **Heinkel, Stanford**
Hennessey, [John] David
Bio-bibliographic data:
Australian Crime Fiction, pp. 111–12.
(207)
Hennissart, Martha. *See* **Lathen, Emma**
Henry, Margaret
Bio-bibliographic data:
Australian Crime Fiction, p. 112. (207)
Henry, O. *Pseud. for* **William Sidney
Porter**
Bio-bibliographic data:
*Critical Survey of Mystery and Detective
Fiction*, pp. 852–58. (41)
*The Encyclopedia of Mystery and
Detection*, pp. 196–97. (7)
*100 Masters of Mystery and Detective
Fiction*, pp. 310–17. (37)
Henry, Sue
Bio-bibliographic data:
By a Woman's Hand, 2nd ed., p. 108.
(884b)
Detecting Women, 1st ed., p. 72. (877a)
Detecting Women 2, p. 93. (877b)
Detecting Women, 3rd ed., p. 130. (877c)
*The Mammoth Encyclopedia of Modern
Crime Fiction*, p. 223. (1)
Web site: http://stopyourekillingme.com/
sue-henry.html
Hensley, Joe L.; i.e., Joseph Louis Hensley
Bio-bibliographic data:
Detecting Men, 1st ed., p. 123. (876)
Encyclopedia Mysteriosa, p. 161. (2)
*The Mammoth Encyclopedia of Modern
Crime Fiction*, pp. 223–24. (1)
*St. James Guide to Crime & Mystery
Writers*, 4th ed., p. 506. (882d)
*Twentieth-Century Crime and Mystery
Writers*, 2nd ed., p. 439. (882b)
*Twentieth-Century Crime and Mystery
Writers*, 3rd ed., pp. 524–25. (882c)
Personal papers in Lilly Library, Indiana
University, Bloomington.

Herald, Beverly Taylor. *See* **McCafferty, Barbara Taylor, and Beverly Taylor Herald**

Herbertson, A. *See* **Batt, Leon**

Heritage, Martin. *See* **Horler, Sydney**

Hernández Luna, Juan
Bio-bibliographic data:
Latin American Mystery Writers: An A to Z Guide. (881)

Herndon, Nancy
Bio-bibliographic data:
Detecting Women 2, pp. 93–94. (877b)
Detecting Women, 3rd ed., p. 130. (877c)
Web site: http://stopyourekillingme.com/ nancy-herndon.html

Herne, Huxley. *See* **Brooker, Bertram**

Heron, Echo
Bio-bibliographic data:
Detecting Women, 3rd ed., pp. 130–31. (877c)

Herron, Shaun
Bio-bibliographic data:
Canadian Crime Fiction, pp. 102–3. (209)
Twentieth-Century Crime and Mystery Writers, 1st ed., pp. 758–60. (882a)
Twentieth-Century Crime and Mystery Writers, 2nd ed., pp. 439–40. (882b)

Herscholt, Wolfe: house pseud. used by G. C. Bleeck and Russell Hausfeld (q.q.v.) among others.

Herscovici, Alan
Bio-bibliographic data:
Canadian Crime Fiction, p. 103. (209)

Hervey, Evelyn. *See* **Keating, H. R. F.; i.e., Henry Reymond Fitzwalter**

Hervey, Michael
Bio-bibliographic data:
Australian Crime Fiction, p. 113. (207)

Hess, Joan
Bio-bibliographic data:
By a Woman's Hand, 1st ed., pp. 101–2. (884a)
By a Woman's Hand, 2nd ed., pp. 108–9. (884b)
Detecting Women, 1st ed., p. 72. (877a)
Detecting Women 2, p. 94. (877b)
Detecting Women, 3rd ed., pp. 119, 131. (877c)
Encyclopedia Mysteriosa, p. 161. (2)
Great Women Mystery Writers, pp. 154–57. (880)
The Mammoth Encyclopedia of Modern Crime Fiction, pp. 224–25. (1)

St. James Guide to Crime & Mystery Writers, 4th ed., pp. 507–8. (882d)
Speaking of Murder, pp. 29–42. (875a)
Twentieth-Century Crime and Mystery Writers, 3rd ed., pp. 525–26. (882c)
Whodunit? A Who's Who in Crime and Mystery Writing, p. 95. (5)
Web site: http://www.joanhess.com; http://www.maggody.com; http:// stopyourekillingme.com/joan-hess. html

Hext, Harrington. *See* **Phillpotts, Eden**

Heyer, Georgette
Bio-bibliographic data:
British Mystery Writers, 1920–1939, pp. 157–61. (867)
Corpus Delicti of Mystery Fiction, pp. 82–83. (879)
Critical Survey of Mystery and Detective Fiction, pp. 859–64. (41)
Detecting Women 2, pp. 94–95. (877b)
Encyclopedia Mysteriosa, pp. 161–62. (2)
The Encyclopedia of Murder and Mystery, pp. 241–42. (6)
The Encyclopedia of Mystery and Detection, pp. 197–98. (7)
Great Women Mystery Writers, pp. 157–60. (880)
The Oxford Companion to Crime and Mystery Writing, p. 205. (4)
St. James Guide to Crime & Mystery Writers, 4th ed., pp. 508–10. (882d)
Twentieth-Century Crime and Mystery Writers, 1st ed., pp. 761–63. (882a)
Twentieth-Century Crime and Mystery Writers, 2nd ed., pp. 441–42. (882b)
Twentieth-Century Crime and Mystery Writers, 3rd ed., pp. 526–27. (882c)
Whodunit? A Who's Who in Crime and Mystery Writing, p. 95. (5)
Web site: http://stopyourekillingme.com/ georgette-heyer.html; http://www. georgette-heyer.com

Hiaasen, Carl
Bio-bibliographic data:
Encyclopedia Mysteriosa, p. 162. (2)
The Encyclopedia of Murder and Mystery, pp. 242–43. (6)
The Mammoth Encyclopedia of Modern Crime Fiction, pp. 226–27. (1)
St. James Guide to Crime & Mystery Writers, 4th ed., pp. 510–11. (882d)
Speaking of Murder, vol. II, pp. 66–77. (875b)

Twentieth-Century Crime and Mystery Writers, 3rd ed., pp. 527–29. (882c)
Whodunit? A Who's Who in Crime and Mystery Writing, pp. 95–96. (5)
Personal papers in Mugar Memorial Library, Boston University.
Web site: http://www.carlhiaasen.com; http://stopyourekillingme.com/ carl-hiassen.html; http://www. thrillingdetective.com/trivia/ hiaasen.html

Hibbert, Eleanor Alice Burford. *See* **Holt, Victoria**

Higgins, George V[incent]
Bio-bibliographic data:
Detecting Men, 1st ed., p. 124. (876)
Encyclopedia Mysteriosa, p. 162. (2)
The Encyclopedia of Murder and Mystery, p. 243. (6)
The Mammoth Encyclopedia of Modern Crime Fiction, pp. 227–28. (1)
Mystery and Suspense Writers, pp. 491–501. (884.2)
The Oxford Companion to Crime and Mystery Writing, p. 205. (4)
St. James Guide to Crime & Mystery Writers, 4th ed., pp. 511–12. (882d)
Twentieth-Century Crime and Mystery Writers, 1st ed., pp. 763–65. (882a)
Twentieth-Century Crime and Mystery Writers, 2nd ed., pp. 442–43. (882b)
Twentieth-Century Crime and Mystery Writers, 3rd ed., pp. 529–30. (882c)
Whodunit? A Who's Who in Crime and Mystery Writing, p. 96. (5)
Web site: http://stopyourekillingme.com/ george-v-higgins.html

Higgins, Jack. *See* **Patterson, Harry**

Highsmith, Domini
Bio-bibliographic data:
Detecting Women 2, p. 95. (877b)
Detecting Women, 3rd ed., pp. 131–32. (877c)

Highsmith, Patricia. *Pseud. for* **Mary Patricia Plangman**
Bio-bibliographic data:
And Then There Were Nine . . . More Women of Mystery, pp. 168–97. (863)
The Big Book of Noir, pp. 291–95. (24)
By a Woman's Hand, 1st ed., pp. 102–4. (884a)
By a Woman's Hand, 2nd ed., pp. 109–10. (884b)

Critical Survey of Mystery and Detective Fiction, pp. 865–71. (41)
Designs of Darkness, pp. 158–71. (873)
Detecting Women, 1st ed., pp. 72–73. (877a)
Detecting Women 2, p. 95. (877b)
Encyclopedia Mysteriosa, p. 163. (2)
The Encyclopedia of Murder and Mystery, p. 243. (6)
The Encyclopedia of Mystery and Detection, p. 198. (7)
Great Women Mystery Writers, pp. 160–64. (880)
The Mammoth Encyclopedia of Modern Crime Fiction, pp. 228–29. (1)
Mystery and Suspense Writers, pp. 503–16. (884.2)
100 Masters of Mystery and Detective Fiction, pp. 318–25. (37)
The Oxford Companion to Crime and Mystery Writing, pp. 205–6. (4)
St. James Guide to Crime & Mystery Writers, 4th ed., pp. 515–17. (882d)
Twentieth-Century Crime and Mystery Writers, 1st ed., p.765–68. (882a)
Twentieth-Century Crime and Mystery Writers, 2nd ed., pp. 445–47. (882b)
Twentieth-Century Crime and Mystery Writers, 3rd ed., pp. 532–34. (882c)
Whodunit? A Who's Who in Crime and Mystery Writing, p. 96. (5)
Women Authors of Detective Series, pp. 98–103. (882.5)
Women of Mystery, pp. 326–39. (874)
Web site: http://stopyourekillingme.com/ patricia-highsmith.html; http://www. wwnorton.com/highsmith

Hightower, Lynn S.
Bio-bibliographic data:
By a Woman's Hand, 2nd ed., pp. 110–11. (884b)
Detecting Women, 1st ed., p. 73. (877a)
Detecting Women 2, pp. 95–96. (877b)
Detecting Women, 3rd ed., p. 132. (877c)
Web site: http://stopyourekillingme.com/ lynn-s-hightower.html

Hilary, Richard. Pseud. of Richard Bodino and Hilary Connors
Bio-bibliographic data
Detecting Men, 1st ed., p. 125. (876)

Hildick, Wallace
Bio-bibliographic data:
Twentieth-Century Crime and Mystery Writers, 1st ed., pp. 768–71. (882a)

Hill, Douglas
Bio-bibliographic data:
Canadian Crime Fiction, p. 103. (209)
Hill, H. Haverstock. *See* **Walsh, J. M.**
Hill, Headon. *Pseud. for* **Francis Edward Grainger**
Bio-bibliographic data:
Canadian Crime Fiction, pp. 255, 256. (209)
The Encyclopedia of Mystery and Detection, p. 198. (7)
Hill, Heather (I). *See* **Carroll, Joy**
Hill, Heather (II)
Bio-bibliographic data:
Canadian Crime Fiction, p. 167. (209)
Hill, John Spencer
Bio-bibliographic data:
Canadian Crime Fiction, p. 103. (209)
Detecting Men, 1st ed., p. 125. (876)
The Mammoth Encyclopedia of Modern Crime Fiction, pp. 229–20. (1)
Hill, R. Lance
Bio-bibliographic data:
Canadian Crime Fiction, pp. 103–4. (209)
Hill, Reginald
Bio-bibliographic data:
Colloquium on Crime, pp. 149–66. (884.1)
Critical Survey of Mystery and Detective Fiction, pp. 872–77. (41)
Detecting Men, 1st ed., pp. 125–26. (876)
Encyclopedia Mysteriosa, p. 164. (2)
The Encyclopedia of Murder and Mystery, p. 244. (6)
The Fatal Art of Entertainment, pp. 194–223. (878)
The Mammoth Encyclopedia of Modern Crime Fiction, pp. 230–31. (1)
The Oxford Companion to Crime and Mystery Writing, p. 206. (4)
St. James Guide to Crime & Mystery Writers, 4th ed., pp. 517–19. (882d)
Twentieth-Century Crime and Mystery Writers, 1st ed., pp. 771–74. (882a)
Twentieth-Century Crime and Mystery Writers, 2nd ed., pp. 447–48. (882b)
Twentieth-Century Crime and Mystery Writers, 3rd ed., pp. 534–35. (882c)
Whodunit? A Who's Who in Crime and Mystery Writing, pp. 96–97. (5)
Personal papers in Mugar Memorial Library, Boston University.
Web site: http://www.randomhouse. com/features/reghill; http://

stopyourekillingme.com/reginald-hill. html
Hillerman, Tony; i.e., Anthony Grove
Bio-bibliographic data:
Colloquium on Crime, pp. 127–47. (884.1)
Critical Survey of Mystery and Detective Fiction, pp. 878–83. (41)
Detecting Men, 1st ed., p. 126. (876)
Encyclopedia Mysteriosa, pp. 164–66. (2)
The Encyclopedia of Murder and Mystery, pp. 244–45. (6)
The Fatal Art of Entertainment, pp. 84–111. (878)
The Mammoth Encyclopedia of Modern Crime Fiction, pp. 232–33. (1)
100 Masters of Mystery and Detective Fiction, pp. 326–32. (37)
The Oxford Companion to Crime and Mystery Writing, p. 206. (4)
St. James Guide to Crime & Mystery Writers, 4th ed., pp. 519–20. (882d)
Speaking of Murder, pp. 143–52. (875a)
Twentieth-Century Crime and Mystery Writers, 1st ed., pp. 774–76. (882a)
Twentieth-Century Crime and Mystery Writers, 2nd ed., pp. 448–50. (882b)
Twentieth-Century Crime and Mystery Writers, 3rd ed., pp. 535–37. (882c)
Whodunit? A Who's Who in Crime and Mystery Writing, p. 97. (5)
Personal papers in Zimmerman Library, University of New Mexico.
Web site: http://stopyourekillingme.com/ tony-hillerman.html; http://www. umsl.edu/~smueller/index.htm
Hilliard, Jan. *See* **Grant, [Hilda] Kay**
Hilton, James
Bio-bibliographic data:
British Mystery Writers, 1920–1939, pp. 162–64. (867)
The Encyclopedia of Murder and Mystery, p. 245. (6)
The Encyclopedia of Mystery and Detection, pp. 198–99. (7)
James Hilton Society
c/o John Hammond, Chairman
49 Beckingthorpe Drive
Borresford, Nottingham
NG13 0DN United Kingdom
Hilton, John Buxton
Bio-bibliographic data:
The Mammoth Encyclopedia of Modern Crime Fiction, pp. 233–34. (1)

St. James Guide to Crime & Mystery Writers, 4th ed., pp. 520–22. (882d)
Twentieth-Century Crime and Mystery Writers, 1st ed., pp. 776–78. (882a)
Twentieth-Century Crime and Mystery Writers, 2nd ed., pp. 450–51. (882b)
Twentieth-Century Crime and Mystery Writers, 3rd ed., pp. 537–39. (882c)
Personal papers in Mugar Memorial Library, Boston University.
Web site: http://stopyourekillingme.com/john-buxton-hilton.html

Himes, Chester [Bomar]
Bio-bibliographic data:
American Hard-Boiled Crime Writers, pp. 216–25. (862)
The Big Book of Noir, pp. 273–80. (24)
Critical Survey of Mystery and Detective Fiction, pp. 884–90. (41)
Encyclopedia Mysteriosa, p. 166. (2)
The Encyclopedia of Murder and Mystery, pp. 245–46. (6)
The Mammoth Encyclopedia of Modern Crime Fiction, pp. 235–36. (1)
100 Masters of Mystery and Detective Fiction, pp. 333–39. (37)
The Oxford Companion to Crime and Mystery Writing, pp. 206–7. (4)
St. James Guide to Crime & Mystery Writers, 4th ed., pp. 522–24. (882d)
Twentieth-Century Crime and Mystery Writers, 1st ed., pp. 778–80. (882a)
Twentieth-Century Crime and Mystery Writers, 2nd ed., pp. 451–52. (882b)
Twentieth-Century Crime and Mystery Writers, 3rd ed., pp. 539–40. (882c)
Whodunit? A Who's Who in Crime and Mystery Writing, pp. 97–98. (5)
Personal papers in the Beinecke Rare Book and Manuscript Library, Yale University.
Personal papers in the Julius Rosenwald Fund, Fisk University, Nashville, Tennessee.
Web site: http://www.math.buffalo.edu/~sww/Himes/Chester.html; http://stopyourekillingme.com/chester-himes.html

Hinch, Derryn
Bio-bibliographic data:
Australian Crime Fiction, pp. 113–14. (207)

Hirschberg, Cornelius
Bio-bibliographic data:

Twentieth-Century Crime and Mystery Writers, 1st ed., pp. 780–81. (882a)

Hitchcock, Alfred [Joseph]
Bio-bibliographic data:
Encyclopedia Mysteriosa, pp. 166–67. (2)
The Encyclopedia of Murder and Mystery, p. 248. (6)
The Encyclopedia of Mystery and Detection, pp. 199–204. (7)

Hitchens, [Julia Clara Catherine] Dolores Birk Olsen
Bio-bibliographic data:
Detecting Women 2, pp. 96, 150–51. (877b)
St. James Guide to Crime & Mystery Writers, 4th ed., pp. 802–03. (882d)
Twentieth-Century Crime and Mystery Writers, 1st ed., pp. 1130–32. (882a)
Twentieth-Century Crime and Mystery Writers, 2nd ed., pp. 684–86. (882b)
Twentieth-Century Crime and Mystery Writers, 3rd ed., pp. 817–18. (882c)
Personal papers in Mugar Memorial Library, Boston University.

Hjerstedt, Gunard. *See* **Keene, Day**
Hoag, Tami
Bio-bibliographic data:
The Mammoth Encyclopedia of Modern Crime Fiction, pp. 236–37. (1)
Web site: http://stopyourekillingme.com/tami-hoag.html

Hobart, Robertson. *See* **Lee, Norman**
Hobson, B.
Bio-bibliographic data:
Australian Crime Fiction, pp. 114, 125. (207)

Hoch, Edward D[entinger]
Bio-bibliographic data:
Critical Survey of Mystery and Detective Fiction, pp. 891–97. (41)
Detecting Men, 1st ed., p. 127. (876)
Encyclopedia Mysteriosa, p. 167. (2)
The Encyclopedia of Mystery and Detection, pp. 204–5. (7)
The Mammoth Encyclopedia of Modern Crime Fiction, pp. 237–39. (1)
100 Masters of Mystery and Detective Fiction, pp. 340–46. (37)
The Oxford Companion to Crime and Mystery Writing, p. 222. (4)
St. James Guide to Crime & Mystery Writers, 4th ed., pp. 524–25. (882d)
Twentieth-Century Crime and Mystery Writers, 1st ed., pp. 781–94. (882a)

Twentieth-Century Crime and Mystery Writers, 2nd ed., pp. 452–60. (882b)
Twentieth-Century Crime and Mystery Writers, 3rd ed., pp. 540–50. (882c)
Whodunit? A Who's Who in Crime and Mystery Writing, pp. 99–100. (5)
Web site: http://stopyourekillingme.com/ edward-d-hoch.html

Hockaby, Stephen. *See* **Mitchell, Gladys**

Hocking, Anne
Bio-bibliographic data:
Twentieth-Century Crime and Mystery Writers, 1st ed., pp. 794–96. (882a)
Twentieth-Century Crime and Mystery Writers, 2nd ed., pp. 460–61. (882b)
Twentieth-Century Crime and Mystery Writers, 3rd ed., pp. 550–51. (882c)

Hodge, Harry [Carver]
Bio-bibliographic data:
Australian Crime Fiction, p. 114. (207)

Hodgson, Barbara
Bio-bibliographic data:
Canadian Crime Fiction, p. 104. (209)

Hodgson, William Hope
Bio-bibliographic data:
British Mystery Writers, 1860–1919, pp. 166–68. (866)
The Encyclopedia of Murder and Mystery, pp. 248–49. (6)
The Encyclopedia of Mystery and Detection, p. 205. (7)
St. James Guide to Crime & Mystery Writers, 4th ed., p. 526. (882d)
Twentieth-Century Crime and Mystery Writers, 1st ed., pp. 797–98. (882a)
Twentieth-Century Crime and Mystery Writers, 2nd ed., p. 462. (882b)
Twentieth-Century Crime and Mystery Writers, 3rd ed., pp. 551–52. (882c)
Web site: http://www.creative.net/ ~alang/lit/horror/whhbio.htm

Hreg, Peter
Bio-bibliographic data:
The Encyclopedia of Murder and Mystery, p. 249. (6)
St. James Guide to Crime & Mystery Writers, 4th ed., pp. 526–28. (882d)

Hoff, B. J.
Bio-bibliographic data:
Detecting Women, 3rd ed., pp. 132–33. (877c)

Hoffman, Kurt: house pseud.
Bio-bibliographic data:
Australian Crime Fiction, p. 114. (207)

Hoffman, William
Bio-bibliographic data:
The Mammoth Encyclopedia of Modern Crime Fiction, p. 239. (1)

Hogan, Margaret
Bio-bibliographic data:
Canadian Crime Fiction, p. 104. (209)

Holbrook, Teri
Bio-bibliographic data:
Detecting Women 2, p. 96. (877b)
Detecting Women, 3rd ed., p. 133. (877c)
Web site: http://stopyourekillingme.com/ teri-holbrook.html; http://members. aol.com/femmesweb/holbrook.htm; http://members.aol.com/atlsinc/ tholbrook

Holden, J. Railton
Bio-bibliographic data:
Canadian Crime Fiction, p. 256. (209)

Holding, Elisabeth Sanxay
Bio-bibliographic data:
The Encyclopedia of Mystery and Detection, p. 205. (7)
St. James Guide to Crime & Mystery Writers, 4th ed., pp. 528–29. (882d)
Twentieth-Century Crime and Mystery Writers, 1st ed., pp. 798–800. (882a)
Twentieth-Century Crime and Mystery Writers, 2nd ed., pp. 462–63. (882b)
Twentieth-Century Crime and Mystery Writers, 3rd ed., pp. 552–53. (882c)

Holding, James
Bio-bibliographic data:
Twentieth-Century Crime and Mystery Writers, 1st ed., pp. 800–802. (882a)
Twentieth-Century Crime and Mystery Writers, 2nd ed., pp. 463–67. (882b)
Twentieth-Century Crime and Mystery Writers, 3rd ed., pp. 553–57. (882c)
Personal papers in University of Minnesota Library, Minneapolis.

Holland, Isabelle
Bio-bibliographic data:
By a Woman's Hand, 1st ed., p. 104. (884a)
By a Woman's Hand, 2nd ed., pp. 111–12. (884b)
Detecting Women, 1st ed., p. 73. (877a)
Detecting Women 2, pp. 96–97. (877b)
Detecting Women, 3rd ed., p. 133. (877c)

Holland, Judith. *See* **Wakefield, Hannah**

Holliday, Joe; i.e., Joseph
Bio-bibliographic data:
Canadian Crime Fiction, p. 104. (209)

Hollier, Robert
Bio-bibliographic data:
Canadian Crime Fiction, p. 104. (209)
Hollingsworth, Gerelyn
Bio-bibliographic data:
Detecting Women, 1st ed., p. 73. (877a)
Detecting Women 2, p. 97. (877b)
Holman, C. Hugh
Bio-bibliographic data:
Twentieth-Century Crime and Mystery Writers, 1st ed., pp. 803–5. (882a)
Holme, Timothy
Bio-bibliographic data:
Twentieth-Century Crime and Mystery Writers, 3rd ed., pp. 557–58. (882c)
Holmes, Gordon. *Pseud. for* Louis Tracy and M. P. Shiel (q.q.v.).
Bio-bibliographic data:
The Encyclopedia of Mystery and Detection, pp. 205–6. (7)
Holmes, H. H. *See* Boucher, Anthony
Holmes, Jeffrey
Bio-bibliographic data:
Canadian Crime Fiction, pp. 104–5. (209)
Holman, Russell
Bio-bibliographic data:
Canadian Crime Fiction, p. 105. (209)
Holms, Joyce
Bio-bibliographic data:
Detecting Women, 3rd ed., pp. 133–34. (877c)
Holt, A. J.: perhaps pseud. for Christopher Hyde (q.v.)
Bio-bibliographic data:
Canadian Crime Fiction, p. 105. (209)
Web site: http://stopyourekillingme.com/a-j-holt.html
Holt, Gavin. *See* Rodda, [Percival] Charles
Holt, Gerald
Bio-bibliographic data:
Canadian Crime Fiction, p. 105. (209)
Holt, Hazel
Bio-bibliographic data:
By a Woman's Hand, 1st ed., p. 105. (884a)
By a Woman's Hand, 2nd ed., p. 112. (884b)
Detecting Women, 1st ed., p. 74. (877a)
Detecting Women 2, p. 97. (877b)
Detecting Women, 3rd ed., p. 134. (877c)
Web site: http://stopyourekillingme.com/hazel-holt.html; http://www.hazelholt.com

Holt, Samuel. *See* Westlake, Donald E.
Holt, Victoria. *Pseud. for* Eleanor Alice Burford Hibbert
Bio-bibliographic data:
Australian Crime Fiction, p. 114. (207)
Corpus Delicti of Mystery Fiction, pp. 83–84. (879)
Encyclopedia Mysteriosa, p. 173. (2)
The Encyclopedia of Mystery and Detection, p. 214. (7)
St. James Guide to Crime & Mystery Writers, 4th ed., pp. 529–32. (882d)
Twentieth-Century Crime and Mystery Writers, 2nd ed., pp. 467–70. (882b)
Twentieth-Century Crime and Mystery Writers, 3rd ed., pp. 558–61. (882c)
Web site: http://stopyourekillingme.com/victoria-holt.html
Holton, Hugh
Bio-bibliographic data:
Detecting Men, 1st ed., p. 127. (876)
Web site: http://stopyourekillingme.com/hugh-holton.html
Holton, Leonard. *Pseud. for* Leonard Patrick O'Connor Wibberley
Bio-bibliographic data:
Critical Survey of Mystery and Detective Fiction, pp. 898–904. (41)
Encyclopedia Mysteriosa, p. 173. (2)
The Encyclopedia of Murder and Mystery, p. 250. (6)
The Encyclopedia of Mystery and Detection, pp. 214–15. (7)
Twentieth-Century Crime and Mystery Writers, 1st ed., pp. 805–9. (882a)
Twentieth-Century Crime and Mystery Writers, 2nd ed., pp. 470–72. (882b)
Twentieth-Century Crime and Mystery Writers, 3rd ed., pp. 561–64. (882c)
Personal papers in University of Southern California, Los Angeles, California.
Holtzer, Susan
Bio-bibliographic data:
Detecting Women, 1st ed., p. 74. (877a)
Detecting Women 2, p. 97. (877b)
Detecting Women, 3rd ed., pp. 134–35. (877c)
Web site: http://stopyourekillingme.com/susan-holtzer.html
Home-Gall, Edward R[eginald]
Bio-bibliographic data:
Canadian Crime Fiction, p. 256. (209)
Homel, David
Bio-bibliographic data:

Hornung, E. W.; i.e., Ernest William
Bio-bibliographic data:
Australian Crime Fiction, pp. 115–16.
   (207)
British Mystery Writers, 1860–1919, pp.
   169–77. (866)
Corpus Delicti of Mystery Fiction, pp.
   84–86. (879)
*Critical Survey of Mystery and Detective
   Fiction*, pp. 905–10. (41)
Encyclopedia Mysteriosa, p. 174. (2)
The Encyclopedia of Murder and Mystery,
   p. 253. (6)
*The Encyclopedia of Mystery and
   Detection*, p. 216. (7)
*100 Masters of Mystery and Detective
   Fiction*, pp. 347–52. (37)
*The Oxford Companion to Crime and
   Mystery Writing*, p. 225. (4)
*St. James Guide to Crime & Mystery
   Writers*, 4th ed., pp. 538–40. (882d)
*Twentieth-Century Crime and Mystery
   Writers,* 1st ed., pp. 816–18. (882a)
*Twentieth-Century Crime and Mystery
   Writers*, 2nd ed., pp. 477–78. (882b)
*Twentieth-Century Crime and Mystery
   Writers*, 3rd ed., pp. 569–71. (882c)
*Whodunit? A Who's Who in Crime and
   Mystery Writing*, p. 101. (5)
Horowitz, Renee B.
Bio-bibliographic data:
Detecting Women, 3rd ed., p. 136. (877c)
Horsfield, Richard Edward. *See* **Gaunt,
   M. B.**
Horwitz, Merle
Bio-bibliographic data:
Detecting Men, 1st ed., p. 128. (876)
Hosier, [J.] Sydney
Bio-bibliographic data:
Canadian Crime Fiction, p. 106. (209)
Hospital, Janette Turner. *See* **Juniper,
   Alex**
Hough, S. B.
Bio-bibliographic data:
*Twentieth-Century Crime and Mystery
   Writers,* 1st ed., pp. 819–21. (882a)
*Twentieth-Century Crime and Mystery
   Writers*, 2nd ed., pp. 478–79. (882b)
*Twentieth-Century Crime and Mystery
   Writers*, 3rd ed., pp. 571–72. (882c)
Personal papers in Archive of
   Contemporary History, University of
   Wyoming, Laramie.

Houle, Mario
Bio-bibliographic data:
Canadian Crime Fiction, p. 106. (209)
Household, Geoffrey
Bio-bibliographic data:
*British Mystery and Thriller Writers since
   1940, First Series*, pp. 194–209. (868)
*Critical Survey of Mystery and Detective
   Fiction*, pp. 911–15. (41)
Encyclopedia Mysteriosa, p. 175. (2)
The Encyclopedia of Murder and Mystery,
   p. 254. (6)
*The Encyclopedia of Mystery and
   Detection*, pp. 216–17. (7)
*The Oxford Companion to Crime and
   Mystery Writing*, p. 228. (4)
*St. James Guide to Crime & Mystery
   Writers*, 4th ed., pp. 540–41. (882d)
*Twentieth-Century Crime and Mystery
   Writers,* 1st ed., pp. 821–23. (882a)
*Twentieth-Century Crime and Mystery
   Writers*, 2nd ed., pp. 479–81. (882b)
*Twentieth-Century Crime and Mystery
   Writers*, 3rd ed., pp. 572–74. (882c)
Personal papers in Lilly Library, Indiana
   University, Bloomington, Indiana.
Housewright, David
Bio-bibliographic data:
Detecting Men, 1st ed., p. 129. (876)
Web site: http://www.
   davidhousewright.com
Hovey, Joan Hall
Bio-bibliographic data:
Canadian Crime Fiction, p. 106. (209)
Web site: http://stopyourekillingme.com/
   joan-hall-hovey.html; http://www.
   joanhallhovey.com
Howard, Clark
Bio-bibliographic data:
Encyclopedia Mysteriosa, p. 175. (2)
*St. James Guide to Crime & Mystery
   Writers*, 4th ed., pp. 541–42. (882d)
*Twentieth-Century Crime and Mystery
   Writers*, 2nd ed., pp. 481–83. (882b)
*Twentieth-Century Crime and Mystery
   Writers*, 3rd ed., pp. 574–76. (882c)
Howard, George Bronson. *See*
   Bronson-Howard, George
Howard, Hartley. *See* **Ognall, Leopold
   Horace**
Howard, Tom. *Pseud. for* **John Thomas
   Howard Reid**
Bio-bibliographic data:

Australian Crime Fiction, pp. 116–17. (207)

Howe, Melodie Johnson
Bio-bibliographic data:
Detecting Women, 1st ed., p. 75. (877a)
Detecting Women 2, p. 99. (877b)
Detecting Women, 3rd ed., pp. 136–37. (877c)

Howell, Lis
Bio-bibliographic data:
Detecting Women, 3rd ed., p. 137. (877c)

Howell, Wayne
Bio-bibliographic data:
Canadian Crime Fiction, p. 107. (209)

Howley, Brendan
Bio-bibliographic data:
Canadian Crime Fiction, p. 107. (209)

Hoyt, Richard
Bio-bibliographic data:
Detecting Men, 1st ed., p. 129. (876)
Encyclopedia Mysteriosa, pp. 175–76. (2)
St. James Guide to Crime & Mystery Writers, 4th ed., pp. 542–43. (882d)
Twentieth-Century Crime and Mystery Writers, 2nd ed., p. 483. (882b)
Twentieth-Century Crime and Mystery Writers, 3rd ed., p. 576. (882c)
Personal papers in Mugar Memorial Library, Boston University.
Web site: http://stopyourekillingme.com/richard-hoyt.html

Hoyte, Henry
Bio-bibliographic data:
Australian Crime Fiction, p. 118. (207)

Hubbard, George [Barron]
Bio-bibliographic data:
Canadian Crime Fiction, pp. 256, 261. (209)

Hubbard, P. M.; i.e., Philip Maitland
Bio-bibliographic data:
The Encyclopedia of Murder and Mystery, p. 255. (6)
St. James Guide to Crime & Mystery Writers, 4th ed., pp. 543–44. (882d)
Twentieth-Century Crime and Mystery Writers, 1st ed., pp. 823–25. (882a)
Twentieth-Century Crime and Mystery Writers, 2nd ed., pp. 483–84. (882b)
Twentieth-Century Crime and Mystery Writers, 3rd ed., pp. 576–78. (882c)

Huberdeau, Madeleine
Bio-bibliographic data:
Canadian Crime Fiction, p. 107. (209)

Hubin, Allen J.
Bio-bibliographic data:
Encyclopedia Mysteriosa, p. 176. (2)
The Encyclopedia of Mystery and Detection, p. 217. (7)

Hudson, Christopher
Bio-bibliographic data:
Australian Crime Fiction, p. 118. (207)

Huebner, Frederick D.
Bio-bibliographic data:
Detecting Men, 1st ed., p. 130. (876)
Web site: http://stopyourekillingme.com/frederick-d-huebner.html

Huff, Tanya [Sue]
Bio-bibliographic data:
By a Woman's Hand, 2nd ed., pp. 113–14. (884b)
Canadian Crime Fiction, pp. 107–8. (209)
Detecting Women 2, p. 99. (877b)
Detecting Women, 3rd ed., p. 137. (877c)
Web site: http://stopyourekillingme.com/tanya-huff.html

Hughes, Carole
Bio-bibliographic data:
Australian Crime Fiction, p. 9. (207)

Hughes, Dorothy B.; i.e., Dorothy Belle Flanagan
Bio-bibliographic data:
Encyclopedia Mysteriosa, p. 176. (2)
The Encyclopedia of Murder and Mystery, pp. 255–56. (6)
The Encyclopedia of Mystery and Detection, pp. 217–18. (7)
Great Women Mystery Writers, pp. 164–66. (880)
St. James Guide to Crime & Mystery Writers, 4th ed., pp. 545–46. (882d)
13 Mistresses of Murder, pp. 53–63. (871)
Twentieth-Century Crime and Mystery Writers, 1st ed., pp. 825–27. (882a)
Twentieth-Century Crime and Mystery Writers, 2nd ed., pp. 485–86. (882b)
Twentieth-Century Crime and Mystery Writers, 3rd ed., pp. 578–79. (882c)

Hughes, Matilda. *See* **MacLeod, Charlotte**

Hughes, Monica
Bio-bibliographic data:
Canadian Crime Fiction, p. 108. (209)

Hughes, Zach. *See* **Zachary, Hugh**

Hugo, Richard
Bio-bibliographic data:
The Encyclopedia of Murder and Mystery, p. 256. (6)

Hugo, Victor[-Marie]
Bio-bibliographic data:
The Encyclopedia of Mystery and Detection, p. 218. (7)
Hull, Richard. *Pseud. for* **Richard Henry Sampson**
Bio-bibliographic data:
British Mystery Writers, 1920–1939, pp. 165–69. (867)
Critical Survey of Mystery and Detective Fiction, pp. 916–21. (41)
Encyclopedia Mysteriosa, p. 176. (2)
The Encyclopedia of Mystery and Detection, pp. 218–19. (7)
St. James Guide to Crime & Mystery Writers, 4th ed., p. 546. (882d)
Twentieth-Century Crime and Mystery Writers, 1st ed., pp. 827–29. (882a)
Twentieth-Century Crime and Mystery Writers, 2nd ed., p. 486. (882b)
Twentieth-Century Crime and Mystery Writers, 3rd ed., pp. 579–80. (882c)
Web site: http://stopyourekillingme.com/richard-hull.html
Hulme, Juliet Marion. *See* **Perry, Anne**
Hume, Fergus; i.e, Fergusson Wright
Bio-bibliographic data:
Australian Crime Fiction, pp. 118–20. (207)
British Mystery Writers, 1860–1919, pp. 178–83. (866)
Encyclopedia Mysteriosa, pp. 176–77. (2)
The Encyclopedia of Murder and Mystery, pp. 256–57. (6)
The Encyclopedia of Mystery and Detection, pp. 219–20. (7)
St. James Guide to Crime & Mystery Writers, 4th ed., pp. 546–49. (882d)
Twentieth-Century Crime and Mystery Writers, 1st ed., pp. 829–33. (882a)
Twentieth-Century Crime and Mystery Writers, 2nd ed., pp. 486–89. (882b)
Twentieth-Century Crime and Mystery Writers, 3rd ed., pp. 580–82. (882c)
Humm, Martin J.
Bio-bibliographic data:
Canadian Crime Fiction, pp. 108, 157. (209)
Hungerford, T. A. G.; i.e., Thomas Arthur Guy
Bio-bibliographic data:
Australian Crime Fiction, p. 120. (207)

Hunt, David. *See* **Bayer, William**
Hunt, E. Howard, Jr.; i.e., Everette Howard
Bio-bibliographic data:
The Big Book of Noir, p. 264. (24)
Encyclopedia Mysteriosa, p. 177. (2)
The Encyclopedia of Mystery and Detection, p. 220. (7)
The Mammoth Encyclopedia of Modern Crime Fiction, pp. 240–41. (1)
St. James Guide to Crime & Mystery Writers, 4th ed., pp. 549–51. (882d)
Twentieth-Century Crime and Mystery Writers, 2nd ed., pp. 489–90. (882b)
Twentieth-Century Crime and Mystery Writers, 3rd ed., pp. 582–83. (882c)
Hunt, Katherine Chandler
Bio-bibliographic data:
Canadian Crime Fiction, pp. 108, 157. (209)
Hunt, Kyle. *See* **Creasey, John**
Hunt, Richard
Bio-bibliographic data:
Detecting Men, 1st ed., p. 130. (876)
Hunter, Alan [James Herbert]
Bio-bibliographic data:
Detecting Men, 1st ed., pp. 130–31. (876)
Encyclopedia Mysteriosa, pp. 177–78. (2)
The Encyclopedia of Murder and Mystery, p. 257. (6)
The Encyclopedia of Mystery and Detection, p. 220. (7)
St. James Guide to Crime & Mystery Writers, 4th ed., pp. 551–53. (882d)
Twentieth-Century Crime and Mystery Writers, 1st ed., pp. 834–36. (882a)
Twentieth-Century Crime and Mystery Writers, 2nd ed., pp. 490–92. (882b)
Twentieth-Century Crime and Mystery Writers, 3rd ed., pp. 584–85. (882c)
Hunter, Evan
Bio-bibliographic data:
Critical Survey of Mystery and Detective Fiction, pp. 1112–17. (41)
The Craft of Crime: Conversations with Crime Writers, pp. 1–23. (872)
Detecting Men, 1st ed., pp. 173–74. (876)
Encyclopedia Mysteriosa, pp. 213–14. (2)
The Encyclopedia of Murder and Mystery, pp. 309–10. (6)
The Encyclopedia of Mystery and Detection, pp. 258–59. (7)
The Mammoth Encyclopedia of Modern Crime Fiction, pp. 305–9. (1)

Mystery and Suspense Writers, pp.
517–26. (884.2)
*100 Masters of Mystery and Detective
Fiction*, pp. 424–30. (37)
*The Oxford Companion to Crime and
Mystery Writing*, pp. 282–83. (4)
*St. James Guide to Crime & Mystery
Writers*, 4th ed., pp. 716–19. (882d)
Speaking of Murder, pp. 43–54. (875a)
Talking Murder, pp. 186–99. (883)
*Twentieth-Century Crime and Mystery
Writers*, 1st ed., pp. 1032–37. (882a)
*Twentieth-Century Crime and Mystery
Writers*, 2nd ed., pp. 618–20. (882b)
*Twentieth-Century Crime and Mystery
Writers*, 3rd ed., pp. 731–34. (882c)
*Whodunit? A Who's Who in Crime and
Mystery Writing*, pp. 128–29. (5)
Personal papers in Mugar Memorial
Library, Boston University
Web site: http://www.edmcbain.com;
http://stopyourekillingme.com/
evan-hunter.html; http://www.
thrillingdetective.com/trivia/
mcbain.html

Hunter, Fred W.
Bio-bibliographic data:
Detecting Men, 1st ed., p. 132. (876)
Web site:
http://home.earthlink.net/~fhunter/
welcome.html

Hunter, James H[ogg]
Bio-bibliographic data:
Canadian Crime Fiction, pp. 108–9. (209)

Hunter, Richard Wilkes
Bio-bibliographic data:
Australian Crime Fiction, pp. 120–21.
(207)

Hunter, Stephen
Bio-bibliographic data:
Detecting Men, 1st ed., p. 132. (876)
Web site: http://stopyourekillingme.com/
stephen-hunter.html; http://wbanet.
com/hunter

Huot, A.
Bio-bibliographic data:
Canadian Crime Fiction, p. 109. (209)

Huot, Alexandre
Bio-bibliographic data:
Canadian Crime Fiction, p. 109. (209)

Hurley, John J. *See* **Rafferty, S. S.**

Hutchins, Hazel
Bio-bibliographic data:
Canadian Crime Fiction, p. 109. (209)

Hutchinson, Bobby
Bio-bibliographic data:
Canadian Crime Fiction, p. 109. (209)

Huxley, Aldous [Leonard]
Bio-bibliographic data:
The Encyclopedia of Murder and Mystery,
p. 257. (6)

Huxley, Elspeth [Josceline Grant]
Bio-bibliographic data:
British Mystery Writers, 1920–1939, pp.
169–75. (867)
Detecting Women 2, p. 99. (877b)
The Encyclopedia of Murder and Mystery,
pp. 257–58. (6)
*The Encyclopedia of Mystery and
Detection*, p. 221. (7)
*St. James Guide to Crime & Mystery
Writers*, 4th ed., pp. 553–55. (882d)
*Twentieth-Century Crime and Mystery
Writers*, 1st ed., pp. 836–39. (882a)
*Twentieth-Century Crime and Mystery
Writers*, 2nd ed., pp. 492–93. (882b)
*Twentieth-Century Crime and Mystery
Writers*, 3rd ed., pp. 585–87. (882c)

Hyde, Anthony
Bio-bibliographic data:
Canadian Crime Fiction, p. 109. (209)

Hyde, Christopher
Bio-bibliographic data:
Canadian Crime Fiction, pp. 105 (?), 109.
(209)

Hyde, Eleanor
Bio-bibliographic data:
Detecting Women 2, p. 100. (877b)
Detecting Women, 3rd ed., pp. 137–38. (877c)

Hyde, Laurence
Bio-bibliographic data:
Canadian Crime Fiction, pp. 109–10.
(209)

Hyland, Stanley
Bio-bibliographic data:
*Twentieth-Century Crime and Mystery
Writers,* 1st ed., pp. 839–40. (882a)

**Hyne, C. J. Cutcliffe; i.e., Charles John
Cutcliffe Wright**
Bio-bibliographic data:
*The Encyclopedia of Mystery and
Detection*, p. 221. (7)

I

Iakovou, Judy. *See* **Iakovou, Takis, and
Judy Iakovou**

Iakovou, Takis, and Judy Iakovou
Bio-bibliographic data:

Detecting Women, 3rd ed., p. 138. (877c)
Web site: http://www.stopyourekillingme.
com/takis-&-judy-iakovou.html
Iams, Jack; i.e., Samuel H. Iams, Jr.
Bio-bibliographic data:
Encyclopedia Mysteriosa, p. 180. (2)
*The Encyclopedia of Mystery and
Detection,* p. 223. (7)
*Twentieth-Century Crime and Mystery
Writers,* 1st ed., pp. 840–41. (882a)
*Twentieth-Century Crime and Mystery
Writers,* 2nd ed., pp. 493–94. (882b)
Personal papers in Princeton University
Library, Princeton, New Jersey.
Iannuzzi, John N.
Bio-bibliographic data:
*Twentieth-Century Crime and Mystery
Writers,* 1st ed., pp. 841–42. (882a)
*Twentieth-Century Crime and Mystery
Writers,* 2nd ed., pp. 494–95. (882b)
Ibargüengoitia, Jorge
Bio-bibliographic data:
*Latin American Mystery Writers: An A to
Z Guide. (881)*
Iles, Francis. *See* **Berkeley, Anthony**
Infante, Anne
Bio-bibliographic data:
Australian Crime Fiction, p. 122. (207)
Inglis, Charles
Bio-bibliographic data:
Australian Crime Fiction, p. 122. (207)
Inigo, Martin. *See* **Marston, Edward**
Inman, H. Escott
Bio-bibliographic data:
Australian Crime Fiction, pp. 122–23.
(207)
Innes, [Ralph] Hammond
Bio-bibliographic data:
Australian Crime Fiction, p. 123. (207)
Canadian Crime Fiction, p. 256. (209)
The Encyclopedia of Murder and Mystery,
p. 261. (6)
*The Encyclopedia of Mystery and
Detection,* pp. 223–24. (7)
*St. James Guide to Crime & Mystery
Writers,* 4th ed., pp. 557–58. (882d)
*Twentieth-Century Crime and Mystery
Writers,* 1st ed., pp. 842–44. (882a)
*Twentieth-Century Crime and Mystery
Writers,* 2nd ed., pp. 495–96. (882b)
*Twentieth-Century Crime and Mystery
Writers,* 3rd ed., pp. 588–89. (882c)
Personal papers in Mugar Memorial
Library, Boston University.

Innes, Michael. *Pseud. for* **John Innes
Mackintosh Stewart**
Bio-bibliographic data:
Australian Crime Fiction, p. 123. (207)
*Critical Survey of Mystery and Detective
Fiction,* pp. 922–27. (41)
Encyclopedia Mysteriosa, pp. 180–81. (2)
The Encyclopedia of Murder and Mystery,
pp. 261–62. (6)
Mystery and Suspense Writers, pp.
527–39. (884.2)
*100 Masters of Mystery and Detective
Fiction,* pp. 353–58. (37)
*The Oxford Companion to Crime and
Mystery Writing,* pp. 236–37. (4)
*St. James Guide to Crime & Mystery
Writers,* 4th ed., pp. 558–60. (882d)
*Twentieth-Century Crime and Mystery
Writers,* 1st ed., pp. 844–48. (882a)
*Twentieth-Century Crime and Mystery
Writers,* 2nd ed., pp. 496–98. (882b)
*Twentieth-Century Crime and Mystery
Writers,* 3rd ed., pp. 589–81. (882c)
*Whodunit? A Who's Who in Crime and
Mystery Writing,* p. 105. (5)
Web site: http://www.stopyourekillingme.
com/michael-innis.html
Innes, Murray M.
Bio-bibliographic data:
Australian Crime Fiction, p. 124. (207)
Ireland, David
Bio-bibliographic data:
Australian Crime Fiction, p. 124. (207)
Irish, William. *See* **Woolrich, Cornell**
Ironside, Elizabeth
Bio-bibliographic data:
*The Mammoth Encyclopedia of Modern
Crime Fiction,* p. 242. (1)
Irvine, Angela. *See* **Davis, Val**
Irvine, E. Marie
Bio-bibliographic data:
Australian Crime Fiction, p. 183. (207)
Irvine, Robert [Ralstone]. *See also* **Davis,
Val**
Bio-bibliographic data:
Detecting Men, 1st ed., pp. 132–33. (876)
*The Mammoth Encyclopedia of Modern
Crime Fiction,* pp. 242–43. (1)
*St. James Guide to Crime & Mystery
Writers,* 4th ed., pp. 560–61. (882d)
*Twentieth-Century Crime and Mystery
Writers,* 3rd ed., pp. 592–93. (882c)
Web site: http://www.stopyourekillingme.
com/robert-irvine.html

Irving, John [Winslow]
Bio-bibliographic data:
Canadian Crime Fiction, p. 279. (209)
The Encyclopedia of Murder and Mystery,
  pp. 264–65 (6)
Irwin, Will. *See* **Burgess, Gelett**
Isaacs, Susan
Bio-bibliographic data:
By a Woman's Hand, 2nd ed., p. 115.
  (884b)
Web site: http://www.stopyourekillingme.
  com/susan-isaacs.html; http://www.
  susanisaacs.com
Ishmael, John
Bio-bibliographic data:
Canadian Crime Fiction, p. 110. (209)
Israel, Charles-E[dward]
Bio-bibliographic data:
Canadian Crime Fiction, p. 110. (209)
Izzi, Eugene [John]
Bio-bibliographic data:
Detecting Men, 1st ed., p. 97. (876)
*The Mammoth Encyclopedia of Modern
  Crime Fiction,* pp. 243–44. (1)

J

JAB. *Pseud. for* **André Blanchard**
Bio-bibliographic data:
Canadian Crime Fiction, p. 110. (209)
Jackman, Stuart
Bio-bibliographic data:
*Twentieth-Century Crime and Mystery
  Writers,* 1st ed., pp. 848–50. (882a)
Jackson, Basil
Bio-bibliographic data:
Canadian Crime Fiction, pp. 256, 279.
  (209)
Jackson, [Walter] Francis
Bio-bibliographic data:
Australian Crime Fiction, pp. 125, 183.
  (207)
Jackson, Hialeah. *See* **Polly Whitney**
Jackson, Hugh Nelson
Bio-bibliographic data:
Australian Crime Fiction, p. 125. (207)
Jackson, Jon A.
Bio-bibliographic data:
Detecting Men, 1st ed., p. 133. (876)
Web site: http://www.stopyourekillingme.
  com/jon-a-jackson.html; http://www.
  jonajackson.com
Jackson, Marian J. A. *Pseud. for* **Marian
  Rogers**
Bio-bibliographic data:

By a Woman's Hand, 1st ed., p. 108.
  (884a)
By a Woman's Hand, 2nd ed., p. 116.
  (884b)
Detecting Women, 1st ed., p. 75. (877a)
Detecting Women 2, p. 100. (877b)
Detecting Women, 3rd ed., pp. 138–39.
  (877c)
Web site: http://www.stopyourekillingme.
  com/marian-j-a-jackson.html
Jackson, Muriel Resnick
Bio-bibliographic data:
Detecting Women, 1st ed., p. 76. (877a)
Detecting Women 2, p. 100. (877b)
Jackson, Shirley
Bio-bibliographic data:
*And then There Were Nine . . . More
  Women of Mystery,* pp. 198–219. (874)
The Encyclopedia of Murder and Mystery,
  p. 267. (6)
*Twentieth-Century Crime and Mystery
  Writers,* 1st ed., pp. 850–52. (882a)
Jacob, Jacques
Bio-bibliographic data:
Canadian Crime Fiction, p. 110. (209)
Jacobs, Jonnie
Bio-bibliographic data:
Detecting Women, 1st ed., p. 76. (877a)
Detecting Women 2, p. 100. (877b)
Detecting Women, 3rd ed., p. 139. (877c)
Web site: http://www.stopyourekillingme.
  com/jonnie-jacobs.html
Jacobs, Nancy Baker
Bio-bibliographic data:
By a Woman's Hand, 1st ed., p. 109.
  (884a)
By a Woman's Hand, 2nd ed., pp. 116–17.
  (884b)
Detecting Women, 1st ed., p. 76. (877a)
Detecting Women 2, pp. 100–1. (877b)
Detecting Women, 3rd ed., p. 139. (877c)
Web site: http://www.stopyourekillingme.
  com/nancy-baker-jacobs.html
Jacobs, T. C. H. *Pseud. for* **Jacques
  Pendower**
Bio-bibliographic data:
*Twentieth-Century Crime and Mystery
  Writers,* 1st ed., pp. 852–55. (882a)
*Twentieth-Century Crime and Mystery
  Writers,* 2nd ed., pp. 498–500. (882b)
Jacobs, W. W.; i.e., William Wymark
Bio-bibliographic data:
*Critical Survey of Mystery and Detective
  Fiction,* pp. 928–31. (41)

*The Encyclopedia of Mystery and
Detection*, p. 224. (7)
Jaffe, Jody
Bio-bibliographic data:
Detecting Women 2, p. 101. (877b)
Detecting Women, 3rd ed., p. 140. (877c)
Web site: http://www.stopyourekillingme.
com/jody-jaffe.html
Jahn, Michael
Bio-bibliographic data:
Detecting Men, 1st ed., p. 133. (876)
Web site: http://www.stopyourekillingme.
com/michael-jahn.html; http://
home.att.net/~medj
Jakeman, Jane
Bio-bibliographic data:
Detecting Women, 3rd ed., p. 140. (877c)
Jakes, John
Bio-bibliographic data:
The Encyclopedia of Murder and Mystery,
p. 268. (6)
James, Bert. *See* **Hobson, B.**
James, Bill. *Pseud. for* **Allan James
Tucker**
Bio-bibliographic data:
Detecting Men, 1st ed., p. 134. (876)
*St. James Guide to Crime & Mystery
Writers*, 4th ed., pp. 563–64. (882d)
Personal papers in Mugar Memorial
Library, Boston University.
Web site: http://www.stopyourekillingme.
com/bill-james.html
James, Henry
Bio-bibliographic data:
The Encyclopedia of Murder and Mystery,
p. 268. (6)
James, Henry Colbert
Bio-bibliographic data:
Australian Crime Fiction, p. 125. (207)
James, Martin
Bio-bibliographic data:
Australian Crime Fiction, p. 125. (207)
**James, P. D.; i.e., Phyllis Dorothy James
White, Baroness James**
Bio-bibliographic data:
*British Mystery and Thriller Writers since
1940, First Series*, pp. 210–27. (868)
By a Woman's Hand, 1st ed., pp. 109–11.
(884a)
By a Woman's Hand, 2nd ed., pp. 117–18.
(884b)
Canadian Crime Fiction, p. 279. (209)
*Critical Survey of Mystery and Detective
Fiction*, pp. 932–38. (41)

Designs of Darkness, pp. 14–32. (873)
Detecting Women, 1st ed., pp. 76–77.
(877a)
Detecting Women 2, p. 101. (877b)
Detecting Women, 3rd ed., pp. 140–41.
(877c)
Encyclopedia Mysteriosa, pp. 182–83. (2)
The Encyclopedia of Murder and Mystery,
pp. 268–69. (6)
*The Encyclopedia of Mystery and
Detection*, p. 225. (7)
The Fatal Art of Entertainment, pp. 54–83.
(878)
Great Women Mystery Writers, pp.
167–70. (880)
Mystery and Suspense Writers, pp.
541–57. (884.2)
*100 Masters of Mystery and Detective
Fiction*, pp. 359–66. (37)
*The Oxford Companion to Crime and
Mystery Writing*, p. 241. (4)
*St. James Guide to Crime & Mystery
Writers*, 4th ed., pp. 564–66. (882d)
10 Women of Mystery, pp. 106–23. (864,
865)
13 Mistresses of Murder, pp. 65–74. (871)
*Twentieth-Century Crime and Mystery
Writers*, 1st ed., pp. 855–57. (882a)
*Twentieth-Century Crime and Mystery
Writers*, 2nd ed., pp. 500–501. (882b)
*Twentieth-Century Crime and Mystery
Writers*, 3rd ed., pp. 594–95. (882c)
*Whodunit? A Who's Who in Crime and
Mystery Writing*, p. 107. (5)
Women Authors of Detective Series, pp.
84–90. (882.5)
Women of Mystery, pp. 340–61. (874)
Web site: http://www.stopyourekillingme.
com/p-d-james.html
James, Trevor
Bio-bibliographic data:
Australian Crime Fiction, p. 9. (207)
Jamieson, Heber Carss
Bio-bibliographic data:
Canadian Crime Fiction, p. 110. (209)
Jance, J. A.; i.e., Judith Ann
Bio-bibliographic data:
By a Woman's Hand, 1st ed., pp. 111–12.
(884a)
By a Woman's Hand, 2nd ed., p. 119.
(884b)
Deadly Women, pp. 281–85. (26.5)
Detecting Women, 1st ed., p. 77. (877a)
Detecting Women 2, p. 102. (877b)

Detecting Women, 3rd ed., p. 141. (877c)
The Encyclopedia of Murder and Mystery, p. 269. (6)
St. James Guide to Crime & Mystery Writers, 4th ed., pp. 566–68. (882d)
Speaking of Murder, vol. II, pp. 44–49. (875b)
Whodunit? A Who's Who in Crime and Mystery Writing, pp. 107–8. (5)
Web site: http://www.stopyourekillingme. com/j-a-jance.html; http://www. jajance.com
Janes, Gene
Bio-bibliographic data:
Australian Crime Fiction, pp. 125–26. (207)
Janes, J. Robert; i.e., Joseph
Bio-bibliographic data:
Canadian Crime Fiction, pp. 110–11. (209)
Detecting Men, 1st ed., p. 134. (876)
The Encyclopedia of Murder and Mystery, p. 269. (6)
Whodunit? A Who's Who in Crime and Mystery Writing, p. 108. (5)
Web site: http://www.stopyourekillingme. com/j-robert-janes.html
Janeshutz, Trish. *See* **MacGregor, T. J.**
Janson, Hank
Web site: http://www.hankjanson.org.uk
Japrisot, Sebastien. *Pseud. for* **Jean Baptiste Rossi**
Bio-bibliographic data:
The Encyclopedia of Murder and Mystery, pp. 269–70. (6)
St. James Guide to Crime & Mystery Writers, 4th ed., pp. 568–69. (882d)
Twentieth-Century Crime and Mystery Writers, 1st ed., pp. 1541–42. (882a)
Twentieth-Century Crime and Mystery Writers, 2nd ed., p. 942. (882b)
Twentieth-Century Crime and Mystery Writers, 3rd ed., pp. 1131–132. (882c)
Whodunit? A Who's Who in Crime and Mystery Writing, p. 108. (5)
Jardin, Red: joint pseud. for Eve Burkhardt and Robert Ferdinand Burkhardt (q.q.v.)
Jardine, Quintin
Bio-bibliographic data:
Detecting Men, 1st ed., p. 135. (876)
Web site: http://www.stopyourekillingme. com/quintin-jardine.html; http://

authorpages.hoddersystems.com/ QuintinJardine/frameset.asp
Jargaille, Louis
Bio-bibliographic data:
Canadian Crime Fiction, p. 111. (209)
Jarrett, Cora [Hardy]
Bio-bibliographic data:
The Encyclopedia of Mystery and Detection, p. 225. (7)
Twentieth-Century Crime and Mystery Writers, 1st ed., pp. 858–59. (882a)
Jarvis, Thomas Stinson
Bio-bibliographic data:
Canadian Crime Fiction, p. 111. (209)
Jarvis, William H[enry] P[ope]
Bio-bibliographic data:
Canadian Crime Fiction, p. 112. (209)
Jasmin, Claude
Bio-bibliographic data:
Canadian Crime Fiction, p. 112. (209)
Jason. *Pseud. for* **G. Stannus and Hugh Munro**
Bio-bibliographic data:
Australian Crime Fiction, p. 126. (207)
Jason, Stuart: unidentified house pseud.
Bio-bibliographic data:
Canadian Crime Fiction, p. 257. (209)
Jaspersohn, William
Bio-bibliographic data:
Detecting Men, 1st ed., p. 135. (876)
Jay, Charlotte. *Pseud. for* **Geraldine Mary Jay Halls**
Bio-bibliographic data:
Australian Crime Fiction, pp. 126–27. (207)
Encyclopedia Mysteriosa, p. 183. (2)
The Encyclopedia of Murder and Mystery, p. 270. (6)
St. James Guide to Crime & Mystery Writers, 4th ed., pp. 569–70. (882d)
Twentieth-Century Crime and Mystery Writers, 1st ed., pp. 859–61. (882a)
Twentieth-Century Crime and Mystery Writers, 2nd ed., pp. 501–2. (882b)
Twentieth-Century Crime and Mystery Writers, 3rd ed., pp. 595–96. (882c)
Jay, Geraldine Mary Jay Halls. *See* **Jay, Charlotte**
Jeannel, Jean-André. *See* **Nel, Jean**
Jecks, Michael
Bio-bibliographic data:
Detecting Men, 1st ed., p. 135. (876)
Web site: http://www.stopyourekillingme. com/michael-jecks.html

Jefferies, William. *See* **Deaver, Jeffery**
Jefferis, Barbara [Tarlton]
 Bio-bibliographic data:
 Australian Crime Fiction, pp. 127–28.
 (207)
Jeffers, H. Paul
 Bio-bibliographic data:
 Detecting Men, 1st ed., p. 136. (876)
Jeffries, Graham Montague. *See* **Graeme,**
 Bruce
Jeffries, Ian. *Pseud. for* **Peter Hays**
 Bio-bibliographic data:
 Detecting Men, 1st ed., p. 136. (876)
Jeffries, Roderic [Graeme]
 Bio-bibliographic data:
 Detecting Men, 1st ed., p. 20, 26, 105–6,
 136–37. (876)
 Encyclopedia Mysteriosa, pp. 183–84, (2)
 The Encyclopedia of Murder and Mystery,
 p. 270. (6)
 The Encyclopedia of Mystery and
 Detection, pp. 225–26. (7)
 The Mammoth Encyclopedia of Modern
 Crime Fiction, pp. 255–58. (1)
 St. James Guide to Crime & Mystery
 Writers, 4th ed., pp. 570–74. (882d)
 Twentieth-Century Crime and Mystery
 Writers, 1st ed., pp. 861–65. (882a)
 Twentieth-Century Crime and Mystery
 Writers, 2nd ed., pp. 503–5. (882b)
 Twentieth-Century Crime and Mystery
 Writers, 3rd ed., pp. 596–600. (882c)
 Personal papers in Mugar Memorial
 Library, Boston University.
 Web site: http://www.stopyourekillingme.
 com/roderic-jeffries.html
Jéhin, Jules
 Bio-bibliographic data:
 Canadian Crime Fiction, p. 113. (209)
Jenkins, Charles C[hristopher].
 Bio-bibliographic data:
 Canadian Crime Fiction, p. 113. (209)
Jenkins, Geoffrey
 Bio-bibliographic data:
 Canadian Crime Fiction, p. 279. (209)
 Detecting Men, 1st ed., p. 137. (876)
Jenkins, Herbert [George]
 Bio-bibliographic data:
 Canadian Crime Fiction, p. 279. (209)
Jenkins, Jerry
 Bio-bibliographic data:
 Detecting Men, 1st ed., pp. 137–38. (876)
 Web site: http://www.stopyourekillingme.
 com/jerry-jenkins.html

Jenkins, Robert Smith
 Bio-bibliographic data:
 Canadian Crime Fiction, p. 113. (209)
Jennings, Maureen
 Bio-bibliographic data:
 Canadian Crime Fiction, pp. 113–14.
 (209)
 Detecting Women, 3rd ed., p. 142. (877c)
 Web site: http://www.stopyourekillingme.
 com/maureen-jennings.html;
 http://www.maureenjennings.com
Jepson, Selwyn
 Bio-bibliographic data:
 Encyclopedia Mysteriosa, p. 184. (2)
 The Encyclopedia of Mystery and
 Detection, p. 226. (7)
 Twentieth-Century Crime and Mystery
 Writers, 1st ed., pp. 865–67. (882a)
 Twentieth-Century Crime and Mystery
 Writers, 2nd ed., pp. 506–7. (882b)
 Twentieth-Century Crime and Mystery
 Writers, 3rd ed., pp. 600–601. (882c)
Jesse, F. Tennyson; i.e., Fryniwyd
 Bio-bibliographic data:
 British Mystery Writers, 1920–1939, pp.
 176–81. (867)
 The Encyclopedia of Murder and Mystery,
 p. 271. (6)
 The Encyclopedia of Mystery and
 Detection, pp. 226–27. (7)
 Twentieth-Century Crime and Mystery
 Writers, 1st ed., pp. 868–70. (882a)
 Twentieth-Century Crime and Mystery
 Writers, 2nd ed., pp. 507–8. (882b)
 Twentieth-Century Crime and Mystery
 Writers, 3rd ed., pp. 601–3. (882c)
Jessup, Audrey
 Bio-bibliographic data:
 Canadian Crime Fiction, p. 36. (209)
Jessup, Richard
 Bio-bibliographic data:
 Twentieth-Century Crime and Mystery
 Writers, 2nd ed., pp. 508–9. (882b)
 Twentieth-Century Crime and Mystery
 Writers, 3rd ed., pp. 603–4. (882c)
Jevons, Marshall. *Pseud. for* **William Breit**
 and Kenneth G. Elzinga
 Bio-bibliographic data:
 Detecting Men, 1st ed., p. 138. (876)
Jiles, Paulette
 Bio-bibliographic data:
 Canadian Crime Fiction, p. 114. (209)
Jillett, Neil
 Bio-bibliographic data:

Australian Crime Fiction, p. 128, 193. (207)
Jobson, A. E.
Bio-bibliographic data:
Australian Crime Fiction, p. 128. (207)
Jobson, Hamilton
Bio-bibliographic data:
Twentieth-Century Crime and Mystery Writers, 1st ed., pp. 870–71. (882a)
Twentieth-Century Crime and Mystery Writers, 2nd ed., pp. 509–10. (882b)
John, Alix. *See* **Jones, Alice**
John, Cathie. *Pseud. for* **Cathie and John Celestri**
Bio-bibliographic data:
Detecting Women, 3rd ed., p. 142. (877c)
Web site: http://www.stopyourekillingme. com/cathie-john.html; http://www. cathiejohn.com
John, Katherine. *Pseud. for* **Karo Nadolny**
Bio-bibliographic data:
Detecting Women, 3rd ed., p. 142. (877c)
John, Owen
Bio-bibliographic data:
Canadian Crime Fiction, p. 257. (209)
Johns, Veronica Parker
Bio-bibliographic data:
Detecting Women 2, p. 102. (877b)
Encyclopedia Mysteriosa, pp. 184–85. (2)
The Encyclopedia of Mystery and Detection, p. 227. (7)
St. James Guide to Crime & Mystery Writers, 4th ed., pp. 574–75. (882d)
Twentieth-Century Crime and Mystery Writers, 2nd ed., pp. 510–11. (882b)
Twentieth-Century Crime and Mystery Writers, 3rd ed., pp. 604–5. (882c)
Johns, W. E.; i.e., William Earl
Bio-bibliographic data:
Canadian Crime Fiction, p. 257. (209)
Johnson, Barbara
Bio-bibliographic data:
Detecting Women, 3rd ed., p. 143. (877c)
Web site: http://www.stopyourekillingme. com/barbara-johnson.html
Johnson, Carl
Bio-bibliographic data:
Australian Crime Fiction, p. 128. (207)
Johnson, Colin. *See* **Mudrooroo**
Johnson, Dolores
Bio-bibliographic data:
Detecting Women, 3rd ed., p. 143. (877c)
Web site: http://www.stopyourekillingme. com/dolores-johnson.html

Johnson, E. Pauline; i.e., Emily
Bio-bibliographic data:
Canadian Crime Fiction, pp. 114–15. (209)
Johnson, E. Richard; i.e., Emil Richard
Bio-bibliographic data:
Detecting Men, 1st ed., p. 138. (876)
Encyclopedia Mysteriosa, p. 185. (2)
The Mammoth Encyclopedia of Modern Crime Fiction, pp. 258–59. (1)
St. James Guide to Crime & Mystery Writers, 4th ed., pp. 575–76. (882d)
Twentieth-Century Crime and Mystery Writers, 1st ed., p. 872. (882a)
Twentieth-Century Crime and Mystery Writers, 2nd ed., p. 511. (882b)
Twentieth-Century Crime and Mystery Writers, 3rd ed., p. 605. (882c)
Personal papers in Mugar Memorial Library, Boston University.
Web site: http://www.stopyourekillingme. com/e-richard-johnson.html
Johnson, Lee. *See* **Johnson, Lillian Beatrice**
Johnson, Lillian Beatrice
Bio-bibliographic data:
Canadian Crime Fiction, p. 115. (209)
Johnson, Owen [McMahon]
Bio-bibliographic data:
The Encyclopedia of Mystery and Detection, p. 227. (7)
Johnson, [Walter] Ryerson
Bio-bibliographic data:
Canadian Crime Fiction, p. 257. (209)
Johnston, George H.; i.e., George Henry
Bio-bibliographic data:
Australian Crime Fiction, p. 129, 175–76. (207)
Johnston, Madeleine
Bio-bibliographic data:
Canadian Crime Fiction, p. 257. (209)
Johnston, Velda
Bio-bibliographic data:
By a Woman's Hand, 1st ed., pp. 112–13. (884a)
By a Woman's Hand, 2nd ed., pp. 119–20. (884b)
Critical Survey of Mystery and Detective Fiction, pp. 939–42. (41)
St. James Guide to Crime & Mystery Writers, 4th ed., pp. 576–77. (882d)
Twentieth-Century Crime and Mystery Writers, 2nd ed., pp. 512–13. (882b)

Twentieth-Century Crime and Mystery Writers, 3rd ed., pp. 606–7. (882c)

Jolley, Elizabeth
Bio-bibliographic data:
Australian Crime Fiction, p. 145, 146. (207)

Jonas, George
Bio-bibliographic data:
Canadian Crime Fiction, pp. 115–16. (209)

Jones, Alice
Bio-bibliographic data:
Canadian Crime Fiction, p. 114, 116. (209)

Jones, D. J. H.: unidentified pseud.
Bio-bibliographic data:
Detecting Women, 3rd ed., p. 143. (877c)

Jones, Dennis
Bio-bibliographic data:
Canadian Crime Fiction, p. 116, 201–2. (209)

Jones, Elwyn
Bio-bibliographic data:
Australian Crime Fiction, p. 129. (207)

Jones, Frank
Bio-bibliographic data:
Canadian Crime Fiction, pp. 116–17. (209)

Jones, Hazel Wynn
Bio-bibliographic data:
Detecting Women 2, pp. 102–3. (877b)

Jones, H[enry James O'Brien]. Bedford. *See* **Bedford-Jones, H[enry James O'Brien].**

Jones, James Thomas. *See* **Leslie, Mary**

Jones, Philip [Mitchell]
Bio-bibliographic data:
Australian Crime Fiction, p. 129. (207)

Jones, Susan Carleton [Morrow]
Bio-bibliographic data:
Canadian Crime Fiction, p. 37, 117. (209)

Jones, Tim Wynne. *See* **Wynne-Jones, Tim**

Jordan, Jennifer
Bio-bibliographic data:
Detecting Women 2, p. 103. (877b)
Detecting Women, 3rd ed., p. 144. (877c)
Web site: http://www.stopyourekillingme.com/jennifer-jordan.html

Jordan, Maureen McAvoy
Bio-bibliographic data:
Canadian Crime Fiction, p. 117. (209)

Jorgensen, Christine T.
Bio-bibliographic data:
Detecting Women 2, p. 103. (877b)

Detecting Women, 3rd ed., p. 144. (877c)
Web site: http://www.stopyourekillingme.com/christine-t-jorgensen.html

Joseph, Alison
Bio-bibliographic data:
Detecting Women, 3rd ed., pp. 144–45. (877c)
Women of Mystery, p. 435. (874)

Joske, Anne Neville. *See* **Neville, Margot**

Joyce, James
Bio-bibliographic data:
The Encyclopedia of Murder and Mystery, p. 272. (6)

Judd, Bob
Bio-bibliographic data:
Detecting Men, 1st ed., p. 139. (876)

Judd, James
Bio-bibliographic data:
Canadian Crime Fiction, p. 117. (209)

Judd, Sara [Hutton] Bowen. *See* **Bowen-Judd, Sara [Hutton]**

Julien, Susanne
Bio-bibliographic data:
Canadian Crime Fiction, p. 113. (209)

Juniper, Alex. *Pseud. for* **Janette Turner Hospital**
Bio-bibliographic data:
Australian Crime Fiction, p.129–30, 146. (207)
Canadian Crime Fiction, p. 106, 117. (209)

Junor, Charles
Bio-bibliographic data:
Australian Crime Fiction, p. 130. (207)

Juteau, Marjolaine
Bio-bibliographic data:
Canadian Crime Fiction, p. 117. (209)

K

Kabal, A. M. *See* **Bhabra, H. S.**

Kaewert, Julie Wallin
Bio-bibliographic data:
Detecting Women, 3rd ed., p. 145. (877c)
Web site: http://stopyourekillingme.com/julie-kaewert.html

Kahn, Mary. *See* **Kahnykevych, Tania Maria**

Kahn, Michael A.
Bio-bibliographic data:
Detecting Men, 1st ed., p. 139. (876)
Web site: http://stopyourekillingme.com/michael-a-kahn.html

Kahn, Sharon
Bio-bibliographic data:

Detecting Women, 3rd ed., p. 145. (877c)
Web site: http://stopyourekillingme.com/
sharon-kahn.html

Kahnykevych, Tania Maria
Bio-bibliographic data:
Canadian Crime Fiction, p. 36, 117–18,
224. (209)

Kakonis, Tom
Bio-bibliographic data:
Detecting Men, 1st ed., p. 139. (876)

Kallen, Lucille
Bio-bibliographic data:
By a Woman's Hand, 1st ed., pp. 114–15.
(884a)
By a Woman's Hand, 2nd ed., pp. 121–22.
(884b)
Detecting Women, 1st ed., p. 77. (877a)
Detecting Women 2, p. 103. (877b)
Detecting Women, 3rd ed., pp. 145–46.
(877c)
Encyclopedia Mysteriosa, p. 188. (2)
Great Women Mystery Writers, pp.
171–73. (880)
*Twentieth-Century Crime and Mystery
Writers,* 2nd ed., pp. 513–14. (882b)
*Twentieth-Century Crime and Mystery
Writers,* 3rd ed., p. 608. (882c)
Web site: http://stopyourekillingme.com/
lucille-kallen.html

Kaminsky, Stuart M[elvin]
Bio-bibliographic data:
Canadian Crime Fiction, p. 280. (209)
*Critical Survey of Mystery and Detective
Fiction,* pp. 943–47. (41)
Detecting Men, 1st ed., p. 140. (876)
Encyclopedia Mysteriosa, p. 188. (2)
The Encyclopedia of Murder and Mystery,
p. 273. (6)
*The Mammoth Encyclopedia of Modern
Crime Fiction,* pp. 259–60. (1)
*St. James Guide to Crime & Mystery
Writers,* 4th ed., pp. 579–81. (882d)
*Twentieth-Century Crime and Mystery
Writers,* 2nd ed., pp. 514–15. (882b)
*Twentieth-Century Crime and Mystery
Writers,* 3rd ed., pp. 609–11. (882c)
Web site:
http://www.stuartkaminsky.com;
http://stopyourekillingme.com/
stuart-m-kaminsky.html

Kane [Martin]. *Pseud. for* **C. J. McKenzie**
Bio-bibliographic data:
Australian Crime Fiction, p. 131. (207)

Kane, Frank
Bio-bibliographic data:
The Encyclopedia of Murder and Mystery,
pp. 273–74. (6)
*St. James Guide to Crime & Mystery
Writers,* 4th ed., pp. 582–83. (882d)
*Twentieth-Century Crime and Mystery
Writers,* 1st ed., pp. 873–75. (882a)
*Twentieth-Century Crime and Mystery
Writers,* 2nd ed., pp. 515–16. (882b)
*Twentieth-Century Crime and Mystery
Writers,* 3rd ed., pp. 611–12. (882c)
Web site: http://www.thrillingdetective.
com/trivia/kane.html

Kane, Henry
Bio-bibliographic data:
Encyclopedia Mysteriosa, p. 188. (2)
*The Encyclopedia of Mystery and
Detection,* p. 228. (7)
*St. James Guide to Crime & Mystery
Writers,* 4th ed., pp. 583–84. (882d)
*Twentieth-Century Crime and Mystery
Writers,* 1st ed., pp. 875–78. (882a)
*Twentieth-Century Crime and Mystery
Writers,* 2nd ed., pp. 516–18. (882b)
*Twentieth-Century Crime and Mystery
Writers,* 3rd ed., pp. 612–14. (882c)
Personal papers in Mugar Memorial
Library, Boston University.

Kane, Jonathan. *See* **Wilson, Derek**

Kantner, Rob; i.e., T. Robin
Bio-bibliographic data:
Detecting Men, 1st ed., p. 141. (876)
*The Mammoth Encyclopedia of Modern
Crime Fiction,* p. 261. (1)
Web site: http://stopyourekillingme.com/
rob-kantner.html; http://www.
robkantner.com

Kantor, [Benjamin] MacKinlay
Bio-bibliographic data:
The Encyclopedia of Murder and Mystery,
p. 274. (6)
*The Encyclopedia of Mystery and
Detection,* p. 228. (7)

Karapanou, Marta
Bio-bibliographic data:
The Encyclopedia of Murder and Mystery,
p. 274. (6)

Karlson, Hans: house pseud.
Bio-bibliographic data:
Australian Crime Fiction, p. 131 (207)

Karni, Michaela. *See* **Berne, Karin**

Karr, Leona
Bio-bibliographic data:

Detecting Women, 1st ed., p. 78. (877a)
Detecting Women 2, p. 104. (877b)
Web site: http://stopyourekillingme.com/
leona-karr.html
Kata, Elizabeth
Bio-bibliographic data:
Australian Crime Fiction, p. 131. (207)
Katz, Jon
Bio-bibliographic data:
Detecting Men, 1st ed., p. 141. (876)
Web site: http://stopyourekillingme.com/
jon-katz.html
Katz, Michael J.
Bio-bibliographic data:
Detecting Men, 1st ed., p. 141. (876)
Kaufelt, David A.
Bio-bibliographic data:
Detecting Men, 1st ed., p. 142. (876)
Kavanagh, Dan. *See* **Barnes, Julian**
Kavanagh, Paul. *See* **Block, Lawrence**
Keane, Kay. *Pseud. for* **Kay [Katherine]
Kearney**
Bio-bibliographic data:
Australian Crime Fiction, p. 132. (207)
Kearney, Kay. *See* **Keane, Kay**
Kearsley, Susanna
Bio-bibliographic data:
Canadian Crime Fiction, p. 118. (209)
**Keating, H. R. F.; i.e, Henry Reymond
Fitzwalter**
Bio-bibliographic data:
*British Mystery and Thriller Writers since
1940, First Series,* pp. 228–39. (868)
*Critical Survey of Mystery and Detective
Fiction,* pp. 948–53. (41)
Detecting Men, 1st ed., p. 124, 142–43.
(876)
Encyclopedia Mysteriosa, pp. 189–90. (2)
The Encyclopedia of Murder and Mystery,
pp. 275–76. (6)
*The Encyclopedia of Mystery and
Detection,* pp. 228–29. (7)
*The Mammoth Encyclopedia of Modern
Crime Fiction,* pp. 262–64. (1)
*The Oxford Companion to Crime and
Mystery Writing,* p. 252. (4)
*St. James Guide to Crime & Mystery
Writers,* 4th ed., pp. 584–87. (882d)
Twelve Englishmen of Mystery, pp.
276–301. (865)
*Twentieth-Century Crime and Mystery
Writers,* 1st ed., pp. 878–81. (882a)
*Twentieth-Century Crime and Mystery
Writers,* 2nd ed., pp. 518–20. (882b)

*Twentieth-Century Crime and Mystery
Writers,* 3rd ed., pp. 615–17. (882c)
*Whodunit? A Who's Who in Crime and
Mystery Writing,* p. 111. (5)
Web site: http://www.twbooks.co.uk/
authors/hrfkeating.html; http://
stopyourekillingme.com/h-r-f-keating.
html
Keegan, Alex
Bio-bibliographic data:
Detecting Men, 1st ed., p. 143. (876)
Web site: http://stopyourekillingme.com/
alex-keegan.html; http://www.
btinternet.com/~alex.keegan1
Keeler, Harry Stephen
Bio-bibliographic data:
*Critical Survey of Mystery and Detective
Fiction,* pp. 954–59. (41)
Encyclopedia Mysteriosa, p. 190. (2)
*The Encyclopedia of Mystery and
Detection,* p. 229. (7)
*St. James Guide to Crime & Mystery
Writers,* 4th ed., pp. 587–88. (882d)
*Twentieth-Century Crime and Mystery
Writers,* 1st ed., pp. 881–84. (882a)
*Twentieth-Century Crime and Mystery
Writers,* 2nd ed., pp. 520–22. (882b)
*Twentieth-Century Crime and Mystery
Writers,* 3rd ed., pp. 617–19. (882c)
Web site: http://members.aol.com/
harryskeeler;
Harry Stephen Keeler Society
c/o Richard Polt
4745 Winton Road
Cincinnati, OH 45232
http://xavier.xu.edu/~polt/
keeler.html
Fender Tucker
c/o Ramble House
443 Gladstone Boulevard
Shreveport, LA 71104
http://www.ramblehouse.bigstep.
com
**Keene, Carolyn. Pseud. for Edward L.
Stratemeyer, Harriet S. Adams, and
many others. The following entries
concentrate on the output of
Stratemeyer and Adams.**
Bio-bibliographic data:
Canadian Crime Fiction, p. 118, 257.
(209)
*The Encyclopedia of Mystery and
Detection,* pp. 229–30. (7)

Keene, Day. *Pseud. for* **Gunard Hjerststedt**
Bio-bibliographic data:
The Big Book of Noir, p. 187. (24)
Encyclopedia Mysteriosa, pp. 190–91. (2)
St. James Guide to Crime & Mystery Writers, 4th ed., pp. 588–89. (882d)
Twentieth-Century Crime and Mystery Writers, 1st ed., pp. 884–86. (882a)
Twentieth-Century Crime and Mystery Writers, 2nd ed., pp. 522–23. (882b)
Twentieth-Century Crime and Mystery Writers, 3rd ed., pp. 619–20. (882c)
http://www.miskatonic.org/rara-avis/biblio/keene.html; http://www.thrillingdetective.com/trivia/keene.html

Keene, Faraday. *See* **Jarrett, Cora**

Keens-Douglas, Ricardo
Bio-bibliographic data:
Canadian Crime Fiction, p. 118. (209)

Keilstrup, Margaret
Bio-bibliographic data:
By a Woman's Hand, 1st ed., pp. 133–34. (884a)
By a Woman's Hand, 2nd ed., p. 143. (884b)
Detecting Women, 1st ed., p. 88. (877a)
Detecting Women 2, p. 121. (877b)
Detecting Women, 3rd ed., p. 161, 167. (877c)

Keirstead, B. S.; i.e., Burton Seely
Bio-bibliographic data:
Canadian Crime Fiction, p. 118. (209)

Keith, J. Kilmeney. *See* **Gilbert, Anthony**

Kelland, Clarence Budington
Bio-bibliographic data:
Canadian Crime Fiction, p. 257. (209)
Twentieth-Century Crime and Mystery Writers, 1st ed., pp. 886–89. (882a)

Kellerman, Faye [Marder]
Bio-bibliographic data:
By a Woman's Hand, 1st ed., pp. 115–16. (884a)
By a Woman's Hand, 2nd ed., p. 122. (884b)
Detecting Women, 1st ed., p. 78. (877a)
Detecting Women 2, p. 104. (877b)
Detecting Women, 3rd ed., p. 146. (877c)
Encyclopedia Mysteriosa, p. 191. (2)
The Encyclopedia of Murder and Mystery, p. 276. (6)
Great Women Mystery Writers, pp. 173–76. (880)

The Mammoth Encyclopedia of Modern Crime Fiction, pp. 264–65. (1)
St. James Guide to Crime & Mystery Writers, 4th ed., pp. 589–91. (882d)
Twentieth-Century Crime and Mystery Writers, 3rd ed., pp. 620–21. (882c)
Whodunit? A Who's Who in Crime and Mystery Writing, p. 111. (5)
Web site: http://stopyourekillingme.com/faye-kellerman.html

Kellerman, Jonathan
Bio-bibliographic data:
Detecting Men, 1st ed., p. 143. (876)
Encyclopedia Mysteriosa, p. 191. (2)
The Encyclopedia of Murder and Mystery, p. 276. (6)
The Mammoth Encyclopedia of Modern Crime Fiction, pp. 265–66. (1)
St. James Guide to Crime & Mystery Writers, 4th ed., pp. 591–92. (882d)
Twentieth-Century Crime and Mystery Writers, 3rd ed., pp. 621–23. (882c)
Whodunit? A Who's Who in Crime and Mystery Writing, pp. 111–12. (5)
Web site http://www.mysterynet.com/jkellerman; http://stopyourekillingme.com/jonathan.kellerman.html

Kelley, Patrick
Bio-bibliographic data:
Detecting Men, 1st ed., p. 144. (876)

Kelley Jr., Thomas P[atrick].
Bio-bibliographic data:
Canadian Crime Fiction, pp. 118–19. (209)

Kellogg, Marne Davis
Bio-bibliographic data:
Detecting Women, 3rd ed., p. 146. (877c)
Web site: http://stopyourekillingme.com/marne-davis-kellogg.html; http://marniedaviskellogg.com

Kellow, Kathleen. *See* **Holt, Victoria**

Kelly, Judith [Sage]
Bio-bibliographic data:
Canadian Crime Fiction, p. 119. (209)

Kelly, Martha Mott. *See* **Quentin, Patrick**

Kelly, Mary [Theresa Coolican]
Bio-bibliographic data:
By a Woman's Hand, 2nd ed., pp. 122–23. (884b)
Critical Survey of Mystery and Detective Fiction, pp. 960–64. (41)
Detecting Women 2, p. 104. (877b)
Detecting Women, 3rd ed., p. 147. (877c)
Encyclopedia Mysteriosa, pp. 191–92. (2)

St. James Guide to Crime & Mystery Writers, 4th ed., pp. 592–93. (882d)
Twentieth-Century Crime and Mystery Writers, 1st ed., pp. 889–90. (882a)
Twentieth-Century Crime and Mystery Writers, 2nd ed., pp. 523–24. (882b)
Twentieth-Century Crime and Mystery Writers, 3rd ed., pp. 623–24. (882c)
Personal papers in Mugar Memorial Library, Boston University.

Kelly, Mary Ann
Bio-bibliographic data:
Detecting Women, 1st ed., p. 78. (877a)
Detecting Women 2, pp. 104–5. (877b)
Detecting Women, 3rd ed., p. 147. (877c)

Kelly, Nora [Hickson]
Bio-bibliographic data:
By a Woman's Hand, 1st ed., p. 116. (884a)
By a Woman's Hand, 2nd ed., pp. 123–24. (884b)
Canadian Crime Fiction, p. 119. (209)
Detecting Women, 1st ed., p. 78. (877a)
Detecting Women 2, p. 105. (877b)
Detecting Women, 3rd ed., pp. 147–48. (877c)
Web site: http://stopyourekillingme.com/ nora-kelly.html

Kelly, Susan
Bio-bibliographic data:
By a Woman's Hand, 1st ed., pp. 116–17. (884a)
By a Woman's Hand, 2nd ed., p. 124. (884b)
Detecting Women, 1st ed., p. 79. (877a)
Detecting Women 2, p. 105. (877b)
Detecting Women, 3rd ed., p. 148. (877c)
Great Women Mystery Writers, pp. 176–78. (880)
Web site: http://stopyourekillingme.com/ susan-kelly.html

Kelly, Susan B.
Bio-bibliographic data:
By a Woman's Hand, 1st ed., pp. 117–18. (884a)
By a Woman's Hand, 2nd ed., pp. 124–25. (884b)
Detecting Women, 1st ed., p. 79. (877a)
Detecting Women 2, p. 105. (877b)
Detecting Women, 3rd ed., p. 148. (877c)
Web site: http://stopyourekillingme.com/ susan-b-kelly.html

Kelly, Vince; i.e., Vincent Gatton
Bio-bibliographic data:

Australian Crime Fiction, p. 132. (207)

Kelman, Judith
Bio-bibliographic data:
By a Woman's Hand, 1st ed., p. 118. (884a)
By a Woman's Hand, 2nd ed., p. 125. (884b)
The Mammoth Encyclopedia of Modern Crime Fiction, pp. 266–67. (1)
Web site: http://www.jkelman.com; http://stopyourekillingme.com/ judith-kelman.html

Kelner, Toni L. P.
Bio-bibliographic data:
By a Woman's Hand, 2nd ed., pp. 125–26. (884b)
Detecting Women, 1st ed., p. 79. (877a)
Detecting Women 2, p. 106. (877b)
Detecting Women, 3rd ed., pp. 148–49. (877c)
Web site: http://stopyourekillingme.com/ toni-l-p-kelner.html

Kemelman, Harry
Bio-bibliographic data:
Critical Survey of Mystery and Detective Fiction, pp. 965–72. (41)
Detecting Men, 1st ed., p. 144. (876)
Encyclopedia Mysteriosa, p. 192. (2)
The Encyclopedia of Murder and Mystery, pp. 277–78. (6)
The Encyclopedia of Mystery and Detection, pp. 230–31. (7)
The Mammoth Encyclopedia of Modern Crime Fiction, pp. 267–68. (1)
100 Masters of Mystery and Detective Fiction, pp. 367–74. (37)
St. James Guide to Crime & Mystery Writers, 4th ed., pp. 593–94. (882d)
Twentieth-Century Crime and Mystery Writers, 1st ed., pp. 891–92. (882a)
Twentieth-Century Crime and Mystery Writers, 2nd ed., pp. 524–25. (882b)
Twentieth-Century Crime and Mystery Writers, 3rd ed., pp. 624–25. (882c)
Whodunit? A Who's Who in Crime and Mystery Writing, p. 112. (5)
Web site: http://stopyourekillingme.com/ harry-kemelman.html

Kemprecos, Paul
Bio-bibliographic data:
Detecting Men, 1st ed., pp. 144–45. (876)
Web site: http://stopyourekillingme.com/ paul-kemprecos.html

Kendall, Ralph S[elwood]
Bio-bibliographic data:
Canadian Crime Fiction, p. 119. (209)
Kendrake, Carleton. *See* **Gardner, Erle Stanley**
Kendrick, Baynard H[ardwick].
Bio-bibliographic data:
Canadian Crime Fiction, p. 280. (209)
Critical Survey of Mystery and Detective Fiction, p. 973. (41)
Encyclopedia Mysteriosa, p. 192. (2)
The Encyclopedia of Murder and Mystery, p. 278. (6)
The Encyclopedia of Mystery and Detection, p. 231. (7)
100 Masters of Mystery and Detective Fiction, pp. 375–80. (37)
St. James Guide to Crime & Mystery Writers, 4th ed., pp. 595–96. (882d)
Twentieth-Century Crime and Mystery Writers, 1st ed., pp. 892–94. (882a)
Twentieth-Century Crime and Mystery Writers, 2nd ed., pp. 525–26. (882b)
Twentieth-Century Crime and Mystery Writers, 3rd ed., pp. 625–26. (882c)
Keneally, Tom; i.e., Thomas Michael
Bio-bibliographic data:
Australian Crime Fiction, pp. 132–33. (207)
The Encyclopedia of Murder and Mystery, p. 278. (6)
Kennealy, Jerry
Bio-bibliographic data:
Detecting Men, 1st ed., p. 145. (876)
Encyclopedia Mysteriosa, p. 192. (2)
The Mammoth Encyclopedia of Modern Crime Fiction, pp. 268–69. (1)
Web site: http://stopyourekillingme.com/jerry-kennealy.html
Kenneally, Jerry. *See* **Kennealy, Jerry**
Kennedy, Howard Angus
Bio-bibliographic data:
Canadian Crime Fiction, pp. 119–20. (209)
Kennedy, John De N[avarre], O.B.E., Q.C.
Bio-bibliographic data:
Canadian Crime Fiction, p. 120. (209)
Kennedy, Milward. *Pseud. for* **Milward Rodon Kennedy Burge**
Bio-bibliographic data:
Canadian Crime Fiction, p. 248, 257. (209)
The Encyclopedia of Mystery and Detection, p. 233. (7)

Twentieth-Century Crime and Mystery Writers, 1st ed., pp. 894–96. (882a)
. *Twentieth-Century Crime and Mystery Writers*, 2nd ed., pp. 526–27. (882b)
Twentieth-Century Crime and Mystery Writers, 3rd ed., pp. 626–27. (882c)
Kennett, Shirley
Bio-bibliographic data:
Detecting Women, 3rd ed., p. 149. (877c)
Web site: http://stopyourekillingme.com/shirley-kennett.html; http://www.shirleykennett.com
Kenney, Susan
Bio-bibliographic data:
By a Woman's Hand, 1st ed., pp. 118–19. (884a)
By a Woman's Hand, 2nd ed., p. 126. (884b)
Detecting Women, 1st ed., p. 80. (877a)
Detecting Women 2, p. 106. (877b)
Detecting Women, 3rd ed., p. 149. (877c)
Great Women Mystery Writers, pp. 178–79. (880)
Kenny, Charles J. *See* **Gardner, Erle Stanley**
Kenny, Robert John
Bio-bibliographic data:
Australian Crime Fiction, p. 133. (207)
Kenrick, Tony; i.e., Anthony Arthur
Bio-bibliographic data:
Australian Crime Fiction, pp. 133–34. (207)
Canadian Crime Fiction, p. 280. (209)
Encyclopedia Mysteriosa, p. 193. (2)
St. James Guide to Crime & Mystery Writers, 4th ed., pp. 596–97. (882d)
Twentieth-Century Crime and Mystery Writers, 1st ed., pp. 896–97. (882a)
Twentieth-Century Crime and Mystery Writers, 2nd ed., pp. 527–28. (882b)
Twentieth-Century Crime and Mystery Writers, 3rd ed., pp. 627–29. (882c)
Kensch, Otto: house pseud.
Bio-bibliographic data:
Australian Crime Fiction, p. 134. (207)
Kent, Bill
Bio-bibliographic data:
Detecting Men, 1st ed., p. 145. (876)
Kent, Larry. Pseud. used by many writers including Don Haring (q.v.)
Bio-bibliographic data:
Australian Crime Fiction, pp. 134–43. (207)

Kent, Paul
Bio-bibliographic data:
Canadian Crime Fiction, p. 120. (209)
Kent, Winona
Bio-bibliographic data:
Canadian Crime Fiction, pp. 120–21.
(209)
Kenyon, Charles R.
Bio-bibliographic data:
Canadian Crime Fiction, p. 121. (209)
Kenyon, Michael
Bio-bibliographic data:
Detecting Men, 1st ed., p. 146. (876)
Encyclopedia Mysteriosa, p. 193. (2)
*The Mammoth Encyclopedia of Modern
Crime Fiction,* pp. 269–70. (1)
*St. James Guide to Crime & Mystery
Writers,* 4th ed., pp. 597–98. (882d)
*Twentieth-Century Crime and Mystery
Writers,* 1st ed., pp. 897–98. (882a)
*Twentieth-Century Crime and Mystery
Writers,* 2nd ed., pp. 528–29. (882b)
*Twentieth-Century Crime and Mystery
Writers,* 3rd ed., pp. 629–30. (882c)
Web site: http://stopyourekillingme.com/
michael-kenyon.html
Kerr, Philip
Bio-bibliographic data:
Detecting Men, 1st ed., p. 146. (876)
The Encyclopedia of Murder and Mystery,
p. 279. (6)
*St. James Guide to Crime & Mystery
Writers,* 4th ed., pp. 598–99. (882d)
Web site: http://stopyourekillingme.com/
philip-kerr.html
Kersh, Gerald
Bio-bibliographic data:
*Critical Survey of Mystery and Detective
Fiction,* pp. 979–984. (41)
The Encyclopedia of Murder and Mystery,
p. 279. (6)
*The Encyclopedia of Mystery and
Detection,* p. 233. (7)
*St. James Guide to Crime & Mystery
Writers,* 4th ed., pp. 599–600. (882d)
*Twentieth-Century Crime and Mystery
Writers,* 1st ed., pp. 899–901. (882a)
*Twentieth-Century Crime and Mystery
Writers,* 2nd ed., pp. 529–30. (882b)
*Twentieth-Century Crime and Mystery
Writers,* 3rd ed., pp. 630–31. (882c)
Kershaw, Valerie
Bio-bibliographic data:
Detecting Women, 3rd ed., p. 150. (877c)

Kettner, Carla
Bio-bibliographic data:
Australian Crime Fiction, p. 9. (207)
Keverne, Richard. *Pseud. for* **Clifford
James Wheeler Hosken**
Bio-bibliographic data:
*Twentieth-Century Crime and Mystery
Writers,* 1st ed., pp. 901–2. (882a)
Key, Sean A. *See* **Coughlin, William J.**
Khalo, Michel
Bio-bibliographic data:
Canadian Crime Fiction, p. 121. (209)
Kiecolt-Glaser, Janice
Bio-bibliographic data:
Detecting Women, 3rd ed., p. 150. (877c)
Kienzle, William X[avier].
Bio-bibliographic data:
Detecting Men, 1st ed., pp. 146–47. (876)
Encyclopedia Mysteriosa, p. 194. (2)
The Encyclopedia of Murder and Mystery,
p. 280. (6)
*The Mammoth Encyclopedia of Modern
Crime Fiction,* p. 270. (1)
*St. James Guide to Crime & Mystery
Writers,* 4th ed., pp. 600–602. (882d)
*Twentieth-Century Crime and Mystery
Writers,* 2nd ed., pp. 530–31. (882b)
*Twentieth-Century Crime and Mystery
Writers,* 3rd ed., pp. 631–32. (882c)
Personal papers in University of Detroit
Library, Michigan.
Web site: http://stopyourekillingme.com/
william-x-kienzle.html
Kiernan, Liam
Bio-bibliographic data:
Canadian Crime Fiction, p. 121. (209)
Kijewski, Karen
Bio-bibliographic data:
By a Woman's Hand, 1st ed., pp. 119–20.
(884a)
By a Woman's Hand, 2nd ed., p. 127.
(884b)
Detecting Women, 1st ed., p. 80. (877a)
Detecting Women 2, p. 106. (877b)
Detecting Women, 3rd ed., pp. 150–51.
(877c)
Great Women Mystery Writers, pp.
179–81. (880)
*The Mammoth Encyclopedia of Modern
Crime Fiction,* pp. 270–71. (1)
*St. James Guide to Crime & Mystery
Writers,* 4th ed., pp. 602–3. (882d)
*Whodunit? A Who's Who in Crime and
Mystery Writing,* p. 112. (5)

Web site: http://stopyourekillingme.com/
karen-kijewski.html

Kilgore, Alex
Bio-bibliographic data:
Canadian Crime Fiction, p. 257. (209)

Kilian, Crawford
Bio-bibliographic data:
Canadian Crime Fiction, p. 121. (209)

Kilian, Michael
Bio-bibliographic data:
Canadian Crime Fiction, pp. 257–58.
(209)

Kilmer, Nicholas
Bio-bibliographic data:
Detecting Men, 1st ed., p. 147. (876)

Kilpatrick, Nancy
Bio-bibliographic data:
Canadian Crime Fiction, p. 121, 122.
(209)

Kimmins, Anthony [Martin]
Bio-bibliographic data:
Australian Crime Fiction, pp. 143–44.
(207)

Kincaid, D. *Pseud. for* Bert Fields
Bio-bibliographic data:
Detecting Men, 1st ed., p. 147. (876)

King, [William Benjamin] Basil
Bio-bibliographic data:
Canadian Crime Fiction, p. 122. (209)

King, C[harles]. Daly
Bio-bibliographic data:
The Encyclopedia of Murder and Mystery,
pp. 281–82. (6)
*The Encyclopedia of Mystery and
Detection,* pp. 233–34. (7)
*Twentieth-Century Crime and Mystery
Writers,* 1st ed., pp. 902–4. (882a)
*Twentieth-Century Crime and Mystery
Writers,* 2nd ed., pp. 531–32. (882b)

King, Frank
Bio-bibliographic data:
Detecting Men, 1st ed., pp. 18, 148. (876)
Detecting Women, 1st ed., p. 19. (877a)
*The Mammoth Encyclopedia of Modern
Crime Fiction,* pp. 27–28. (1)
Web site: http://stopyourekillingme.com/
frank-king.html

King, Laurie R.
Bio-bibliographic data:
By a Woman's Hand, 2nd ed., pp. 127–28.
(884b)
Deadly Women, pp. 341–45. (26.5)
Detecting Women, 1st ed., p. 80. (877a)
Detecting Women 2, pp. 106–7. (877b)

Detecting Women, 3rd ed., p. 151. (877c)
The Encyclopedia of Murder and Mystery,
p. 282. (6)
*The Mammoth Encyclopedia of Modern
Crime Fiction,* pp. 271–72. (1)
*St. James Guide to Crime & Mystery
Writers,* 4th ed., pp. 603–4. (882d)
Speaking of Murder, vol. II, pp. 173–83.
(875b)
Talking Murder, pp. 142–54. (883)
Women of Mystery, p. 436. (874)
Web site: http://stopyourekillingme.com/
laurie-r-king.html; http://www.
laurierking.com

King, Peter
Bio-bibliographic data:
Detecting Men, 1st ed., p. 148. (876)
Web site: http://stopyourekillingme.com/
peter-king.html

King, Rufus [Frederick]
Bio-bibliographic data:
Canadian Crime Fiction, pp. 280–81.
(209)
Encyclopedia Mysteriosa, pp. 194–95. (2)
The Encyclopedia of Murder and Mystery,
pp. 282–83. (6)
*The Encyclopedia of Mystery and
Detection,* pp. 234–35. (7)
*Twentieth-Century Crime and Mystery
Writers,* 1st ed., pp. 904–6. (882a)
*Twentieth-Century Crime and Mystery
Writers,* 2nd ed., pp. 532–33. (882b)
*Twentieth-Century Crime and Mystery
Writers,* 3rd ed., pp. 632–33. (882c)

King, Sara
Bio-bibliographic data:
Canadian Crime Fiction, pp. 121–22.
(209)

King, Stephen [Edwin]
Bio-bibliographic data:
*Critical Survey of Mystery and Detective
Fiction,* pp. 985–89. (41)
Speaking of Murder, pp. 1–14. (875a)

King, Wal
Bio-bibliographic data:
Australian Crime Fiction, p. 144. (207)

**Kingsbury, Kate. *Pseud. for* Doreen
Roberts**
Bio-bibliographic data:
By a Woman's Hand, 2nd ed., p. 128.
(884b)
Detecting Women, 1st ed., p. 80. (877a)
Detecting Women 2, p. 107. (877b)

Detecting Women, 3rd ed., pp. 151–52.
(877c)
Web site: http://stopyourekillingme.com/
kate-kingsbury.html
Kirby, Paul
Bio-bibliographic data:
Australian Crime Fiction, p. 144. (207)
Kirby, Reginald
Bio-bibliographic data:
Australian Crime Fiction, pp. 144–45.
(207)
Kirk, Michael. *See* **Knox, Bill**
Kirst, Hans Hellmut
Bio-bibliographic data:
*St. James Guide to Crime & Mystery
Writers,* 4th ed., pp. 604–5. (882d)
*Twentieth-Century Crime and Mystery
Writers,* 1st ed., pp. 1542–43. (882a)
*Twentieth-Century Crime and Mystery
Writers,* 2nd ed., pp. 942–43. (882b)
*Twentieth-Century Crime and Mystery
Writers,* 3rd ed., pp. 1132–33. (882c)
Kirton, Bill
Bio-bibliographic data:
Detecting Men, 1st ed., p. 148. (876)
**Kitchin, C. H. B.; i.e., Clifford Henry
Benn**
Bio-bibliographic data:
British Mystery Writers, 1920–1939, pp.
182–85. (867)
*The Encyclopedia of Mystery and
Detection,* p. 235. (7)
*St. James Guide to Crime & Mystery
Writers,* 4th ed., pp. 605–6. (882d)
*Twentieth-Century Crime and Mystery
Writers,* 1st ed., pp. 906–8. (882a)
*Twentieth-Century Crime and Mystery
Writers,* 2nd ed., pp. 533–34. (882b)
*Twentieth-Century Crime and Mystery
Writers,* 3rd ed., pp. 633–34. (882c)
Kittredge, Mary
Bio-bibliographic data:
By a Woman's Hand, 1st ed., p. 120.
(884a)
By a Woman's Hand, 2nd ed., pp. 128–29.
(884b)
Detecting Women, 1st ed., p. 81. (877a)
Detecting Women 2, p. 107. (877b)
Detecting Women, 3rd ed., p. 111, 152.
(877c)
Web site: http://www.sarahgraves.org

Kiyoharu, Matsumoto. *See* **Matsumoto,
Seicho**
Klang, Gary
Bio-bibliographic data:
Canadian Crime Fiction, p. 169 (209)
Klavan, Andrew
Bio-bibliographic data:
*St. James Guide to Crime & Mystery
Writers,* 4th ed., pp. 606–7. (882d)
Klein, A. M.; i.e., Abraham Moses
Bio-bibliographic data:
Canadian Crime Fiction, p. 122. (209)
Kline, Victor
Bio-bibliographic data:
Australian Crime Fiction, p. 9. (207)
Klinger, Henry
Bio-bibliographic data:
*Twentieth-Century Crime and Mystery
Writers,* 1st ed., p. 908. (882a)
Kneale, Bruce
Bio-bibliographic data:
Australian Crime Fiction, p. 145. (207)
Knight, Alanna
Bio-bibliographic data:
By a Woman's Hand, 1st ed., pp. 120–21.
(884a)
By a Woman's Hand, 2nd ed., pp. 129–30.
(884b)
Detecting Women, 1st ed., p. 81. (877a)
Detecting Women 2, p. 108. (877b)
Detecting Women, 3rd ed., pp. 152–53.
(877c)
*The Mammoth Encyclopedia of Modern
Crime Fiction,* pp. 272–73. (1)
Web site: http://www.alannaknight.com
Knight, Amarantha. *See* **Kilpatrick,
Nancy**
Knight, Clifford [Reynolds]
Bio-bibliographic data:
Australian Crime Fiction, p. 145. (207)
*Twentieth-Century Crime and Mystery
Writers,* 2nd ed., pp. 534–35. (882b)
*Twentieth-Century Crime and Mystery
Writers,* 3rd ed., pp. 634–35. (882c)
Knight, David
Bio-bibliographic data:
Canadian Crime Fiction, pp. 122–23.
(209)
Knight, J. D.
Bio-bibliographic data:
Detecting Men, 1st ed., p. 149. (876)
Knight, Kathleen Moore
Bio-bibliographic data:

Critical Survey of Mystery and Detective Fiction, pp. 990–95. (41)
Detecting Women 2, p. 108. (877b)
St. James Guide to Crime & Mystery Writers, 4th ed., pp. 607–9. (882d)
Twentieth-Century Crime and Mystery Writers, 2nd ed., pp. 535–36. (882b)
Twentieth-Century Crime and Mystery Writers, 3rd ed., pp. 635–36. (882c)
Knight, Kathryn Lasky
Bio-bibliographic data:
By a Woman's Hand, 1st ed., pp. 121–22. (884a)
By a Woman's Hand, 2nd ed., p. 130. (884b)
Detecting Women, 1st ed., p. 81. (877a)
Detecting Women 2, p. 109. (877b)
Detecting Women, 3rd ed., p. 153. (877c)
Web site: http://stopyourekillingme.com/ kathryn-lasky-knight.html
Knight, Phyllis
Bio-bibliographic data:
Canadian Crime Fiction, p. 281. (209)
Detecting Women, 1st ed., p. 82. (877a)
Detecting Women 2, p. 109. (877b)
Detecting Women, 3rd ed., p. 153. (877c)
Knight, Stephen Thomas
Bio-bibliographic data:
Australian Crime Fiction, pp. 145–46. (207)
Knott, Frederick M. P.
Bio-bibliographic data:
Encyclopedia Mysteriosa, p. 195. (2)
The Encyclopedia of Murder and Mystery, p. 283. (6)
The Encyclopedia of Mystery and Detection, pp. 235–36. (7)
Knott, James
Bio-bibliographic data:
Australian Crime Fiction, p. 146. (207)
Knott, Will C.
Bio-bibliographic data:
Canadian Crime Fiction, p. 254, 258. (209)
Knox, [William] Alexander
Bio-bibliographic data:
Canadian Crime Fiction, p. 23, 52, 123. (209)
Knox, Bill; i.e., William Knox
Bio-bibliographic data:
Canadian Crime Fiction, p. 281, 282, 286. (209)
Detecting Men, 1st ed., pp. 149–50, 164–65. (876)

Encyclopedia Mysteriosa, pp. 195–96. (2)
The Encyclopedia of Murder and Mystery, pp. 283–84. (6)
The Mammoth Encyclopedia of Modern Crime Fiction, pp. 273–75. (1)
St. James Guide to Crime & Mystery Writers, 4th ed., pp. 609–11. (882d)
Twentieth-Century Crime and Mystery Writers, 1st ed., pp. 908–12. (882a)
Twentieth-Century Crime and Mystery Writers, 2nd ed., pp. 536–38. (882b)
Twentieth-Century Crime and Mystery Writers, 3rd ed., pp. 636–38. (882c)
Personal papers in Mugar Memorial Library, Boston University.
Web site: http://stopyourekillingme.com/ bill-knox.html
Knox, [Monsignor] Ronald A[rbuthnot].
Bio-bibliographic data:
British Mystery Writers, 1920–1939, pp. 186–91. (867)
Critical Survey of Mystery and Detective Fiction, pp. 996–1004. (41)
Encyclopedia Mysteriosa, p. 196. (2)
The Encyclopedia of Murder and Mystery, p. 284. (6)
The Encyclopedia of Mystery and Detection, p. 236. (7)
Mystery and Suspense Writers, pp. 559–68. (884.2)
The Oxford Companion to Crime and Mystery Writing, p. 254. (4)
St. James Guide to Crime & Mystery Writers, 4th ed., pp. 611–14. (882d)
Twentieth-Century Crime and Mystery Writers, 1st ed., pp. 912–17. (882a)
Twentieth-Century Crime and Mystery Writers, 2nd ed., pp. 538–41. (882b)
Twentieth-Century Crime and Mystery Writers, 3rd ed., pp. 638–41. (882c)
Whodunit? A Who's Who in Crime and Mystery Writing, p. 112. (5)
Koch, Eric
Bio-bibliographic data:
Canadian Crime Fiction, pp. 123–24. (209)
Kohler, Vince
Bio-bibliographic data:
Detecting Men, 1st ed., p. 150. (876)
Komo, Dolores
Bio-bibliographic data:
Detecting Women 2, p. 109. (877b)
Web site: http://stopyourekillingme.com/ dolores-komo.html

Kong, Debra Purdy
Bio-bibliographic data:
Canadian Crime Fiction, p. 124. (209)
Konkel, Chuck; i.e., Kazimierz [Gerard Edward]
Bio-bibliographic data:
Canadian Crime Fiction, p. 124. (209)
Koontz, Dean R[ay]
Bio-bibliographic data:
Critical Survey of Mystery and Detective Fiction, pp. 1005–9. (41)
St. James Guide to Crime & Mystery Writers, 4th ed., pp. 614–17. (882d)
Speaking of Murder, vol. II, pp. 1–15. (875b)
Twentieth-Century Crime and Mystery Writers, 2nd ed., pp. 541–43. (882b)
Twentieth-Century Crime and Mystery Writers, 3rd ed., pp. 641–43. (882c)
Web site: http://stopyourekillingme.com/ dean-r-koontz.html; http://www. deankoontz.com
Korzenioski, Jósef Teodor Konrad. *See* **Conrad, Joseph**
Kosak, Carl. *See* **Constantine, K. C.**
Kotzwinkle, William
Bio-bibliographic data:
Canadian Crime Fiction, p. 281. (209)
Kraft, Gabrielle
Bio-bibliographic data:
By a Woman's Hand, 1st ed., p. 122. (884a)
By a Woman's Hand, 2nd ed., pp. 130–31. (884b)
Detecting Women, 1st ed., p. 82. (877a)
Detecting Women 2, p. 109. (877b)
Detecting Women, 3rd ed., pp. 153–54. (877c)
Kramer, Greg
Bio-bibliographic data:
Canadian Crime Fiction, p. 124. (209)
Krauth, Nigel [Lawrence]
Bio-bibliographic data:
Australian Crime Fiction, p. 145, 146. (207)
Krentz, Jayne Ann. *See* **Castle, Jayne**
Kreuter, Katherine E.
Bio-bibliographic data:
Detecting Women 2, p. 110. (877b)
Krich, Rochelle Majer
Bio-bibliographic data:
By a Woman's Hand, 1st ed., pp. 122–23. (884a)

By a Woman's Hand, 2nd ed., pp. 131–32. (884b)
Detecting Women, 1st ed., p. 82. (877a)
Detecting Women 2, p. 110. (877b)
Detecting Women, 3rd ed., p. 154. (877c)
The Mammoth Encyclopedia of Modern Crime Fiction, pp. 275–76. (1)
Web site: http://www.rochellekrich.com; http://stopyourekillingme.com/ rochelle-krich.html
Kristeva, Julia
Bio-bibliographic data:
The Encyclopedia of Murder and Mystery, p. 285. (6)
Kroetsch, Robert
Bio-bibliographic data:
Canadian Crime Fiction, pp. 124–25. (209)
Kruger, Mary
Bio-bibliographic data:
Detecting Women 2, p. 110. (877b)
Detecting Women, 3rd ed., p. 154. (877c)
Web site: http://stopyourekillingme.com/ mary-kruger.html
Krumgold, Joseph
Bio-bibliographic data:
The Encyclopedia of Mystery and Detection, p. 237. (7)
Krumm, Stan
Bio-bibliographic data:
Canadian Crime Fiction, p. 125. (209)
Kuhfeld, Mary Pulver. *See also* **Kuhfeld, Mary Pulver, and Gail Bacon**
Bio-bibliographic data:
Detecting Women, 3rd ed., p. 93, 225. (877c)
The Mammoth Encyclopedia of Modern Crime Fiction, pp. 399–400. (1)
Web site: http://www.soncom.com/ fenyx.index.htm
Kuhfeld, Mary Pulver, and Gail Bacon
Bio-bibliographic data:
By a Woman's Hand, 1st ed., p. 175. (884a)
By a Woman's Hand, 2nd ed., p. 189. (884b)
Detecting Women, 1st ed., p. 58, 119. (877a)
Detecting Women 2, p. 71, 160. (877b)
Detecting Women, 3rd ed., p. 98. (877c)
Kuhlken, Ken
Bio-bibliographic data:
Detecting Men, 1st ed., p. 150. (876)

Web site: http://stopyourekillingme.com/
ken-kuhlken.html; http://www.
kenkulhken.net

Kunz, Kathleen
Bio-bibliographic data:
Detecting Women, 1st ed., p. 82. (877a)
Detecting Women 2, p. 110. (877b)

Kurland, Michael
Bio-bibliographic data:
Detecting Men, 1st ed., p. 151. (876)
*The Mammoth Encyclopedia of Modern
Crime Fiction,* pp. 276–77. (1)
Web site: http://www.michaelkurland.com

Kurnitz, Harry. *See* Page, Marco

Kurtz, R.
Bio-bibliographic data:
Canadian Crime Fiction, p. 51. (209)

Kutscher, Teddy
Bio-bibliographic data:
Canadian Crime Fiction, p. 125, 222.
(209)

**Kuttner, Henry. *See* Moore, Catherine
Lucille, and Henry Kuttner**

**Kyd, Thomas. *Pseud. for* Alfred Bennett
Harbage**
Bio-bibliographic data:
*Critical Survey of Mystery and Detective
Fiction,* pp. 1010–16. (41)
The Encyclopedia of Murder and Mystery,
p. 286. (6)
*The Encyclopedia of Mystery and
Detection,* p. 237. (7)
*St. James Guide to Crime & Mystery
Writers,* 4th ed., pp. 617–18. (882d)
*Twentieth-Century Crime and Mystery
Writers,* 1st ed., pp. 917–19. (882a)
*Twentieth-Century Crime and Mystery
Writers,* 2nd ed., pp. 543–44. (882b)
*Twentieth-Century Crime and Mystery
Writers,* 3rd ed., pp. 643–45. (882c)

**Kyle, Duncan. *Pseud. for* John Franklin
Broxholme**
Bio-bibliographic data:
Australian Crime Fiction, pp. 146–47.
(207)
Canadian Crime Fiction, p. 248, 258.
(209)
Encyclopedia Mysteriosa, p. 197. (2)
*St. James Guide to Crime & Mystery
Writers,* 4th ed., pp. 618–19. (882d)
*Twentieth-Century Crime and Mystery
Writers,* 2nd ed., pp. 544–45. (882b)
*Twentieth-Century Crime and Mystery
Writers,* 3rd ed., pp. 645–46. (882c)

Kyle, Robert. *Pseud. for* Robert Terrall
Bio-bibliographic data:
The Big Book of Noir, p. 265. (24)

Kyle, Sefton. *See* Vickers, Roy

L

La Bern, Arthur
Bio-bibliographic data:
*Twentieth-Century Crime and Mystery
Writers,* 1st ed., pp. 919–22. (882a)

**Labrecque, Madeleine Gaudreault. *See*
Gaudreault-Labrecque, Madeleine**

Lacasse, Lise
Bio-bibliographic data:
Canadian Crime Fiction, p. 125. (209)

Lacey, Sarah. *See* Mitchell, Kay

Lachaine, Richard
Bio-bibliographic data:
Canadian Crime Fiction, p. 125. (209)

Lachnit, Carroll
Bio-bibliographic data:
Detecting Women 2, p. 111. (877b)
Detecting Women, 3rd ed., p. 155. (877c)
Web site: http://stopyourekillingme.com/
carroll-lachnit.html

Lackey, Mercedes
Bio-bibliographic data:
By a Woman's Hand, 2nd ed., pp. 133–34.
(884b)
Detecting Women 2, p. 111. (877b)
Detecting Women, 3rd ed., p. 155. (877c)
Web site: http://stopyourekillingme.com/
mercedes-lackey.html

Lacy, Ed. *Pseud. for* Leonard S. Zinberg
Bio-bibliographic data:
American Hard-Boiled Crime Writers, pp.
226–32. (862)
*Critical Survey of Mystery and Detective
Fiction,* pp. 1017–20. (41)
Encyclopedia Mysteriosa, p. 198. (2)
The Encyclopedia of Murder and Mystery,
p. 287. (6)
*The Encyclopedia of Mystery and
Detection,* p. 238. (7)
*The Mammoth Encyclopedia of Modern
Crime Fiction,* pp. 279–80. (1)
*Murder off the Rack: Critical Studies of
Ten Paperback Masters,* pp. 15–34.
(869)
*St. James Guide to Crime & Mystery
Writers,* 4th ed., pp. 621–22. (882d)
*Twentieth-Century Crime and Mystery
Writers,* 1st ed., pp. 922–24. (882a)

Twentieth-Century Crime and Mystery Writers, 2nd ed., pp. 545–47. (882b)
Twentieth-Century Crime and Mystery Writers, 3rd ed., pp. 647–49. (882c)
Personal papers in Mugar Memorial Library, Boston University.
Web site: http://www.thrillingdetective. com/trivia/lacy.html

Ladouceur, Pierre
Bio-bibliographic data:
Canadian Crime Fiction, p. 125. (209)

Laffin, John [Alfred Charles]
Bio-bibliographic data:
Australian Crime Fiction, pp. 148–49. (207)

Laflamme, H.
Bio-bibliographic data:
Canadian Crime Fiction, p. 125. (209)

La France, Micheline
Bio-bibliographic data:
Canadian Crime Fiction, p. 125. (209)

Lafritte, Sam: unidentified pseud.
Bio-bibliographic data:
Canadian Crime Fiction, p. 125. (209)

Lagacé, Loraine
Bio-bibliographic data:
Canadian Crime Fiction, p. 125. (209)

La Haye, Alexander M.
Bio-bibliographic data:
Canadian Crime Fiction, p. 125. (209)

Lake, Deryn. *Pseud. for* **Dinah Lampitt**
Bio-bibliographic data:
Detecting Women, 3rd ed., p. 156. (877c)
The Mammoth Encyclopedia of Modern Crime Fiction, pp. 280–81. (1)
Web site: http://www.twbooks.co.uk/ authors/derynlake.html

Lake, M. D. *Pseud. for* **James Allen Simpson**
Bio-bibliographic data:
Detecting Men, 1st ed., p. 151. (876)
The Mammoth Encyclopedia of Modern Crime Fiction, p. 281. (1)
Web site: http://stopyourekillingme.com/ m-d-lake.html

Lalane-Cassou, Jean-Claude
Bio-bibliographic data:
Canadian Crime Fiction, p. 125. (209)

Lamarre, Tatiana
Bio-bibliographic data:
Canadian Crime Fiction, p. 126. (209)

Lamb, J. Dayne
Bio-bibliographic data:
Detecting Women, 1st ed., p. 83. (877a)

Detecting Women 2, p. 111. (877b)
Detecting Women, 3rd ed., p. 156. (877c)
Web site: http://stopyourekillingme.com/ j-dayne.lamb.html

Lamb, J. J.
Bio-bibliographic data:
Canadian Crime Fiction, p. 258. (209)

Lamb, James B.
Bio-bibliographic data:
Canadian Crime Fiction, p. 126. (209)

Lambert, Derek [William]
Bio-bibliographic data:
Encyclopedia Mysteriosa, p. 199. (2)
St. James Guide to Crime & Mystery Writers, 4th ed., pp. 622–23. (882d)
Twentieth-Century Crime and Mystery Writers, 2nd ed., pp. 547–48. (882b)
Twentieth-Century Crime and Mystery Writers, 3rd ed., pp. 649–50. (882c)
Personal papers in Mugar Memorial Library, Boston University.

Lambert, Elisabeth
Bio-bibliographic data:
Australian Crime Fiction, p. 149. (207)

Lambert, Eric
Bio-bibliographic data:
Australian Crime Fiction, pp. 149–50. (207)

Lambert, Mercedes: unidentified pseud.
Bio-bibliographic data:
Detecting Women, 1st ed., p. 83. (877a)
Detecting Women 2, p. 112. (877b)
Detecting Women, 3rd ed., p. 156. (877c)
Web site: http://stopyourekillingme.com/ mercedes-lambert.html

Lambton, A. H.
Bio-bibliographic data:
Australian Crime Fiction, p. 150. (207)

Lamiel, Miguel
Bio-bibliographic data:
Canadian Crime Fiction, p. 126. (209)

Lamirande, Claire de
Bio-bibliographic data:
Canadian Crime Fiction, p. 126. (209)

Lamoreux, Henri
Bio-bibliographic data:
Canadian Crime Fiction, p. 126. (209)

Lampitt, Dina. *See* **Lake, Deryn**
Lamprey, A. C. *See* **Fish, Robert L.**
Lancaster, G. B. *Pseud. for* **Edith J. Lyttleton**
Bio-bibliographic data:
Canadian Crime Fiction, p. 126, 135. (209)

Landreth, Marsha
Bio-bibliographic data:
By a Woman's Hand, 2nd ed., p. 134.
(884b)
Detecting Women, 1st ed., p. 83. (877a)
Detecting Women 2, p. 112. (877b)
Detecting Women, 3rd ed., p. 157. (877c)
Web site: http://stopyourekillingme.com/
marsha-landreth.html

Landry, François
Bio-bibliographic data:
Canadian Crime Fiction, p. 126. (209)

Landry, Hughette
Bio-bibliographic data:
Canadian Crime Fiction, p. 126. (209)

Lane, Barbara Ann
Bio-bibliographic data:
Canadian Crime Fiction, p. 126. (209)

Lane, Grant. *See* **Fisher, Steve**

Lang, Fritz
Bio-bibliographic data:
The Encyclopedia of Murder and Mystery,
pp. 288–89. (6)
*The Encyclopedia of Mystery and
Detection,* pp. 238–40. (7)

Lang, John George
Bio-bibliographic data:
Australian Crime Fiction, p. 150. (207)

Langton, Jane [Gillson]
Bio-bibliographic data:
*The Craft of Crime: Conversations with
Crime Writers,* pp. 79–103. (872)
*The Mammoth Encyclopedia of Modern
Crime Fiction,* pp. 281–82. (1)
*Whodunit? A Who's Who in Crime and
Mystery Writing,* p. 113. (5)
Web site: http://stopyourekillingme.com/
jane-langton.html

Langdon, Kenneth
Bio-bibliographic data:
Canadian Crime Fiction, p. 126. (209)

Langford, Ernest
Bio-bibliographic data:
Canadian Crime Fiction, p. 127. (209)

Langford, [J.] Stuart
Bio-bibliographic data:
Canadian Crime Fiction, p. 127. (209)

Langton, Jane [Gillson]
Bio-bibliographic data:
By a Woman's Hand, 1st ed., pp. 124–25.
(884a)
By a Woman's Hand, 2nd ed., pp. 134–35.
(884b)
Detecting Women, 1st ed., p. 84. (877a)

Detecting Women 2, p. 112. (877b)
Detecting Women, 3rd ed., p. 157. (877c)
Encyclopedia Mysteriosa, pp. 199–200.
(2)
The Fatal Art of Entertainment, pp.
224–49. (878)
Great Women Mystery Writers, pp.
183–85. (880)
*St. James Guide to Crime & Mystery
Writers,* 4th ed., pp. 623–25. (882d)
*Twentieth-Century Crime and Mystery
Writers,* 2nd ed., pp. 549–50. (882b)
*Twentieth-Century Crime and Mystery
Writers,* 3rd ed., pp. 650–52. (882c)
Personal papers in Mugar Memorial
Library, Boston University.
Personal papers in Kerlan Collection,
University of Minnesota,
Minneapolis.

Lanier, Virginia
Bio-bibliographic data:
Detecting Women, 3rd ed., pp. 157–58.
(877c)
Web site: http://stopyourekillingme.com/
virginia-lanier.html; http://www.
geocities.com/Heartland/Meadows/
1442/vlanier.htm

Lansdale, Joe R.
Bio-bibliographic data:
The Big Book of Noir, p. 325. (24)
Detecting Men, 1st ed., p. 152. (876)
*The Mammoth Encyclopedia of Modern
Crime Fiction,* pp. 282–83. (1)
*St. James Guide to Crime & Mystery
Writers,* 4th ed., pp. 625–26. (882d)
*Twentieth-Century Crime and Mystery
Writers,* 3rd ed., p. 652. (882c)
Personal papers in Southwest Texas State
University, San Marcos, Texas.
Web site: http://www.joerlansdale.com;
http://stopyourekillingme.com/
joe-r-lansdale.html

Lapalme, Michel
Bio-bibliographic data:
Canadian Crime Fiction, p. 127. (209)

La Pierre, Janet
Bio-bibliographic data:
By a Woman's Hand, 1st ed., p. 125.
(884a)
By a Woman's Hand, 2nd ed., pp. 135–36.
(884b)
Detecting Women, 1st ed., p. 84. (877a)
Detecting Women 2, p. 113. (877b)
Detecting Women, 3rd ed., p. 158. (877c)

Web site: http://stopyourekillingme.com/
jane-la-pierre.html; http://www.
janetlapierre.com

La Plante, Lynda
Bio-bibliographic data:
Detecting Women, 1st ed., p. 84. (877a)
Detecting Women 2, p. 113. (877b)
Detecting Women, 3rd ed., pp. 158–59.
(877c)
*The Mammoth Encyclopedia of Modern
Crime Fiction,* pp. 277–79. (1)
Web site: http://www.laplanteproductions.
com; http://stopyourekillingme.com/
lynda-la-plante.html

Larche, Marcel
Bio-bibliographic data:
Canadian Crime Fiction, p. 127. (209)

Larivière, Jules
Bio-bibliographic data:
Canadian Crime Fiction, p. 127. (209)

LaRue, Monique
Bio-bibliographic data:
Canadian Crime Fiction, p. 127. (209)

Lashner, William
Bio-bibliographic data:
Detecting Men, 1st ed., p. 152. (876)

Lathen, Emma. *Pseud. for* **Mary Jane
Latsis and Martha Henissart**
Bio-bibliographic data:
By a Woman's Hand, 1st ed., pp. 125–26.
(884a)
By a Woman's Hand, 2nd ed., pp. 136–37.
(884b)
Corpus Delicti of Mystery Fiction, pp.
86–87. (879)
*The Craft of Crime: Conversations with
Crime Writers,* pp. 176–201. (872)
*Critical Survey of Mystery and Detective
Fiction,* pp. 1021–26. (41)
Detecting Women, 1st ed., p. 51, 85.
(877a)
Detecting Women 2, p. 56, 113–14. (877b)
Detecting Women, 3rd ed., pp. 77–78, 159.
(877c)
Encyclopedia Mysteriosa, p. 201. (2)
The Encyclopedia of Murder and Mystery,
pp. 290–91. (6)
*The Encyclopedia of Mystery and
Detection,* p. 241. (7)
Great Women Mystery Writers, pp.
185–89. (880)
*The Mammoth Encyclopedia of Modern
Crime Fiction,* pp. 283–85. (1)

*The Oxford Companion to Crime and
Mystery Writing,* p. 255. (4)
*St. James Guide to Crime & Mystery
Writers,* 4th ed., pp. 626–28. (882d)
10 Women of Mystery, pp. 248–67. (864,
865)
13 Mistresses of Murder, pp. 75–85. (871)
*Twentieth-Century Crime and Mystery
Writers,* 1st ed., pp. 924–26. (882a)
*Twentieth-Century Crime and Mystery
Writers,* 2nd ed., pp. 550–51. (882b)
*Twentieth-Century Crime and Mystery
Writers,* 3rd ed., pp. 652–54. (882c)
*Whodunit? A Who's Who in Crime and
Mystery Writing,* p. 113. (5)
Women of Mystery, pp. 406–11. (874)
Web site: http://stopyourekillingme.com/
emma-lathen.html

Lathrop, West
Bio-bibliographic data:
Canadian Crime Fiction, p. 258. (209)

Latimer, Jonathan [Wyatt]
Bio-bibliographic data:
*Critical Survey of Mystery and Detective
Fiction,* pp. 1027–32. (41)
Encyclopedia Mysteriosa, p. 201. (2)
The Encyclopedia of Murder and Mystery,
p. 291. (6)
*The Encyclopedia of Mystery and
Detection,* p. 241. (7)
*St. James Guide to Crime & Mystery
Writers,* 4th ed., pp. 628–29. (882d)
*Twentieth-Century Crime and Mystery
Writers,* 1st ed., pp. 926–28. (882a)
*Twentieth-Century Crime and Mystery
Writers,* 2nd ed., pp. 551–52. (882b)
*Twentieth-Century Crime and Mystery
Writers,* 3rd ed., pp. 654–55. (882c)
Web site: http://stopyourekillingme.com/
jonathan-latimer.html; http://www.
miskatonic.org/rara-avis/biblio/
latimer.html; http://www.
thrillingdetective.com/trivia/
latimer.html

Latraverse, Plume
Bio-bibliographic data:
Canadian Crime Fiction, p. 127. (209)

Latsis, Mary J. *See* **Lathen, Emma**

Latta, David
Bio-bibliographic data:
Australian Crime Fiction, p. 150. (207)

Laughlin, Catherine
Bio-bibliographic data:
Australian Crime Fiction, p. 9. (207)

Laurence, Janet
Bio-bibliographic data:
By a Woman's Hand, 1st ed., pp. 126–27.
(884a)
By a Woman's Hand, 2nd ed., p. 137.
(884b)
Detecting Women, 1st ed., p. 85. (877a)
Detecting Women 2, p. 114. (877b)
Detecting Women, 3rd ed., p. 160. (877c)
*The Mammoth Encyclopedia of Modern
Crime Fiction,* p. 285. (1)
Web site: http://stopyourekillingme.com/
janet-laurence.html

Laurini, Myriam
Bio-bibliographic data:
*Latin American Mystery Writers: An A to
Z Guide. (881)*

Lauriston, Victor
Bio-bibliographic data:
Canadian Crime Fiction, pp. 127–28.
(209)

Lavigne, Guy
Bio-bibliographic data:
Canadian Crime Fiction, p. 128. (209)

Law, Alexander
Bio-bibliographic data:
Canadian Crime Fiction, p. 128. (209)

**Law, Janice. *Pseud. for* Janice Law
Trecker**
Bio-bibliographic data:
By a Woman's Hand, 1st ed., pp. 127–28.
(884a)
By a Woman's Hand, 2nd ed., pp. 137–38.
(884b)
Detecting Women, 1st ed., p. 86. (877a)
Detecting Women 2, pp. 114–15. (877b)
Detecting Women, 3rd ed., p. 160. (877c)
Web site: http://stopyourekillingme.com/
janice-law.html; http://www.
janicelaw.com

Law, Marjorie [Jean]: unidentified pseud.
Bio-bibliographic data:
Australian Crime Fiction, pp. 150–51.
(207)

Lawless, Anthony. *See* Macdonald, Philip
Lawrence, Hilda
Bio-bibliographic data:
Detecting Women 2, p. 115. (877b)
Detecting Women, 3rd ed., p. 161. (877c)
Encyclopedia Mysteriosa, p. 202. (2)
The Encyclopedia of Murder and Mystery,
pp. 291–92. (6)
*The Encyclopedia of Mystery and
Detection,* p. 242. (7)

*Twentieth-Century Crime and Mystery
Writers,* 1st ed., pp. 928–30. (882a)
*Twentieth-Century Crime and Mystery
Writers,* 2nd ed., pp. 552–53. (882b)
*Twentieth-Century Crime and Mystery
Writers,* 3rd ed., pp. 655–56. (882c)

Lawrence, John
Bio-bibliographic data:
Australian Crime Fiction, p. 151. (207)

Lawrence, John Frederick Brock
Bio-bibliographic data:
Canadian Crime Fiction, p. 128. (209)

**Lawrence, Margaret. *See* Keilstrup,
Margaret**
Lawrence, Martha
Bio-bibliographic data:
Detecting Women 2, p. 115. (877b)
Detecting Women, 3rd ed., p. 161. (877c)
Web site: http://stopyourekillingme.com/
martha-lawrence.html; http://www.
marthalawrence.com

Layhew, Mrs. Jane
Bio-bibliographic data:
Canadian Crime Fiction, p. 128. (209)

Leacock, Stephen [Butler]
Bio-bibliographic data:
The Encyclopedia of Murder and Mystery,
p. 292. (6)

Lear, Peter. *See* Lovesey, Peter
Learning, Walter
Bio-bibliographic data:
Canadian Crime Fiction, p. 128, 160.
(209)

Leasor, [Thomas] James
Bio-bibliographic data:
Canadian Crime Fiction, p. 281. (209)
Encyclopedia Mysteriosa, p. 203. (2)
The Encyclopedia of Murder and Mystery,
p. 293. (6)
*St. James Guide to Crime & Mystery
Writers,* 4th ed., pp. 629–32. (882d)
*Twentieth-Century Crime and Mystery
Writers,* 1st ed., pp. 930–32. (882a)
*Twentieth-Century Crime and Mystery
Writers,* 2nd ed., pp. 553–54. (882b)
*Twentieth-Century Crime and Mystery
Writers,* 3rd ed., pp. 656–58. (882c)

**Leather, Sir Edwin "Ted" [Hartley
Cameron], KCMG, KCVO, LL.D.**
Bio-bibliographic data:
Canadian Crime Fiction, p. 129. (209)

Leaver, Harold R.
Bio-bibliographic data:
Canadian Crime Fiction, p. 129. (209)

Leavitt, Thaddeus [W. H.]
Bio-bibliographic data:
Canadian Crime Fiction, p. 129. (209)
Lebel, Joseph-Marc-Octave-Antoine. *See*
Feron, Jean
Leblanc, Louise
Bio-bibliographic data:
Canadian Crime Fiction, p. 129. (209)
Leblanc, Maurice
Bio-bibliographic data:
Corpus Delicti of Mystery Fiction, pp.
87–89. (879)
*Critical Survey of Mystery and Detective
Fiction*, pp. 1033–40. (41)
Encyclopedia Mysteriosa, p. 203. (2)
The Encyclopedia of Murder and Mystery,
p. 293. (6)
*The Encyclopedia of Mystery and
Detection*, p. 242. (7)
*The Oxford Companion to Crime and
Mystery Writing*, p. 260. (4)
*St. James Guide to Crime & Mystery
Writers*, 4th ed., pp. 632–33. (882d)
*Twentieth-Century Crime and Mystery
Writers,* 1st ed., pp. 1543–45. (882a)
*Twentieth-Century Crime and Mystery
Writers,* 2nd ed., pp. 943–44. (882b)
*Twentieth-Century Crime and Mystery
Writers,* 3rd ed., p. 1133. (882c)
*Whodunit? A Who's Who in Crime and
Mystery Writing*, p. 116. (5)
Leblond, Robert
Bio-bibliographic data:
Canadian Crime Fiction, p. 129. (209)
Lebugle, André
Bio-bibliographic data:
Canadian Crime Fiction, p. 130. (209)
le Carré, John. *Pseud. for* **David John
Moore Cornwell**
Bio-bibliographic data:
*British Mystery and Thriller Writers since
1940, First Series*, pp. 240–55. (868)
Canadian Crime Fiction, p. 281. (209)
Corpus Delicti of Mystery Fiction, p. 89.
(879)
*Critical Survey of Mystery and Detective
Fiction*, pp. 1041–47. (41)
Detecting Men, 1st ed., pp. 152–53. (876)
Encyclopedia Mysteriosa, p. 203. (2)
The Encyclopedia of Murder and Mystery,
pp. 293–94. (6)
*The Encyclopedia of Mystery and
Detection*, pp. 242–43. (7)

Mystery and Suspense Writers, pp.
569–87. (884.2)
*100 Masters of Mystery and Detective
Fiction*, pp. 381–89. (37)
*The Oxford Companion to Crime and
Mystery Writing*, pp. 260–61. (4)
*St. James Guide to Crime & Mystery
Writers*, 4th ed., pp. 633–35. (882d)
*Twentieth-Century Crime and Mystery
Writers,* 1st ed., pp. 933–35. (882a)
*Twentieth-Century Crime and Mystery
Writers,* 2nd ed., pp. 555–56. (882b)
*Twentieth-Century Crime and Mystery
Writers,* 3rd ed., pp. 658–60. (882c)
*Whodunit? A Who's Who in Crime and
Mystery Writing*, pp. 116–17. (5)
Web site: http://stopyourekillingme.com/
john-le-carre.html;
http://www.bdd.com/features/lecarre/
author.html
Leckie, Keith [Ross]
Bio-bibliographic data:
Canadian Crime Fiction, p. 130. (209)
L'écuyer, [Pascal-François] EugPne
Bio-bibliographic data:
Canadian Crime Fiction, p. 130. (209)
Lee, Albert
Bio-bibliographic data:
Australian Crime Fiction, p. 9. (207)
Lee, Barbara
Bio-bibliographic data:
Detecting Women 2, p. 115. (877b)
Detecting Women, 3rd ed., p. 162. (877c)
Web site: http://stopyourekillingme.com/
barbara-lee-html
Lee, Christopher
Bio-bibliographic data:
Detecting Men, 1st ed., p. 153. (876)
Lee, Gypsy Rose. *See also* **Rice, Craig,
who ghostwrote the novels published
under this name.**
Bio-bibliographic data:
The Encyclopedia of Murder and Mystery,
p. 294. (6)
Web site: http://stopyourekillingme.com/
gypsy-rose-lee.html
Lee, Herbert Patrick
Bio-bibliographic data:
Canadian Crime Fiction, p. 130. (209)
Lee, Manfred B. *See* **Queen, Ellery**
Lee, Marie
Bio-bibliographic data:
Detecting Women 2, p. 115. (877b)
Detecting Women, 3rd ed., p. 162. (877c)

Lee, Norman
Bio-bibliographic data:
Australian Crime Fiction, pp. 151–52.
(207)
Lee, Thomas
Bio-bibliographic data:
Canadian Crime Fiction, p. 258. (209)
Lee, W. W.; i.e., Wendi W.
Bio-bibliographic data:
Detecting Women 2, p. 116. (877b)
Detecting Women, 3rd ed., pp. 162–63.
(877c)
Web site: http://stopyourekillingme.com/
wendi-lee.html
Leek, Margaret. *See* **Bowen-Judd, Sara
Hutton**
Lees, Jack; i.e., John Garfield
Bio-bibliographic data:
Canadian Crime Fiction, p. 130. (209)
le Fanu, Joseph Sheridan
Bio-bibliographic data:
British Mystery Writers, 1860–1919, pp.
184–90. (866)
*Critical Survey of Mystery and Detective
Fiction*, pp. 1049–52. (41)
The Encyclopedia of Murder and Mystery,
pp. 294–95. (6)
*The Encyclopedia of Mystery and
Detection*, p. 243. (7)
*St. James Guide to Crime & Mystery
Writers*, 4th ed., pp. 635–36. (882d)
*Twentieth-Century Crime and Mystery
Writers*, 1st ed., pp. 1528–29. (882a)
*Twentieth-Century Crime and Mystery
Writers*, 2nd ed., p. 933. (882b)
*Twentieth-Century Crime and Mystery
Writers*, 3rd ed., p. 1123. (882c)
Personal papers in National Library of
Ireland.
Personal papers in Trinity College,
Dublin.
Legault, Josée
Bio-bibliographic data:
Canadian Crime Fiction, p. 130. (209)
Le Grand, Leon
Bio-bibliographic data:
Australian Crime Fiction, p. 152. (207)
Lehane, Dennis
Bio-bibliographic data:
Detecting Men, 1st ed., p. 153. (876)
The Encyclopedia of Murder and Mystery,
p. 296. (6)
*The Mammoth Encyclopedia of Modern
Crime Fiction*, p. 286. (1)

*Whodunit? A Who's Who in Crime and
Mystery Writing*, p. 117. (5)
Web site:
http://www.denislehanebooks.com;
http://stopyourekillingme.com/
dennis-lehane.html
Lehner, Adolph
Bio-bibliographic data:
Canadian Crime Fiction, p. 130. (209)
Leighton, Robert
Bio-bibliographic data:
Canadian Crime Fiction, p. 258. (209)
Leith, Linda
Bio-bibliographic data:
Canadian Crime Fiction, p. 130. (209)
Leitz, David
Bio-bibliographic data:
Detecting Men, 1st ed., p. 153. (876)
Web site: http://stopyourekillingme.com/
david-leith.html
Lejeune, Anthony. *Pseud. for* **Edward
Anthony Thompson**
Bio-bibliographic data:
Detecting Men, 1st ed., p. 154. (876)
*St. James Guide to Crime & Mystery
Writers*, 4th ed., pp. 636–37. (882d)
*Twentieth-Century Crime and Mystery
Writers*, 1st ed., pp. 935–37. (882a)
*Twentieth-Century Crime and Mystery
Writers*, 2nd ed., pp. 556–57. (882b)
*Twentieth-Century Crime and Mystery
Writers*, 3rd ed., pp. 660–61. (882c)
Lemarchand, Elizabeth
Bio-bibliographic data:
By a Woman's Hand, 1st ed., pp. 128–29.
(884a)
By a Woman's Hand, 2nd ed., p. 138.
(884b)
Detecting Women 2, pp. 116–17. (877b)
Detecting Women, 3rd ed., p. 163. (877c)
Great Women Mystery Writers, pp.
189–91. (880)
*St. James Guide to Crime & Mystery
Writers*, 4th ed., pp. 637–39. (882d)
*Twentieth-Century Crime and Mystery
Writers*, 1st ed., pp. 937–39. (882a)
*Twentieth-Century Crime and Mystery
Writers*, 2nd ed., pp. 557–58. (882b)
*Twentieth-Century Crime and Mystery
Writers*, 3rd ed., pp. 661–62. (882c)
Web site: http://stopyourekillingme.com/
elizabeth-lemarchand.html
Lemelin, Roger
Bio-bibliographic data:

Canadian Crime Fiction, pp. 130–31. (209)

Lemieux, Jean
Bio-bibliographic data:
Canadian Crime Fiction, p. 131. (209)

Lemieux, Kenneth. *See* **Orvis, Kenneth**

LeZero, Vicente
Bio-bibliographic data:
Latin American Mystery Writers: An A to Z Guide. (881)

Leon, Donna
Bio-bibliographic data:
By a Woman's Hand, 1st ed., p. 129. (884a)
By a Woman's Hand, 2nd ed., pp. 138–39. (884b)
Detecting Women, 1st ed., p. 86. (877a)
Detecting Women 2, p. 117. (877b)
Detecting Women, 3rd ed., pp. 163–64. (877c)
The Mammoth Encyclopedia of Modern Crime Fiction, pp. 286–87. (1)
Web site:
http://www.phys.uni-paderborn.de/~stern/leon/; http://www.twbooks.co.uk/ajthors/donnaleon.html; http://stopyourekillingme.com/donna-leon.html

Leon, Henry Cecil. *See* **Cecil, Henry**

Léon, Sergio
Bio-bibliographic data:
Canadian Crime Fiction, p. 131. (209)

Leonard, Charles L. *See* **Heberden, Mary Violet**

Leonard, Elmore [John]
Bio-bibliographic data:
American Hard-Boiled Crime Writers, pp. 233–46. (862)
Canadian Crime Fiction, p. 258. (209)
Critical Survey of Mystery and Detective Fiction, pp. 1053–57. (41)
Detecting Men, 1st ed., p. 154. (876)
Encyclopedia Mysteriosa, p. 204. (2)
The Encyclopedia of Murder and Mystery, p. 296. (6)
The Mammoth Encyclopedia of Modern Crime Fiction, pp. 287–89. (1)
Mystery and Suspense Writers, pp. 589–603. (884.2)
100 Masters of Mystery and Detective Fiction, pp. 390–95. (37)
The Oxford Companion to Crime and Mystery Writing, pp. 264–65. (4)

St. James Guide to Crime & Mystery Writers, 4th ed., pp. 639–40. (882d)
Talking Murder, pp. 155–72. (883)
Twentieth-Century Crime and Mystery Writers, 2nd ed., pp. 558–59. (882b)
Twentieth-Century Crime and Mystery Writers, 3rd ed., pp. 662–64. (882c)
Whodunit? A Who's Who in Crime and Mystery Writing, pp. 117–18. (5)
Personal papers in University of Detroit Library, Michigan.
Web site: http://www.elmoreleonard.html; http://stopyourekillingme.com/elmer-leonard.html; http://www.thrillingdetective.com/trivia/leonard.html

Leonov, Leonid Maksimovich
Bio-bibliographic data:
Critical Survey of Mystery and Detective Fiction, pp. 1058–64. (41)

Lepage, Monique
Bio-bibliographic data:
Canadian Crime Fiction, p. 131. (209)

Le Queux, William [Tufnell]
Bio-bibliographic data:
British Mystery Writers, 1860–1919, pp. 191–98. (866)
Critical Survey of Mystery and Detective Fiction, pp. 1065–70. (41)
Encyclopedia Mysteriosa, pp. 204–5. (2)
The Encyclopedia of Murder and Mystery, pp. 297–98. (6)
The Encyclopedia of Mystery and Detection, pp. 243–44. (7)
Twentieth-Century Crime and Mystery Writers, 1st ed., pp. 939–44. (882a)
Twentieth-Century Crime and Mystery Writers, 2nd ed., pp. 559–62. (882b)
Twentieth-Century Crime and Mystery Writers, 3rd ed., pp. 664–67.

Leroux, Gaston
Bio-bibliographic data:
Critical Survey of Mystery and Detective Fiction, pp. 1071–77. (41)
Encyclopedia Mysteriosa, p. 205. (2)
The Encyclopedia of Murder and Mystery, p. 298. (6)
The Encyclopedia of Mystery and Detection, pp. 244–45. (7)
100 Masters of Mystery and Detective Fiction, pp. 396–402. (37)
St. James Guide to Crime & Mystery Writers, 4th ed., pp. 640–41. (882d)

Twentieth-Century Crime and Mystery Writers, 2nd ed., pp. 564–65. (882b)
Twentieth-Century Crime and Mystery Writers, 3rd ed., pp. 670–71. (882c)
Web site: http://stopyourekillingme.com/ roy-lewis.html
Lewis, Roy H.
Bio-bibliographic data:
Detecting Men, 1st ed., p. 158. (876)
Web site: http://stopyourekillingme.com/ roy-h-lewis.html
Lewis, Sherry
Bio-bibliographic data:
Detecting Women 2, p. 118. (877b)
Detecting Women, 3rd ed., p. 164. (877c)
Web site: http://stopyourekillingme.com/ sherry-lewis.html
Lewis, Ted
Bio-bibliographic data:
Detecting Men, 1st ed., p. 158. (876)
The Mammoth Encyclopedia of Modern Crime Fiction, pp. 293–94. (1)
Lexander, Ren
Bio-bibliographic data:
Australian Crime Fiction, p. 153. (207)
Lichtenstein, Peter. *See* **Peters, Lance**
Licione, Jean-Pierre. *See* **Malacci, Robert**
Liggett, Walter W.
Bio-bibliographic data:
Canadian Crime Fiction, p. 259. (209)
Limoges, Victor
Bio-bibliographic data:
Canadian Crime Fiction, p. 132. (209)
Lin-Chandler, Irene
Bio-bibliographic data:
Detecting Women, 3rd ed., p. 164. (877c)
Lincoln, Victoria [Endicott]
Bio-bibliographic data:
Canadian Crime Fiction, p. 259. (209)
Lindall, Edward. *Pseud. for* **Edward Ernest Smith**
Bio-bibliographic data:
Australian Crime Fiction, pp. 153–54. (207)
Lindblad, John
Bio-bibliographic data:
Canadian Crime Fiction, p. 132. (209)
Lindsay, Douglas
Bio-bibliographic data:
The Mammoth Encyclopedia of Modern Crime Fiction, pp. 294–95. (1)
Web site: http://www.barney-thomson. com

Lindsay, Hilarie
Bio-bibliographic data:
Australian Crime Fiction, p. 154. (207)
Lindsay, Joan [Beckett]
Bio-bibliographic data:
Australian Crime Fiction, pp. 154–55. (207)
Lindsay, Paul
Bio-bibliographic data:
Detecting Men, 1st ed., p. 158. (876)
Web site: http://stopyourekillingme.com/ paul-lindsay.html
Lindsay, R. H.; i.e., Robert Howard
Bio-bibliographic data:
Canadian Crime Fiction, p. 132. (209)
Lindsey, David L.
Bio-bibliographic data:
Detecting Men, 1st ed., p. 159. (876)
Web site: http://stopyourekillingme.com/ david-l-lindsey.html
Linington, [Barbara] Elizabeth
Bio-bibliographic data:
By a Woman's Hand, 1st ed., p. 130. (884a)
By a Woman's Hand, 2nd ed., pp. 139–40. (884b)
Critical Survey of Mystery and Detective Fiction, pp. 1078–85. (41)
Detecting Women, 1st ed., pp. 129–30. (877a)
Detecting Women 2, p. 62, 118, 172–73. (877b)
Encyclopedia Mysteriosa, pp. 206–7. (2)
The Encyclopedia of Murder and Mystery, pp. 299–300. (6)
The Encyclopedia of Mystery and Detection, pp. 247–48. (7)
Great Women Mystery Writers, pp. 192–97. (880)
The Mammoth Encyclopedia of Modern Crime Fiction, pp. 295–96. (1)
The Oxford Companion to Crime and Mystery Writing, p. 268. (4)
St. James Guide to Crime & Mystery Writers, 4th ed., pp. 648–50. (882d)
Twentieth-Century Crime and Mystery Writers, 1st ed., pp. 950–52. (882a)
Twentieth-Century Crime and Mystery Writers, 2nd ed., pp. 565–68. (882b)
Twentieth-Century Crime and Mystery Writers, 3rd ed., pp. 671–73. (882c)
Whodunit? A Who's Who in Crime and Mystery Writing, p. 119. (5)

Personal papers in Mugar Memorial
Library, Boston University
Web site: http://stopyourekillingme.com/
elizabeth-linington.html
Elizabeth Linington Society
c/o Rinehart S. Potts
1223 Glen Terrace
Glassboro, NJ 08028

Link, William. *See* **Levinson, Richard, and William Link**

Links, J. G. *See* **Wheatley, Dennis**

Linscott, Gillian
Bio-bibliographic data:
By a Woman's Hand, 1st ed., pp. 130–31. (884a)
By a Woman's Hand, 2nd ed., pp. 140–41. (884b)
Detecting Women, 1st ed., p. 86. (877a)
Detecting Women 2, pp. 118–19. (877b)
Detecting Women, 3rd ed., p. 165. (877c)
The Mammoth Encyclopedia of Modern Crime Fiction, pp. 296–97. (1)
Web site: http://www.gillianlinscott. co.uk; http://www.twbooks.co. uk/authors/glinscott.html; http://stopyourekillingme.com/ gillian-linscott.html

Lion, Kate
Bio-bibliographic data:
Australian Crime Fiction, p. 9. (207)

Lipinski, Thomas
Bio-bibliographic data:
Detecting Men, 1st ed., p. 159. (876)
Web site: http://stopyourekillingme.com/ thomas-lipinski.html

Lippman, Laura
Bio-bibliographic data:
Detecting Women, 3rd ed., p. 165. (877c)
The Mammoth Encyclopedia of Modern Crime Fiction, pp. 297–98. (1)
Web site: http://www.lauralippman. com; http://stopyourekillingme. com/laura-lippman.html

Lips, André M.
Bio-bibliographic data:
Canadian Crime Fiction, p. 132. (209)

Littell, Robert
Bio-bibliographic data:
St. James Guide to Crime & Mystery Writers, 4th ed., pp. 650–51. (882d)
Twentieth-Century Crime and Mystery Writers, 2nd ed., p. 568. (882b)
Twentieth-Century Crime and Mystery Writers, 3rd ed., pp. 673–74. (882c)

Web site: http://stopyourekillingme.com/ robert-littell.html

Little, Conyth. *See* **Little, Constance, and Gwyneth Little**

Little, Constance, and Gwyneth Little
Bio-bibliographic data:
Australian Crime Fiction, p. 155. (207)
Twentieth-Century Crime and Mystery Writers, 1st ed., p. 953. (882a)
Twentieth-Century Crime and Mystery Writers, 2nd ed., pp. 568–69. (882b)

Litvinov, Ivy
Bio-bibliographic data:
The Encyclopedia of Murder and Mystery, p. 302. (6)
Twentieth-Century Crime and Mystery Writers, 1st ed., pp. 954–55. (882a)

Livesay, Ann. *Pseud. for* **Ann Sutton**
Bio-bibliographic data:
Detecting Women, 3rd ed., p. 166. (877c)

Livesey, Margot
Bio-bibliographic data:
Canadian Crime Fiction, p. 282. (209)

Livingston, Jack. *Pseud. for* **James L. Nusser**
Bio-bibliographic data:
Detecting Men, 1st ed., p. 159. (876)

Livingston, Nancy
Bio-bibliographic data:
Australian Crime Fiction, p. 155 (207)
By a Woman's Hand, 1st ed., pp. 131–32. (884a)
By a Woman's Hand, 2nd ed., p. 141. (884b)
Detecting Women 2, p. 119. (877b)
The Mammoth Encyclopedia of Modern Crime Fiction, p. 298. (1)
St. James Guide to Crime & Mystery Writers, 4th ed., pp. 651–53. (882d)
Twentieth-Century Crime and Mystery Writers, 3rd ed., pp. 674–76. (882c)
Web site: http://stopyourekillingme.com/ nancy-livingston.html

Livingstone, Nancy. *See* **Livingston, Nancy**

Llewellyn, Caroline. *Pseud. for* **Caroline Llewellyn Champlin**
Bio-bibliographic data:
By a Woman's Hand, 1st ed., p. 132. (884a)
By a Woman's Hand, 2nd ed., pp. 141–42. (884b)
Canadian Crime Fiction, p. 40, 132. (209)

Llewellyn, Sam
Bio-bibliographic data:

The Encyclopedia of Murder and Mystery,
p. 302. (6)
Lloyd, MacDonald. *See* **Winslow, Don**
Lloyd, Victor [Henry]
Bio-bibliographic data:
Australian Crime Fiction, p. 155. (207)
Lloyd, Wallace. *See* **Algie, James**
Lochte, Dick; i.e., Richard Samuel
Bio-bibliographic data:
Detecting Men, 1st ed., p. 160. (876)
*The Mammoth Encyclopedia of Modern
Crime Fiction*, p. 299. (1)
*St. James Guide to Crime & Mystery
Writers*, 4th ed., pp. 653–55. (882d)
*Twentieth-Century Crime and Mystery
Writers*, 3rd ed., pp. 676–77. (882c)
Web site: http://stopyourekillingme.com/
dick-lochte.html
Lock, Arnold Charles Cooper. *See*
Cooper, Charles
Lockridge, Frances. *See* **Lockridge,
Richard, and Frances**
**Lockridge, Richard [Orson], and Frances
[Louise Davis]**
Bio-bibliographic data:
Corpus Delicti of Mystery Fiction, pp.
89–92. (879)
*Critical Survey of Mystery and Detective
Fiction*, pp. 1086–92. (41)
Detecting Women, 1st ed., pp. 86–87.
(877a)
Detecting Women 2, pp. 119–20. (877b)
Encyclopedia Mysteriosa, p. 207. (2)
The Encyclopedia of Murder and Mystery,
pp. 302–3. (6)
*The Encyclopedia of Mystery and
Detection*, pp. 248–49. (7)
*100 Masters of Mystery and Detective
Fiction*, pp. 404–9. (37)
*St. James Guide to Crime & Mystery
Writers*, 4th ed., pp. 655–57. (882d)
*Twentieth-Century Crime and Mystery
Writers*, 1st ed., pp. 955–60. (882a)
*Twentieth-Century Crime and Mystery
Writers*, 2nd ed., pp. 569–72. (882b)
*Twentieth-Century Crime and Mystery
Writers*, 3rd ed., pp. 677–80. (882c)
Web site:
http://stopyourekillingme.
com/francis-lockridge.html;
http://stopyourekillingme.com/
richard-lockridge.html
Lofts, Norah
Bio-bibliographic data:

*Twentieth-Century Crime and Mystery
Writers*, 1st ed., pp. 960–63. (882a)
Logan, Margaret
Bio-bibliographic data:
By a Woman's Hand, 1st ed., p. 133.
(884a)
By a Woman's Hand, 2nd ed., p. 142.
(884b)
Detecting Women 2, p. 121. (877b)
Detecting Women, 3rd ed., p. 166. (877c)
Logue, John
Bio-bibliographic data:
Detecting Men, 1st ed., p. 160. (876)
Logue, Mary
Bio-bibliographic data:
Detecting Women, 1st ed., p. 87. (877a)
Detecting Women 2, p. 121. (877b)
Web site: http://stopyourekillingme.com/
mary-logue.html
Loiselet, André
Bio-bibliographic data:
Canadian Crime Fiction, p. 132. (209)
Lombino, Salvatore. *See* **Hunter, Evan**
London, Jack
Bio-bibliographic data:
Canadian Crime Fiction, p. 259. (209)
Long, Lydia. *See* **Blackmur, L. L.**
Long, Martin [Merrick]
Bio-bibliographic data:
Australian Crime Fiction, p. 145, 146,
155–56. (207)
Longrigg, Roger Erskine
Bio-bibliographic data:
Detecting Men, 1st ed., p. 81, 199. (876)
Encyclopedia Mysteriosa, p. 270. (2)
*The Mammoth Encyclopedia of Modern
Crime Fiction*, pp. 299–301. (1)
*St. James Guide to Crime & Mystery
Writers*, 4th ed., pp. 820–22. (882d)
*Twentieth-Century Crime and Mystery
Writers*, 1st ed., pp. 506–8. (882a)
*Twentieth-Century Crime and Mystery
Writers*, 2nd ed., pp. 285–86. (882b)
*Twentieth-Century Crime and Mystery
Writers*, 3rd ed., pp. 831–33. (882c)
Web site: http://stopyourekillingme.com/
roger-erskine-longrigg.html
Longstreth, T. Morris; i.e., Thomas
Bio-bibliographic data:
Canadian Crime Fiction, p. 259. (209)
Loomis, J. Paul
Bio-bibliographic data:
Canadian Crime Fiction, p. 132. (209)

Lorac, E. C. R. *See* **Carnac, Carol**
Loraine, Philip. *Pseud. for* **Robin Estridge**
Bio-bibliographic data:
St. James Guide to Crime & Mystery
Writers, 4th ed., p. 658. (882d)
Twentieth-Century Crime and Mystery
Writers, 1st ed., pp. 963–64. (882a)
Twentieth-Century Crime and Mystery
Writers, 2nd ed., pp. 572–73. (882b)
Twentieth-Century Crime and Mystery
Writers, 3rd ed., pp. 680–81. (882c)
Loranger, Francine
Bio-bibliographic data:
Canadian Crime Fiction, p. 132. (209)
Lord, Gabrielle [Craig]
Bio-bibliographic data:
Australian Crime Fiction, p. 156. (207)
Lordon, Randye
Bio-bibliographic data:
Detecting Women, 1st ed., p. 87. (877a)
Detecting Women 2, p. 121. (877b)
Detecting Women, 3rd ed., pp. 166–67.
(877c)
Web site: http://stopyourekillingme.com/
randye-lorden.html; http://www.
barkinfish.com/lordon
Lorens, M. K. *See* **Keilstrup, Margaret**
Lostal, Sauli
Bio-bibliographic data:
Latin American Mystery Writers: An A to
Z Guide. (881)
Lotz, Jim; i.e., James Robert
Bio-bibliographic data:
Canadian Crime Fiction, pp. 132–33.
(209)
Louis, Joseph: unidentified pseud.
Bio-bibliographic data:
Canadian Crime Fiction, p. 133. (209)
Love, Ann
Bio-bibliographic data:
Canadian Crime Fiction, p. 133. (209)
Loveday, Gordon Keith
Bio-bibliographic data:
Canadian Crime Fiction, p. 133. (209)
Lovell, Marc. *See* **McShane, Mark**
Lovesey, Peter
Bio-bibliographic data:
British Mystery and Thriller Writers since
1940, First Series, pp. 256–74. (868)
The Craft of Crime: Conversations with
Crime Writers, pp. 258–88. (872)
Critical Survey of Mystery and Detective
Fiction, pp. 1093–98. (41)
Designs of Darkness, pp. 52–65. (873)

Detecting Men, 1st ed., pp. 160–61. (876)
Encyclopedia Mysteriosa, p. 210. (2)
The Encyclopedia of Murder and Mystery,
p. 305. (6)
The Encyclopedia of Mystery and
Detection, p. 252. (7)
The Mammoth Encyclopedia of Modern
Crime Fiction, pp. 301–2. (1)
St. James Guide to Crime & Mystery
Writers, 4th ed., pp. 659–60. (882d)
Speaking of Murder, pp. 73–85. (875a)
Talking Murder, pp. 173–85. (883)
Twentieth-Century Crime and Mystery
Writers, 1st ed., pp. 965–66. (882a)
Twentieth-Century Crime and Mystery
Writers, 2nd ed., pp. 573–74. (882b)
Twentieth-Century Crime and Mystery
Writers, 3rd ed., pp. 681–82. (882c)
Whodunit? A Who's Who in Crime and
Mystery Writing, pp. 119–20. (5)
Web site: http://www.twbooks.co.uk/
authors/peterlovesey.html; http://
stopyourekillingme.com/
Lovesey, Phil; i.e., Philip
Bio-bibliographic data:
The Mammoth Encyclopedia of Modern
Crime Fiction, p. 303. (1)
Web site: http://www.twbooks.co.uk/
authors/phillovesey.html
Lovett, Sarah
Bio-bibliographic data:
Detecting Women 2, pp. 121–22. (877b)
Detecting Women, 3rd ed., p. 167. (877c)
Web site: http://stopyourekillingme.com/
sarah-lovett.html; http://www.
sarahlovett.com
Low, Gardner. *See* **Rodda, [Percival]**
Charles
Lowndes, Marie [Adelaide] Belloc
Bio-bibliographic data:
British Mystery Writers, 1860–1919, pp.
199–204. (866)
Critical Survey of Mystery and Detective
Fiction, pp. 1099–1105. (41)
Encyclopedia Mysteriosa, p.210. (2)
The Encyclopedia of Murder and Mystery,
pp. 305–6. (6)
The Encyclopedia of Mystery and
Detection, pp. 252–53. (7)
Great Women Mystery Writers, pp.
197–200. (880)
100 Masters of Mystery and Detective
Fiction, pp. 410–16. (37)

The Oxford Companion to Crime and Mystery Writing, p. 37. (4)
St. James Guide to Crime & Mystery Writers, 4th ed., pp. 660–62. (882d)
Twentieth-Century Crime and Mystery Writers, 1st ed., pp. 967–70. (882a)
Twentieth-Century Crime and Mystery Writers, 2nd ed., pp. 574–76. (882b)
Twentieth-Century Crime and Mystery Writers, 3rd ed., pp. 682–84. (882c)
Whodunit? A Who's Who in Crime and Mystery Writing, p. 18. (5)

Lowry, [Clarence] Malcolm [Boden]
Bio-bibliographic data:
Canadian Crime Fiction, pp. 133–34. (209)

Luard, Nicholas
Bio-bibliographic data:
Twentieth-Century Crime and Mystery Writers, 2nd ed., pp. 576–77. (882b)
Twentieth-Century Crime and Mystery Writers, 3rd ed., pp. 684–85. (882c)

Luber, Philip
Bio-bibliographic data:
Detecting Men, 1st ed., p. 161. (876)

Lucke, Margaret
Bio-bibliographic data:
Detecting Women, 1st ed., p. 88. (877a)
Detecting Women 2, p. 122. (877b)

Ludlum, Robert
Bio-bibliographic data:
Critical Survey of Mystery and Detective Fiction, pp. 1106–11. (41)
Encyclopedia Mysteriosa, pp. 210–11. (2)
Mystery and Suspense Writers, pp. 605–13. (884.2)
100 Masters of Mystery and Detective Fiction, pp. 417–23. (37)
St. James Guide to Crime & Mystery Writers, 4th ed., pp. 662–64. (882d)
Twentieth-Century Crime and Mystery Writers, 1st ed., pp. 970–71. (882a)
Twentieth-Century Crime and Mystery Writers, 2nd ed., pp. 577–78. (882b)
Twentieth-Century Crime and Mystery Writers, 3rd ed., pp. 685–86. (882c)
Web site: http://stopyourekillingme.com/robert-ludlum.html; http://ludlumbooks.com

Ludwig, Boris: house pseud.
Bio-bibliographic data:
Australian Crime Fiction, p. 157. (207)

Luigi, Belli: house pseud. used by G. C. Bleeck (q.v.) among others
Bio-bibliographic data:
Australian Crime Fiction, pp. 157–58. (207)

Lund, T[rygve].
Bio-bibliographic data:
Canadian Crime Fiction, p. 134. (209)

Lupica, Mike
Bio-bibliographic data:
Detecting Men, 1st ed., p. 161. (876)

Lupoff, Richard A.
Bio-bibliographic data:
Detecting Men, 1st ed., p. 162. (876)

Lusby, Jim
Bio-bibliographic data:
Detecting Men, 1st ed., p. 162. (876)

Lustgarten, Edgar [Marcus]
Bio-bibliographic data:
The Encyclopedia of Mystery and Detection, p. 255. (7)
St. James Guide to Crime & Mystery Writers, 4th ed., pp. 664–65. (882d)
Twentieth-Century Crime and Mystery Writers, 1st ed., pp. 971–73. (882a)
Twentieth-Century Crime and Mystery Writers, 2nd ed., pp. 578–79. (882b)
Twentieth-Century Crime and Mystery Writers, 3rd ed., pp. 686–87. (882c)

Lutz, Giles A[lfred].
Bio-bibliographic data:
Canadian Crime Fiction, p. 259. (209)

Lutz, John [Thomas]
Bio-bibliographic data:
The Big Book of Noir, p. 326. (24)
Detecting Men, 1st ed., pp. 162–63. (876)
Encyclopedia Mysteriosa, pp. 211–12. (2)
The Encyclopedia of Murder and Mystery, pp. 307–8. (6)
The Mammoth Encyclopedia of Modern Crime Fiction, pp. 303–4. (1)
St. James Guide to Crime & Mystery Writers, 4th ed., pp. 665–66. (882d)
Twentieth-Century Crime and Mystery Writers, 1st ed., pp. 973–77. (882a)
Twentieth-Century Crime and Mystery Writers, 2nd ed., pp. 579–81. (882b)
Twentieth-Century Crime and Mystery Writers, 3rd ed., pp. 687–90. (882c)
Web site: http://stopyourekillingme.com/john-lutz.html

Lyall, Gavin [Tudor]
Bio-bibliographic data:

*British Mystery and Thriller Writers since
  1940, First Series*, pp. 275–83. (868)
Canadian Crime Fiction, p. 282. (209)
Encyclopedia Mysteriosa, p. 212. (2)
The Encyclopedia of Murder and Mystery,
  p. 308. (6)
*The Encyclopedia of Mystery and
  Detection,* p. 255. (7)
*St. James Guide to Crime & Mystery
  Writers,* 4th ed., pp. 666–67. (882d)
*Twentieth-Century Crime and Mystery
  Writers,* 1st ed., pp. 977–79. (882a)
*Twentieth-Century Crime and Mystery
  Writers,* 2nd ed., pp. 581–82. (882b)
*Twentieth-Century Crime and Mystery
  Writers,* 3rd ed., pp. 690–91. (882c)
Web site: http://stopyourekillingme.com/
  gavin-lyall.html
Lyle-Smith, Alan
  Bio-bibliographic data:
  Canadian Crime Fiction, p. 282. (209)
Lynch, Gerald
  Bio-bibliographic data:
  Canadian Crime Fiction, p. 134. (209)
Lynch, Jack
  Bio-bibliographic data:
  Detecting Men, 1st ed., p. 163. (876)
Lynch, Lawrence L. *Pseud. for* **Emma
  Murdock Van Deventer**
  Bio-bibliographic data:
  *The Encyclopedia of Mystery and
  Detection,* pp. 255–56. (7)
Lynde, Francis
  Bio-bibliographic data:
  *The Encyclopedia of Mystery and
  Detection,* p. 256. (7)
Lynds, Dennis
  Bio-bibliographic data:
  *Critical Survey of Mystery and Detective
  Fiction,* pp. 379–86. (41)
  Detecting Men, 1st ed., p. 25, 59–60, 69,
  107, 224–25. (876)
  Encyclopedia Mysteriosa, p. 70. (2)
  *The Encyclopedia of Mystery and
  Detection,* pp. 96–97. (7)
  *The Mammoth Encyclopedia of Modern
  Crime Fiction,* pp. 102–5. (1)
  *St. James Guide to Crime & Mystery
  Writers,* 4th ed. pp. 218–21. (882d)
  *Twentieth-Century Crime and Mystery
  Writers,* 1st ed., pp. 339–44. (882a)
  *Twentieth-Century Crime and Mystery
  Writers,* 2nd ed., pp. 187–90. (882b)

*Twentieth-Century Crime and Mystery
  Writers,* 3rd ed., pp. 233–37. (882c)
Personal papers in Center for the Study of
  Popular Culture, Bowling Green State
  University, Bowling Green, Ohio
Web site: http://stopyourekillingme.com/
  dennis-lynds.html;
  http://www.dennislynds.com; http://
  www.thrillingdetective.com/trivia/
  collins.html
Lynds, Gayle
  Bio-bibliographic data:
  Detecting Women, 3rd ed., pp. 167–68.
  (877c)
  Web site: http://www.gaylelynds.com
Lynford, Richard
  Bio-bibliographic data:
  Australian Crime Fiction, p. 158. (207)
Lynn, David
  Bio-bibliographic data:
  Australian Crime Fiction, pp. 158–59.
  (207)
Lynravn, N. S. *See* **Martin, L. W., and N.
  S. Lynravn**
Lyons, Arthur. *See also* **Noguchi, Thomas
  T. with Arthur Lyons**
  Bio-bibliographic data:
  Detecting Men, 1st ed., pp. 163–64. (876)
  Encyclopedia Mysteriosa, p. 212. (2)
  *The Mammoth Encyclopedia of Modern
  Crime Fiction,* p. 305. (1)
  *St. James Guide to Crime & Mystery
  Writers,* 4th ed., pp. 667–69. (882d)
  *Twentieth-Century Crime and Mystery
  Writers,* 2nd ed., p. 583. (882b)
  *Twentieth-Century Crime and Mystery
  Writers,* 3rd ed., pp. 691–92. (882c)
Web site: http://stopyourekillingme.com/
  arthur-lyons.html
Lyons, Ivan. *See* **Lyons, Nan, and Ivan
  Lyons**
Lyons, Nan, and Ivan Lyons
  Bio-bibliographic data:
  Detecting Women, 1st ed., p. 88 (877a)
  Detecting Women 2, p. 122. (877b)
  Detecting Women, 3rd ed., p. 168. (877c)
Lyttleton, Edith J. *See* **Lancaster, G. B.**

M
MacAlan, Peter. *See* **Tremayne, Peter**
Mac Anthony, Joseph
  Bio-bibliographic data:
  Canadian Crime Fiction, p. 135. (209)

Macdonald, Alistair [A.]
Bio-bibliographic data:
Canadian Crime Fiction, p. 136. (209)
Macdonald, John: name used by Kenneth Millar before he settled on Ross Macdonald (q.v.)
Macdonald, John B[arfoot].
Bio-bibliographic data:
Canadian Crime Fiction, p. 136. (209)
MacDonald, John D[ann].
Bio-bibliographic data:
The Big Book of Noir, p. 184, 209–11. (24)
Corpus Delicti of Mystery Fiction, pp. 92–94. (879)
Critical Survey of Mystery and Detective Fiction, pp. 1130–34. (41)
Encyclopedia Mysteriosa, pp. 216–17. (2)
The Encyclopedia of Murder and Mystery, pp. 313–14. (6)
The Encyclopedia of Mystery and Detection, pp. 260–61. (7)
The Mammoth Encyclopedia of Modern Crime Fiction, pp. 313–16. (1)
Mystery and Suspense Writers, pp. 615–31. (884.2)
100 Masters of Mystery and Detective Fiction, pp. 437–42. (37)
The Oxford Companion to Crime and Mystery Writing, p. 274. (4)
St. James Guide to Crime & Mystery Writers, 4th ed., pp. 671–74. (882d)
Twentieth-Century Crime and Mystery Writers, 1st ed., pp. 979–83. (882a)
Twentieth-Century Crime and Mystery Writers, 2nd ed., pp. 583–86. (882b)
Twentieth-Century Crime and Mystery Writers, 3rd ed., pp. 693–95. (882c)
Whodunit? A Who's Who in Crime and Mystery Writing, p. 121. (5)
Personal papers in University of Florida Library, Gainesville.
Web site: http://stopyourekillingme.com/ john-d-macdonald; http://www. miskatonic.org/rara-avis/biblio/ jdmacdonald.html; http://www. thrillingdetective.com/trivia/jdm.html ; http://members.bellatlantic.net/~ mwarble/slipf18.home.htm; http:// www.home.earthlink.net/~rufener/ homepage.html; http://www.kruse. demon.co.uk/johnd.htm
   The JDM Bibliophile
   c/o Ed Hirshberg
   University of South Florida

   4202 East Fowler Avenue, Stop
   USF0107
   Tampa, FL 33620
Macdonald, John Ross: name used by Kenneth Millar before he settled on Ross Macdonald (q.v.)
MacDonald, Marianne
Bio-bibliographic data:
Detecting Women, 3rd ed., p. 168. (877c)
Web site: http://stopyourekillingme.com/ marianne-macdonald.html; http:// www.marianne-macdonald.com
MacDonald, Patricia
Bio-bibliographic data:
Encyclopedia Mysteriosa, p. 217. (2)
MacDonald, Philip
Bio-bibliographic data:
British Mystery Writers, 1920–1939, pp. 192–97. (867)
Canadian Crime Fiction, p. 282. (209)
Encyclopedia Mysteriosa, p. 217. (2)
The Encyclopedia of Murder and Mystery, p. 314. (6)
The Encyclopedia of Mystery and Detection, pp. 261–62. (7)
The Oxford Companion to Crime and Mystery Writing, pp. 274–75. (4)
St. James Guide to Crime & Mystery Writers, 4th ed., pp. 674–76. (882d)
Twentieth-Century Crime and Mystery Writers, 1st ed., pp. 984–87. (882a)
Twentieth-Century Crime and Mystery Writers, 2nd ed., pp. 586–88. (882b)
Twentieth-Century Crime and Mystery Writers, 3rd ed., pp. 695–97. (882c)
Whodunit? A Who's Who in Crime and Mystery Writing, pp. 121–22. (5)
Web site: http://stopyourekillingme.com/ philip-macdonald.html
MacDonald, Ronald. See MacDonald, Philip
Macdonald, Ross. *Pseud. for* Kenneth Millar
Bio-bibliographic data:
American Hard-Boiled Crime Writers, pp. 247–66. (862)
The Big Book of Noir, pp. 245–50. (24)
Canadian Crime Fiction, pp. 136–37, 149–50. (209)
Corpus Delicti of Mystery Fiction, pp. 94–96. (879)
Critical Survey of Mystery and Detective Fiction, pp. 1135–40. (41)
Designs of Darkness, pp. 82–100. (873)

Encyclopedia Mysteriosa, p. 217. (2)
The Encyclopedia of Murder and Mystery,
pp. 314–16. (6)
*The Encyclopedia of Mystery and
Detection,* pp. 262–63. (7)
Hardboiled Mystery Writers, pp. 243–318.
(870a)
*The Mammoth Encyclopedia of Modern
Crime Fiction,* pp. 316–18. (1)
Mystery and Suspense Writers, pp.
633–50. (884.2)
*100 Masters of Mystery and Detective
Fiction,* pp. 443–48. (37)
*The Oxford Companion to Crime and
Mystery Writing,* p. 275. (4)
*St. James Guide to Crime & Mystery
Writers,* 4th ed., pp. 676–78. (882d)
*Twentieth-Century Crime and Mystery
Writers,* 1st ed., pp. 987–89. (882a)
*Twentieth-Century Crime and Mystery
Writers,* 2nd ed., pp. 588–90. (882b)
*Twentieth-Century Crime and Mystery
Writers,* 3rd ed., pp. 697–99. (882c)
*Whodunit? A Who's Who in Crime and
Mystery Writing,* pp. 122–23. (5)
Personal papers in University of California
Library, Irvine.
Web site: http://stopyourekillingme.com/
ross-macdonald.html; http://hem.
passagen.se/caltex/index.html; http://
www.miskatonic.org/rara-avis/biblio/
rossmacdonald.html; http://www.
thrillingdetective.com/trivia/
kenmillar.html
Macdonnell, J. E.; i.e., James Edmond
Bio-bibliographic data:
Australian Crime Fiction, pp. 161–62.
(207)
MacDougal, Bonnie
Bio-bibliographic data:
Detecting Women, 3rd ed., pp. 168–69.
(877c)
MacDougall, Lee
Bio-bibliographic data:
Canadian Crime Fiction, pp. 137–38.
(209)
Mace, Helen. *Pseud. for* M. Helen Hall
Bio-bibliographic data:
Australian Crime Fiction, p. 160. (207)
MacGregor, Roy
Bio-bibliographic data:
Canadian Crime Fiction, pp. 138–39.
(209)

MacGregor, T. J.; i.e., Patricia Janeshutz
Bio-bibliographic data:
By a Woman's Hand, 1st ed., pp. 135–36.
(884a)
By a Woman's Hand, 2nd ed., pp. 144–45.
(884b)
Detecting Women, 1st ed., p. 52, 88–89.
(877a)
Detecting Women 2, p. 57, 122. (877b)
Detecting Women, 3rd ed., pp. 79–80, 169.
(877c)
Encyclopedia Mysteriosa, p. 220. (2)
Web site: http://stopyourekillingme.com/
t-j-macgregor.html
MacHarg, William [Briggs]
Bio-bibliographic data:
Encyclopedia Mysteriosa, p. 220. (2)
The Encyclopedia of Murder and Mystery,
p. 318. (6)
*The Encyclopedia of Mystery and
Detection,* p. 266. (7)
**Machen, Arthur. *Pseud.* (later name
change) *for* Arthur Llewellyn Jones**
Bio-bibliographic data:
The Encyclopedia of Murder and Mystery,
p. 318. (6)
*The Encyclopedia of Mystery and
Detection,* pp. 266–67. (7)
MacInnes, Helen [Clark]
Bio-bibliographic data:
*British Mystery and Thriller Writers since
1940, First Series,* pp. 284–94. (868)
Corpus Delicti of Mystery Fiction, pp.
96–97. (879)
*Critical Survey of Mystery and Detective
Fiction,* pp. 1167–71. (41)
Encyclopedia Mysteriosa, p. 221. (2)
*The Encyclopedia of Mystery and
Detection,* p. 267. (7)
Mystery and Suspense Writers, pp.
651–64. (884.2)
*100 Masters of Mystery and Detective
Fiction,* pp. 455–59. (37)
*St. James Guide to Crime & Mystery
Writers,* 4th ed., pp. 678–79. (882d)
*Twentieth-Century Crime and Mystery
Writers,* 1st ed., pp. 990–92. (882a)
*Twentieth-Century Crime and Mystery
Writers,* 2nd ed., pp. 590–91. (882b)
*Twentieth-Century Crime and Mystery
Writers,* 3rd ed., pp. 699–701. (882c)
Personal papers in Princeton University
Library, Princeton, New Jersey.

Web site: http://stopyourekillingme.com/
helen-macinnes.html
MacIntyre, David
Bio-bibliographic data:
Canadian Crime Fiction, p. 139. (209)
Mack, Willard
Bio-bibliographic data:
Canadian Crime Fiction, p. 139. (209)
**MacKay, Amanda. *Pseud. for* Amanda
Joan MacKay Smith**
Bio-bibliographic data:
Detecting Women 2, pp. 122–23. (877b)
Detecting Women, 3rd ed., p. 169. (877c)
MacKay, Scott
Bio-bibliographic data:
Canadian Crime Fiction, p. 139. (209)
MacKenzie, Donald
Bio-bibliographic data:
Canadian Crime Fiction, pp. 139–40.
(209)
Detecting Men, 1st ed., p. 164. (876)
Encyclopedia Mysteriosa, p. 222. (2)
*The Mammoth Encyclopedia of Modern
Crime Fiction,* pp. 321–22. (1)
*St. James Guide to Crime & Mystery
Writers,* 4th ed., pp. 679–80. (882d)
*Twentieth-Century Crime and Mystery
Writers,* 1st ed., pp. 992–93. (882a)
*Twentieth-Century Crime and Mystery
Writers,* 2nd ed., pp. 591–92. (882b)
*Twentieth-Century Crime and Mystery
Writers,* 3rd ed., pp. 701–2. (882c)
Personal papers in Mugar Memorial
Library, Boston University.
**Mackenzie, Kenneth. *See* Mackenzie,
Seaforth**
MacKenzie, Nadine
Bio-bibliographic data:
Canadian Crime Fiction, p. 140. (209)
MacKenzie, Nigel
Bio-bibliographic data:
Australian Crime Fiction, p. 166. (207)
Mackenzie, Seaforth
Bio-bibliographic data:
Australian Crime Fiction, p. 166. (207)
Mackie, John
Bio-bibliographic data:
Canadian Crime Fiction, pp. 140–41.
(209)

**MacKintosh, Elizabeth. *See* Tey,
Josephine**
Macklin, Robert. *See* Galbally, Frank
MacLane, Jack. *See* Crider, Bill
MacLean, Alistair [Stuart]
Bio-bibliographic data:
Canadian Crime Fiction, p. 260. (209)
*Critical Survey of Mystery and Detective
Fiction,* pp. 1172–76. (41)
*St. James Guide to Crime & Mystery
Writers,* 4th ed., pp. 680–82. (882d)
*Twentieth-Century Crime and Mystery
Writers,* 1st ed., pp. 994–95. (882a)
*Twentieth-Century Crime and Mystery
Writers,* 2nd ed., pp. 592–93. (882b)
*Twentieth-Century Crime and Mystery
Writers,* 3rd ed., pp. 702–3. (882c)
Web site: http://stopyourekillingme.com/
alistair-maclean.html
MacLean, Julia
Bio-bibliographic data:
Canadian Crime Fiction, p. 141. (209)
MacLean, Robert
Bio-bibliographic data:
Canadian Crime Fiction, p. 141. (209)
MacLeish, Dougal. *See* Goodspeed, D. J.
MacLennan, [John] Hugh
Bio-bibliographic data:
Canadian Crime Fiction, p. 142. (209)
MacLeod, Angus
Bio-bibliographic data:
The Encyclopedia of Murder and Mystery,
p. 319. (6)
MacLeod, Charlotte [Matilda Hughes]
Bio-bibliographic data:
By a Woman's Hand, 1st ed., pp. 136–37.
(884a)
By a Woman's Hand, 2nd ed., p. 145.
(884b)
Canadian Crime Fiction, pp. 49–50, 108,
142–43. (209)
*Critical Survey of Mystery and Detective
Fiction,* pp. 1177–83. (41)
Deadly Women, pp. 346–51. (26.5)
Detecting Women, 1st ed., pp. 42–43, 89.
(877a)
Detecting Women 2, p. 46, 123. (877b)
Detecting Women, 3rd ed., pp. 62–63, 170.
(877c)
Encyclopedia Mysteriosa, pp. 222–23. (2)
The Encyclopedia of Murder and Mystery,
pp. 319–20. (6)
Great Women Mystery Writers, pp.
208–11. (880)

The Mammoth Encyclopedia of Modern Crime Fiction, pp. 322– (1)

St. James Guide to Crime & Mystery Writers, 4th ed., pp. 682–84. (882d)

Twentieth-Century Crime and Mystery Writers, 2nd ed., pp. 593–94. (882b)

Twentieth-Century Crime and Mystery Writers, 3rd ed., pp. 703–5. (882c)

Whodunit? A Who's Who in Crime and Mystery Writing, p. 123. (5)

Personal papers in Mugar Memorial Library, Boston University.

Web site: http://stopyourekillingme.com/charlotte-macleod.html

MacLeod, Robert. *See* **Knox, Bill**

Macmillan, Anne [Morton]

Bio-bibliographic data:

Canadian Crime Fiction, p. 143. (209)

MacPherson, Rett. *Pseud. for* **Lauretta Allen**

Bio-bibliographic data:

Detecting Women, 3rd ed., pp. 170–71. (877c)

Web site: http://stopyourekillingme.com/rett-macpherson.html

MacSkimming, Roy

Bio-bibliographic data:

Canadian Crime Fiction, p. 144. (209)

Mactaggart, Morna Doris Brown. *See* **Ferrars, E. X.**

Madden, E. S.; i.e., Edward Stanislaus

Bio-bibliographic data:

Australian Crime Fiction, p. 169. (207)

Maddock, Stephen. *See* **Walsh, J. M.**

Mahoney, Dan

Bio-bibliographic data:

Detecting Men, 1st ed., p. 165. (876)

Web site: http://stopyourekillingme.com/dan-mahoney.html

Maiden, Jennifer [Margaret]

Bio-bibliographic data:

Australian Crime Fiction, p. 170. (207)

Mailer, Norman

Bio-bibliographic data:

The Encyclopedia of Murder and Mystery, p. 323. (6)

Maillard, Keith

Bio-bibliographic data:

Canadian Crime Fiction, p. 144. (209)

Maillé, Albert. *See* **Dreux, Albert**

Maiman, Jaye

Bio-bibliographic data:

By a Woman's Hand, 2nd ed., p. 146. (884b)

Detecting Women 2, p. 123. (877b)

Detecting Women, 3rd ed., p. 171. (877c)

Mainwaring, Daniel. *See* **Homes, Geoffrey**

Maitland, Barry

Bio-bibliographic data:

Detecting Men, 1st ed., p. 165. (876)

The Mammoth Encyclopedia of Modern Crime Fiction, pp. 325–26. (1)

Web site: http://stopyourekillingme.com/barry-maitland.html

Maitland, Derek

Bio-bibliographic data:

Australian Crime Fiction, p. 170. (207)

Major, Andre

Bio-bibliographic data:

Canadian Crime Fiction, pp. 144–45. (209)

Makins, Clifford. *See* **Dexter, Ted**

Malacci, Robert. *Pseud. for* **Jean-Pierre Licione**

Bio-bibliographic data:

Canadian Crime Fiction, p. 145. (209)

Malcolm, John. *Pseud. for* **John Malcolm Andrews**

Bio-bibliographic data:

Detecting Men, 1st ed., p. 166. (876)

The Mammoth Encyclopedia of Modern Crime Fiction, p. 326. (1)

St. James Guide to Crime & Mystery Writers, 4th ed., pp. 684–85. (882d)

Twentieth-Century Crime and Mystery Writers, 3rd ed., pp. 705–6. (882c)

Web site: http://stopyourekillingme.com/john-malcolm.html

Malet, Léo

Bio-bibliographic data:

The Encyclopedia of Murder and Mystery, p. 324. (6)

Maling, Arthur [Gordon]

Bio-bibliographic data:

Canadian Crime Fiction, p. 260. (209)

Encyclopedia Mysteriosa, pp. 226–27. (2)

The Encyclopedia of Murder and Mystery, p. 325. (6)

Twentieth-Century Crime and Mystery Writers, 1st ed., pp. 996–97. (882a)

Twentieth-Century Crime and Mystery Writers, 2nd ed., pp. 594–95. (882b)

Twentieth-Century Crime and Mystery Writers, 3rd ed., pp. 706–7. (882c)

Personal papers in Mugar Memorial Library, Boston University.

Malleson, Lucy Beatrice. *See* **Gilbert, Anthony**
Mallett, Lyndon
Bio-bibliographic data:
Detecting Men, 1st ed., p. 166. (876)
Mallette, Gertrude E[thel].
Bio-bibliographic data:
Canadian Crime Fiction, p. 93, 145. (209)
Malloch, Peter. *See* **Dunan, W. Murdoch**
Mallon, Maurus E[dward].
Bio-bibliographic data:
Canadian Crime Fiction, p. 145. (209)
Malloy, Lester. *See* **Meares, Leonard**
Malmont, Valerie S.
Bio-bibliographic data:
Detecting Women, 1st ed., p. 89. (877a)
Detecting Women 2, p. 124. (877b)
Detecting Women, 3rd ed., p. 171. (877c)
Web site: http://stopyourekillingme.com/
valerie-s-malmont.html; http://
members.aol.com/malmont
Malone, Michael
Bio-bibliographic data:
*The Mammoth Encyclopedia of Modern
Crime Fiction*, pp. 326–27. (1)
Web site: http://stopyourekillingme.com/
michael-malone.html
Malone, Paul. *See* **Newton, Michael**
Maloney, Shane
Bio-bibliographic data:
*The Mammoth Encyclopedia of Modern
Crime Fiction*, pp. 327–28. (1)
Web site: http://stopyourekillingme.com/
shane-maloney.html
Malzberg, Barry N[athaniel].
Bio-bibliographic data:
Encyclopedia Mysteriosa, p. 228. (2)
*St. James Guide to Crime & Mystery
Writers*, 4th ed., pp. 686–89. (882d)
*Twentieth-Century Crime and Mystery
Writers*, 2nd ed., pp. 595–98. (882b)
*Twentieth-Century Crime and Mystery
Writers*, 3rd ed., pp. 707–9. (882c)
Mander, Christine
Bio-bibliographic data:
Canadian Crime Fiction, p. 145. (209)
Maness, Larry
Bio-bibliographic data:
Detecting Men, 1st ed., p. 167. (876)
Web site: http://stopyourekillingme.com/
larry-maness.html
Maney, Mabel
Bio-bibliographic data:
Detecting Women 2, p. 124. (877b)

Detecting Women, 3rd ed., pp. 171–72.
(877c)
Manguel, Alberto
Bio-bibliographic data:
Canadian Crime Fiction, p. 145. (209)
Mann, Jessica
Bio-bibliographic data:
By a Woman's Hand, 1st ed., pp. 137–38.
(884a)
By a Woman's Hand, 2nd ed., pp. 146–47.
(884b)
Detecting Women, 1st ed., p. 90. (877a)
Detecting Women 2, p. 124. (877b)
Detecting Women, 3rd ed., p. 172. (877c)
*The Mammoth Encyclopedia of Modern
Crime Fiction*, pp. 328–29. (1)
*St. James Guide to Crime & Mystery
Writers*, 4th ed., pp. 689–90. (882d)
*Twentieth-Century Crime and Mystery
Writers*, 1st ed., pp. 997–98. (882a)
*Twentieth-Century Crime and Mystery
Writers*, 2nd ed., p. 598. (882b)
*Twentieth-Century Crime and Mystery
Writers*, 3rd ed., p. 710. (882c)
Mann, Leonard
Bio-bibliographic data:
Australian Crime Fiction, p. 170. (207)
Mann, Paul
Bio-bibliographic data:
Australian Crime Fiction, p. 171. (207)
Detecting Men, 1st ed., p. 167. (876)
Manners, Carol. *See* **Clarement, Ruth**
Manners, Gordon. *Pseud. for* **Mary Eliza
Fullerton**
Bio-bibliographic data:
Australian Crime Fiction, p. 171. (207)
Manning, Adelaide Frances Oke. *See*
Coles, Manning
Manning, Bruce. *See* **Bristow, Gwen**
Manseau, Pierre
Bio-bibliographic data:
Canadian Crime Fiction, p. 145. (209)
Mant, Janice [Elba] MacDonald
Bio-bibliographic data:
Canadian Crime Fiction, pp. 145–46.
(209)
Manthorne, Jackie
Bio-bibliographic data:
Canadian Crime Fiction, p. 146. (209)
Detecting Women 2, p. 124. (877b)
Detecting Women, 3rd ed., pp. 172–73.
(877c)
Manzur, Jorge
Bio-bibliographic data:

Latin American Mystery Writers: An A to Z Guide. (881)

Mara, Bernard. *See* **Moore, Brian**

Maracotta, Lindsay
Bio-bibliographic data:
Detecting Women, 3rd ed., p. 173. (877c)
Web site: http://stopyourekillingme.com/
lindsay-maracotta.html

Marceau, Claude
Bio-bibliographic data:
Canadian Crime Fiction, p. 146. (209)

Marchand, Philip
Bio-bibliographic data:
Canadian Crime Fiction, p. 146. (209)

Marchildon, Daniel
Bio-bibliographic data:
Canadian Crime Fiction, p. 146. (209)

Marcin, Max
Bio-bibliographic data:
The Encyclopedia of Mystery and Detection, p. 274. (7)

Marcott, James. *Pseud. for* **Duane R. Schermerhorn**
Bio-bibliographic data:
Canadian Crime Fiction, p. 260. (209)

Marcy, Jean. *Pseud. for* **Jean Hutchinson and Marcy Jacobs**
Bio-bibliographic data:
Detecting Women, 3rd ed., p. 173. (877c)

Margolis, Seth
Bio-bibliographic data:
Detecting Men, 1st ed., p. 167. (876)

Marineau, MichPle
Bio-bibliographic data:
Canadian Crime Fiction, p. 146. (209)

Mariz, Linda French
Bio-bibliographic data:
Detecting Women, 1st ed., p. 90. (877a)
Detecting Women 2, p. 125. (877b)
Detecting Women, 3rd ed., pp. 173–74. (877c)

Markham, Robert. *See* **Amis, Kingsley**

Markowitz, Murray:
Bio-bibliographic data:
Canadian Crime Fiction, p. 146. (209)

Marks, Alan. *See* **Annand, Alan**

Marks, Stanley
Bio-bibliographic data:
Australian Crime Fiction, p. 171. (207)

Markson, David
Bio-bibliographic data:
The Big Book of Noir, p. 265. (24)

Markstein, George
Bio-bibliographic data:

Twentieth-Century Crime and Mystery Writers, 2nd ed., p. 599. (882b)

Marlowe, Dan J[ames].
Bio-bibliographic data:
Encyclopedia Mysteriosa, p. 231. (2)
The Encyclopedia of Mystery and Detection, p. 274. (7)
The Mammoth Encyclopedia of Modern Crime Fiction, pp. 329–30. (1)
St. James Guide to Crime & Mystery Writers, 4th ed., pp. 690–91. (882d)
Twentieth-Century Crime and Mystery Writers, 1st ed., pp. 999–1000. (882a)
Twentieth-Century Crime and Mystery Writers, 2nd ed., pp. 599–601. (882b)
Twentieth-Century Crime and Mystery Writers, 3rd ed., pp. 710–12. (882c)

Marlowe, Derek
Bio-bibliographic data:
St. James Guide to Crime & Mystery Writers, 4th ed., pp. 691–92. (882d)
Twentieth-Century Crime and Mystery Writers, 1st ed., pp. 1000–1002. (882a)
Twentieth-Century Crime and Mystery Writers, 2nd ed., pp. 601–2. (882b)
Twentieth-Century Crime and Mystery Writers, 3rd ed., pp. 712–13. (882c)

Marlowe, Greg
Bio-bibliographic data:
Canadian Crime Fiction, p. 260. (209)

Marlowe, Hugh. *Pseud. for* **Henry Patterson**
Bio-bibliographic data:
Twentieth-Century Crime and Mystery Writers, 1st ed., pp. 1002–5. (882a)
Web site: http://stopyourekillingme.com/
hugh-marlowe.html

Marlowe, Mary. *Pseud. for* **Margaret Mary Shanahan**
Bio-bibliographic data:
Australian Crime Fiction, pp. 171–72. (207)

Marlowe, Rufus. *See* **Sheltus, John Ashley**

Marlowe, Stephen: name changed from Milton Lesser
Bio-bibliographic data:
Detecting Men, 1st ed., p. 168, 216. (876)
The Encyclopedia of Murder and Mystery, p. 329. (6)
St. James Guide to Crime & Mystery Writers, 4th ed., pp. 692–94. (882d)
Twentieth-Century Crime and Mystery Writers, 1st ed., pp. 1005–7. (882a)

Twentieth-Century Crime and Mystery Writers, 2nd ed., pp. 602–3. (882b)
Twentieth-Century Crime and Mystery Writers, 3rd ed., pp. 713–14. (882c)
Personal papers in College of William and Mary, Williamsburg, Virginia.

Maron, Margaret
Bio-bibliographic data:
By a Woman's Hand, 1st ed., p. 138. (884a)
By a Woman's Hand, 2nd ed., p. 147. (884b)
Detecting Women, 1st ed., pp. 90–91. (877a)
Detecting Women 2, p. 125. (877b)
Detecting Women, 3rd ed., p. 174. (877c)
The Encyclopedia of Murder and Mystery, pp. 329–30. (6)
Great Women Mystery Writers, pp. 213–15. (880)
The Mammoth Encyclopedia of Modern Crime Fiction, pp. 330–31. (1)
St. James Guide to Crime & Mystery Writers, 4th ed., pp. 694–95. (882d)
Speaking of Murder, vol. II, pp. 102–14. (875b)
Whodunit? A Who's Who in Crime and Mystery Writing, pp. 124–25. (5)
Women of Mystery, p. 436. (874)
Web site: http://www.margaretmaron. com; http://stopyourekillingme. com/margaret-maron.html

Marquand, John P[hillips].
Bio-bibliographic data:
Critical Survey of Mystery and Detective Fiction, pp. 1184–88. (41)
Encyclopedia Mysteriosa, p. 234. (2)
The Encyclopedia of Murder and Mystery, pp. 330–31. (6)
The Encyclopedia of Mystery and Detection, pp. 277–78. (7)
St. James Guide to Crime & Mystery Writers, 4th ed., pp. 695–97. (882d)
Twentieth-Century Crime and Mystery Writers, 1st ed., pp. 1007–10. (882a)
Twentieth-Century Crime and Mystery Writers, 2nd ed., pp. 603–5. (882b)
Twentieth-Century Crime and Mystery Writers, 3rd ed., pp. 714–16. (882c)

Marquis, Max
Bio-bibliographic data:
Detecting Men, 1st ed., p. 168. (876)

Marric, J. J. *See* **Creasey, John**
Marris, Kathrine. *See* **Beck, K. K.**
Marsh, [Dame Edith] Ngaio
Bio-bibliographic data:
British Mystery Writers, 1920–1939, pp. 198–213. (867)
Corpus Delicti of Mystery Fiction, pp. 98–99. (879)
Critical Survey of Mystery and Detective Fiction, pp. 1189–94. (41)
Detecting Women, 1st ed., pp. 91–92. (877a)
Detecting Women 2, pp. 125–26. (877b)
Encyclopedia Mysteriosa, pp. 234–35. (2)
The Encyclopedia of Murder and Mystery, pp. 331–32. (6)
The Encyclopedia of Mystery and Detection, pp. 278–79. (7)
Great Women Mystery Writers, pp. 215–19. (880)
Mystery and Suspense Writers, pp. 665–77. (884.2)
100 Masters of Mystery and Detective Fiction, pp. 460–66. (37)
The Oxford Companion to Crime and Mystery Writing, pp. 279–80. (4)
St. James Guide to Crime & Mystery Writers, 4th ed., pp. 697–99. (882d)
10 Women of Mystery, pp. 78–105. (864, 865)
Twentieth-Century Crime and Mystery Writers, 1st ed., p. 1010–13. (882a)
Twentieth-Century Crime and Mystery Writers, 2nd ed., pp. 605–7. (882b)
Twentieth-Century Crime and Mystery Writers, 3rd ed., pp. 716–18. (882c)
Whodunit? A Who's Who in Crime and Mystery Writing, pp. 125–26. (5)
Women Authors of Detective Series, pp. 50–58. (882.5)
Women of Mystery, pp. 225–61. (874)
Personal papers in Mugar Memorial Library, Boston University.
Personal papers in Alexander Turnbull Library, Wellington, New Zealand.
Web site: http://stopyourekillingme.com/ ngaio-marsh.html; http://www. ngaio-marsh.org.nz
Ngaio Marsh Society International
c/o Nicole St. John
103 Godwin Avenue, #299
Midland Park, NJ 07432
http://www.chipmunkcrossing. com/activities/nmsi.html

Marsh, Richard. *Pseud. for* **Bernard Heldmann**
Bio-bibliographic data:
The Encyclopedia of Murder and Mystery, p. 332. (6)
Marshall, Archibald
Bio-bibliographic data:
The Encyclopedia of Mystery and Detection, p. 279. (7)
Marshall, Bill; i.e., William
Bio-bibliographic data:
Canadian Crime Fiction, p. 8, 147. (209)
Marshall, Charles or Charlee
Bio-bibliographic data:
Australian Crime Fiction, p. 9. (207)
Marshall, [P. O.] Douglas
Bio-bibliographic data:
Canadian Crime Fiction, p. 147. (209)
Marshall, Mel
Bio-bibliographic data:
Canadian Crime Fiction, p. 254, 260. (209)
Marshall, Raymond. *See* **Chase, James Hadley**
Marshall, Robin
Bio-bibliographic data:
Canadian Crime Fiction, p. 147. (209)
Marshall, Tom
Bio-bibliographic data:
Canadian Crime Fiction, p. 147. (209)
Marshall, William (I). *See* **Marshall, Bill**
Marshall, William [Leonard] (II)
Bio-bibliographic data:
Australian Crime Fiction, pp. 172–74. (207)
Detecting Men, 1st ed., pp. 168–69. (876)
Encyclopedia Mysteriosa, p. 235. (2)
The Encyclopedia of Murder and Mystery, p. 332. (6)
The Mammoth Encyclopedia of Modern Crime Fiction, pp. 331–32. (1)
St. James Guide to Crime & Mystery Writers, 4th ed., pp. 699–700. (882d)
Twentieth-Century Crime and Mystery Writers, 2nd ed., pp. 607–8. (882b)
Twentieth-Century Crime and Mystery Writers, 3rd ed., pp. 718–19. (882c)
Web site: http://stopyourekillingme.com/ william-marshall.html
Marsten, Richard. *See* **Hunter, Evan**
Marston, A. E. *See* **Miles, Keith**
Marston, Edward. *See* **Miles, Keith**
Martel, Jean-Marc
Bio-bibliographic data:

Canadian Crime Fiction, p. 147. (209)
Martel, Charles. *Pseud. for* **Thomas Delf?**
Bio-bibliographic data:
The Encyclopedia of Murder and Mystery, p. 333. (6)
Martell, Dominc. *See* **Reaves, Sam**
Marten, Jon Chisholm. *See* **Conyn, Cornelius, and Jon Chisholm Marten**
Martin, A. E.; i.e., Archibald Edward
Bio-bibliographic data:
Australian Crime Fiction, pp. 174–75. (207)
Martin, Allana
Bio-bibliographic data:
Detecting Women, 3rd ed., p. 174. (877c)
Web site: http://stopyourekillingme.com/ allana-martin.html
Martin, Clarence W.
Bio-bibliographic data:
Australian Crime Fiction, p. 175. (207)
Martin, Ian Kennedy
Bio-bibliographic data:
Canadian Crime Fiction, p. 260. (209)
Martin, James E.
Bio-bibliographic data:
Detecting Men, 1st ed., p. 170. (876)
Martin, L. W.; i.e., Lincoln William and N[orman]. S[oren]. Lynravn
Bio-bibliographic data:
Australian Crime Fiction, p. 175. (207)
Martin, Lee. *See* **Wingate, Anne**
Martin, Quinn
Bio-bibliographic data:
Encyclopedia Mysteriosa, p. 235. (2)
Martin, Roy Peter. *See* **Melville, James**
Martin, Shane. *See* **Johnston, George H.**
Martin, Thomas Hector. *See* **Saxon, Peter**
Martinez de la Vega, Jose
Bio-bibliographic data:
Latin American Mystery Writers: An A to Z Guide. (881)
Martini, Juan Carlos
Bio-bibliographic data:
Latin American Mystery Writers: An A to Z Guide. (881)
Martini, Steve
Bio-bibliographic data:
Detecting Men, 1st ed., p. 170. (876)
St. James Guide to Crime & Mystery Writers, 4th ed., p. 703. (882d)
Web site: http://stopyourekillingme.com/ steve-martini.html; http://www. stevemartini.com

Martyn, Wyndham
Bio-bibliographic data:
Canadian Crime Fiction, p. 260. (209)
Marvin, Susan. *See* **Ellis, Julie [M.]**
Mason, A. E. W.; i.e., Alfred Edward Woodley
Bio-bibliographic data:
British Mystery Writers, 1860–1919, pp. 205–11. (866)
Critical Survey of Mystery and Detective Fiction, pp. 1195–99. (41)
Encyclopedia Mysteriosa, p. 236. (2)
The Encyclopedia of Murder and Mystery, p. 334. (6)
The Encyclopedia of Mystery and Detection, pp. 279–80. (7)
The Oxford Companion to Crime and Mystery Writing, p. 280. (4)
St. James Guide to Crime & Mystery Writers, 4th ed., p.703–5. (882d)
Twelve Englishmen of Mystery, pp. 34–63. (865)
Twentieth-Century Crime and Mystery Writers, 1st ed., pp. 1014–17. (882a)
Twentieth-Century Crime and Mystery Writers, 2nd ed., pp. 608–9. (882b)
Twentieth-Century Crime and Mystery Writers, 3rd ed., pp. 719–21. (882c)
Whodunit? A Who's Who in Crime and Mystery Writing, p. 126. (5)
Mason, Colin
Bio-bibliographic data:
Australian Crime Fiction, p. 176. (207)
Mason, F[rancis]. Van Wyck
Bio-bibliographic data:
Encyclopedia Mysteriosa, p. 236. (2)
The Encyclopedia of Mystery and Detection, pp. 282–83. (7)
St. James Guide to Crime & Mystery Writers, 4th ed., pp. 705–7. (882d)
Twentieth-Century Crime and Mystery Writers, 1st ed., pp. 1017–20. (882a)
Twentieth-Century Crime and Mystery Writers, 2nd ed., pp. 609–11. (882b)
Twentieth-Century Crime and Mystery Writers, 3rd ed., pp. 721–23. (882c)
Mason, Sarah J[ill].
Bio-bibliographic data:
By a Woman's Hand, 1st ed., pp. 138–39. (884a)
By a Woman's Hand, 2nd ed., pp. 147–48. (884b)
Detecting Women, 1st ed., p. 44, 92. (877a)

Detecting Women 2, p. 47, 127. (877b)
Detecting Women, 3rd ed., pp. 63–64, 175. (877c)
The Mammoth Encyclopedia of Modern Crime Fiction, pp. 334–35. (1)
Web site: http://stopyourekillingme.com/sarah-j-mason.html
Mason, Tally. *See* **Derleth, August**
Massey, Ruth. *Pseud. for* **Ruth [Lillian Massey] Tovell**
Bio-bibliographic data:
Canadian Crime Fiction, pp. 147–48, 223. (209)
Massey, Sujata
Bio-bibliographic data:
Detecting Women, 3rd ed., pp. 175–76. (877c)
The Mammoth Encyclopedia of Modern Crime Fiction, pp. 335–36. (1)
Web site: http://www.interbridge.com/sujata/index.html; http://stopyourekillingme.com/sujata-massey.html
Massie, Sonja. *See* **McKevett, G. A**
Masterman, John
Bio-bibliographic data:
St. James Guide to Crime & Mystery Writers, 4th ed., pp. 707–8. (882d)
Twentieth-Century Crime and Mystery Writers, 3rd ed., pp. 723–24. (882c)
Masters, J. D.
Bio-bibliographic data:
Detecting Men, 1st ed., pp. 170–71. (876)
Masters, Priscilla
Bio-bibliographic data:
Detecting Women, 3rd ed., p. 176. (877c)
Web site: http://stopyourekillingme.com/priscilla-masters.html
Masterson, Whit. *See* **Miller, Wade**
Masur, Harold Q.
Bio-bibliographic data:
Detecting Men, 1st ed., p. 171. (876)
Encyclopedia Mysteriosa, p. 239. (2)
The Encyclopedia of Murder and Mystery, p. 336. (6)
The Encyclopedia of Mystery and Detection, p. 283. (7)
St. James Guide to Crime & Mystery Writers, 4th ed., pp. 708–9. (882d)
Twentieth-Century Crime and Mystery Writers, 1st ed., pp. 1020–22. (882a)
Twentieth-Century Crime and Mystery Writers, 2nd ed., pp. 611–13. (882b)

Twentieth-Century Crime and Mystery Writers, 3rd ed., pp. 724–26. (882c)

Matera, Lia
Bio-bibliographic data:
By a Woman's Hand, 1st ed., pp. 139–40. (884a)
By a Woman's Hand, 2nd ed., pp. 148–49. (884b)
Canadian Crime Fiction, p. 148. (209)
Detecting Women, 1st ed., pp. 92–93. (877a)
Detecting Women 2, p. 127. (877b)
Detecting Women, 3rd ed., pp. 176–77. (877c)
Encyclopedia Mysteriosa, p. 240. (2)
Great Women Mystery Writers, pp. 219–21. (880)
The Mammoth Encyclopedia of Modern Crime Fiction, p. 336. (1)
St. James Guide to Crime & Mystery Writers, 4th ed., p. 710. (882d)
Web site: http://www.scruz.net/ ~lmatera/liamatera.html; http:// stopyourekillingme.com/lia-matera. html

Mather, Berkely. *Pseud. for* **John Evan Weston Davies**
Bio-bibliographic data:
Australian Crime Fiction, p. 177. (207)
Canadian Crime Fiction, p. 275, 283. (209)
Twentieth-Century Crime and Mystery Writers, 1st ed., pp. 1022–25. (882a)
Twentieth-Century Crime and Mystery Writers, 2nd ed., pp. 613–14. (882b)
Twentieth-Century Crime and Mystery Writers, 3rd ed., pp. 726–27. (882c)

Mather, Linda. *Pseud. for* **Linda Ainsbury**
Bio-bibliographic data:
Detecting Women, 1st ed., p. 93. (877a)
Detecting Women 2, p. 127. (877b)
Detecting Women, 3rd ed., p. 177. (877c)

Mather, Richard Arthur
Bio-bibliographic data:
Australian Crime Fiction, pp. 176–77. (207)

Mathers, Helen [Buckingham]
Bio-bibliographic data:
The Encyclopedia of Mystery and Detection, p. 283. (7)

Mathews, Francine
Bio-bibliographic data:
Detecting Women, 1st ed., p. 93. (877a)
Detecting Women 2, pp. 127–28. (877b)

Detecting Women, 3rd ed., p. 177. (877c)
Web site: http://stopyourekillingme.com/ francine-mathews.html; http://www. francinemathews.com

Mathieu, André
Bio-bibliographic data:
Canadian Crime Fiction, p. 148. (209)

Matsumoto, Seicho. *Pseud. for* **Matsumoto Kiyoharu**
Bio-bibliographic data:
The Encyclopedia of Murder and Mystery, p. 337. (6)
The Mammoth Encyclopedia of Modern Crime Fiction, p. 337. (1)
The Oxford Companion to Crime and Mystery Writing, pp. 281–82. (4)
St. James Guide to Crime & Mystery Writers, 4th ed., pp. 710–11. (882d)
Twentieth-Century Crime and Mystery Writers, 3rd ed., p. 1134. (882c)
Whodunit? A Who's Who in Crime and Mystery Writing, pp. 127–28. (5)

Matteson, Stefanie
Bio-bibliographic data:
By a Woman's Hand, 1st ed., pp. 140–41. (884a)
By a Woman's Hand, 2nd ed., pp. 149–50. (884b)
Detecting Women, 1st ed., p. 93. (877a)
Detecting Women 2, p. 128. (877b)
Detecting Women, 3rd ed., p. 178. (877c)
Web site: http://stopyourekillingme.com/ stefanie-matteson.html

Matthews, Alex
Bio-bibliographic data:
Detecting Women 2, p. 128. (877b)
Detecting Women, 3rd ed., p. 178. (877c)
Web site: http://stopyourekillingme.com/ alex-matthews.html

Matthews, Patricia
Bio-bibliographic data:
Detecting Women, 3rd ed., pp. 178–79. (877c)

Matthews, Lew. *See* **Lewin, Matthew Z.**

Maugham, Robin
Bio-bibliographic data:
Twentieth-Century Crime and Mystery Writers, 1st ed., pp. 1025–27. (882a)

Maugham, W[illiam]. Somerset
Bio-bibliographic data:
British Mystery Writers, 1920–1939, pp. 214–20. (867)
Critical Survey of Mystery and Detective Fiction, pp. 1200–1206. (41)

Encyclopedia Mysteriosa, p. 240. (2)
The Encyclopedia of Murder and Mystery,
pp. 337–38. (6)
*The Encyclopedia of Mystery and
Detection,* pp. 283–84. (7)
*St. James Guide to Crime & Mystery
Writers,* 4th ed., pp. 711–14. (882d)
*Twentieth-Century Crime and Mystery
Writers,* 1st ed., pp. 1028–32. (882a)
*Twentieth-Century Crime and Mystery
Writers,* 2nd ed., pp. 614–17. (882b)
*Twentieth-Century Crime and Mystery
Writers,* 3rd ed., pp. 727–30. (882c)
Personal papers in Humanities Research
Center, University of Texas at Austin.
Personal papers in Beinecke Library, Yale
University
Personal papers in Berg Collection, New
York Public Library.
Personal papers in Special Collections,
Stanford University, California.
Personal papers in Houghton Library,
Harvard University, Cambridge,
Massachusetts.
Personal papers in Special Collections,
University of Michigan Libraries.
Personal papers in Butler Library,
Columbia University, New York City.
Personal papers in Fales Collection, New
York University, New York City.
Personal papers in Cornell University,
Ithaca, New York.
Maupassant, Guy de
Bio-bibliographic data:
*Critical Survey of Mystery and Detective
Fiction,* pp. 1207–12. (41)
The Encyclopedia of Murder and Mystery,
p. 338. (6)
Maurensig, Paolo
Bio-bibliographic data:
The Encyclopedia of Murder and Mystery,
p. 338. (6)
Maxim, John
Bio-bibliographic data:
Detecting Men, 1st ed., p. 172. (876)
Web site: http://stopyourekillingme.com/
john-r-maxim.html; http://www.
geocities.com/john_r_maxim
**Maxwell, A. E. Pseud. of Ann Maxwell
and Evan Maxwell**
Bio-bibliographic data:
By a Woman's Hand, 1st ed., pp. 141–42.
(884a)

By a Woman's Hand, 2nd ed., p. 150.
(884b)
Detecting Women, 1st ed., p. 94. (877a)
Detecting Women 2, p. 128. (877b)
Detecting Women, 3rd ed., p. 179. (877c)
Web site: http://stopyourekillingme.com/
a-e-maxwell.html
Maxwell, Helen K. *See* **Foley, Rae**
Maxwell, Kurt. *See* **Palka, Kurt Maxwell**
Maxwell, M. E. Braddon. *See* **Braddon, M.
E.**
Mayer, Jeni
Bio-bibliographic data:
Canadian Crime Fiction, p. 148. (209)
Maynard, Kevin H.
Bio-bibliographic data:
Canadian Crime Fiction, p. 148. (209)
Mayo, J. K.
Bio-bibliographic data:
Canadian Crime Fiction, p. 260, 283.
(209)
Detecting Men, 1st ed., p. 172. (876)
Mayor, Archer [Huntington]
Bio-bibliographic data:
Detecting Men, 1st ed., p. 172. (876)
*St. James Guide to Crime & Mystery
Writers,* 4th ed., pp. 715–16. (882d)
*Whodunit? A Who's Who in Crime and
Mystery Writing,* p. 128. (5)
Web site: http://stopyourekillingme.com/
archer-mayor.html; http://www.
archermayor.com
Mayse, Arthur [William Caswell]
Bio-bibliographic data:
Canadian Crime Fiction, p. 148. (209)
Mayse, Susan
Bio-bibliographic data:
Canadian Crime Fiction, pp. 148–49.
(209)
McAllester, Melanie
Bio-bibliographic data:
Detecting Women, 1st ed., p. 94. (877a)
Detecting Women 2, p. 129. (877b)
Detecting Women, 3rd ed., p. 179. (877c)
McAllister, Alister. *See* **Brock, Lynn**
McAuliffe, Frank
Bio-bibliographic data:
*Twentieth-Century Crime and Mystery
Writers,* 2nd ed., pp. 617–18. (882b)
*Twentieth-Century Crime and Mystery
Writers,* 3rd ed., pp. 730–31. (882c)

McBain, Ed. *See* **Hunter, Evan**
McBride, James R., and Margaret McBride
Bio-bibliographic data:
Canadian Crime Fiction, p. 135. (209)
McBride, Margaret. *See* **McBride, James R., and Margaret McBride**
McCabe, Cameron. *See* **Borneman, Ernest [William Julius]**
McCafferty, Barbara Taylor. *See also* **McCafferty, Barbara Taylor, and Beverly Taylor Herald**
Bio-bibliographic data:
By a Woman's Hand, 1st ed., p. 142. (884a)
By a Woman's Hand, 2nd ed., pp. 150–51. (884b)
Detecting Women, 1st ed., p. 94. (877a)
Detecting Women 2, p. 129. (877b)
Detecting Women, 3rd ed., p. 180, 181. (877c)
The Mammoth Encyclopedia of Modern Crime Fiction, p. 309. (1)
Web site: http://www.mysterytwins.com; http://stopyourekillingme.com/ barbara-taylor-mccafferty.html; http://members.tripod.com/ TaylorMac/index.htm
McCafferty, Barbara Taylor, and Beverly Taylor Herald
Bio-bibliographic data:
Detecting Women, 3rd ed., pp. 179–80. (877c)
McCafferty, Jeanne
Bio-bibliographic data:
Detecting Women, 3rd ed., p. 180. (877c)
McCafferty, Taylor. *See* **Barbara Taylor McCafferty**
McCall, K. T. *Pseud. for* **Audrey Armitage and Muriel Watkins**
Bio-bibliographic data:
Australian Crime Fiction, pp. 160–61. (207)
McCall, Thomas
Bio-bibliographic data:
Detecting Men, 1st ed., p. 174. (876)
McCall, Wendell. *See* **Pearson, Ridley**
McCann, Will
Bio-bibliographic data:
Canadian Crime Fiction, p. 135. (209)
McCarry, Charles
Bio-bibliographic data:
Encyclopedia Mysteriosa, p. 214. (2)

The Encyclopedia of Murder and Mystery, pp. 310–11. (6)
Twentieth-Century Crime and Mystery Writers, 1st ed., pp. 1037–38. (882a)
Twentieth-Century Crime and Mystery Writers, 2nd ed., p. 621. (882b)
Twentieth-Century Crime and Mystery Writers, 3rd ed., pp. 734–35. (882c)
Web site: http://stopyourekillingme.com/ charles-mccarry.html
McCarter, Jim; i.e., James Walsh
Bio-bibliographic data:
Australian Crime Fiction, p. 161. (207)
McClean, J. Sloan
Bio-bibliographic data:
Canadian Crime Fiction, p. 259. (209)
McClellan, Janet
Bio-bibliographic data:
Detecting Women, 3rd ed., p. 181. (877c)
Web site: http://www.janetmcclellan.com
McClellan, Tierney. *See* **McCafferty, Barbara Taylor**
McClendon, Lise
Bio-bibliographic data:
Detecting Women, 1st ed., p. 94. (877a)
Detecting Women 2, p. 129. (877b)
Detecting Women, 3rd ed., p. 181. (877c)
Web site: http://stopyourekillingme.com/ lise-mcclendon.html; http://www. lisemcclendon.com
McClintock, Gray
Bio-bibliographic data:
Canadian Crime Fiction, p. 135. (209)
McClintock, Norah
Bio-bibliographic data:
Canadian Crime Fiction, p. 135. (209)
McCloy, Helen [Worrell Clarkson]
Bio-bibliographic data:
Detecting Women, 1st ed., p. 95. (877a)
Detecting Women 2, p. 130. (877b)
Encyclopedia Mysteriosa, p. 215. (2)
The Encyclopedia of Murder and Mystery, p. 311. (6)
The Encyclopedia of Mystery and Detection, pp. 259–60. (7)
St. James Guide to Crime & Mystery Writers, 4th ed., pp. 719–21. (882d)
Twentieth-Century Crime and Mystery Writers, 1st ed., pp. 1039–42. (882a)
Twentieth-Century Crime and Mystery Writers, 2nd ed., pp. 622–23. (882b)
Twentieth-Century Crime and Mystery Writers, 3rd ed., pp. 735–37. (882c)

Personal papers in Mugar Memorial
Library, Boston University.

McClure, James [Howe]
Bio-bibliographic data:
Colloquium on Crime, pp. 167–88. (884.1)
*The Craft of Crime: Conversations with
Crime Writers*, pp. 24–55. (872)
*Critical Survey of Mystery and Detective
Fiction*, pp. 1118–23. (41)
Detecting Men, 1st ed., pp. 174–75. (876)
Encyclopedia Mysteriosa, p. 215. (2)
The Encyclopedia of Murder and Mystery,
pp. 311–12. (6)
*The Mammoth Encyclopedia of Modern
Crime Fiction*, p. 310. (1)
*100 Masters of Mystery and Detective
Fiction*, pp. 431–36. (37)
*The Oxford Companion to Crime and
Mystery Writing*, p. 283. (4)
*St. James Guide to Crime & Mystery
Writers*, 4th ed., pp. 721–23. (882d)
*Twentieth-Century Crime and Mystery
Writers,* 1st ed., pp. 1042–43. (882a)
*Twentieth-Century Crime and Mystery
Writers,* 2nd ed., pp. 623–24. (882b)
*Twentieth-Century Crime and Mystery
Writers,* 3rd ed., pp. 737–38. (882c)
*Whodunit? A Who's Who in Crime and
Mystery Writing*, p. 129. (5)
Web site: http://stopyourekillingme.com/
james-mcclure.html

McConnell, Frank
Bio-bibliographic data:
Detecting Men, 1st ed., p. 175. (876)

McConnell, James Douglas Rutherford.
See Rutherford, Douglas

McConnell, Vicki P.
Bio-bibliographic data:
By a Woman's Hand, 1st ed., pp. 142–43.
(884a)
Detecting Women 2, p. 130. (877b)
Detecting Women, 3rd ed., p. 182. (877c)

McCormack, Eric
Bio-bibliographic data:
Canadian Crime Fiction, p. 135. (209)

McCormick, Claire. *Pseud. for* **Marta
Haake Labus**
Bio-bibliographic data:
Detecting Women, 3rd ed., p. 182. (877c)

McCourt, Edward A[lexander].
Bio-bibliographic data:
Canadian Crime Fiction, pp. 135–36.
(209)

McCoy, Horace
Bio-bibliographic data:
The Encyclopedia of Murder and Mystery,
p. 312. (6)
*St. James Guide to Crime & Mystery
Writers*, 4th ed., pp. 723–24. (882d)
*Twentieth-Century Crime and Mystery
Writers,* 1st ed., pp. 1044–45. (882a)
*Twentieth-Century Crime and Mystery
Writers,* 2nd ed., pp. 624–25. (882b)
*Twentieth-Century Crime and Mystery
Writers,* 3rd ed., pp. 738–39. (882c)
Personal papers in University of
California, Los Angeles.

McCreede, Jess. *Pseud. for* **Jerry O'Neal**
Bio-bibliographic data:
Canadian Crime Fiction, pp. 259–60.
(209)

McCrumb, Sharyn [Arwood]
Bio-bibliographic data:
By a Woman's Hand, 1st ed., pp. 143–44.
(884a)
By a Woman's Hand, 2nd ed., pp. 151–52.
(884b)
Detecting Women, 1st ed., pp. 95–96.
(877a)
Detecting Women 2, pp. 130–31. (877b)
Detecting Women, 3rd ed., pp. 182–83.
(877c)
The Encyclopedia of Murder and Mystery,
pp. 312–13. (6)
Great Women Mystery Writers, pp. 201–3.
(880)
*St. James Guide to Crime & Mystery
Writers*, 4th ed., pp. 724–25. (882d)
Speaking of Murder, pp. 191–204. (875a)
*Whodunit? A Who's Who in Crime and
Mystery Writing*, p. 129. (5)
Web site: http://stopyourekillingme.com/
sharyn-mccrumb.html; http://www.
sharynmccrumb.com

McCurtin, Peter. *See* **Curry, Gene**
McCutchan, Philip Donald
Bio-bibliographic data:
Australian Crime Fiction, p. 161. (207)
Detecting Men, 1st ed., p. 97, 175–76,
(876)
*St. James Guide to Crime & Mystery
Writers*, 4th ed., pp. 725–29. (882d)
*Twentieth-Century Crime and Mystery
Writers,* 1st ed., pp. 1045–48. (882a)
*Twentieth-Century Crime and Mystery
Writers,* 2nd ed., pp. 625–27. (882b)

*Twentieth-Century Crime and Mystery
Writers,* 3rd ed., pp. 739–42. (882c)
McCutcheon, George Barr
Bio-bibliographic data:
*The Encyclopedia of Mystery and
Detection,* p. 260. (7)
McDaniel, David [Edward]
Bio-bibliographic data:
Australian Crime Fiction, p. 161. (207)
McDermid, Val
Bio-bibliographic data:
By a Woman's Hand, 1st ed., pp. 144–45.
(884a)
By a Woman's Hand, 2nd ed., pp. 152–53.
(884b)
Deadly Women, pp. 115–18. (26.5)
Detecting Women, 1st ed., p. 96. (877a)
Detecting Women 2, p. 131. (877b)
Detecting Women, 3rd ed., pp. 183–84.
(877c)
Great Women Mystery Writers, pp. 203–5.
(880)
*The Mammoth Encyclopedia of Modern
Crime Fiction,* pp. 311–12. (1)
*St. James Guide to Crime & Mystery
Writers,* 4th ed., pp. 729–30. (882d)
*Whodunit? A Who's Who in Crime and
Mystery Writing,* pp. 129–30. (5)
Women of Mystery, p. 436. (874)
Web site: http://www.twbooks.co.uk/
authors/valmcdermid.html; http://
stopyourekillingme.com/
val-mcdermid.html
McDonald, Alice
Bio-bibliographic data:
Canadian Crime Fiction, p. 136. (209)
McDonald, Gregory [Christopher]
Bio-bibliographic data:
*The Craft of Crime: Conversations with
Crime Writers,* pp. 104–42. (872)
*Critical Survey of Mystery and Detective
Fiction,* pp. 1124–29. (41)
Detecting Men, 1st ed., pp. 176–77. (876)
Encyclopedia Mysteriosa, p. 216. (2)
*The Mammoth Encyclopedia of Modern
Crime Fiction,* pp. 312–13. (1)
*St. James Guide to Crime & Mystery
Writers,* 4th ed., pp. 730–31. (882d)
*Twentieth-Century Crime and Mystery
Writers,* 1st ed., pp. 1048–49. (882a)
*Twentieth-Century Crime and Mystery
Writers,* 2nd ed., pp. 627–28. (882b)
*Twentieth-Century Crime and Mystery
Writers,* 3rd ed., pp. 742–44. (882c)

Personal papers in Mugar Memorail
Library, Boston University.
Web site:
http://www.gregorymcdonald.com;
http://stopyourekillingme.com/
gregory-mcdonald.html; http://
fletch.spencerryan.net
McDuff, E. M.; i.e., Eileen May
Bio-bibliographic data:
Australian Crime Fiction, p. 162. (207)
McDuffie, Harry R.
Bio-bibliographic data:
Australian Crime Fiction, p. 162. (207)
McEldowney, Eugene
Bio-bibliographic data:
Detecting Men, 1st ed., p. 177. (876)
McElwain, Miranda
Bio-bibliographic data:
Australian Crime Fiction, p. 162. (207)
McEwen, Jessie Evelyn
Bio-bibliographic data:
Canadian Crime Fiction, p. 138. (209)
McFall, Patricia
Bio-bibliographic data:
Detecting Women, 1st ed., p. 96. (877a)
Detecting Women 2, pp. 131–32. (877b)
McFarlane, Arthur E[merson]
Bio-bibliographic data:
Canadian Crime Fiction, p. 138. (209)
McFarlane, Ian
Bio-bibliographic data:
Australian Crime Fiction, p. 162. (207)
McFarlane, [Charles] Leslie
Bio-bibliographic data:
Canadian Crime Fiction, p. 138, 183.
(209)
McGarrity, Mark. *See* **Gill, Bartholomew**
McGarrity, Michael
Bio-bibliographic data:
Detecting Men, 1st ed., p. 177. (876)
Web site: http://stopyourekillingme.com/
michael-mcgarrity.html; http://
michaelmcgarrity.tripod.com/defaul.
htm; http://www.michaelmcgarrity.
net
McGaughey, Neil
Bio-bibliographic data:
Detecting Men, 1st ed., p. 177. (876)
McGerr, Patricia
Bio-bibliographic data:
*Critical Survey of Mystery and Detective
Fiction,* pp. 1141–47. (41)
Detecting Women, 1st ed., p. 96. (877a)
Detecting Women 2, p. 132. (877b)

Encyclopedia Mysteriosa, p. 219. (2)
Twentieth-Century Crime and Mystery Writers, 1st ed., pp. 1049–52. (882a)
St. James Guide to Crime & Mystery Writers, 4th ed., pp. 732–33. (882d)
Twentieth-Century Crime and Mystery Writers, 2nd ed., pp. 628–29. (882b)
Twentieth-Century Crime and Mystery Writers, 3rd ed., pp. 744–45. (882c)
Personal papers in Institute for Popular Culture, Bowling Green University, Bowling Green, Ohio.
Personal papers in Trinity College, Washington, D.C.

McGiffin, Janet
Bio-bibliographic data:
By a Woman's Hand, 2nd ed., p. 153. (884b)
Detecting Women, 1st ed., p. 97. (877a)
Detecting Women 2, p. 132. (877b)
Detecting Women, 3rd ed., p. 184. (877c)

McGillivray, James
Bio-bibliographic data:
Canadian Crime Fiction, p. 138. (209)

McGinley, Patrick
Bio-bibliographic data:
Critical Survey of Mystery and Detective Fiction, pp. 1148–53. (41)

McGirr, Edmund. *Pseud. for* **Kenneth Giles**
Bio-bibliographic data:
Twentieth-Century Crime and Mystery Writers, 1st ed., pp. 1052–54. (882a)
Twentieth-Century Crime and Mystery Writers, 2nd ed., pp. 630–31. (882b)
Twentieth-Century Crime and Mystery Writers, 3rd ed., pp. 745–47. (882c)

McGivern, William P[eter].
Bio-bibliographic data:
Critical Survey of Mystery and Detective Fiction, pp. 1154–59. (41)
Encyclopedia Mysteriosa, pp. 219–20. (2)
The Encyclopedia of Murder and Mystery, p. 317. (6)
The Encyclopedia of Mystery and Detection, pp. 264–65. (7)
100 Masters of Mystery and Detective Fiction, pp. 449–54. (37)
St. James Guide to Crime & Mystery Writers, 4th ed., pp. 733–34. (882d)
Twentieth-Century Crime and Mystery Writers, 1st ed., pp. 1055–57. (882a)
Twentieth-Century Crime and Mystery Writers, 2nd ed., pp. 631–32. (882b)

Twentieth-Century Crime and Mystery Writers, 3rd ed., pp. 747–48. (882c)
Personal papers in Mugar Memorial Library, Boston University.
Web site: http://stopyourekillingme.com/ william-mcgivern.html; http://www.miskatonic.org/rara-avis/b iblio/mcgivern.html

McGown, Jill
Bio-bibliographic data:
By a Woman's Hand, 1st ed., p. 145. (884a)
By a Woman's Hand, 2nd ed., pp. 153–54. (884b)
Detecting Women, 1st ed., p. 97. (877a)
Detecting Women 2, p. 132. (877b)
Detecting Women, 3rd ed., p. 184. (877c)
Great Women Mystery Writers, pp. 205–8. (880)
The Mammoth Encyclopedia of Modern Crime Fiction, pp. 318–19. (1)
St. James Guide to Crime & Mystery Writers, 4th ed., pp. 734–36. (882d)
Twentieth-Century Crime and Mystery Writers, 3rd ed., pp. 748–49. (882c)
Web site: http://www.jillmcgown.com; http://www.twbooks.co.uk/authors/jill mcgown.html; http://stopyourekillingme.com/jill-mc gown.html

McGrew, Julia
Bio-bibliographic data:
Canadian Crime Fiction, p. 139. (209)

McGuire, Christine
Bio-bibliographic data:
Detecting Women, 1st ed., p. 97. (877a)
Detecting Women 2, p. 132. (877b)
Detecting Women, 3rd ed., pp. 184–85. (877c)
Web site: http://stopyourekillingme.com/ christine-mcguire.html

McGuire, Frances Margaret
Bio-bibliographic data:
Australian Crime Fiction, p. 163. (207)

McGuire, Patrick O. *See* **Mitchell, James**

McGuire, [Dominic] Paul
Bio-bibliographic data:
Australian Crime Fiction, pp. 163–65. (207)
The Encyclopedia of Murder and Mystery, p. 317. (6)
The Encyclopedia of Mystery and Detection, pp. 265–66. (7)

St. James Guide to Crime & Mystery Writers, 4th ed., pp. 736–37. (882d)
Twentieth-Century Crime and Mystery Writers, 1st ed., pp. 1057–59. (882a)
Twentieth-Century Crime and Mystery Writers, 2nd ed., pp. 632–33. (882b)
Twentieth-Century Crime and Mystery Writers, 3rd ed., pp. 749–50. (882c)
McHale, Tom
Bio-bibliographic data:
The Encyclopedia of Murder and Mystery, pp. 317–18. (6)
McIlvanney, William
Bio-bibliographic data:
Detecting Men, 1st ed., p. 178. (876)
Encyclopedia Mysteriosa, p. 220. (2)
The Encyclopedia of Murder and Mystery, p. 318. (6)
The Mammoth Encyclopedia of Modern Crime Fiction, p. 319. (1)
St. James Guide to Crime & Mystery Writers, 4th ed., pp. 737–38. (882d)
Twentieth-Century Crime and Mystery Writers, 2nd ed., pp. 633–34. (882b)
Twentieth-Century Crime and Mystery Writers, 3rd ed., pp. 750–52. (882c)
Web site: http://stopyourekillingme.com/ william-mcilvanney.html
McInerny, Ralph [Matthew]
Bio-bibliographic data:
Critical Survey of Mystery and Detective Fiction, pp. 1160–66. (41)
Detecting Men, 1st ed., pp. 178–79, 210–11. (876)
Encyclopedia Mysteriosa, pp. 220–21. (2)
The Encyclopedia of Murder and Mystery, pp. 318–19. (6)
The Mammoth Encyclopedia of Modern Crime Fiction, pp. 320–21. (1)
St. James Guide to Crime & Mystery Writers, 4th ed., pp. 738–40. (882d)
Twentieth-Century Crime and Mystery Writers, 2nd ed., pp. 634–36. (882b)
Twentieth-Century Crime and Mystery Writers, 3rd ed., pp. 752–53. (882c)
Personal papers in University of Notre Dame Library, Indiana.
Web site: http://stopyourekillingme.com/ ralph-m-mcinerny.html
McIntosh, Kinn Hamilton. *See* **Aird, Catherine**
McKay, John George
Bio-bibliographic data:
Canadian Crime Fiction, p. 139. (209)

McKechnie, N. K.; i.e., Neil Kenneth
Bio-bibliographic data:
Canadian Crime Fiction, p. 139. (209)
McKee-Wright, April
Bio-bibliographic data:
Australian Crime Fiction, p. 163. (207)
McKemmish, Jan
Bio-bibliographic data:
Australian Crime Fiction, p. 166. (207)
McKenna, Bridget
Bio-bibliographic data:
By a Woman's Hand, 2nd ed., pp. 154–55. (884b)
Detecting Women, 1st ed., p. 97. (877a)
Detecting Women 2, p. 133. (877b)
Detecting Women, 3rd ed., p. 185. (877c)
McKenzie, C. J. *See* **Kane, Martin**
McKenzie, Valerie
Bio-bibliographic data:
Australian Crime Fiction, p. 166. (207)
McKernan, Victoria
Bio-bibliographic data:
Detecting Women 2, p. 133. (877b)
Detecting Women, 3rd ed., p. 185. (877c)
McKevett, G. A. *Pseud. for* **Sonja Massie**
Bio-bibliographic data:
Detecting Women 2, p. 133. (877b)
Detecting Women, 3rd ed., p. 186. (877c)
Web site: http://stopyourekillingme.com/ g-a-mckevett.html
McKim, Audrey
Bio-bibliographic data:
Canadian Crime Fiction, p. 141. (209)
McKimmey, James
Bio-bibliographic data:
The Big Book of Noir, p. 265. (24)
McKinnon, Keith
Bio-bibliographic data:
Canadian Crime Fiction, p. 141. (209)
McKinnon, Marion Crook. *See* **Crook, Marion**
McKitterick, Molly
Bio-bibliographic data:
Detecting Women, 3rd ed., p. 186. (877c)
McLachlan, Ian
Bio-bibliographic data:
Canadian Crime Fiction, p. 141. (209)
McLaughlin, Norrie
Bio-bibliographic data:
Canadian Crime Fiction, p. 141. (209)
McLean, Benjamin
Bio-bibliographic data:
Canadian Crime Fiction, p. 141. (209)

McMullen, Mary
Bio-bibliographic data:
Encyclopedia Mysteriosa, pp. 223–24. (2)
*The Encyclopedia of Mystery and
Detection,* p. 269. (7)
*Twentieth-Century Crime and Mystery
Writers,* 1st ed., pp. 1059–60. (882a)
*Twentieth-Century Crime and Mystery
Writers,* 2nd ed., pp. 636–37. (882b)
*Twentieth-Century Crime and Mystery
Writers,* 3rd ed., pp. 753–54. (882c)
McNab, Claire. *Pseud. for* **Claire
Carmichael**
Bio-bibliographic data:
Australian Crime Fiction, p. 146, 166–67.
(207)
By a Woman's Hand, 1st ed., pp. 145–46.
(884a)
By a Woman's Hand, 2nd ed., p. 155.
(884b)
Detecting Women 2, p. 133. (877b)
Detecting Women, 3rd ed., pp. 186–87.
(877c)
Great Women Mystery Writers, pp.
211–12. (880)
Web site: http://stopyourekillingme.com/
claire-mcnab.html
McNamee, James
Bio-bibliographic data:
Canadian Crime Fiction, p. 143. (209)
McNaught, Eleanor [Mildred Sanderson]
Bio-bibliographic data:
Canadian Crime Fiction, p. 143. (209)
McNeil, Florence
Bio-bibliographic data:
Canadian Crime Fiction, pp. 143–44.
(209)
McNeile, Herman Cyril. *See* **Sapper**
McNeilly, Wilfred [Glassford]
Bio-bibliographic data:
Australian Crime Fiction, p. 201, 211.
(207)
McPherson, Michael C.
Bio-bibliographic data:
Canadian Crime Fiction, p. 144. (209)
McQueen, James [Stuart]
Bio-bibliographic data:
Australian Crime Fiction, p. 167. (207)
McQuillan, Karin
Bio-bibliographic data:
By a Woman's Hand, 2nd ed., pp. 155–56.
(884b)
Detecting Women, 1st ed., p. 98. (877a)
Detecting Women 2, pp. 133–34. (877b)

Detecting Women, 3rd ed., p. 187. (877c)
Web site: http://stopyourekillingme.com/
karin-mcquillan.html
McShane, Mark
Bio-bibliographic data:
Australian Crime Fiction, pp. 168–69.
(207)
Canadian Crime Fiction, p. 259, 260.
(209)
Encyclopedia Mysteriosa, p. 224. (2)
*The Mammoth Encyclopedia of Modern
Crime Fiction,* pp. 324–25. (1)
*St. James Guide to Crime & Mystery
Writers,* 4th ed., pp. 741–43. (882d)
*Twentieth-Century Crime and Mystery
Writers,* 1st ed., pp. 1060–62. (882a)
*Twentieth-Century Crime and Mystery
Writers,* 2nd ed., pp. 637–38. (882b)
*Twentieth-Century Crime and Mystery
Writers,* 3rd ed., pp. 754–56. (882c)
Personal papers in Mugar Memorial
Library, Boston University.
Personal papers in University of Wyoming
Library, Laramie, Wyoming.
Personal papers in Sydney University,
Sydney, Australia.
McShea, Susanna Hoffmann
Bio-bibliographic data:
Detecting Women 2, p. 134. (877b)
Detecting Women, 3rd ed., p. 187. (877c)
**Meade, L. T.; i.e, Lillie Thomas; pseud.
for Elizabeth Thomasina Meade
Smith**
Bio-bibliographic data:
Australian Crime Fiction, p. 177. (207)
Encyclopedia Mysteriosa, p. 241. (2)
The Encyclopedia of Murder and Mystery,
p. 339. (6)
*The Encyclopedia of Mystery and
Detection,* pp. 284–85. (7)
*Twentieth-Century Crime and Mystery
Writers,* 1st ed., pp. 1063–69. (882a)
*Twentieth-Century Crime and Mystery
Writers,* 2nd ed., pp. 638–42. (882b)
*Twentieth-Century Crime and Mystery
Writers,* 3rd ed., pp. 756–60. (882c)
Meares, Leonard
Bio-bibliographic data:
Australian Crime Fiction, pp. 177–78.
(207)
Medawar, Mardi Oakley
Bio-bibliographic data:
Detecting Women, 3rd ed., pp. 187–88.
(877c)

Web site: http://stopyourekillingme.com/
mardi-oakley-medawar.html
**Meek, M. R. D.; i.e., Margaret Reid
Duncan**
Bio-bibliographic data:
By a Woman's Hand, 1st ed., pp. 146–47.
(884a)
By a Woman's Hand, 2nd ed., p. 156.
(884b)
Detecting Women, 1st ed., p. 98. (877a)
Detecting Women 2, p. 134. (877b)
Detecting Women, 3rd ed., p. 188. (877c)
Great Women Mystery Writers, pp.
221–23. (880)
*The Mammoth Encyclopedia of Modern
Crime Fiction,* pp. 337–38. (1)
*St. James Guide to Crime & Mystery
Writers,* 4th ed., pp. 743–44. (882d)
*Twentieth-Century Crime and Mystery
Writers,* 3rd ed., pp. 760–61. (882c)
Web site: http://stopyourekillingme.com/
m-r-d-meek.html
Meggs, Brown
Bio-bibliographic data:
*Twentieth-Century Crime and Mystery
Writers,* 1st ed., pp. 1069–70. (882a)
Meier, Leslie
Bio-bibliographic data:
Detecting Women, 1st ed., p. 98. (877a)
Detecting Women 2, p. 134. (877b)
Detecting Women, 3rd ed., pp. 188–89.
(877c)
Web site: http://stopyourekillingme.com/
leslie-meier.html
Melançon, André
Bio-bibliographic data:
Canadian Crime Fiction, p. 149. (209)
Melfi, Mary
Bio-bibliographic data:
Canadian Crime Fiction, p. 149. (209)
**Melville, James. *Pseud. for* Roy Peter
Martin**
Bio-bibliographic data:
*Critical Survey of Mystery and Detective
Fiction,* pp. 1213–18. (41)
Detecting Men, 1st ed., p. 179. (876)
Encyclopedia Mysteriosa, p. 241. (2)
The Encyclopedia of Murder and Mystery,
p. 340. (6)
*The Mammoth Encyclopedia of Modern
Crime Fiction,* pp. 338–39. (1)
*St. James Guide to Crime & Mystery
Writers,* 4th ed., pp. 744–45. (882d)

*Twentieth-Century Crime and Mystery
Writers,* 2nd ed., pp. 642–43. (882b)
*Twentieth-Century Crime and Mystery
Writers,* 3rd ed., pp. 761–62. (882c)
Personal papers in Mugar Memorial
Library, Boston University.
Web site: http://stopyourekillingme.com/
james-melville.html
**Melville, Jean-Pierre. *Pseud. for*
Jean-Pierre Grumbach**
Bio-bibliographic data:
The Encyclopedia of Murder and Mystery,
p. 340. (6)
Melville, Jennie. *See* Butler, Gwendoline
**Melvin, L[ewis]. David St. C[olumb].
Skene. *See* Skene-Melvin, L[ewis].
David St. C[olumb].**
Mencken, H. L.; i.e., Henry Louis
Bio-bibliographic data:
The Encyclopedia of Murder and Mystery,
pp. 340–41. (6)
Mendaham, Roy
Bio-bibliographic data:
Australian Crime Fiction, p. 178. (207)
Mendoza, Eduoardo
Bio-bibliographic data:
The Encyclopedia of Murder and Mystery,
p. 341. (6)
**Mercer, Cecil William. *See* Yates,
Dornford**
Mercer, Judy
Bio-bibliographic data:
Detecting Women, 3rd ed., pp. 189–90.
(877c)
Web site: http://stopyourekillingme.com/
judy-mercer.html
Meredith, Anne. *See* Gilbert, Anthony
Meredith, D. R.; i.e., Doris R.
Bio-bibliographic data:
By a Woman's Hand, 1st ed., pp. 147–48.
(884a)
By a Woman's Hand, 2nd ed., p. 157.
(884b)
Detecting Women, 1st ed., p. 99. (877a)
Detecting Women 2, p. 135. (877b)
Detecting Women, 3rd ed., p. 190. (877c)
Web site: http://stopyourekillingme.com/
d-r-meredith.html
Meredith, Wendy A. D. M.
Bio-bibliographic data:
Canadian Crime Fiction, p. 149. (209)
Merington, Marguerite
Bio-bibliographic data:
Canadian Crime Fiction, p. 260. (209)

Merrill, P. J. *See* **Roth, Holly**
Merriman, Pat. *See* **Perowne, Barry**
Mertz, Barbara Louise Gross
  Bio-bibliographic data:
  By a Woman's Hand, 1st ed., pp. 169–70.
    (884a)
  By a Woman's Hand, 2nd ed., pp. 182–83.
    (884b)
  *Critical Survey of Mystery and Detective
    Fiction,* pp. 1311–17. (41)
  Deadly Women, pp. 81–86. (26.5)
  Detecting Women, 1st ed., pp. 115–16.
    (877a)
  Detecting Women 2, p. 136, 155. (877b)
  Detecting Women, 3rd ed., p. 191, 220.
    (877c)
  Encyclopedia Mysteriosa, p. 273. (2)
  The Encyclopedia of Murder and Mystery,
    pp. 389–90. (6)
  Great Women Mystery Writers, pp.
    275–79. (880)
  *The Mammoth Encyclopedia of Modern
    Crime Fiction,* pp. 388–89. (1)
  *100 Masters of Mystery and Detective
    Fiction,* pp. 502–10. (37)
  *St. James Guide to Crime & Mystery
    Writers,* 4th ed., pp. 835–37. (882d)
  Speaking of Murder, pp. 163–69. (875a)
  *Twentieth-Century Crime and Mystery
    Writers,* 1st ed., pp. 1170–72. (882a)
  *Twentieth-Century Crime and Mystery
    Writers,* 2nd ed., pp. 706–7. (882b)
  *Twentieth-Century Crime and Mystery
    Writers,* 3rd ed., pp. 844–46. (882c)
  *Whodunit? A Who's Who in Crime and
    Mystery Writing,* pp. 150–51. (5)
  Personal papers in Hood College,
    Frederick, Maryland.
  Personal papers in Mugar Memorial
    Library, Boston University.
  Personal papers in University of
    Wyoming, Laramie, Wyoming.
  Web site: http://www.mpmbookscom;
    http://stopyourekillingme.com/
    barbara-michaels.html; http://www.
    autopen.com/elizabeth.peters.shtml
Meryon, Edward. *Pseud. for* **Edward
  Meryon Webb**
  Bio-bibliographic data:
  Australian Crime Fiction, p. 178. (207)
Messier, Julie
  Bio-bibliographic data:
  Canadian Crime Fiction, p. 149. (209)

Messmann, Jon
  Bio-bibliographic data:
  Australian Crime Fiction, p. 202. (207)
  Canadian Crime Fiction, p. 260, 261.
    (209)
Methold, Ken
  Bio-bibliographic data:
  Australian Crime Fiction, p. 179. (207)
Metzenthen, Dave
  Bio-bibliographic data:
  Australian Crime Fiction, p. 9. (207)
Meyer, Charles
  Bio-bibliographic data:
  Detecting Men, 1st ed., p. 179. (876)
  Web site: http://stopyourekillingme.com/
    charles-meyer.html
Meyer, Nicholas
  Bio-bibliographic data:
  *Twentieth-Century Crime and Mystery
    Writers,* 1st ed., pp. 1071–72. (882a)
  *Twentieth-Century Crime and Mystery
    Writers,* 2nd ed., pp. 643–44. (882b)
  *Twentieth-Century Crime and Mystery
    Writers,* 3rd ed., pp. 762–63. (882c)
Meyers, Annette, and Martin Meyers. *See
  also* **Meyers, Martin**
  Bio-bibliographic data:
  By a Woman's Hand, 1st ed., p. 148.
    (884a)
  By a Woman's Hand, 2nd ed., pp. 157–68.
    (884b)
  Detecting Women, 1st ed., p. 100. (877a)
  Detecting Women 2, pp. 135–36. (877b)
  Detecting Women, 3rd ed., pp. 190–91.
    (877c)
  Encyclopedia Mysteriosa, p. 243. (2)
  Great Women Mystery Writers, pp.
    223–25. (880)
  *The Mammoth Encyclopedia of Modern
    Crime Fiction,* pp. 339–40. (1)
  Web site:
    http://www.meyersmysteries.com;
    http://stopyourekillingme.com/
    annette-meyers.html
Meyers, Maan. *See* **Meyers, Annette, and
  Martin Meyers**
Meyers, Martin
  Bio-bibliographic data:
  Detecting Men, 1st ed., p. 180. (876)
  Web site: http://stopyourekillingme.com/
    martin-meyers.html
Meyers, Ric; i.e., Richard Sam
  Bio-bibliographic data:
  Encyclopedia Mysteriosa, p. 243. (2)

Meynell, Laurence
Bio-bibliographic data:
*St. James Guide to Crime & Mystery
Writers,* 4th ed., pp. 746–48. (882d)
*Twentieth-Century Crime and Mystery
Writers,* 1st ed., pp. 1072–77. (882a)
*Twentieth-Century Crime and Mystery
Writers,* 2nd ed., pp. 644–46. (882b)
*Twentieth-Century Crime and Mystery
Writers,* 3rd ed., pp. 763–66. (882c)
Personal papers in Mugar Memorial
Library, Boston University.
Michael, Ian [David Lewis]. *See* **Serafin,
David**
Michaelis, Alan
Bio-bibliographic data:
Australian Crime Fiction, p. 179. (207)
Michaels, Barbara. *See* **Mertz, Barbara
Louise Gross**
Michaels, Grant. *Pseud. for* **Michael
Mesrobian**
Bio-bibliographic data:
Detecting Men, 1st ed., p. 180. (876)
Michaels, Melisa
Bio-bibliographic data:
Detecting Women, 3rd ed., pp. 191–92.
(877c)
Michaels, Philip. *See* **van Rjndt, Philippe**
Michaud, Nando
Bio-bibliographic data:
Canadian Crime Fiction, p. 149. (209)
Michaud, Denys Hardy
Bio-bibliographic data:
Canadian Crime Fiction, p. 149. (209)
Michels, [Sharry] Christine
Bio-bibliographic data:
Canadian Crime Fiction, p. 149. (209)
Mickelbury, Penny
Bio-bibliographic data:
Detecting Women 2, p. 136. (877b)
Detecting Women, 3rd ed., p. 192. (877c)
Web site: http://stopyourekillingme.com/
penny-mickelbury.html
Mickle, Alan D[urward].
Bio-bibliographic data:
Australian Crime Fiction, p. 179. (207)
Middleton, Elizabeth. *See* **Antill, Elizabeth**
Middleton, L. J.
Bio-bibliographic data:
Canadian Crime Fiction, p. 149. (209)
Mikulski, Barbara, and Marylouise Oates
Bio-bibliographic data:
Detecting Women, 3rd ed., p. 192. (877c)

Milan, Borton. *Pseud. for* **Jeff Collignon**
Bio-bibliographic data:
Detecting Men, 1st ed., p. 180. (876)
Miles, John. *See* **Bickham, Jack**
Miles, Keith. *Pseud. for* **Edward Marston**
Bio-bibliographic data:
Australian Crime Fiction, p. 180. (207)
Detecting Men, 1st ed., pp. 169–70, 181.
(876)
*The Mammoth Encyclopedia of Modern
Crime Fiction,* pp. 332–34. (1)
*St. James Guide to Crime & Mystery
Writers,* 4th ed., pp. 700–703. (882d)
Web site:
http://www.twbooks.co.uk/authors/
aemarston.html; http://
stopyourekillingme.com/keith-miles.
html
Miles, Margaret
Bio-bibliographic data:
Detecting Women, 3rd ed., p. 193. (877c)
Web site: http://stopyourekillingme.com/
margaret-miles.html; http://
margaretmiles.com
Milewski, Arthur
Bio-bibliographic data
Canadian Crime Fiction, p. 149. (209)
Millar, Kenneth. *See* **Macdonald, Ross**
Millar, Margaret [Ellis Sturm]
Bio-bibliographic data:
By a Woman's Hand, 1st ed., p. 149.
(884a)
By a Woman's Hand, 2nd ed., pp. 158–59.
(884b)
Canadian Crime Fiction, pp. 150–51.
(209)
*Critical Survey of Mystery and Detective
Fiction,* pp. 1219–23. (41)
Designs of Darkness, pp. 66–81. (873)
Detecting Women, 1st ed., p. 100. (877a)
Detecting Women 2, p. 137. (877b)
Encyclopedia Mysteriosa, pp. 244–45. (2)
The Encyclopedia of Murder and Mystery,
pp. 343–44. (6)
*The Encyclopedia of Mystery and
Detection,* pp. 287–88. (7)
Great Women Mystery Writers, pp.
225–28. (880)
*The Mammoth Encyclopedia of Modern
Crime Fiction,* pp. 340–42. (1)
Mystery and Suspense Writers, pp.
679–87. (884.2)
*100 Masters of Mystery and Detective
Fiction,* pp. 467–73. (37)

The Oxford Companion to Crime and Mystery Writing, p. 291. (4)
St. James Guide to Crime & Mystery Writers, 4th ed., pp. 749–50. (882d)
10 Women of Mystery, pp. 223–46. (864, 865)
13 Mistresses of Murder, pp. 87–96. (871)
Twentieth-Century Crime and Mystery Writers, 1st ed., pp. 1077–79. (882a)
Twentieth-Century Crime and Mystery Writers, 2nd ed., pp. 646–48. (882b)
Twentieth-Century Crime and Mystery Writers, 3rd ed., pp. 766–67. (882c)
Whodunit? A Who's Who in Crime and Mystery Writing, p. 133. (5)
Women of Mystery, pp. 412–18. (874)

Millar, Thomas P[almer].
Bio-bibliographic data:
Canadian Crime Fiction, p. 151. (209)

Miller, Albert G[riffith]. *See* **O'Brien, Jack**

Miller, Bill. *See* **Miller, Wade**

Miller, Gordon [Eric]
Bio-bibliographic data:
Australian Crime Fiction, p. 180. (207)

Miller, [Hanson] Orlo
Bio-bibliographic data:
Canadian Crime Fiction, p. 151. (209)

Miller, Rex
Bio-bibliographic data:
Detecting Men, 1st ed., p. 181. (876)

Miller, Robert
Bio-bibliographic data:
Canadian Crime Fiction, p. 8, 151. (209)

Miller, Victor B.
Bio-bibliographic data:
Detecting Men, 1st ed., p. 182. (876)

Miller, Wade. *Pseud. for* **Robert Wade and Bill Miller**
Bio-bibliographic data:
The Big Book of Noir, pp. 185–86. (24)
Detecting Men, 1st ed., p. 182. (876)
Encyclopedia Mysteriosa, p. 245. (2)
The Encyclopedia of Murder and Mystery, pp. 344–45. (6)
The Encyclopedia of Mystery and Detection, p. 288. (7)
St. James Guide to Crime & Mystery Writers, 4th ed., pp. 750–52. (882d)
Twentieth-Century Crime and Mystery Writers, 1st ed., pp. 1079–82. (882a)
Twentieth-Century Crime and Mystery Writers, 2nd ed., pp. 648–49. (882b)

Twentieth-Century Crime and Mystery Writers, 3rd ed., pp. 767–69. (882c)

Millet, J.
Bio-bibliographic data:
Canadian Crime Fiction, p. 151. (209)

Millhiser, Marlys
Bio-bibliographic data:
By a Woman's Hand, 2nd ed., pp. 159–60. (884b)
Detecting Women, 1st ed., p. 101. (877a)
Detecting Women 2, p. 137. (877b)
Detecting Women, 3rd ed., p. 193. (877c)
Web site: http://stopyourekillingme.com/marlys-millhiser.html; http://members.aol.com/femmesweb/marlys.htm

Mills, Arthur [Hobart]
Bio-bibliographic data:
Australian Crime Fiction, p. 180. (207)

Mills, D. F.
Bio-bibliographic data:
By a Woman's Hand, 1st ed., p. 150. (884a)
By a Woman's Hand, 2nd ed., pp. 160–61. (884b)

Mills, John
Bio-bibliographic data:
Canadian Crime Fiction, pp. 151–52. (209)

Milne, A. A.; i.e., Alan Alexander
Bio-bibliographic data:
British Mystery Writers, 1920–1939, pp. 227–31. (867)
Critical Survey of Mystery and Detective Fiction, pp. 1224–30. (41)
The Encyclopedia of Murder and Mystery, p. 345. (6)
The Encyclopedia of Mystery and Detection, pp. 288–89. (7)
St. James Guide to Crime & Mystery Writers, 4th ed., pp. 752–54. (882d)
Twentieth-Century Crime and Mystery Writers, 1st ed., pp. 1082–86. (882a)
Twentieth-Century Crime and Mystery Writers, 2nd ed., pp. 649–51. (882b)
Twentieth-Century Crime and Mystery Writers, 3rd ed., pp. 769–71. (882c)
Personal papers in Humanities Research Center, University of Texas at Austin.
Web site: http://stopyourckillingme.com/a-a-milne.html

Milne, John
Bio-bibliographic data:
Detecting Men, 1st ed., pp. 182–83. (876)

*St. James Guide to Crime & Mystery
Writers*, 4th ed., pp. 754–55. (882d)
*Twentieth-Century Crime and Mystery
Writers,* 3rd ed., pp. 771–72. (882c)
Web site: http://stopyourekillingme.com/
john-milne.html

Mina, Denise
Bio-bibliographic data:
*The Mammoth Encyclopedia of Modern
Crime Fiction,* p. 342. (1)
Web site: http://stopyourekillingme.com/
denise-mina.html

Minchin, Devon [George]
Bio-bibliographic data:
Australian Crime Fiction, p. 180. (207)

Minichino, Camille
Bio-bibliographic data:
Detecting Women, 3rd ed., pp. 193–94.
(877c)
Web site: http://stopyourekillingme.com/
camille-minichino.html; http://www.
minichino.com

Mitchell, Gladys [Maude Winifred]
Bio-bibliographic data:
British Mystery Writers, 1920–1939, pp.
232–38. (867)
*Critical Survey of Mystery and Detective
Fiction,* pp. 1231–35. (41)
Detecting Women, 1st ed., p. 101. (877a)
Detecting Women 2, pp. 137–39, 185.
(877b)
Encyclopedia Mysteriosa, p. 246. (2)
The Encyclopedia of Murder and Mystery,
pp. 346–47. (6)
*The Encyclopedia of Mystery and
Detection,* p. 289. (7)
Great Women Mystery Writers, pp.
228–33. (880)
*The Oxford Companion to Crime and
Mystery Writing,* p. 293. (4)
*St. James Guide to Crime & Mystery
Writers,* 4th ed., pp. 755–57. (882d)
*Twentieth-Century Crime and Mystery
Writers,* 1st ed., pp. 1086–89. (882a)
*Twentieth-Century Crime and Mystery
Writers,* 2nd ed., pp. 651–53. (882b)
*Twentieth-Century Crime and Mystery
Writers,* 3rd ed., pp. 772–74. (882c)
*Whodunit? A Who's Who in Crime and
Mystery Writing,* p. 134. (5)
Women Authors of Detective Series, pp.
59–64. (882.5)

Web site: http://stopyourekillingme.com/
gladys-mitchell.html; http://www.
gladysmitchell.com

Mitchell, James [William]
Bio-bibliographic data:
Encyclopedia Mysteriosa, p. 246. (2)
*The Mammoth Encyclopedia of Modern
Crime Fiction,* pp. 342–43. (1)
*St. James Guide to Crime & Mystery
Writers,* 4th ed., pp. 757–58. (882d)
*Twentieth-Century Crime and Mystery
Writers,* 2nd ed., pp. 653–54. (882b)
*Twentieth-Century Crime and Mystery
Writers,* 3rd ed., pp. 774–76. (882c)

Mitchell, Kay
Bio-bibliographic data:
By a Woman's Hand, 1st ed., pp. 150–51.
(884a)
By a Woman's Hand, 2nd ed., pp. 161–62.
(884b)
Detecting Women, 1st ed., p. 83. (877a)
Detecting Women 2, pp. 110–11, 139.
(877b)
Detecting Women, 3rd ed., p. 155, 194.
(877c)
*The Mammoth Encyclopedia of Modern
Crime Fiction,* pp. 343–44. (1)
Web site:
http://www.twbooks.co.uk/authors/
kaymitchell.html; http://
stopyourekillingme.com/
kay-mitchell.html

Mitchell, Ken; i.e., Kenneth Ronald
Bio-bibliographic data:
Canadian Crime Fiction, p. 152. (209)

Mitchell, Kirk
Bio-bibliographic data:
Detecting Men, 1st ed., p. 183. (876)

Mitchell, Mary. *See* **Plain, Josephine**

Mitchell, W. O.; i.e., William Ormond
Bio-bibliographic data:
Canadian Crime Fiction, pp. 152–53.
(209)

Miville-Deschênes, Jean
Bio-bibliographic data:
Canadian Crime Fiction, p. 153. (209)

Moen, Ruth Raby
Bio-bibliographic data:
Detecting Women, 3rd ed., p. 194. (877c)

Moffat, Gwen
Bio-bibliographic data:
By a Woman's Hand, 1st ed., p. 151.
(884a)

By a Woman's Hand, 2nd ed., p. 162.
(884b)
Detecting Women, 1st ed., p. 102. (877a)
Detecting Women 2, pp. 139–40. (877b)
Detecting Women, 3rd ed., pp. 194–95.
(877c)
Great Women Mystery Writers, pp.
233–35. (880)
*The Mammoth Encyclopedia of Modern
Crime Fiction,* pp. 344–45. (1)
*St. James Guide to Crime & Mystery
Writers,* 4th ed., pp. 758–60. (882d)
*Twentieth-Century Crime and Mystery
Writers,* 1st ed., pp. 1089–91. (882a)
*Twentieth-Century Crime and Mystery
Writers,* 2nd ed., pp. 654–55. (882b)
*Twentieth-Century Crime and Mystery
Writers,* 3rd ed., pp. 776–77. (882c)
Web site:
www.twbooks.co.uk/authors/gmoffat.
html
Moffatt, James
Bio-bibliographic data:
Canadian Crime Fiction, p. 153. (209)
Moffett, Cleveland [Langston]
Bio-bibliographic data:
*The Encyclopedia of Mystery and
Detection,* p. 289. (7)
Moffitt, Ian
Bio-bibliographic data:
Australian Crime Fiction, p. 145, 181.
(207)
Molesworth, Voltaire
Bio-bibliographic data:
Australian Crime Fiction, p. 181. (207)
Monfredo, Miriam Grace
Bio-bibliographic data:
By a Woman's Hand, 1st ed., pp. 151–52.
(884a)
By a Woman's Hand, 2nd ed., pp. 162–63.
(884b)
Detecting Women, 1st ed., p. 102. (877a)
Detecting Women 2, p. 140. (877b)
Detecting Women, 3rd ed., p. 195. (877c)
*The Mammoth Encyclopedia of Modern
Crime Fiction,* p. 345. (1)
Web site: http://www.
miriamgracemonfredo.com; http://
stopyourekillingme.com/
miriam-grace-monfredo.html
Monpetit, Charles
Bio-bibliographic data:
Canadian Crime Fiction, p. 153. (209)

Monsarrat, Nicholas [John Turney]
Bio-bibliographic data:
Canadian Crime Fiction, p. 261. (209)
Montalbán, Manuel Vázquez
Bio-bibliographic data:
*The Mammoth Encyclopedia of Modern
Crime Fiction,* pp. 345–46. (1)
Web site: http://www.vespito.net/
mcm.html
Monteilhet, Hubert
Bio-bibliographic data:
*St. James Guide to Crime & Mystery
Writers,* 4th ed., pp. 760–61. (882d)
*Twentieth-Century Crime and Mystery
Writers,* 1st ed., p. 1546. (882a)
*Twentieth-Century Crime and Mystery
Writers,* 2nd ed., p. 944. (882b)
*Twentieth-Century Crime and Mystery
Writers,* 3rd ed., pp. 1134–35. (882c)
Montgomery, Robert Bruce. *See* **Crispin,
Edmund**
Montgomery, Yvonne E.
Bio-bibliographic data:
Detecting Women, 1st ed., p. 102. (877a)
Detecting Women 2, p. 140. (877b)
Detecting Women, 3rd ed., pp. 195–96.
(877c)
Montrose, David. *Pseud. for* **Charles R.
Graham**
Bio-bibliographic data:
Canadian Crime Fiction, p. 91, 153. (209)
Moody, Bill
Bio-bibliographic data:
Detecting Men, 1st ed., p. 183. (876)
Moody, Skye Kathleen
Bio-bibliographic data:
Detecting Women, 3rd ed., p. 196. (877c)
Web site: http://stopyourekillingme.com/
skye-kathleen-moody.html
Moody, Susan [Elizabeth]
Bio-bibliographic data:
By a Woman's Hand, 1st ed., pp. 152–53.
(884a)
By a Woman's Hand, 2nd ed., p. 163.
(884b)
Detecting Women, 1st ed., p. 103. (877a)
Detecting Women 2, pp. 140–41. (877b)
Detecting Women, 3rd ed., pp. 196–97.
(877c)
Encyclopedia Mysteriosa, p. 247. (2)
Great Women Mystery Writers, pp.
236–38. (880)
*The Mammoth Encyclopedia of Modern
Crime Fiction,* pp. 346–47. (1)

St. James Guide to Crime & Mystery Writers, 4th ed., pp. 761–63. (882d)
Twentieth-Century Crime and Mystery Writers, 3rd ed., pp. 777–78. (882c)
Whodunit? A Who's Who in Crime and Mystery Writing, pp. 134–35. (5)
Web site: http://stopyourekillingme.com/susan-moody.html

Mooney, Ray
Bio-bibliographic data:
Australian Crime Fiction, pp. 181–82. (207)

Moore, Amos. *See* **Hubbard, George [Barron]**

Moore, Barbara
Bio-bibliographic data:
Detecting Women 2, p. 141. (877b)
Detecting Women, 3rd ed., p. 197. (877c)
Web site: http://stopyourekillingme.com/barbara-moore.html

Moore, Brian
Bio-bibliographic data:
Canadian Crime Fiction, p. 32, 146, 153–54, 235. (209)
The Encyclopedia of Murder and Mystery, p. 348. (6)

Moore, Catherine Lucille and Henry Kuttner
Bio-bibliographic data:
The Encyclopedia of Murder and Mystery, pp. 285–86. (6)
The Encyclopedia of Mystery and Detection, p. 237. (7)

Moore, Christopher [G.]
Bio-bibliographic data:
Canadian Crime Fiction, p. 154. (209)
Web site: http://stopyourekillingme.com/christopher-g-moore.html; http://cgmoore.com

Moore, J. Mavor
Bio-bibliographic data:
Canadian Crime Fiction, p. 154, 207. (209)

Moore, Margaret
Bio-bibliographic data:
Detecting Women, 3rd ed., p. 197. (877c)

Moore, Maureen [Audrey]
Bio-bibliographic data:
Canadian Crime Fiction, p. 154. (209)

Moore, Miriam Ann
Bio-bibliographic data:
Detecting Women, 3rd ed., pp. 197–98. (877c)

Moore, P. S.; i.e., Phyllis S.
Bio-bibliographic data:
Canadian Crime Fiction, p. 154. (209)

Moore, Richard A.
Bio-bibliographic data:
Detecting Men, 1st ed., p. 183. (876)

Moore, Roy
Bio-bibliographic data:
Canadian Crime Fiction, p. 154. (209)

Moorhead, Finola
Bio-bibliographic data:
Australian Crime Fiction, p. 182. (207)

Moorhouse, [Arthur] Herbert Joseph. *See* **Moorehouse, Hopkins**

Moorehouse, Hopkins. *Pseud. for* **[Arthur] Herbert Joseph Moorhouse**
Bio-bibliographic data:
Canadian Crime Fiction, pp. 154–55. (209)

Moreau, Gerald
Bio-bibliographic data:
Canadian Crime Fiction, p. 155. (209)

Morel, Lucie F.
Bio-bibliographic data:
Canadian Crime Fiction, p. 155. (209)

Morelle, Gaston. *Pseud. for* **Benjamin Richaud**
Bio-bibliographic data:
Canadian Crime Fiction, p. 155. (209)

Morell, Mary
Bio-bibliographic data:
Detecting Women 2, p. 141. (877b)
Detecting Women, 3rd ed., p. 198. (877c)

Morgan, D. Miller
Bio-bibliographic data:
Detecting Women, 3rd ed., p. 198. (877c)

Morgan, Kate. *Pseud. for* **Ann Hamilton Whitman**
Bio-bibliographic data:
By a Woman's Hand, 1st ed., p. 153. (884a)
By a Woman's Hand, 2nd ed., p. 164. (884b)
Detecting Women, 1st ed., p. 103. (877a)
Detecting Women 2, p. 141. (877b)
Detecting Women, 3rd ed., pp. 198–99. (877c)

Morgan, Patrick. *Pseud. for* **George Snyder**
Bio-bibliographic data:
Australian Crime Fiction, p. 182, 202 (207)

Morice, Anne. *Pseud. for* **Felicity Shaw**
Bio-bibliographic data:

And Then There Were Nine . . . More Women of Mystery, pp. 58–79. (863)
By a Woman's Hand, 1st ed., p. 154. (884a)
By a Woman's Hand, 2nd ed., pp. 164–65. (884b)
Critical Survey of Mystery and Detective Fiction, pp. 1236–40. (41)
Detecting Women, 1st ed., p. 104. (877a)
Detecting Women 2, p. 142. (877b)
Great Women Mystery Writers, pp. 238–41. (880)
St. James Guide to Crime & Mystery Writers, 4th ed., pp. 763–64. (882d)
Twentieth-Century Crime and Mystery Writers, 1st ed., pp. 1091–93. (882a)
Twentieth-Century Crime and Mystery Writers, 2nd ed., pp. 656–57. (882b)
Twentieth-Century Crime and Mystery Writers, 3rd ed., pp. 778–80. (882c)
Personal papers in Mugar Memorial Library, Boston University.
Web site: http://stopyourekillingme.com/anne-morice.html

Morin, Louise
Bio-bibliographic data:
Canadian Crime Fiction, p. 155. (209)

Morison, B. J.; i.e, Betty Jane
Bio-bibliographic data:
By a Woman's Hand, 1st ed., pp. 154–55. (884a)
By a Woman's Hand, 2nd ed., p. 165. (884b)
Detecting Women 2, p. 142. (877b)
Detecting Women, 3rd ed., p. 199. (877c)

Morland, Nigel
Bio-bibliographic data:
Encyclopedia Mysteriosa, pp. 247–48. (2)
The Encyclopedia of Mystery and Detection, p. 290. (7)
St. James Guide to Crime & Mystery Writers, 4th ed., pp. 764–67. (882d)
Twentieth-Century Crime and Mystery Writers, 1st ed., pp. 1093–97. (882a)
Twentieth-Century Crime and Mystery Writers, 2nd ed., pp. 657–59. (882b)
Twentieth-Century Crime and Mystery Writers, 3rd ed., pp. 780–82. (882c)

Morley, Christopher [Darlington]
Bio-bibliographic data:
The Encyclopedia of Murder and Mystery, p. 348. (6)
Christopher Morley Knothole Association

c/o Bryant Library
2 Paper Mill Road
Roslyn, NY 11576

Morrison, Arthur
Bio-bibliographic data:
British Mystery Writers, 1860–1919, pp. 212–18. (866)
Critical Survey of Mystery and Detective Fiction, pp. 1241–45. (41)
Encyclopedia Mysteriosa, p. 248. (2)
The Encyclopedia of Murder and Mystery, pp. 348–49. (6)
The Encyclopedia of Mystery and Detection, p. 291. (7)
The Oxford Companion to Crime and Mystery Writing, pp. 293–94. (4)
St. James Guide to Crime & Mystery Writers, 4th ed., pp. 767–68. (882d)
Twentieth-Century Crime and Mystery Writers, 1st ed., pp. 1097–99. (882a)
Twentieth-Century Crime and Mystery Writers, 2nd ed., pp. 659–60. (882b)
Twentieth-Century Crime and Mystery Writers, 3rd ed., pp. 782–83. (882c)
Whodunit? A Who's Who in Crime and Mystery Writing, p. 135. (5)
Web site: http://stopyourekillingme.com/arthur-morrison.html

Morrison, H. S.
Bio-bibliographic data:
Australian Crime Fiction, p. 182. (207)

Morrone, Wenda Wardell
Bio-bibliographic data:
Detecting Women, 3rd ed., p. 199. (877c)

Morse, L. A.; i.e., Larry Alan
Bio-bibliographic data:
Canadian Crime Fiction, p. 71, 155. (209)
Detecting Men, 1st ed., p. 184 (876)
Twentieth-Century Crime and Mystery Writers, 3rd ed., pp. 783–84. (882c)

Morse, Murray N.
Bio-bibliographic data:
Canadian Crime Fiction, p. 155. (209)

Morson, Ian
Bio-bibliographic data:
Detecting Men, 1st ed., p. 184. (876)
The Mammoth Encyclopedia of Modern Crime Fiction, p. 348. (1)
Web site: http://website.lineone.net/~ian.morson; http://stopyourekillingme.com/ian-morson.html

Mortimer, John [Clifford]
Bio-bibliographic data:

Critical Survey of Mystery and Detective Fiction, pp. 1246–51. (41)
Encyclopedia Mysteriosa, p. 248. (2)
The Fatal Art of Entertainment, pp. 112–35. (878)
The Mammoth Encyclopedia of Modern Crime Fiction, pp. 348–49. (1)
Mystery and Suspense Writers, pp. 689–98. (884.2)
The Oxford Companion to Crime and Mystery Writing, p. 294. (4)
St. James Guide to Crime & Mystery Writers, 4th ed., pp. 768–70. (882d)
Twentieth-Century Crime and Mystery Writers, 2nd ed., pp. 660–62. (882b)
Twentieth-Century Crime and Mystery Writers, 3rd ed., pp. 784–86. (882c)
Whodunit? A Who's Who in Crime and Mystery Writing, pp. 135–36. (5)
Personal papers in Mugar Memorial Library, Boston University.
Personal papers in Special Collections, University of California, Los Angeles.
Web site: http://stopyourekillingme.com/john-mortimer.html; http://www.law4u.com.au./lil/tv_rumpole.html; http:///www.csee.umbc.edu/~schott/rumpole;

Morton, Anthony. *See* **Creasey, John**
Morton, Guy [Eugene]
Bio-bibliographic data:
Canadian Crime Fiction, pp. 155–56, 223–24. (209)
Mosley, Walter E.
Bio-bibliographic data:
Detecting Men, 1st ed., pp. 184–85. (876)
Encyclopedia Mysteriosa, pp. 248–49. (2)
The Encyclopedia of Murder and Mystery, pp. 350–51. (6)
The Mammoth Encyclopedia of Modern Crime Fiction, pp. 350–51. (1)
The Oxford Companion to Crime and Mystery Writing, pp. 294–95. (4)
St. James Guide to Crime & Mystery Writers, 4th ed., pp. 771–72. (882d)
Speaking of Murder, vol. II, pp. 89–101. (875b)
Talking Murder, pp. 200–206. (883)
Whodunit? A Who's Who in Crime and Mystery Writing, p. 136. (5)
Web site: http://stopyourekillingme.com/walter-mosley.html
Most, Bruce W.
Bio-bibliographic data:

Detecting Men, 1st ed., p. 185. (876)
Mott, Laurance
Bio-bibliographic data:
Canadian Crime Fiction, p. 261. (209)
Mounce, D. R.; i.e., David R.
Bio-bibliographic data:
Canadian Crime Fiction, p. 156. (209)
Mountcastle, Clara H.
Bio-bibliographic data:
Canadian Crime Fiction, p. 156, 201. (209)
Mountjoy, Christopher T. *See* **Miles, Keith**
Mowat, Farley
Bio-bibliographic data:
Canadian Crime Fiction, pp. 156–57. (209)
Mowery, William Byron
Bio-bibliographic data:
Canadian Crime Fiction, p. 261. (209)
Moyes, Patricia
Bio-bibliographic data:
By a Woman's Hand, 1st ed., pp. 155–56. (884a)
By a Woman's Hand, 2nd ed., pp. 165–66. (884b)
Critical Survey of Mystery and Detective Fiction, pp. 1252–57. (41)
Detecting Women, 1st ed., pp. 104–5. (877a)
Detecting Women 2, p. 143. (877b)
Detecting Women, 3rd ed., p. 200. (877c)
Encyclopedia Mysteriosa, pp. 249–50. (2)
The Encyclopedia of Murder and Mystery, p. 352. (6)
The Encyclopedia of Mystery and Detection, pp. 292–93. (7)
Great Women Mystery Writers, pp. 241–44. (880)
The Mammoth Encyclopedia of Modern Crime Fiction, pp. 351–2. (1)
St. James Guide to Crime & Mystery Writers, 4th ed., pp. 772–74. (882d)
Twentieth-Century Crime and Mystery Writers, 1st ed., pp. 1099–1102. (882a)
Twentieth-Century Crime and Mystery Writers, 2nd ed., pp. 662–64. (882b)
Twentieth-Century Crime and Mystery Writers, 3rd ed., pp. 786–88. (882c)
Whodunit? A Who's Who in Crime and Mystery Writing, p. 137. (5)
Personal papers in University of Wyoming.

Web site: http://stopyourekillingme.com/
patricia-moyes.html

Muddock, Joyce Emmerson Preston. *See*
Donovan, Dick

Mudrooroo
Bio-bibliographic data:
Australian Crime Fiction, p. 145, 146,
182–83. (207)

Mudrooroo Narogin. *See* **Mudrooroo**

Muir, Dexter. *See* **Gribble, Leonard R.**

Mullen, Jack
Bio-bibliographic data:
Detecting Men, 1st ed., p. 185. (876)

Muller, Marcia
Bio-bibliographic data:
American Hard-Boiled Crime Writers, pp.
267–82. (862)
By a Woman's Hand, 1st ed., pp. 156–57.
(884a)
By a Woman's Hand, 2nd ed., pp. 166–67.
(884b)
Deadly Women, pp. 306–13. (26.5)
Detecting Women, 1st ed., pp. 105–6.
(877a)
Detecting Women 2, pp. 143–44. (877b)
Detecting Women, 3rd ed., pp. 200–201.
(877c)
Encyclopedia Mysteriosa, p. 251. (2)
The Encyclopedia of Murder and Mystery,
pp. 352–53. (6)
Great Women Mystery Writers, pp.
244–47. (880)
*The Mammoth Encyclopedia of Modern
Crime Fiction*, pp. 352–53. (1)
*The Oxford Companion to Crime and
Mystery Writing*, p. 299. (4)
*St. James Guide to Crime & Mystery
Writers*, 4th ed., pp. 774–76. (882d)
Speaking of Murder, pp. 103–12. (875a)
*Twentieth-Century Crime and Mystery
Writers*, 2nd ed., pp. 664–65. (882b)
*Twentieth-Century Crime and Mystery
Writers*, 3rd ed., pp. 788–90. (882c)
*Whodunit? A Who's Who in Crime and
Mystery Writing*, p. 137. (5)
Personal papers in Popular Culture
Collection, Bowling Green State
University, Bowling Green, Ohio.
Web site: http://stopyourekillingme.com/
marcia-muller.html; http://www.
interbridge.com/marciamuller

Müllner, Adolf
Bio-bibliographic data:

*Critical Survey of Mystery and Detective
Fiction*, pp. 1258–63. (41)

Munger, Katy. *See* **Gray, Gallagher**

Munro, Hector Hugh. *See* **Saki**

Munro, Hugh. *See* **Jason**

Munro, James. *See* **Mitchell, James**

Munro, John
Bio-bibliographic data:
Australian Crime Fiction, p. 9. (207)

Murdoch, Bruce. *See* **Creasey, John**

Murdoch, Walter [Logie Forbes]
Bio-bibliographic data:
Australian Crime Fiction, p. 183. (207)

Murphy, Dallas
Bio-bibliographic data:
Detecting Men, 1st ed., p. 185. (876)

Murphy, Haughton. *Pseud. for* **James
Duffy**
Bio-bibliographic data:
Detecting Men, 1st ed., p. 186. (876)
Web site: http://stopyourekillingme.com/
haughton-murphy.html

Murphy, Ida Mary. *See* **Spence, Ainslie**

Murphy, Shirley Rousseau
Bio-bibliographic data:
Detecting Women, 3rd ed., pp. 201–2.
(877c)
Web site: http://stopyourekillingme.com/
shirley-rousseau-murphy.html; http://
www.joegray.com

Murphy, W. Leo; i.e., William Leo
Bio-bibliographic data:
Canadian Crime Fiction, p. 157. (209)

**Murphy, Warren [Burton] (and Richard
Sapir)**
Bio-bibliographic data:
Detecting Men, 1st ed., pp. 186–88. (876)
Encyclopedia Mysteriosa, p. 253. (2)
*The Mammoth Encyclopedia of Modern
Crime Fiction*, pp. 353–55. (1)
*Murder off the Rack: Critical Studies of
Ten Paperback Masters*, pp. 145–65.
(869)
*St. James Guide to Crime & Mystery
Writers*, 4th ed., pp. 776–79. (882d)
*Twentieth-Century Crime and Mystery
Writers*, 3rd ed., pp. 790–93. (882c)
Web site: www.sinanju.com and
http://warrenmurphy.tripod.com

Murray, Alma
Bio-bibliographic data:
Australian Crime Fiction, p. 9. (207)

Murray, David Christie
Bio-bibliographic data:

Narogin, Mudrooroo. *See* Mudrooroo
Nash, Chandler. *See* Hunt, Katherine Chandler
Nash, Simon
  Bio-bibliographic data:
  The Encyclopedia of Murder and Mystery, pp. 363–63. (6)
Nassim, Liza. *See* Cody, Liza
Nathan, Paul
  Bio-bibliographic data:
  Detecting Men, 1st ed., p. 189. (876)
Nations, Opal L. *See* Humm, Martin J.
Natsuki, Shizuko
  Bio-bibliographic data:
  Great Women Mystery Writers, pp. 251–54. (880)
  The Mammoth Encyclopedia of Modern Crime Fiction, p. 358. (1)
  Twentieth-Century Crime and Mystery Writers, 3rd ed., p. 1135. (882c)
Naud, Martin
  Bio-bibliographic data:
  Canadian Crime Fiction, p. 158. (209)
Nava, Michael
  Bio-bibliographic data:
  Detecting Men, 1st ed., p. 190. (876)
  The Mammoth Encyclopedia of Modern Crime Fiction, pp. 358–59. (1)
  Web site: http://www.stopyourekillingme. com/michael-nava.html
Navratilova, Martina and Liz Nickles
  Bio-bibliographic data:
  Detecting Women, 3rd ed., pp. 204–5. (877c)
Nebel, [Louis] Frederick
  Bio-bibliographic data:
  American Hard-Boiled Crime Writers, pp. 283–88. (862)
  Critical Survey of Mystery and Detective Fiction, pp. 1264–68. (41)
  Encyclopedia Mysteriosa, p. 258. (2)
  The Encyclopedia of Murder and Mystery, p. 364. (6)
  St. James Guide to Crime & Mystery Writers, 4th ed., pp. 782–83. (882d)
  Twentieth-Century Crime and Mystery Writers, 1st ed., pp. 1104–5. (882a)
  Twentieth-Century Crime and Mystery Writers, 2nd ed., pp. 666–67. (882b)
  Twentieth-Century Crime and Mystery Writers, 3rd ed., pp. 795–96. (882c)
  Personal papers in University of Oregon Library, Eugene, Oregon.

  Web site: http://www.stopyourekillingme. com/frederick-nebel.html; http:// www.miskatonic.org/rara-avis/ biblio/nebel.html; http://www. thrillingdetective.com/trivia/nebel.ht ml
Neel, Janet. *Pseud. for* Janet Cohen
  Bio-bibliographic data:
  By a Woman's Hand, 1st ed., p. 159. (884a)
  By a Woman's Hand, 2nd ed., p. 169. (884b)
  Detecting Women, 1st ed., p. 107. (877a)
  Detecting Women 2, p. 145. (877b)
  Detecting Women, 3rd ed., p. 205. (877c)
  The Mammoth Encyclopedia of Modern Crime Fiction, p. 359. (1)
  St. James Guide to Crime & Mystery Writers, 4th ed., pp. 783–84. (882d)
  Web site: http://www.stopyourekillingme. com/janet-neel.html
Neely, Barbara
  Bio-bibliographic data:
  By a Woman's Hand, 2nd ed., pp. 169–70. (884b)
  Detecting Women, 1st ed., p. 107. (877a)
  Detecting Women 2, p. 146. (877b)
  Detecting Women, 3rd ed., p. 205. (877c)
  The Encyclopedia of Murder and Mystery, pp. 364–65. (6)
  The Fatal Art of Entertainment, pp. 326–51. (878)
  The Mammoth Encyclopedia of Modern Crime Fiction, pp. 359–60. (1)
  St. James Guide to Crime & Mystery Writers, 4th ed., pp. 784–86. (882d)
  Whodunit? A Who's Who in Crime and Mystery Writing, p. 140. (5)
  Web site: http://www.blanchewhite.com; http://www.stopyourekillingme.com/ barbara-neely.html
Neely, Richard
  Bio-bibliographic data:
  Critical Survey of Mystery and Detective Fiction, pp. 1269–72. (41)
  The Encyclopedia of Murder and Mystery, p. 365. (6)
  St. James Guide to Crime & Mystery Writers, 4th ed., pp. 786–87. (882d)
  Twentieth-Century Crime and Mystery Writers, 2nd ed., pp. 667–68. (882b)
  Twentieth-Century Crime and Mystery Writers, 3rd ed., pp. 796–97. (882c)

Neiryunck, Jacques
Bio-bibliographic data:
Canadian Crime Fiction, p. 158. (209)
Nel, Jean. *Pseud. for* **Jean-André Jeannel**
Bio-bibliographic data:
Canadian Crime Fiction, p. 158. (209)
Nessen, Ron and Johanna Neuman
Bio-bibliographic data:
Detecting Women, 3rd ed., p. 206 (877c)
Web site: http://www.stopyourekillingme.
com/ron-nessen.html
Neuman, Johanna. *See* **Nessen, Ron, and Johanna Neuman**
Neville, Barbara Alison. *See* **Candy, Edward**
Neville, Margot. *Pseud. for* **Margot Goyder and Anne Neville Goyder Joske**
Bio-bibliographic data:
Australian Crime Fiction, pp. 185–87. (207)
Twentieth-Century Crime and Mystery Writers, 1st ed., pp. 1106–7. (882a)
Twentieth-Century Crime and Mystery Writers, 2nd ed., pp. 668–69. (882b)
Twentieth-Century Crime and Mystery Writers, 3rd ed., pp. 797–98. (882c)
Nevins, Francis M[ichael]., Jr.
Bio-bibliographic data:
Detecting Men, 1st ed., p. 190. (876)
Encyclopedia Mysteriosa, pp. 258–59. (2)
The Encyclopedia of Murder and Mystery, p. 365. (6)
The Encyclopedia of Mystery and Detection, p. 294. (7)
The Mammoth Encyclopedia of Modern Crime Fiction, pp. 360–61. (1)
St. James Guide to Crime & Mystery Writers, 4th ed., pp. 787–89. (882d)
Twentieth-Century Crime and Mystery Writers, 1st ed., pp. 1107–9. (882a)
Twentieth-Century Crime and Mystery Writers, 2nd ed., pp. 669–70. (882b)
Twentieth-Century Crime and Mystery Writers, 3rd ed., pp. 798–99. (882c)
Newland, Simpson
Bio-bibliographic data:
Australian Crime Fiction, p. 187. (207)
Newman, Bernard
Bio-bibliographic data:
Twentieth-Century Crime and Mystery Writers, 1st ed., pp. 1109–13. (882a)
Twentieth-Century Crime and Mystery Writers, 2nd ed., pp. 670–73. (882b)

Twentieth-Century Crime and Mystery Writers, 3rd ed., pp. 800–802. (882c)
Newman, Christopher
Bio-bibliographic data:
Detecting Men, 1st ed., pp. 190–91. (876)
Web site: http://www.stopyourekillingme.
com/christopher-newman.html
Newman, G. F.; i.e., Gordon Frank
Bio-bibliographic data:
Detecting Men, 1st ed., p. 191. (876)
The Mammoth Encyclopedia of Modern Crime Fiction, pp. 361–62. (1)
St. James Guide to Crime & Mystery Writers, 4th ed., pp. 789–90. (882d)
Twentieth-Century Crime and Mystery Writers, 2nd ed., pp. 673–74. (882b)
Twentieth-Century Crime and Mystery Writers, 3rd ed., pp. 802–3. (882c)
Newman, Joel
Bio-bibliographic data:
Canadian Crime Fiction, p. 158. (209)
Newman, Sharan
Bio-bibliographic data:
By a Woman's Hand, 2nd ed., p. 170. (884b)
Deadly Women, pp. 89–91. (26.5)
Detecting Women, 1st ed., p. 107. (877a)
Detecting Women 2, p. 146. (877b)
Detecting Women, 3rd ed., p. 206. (877c)
The Mammoth Encyclopedia of Modern Crime Fiction, pp. 362–63. (1)
Web site: http://www.hevanet.com/
sharan/Levendeur.html; http://www.
stopyourekillingme.com/
sharan-newman.html
Newton, [Wilfrid] Douglas
Bio-bibliographic data:
Canadian Crime Fiction, p. 261. (209)
Newton, Michael
Bio-bibliographic data:
Detecting Men, 1st ed., pp. 166–67, 191. (876)
Nichol, James W.
Bio-bibliographic data:
Canadian Crime Fiction, p. 158. (209)
Nichols, Beverley
Bio-bibliographic data:
St. James Guide to Crime & Mystery Writers, 4th ed., pp. 790–92. (882d)
Twentieth-Century Crime and Mystery Writers, 1st ed., pp. 1114–16. (882a)
Twentieth-Century Crime and Mystery Writers, 2nd ed., pp. 674–75. (882b)

*Twentieth-Century Crime and Mystery
  Writers,* 3rd ed., pp. 803–5. (882c)
Personal papers in Humanities Research
  Center, University of Texas at Austin.
Nicholson, Margaret Beda Larminie. *See*
  Yorke, Margaret
Nickels, Liz. *See* **Navratilova, Martina,
  and Liz Nickels**
Nickson, Elizabeth
  Bio-bibliographic data:
  Canadian Crime Fiction, p. 158. (209)
Nicol, Eric
  Bio-bibliographic data:
  Canadian Crime Fiction, p. 158. (209)
Nicole, Claudette. *See* **Messmann, Jon**
Nicolov, Borislav
  Bio-bibliographic data:
  Canadian Crime Fiction, p. 158. (209)
Nielsen, Helen [Berniece]
  Bio-bibliographic data:
  Detecting Women 2, p. 146. (877b)
  Detecting Women, 3rd ed., pp. 206–7.
    (877c)
  Encyclopedia Mysteriosa, p. 259. (2)
  *The Encyclopedia of Mystery and
    Detection,* p. 294. (7)
  *St. James Guide to Crime & Mystery
    Writers,* 4th ed., pp. 792–93. (882d)
  *Twentieth-Century Crime and Mystery
    Writers,* 1st ed., pp. 1117–19. (882a)
  *Twentieth-Century Crime and Mystery
    Writers,* 2nd ed., pp. 675–77. (882b)
  *Twentieth-Century Crime and Mystery
    Writers,* 3rd ed., pp. 805–7. (882c)
  Personal papers in Mugar Memorial
    Library, Boston University.
Nighbert, David F.
  Bio-bibliographic data:
  Detecting Men, 1st ed., p. 192. (876)
Niles, Chris
  Bio-bibliographic data:
  Detecting Women, 3rd ed., p. 207. (877c)
Nisbet, [James] Hume
  Bio-bibliographic data:
  Australian Crime Fiction, pp. 187–88.
    (207)
Nitsua, Benjamin. *See* **Austin, Rev.
  Benjamin Fish**
Niven, Frederick [John]
  Bio-bibliographic data:
  Canadian Crime Fiction, pp. 158–59.
    (209)
Nixon, Joan Lowery
  Bio-bibliographic data:

Deadly Women, pp. 251–53. (26.5)
Noel, Mireille
  Bio-bibliographic data:
  Canadian Crime Fiction, p. 159. (209)
Noguchi, Thomas T. with Arthur Lyons.
  See also **Lyons, Arthur**
  Bio-bibliographic data:
  Detecting Men, 1st ed., p. 192. (876)
Nolan, William F.
  Bio-bibliographic data:
  Detecting Men, 1st ed., p. 192. (876)
  *The Encyclopedia of Mystery and
    Detection,* pp. 294–95. (7)
  *St. James Guide to Crime & Mystery
    Writers,* 4th ed., pp. 793–95. (882d)
  *Twentieth-Century Crime and Mystery
    Writers,* 1st ed., pp. 1119–21. (882a)
  *Twentieth-Century Crime and Mystery
    Writers,* 2nd ed., pp. 677–79. (882b)
  *Twentieth-Century Crime and Mystery
    Writers,* 3rd ed., pp. 807–9. (882c)
  Personal papers in Center for Popular
    Culture, Bowling Green State
    University, Bowling Green, Ohio
  Web site: http://www.stopyourekillingme.
    com/william-f-nolan.html
Noll, Ingrid
  Bio-bibliographic data:
  *The Mammoth Encyclopedia of Modern
    Crime Fiction,* p. 363. (1)
Nordan, Robert
  Bio-bibliographic data:
  Detecting Men, 1st ed., p. 193. (876)
Norman, Howard
  Bio-bibliographic data:
  Canadian Crime Fiction, p. 261. (209)
Norman, James (I)
  Bio-bibliographic data:
  *Twentieth-Century Crime and Mystery
    Writers,* 1st ed., pp. 1122–23. (882a)
  *Twentieth-Century Crime and Mystery
    Writers,* 2nd ed., pp. 679–80. (882b)
Norman, James (II)
  Bio-bibliographic data:
  Canadian Crime Fiction, p. 159. (209)
North, Dick
  Bio-bibliographic data:
  Canadian Crime Fiction, p. 159. (209)
North, Eric. *See* **Cronin, Bernard**
North, Gerry
  Bio-bibliographic data:
  Australian Crime Fiction, p. 188. (207)
North, Gil. *Pseud. for* **Geoffrey Horne**
  Bio-bibliographic data:

Detecting Men, 1st ed., p. 193. (876)
St. James Guide to Crime & Mystery Writers, 4th ed., p. 796. (882d)
Twentieth-Century Crime and Mystery Writers, 1st ed., pp. 1123–25. (882a)
Twentieth-Century Crime and Mystery Writers, 2nd ed., pp. 680–81. (882b)
Twentieth-Century Crime and Mystery Writers, 3rd ed., pp. 809–10. (882c)

North, Jessica: unidentified pseud.
Bio-bibliographic data:
Canadian Crime Fiction, p. 261. (209)

North, Suzanne
Bio-bibliographic data:
Canadian Crime Fiction, pp. 159–60. (209)
Detecting Women, 1st ed., p. 107. (877a)
Detecting Women 2, p. 146. (877b)
Detecting Women, 3rd ed., p. 207. (877c)

Northfield, Diane
Bio-bibliographic data:
Canadian Crime Fiction, p. 160. (209)

Norway, Nevil Shute. *See* **Shute, Nevil**

Notar, Stephen
Bio-bibliographic data:
Canadian Crime Fiction, p. 160. (209)

Nottingham, Poppy
Bio-bibliographic data:
Australian Crime Fiction, p. 188. (207)

Nowlan, Alden [Albert]
Bio-bibliographic data:
Canadian Crime Fiction, p. 160. (209)

Nunn, Frank
Bio-bibliographic data:
Australian Crime Fiction, p. 189. (207)

Nunnally, Tiina
Bio-bibliographic data:
Detecting Women, 3rd ed., pp. 207–8. (877c)
Web site: http://www.stopyourekillingme. com/tiina-nunnally.html

Nyoongah, Mudrooroo Narogin. *See* **Mudrooroo**

O

Oakes, Leslie Manton
Bio-bibliographic data:
Australian Crime Fiction, p. 190. (207)

Oakley, E. D.
Bio-bibliographic data:
Australian Crime Fiction, p. 190. (207)

Oates, Joyce Carol
Bio-bibliographic data:

By a Woman's Hand, 1st ed., pp. 199–200. (884a)
By a Woman's Hand, 2nd ed., pp. 211–12. (884b)
The Mammoth Encyclopedia of Modern Crime Fiction, pp. 363–64. (1)
Talking Murder, pp. 229–39. (883)
Whodunit? A Who's Who in Crime and Mystery Writing, p. 143. (5)
Web site: http://www.usfca.edu/~southerr

Oates, Marylouise. *See* **Mikulski, Barbara, and Marylouise Oates**

Oatley, Keith
Bio-bibliographic data:
Canadian Crime Fiction, p. 161. (209)

Oblinger, Milo Milton. *See* **Richards, Milton**

O'Brien, Jack
Bio-bibliographic data:
Canadian Crime Fiction, p. 262. (209)

O'Brien, Meg
Bio-bibliographic data:
By a Woman's Hand, 1st ed., pp. 160–61. (884a)
By a Woman's Hand, 2nd ed., pp. 171–72. (884b)
Detecting Women, 1st ed., p. 108. (877a)
Detecting Women 2, pp. 146–47. (877b)
Detecting Women, 3rd ed., p. 208. (877c)

O'Callaghan, [Helen] Maxine
Bio-bibliographic data:
By a Woman's Hand, 1st ed., p. 161. (884a)
By a Woman's Hand, 2nd ed., p. 172. (884b)
Detecting Women, 1st ed., p. 108. (877a)
Detecting Women 2, p. 147. (877b)
Detecting Women, 3rd ed., pp. 208–9. (877c)
The Mammoth Encyclopedia of Modern Crime Fiction, p. 365. (1)
Web site: http://www.stopyourekillingme. com/maxine-ocallaghan.html; http:// users.aol.com/maxineoc/max1.htm

O'Connell, Carol
Bio-bibliographic data:
By a Woman's Hand, 2nd ed., pp. 172–73. (884b)
Detecting Women, 1st ed., p. 108. (877a)
Detecting Women 2, p. 147. (877b)
Detecting Women, 3rd ed., p. 209. (877c)
The Mammoth Encyclopedia of Modern Crime Fiction, pp. 365–66. (1)

St. James Guide to Crime & Mystery
  Writers, 4th ed., pp. 797–98. (882d)
Women of Mystery, pp. 436–37. (874)
Web site: http://www.twbooks.co.uk/
  authors/coconnl.html; http://www.
  stopyourekillingme.com/
  carol-oconnell.html
O'Connell, Catherine
  Bio-bibliographic data:
  Detecting Women 2, p. 148. (877b)
O'Connell, Jack
  Bio-bibliographic data:
  Detecting Men, 1st ed., p. 193. (876)
O'Connor, Maureen. *See* **Hall, Patricia**
O'Connor, Michael
  Bio-bibliographic data:
  Australian Crime Fiction, p. 190. (207)
O'Connor, Patrick. *See* **Holton, Leonard**
O'Connor, Richard
  Bio-bibliographic data:
  Canadian Crime Fiction, p. 262, 269.
  (209)
  Twentieth-Century Crime and Mystery
    Writers, 1st ed., pp. 1448–51. (882a)
  Personal papers in University of Maine
    Library, Orono.
OCork, Shannon
  Bio-bibliographic data:
  Detecting Women, 1st ed., p. 110. (877a)
  Detecting Women 2, p. 149. (877b)
  Detecting Women, 3rd ed., p. 211. (877c)
  13 Mistresses of Murder, pp. 97–104.
    (871)
  Web site: http://www.stopyourekillingme.
    com/shannon-ocork.html
Odier, Daniel
  Bio-bibliographic data:
  The Mammoth Encyclopedia of Modern
    Crime Fiction, pp. 366–67. (1)
O'Donnell, Lillian
  Bio-bibliographic data:
  And Then There Were Nine . . . More
    Women of Mystery, pp. 100–19. (863)
  By a Woman's Hand, 1st ed., pp. 161–62.
    (884a)
  By a Woman's Hand, 2nd ed., pp. 173–74.
    (884b)
  Canadian Crime Fiction, p. 262. (209)
  Detecting Women, 1st ed., p. 109. (877a)
  Detecting Women 2, p. 148. (877b)
  Detecting Women, 3rd ed., pp. 209–10.
    (877c)
  Encyclopedia Mysteriosa, p. 262. (2)

The Encyclopedia of Murder and Mystery,
  p. 372. (6)
Great Women Mystery Writers, pp.
  255–58. (880)
The Mammoth Encyclopedia of Modern
  Crime Fiction, pp. 367–68. (1)
St. James Guide to Crime & Mystery
  Writers, 4th ed., pp. 798–99. (882d)
Twentieth-Century Crime and Mystery
  Writers, 1st ed., pp. 1125–27. (882a)
Twentieth-Century Crime and Mystery
  Writers, 2nd ed., pp. 681–82. (882b)
Twentieth-Century Crime and Mystery
  Writers, 3rd ed., pp. 811–12. (882c)
Personal papers in Mugar Memorial
  Library, Boston University.
Web site: http://www.stopyourekillingme.
  com/lillian-odonnell.html
O'Donnell, Peter
  Bio-bibliographic data:
  British Mystery and Thriller Writers since
    1940, First Series, pp. 295–304. (868)
  Detecting Men, 1st ed., p. 194. (876)
  Encyclopedia Mysteriosa, p. 263. (2)
  St. James Guide to Crime & Mystery
    Writers, 4th ed., pp. 799–800. (882d)
  Twentieth-Century Crime and Mystery
    Writers, 1st ed., pp. 1127–28. (882a)
  Twentieth-Century Crime and Mystery
    Writers, 2nd ed., p. 682. (882b)
  Twentieth-Century Crime and Mystery
    Writers, 3rd ed., pp. 812–13. (882c)
  Web site: http://www.stopyourekillingme.
    com/peter-odonnell.html
O'Farrell, William
  Bio-bibliographic data:
  Twentieth-Century Crime and Mystery
    Writers, 2nd ed., pp. 682–83. (882b)
  Twentieth-Century Crime and Mystery
    Writers, 3rd ed., pp. 813–14. (882c)
Offord, Lenore Glen
  Bio-bibliographic data:
  Detecting Women 2, p. 149. (877b)
  Encyclopedia Mysteriosa, p. 262. (2)
  Twentieth-Century Crime and Mystery
    Writers, 1st ed., pp. 1128–29. (882a)
  Twentieth-Century Crime and Mystery
    Writers, 2nd ed., p. 684. (882b)
  Twentieth-Century Crime and Mystery
    Writers, 3rd ed., pp. 814–15. (882c)
  Personal papers in Bancroft Library,
    University of California, Berkeley.
  Personal papers in University of Oregon
    Library, Eugene, Oregon.

Ogden, Julie. *See* **Coupe, Stuart, and Julie Ogden**

Ognall, Leopold Horace
Bio-bibliographic data:
Canadian Crime Fiction, p. 37, 106–7, 161. (209)
Critical Survey of Mystery and Detective Fiction, pp. 262–66. (41)
St. James Guide to Crime & Mystery Writers, 4th ed. pp. 152–53. (882d)
Twentieth-Century Crime and Mystery Writers, 1st ed., pp. 256–58. (882a)
Twentieth-Century Crime and Mystery Writers, 2nd ed., pp. 139–40. (882b)
Twentieth-Century Crime and Mystery Writers, 3rd ed., pp. 170–72. (882c)

O'Grady, Rohan. *Pseud. for* **June O'Grady Skinner**
Bio-bibliographic data:
Canadian Crime Fiction, p. 161, 204. (209)

O'Hagan, Joan
Bio-bibliographic data:
Australian Crime Fiction, p. 190. (207)
Twentieth-Century Crime and Mystery Writers, 3rd ed., p. 815. (882c)

O'Higgins, Harvey J[errold].
Bio-bibliographic data:
Canadian Crime Fiction, pp. 161–62. (209)
The Encyclopedia of Mystery and Detection, pp. 297–98. (7)

o'huigin, sean [*sic*]
Bio-bibliographic data:
Canadian Crime Fiction, p. 162. (209)

O'Kane, Leslie
Bio-bibliographic data:
Detecting Women, 3rd ed., p. 210. (877c)
Web site: http://www.stopyourekillingme. com/leslie-okane.html; http:// members.aol.com/LESOKANE

O'Leary, Ann
Bio-bibliographic data:
Australian Crime Fiction, p. 9. (207)

Oleksiw, Susan
Bio-bibliographic data:
By a Woman's Hand, 2nd ed., p. 174. (884b)
Detecting Women, 1st ed., p. 110. (877a)
Detecting Women 2, p. 149. (877b)
Detecting Women, 3rd ed., p. 212. (877c)
Web site: http://www.stopyourekillingme. com/susan-oleksiw.html

Oligny, Odette. *See* **Vaubert, Michelle de**

Oliphant, B. J. *Pseud. for* **Sheri S. Tepper**
Bio-bibliographic data:
By a Woman's Hand, 1st ed., pp. 162–63. (884a)
By a Woman's Hand, 2nd ed., pp. 174–75. (884b)
Detecting Women, 1st ed., p. 110, 111. (877a)
Detecting Women 2, p. 150, 151. (877b)
Detecting Women, 3rd ed., p. 212, 213. (877c)
Web site: http://stopyourekillingme.com/ sheri-s-tepper.html

Oliver, Anthony
Bio-bibliographic data:
St. James Guide to Crime & Mystery Writers, 4th ed., pp. 800–802. (882d)
Twentieth-Century Crime and Mystery Writers, 3rd ed., pp. 815–17. (882c)

Oliver, Maria Antònia
Bio-bibliographic data:
Australian Crime Fiction, p. 191. (207)
Detecting Women, 1st ed., p. 110. (877a)
Detecting Women 2, p. 150. (877b)
Detecting Women, 3rd ed., pp. 212–13. (877c)

Oliver, Marie. *See* **Beck, K. K.**

Oliver, Steve
Bio-bibliographic data:
Detecting Men, 1st ed., p. 194. (876)

Olsen, D. B. *See* **Hitchens, Julia Clara Catherine Dolores Birk Olsen (pseud.)**

Olson, Oscar Nils
Bio-bibliographic data:
Canadian Crime Fiction, p. 162. (209)

O'Malley, Lady Mary Dolling Saunders. *See* **Bridge, Ann**

O'Marie, [Sister] Carol Anne
Bio-bibliographic data:
By a Woman's Hand, 1st ed., pp. 163–64. (884a)
By a Woman's Hand, 2nd ed., pp. 175–76. (884b)
Detecting Women, 1st ed., p. 109. (877a)
Detecting Women 2, pp. 148–49. (877b)
Detecting Women, 3rd ed., pp. 210–11. (877c)
Encyclopedia Mysteriosa, pp. 263–64. (2)
The Mammoth Encyclopedia of Modern Crime Fiction, p. 368. (1)
St. James Guide to Crime & Mystery Writers, 4th ed., pp. 803–4. (882d)

Twentieth-Century Crime and Mystery Writers, 3rd ed., pp. 818–19. (882c)
Personal papers in Mt. St. Mary's College, Los Angeles, California.
Web site: http://www.stopyourekillingme.com/carol-anne-omarie.html
Ondaatje, Michael
Bio-bibliographic data:
Canadian Crime Fiction, p. 163. (209)
O'Neal, Jerry. *See* **McCreede, Jess**
O'Neill, Egan. *See* **Linington, Elizabeth**
Onge, Daniel Saint. *See* **Saint-Onge, Daniel**
Oppenheim, E. Phillips; i.e., Edward Phillips
Bio-bibliographic data:
British Mystery Writers, 1860–1919, pp. 219–29. (866)
Corpus Delicti of Mystery Fiction, pp. 99–104. (879)
Critical Survey of Mystery and Detective Fiction, pp. 1273–78. (41)
Encyclopedia Mysteriosa, p. 264. (2)
The Encyclopedia of Murder and Mystery, p. 375. (6)
The Encyclopedia of Mystery and Detection, pp. 299–300. (7)
100 Masters of Mystery and Detective Fiction, pp. 474–79. (37)
The Oxford Companion to Crime and Mystery Writing, pp. 318–19. (4)
St. James Guide to Crime & Mystery Writers, 4th ed., pp. 804–8. (882d)
Twentieth-Century Crime and Mystery Writers, 1st ed., pp. 1132–39. (882a)
Twentieth-Century Crime and Mystery Writers, 2nd ed., pp. 686–89. (882b)
Twentieth-Century Crime and Mystery Writers, 3rd ed., pp. 819–23. (882c)
Whodunit? A Who's Who in Crime and Mystery Writing, pp. 143–44. (5)
Orczy, Baroness Emmuska; i.e., Emma Magdalena Rosalia Maria Josefa Barbara Orczy
Bio-bibliographic data:
British Mystery Writers, 1860–1919, pp. 229–34. (866)
Critical Survey of Mystery and Detective Fiction, pp. 1279–85. (41)
Encyclopedia Mysteriosa, p. 264. (2)
The Encyclopedia of Murder and Mystery, pp. 375–76. (6)
The Encyclopedia of Mystery and Detection, p. 300. (7)

Great Women Mystery Writers, pp. 259–61. (880)
100 Masters of Mystery and Detective Fiction, pp. 480–86. (37)
The Oxford Companion to Crime and Mystery Writing, p. 319. (4)
St. James Guide to Crime & Mystery Writers, 4th ed., pp. 808–10. (882d)
Twentieth-Century Crime and Mystery Writers, 1st ed., pp. 1139–42. (882a)
Twentieth-Century Crime and Mystery Writers, 2nd ed., pp. 690–91. (882b)
Twentieth-Century Crime and Mystery Writers, 3rd ed., pp. 823–24. (882c)
Whodunit? A Who's Who in Crime and Mystery Writing, p. 144. (5)
Orde, A. J. *See* **Oliphant, B. J.**
Orde, Lewis
Bio-bibliographic data:
Canadian Crime Fiction, p. 283. (209)
O'Reilly, John Boyle
Bio-bibliographic data:
Australian Crime Fiction, p. 191. (207)
Orenstein, Frank
Bio-bibliographic data:
Detecting Men, 1st ed., pp. 194–95. (876)
Ormerod, Roger
Bio-bibliographic data:
Detecting Men, 1st ed., p. 195. (876)
The Mammoth Encyclopedia of Modern Crime Fiction, pp. 368–70. (1)
St. James Guide to Crime & Mystery Writers, 4th ed., pp. 810–11. (882d)
Twentieth-Century Crime and Mystery Writers, 1st ed., pp. 1142–43. (882a)
Twentieth-Century Crime and Mystery Writers, 2nd ed., pp. 691–92. (882b)
Twentieth-Century Crime and Mystery Writers, 3rd ed., pp. 824–25. (882c)
Orson, Richard. *See* **Lockridge, Richard and Frances**
Ørum, Poul
Bio-bibliographic data:
Twentieth-Century Crime and Mystery Writers, 1st ed., pp. 1546–47. (882a)
Twentieth-Century Crime and Mystery Writers, 2nd ed., p. 945. (882b)
Twentieth-Century Crime and Mystery Writers, 3rd ed., pp. 1135–36. (882c)
Orvis, Kenneth. *Pseud. for* **Kenneth Lemieux**
Bio-bibliographic data:
Canadian Crime Fiction, p. 131, 163. (209)

Detecting Men, 1st ed., p. 196. (876)
Osborn, David D.
Bio-bibliographic data:
Detecting Men, 1st ed., p. 196. (876)
Web site: http://www.stopyourekillingme.
com/david-osborn.html
Osborne, Denise
Bio-bibliographic data:
Detecting Women, 1st ed., p. 111. (877a)
Detecting Women 2, p. 151. (877b)
Detecting Women, 3rd ed., p. 213. (877c)
Web site: http://www.stopyourekillingme.
com/denise-osborne.html; http://
www.deniseosbornemysteries.com
Osborne, Dorothy
Bio-bibliographic data:
Canadian Crime Fiction, p. 262. (209)
Osborne, Louise
Bio-bibliographic data:
Canadian Crime Fiction, p. 262. (209)
O'Shaughnessy, Perri. *Pseud. for* **Pamela**
O'Shaughnessy and Mary
O'Shaughnessy
Bio-bibliographic data:
Detecting Women, 3rd ed., p. 211. (877c)
Web site: http://www.stopyourekillingme.
com/perri-oshaughnessy.html;
http://www.perrio.com
Osler, Eric Richard. *See* **Dick, T.**
Oster, Jerry
Bio-bibliographic data:
Detecting Men, 1st ed., p. 196. (876)
Ostrovsky, Victor
Bio-bibliographic data:
Canadian Crime Fiction, p. 163. (209)
Otis, Gaston
Bio-bibliographic data:
Canadian Crime Fiction, p. 164. (209)
Ouelle, Laurie
Bio-bibliographic data:
Canadian Crime Fiction, p. 164. (209)
Oursler, Fulton. *See* **Abbot, Anthony**
Owen, [Albert John] Harrison
Bio-bibliographic data:
Australian Crime Fiction, p. 191. (207)
Owens, Louis
Bio-bibliographic data:
Detecting Men, 1st ed., p. 197. (876)
Oxlade, Boyd
Bio-bibliographic data:
Australian Crime Fiction, p. 191. (207)
Oxley, J. Macdonald
Bio-bibliographic data:
Canadian Crime Fiction, p. 262. (209)

P

Packard, Frank L[ucius].
Bio-bibliographic data:
Canadian Crime Fiction, pp. 164–65.
(209)
Encyclopedia Mysteriosa, p. 267. (2)
The Encyclopedia of Murder and Mystery,
p. 379. (6)
*The Encyclopedia of Mystery and
Detection*, p. 305. (7)
*Twentieth-Century Crime and Mystery
Writers*, 1st ed., pp. 1143–45. (882a)
*Twentieth-Century Crime and Mystery
Writers*, 2nd ed., pp. 692–93. (882b)
*Twentieth-Century Crime and Mystery
Writers*, 3rd ed., p. 826. (882c)
Packer, Vin. *Pseud. for* **Marijane Meaker**
Bio-bibliographic data:
The Big Book of Noir, p. 186. (24)
*Murder off the Rack: Critical Studies of
Ten Paperback Masters*, pp. 55–69.
(869)
Padgett, [Mary] Abigail
Bio-bibliographic data:
By a Woman's Hand, 2nd ed., pp. 177–78.
(884b)
Canadian Crime Fiction, pp. 283–84.
(209)
Detecting Women, 1st ed., p. 111. (877a)
Detecting Women 2, pp. 151–52. (877b)
Detecting Women, 3rd ed., pp. 213–14.
(877c)
*The Mammoth Encyclopedia of Modern
Crime Fiction*, p. 370. (1)
*St. James Guide to Crime & Mystery
Writers*, 4th ed., pp. 813–14. (882d)
Web site:
http://www.twbookmark.com/authors/
66/264/index.html http://
stopyourekillingme.com/
Abigail-Padgett.html
Padgett, Lewis. *See* **Kuttner, Henry**
Padura Fuentes, Leonardo
Bio-bibliographic data:
*Latin American Mystery Writers: An A to
Z Guide. (881)*
Page, Emma. *Pseud. for* **Honoria Tirbutt**
Bio-bibliographic data:
Detecting Women 2, p. 152. (877b)
Detecting Women, 3rd ed., p. 214. (877c)
*The Mammoth Encyclopedia of Modern
Crime Fiction*, pp. 370–71. (1)
*Twentieth-Century Crime and Mystery
Writers*, 1st ed., pp. 1145–46. (882a)

Page, Jake
Bio-bibliographic data:
Detecting Men, 1st ed., p. 197. (876)
Web site: http://stopyourekillingme.com/
jake-page.html
Page, Katherine Hall
Bio-bibliographic data:
By a Woman's Hand, 1st ed., p. 165.
(884a)
By a Woman's Hand, 2nd ed., p. 178.
(884b)
Detecting Women, 1st ed., p. 112. (877a)
Detecting Women 2, p. 152. (877b)
Detecting Women, 3rd ed., pp. 214–15.
(877c)
Web site: http://stopyourekillingme.com/
katherine-hall-page.html
Page, Marco. *Pseud. for* **Harry Kurnitz**
Bio-bibliographic data:
The Encyclopedia of Murder and Mystery,
p. 379. (6)
*The Encyclopedia of Mystery and
Detection,* p. 304. (7)
*Twentieth-Century Crime and Mystery
Writers,* 1st ed., pp. 1146–47. (882a)
*Twentieth-Century Crime and Mystery
Writers,* 2nd ed., pp. 693–94. (882b)
*Twentieth-Century Crime and Mystery
Writers,* 3rd ed., p. 827. (882c)
Page, Norvell W. *See* **Stockbridge, Grant**
Paige, Robin. *See* **Albert, Susan Wittig,
and Bill Albert**
Pain, Barry [Eric Odell]
Bio-bibliographic data:
*The Encyclopedia of Mystery and
Detection,* pp. 305–6. (7)
Pairo, Preston, III
Bio-bibliographic data:
Detecting Men, 1st ed., p. 197. (876)
Palk, Arthur [Joseph]
Bio-bibliographic data:
Australian Crime Fiction, p. 192. (207)
Palka, Kurt Maxwell
Bio-bibliographic data:
Canadian Crime Fiction, p. 148, 165.
(209)
Palmer, Frank
Bio-bibliographic data:
Detecting Men, 1st ed., p. 198. (876)
Palmer, Madelyn
Bio-bibliographic data:
Australian Crime Fiction, pp. 192–93.
(207)

Palmer, John Leslie. *See* **Beeding, Francis**
Palmer, [Charles] Stuart
Bio-bibliographic data:
*Critical Survey of Mystery and Detective
Fiction,* pp. 1286–92. (41)
Encyclopedia Mysteriosa, p. 267. (2)
The Encyclopedia of Murder and Mystery,
p. 380. (6)
*The Encyclopedia of Mystery and
Detection,* p. 306. (7)
*St. James Guide to Crime & Mystery
Writers,* 4th ed., pp. 814–15. (882d)
*Twentieth-Century Crime and Mystery
Writers,* 1st ed., pp. 1148–50. (882a)
*Twentieth-Century Crime and Mystery
Writers,* 2nd ed., pp. 694–95. (882b)
*Twentieth-Century Crime and Mystery
Writers,* 3rd ed., pp. 827–28. (882c)
Web site: http://stopyourekillingme.com/
stuart-palmer.html
Palmer, William J.
Bio-bibliographic data:
Detecting Men, 1st ed., p. 198. (876)
Papazoglou, Orania
Bio-bibliographic data:
By a Woman's Hand, 1st ed., pp. 94–95.
(884a)
By a Woman's Hand, 2nd ed., pp.
100–101. (884b)
Detecting Women, 1st ed., pp. 66–67, 112.
(877a)
Detecting Women 2, p. 86, 152–53. (877b)
Detecting Women, 3rd ed., pp. 118–19,
215. (877c)
Encyclopedia Mysteriosa, p. 146. (2)
The Encyclopedia of Murder and Mystery,
pp. 225–26. (6)
Great Women Mystery Writers, pp.
263–66. (880)
*The Mammoth Encyclopedia of Modern
Crime Fiction,* pp. 371–72. (1)
*St. James Guide to Crime & Mystery
Writers,* 4th ed., pp. 815–17. (882d)
Web site: http://stopyourekillingme.com/
orania-papazoglou.html; http://
www.janehaddam.com
Pape, Gordon
Bio-bibliographic data:
Canadian Crime Fiction, p. 165. (209)
Paquette, Claire
Bio-bibliographic data:
Canadian Crime Fiction, p. 165. (209)
Paquin, Ubald
Bio-bibliographic data:

Canadian Crime Fiction, p. 165. (209)
Paretsky, Sara
Bio-bibliographic data:
By a Woman's Hand, 1st ed., pp. 166–67.
(884a)
By a Woman's Hand, 2nd ed., p. 179.
(884b)
*Critical Survey of Mystery and Detective
Fiction*, pp. 1293–98. (41)
Deadly Women, pp. 286–90. (26.5)
Detecting Women, 1st ed., p. 113. (877a)
Detecting Women 2, p. 153. (877b)
Detecting Women, 3rd ed., p. 216. (877c)
Encyclopedia Mysteriosa, p. 269. (2)
The Encyclopedia of Murder and Mystery,
p. 381. (6)
Great Women Mystery Writers, pp.
266–69. (880)
*The Mammoth Encyclopedia of Modern
Crime Fiction*, pp. 372–74. (1)
Mystery and Suspense Writers, pp.
699–713. (884.2)
*100 Masters of Mystery and Detective
Fiction*, pp. 487–93. (37)
*The Oxford Companion to Crime and
Mystery Writing*, p. 324. (4)
*St. James Guide to Crime & Mystery
Writers*, 4th ed., pp. 817–18. (882d)
*Twentieth-Century Crime and Mystery
Writers,* 3rd ed., pp. 829–30. (882c)
*Whodunit? A Who's Who in Crime and
Mystery Writing*, p. 147. (5)
Women Authors of Detective Series, pp.
139–44. (882.5)
Web site: http://www.saraparetsky.com;
http://stopyourekillingme.com/
sara-paretsky.html
Pargeter, Edith Mary. *See* **Peters, Ellis**
Paris, Ann. *See* **Papazoglou, Orania**
Parker, Barbara
Bio-bibliographic data:
Detecting Women, 1st ed., p. 114. (877a)
Detecting Women 2, p. 153. (877b)
Detecting Women, 3rd ed., p. 216. (877c)
Speaking of Murder, vol. II, pp. 126–32.
(875b)
Web site: http://stopyourekillingme.com/
barbara-parker.html; http://www.
barbaraparker.com
Parker, Sir [Horatio] Gilbert, Bart
Bio-bibliographic data:
Canadian Crime Fiction, pp. 165–66.
(209)

Parker, Richard
Bio-bibliographic data:
Australian Crime Fiction, p. 193. (207)
Parker, Robert B[rown]
Bio-bibliographic data:
The Big Book of Noir, pp. 328–29. (24)
Colloquium on Crime, pp. 189–203. (884.1)
*The Craft of Crime: Conversations with
Crime Writers*, pp. 143–75. (872)
*Critical Survey of Mystery and Detective
Fiction*, pp. 1299–1304. (41)
Detecting Men, 1st ed., pp. 198–99. (876)
Encyclopedia Mysteriosa, p. 270. (2)
The Encyclopedia of Murder and Mystery,
pp. 382–83. (6)
*The Mammoth Encyclopedia of Modern
Crime Fiction*, pp. 374–76. (1)
Mystery and Suspense Writers, pp.
715–32. (884.2)
*100 Masters of Mystery and Detective
Fiction*, pp. 494–501. (37)
*The Oxford Companion to Crime and
Mystery Writing*, p. 325. (4)
*St. James Guide to Crime & Mystery
Writers*, 4th ed., pp. 818–20. (882d)
Speaking of Murder, vol. II, pp. 211–24.
(875b)
Talking Murder, pp. 207–14. (883)
*Twentieth-Century Crime and Mystery
Writers,* 1st ed., pp. 1150–52. (882a)
*Twentieth-Century Crime and Mystery
Writers,* 2nd ed., pp. 695–96. (882b)
*Twentieth-Century Crime and Mystery
Writers,* 3rd ed., pp. 830–31. (882c)
*Whodunit? A Who's Who in Crime and
Mystery Writing*, pp. 147–48. (5)
Personal papers in Colby College,
Waterville, Maine.
Web site:
http://www.mindspring.com/~boba4;
http://www.geocities.com/Athens/
Academy/5473;
http://stopyourekillingme.
com/robert-b-parker.html; http://
www.thrillingdetective.com/trivia/par
ker.html; http://www.bookreporter.
com/authors/au-parker-robert.asp;
http://www.mindspring.com/~boba4;
http://www.noexit.co.uk/parker.htm
<P9>

Parr, Angelica. *See* Papazoglou, Orania
Parr, Robert. *See* Gardner, Erle Stanley
Parrish, Frank. *See* Longrigg, Roger
  Erskine
Parrish, Richard
  Bio-bibliographic data:
  Detecting Men, 1st ed., p. 200. (876)
Parry, David
  Bio-bibliographic data:
  Canadian Crime Fiction, p. 166. (209)
Parsons, Robert. *See* Jillett, Neil
Partridge, Anthony. *See* Oppenheim, E.
  Phillips
Partridge, Eric [Honeywood]
  Bio-bibliographic data:
  The Encyclopedia of Murder and Mystery,
    p. 384. (6)
Pasquet, Jacques
  Bio-bibliographic data:
  Canadian Crime Fiction, p. 167. (209)
Paterson, Andrew James
  Bio-bibliographic data:
  Canadian Crime Fiction, p. 167. (209)
Paton Walsh, Jill
  Bio-bibliographic data:
  Detecting Women, 1st ed., p. 143. (877a)
  Detecting Women 2, p. 189. (877b)
  Detecting Women, 3rd ed., pp. 216–17.
    (877c)
Patrick, Q. *See* Quentin, Patrick
Patterson, Harry
  Bio-bibliographic data:
  Canadian Crime Fiction, p. 279, 284.
    (209)
  Detecting Men, 1st ed., p. 89, 124–25.
    (876)
  Encyclopedia Mysteriosa, pp. 162–63. (2)
  *St. James Guide to Crime & Mystery
    Writers*, 4th ed., pp. 512–15. (882d)
  *Twentieth-Century Crime and Mystery
    Writers*, 2nd ed., pp. 443–45. (882b)
  *Twentieth-Century Crime and Mystery
    Writers*, 3rd ed., pp. 530–32. (882c)
  Web site: http://stopyourekillingme.com/
    harry-patterson.html; http://www.
    scintilla.utwente.nl/users/gert/higgins
Patterson, James
  Bio-bibliographic data:
  Detecting Men, 1st ed., p. 200. (876)
  *The Mammoth Encyclopedia of Modern
    Crime Fiction*, pp. 376–77. (1)
  Web site:
    http://www.twbookmark.com/features
    / jamespatterson/index.html; http://

stopyourekillingme.com/
  james-patterson.html
Patterson, Richard North
  Bio-bibliographic data:
  Detecting Men, 1st ed., p. 200. (876)
  *The Mammoth Encyclopedia of Modern
    Crime Fiction*, pp. 377–78. (1)
  Web site: http://stopyourekillingme.com/
    richard-north-patterson.html;
    http://www.bdd.com/features/
    patterson
Pattinson, Lee. *See* Farr, Caroline
Pattullo, George Robson
  Bio-bibliographic data:
  Canadian Crime Fiction, p. 167. (209)
Paul, Barbara: listed by some as an
  unidentified pseud., although others
  state that this is her full name.
  Bio-bibliographic data:
  By a Woman's Hand, 1st ed., p. 167.
    (884a)
  By a Woman's Hand, 2nd ed., pp. 179–80.
    (884b)
  Detecting Women, 1st ed., p. 114. (877a)
  Detecting Women 2, p. 154. (877b)
  Detecting Women, 3rd ed., p. 217. (877c)
  Encyclopedia Mysteriosa, p. 271. (2)
  The Encyclopedia of Murder and Mystery,
    p. 384. (6)
  Great Women Mystery Writers, pp.
    269–71. (880)
  *The Mammoth Encyclopedia of Modern
    Crime Fiction*, pp. 378–79. (1)
  *St. James Guide to Crime & Mystery
    Writers*, 4th ed., pp. 822–23. (882d)
  Personal papers in Mugar Memorial
    Library, Boston University.
  Web site: http://www.barbarapaul.com;
    http://stopyourekillingme.com/
    barbara-paul.html
Paul, Elliot [Harold]
  Bio-bibliographic data:
  Encyclopedia Mysteriosa, p. 271. (2)
  The Encyclopedia of Murder and Mystery,
    p. 385. (6)
  *The Encyclopedia of Mystery and
    Detection*, p. 306. (7)
  *St. James Guide to Crime & Mystery
    Writers*, 4th ed., pp. 823–24. (882d)
  *Twentieth-Century Crime and Mystery
    Writers*, 1st ed., pp. 1153–55. (882a)
  *Twentieth-Century Crime and Mystery
    Writers*, 2nd ed., pp. 697–98. (882b)

*Twentieth-Century Crime and Mystery
Writers,* 1st ed., pp. 1155–58. (882a)
Pence, Joanne
Bio-bibliographic data:
By a Woman's Hand, 2nd ed., pp. 180–81.
(884b)
Detecting Women, 1st ed., p. 114. (877a)
Detecting Women 2, p. 154. (877b)
Detecting Women, 3rd ed., p. 218. (877c)
Web site: http://stopyourekillingme.com/
joanne-pence.html; http://members.
aol.com/jopence; http://www.
joannepence.com
Pendleton, Don; i.e., Donald Eugene
Bio-bibliographic data:
Canadian Crime Fiction, p. 263. (209)
Encyclopedia Mysteriosa, p. 272. (2)
*The Mammoth Encyclopedia of Modern
Crime Fiction,* pp. 383–84. (1)
*Murder off the Rack: Critical Studies of
Ten Paperback Masters,* pp. 135–44.
(869)
*St. James Guide to Crime & Mystery
Writers,* 4th ed., pp. 825–28. (882d)
*Twentieth-Century Crime and Mystery
Writers,* 1st ed., pp. 1158–61. (882a)
*Twentieth-Century Crime and Mystery
Writers,* 2nd ed., pp. 699–701. (882b)
*Twentieth-Century Crime and Mystery
Writers,* 3rd ed., pp. 835–37. (882c)
Personal papers in Lilly Library, Indiana
University, Bloomington, Indiana.
Web site: http://www.donpendleton.com;
http://stopyourekillingme.com/
don-pendleton.html; http://www.
mackbolan.com; http://www.
stormy-night.org/stonyland/index.htm
l
Penman, Sharon Kay
Bio-bibliographic data:
Detecting Women, 3rd ed., p. 218. (877c)
Web site: http://stopyourekillingme.com/
sharon-kay-penman.html; http://www.
sharonkaypenman.com
Penn, John. *Pseud. for* **Palma Harcourt
and Jack H. Trotman**
Bio-bibliographic data:
Detecting Women, 3rd ed., pp. 218–19.
(877c)
Pennac, Daniel. *Pseud. for* **Daniel
Pennachioni**
Bio-bibliographic data:
The Encyclopedia of Murder and Mystery,
pp. 387–88. (6)

*The Mammoth Encyclopedia of Modern
Crime Fiction,* pp. 384–85. (1)
Pennachioni, Daniel. *See* **Pennac, Daniel**
Pentecost, Hugh. *Pseud. for* **Judson
Pentecost Philips**
Bio-bibliographic data:
*Critical Survey of Mystery and Detective
Fiction,* pp. 1305–10. (41)
Encyclopedia Mysteriosa, pp. 275–76. (2)
The Encyclopedia of Murder and Mystery,
pp. 391–92. (6)
*The Encyclopedia of Mystery and
Detection,* pp. 308–9. (7)
*The Oxford Companion to Crime and
Mystery Writing,* p. 328. (4)
*St. James Guide to Crime & Mystery
Writers,* 4th ed., pp. 828–31. (882d)
*Twentieth-Century Crime and Mystery
Writers,* 1st ed., pp. 1162–67. (882a)
*Twentieth-Century Crime and Mystery
Writers,* 2nd ed., pp. 701–4. (882b)
*Twentieth-Century Crime and Mystery
Writers,* 3rd ed., pp. 837–41. (882c)
*Whodunit? A Who's Who in Crime and
Mystery Writing,* pp. 149–50. (5)
Web site: http://stopyourekillingme.com/
hugh-pentecost.html
Penzler, Otto
Bio-bibliographic data:
Encyclopedia Mysteriosa, pp. 272–73. (2)
The Encyclopedia of Murder and Mystery,
p. 388. (6)
Percy, H. R.; i.e., Herbert Roland
Bio-bibliographic data:
Canadian Crime Fiction, p. 168. (209)
Perdue, Ame. *See* **Carroll, W. J.**
Perez, Nora
Bio-bibliographic data:
Canadian Crime Fiction, p. 168. (209)
Perez-Reverte, Arturo
Bio-bibliographic data:
The Encyclopedia of Murder and Mystery,
p. 388. (6)
*Whodunit? A Who's Who in Crime and
Mystery Writing,* p. 150. (5)
Web site: http://stopyourekillingme.com/
arturo-perez-reverte.html
Pérez Zelaschi, Adolfo
Bio-bibliographic data:
*Latin American Mystery Writers: An A to
Z Guide. (881)*
Perowne, Barry. *Pseud. for* **Philip Atkey**
Bio-bibliographic data:
Encyclopedia Mysteriosa, p. 273. (2)

The Encyclopedia of Murder and Mystery,
    p. 388. (6)
*The Encyclopedia of Mystery and
    Detection*, pp. 307–8. (7)
*St. James Guide to Crime & Mystery
    Writers*, 4th ed., pp. 831–32. (882d)
*Twentieth-Century Crime and Mystery
    Writers,* 1st ed., pp. 1167–68. (882a)
*Twentieth-Century Crime and Mystery
    Writers,* 2nd ed., pp. 704–5. (882b)
*Twentieth-Century Crime and Mystery
    Writers,* 3rd ed., pp. 841–42. (882c)
Perrault, E. G.; i.e., Ernest G.
Bio-bibliographic data:
Canadian Crime Fiction, p. 168. (209)
**Perry, Anne: name adopted by Juliet
    Marion Hulme**
Bio-bibliographic data:
By a Woman's Hand, 1st ed., pp. 168–69.
    (884a)
By a Woman's Hand, 2nd ed., pp. 181–82.
    (884b)
Designs of Darkness, pp. 204–23. (873)
Detecting Women, 1st ed., pp. 114–15.
    (877a)
Detecting Women 2, pp. 154–55. (877b)
Detecting Women, 3rd ed., pp. 219–20.
    (877c)
Encyclopedia Mysteriosa, p. 273. (2)
Great Women Mystery Writers, pp.
    271–74. (880)
*The Mammoth Encyclopedia of Modern
    Crime Fiction*, pp. 385–86. (1)
*St. James Guide to Crime & Mystery
    Writers*, 4th ed., pp. 823–34. (882d)
Speaking of Murder, pp. 223–34. (875a)
*Twentieth-Century Crime and Mystery
    Writers,* 3rd ed., pp. 842–43. (882c)
*Whodunit? A Who's Who in Crime and
    Mystery Writing*, p. 150. (5)
Women of Mystery, pp. 425–32. (874)
Personal papers in Mugar Memorial
    Library, Boston University.
Web site: http://www.anneperry.com;
    http://stopyourekillingme.com/
    anne-perry.html
Perry, Douglas C.
Bio-bibliographic data:
Canadian Crime Fiction, p. 168. (209)
Perry, Ritchie
Bio-bibliographic data:
Detecting Men, 1st ed., pp. 203–4. (876)
*St. James Guide to Crime & Mystery
    Writers*, 4th ed., pp. 834–35. (882d)

*Twentieth-Century Crime and Mystery
    Writers,* 1st ed., pp. 1169–70. (882a)
*Twentieth-Century Crime and Mystery
    Writers,* 2nd ed., pp. 705–6. (882b)
*Twentieth-Century Crime and Mystery
    Writers,* 3rd ed., pp. 843–44. (882c)
Personal papers in Mugar Memorial
    Library, Boston University.
Perry, Roland
Bio-bibliographic data:
Australian Crime Fiction, p. 193. (207)
Perry, Thomas
Bio-bibliographic data:
Detecting Men, 1st ed., p. 204. (876)
The Encyclopedia of Murder and Mystery,
    pp. 388–89. (6)
*The Mammoth Encyclopedia of Modern
    Crime Fiction*, pp. 387–88. (1)
Web site: http://stopyourekillingme.com/
    thomas-perry.html
Perutz, Leo
Bio-bibliographic data:
The Encyclopedia of Murder and Mystery,
    p. 389. (6)
Peters, Bill. *See* McGivern, William P.
**Peters, Elizabeth. *See* Mertz, Barbara
    Louise Gross**
**Peters, Ellis. *Pseud. for* Edith Mary
    Pargeter**
Bio-bibliographic data:
By a Woman's Hand, 1st ed., pp. 170–71.
    (884a)
By a Woman's Hand, 2nd ed., pp. 183–84.
    (884b)
*Critical Survey of Mystery and Detective
    Fiction*, pp. 1318–24. (41)
Detecting Women, 1st ed., p. 113, 116–17.
    (877a)
Detecting Women 2, p. 156. (877b)
Encyclopedia Mysteriosa, pp. 273–74. (2)
The Encyclopedia of Murder and Mystery,
    p. 390. (6)
Great Women Mystery Writers, pp.
    279–83. (880)
*The Mammoth Encyclopedia of Modern
    Crime Fiction*, pp. 389–92. (1)
*100 Masters of Mystery and Detective
    Fiction*, pp. 511–18. (37)
*The Oxford Companion to Crime and
    Mystery Writing*, p. 329. (4)
*St. James Guide to Crime & Mystery
    Writers*, 4th ed., pp. 837–41. (882d)
*Twentieth-Century Crime and Mystery
    Writers,* 1st ed., pp. 1172–76. (882a)

*Twentieth-Century Crime and Mystery
Writers,* 2nd ed., pp. 707–10. (882b)
*Twentieth-Century Crime and Mystery
Writers,* 3rd ed., pp. 846–49. (882c)
*Whodunit? A Who's Who in Crime and
Mystery Writing,* p. 151. (5)
Women Authors of Detective Series, pp.
74–83. (882.5)
Web site: http://stopyourekillingme.com/
ellis-peters.html; http://www.iw.
net/~csonne; http://user.chollian.net/
~beringar; http://wellscs.com/ann/
reading/cadfael.htm
Peters, Geoffrey. *See* **Palmer, Madelyn**
Peters, Ludovic. *Pseud. for* **Peter Ludwig
Brent**
Bio-bibliographic data:
*Twentieth-Century Crime and Mystery
Writers,* 1st ed., pp. 1176–78. (882a)
*Twentieth-Century Crime and Mystery
Writers,* 2nd ed., p. 710. (882b)
Peters, Lance. *Pseud. for* **Peter
Lichtenstein**
Bio-bibliographic data:
Australian Crime Fiction, pp. 193–94.
(207)
Peters, Maureen. *See* **Black, Veronica**
Peterson, Audrey: unidentified pseud.
Bio-bibliographic data:
By a Woman's Hand, 1st ed., pp. 171–72.
(884a)
By a Woman's Hand, 2nd ed., pp. 184–85.
(884b)
Detecting Women, 1st ed., p. 117. (877a)
Detecting Women 2, p. 257. (877b)
Detecting Women, 3rd ed., p. 221. (877c)
Web site: http://stopyourekillingme.com/
audrey-peterson.html
Peterson, Gary
Bio-bibliographic data:
Canadian Crime Fiction, p. 168. (209)
Peterson, Keith
Bio-bibliographic data:
Detecting Men, 1st ed., p. 204. (876)
Petievich, Gerald
Bio-bibliographic data:
Detecting Men, 1st ed., pp. 204–5. (876)
Encyclopedia Mysteriosa, pp. 274–75. (2)
*St. James Guide to Crime & Mystery
Writers,* 4th ed., pp. 841–42. (882d)
*Twentieth-Century Crime and Mystery
Writers,* 3rd ed., pp. 849–50. (882c)
Personal papers in Mugar Memorial
Library, Boston University.

Petit, Diane
Bio-bibliographic data:
Detecting Women, 3rd ed., p. 221. (877c)
Petitdidier, Maurice
Bio-bibliographic data:
Canadian Crime Fiction, p. 168. (209)
Petrie, Rhona. *See* **Curzon, Clare
Pétrin, Léa**
Bio-bibliographic data:
Canadian Crime Fiction, p. 169. (209)
Peyrou, Manuel
Bio-bibliographic data:
*Latin American Mystery Writers: An A to
Z Guide. (881)*
Phelps, Anthony
Bio-bibliographic data:
Canadian Crime Fiction, p. 169. (209)
Philby, Charles G.: unidentified pseud.
Bio-bibliographic data:
Canadian Crime Fiction, p. 169. (209)
Philbin, Tom
Bio-bibliographic data:
Detecting Men, 1st ed., p. 205. (876)
Philbrick, W. R.; i.e., W. Rodman
Bio-bibliographic data:
Detecting Men, 1st ed., p. 205. (876)
Philips, Judson P[entecost]. *See* **Pentecost,
Hugh**
Philipps, Maurice
Bio-bibliographic data:
Canadian Crime Fiction, p. 169. (209)
Phillips, Arthur
Bio-bibliographic data:
Canadian Crime Fiction, p. 169. (209)
Phillips, Dennis. *See* **Daniels, Philip**
Phillips, Edward O[ppenshaw].
Bio-bibliographic data:
Canadian Crime Fiction, p. 169. (209)
Phillips, Gary
Bio-bibliographic data:
Detecting Men, 1st ed., p. 206. (876)
Web site: http://stopyourekillingme.com/
gary-phillips.html
Phillips, James Atlee. *See* **Atlee, Philip**
Phillips, Mike
Bio-bibliographic data:
Detecting Men, 1st ed., p. 206. (876)
*The Mammoth Encyclopedia of Modern
Crime Fiction,* pp. 392–93. (1)
Web site:
http://www.twbooks.co.uk/authors/
mikephillips.html; http://
stopyourekillingme.com/
mike-phillips.html

Phillips, T. J. *Pseud. for* **Tom Savage**
Bio-bibliographic data:
Detecting Men, 1st ed., p. 206. (876)
Web site: http://stopyourekillingme.com/
t-j-phillips.html
Phillips, Vic
Bio-bibliographic data:
Canadian Crime Fiction, p. 169. (209)
Phillipps-Wooley, Sir Clive [Oldnall Long], F. R. G. S.
Bio-bibliographic data:
Canadian Crime Fiction, pp. 169–70.
(209)
Phillpotts, Eden
Bio-bibliographic data:
British Mystery Writers, 1860–1919, pp.
242–52. (866)
Critical Survey of Mystery and Detective Fiction, pp. 1325–30. (41)
Encyclopedia Mysteriosa, p. 276. (2)
The Encyclopedia of Murder and Mystery,
p. 392. (6)
The Encyclopedia of Mystery and Detection, p. 309. (7)
Twentieth-Century Crime and Mystery Writers, 1st ed., pp. 1179–87. (882a)
Twentieth-Century Crime and Mystery Writers, 2nd ed., pp. 711–15. (882b)
Twentieth-Century Crime and Mystery Writers, 3rd ed., pp. 850–55. (882c)
Picard, Francine
Bio-bibliographic data:
Canadian Crime Fiction, p. 170. (209)
Pickard, Nancy
Bio-bibliographic data:
By a Woman's Hand, 1st ed., pp. 172–73.
(884a)
By a Woman's Hand, 2nd ed., p. 185.
(884a)
Deadly Women, pp. 243–47. (26.5)
Detecting Women, 1st ed., p. 117. (877a)
Detecting Women 2, pp. 157–58. (877b)
Detecting Women, 3rd ed., p. 222. (877c)
Encyclopedia Mysteriosa, pp. 276–77. (2)
Great Women Mystery Writers, pp.
283–86. (880)
The Mammoth Encyclopedia of Modern Crime Fiction, pp. 393–94. (1)
St. James Guide to Crime & Mystery Writers, 4th ed., pp. 842–43. (882d)
Speaking of Murder, vol. II, pp. 225–32.
(875b)
Twentieth-Century Crime and Mystery Writers, 3rd ed., pp. 855–56. (882c)

Whodunit? A Who's Who in Crime and Mystery Writing, p. 151. (5)
Web site: http://stopyourekillingme.com/
nancy-pickard.html
Pidgin, Charles Felton
Bio-bibliographic data:
The Encyclopedia of Mystery and Detection, pp. 309–10. (7)
Pierce, David M.
Bio-bibliographic data:
Canadian Crime Fiction, p. 170. (209)
Detecting Men, 1st ed., p. 207. (876)
Piesman, Marissa
Bio-bibliographic data:
By a Woman's Hand, 1st ed., pp. 173–74.
(884a)
By a Woman's Hand, 2nd ed., p. 186.
(884b)
Detecting Women, 1st ed., p. 118. (877a)
Detecting Women 2, p. 158. (877b)
Detecting Women, 3rd ed., p. 223. (877c)
Web site: http://stopyourekillingme.com/
marissa-piesman.html
Pigeon, Pierre
Bio-bibliographic data:
Canadian Crime Fiction, p. 170. (209)
Piglia, Ricardo
Bio-bibliographic data:
Latin American Mystery Writers: An A to Z Guide. (881)
Pike, Robert L. *See* **Fish, Robert L.**
Pilarski, Jan
Bio-bibliographic data:
Canadian Crime Fiction, p. 155. (209)
Pincus, Elizabeth
Bio-bibliographic data:
By a Woman's Hand, 2nd ed., pp. 186–87.
(884b)
Detecting Women, 1st ed., p. 118. (877a)
Detecting Women 2, p. 158. (877b)
Detecting Women, 3rd ed., p. 223. (877c)
Piner, Jack
Bio-bibliographic data:
Canadian Crime Fiction, p. 170. (209)
Pinkerton, Allan
Bio-bibliographic data:
The Encyclopedia of Murder and Mystery,
pp. 393–94. (6)
The Encyclopedia of Mystery and Detection, p. 310. (7)
Pitcairn, John James. *See* **Ashdown, Clifford**
Piper, Evelyn. *Pseud. for* **Merriam Modell**
Bio-bibliographic data:

*Twentieth-Century Crime and Mystery
    Writers,* 1st ed., pp. 1187–88. (882a)
*Twentieth-Century Crime and Mystery
    Writers,* 2nd ed., pp. 715–16. (882b)
*Twentieth-Century Crime and Mystery
    Writers,* 3rd ed., pp. 856–57. (882c)
Personal papers in Mugar Memorial
    Library, Boston University.
Pirkis, C. L.; i.e., Catherine Louisa
Bio-bibliographic data:
The Encyclopedia of Murder and Mystery,
    p. 394. (6)
Piuze, Simone
Bio-bibliographic data:
Canadian Crime Fiction, p. 170. (209)
Plain, Josephine. *Pseud. for* **Mary Mitchell**
Bio-bibliographic data:
Australian Crime Fiction, p. 194. (207)
Plangman, Mary Patricia. *See* **Highsmith,
    Patricia**
Plante, Marie
Bio-bibliographic data:
Canadian Crime Fiction, p. 171. (209)
Plante, Raymond
Bio-bibliographic data:
Canadian Crime Fiction, p. 149, 171.
    (209)
Plaut, W. Gunter; i.e., Wolf
Bio-bibliographic data:
Canadian Crime Fiction, p. 171. (209)
Player, Robert. *Pseud. for* **Robert
    Furneaux Jordan**
Bio-bibliographic data:
*Twentieth-Century Crime and Mystery
    Writers,* 1st ed., pp. 1188–89. (882a)
*Twentieth-Century Crime and Mystery
    Writers,* 2nd ed., pp. 716–17. (882b)
Ploese, Mónica
Bio-bibliographic data:
*Latin American Mystery Writers: An A to
    Z Guide. (881)*
Plummer, Norman M.
Bio-bibliographic data:
Canadian Crime Fiction, p. 171. (209)
Plunkett, Edward John Moreton Drax.
    See **Dunsany, Lord**
Pocock, [Henry] Roger [Ashwell]
Bio-bibliographic data:
Canadian Crime Fiction, pp. 171–72.
    (209)
Poe, Edgar Allan
Bio-bibliographic data:
*Critical Survey of Mystery and Detective
    Fiction,* pp. 1331–37. (41)

Encyclopedia Mysteriosa, pp. 277–78. (2)
The Encyclopedia of Murder and Mystery,
    pp. 394–95. (6)
*The Encyclopedia of Mystery and
    Detection,* pp. 310–15. (7)
Mystery and Suspense Writers, pp.
    733–55. (884.2)
*100 Masters of Mystery and Detective
    Fiction,* pp. 519–26. (37)
*The Oxford Companion to Crime and
    Mystery Writing,* pp. 332–33. (4)
*St. James Guide to Crime & Mystery
    Writers,* 4th ed., pp. 843–45. (882d)
*Twentieth-Century Crime and Mystery
    Writers,* 1st ed., pp. 1530–31. (882a)
*Twentieth-Century Crime and Mystery
    Writers,* 2nd ed., pp. 933–34. (882b)
*Twentieth-Century Crime and Mystery
    Writers,* 3rd ed., pp. 1123–24. (882c)
*Whodunit? A Who's Who in Crime and
    Mystery Writing,* pp. 152–53. (5)
Personal papers in Humanities Research
    Center, University of Texas at Austin.
Personal papers in Pierpont Morgan
    Library, New York City.
Personal papers in Free Library of
    Philadelphia.
Personal papers in Henry E. Huntington
    Library and Art Gallery, San Marino,
    California.
Personal papers in Lilly Library, Indiana
    University.
Personal papers in New York Public
    Library.
Personal papers in University of Virginia.
Personal papers in Enoch Pratt Free
    Library, Baltimore, Maryland.
Personal papers in Poe Foundation,
    Richmond, Virginia.
Personal papers in Boston Public Library.
Personal papers in Library of Congress.
Personal papers in Columbia University
    Libraries.
Personal papers in Duke University
    Libraries.
Personal papers in Beinecke Library, Yale
    University.
Web site: http://stopyourekillingme.com/
    edgar-allan-poe.html;
    http://www.poedecoder.com
        Edgar Allan Poe Society of
            Baltimore
        c/o Jeffrey Savoye
        3301 Woodside Avenue

Baltimore, MD 21235
http://www.eapoe.org
Poe Museum
c/o Steven Hicks
1914–16 Main Street
Richmond, VA 23223
http://www.poemuseum.org
Poe Studies Association
c/o Carole Shaffer-Koros
CAHSSJ 106
Union, NJ 07083

Poissant, Marc-André. *See* **Fisher, Mark**

Poletti, Syria
Bio-bibliographic data:
Latin American Mystery Writers: An A to Z Guide. (881)

Pollard, [Joseph] Percival
Bio-bibliographic data:
The Encyclopedia of Mystery and Detection, p. 317. (7)

Pollock, Donald
Bio-bibliographic data:
Canadian Crime Fiction, p. 172. (209)

Pollock, Francis Lillie
Bio-bibliographic data:
Canadian Crime Fiction, p. 172. (209)

Pollock, J. C.
Bio-bibliographic data:
Canadian Crime Fiction, p. 263. (209)

Pomidor, Bill
Bio-bibliographic data:
Detecting Men, 1st ed., p. 207. (876)
Web site: http://stopyourekillingme.com/bill-pomidor.html

Ponson du Terail, Pierre Alexis
Bio-bibliographic data:
The Encyclopedia of Murder and Mystery, p. 397. (6)

Popkin, Zelda
Bio-bibliographic data:
Detecting Women, 1st ed., p. 118. (877a)
Detecting Women 2, p. 158. (877b)
Twentieth-Century Crime and Mystery Writers, 1st ed., pp. 1190–91. (882a)

Pople, Maureen
Bio-bibliographic data:
Australian Crime Fiction, p. 9. (207)

Porath, Sharon
Bio-bibliographic data:
Detecting Women 2, p. 159. (877b)

Porée-Kurrer, Philippe
Bio-bibliographic data:
Canadian Crime Fiction, pp. 172–73. (209)

Portal, Ellis. *See* **Powe, Bruce Allan**

Porter, Anna [Szigethy]
Bio-bibliographic data:
Canadian Crime Fiction, p. 173. (209)
Detecting Women, 1st ed., p. 118. (877a)
Detecting Women 2, p. 159. (877b)
Detecting Women, 3rd ed., pp. 223–24. (877c)

Porter, Dorothy
Bio-bibliographic data:
The Encyclopedia of Murder and Mystery, p. 397. (6)

Porter, Joyce
Bio-bibliographic data:
Detecting Women 2, pp. 159–60. (877b)
Critical Survey of Mystery and Detective Fiction, pp. 1338–41. (41)
Encyclopedia Mysteriosa, p. 281. (2)
The Encyclopedia of Murder and Mystery, pp. 397–98. (6)
The Encyclopedia of Mystery and Detection, p. 318. (7)
Great Women Mystery Writers, pp. 286–89. (880)
The Oxford Companion to Crime and Mystery Writing, p. 349. (4)
St. James Guide to Crime & Mystery Writers, 4th ed., pp. 845–47. (882d)
Twentieth-Century Crime and Mystery Writers, 1st ed., pp. 1191–93. (882a)
Twentieth-Century Crime and Mystery Writers, 2nd ed., pp. 717–18. (882b)
Twentieth-Century Crime and Mystery Writers, 3rd ed., pp. 857–58. (882c)
Whodunit? A Who's Who in Crime and Mystery Writing, p. 156. (5)
Web site: http://stopyourekillingme.com/joyce-porter.html

Porter, William Sydney. *See* **Henry, O.**

Portus, Professor G. V.
Bio-bibliographic data:
Australian Crime Fiction, p. 183. (207)

Post, Melville Davisson
Bio-bibliographic data:
Critical Survey of Mystery and Detective Fiction, pp. 1342–48. (41)
Encyclopedia Mysteriosa, pp. 281–82. (2)
The Encyclopedia of Murder and Mystery, pp. 398–99. (6)
The Encyclopedia of Mystery and Detection, p. 319. (7)
The Oxford Companion to Crime and Mystery Writing, p. 349. (4)

St. James Guide to Crime & Mystery
  Writers, 4th ed., pp. 847–48. (882d)
Twentieth-Century Crime and Mystery
  Writers, 1st ed., pp. 1194–95. (882a)
Twentieth-Century Crime and Mystery
  Writers, 2nd ed., pp. 718–19. (882b)
Twentieth-Century Crime and Mystery
  Writers, 3rd ed., pp. 858–59. (882c)
Whodunit? A Who's Who in Crime and
  Mystery Writing, p. 156. (5)
Postgate, Raymond
Bio-bibliographic data:
The Encyclopedia of Murder and Mystery,
  p. 399. (6)
The Encyclopedia of Mystery and
  Detection, pp. 319–20. (7)
Twentieth-Century Crime and Mystery
  Writers, 1st ed., pp. 1196–98. (882a)
Twentieth-Century Crime and Mystery
  Writers, 2nd ed., pp. 719–21. (882b)
Twentieth-Century Crime and Mystery
  Writers, 3rd ed., pp. 859–61. (882c)
Potter, Jeremy
Bio-bibliographic data:
The Mammoth Encyclopedia of Modern
  Crime Fiction, pp. 394–95. (1)
Potts, Jean
Bio-bibliographic data:
Critical Survey of Mystery and Detective
  Fiction, pp. 1349–54. (41)
Encyclopedia Mysteriosa, p. 282. (2)
The Encyclopedia of Murder and Mystery,
  pp. 399–400. (6)
The Encyclopedia of Mystery and
  Detection, p. 320. (7)
St. James Guide to Crime & Mystery
  Writers, 4th ed., pp. 848–49. (882d)
Twentieth-Century Crime and Mystery
  Writers, 1st ed., pp. 1198–1200.
  (882a)
Twentieth-Century Crime and Mystery
  Writers, 2nd ed., pp. 721–22. (882b)
Twentieth-Century Crime and Mystery
  Writers, 3rd ed., pp. 861–62. (882c)
Poulin, Richard
Bio-bibliographic data:
Canadian Crime Fiction, p. 173. (209)
Poupart, Jean-Marie
Bio-bibliographic data:
Canadian Crime Fiction, p. 173. (209)
Powe, Bruce Allan:
Bio-bibliographic data:
Canadian Crime Fiction, pp. 173–74.
  (209)

Powell, Deborah
Bio-bibliographic data:
By a Woman's Hand, 1st ed., pp. 174–75.
  (884a)
Detecting Women 2, p. 160. (877b)
Detecting Women, 3rd ed., p. 224. (877c)
Powell, James
Bio-bibliographic data:
Canadian Crime Fiction, p. 174. (209)
Encyclopedia Mysteriosa, pp. 282–83. (2)
St. James Guide to Crime & Mystery
  Writers, 4th ed., p. 849. (882d)
Twentieth-Century Crime and Mystery
  Writers, 1st ed., pp. 1200–1202.
  (882a)
Twentieth-Century Crime and Mystery
  Writers, 2nd ed., pp. 722–23. (882b)
Twentieth-Century Crime and Mystery
  Writers, 3rd ed., pp. 862–64. (882c)
Personal papers in University of
  Wyoming, Laramie, Wyoming.
Powell, Richard
Bio-bibliographic data:
The Encyclopedia of Murder and Mystery,
  p. 400. (6)
Powell, Talmage
Bio-bibliographic data:
Encyclopedia Mysteriosa, p. 283. (2)
Twentieth-Century Crime and Mystery
  Writers, 2nd ed., pp. 723–26. (882b)
Twentieth-Century Crime and Mystery
  Writers, 3rd ed., pp. 864–69. (882c)
Personal papers in University of North
  Carolina Library, Chapel Hill.
Power, Patricia
Bio-bibliographic data:
Canadian Crime Fiction, p. 174. (209)
Powley, Jean [Makins]
Bio-bibliographic data:
Canadian Crime Fiction, p. 36, 174. (209)
Poyer, David
Bio-bibliographic data:
Detecting Men, 1st ed., p. 207. (876)
Pozzessere, Heather Graham
Bio-bibliographic data:
Canadian Crime Fiction, p. 174. (209)
Pradel, Roger
Bio-bibliographic data:
Canadian Crime Fiction, p. 174. (209)
Praed, Rosa [Caroline Murray-Prior
  Praed]
Bio-bibliographic data:
Australian Crime Fiction, pp. 194–95.
  (207)

Prather, Richard S[cott]
Bio-bibliographic data:
Corpus Delicti of Mystery Fiction, pp.
104–5. (879)
Detecting Men, 1st ed., p. 208. (876)
Encyclopedia Mysteriosa, p. 283. (2)
The Encyclopedia of Murder and Mystery,
p. 400. (6)
*The Mammoth Encyclopedia of Modern
Crime Fiction*, pp. 395–96. (1)
*St. James Guide to Crime & Mystery
Writers*, 4th ed., pp. 849–51. (882d)
*Twentieth-Century Crime and Mystery
Writers*, 1st ed., pp. 1202–4. (882a)
*Twentieth-Century Crime and Mystery
Writers*, 2nd ed., pp. 726–28. (882b)
*Twentieth-Century Crime and Mystery
Writers*, 3rd ed., pp. 869–70. (882c)
Personal papers in Rare Books and Special
Collections, University of Wyoming,
Laramie.
Web site: http://stopyourekillingme.com/
richard-prather.html
Pratt, Ambrose [Goddard Hesketh]
Bio-bibliographic data:
Australian Crime Fiction, p. 195. (207)
Pratt, Bruce W.
Bio-bibliographic data:
Australian Crime Fiction, p. 183. (207)
Préfontaine, de Fernand. *See* **Berton, Dick**
Prentice, Jim
Bio-bibliographic data:
Canadian Crime Fiction, p. 174. (209)
Preston, James
Bio-bibliographic data:
Australian Crime Fiction, pp. 196–97.
(207)
Price, Anthony
Bio-bibliographic data:
Canadian Crime Fiction, p. 284. (209)
Detecting Men, 1st ed., p. 209. (876)
Encyclopedia Mysteriosa, pp. 283–84. (2)
*St. James Guide to Crime & Mystery
Writers*, 4th ed., pp. 851–52. (882d)
*Twentieth-Century Crime and Mystery
Writers*, 1st ed., pp. 1204–6. (882a)
*Twentieth-Century Crime and Mystery
Writers*, 2nd ed., pp. 728–29. (882b)
*Twentieth-Century Crime and Mystery
Writers*, 3rd ed., pp. 870–72. (882c)
Web site: http://stopyourekillingme.com/
anthony-price.html
Prichard, Hesketh [Vernon Hesketh]
Bio-bibliographic data:

Canadian Crime Fiction, p. 263. (209)
The Encyclopedia of Murder and Mystery,
p. 401. (6)
*The Encyclopedia of Mystery and
Detection*, p. 320. (7)
Priestly, J. B.; i.e., John Boynton
Bio-bibliographic data:
British Mystery Writers, 1920–1939, pp.
239–45. (867)
Canadian Crime Fiction, p. 284. (209)
*Critical Survey of Mystery and Detective
Fiction*, pp. 1355–62. (41)
Encyclopedia Mysteriosa, pp. 284–85. (2)
The Encyclopedia of Murder and Mystery,
p. 402. (6)
*The Encyclopedia of Mystery and
Detection*, pp. 321–22. (7)
*Twentieth-Century Crime and Mystery
Writers*, 1st ed., pp. 1206–13. (882a)
*Twentieth-Century Crime and Mystery
Writers*, 2nd ed., pp. 729–33. (882b)
*Twentieth-Century Crime and Mystery
Writers*, 3rd ed., pp. 872–75. (882c)
Personal papers in Humanities Research
Center, University of Texas at Austin.
Prior, Allan
Bio-bibliographic data:
*Twentieth-Century Crime and Mystery
Writers*, 1st ed., pp. 1213–15. (882a)
*Twentieth-Century Crime and Mystery
Writers*, 2nd ed., pp. 733–34. (882b)
*Twentieth-Century Crime and Mystery
Writers*, 3rd ed., pp. 876–77. (882c)
Personal papers in Mugar Memorial
Library, Boston University.
Procter, Maurice
Bio-bibliographic data:
Encyclopedia Mysteriosa, p. 285. (2)
The Encyclopedia of Murder and Mystery,
pp. 404–5. (6)
*The Encyclopedia of Mystery and
Detection*, p. 322. (7)
*St. James Guide to Crime & Mystery
Writers*, 4th ed., pp. 852–53. (882d)
*Twentieth-Century Crime and Mystery
Writers*, 1st ed., pp. 1215–17. (882a)
*Twentieth-Century Crime and Mystery
Writers*, 2nd ed., pp. 734–35. (882b)
*Twentieth-Century Crime and Mystery
Writers*, 3rd ed., pp. 877–78. (882c)
Personal papers in Mugar Memorial
Library, Boston University.
Prokich, Alex
Bio-bibliographic data:

Canadian Crime Fiction, pp. 174–75. (209)

Pronzini, Bill; i.e., William John
Bio-bibliographic data:
American Hard-Boiled Crime Writers, pp. 289–300. (862)
The Big Book of Noir, p. 326. (24)
Canadian Crime Fiction, p. 263. (209)
Critical Survey of Mystery and Detective Fiction, pp. 1363–69. (41)
Detecting Men, 1st ed., p. 93, 209–10. (876)
Encyclopedia Mysteriosa, pp. 285–86. (2)
The Encyclopedia of Murder and Mystery, pp. 405–6. (6)
The Mammoth Encyclopedia of Modern Crime Fiction, pp. 396–99. (1)
100 Masters of Mystery and Detective Fiction, pp. 527–36. (37)
St. James Guide to Crime & Mystery Writers, 4th ed., pp. 853–57. (882d)
Speaking of Murder, pp. 153–62. (875a)
Twentieth-Century Crime and Mystery Writers, 1st ed., pp. 1217–23. (882a)
Twentieth-Century Crime and Mystery Writers, 2nd ed., pp. 735–39. (882b)
Twentieth-Century Crime and Mystery Writers, 3rd ed., pp. 878–83. (882c)
Whodunit? A Who's Who in Crime and Mystery Writing, pp. 159–60. (5)
Personal papers in Mugar Memorial Library, Boston University.
Web site: http://stopyourekillingme.com/bill-pronzini.html; http://www.thrillingdetective.com/trivia/pronzini.html

Propper, Milton [Morris]
Bio-bibliographic data:
Encyclopedia Mysteriosa, p. 286. (2)
The Encyclopedia of Mystery and Detection, pp. 322–23. (7)
Twentieth-Century Crime and Mystery Writers, 1st ed., pp. 1224–25. (882a)
Twentieth-Century Crime and Mystery Writers, 2nd ed., pp. 739–40. (882b)
Twentieth-Century Crime and Mystery Writers, 3rd ed., pp. 883–84. (882c)

Prowell, Sandra West
Bio-bibliographic data:
By a Woman's Hand, 2nd ed., pp. 187–88. (884b)
Detecting Women, 1st ed., p. 119. (877a)
Detecting Women 2, p. 160. (877b)
Detecting Women, 3rd ed., p. 224. (877c)

Web site: http://stopyourekillingme.com/sandra-west-prowell.html; http://www.imt.net/~gedison/prowell.html

Puccetti, Roland
Bio-bibliographic data:
Canadian Crime Fiction, p. 175. (209)

Puckett, Andrew
Bio-bibliographic data:
Detecting Men, 1st ed., p. 210. (876)

Pugh, Dianne G.
Bio-bibliographic data:
By a Woman's Hand, 2nd ed., pp. 188–89. (884b)
Detecting Women, 1st ed., p. 119. (877a)
Detecting Women 2, p. 160. (877b)
Detecting Women, 3rd ed., pp. 224–25. (877c)
Web site: http://stopyourekillingme.com/dianne-g-pugh.html

Puig, Manuel
Bio-bibliographic data:
Critical Survey of Mystery and Detective Fiction, pp. 1370–74. (41)

Pulver, Mary Monica. *See* **Kuhfeld, Mary Pulver; Kuhfeld, Mary Pulver, and Gail Bacon**

Punshon, E. R.; i.e., Ernest Robertson
Bio-bibliographic data:
Australian Crime Fiction, p. 197. (207)
The Encyclopedia of Mystery and Detection, p. 324. (7)
St. James Guide to Crime & Mystery Writers, 4th ed., pp. 857–58. (882d)
Twentieth-Century Crime and Mystery Writers, 3rd ed., pp. 884–85. (882c)

Purser, Philip
Bio-bibliographic data:
Twentieth-Century Crime and Mystery Writers, 3rd ed., pp. 885–87. (882c)

Puzo, Mario
Bio-bibliographic data:
The Mammoth Encyclopedia of Modern Crime Fiction, pp. 400–2. (1)
Web site: http://www.jgeoff.com/puzo; http://stopyourekillingme.com/mario-puzo.html

Pyke, John
Bio-bibliographic data:
Australian Crime Fiction, p. 197. (207)

Q

Quaife, Darlene Barry
Bio-bibliographic data:
Canadian Crime Fiction, p. 175. (209)

Queen, Ellery. *Pseud. for* **Manfred Bennington Lee and Frederic Dannay and others. Those curious about the others are referred to Francis M. Nevins, "Death and Ghosts: The Ellery Queen Paperback Originals,"** *Dime Novel Round-Up* **67, no. 1 (1998): 3–17.**
Bio-bibliographic data:
Corpus Delicti of Mystery Fiction, pp. 105–7. (879)
Critical Survey of Mystery and Detective Fiction, pp. 1375–83. (41)
Encyclopedia Mysteriosa, pp. 291–92. (2)
The Encyclopedia of Murder and Mystery, pp. 412–13. (6)
The Encyclopedia of Mystery and Detection, pp. 325–28. (7)
Mystery and Suspense Writers, pp. 757–71. (884.2)
100 Masters of Mystery and Detective Fiction, pp. 537–45. (37)
The Oxford Companion to Crime and Mystery Writing, pp. 367–68. (4)
St. James Guide to Crime & Mystery Writers, 4th ed., pp. 859–63. (882d)
Twentieth-Century Crime and Mystery Writers, 1st ed., pp. 1225–31. (882a)
Twentieth-Century Crime and Mystery Writers, 2nd ed., pp. 740–44. (882b)
Twentieth-Century Crime and Mystery Writers, 3rd ed., pp. 888–92. (882c)
Whodunit? A Who's Who in Crime and Mystery Writing, pp. 161–62. (5)
Personal papers in Humanities Research Center, University of Texas at Austin
Web site: http://www.stopyourekillingme. com/ellery-queen.html; http://neptune. spaceports.com/~queen/index.html
Quentin, Patrick. *Pseud. for* **four authors, Hugh Callingham Wheeler and others: Richard Wilson Webb and Martha Mott Kelly; Richard Wilson Webb and Mary Louise Aswell; Webb by himself; Webb and Wheeler; and Wheeler by himself.**
Bio-bibliographic data:
Critical Survey of Mystery and Detective Fiction, pp. 1384–88. (41)
Encyclopedia Mysteriosa, pp. 294–95. (2)
The Encyclopedia of Murder and Mystery, p. 415. (6)

The Encyclopedia of Mystery and Detection, pp. 331–32. (7)
St. James Guide to Crime & Mystery Writers, 4th ed., pp. 863–65. (882d)
Twentieth-Century Crime and Mystery Writers, 1st ed., pp. 1232–36. (882a)
Twentieth-Century Crime and Mystery Writers, 2nd ed., pp. 744–47. (882b)
Twentieth-Century Crime and Mystery Writers, 3rd ed., pp. 892–94. (882c)
Quest, Erica. *Pseud. for* **Nancy Buckingham Sawyer and John Sawyer**
Bio-bibliographic data:
By a Woman's Hand, 1st ed., pp. 176–77. (884a)
Detecting Women 2, p. 161. (877b)
Detecting Women, 3rd ed., p. 225. (877c)
Quill, Monica. *See* **McInerny, Ralph**
Quin-Harken, Janet. *See* **Bowen, Rhys**
Quinn, Elizabeth. *Pseud. for* **Elizabeth Quinn Barnard**
Bio-bibliographic data:
Detecting Women, 1st ed., p. 119. (877a)
Detecting Women 2, p. 161. (877b)
Detecting Women, 3rd ed., pp. 225–26. (877c)
Web site: http://www.stopyourekillingme. com/elizabeth-quinn.html
Quinn, Monica. *See* **McInerny, Ralph**
Quinn, Patrick Edward
Bio-bibliographic data:
Australian Crime Fiction, p. 198. (207)
Quinn, Simon. *See* **Smith, Martin Cruz**
Quinton, Ann
Bio-bibliographic data:
Detecting Women, 3rd ed., p. 226. (877c)
Quogan, Anthony. *Pseud. for* **Anthony Stephenson**
Bio-bibliographic data:
Canadian Crime Fiction, p. 175, 212–13. (209)

R

Rabe, Peter
Bio-bibliographic data:
The Big Book of Noir, p. 184, 255–62. (24)
Encyclopedia Mysteriosa, p. 297. (2)
Murder off the Rack: Critical Studies of Ten Paperback Masters, pp. 113–33. (869)
St. James Guide to Crime & Mystery Writers, 4th ed., pp. 867–68. (882d)

*Twentieth-Century Crime and Mystery
Writers,* 2nd ed., pp. 747–48. (882b)
*Twentieth-Century Crime and Mystery
Writers,* 3rd ed., pp. 895–96. (882c)
Raby, Georges
Bio-bibliographic data:
Canadian Crime Fiction, p. 175. (209)
Radall, Thomas [Head]
Bio-bibliographic data:
Canadian Crime Fiction, pp. 175–76.
(209)
Radcliffe, Ann [Ward]
Bio-bibliographic data:
*Critical Survey of Mystery and Detective
Fiction,* pp. 1389–94. (41)
*The Encyclopedia of Mystery and
Detection,* p. 333. (7)
Radford, E., and M. A. Radford
Bio-bibliographic data:
*Twentieth-Century Crime and Mystery
Writers,* 1st ed., pp. 1236–37. (882a)
*Twentieth-Century Crime and Mystery
Writers,* 2nd ed., p. 748. (882b)
**Radley, Sheila. *Pseud. for* Sheila Mary
Robinson**
Bio-bibliographic data:
By a Woman's Hand, 1st ed., pp. 178–79.
(884a)
By a Woman's Hand, 2nd ed., p. 190.
(884b)
Detecting Women, 1st ed., p. 120. (877a)
Detecting Women 2, p. 161. (877b)
Detecting Women, 3rd ed., pp. 226–27.
(877c)
Encyclopedia Mysteriosa, p. 297. (2)
Great Women Mystery Writers, pp.
291–93. (880)
*The Mammoth Encyclopedia of Modern
Crime Fiction,* p. 402. (1)
*St. James Guide to Crime & Mystery
Writers,* 4th ed., pp. 868–69. (882d)
*Twentieth-Century Crime and Mystery
Writers,* 3rd ed., pp. 896–97. (882c)
Web site: http://stopyourekillingme.com/
sheila-radley.html
Rae, Hugh C.
Bio-bibliographic data:
*Twentieth-Century Crime and Mystery
Writers,* 1st ed., pp. 1238–39. (882a)
*Twentieth-Century Crime and Mystery
Writers,* 2nd ed., pp. 749–50. (882b)
*Twentieth-Century Crime and Mystery
Writers,* 3rd ed., pp. 897–98. (882c)

Raffery, Roger
Bio-bibliographic data:
Australian Crime Fiction, p. 199. (207)
Rafferty, S. S. *Pseud. for* John J. Hurley
Bio-bibliographic data:
*Twentieth-Century Crime and Mystery
Writers,* 1st ed., pp. 1240–41. (882a)
**Raimond, C. E. *Pseud. for* Elizabeth
Robins**
Bio-bibliographic data:
Canadian Crime Fiction, p. 264, 265.
(209)
Raine, William MacLeod
Bio-bibliographic data:
Canadian Crime Fiction, p. 264. (209)
Raleigh, Michael
Bio-bibliographic data:
Detecting Men, 1st ed., p. 211. (876)
Web site: http://stopyourekillingme.com/
michael-raleigh.html
Ramírez Heredia, Rafael
Bio-bibliographic data:
*Latin American Mystery Writers: An A to
Z Guide. (881)*
Ramos, Manuel
Bio-bibliographic data:
Detecting Men, 1st ed., p. 211. (876)
Web site: http://stopyourekillingme.com/
manuel-ramos.html; http://www.
manuelramos.com
Randall, Diane. *See* Ross, W. E. D.
Randisi, Robert J[oseph].
Bio-bibliographic data:
Canadian Crime Fiction, p. 264, 265.
(209)
Detecting Men, 1st ed., pp. 211–12. (876)
Encyclopedia Mysteriosa, p. 298. (2)
The Encyclopedia of Murder and Mystery,
p. 417. (6)
*The Mammoth Encyclopedia of Modern
Crime Fiction,* pp. 403–4. (1)
*St. James Guide to Crime & Mystery
Writers,* 4th ed., pp. 869–70. (882d)
*Twentieth-Century Crime and Mystery
Writers,* 2nd ed., pp. 750–51. (882b)
*Twentieth-Century Crime and Mystery
Writers,* 3rd ed., pp. 898–900. (882c)
*Whodunit? A Who's Who in Crime and
Mystery Writing,* pp. 163–64. (5)
Web site: http://stopyourekillingme.com/
robert-j-randisi.html; http://www.
thrillingdetective.com/trivia/randisi.ht
ml

Randolph, Ellen. *See* Ross, W. E. D.
Randolph, Georgianna Ann. *See* Rice, Craig
Randolph, Marion. *Pseud. for* Marie Fried Rodell
Bio-bibliographic data:
Twentieth-Century Crime and Mystery Writers, 1st ed., pp. 1241–43. (882a)
Twentieth-Century Crime and Mystery Writers, 2nd ed., pp. 751–52. (882b)
Ranken, J. L. *See* Rankin, J. L.
Rankin, Ian
Bio-bibliographic data:
Detecting Men, 1st ed., p. 212. (876)
The Encyclopedia of Murder and Mystery, pp. 417–18. (6)
The Mammoth Encyclopedia of Modern Crime Fiction, pp. 404–6. (1)
St. James Guide to Crime & Mystery Writers, 4th ed., pp. 870–71. (882d)
Speaking of Murder, pp. 127–34. (875a)
Whodunit? A Who's Who in Crime and Mystery Writing, p. 164. (5)
Web site: http://www.ianrankin.com; http://stopyourekillingme.com/ian-rankin.html
Rankin, J. L.; i.e., Jean Logan
Bio-bibliographic data:
Australian Crime Fiction, p. 183, 199. (207)
Ransom, Daniel. *See* Gorman, Ed
Raphael, Chaim. *See* Davey, Jocelyn
Raphael, Lev
Bio-bibliographic data:
Detecting Men, 1st ed., p. 212. (876)
Web site: http://stopyourekillingme.com/lev-raphael.html; http://www.levraphael.com
Rathbone, Julian
Bio-bibliographic data:
The Mammoth Encyclopedia of Modern Crime Fiction, pp. 406–7. (1)
St. James Guide to Crime & Mystery Writers, 4th ed., pp. 871–73. (882d)
Speaking of Murder, vol. II, pp. 153–61. (875b)
Twentieth-Century Crime and Mystery Writers, 1st ed., pp. 1243–45. (882a)
Twentieth-Century Crime and Mystery Writers, 2nd ed., pp. 752–53. (882b)
Twentieth-Century Crime and Mystery Writers, 3rd ed., pp. 900–902. (882c)
Web site: http://www.julianrathbone.html

Ratton, John
Bio-bibliographic data:
Australian Crime Fiction, p. 199. (207)
Rawlings, Ellen
Bio-bibliographic data:
Detecting Women, 3rd ed., p. 227. (877c)
Web site: http://stopyourekillingme.com/ellen-rawlings.html
Rawlins, Eustace. *See* Eustace, Robert
Rawson, Clayton
Bio-bibliographic data:
Encyclopedia Mysteriosa, p. 299. (2)
The Encyclopedia of Murder and Mystery, pp. 418–19. (6)
The Encyclopedia of Mystery and Detection, p. 339. (7)
St. James Guide to Crime & Mystery Writers, 4th ed., pp. 873–74. (882d)
Twentieth-Century Crime and Mystery Writers, 1st ed., pp. 1245–46. (882a)
Twentieth-Century Crime and Mystery Writers, 2nd ed., pp. 753–54. (882b)
Twentieth-Century Crime and Mystery Writers, 3rd ed., pp. 902–3. (882c)
Raymond. *Pseud. for* Raymond Robichaud
Bio-bibliographic data:
Canadian Crime Fiction, p. 176. (209)
Raymond, Derek. *Pseud. for* Robin Robert William Arthur Cook
Bio-bibliographic data:
The Mammoth Encyclopedia of Modern Crime Fiction, pp. 407–8. (1)
St. James Guide to Crime & Mystery Writers, 4th ed., pp. 874–75. (882d)
Twentieth-Century Crime and Mystery Writers, 3rd ed., pp. 903–4. (882c)
Personal papers in Mugar Memorial Library, Boston University.
Raymond, René. *See* Chase, James Hadley
Raymond, Trevor
Bio-bibliographic data:
Canadian Crime Fiction, p. 176. (209)
Raymonde, A. P.
Bio-bibliographic data:
Australian Crime Fiction, p. 199. (207)
Rayner, Claire
Bio-bibliographic data:
Detecting Women, 3rd ed., p. 227. (877c)
Reach, Angus [Bethune]
Bio-bibliographic data:
British Mystery Writers, 1860–1919, pp. 253–57. (866)
The Encyclopedia of Mystery and Detection, p. 339. (7)

Reaney, James [Crerar]
Bio-bibliographic data:
Canadian Crime Fiction, pp. 176–77.
(209)
Reardon, Mitch
Bio-bibliographic data:
Australian Crime Fiction, p. 9. (207)
Reasoner, James, and L. J. Washburn
Bio-bibliographic data:
The Big Book of Noir, p. 325. (24)
**Reaves, Sam. *Pseud. for* Samuel Allen
Salter**
Bio-bibliographic data:
*The Mammoth Encyclopedia of Modern
Crime Fiction*, pp. 408–9. (1)
Web site: http://www.martell-reaves.com;
http://stopyourekillingme.com/
sam-reaves.html
Recio Tenorio, Bertha
Bio-bibliographic data:
*Latin American Mystery Writers: An A to
Z Guide. (881)*
Recknor, Ellen. *See* Bryan, Kate
Redmann, J. M.; i.e., Jean M.
Bio-bibliographic data:
By a Woman's Hand, 1st ed., p. 179.
(884a)
By a Woman's Hand, 2nd ed., p. 191.
(884b)
Detecting Women 2, p. 162. (877b)
Detecting Women, 3rd ed., pp. 227–28.
(877c)
Web site: http://stopyourekillingme.com/
jean-m-redmann.html
Reed, Barry
Bio-bibliographic data:
Detecting Men, 1st ed., p. 213. (876)
Web site: http://stopyourekillingme.com/
barry-read.html
Reed, Bill
Bio-bibliographic data:
Australian Crime Fiction, p. 199. (207)
Reed, Eliot. *See* Rodda, Percival Charles
Reed, Ishmael
Bio-bibliographic data:
*Twentieth-Century Crime and Mystery
Writers*, 1st ed., pp. 1246–48. (882a)
Personal papers in University of Delaware
Library, Special Collections
Web site:
http://www.math.buffalo.edu/~sww/
reed_ishmael0.html; http://www.
english.uiuc.edu/maps/poets/m_r/
reed/reed.htm

Rees, Arthur J[ohn].
Bio-bibliographic data:
Australian Crime Fiction, p. 200. (207)
Rees, Dilwyn. *See* Daniel, Glyn E.
Reeve, Arthur B[enjamin].
Bio-bibliographic data:
*Critical Survey of Mystery and Detective
Fiction*, pp. 1395–1400. (41)
Encyclopedia Mysteriosa, p. 300. (2)
The Encyclopedia of Murder and Mystery,
p. 421. (6)
*The Encyclopedia of Mystery and
Detection*, p. 340. (7)
*The Oxford Companion to Crime and
Mystery Writing*, p. 378. (4)
*Twentieth-Century Crime and Mystery
Writers*, 1st ed., pp. 1248–51. (882a)
*Twentieth-Century Crime and Mystery
Writers*, 2nd ed., pp. 754–56. (882b)
*Twentieth-Century Crime and Mystery
Writers*, 3rd ed., pp. 904–6. (882c)
*Whodunit? A Who's Who in Crime and
Mystery Writing*, p. 165. (5)
Reeves, John
Bio-bibliographic data:
Canadian Crime Fiction, p. 177. (209)
Reeves, Robert
Bio-bibliographic data:
Detecting Men, 1st ed., p. 213. (876)
Web site: http://stopyourekillingme.com/
robert-reeves.html
Reeves-Stevens, Garfield
Bio-bibliographic data:
Canadian Crime Fiction, p. 177. (209)
**Regester, Seeley. *Pseud. for* Metta Victoria
Fuller Victor**
Bio-bibliographic data:
Encyclopedia Mysteriosa, p. 300. (2)
The Encyclopedia of Murder and Mystery,
p. 421. (6)
*The Encyclopedia of Mystery and
Detection*, p. 340. (7)
Great Women Mystery Writers, pp.
293–95. (880)
*The Oxford Companion to Crime and
Mystery Writing*, pp. 380–81. (4)
*Whodunit? A Who's Who in Crime and
Mystery Writing*, pp. 165–66. (5)
Reichs, Kathy
Bio-bibliographic data:
Detecting Women, 3rd ed., p. 228. (877c)
*The Mammoth Encyclopedia of Modern
Crime Fiction*, p. 409. (1)

Web site: http://literati.net/Reichs; http://
stopyourekillingme.com/kathy-reichs.
html

**Reid, Desmond: house pseud. used by
Wilfred [Glassford] McNeilly (q.v.)
and others**
Bio-bibliographic data:
Australian Crime Fiction, p. 200. (207)
Reid, John Thomas Howard. *See* **Howard,
Tom**
Reid, Robert Sims
Bio-bibliographic data:
Detecting Men, 1st ed., p. 213. (876)
Reid, Wallace Q. *See* **Goodchild, George**
Reilly, Helen [Kieran]
Bio-bibliographic data:
Canadian Crime Fiction, p. 264. (209)
*Critical Survey of Mystery and Detective
Fiction,* pp. 1401–5. (41)
Detecting Women, 1st ed., pp. 120–21.
(877a)
Detecting Women 2, pp. 162–63. (877b)
Encyclopedia Mysteriosa, p. 301. (2)
The Encyclopedia of Murder and Mystery,
pp. 421–22. (6)
*The Encyclopedia of Mystery and
Detection,* pp. 340–41. (7)
*St. James Guide to Crime & Mystery
Writers,* 4th ed., pp. 876–77. (882d)
*Twentieth-Century Crime and Mystery
Writers,* 1st ed., pp. 1251–54. (882a)
*Twentieth-Century Crime and Mystery
Writers,* 2nd ed., pp. 756–57. (882b)
*Twentieth-Century Crime and Mystery
Writers,* 3rd ed., pp. 906–7. (882c)
Renaud, Jacques
Bio-bibliographic data:
Canadian Crime Fiction, pp. 177–78.
(209)
Rendell, Ruth [Barbara]
Bio-bibliographic data:
*British Mystery and Thriller Writers since
1940, First Series,* pp. 305–27. (868)
By a Woman's Hand, 1st ed., pp. 179–80.
(884a)
By a Woman's Hand, 2nd ed., pp. 191–92.
(884b)
*The Craft of Crime: Conversations with
Crime Writers,* pp. 227–57. (872)
*Critical Survey of Mystery and Detective
Fiction,* pp. 1406–11. (41)
Designs of Darkness, pp. 124–42. (873)
Detecting Women, 1st ed., p. 121. (877a)
Detecting Women 2, p. 163. (877b)

Detecting Women, 3rd ed., pp. 228–29.
(877c)
Encyclopedia Mysteriosa, pp. 301–2. (2)
The Encyclopedia of Murder and Mystery,
pp. 422–23. (6)
Great Women Mystery Writers, pp.
295–99. (880)
*The Mammoth Encyclopedia of Modern
Crime Fiction,* pp. 409–12. (1)
Mystery and Suspense Writers, pp.
773–90. (884.2)
*100 Masters of Mystery and Detective
Fiction,* pp. 546–52. (37)
*The Oxford Companion to Crime and
Mystery Writing,* p. 384. (4)
*St. James Guide to Crime & Mystery
Writers,* 4th ed., pp. 877–79. (882d)
10 Women of Mystery, pp. 124–49. (864,
865)
13 Mistresses of Murder, pp. 105–13.
(871)
*Twentieth-Century Crime and Mystery
Writers,* 1st ed., pp. 1254–56. (882a)
*Twentieth-Century Crime and Mystery
Writers,* 2nd ed., pp. 757–58. (882b)
*Twentieth-Century Crime and Mystery
Writers,* 3rd ed., pp. 907–9. (882c)
*Whodunit? A Who's Who in Crime and
Mystery Writing,* p. 166. (5)
Women Authors of Detective Series, pp.
111–18. (882.5)
Women of Mystery, pp. 362–73. (874)
Web site:
http://www.twbooks.co.uk/authors/
rendell.html; http://
stopyourekillingme.com/ruth-rendell.
html
Rennie, James A[lan].
Bio-bibliographic data:
Canadian Crime Fiction, p. 264. (209)
Renshaw, Anthony
Bio-bibliographic data:
Canadian Crime Fiction, p. 178. (209)
Renwick, Peter
Bio-bibliographic data:
Australian Crime Fiction, p. 200. (207)
Resnicow, Herbert
Bio-bibliographic data:
Detecting Men, 1st ed., p. 214. (876)
Encyclopedia Mysteriosa, p. 302. (2)
*St. James Guide to Crime & Mystery
Writers,* 4th ed., pp. 879–80. (882d)
*Twentieth-Century Crime and Mystery
Writers,* 3rd ed., pp. 909–10. (882c)

Reuben, Shelly
Bio-bibliographic data:
Detecting Women, 3rd ed., p. 229. (877c)
Reynolds, Dickson. *See* **Reynolds, Helen Mary Greenwood [Campbell Dickson]**
Reynolds, Helen Mary Greenwood [Campbell Dickson]
Bio-bibliographic data:
Canadian Crime Fiction, p. 178. (209)
Reynolds, John Lawrence
Bio-bibliographic data:
Canadian Crime Fiction, p. 178. (209)
Reynolds, William J.
Bio-bibliographic data:
Detecting Men, 1st ed., p. 214. (876)
St. James Guide to Crime & Mystery Writers, 4th ed., pp. 880–82. (882d)
Twentieth-Century Crime and Mystery Writers, 3rd ed., pp. 910–12. (882c)
Web site: http://stopyourekillingme.com/
william-j-reynolds.html
Rhea, Nicholas. *See* **Walker, Peter N.**
Rhode, John. *Pseud. for* **Cecil John Charles Street**
Bio-bibliographic data:
Australian Crime Fiction, p. 216. (207)
British Mystery Writers, 1920–1939, pp. 246–55. (867)
Canadian Crime Fiction, p. 264, 267. (209)
Critical Survey of Mystery and Detective Fiction, pp. 1412–19. (41)
Encyclopedia Mysteriosa, p. 303. (2)
The Encyclopedia of Murder and Mystery, pp. 423–24. (6)
The Encyclopedia of Mystery and Detection, pp. 341–42. (7)
The Oxford Companion to Crime and Mystery Writing, p. 387. (4)
St. James Guide to Crime & Mystery Writers, 4th ed., pp. 882–85. (882d)
Twentieth-Century Crime and Mystery Writers, 1st ed., pp. 1256–62. (882a)
Twentieth-Century Crime and Mystery Writers, 2nd ed., pp. 758–62. (882b)
Twentieth-Century Crime and Mystery Writers, 3rd ed., pp. 912–15. (882c)
Whodunit? A Who's Who in Crime and Mystery Writing, p. 166. (5)
Web site: http://stopyourekillingme.com/
john-rhode.html

Ribas, Jacques Folch. *See* **Folch-Ribas, Jacques**
Rice, Craig. *Pseud. for* **Georgiana Ann Randolph Craig; pseud. also used once by Lawrence Block (q.v.).**
Bio-bibliographic data:
And Then There Were Nine . . . More Women of Mystery, (863)
Women of Mystery, pp. 120–45. (874)
Critical Survey of Mystery and Detective Fiction, pp. 1420–26. (41)
Detecting Women 2, pp. 163–64, 187. (877b)
Encyclopedia Mysteriosa, pp. 303–4. (2)
The Encyclopedia of Murder and Mystery, pp. 424–25. (6)
The Encyclopedia of Mystery and Detection, p. 342. (7)
Great Women Mystery Writers, pp. 299–302. (880)
The Oxford Companion to Crime and Mystery Writing, p. 387. (4)
St. James Guide to Crime & Mystery Writers, 4th ed., pp. 885–87. (882d)
Twentieth-Century Crime and Mystery Writers, 1st ed., pp. 1262–65. (882a)
Twentieth-Century Crime and Mystery Writers, 2nd ed., pp. 762–64. (882b)
Twentieth-Century Crime and Mystery Writers, 3rd ed., pp. 915–17. (882c)
Whodunit? A Who's Who in Crime and Mystery Writing, pp. 166–67. (5)
Web site: http://stopyourekillingme.com/
craig-rice.html; http://jeffreymarks.
com/rice; http://www.
thrillingdetective.com/trivia/rice.html
Rice, Dixon
Bio-bibliographic data:
Australian Crime Fiction, p. 201. (207)
Rice, Linda
Bio-bibliographic data:
Canadian Crime Fiction, p. 264, 269. (209)
Rice, Walter
Bio-bibliographic data:
Canadian Crime Fiction, p. 264, 269. (209)
Rich, Nicholas
Bio-bibliographic data:
Australian Crime Fiction, p. 201. (207)
Rich, Virginia
Bio-bibliographic data:
By a Woman's Hand, 1st ed., pp. 180–81. (884a)

By a Woman's Hand, 2nd ed., pp. 192–93. (884b)
Detecting Women, 1st ed., p. 122. (877a)
Detecting Women 2, p. 164. (877b)
Great Women Mystery Writers, pp. 302–3. (880)
Web site: http://stopyourekillingme.com/ virginia-rich.html

Richard, Susan. *See* **Ellis, Julie [M.]**

Richards, David Adams
Bio-bibliographic data:
Canadian Crime Fiction, p. 179. (209)

Richards, Francis. *See* **Lockridge, Richard, and Frances**

Richards, Hank
Bio-bibliographic data:
Australian Crime Fiction, p. 201. (207)

Richards, Kel; i.e., Kelvin Barry
Bio-bibliographic data:
Australian Crime Fiction, p. 146, 201. (207)

Richards, Michael
Bio-bibliographic data:
Australian Crime Fiction, p. 9. (207)

Richards, Milton. *Pseud. for* **Milo Milton Oblinger**
Bio-bibliographic data:
Canadian Crime Fiction, pp. 264–65. (209)

Richards, Paul: house pseud.
Bio-bibliographic data:
Australian Crime Fiction, p. 202. (207)

Richardson, Robert
Bio-bibliographic data:
Detecting Men, 1st ed., p. 215. (876)
The Mammoth Encyclopedia of Modern Crime Fiction, p. 414. (1)
St. James Guide to Crime & Mystery Writers, 4th ed., pp. 887–88. (882d)
Web site: http://www.twbooks.co.uk/ authors/rrichardson.html

Richardson, Tracey
Bio-bibliographic data:
Canadian Crime Fiction, p. 179. (209)
Detecting Women, 3rd ed., p. 229. (877c)

Richaud, Benjamin. *See* **Morelle, Gaston**

Richley, Mordecai
Bio-bibliographic data:
Canadian Crime Fiction, p. 179. (209)

Richman, Phyllis
Bio-bibliographic data:
Detecting Women, 3rd ed., pp. 229–30. (877c)

Web site: http://stopyourekillingme.com/ phyllis-richman.html

Richmond
Bio-bibliographic data:
St. James Guide to Crime & Mystery Writers, 4th ed., p. 888. (882d)
Twentieth-Century Crime and Mystery Writers, 1st ed., p. 1531. (882a)
Twentieth-Century Crime and Mystery Writers, 2nd ed., p. 934. (882b)
Twentieth-Century Crime and Mystery Writers, 3rd ed., p. 1124. (882c)

Richmond, Philip
Bio-bibliographic data:
Australian Crime Fiction, p. 202. (207)

Rider, J. W. *See* **Stevens, Shane**

Ridgway, Jason. *See* **Marlowe, Stephen**

Ridley, Nat, Jr.: house pseud.
Bio-bibliographic data:
Canadian Crime Fiction, p. 265. (209)

Riel, Louis. *Pseud. for* **Edouard Garand**
Bio-bibliographic data:
Canadian Crime Fiction, p. 179. (209)

Rienits, Rex
Bio-bibliographic data:
Australian Crime Fiction, p. 202. (207)

Rigelhof, T. F.
Bio-bibliographic data:
Canadian Crime Fiction, p. 179. (209)

Riggs, John R.
Bio-bibliographic data:
Detecting Men, 1st ed., p. 216. (876)
Web site: http://stopyourekillingme.com/ john-r-riggs.html

Rigoni, Orlando Joseph
Bio-bibliographic data:
Canadian Crime Fiction, p. 5, 179. (209)

Riley, Len
Bio-bibliographic data:
Australian Crime Fiction, p. 202. (207)

Riley, Louise
Bio-bibliographic data:
Canadian Crime Fiction, p. 180. (209)

Riley, Wilma
Bio-bibliographic data:
Canadian Crime Fiction, p. 180. (209)

Rinehart, Mary Roberts
Bio-bibliographic data:
Corpus Delicti of Mystery Fiction, pp. 107–9. (879)
Critical Survey of Mystery and Detective Fiction, pp. 1427–33. (41)
Detecting Women, 1st ed., p. 122. (877a)
Detecting Women 2, p. 164. (877b)

Encyclopedia Mysteriosa, pp. 304–5. (2)
The Encyclopedia of Murder and Mystery, pp. 426–28. (6)
The Encyclopedia of Mystery and Detection, pp. 342–44. (7)
Great Women Mystery Writers, pp. 303–7. (880)
100 Masters of Mystery and Detective Fiction, pp. 553–60. (37)
The Oxford Companion to Crime and Mystery Writing, pp. 387–88. (4)
St. James Guide to Crime & Mystery Writers, 4th ed., pp. 888–91. (882d)
10 Women of Mystery, pp. 183–220. (864, 865)
Twentieth-Century Crime and Mystery Writers, 1st ed., pp. 1265–70. (882a)
Twentieth-Century Crime and Mystery Writers, 2nd ed., pp. 764–66. (882b)
Twentieth-Century Crime and Mystery Writers, 3rd ed., pp. 917–20. (882c)
Whodunit? A Who's Who in Crime and Mystery Writing, p. 167. (5)
Women of Mystery, pp. 18–72. (874)
Personal papers in University of Pittsburgh Library.
Web site: http://stopyourekillingme.com/ mary-roberts-rinehart.html
Ring, Raymond H.
Bio-bibliographic data:
Detecting Men, 1st ed., pp. 216–17. (876)
Riordan, Rick
Bio-bibliographic data:
The Mammoth Encyclopedia of Modern Crime Fiction, p. 415. (1)
Web site: http://www.rickriordan.com; http://stopyourekillingme.com/ rick-riordan.html
Ripley, Ann
Bio-bibliographic data:
Detecting Women 2, p. 165. (877b)
Detecting Women, 3rd ed., p. 230. (877c)
Web site: http://stopyourekillingme.com/ ann-ripley.html
Ripley, Jack. *See* **Wainwright, John**
Ripley, Mike
Bio-bibliographic data:
Detecting Men, 1st ed., p. 217. (876)
The Mammoth Encyclopedia of Modern Crime Fiction, pp. 415–16. (1)
Web site: http://www.twbooks.co.uk/ authors/mikeripley1.html; http:// stopyourekillingme.com/ mike-ripley.html

Ripley, W. L.
Bio-bibliographic data:
Detecting Men, 1st ed., p. 218. (876)
Web site: http://stopyourekillingme.com/ w-l-ripley.html
Rippon, Marion [Edith Simpson]
Bio-bibliographic data:
Canadian Crime Fiction, p. 180. (209)
Detecting Women, 3rd ed., p. 230. (877c)
Ritchie, Jack. *Pseud. for* **John George Reitci**
Bio-bibliographic data:
St. James Guide to Crime & Mystery Writers, 4th ed., p. 891. (882d)
Twentieth-Century Crime and Mystery Writers, 1st ed., pp. 1270–72. (882a)
Twentieth-Century Crime and Mystery Writers, 2nd ed., pp. 766–69. (882b)
Twentieth-Century Crime and Mystery Writers, 3rd ed., pp. 920–23. (882c)
Ritchie, Simon. *See* **Fodden, Simon [Ritchie]**
Rivest, Brigitte
Bio-bibliographic data:
Canadian Crime Fiction, p. 180. (209)
Rivett, Edith Caroline. *See* **Carnac, Carol**
Rixon, Annie Louisa. *Pseud. for* **Mrs. Richard de Clare Studdert**
Bio-bibliographic data:
Australian Crime Fiction, p. 202. (207)
Roat, Ronald Clair
Bio-bibliographic data:
Detecting Men, 1st ed., p. 218. (876)
Web site: http://stopyourekillingme.com/ ronald-clair-roat.html
Robb, Candace M.
Bio-bibliographic data:
By a Woman's Hand, 2nd ed., p. 193. (884b)
Detecting Women, 1st ed., p. 122. (877a)
Detecting Women 2, p. 165. (877b)
Detecting Women, 3rd ed., pp. 230–31. (877c)
The Mammoth Encyclopedia of Modern Crime Fiction, p. 416. (1)
Web site: http://www.candacerobb.com; http://stopyourekillingme.com/ candace-robb.html
Robb, J. D. *Pseud. for* **Nora Roberts**
Bio-bibliographic data:
Detecting Women 2, p. 165. (877b)
Detecting Women, 3rd ed., p. 231. (877c)
Web site: http://stopyourekillingme.com/ j-d-robb.html;

http://www.noraroberts.
com/jdrobb.htm

Robbe-Grillet, Alain
Bio-bibliographic data:
*Critical Survey of Mystery and Detective
Fiction*, pp. 1434–41. (41)
*Twentieth-Century Crime and Mystery
Writers*, 1st ed., pp. 1547–48. (882a)
*Twentieth-Century Crime and Mystery
Writers*, 2nd ed., p. 945. (882b)
*Twentieth-Century Crime and Mystery
Writers*, 3rd ed., p. 1136. (882c)

Robbins, Kay. *See* Hooper, Kay

Robens, Howard
Bio-bibliographic data:
Canadian Crime Fiction, p. 180. (209)

Roberge, Marc
Bio-bibliographic data:
Canadian Crime Fiction, p. 180. (209)

Roberts, Carey
Bio-bibliographic data:
Detecting Women, 1st ed., p. 123. (877a)
Detecting Women 2, p. 165. (877b)
Detecting Women, 3rd ed., pp. 231–32.
(877c)

Roberts, Gildas Jack
Bio-bibliographic data:
Canadian Crime Fiction, pp. 180–81.
(209)

Roberts, Gillian. *Pseud. for* Judith Greber
Bio-bibliographic data:
By a Woman's Hand, 1st ed., pp. 181–82.
(884a)
By a Woman's Hand, 2nd ed., pp. 193–94.
(884b)
Detecting Women, 1st ed., p. 123. (877a)
Detecting Women 2, pp. 165–66. (877b)
Detecting Women, 3rd ed., p. 232. (877c)
*The Mammoth Encyclopedia of Modern
Crime Fiction*, p. 417. (1)
*St. James Guide to Crime & Mystery
Writers*, 4th ed., pp. 892–93. (882d)
Web site: http://www.gillianroberts.com;
http://stopyourekillingme.com/
gillian-roberts.html

Roberts, J. R. *See* Randisi, Robert Joseph
**Roberts, James Hall. *Pseud. for* Robert
Lipscomb Duncan**
Bio-bibliographic data:
*Critical Survey of Mystery and Detective
Fiction*, pp. 1442–47. (41)
*Twentieth-Century Crime and Mystery
Writers*, 1st ed., pp. 1272–73. (882a)

*Twentieth-Century Crime and Mystery
Writers*, 2nd ed., pp. 770–71. (882b)
*Twentieth-Century Crime and Mystery
Writers*, 3rd ed., pp. 923–24. (882c)
Personal papers in Mugar Memorial
Library, Boston University.

Roberts, John Maddox
Bio-bibliographic data:
Detecting Men, 1st ed., p. 218. (876)

Roberts, Julian. *See* Jeffries, Roderic
Roberts, Ken
Bio-bibliographic data:
Canadian Crime Fiction, p. 181. (209)

Roberts, Les
Bio-bibliographic data:
Detecting Men, 1st ed., p. 219. (876)
Encyclopedia Mysteriosa, p. 306. (2)
*The Mammoth Encyclopedia of Modern
Crime Fiction*, pp. 418–19. (1)
*St. James Guide to Crime & Mystery
Writers*, 4th ed., pp. 893–95. (882d)
*Twentieth-Century Crime and Mystery
Writers*, 3rd ed., pp. 924–26. (882c)
Personal papers in Institute for Popular
Culture, Bowling Green State
University, Bowling Green, Ohio
Web site: http://www.lesroberts.com;
http://stopyourekillingme.com/
les-roberts.html

Roberts, Lillian M.
Bio-bibliographic data:
Detecting Women, 3rd ed., p. 232. (877c)

Roberts, Lora
Bio-bibliographic data:
By a Woman's Hand, 2nd ed., pp. 194–95.
(884b)
Detecting Women, 1st ed., p. 123. (877a)
Detecting Women 2, p. 166. (877b)
Detecting Women, 3rd ed., p. 233. (877c)

Roberts, Mark K.
Bio-bibliographic data:
Canadian Crime Fiction, p. 252, 265.
(209)

Roberts, Nora. *See* Robb, J. D.
Roberts, Paul William
Bio-bibliographic data:
Canadian Crime Fiction, p. 181. (209)

Roberts, Willo Davis
Bio-bibliographic data:
*St. James Guide to Crime & Mystery
Writers*, 4th ed., pp. 895–96. (882d)
*Twentieth-Century Crime and Mystery
Writers*, 2nd ed., pp. 771–72. (882b)

Twentieth-Century Crime and Mystery Writers, 3rd ed., pp. 926–27. (882c)
Personal papers in Institute for Popular Culture, Bowling Green State University, Bowling Green, Ohio.
Personal papers in de Grummond Collection, University of Southern Mississippi, Hattiesburg.
Personal papers in Central Missouri State University, Arrensburg, Missouri.
Roberts, Zelma [Oakley], and Hal Saunders
Bio-bibliographic data:
Australian Crime Fiction, p. 203. (207)
Robertson, Andrew
Bio-bibliographic data:
Australian Crime Fiction, p. 203. (207)
Robertson, Douglas S.
Bio-bibliographic data:
Canadian Crime Fiction, p. 181. (209)
Robertson, Ellison
Bio-bibliographic data:
Canadian Crime Fiction, p. 181. (209)
Robertson, Heather [Margaret]
Bio-bibliographic data:
Canadian Crime Fiction, pp. 181–82. (209)
Robertson, Marjorie
Bio-bibliographic data:
Australian Crime Fiction, p. 203. (207)
Robeson, Kenneth: house pseud. used by Street and Smith primarily for their *Doc Savage* pulp magazines. The majority of the *Doc Savage* novels was written by Lester Dent (q.v.).
Robichaud, Raymond. *See* **Raymond**
Robins, Elizabeth. *See* **Raimond, C. E.**
Robins, Monty
Bio-bibliographic data:
Canadian Crime Fiction, p. 182. (209)
Robinson, Brad
Bio-bibliographic data:
Canadian Crime Fiction, p. 97, 182. (209)
Robinson, Kevin
Bio-bibliographic data:
Detecting Men, 1st ed., p. 219. (876)
Web site: http://stopyourekillingme.com/kevin-robinson.html
Robinson, Leah Ruth: unidentified pseud.
Bio-bibliographic data:
Detecting Women, 3rd ed., p. 233. (877c)
Robinson, Lynda S.
Bio-bibliographic data:

By a Woman's Hand, 2nd ed., p. 195. (884b)
Detecting Women 2, p. 166. (877b)
Detecting Women, 3rd ed., pp. 233–34. (877c)
Web site: http://stopyourekillingme.com/lynda-s-robinson.html; http://www.meren.com
Robinson, Peter
Bio-bibliographic data:
Canadian Crime Fiction, p. 182. (209)
Detecting Men, 1st ed., p. 220. (876)
The Mammoth Encyclopedia of Modern Crime Fiction, pp. 419–20. (1)
St. James Guide to Crime & Mystery Writers, 4th ed., pp. 896–98. (882d)
Whodunit? A Who's Who in Crime and Mystery Writing, p. 169. (5)
Web site: http://www.inspectorbanks.com; http://stopyourekillingme.com/peter-robinson.html
Robinson, Sheila Mary. *See* **Radley, Sheila**
Robinson, Spider
Bio-bibliographic data:
Canadian Crime Fiction, p. 183. (209)
Web site: http://www.spiderrobinson.com
Robitaille, Julie
Bio-bibliographic data:
Detecting Women, 1st ed., p. 123. (877a)
Detecting Women 2, p. 166. (877b)
Detecting Women, 3rd ed., p. 234. (877c)
Robitaille, Louis-Bernard
Bio-bibliographic data:
Canadian Crime Fiction, p. 183. (209)
Rochette, André
Bio-bibliographic data:
Canadian Crime Fiction, p. 183. (209)
Rockwood, Roy: house pseud. for the Stratemeyer Syndicate. In this case, the reference is to work written by Leslie McFarlane (q.v.).
Rodda, [Percival] Charles
Bio-bibliographic data:
Australian Crime Fiction, pp. 203–6. (207)
Web site: http://stopyourekillingme.com/charles-rodda.html
Rodda, Emily. *See* **Rowe, Jennifer [June]**
Roddy, Ray; i.e., Raymond N.
Bio-bibliographic data:
Canadian Crime Fiction, p. 183. (209)
Roderus, Frank
Bio-bibliographic data:
Detecting Men, 1st ed., p. 220. (876)

Roe, C. F.; i.e., C. Francis
Bio-bibliographic data:
Detecting Men, 1st ed., pp. 220–21. (876)
Web site: http://stopyourekillingme.com/
c-f-roe.html

Roe, Caroline [Medora]
Bio-bibliographic data:
By a Woman's Hand, 1st ed., pp. 185–86.
(884a)
By a Woman's Hand, 2nd ed., pp.
199–200. (884b)
Canadian Crime Fiction, pp. 190–91.
(209)
Detecting Women, 1st ed., p. 125. (877a)
Detecting Women 2, p. 168, (877b)
Detecting Women, 3rd ed., p. 234, 240–41.
(877c)
*The Mammoth Encyclopedia of Modern
Crime Fiction*, p. 420. (1)
Web site: http://stopyourekillingme.com/
caroline-roe.html

Rogers, Chris
Bio-bibliographic data:
Detecting Women, 3rd ed., pp. 234–35.
(877c)
Web site: http://stopyourekillingme.com/
chris-rogers.html

Rogers, Joel Townsley
Bio-bibliographic data:
Encyclopedia Mysteriosa, p. 307. (2)
*The Encyclopedia of Mystery and
Detection*, p. 344. (7)
*St. James Guide to Crime & Mystery
Writers*, 4th ed., p. 898. (882d)
*Twentieth-Century Crime and Mystery
Writers*, 1st ed., p. 1274. (882a)
*Twentieth-Century Crime and Mystery
Writers*, 2nd ed., p. 772. (882b)
*Twentieth-Century Crime and Mystery
Writers*, 3rd ed., p. 927. (882c)

Rogow, Roberta
Bio-bibliographic data:
Detecting Women, 3rd ed., p. 235. (877c)

Rohlfs, Anna Katharine Green. *See*
Green, Anna Katharine

Rohmer, Richard [Heath]
Bio-bibliographic data:
Canadian Crime Fiction, pp. 183–84.
(209)

**Rohmer, Sax: pseud., later name change
for Arthur Henry Sarsfield Ward**
Bio-bibliographic data:
British Mystery Writers, 1860–1919, pp.
258–68. (866)

Corpus Delicti of Mystery Fiction, pp.
111–13. (879)
*Critical Survey of Mystery and Detective
Fiction*, pp. 1448–53. (41)
Encyclopedia Mysteriosa, p. 307. (2)
The Encyclopedia of Murder and Mystery,
p. 430. (6)
*The Encyclopedia of Mystery and
Detection*, pp. 345–47. (7)
Mystery and Suspense Writers, pp.
791–804. (884.2)
*The Oxford Companion to Crime and
Mystery Writing*, p. 389. (4)
*St. James Guide to Crime & Mystery
Writers*, 4th ed., pp. 898–901. (882d)
*Twentieth-Century Crime and Mystery
Writers*, 1st ed., pp. 1274–79. (882a)
*Twentieth-Century Crime and Mystery
Writers*, 2nd ed., pp. 772–75. (882b)
*Twentieth-Century Crime and Mystery
Writers*, 3rd ed., 927–30. (882c)
*Whodunit? A Who's Who in Crime and
Mystery Writing*, p. 169. (5)
Web site: http://stopyourekillingme.com/
sax-rohmer.html; http://kirjasto.
sci.fi/rohmer.htm; http://home.freeuk.
com/castlegates/rohmer.htm; http://
www.njedge.net/~knapp/FuFrames.
htm

Rolls, Anthony. *See* **Vulliamy, C. E.**
Romanoff, Alexander Nicholayevitch. *See*
Abdullah, Achmed
Romberg, Nina: unidentified pseud.
Bio-bibliographic data:
Detecting Women, 1st ed., p. 123. (877a)
Detecting Women 2, p. 166. (877b)
Detecting Women, 3rd ed., p. 235. (877c)
Rome, Anthony. *See* **Albert, Marvin**
Ronan, Tom
Bio-bibliographic data:
Australian Crime Fiction, p. 206. (207)
Ronns, Edward. *See* **Aarons, Edward S.**
Ronquillo, Víctor
Bio-bibliographic data:
*Latin American Mystery Writers: An A to
Z Guide. (881)*
Roome, Annette
Bio-bibliographic data:
By a Woman's Hand, 1st ed., pp. 182–83.
(884a)
Detecting Women, 1st ed., p. 124. (877a)
Detecting Women 2, p. 166. (877b)
Detecting Women, 3rd ed., pp. 235–36.
(877c)

Web site: http://stopyourekillingme.com/
annette-roome.html

Roos, Kelley. *Pseud. for* **Audrey Roos and William Roos**
Bio-bibliographic data:
Encyclopedia Mysteriosa, p. 308. (2)
*Twentieth-Century Crime and Mystery
Writers,* 1st ed., pp. 1279–81. (882a)
*Twentieth-Century Crime and Mystery
Writers,* 2nd ed., pp. 775–76. (882b)
*Twentieth-Century Crime and Mystery
Writers,* 3rd ed., 930–31. (882c)
Personal papers in Mugar Memorial
Library, Boston University.

Roosevelt, Elliott
Bio-bibliographic data:
Detecting Men, 1st ed., p. 221. (876)
Web site: http://stopyourekillingme.com/
elliott-roosevelt.html

Roper, Gayle G.
Bio-bibliographic data:
Canadian Crime Fiction, p. 265. (209)

Roquebrune, Robert Laroque de. *See*
Berton, Dick

Roscoe, Patrick
Bio-bibliographic data:
Canadian Crime Fiction, p. 184. (209)

Rosen, Richard D.
Bio-bibliographic data:
Detecting Men, 1st ed., p. 222. (876)
*St. James Guide to Crime & Mystery
Writers,* 4th ed., pp. 901–2. (882d)
*Twentieth-Century Crime and Mystery
Writers,* 3rd ed., 931–32. (882c)
Web site: http://stopyourekillingme.com/
richard-rosen.html

Rosenberg, Nancy Taylor
Bio-bibliographic data:
By a Woman's Hand, 2nd ed., pp. 195–96.
(884b)
*The Mammoth Encyclopedia of Modern
Crime Fiction,* p. 421. (1)
*St. James Guide to Crime & Mystery
Writers,* 4th ed., p. 902. (882d)
Web site: http://www.nancytrosenberg.
com; http://stopyourekillingme.
com/nancy-taylor-rosenberg.html

Rosenberg, Robert
Bio-bibliographic data:
Detecting Men, 1st ed., p. 222. (876)
Web site: http://stopyourekillingme.com/
robert-rosenberg.html; http://www.
ariga.com/cohen/pr4rbr.htm

Rosenkrantz, Palle [Adam Vilhelm von]
Bio-bibliographic data:
The Encyclopedia of Murder and Mystery,
pp. 431–32. (6)

Rosenstock, [Patricia] Janet [Stearns]
Bio-bibliographic data:
Canadian Crime Fiction, p. 184. (209)

Ross, Alan Clunies
Bio-bibliographic data:
Australian Crime Fiction, p. 183. (207)

Ross, Angus. *Pseud. for* **Kenneth Giggal**
Bio-bibliographic data:
*Twentieth-Century Crime and Mystery
Writers,* 1st ed., pp. 1281–83. (882a)
*Twentieth-Century Crime and Mystery
Writers,* 2nd ed., pp. 776–77. (882b)
*Twentieth-Century Crime and Mystery
Writers,* 3rd ed., 932–34. (882c)
Personal papers in University of
Wyoming, Laramie, Wyoming.

Ross, Annie: unidentified pseud.
Bio-bibliographic data:
Detecting Women, 3rd ed., p. 236. (877c)

Ross, Barnaby. *See* **Queen, Ellery**

Ross, Clarissa. *See* **Ross, W. E. D.**

Ross, Dan. *See* **Ross, W. E. D.**

Ross, Dana. *See* **Ross, W. E. D.**

Ross, Gary
Bio-bibliographic data:
Canadian Crime Fiction, pp. 185–86.
(209)

Ross, H. Williamson. *Pseud. for*
Williamson Hope
Bio-bibliographic data:
Australian Crime Fiction, p. 207. (207)

Ross, Hal
Bio-bibliographic data:
Canadian Crime Fiction, p. 186. (209)

Ross, James
Bio-bibliographic data:
The Encyclopedia of Murder and Mystery,
p. 432. (6)

Ross, Jane Clunies
Bio-bibliographic data:
Australian Crime Fiction, p. 183. (207)

Ross, Jonathan. *See* **Rossiter, John**

Ross, Kate; i.e., Katherine
Bio-bibliographic data:
By a Woman's Hand, 2nd ed., p. 196.
(884b)
Detecting Women, 1st ed., p. 124. (877a)
Detecting Women 2, p. 167. (877b)
Detecting Women, 3rd ed., p. 236. (877c)

*The Mammoth Encyclopedia of Modern
Crime Fiction*, pp. 422–23. (1)
*St. James Guide to Crime & Mystery
Writers,* 4th ed., pp. 904–5. (882d)
Web site: http://stopyourekillingme.com/
kate-ross.html; http://www.
iwillfollow.com/kjr
Ross, Marilyn. *See* **Ross, W. E. D.**
Ross, Philip. *Pseud. for* **Philip R. Eck**
Bio-bibliographic data:
Detecting Men, 1st ed., p. 223. (876)
Ross, Veronica [Flechtman]
Bio-bibliographic data:
Canadian Crime Fiction, p. 188. (209)
**Ross, W. E. D.; i.e., William Edward
Daniel**
Bio-bibliographic data:
Canadian Crime Fiction, p. 5, 31, 44–45,
53, 54, 176, 185, 186–88, 188–89.
(209)
Rossi, Jean Baptiste. *See* **Japrisot,
Sébastien**
Rossiter, John
Bio-bibliographic data:
Detecting Men, 1st ed., pp. 222– 223.
(876)
*The Mammoth Encyclopedia of Modern
Crime Fiction*, pp. 421–22. (1)
*St. James Guide to Crime & Mystery
Writers,* 4th ed., pp. 903–4. (882d)
*Twentieth-Century Crime and Mystery
Writers,* 1st ed., pp. 1283–85. (882a)
*Twentieth-Century Crime and Mystery
Writers,* 2nd ed., pp. 777–78. (882b)
*Twentieth-Century Crime and Mystery
Writers,* 3rd ed., pp. 934–35. (882c)
Roth, Holly
Bio-bibliographic data:
Encyclopedia Mysteriosa, p. 309. (2)
*The Encyclopedia of Mystery and
Detection,* p. 347. (7)
*St. James Guide to Crime & Mystery
Writers,* 4th ed., pp. 905–6. (882d)
*Twentieth-Century Crime and Mystery
Writers,* 1st ed., pp. 1285–87. (882a)
*Twentieth-Century Crime and Mystery
Writers,* 2nd ed., pp. 778–79. (882b)
*Twentieth-Century Crime and Mystery
Writers,* 3rd ed., pp. 935–36. (882c)
Rothenberg, Rebecca
Bio-bibliographic data:
By a Woman's Hand, 2nd ed., p. 197.
(884b)
Detecting Women, 1st ed., p. 124. (877a)

Detecting Women 2, p. 167. (877b)
Detecting Women, 3rd ed., p. 237. (877c)
Web site: http://stopyourekillingme.com/
rebecca-rothenberg.html
Rothwell, Barbara Yates
Bio-bibliographic data:
Australian Crime Fiction, p. 9. (207)
Rothwell, Una
Bio-bibliographic data:
Australian Crime Fiction, p. 207. (207)
Roughead, William
Bio-bibliographic data:
The Encyclopedia of Murder and Mystery,
p. 432. (6)
Rousseau, Alfred
Bio-bibliographic data:
Canadian Crime Fiction, p. 189. (209)
Rowbotham, David [Harold]
Bio-bibliographic data:
Australian Crime Fiction, p. 207. (207)
Rowe, Jennifer [June]
Bio-bibliographic data:
Australian Crime Fiction, p. 9, 145–46,
208. (207)
By a Woman's Hand, 1st ed., p. 183.
(884a)
By a Woman's Hand, 2nd ed., pp. 197–98.
(884b)
Detecting Women, 1st ed., p. 124. (877a)
Detecting Women 2, p. 167. (877b)
Detecting Women, 3rd ed., p. 237. (877c)
*The Mammoth Encyclopedia of Modern
Crime Fiction*, pp. 423–24. (1)
Web site: http://stopyourekillingme.com/
jennifer-rowe.html
Rowe, John G[abriel]
Bio-bibliographic data:
Canadian Crime Fiction, p. 265. (209)
Rowe, John [Seymour]
Bio-bibliographic data:
Australian Crime Fiction, p. 208. (207)
Rowland, Laura Joh
Bio-bibliographic data:
Detecting Women, 3rd ed., pp. 237–38.
(877c)
*The Mammoth Encyclopedia of Modern
Crime Fiction*, p. 424. (1)
Web site:
http://ourworld.compuserve.com/
homepages.laurajohrowland.ljr.html;
http://stopyourekillingme.com/
laura-joh-rowland.html
Rowlands, Betty
Bio-bibliographic data:

By a Woman's Hand, 1st ed., pp. 183–84. (884a)
By a Woman's Hand, 2nd ed., p. 198. (884b)
Detecting Women, 1st ed., p. 125. (877a)
Detecting Women 2, p. 167. (877b)
Detecting Women, 3rd ed., p. 238. (877c)
Web site: http://stopyourekillingme.com/ betty-rowlands.html

Rowlandson, H.
Bio-bibliographic data:
Australian Crime Fiction, p. 208. (207)

Royce, Kenneth. *Pseud. for* **Kenneth Royce Gandley**
Bio-bibliographic data:
St. James Guide to Crime & Mystery Writers, 4th ed., pp. 906–7. (882d)
Twentieth-Century Crime and Mystery Writers, 1st ed., pp. 1287–88. (882a)
Twentieth-Century Crime and Mystery Writers, 2nd ed., pp. 779–80. (882b)
Twentieth-Century Crime and Mystery Writers, 3rd ed., pp. 936–37. (882c)

Rozan, S. J.; i.e., Shira Judith
Bio-bibliographic data:
Detecting Women 2, p. 168. (877b)
Detecting Women, 3rd ed., pp. 238–39. (877c)
The Mammoth Encyclopedia of Modern Crime Fiction, pp. 424–25. (1)
Web site: http://www.sjrozan.com; http://stopyourekillingme.com/s-j-rozan.html

Rubino, Jane
Bio-bibliographic data:
Detecting Women, 3rd ed., p. 239. (877c)
Web site: http://stopyourekillingme.com/ jane-rubino.html; http://www.rujane.com

Ruddy, Jon
Bio-bibliographic data:
Canadian Crime Fiction, p. 189. (209)

Rudel-Tessier, J.
Bio-bibliographic data:
Canadian Crime Fiction, p. 189. (209)

Rudman, Anne. *See* **Barrett, Margaret**

Ruesch, Hans
Bio-bibliographic data:
Canadian Crime Fiction, p. 265. (209)

Ruell, Patrick. *See* **Hill, Reginald**

Ruffiange, André
Bio-bibliographic data:
Canadian Crime Fiction, p. 189. (209)

Ruhen, Carl. *See* **Farr, Caroline**

Running, Arnold
Bio-bibliographic data:
Canadian Crime Fiction, p. 189. (209)

Runyon, [Alfred] Damon
Bio-bibliographic data:
The Encyclopedia of Murder and Mystery, p. 434. (6)
The Encyclopedia of Mystery and Detection, pp. 347–48. (7)

Ruryk, Jean
Bio-bibliographic data:
Canadian Crime Fiction, p. 189. (209)
Detecting Women 2, p. 168. (877b)
Detecting Women, 3rd ed., p. 239. (877c)
Web site: http://stopyourekillingme.com/ jean-ruryk.html

Rushford, Patricia H.
Bio-bibliographic data:
Detecting Women, 3rd ed., p. 240. (877c)

Rushton, William [George]
Bio-bibliographic data:
Australian Crime Fiction, pp. 208–9. (207)

Russell, Alan
Bio-bibliographic data:
Detecting Men, 1st ed., p. 224. (876)
St. James Guide to Crime & Mystery Writers, 4th ed., pp. 907–9. (882d)

Russell, Arthur. *Pseud. for* **Arthur Russell Goode**
Bio-bibliographic data:
Australian Crime Fiction, p. 209. (207)

Russell, John
Bio-bibliographic data:
The Encyclopedia of Mystery and Detection, p. 348. (7)

Russell, Martin
Bio-bibliographic data:
Detecting Men, 1st ed., p. 224. (876)
St. James Guide to Crime & Mystery Writers, 4th ed., pp. 909–10. (882d)
Twentieth-Century Crime and Mystery Writers, 1st ed., pp. 1289–90. (882a)
Twentieth-Century Crime and Mystery Writers, 2nd ed., pp. 780–81. (882b)
Twentieth-Century Crime and Mystery Writers, 3rd ed., pp. 937–38. (882c)

Russell, Ray
Bio-bibliographic data:
Twentieth-Century Crime and Mystery Writers, 1st ed., pp. 1290–92. (882a)
Personal papers in University of Wyoming Library, Cheyenne.

Russell, W. Clark; i.e., William Clark
Bio-bibliographic data:
*The Encyclopedia of Mystery and
Detection*, p. 348. (7)
Russell, William. *See* **Waters**
Rust, Megan Mallory
Bio-bibliographic data:
Detecting Women, 3rd ed., p. 240. (877c)
Women Authors of Detective Series, pp.
160–65. (882.5)
Web site: http://stopyourekillingme.com/
megan-mallory.html; http://www.
meganrust.com
Rutherford, Douglas. *Pseud. for* **James
Douglas Rutherford McConnell**
Bio-bibliographic data:
Encyclopedia Mysteriosa, p. 310. (2)
*Twentieth-Century Crime and Mystery
Writers*, 1st ed., pp. 1292–93. (882a)
*Twentieth-Century Crime and Mystery
Writers*, 2nd ed., pp. 781–82. (882b)
*Twentieth-Century Crime and Mystery
Writers*, 3rd ed., pp. 938–39. (882c)
Rydell, Helen. *See* **Forbes, [DeLoris
Florine] Stanton**
Rydell, Stanton. *See* **Forbes, [DeLoris
Florine] Stanton**
Ryga, George
Bio-bibliographic data:
Canadian Crime Fiction, p. 189. (209)

S

Sabella, Monique
Bio-bibliographic data:
Canadian Crime Fiction, p. 190. (209)
Sabre, Dirk. *See* **Laffin, John**
Sadler, Mark. *See* **Lynds, Dennis**
Sadleir, Anna T[heresa].
Bio-bibliographic data:
Canadian Crime Fiction, p. 190. (209)
Saint, Eddie; i.e., Edward Carver
Bio-bibliographic data:
Australian Crime Fiction, p. 210. (207)
St. John, Daniel
Bio-bibliographic data:
Canadian Crime Fiction, p. 266. (209)
St. John, David. *See* **Hunt, E. Howard**
Saint Maur, Harry
Bio-bibliographic data:
Australian Crime Fiction, p. 210. (207)
Saint-Onge, Daniel
Bio-bibliographic data:
Canadian Crime Fiction, p. 190. (209)

St. Pierre, Paul
Bio-bibliographic data:
Canadian Crime Fiction, p. 190. (209)
Saint-Thomas, Harold
Bio-bibliographic data:
Australian Crime Fiction, p. 210. (207)
Saki. *Pseud. for* **Hector Hugh Munro**
Bio-bibliographic data:
*Critical Survey of Mystery and Detective
Fiction*, pp. 1454–59. (41)
Sale, David
Bio-bibliographic data:
Australian Crime Fiction, p. 210. (207)
Sale, Medora. *See* **Roe, Caroline [Medora]**
Sale, Richard
Bio-bibliographic data:
*The Encyclopedia of Mystery and
Detection*, pp. 351–52. (7)
*St. James Guide to Crime & Mystery
Writers*, 4th ed., pp. 911–12. (882d)
*Twentieth-Century Crime and Mystery
Writers*, 1st ed., pp. 1294–95. (882a)
*Twentieth-Century Crime and Mystery
Writers*, 2nd ed., pp. 782–84. (882b)
*Twentieth-Century Crime and Mystery
Writers*, 3rd ed., pp. 940–42. (882c)
Personal papers in University of Southern
California, Los Angeles.
Sallis, James
Bio-bibliographic data:
The Big Book of Noir, p. 326. (24)
Detecting Men, 1st ed., p. 225. (876)
*The Mammoth Encyclopedia of Modern
Crime Fiction*, pp. 425–26. (1)
*St. James Guide to Crime & Mystery
Writers*, 4th ed., pp. 912–13. (882d)
Talking Murder, pp. 215–28. (883)
*Whodunit? A Who's Who in Crime and
Mystery Writing*, p. 171. (5)
Web site:
http://www.btinternet.com/~richnabi;
http://stopyourekillingme.com/
james-sallis.html
Salter, Anna
Bio-bibliographic data:
Detecting Women, 3rd ed., p. 241. (877c)
Web site: http://stopyourekillingme.com/
anna-salter.html
Salter, Elizabeth [Fulton]
Bio-bibliographic data:
Australian Crime Fiction, pp. 210–11.
(207)

Salter, Samuel Allen. *See* Reaves, Sam
Sambrano, Kevin George
Bio-bibliographic data:
Canadian Crime Fiction, p. 191. (209)
Sampson, Richard Henry. *See* Hull,
Richard
Sanborn, B. X. *See* Ballinger, Bill S.
Sandaval, Jaime. *See* Marlowe, Dan J.
Sandberg, Theresa. *See* Arnold, Catherine
Sanders, Daphne. *See* Rice, Craig
Sanders, George. *See* Rice, Craig
Sanders, Lawrence
Bio-bibliographic data:
*Critical Survey of Mystery and Detective
Fiction*, pp. 1460–66. (41)
Detecting Men, 1st ed., p. 225. (876)
Encyclopedia Mysteriosa, p. 315. (2)
*The Mammoth Encyclopedia of Modern
Crime Fiction*, pp. 426–28. (1)
*100 Masters of Mystery and Detective
Fiction*, pp. 561–68. (37)
*St. James Guide to Crime & Mystery
Writers*, 4th ed., pp. 914–15. (882d)
*Twentieth-Century Crime and Mystery
Writers*, 1st ed., pp. 1296–97. (882a)
*Twentieth-Century Crime and Mystery
Writers*, 2nd ed., pp. 784–85. (882b)
*Twentieth-Century Crime and Mystery
Writers*, 3rd ed., pp. 942–44. (882c)
Web site: http://stopyourekillingme.com/
lawrence-sanders.html; http://www.
thrillingdetective.com/trivia/sanders.
html
Sanders, William
Bio-bibliographic data:
Detecting Men, 1st ed., p. 226. (876)
Sanderson, [Ronald] Douglas
Bio-bibliographic data:
Canadian Crime Fiction, p. 30, 64, 191.
(209)
Sandford, John. *Pseud. for* John Camp
Bio-bibliographic data:
Detecting Men, 1st ed., p. 226. (876)
Web site: http://stopyourekillingme.com/
john-sandford.html; http://www.
johnsandford.org
Sandford, Lionel E.
Bio-bibliographic data:
Canadian Crime Fiction, p. 266. (209)
Sandoe, James
Bio-bibliographic data:
The Encyclopedia of Murder and Mystery,
pp. 437–38. (6)

*The Encyclopedia of Mystery and
Detection*, p. 352. (7)
Sandstrom, Eve K.
Bio-bibliographic data:
By a Woman's Hand, 1st ed., p. 186.
(884a)
By a Woman's Hand, 2nd ed., p. 200.
(884b)
Detecting Women, 1st ed., p. 125. (877a)
Detecting Women 2, pp. 168–69. (877b)
Detecting Women, 3rd ed., p. 241. (877c)
Web site: http://stopyourekillingme.com/
eve-k-standstrom.html
Santini, Rosemarie
Bio-bibliographic data:
Detecting Women, 3rd ed., p. 242. (877c)
Sanxay, Elizabeth. *See* Holding, Elizabeth
Sanxay
Sapir, Richard [Ben], and Warren
Murphy
Bio-bibliographic data:
Encyclopedia Mysteriosa, p. 315. (2)
*Twentieth-Century Crime and Mystery
Writers*, 2nd ed., pp. 785–87. (882b)
Sapper: pseud. used first by Herman Cyril
McNeile, later by Gerard Fairlie (q.v.)
Bio-bibliographic data:
British Mystery Writers, 1920–1939, pp.
221–26. (867)
Canadian Crime Fiction, p. 284. (209)
*Critical Survey of Mystery and Detective
Fiction*, pp. 1467–71. (41)
Encyclopedia Mysteriosa, pp. 315–16. (2)
The Encyclopedia of Murder and Mystery,
p. 438. (6)
*The Encyclopedia of Mystery and
Detection*, p. 269. (7)
*The Oxford Companion to Crime and
Mystery Writing*, pp. 283–84. (4)
*St. James Guide to Crime & Mystery
Writers*, 4th ed., pp. 915–17. (882d)
*Twentieth-Century Crime and Mystery
Writers*, 1st ed., pp. 1297–99. (882a)
*Twentieth-Century Crime and Mystery
Writers*, 2nd ed., pp. 787–88. (882b)
*Twentieth-Century Crime and Mystery
Writers*, 3rd ed., pp. 943–45. (882c)
*Whodunit? A Who's Who in Crime and
Mystery Writing*, p. 130. (5)
Web site: http://www.
bulldogdrummond.com
Sarrantonio, Al
Bio-bibliographic data:
Detecting Men, 1st ed., p. 227. (876)

Sarto, Ben. *See* **Fawcett, Frank Dubrez**
Sasturain, Juan
Bio-bibliographic data:
Latin American Mystery Writers: An A to Z Guide. (881)
Satterthwait, Walter
Bio-bibliographic data:
Detecting Men, 1st ed., p. 227. (876)
The Mammoth Encyclopedia of Modern Crime Fiction, pp. 428–29. (1)
St. James Guide to Crime & Mystery Writers, 4th ed., pp. 917–18. (882d)
Web site: http://freenet.vcu.edu/ education/literature/Walter_ Satterthwait.html; http:// stopyourekillingme.com/ walter-satterthwait.html
Saucier, Guylène
Bio-bibliographic data:
Canadian Crime Fiction, p. 191. (209)
Saul, John Ralston
Bio-bibliographic data:
Canadian Crime Fiction, p. 191. (209)
Saum, Karen
Bio-bibliographic data:
Detecting Women 2, p. 169. (877b)
Detecting Women, 3rd ed., p. 242. (877c)
Saunders, Hal. *See* **Roberts, Zelma [Oakley] and Hal Saunders**
Saunders, Hilary Aidan St. George. *See* **Beeding, Francis**
Saurel, Pierre
Bio-bibliographic data:
Canadian Crime Fiction, p. 192. (209)
Sauriol, Jacques
Bio-bibliographic data:
Canadian Crime Fiction, p. 192. (209)
Sauter, Eric
Bio-bibliographic data:
Detecting Men, 1st ed., p. 227. (876)
St. James Guide to Crime & Mystery Writers, 4th ed., pp. 918–19. (882d)
Twentieth-Century Crime and Mystery Writers, 3rd ed., pp. 945–46. (882c)
Savage, Ernest
Bio-bibliographic data:
Twentieth-Century Crime and Mystery Writers, 2nd ed., pp. 789–90. (882b)
Twentieth-Century Crime and Mystery Writers, 3rd ed., pp. 946–47. (882c)
Savile, Andrew. *See* **Taylor, Andrew**
Savoie, Jean-Yves
Bio-bibliographic data:
Canadian Crime Fiction, p. 192. (209)

Sawkins, Raymond Harold. *See* **Forbes, Colin**
Sawyer, Corinne Holt
Bio-bibliographic data:
By a Woman's Hand, 1st ed., pp. 186–87. (884a)
By a Woman's Hand, 2nd ed., pp. 200–201. (884b)
Detecting Women, 1st ed., p. 126. (877a)
Detecting Women 2, p. 169. (877b)
Detecting Women, 3rd ed., pp. 242–43. (877c)
Web site: http://stopyourekillingme.com/ corinne-holt-sawyer.html
Sawyer, John. *See* **Quest, Erica**
Sawyer, Nancy Buckingham. *See* **Quest, Erica**
Sawyer, Robert J.
Bio-bibliographic data:
Canadian Crime Fiction, pp. 192–93. (209)
Saxby, Argyll
Bio-bibliographic data:
Canadian Crime Fiction, p. 266. (209)
Saxe, Peter. *See* **Chaffer, Frederic[k?]**
Saxon, Peter: house pseud. used by William Arthur Howard Barker, Thomas Hector Martin, and William Glassford McNeilly (q.v.)
Bio-bibliographic data:
Australian Crime Fiction, p. 211. (207)
Sayers, Dorothy L[eigh].
Bio-bibliographic data:
British Mystery Writers, 1920–1939, pp. 254–72. (867)
Corpus Delicti of Mystery Fiction, pp. 113–14. (879)
Critical Survey of Mystery and Detective Fiction, pp. 1472–81. (41)
Detecting Women, 1st ed., p. 126. (877a)
Detecting Women 2, pp. 169–70. (877b)
Encyclopedia Mysteriosa, pp. 316–17. (2)
The Encyclopedia of Murder and Mystery, pp. 438–40. (6)
The Encyclopedia of Mystery and Detection, pp. 352–54. (7)
Great Women Mystery Writers, pp. 309–13. (880)
Mystery and Suspense Writers, pp. 805–28. (884.2)
100 Masters of Mystery and Detective Fiction, pp. 569–78. (37)
The Oxford Companion to Crime and Mystery Writing, pp. 396–97. (4)

St. James Guide to Crime & Mystery Writers, 4th ed., pp. 919–22. (882d)
10 Women of Mystery, pp. 8–39. (864, 865)
Twentieth-Century Crime and Mystery Writers, 1st ed., pp. 1300–4. (882a)
Twentieth-Century Crime and Mystery Writers, 2nd ed., pp. 790–92. (882b)
Twentieth-Century Crime and Mystery Writers, 3rd ed., pp. 947–50. (882c)
Whodunit? A Who's Who in Crime and Mystery Writing, pp. 171–72. (5)
Women Authors of Detective Series, pp. 33–44. (882.5)
Women of Mystery, pp. 161–224. (874)
Personal papers in Humanities Research Center, University of Texas at Austin.
Personal papers in Marion E. Wade Collection, Wheaton College, Illinois.
Web site:
http://www.wheaton.edu/learnres/ wade; http://www.miltonroad. demon.co.uk; http://www.greenbay. co.uk; http://stopyourekillingme.com/ dorothy-l-sayers.html
Dorothy L. Sayers Society
c/o Christopher Dean
Rose Cottage
Malthouse Lane
Hassocks BN6 9JY
United Kingdom
http://www.sayers.org.uk

Saylor, Steven
Bio-bibliographic data:
Detecting Men, 1st ed., p. 228. (876)
The Mammoth Encyclopedia of Modern Crime Fiction, pp. 429–30. (1)
St. James Guide to Crime & Mystery Writers, 4th ed., pp. 922–23. (882d)
Web site: http://www.stevensaylor.com; http://stopyourekillingme.com/ steven-saylor.html

Scarborough, Elizabeth
Bio-bibliographic data:
Canadian Crime Fiction, p. 266. (209)

Schallinger, Sophie
Bio-bibliographic data:
Canadian Crime Fiction, p. 193. (209)

Schenkel, S. E.; i.e., Shirley
Bio-bibliographic data:
Detecting Women, 1st ed., p. 127. (877a)
Detecting Women 2, p. 170. (877b)

Scherf, Margaret
Bio-bibliographic data:

Detecting Women, 1st ed., p. 127. (877a)
Detecting Women 2, p. 170. (877b)
The Encyclopedia of Mystery and Detection, pp. 355–56. (7)
St. James Guide to Crime & Mystery Writers, 4th ed., p.924. (882d)
Twentieth-Century Crime and Mystery Writers, 1st ed., pp. 1304–5. (882a)
Twentieth-Century Crime and Mystery Writers, 2nd ed., pp. 793–94. (882b)
Twentieth-Century Crime and Mystery Writers, 3rd ed., pp. 950–51. (882c)
Personal papers in University of Oregon Library, Eugene, Oregon.
Web site: http://stopyourekillingme.com/ margaret-scherf.html

Schermerhorn, Duane R. *See* **Marcott, James**

Schier, Norma
Bio-bibliographic data:
Detecting Women, 1st ed., p. 127. (877a)
Detecting Women 2, p. 171. (877b)
Detecting Women, 3rd ed., p. 243. (877c)

Schmidt, Carol
Bio-bibliographic data:
Detecting Women 2, p. 171. (877b)
Detecting Women, 3rd ed., p. 243. (877c)

Schinkel, David
Bio-bibliographic data:
Canadian Crime Fiction, p. 193. (209)

Scholefield, Alan
Bio-bibliographic data:
Detecting Men, 1st ed., p. 228. (876)

Schoonover, Jason
Bio-bibliographic data:
Canadian Crime Fiction, p. 193. (209)

Schoonover, Winston. *Pseud. for* **Charles Sevilla**
Bio-bibliographic data:
Detecting Men, 1st ed., p. 229. (876)

Schopen, Bernard
Bio-bibliographic data:
Detecting Men, 1st ed., p. 229. (876)
Web site: http://stopyourekillingme.com/ bernard-schopen.html; http:// members.tripod.com/~bernardschope n

Schorr, Mark
Bio-bibliographic data:
Detecting Men, 1st cd., p. 229. (876)
Encyclopedia Mysteriosa, p. 318. (2)
St. James Guide to Crime & Mystery Writers, 4th ed., pp. 924–25. (882d)

Twentieth-Century Crime and Mystery Writers, 3rd ed., pp. 951–52. (882c)

Schumacher, Aileen
Bio-bibliographic data:
Detecting Women, 3rd ed., pp. 243–44. (877c)
Web site: http://stopyourekillingme.com/ aileen-schumacher.html; http://aliken. com/aileen

Schutz, Benjamin M.
Bio-bibliographic data:
Detecting Men, 1st ed., p. 230 (876)
Encyclopedia Mysteriosa, p. 318. (2)
The Mammoth Encyclopedia of Modern Crime Fiction, p. 430. (1)

Sciascia, Leonardo
Bio-bibliographic data:
The Encyclopedia of Murder and Mystery, pp. 441–42. (6)
The Mammoth Encyclopedia of Modern Crime Fiction, pp. 430–31. (1)
Twentieth-Century Crime and Mystery Writers, 3rd ed., pp. 1136–37. (882c)
Whodunit? A Who's Who in Crime and Mystery Writing, pp. 172–73. (5)

Scobie, Alastair
Bio-bibliographic data:
Australian Crime Fiction, pp. 211–12. (207)

Scoppettone, Sandra
Bio-bibliographic data:
By a Woman's Hand, 1st ed., pp. 187–88. (884a)
By a Woman's Hand, 2nd ed., pp. 201–2. (884b)
Detecting Women, 1st ed., p. 127. (877a)
Detecting Women 2, p. 171. (877b)
Detecting Women, 3rd ed., p. 244. (877c)
Encyclopedia Mysteriosa, p. 319. (2)
The Mammoth Encyclopedia of Modern Crime Fiction, pp. 432–33. (1)
Web site: http://www.imt.net/~gedison/ scoppett.html; http:// stopyourekillingme.com /sandra-scoppetone.html

Scot-Bernard, P.; i.e., Patricia Scot Bernard
Bio-bibliographic data:
Australian Crime Fiction, p. 212. (207)

Scott, Anthony. *See* **Halliday, Brett**

Scott, Barbara A.
Bio-bibliographic data:
Detecting Women, 3rd ed., p. 244. (877c)

Scott, Chris
Bio-bibliographic data:
Canadian Crime Fiction, p. 193. (209)

Scott, G. Firth; i.e., George Firth
Bio-bibliographic data:
Australian Crime Fiction, p. 212. (207)

Scott, [John] Gavin
Bio-bibliographic data:
Canadian Crime Fiction, p. 193. (209)

Scott, J. M.; i.e., James Maurice
Bio-bibliographic data:
Canadian Crime Fiction, p. 266. (209)

Scott, Jack S. *Pseud. for* **Jonathan Escott**
Bio-bibliographic data:
Encyclopedia Mysteriosa, pp. 319–20. (2)
Twentieth-Century Crime and Mystery Writers, 2nd ed., pp. 794–95. (882b)
Twentieth-Century Crime and Mystery Writers, 3rd ed., pp. 952–53. (882c)
Personal papers in Mugar Memorial Library, Boston University.

Scott, Justin
Bio-bibliographic data:
Detecting Men, 1st ed., p. 230. (876)

Scott, Margaret [Daphne]
Bio-bibliographic data:
Australian Crime Fiction, pp. 212–13. (207)

Scott, Mary Ann
Bio-bibliographic data:
Canadian Crime Fiction, pp. 193–94. (209)

Scott, Michael
Bio-bibliographic data:
Australian Crime Fiction, p. 213. (207)

Scott, R. T. M.; i.e., Reginald Thomas Maitland
Bio-bibliographic data:
Canadian Crime Fiction, p. 194. (209)
Twentieth-Century Crime and Mystery Writers, 1st ed., pp. 1306–7. (882a)

Scott II, R. T. M.; i.e., Reginald Thomas Maitland
Bio-bibliographic data:
Canadian Crime Fiction, p. 194. (209)

Scott, Rosie
Bio-bibliographic data:
Detecting Women, 1st ed., p. 128. (877a)
Detecting Women 2, p. 171. (877b)

Scott, Will; i.e., William Matthew
Bio-bibliographic data:
The Encyclopedia of Mystery and Detection, p. 357. (7)

Scottoline, Lisa
Bio-bibliographic data:
By a Woman's Hand, 2nd ed., pp. 202–3. (884b)
Detecting Women, 1st ed., p. 128. (877a)
Detecting Women 2, p. 171. (877b)
Detecting Women, 3rd ed., p. 245. (877c)
The Mammoth Encyclopedia of Modern Crime Fiction, p. 433. (1)
Web site: http://www.scottoline.com; http://stopyourekillingme.com/lisa-scottoline.html
Scutt, Jocelynn Annette. *See* Chan, Melissa
Seager, Joan
Bio-bibliographic data:
Canadian Crime Fiction, p. 195. (209)
Sedley, Kate. *Pseud. for* Brenda Margaret Lilian Honeyman Clarke
Bio-bibliographic data:
By a Woman's Hand, 1st ed., pp. 188–89. (884a)
By a Woman's Hand, 2nd ed., p. 203. (884b)
Detecting Women, 1st ed., p. 128. (877a)
Detecting Women 2, p. 172. (877b)
Detecting Women, 3rd ed., p. 245. (877c)
The Mammoth Encyclopedia of Modern Crime Fiction, pp. 433–34. (1)
Web site: http://stopyourekillingme.com/kate-sedley.html
Seeley, Mabel [Hodnefield]
Bio-bibliographic data:
Encyclopedia Mysteriosa, p. 321. (2)
The Encyclopedia of Murder and Mystery, pp. 445–46. (6)
The Encyclopedia of Mystery and Detection, pp. 357–58. (7)
Twentieth-Century Crime and Mystery Writers, 1st ed., pp. 1308–9. (882a)
Twentieth-Century Crime and Mystery Writers, 2nd ed., pp. 795–96. (882b)
Twentieth-Century Crime and Mystery Writers, 3rd ed., pp. 953–54. (882c)
Web site: http://stopyourekillingme.com/mabel-seeley.html
Sehler, Raoul Stephen. *See* Burns, Rex
Sehler, Tom. *See* Burns, Rex
Sela, Owen
Bio-bibliographic data:
Canadian Crime Fiction, pp. 284–85. (209)
Sellars, Rev. Walter
Bio-bibliographic data:

Canadian Crime Fiction, p. 195. (209)
Sellers, Peter A.
Bio-bibliographic data:
Canadian Crime Fiction, p. 195. (209)
Selwyn, Francis. *See* Thomas, Donald
Serafín, David. *Pseud. for* Ian David Lewis Michael
Bio-bibliographic data:
Detecting Men, 1st ed., p. 231. (876)
The Mammoth Encyclopedia of Modern Crime Fiction, pp. 434–35. (1)
St. James Guide to Crime & Mystery Writers, 4th ed., pp. 926–27. (882d)
Twentieth-Century Crime and Mystery Writers, 3rd ed., pp. 955–56. (882c)
Seranus. *Pseud. for* Susan Frances Harrison
Bio-bibliographic data:
Canadian Crime Fiction, p. 98, 195. (209)
Serna, Enrique
Bio-bibliographic data:
Latin American Mystery Writers: An A to Z Guide. (881)
Sernine, Daniel
Bio-bibliographic data:
Canadian Crime Fiction, p. 195. (209)
Service, Robert W[illiam].
Bio-bibliographic data:
Canadian Crime Fiction, pp. 195–97. (209)
Seton, Georgina
Bio-bibliographic data:
Australian Crime Fiction, p. 213. (207)
Sexton, Michael
Bio-bibliographic data:
Australian Crime Fiction, p. 213. (207)
Seymour, Gerald
Bio-bibliographic data:
St. James Guide to Crime & Mystery Writers, 4th ed., pp. 927–28. (882d)
Twentieth-Century Crime and Mystery Writers, 2nd ed., pp. 796–97. (882b)
Twentieth-Century Crime and Mystery Writers, 3rd ed., p. 956. (882c)
Shaber, Sarah R.
Bio-bibliographic data:
Detecting Women, 3rd ed., pp. 245–46. (877c)
Web site: http://stopyourekillingme.com/sarah-r-shaber.html; http://www.sarahshaber.com
Shaffer, Anthony. *See* Anthony, Peter
Shaffer, Ivan
Bio-bibliographic data:

Canadian Crime Fiction, p. 198. (209)

Shaffer, Louise
Bio-bibliographic data:
Detecting Women 2, p. 172. (877b)
Detecting Women, 3rd ed., p. 246. (877c)
Web site: http://stopyourekillingme.com/
louise-shaffer.html

Shaffer, Peter, and Anthony. *See* **Antony,**
Peter

Shah, Diane K.
Bio-bibliographic data:
By a Woman's Hand, 1st ed., pp. 189–90.
(884a)
Detecting Women, 1st ed., p. 128. (877a)
Detecting Women 2, p. 172. (877b)
Detecting Women, 3rd ed., p. 246. (877c)

Shakespeare, William
Bio-bibliographic data:
The Oxford Companion to Crime and
Mystery Writing, pp. 407–9. (4)
Whodunit? A Who's Who in Crime and
Mystery Writing, pp. 174–76. (5)

Shames, Laurence
Bio-bibliographic data:
The Mammoth Encyclopedia of Modern
Crime Fiction, pp. 436–37. (1)
Web site: http://www.twbooks.co.uk/
authors/lshames.html; http://
stopyourekillingme.com/
laurence-shames.html

Shanahan, Margaret Mary. *See* **Marlowe,**
Mary

Shankman, Sarah
Bio-bibliographic data:
By a Woman's Hand, 1st ed., pp. 190–91.
(884a)
By a Woman's Hand, 2nd ed., pp. 203–4.
(884b)
Detecting Women, 1st ed., pp. 128–29.
(877a)
Detecting Women 2, p. 172. (877b)
Detecting Women, 3rd ed., p. 246-247.
(877c)
Great Women Mystery Writers, pp.
314–15. (880)
Web site: http://stopyourekillingme.com/
sarah-shankman.html

Shannon, Dell. *See* **Linington, Elizabeth**

Shannon, Doris [Giroux]. *See* **Giroux, E.**
X.

Shapiro, Lionel [Sebastian Berk]
Bio-bibliographic data:
Canadian Crime Fiction, p. 198. (209)

Sharam, Norman. *See* **Steed, Neville**

Sharkey, Joe. *See* **Amato, Angela, and Joe**
Sharkey

Sharp, Luke. *See* **Barr, Robert**

Shatner, William
Bio-bibliographic data:
Canadian Crime Fiction, pp. 198–99.
(209)
Detecting Men, 1st ed., p. 231. (876)
Web site: http://stopyourekillingme.com/
william-shatner.html

Shave, Lionel
Bio-bibliographic data:
Australian Crime Fiction, pp. 213–14.
(207)

Shaw, Charles
Bio-bibliographic data:
Australian Crime Fiction, p. 214. (207)

Shaw, Herbert
Bio-bibliographic data:
Canadian Crime Fiction, p. 199, 285.
(209)

Shaw, Joseph T.
Bio-bibliographic data:
The Encyclopedia of Murder and Mystery,
p. 448. (6)

Shaw, Simon
Bio-bibliographic data:
Detecting Men, 1st ed., p. 231. (876)
The Mammoth Encyclopedia of Modern
Crime Fiction, p. 437. (1)
Web site: http://stopyourekillingme.com/
simon-shaw.html

Shea, Shirley
Bio-bibliographic data:
Canadian Crime Fiction, pp. 77–78, 199.
(209)

Shearing, Joseph. *Pseud. for* **Gabrielle**
Margaret Vere Campbell
Bio-bibliographic data:
British Mystery Writers, 1860–1919, pp.
269–76. (866)
Twentieth-Century Crime and Mystery
Writers, 1st ed., pp. 1311–17. (882a)
Twentieth-Century Crime and Mystery
Writers, 2nd ed., pp. 797–801. (882b)
Twentieth-Century Crime and Mystery
Writers, 3rd ed., pp. 957–60. (882c)

Shears, Richard [John]
Bio-bibliographic data:
Australian Crime Fiction, p. 214. (207)

Sheldon, [Frank] Michael
Bio-bibliographic data:
Canadian Crime Fiction, p. 199. (209)

Shelley, Mary
Bio-bibliographic data:
The Encyclopedia of Mystery and Detection, pp. 361–62. (7)
Shelley, Sidney [Joseph]
Bio-bibliographic data:
Canadian Crime Fiction, p. 266. (209)
Shelton, Connie
Bio-bibliographic data:
Detecting Women 2, pp. 173–74. (877b)
Detecting Women, 3rd ed., p. 247. (877c)
Web site: http://stopyourekillingme.com/
connie-shelton.html; http://www.
connieshelton.com
Sheltus, John Ashley
Bio-bibliographic data:
Canadian Crime Fiction, p. 147, 199.
(209)
Shepherd, Stella
Bio-bibliographic data:
By a Woman's Hand, 1st ed., pp. 191–92.
(884a)
By a Woman's Hand, 2nd ed., pp. 204–5.
(884b)
Detecting Women, 1st ed., p. 130. (877a)
Detecting Women 2, p. 174. (877b)
Detecting Women, 3rd ed., pp. 247–48.
(877c)
Sheppard, E. E.; i.e., Edmund Ernest
Bio-bibliographic data:
Canadian Crime Fiction, pp. 199–200.
(209)
Sherburne, James
Bio-bibliographic data:
Detecting Men, 1st ed., p. 232. (876)
Sherer, Michael W.
Bio-bibliographic data:
Detecting Men, 1st ed., p. 232. (876)
Web site: http://stopyourekillingme.com/
michael-w-sherer.html; http://
fooddotcomm.com/books.htm
Sheridan, Juanita
Bio-bibliographical data:
Detecting Women 2, p. 174. (877b)
Detecting Women, 3rd ed., p. 248. (877c)
Sherlock, A. B.
Bio-bibliographic data:
Australian Crime Fiction, pp. 214–15.
(207)
Sherman, Beth
Bio-bibliographic data:
Detecting Women, 3rd ed., p. 248. (877c)
Web site: http://stopyourekillingme.com/
beth-sherman.html

Sherman, Jason
Bio-bibliographic data:
Canadian Crime Fiction, p. 200. (209)
Sherwood, John
Bio-bibliographic data:
St. James Guide to Crime & Mystery Writers, 4th ed., pp. 928–30. (882d)
Twentieth-Century Crime and Mystery Writers, 3rd ed., pp. 960–61. (882c)
Web site: http://stopyourekillingme.com/
john-sherwood.html
Shiel, M. P.; i.e., Matthew Phipps
Bio-bibliographic data:
Encyclopedia Mysteriosa, p. 330. (2)
The Encyclopedia of Murder and Mystery,
pp. 449–50. (6)
The Encyclopedia of Mystery and Detection, pp. 362–63. (7)
Twentieth-Century Crime and Mystery Writers, 2nd ed., pp. 801–2. (882b)
Twentieth-Century Crime and Mystery Writers, 3rd ed., pp. 961–63. (882c)
Shields, Carol [Warner]
Bio-bibliographic data:
Canadian Crime Fiction, p. 200. (209)
Shields, Dinah
Bio-bibliographic data:
Canadian Crime Fiction, p. 200. (209)
Shipley, Nan; i.e., Nancy Sommerville
Bio-bibliographic data:
Canadian Crime Fiction, pp. 200–201.
(209)
Shoemaker, Bill
Bio-bibliographic data:
Detecting Men, 1st ed., p. 232. (876)
Web site: http://stopyourekillingme.com/
bill-shoemaker.html
Shone, Anna. *Pseud. for* Bridget Ann Shone
Bio-bibliographic data:
Detecting Women 2, p. 174. (877b)
Detecting Women, 3rd ed., pp. 248–49.
(877c)
Web site: http://stopyourekillingme.com/
anna-shone.html
Short, Sharon Gwyn
Bio-bibliographic data:
Detecting Women, 1st ed., p. 130. (877a)
Detecting Women 2, p. 174. (877b)
Detecting Women, 3rd ed., p. 249. (877c)
Web site: http://stopyourekillingme.com/
sharon-gwyn-short.html
Shurtleff, Bertrand
Bio-bibliographic data:

Canadian Crime Fiction, p. 266. (209)
Shute, Nevil. *Pseud. for* **Nevil Shute Norway**
Bio-bibliographic data:
Australian Crime Fiction, p. 215. (207)
Canadian Crime Fiction, p. 266. (209)
Twentieth-Century Crime and Mystery Writers, 1st ed., pp. 1317–18. (882a)
Sibley, Celestine
Bio-bibliographic data:
By a Woman's Hand, 1st ed., p. 192. (884a)
By a Woman's Hand, 2nd ed., p. 205. (884b)
Detecting Women, 1st ed., p. 130. (877a)
Detecting Women 2, p. 175. (877b)
Detecting Women, 3rd ed., p. 249. (877c)
Web site: http://stopyourekillingme.com/celestine-sibley.html
Siller, Van. *Pseud. for* **Hilda van Siller**
Bio-bibliographic data:
Twentieth-Century Crime and Mystery Writers, 1st ed., pp. 1319–20. (882a)
Twentieth-Century Crime and Mystery Writers, 2nd ed., pp. 802–3. (882b)
Silva, Linda Kay
Bio-bibliographic data:
Detecting Women 2, p. 175. (877b)
Detecting Women, 3rd ed., pp. 249–50. (877c)
Silver, Alfred
Bio-bibliographic data:
Canadian Crime Fiction, p. 201. (209)
Silver, Rodney
Bio-bibliographic data:
Australian Crime Fiction, p. 9. (207)
Sim, Georges. *See* **Simenon, Georges**
Sima, Caris. *See* **Mountcastle, Clara H.**
Simard, Bertrand
Bio-bibliographic data:
Canadian Crime Fiction, p. 201. (209)
Simard, Ludovic
Bio-bibliographic data:
Canadian Crime Fiction, p. 201. (209)
Simard, Rémy
Bio-bibliographic data:
Canadian Crime Fiction, p. 201. (209)
Simenon, Georges [Joseph Christian]
Bio-bibliographic data:
Corpus Delicti of Mystery Fiction, pp. 114–17. (879)
Critical Survey of Mystery and Detective Fiction, pp. 1482–94. (41)
Encyclopedia Mysteriosa, p. 331. (2)

The Encyclopedia of Murder and Mystery, pp. 452–54. (6)
The Encyclopedia of Mystery and Detection, pp. 363–65. (7)
Mystery and Suspense Writers, pp. 829–51. (884.2)
100 Masters of Mystery and Detective Fiction, pp. 579–92. (37)
The Oxford Companion to Crime and Mystery Writing, p. 415. (4)
St. James Guide to Crime & Mystery Writers, 4th ed., pp. 930–33. (882d)
Twentieth-Century Crime and Mystery Writers, 1st ed., pp. 1548–51. (882a)
Twentieth-Century Crime and Mystery Writers, 2nd ed., pp. 945–47. (882b)
Twentieth-Century Crime and Mystery Writers, 3rd ed., pp. 1137–38. (882c)
Whodunit? A Who's Who in Crime and Mystery Writing, pp. 178–79. (5)
Personal papers in Centre d'Etudes Georges Simenon, Liège, Belgium.
Personal papers in Simenon Center, Drew University, Madison, New Jersey.
Web site: http://stopyourekillingme.com/georges-simenon.html;
Les Amis de Georges Simenon
c/o Michael Schepens
Beigemsesteenweg 291
1852 Beigem (Grimbergen)
Belgium
Le Centre d'Etudes Georges
Simenon
c/o Prof. Danielle Bajomee
Université de Liège
Place Cockerill, 3
B-400 Liège Belgium
http://www.ulg.ac.be/libnet/simenon.htm
Simmie, Lois [Binns]
Bio-bibliographic data:
Canadian Crime Fiction, p. 201. (209)
Simon, Jean-François
Bio-bibliographic data:
Canadian Crime Fiction, p. 201. (209)
Simon, Robin
Bio-bibliographic data:
Australian Crime Fiction, p. 216. (207)
Simon, Roger L[ichtenberg].
Bio-bibliographic data:
Detecting Men, 1st ed., p. 233. (876)
Encyclopedia Mysteriosa, p. 332. (2)
The Encyclopedia of Murder and Mystery, p. 454. (6)

The Mammoth Encyclopedia of Modern Crime Fiction, pp. 437–38. (1)
St. James Guide to Crime & Mystery Writers, 4th ed., pp. 933–34. (882d)
Twentieth-Century Crime and Mystery Writers, 1st ed., pp. 1320–21. (882a)
Twentieth-Century Crime and Mystery Writers, 2nd ed., p. 803. (882b)
Twentieth-Century Crime and Mystery Writers, 3rd ed., p. 963. (882c)
Web site: http://stopyourekillingme.com/roger-l-simon.html
Simon, Ted. *See* **Jones, Dennis**
Simonds, Merilyn
Bio-bibliographic data:
Canadian Crime Fiction, p. 202. (209)
Simonds, Peter
Bio-bibliographic data:
Canadian Crime Fiction, p. 92, 202. (209)
Simonson, Sheila
Bio-bibliographic data:
By a Woman's Hand, 2nd ed., pp. 205–6. (884b)
Detecting Women, 1st ed., p. 131. (877a)
Detecting Women 2, p. 175. (877b)
Detecting Women, 3rd ed., p. 250. (877c)
Web site: http://stopyourekillingme.com/sheila-simonson.html
Simpson, Dorothy
Bio-bibliographic data:
By a Woman's Hand, 1st ed., p. 193. (884a)
By a Woman's Hand, 2nd ed., pp. 206–7. (884b)
Detecting Women, 1st ed., p. 131. (877a)
Detecting Women 2, p. 175. (877b)
Detecting Women, 3rd ed., pp. 250–51. (877c)
The Encyclopedia of Murder and Mystery, p. 455. (6)
Great Women Mystery Writers, pp. 316–18. (880)
The Mammoth Encyclopedia of Modern Crime Fiction, pp. 438–39. (1)
St. James Guide to Crime & Mystery Writers, 4th ed., pp. 934–36. (882d)
Twentieth-Century Crime and Mystery Writers, 2nd ed., pp. 803–4. (882b)
Twentieth-Century Crime and Mystery Writers, 3rd ed., pp. 963–65. (882c)
Women of Mystery, p. 437. (874)
Web site: http://stopyourekillingme.com/dorothy-simpson.html

Simpson, Harold
Bio-bibliographic data:
Canadian Crime Fiction, p. 202. (209)
Simpson, Helen [middle name given as Deguerry and de Guerry]
Bio-bibliographic data:
Australian Crime Fiction, p. 216. (207)
British Mystery Writers, 1920–1939, pp. 273–76. (867)
The Encyclopedia of Mystery and Detection, p. 365. (7)
Twentieth-Century Crime and Mystery Writers, 1st ed., pp. 1321–23. (882a)
Simpson, James Allen. *See* **Lake, M. D.**
Simpson, Leo
Bio-bibliographic data:
Canadian Crime Fiction, p. 202. (209)
Simpson, Roger. *See* **Shears, Richard**
Sims, George R[obert].
Bio-bibliographic data:
British Mystery Writers, 1860–1919, pp. 277–82. (866)
British Mystery and Thriller Writers since 1940, First Series, pp. 328–32. (868)
The Encyclopedia of Mystery and Detection, p. 365. (7)
St. James Guide to Crime & Mystery Writers, 4th ed., pp. 936–37. (882d)
Twentieth-Century Crime and Mystery Writers, 1st ed., pp. 1324–25. (882a)
Twentieth-Century Crime and Mystery Writers, 2nd ed., pp. 804–5. (882b)
Twentieth-Century Crime and Mystery Writers, 3rd ed., pp. 965–66. (882c)
Sims, L. V.
Bio-bibliographic data:
By a Woman's Hand, 1st ed., pp. 193–94. (884a)
Detecting Women, 1st ed., p. 131. (877a)
Detecting Women 2, p. 176. (877b)
Detecting Women, 3rd ed., p. 251. (877c)
Sinay, Sergio
Bio-bibliographic data:
Latin American Mystery Writers: An A to Z Guide. (881)
Sinclair, Bertrand W[illiam].
Bio-bibliographic data:
Canadian Crime Fiction, pp. 202–3. (209)
Sinclair, Dennis. *See* **Brown, Carter**
Singer, Bant. *See* **Shaw, Charles**
Singer, Shelley
Bio-bibliographic data:
By a Woman's Hand, 1st ed., pp. 194–95. (884a)

By a Woman's Hand, 2nd ed., p. 207.
(884b)
Detecting Women, 1st ed., p. 132. (877a)
Detecting Women 2, p. 176. (877b)
Detecting Women, 3rd ed., pp. 251–52.
(877c)
Web site: http://stopyourekillingme.com/
shelley-singer.html
Sjöwall, Maj. *See* **Wahlöö, Per, and Maj
Sjöwall**
**Skene-Melvin, L[ewis]. David St.
C[olumb].**
Bio-bibliographic data:
Canadian Crime Fiction, p. 203. (209)
Skinner, Constance L[indsay].
Bio-bibliographic data:
Canadian Crime Fiction, pp. 203–4. (209)
Skinner, June O'Grady. *See* **O'Grady,
Rohan**
Sklepowich, Edward
Bio-bibliographic data:
Detecting Men, 1st ed., p. 233. (876)
Skoggard, Bruno
Bio-bibliographic data:
Canadian Crime Fiction, p. 285. (209)
Skom, Edith
Bio-bibliographic data:
Detecting Women, 1st ed., p. 132. (877a)
Detecting Women 2, p. 177. (877b)
Detecting Women, 3rd ed., p. 252. (877c)
Skvorecky, Josef [Vaclav]
Bio-bibliographic data:
Canadian Crime Fiction, pp. 204–5, 242.
(209)
The Encyclopedia of Murder and Mystery,
p. 457. (6)
*The Mammoth Encyclopedia of Modern
Crime Fiction,* pp. 439–40. (1)
Slade, Bernard
Bio-bibliographic data:
Canadian Crime Fiction, p. 205. (209)
Slade, Michael
Bio-bibliographic data:
Canadian Crime Fiction, p. 205. (209)
Web site: http://stopyourekillingme.com/
michael-slade.html
Slater, Ian [David]
Bio-bibliographic data:
Canadian Crime Fiction, p. 205. (209)
Slatter, Kevin M.
Bio-bibliographic data:
Australian Crime Fiction, p. 217. (207)
Sleem, Patty
Bio-bibliographic data:

Detecting Women, 3rd ed., p. 253. (877c)
Slesar, Henry
Bio-bibliographic data:
Encyclopedia Mysteriosa, p. 332. (2)
*The Mammoth Encyclopedia of Modern
Crime Fiction,* pp. 440–41. (1)
*St. James Guide to Crime & Mystery
Writers,* 4th ed., pp. 937–38. (882d)
*Twentieth-Century Crime and Mystery
Writers,* 1st ed., pp. 1326–28. (882a)
*Twentieth-Century Crime and Mystery
Writers,* 2nd ed., pp. 806–9. (882b)
*Twentieth-Century Crime and Mystery
Writers,* 3rd ed., pp. 966–69. (882c)
Sligo, John
Bio-bibliographic data:
Australian Crime Fiction, p. 145. (207)
**Slim, Iceberg; i.e., Robert Maupin Beck
III**
Bio-bibliographic data:
*The Mammoth Encyclopedia of Modern
Crime Fiction,* pp. 441–42. (1)
Slovo, Gillian
Bio-bibliographic data:
By a Woman's Hand, 1st ed., p. 195.
(884a)
By a Woman's Hand, 2nd ed., p. 208.
(884b)
Detecting Women, 1st ed., p. 132. (877a)
Detecting Women 2, p. 177. (877b)
Detecting Women, 3rd ed., p. 253. (877c)
Great Women Mystery Writers, pp.
318–19. (880)
*The Mammoth Encyclopedia of Modern
Crime Fiction,* pp. 442–43. (1)
*St. James Guide to Crime & Mystery
Writers,* 4th ed., pp. 938–39. (882d)
*Twentieth-Century Crime and Mystery
Writers,* 3rd ed., pp. 969–70. (882c)
Web site: http://www.twbooks.co.uk/
authors/gillianslovo.html; http://
stopyourekillingme.com/
gillian-slovo.html
Sluman, Norma [Pauline Hardman]
Bio-bibliographic data:
Canadian Crime Fiction, p. 206. (209)
Slusher, William S.
Bio-bibliographic data:
Detecting Men, 1st ed., p. 233. (876)
Smart, Hawley
Bio-bibliographic data:
The Encyclopedia of Murder and Mystery,
p. 459. (6)

Smiley, Virginia [Kester]
Bio-bibliographic data:
Canadian Crime Fiction, p. 266. (209)
Smith, A. [W.] de Herries
Bio-bibliographic data:
Canadian Crime Fiction, p. 206. (209)
Smith, Alexander McCall
Bio-bibliographic data:
*Whodunit? A Who's Who in Crime and
Mystery Writing,* pp. 183–84. (5)
Smith, Alison
Bio-bibliographic data:
Detecting Women, 3rd ed., p. 253. (877c)
Smith, André
Bio-bibliographic data:
Canadian Crime Fiction, p. 206. (209)
Smith, April
Bio-bibliographic data:
Detecting Women 2, p. 177. (877b)
Web site: http://stopyourekillingme.com/
april-smith.html; http://www.
aprilsmith.net
Smith, Barbara Burnett
Bio-bibliographic data:
Detecting Women, 1st ed., p. 133. (877a)
Detecting Women 2, p. 177. (877b)
Detecting Women, 3rd ed., p. 254. (877c)
Web site: http://stopyourekillingme.com/
barbara-burnett-smith.html; http://
www.io.com/Purple_Sage
Smith, Caesar. *See* **Trevor, Elleston**
Smith, Cynthia
Bio-bibliographic data:
Detecting Women, 3rd ed., p. 254. (877c)
Smith, David [Gordon]
Bio-bibliographic data:
Australian Crime Fiction, p. 218. (207)
Smith, Edward Ernest. *See* **Lindall,
Edward**
Smith, Elizabeth Thomasina Meade. *See*
Meade, L. T.
Smith, Ernest Bramah. *See* **Bramah,
Ernest**
Smith, Evelyn E.
Bio-bibliographic data:
By a Woman's Hand, 1st ed., pp. 195–96.
(884a)
By a Woman's Hand, 2nd ed., pp. 208–9.
(884b)
Detecting Women 2, p. 177. (877b)
Detecting Women, 3rd ed., pp. 254–55.
(877c)
Smith, Frank A[llen].
Bio-bibliographic data:

Detecting Men, 1st ed., p. 234. (876)
Canadian Crime Fiction, p. 206. (209)
Web site: http://stopyourekillingme.com/
frank-a-smith.html
Smith, Frank E. *See* **Craig, Jonathan**
Smith, J. C. S.; i.e., Jane S.
Bio-bibliographic data:
Detecting Women 2, p. 178. (877b)
Detecting Women, 3rd ed., p. 255. (877c)
Smith, Janet L.
Bio-bibliographic data:
By a Woman's Hand, 1st ed., pp. 196–97.
(884a)
By a Woman's Hand, 2nd ed., p. 209.
(884b)
Detecting Women, 1st ed., p. 133. (877a)
Detecting Women 2, p. 178. (877b)
Detecting Women, 3rd ed., p. 255. (877c)
Web site: http://stopyourekillingme.com/
janet-smith.html
Smith, Joan
Bio-bibliographic data:
By a Woman's Hand, 1st ed., pp. 197–98.
(884a)
By a Woman's Hand, 2nd ed., pp. 209–10.
(884b)
Canadian Crime Fiction, p. 206. (209)
Detecting Women, 1st ed., p. 133. (877a)
Detecting Women 2, p. 178. (877b)
Detecting Women, 3rd ed., pp. 255–56.
(877c)
Great Women Mystery Writers, pp.
320–21. (880)
*The Mammoth Encyclopedia of Modern
Crime Fiction,* pp. 443–44. (1)
*St. James Guide to Crime & Mystery
Writers,* 4th ed., pp. 939–40. (882d)
Women of Mystery, p. 437. (874)
Web site: http://stopyourekillingme.com/
joan-smith.html
Smith, Joan G.; i.e., Joan Gerda
Bio-bibliographic data:
Detecting Women 2, p. 178. (877b)
Detecting Women, 3rd ed., p. 256. (877c)
Smith, Julie; i.e., Julienne Drew Smith
Bio-bibliographic data:
By a Woman's Hand, 1st ed., pp. 198–99.
(884a)
By a Woman's Hand, 2nd ed., pp. 210–11.
(884b)
Detecting Women, 1st ed., p. 133. (877a)
Detecting Women 2, pp. 178–79. (877b)
Detecting Women, 3rd ed., pp. 256–57.
(877c)

Encyclopedia Mysteriosa, p. 334. (2)
Great Women Mystery Writers, pp. 321–23. (880)
The Mammoth Encyclopedia of Modern Crime Fiction, pp. 444–45. (1)
St. James Guide to Crime & Mystery Writers, 4th ed., pp. 940–42. (882d)
Twentieth-Century Crime and Mystery Writers, 3rd ed., pp. 970–71. (882c)
Web site:
http://www.juliesmithauthor.com;
http://stopyourekillingme.com/
julie-smith.html

Smith, Kay Nolte
Bio-bibliographic data:
Encyclopedia Mysteriosa, p. 334. (2)
St. James Guide to Crime & Mystery Writers, 4th ed., pp. 942–43. (882d)
Twentieth-Century Crime and Mystery Writers, 2nd ed., pp. 809–10. (882b)
Twentieth-Century Crime and Mystery Writers, 3rd ed., pp. 971–72. (882c)

Smith, Lora R. *See* **Roberts, Lora**

Smith, Mark
Bio-bibliographic data:
The Craft of Crime: Conversations with Crime Writers, pp. 322–49. (872)

Smith, Martin Cruz
Bio-bibliographic data:
Critical Survey of Mystery and Detective Fiction, pp. 1502–7. (41)
Detecting Men, 1st ed., p. 234. (876)
Encyclopedia Mysteriosa, pp. 334–35. (2)
The Mammoth Encyclopedia of Modern Crime Fiction, pp. 445–46. (1)
100 Masters of Mystery and Detective Fiction, pp. 601–7. (37)
St. James Guide to Crime & Mystery Writers, 4th ed., pp. 943–45. (882d)
Twentieth-Century Crime and Mystery Writers, 2nd ed., pp. 810–11. (882b)
Twentieth-Century Crime and Mystery Writers, 3rd ed., pp. 973–74. (882c)
Web site: http://literati.net/MCSmith/
Smithbooks.htm; http://
stopyourekillingme.com/
martin-cruz-smith.html

Smith, Peter Claudius Gautier. *See* **Conway, Peter**

Smith, Rebecca. *See* **Tope, Rebecca**

Smith, Robert A[rthur].
Bio-bibliographic data:
Canadian Crime Fiction, pp. 206–7. (209)

Smith, Rosamond. *See* **Oates, Joyce Carol**

Smith, Sarah
Bio-bibliographic data:
Detecting Women, 3rd ed., p. 257. (877c)
Web site: http://world.std.com/~swrs

Smith, Shelley. *Pseud. for* **Nancy Hermione Bodington**
Bio-bibliographic data:
St. James Guide to Crime & Mystery Writers, 4th ed., pp. 945–46. (882d)
Twentieth-Century Crime and Mystery Writers, 1st ed., pp. 1328–30. (882a)
Twentieth-Century Crime and Mystery Writers, 2nd ed., pp. 811–12. (882b)
Twentieth-Century Crime and Mystery Writers, 3rd ed., pp. 974–75. (882c)

Smith, Spenser
Bio-bibliographic data:
Australian Crime Fiction, p. 218. (207)

Smith, Taylor
Bio-bibliographic data:
Canadian Crime Fiction, p. 207. (209)
Web site: http://stopyourekillingme.com/
taylor-smith.html; http://www.
taylorsmith.org

Smith, Thomas David. *See* **Hawthorn, Clyde**

Smith-Levin, Judith
Bio-bibliographic data:
Detecting Women, 3rd ed., p. 257. (877c)

Snell, LeRoy W.
Bio-bibliographic data:
Canadian Crime Fiction, p. 266. (209)

Snell, Roy Judson. *See* **Craig, James**

Snow, C. P.; i.e., Charles Percy Snow, Baron Snow of Leicester
Bio-bibliographic data:
British Mystery Writers, 1920–1939, pp. 277–83. (867)
The Encyclopedia of Murder and Mystery, p. 460. (6)
The Encyclopedia of Mystery and Detection, p. 366. (7)

Snyder, George. *See* **Morgan, Patrick**

Soiza Reilly, Juan José de
Bio-bibliographic data:
Latin American Mystery Writers: An A to Z Guide. (881)

Solomita, Stephen
Bio-bibliographic data:
Detecting Men, 1st ed., p. 234. (876)
Web site: http://stopyourekillingme.com/
stephen-solomita.html

Somain, Jean-François. *See* **Somcynsky, Jean-François**

Somcynsky, Jean-François
Bio-bibliographic data:
Canadian Crime Fiction, p. 207. (209)

Somers, Harry
Bio-bibliographic data:
Canadian Crime Fiction, p. 207. (209)

Somers, Paul. *See* **Garve, Andrew**

Songer, C. J.; i.e., Christine J.
Bio-bibliographic data:
Detecting Women, 3rd ed., pp. 257–58. (877c)
Web site: http://stopyourekillingme.com/ c-j-songer.html

Sonin, Ray
Bio-bibliographic data:
Canadian Crime Fiction, p. 207. (209)

Soos, Troy
Bio-bibliographic data:
Detecting Men, 1st ed., p. 235. (876)
Web site: http://stopyourekillingme.com/ troy-soos.html; http://members. aol.com/TroySoos/index.html

Soren, Marco
Bio-bibliographic data:
Canadian Crime Fiction, p. 207. (209)

Sorrells, Walter
Bio-bibliographic data:
The Mammoth Encyclopedia of Modern Crime Fiction, pp. 446–47. (1)

Soulières, Robert
Bio-bibliographic data:
Canadian Crime Fiction, p. 207. (209)

Southouse, Reginald Evelyn Peter. *See* **Cheney, Peter**

Souvestre, Pierre
Bio-bibliographic data:
The Encyclopedia of Murder and Mystery, p. 462. (6)

Spain, Nancy
Bio-bibliographic data:
St. James Guide to Crime & Mystery Writers, 4th ed., pp. 946–47. (882d)
Twentieth-Century Crime and Mystery Writers, 3rd ed., pp. 975–76. (882c)

Sparling, S. L.; i.e., Sharon L.
Bio-bibliographic data:
Canadian Crime Fiction, p. 207. (209)

Speart, Jessica
Bio-bibliographic data:
Detecting Women, 3rd ed., p. 258. (877c)

Web site: http://stopyourekillingme.com/ jessica-speart.html; http://www. jessicaspeart.com

Spehner, Norbert
Bio-bibliographic data:
Canadian Crime Fiction, p. 208. (209)

Spence, Ainslie. *Pseud. for* **Ida Mary Murphy**
Bio-bibliographic data:
Australian Crime Fiction, p. 218. (207)

Spencer, John B.
Bio-bibliographic data:
Detecting Men, 1st ed., p. 235. (876)

Spencer, Julian
Bio-bibliographic data:
Australian Crime Fiction, pp. 218–19. (207)

Spencer, Ross H.
Bio-bibliographic data:
Detecting Men, 1st ed., p. 235. (876)

Spender, J. M.; i.e., Jean Maud
Bio-bibliographic data:
Australian Crime Fiction, p. 219. (207)

Spetigue, D. O.; i.e., Donald O.
Bio-bibliographic data:
Canadian Crime Fiction, p. 208. (209)

Spicer, Bart
Bio-bibliographic data:
Encyclopedia Mysteriosa, p. 336. (2)
St. James Guide to Crime & Mystery Writers, 4th ed., pp. 947–48. (882d)
Twentieth-Century Crime and Mystery Writers, 1st ed., pp. 1331–32. (882a)
Twentieth-Century Crime and Mystery Writers, 2nd ed., pp. 812–13. (882b)
Twentieth-Century Crime and Mystery Writers, 3rd ed., pp. 976–77. (882c)

Spicer, Michael
Bio-bibliographic data:
Detecting Men, 1st ed., p. 236. (876)

Spillane, Mickey: i.e., Frank Morrison Spillane
Bio-bibliographic data:
American Hard-Boiled Crime Writers, pp. 301–9. (862)
The Big Book of Noir, pp. 231–36. (24)
Corpus Delicti of Mystery Fiction, pp. 117–18. (879)
Critical Survey of Mystery and Detective Fiction, pp. 1508–13. (41)
Detecting Men, 1st ed., p. 236. (876)
Encyclopedia Mysteriosa, pp. 336–37. (2)
The Encyclopedia of Mystery and Detection, pp. 367–70. (7)

The Mammoth Encyclopedia of Modern Crime Fiction, pp. 447–49. (1)
Mystery and Suspense Writers, pp. 869–84. (884.2)
100 Masters of Mystery and Detective Fiction, pp. 608–14. (37)
The Oxford Companion to Crime and Mystery Writing, p. 423. (4)
St. James Guide to Crime & Mystery Writers, 4th ed., pp. 948–49. (882d)
Speaking of Murder, pp. 113–25. (875a)
Twentieth-Century Crime and Mystery Writers, 1st ed., pp. 1332–35. (882a)
Twentieth-Century Crime and Mystery Writers, 2nd ed., pp. 813–15. (882b)
Twentieth-Century Crime and Mystery Writers, 3rd ed., pp. 977–78. (882c)
Whodunit? A Who's Who in Crime and Mystery Writing, pp. 184–85. (5)
Web site: http://stopyourekillingme.com/ mickey-spillane.html; http://www. interlog.com/~roco/hammer.html; http://www.thrillingdetective.com/ trivia/spillane.html

Sprague, Gretchen
Bio-bibliographic data:
Detecting Women, 3rd ed., p. 258. (877c)

Sprigg, Christopher St. John
Bio-bibliographic data:
The Encyclopedia of Mystery and Detection, p. 370. (7)
Twentieth-Century Crime and Mystery Writers, 1st ed., pp. 1335–37. (882a)

Spring, Michelle
Bio-bibliographic data:
Canadian Crime Fiction, p. 208. (209)
Detecting Women, 1st ed., p. 134. (877a)
Detecting Women 2, p. 179. (877b)
Detecting Women, 3rd ed., pp. 258–59. (877c)
Web site: http://stopyourekillingme.com/ michelle-spring.html

Sprinkle, Patricia H[ouck].
Bio-bibliographic data:
By a Woman's Hand, 1st ed., p. 200. (884a)
By a Woman's Hand, 2nd ed., p. 212. (884b)
Detecting Women 2, p. 179. (877b)
Detecting Women, 3rd ed., p. 259. (877c)
Web site: http://stopyourekillingme.com/ patricia-houck-sprinkle.html

Squire, Elizabeth Daniels
Bio-bibliographic data:

By a Woman's Hand, 2nd ed., pp. 212–13. (884b)
Detecting Women, 1st ed., p. 135. (877a)
Detecting Women 2, pp. 179–80. (877b)
Detecting Women, 3rd ed., pp. 259–60. (877c)
The Mammoth Encyclopedia of Modern Crime Fiction, pp. 449–50. (1)
Web site:
http://www.booktalk.com/edsquire; http://stopyourekillingme.com/ elizabeth-daniels-squire.html; http:// members.aol.com/femmesweb/ squire.htm

Stabenow, Dana [Helen]
Bio-bibliographic data:
By a Woman's Hand, 1st ed., pp. 200–201. (884a)
By a Woman's Hand, 2nd ed., pp. 213–14. (884b)
Detecting Women, 1st ed., p. 135. (877a)
Detecting Women 2, p. 180. (877b)
Detecting Women, 3rd ed., p. 260. (877c)
The Mammoth Encyclopedia of Modern Crime Fiction, pp. 450–51. (1)
St. James Guide to Crime & Mystery Writers, 4th ed., pp. 950–52. (882d)
Whodunit? A Who's Who in Crime and Mystery Writing, p. 186. (5)
Web site: http://www.stabenow.com; http://stopyourekillingme.com/ dana-stabenow.html

Stacey, Susannah. *See* **Staynes, Jill, and Margaret Storey**

Stagge, Jonathan. *See* **Quentin, Patrick**

Staincliffe, Cath
Bio-bibliographic data:
Detecting Women, 3rd ed., p. 261. (877c)
Web site: http://stopyourekillingme.com/ cath-staincliffe.html

Stallwood, Veronica
Bio-bibliographic data:
By a Woman's Hand, 2nd ed., pp. 215–16. (884b)
Detecting Women, 1st ed., p. 135. (877a)
Detecting Women 2, p. 180. (877b)
Detecting Women, 3rd ed., p. 261. (877c)
The Mammoth Encyclopedia of Modern Crime Fiction, p. 451. (1)
Web site: http://stopyourekillingme.com/ veronica-stallwood.html

Standiford, Les
Bio-bibliographic data:
Detecting Men, 1st ed., p. 237. (876)

Web site: http://stopyourekillingme.com/
les-standiford.html

Stannus, G. *See* **Jason**

Star, Nancy
Bio-bibliographic data:
Detecting Women, 3rd ed., p. 262. (877c)

Stark, [T.] James
Bio-bibliographic data:
Canadian Crime Fiction, p. 208. (209)

Stark, Richard. *See* **Westlake, Donald E.**

Starnes, John
Bio-bibliographic data:
Canadian Crime Fiction, pp. 208–9. (209)

Starr, Patti
Bio-bibliographic data:
Canadian Crime Fiction, p. 209. (209)

Starrett, [Charles] Vincent [Emerson]
Bio-bibliographic data:
Canadian Crime Fiction, pp. 209–11.
(209)
*Critical Survey of Mystery and Detective
Fiction,* pp. 1514–20. (41)
Encyclopedia Mysteriosa, pp. 337–38. (2)
The Encyclopedia of Murder and Mystery,
p. 464. (6)
*The Encyclopedia of Mystery and
Detection,* p. 370. (7)
*The Oxford Companion to Crime and
Mystery Writing,* p. 429. (4)
*St. James Guide to Crime & Mystery
Writers,* 4th ed., pp. 952–54. (882d)
*Twentieth-Century Crime and Mystery
Writers,* 1st ed., pp. 1337–41. (882a)
*Twentieth-Century Crime and Mystery
Writers,* 2nd ed., pp. 815–17. (882b)
*Twentieth-Century Crime and Mystery
Writers,* 3rd ed., pp. 978–80. (882c)
*Whodunit? A Who's Who in Crime and
Mystery Writing,* p. 186. (5)

Staynes, Jill, and Margaret Storey
Bio-bibliographic data:
By a Woman's Hand, 1st ed., pp. 201–2.
(884a)
By a Woman's Hand, 2nd ed., pp. 214–15.
(884b)
Detecting Women, 1st ed., p. 55, 135.
(877a)
Detecting Women 2, p. 64, 180. (877b)
Detecting Women, 3rd ed., pp. 89–90,
260–61. (877c)
Great Women Mystery Writers, pp.
324–25. (880)
*The Mammoth Encyclopedia of Modern
Crime Fiction,* pp. 451–52. (1)

**Stead, Robert J. C.; i.e., Robert James
Campbell**
Bio-bibliographic data:
Canadian Crime Fiction, p. 211. (209)

Steed, Neville
Bio-bibliographic data:
Detecting Men, 1st ed., p. 238. (876)
*The Mammoth Encyclopedia of Modern
Crime Fiction,* pp. 452–53. (1)

Steel, Kurt. *Pseud. for* **Rudolf Hornaday
Kagey**
Bio-bibliographic data:
*Twentieth-Century Crime and Mystery
Writers,* 2nd ed., pp. 817–18. (882b)
*Twentieth-Century Crime and Mystery
Writers,* 3rd ed., pp. 980–81. (882c)

Steele, Harwood [Robert Elmes], Lt.-Col.
Bio-bibliographic data:
Canadian Crime Fiction, pp. 211–12.
(209)

Steele, Tedd
Bio-bibliographic data:
Canadian Crime Fiction, p. 212. (209)

Steeves, Harrison R[oss].
Bio-bibliographic data:
*The Encyclopedia of Mystery and
Detection,* p. 371. (7)

Stegner, Wallace
Bio-bibliographic data:
Canadian Crime Fiction, p. 267. (209)

Stein, Aaron Marc
Bio-bibliographic data:
Encyclopedia Mysteriosa, p. 338. (2)
The Encyclopedia of Murder and Mystery,
p. 465. (6)
*The Encyclopedia of Mystery and
Detection,* p. 371. (7)
*St. James Guide to Crime & Mystery
Writers,* 4th ed., pp. 954–57. (882d)
*Twentieth-Century Crime and Mystery
Writers,* 1st ed., pp. 1341–45. (882a)
*Twentieth-Century Crime and Mystery
Writers,* 2nd ed., pp. 818–21. (882b)
*Twentieth-Century Crime and Mystery
Writers,* 3rd ed., pp. 981–84. (882c)
Personal papers in Firestone Library,
Princeton University, New Jersey.

Stein, Triss
Bio-bibliographic data:
Detecting Women, 1st ed., p. 136. (877a)
Detecting Women 2, pp. 180–81. (877b)
Detecting Women, 3rd ed., p. 262. (877c)

Steinberg, Janice
Bio-bibliographic data:

Detecting Women 2, p. 181. (877b)
Detecting Women, 3rd ed., p. 262. (877c)
Web site: http://stopyourekillingme.com/
janice-steinberg.html; http://www.
janicesteinberg.com

Steinbrenner, [Peter] Chris[tian]
Bio-bibliographic data:
Encyclopedia Mysteriosa, p. 338. (2)

Steiner, Susan
Bio-bibliographic data:
Detecting Women, 1st ed., p. 136. (877a)
Detecting Women 2, p. 181. (877b)
Detecting Women, 3rd ed., p. 263. (877c)

Stenstreem, Ruth. *See* **Babson, Marian**

Stephens, Kate
Bio-bibliographic data:
Australian Crime Fiction, p. 9, 145, 146.
(207)

Stephens, Reed. *Pseud. for* **Stephen R.
Donaldson**
Bio-bibliographic data:
Detecting Men, 1st ed., p. 238. (876)

Stephenson, Anne
Bio-bibliographic data:
Canadian Crime Fiction, p. 212. (209)

Stephenson, Anthony. *See* **Quogan,
Anthony**

Sterling, Stewart. *Pseud. for* **Prentice
Winchell**
Bio-bibliographic data:
Encyclopedia Mysteriosa, p. 339. (2)
The Encyclopedia of Murder and Mystery,
pp. 465–66. (6)
*Twentieth-Century Crime and Mystery
Writers,* 2nd ed., pp. 821–22. (882b)
*Twentieth-Century Crime and Mystery
Writers,* 3rd ed., pp. 984–86. (882c)

Stern, Richard Martin
Bio-bibliographic data:
*The Mammoth Encyclopedia of Modern
Crime Fiction*, pp. 453–54. (1)
*St. James Guide to Crime & Mystery
Writers,* 4th ed., pp. 957–58. (882d)
*Twentieth-Century Crime and Mystery
Writers,* 1st ed., pp. 1346–47. (882a)
*Twentieth-Century Crime and Mystery
Writers,* 2nd ed., pp. 822–23. (882b)
*Twentieth-Century Crime and Mystery
Writers,* 3rd ed., pp. 986–87. (882c)
Personal papers in Mugar Memorial
Library, Boston University.
Web site: http://stopyourekillingme.com/
richard-martin-stern.html

Stevens, David
Bio-bibliographic data:
Canadian Crime Fiction, p. 213. (209)

Stevens, Joan M.
Bio-bibliographic data:
Australian Crime Fiction, p. 220. (207)

Stevens, Serita
Bio-bibliographic data:
Detecting Women, 1st ed., p. 136. (877a)
Detecting Women 2, p. 181. (877b)
Detecting Women, 3rd ed., p. 263. (877c)

Stevens, Shane
Bio-bibliographic data:
Detecting Men, 1st ed., p. 215 (876)

Stevenson, John
Bio-bibliographic data:
Australian Crime Fiction, p. 50. (207)

Stevenson, Richard. *Pseud. for* **Richard
Lipez**
Bio-bibliographic data:
Detecting Men, 1st ed., pp. 238–39. (876)
Web site: http://stopyourekillingme.com/
richard-stevenson.html

Stevenson, Robert Louis
Bio-bibliographic data:
*Critical Survey of Mystery and Detective
Fiction*, pp. 1521–26. (41)
The Encyclopedia of Murder and Mystery,
pp. 466–67. (6)
*The Encyclopedia of Mystery and
Detection*, pp. 371–74. (7)
*100 Masters of Mystery and Detective
Fiction*, pp. 615–20. (37)

Stevenson, William
Bio-bibliographic data:
Canadian Crime Fiction, p. 213. (209)

Stewardson, Dawn
Bio-bibliographic data:
Canadian Crime Fiction, p. 213. (209)

Stewart, Alfred Walter. *See* **Connington,
J. J.**

Stewart, John Innes Mackintosh. *See*
Innes, Michael

Stewart, Mary [Florence Elinor]
Bio-bibliographic data:
By a Woman's Hand, 1st ed., pp. 202–3.
(884a)
By a Woman's Hand, 2nd ed., pp. 216–17.
(884b)
Corpus Delicti of Mystery Fiction, pp.
118–19. (879)
*Critical Survey of Mystery and Detective
Fiction*, pp. 1527–32. (41)
Encyclopedia Mysteriosa, p. 339. (2)

*The Encyclopedia of Mystery and
Detection*, pp. 374–75. (7)
*100 Masters of Mystery and Detective
Fiction*, pp. 621–26. (37)
*The Oxford Companion to Crime and
Mystery Writing*, p. 431. (4)
*St. James Guide to Crime & Mystery
Writers*, 4th ed., pp. 958–60. (882d)
*Twentieth-Century Crime and Mystery
Writers*, 1st ed., pp. 1347–49. (882a)
*Twentieth-Century Crime and Mystery
Writers*, 2nd ed., pp. 823–24. (882b)
*Twentieth-Century Crime and Mystery
Writers*, 3rd ed., pp. 987–88. (882c)
*Whodunit? A Who's Who in Crime and
Mystery Writing*, pp. 186–87. (5)
Personal papers in National Library of
Scotland, Edinburgh.
Web site: http://stopyourekillingme.com/
mary-stewart.html
Stewart, Sean
Bio-bibliographic data:
Canadian Crime Fiction, p. 214. (209)
Stewart, W. T.; i.e., William Thomas
Bio-bibliographic data:
Australian Crime Fiction, p. 220. (207)
Stewart, Walter
Bio-bibliographic data:
Canadian Crime Fiction, p. 214. (209)
Stinson, Jim
Bio-bibliographic data:
Detecting Men, 1st ed., p. 239. (876)
Stirling, Donald
Bio-bibliographic data:
Canadian Crime Fiction, p. 214. (209)
Stivens, Dal; i.e., Dallas George
Bio-bibliographic data:
Australian Crime Fiction, p. 220. (207)
**Stockbridge, Grant: house pseud. used by
Norvell W. Page and R. T. M. Scott
(q.v.)**
Stockley, Grif
Bio-bibliographic data:
Detecting Men, 1st ed., p. 239. (876)
Web site: http://stopyourekillingme.com/
grif-stockley.html
Stockton, Frank R.; i.e., Francis Richard
Bio-bibliographic data:
*Critical Survey of Mystery and Detective
Fiction*, pp. 1533–39. (41)
*The Encyclopedia of Mystery and
Detection*, p. 375. (7)

Stoddard, Charles. *See* **Strong, Charles
Stanley**
Stoker, Bram; i.e., Abraham
Bio-bibliographic data:
British Mystery Writers, 1860–1919, pp.
283–89. (866)
*The Encyclopedia of Mystery and
Detection*, p. 375. (7)
*Twentieth-Century Crime and Mystery
Writers*, 1st ed., pp. 1349–51. (882a)
    Bram Stoker Club
    c/o David Lass
    Regent House
    Dublin 2 Ireland
    Bram Stoker Memorial Association
    c/o Jenny O'Casey
    29 Washington Square West,
    Penthouse N
    New York, NY 10011
Stone, Hampton. *See* **Stein, Aaron Marc**
Stone, Louis
Bio-bibliographic data:
Australian Crime Fiction, pp. 220–21.
(207)
Stone, Michael
Bio-bibliographic data:
Detecting Men, 1st ed., p. 239. (876)
Web site: http://stopyourekillingme.com/
michael-stone.html
Stone, Thomas H. *See* **Harknett, Terry
Williams**
Stoneham, C. T.; i.e., Charles Thurley. *See*
Thurley, Norgrove
Storey, Alice. *See* **Shankman, Sarah**
Storey, Margaret. *See* **Staynes, Jill, and
Margaret Storey**
Stout, Rex [Todhunter]
Bio-bibliographic data:
Corpus Delicti of Mystery Fiction, pp.
119–22. (879)
*Critical Survey of Mystery and Detective
Fiction*, pp. 1540–47. (41)
Encyclopedia Mysteriosa, pp. 340–41. (2)
The Encyclopedia of Murder and Mystery,
pp. 468–70. (6)
*The Encyclopedia of Mystery and
Detection*, pp. 376–77. (7)
Mystery and Suspense Writers, pp.
885–99. (884.2)
*100 Masters of Mystery and Detective
Fiction*, pp. 627–34. (37)
*The Oxford Companion to Crime and
Mystery Writing*, pp. 431–32. (4)

St. James Guide to Crime & Mystery Writers, 4th ed., pp. 960–62. (882d)
Twentieth-Century Crime and Mystery Writers, 1st ed., pp. 1351–55. (882a)
Twentieth-Century Crime and Mystery Writers, 2nd ed., pp. 824–27. (882b)
Twentieth-Century Crime and Mystery Writers, 3rd ed., pp. 988–91. (882c)
Whodunit? A Who's Who in Crime and Mystery Writing, p. 187. (5)
Personal papers in University of North Carolina Libraries, Chapel Hill, North Carolina
Web site: http://stopyourekillingme.com/rex-stout.html; http://www.geocities.com/Athens/8907/nero.html; http://www.thrillingdetective.com/wolfe.html; http://www.things.org/~muffy/pages/books/rex_stout/nero_wolfe.html; http://www.cs.rit.edu/~lac/nero/charsearch.html; http://www.nerowolfe.org; http://www.nerowolfe.freeservers.com/indexnw.html
The Wolfe Pack
c/o Mary A. Glascock
P.O. Box 1230822
Ansonia Station
New York, NY 10023
http://www.nerowolfe.org
Publishes the *Gazette* (ISSN 0193–533X).

Stow, [Julian] Randolph
Bio-bibliographic data:
Australian Crime Fiction, p. 221. (207)

Straker, J. F.
Bio-bibliographic data:
Twentieth-Century Crime and Mystery Writers, 1st ed., pp. 1356–57. (882a)
Twentieth-Century Crime and Mystery Writers, 2nd ed., p. 827. (882b)
Twentieth-Century Crime and Mystery Writers, 3rd ed., p. 991. (882c)

Straley, John
Bio-bibliographic data:
Detecting Men, 1st ed., p. 240. (876)
Web site: http://stopyourekillingme.com/john-straley.html; http://www.johnstraley.com

Strange, John Stephen. *Pseud. for* **Dorothy Stockbridge Tillet**
Bio-bibliographic data:
Twentieth-Century Crime and Mystery Writers, 1st ed., pp. 1357–59. (882a)

Twentieth-Century Crime and Mystery Writers, 2nd ed., pp. 827–28. (882b)
Twentieth-Century Crime and Mystery Writers, 3rd ed., pp. 991–92. (882c)

Stranger, L. D.
Bio-bibliographic data:
Australian Crime Fiction, p. 221. (207)

Stratemeyer, Edward L.
Bio-bibliographic data:
The Encyclopedia of Murder and Mystery, pp. 471–72. (6)

Straub, Peter
Web site: http://www.net-site.com/straub

Street, Cecil John Charles. *See* **Rhode, John**

Streib, Dan; i.e., Daniel T.
Bio-bibliographic data:
Canadian Crime Fiction, p. 267. (209)

Stribling, T. S.; i.e., Thomas Sigismund
Bio-bibliographic data:
Encyclopedia Mysteriosa, p. 342. (2)
The Encyclopedia of Murder and Mystery, p. 472. (6)
The Encyclopedia of Mystery and Detection, p. 377. (7)
The Oxford Companion to Crime and Mystery Writing, p. 433. (4)
St. James Guide to Crime & Mystery Writers, 4th ed., pp. 962–63. (882d)
Twentieth-Century Crime and Mystery Writers, 1st ed., pp. 1359–61. (882a)
Twentieth-Century Crime and Mystery Writers, 2nd ed., pp. 828–30. (882b)
Twentieth-Century Crime and Mystery Writers, 3rd ed., pp. 992–94. (882c)
Whodunit? A Who's Who in Crime and Mystery Writing, pp. 187–88. (5)

Striker, Fran; i.e., Francis Hamilton
Bio-bibliographic data:
Canadian Crime Fiction, p. 267. (209)

Stringer, Arthur [John Arbuthnott]
Bio-bibliographic data:
Canadian Crime Fiction, pp. 214–16. (209)
The Encyclopedia of Mystery and Detection, pp. 377–78. (7)

Strong, Charles Stanley
Bio-bibliographic data:
Canadian Crime Fiction, p. 267. (209)

Strong, L. A. G.; i.e., Leonard Alfred George
Bio-bibliographic data:
The Encyclopedia of Murder and Mystery, p. 472. (6)

Strongman, Mike: unidentified pseud.
Bio-bibliographic data:
Australian Crime Fiction, p. 71, 221–22.
(207)
Stroud, Carsten
Bio-bibliographic data:
Canadian Crime Fiction, pp. 216–17.
(209)
*The Mammoth Encyclopedia of Modern
Crime Fiction,* p. 454. (1)
Strunk, Frank C.
Bio-bibliographic data:
Detecting Men, 1st ed., p. 240. (876)
**Struthers, Betsy; i.e., Elizabeth [Jane
Porter]**
Bio-bibliographic data:
Canadian Crime Fiction, p. 217. (209)
Detecting Women, 3rd ed., p. 263. (877c)
Stryker, George. *See* **Darrigo, Dave**
Stuart, Ian
Bio-bibliographic data:
*Twentieth-Century Crime and Mystery
Writers,* 2nd ed., p. 830. (882b)
*Twentieth-Century Crime and Mystery
Writers,* 3rd ed., pp. 994–95. (882c)
Web site: http://stopyourekillingme.com/
ian-stuart.html
Stubbs, Jean
Bio-bibliographic data:
*Critical Survey of Mystery and Detective
Fiction,* pp. 1548–52. (41)
Designs of Darkness, pp. 35–50. (873)
Detecting Women, 3rd ed., p. 264. (877c)
*St. James Guide to Crime & Mystery
Writers,* 4th ed., pp. 964–65. (882d)
*Twentieth-Century Crime and Mystery
Writers,* 1st ed., pp. 1361–64. (882a)
*Twentieth-Century Crime and Mystery
Writers,* 2nd ed., pp. 830–32. (882b)
*Twentieth-Century Crime and Mystery
Writers,* 3rd ed., pp. 996–97. (882c)
Studdert, Mrs. Richard de Clare. *See*
Rixon, Annie Louisa
Stuewe, Paul
Bio-bibliographic data:
Canadian Crime Fiction, p. 217. (209)
**Stutley, S. J., and A. E. Copp; i.e., Sydney
James [Dacres] and Alf. E.**
Bio-bibliographic data:
Australian Crime Fiction, p. 222. (207)
Sturrock, Jeremy. *Pseud. for* **Benjamin
James Healey**
Bio-bibliographic data:

*Twentieth-Century Crime and Mystery
Writers,* 1st ed., pp. 1364–65. (882a)
*Twentieth-Century Crime and Mystery
Writers,* 2nd ed., pp. 832–33. (882b)
*Twentieth-Century Crime and Mystery
Writers,* 3rd ed., pp. 997–98. (882c)
Personal papers in Mugar Memorial
Library, Boston University.
Stuyck, Karen Hanson
Bio-bibliographic data:
Detecting Women, 3rd ed., p. 264. (877c)
Styles, Lesley [Emily]
Bio-bibliographic data:
Australian Crime Fiction, p. 222. (207)
Sublett, Jesse
Bio-bibliographic data:
Detecting Men, 1st ed., p. 241. (876)
Web site: http://stopyourekillingme.com/
jesse-sublett.html; http://www.
overbooked.org/Sublett.html
Such, Peter
Bio-bibliographic data:
Canadian Crime Fiction, p. 217. (209)
Sucher, Dorothy
Bio-bibliographic data:
By a Woman's Hand, 1st ed., pp. 203–4.
(884a)
Detecting Women, 1st ed., p. 136. (877a)
Detecting Women 2, p. 181. (877b)
Detecting Women, 3rd ed., p. 264. (877c)
Great Women Mystery Writers, pp.
325–27. (880)
Web site: http://stopyourekillingme.com/
dorothy-sucher.html; http://www.
sovernet.net/~jsucher/dot
Sue, Eugène. *Pseud. for* **Marie Joseph
Marie Sue**
Bio-bibliographic data:
*Critical Survey of Mystery and Detective
Fiction,* pp. 1553–59. (41)
The Encyclopedia of Murder and Mystery,
p. 473. (6)
*The Encyclopedia of Mystery and
Detection,* p. 378. (7)
Sullivan, [Edward] Alan
Bio-bibliographic data:
Canadian Crime Fiction, p. 157, 217–18.
(209)
Sullivan, Winona
Bio-bibliographic data:
Detecting Women, 1st ed., pp. 136–37.
(877a)
Detecting Women 2, p. 181. (877b)
Detecting Women, 3rd ed., p. 265. (877c)

Web site: http://stopyourekillingme.com/
winona-sullivan.html

Summers, Jaron
Bio-bibliographic data:
Canadian Crime Fiction, p. 218. (209)

Summerton, Margaret
Bio-bibliographic data:
*Twentieth-Century Crime and Mystery
Writers,* 1st ed., pp. 1365–67. (882a)
*Twentieth-Century Crime and Mystery
Writers,* 2nd ed., pp. 833–34. (882b)

Sumner, Penny
Bio-bibliographic data:
Australian Crime Fiction, p. 222. (207)
Detecting Women 2, p. 182. (877b)
Detecting Women, 3rd ed., p. 265. (877c)

Surrey, George
Bio-bibliographic data:
Canadian Crime Fiction, p. 268. (209)

Sutherland, Robert
Bio-bibliographic data:
Canadian Crime Fiction, p. 218. (209)

Sutherland, Ronald
Bio-bibliographic data:
Canadian Crime Fiction, pp. 218–19.
(209)

Swain, Dwight V.
Bio-bibliographic data:
Australian Crime Fiction, p. 158. (207)

Swan, Susan [Elizabeth]
Bio-bibliographic data:
Canadian Crime Fiction, p. 219. (209)

Swan, Thomas
Bio-bibliographic data:
Detecting Men, 1st ed., p. 241. (876)
Web site: http://stopyourekillingme.com/
thomas-swan.html

Swanson, Doug J.
Bio-bibliographic data:
Detecting Men, 1st ed., p. 241. (876)
*The Mammoth Encyclopedia of Modern
Crime Fiction,* pp. 454–55. (1)
Web site: http://www.dougswanson.com;
http://stopyourekillingme.com/
doug-j-swanson.html

Sweatman, Margaret
Bio-bibliographic data:
Canadian Crime Fiction, p. 219. (209)

Swede, George
Bio-bibliographic data:
Canadian Crime Fiction, pp. 219–20.
(209)

Switzer, Robert
Bio-bibliographic data:

Canadian Crime Fiction, p. 220. (209)

Sylvestre, Danielle. *See* **Chevrette,
Christiane, and Danielle Sylvestre**

Sylvestre, Paul-François
Bio-bibliographic data:
Canadian Crime Fiction, p. 220. (209)

Symons, Julian [Gustave]
Bio-bibliographic data:
*British Mystery and Thriller Writers since
1940, First Series,* pp. 333–44. (868)
*Critical Survey of Mystery and Detective
Fiction,* pp. 1560–66. (41)
Designs of Darkness, pp. 172–85. (873)
Encyclopedia Mysteriosa, pp. 343–44. (2)
The Encyclopedia of Murder and Mystery,
pp. 475–76. (6)
*The Encyclopedia of Mystery and
Detection,* pp. 378–79. (7)
The Fatal Art of Entertainment, pp.
[xx]–27. (878)
*The Mammoth Encyclopedia of Modern
Crime Fiction,* pp. 455–56. (1)
Mystery and Suspense Writers, pp.
901–10. (884.2)
*100 Masters of Mystery and Detective
Fiction,* pp. 635–43. (37)
*The Oxford Companion to Crime and
Mystery Writing,* pp. 441–42. (4)
*St. James Guide to Crime & Mystery
Writers,* 4th ed., pp. 965–68. (882d)
Twelve Englishmen of Mystery, pp.
196–221. (865)
*Twentieth-Century Crime and Mystery
Writers,* 1st ed., pp. 1367–70. (882a)
*Twentieth-Century Crime and Mystery
Writers,* 2nd ed., pp. 834–36. (882b)
*Twentieth-Century Crime and Mystery
Writers,* 3rd ed., pp. 998–1001. (882c)
*Whodunit? A Who's Who in Crime and
Mystery Writing,* p. 189. (5)
Personal papers in Humanities Research
Center, University of Texas at Austin.
Web site: http://stopyourekillingme.com/
julian-symons.html

Szanto, George [H.]
Bio-bibliographic data:
Canadian Crime Fiction, p. 220. (209)

Szymanski, Therese
Bio-bibliographic data:
Detecting Women, 3rd ed., p. 265. (877c)
Web site: http://stopyourekillingme.com/
therese-szymanski.html

T

Taibo II, Pasco Ignacio
Bio-bibliographic data:
Detecting Men, 1st ed., p. 242. (876)
The Encyclopedia of Murder and Mystery,
p. 477. (6)
*Latin American Mystery Writers: An A to
Z Guide. (881)*
*Whodunit? A Who's Who in Crime and
Mystery Writing,* p. 191. (5)
Web site: http://www.thrillingdetective.
com/trivia/;
http://www.thrillingdetective.
com/trivia/taibo.html
Taibo III, Pasco Ignacio. *See* **Taibo II,
Paco Ignacio**
Tan, Maureen
Bio-bibliographic data:
Detecting Women, 3rd ed., p. 266. (877c)
Tanenbaum, Robert K.
Bio-bibliographic data:
Detecting Men, 1st ed., p. 242. (876)
*The Mammoth Encyclopedia of Modern
Crime Fiction,* pp. 457–58. (1)
*St. James Guide to Crime & Mystery
Writers,* 4th ed., p. 969. (882d)
Web site: http://stopyourekillingme.com/
robert-k-tanenbaum.html
Tapply, William G[eorge].
Bio-bibliographic data:
Detecting Men, 1st ed., pp. 242–43. (876)
Encyclopedia Mysteriosa, pp. 345–46. (2)
*The Mammoth Encyclopedia of Modern
Crime Fiction,* p. 458. (1)
*St. James Guide to Crime & Mystery
Writers,* 4th ed., pp. 969–71. (882d)
*Twentieth-Century Crime and Mystery
Writers,* 3rd ed., pp. 1002–3. (882c)
*Whodunit? A Who's Who in Crime and
Mystery Writing,* p. 191. (5)
Web site: http://www.williamgtapply.com;
http://stopyourekillingme.com/
william-g-tapply.html
Tard, Louis-Martin
Bio-bibliographic data:
Canadian Crime Fiction, p. 220. (209)
Tardif, Louis
Bio-bibliographic data:
Canadian Crime Fiction, p. 220. (209)
Taschdjian, Claire [Louise]
Bio-bibliographic data:
Canadian Crime Fiction, p. 285. (209)

Tate, Ellalice. *See* **Holt, Victoria**
Tate, Frank
Bio-bibliographic data:
Canadian Crime Fiction, p. 220. (209)
Taylor, Alison G.: unidentified pseud.
Bio-bibliographic data:
Detecting Women, 3rd ed., p. 266. (877c)
Web site: http://stopyourekillingme.com/
alison-g-taylor.html
Taylor, Andrew [John Robert]
Bio-bibliographic data:
Detecting Men, 1st ed., p. 243. (876)
The Encyclopedia of Murder and Mystery,
p. 478. (6)
*The Mammoth Encyclopedia of Modern
Crime Fiction,* pp. 459–60. (1)
*St. James Guide to Crime & Mystery
Writers,* 4th ed., pp. 971–72. (882d)
*Twentieth-Century Crime and Mystery
Writers,* 3rd ed., pp. 1003–4. (882c)
Web site:
http://www.lydmouth.demon.co.uk/
atylor1.htm;
http://stopyourekillingme.
com/andrew-taylor.html
Taylor, Domini. *See* **Longrigg, Roger**
Taylor, Elizabeth Atwood
Bio-bibliographic data:
By a Woman's Hand, 1st ed., pp. 205–6.
(884a)
By a Woman's Hand, 2nd ed., pp. 218–19.
(884b)
Detecting Women, 1st ed., p. 137. (877a)
Detecting Women 2, p. 182. (877b)
Detecting Women, 3rd ed., p. 266. (877c)
Web site: http://stopyourekillingme.com/
elizabeth-atwood-taylor.html
Taylor, H. Baldwin. *See* **Waugh, Hillary**
Taylor, Jean
Bio-bibliographic data:
Detecting Women 2, p. 182. (877b)
Detecting Women, 3rd ed., p. 267. (877c)
Web site: http://stopyourekillingme.com/
jean-taylor.html
Taylor, John M. *See* **Pidgin, Charles
Felton**
Taylor, Kathleen
Bio-bibliographic data:
Detecting Women, 3rd ed., p. 267. (877c)
Web site: http://stopyourckillingme.com/
kathleen-taylor.html; http://www.
basec.net/~ktaylor
Taylor, L. A.; i.e., Laurie Aylma
Bio-bibliographic data:

Detecting Women, 1st ed., p. 137. (877a)
Detecting Women 2, p. 182. (877b)
Detecting Women, 3rd ed., pp. 267–68.
    (877c)
Taylor, May
Bio-bibliographic data:
Australian Crime Fiction, p. 223. (207)
Taylor, Philip Neville Walker. *See*
    Walker-Taylor, Philip Neville
Taylor, Phoebe Atwood
Bio-bibliographic data:
Corpus Delicti of Mystery Fiction, pp.
    122–24. (879)
Critical Survey of Mystery and Detective
    Fiction, pp. 1567–72. (41)
Detecting Women, 1st ed., pp. 137–38,
    139. (877a)
Detecting Women 2, pp. 182–83, 185.
    (877b)
Encyclopedia Mysteriosa, p. 346. (2)
The Encyclopedia of Murder and Mystery,
    pp. 478–79. (6)
The Encyclopedia of Mystery and
    Detection, p. 380. (7)
Great Women Mystery Writers, pp.
    329–32. (880)
The Oxford Companion to Crime and
    Mystery Writing, p. 445. (4)
St. James Guide to Crime & Mystery
    Writers, 4th ed., pp. 972–74. (882d)
Twentieth-Century Crime and Mystery
    Writers, 1st ed., pp. 1371–73. (882a)
Twentieth-Century Crime and Mystery
    Writers, 2nd ed., pp. 836–38. (882b)
Twentieth-Century Crime and Mystery
    Writers, 3rd ed., pp. 1004–6. (882c)
Whodunit? A Who's Who in Crime and
    Mystery Writing, p. 191. (5)
Personal papers in Mugar Memorial
    Library, Boston University.
Web site: http://stopyourekillingme.com/
    phoebe-atwood-taylor.html
Taylor, Tom. *See* **Bullivant, Cecil Henry**
Taylor, "Toso"; i.e., Rev. Thomas
    Hilhouse
Bio-bibliographic data:
Australian Crime Fiction, p. 223. (207)
Taylor, Wendell Hertig
Bio-bibliographic data:
Encyclopedia Mysteriosa, p. 346. (2)
The Encyclopedia of Murder and Mystery,
    p. 479. (6)
The Encyclopedia of Mystery and
    Detection, p. 380. (7)

Taylor Gray, Elayne
Bio-bibliographic data:
Canadian Crime Fiction, p. 220. (209)
Teilhet, Darwin LeOra
Bio-bibliographic data:
Critical Survey of Mystery and Detective
    Fiction, pp. 1573–78. (41)
Tekahionwake. *See* **Johnson, E. Pauline**
Telenga, Suzette. *See* **Yorke, Susan**
Tell, Dorothy
Bio-bibliographic data:
Detecting Women 2, p. 183. (877b)
Detecting Women, 3rd ed., p. 268. (877c)
Temple, Lou Jane
Bio-bibliographic data:
Detecting Women, 3rd ed., p. 268. (877c)
Web site: http://stopyourekillingme.com/
    lou-jane-temple.html
Temple, Peter
Bio-bibliographic data:
The Mammoth Encyclopedia of Modern
    Crime Fiction, p. 460. (1)
Templeton, Charles B[radley].
Bio-bibliographic data:
Canadian Crime Fiction, p. 221. (209)
Templeton, George
Bio-bibliographic data:
Canadian Crime Fiction, p. 221. (209)
Templeton, Jesse. *See* **Goodchild, George**
Tench, C. V.
Bio-bibliographic data:
Canadian Crime Fiction, p. 221. (209)
Tepper, Sheri S. *See* **Oliphant, B. J.**
Terman, Douglas
Bio-bibliographic data:
Canadian Crime Fiction, p. 268. (209)
Terrall, Robert. *See* **Kyle, Robert**
Terry, Joe
Bio-bibliographic data:
Australian Crime Fiction, p. 223. (207)
Tesler, Nancy
Bio-bibliographic data:
Detecting Women, 3rd ed., pp. 268–69.
    (877c)
Web site: http://stopyourekillingme.com/
    nancy-tesler.html; http://www.
    nancytesler.com
Tessier, J. Rudel. *See* **Rudel-Tessier, J.**
Tessier, Vanna
Bio-bibliographic data:
Canadian Crime Fiction, p. 221. (209)
Tey, Josephine. *Pseud. for* **Elizabeth**
    MacKintosh
Bio-bibliographic data:

British Mystery Writers, 1920–1939, pp. 284–95. (867)
Corpus Delicti of Mystery Fiction, pp. 124–25. (879)
Critical Survey of Mystery and Detective Fiction, pp. 1579–83. (41)
Detecting Women, 1st ed., p. 138. (877a)
Detecting Women 2, p. 183. (877b)
Encyclopedia Mysteriosa, p. 347. (2)
The Encyclopedia of Murder and Mystery, p. 480. (6)
The Encyclopedia of Mystery and Detection, pp. 384–85. (7)
Great Women Mystery Writers, pp. 332–35. (880)
Mystery and Suspense Writers, pp. 911–21. (884.2)
100 Masters of Mystery and Detective Fiction, pp. 644–49. (37)
The Oxford Companion to Crime and Mystery Writing, pp. 450–51. (4)
St. James Guide to Crime & Mystery Writers, 4th ed., pp. 974–75. (882d)
10 Women of Mystery, pp. 40–76. (864, 865)
Twentieth-Century Crime and Mystery Writers, 1st ed., pp. 1373–76. (882a)
Twentieth-Century Crime and Mystery Writers, 2nd ed., pp. 838–39. (882b)
Twentieth-Century Crime and Mystery Writers, 3rd ed., pp. 1006–7. (882c)
Whodunit? A Who's Who in Crime and Mystery Writing, pp. 191–92. (5)
Women Authors of Detective Series, pp. 45–49. (882.5)
Women of Mystery, pp. 262–79. (874)
Web site: http://stopyourekillingme.com/josephine-tey.html

Thayer, [Emma Redington] Lee
Bio-bibliographic data:
Canadian Crime Fiction, p. 268. (209)
Encyclopedia Mysteriosa, p. 348. (2)
The Encyclopedia of Murder and Mystery, p. 481. (6)
The Encyclopedia of Mystery and Detection, p. 386. (7)
Twentieth-Century Crime and Mystery Writers, 1st ed., pp. 1376–79. (882a)
Twentieth-Century Crime and Mystery Writers, 2nd ed., pp. 839–41. (882b)
Twentieth-Century Crime and Mystery Writers, 3rd ed., pp. 1008–9. (882c)

Thayer, Tiffany [Ellsworth]
Bio-bibliographic data:

Canadian Crime Fiction, p. 285. (209)
Thériault, Claude
Bio-bibliographic data:
Canadian Crime Fiction, p. 221. (209)
Thériault, Yves
Bio-bibliographic data:
Canadian Crime Fiction, pp. 221–22. (209)
Thibault, André
Bio-bibliographic data:
Canadian Crime Fiction, p. 222. (209)
Thomas, Donald [Serrell]
Bio-bibliographic data:
Detecting Men, 1st ed., p. 230. (876)
The Mammoth Encyclopedia of Modern Crime Fiction, pp. 461–62. (1)
St. James Guide to Crime & Mystery Writers, 4th ed., pp. 925–26. (882d)
Twentieth-Century Crime and Mystery Writers, 1st ed., pp. 1309–10. (882a)
Twentieth-Century Crime and Mystery Writers, 2nd ed., p. 796. (882b)
Twentieth-Century Crime and Mystery Writers, 3rd ed., pp. 954–55. (882c)
Thomas, Paul
Bio-bibliographic data:
The Mammoth Encyclopedia of Modern Crime Fiction, p. 462. (1)
Thomas, Ross [Elmore]
Bio-bibliographic data:
Critical Survey of Mystery and Detective Fiction, pp. 1584–89. (41)
Encyclopedia Mysteriosa, pp. 349–50. (2)
The Encyclopedia of Murder and Mystery, pp. 483–84. (6)
The Encyclopedia of Mystery and Detection, pp. 386–87. (7)
The Mammoth Encyclopedia of Modern Crime Fiction, pp. 462–64. (1)
100 Masters of Mystery and Detective Fiction, pp. 650–56. (37)
St. James Guide to Crime & Mystery Writers, 4th ed., pp. 976–77. (882d)
Twentieth-Century Crime and Mystery Writers, 1st ed., pp. 1379–80. (882a)
Twentieth-Century Crime and Mystery Writers, 2nd ed., pp. 841–42. (882b)
Twentieth-Century Crime and Mystery Writers, 3rd ed., pp. 1009–10. (882c)
Web site: http://stopyourekillingme.com/ross-thomas.html
Thomas, Ted. *See* Kutscher, Teddy
Thomas-Graham, Pamela
Bio-bibliographic data:

Detecting Women, 3rd ed., p. 269. (877c)
Web site: http://stopyourekillingme.com/
pamela-thomas-graham.html
Thomes, William H[enry].
Bio-bibliographic data:
Australian Crime Fiction, p. 224. (207)
Thompson, Charles Kenneth
Bio-bibliographic data:
Australian Crime Fiction, p. 224. (207)
Thompson, David
Bio-bibliographic data:
Canadian Crime Fiction, pp. 222–23.
(209)
Thompson, Estelle [May]
Bio-bibliographic data:
Australian Crime Fiction, pp. 224–25.
(207)
Thompson, Jim; i.e., James Myers
Bio-bibliographic data:
American Hard-Boiled Crime Writers, pp.
310–28. (862)
The Big Book of Noir, pp. 177–82, 185.
(24)
*Critical Survey of Mystery and Detective
Fiction,* pp. 1590–95. (41)
Encyclopedia Mysteriosa, p. 350. (2)
The Encyclopedia of Murder and Mystery,
p. 484. (6)
*The Mammoth Encyclopedia of Modern
Crime Fiction,* pp. 464–65. (1)
*Murder off the Rack: Critical Studies of
Ten Paperback Masters,* pp. 35–54.
(869)
*100 Masters of Mystery and Detective
Fiction,* pp. 657–62. (37)
*The Oxford Companion to Crime and
Mystery Writing,* pp. 459–60. (4)
*St. James Guide to Crime & Mystery
Writers,* 4th ed., pp. 978–79. (882d)
*Twentieth-Century Crime and Mystery
Writers,* 2nd ed., pp. 842–43. (882b)
*Twentieth-Century Crime and Mystery
Writers,* 3rd ed., pp. 1010–12. (882c)
*Whodunit? A Who's Who in Crime and
Mystery Writing,* pp. 192–93. (5)
Web site: http://stopyourekillingme.com/
jim-thompson.html; http://geocities.
com/SoHo/Lofts6437/jim.htm;
http://www.miskatonic.org/rara-avis/
biblio/thompson.html
Thompson, Joyce
Bio-bibliographic data:
Detecting Women, 1st ed., pp. 138–39.
(877a)

Detecting Women 2, p. 184. (877b)
Thomson, Basil
Bio-bibliographic data:
*Twentieth-Century Crime and Mystery
Writers,* 1st ed., pp. 1381–82. (882a)
*Twentieth-Century Crime and Mystery
Writers,* 2nd ed., p. 844. (882b)
*Twentieth-Century Crime and Mystery
Writers,* 3rd ed., pp. 1012–13. (882c)
Thomson, David Landsborough
Bio-bibliographic data:
Canadian Crime Fiction, p. 54, 223. (209)
Thomson, June
Bio-bibliographic data:
By a Woman's Hand, 1st ed., p. 206.
(884a)
By a Woman's Hand, 2nd ed., p. 219.
(884b)
*The Craft of Crime: Conversations with
Crime Writers,* pp. 56–78. (872)
Detecting Women, 1st ed., p. 139. (877a)
Detecting Women 2, p. 184. (877b)
Detecting Women, 3rd ed., pp. 269–70.
(877c)
Encyclopedia Mysteriosa, pp. 350–51. (2)
The Encyclopedia of Murder and Mystery,
pp. 484–85. (6)
Great Women Mystery Writers, pp.
335–38. (880)
*The Mammoth Encyclopedia of Modern
Crime Fiction,* pp. 465–66. (1)
*St. James Guide to Crime & Mystery
Writers,* 4th ed., pp. 979–80. (882d)
*Twentieth-Century Crime and Mystery
Writers,* 1st ed., pp. 1382–84. (882a)
*Twentieth-Century Crime and Mystery
Writers,* 2nd ed., p. 845. (882b)
*Twentieth-Century Crime and Mystery
Writers,* 3rd ed., pp. 1013–14. (882c)
Web site: http://stopyourekillingme.com/
june-thomson.html
Thomson, Maynard F.
Bio-bibliographic data:
Detecting Men, 1st ed., p. 244. (876)
Thornburg, Newton
Bio-bibliographic data:
*St. James Guide to Crime & Mystery
Writers,* 4th ed., pp. 980–81. (882d)
*Twentieth-Century Crime and Mystery
Writers,* 3rd ed., pp. 1014–15. (882c)
Thrasher, L. L. *Pseud. for* Linda Baty
Bio-bibliographic data:
Detecting Women, 3rd ed., p. 270. (877c)

Web site: http://stopyourekillingme.com/
l-l-thrasher.html

Thurley, Norgrove. *Pseud. for* **Charles Thurley Stoneham**
Bio-bibliographic data:
Canadian Crime Fiction, p. 267, 268. (209)

Thurlo, Aimée, and David Thurlo
Bio-bibliographic data:
Detecting Women 2, p. 184. (877b)
Detecting Women, 3rd ed., p. 270. (877c)
Web site: http://www.comet.net/writersm/
thurlo.htm; http://stopyourekillingme.
com/aimee-thurlo.html; http://www.
aimeeanddavidthurlo.com

Thurlo, David. *See* **Thurlo, Aimée, and David Thurlo**

Thurston, Robert
Bio-bibliographic data:
Detecting Men, 1st ed., p. 244. (876)
Web site: http://stopyourekillingme.com/
robert-thurston.html

Thynne, Robert
Bio-bibliographic data:
Australian Crime Fiction, p. 228. (207)

Tidyman, Ernest
Bio-bibliographic data:
Encyclopedia Mysteriosa, p. 352. (2)
The Mammoth Encyclopedia of Modern Crime Fiction, pp. 466–67. (1)
Twentieth-Century Crime and Mystery Writers, 1st ed., pp. 1384–85. (882a)
Twentieth-Century Crime and Mystery Writers, 2nd ed., pp. 845–46. (882b)
Twentieth-Century Crime and Mystery Writers, 3rd ed., p. 1015. (882c)

Tierney, Ronald
Bio-bibliographic data:
Detecting Men, 1st ed., pp. 244–45. (876)

Tillet, Dorothy Stockbridge. *See* **Strange, John Stephen**

Tillray, Les. *See* **Gardner, Erle Stanley**

Tilton, Alice. *See* **Taylor, Phoebe Atwood**

Timlin, Mark
Bio-bibliographic data:
Detecting Men, 1st ed., p. 245. (876)
The Mammoth Encyclopedia of Modern Crime Fiction, pp. 467–68. (1)
Web site: http://www.nicksharman.co.uk;
http://stopyourekillingme.com/
mark-timlin.html; http://www.users.
totalise.co.uk/~slider

Timms, Kathleen
Bio-bibliographic data:

Canadian Crime Fiction, p. 223. (209)

Tirbutt, Honoria. *See* **Page, Emma**

Tishy, Cecilia. *Pseud. for* **Cecilia Tichi**
Bio-bibliographic data:
Detecting Women, 3rd ed., p. 271. (877c)
Web site: http://stopyourekillingme.com/
cecilia-tishy.html; http://www.
tishy.com

Todd, Charles: joint pseud. of Caroline and Charles, last name not revealed
Bio-bibliographic data:
The Mammoth Encyclopedia of Modern Crime Fiction, pp. 468–69. (1)
Web site: http://www.charlestodd.com;
http://stopyourekillingme.com/
charles-todd.html

Todd, Janice
Bio-bibliographic data:
Australian Crime Fiction, p. 228. (207)

Todd, Marilyn
Bio-bibliographic data:
Detecting Women, 3rd ed., p. 271. (877c)
The Mammoth Encyclopedia of Modern Crime Fiction, p. 469. (1)
Web site: http://stopyourekillingme.com/
marilyn-todd.html

Todd, Robert Henry
Bio-bibliographic data:
Canadian Crime Fiction, p. 223. (209)

Togawa, Masako
Bio-bibliographic data:
Great Women Mystery Writers, pp. 338–40. (880)
The Mammoth Encyclopedia of Modern Crime Fiction, pp. 469–70. (1)
St. James Guide to Crime & Mystery Writers, 4th ed., pp. 981–82. (882d)
Twentieth-Century Crime and Mystery Writers, 3rd ed., pp. 1138–39. (882c)

Tolley, Michael J.
Bio-bibliographic data:
Australian Crime Fiction, p. 228. (207)

Tone, Teona
Bio-bibliographic data:
Detecting Women 2, p. 185. (877b)
Detecting Women, 3rd ed., p. 271. (877c)

Toole, D. H.; i.e., David H.
Bio-bibliographic data:
Canadian Crime Fiction, p. 223. (209)

Toombs, Jane Jenke
Bio-bibliographic data:
Canadian Crime Fiction, p. 268. (209)

Tope, Rebecca. *Pseud. for* **Rebecca Smith**
Bio-bibliographic data:

*The Mammoth Encyclopedia of Modern
Crime Fiction*, p. 470. (1)
Web site: www.rebeccatope.com
Topor, Tom
Bio-bibliographic data:
Detecting Men, 1st ed., p. 245. (876)
Torday, Ursula. *See* **Blackstock, Charity**
Torgerson, Edwin Dial
Bio-bibliographic data:
Canadian Crime Fiction, p. 268. (209)
Torrie, Malcolm. *See* **Mitchell, Gladys**
Tourigny, François
Bio-bibliographic data:
Canadian Crime Fiction, p. 223. (209)
Tourney, Leonard
Bio-bibliographic data:
Detecting Men, 1st ed., p. 246. (876)
*St. James Guide to Crime & Mystery
Writers,* 4th ed., pp. 982–83. (882d)
Web site: http://stopyourekillingme.com/
leonard-tourney.html
Tovell, Ruth. *See* **Massey, Ruth**
Towne, Stuart. *See* **Rawson, Clayton**
Townend, Peter R.
Bio-bibliographic data:
Detecting Men, 1st ed., p. 246. (876)
Tracy, Louis
Bio-bibliographic data:
*The Encyclopedia of Mystery and
Detection,* p.392. (7)
Traill, Peter. *See* **Morton, Guy [Eugene]**
Train, Arthur C[heyney].
Bio-bibliographic data:
The Encyclopedia of Murder and Mystery,
p. 491. (6)
*The Encyclopedia of Mystery and
Detection,* pp. 392–93. (7)
*Twentieth-Century Crime and Mystery
Writers,* 1st ed., pp. 1385–87. (882a)
*Twentieth-Century Crime and Mystery
Writers,* 2nd ed., pp. 846–47. (882b)
*Twentieth-Century Crime and Mystery
Writers,* 3rd ed., pp. 1016–17. (882c)
Trainor, J. F.; i.e., Joseph F.
Bio-bibliographic data:
Detecting Men, 1st ed., p. 246. (876)
Web site: http://stopyourekillingme.com/
j-f-trainor.html
Trait, E. J.
Bio-bibliographic data:
Australian Crime Fiction, p. 229. (207)
Travis, Elizabeth
Bio-bibliographic data:

By a Woman's Hand, 1st ed., p. 207.
(884a)
Detecting Women 2, p. 185. (877b)
Detecting Women, 3rd ed., p. 272. (877c)
Treat, Lawrence. *Pseud. for* **Lawrence
Arthur Goldstone**
Bio-bibliographic data:
*Critical Survey of Mystery and Detective
Fiction,* pp. 1596–1601. (41)
Encyclopedia Mysteriosa, p. 356. (2)
The Encyclopedia of Murder and Mystery,
p. 493. (6)
*100 Masters of Mystery and Detective
Fiction,* pp. 663–69. (37)
*The Oxford Companion to Crime and
Mystery Writing,* pp. 468–69. (4)
*St. James Guide to Crime & Mystery
Writers,* 4th ed., pp. 983–85. (882d)
*Twentieth-Century Crime and Mystery
Writers,* 1st ed., pp. 1387–90. (882a)
*Twentieth-Century Crime and Mystery
Writers,* 2nd ed., pp. 847–50. (882b)
*Twentieth-Century Crime and Mystery
Writers,* 3rd ed., pp. 1017–20. (882c)
Treble, Donald
Bio-bibliographic data:
Australian Crime Fiction, p. 229. (207)
Trecker, Janice Law. *See* **Law, Janice**
Tremayne, Peter. *Pseud. for* **Peter [John
Philip] Berresford Ellis**
Bio-bibliographic data:
Detecting Men, 1st ed., p. 247. (876)
*The Mammoth Encyclopedia of Modern
Crime Fiction,* p. 471. (1)
Web site: http://www.sisterfidelma.com;
http://stopyourekillingme.com/
peter-tremayne.html
Tremblay, Carole
Bio-bibliographic data:
Canadian Crime Fiction, p. 224. (209)
Trench, John
Bio-bibliographic data:
Detecting Men, 1st ed., p. 247. (876)
*Twentieth-Century Crime and Mystery
Writers,* 1st ed., p. 1391. (882a)
*Twentieth-Century Crime and Mystery
Writers,* 2nd ed., pp. 850–51. (882b)
*Twentieth-Century Crime and Mystery
Writers,* 3rd ed., p. 1020. (882c)
*St. James Guide to Crime & Mystery
Writers,* 4th ed., pp. 985–86. (882d)
Trenhaile, John
Bio-bibliographic data:
Detecting Men, 1st ed., p. 247. (876)

St. James Guide to Crime & Mystery Writers, 4th ed., p. 986. (882d)
Twentieth-Century Crime and Mystery Writers, 3rd ed., pp. 1020–21. (882c)
Trent, Martha
Bio-bibliographic data:
Canadian Crime Fiction, p. 268. (209)
Trevanian. *Pseud. for* **Rodney H. Whitaker**
Bio-bibliographic data:
Canadian Crime Fiction, p. 224, 231. (209)
Encyclopedia Mysteriosa, p. 357. (2)
St. James Guide to Crime & Mystery Writers, 4th ed., pp. 987–88. (882d)
Twentieth-Century Crime and Mystery Writers, 1st ed., p. 1392. (882a)
Twentieth-Century Crime and Mystery Writers, 2nd ed., pp. 851–52. (882b)
Twentieth-Century Crime and Mystery Writers, 3rd ed., pp. 1021–22. (882c)
Web site: http://stopyourekillingme.com/trevanian.html
Trevor, Elleston; born Trevor Dudley-Smith, name changed to Elleston Trevor
Bio-bibliographic data:
Critical Survey of Mystery and Detective Fiction, pp. 1602–8. (41)
Encyclopedia Mysteriosa, pp. 146–47. (2)
The Encyclopedia of Murder and Mystery, p. 227. (6)
The Encyclopedia of Mystery and Detection, pp. 180–81. (7)
St. James Guide to Crime & Mystery Writers, 4th ed., pp. 469–72. (882d)
Twentieth-Century Crime and Mystery Writers, 1st ed., pp. 1393–96. (882a)
Twentieth-Century Crime and Mystery Writers, 2nd ed., pp. 852–54. (882b)
Twentieth-Century Crime and Mystery Writers, 3rd ed., pp. 486–88. (882c)
Personal papers in Mugar Memorial Library, Boston University.
Web site: http://www.quiller.net
Trevor, Glen. *Pseud. for* **James Hilton**
Bio-bibliographic data:
Twentieth-Century Crime and Mystery Writers, 1st ed., pp. 1396–98. (882a)
Treynor, Albert M.
Bio-bibliographic data:
Canadian Crime Fiction, p. 224. (209)

Trimble, Jacquelyn Whitney. *See* **Whitney, J. L. H.**
Tripp, Miles Barton
Bio-bibliographic data:
Detecting Men, 1st ed., p. 44, 248. (876)
The Encyclopedia of Murder and Mystery, p. 62. (6)
The Mammoth Encyclopedia of Modern Crime Fiction, pp. 472–73. (1)
St. James Guide to Crime & Mystery Writers, 4th ed., pp. 988–89. (882d)
Twentieth-Century Crime and Mystery Writers, 1st ed., pp. 1398–1400. (882a)
Twentieth-Century Crime and Mystery Writers, 2nd ed., pp. 854–55. (882b)
Twentieth-Century Crime and Mystery Writers, 3rd ed., pp. 1022–23. (882c)
Trocheck, Kathy Hogan
Bio-bibliographic data:
By a Woman's Hand, 1st ed., pp. 207–8. (884a)
By a Woman's Hand, 2nd ed., pp. 219–20. (884b)
Detecting Women, 1st ed., p. 140. (877a)
Detecting Women 2, p. 186. (877b)
Detecting Women, 3rd ed., p. 272. (877c)
Web site: http://stopyourekillingme.com/kathy-hogan-trocheck.html; http://www.kathytrocheck.com
Trow, M.J.; i.e., Meirion James
Bio-bibliographic data:
Detecting Men, 1st ed., pp. 248–49. (876)
The Mammoth Encyclopedia of Modern Crime Fiction, p. 473. (1)
Web site: http://stopyourekillingme.com/m-j-trow.html
Troy, Amanda. *See* **Kahnykevych, Tania Maria**
Trudeau, Hélène
Bio-bibliographic data:
Canadian Crime Fiction, p. 224. (209)
Trudel, Jacques
Bio-bibliographic data:
Canadian Crime Fiction, p. 224. (209)
Truffaut, François
Bio-bibliographic data:
The Encyclopedia of Murder and Mystery, p. 495. (6)
Trujillo Muñoz, Gabriel
Bio-bibliographic data:
Latin American Mystery Writers: An A to Z Guide. (881)

Truman, Margaret
Bio-bibliographic data:
By a Woman's Hand, 1st ed., pp. 208–9.
(884a)
By a Woman's Hand, 2nd ed., pp. 220–21.
(884b)
Detecting Women, 1st ed., p. 140. (877a)
Detecting Women 2, p. 186. (877b)
Detecting Women, 3rd ed., pp. 272–73.
(877c)
Great Women Mystery Writers, pp.
340–41. (880)
Web site: http://stopyourekillingme.com/
margaret-truman.html
Tucker, Allan James. *See* **James, Bill**
Tucker, James. *See* **James, Bill**
Tucker, Kerry
Bio-bibliographic data:
By a Woman's Hand, 1st ed., p. 209.
(884a)
By a Woman's Hand, 2nd ed., p. 221.
(884b)
Detecting Women, 1st ed., p. 140. (877a)
Detecting Women 2, p. 186. (877b)
Detecting Women, 3rd ed., p. 273. (877c)
Web site: http://stopyourekillingme.com/
kerry-tucker.html
Tucker, Wilson
Web site: http://www.printstations.
com/WTucker.htm
Turcotte, Diane
Bio-bibliographic data:
Canadian Crime Fiction, p. 224. (209)
Turgeon, Pierre
Bio-bibliographic data:
Canadian Crime Fiction, p. 224. (209)
Turnbull, Dora Amy Elles Dillon. *See*
Wentworth, Patricia
Turnbull, Peter
Bio-bibliographic data:
Detecting Men, 1st ed., p. 249. (876)
Encyclopedia Mysteriosa, p. 358. (2)
*The Mammoth Encyclopedia of Modern
Crime Fiction,* p. 474. (1)
*St. James Guide to Crime & Mystery
Writers,* 4th ed., pp. 989–90. (882d)
*Twentieth-Century Crime and Mystery
Writers,* 3rd ed., pp. 1023–24. (882c)
Web site: http://stopyourekillingme.com/
peter-turnbull.html
Turner, Anthony
Bio-bibliographic data:
Australian Crime Fiction, p. 229. (207)

Turner, D. Harold; i.e., David
Bio-bibliographic data:
Canadian Crime Fiction, pp. 224–25.
(209)
Turner, Ethel
Bio-bibliographic data:
Australian Crime Fiction, p. 183. (207)
Turow, Scott
Bio-bibliographic data:
*The Mammoth Encyclopedia of Modern
Crime Fiction,* p. 475. (1)
*St. James Guide to Crime & Mystery
Writers,* 4th ed., pp. 990–92. (882d)
*Twentieth-Century Crime and Mystery
Writers,* 3rd ed., pp. 1024–26. (882c)
*Whodunit? A Who's Who in Crime and
Mystery Writing,* p. 195. (5)
Web site: http://www.scottturow.com;
http://stopyourekillingme.com/
scott-turow.html
Twain, Mark: *See* **Clemens, Samuel
Langhorne**
Tweedsmuir, First Baron. *See* **Buchan,
John**
Twohy, Robert
Bio-bibliographic data:
*Twentieth-Century Crime and Mystery
Writers,* 2nd ed., pp. 855–56. (882b)
*Twentieth-Century Crime and Mystery
Writers,* 3rd ed., pp. 1026–27. (882c)
Tyre, Nedra
Bio-bibliographic data:
*The Encyclopedia of Mystery and
Detection,* p. 394. (7)
*Twentieth-Century Crime and Mystery
Writers,* 1st ed., pp. 1400–1403.
(882a)
*Twentieth-Century Crime and Mystery
Writers,* 2nd ed., pp. 856–58. (882b)
*Twentieth-Century Crime and Mystery
Writers,* 3rd ed., pp. 1028–29. (882c)
Tyre, Peg
Bio-bibliographic data:
Detecting Women, 1st ed., p. 141. (877a)
Detecting Women 2, p. 186. (877b)
Detecting Women, 3rd ed., p. 273. (877c)

U
Uhnak, Dorothy
Bio-bibliographic data:
*And Then There Were Nine . . . More
Women of Mystery,* pp. 80–99. (863)
By a Woman's Hand, 2nd ed., pp. 222–23.
(884a)

By a Woman's Hand, 1st ed., pp. 210–11.
(884b)
Detecting Women, 1st ed., p. 141. (877a)
Detecting Women 2, p. 187. (877b)
Detecting Women, 3rd ed., p. 274. (877c)
Encyclopedia Mysteriosa, p. 359. (2)
The Encyclopedia of Murder and Mystery,
p. 499. (6)
*The Encyclopedia of Mystery and
Detection,* p. 395. (7)
Great Women Mystery Writers, pp.
343–45. (880)
*The Mammoth Encyclopedia of Modern
Crime Fiction,* pp. 475–76. (1)
*St. James Guide to Crime & Mystery
Writers,* 4th ed., p. 993. (882d)
13 Mistresses of Murder, pp. 115–24.
(871)
*Twentieth-Century Crime and Mystery
Writers,* 1st ed., pp. 1403–4. (882a)
*Twentieth-Century Crime and Mystery
Writers,* 2nd ed., p. 858. (882b)
*Twentieth-Century Crime and Mystery
Writers,* 3rd ed., p. 1030. (882c)
Personal papers in Mugar Memorial
Library, Boston University.
Web site: http://www.stopyourekillingme.
com/dorothy-uhnak.html
Underwood, Michael. *Pseud. for* **John
Michael Evelyn**
Bio-bibliographic data:
Encyclopedia Mysteriosa, p. 359. (2)
The Encyclopedia of Murder and Mystery,
pp. 499–500. (6)
*The Mammoth Encyclopedia of Modern
Crime Fiction,* pp. 476–77. (1)
*St. James Guide to Crime & Mystery
Writers,* 4th ed., pp. 994–95. (882d)
*Twentieth-Century Crime and Mystery
Writers,* 1st ed., pp. 1404–6. (882a)
*Twentieth-Century Crime and Mystery
Writers,* 2nd ed., pp. 858–60. (882b)
*Twentieth-Century Crime and Mystery
Writers,* 3rd ed., pp. 1031–32. (882c)
Personal papers in Mugar Memorial
Library, Boston University.
Unruh, Daile
Bio-bibliographic data:
Canadian Crime Fiction, p. 225. (209)
Upfield, Arthur W[illiam].
Bio-bibliographic data:
Australian Crime Fiction, pp. 230–36.
(207)

Corpus Delicti of Mystery Fiction, pp.
125–26. (879)
*Critical Survey of Mystery and Detective
Fiction,* pp. 1616–21. (41)
Encyclopedia Mysteriosa, p. 360. (2)
The Encyclopedia of Murder and Mystery,
pp. 500–501. (6)
*The Encyclopedia of Mystery and
Detection,* p. 396. (7)
*The Oxford Companion to Crime and
Mystery Writing,* pp. 473–74. (4)
*St. James Guide to Crime & Mystery
Writers,* 4th ed., pp. 995–97. (882d)
*Twentieth-Century Crime and Mystery
Writers,* 1st ed., pp. 1406–9. (882a)
*Twentieth-Century Crime and Mystery
Writers,* 2nd ed., pp. 860–61. (882b)
*Twentieth-Century Crime and Mystery
Writers,* 3rd ed., pp. 1032–34. (882c)
*Whodunit? A Who's Who in Crime and
Mystery Writing,* p. 198. (5)
Web site: http://www.stopyourekillingme.
com/arthur-upfield.html
Upton, Robert
Bio-bibliographic data:
The Encyclopedia of Murder and Mystery,
p. 501. (6)
Urbanel, Robert
Bio-bibliographic data:
Canadian Crime Fiction, p. 225. (209)
Urbanyi, Pablo
Bio-bibliographic data:
Canadian Crime Fiction, p. 225. (209)
*Latin American Mystery Writers: An A to
Z Guide. (881)*

V

Vac, Bertrand. *Pseud. for* **Aimé Pelletier**
Bio-bibliographic data:
Canadian Crime Fiction, p. 167, 225.
(209)
Vachell, Horace Annesley
Bio-bibliographic data:
*The Encyclopedia of Mystery and
Detection,* p. 396. (7)
Vachss, Andrew [Henry]
Bio-bibliographic data:
Canadian Crime Fiction, p. 285. (209)
Detecting Men, 1st ed., p. 249. (876)
Encyclopedia Mysteriosa, p. 361. (2)
The Encyclopedia of Murder and Mystery,
p. 503. (6)
*The Mammoth Encyclopedia of Modern
Crime Fiction,* p. 478. (1)

St. James Guide to Crime & Mystery Writers, 4th ed., pp. 999–1000. (882d)
Talking Murder, pp. 240–57. (883)
Twentieth-Century Crime and Mystery Writers, 3rd ed., pp. 1035–36. (882c)
Web site: http://www.vachss.com; http://www.stopyourekillingme.com/andrew-vachss.html

Vaczek, Louis Charles
Bio-bibliographic data:
Canadian Crime Fiction, p. 255, 268, 278, 285. (209)

Vaillancourt, Madeleine
Bio-bibliographic data:
Canadian Crime Fiction, p. 225. (209)

Valcour, Gary F.
Bio-bibliographic data:
Canadian Crime Fiction, p. 225. (209)

Valdez, Paul: house pseud., possibly used exclusively by Carter Brown (q.v.)
Bio-bibliographic data:
Australian Crime Fiction, pp. 237–38. (207)

Valentine, Deborah
Bio-bibliographic data:
By a Woman's Hand, 1st ed., pp. 212–13. (884a)
Detecting Women, 1st ed., p. 141. (877a)
Detecting Women 2, p. 187. (877b)
Detecting Women, 3rd ed., p. 274. (877c)

Valentine, Jo. See Armstrong, Charlotte

Valin, Jonathan [Louis]
Bio-bibliographic data:
Critical Survey of Mystery and Detective Fiction, pp. 1622–27. (41)
Detecting Men, 1st ed., p. 250. (876)
Encyclopedia Mysteriosa, p. 361. (2)
The Encyclopedia of Murder and Mystery, p. 503. (6)
The Mammoth Encyclopedia of Modern Crime Fiction, p. 479. (1)
St. James Guide to Crime & Mystery Writers, 4th ed., pp. 1000–1001. (882d)
Twentieth-Century Crime and Mystery Writers, 2nd ed., pp. 861–62. (882b)
Twentieth-Century Crime and Mystery Writers, 3rd ed., pp. 1036–37. (882c)
Web site: http://www.stopyourekillingme.com/jonathan-valin.html

Vallée, Brian
Bio-bibliographic data:
Canadian Crime Fiction, pp. 225–26. (209)

Vallings, Gabrielle [Francesca Lillian May]
Bio-bibliographic data:
Australian Crime Fiction, p. 238. (207)

Vanardy, Varick. See Dey, Frederic Van Rensselaer

Van Belkom, Edo
Bio-bibliographic data:
Canadian Crime Fiction, p. 226. (209)

Vance, Jack. See Vance, John Holbrook

Vance, John Holbrook
Bio-bibliographic data:
Detecting Men, 1st ed., p. 251. (876)
The Encyclopedia of Mystery and Detection, p. 398. (7)
St. James Guide to Crime & Mystery Writers, 4th ed., pp. 1001–3. (882d)
Twentieth-Century Crime and Mystery Writers, 1st ed., pp. 1409–12. (882a)
Twentieth-Century Crime and Mystery Writers, 2nd ed., pp. 862–64. (882b)
Twentieth-Century Crime and Mystery Writers, 3rd ed., pp. 1037–38. (882c)
Personal papers in Mugar Memorial Library, Boston University.

Vance, Louis Joseph
Bio-bibliographic data:
Encyclopedia Mysteriosa, p. 362. (2)
The Encyclopedia of Mystery and Detection, pp. 398–99. (7)
St. James Guide to Crime & Mystery Writers, 4th ed., pp. 1003–4. (882d)
Twentieth-Century Crime and Mystery Writers, 1st ed., pp. 1412–13. (882a)
Twentieth-Century Crime and Mystery Writers, 2nd ed., pp. 864–65. (882b)
Twentieth-Century Crime and Mystery Writers, 3rd ed., pp. 1038–39. (882c)

Vandercook, John W[omack].
Bio-bibliographic data:
Australian Crime Fiction, p. 238. (207)
The Encyclopedia of Mystery and Detection, p. 401. (7)

Van Deventer, Emma Murdock. See Lynch, Lawrence L.

Van de Water, Frederic F[ranklyn].
Bio-bibliographic data:
Canadian Crime Fiction, pp. 268–69, 285. (209)

van de Wetering, Janwillem; sometimes given as Jan Willem
Bio-bibliographic data:
The Craft of Crime: Conversations with Crime Writers, pp. 289–321. (872)

Critical Survey of Mystery and Detective Fiction, pp. 1628–33. (41)
Designs of Darkness, pp. 144–57. (873)
Detecting Men, 1st ed., p. 250. (876)
Encyclopedia Mysteriosa, p. 363. (2)
The Encyclopedia of Murder and Mystery, pp. 505–6. (6)
The Mammoth Encyclopedia of Modern Crime Fiction, pp. 479–81. (1)
The Oxford Companion to Crime and Mystery Writing, pp. 476–77. (4)
St. James Guide to Crime & Mystery Writers, 4th ed., pp. 1004–6. (882d)
Twentieth-Century Crime and Mystery Writers, 1st ed., p. 1551. (882a)
Twentieth-Century Crime and Mystery Writers, 2nd ed., pp. 865–66. (882b)
Twentieth-Century Crime and Mystery Writers, 3rd ed., pp. 1039–41. (882c)
Whodunit? A Who's Who in Crime and Mystery Writing, pp. 199–200. (5)
Web site:
    http://www.dpbooks.com/vandewet.
    htm; http://www.stopyourekillingme.
    com/janwillem-van-de-wetering.html
Van Dine, S. S. *Pseud. for* **Willard Huntington Wright**
Bio-bibliographic data:
Corpus Delicti of Mystery Fiction, pp. 126–8. (879)
Critical Survey of Mystery and Detective Fiction, pp. 1634–40. (41)
Encyclopedia Mysteriosa, pp. 363–64. (2)
The Encyclopedia of Murder and Mystery, pp. 506–7. (6)
The Encyclopedia of Mystery and Detection, pp. 401–2. (7)
Mystery and Suspense Writers, pp. 923–32. (884.2)
100 Masters of Mystery and Detective Fiction, pp. 670–76. (37)
The Oxford Companion to Crime and Mystery Writing, p. 477. (4)
St. James Guide to Crime & Mystery Writers, 4th ed., pp. 1006–7. (882d)
Twentieth-Century Crime and Mystery Writers, 1st ed., pp. 1414–16. (882a)
Twentieth-Century Crime and Mystery Writers, 2nd ed., pp. 866–68. (882b)
Twentieth-Century Crime and Mystery Writers, 3rd ed., pp. 1041–42. (882c)
Whodunit? A Who's Who in Crime and Mystery Writing, p. 200. (5)

Personal papers in Princeton University Library, New Jersey.
Web site: http://www.stopyourekillingme.
    com/s-s-van-dine.html
Van Druten, John [William]
Bio-bibliographic data:
Canadian Crime Fiction, p. 285. (209)
Van Gieson, Judith
Bio-bibliographic data:
By a Woman's Hand, 1st ed., p. 213. (884a)
By a Woman's Hand, 2nd ed., pp. 224–25. (884b)
Detecting Women, 1st ed., p. 141. (877a)
Detecting Women 2, p. 187. (877b)
Detecting Women, 3rd ed., pp. 274–75. (877c)
St. James Guide to Crime & Mystery Writers, 4th ed., pp. 1007–8. (882d)
Web site: http://www.stopyourekillingme.
    com/judith-van-gieson.html; http://
    www.judithvangieson.com
van Greenaway, Peter
Bio-bibliographic data:
St. James Guide to Crime & Mystery Writers, 4th ed., pp. 1008–9. (882d)
Twentieth-Century Crime and Mystery Writers, 2nd ed., p. 868. (882b)
Twentieth-Century Crime and Mystery Writers, 3rd ed., p. 1043. (882c)
van Gulik, Robert H[ans].
Bio-bibliographic data:
Corpus Delicti of Mystery Fiction, pp. 76–77. (879)
Critical Survey of Mystery and Detective Fiction, pp. 1641–47. (41)
Encyclopedia Mysteriosa, p. 364. (2)
The Encyclopedia of Murder and Mystery, pp. 507–8. (6)
The Encyclopedia of Mystery and Detection, pp. 402–3. (7)
The Mammoth Encyclopedia of Modern Crime Fiction, pp. 481–82. (1)
Mystery and Suspense Writers, pp. 933–41. (884.2)
100 Masters of Mystery and Detective Fiction, pp. 677–83. (37)
The Oxford Companion to Crime and Mystery Writing, p. 478. (4)
St. James Guide to Crime & Mystery Writers, 4th ed., pp. 1009–10. (882d)
Twentieth-Century Crime and Mystery Writers, 1st ed., pp. 1552–53. (882a)

Twentieth-Century Crime and Mystery Writers, 2nd ed., p. 947. (882b)
Twentieth-Century Crime and Mystery Writers, 3rd ed., pp. 1139–40. (882c)
Whodunit? A Who's Who in Crime and Mystery Writing, p. 201. (5)
Web site: http://www.stopyourekillingme.com/robert-van-gulik.html

Van Hook, Beverly
Bio-bibliographic data:
Detecting Women, 3rd ed., p. 275. (877c)

Vanier-Bellemare, Pauline
Bio-bibliographic data:
Canadian Crime Fiction, p. 226. (209)

van Rjndt, Philippe
Bio-bibliographic data:
Canadian Crime Fiction, p. 149, 226. (209)

Van Til, Reinder. *See* **Evers, Crabbe**

Varela, Luis V.
Bio-bibliographic data:
Latin American Mystery Writers: An A to Z Guide. (881)

Vargas Llosa, Mario
Bio-bibliographic data:
The Encyclopedia of Murder and Mystery, p. 508. (6)

Vassilikos, Vassilis
Bio-bibliographic data:
The Encyclopedia of Murder and Mystery, p. 508. (6)

Vaubert, Michelle de. *Pseud. for* **Odette Oligny**
Bio-bibliographic data:
Canadian Crime Fiction, p. 226. (209)

Vázquez Montalbán, Manuel
Bio-bibliographic data:
The Encyclopedia of Murder and Mystery, pp. 508–9. (6)

Vedder, John K. *See* **Gruber, Frank**

Veitch, Anthony Scott
Bio-bibliographic data:
Australian Crime Fiction, p. 238. (207)

Venables, Terry. *See* **Yuill, P. B.**

Venning, Michael. *See* **Rice, Craig**

Vergara, René
Bio-bibliographic data:
Latin American Mystery Writers: An A to Z Guide. (881)

Verkoczy, Elizabeth
Bio-bibliographic data:
Canadian Crime Fiction, p. 226. (209)

Vermandel, Janet Gregory
Bio-bibliographic data:

Canadian Crime Fiction, p. 226. (209)

Vernal, François de
Bio-bibliographic data:
Canadian Crime Fiction, p. 226. (209)

Verne, Jules
Bio-bibliographic data:
Canadian Crime Fiction, p. 269. (209)

Verner, Gerald. *Pseud. for* **Donald William Steward (?)**
Bio-bibliographic data:
Twentieth-Century Crime and Mystery Writers, 3rd ed., pp. 1044–46. (882c)

Vernon, Henry
Bio-bibliographic data:
Canadian Crime Fiction, p. 269. (209)

Verral, Charles Spain
Bio-bibliographic data:
Canadian Crime Fiction, p. 226. (209)

Vertolli, Lou
Bio-bibliographic data:
Canadian Crime Fiction, p. 227. (209)

Vickers, Roy C.
Bio-bibliographic data:
British Mystery Writers, 1920–1939, pp. 296–301. (867)
Encyclopedia Mysteriosa, p. 365. (2)
The Encyclopedia of Mystery and Detection, p. 403. (7)
St. James Guide to Crime & Mystery Writers, 4th ed., pp. 1011–12. (882d)
Twentieth-Century Crime and Mystery Writers, 1st ed., pp. 1417–19. (882a)
Twentieth-Century Crime and Mystery Writers, 2nd ed., pp. 868–70. (882b)
Twentieth-Century Crime and Mystery Writers, 3rd ed., pp. 1047–48. (882c)

Victor, Leslie
Bio-bibliographic data:
Australian Crime Fiction, p. 183. (207)

Victor, Mrs. Metta Victoria Fuller. *See* **Regester, Seeley**

Vidal, Gore. *See* **Box, Edgar**

Vidocq, Eugène François
Bio-bibliographic data:
Critical Survey of Mystery and Detective Fiction, pp. 1648–53. (41)
The Encyclopedia of Murder and Mystery, p. 509. (6)
The Encyclopedia of Mystery and Detection, p. 403. (7)
The Oxford Companion to Crime and Mystery Writing, p. 479. (4)
Whodunit? A Who's Who in Crime and Mystery Writing, p. 202. (5)

Viets, Elaine
Bio-bibliographic data:
Detecting Women, 3rd ed., p. 275. (877c)
Web site: http://www.stopyourekillingme.
com/elaine-viets.html; http://www.
elaineviets.com
Villemain, Charles
Bio-bibliographic data:
Canadian Crime Fiction, p. 227. (209)
Villemaire, Yolande
Bio-bibliographic data:
Canadian Crime Fiction, p. 227. (209)
Villon, Christiane
Bio-bibliographic data:
Canadian Crime Fiction, p. 227. (209)
Vincent, Lawrence M.
Bio-bibliographic data:
Detecting Men, 1st ed., p. 251. (876)
Vincent, Pauline
Bio-bibliographic data:
Canadian Crime Fiction, p. 227. (209)
Vine, Barbara. *See* **Rendell, Ruth**
Vipond, Don [Harry]
Bio-bibliographic data:
Canadian Crime Fiction, p. 269. (209)
Vlasopolos, Anca
Bio-bibliographic data:
Detecting Women, 1st ed., p. 142. (877a)
Detecting Women 2, p. 188. (877b)
Vogel, Harry B[enjamin].
Bio-bibliographic data:
Australian Crime Fiction, p. 238. (207)
Voltaire. *Pseud. for* **François-Marie Arouet**
Bio-bibliographic data:
Critical Survey of Mystery and Detective Fiction, pp. 1654–58. (41)
von Doderer, Heimito. *See* **Doderer, Heimito von**
von Droste-Hülshoff, Annette. *See* **Droste-Hülshoff, Annette von**
Voukirakis: unidentified pseud.
Bio-bibliographic data:
Canadian Crime Fiction, p. 227. (209)
Vulliamy, C. E.; i.e., Colwyn Edward
Bio-bibliographic data:
Critical Survey of Mystery and Detective Fiction, pp. 1659–64. (41)
The Encyclopedia of Mystery and Detection, pp. 403–4. (7)
Twentieth-Century Crime and Mystery Writers, 1st ed., pp. 1420–22. (882a)

W

W. W.; i.e., Waif Wander. *See* **Fortune, Mrs. Mary Helena**
Waddell, Martin
Bio-bibliographic data:
Detecting Men, 1st ed., p. 252. (876)
Wade, Alan. *See* **Vance, John Holbrook**
Wade, Henry. *Pseud. for* **Sir Henry Lancelot Aubrey-Fletcher, 6th Baronet**
Bio-bibliographic data:
British Mystery Writers, 1920–1939, pp. 302–7. (867)
Critical Survey of Mystery and Detective Fiction, pp. 1665–70. (41)
Encyclopedia Mysteriosa, p. 366. (2)
The Encyclopedia of Murder and Mystery, p. 511. (6)
The Encyclopedia of Mystery and Detection, pp. 405–6. (7)
The Oxford Companion to Crime and Mystery Writing, p. 489. (4)
St. James Guide to Crime & Mystery Writers, 4th ed., pp. 1013–14. (882d)
Twentieth-Century Crime and Mystery Writers, 1st ed., pp. 1422–1324. (882a)
Twentieth-Century Crime and Mystery Writers, 2nd ed., pp. 870–71. (882b)
Twentieth-Century Crime and Mystery Writers, 3rd ed., pp. 1049–50. (882c)
Whodunit? A Who's Who in Crime and Mystery Writing, p. 205. (5)
Wade, Robert. *See* **Miller, Wade**
Wade-Farrel, R.: apparently not the same person as John Wade Farrell, a pseud. of John D. MacDonald
Bio-bibliographic data:
Australian Crime Fiction, p. 239. (207)
Wahlöö, Per, and Maj Sjöwall
Bio-bibliographic data:
Critical Survey of Mystery and Detective Fiction, pp. 1495–1501. (41)
Detecting Women 2, p. 176. (877b)
Detecting Women, 3rd ed., p. 252. (877c)
Encyclopedia Mysteriosa, p. 332. (2)
The Encyclopedia of Murder and Mystery, p. 456. (6)
The Encyclopedia of Mystery and Detection, p. 406. (7)
The Mammoth Encyclopedia of Modern Crime Fiction, pp. 482–83. (1)
Mystery and Suspense Writers, pp. 853–68. (884.2)

100 Masters of Mystery and Detective Fiction, pp. 593–600. (37)

The Oxford Companion to Crime and Mystery Writing, pp. 416–17. (4)

St. James Guide to Crime & Mystery Writers, 4th ed., pp. 1014–15. (882d)

Twentieth-Century Crime and Mystery Writers, 1st ed., pp. 1553–54. (882a)

Twentieth-Century Crime and Mystery Writers, 2nd ed., pp. 947–48. (882b)

Twentieth-Century Crime and Mystery Writers, 3rd ed., p. 1140. (882c)

Whodunit? A Who's Who in Crime and Mystery Writing, p. 180. (5)

Web site: http://stopyourekillingme.com/per-wahloo.html

Waif Wander. *See* **Fortune, Mrs. Mary Helena**

Wain, Alan
Bio-bibliographic data:
Canadian Crime Fiction, p. 227. (209)

Wainer, Cord. *See* **Dewey, Thomas B.**

Wainewright, Thomas Griffiths
Bio-bibliographic data:
The Encyclopedia of Murder and Mystery, p. 511. (6)

Wainwright, John [William]
Bio-bibliographic data:
Detecting Men, 1st ed., p. 217, 252–53. (876)

Encyclopedia Mysteriosa, pp. 366–67. (2)

The Encyclopedia of Murder and Mystery, p. 511. (6)

The Mammoth Encyclopedia of Modern Crime Fiction, pp. 483–84. (1)

St. James Guide to Crime & Mystery Writers, 4th ed., pp. 1015–18. (882d)

Twentieth-Century Crime and Mystery Writers, 1st ed., pp. 1424–27. (882a)

Twentieth-Century Crime and Mystery Writers, 2nd ed., pp. 871–73. (882b)

Twentieth-Century Crime and Mystery Writers, 3rd ed., pp. 1050–52. (882c)

Wakefield, Hannah. *Pseud. for* **Sarah Burton and Judy Holland**
Bio-bibliographic data:
Detecting Women, 1st ed., p. 142. (877a)

Detecting Women 2, p. 188. (877b)

Detecting Women, 3rd ed., pp. 275–76. (877c)

Twentieth-Century Crime and Mystery Writers, 3rd ed., pp. 1052–53. (882c)

Walford, Frank
Bio-bibliographic data:

Australian Crime Fiction, pp. 239–40. (207)

Walker, Brenda
Bio-bibliographic data:
Australian Crime Fiction, p. 240. (207)

Walker, David [Harry]
Bio-bibliographic data:
Canadian Crime Fiction, pp. 227–28. (209)

Walker, David J.
Bio-bibliographic data:
Detecting Men, 1st ed., p. 253. (876)

Web site: http://stopyourekillingme.com/david-j-walker.html; http://members.aol.com/wfksoft/djwalker/mystery.htm

Walker, Harry. *See* **Waugh, Hillary**

Walker, Mary Willis
Bio-bibliographic data:
By a Woman's Hand, 2nd ed., pp. 226–27. (884b)

Detecting Women, 1st ed., p. 142. (877a)

Detecting Women 2, p. 188. (877b)

Detecting Women, 3rd ed., p. 276. (877c)

The Mammoth Encyclopedia of Modern Crime Fiction, p. 485. (1)

St. James Guide to Crime & Mystery Writers, 4th ed., pp. 1018–19. (882d)

Web site:
http://www.twbooks.co.uk/authors/mwwalker.html; http://stopyourekillingme.com/mary-willis.walker.html

Walker, Peter N.
Bio-bibliographic data:
Detecting Men, 1st ed., pp. 214–15, 253. (876)

The Mammoth Encyclopedia of Modern Crime Fiction, pp. 412–14. (1)

Web site: www.heartbeat.demon.co.uk; www.twbooks.co.uk/authors/nrhea.htm

Walker, Robert W.
Bio-bibliographic data:
Detecting Men, 1st ed., p. 254. (876)

Web site: http://stopyourekillingme.com/robert-w-walker.html

Walker, Rowland
Bio-bibliographic data:
Canadian Crime Fiction, p. 269. (209)

Walker, Thomas
Bio-bibliographic data:
Australian Crime Fiction, p. 240. (207)

Walker, William Silvester ("Coo-ee")
Bio-bibliographic data:
Australian Crime Fiction, p. 240. (207)
Walker-Taylor, Philip Neville
Bio-bibliographic data:
Australian Crime Fiction, pp. 240–41.
(207)
Wall, Robert [E.]
Bio-bibliographic data:
Canadian Crime Fiction, p. 286. (209)
Wallace, Clarke
Bio-bibliographic data:
Canadian Crime Fiction, p. 228. (209)
Wallace, [Richard Horatio] Edgar
Bio-bibliographic data:
Australian Crime Fiction, p. 241. (207)
British Mystery Writers, 1860–1919, pp.
290–302. (866)
Canadian Crime Fiction, p. 286. (209)
*Critical Survey of Mystery and Detective
Fiction,* pp. 1671–77. (41)
Encyclopedia Mysteriosa, p. 367. (2)
The Encyclopedia of Murder and Mystery,
pp. 512–513. (6)
*The Encyclopedia of Mystery and
Detection,* p. 406–411. (7)
Mystery and Suspense Writers, pp.
943–55. (884.2)
*100 Masters of Mystery and Detective
Fiction,* pp. 684–91. (37)
*The Oxford Companion to Crime and
Mystery Writing,* p. 489. (4)
*St. James Guide to Crime & Mystery
Writers,* 4th ed., pp. 1019–23. (882d)
*Twentieth-Century Crime and Mystery
Writers,* 1st ed., pp. 1428–35. (882a)
*Twentieth-Century Crime and Mystery
Writers,* 2nd ed., pp. 873–77. (882b)
*Twentieth-Century Crime and Mystery
Writers,* 3rd ed., pp. 1053–57. (882c)
*Whodunit? A Who's Who in Crime and
Mystery Writing,* pp. 205–6. (5)
Edgar Wallace Society
c/o Penny Wyrd
84 Ridgefield Rd
Oxford, OX4 3DA
United Kingdom
http://www.EdgarWallace.org
Wallace, John
Bio-bibliographic data:
Australian Crime Fiction, pp. 241–43.
(207)
Wallace, Marilyn
Bio-bibliographic data:

By a Woman's Hand, 1st ed., pp. 214–15.
(884a)
By a Woman's Hand, 2nd ed., p. 227.
(884b)
Detecting Women, 1st ed., p. 142. (877a)
Detecting Women 2, p. 188. (877b)
Detecting Women, 3rd ed., p. 276. (877c)
*The Mammoth Encyclopedia of Modern
Crime Fiction,* pp. 485–86. (1)
*St. James Guide to Crime & Mystery
Writers,* 4th ed., pp. 1023–24. (882d)
*Twentieth-Century Crime and Mystery
Writers,* 3rd ed., pp. 1057–58. (882c)
Web site: http://stopyourekillingme.com/
marilyn-wallace.html
Wallace, Patricia. *Pseud. for* **Patricia
Wallace Estrada**
Bio-bibliographic data:
Detecting Women, 1st ed., p. 143. (877a)
Detecting Women 2, pp. 188–89. (877b)
Detecting Women, 3rd ed., p. 277. (877c)
Wallace, Robert. *Pseud. for* **Robin
Wallace-Crabbe**
Bio-bibliographic data:
Australian Crime Fiction, p. 146, 243–44.
(207)
Detecting Men, 1st ed., p. 254. (876)
Wallace-Crabbe, Robin. *See* **Wallace,
Robert**
Walling, R. A. J.; i.e., Robert Alfred John
Bio-bibliographic data:
*The Encyclopedia of Mystery and
Detection,* p. 411. (7)
*Twentieth-Century Crime and Mystery
Writers,* 1st ed., pp. 1435–37. (882a)
Wallingford, Lee
Bio-bibliographic data:
Detecting Women, 1st ed., p. 143. (877a)
Detecting Women 2, p. 189. (877b)
Detecting Women, 3rd ed., p. 277. (877c)
Wallis, J. H.; i.e., James Harold
Bio-bibliographic data:
*The Encyclopedia of Mystery and
Detection,* p. 412. (7)
Walmsley, Tom; i.e., Thomas
Bio-bibliographic data:
Canadian Crime Fiction, p. 228. (209)
Walsh, J. M.; i.e., James Morgan
Bio-bibliographic data:
Australian Crime Fiction, p. 48, 244–46.
(207)
Walsh, Jill Paton. *See* **Paton Walsh, Jill**
Walsh, Rodolfo
Bio-bibliographic data:

Latin American Mystery Writers: An A to Z Guide. (881)

Walsh, Thomas [Francis Morgan]
Bio-bibliographic data:
Encyclopedia Mysteriosa, pp. 367–68. (2)
St. James Guide to Crime & Mystery Writers, 4th ed., p. 1024. (882d)
Twentieth-Century Crime and Mystery Writers, 1st ed., pp. 1437–40. (882a)
Twentieth-Century Crime and Mystery Writers, 2nd ed., pp. 877–79. (882b)
Twentieth-Century Crime and Mystery Writers, 3rd ed., pp. 1058–59. (882c)

Waltch, Lilla M.
Bio-bibliographic data:
Detecting Women 2, p. 189. (877b)
Detecting Women, 3rd ed., p. 277. (877c)

Walters, Linda. *See* **Rice, Linda, and Rice, Walter**

Walters, Minette [Caroline Mary Jebb]
Bio-bibliographic data:
By a Woman's Hand, 1st ed., pp. 215–16. (884a)
By a Woman's Hand, 2nd ed., pp. 227–28. (884b)
Deadly Women, pp. 195–98. (26.5)
The Mammoth Encyclopedia of Modern Crime Fiction, pp. 486–87. (1)
St. James Guide to Crime & Mystery Writers, 4th ed., pp. 1024–25. (882d)
Speaking of Murder, pp. 171–80. (875a)
Women of Mystery, pp. 400–405. (874)
Whodunit? A Who's Who in Crime and Mystery Writing, p. 206. (5)
Web site: http://stopyourekillingme.com/minette-walters.html

Walton, Francis. *See* **Flynt, Josiah**

Walworth, Bob
Bio-bibliographic data:
Canadian Crime Fiction, p. 269. (209)

Walz, Audrey. *See* **Bonnamy, Francis**

Wambaugh, Joseph
Bio-bibliographic data:
Critical Survey of Mystery and Detective Fiction, pp. 1678–82. (41)
The Encyclopedia of Murder and Mystery, p. 514. (6)
The Mammoth Encyclopedia of Modern Crime Fiction, pp. 487–88. (1)
100 Masters of Mystery and Detective Fiction, pp. 692–99. (37)
St. James Guide to Crime & Mystery Writers, 4th ed., pp. 1025–28. (882d)

Twentieth-Century Crime and Mystery Writers, 1st ed., pp. 1440–41. (882a)
Twentieth-Century Crime and Mystery Writers, 2nd ed., pp. 879–80. (882b)
Twentieth-Century Crime and Mystery Writers, 3rd ed., pp. 1059–61. (882c)
Web site: http://stopyourekillingme.com/joseph-wambaugh.html

Wander, Waif. *See* **Fortune, Mrs. Mary Helena**

Wanock, William
Bio-bibliographic data:
Australian Crime Fiction, p. 246. (207)

Ward, Arthur Henry Sarsfield. *See* **Rohmer, Sax**

Ward, Gergory
Bio-bibliographic data:
Canadian Crime Fiction, p. 228. (209)

Warga, Wayne
Bio-bibliographic data:
Detecting Men, 1st ed., p. 254. (876)

Warmbold, Jean
Bio-bibliographic data:
Detecting Women 2, p. 189. (877b)
Detecting Women, 3rd ed., p. 278. (877c)

Warne, Leona. *See* **Batt, Leon**

Warner, Mignon
Bio-bibliographic data:
Australian Crime Fiction, p. 246. (207)
Detecting Women, 1st ed., p. 143. (877a)
Detecting Women 2, p. 190. (877b)
Detecting Women, 3rd ed., p. 278. (877c)
Web site: http://stopyourekillingme.com/mignon-warner.html

Warner, Penny
Bio-bibliographic data:
Detecting Women, 3rd ed., pp. 278–79. (877c)
The Mammoth Encyclopedia of Modern Crime Fiction, pp. 488–89. (1)
Web site:
http://home.netcom.com/~tpwarner;
http://stopyourekillingme.com/penny-warner.html; http://www.pennywarner.com

Warren, Arnold
Bio-bibliographic data:
Canadian Crime Fiction, p. 228. (209)

Warren, Dianne
Bio-bibliographic data:
Canadian Crime Fiction, p. 228. (209)

Warriner, Thurman
Bio-bibliographic data:

Twentieth-Century Crime and Mystery Writers, 1st ed., pp. 1441–43. (882a)
Twentieth-Century Crime and Mystery Writers, 2nd ed., pp. 880–81. (882b)
Twentieth-Century Crime and Mystery Writers, 3rd ed., pp. 1061–62. (882c)
Washburn, L. J. *See* **Reasoner, James, and L. J. Washburn**
Washburn, Stan
Bio-bibliographic data:
Detecting Men, 1st ed., p. 255. (876)
Web site: http://stopyourekillingme.com/
stan-washburn.html
Wasserman, Jack
Bio-bibliographic data:
Canadian Crime Fiction, p. 180, 228.
(209)
Waten, Judah [Leon]
Bio-bibliographic data:
Australian Crime Fiction, p. 246. (207)
Waterhouse, Jane
Bio-bibliographic data:
Detecting Women, 3rd ed., p. 279. (877c)
Waters. *Pseud. for* **William Russell**
Bio-bibliographic data:
Encyclopedia Mysteriosa, pp. 368–69. (2)
The Encyclopedia of Murder and Mystery,
pp. 515–16. (6)
*The Encyclopedia of Mystery and
Detection*, p. 412. (7)
*St. James Guide to Crime & Mystery
Writers*, 4th ed., p. 1028. (882d)
*Twentieth-Century Crime and Mystery
Writers*, 1st ed., p. 1532. (882a)
*Twentieth-Century Crime and Mystery
Writers*, 2nd ed., pp. 934–35. (882b)
*Twentieth-Century Crime and Mystery
Writers*, 3rd ed., pp. 1124–25. (882c)
Waterton, Betty
Bio-bibliographic data:
Canadian Crime Fiction, p. 229. (209)
Watkins, A. C. *See* **Watkins, Alan
[Clarence]**
Watkins, Alan [Clarence]
Bio-bibliographic data:
Australian Crime Fiction, p. 246. (207)
Watkins, Muriel. *See* **McCall, K. T.**
Watson, Clarissa
Bio-bibliographic data:
Detecting Women, 1st ed., p. 144. (877a)
Detecting Women 2, p. 190. (877b)
Detecting Women, 3rd ed., p. 279. (877c)
Watson, Colin
Bio-bibliographic data:

Encyclopedia Mysteriosa, p. 369. (2)
*The Encyclopedia of Mystery and
Detection*, p. 412. (7)
*The Mammoth Encyclopedia of Modern
Crime Fiction*, p. 489. (1)
*The Oxford Companion to Crime and
Mystery Writing*, p. 491. (4)
*St. James Guide to Crime & Mystery
Writers*, 4th ed., pp. 1028–30. (882d)
*Twentieth-Century Crime and Mystery
Writers*, 1st ed., pp. 1443–45. (882a)
*Twentieth-Century Crime and Mystery
Writers*, 2nd ed., pp. 881–82. (882b)
*Twentieth-Century Crime and Mystery
Writers*, 3rd ed., pp. 1062–63. (882c)
*Whodunit? A Who's Who in Crime and
Mystery Writing*, p. 206. (5)
Web site: http://stopyourekillingme.com/
colin-watson.html
Watson, John Reay
Bio-bibliographic data:
Australian Crime Fiction, p. 247. (207)
Watson, Patrick
Bio-bibliographic data:
Canadian Crime Fiction, p. 229. (209)
Watson, Robert
Bio-bibliographic data:
Canadian Crime Fiction, p. 229. (209)
Watson, Sheila
Bio-bibliographic data:
Canadian Crime Fiction, p. 229. (209)
Watts, Leslie [E.]
Bio-bibliographic data:
Canadian Crime Fiction, pp. 229–30.
(209)
Waugh, Hillary [Baldwin]
Bio-bibliographic data:
Detecting Men, 1st ed., p. 244, 255–56.
(876)
*Critical Survey of Mystery and Detective
Fiction*, pp. 1683–88. (41)
Encyclopedia Mysteriosa, p. 369. (2)
The Encyclopedia of Murder and Mystery,
pp. 516–17. (6)
*The Encyclopedia of Mystery and
Detection*, pp. 413–14. (7)
*100 Masters of Mystery and Detective
Fiction*, pp. 700–705. (37)
*The Oxford Companion to Crime and
Mystery Writing*, pp. 491–92. (4)
*St. James Guide to Crime & Mystery
Writers*, 4th ed., pp. 1030–32. (882d)
*Twentieth-Century Crime and Mystery
Writers*, 1st ed., pp. 1445–48. (882a)

Twentieth-Century Crime and Mystery Writers, 2nd ed., pp. 882–84. (882b)
Twentieth-Century Crime and Mystery Writers, 3rd ed., pp. 1063–65. (882c)
Whodunit? A Who's Who in Crime and Mystery Writing, p. 207. (5)
Personal papers in Mugar Memorial Library, Boston University.

Waugh, Michael
Bio-bibliographic data:
Australian Crime Fiction, p. 247. (207)

Wayland, Patrick. *See* **O'Connor, Richard**

Wayne, Anderson. *See* **Halliday, Brett**

Webb, Christopher. *See* **Holton, Leonard**

Webb, Edward Meryon. *See* **Meryon, Edward**

Webb, Jack; i.e., John Randolph Webb
Bio-bibliographic data:
Critical Survey of Mystery and Detective Fiction, pp. 1689–93. (41)
Detecting Men, 1st ed., p. 256. (876)
Encyclopedia Mysteriosa, pp. 369–70. (2)
St. James Guide to Crime & Mystery Writers, 4th ed., pp. 1032–33. (882d)
Twentieth-Century Crime and Mystery Writers, 1st ed., pp. 1451–52. (882a)
Twentieth-Century Crime and Mystery Writers, 2nd ed., pp. 884–85. (882b)
Twentieth-Century Crime and Mystery Writers, 3rd ed., pp. 1065–66. (882c)

Webb, Jonathan
Bio-bibliographic data:
Canadian Crime Fiction, p. 230. (209)

Webb, Martha G. *See* **Wingate, Anne**

Webb, Richard Wilson. *See* **Quentin, Patrick**

Weber, Janice
Bio-bibliographic data:
Detecting Women, 3rd ed., p. 280. (877c)
Web site: http://stopyourekillingme.com/janice-weber.html

Webley, Jonathan. *See* **Batt, Leon**

Webster, Henry Kitchell
Bio-bibliographic data:
The Encyclopedia of Murder and Mystery, p. 517. (6)
The Encyclopedia of Mystery and Detection, p. 414. (7)

Webster, Noah. *See* **Knox, Bill**

Wees, Frances Shelley [Johnson]; Mrs. Wilfred Rusk
Bio-bibliographic data:
Canadian Crime Fiction, p. 230. (209)

Weesner, Theodore
Bio-bibliographic data:
The Encyclopedia of Murder and Mystery, pp. 517–18. (6)

Weintraub, William
Bio-bibliographic data:
Canadian Crime Fiction, p. 230. (209)

Weir, Charlene
Bio-bibliographic data:
By a Woman's Hand, 2nd ed., pp. 228–29. (884b)
Detecting Women, 1st ed., p. 144. (877a)
Detecting Women 2, p. 190. (877b)
Detecting Women, 3rd ed., p. 280. (877c)
Web site: http://stopyourekillingme.com/charlene-weir.html

Welch, Pat
Bio-bibliographic data:
Detecting Women, 1st ed., p. 144. (877a)
Detecting Women 2, pp. 190–91. (877b)
Detecting Women, 3rd ed., p. 281. (877c)

Welcome, John. *Pseud. for* **John Needham Huggard Brennan**
Bio-bibliographic data:
Detecting Men, 1st ed., p. 256. (876)
The Encyclopedia of Murder and Mystery, p. 518. (6)
St. James Guide to Crime & Mystery Writers, 4th ed., pp. 1033–34. (882d)
Twentieth-Century Crime and Mystery Writers, 1st ed., pp. 1453–54. (882a)
Twentieth-Century Crime and Mystery Writers, 2nd ed., pp. 885–86. (882b)
Twentieth-Century Crime and Mystery Writers, 3rd ed., pp. 1066–67. (882c)

Weller, Archie
Bio-bibliographic data:
Australian Crime Fiction, p. 145, 146. (207)

Wellman, Manly Wade
Bio-bibliographic data:
The Encyclopedia of Murder and Mystery, p. 518. (6)
The Encyclopedia of Mystery and Detection, p. 414. (7)

Wells, Carolyn
Bio-bibliographic data:
Detecting Women, 1st ed., pp. 144–46. (877a)
Detecting Women 2, pp. 191–92. (877b)
Encyclopedia Mysteriosa, p. 370. (2)
The Encyclopedia of Murder and Mystery, pp. 518–19. (6)

*The Encyclopedia of Mystery and
    Detection*, pp. 414–15. (7)
*St. James Guide to Crime & Mystery
    Writers,* 4th ed., pp. 1034–37. (882d)
*Twentieth-Century Crime and Mystery
    Writers,* 1st ed., pp. 1454–59. (882a)
*Twentieth-Century Crime and Mystery
    Writers,* 2nd ed., pp. 886–89. (882b)
*Twentieth-Century Crime and Mystery
    Writers,* 3rd ed., pp. 1067–70. (882c)
Wells, H. G.; i.e., Herbert George
Bio-bibliographic data:
British Mystery Writers, 1860–1919, pp.
    303–16. (866)
The Encyclopedia of Murder and Mystery,
    p. 519. (6)
*The Encyclopedia of Mystery and
    Detection,* pp. 415–16. (7)
Wells, Tobias. *See* for Forbes, [DeLoris
    Florine] Stanton
Wender, Theodora
Bio-bibliographic data:
Detecting Women 2, p. 193. (877b)
Detecting Women, 3rd ed., p. 282. (877c)
Wentworth, Patricia. *Pseud. for* **Dora Amy
    Turnbull, sometimes carried as Dora
    Amy Elles**
Bio-bibliographic data:
British Mystery Writers, 1920–1939, pp.
    309–14. (867)
*Critical Survey of Mystery and Detective
    Fiction,* pp. 1694–99. (41)
Detecting Women, 1st ed., p. 146. (877a)
Detecting Women 2, pp. 193–94. (877b)
Encyclopedia Mysteriosa, p. 370. (2)
The Encyclopedia of Murder and Mystery,
    pp. 519–20. (6)
*The Encyclopedia of Mystery and
    Detection,* pp. 416–17. (7)
Great Women Mystery Writers, pp.
    347–52. (880)
*100 Masters of Mystery and Detective
    Fiction,* pp. 706–11. (37)
*The Oxford Companion to Crime and
    Mystery Writing,* p. 493. (4)
*St. James Guide to Crime & Mystery
    Writers,* 4th ed., pp. 1037–39. (882d)
*Twentieth-Century Crime and Mystery
    Writers,* 1st ed., pp. 1459–63. (882a)
*Twentieth-Century Crime and Mystery
    Writers,* 2nd ed., pp. 889–91. (882b)
*Twentieth-Century Crime and Mystery
    Writers,* 3rd ed., pp. 1070–72. (882c)

*Whodunit? A Who's Who in Crime and
    Mystery Writing,* pp. 207–8. (5)
Women Authors of Detective Series, pp.
    9–15. (882.5)
Web site: http://stopyourekillingme.com/
    patricia-wentworth.html
Wenzel, Barbara [Ann]. *See* **Fitzpatrick,
    Peter [Henry], and Barbara [Ann]
    Wenzel**
Wesley, Valerie Wilson
Bio-bibliographic data:
By a Woman's Hand, 2nd ed., pp. 229–30.
    (884b)
Detecting Women, 1st ed., p. 147. (877a)
Detecting Women 2, p. 194. (877b)
Detecting Women, 3rd ed., p. 282. (877c)
Web site: http://stopyourekillingme.com/
    valerie-wilson-wesley.html; http://
    www.tamarahayle.com/welcome.htm
West, Charles
Bio-bibliographic data:
Australian Crime Fiction, pp. 247–48.
    (207)
West, Chassie
Bio-bibliographic data:
Detecting Women 2, p. 194. (877b)
Web site: http://www.chassiewest.com;
    http://stopyourekillingme.com/
    chassie-west.html
West, Christopher
Bio-bibliographic data:
Detecting Men, 1st ed., p. 257. (876)
Web site: http://www.twbooks.co.uk/
    authors/cwest.html; http://
    stopyourekillingme.com/
    christopher-west.html
West, John B.
Bio-bibliographic data:
Encyclopedia Mysteriosa, p. 371. (2)
West, Morris [Langlo]
Bio-bibliographic data:
Australian Crime Fiction, p. 248. (207)
West, V. C. *Pseud. for* **Leslie Loval
    Woolacott**
Westermann, John
Bio-bibliographic data:
Detecting Men, 1st ed., p. 257. (876)
Westfall, Patricia Tichenor
Bio-bibliographic data:
Detecting Women, 3rd ed., p. 282. (877c)
Westlake, Donald E[dwin].
Bio-bibliographic data:
The Big Book of Noir, pp. 267–72. (24)

Canadian Crime Fiction, p. 267, 269. (209)

Critical Survey of Mystery and Detective Fiction, pp. 1700–1706. (41)

Detecting Men, 1st ed., p. 58, 237, 257. (876)

Encyclopedia Mysteriosa, pp. 371–72. (2)

The Encyclopedia of Murder and Mystery, p. 522. (6)

The Encyclopedia of Mystery and Detection, pp. 417–18. (7)

The Mammoth Encyclopedia of Modern Crime Fiction, pp. 489–93. (1)

Mystery and Suspense Writers, pp. 957–65. (884.2)

100 Masters of Mystery and Detective Fiction, pp. 712–20. (37)

St. James Guide to Crime & Mystery Writers, 4th ed., pp. 1039–41. (882d)

Speaking of Murder, vol. II, pp. 16–37. (875b)

Talking Murder, pp. 258–67. (883)

Twentieth-Century Crime and Mystery Writers, 1st ed., pp. 1463–67. (882a)

Twentieth-Century Crime and Mystery Writers, 2nd ed., pp. 891–93. (882b)

Twentieth-Century Crime and Mystery Writers, 3rd ed., pp. 1072–75. (882c)

Whodunit? A Who's Who in Crime and Mystery Writing, p. 208. (5)

Personal papers in Mugar Memorial Library, Boston University.

Web site: http://www.donaldwestlake. com; http://stopyourekillingme. com/donald-e-westlake.html; http:// www.thrillingdetective.com/trivia/ westlake.html

Westlaw, Steven. *See* **Pyke, John**

Westmacott, Mary. *See* **Christie, Agatha**

Weston, Carolyn

Bio-bibliographic data:

Detecting Women 2, pp. 194–95. (877b)

Detecting Women, 3rd ed., p. 283. (877c)

Twentieth-Century Crime and Mystery Writers, 1st ed., pp. 1467–68. (882a)

Weston, Garnett [James]

Bio-bibliographic data:

Canadian Crime Fiction, p. 230. (209)

Weyman, Ronald C.

Bio-bibliographic data:

Canadian Crime Fiction, p. 231. (209)

Whalley, Peter

Bio-bibliographic data:

St. James Guide to Crime & Mystery Writers, 4th ed., pp. 1041–42. (882d)

Twentieth-Century Crime and Mystery Writers, 3rd ed., pp. 1075–76. (882c)

Wharton, Anthony. *See* **Brock, Lynn**

Wheat, Carolyn

Bio-bibliographic data:

By a Woman's Hand, 1st ed., p. 216. (884a)

By a Woman's Hand, 2nd ed., p. 230. (884b)

Detecting Women, 1st ed., p. 147. (877a)

Detecting Women 2, p. 195. (877b)

Detecting Women, 3rd ed., p. 283. (877c)

The Mammoth Encyclopedia of Modern Crime Fiction, p. 493. (1)

St. James Guide to Crime & Mystery Writers, 4th ed., p. 1043. (882d)

Twentieth-Century Crime and Mystery Writers, 3rd ed., pp. 1076–77. (882c)

Web site: http://stopyourekillingme.com/ carolyn-wheat.html

Wheatley, Dennis [Yates]

Bio-bibliographic data:

British Mystery Writers, 1920–1939, pp. 315–21. (867)

Canadian Crime Fiction, pp. 269–70. (209)

Critical Survey of Mystery and Detective Fiction, pp. 1707–12. (41)

Encyclopedia Mysteriosa, p. 373. (2)

The Encyclopedia of Murder and Mystery, pp. 523–24. (6)

The Encyclopedia of Mystery and Detection, p. 418. (7)

St. James Guide to Crime & Mystery Writers, 4th ed., pp. 1043–46. (882d)

Twentieth-Century Crime and Mystery Writers, 1st ed., pp. 1468–72. (882a)

Twentieth-Century Crime and Mystery Writers, 2nd ed., pp. 893–95. (882b)

Twentieth-Century Crime and Mystery Writers, 3rd ed., pp. 1077–79. (882c)

Wheeler, Edward L[ytton].

Bio-bibliographic data:

The Encyclopedia of Mystery and Detection, pp. 418–19. (7)

Wheeler, Hugh Callingham. *See* **Quentin, Patrick**

Whitaker, Rodney H. *See* **Trevanian**

White, Alan. *See* **Fraser, James**

White, Babington. *See* **Braddon, Mary Elizabeth**

White, Ethel Lina

Bio-bibliographic data:

*The Encyclopedia of Mystery and
Detection*, p. 419. (7)
*Twentieth-Century Crime and Mystery
Writers*, 1st ed., pp. 1472–73. (882a)
White, George M. *See* **Walsh, J. M.**
White, Gloria
Bio-bibliographic data:
By a Woman's Hand, 2nd ed., pp. 230–31.
(884b)
Detecting Women, 1st ed., p. 147. (877a)
Detecting Women 2, p. 195. (877b)
Detecting Women, 3rd ed., pp. 283–84.
(877c)
White, Jon Manchip
Bio-bibliographic data:
*St. James Guide to Crime & Mystery
Writers*, 4th ed., pp. 1046–48. (882d)
*Twentieth-Century Crime and Mystery
Writers*, 1st ed., pp. 1473–76. (882a)
*Twentieth-Century Crime and Mystery
Writers*, 2nd ed., pp. 896–97. (882b)
*Twentieth-Century Crime and Mystery
Writers*, 3rd ed., pp. 1079–80. (882c)
White, Leslie T[urner].
Bio-bibliographic data:
Canadian Crime Fiction, p. 231. (209)
White, Lionel
Bio-bibliographic data:
The Big Book of Noir, pp. 188–89. (24)
Encyclopedia Mysteriosa, pp. 373–74. (2)
*Twentieth-Century Crime and Mystery
Writers*, 1st ed., pp. 1476–78. (882a)
*Twentieth-Century Crime and Mystery
Writers*, 2nd ed., pp. 897–98. (882b)
*Twentieth-Century Crime and Mystery
Writers*, 3rd ed., pp. 1080–82. (882c)
White, Osmar [Egmont Dorkin]
Bio-bibliographic data:
Australian Crime Fiction, p. 249. (207)
White, Randy Wayne
Bio-bibliographic data:
Detecting Men, 1st ed., p. 258. (876)
Web site: http://stopyourekillingme.com/
randy-wayne-white.html; http://www.
rwwhite.com
White, Ronald
Bio-bibliographic data:
Canadian Crime Fiction, p. 231. (209)
White, Samuel Alexander
Bio-bibliographic data:
Canadian Crime Fiction, pp. 231–32.
(209)
White, Stephen
Bio-bibliographic data:

Detecting Men, 1st ed., p. 258. (876)
Web site: http://stopyourekillingme.com/
stephen-white.html; http://www.
authorstephenwhite.com
White, Stewart Edward
Bio-bibliographic data:
Canadian Crime Fiction, p. 270. (209)
White, Teri [Honohan]
Bio-bibliographic data:
By a Woman's Hand, 1st ed., pp. 216–17.
(884a)
By a Woman's Hand, 2nd ed., pp. 231–32.
(884b)
Detecting Women, 1st ed., p. 147. (877a)
Detecting Women 2, pp. 195–96. (877b)
Detecting Women, 3rd ed., p. 284. (877c)
Encyclopedia Mysteriosa, p. 374. (2)
*The Mammoth Encyclopedia of Modern
Crime Fiction*, pp. 493–94. (1)
*St. James Guide to Crime & Mystery
Writers*, 4th ed., pp. 1049–50. (882d)
*Twentieth-Century Crime and Mystery
Writers*, 3rd ed., pp. 1082–83. (882c)
Web site: http://www.comlink.ne.
jp~winkie.html
White, William Anthony Parker. *See*
Boucher, Anthony
Whitechurch, Victor L[orenzo].
Bio-bibliographic data:
British Mystery Writers, 1860–1919, pp.
317–22. (866)
*Critical Survey of Mystery and Detective
Fiction*, pp. 1713–716. (41)
The Encyclopedia of Murder and Mystery,
p. 524. (6)
*The Encyclopedia of Mystery and
Detection*, p. 419. (7)
*Twentieth-Century Crime and Mystery
Writers*, 1st ed., pp. 1478–80. (882a)
Whitehead, Barbara
Bio-bibliographic data:
By a Woman's Hand, 1st ed., pp. 217–18.
(884a)
By a Woman's Hand, 2nd ed., p. 232.
(884b)
Detecting Women, 3rd ed., p. 284. (877c)
Whitehouse, Wesley L[eonard].
Bio-bibliographic data:
Australian Crime Fiction, p. 249. (207)
Whiteson, Leon
Bio-bibliographic data:
Canadian Crime Fiction, p. 286. (209)
Whitfield, Raoul [Fauconnier]
Bio-bibliographic data:

American Hard-Boiled Crime Writers, pp. 329–35. (862)
Encyclopedia Mysteriosa, p. 374. (2)
The Encyclopedia of Murder and Mystery, p. 525. (6)
The Encyclopedia of Mystery and Detection, pp. 419–20. (7)
St. James Guide to Crime & Mystery Writers, 4th ed., pp. 1050–51. (882d)
Twentieth-Century Crime and Mystery Writers, 1st ed., pp. 1480–83. (882a)
Twentieth-Century Crime and Mystery Writers, 2nd ed., pp. 898–900. (882b)
Twentieth-Century Crime and Mystery Writers, 3rd ed., pp. 1083–84. (882c)
Web site:
http://www.cwru.edu/artsci/engl/
marling/hardboiled/Whitfield.HTM;
http://pulprack.com/index3.html

Whitman, Charles
Bio-bibliographic data:
Australian Crime Fiction, pp. 249–50. (207)

Whitney, J. L. H. *Pseud. for* **Jacquelyn Whitney Trimble**
Bio-bibliographic data:
Canadian Crime Fiction, p. 268, 270. (209)

Whitney, Phyllis A[yame].
Bio-bibliographic data:
By a Woman's Hand, 1st ed., pp. 218–19. (884a)
By a Woman's Hand, 2nd ed., pp. 232–33. (884b)
Critical Survey of Mystery and Detective Fiction, pp. 1717–22. (41)
Encyclopedia Mysteriosa, p. 374. (2)
The Encyclopedia of Mystery and Detection, p. 420. (7)
The Oxford Companion to Crime and Mystery Writing, p. 495. (4)
St. James Guide to Crime & Mystery Writers, 4th ed., pp. 1051–53. (882d)
13 Mistresses of Murder, pp. 125–35. (871)
Twentieth-Century Crime and Mystery Writers, 1st ed., pp. 1483–86. (882a)
Twentieth-Century Crime and Mystery Writers, 2nd ed., pp. 900–902. (882b)
Twentieth-Century Crime and Mystery Writers, 3rd ed., pp. 1084–86. (882c)
Whodunit? A Who's Who in Crime and Mystery Writing, pp. 208–9. (5)

Personal papers in Mugar Memorial Library, Boston University.
Web site:
http://www.phyllisawhitney.com

Whitney, Polly
Bio-bibliographic data:
Detecting Women 2, p. 196. (877b)
Detecting Women, 3rd ed., p. 138, 284–85. (877c)
Web site: http://members.aol.com/
mystfield/kitchen/polly.html; http://
stopyourekillingme.com/
polly-whitney.html

Whittington, Harry
Bio-bibliographic data:
The Big Book of Noir, p. 187, 201–8. (24)
Canadian Crime Fiction, p. 254, 270. (209)
The Encyclopedia of Murder and Mystery, p. 525. (6)
Murder off the Rack: Critical Studies of Ten Paperback Masters, pp. 1–14. (869)
St. James Guide to Crime & Mystery Writers, 4th ed., pp. 1053–55. (882d)
Twentieth-Century Crime and Mystery Writers, 1st ed., pp. 1486–89. (882a)
Twentieth-Century Crime and Mystery Writers, 2nd ed., pp. 902–4. (882b)
Twentieth-Century Crime and Mystery Writers, 3rd ed., pp. 1086–89. (882c)
Personal papers in Florida State University, Tallahassee.

Wibberley, Leonard Patrick O'Connor. *See* **Holton, Leonard**

Wicking, G. W.; i.e., George Walter
Bio-bibliographic data:
Australian Crime Fiction, p. 250. (207)

Wiebe, Armin
Bio-bibliographic data:
Canadian Crime Fiction, p. 232. (209)

Wiebe, Rudy
Bio-bibliographic data:
Canadian Crime Fiction, p. 232. (209)

Wiegand, William
Bio-bibliographic data:
Twentieth-Century Crime and Mystery Writers, 1st ed., pp. 1489–90. (882a)

Wiens, Ernst
Bio-bibliographic data:
Canadian Crime Fiction, p. 232. (209)

Wilcox, Collin
Bio-bibliographic data:
Detecting Men, 1st ed., pp. 258–59. (876)

Twentieth-Century Crime and Mystery Writers, 3rd ed., pp. 1091–93. (882c)
Web site: http://www.twbooks.co/authors/davidwilliams.html; http://stopyourekillingme.com/david-williams.html

Williams, David R[icardo]., Q.C.
Bio-bibliographic data:
Canadian Crime Fiction, pp. 232–33. (209)

Williams, Edward Huntington
Bio-bibliographic data:
Canadian Crime Fiction, p. 270. (209)

Williams, [George] Emlyn
Bio-bibliographic data:
British Mystery Writers, 1920–1939, pp. 326–30. (867)
Encyclopedia Mysteriosa, p. 376. (2)
The Encyclopedia of Mystery and Detection, p. 421. (7)

Williams, Gordon. *See* Yuill, P. B., and Terry Venables

Williams, Gwyn Paul
Bio-bibliographic data:
Canadian Crime Fiction, p. 233. (209)

Williams, Linda V. *See* Grant, Linda

Williams, Margaret Wetherby. *See* Erskine, Margaret

Williams, Timothy
Bio-bibliographic data:
The Mammoth Encyclopedia of Modern Crime Fiction, p. 500. (1)
Web site: http://www.twbooks.co.uk/authors/twilliams.html

Williams, [George] Valentine
Bio-bibliographic data:
British Mystery Writers, 1920–1939, pp. 331–38. (867)
Canadian Crime Fiction, p. 270. (209)
The Encyclopedia of Murder and Mystery, p. 528. (6)
The Encyclopedia of Mystery and Detection, p. 422. (7)
St. James Guide to Crime & Mystery Writers, 4th ed., pp. 1060–61. (882d)
Twentieth-Century Crime and Mystery Writers, 1st ed., pp. 1494–96. (882a)
Twentieth-Century Crime and Mystery Writers, 2nd ed., pp. 907–8. (882b)
Twentieth-Century Crime and Mystery Writers, 3rd ed., pp. 1093–94. (882c)

Williams, W. H. [Bill]. *See* Brody, Marc

Williamson, [Grahame] Moncrieff
Bio-bibliographic data:

Canadian Crime Fiction, p. 233. (209)

Willis, George Anthony Armstrong. *See* Armstrong, Anthony

Willis, Ted;. i.e., Baron Edward Henry Wills
Bio-bibliographic data:
Encyclopedia Mysteriosa, p. 376. (2)
The Encyclopedia of Murder and Mystery, p. 529. (6)
St. James Guide to Crime & Mystery Writers, 4th ed., pp. 1061–63. (882d)
Twentieth-Century Crime and Mystery Writers, 1st ed., pp. 1497–1500. (882a)
Twentieth-Century Crime and Mystery Writers, 2nd ed., pp. 908–10. (882b)
Twentieth-Century Crime and Mystery Writers, 3rd ed., pp. 1094–96. (882c)

Willoughby, Lee Davis. *See* Myers, Barry

Wills, Cecil M.
Bio-bibliographic data:
Twentieth-Century Crime and Mystery Writers, 1st ed., pp. 1500–1501. (882a)
Twentieth-Century Crime and Mystery Writers, 2nd ed., pp. 910–11. (882b)
Twentieth-Century Crime and Mystery Writers, 3rd ed., pp. 1096–97. (882c)

Wilmer, Dale. *See* Miller, Wade

Wilson, Anne
Bio-bibliographic data:
Detecting Women, 3rd ed., p. 286. (877c)

Wilson, Barbara
Bio-bibliographic data:
By a Woman's Hand, 1st ed., pp. 219–20. (884a)
By a Woman's Hand, 2nd ed., pp. 234–35. (884b)
Detecting Women, 1st ed., p. 148. (877a)
Detecting Women 2, pp. 196–97. (877b)
Detecting Women, 3rd ed., pp. 286–87. (877c)
Great Women Mystery Writers, pp. 352–54. (880)
St. James Guide to Crime & Mystery Writers, 4th ed., pp. 1064–65. (882d)
Twentieth-Century Crime and Mystery Writers, 3rd ed., pp. 1097–98. (882c)
Web site: http://stopyourekillingme.com/barbara-wilson.html

Wilson, Barbara Jaye
Bio-bibliographic data:
Detecting Women, 3rd ed., p. 287. (877c)

Web site: http://stopyourekillingme.com/
barbara-jaye-wilson.html
Wilson, Colin
Bio-bibliographic data:
*St. James Guide to Crime & Mystery
Writers,* 4th ed., pp. 1065–68. (882d)
*Twentieth-Century Crime and Mystery
Writers,* 1st ed., pp. 1502–5. (882a)
*Twentieth-Century Crime and Mystery
Writers,* 2nd ed., pp. 911–13. (882b)
*Twentieth-Century Crime and Mystery
Writers,* 3rd ed., pp. 1098–1. (882c)
Personal papers in Humanities Research
Center, University of Texas at Austin.
Wilson, Derek
Bio-bibliographic data:
Detecting Men, 1st ed., p. 260. (876)
*The Mammoth Encyclopedia of Modern
Crime Fiction,* pp. 500–501. (1)
Web site: http://www.derekwilson.com;
http://www.twbooks.co.uk/authors/
dwilson.html
Wilson, Edmund
Bio-bibliographic data:
The Encyclopedia of Murder and Mystery,
p. 529. (6)
Wilson, Eric [Hamilton]
Bio-bibliographic data:
Canadian Crime Fiction, pp. 233–34.
(209)
Wilson, Jacqueline
Bio-bibliographic data:
*Twentieth-Century Crime and Mystery
Writers,* 2nd ed., pp. 913–14. (882b)
Wilson, John Morgan
Bio-bibliographic data:
*The Mammoth Encyclopedia of Modern
Crime Fiction,* pp. 501–2. (1)
Web site: http://www.
johnmorganwilson.com; http://
stopyourekillingme.com/
john-morgan-wilson.html
Wilson, Karen Ann
Bio-bibliographic data:
Detecting Women 2, p. 197. (877b)
Detecting Women, 3rd ed., p. 287. (877c)
Web site: http://stopyourekillingme.com/
karen-ann-wilson.html
Wilson, Rob
Bio-bibliographic data:
Canadian Crime Fiction, p. 234. (209)
Wilson, Robert
Bio-bibliographic data:

*The Mammoth Encyclopedia of Modern
Crime Fiction,* pp. 502–3. (1)
Web site: http://www.twbooks.co.uk/
authors/rwilson.html; http://
stopyourekillingme.com/
robert-wilson.html
Wilson, Serge
Bio-bibliographic data:
Canadian Crime Fiction, p. 234. (209)
Wiltse, David
Bio-bibliographic data:
Detecting Men, 1st ed., p. 261. (876)
Web site: http://stopyourekillingme.com/
david-wiltse.html; http://pw2.netcom.
com/~luckyman/wiltse/wiltse.html
Wiltz, Chris
Bio-bibliographic data:
By a Woman's Hand, 1st ed., pp. 220–21.
(884a)
By a Woman's Hand, 2nd ed., p. 235.
(884b)
Detecting Women 2, p. 197. (877b)
Detecting Women, 3rd ed., p. 288. (877c)
Great Women Mystery Writers, pp.
354–55. (880)
Winchell, Prentice. *See* **Sterling, Stewart**
Wing, Willis Kingsley. *See* **Moore, Brian**
Wingate, Anne
Bio-bibliographic data:
By a Woman's Hand, 1st ed., pp. 221–22.
(884a)
By a Woman's Hand, 2nd ed., pp. 235–36.
(884b)
Detecting Women, 1st ed., p. 92, 148–49.
(877a)
Detecting Women 2, p. 126, 190, 197.
(877b)
Detecting Women, 3rd ed., p. 175, 279–80,
288. (877c)
Web site: http://stopyourekillingme.com/
anne-wingate.html
Wingfield, R. D.; i.e, Rodney D.
Bio-bibliographic data:
Detecting Men, 1st ed., p. 261. (876)
*The Mammoth Encyclopedia of Modern
Crime Fiction,* pp. 503–4. (1)
Web site: http://stopyourekillingme.com/
r-d-wingfield.html
Wings, Mary
Bio-bibliographic data:
By a Woman's Hand, 1st ed., pp. 222–23.
(884a)
By a Woman's Hand, 2nd ed., pp. 236–37.
(884b)

Deadly Women, pp. 275–79. (26.5)
Detecting Women, 1st ed., p. 149. (877a)
Detecting Women 2, p. 197. (877b)
Detecting Women, 3rd ed., pp. 288–89. (877c)
Great Women Mystery Writers, pp. 356–57. (880)
The Mammoth Encyclopedia of Modern Crime Fiction, p. 504. (1)
St. James Guide to Crime & Mystery Writers, 4th ed., pp. 1068–69. (882d)
Twentieth-Century Crime and Mystery Writers, 3rd ed., pp. 1101–2. (882c)
Web site: http://www.twbooks.co.uk/ authors/mwings.html; http:// stopyourekillingme.com/mary-wings. html

Winn, Patrick
Bio-bibliographic data:
Australian Crime Fiction, p. 251. (207)

Winslow, Don
Bio-bibliographic data:
Detecting Men, 1st ed., p. 261. (876)
The Mammoth Encyclopedia of Modern Crime Fiction, pp. 504–5. (1)
Web site: http://www.donwinslow.com; http://stopyourekillingme.com/ don-winslow.html

Winslow, Pauline Glen
Bio-bibliographic data:
Detecting Women 2, p. 198. (877b)
Detecting Women, 3rd ed., p. 289. (877c)
Encyclopedia Mysteriosa, p. 379. (2)
St. James Guide to Crime & Mystery Writers, 4th ed., pp. 1069–71. (882d)
Twentieth-Century Crime and Mystery Writers, 2nd ed., pp. 914–16. (882b)
Twentieth-Century Crime and Mystery Writers, 3rd ed., pp. 1102–3. (882c)

Winter, Frank
Bio-bibliographic data:
Australian Crime Fiction, p. 252. (207)

Winterton, Paul. *See* **Garve, Andrew**

Winton, Tim[othy] John
Bio-bibliographic data:
Australian Crime Fiction, p. 252. (207)

Wiper, David William. *See* **Fennario, David**

Wise, Arthur
Bio-bibliographic data:
Twentieth-Century Crime and Mystery Writers, 2nd ed., pp. 916–17. (882b)

Wiseman, Adele
Bio-bibliographic data:

Canadian Crime Fiction, p. 235. (209)

Withrow, Patrick:
Bio-bibliographic data:
Canadian Crime Fiction, p. 166, 235. (209)

Witting, Clifford
Bio-bibliographic data:
Twentieth-Century Crime and Mystery Writers, 1st ed., pp. 1505–6. (882a)
Twentieth-Century Crime and Mystery Writers, 2nd ed., pp. 917–18. (882b)

Wolfe, Susan
Bio-bibliographic data:
Detecting Women, 1st ed., p. 149. (877a)
Detecting Women 2, p. 198. (877b)
Web site: http://stopyourekillingme.com/ susan-wolfe.html

Wolley, Sir Clive Phillipps. *See* **Phillipps-Wolley, Sir Clive**

Wolzien, Valerie
Bio-bibliographic data:
By a Woman's Hand, 1st ed., p. 223. (884a)
By a Woman's Hand, 2nd ed., p. 237. (884b)
Detecting Women, 1st ed., p. 149. (877a)
Detecting Women 2, p. 198. (877b)
Detecting Women, 3rd ed., pp. 289–90. (877c)
Web site: http://stopyourekillingme.com/ valerie-wolzien.html

Womack, Steven
Bio-bibliographic data:
Detecting Men, 1st ed., p. 262. (876)
The Mammoth Encyclopedia of Modern Crime Fiction, pp. 505–6. (1)
Web site: http://www.womackbooks.com; http://stopyourekillingme.com/ steven-womack.html

Wood, Christopher [Hovelle]
Bio-bibliographic data:
Australian Crime Fiction, p. 252. (207)

Wood, Edward John. *See* **Wood, Ted**

Wood, Ellen Price [Mrs. Henry]
Bio-bibliographic data:
The Encyclopedia of Murder and Mystery, pp. 534–35. (6)
The Oxford Companion to Crime and Mystery Writing, p. 502. (4)
St. James Guide to Crime & Mystery Writers, 4th ed., p. 1071. (882d)
Twentieth-Century Crime and Mystery Writers, 1st ed., pp. 1532–33. (882a)

Twentieth-Century Crime and Mystery Writers, 2nd ed., p. 935. (882b)
Twentieth-Century Crime and Mystery Writers, 3rd ed., p. 1125. (882c)
Whodunit? A Who's Who in Crime and Mystery Writing, p. 211. (5)
Wood, Mrs. Henry. *See* **Wood, Ellen Price [Mrs. Henry]**
Wood, Peter H[arry].
Bio-bibliographic data:
Canadian Crime Fiction, pp. 235–36. (209)
Wood, Ted. *Pseud. for* **Edward John Wood**
Bio-bibliographic data:
Canadian Crime Fiction, p. 235. (209)
Detecting Men, 1st ed., p. 29, 262. (876)
Encyclopedia Mysteriosa, p. 383. (2)
The Mammoth Encyclopedia of Modern Crime Fiction, pp. 506–7. (1)
St. James Guide to Crime & Mystery Writers, 4th ed., pp. 1071–73. (882d)
Twentieth-Century Crime and Mystery Writers, 3rd ed., pp. 1103–4. (882c)
Web site: http://www.stopyourekillingme. com/ted-wood.html
Woodbury, Mary
Bio-bibliographic data:
Canadian Crime Fiction, p. 236. (209)
Woodhouse, Arthur
Bio-bibliographic data:
Australian Crime Fiction, p. 252. (207)
Woodrell, Daniel
Bio-bibliographic data:
Detecting Men, 1st ed., pp. 262–63. (876)
The Mammoth Encyclopedia of Modern Crime Fiction, p. 507. (1)
Web site: http://www.twbooks.co.uk/ authors.dwoodrel.html
Woods, Paula L.
Bio-bibliographic data:
Detecting Women, 3rd ed., p. 290. (877c)
Web site: http://stopyourekillingme.com/ paula-woods.html; http://www. woodsontheweb.com
Woods, Sara. *See* **Bowen-Judd, Sara Hutton**
Woods, Sherryl
Bio-bibliographic data:
By a Woman's Hand, 1st ed., pp. 224–25. (884a)
By a Woman's Hand, 2nd ed., p. 238. (884b)
Detecting Women, 1st ed., p. 151. (877a)

Detecting Women 2, p. 200. (877b)
Detecting Women, 3rd ed., p. 290. (877c)
Web site: http://stopyourekillingme.com/ sherryl-woods.html
Woods, Stuart
Bio-bibliographic data:
Detecting Men, 1st ed., p. 263. (876)
The Mammoth Encyclopedia of Modern Crime Fiction, pp. 507–9. (1)
Web site: http://www.stuartwoods.com; http://stopyourekillingme.com/ stuart-woods.html
Woodward, Ann
Bio-bibliographic data:
Detecting Women, 3rd ed., p. 291. (877c)
Woodward, Caroline [Hendrika]
Bio-bibliographic data:
Canadian Crime Fiction, p. 237. (209)
Woodward, Lucy Berton
Bio-bibliographic data:
Canadian Crime Fiction, p. 237. (209)
Woodworth, Deborah
Bio-bibliographic data:
Detecting Women, 3rd ed., p. 291. (877c)
Web site: http://stopyourekillingme.com/ deborah-woodworth.html
Woolacott, Leslie Loval. *See* **West, V. C.**
Woolf, F. X[erxes].: joint pseud. for Howard Engel and his second wife, Jane [Evelyn] Hamilton (q.q.v.)
Woolrich, Cornell [George Hopley]
Bio-bibliographic data:
American Hard-Boiled Crime Writers, pp. 349–64. (862)
The Big Book of Noir, pp. 163–69. (24)
Critical Survey of Mystery and Detective Fiction, pp. 1723–29. (41)
Encyclopedia Mysteriosa, pp. 383–84. (2)
The Encyclopedia of Murder and Mystery, pp. 535–36. (6)
The Encyclopedia of Mystery and Detection, pp. 429–34. (7)
Mystery and Suspense Writers, pp. 967–82. (884.2)
100 Masters of Mystery and Detective Fiction, pp. 721–27. (37)
The Oxford Companion to Crime and Mystery Writing, pp. 502–3. (4)
St. James Guide to Crime & Mystery Writers, 4th ed., pp. 1075–77. (882d)
Twentieth-Century Crime and Mystery Writers, 1st ed., pp. 1509–12. (882a)
Twentieth-Century Crime and Mystery Writers, 2nd ed., pp. 919–21. (882b)

Twentieth-Century Crime and Mystery Writers, 3rd ed., pp. 1106–8. (882c)
Whodunit? A Who's Who in Crime and Mystery Writing, pp. 211–12. (5)
Web site: http://stopyourekillingme.com/cornell-woolrich.html; http://www.miskatonic.org/rara-avis/biblio/woolrich.html

Workman, James
Bio-bibliographic data:
Australian Crime Fiction, p. 253. (207)

Wormser, Richard
Bio-bibliographic data:
Twentieth-Century Crime and Mystery Writers, 2nd ed., pp. 921–22. (882b)
Twentieth-Century Crime and Mystery Writers, 3rd ed., pp. 1108–9. (882c)

Wren, M. K. *Pseud. for* **Martha Kay Renfroe**
Bio-bibliographic data:
By a Woman's Hand, 1st ed., pp. 225–26. (884a)
By a Woman's Hand, 2nd ed., pp. 238–39. (884b)
Detecting Women, 1st ed., p. 152. (877a)
Detecting Women 2, p. 200. (877b)
Detecting Women, 3rd ed., pp. 291–92. (877c)
The Encyclopedia of Murder and Mystery, p. 536. (6)
Web site: http://stopyourekillingme.com/m-k-wren.html; http://www.mkwren.com

Wright, April McKee. *See* **McKee-Wright, April**

Wright, Arthur
Bio-bibliographic data:
Australian Crime Fiction, pp. 253–54. (207)

Wright, Eric
Bio-bibliographic data:
Canadian Crime Fiction, pp. 237–38. (209)
Detecting Men, 1st ed., p. 263. (876)
Encyclopedia Mysteriosa, p. 384. (2)
The Mammoth Encyclopedia of Modern Crime Fiction, pp. 509–10. (1)
St. James Guide to Crime & Mystery Writers, 4th ed., pp. 1077–78. (882d)
Twentieth-Century Crime and Mystery Writers, 3rd ed., pp. 1109–10. (882c)
Whodunit? A Who's Who in Crime and Mystery Writing, p. 212. (5)

Personal papers in the University of Toronto.
Web site: http://stopyourekillingme.com/eric-wright.html

Wright, June
Bio-bibliographic data:
Australian Crime Fiction, pp. 254–55. (207)

Wright, L. R.; i.e., Laurali Rose
Bio-bibliographic data:
By a Woman's Hand, 1st ed., p. 226. (884a)
By a Woman's Hand, 2nd ed., pp. 239–40. (884b)
Canadian Crime Fiction, p. 238. (209)
Detecting Women, 1st ed., p. 152. (877a)
Detecting Women 2, pp. 200–201. (877b)
Detecting Women, 3rd ed., p. 292. (877c)
Encyclopedia Mysteriosa, pp. 384–85. (2)
The Encyclopedia of Murder and Mystery, p. 536. (6)
Great Women Mystery Writers, pp. 361–63. (880)
The Mammoth Encyclopedia of Modern Crime Fiction, pp. 510–11. (1)
St. James Guide to Crime & Mystery Writers, 4th ed., pp. 1078–79. (882d)
Twentieth-Century Crime and Mystery Writers, 3rd ed., pp. 1110–11. (882c)
Web site: http://stopyourekillingme.com/l-r-wright.html

Wright, Nancy Means
Bio-bibliographic data:
Detecting Women, 3rd ed., p. 292. (877c)
Web site: http://stopyourekillingme.com/nancy-means-wright.html; http://www.nancymeanswright.com

Wright, Richard B[ruce].
Bio-bibliographic data:
Canadian Crime Fiction, p. 239. (209)

Wright, Rowland. *See* **Wells, Carolyn**

Wright, Sally S.
Bio-bibliographic data:
Detecting Women, 3rd ed., p. 293. (877c)
Web site: http://stopyourekillingme.com/sally-s-wright.html

Wright, Steve; i.e., Stephen William
Bio-bibliographic data:
Australian Crime Fiction, p. 146, 255. (207)

Wright, Willard Huntington. *See* **Van Dine, S. S.**

Wuorio, Eva-Lis
Bio-bibliographic data:

Canadian Crime Fiction, p. 239. (209)
Wyatt, D. B. *See* **Robinson, Spider**
Wyatt, Daniel
Bio-bibliographic data:
Canadian Crime Fiction, p. 239. (209)
Wyl, Jean-Michel
Bio-bibliographic data:
Canadian Crime Fiction, p. 239. (209)
Wylie, Philip [Gordon]
Bio-bibliographic data:
The Encyclopedia of Murder and Mystery,
p. 538. (6)
*The Encyclopedia of Mystery and
Detection,* p. 434. (7)
Wyllie, John [Vectis Carew]
Bio-bibliographic data:
Canadian Crime Fiction, pp. 239–40.
(209)
The Encyclopedia of Murder and Mystery,
p. 538. (6)
Wynd, Oswald Morris. *See* **Black, Gavin**
Wynne-Jones, Tim[othy]
Bio-bibliographic data:
Canadian Crime Fiction, p. 240. (209)
Wyrick, E. L.; i.e., Edward L.
Bio-bibliographic data:
Detecting Men, 1st ed., p. 264. (876)

Y

Yaffe, James
Bio-bibliographic data:
Detecting Men, 1st ed., p. 264. (876)
The Encyclopedia of Murder and Mystery,
p. 539. (6)
*The Encyclopedia of Mystery and
Detection,* p. 435. (7)
Web site: http://www.stopyourekillingme.
com/james-yaffe.html
Yakir, Leonard
Bio-bibliographic data:
Canadian Crime Fiction, p. 240. (209)
Yarborough, Charlotte
Bio-bibliographic data:
Australian Crime Fiction, p. 256. (207)
Yarbro, Chelsea Quinn. *See also* **Yarbro,
Chelsea Quinn, and Bill Fawcett**
Bio-bibliographic data:
By a Woman's Hand, 1st ed., pp. 227–28.
(884a)
By a Woman's Hand, 2nd ed., p. 241.
(884b)
Canadian Crime Fiction, p. 287. (209)
Detecting Women, 1st ed., p. 55, 152.
(877a)

Detecting Women 2, p. 65, 201. (877b)
Detecting Women, 3rd ed., p. 293. (877c)
Web site: http://www.stopyourekillingme.
com/chelsea-quinn-yarbro.html;
http://www.chelseaquinnyarbro.com
Yarbro, Chelsea Quinn, and Bill Fawcett
Bio-bibliographic data:
Detecting Women, 3rd ed., pp. 91–92.
(877c)
Yates, Alan Geoffrey. *See* **Brown, Carter**
Yates, Brock [Wendell]
Bio-bibliographic data:
Canadian Crime Fiction, p. 270. (209)
Yates, Dornford. *Pseud. for* **Cecil William
Mercer**
Bio-bibliographic data:
British Mystery Writers, 1920–1939, pp.
339–44. (867)
Encyclopedia Mysteriosa, p. 386. (2)
*The Encyclopedia of Mystery and
Detection,* p. 435. (7)
*The Oxford Companion to Crime and
Mystery Writing,* p. 504. (4)
*Twentieth-Century Crime and Mystery
Writers,* 3rd ed., pp. 1112–13. (882c)
*Whodunit? A Who's Who in Crime and
Mystery Writing,* p. 213. (5)
Yates, Margaret Evelyn Tayler
Bio-bibliographic data:
Detecting Women 2, p. 201. (877b)
**Yates, Margaret [Polk], and Paula
Bramlette**
Bio-bibliographic data:
Australian Crime Fiction, p. 257. (207)
Yates, Renate
Bio-bibliographic data:
Australian Crime Fiction, p. 145, 257–58.
(207)
Yeager, Dorian
Bio-bibliographic data:
By a Woman's Hand, 2nd ed., p. 242.
Detecting Women, 1st ed., p. 153. (877a)
Detecting Women 2, pp. 201–2. (877b)
Detecting Women, 3rd ed., pp. 293–94.
(877c)
Web site: http://www.stopyourekillingme.
com/dorian-yeager.html
Yeldham, Peter
Bio-bibliographic data:
Australian Crime Fiction, p. 258. (207)
Yetman, Derek
Bio-bibliographic data:
Canadian Crime Fiction, pp. 240–41.
(209)

Yin, Leslie Charles Bowyer. *See*
    Charteris, Leslie
York, Andrew. *Pseud. for* **Christopher**
    Robin Nicole
Bio-bibliographic data:
Detecting Men, 1st ed., pp. 264–65. (876)
St. James Guide to Crime & Mystery
    Writers, 4th ed., pp. 1081–83. (882d)
Twentieth-Century Crime and Mystery
    Writers, 1st ed., pp. 1513–15. (882a)
Twentieth-Century Crime and Mystery
    Writers, 2nd ed., pp. 923–24. (882b)
Twentieth-Century Crime and Mystery
    Writers, 3rd ed., pp. 1113–15. (882c)
York, Jeremy. *See* **Creasey, John**
York, Kieran
Bio-bibliographic data:
Detecting Women, 3rd ed., p. 294. (877c)
York, [Rev.] Thomas [Lee]
Bio-bibliographic data:
Canadian Crime Fiction, p. 241. (209)
Yorke, Margaret. *Pseud. for* **Margaret**
    Beda Larminie Nicholson
Bio-bibliographic data:
By a Woman's Hand, 1st ed., p. 228.
    (884a)
By a Woman's Hand, 2nd ed., pp. 242–43.
    (884b)
Detecting Women, 1st ed., p. 153. (877a)
Detecting Women 2, p. 202. (877b)
Detecting Women, 3rd ed., p. 294. (877c)
Encyclopedia Mysteriosa, p. 386. (2)
The Encyclopedia of Murder and Mystery,
    p. 540. (6)
Great Women Mystery Writers, pp.
    365–68. (880)
The Mammoth Encyclopedia of Modern
    Crime Fiction, pp. 511–12. (1)
St. James Guide to Crime & Mystery
    Writers, 4th ed., pp. 1083–85. (882d)
Speaking of Murder, vol. II, pp. 50–65.
    (875b)
Twentieth-Century Crime and Mystery
    Writers, 1st ed., pp. 1515–17. (882a)
Twentieth-Century Crime and Mystery
    Writers, 2nd ed., pp. 924–25. (882b)
Twentieth-Century Crime and Mystery
    Writers, 3rd ed., pp. 1115–17. (882c)
Whodunit? A Who's Who in Crime and
    Mystery Writing, p. 213. (5)
Women of Mystery, p. 437. (874)
Personal papers in Mugar Memorial
    Library, Boston University.

Web site:
    http://www.twbooks.co.uk/authors/
    margaretyorke.html; http://www.
    stopyourekillingme.com/
    margaret-yorke.html
Yorke, Susan. *Pseud. for* **Suzette Telenga**
Bio-bibliographic data:
Australian Crime Fiction, p. 258. (207)
Yost, Elwy
Bio-bibliographic data:
Canadian Crime Fiction, p. 241. (209)
Youmans, Claire
Bio-bibliographic data:
Detecting Women, 3rd ed., pp. 294–95.
    (877c)
Young, Collier. *See* **Bloch, Robert**
Young, David
Bio-bibliographic data:
Canadian Crime Fiction, p. 241. (209)
Young, Kendal. *See* **Young, Phyllis Brett**
Young, Madelaine
Bio-bibliographic data:
Canadian Crime Fiction, p. 241. (209)
Young, Phyllis Brett
Bio-bibliographic data:
Canadian Crime Fiction, p. 241. (209)
Young, Samuel Hall
Bio-bibliographic data:
Canadian Crime Fiction, p. 241. (209)
Young, Scott [Alexander]
Bio-bibliographic data:
Canadian Crime Fiction, pp. 241–42.
    (209)
Detecting Men, 1st ed., p. 265. (876)
Yuill, P. B. *Pseud. for* **Gordon Maclean**
    Williams and Terry Venables
Bio-bibliographic data:
The Mammoth Encyclopedia of Modern
    Crime Fiction, pp. 499–500. (1)
Twentieth-Century Crime and Mystery
    Writers, 1st ed., pp. 1517–19. (882a)
Twentieth-Century Crime and Mystery
    Writers, 2nd ed., pp. 926–27. (882b)
Twentieth-Century Crime and Mystery
    Writers, 3rd ed., pp. 1117–18. (882c)

Z

Zabrana, Jan:
Bio-bibliographic data:
Canadian Crime Fiction, p. 242. (209)
Zachary, Fay
Bio-bibliographic data:
Detecting Women 2, p. 202. (877b)
Detecting Women, 3rd ed., p. 295. (877c)

Zachary, Hugh
Bio-bibliographic data:
Canadian Crime Fiction, p. 279, 287.
(209)
Zangwill, Israel
Bio-bibliographic data:
Critical Survey of Mystery and Detective Fiction, pp. 1730–34. (41)
Encyclopedia Mysteriosa, p. 387. (2)
The Encyclopedia of Murder and Mystery, pp. 541–42. (6)
The Encyclopedia of Mystery and Detection, p. 436. (7)
100 Masters of Mystery and Detective Fiction, pp. 728–32. (37)
The Oxford Companion to Crime and Mystery Writing, p. 505. (4)
St. James Guide to Crime & Mystery Writers, 4th ed., pp. 1085–86. (882d)
Twentieth-Century Crime and Mystery Writers, 1st ed., pp. 1519–22. (882a)
Twentieth-Century Crime and Mystery Writers, 2nd ed., pp. 927–28. (882b)
Twentieth-Century Crime and Mystery Writers, 3rd ed., p. 1125. (882c)
Whodunit? A Who's Who in Crime and Mystery Writing, p. 215. (5)
Personal papers in Central Zionist Archives, Jerusalem.
Personal papers in British Library.
Personal papers in Moccata Library of University College, London.
Personal papers in University of London Library.
Zaremba, Eve
Bio-bibliographic data:
By a Woman's Hand, 2nd ed., pp. 244–45. (884b)

Canadian Crime Fiction, pp. 242–43. (209)
Detecting Women, 3rd ed., p. 295. (877c)
The Mammoth Encyclopedia of Modern Crime Fiction, p. 512. (1)
Zigal, Thomas
Bio-bibliographic data:
Detecting Men, 1st ed., p. 265. (876)
Zimmerman, Bruce
Bio-bibliographic data:
Detecting Men, 1st ed., p. 265. (876)
Zimmerman, R. D.; i.e., Robert Dingwall
Bio-bibliographic data:
Detecting Men, 1st ed., p. 266. (876)
Web site: http://www.stopyourekillingme. com/r-d-zimmerman.html
Zinbert, Leonard S. *See* **Lacy, Ed**
Zubro, Mark Richard
Bio-bibliographic data:
Detecting Men, 1st ed., p. 266. (876)
The Mammoth Encyclopedia of Modern Crime Fiction, p. 513. (1)
Web site: http://www.stopyourekillingme. com/mark-richard-zubro.html
Zukowski, Sharon
Bio-bibliographic data:
By a Woman's Hand, 2nd ed., p. 245. (884b)
Detecting Women, 1st ed., p. 153. (877a)
Detecting Women 2, p. 202. (877b)
Detecting Women, 3rd ed., p. 296. (877c)
The Mammoth Encyclopedia of Modern Crime Fiction, pp. 513–14. (1)
Web site: http://www.stopyourekillingme. com/sharon-zukowski.html
Zweig, Eric
Bio-bibliographic data:
Canadian Crime Fiction, p. 243. (209)

Index

The numbers beside the entries refer to annotations, not pages. Characters are listed under their last names (Holmes, Sherlock) unless they do not have a name and are described by their profession (the Continental Op) or their calling (the Green Lama). Honorifics and titles are not listed unless they comprise an essential portion of the name (i.e., Mr. Moto, Father Brown, and Rabbi Small). Numbers are filed as they are pronounced (*19 Tales of Intrigue, Mystery and Adventure* is *Nineteen Tales of Intrigue, Mystery and Adventure* and *10 Women of Mystery* is *Ten Women of Mystery*), and abbreviations (Mr. and Dr.) are treated as they are pronounced (Mister and Doctor.) Items in quote marks reference the chapters and short stories mentioned in the annotations; not all of these are listed.

Black Mask, 9, 12, 25, 116, 205, 313, 367a, 367b, 367c, 367d, 913a, 913b, 913c, 923c, 932a, 932e, 1011, 1018
The Black Mountain (Stout), 962b
Black Orchids (Stout), 962b
Black, Terry "Bulldog," 977
Blackie, Boston, 1044a, 1044b
"Blackmail Bay" (Gibson), 728i
Blackman, Lawrence, 313
Blackstone, Harry, 924
Blackwill, 206
Blackwood, Algernon, 775
Blackwood's Magazine, 916b, 916c
Blade Runner (movie), 1043
Blaine, Torchy, 1044a, 1044b
Blaise, Modesty, 64
Blake, Nicholas, 30a, 30b, 259, 261, 775, 865, 894
Blake, Rodney, 891
Blake, Sexton, 301, 991, 1044a, 1044b
Blanchard, Robert G., 901a
Blanck, Jacob, 949f, 949g
Bleak House (Dickens), 102a, 102b.
Bleeck, Oliver, 965b
Blei, Norbert, 914f
Bleiler, Everett F., 6, 915a, 916t,1010a, 1010b
The Blessing Way (Hillerman), 933a, 933j
Blincoe, Nicholas, 55
Blind-Accessible Mysteries, 84a, 84b
Bloch, Robert, 25, 52, 848a, 895a, 895b, 895c, 949d, 1049
Blochman, Lawrence G., 313
Block, Lawrence, 21, 25, 55, 81, 862, 858a, 875b, 896, 1016
Blonde Crazy (movie), 1035
Blood & Ink (Borowitz), 186
Blood, Captain, 1001a
Bloodhound Detective Story Magazine (British), 368a, 368b
Bloodhounds of Hell (Ousby), 49
Bloods, 1028, 1029a, 1029b, 1029c
Bloody Dagger Reference (Pappas), 1060
Bloody Murder (Symons), 27, 63a, 63b, 63c, 63d, 63e, 63f
Bloom, Harold, 1011, 1012
Bloomsbury Good Reading Guide to Murder, Crime Fiction, and Thrillers (McLeish and McLeish), 42
Blue Belle (Vachss), 217
Blue Book, 39
"The Blue Geranium" (Christie), 906o
The Blue Hammer (Macdonald), 943d
Blue Ribbon Publishing, 265

Blue Rose Series (Straub), 963
Blue Steel Magazine, 369a, 369b, 369c
The Blues Detective (Soitos), 67
Blurbs, 51
Blyth, Harry, 297
Boardman Books, 266, 267
Boardman Crime and Science Fiction (Greenslae, Lesser, and Williams), 266
Boating and Sailing Mysteries (Reader's Advice), 85
Bob Brooks Library , 370
Bob's Your Uncle (Turner-Lord), 8
Bobbsey Twins, 997a, 997b
Bodenheimer, Daniel, 904d
Bodkin, M. McDonnell, 866
The Body in the Library (Christie), 906j, 906k, 1012
Boettcher, Bonna J., 154
Bogar, Jeff, 284
Bogard, Dale, 298
Bogart, Humphrey , 3
Bolton, Judy, 26.5, 1003
Bonaparte, Napoleon, 7, 967c
Bond, James, 7, 983, 1028
Bondage, 371
Bony Bulletin, 314, 372
Book of Common Prayer, 915b
The Book of Etiquette (Brown), 269
Book of First Aid and Home Nursing, 999
The Book of Murder (Anderson), 890
Book of Prefaces to Fifty Classics of Crime Fiction (Barzun and Taylor), 13
The Book of Sleuths (Pate), 991
Book of Terror, 373
"The Book, the Bibliographer, and the Absence of Mind" (Barzun), 197
BookFinder (used and antiquarian book web metasite), 1070
Booking Hawaii Five-O (Rhodes), 1052
Books and Collectibles (used and antiquarian book Web site), 1062, 1071
Books and Publishing Industry Mysteries (Reader's Advice), 83
Books Go to War, 260
Books in Action (Cole), 261
"Books Yet to Appear" (Lovisi), 916d
Booth, Irwin, 935
Borden, Elizabeth "Lizzie," 145, 186
The Borden Murders, 145
Borges, Jorge Luis, 41, 884.2
Borges, Jorges [*sic*] Luis, 197
Borowitz, Albert, 186
Boston Public Library, 243

Gibson, John Michael, 916a, 916b, 916c, 916e
Gibson, Walter, 316, 728g, 728h, 728i, 924, 992, 1007
Giff, Patricia, 997a, 997b
The Gift, 949
"The Gift" (Francis), 921b
Gilbert, Anthony, 10
Gilbert, Colleen B., 957c, 957d
Gilbert, Michael, 36, 865, 884.1, 925
Gilman, Charlotte Perkins, 33
Gilman, Dorothy, 96
Ginna, Peter, 21
Girasol, 728i
"The Girl behind the Hedge" (Spillane), 959a
Girl from U.N.C.L.E. Magazine, 534a, 534b
The Girl in the Pictorial Wrapper (Breen), 1013
Girl Rackets, 535
Girl's Detective Mysteries, 536a, 536b
Girls Series Books (University of Minnesota), 987
Girls Series Books: A Checklist of Hardback Books Published 1900–1975 (University of Minnesota), 997a
Girls Series Books: A Checklist of Titles Published 1840–1991 (University of Minnesota), 997b
Gladstone, William Ewart, 38
The Glass Key (Hammett), 63a, 63b, 63c, 63d, 63e, 63f
Glass Key Award, 257.5q
Glauser Award, 257.5r
Glazed Thundermug Award, 27
"Gloria Scott" (Doyle), 916l
Glover, Dorothy, 59, 203
G-Men, 1000
G-Men Detective, 521a, 521b, 521c, 1000
The Goblin Tower (Long), 114
The Golden Spiders (Stout), 962b
Godey's Lady's Book, 949
Goddu, Teresa A., 949e
"The Godfather and the Father" (Keating), 36
Godwin, William , 10, 11, 63a, 63b, 63c, 63d, 63e, 63f, 202, 949, 1009b
"The Gold-Bug" (Poe), 949
Gold Dagger Award, 44, 55
Gold Seal Detective, 537a, 537b, 537c
Golden Age of Detective Stories (Shortling), 147
"Golden Era" (Dubose and Thomas), 874
Golden Fleece, 538a, 538b

Golden Library of Indian and Detective Adventures (British), 539
"Golden Vulture," 728i
Goldsborough, Robert, 962a
Goldscheider, Gaby, 916a
Goldsmith Publishing Company, 265
The Golf Murders Collection (Taylor), 178
Golf Mysteries (Leininger), 177
Golfing Mysteries (Waterboro Public Library), 179
Gollancz Books, 282
Gollancz Crime Fiction (Williams and Spurrier), 282
Gonda, Manji, 217, 1021
Good Old Index (Ross), 916p
"Goodbye to the Gentleman" (Pate), 991
Goodis, David, 287, 285, 926
Goodwin, Archie, 113, 962b
Gordon, Hava, 290
Gordon, Spike, 290
Gorey, Edward, 1054a, 1054b
Gorman, Ed , 24, 25, 26.5, 869, 875a, 875b
Gorot, Charles, 916p
"The Gothic" (Slung), 36
Gothic Fiction, 41
Gothic Novels of the Twentieth Century (Radcliffe), 114
The Gothic Quest (Summers), 114
Gotwald, Frederick G., 962b
Gouden Strop, 257.5s
Goulart, Ron, 24, 115
Gould, Chester, 265, 992
Goyne, Richard, 955
Grafton, C. W., 13, 878
Grafton, Sue, 21, 42, 120a, 120b, 202, 862, 874, 875a, 875b, 878, 884.2, 927, 1016
Graham Greene: An Annotated Bibliography of Criticism (Cassis), 929a
Graham Greene: A Character Index and Guide (Hoskins), 929c
Graham Greene: A Checklist of Criticism (Vann), 929d
Graham Greene: A Bibliography and Guide to Research (Wobbe), 929e
Graham Greene on Film, 1009b
Graham, Billy, 908
Graham, Philip, 36
Graham, Ruth Bell, 908
Graham, Winston, 867
Graham's Lady's and Gentleman's Magazine, 204, 206, 949, 1028
Graham's Magazine, 949, 1028
Gramol Group Books, 283

Vanderburgh, George A., 914f, 916i, 916j, 916k
The Vanishing Shadow (Sutton), 1003
Vann, J. Don, 929d
Variety Detective Magazine, 841a, 841b, 841c
Veendam, S. S., 30a, 30b
"The Veiled Woman" (Browne/Spillane), 959a
Venture Action Stories, 842
Verbrecher aus Infamie (Schiller), 202
Verdict, 843a, 843b, 843c
*Verdict Crime Detection Magazine, 3*12, 844a, 844b
Verne, Jules, 203
Véry, Pierre, 30a, 30b
Vicarel, Jo Ann, 163, 166
Vice Squad Detective, 845a, 845b, 845c
Vickers, Roy, 1049
Victor, Metta, 248
Victoria, Queen, 988
Victorian Detective Fiction (Glover and Greene), 59
Victorian Detective Fiction (Osborne), 203
Vidal, Gore, 27
Vidocq, EugPne François, 10, 11, 63a, 63b, 63c, 63d, 63e, 63f
Viking Books, 298
Viking/W[orld] D[istributors] L[td] (Holland and Williams), 298
Vincent Starrett (Stewart), 960e
A Vincent Starrett Catalogue (Norfolk-Hall), 960b
A Vincent Starrett Library (Honce), 960a
Vine, Barbara, 954
Vining, Keith, 258
Viva Zapata! (movie), 1035
The Voice on the Radio (Cooney), 193
Le Voleur de Maigret (Simenon), 958f
Voltaire, 46, 54a, 54b, 202
von Droste-Hülshoff, Annette, 66
Voodoo, 40
Le Voyage et les aventures des Trois Princes de Serendip (De Mailly), 46

Wade, Henry, 867
Wahlöö, Per, 4, 6, 18, 52, 880, 884.2, 1017
Waif Wander, 920
Waldman and Son Publishing Company, 265
Walker, Peter, 1053
Walkhoff-Jordan, Klaus-Dieter, 213, 214, 215
Wallace, Edgar, 9, 26.5, 34, 44, 49, 64,184, 186, 211, 259, 265, 270, 272, 273, 279,

280, 285, 286, 866, 884.2, 931, 971a, 971b, 971c, 971d, 971e, 971f, 971g, 971h, , 975a, 975b, 975c, 1012, 1033
Wallace, Penelope, 64
Wallenfeldt, Jeffrey H., 1041
Walpole, Horace, 206
Walsdorf, John J., 964
Walter, Klaus-Peter, 9
Walters, Minette, 26.5, 37, 874, 875a, 875b, 877a, 877b, 877c
Wambaugh, Joseph, 21
Wander, Waif, 920
Wanderer Books, 997a, 997b
Wandrei, Donald, 914b, 914c, 914d, 914e
War Stories, 42
Ward, Christopher, 30a, 30b
Ward, Elizabeth, 237
WarLetters (Carroll), 263
Warletters.com, 263
Warren, Alan, 1055
Waterboro Public Library, 179
Waters, 1028
Waterstone's Guide to Crime Fiction (Rennison and Shepard), 55
Watson, Doctor, 916v, 916w, 916x
Watson, John, 48
"Watson Was a Woman" (Stout), 30a, 30b
Waugh, Hillary, 36, 167, 282
"Wave those Tags" (Dent), 913a
Webb, Jean Francis, 977
Webb, Paul, 901c
Webster, Henry Kitchell, 13
Weddings and Honeymoons, 43a, 43b
Weinberg, Robert, 317a, 317b, 728g, 848c, 895a, 913c
Weird Mystery, 846a, 846b
Weird Tales, 848a, 848b, 848c, 848d, 848e
Weird Tales Collector, 847
Weird Tales Story, 848c
Weird Terror Tales, 849a, 849b
Wellman, Manly Wade, 1000
Wells, Carolyn, 37, 41, 880
Wells, H. G., 775
Wells, Professor, 986
Wer war der Mörder? (Temme), 66
Werremeier, Friedhelm, 214, 215
Wertham, Fredric, 1025
West, Nathaniel, 932b
West, Paul, 99
Westlake, Donald E., 24, 64, 120a, 120b, 226, 266, 282, 293, 295, 869, 875a, 875b, 883, 884.2, , 1016
Westmacott, Mary, 906b, 906j, 906k

About the Author

RICHARD J. BLEILER is Humanities Reference Librarian, Babbidge Library, University of Connecticut, Storrs.